J. Luther (John Luther) Ringwalt

American Encyclopaedia of Printing

J. Luther (John Luther) Ringwalt

American Encyclopaedia of Printing

ISBN/EAN: 9783742881991

Manufactured in Europe, USA, Canada, Australia, Japa

Cover: Foto ©Thomas Meinert / pixelio.de

Manufactured and distributed by brebook publishing software
(www.brebook.com)

J. Luther (John Luther) Ringwalt

American Encyclopaedia of Printing

AMERICAN

ENCYCLOPÆDIA

OF

PRINTING.

Edited by J. LUTHER RINGWALT.

PHILADELPHIA:
MENAMIN & RINGWALT, 517 MINOR STREET.
J. B. LIPPINCOTT & CO., 715 MARKET ST.
1871.

PREFACE.

In the title of this work the term Printing is used in its oldest and widest sense, so as to include not only all the established methods of multiplying fac-similes, but also all the auxiliary processes essential to the production of a folded newspaper or a bound book. As an Encyclopædia, it aims to traverse the circle of the art to which it relates, and therefore to describe its history, as well as its implements, its processes, and its products. In endeavoring to discharge this task, no available source of information has been neglected, but, while much instruction has been gleaned from periodical and standard typographical publications, the plan, arrangement, and a large portion of the contents are so thoroughly original as to induce the belief that it will fill an important vacancy, as a book of reference in printing-offices, as an assistant and instructor to every apprentice, journeyman, and amateur printer, and as an attractive addition to the libraries of all who are interested in the art of printing. Special attention has been given to the inventors, implements, history, statistics, and processes of printing in the United States; as will be seen from the abstract of specifications of American patents relating to printing, the numerous descriptions and illustrations of American presses and all other American implements, and the large proportion of the historical and biographical divisions which is devoted to the inventors and the early and distinguished printers and type-founders of this country.

No class of subjects bearing upon printing, however remotely, has been intentionally excluded, while no class has been admitted that is not directly or indirectly allied to it. This rule necessitates the discussion of a wide range of topics. The stereotyped phrase that printing is the art preservative of all arts, conveys a totally inadequate idea of its present position and utility, for it now not only preserves a record of all arts, but also converts them into useful auxiliaries, in the performance of its grand duties as the most beneficent, useful, and indispensable agent employed in human affairs; and the ever-increasing extension of its realm, which characterizes the nineteenth century, has added greatly to the difficulty of a comprehensive presentation of all its ramifications.

The numerous illustrations faithfully portray almost every object that admits of pictorial representation. So far as they require explanation, it will be found in accompanying passages of the text. The frontispiece reproduces in colors the design of the beautiful vignette upon the certificate of membership issued by the Philadelphia Typographical Society.

The value of the work has been greatly enhanced by the assistance of co-laborers. The biographical and literary articles were prepared chiefly by Jessie E. Ringwalt. The article on Lithography was contributed by Peter S. Duval, of Philadelphia. The articles on Paper, Parchment Paper, Safety-Paper, Splitting-Paper, Staining and Spotting of Paper, Writing-Ink, and the biographical notices of Louis Piette and Dr. J. C. Schaeffer, were written by George C. Schaeffer, Librarian of the United States Patent Office. Stereotyping was contributed by John Fagan; Job-Letter, by Eugene H. Munday; a large portion of the article on Wood Engraving, by William C. Probasco; Envelopes, by E. D. Lockwood; Printing for the Blind, by Napoleon B. Kneass, Jr.; while Eugene H. Munday, Jacob Glaser, James S. Montgomery, and W. S. Syckelmoore, of Philadelphia, and J. J. Jones, of Washington, rendered valuable assistance in the preparation of several articles on important practical subjects. Special acknowledgments are due, also, to Mackellar, Smiths & Jordan, and Collins & M'Leester, type-founders, for helpful courtesies gracefully extended, as well as to those who have aided in the mechanical production of the volume, Messrs. Duval & Hunter, Lithographers, and Messrs. Jas. B. Rodgers Co., Printers.

I hope that this work will excite in the minds of its readers the same interest that stimulated the labors involved in its preparation; that it will help to spread abroad a knowledge of the trials, struggles, and sufferings that have advanced printing to its present position; and that it will aid in arousing the enthusiastic and reverent spirit which prompts the traveling German journeyman to utter, whenever he enters a printing-office, the salutation, GOD GREET THE ART!   J. L. R.

PHILADELPHIA, July, 1871.

HOW A BOOK IS MADE.

ELSEWHERE in this work are described, with minute care and technical exactitude, the sundry styles of type, presses, paper, and all the varied material and labor which enter into the composition of a book; but this careful subdivision has offered no opportunity for a plain, general description of all the processes as they would be observed in their entirety by persons not practically familiar with printing. Such a description is here offered, while the reader is referred to the special subdivisions in the body of the work for the more minute and scientific examination of each department or process, as well as the numerous methods now employed by different printers for accomplishing each result.

In the composing-room are ranged, in rows, stands with slanting tops. Each stand supports two wooden frame-works, one resting above the other, distinguished as the upper and the lower-case. These in turn are subdivided into numerous small compartments, those in the upper-case containing capital and small capital letters, and those in the lower-case containing the small letters, punctuation marks, etc., so arranged that the characters most frequently used are placed nearest the hand of the workman.

Disregarding all technical description of types, they may be considered as oblong pieces of metal, upon one end of which, called the face, stands the letter, figure, or mark of whatever kind, raised from the surface and so reversed that the impression taken from it upon the paper will present the letter or mark in its true position to the eye.

The compositor, standing at his case, fixes the copy, or document which he is to repeat in type, in a convenient place before his eye, so that it either rests upon a rarely-used portion of the case, or is placed on a guide, or fixed in an instrument called a copy-holder. In his left hand is a small metal implement called a composing-stick, capable of holding a number of lines of type, and furnished with a slide by which the required length of the line can be fixed. Into this stick the compositor places with his right hand the type required to set the prescribed copy, using the thumb of his left hand to steady them, and arranging them on a thin brass or steel plate called the rule, which, being removed from line to line as each is completed, serves also to keep the type in place.

The setting-rule is one of the most essential articles belonging to the printer; and newspaper compositors usually own it individually, preserving the same one for years, and regarding it as the distinctive badge of their calling. The primary utility of the rule appears to have been acknowledged in the very origin of typography, for it is placed on the coat of arms of both Fust and Schoeffer, while the composing-stick and copy-holder figure conspicuously on the printer's arms granted to the craft by the Emperor of Germany.

When as many words and parts of words as will fill a line have been set up, it is made of the exact length required by increasing or diminishing the space between the several words. This process is called justifying the line, and it is effected by the use of type of various thicknesses, called spaces. When it is desired that the pages of a book shall present an open appearance, small plates of metal called leads, lower than the type, are inserted between the lines. When the composing-stick is filled, the type is deftly lifted from its position and placed on a galley, or plate of wood or metal with a raised margin at two or three sides, which becomes the receptacle of the set type, until it is in turn filled from the stick.

After a considerable quantity of type has been composed, a proof is obtained, that is, a printed impression in which the errors in composition can be readily detected. Proofs are often taken from galleys, but in ordinary book-printing the type is generally taken from the galley before it is proved, by a workman, whose special business it is to make up the type, that is, to divide it into the lengths required for the pages. To each page he adds the running head, or words placed at the top to indicate the subject, with the number denoting the page, technically called its folio, and under the last line of the first page of every sheet the letter or number called the signature, used to mark the position of the sheet in the work. As each page is made up, a cord, or thin, strong twine, is carried skillfully around the type, tying it into a compact mass.

A proof—known as the first proof—is then taken from these tied-up pages. After being read by the proof-reader, who compares the sheet carefully with the copy used by the compositor, this proof is returned to the compositor, who rectifies all the mistakes noted. Another proof is then taken, which, being in great measure free from mere mechanical or technical errors, is called the author's proof, and is sent to the editor or author to undergo a further revision.

When the author's emendations have been followed in the type, another proof is struck off, to be read again by the proof-reader, and in case of necessity, after these alterations, another proof, called the author's revise, is taken for his use. Three proof-readings are usually deemed sufficient, but in careful or difficult work seven revisions are sometimes required.

The pages of tied-up matter are carried to a stone table called the imposing-stone, upon which they are arranged as they will appear upon the printed sheet. The arrangement of these pages, technically called imposition, appears curiously difficult to the casual observer; and an idea of the peculiarities of the art may be readily gained by examining a common eight-page newspaper, which is in fact one quarto sheet, and observing in what manner the pages are arranged upon each side of the sheet so as to make them follow in successive order after the paper is folded into its allotted shape. In the smaller book-sizes, where many pages are printed upon one sheet, the arrangement or imposition becomes proportionately complex.

The pages thus arranged are fixed in place by pieces of wood and metal which secure them from falling into pi, or out of place, a disaster which may occur at any moment, from the time that the compositor's skilled fingers first transfer them from the stick to the galley, until they are closely clamped to receive the final pressure of the press. These interposed pieces bear various names, but are known under the general term of furniture, and perform the office of securing the pages in their allotted places and maintaining the required margins. The whole is now fastened within an outer iron frame, called a chase, and is known as the form, or the material for one side of a sheet. The process of tightening the form is called locking up, and is effected by the graduated pressure of wedge-shaped quoins, between slanting pieces of furniture, called side-sticks, and the chase.

In press-work, the same result is produced by different presses in different manners, but, in order to maintain simplicity and clearness in the description, we have chosen the Adams press as one in standard use for book-printing, and bearing in its structure the closest resemblance to the hand-press.

Near one end of this press is an interior section, into which the form is placed with the type facing upwards, resting securely upon what is styled the bed of the press, and maintaining its position, with the exception of a direct motion upwards and downwards conveyed to it by the bed of the press, which rises and falls with the mechanical regularity of a heart-beat, from the impulsion of steam-power.

At the end of the press, or, as it may be said, behind the form, is, on the outside, an ink-trough, in which a large roller revolves, lifting the ink in its rotations, and conveying a portion of it to another roller, which repeats this movement to another, until the final rollers of the series, covered with a thin equal coating of ink, sufficient for one impression, move forward over the form, distributing the ink evenly upon the surface of the type.

At the top of the press, above and a little in front of the chamber containing the form, is fixed an inclined table, upon which the workman called the feeder lays the paper, sheet by sheet, while from beneath this table comes a frisky little apparatus appropriately called the frisket, which, resembling an animated window-frame, starts from the front of the press, and in its progress backwards receives the sheet of paper from the inclined table, its edge being firmly grasped at the margin by two closing fingers or nippers, the sheet being thus conveyed backwards to the form.

The bed of the press then, rising, carries the inked form upwards, and the paper is impressed against the tympan, which is a frame covered with a sheet of muslin or gum cloth lined with sheets of paper or cloth called the blankets, and intended to break the force with which the whole is struck against the iron plate or platen, the pressure from which completes the impression.

In other words, the essential parts of the press are the platen and the bed on which the form rests, the other machinery being only the accessories by which the paper is placed between the type and platen, and the necessary ink supplied; the frisket being the instrument for readily conveying the sheet to and from the form, and for preserving the margins of the paper from coming in contact with the furniture; and the tympan, with the blanket, serving to soften the force of the blow and to prevent the type from cutting the paper.

A simple lever action has the effect of slackening the grasp of the nippers, and, by the time the frisket has in its forward course reached just beyond the table, a bellows, concealed below, gives a soft sigh or breath, just sufficient to lift the sheet of paper upwards upon a series of tapes which smoothly carry it to a fly by which the sheet is discharged upon a table. This operation, however, prints only one side of the sheet, and a second impression is necessary to perfect it.

The register, or the accurate backing of one page upon another, is secured by two metallic points in the inclined table, upon which the paper is laid previous to entering the press; the punctures made at the first impression by these points being placed upon them again, the sheet must be held by the nippers in exactly the same position as during the first impression.

Usually the paper is prepared for the press by wetting, an operation frequently accomplished simply by immersing a quire of paper in a tank of water for an instant by hand, and then piling it up with alternate quires of dry and wet paper until the whole is thoroughly dampened. This is also accomplished by machinery. Considerable moisture remains in the paper after it comes from the press, and, to allow it to evaporate, as well as to permit the ink to sink well into the paper, the sheets are dried, usually by hanging them on horizontal poles in a heated room.

Careful examination will disclose a slight roughness upon the surface of the paper, produced by the pressure of the sharp edges of the type: to remove this the sheets are now placed between large pieces of fine smooth Bristol board, and exposed to the immense pressure of a hydraulic press.

It will be observed that all mention of stereotyping and other similar processes in general use, and also the introduction of illustrations or pictures, have been avoided, in order to prevent further complexity of detail, in a manufacture strikingly complicated even in its simplest form, and infinitely varied in minutiæ by the necessities of different establishments and by the tastes or habits both of the directors and the operatives.

The printed sheets are now ready for the bindery, and are first conveyed to the folding-room, where they are ranged in successive piles, each pile containing copies of the same sheet.

The folding is frequently done by machinery, but much is still done by hand, the work-woman laying the sheet on the table before her, so doubled that the folios rest upon one another with absolute precision, and repeating the folding as demanded by the size of the book.

The folded sheets are laid in separate piles, and are distinguished as signatures, each sheet having been marked at the foot of the first page, as has been already stated, in the first preparation of the page of type. This nomenclature of signature, for sheet, is usual among printers and binders through every stage of their operations.

A workwoman then passes from pile to pile, lifting a signature from each. After all the signatures required for the volume have been thus gathered, they are collated by a careful reading of the successive signatures, to make it certain that the pages of the future book will follow one another in due succession. The matter of the volume is now complete, and the sheets are subjected to the operation of a pressing machine to make the pages lie compactly together.

If the work is intended to have either a common or a spring back, it is now taken to the sawing-machine, which makes several shallow cuts into the folded edges of the paper, at the back of the book, as a preliminary to the sewing; but if a flexible back is required, a slight depression is made with an awl to guide the sewer,—sometimes simply a pencil-mark. The book is now ready to be sewed.

The operator in this department sits upon the right hand of an upright frame, upon which lines of strong cord are tied perpendicularly at intervals corresponding to the cuts already made in the sheet. The signatures are then taken one by one, and laid with their backs so that the upright cord enters the slit or cut: the operator then opens the sheet at the middle, and with a needle and strong thread sews the sheet from end to end, passing the thread in the needle securely around the upright twine. The next signature is then laid on, and sewed in the same way, alternating in direction with each sheet, as the sewing must reverse its course, and increasing the strength of the back by doubling alternately from end to end.

In the flexible backs the upright twine is allowed to lie on the outside of the sheets, and the sewing is done through the prepared punctures, making a strong cord of sewing upon the outside of the back by the interlacing of the two twines. When the sewing of the volume is completed, another volume is commenced, leaving a space of the upright cord vacant between the books, until the frame is filled. The upright cords are then loosened, and the volumes cut apart, each being completely secured by the sewing, with a short loose end of the cord projecting to assist in the future operations of the binding. Several extra pages for fly-leaves are generally placed at the beginning of a bound volume, with a couple of leaves of colored paper at the beginning and end of the book, and several of these are at this stage pasted together, that they may subsequently serve to strengthen the connection between the book and its case.

The volume is now placed in a cutting-machine, which trims the edge exactly according to the intended margin.

The back is next pounded with a hammer by hand, so as to round it as a preliminary to what is styled the backing,—an operation performed by placing the volume in a clamp, in such a manner that the back of the book projects above the clamp, exactly the distance needed for the joint or groove into which the sides of the cover will play. A roller works backward and forward above this clamp, with the effect of making the back rounded. A head-band, or strip of folded silk or muslin, is afterwards glued securely across the back at the top and foot of the volume, so as to project slightly beyond the paper. A strip of paper or muslin, exactly the length and width of the back, is next glued firmly over it, followed by another strip made wide enough to extend about half an inch upon the fly-leaves and render the volume compact. The book is now entirely ready for its case, the only exception being that if a spring back is to be added, a piece of paper or muslin is so pasted upon the back that it can be again folded or doubled across, the outer fold being left loose to constitute the spring.

If gilt edges are required, they are added at this stage: the volume is fixed in a vise, and the edges of the leaves are gently touched with glair, or white of egg, upon which is placed the delicate sheet of gold-leaf,—after which the surface of the gilding is thoroughly polished by strong friction from an agate burnisher held in the hand.

Marbled edges are produced by an apparently simple, but in fact very difficult, operation. The edges of the paper are gently and evenly dipped into a trough of mucilage, upon which a trained workman has sprinkled liquid colors in such a manner as to produce the spots, figures, or waved lines displayed in what is called marbling. An instrument is sometimes used to assist in the formation of the figures.

In full muslin, and in a large proportion of half-bound books, the covers are made and completely finished separately from the volume. These cases or covers consist of two pieces of strong pasteboard, the exact size of the sides of the book, which are connected, in the first place, by a strip of cloth or morocco, of the width required for the back of the book.

A full muslin case is completed by covering this back piece and the sides with the muslin, which is firmly glued over the whole outer surface, and turned down neatly upon the inside; the flexible portion for the back being lined to give it additional strength. A slight indentation is made at the edge of the back to form the groove or joint upon which the sides must play, and the muslin cover is ready for ornamentation.

In muslin cases, the figures or arabesques upon the cover are formed by a die fixed in a stamping-press, which makes what is called the blind ornaments, or merely raised figures in the material of the binding; but when gold lettering or figures, are to be added another process is required.

Glair is applied to that part of the surface which is to be gilt, and gold-leaf is afterwards laid on in pieces of sufficient size to embrace the whole ornament. A brass die of the required design is then placed in a stamping-machine, heated by steam, and the heated die is brought down with force upon the gold-leaf; the pressure affixing the gold under the die firmly to the cover, and leaving the rest of the gold-leaf so loose that it can be wiped away with a slight touch.

The muslin cover is then complete, and is attached to the book by pasting the fly-leaves, and generally one of those in colored or toned paper, down upon the inside of the cover.

Half-bound cases are made in exactly the same manner, except that the back is formed of a strip of leather or ornamental morocco, instead of being a portion of the continuous cover of muslin, and to complete the covering of the sides, either muslin or paper is afterwards pasted on the pasteboard; corner-pieces being added when necessary.

Full-bound volumes, or the higher styles covered with leather or morocco, are bound in an entirely different and stronger manner. The ends of cord, which were described as projecting from the sides of the volume after the sewing, are now stiffened with paste, so that they can be threaded in and out through several punctures made for the purpose in the pasteboards intended to form the sides. In this style of binding, the book is now placed in the cutting-machine, with the pasteboard sides so pushed back that they remain untouched by the knife, and continue considerably larger than the printed page, beyond which they are intended to project. The headband, already described in the muslin books, is added at this stage in the full-bound volumes, being pasted at the top and foot of the volume, and extending over upon the boards. The boards of the sides are now pared carefully towards the outer edges, so that the morocco can be folded neatly over upon the inside. Finally, a coating of glue prepares the boards for the morocco, which is pasted over the whole. All these latter operations are embraced under the general term of forwarding, and when they are completed the volume is ready for the finishing.

In the common styles of leather binding, a coat of glair is at this stage placed over the whole surface of the case, but in the finer kinds of morocco, etc., the glair is applied only where gold-leaf or pieces of tinted leather are used. Upon this fresh glair the strips of tinted leather used for the lettering-pieces or other ornamentation are now placed, after which the gold-leaf is added. The finer ornamentation of morocco is done by hand, with brass wheels or dies, heated and impressed, or stamped upon the gold-leaf. After the binding is completed, the books have a final pressing between boards covered on both sides with tin, in order to render them absolutely smooth.

The concluding processes of bookbinding are curious and attractive, not only for the artistic delicacy and precision of the manipulation, but for the beauty of the materials, the lustrous tints of the morocco gleaming with all the gorgeous colors of the rainbow, and the soft depths of the tinted velvets, heightened by the sheen of the gold and silver.

During this epoch of the diversification of industry, it rarely occurs that all the complicated labors of printing, binding, and publishing can be seen within the walls of one building; but in the splendid house of J. B. Lippincott & Co., of Philadelphia, all the processes can be traced, from the setting of the type until the final touch of beauty is given to that fitting framework in which mechanical industry adds its tribute to the labors of intellect, by enshrining literature in the choicest products of its handiwork. In other parts of this work will be found descriptions of various celebrated printing-offices, and of some of the famous European publishers, who are known to the reading public by the celebrity acquired in general literature, not only for the excellence of their workmanship, but also for the devotion of the labor of successive generations to the same industry. In America no house can yet hope to rival the Elzevirs of Holland, or the Stephens, De Tournes, and Didots of France, in duration of existence, but the Lippincott establishment, as the lineal successor of publishers of the last century, may probably claim the dignity of being the oldest printing and publishing house in the United States, in addition to their more recently won honors of being the largest book-distributing office in the world.

Upon the shelves of the salesroom of this establishment is displayed the whole realm of current literature, and after descending from story to story of the huge edifice, following the book through every stage of its growth, it is at length found ranged side by side with representatives from the other great publishers, both in this country and abroad, and, after teaching how the book is made, the establishment completes the work by showing how it is sold.

As exhibiting beneath one roof the methods by which the whole of this important industry is now conducted, a brief description will serve to show the peculiarities of a great American establishment, which is entitled to call itself the largest publishing, bookselling, importing, and stationery house in the world. The building is of peculiar construction, being continuous in extent in the cellarage and first floor, but separated in the upper stories into two distinct buildings, by a space of forty feet, which is bridged between the stories,—the open area giving great advantages of light and air. The building extends from street to street, a distance of 365 feet, having a frontage upon one street of 100 feet, with a depth of 150, while the other front is 50 feet, with a depth of over 200.

In a second or lower cellar, steam-engines produce the motor power required in all parts of the building; while in the first or upper cellar, or basement, the whole space is used for the storage of boxes received, and the packing of boxes which are to be sent away, and which are conveyed up and down by elevators, that receive and discharge these great bulks upon the sidewalk in front of the building. The ground, or first floor, is the salesroom, presenting a perfect literary cosmos; on one side, the publications of the house are ranged in due order, while on the other, in distinct compartments, appear the books of the other publishers, showing at a glance a view of the vast library now presented for the service of the reading world.

The stationery department is disposed in the second floor, embracing all the multitudinous details of blank books, paper, envelopes, games, and fancy articles, included under that general term. Above, or upon the third floor, are smaller apartments employed for the collateral branches of the business. On the fourth floor are the composition and press-rooms, with neat little apartments in the furthest and quietest corner, for the security and peace of the proof-readers; while on every story a small fire-proof room has been so constructed as to be used as a safe for the preservation of the various treasures of the establishment, such as a half-million dollars' worth of stereotype plates, the rich rolls of lustrous Levant morocco, and the many other expensive adornments which assist in the completion of the exquisitely bound work for which this house is so widely known.

Directly as they leave the press, the printed sheets are lifted by an elevator to the seventh story, where all necessary apparatus is prepared for drying them, and after this is accomplished they are let down to the sixth story.

Here the busy folders seize them, and, after the necessary manipulation, forward them to the sewers, from whom the volumes are convoyed to the story beneath, or the fifth floor, where are performed the various labors of the forwarding and finishing, and from it the completed book, whether a paper-covered novel or a magnificent pulpit Bible, departs, either to take its share in the glories of the salesroom, or to be boxed up in the cellar for immediate transportation.

AMERICAN

ENCYCLOPÆDIA OF PRINTING.

A is the first letter of the English Alphabet, and also of the Alphabets of many other modern and ancient languages. In type-founders' specimen books and circulars it is used to designate the size of small fonts of letter, which are called three A, four A, five A fonts, etc., to indicate that they contain the annexed number of A's and a proportionate number of the other letters. It is also used sometimes, in common with the other letters, as a signature; but numeral signatures are generally adopted in the United States.

Abbreviation.—The form to which a word or phrase is reduced by contraction or omission; a letter or a combination of letters, standing for a word or phrase of which they are a part; as, Gen. for Genesis; U. S. A. for United States of America.

In the early Hebrew manuscripts the custom of abbreviating words was carried to such an extent that sometimes only the initial letters of long sentences were used. Among the Romans the same custom was so general that an ancient writer made a list of five thousand of their abbreviations of words and phrases. The manuscript writers who immediately preceded the printers followed in many of their works the same system of consulting their own convenience rather than the interest of their readers; and the early printers adopted this vicious practice in imitating manuscripts. Relics of the old system abound in books printed less than two centuries ago, when yᵉ was used as the printed representation of the, and that appeared in type as yᵗ. In the time of Moxon (1683) the abbreviations just referred to were still used, but the printers of his day had abandoned the more inconvenient practice which had previously prevailed, of using straight strokes over the vowels as indications that m or n, and sometimes other letters, were omitted; and in the eighteenth century the abbreviations of the and that also ceased.

In a number of standard works of reference, as well as catalogues of various kinds, abbreviations are justifiable to avoid lengthy repetitions of words in very frequent use. Thus, in biographical dictionaries b. is made to do duty as born, and d. as died; while in dictionaries of language, it is better to explain at the outset of the work that a. represents adjective, n. noun, etc., than to print these words at full length. Another class of abbreviations—those used in newspaper advertisements, to indicate the time during which they are to be inserted, as tf. for till forbid, and 3m for three months—are also justifiable, because they are mere office directions and are sure to be understood by the limited circle for whose enlightenment they are intended. But in printing sentences designed for general instruction it is better to be as explicit as possible, and to leave no doubt of the exact meaning of copy in the mind of the reader.

Long lists of the abbreviations in frequent use in this country are to be found in various publications, among which are Webster's Dictionary, Worcester's Dictionary, The American Printer, and Wilson's Treatise on Punctuation; but it is impossible to construct a complete list of the words that have been or may be condensed, and printers should constantly remember that this capricious custom is more honored in the breach than in the observance. In epistolary correspondence, abbreviations in the body of the text are regarded as vulgarisms, and they are equally repulsive in printed matter.

As abbreviations sometimes become necessary, however, in spite of the most anxious desire to maintain the legibility of the text, which is a fundamental principle of printing, it is observable that nearly all the words selected for abbreviation are nouns; but this custom is not universal, as other parts of speech are occasionally subjected to the shortening process. And, whether words are abbreviated by apocope or syncope, it is the general custom, in the English language, to affix a period to their termination. Thus, District Attorney in its abbreviated form is printed Dist. Atty., although the first word is shortened by the cutting off of closing letters, while the last word is shortened by the omission of middle letters. The exceptions to this custom come under the category of elisions rather than abbreviations proper, for to this class belong such printed words as the contracted form of the (th') which is sometimes used in poetical works, as well as the contractions representing conversational phrases, such as can't and don't.

Abridgment.—An epitome or compend of a book; as, an abridgment of some history. An abridgment is made by omitting the less important parts of some larger work; as, an abridgment of a dictionary.

Absies.—The name, by quick pronunciation, of the A B C books which were written before the invention of printing, by the London stationers or text-writers who were the English predecessors of booksellers and printers.

Abstract.—An inventory, summary, or epitome, as of a treatise or book. Thus, an Abstract of Title is an epitome of the evidences of ownership.

Accent, as defined by Webster, is: 1. The modulation of the voice in reading or speaking, as practiced by the ancient Greeks, which rendered their rehearsal musical. More strictly, in English, a particular stress or force of voice upon certain syllables of words, which distinguishes them from the others. 2. A mark or character used in writing to direct the stress of the voice in pronunciation. Our ancestors borrowed from the Greek language three of these characters, the acute ('), the grave (`), and the circumflex (˝, or ^). In the Greek, the first shows when the voice is to be raised; the second, when it is to be depressed; and the third, when the vowel is to be uttered with an undulating sound. 3. In mathematics, accents are used to distinguish magnitudes of the same or similar kind, expressed by the same letter, but differing in value; as a', a".

In addition to the accents named above, as derived from the Greek, other signs are used for similar purposes, and although it may be a debatable question whether they should, strictly speaking, be regarded otherwise than as prosodial marks, yet as they form accented letters when they are attached to various members of the alphabet, they are practically accents, especially if free scope is given to Webster's definition. The most important of these marks are those which respectively lengthen, shorten, or prevent a blending of the sound of vowels; although others are employed in printing words in foreign languages. It is one of the glories of the English language, and one of the blessings of English compositors, that accents are rarely used except in works on Elocution, Spelling-Books, Pronouncing Gazetteers, and Dictionaries. A wise custom has decreed that it is not the office of the printer to designate with literal accuracy, in ordinary works, the pronunciation of each word, and American printers are thus saved from one of the most constant and serious annoyances of French and Spanish printers. The manner in which the leading words are printed in our standard dictionaries forcibly illustrates the serious nature of the task involved in printed representations of pronunciation; for, in addition to the ordinary grave, acute, circumflex, long, short, and diæresis marks or accents, a number of other marks are pressed into service to designate peculiar sounds represented at times by some of the consonants as well as the vowels.

A French writer on printing makes the broad assertion that the English language admits of no accent; but the very reverse of this assertion is true, for it would require more accents, or accented letters, in the English language than in any other to make its Alphabet faithfully represent, in all cases, proper pronunciation.

Accented Letters.—A font of accented letters (exclusive of those specially required for Dictionaries, Spelling-Books, Pronouncing Gazetteers, etc.) embraces the following:

Acute	á	é	í	ó	ú	ý
Grave	à	è	ì	ò	ù	ỳ
Circumflex	â	ê	î	ô	û	ŷ
Diæresis	ä	ë	ï	ö	ü	ÿ
Long	ā	ē	ī	ō	ū	ȳ
Short	ă	ĕ	ĭ	ŏ	ŭ	y̆

The Spanish ñ, which signifies that the letter should be pronounced as if written ny.

And the French ç, which gives the letter a sound like that of the English s.

The object of the acute accent is to denote that, in pronouncing the letter to which it is attached, the voice should be elevated or sharpened. It is very frequently used for this purpose in dictionaries of the English language, while the grave accent, denoting a fall or depression of the voice, is used chiefly in Latin, where it serves an important purpose in establishing distinctions between different parts of speech, thus elucidating the meaning as well as the pronunciation. The circumflex denotes a rise and fall of the voice in the same long syllable, and thus combines the power of the acute and grave accents. The diæresis, which is used only when vowels are in conjunction, denotes that the diphthong must be dissolved, or that the vowels must be pronounced as distinct letters. It is coming into comparatively frequent use in the English language, in such words as coöperate and coördination, but its employment for this purpose is furnishing a dangerous precedent; for if the work

ACME SELF-CLAMPING PAPER-CUTTING MACHINE.

ACME NEWSPAPER AND JOB PRESS.

of indicating by accented letters the proper pronunciation of each word is fairly commenced, it is impossible to tell where it is to end; and readers may as well be left to learn for themselves the proper pronunciation of words in which two vowels come together, without a blending of their sounds, as to fathom the innumerable other mysteries of pronunciation in our language. If a diæresis is used, care should be taken to apply it to the second vowel, and not to the first, for, though the last-named custom seems to prevail in a few printing-offices, it is certainly not sanctioned by modern usage, and if it has any foundation whatever it must be sought in antiquated theories.

Exclusive of the diæresis, the other accents proper rarely appear in English words, except in poetry, where they are sometimes employed to give increased dignity to the text by peculiar pronunciation, as in the following lines from Milton:

> By attributing overmuch to things
> Beyond all past example and future.

The long and short accents or prosodial marks are used chiefly in dictionaries and spelling-books to distinguish the variable sounds of vowels.

The French freely use the grave à and è, the acute é, the circumflex â, ê, î, ô, û, and the diæresis ë, ï, and û. In Latin, the grave à, è, î, ô, ù, the circumflex â, ê, î, ô, û, and the diæresis ë, ï, ü, are employed. The Italians use both the grave and acute accented letters. The Spaniards and Portuguese use the acute and circumflex accented vowels a, e, i, o, u, and while the Spanish confine themselves to their ñ, the Portuguese apply a similar mark to a, e and o. The Germans use the ä, ö, ü. The accented w and y are used by the Welsh.

Account-Book Headings.—See JOB PRINTING.

Acme Newspaper and Job Press.—A press invented by C. W. S. Montague, and now manufactured in Boston, intended mainly to meet the requirements of country newspaper offices. The manufacturer claims that it combines the following qualities, viz.: such ease of operation that hand power can be practically and profitably substituted for steam; such simplicity of construction and adjustment that any printer of reasonable intelligence can keep it in order; a capacity for speed and fine work which will render the press profitable, and the lowest price consistent with the first-class construction of a complete press. (See page 19.)

Acme Self-Clamping Paper-Cutting Machine.—A paper-cutting machine, manufactured in Boston, which is self-clamping, and whose arrangements for self-clamping, it is claimed, are superior to those of any other paper-cutter. It is also said to combine, in a high degree, the essential features of strength, accuracy, rapidity, and convenience. (See page 19.)

Acta Diurna.—A term equivalent to the daily news or acts, used as the title of the newspaper or gazette established by the Romans before the Christian era. The intelligence was supplied, as at present, by reporters, styled actuarii; and the items published resembled the contents of a modern journal, embracing the proceedings of the courts of law and public assemblies; descriptions of public works and buildings in progress; lists of deaths, births, and marriages; and trials for divorces, which were of frequent occurrence among the Romans, were very fully reported. Julius Cæsar, on entering upon his Consulate, B. C. 59, authorized the publication of the proceedings of the Senate, upon which there had been previously an injunction of secrecy. The following items extracted from one of these early journals furnish a specimen of their contents:

On the 26th of July, thirty boys and forty girls were born at Trimalchi's estate at Cumæ.

At the same time, a slave was put to death for uttering disrespectful words against his lord.

The same day, a fire broke out in Pompey's gardens, which began in the night, in the steward's apartment.

Adams, Joseph A., of New York, who was formerly a printer, but became a wood-engraver some time before 1830, brought the art of electrotyping, in 1839–41, to a higher degree of perfection than it had ever before obtained; he is the inventor of the Adams electric battery, which, by many electrotypers, is deemed superior to all others. In January, 1870, he obtained a patent for a new method of preparing electrotype moulds, which is a valuable improvement. Besides these achievements, Adams is accredited with the high honor of being the first to execute a superior style of fine printing, in the English sense of the phrase, in the United States. We give below an interesting and instructive account of this important event, which was read by a prominent New York printer at a meeting of the New York Typographical Society in January, 1864:

Mr. J. A. Adams, of this city, was first a printer, then a wood engraver—always an artist and a gentleman—and, finally, a retired, happy man of wealth and leisure. Some twenty-five years ago, this gentleman resolved to illustrate the Bible with very fine wood cuts, interspersed with the text, and have the whole printed much better than anything had been done in this country. After explaining his idea to several publishers, who gave it the cold shoulder, he eventually made an arrangement with Messrs. Harper & Brothers to publish an edition, stipulating that the printing should be done according to his own directions, fully appreciating (and the first man here to appreciate) that engravings so fine must be well printed to give their full value to a book; and believing that the American public, destitute of taste in all matters pertaining to the beautiful as book publishers considered it, would purchase a really beautiful book, if it could be offered, and pay for it a remunerative price.

In due time a goodly number of the wood cuts were completed, a few pages of the work were stereotyped, a set of combination blocks made, a form made up, and the cuts inserted in their proper places in the stereotype plates, by means of the combination blocks. At this stage of the proceedings, Mr. Adams left the engraving room and took off his coat among the printers; and that hour marks an era in the history of printing in this country. He took the two-roller, self-flying Adams press, which had then been in use but a short time, fitted his tympan so nicely to the platen that there could be no play, covered it with fine thin muslin, then secured his form upon the bed, and took an impression. After making his impression as even as possible by the usual method of underlaying, he laid a sheet of smooth, thick paper upon the face of his tympan, secured it in all the margins, both outside and inside, with paste, and then printed his form upon it. Now he commenced overlaying the cuts by a process which is pretty well understood by most wood-cut printers at the present time, but which had never been applied before, either in this country or in Europe. I will not go into the details of it here, but merely say it was the building-up process; slow, tedious, and very trying to the patience, but infallibly correct. Day after day he cut, scraped, rubbed, strained a new sheet over the whole, a little thinner than the first, printed again, and then proceeded with his cutting, pasting, scraping, and rubbing, and then straining on a new sheet, thinner than the last, and so on, course after course, day after day, until the pressmen in the office began to be amused, hinting that there might be such things as humbugs, even in large establishments; and the proprietors discovered evident signs of alarm, according to the peculiarities of each, counted the days already spent upon the form, and very anxiously but respectfully inquired as to the prospects of the future. The humorous brother joked, the serious brother expostulated, the amiable brother suggested the plan of starting the press on some given day, and then touching up the work a little, from time to time, as it progressed (but Mr. A. couldn't possibly see it in that light), and the judicious brother rolled up his clear and eloquent eyes in the agony of despair. Then all the brothers, with one accord, retired to the inner office, and in solemn conclave deliberated; voted that the Colonel should read the contract aloud for the edification of the whole, for verily he had made it, and after the reading they resolved unanimously, all four of them, that Mr. Adams had the right to print the Illustrated Bible according to the dictates of his own conscience. Then they smiled and went home to dinner, for they were philosophers, every one, and knew how to look upon the bright side of such events as could not be altered.

Well, Mr. Adams, with the most skillful pressmen in the office to assist him, labored industriously over this one form for two weeks, and then produced impressions which astonished everybody in America but himself, for he knew from the beginning just what he could do. As soon as the press began to throw off the most beautiful work any of them had ever seen, the Messrs. Harper were satisfied that the enterprise was a success, and that they had not made a mistake in giving Mr. Adams the control of the printing; and as soon as the first number of the Illustrated Bible was offered for sale the question whether fine printing could be made to pay in the United States of America was decided in the affirmative.

Mr. Adams next proceeded to instruct a few of the most tractable pressmen in the office in his system of preparing wood cuts, but he found that not many could learn it; for it requires the genius of an artist to know what an artist expects from his picture. A mere mechanic can never become a good wood-cut printer, be he ever so expert in other branches of the business.

Several of the first numbers of the Bible were printed upon two-roller presses by rolling three times for each impression, but the success of this work rendered it necessary to have a machine which could give a greater amount of rolling and a more perfect distribution of the ink, and the six-roller press was very soon produced by the combined skill of Isaac Adams, of Boston, and J. A. Adams, of New York. After this very perfect machine was built (about which so little was said, but which ought to have secured a resolution of thanks from the mass of sensible printers to the father of all the Adamses), the printing progressed quite rapidly, each revolution printing a sheet, and six presses being put upon it as fast as they could be built and the men instructed. Then followed the Illustrated Shakspeare, Lossing's Field Book of the Revolution, and other works equally beautiful, from the same establishment, and all the friends of progress were gratified to learn that a forward movement had been made, and that the American public was not incurably prejudiced against native skill. Fifty thousand copies of this magnificent work were sold, at twenty-five cents per number, enriching the projector of the enterprise and almost making the publishers comfortable.

Adams Press.—Of the Adams Presses, or Bed and Platen Printing Machines, invented by Isaac Adams of Boston, in 1830, and subsequently improved by himself, his brother, Seth Adams, by the present manufacturers, R. Hoe & Co., as well as by other inventors, Hoe's Catalogue says that for letter-press and cut work of the finest quality, these presses cannot be equaled; and, in spite of the numerous improvements in cylinder presses, this assertion is believed by many experienced book-printers. The Adams Press first solved the great difficulty attending an incorporation of all the advantages of the old hand press for fine work, in a machine which dispensed with hard human labor, and it has been improved so frequently, from time to time, that it has steadily maintained its favorite position in American book offices. It differs widely from other power-presses in use in this country in the fact that it has not only a flat bed, but that the paper receives a flat or platen instead of a cylinder impression, and its devices for insuring accuracy of register have probably never been equaled. In 1860, a writer and printer, in summing up its merits, says they can be traced to three principal points, viz.: 1, the combination of stationary fly-frames with points for making register; 2, periodical and harmoniously concurrent movements between the inking-rollers and the friskets; 3, the masterly application and governing influence of the declension lever. Since 1860 new improvements have been added to lighten the labors of feeders as well as to insure accurate feeding, and also to improve the rolling apparatus, so as to make the distribution of the ink as perfect as possible. Fifty-four numbers of the Adams Press, varying in size or in the number of rollers attached, are now made by Hoe & Co. For its appearance see the accompanying cut.

ADAMS PRESS.

Admiration, Note of.—A term formerly applied to the Exclamation Point (!), but discarded by the best modern authorities.

Adolphus of Nassau enters into the early history of printing as the author of the sack of Mentz in 1462, which event, by dispersing the printers engaged in that city, led to the promulgation of the processes of the art previously unknown. In this first public event in which typography appears, the printers seem, as in after-times, to have been deeply involved in the current affairs. As a competitor for the archbishopric of Mentz, Adolphus of Nassau attacked the city, then in the possession of his rival, the Archbishop Diether von Isenburg. Diether, compelled to retire from the city, affixed a declaration of his rights to the portico of the palace and upon the church, sending it also to the magistrates of Spire.

This was a printed document, styled The Declaration of the Elector Diether against Adolphus, Count of Nassau, with the date 1462, and is unquestionably from the press of Fust and Schoeffer. The document consisted of a sheet two feet in length and nearly sixteen inches in breadth, printed only on one side, and it is probably the earliest printed poster. The text embraced one hundred and six lines, the printed surface being 18¼ inches in length by 12½ inches in width.

The press of Fust seems to have been unemployed from 1462 to 1465, and probably his absence from the city arose from his being considered a partisan of the unsuccessful Diether, while we find that Gutenberg was in 1465 honored with marks of distinction by the successful Archbishop Adolphus, admitted to the court, with a pension, privileges, etc. Gutenberg died only two years afterward (February, 1468), and was then the owner of a press which was purchased by Conrad Humery under the engagement to Archbishop Adolphus that it should not be sold to any one but a citizen of Mentz. From the fact that Gutenberg was impoverished by the result of the lawsuit with Fust in 1455, it seems fair to assume that the favor of Adolphus had assisted him in erecting a new press, which must have been a matter of considerable expense.

Adversaria.—Books in which all matters are temporarily entered as they occur. A miscellaneous collection of notes, remarks, or selections; hence a commonplace-book. A title used for books or papers of such character. The term was originally applied to the adverse or blank side of manuscripts, which, on account of the scarcity of vellum or paper, were frequently used for commonplace-books or journals.

Advertisement.—The act of informing or making known. . . A publication intended to give notice, especially a paid notice in some public print; as, a newspaper containing many advertisements.— *Webster.*

Among printers they are generally called ads. or advers.

Nothing has given such an impetus to the art of printing as the discovery that it could be extensively and profitably applied to business purposes, and that the press could not only disseminate stores of learning and transmit them from one age to another, but be made a useful agent in the affairs of every-day life, alike to the banker who solicits a loan of millions and to the servant out of place who seeks a situation. If the revenue derived by the printers of the present day from varied forms of advertising were cut off, more than half their occupation would be gone, and many newspapers and job offices would instantly become unremunerative.

Although some forms of advertising were practiced by the Greeks and Romans, and others existed in the time of the first printers, it is a comparatively modern idea to press printers into the service of every member of the community who has wares to sell or wants to satisfy, and to make the art of printing perpetually photograph the current transactions of life.

It is a matter of controversy what advertisement first appeared in an English newspaper. In an early number of a paper called the Impartial Intelligencer, published in the year 1648, appears an advertisement referring to the theft of two horses, and this is commonly quoted as the first. A writer in the Newspaper Press, however, claims that he has in his possession a copy of the Mercurius Civicus or London's Intelligencer, printed August 11, 1643, which contains an advertisement of a book on the Sovereign Power of Parliament, and this antedates the horse-theft advertisement five years. After the appearance of these early advertisements, similar announcements were for a time made only at rare intervals. By slow degrees the practice of invoking the printer's aid gradually became prevalent, until at the beginning of the eighteenth century the germ of advertising, as it now exists, became fairly developed. In The Observator Reformed, a London journal, of September 10, 1704, which inserted advertisements of eight lines for a shilling, and at the same time became, through its editor, the medium of communication between advertisers, a series of notices appeared which gave good promise of the better days that were to come after the Observator had passed into oblivion. Its advertisements furnish so good an epitome of staple wants that we reproduce them here, viz.:

If any Hamburgh or other merchant, who shall deserve £200 with an apprentice, wants one, I can help.

One has a pert boy, about 10 years old, can write, read, and be very well recommended; she is willing he should serve some lady or gentleman.

I want a cook-maid for a merchant.

I sell chocolate made of the best nuts, without spice or perfume, and with vinelloes and spice, from four to ten shillings the pound, and I know them to be a great helper of bad stomachs, and restorative to weak people, and I'll insure for their goodness.

If any will sell a free estate, within thirty miles of London, with or without a house, to the value of £100 the year, or thereabout, I can help to a customer.

If any have a place belonging to the law, or otherwise, that is worth £1000 or £2000, I can help to a customer.

If any divines or their relicts have complete sets of manu-

script sermons upon the Epistles and Gospels, the Catechisms or Festivals, I can help to a customer.

A fair house in Eastcheap, next to the Flower-de-lis, now in the tenure of a smith, with a fair yard, laid with free stone, and a vault underneath, with a cellar under the shop, done with the same stone, is to be sold; I have the disposal of it.

I believe I could furnish all the nobility and gentry in England with valuable servants, and such as can have very good recommendation.

Mr. David Rose, chirurgeon and man-midwife, lives at the first brick house on the right hand in Gun-yard, Houndsditch, near Aldgate, London. I have known him these twenty years.

I want an apprentice for an eminent tallow-chandler.

If any want all kind of necessaries for corps, or funerals, I can help to one who does assure me he will use them kindly; and whoever can keep their corps till they get to London, and have a coffin set down, may have them afterwards kept any reasonable time.

About forty miles from London is a schoolmaster, has had such success with boys, as there are almost forty ministers and schoolmasters that were his scholars. His wife also teaches girls lace-making, plain work, raising paste, sauces, and cookery, to the degree of exactness. His price is £10 to £11 the year, with a pair of sheets and one spoon; to be returned. If desired; coaches and other conveniences pass every day within half a mile of the house; and 'tis but an easy day's journey to or from London.

I know of several men and women whose friends would gladly have them match'd; which I'll endeavor to do, as from time to time I shall hear of such whose circumstances are likely to agree; and I'll assure such as will come to me, it shall be done with all the honor and secrecy imaginable. Their own parents shall not manage it more to their satisfaction; and the more comes to me, the better I shall be able to serve 'em.

In the same year that the above announcements appeared in the Observator (1704), John Campbel of Boston, in publishing the first number of the first successful American newspaper, the Boston News-Letter, advertised for advertisements, and gave circulation to the first newspaper advertisement in this country, as follows:

This News-Letter is to be continued Weekly; and all Persons who have any Houses, Lands, Tenements, Farms, Ships, Vessels, Goods, Wares, or Merchandizes, &c. to be Sold, or Let; or servants Run-away, or Goods Stole or Lost; may have the same Inserted at a Reasonable Rate, from Twelve Pence, to Five Shillings, and not to exceed: Who may agree with John Campbel Postmaster of Boston.

This appeal met with but a faint response. Many numbers of the News-Letter contained but two or three advertisements, and a similar dearth afflicted all the early colonial newspapers, until gradually wealth accumulated, wants multiplied, the habit of advertising became established, and the fact that it could be made in many instances a source of profit and advantage was at last so clearly demonstrated, that British newspapers, shortly after the Revolutionary era, noted with surprise the extensive advertising patronage of the leading American cities.

It is only during the present century, however, that the utility of advertising has become well understood in any locality, and at the present day so many thousands neglect to avail themselves fully of its advantages, that it is even now only in its infancy, and the rapid increase in the revenue derived by printers and publishers for advertising during the last quarter of a century foreshadows a still more rapid increase hereafter.

It does not fall within the scope of this work to discuss the general subject of advertisements, except so far as it directly concerns printers, and no attempt will be made here to describe the most effective method of writing them, or to dilate upon the various systems that are tried in turn by advertisers. After they have done their best to arrest public attention by the wording of their copy, a wide scope is often left for the genius of the printer either in displaying them tastefully and effectively, or, when display type is not permissible, in classifying and arranging them to good advantage. Circumstances vary so much that it is impossible to lay down any general rule applicable to this subject, unless it be the obvious one that the compositor should seek to comprehend fully the leading idea or ideas which the advertiser wishes to impress upon the public, and put forth his best efforts to give typographical prominence to them.

The tax on advertisements collected in the United States under the Internal Revenue Law, in the years named below, was as follows: 1863, $40,628.59; 1864, $133,315.11; 1865, $227,530.21; 1866, $290,605.31; 1867, $288,009.80. As the rate charged was three per cent., it indicated that nearly ten millions of dollars per annum were paid for newspaper advertising alone, and it is probable that at the present time $15,000,000 per annum are expended in this country for this purpose.

We give below the returns, by States and Cities, of the Internal Revenue tax on advertisements which was collected for the fiscal year ending June 30, 1867, that being the last year this tax was imposed. It will be seen that tax was paid on advertising receipts amounting to $9,600,323; and the tax paid in the respective States and Cities furnishes a good indication of the distribution of advertising patronage during the year:

BY STATES.

Alabama	$1,584 58	New Hampshire	$706 38
California	10,218 08	New Jersey	1,385 62
Connecticut	2,421 51	New York	99,552 47
Delaware	43 44	Ohio	20,614 61
Dist. of Columbia	4,925 11	Oregon	854 83
Georgia	1,050 51	Pennsylvania	39,343 69
Illinois	15,806 14	Rhode Island	1,935 75
Indiana	1,447 42	South Carolina	3,023 03
Iowa	681 49	Tennessee	5,269 71
Kentucky	5,999 71	Utah Territory	92 07
Louisiana	13,741 85	Vermont	163 53
Maine	1,363 63	Virginia	2,332 62
Maryland	6,898 93	West Virginia	670 32
Massachusetts	25,199 72	Wisconsin	2,928 66
Michigan	3,175 10		
Minnesota	1,116 84	Total	$288,009 80
Missouri	13,470 45		

BY CITIES.

Baltimore, Md.	$6,898 93	Chicago, Ill.	$14,700 91
Boston	22,975 76	Cincinnati, Ohio	15,804 33
Charleston, S. C.	3,923 03	Cleveland, Ohio	3,099 15

Detroit, Mich	3,175 10	Philadelphia	29,630 49
Hartford, Conn	1,945 23	Pittsburgh	6,830 67
Louisville, Ky.	5,999 71	Portland, Me	1,138 48
Memphis, Tenn	2,670 72	Providence, R. I.	1,935 75
Milwaukie, Wis.	2,267 13	Richmond, Va.	2,272 14
Mobile, Ala.	1,584 58	Sacramento, Cal.	1,976 92
Nashville, Tenn	2,598 99	San Francisco, Cal.	8,233 16
New Orleans, La.	13,620 79	St. Louis, Mo.	13,412 90
New York City	82,661 96	Washington, D. C.	4,925 11

Affiche.—A French word for placard, bill, or hand-bill, which has been adopted by some English authorities. Literally, a paper or bill affixed to a wall.

Affix, more generally styled Suffix.—A letter or syllable added at the end of a word, as print-er, one who prints, writ-er, one who writes.

Agate.—The name of a body type. It is chiefly used in newspaper work, and is of modern introduction. It is the next size smaller than Nonpareil, and larger than Pearl. There are about fourteen ems to the inch. It probably originated in the necessities of newspaper publishers. As patronage increased, it became desirable to have a type less in size than Nonpareil, for the advertisements, shipping news, markets, etc.; and Agate was made to meet the emergency. It is now extensively used for pocket editions of the Bible and Prayer Books. (See TYPE.)

Alauzet, P., of Paris, is the inventor of a printing press which has attracted attention in France of late years. Its special aim is to apply the pressure deliberately, and at the same time to insure a quick movement of the form after the impression has been made.

Alden, Timothy, the inventor of the Alden Type-Setting and Distributing Machine, was born at Yarmouth, Massachusetts, June 14, 1819, and died in the city of New York, December 4, 1858. At the age of sixteen he entered the office of the Barre Gazette, published in Barre, Massachusetts, where he learned to be a compositor, and continued laboring as a practical printer until 1846. When only nineteen years of age (1838), he announced his purpose of inventing a type-setting machine, and although his project was ridiculed as visionary he continued to devote his best thoughts and energies to its realization. He removed to New York in 1846, and thenceforth applied himself sedulously to his favorite idea with such success that a practical (although not a perfect) machine was completed and patented in this and other countries in 1856. By this time incessant toil and mental anxiety had so pressed upon his spirits, that his vitality gave way, and his health rapidly declined until the day of his death.

Alden Type-Setting and Distributing Machine.—More money and labor have been lavished upon this machine than upon any other similar effort. The life-long labors of the inventor have been supplemented by many efforts to simplify the ingenious mechanism he devised, to increase its effectiveness, and to adapt it to diversified typographical purposes. And yet, while the fact that it can set and distribute type with great rapidity has been clearly and repeatedly demonstrated, it has not attained, in a commercial sense, practical success. Perhaps nothing will give a better idea, in brief space, of the complicated character of its mechanism, than the statement that it contains 14,626 parts or pieces, and weighs more than 1460 pounds, while the price for which it could be manufactured, as estimated in a report to the stockholders in 1865, was $2000. It is claimed that it can set up more than 4000 ems per hour, and asserted that it has set up and distributed 1000 ems, solid, in ten minutes, without making a single error; but it is acknowledged to be difficult to have more than 4000 ems per hour justified. The machine has been tested in apartments connected with the leading newspaper offices of New York, but it has not supplemented compositors in any of them, and it remains to be seen whether the varied obstacles its projectors have encountered from time to time will ever be fully surmounted. The statements given above are based upon information contained in an elaborate and handsomely printed report made to the stockholders in 1865 (the printing of which, alone, is said to have cost $11,000); but we learn that since that period the machine has been remodeled and simplified, the number of pieces or parts greatly diminished, the Type-Setting and Distributing Machines separated so that each is distinct in itself, and that now (1871) the machine as reconstructed is believed by those who have it in charge, to be on the point of attaining complete practical success. (See ALDEN, TIMOTHY and TYPE-SETTING MACHINES.)

Aldine Editions.—The works published by the famous family of Manutius at Venice and Rome from 1494 to 1597. The Greek and Latin works of this house were so celebrated for their accuracy and commanded such high prices that the emblem of the Aldi, a dolphin twined around an anchor, was frequently counterfeited by other early printers. The Aldi also published the works of Petrarch, Boccaccio, and Dante. The Greek text of the Aldi was very fine, but their books are most celebrated for the introduction of Italic, first used in the Virgil of 1501.

Aldus.—The popular contraction of the name of Theobaldus Manutius (born 1446, died 1515), the head of the family of great Italian typographers generally styled the Aldi,—the name being written Manutius with the plural Manutii, also as Aldus, Aldi, with the anglicized form of Alduses, and in French des Aldes, and Manuce.

Theobaldus Manutius, a man of great learning, was born at Bassiano, in the Papal States, in 1446, and became the tutor of Albertus Pius, a prince of the house of Carpi. When on a visit with his pupil to the famous Mirandola, his attention was first drawn to the new art of printing as the best means of popularizing the learning then restricted to the few. Under the influence of this motive, Manutius went to Venice in 1488, selecting this city as best suited to the completion of his design, and in 1494 commenced the celebrated editions that bear his name.

The remarkable learning of Manutius attracted to him many pupils and the friendship of the distinguished scholars of many countries, while his generosity and wealth made his house a refuge to numbers of the learned fugitives who fled from Constantinople when it was captured by the Turks in the year 1500. These Grecians assisted much in perfecting his Greek publications, and aided him in the laborious and expensive task of collecting the most perfect manuscripts.

Aldus modified the Roman text into the beautiful form now known as the Italic. This character was at first called Venetian, and by the Germans Cursiv or running type, and was intended to distinguish the portions not belonging to the body of the book, such as prefaces, introductions, annotations, etc. The first book printed in Italic type was published in 1501, and had the following title: Virgilius; Venet: Apud Aldum. Aldus also improved punctuation. His Greek type was large, rounded, and elegant, adorned with frequent ligatures, adding great beauty to the appearance. Many of his Greek works were interleaved with the Latin translation, a method followed by the house of Foulis, in Glasgow.

About the year 1500 Aldus printed the first leaf of a proposed edition of the Bible in the Hebrew, Greek, and Latin languages; the work was never completed, but it must be considered as the precursor of the modern Polyglot Bible.

Manutius was indefatigable in his endeavors to render his text perfect, and, besides welcoming the assistance of other scholars, devoted himself zealously to the correction of the press, a duty then requiring much learning, from the imperfect condition of the manuscripts upon which the printer was compelled to depend, and especially from the numerous abbreviations commonly used by the scribes, which Aldus endeavored to diminish. In order to assure to himself the leisure necessary for his labors, Manutius inscribed over his door: WHOEVER YOU ARE, ALDUS EARNESTLY ENTREATS YOU TO DISPATCH YOUR BUSINESS AS SOON AS POSSIBLE, AND THEN DEPART; UNLESS YOU COME HITHER, LIKE ANOTHER HERCULES, TO LEND HIM FRIENDLY ASSISTANCE; FOR HERE WILL BE WORK SUFFICIENT TO EMPLOY YOU, AND AS MANY AS ENTER THIS PLACE—which would be a good inscription for many modern printing-offices.

The disturbed condition of Italy is supposed to have suspended the publications of the Aldine Press from 1510 to 1515, and in the latter year Aldus Manutius died, leaving behind him the renown of having devoted the best years of his life and the whole of a large fortune to rescuing the literature of Greece and Rome from the oblivion of the middle ages.

After the death of Aldus his business was continued for nearly a century, first by his father-in-law, and subsequently by his sons, and their descendants, several of whom became scarcely less famous than their great progenitor.

Alexander, History of.—The first book printed in Europe, according to the authority of Papillon. The fact has been disputed, but he alleges that a twin brother and sister of Ravenna, known as the two Cunio, executed in the year 1284, 1285, or 1286, a series of eight blocks, representing, by pictures and verses, the life of Alexander the Great. Its frontispiece was as follows:

THE HEROIC ACTIONS, REPRESENTED IN FIGURES, of the great and magnanimous Macedonian King, the bold and valiant Alexander; dedicated, presented, and humbly offered to the most holy father Pope Honorius IV., the glory and support of the Church, and to our illustrious and generous father and mother, by us, Alessandro Alberico Cunio, Cavaliere, and Isabella Cunio, twin brother and sister: first reduced, imagined, and attempted to be executed in relief, with a small knife, on blocks of wood, made even and polished by this learned and dear sister, continued and finished by us together, at Ravenna, from the eight pictures of our invention, painted six times larger than here represented; engraved, explained by verses, and thus marked upon the paper to perpetuate the number of them, and to enable us to present them to our relations and friends, in testimony of gratitude, friendship, and affection. All this was done and finished by us, when only sixteen years of age.

Algebra, Composition of.—This is the most difficult description of work which a compositor has to perform, both on account of the accuracy required in justification, and the want of the necessary sorts in almost every printing-office.

The lower-case letters a, b, c, x, y, z, etc., are used in the formulas. They should be set in italic, if the lines in which they are placed be Roman, and vice versa. When capital letters are inserted, the Roman should be employed in all cases.

In setting two or more lines, the similar expressions in each should be placed one above the other, as:

$$8x + 9y + 8z = 2700$$
$$12x + 12y + 10z = 3600$$
$$ax + by + cz = d$$
$$a'x + b'y + c'z = d'$$
$$a''x + b''y + c''z = d''$$

When an equation is too long for the measure of the page, it should be divided either at the × or =, and each part must be justified in the centre of the line which it occupies.

Such words as Hence or Therefore, when used in this kind of work, should be placed at the commencement of the line, and when a figure is put in as a direction to some other formula, it should be put between parentheses or brackets, at the outer end of the line.

The short part of a fraction should be justified in the centre of the long, without reference to either being divisor or dividend, and the space-rule which separates them should be equal in length to the larger part, as:

$$\frac{cb - y}{a} = \frac{B}{0.00001}$$

In putting together such examples as the above, the most expeditious method of proceeding is, to look along the line, and compose the longer part of each fraction, with the signs which may be between them, as:

$$cb - y = 0.00001$$

The line so composed should be placed on a galley, and each of these portions can be put in the composing-stick, as required, and the remainder of the compound line can be finished with very little trouble and without loss of time.—*Lynch's Manual.*

Algebraic Signs.—See SIGNS.

Almanac.—A table or book containing a calendar of days, weeks, and months, to which are usually added astronomical data, such as the rising and setting of the sun, moon, and planets, the changes of the moon, eclipses, times of the tides, church and national festivals, terms of court, and other matters of general interest. In distinguishing between the terms calendar and almanac, the former is a word received from the Greeks and Romans, signifying an orderly arrangement of the divisions of time, as days, weeks, etc., adapted to the purposes of civil life, and forming part of the almanac; while the latter, derived from the Arabic, is a measure of time, or a diary, and may therefore include miscellaneous matter of public or local interest.

The belief in astrology among the Arabians and Mohammedans created a demand for books which could be consulted for lucky or unlucky days, the planetary influences upon the human body, astrological and medicinal formula, etc. These works were brought by the Arabs into Spain, whence they spread through Europe. Many manuscript almanacs of the middle ages are preserved in libraries of Germany, France, and England.

From the very initiation of the art of typography, almanacs have furnished one of the most considerable items in printing. In primitive communities they are considered works of standard importance; and, as one of the best methods of advertising, they have been used of late years especially by the proprietors of patent medicines. Calendars or card almanacs are also considered a very effective business card by fancy or decorative printers and others.

Almanacs have been intimately connected with the history of typography from the earliest times: it is held by many authorities that the almanac of 1457 was the first specimen of printing, and it has been variously credited to Gutenberg, Schoeffer, and Pfister of Bamberg. The fabulous Dr. Faustus, whose story became so strangely blended with that of Fust, was the accredited author of almanacs containing necromantic secrets; in our own country Poor Richard was one of Benjamin Franklin's strongest claims to the gratitude of the mass of the people, who found it a treasury of wit and wisdom; and one of the greatest authors of modern Germany, Auerbach, first won his way to popular esteem by using this form as a means of instruction and entertainment, by adding to the almanac sketches and stories of current life and manners, and this example has been substantially followed by a number of English and American publishers.

Regiomontanus, a famous German mathematician under the patronage of Matthias Corvinus, King of Hungary, published a series of almanacs from 1475 to 1506, and yearly almanacs became an established custom in the sixteenth century. Henry III. of France, in 1579, enacted that the almanac should not be made the instrument of partisan politics by the introduction of prophecies against parties and individuals in the state. The first almanac in the modern shape appeared in England in 1673; it was compiled by Maurice Wheeler, Canon of Christ Church, Oxford, and was printed in that city. The sale was so great that the booksellers of London bought off the copyright in order to monopolize its subsequent sales. The Almanac Royal of Paris, 1679, contained notices of past times, court reception days, fairs, and markets, to which were added soon afterward the genealogy of the reigning house, a list of the clergy, etc. In England James I. granted a monopoly of the trade to the Universities and the Stationers' Company, subject to the censorship of the Archbishop of Canterbury and the Bishop of London. The Universities accepted an annuity from their colleagues, and resigned the active exercise of their privilege into the hands of the Stationers. Under their supervision were conducted the popular almanacs known as Moore's and Partridge's, the latter of which was attacked with great humor by Swift. Poor Robin's Almanac, published from 1652 to 1828, may probably have furnished a sort of model, at least in title, for Dr. Franklin's Poor Richard, a name chosen perhaps by that preacher of common sense to correct the evil effects of that ancient and most worthy legend of Robin and Richard, who were two pretty men, although they persisted in lying in bed till the clock struck ten, in utter defiance of his own precept of

> Early to bed and early to rise
> Makes a man healthy, wealthy, and wise.

Popular superstitions and the extravagancies of astrology found room in these almanacs; the Stationers, like a genuine corporation, having no personality of their own and exhibiting no special bias except for what would sell, as was particularly proved in 1624, when they issued the usual predictions in one almanac and contradicted them most contemptuously in another. The heathenish character of these superstitions was severely reprobated by the Puritans, for whom the almanac of Allstree was prepared, as was asserted, to

> Leave lying astrology
> And write true astronomy.

The popular Moore's Almanac purported to be edited by Francis Moore, physician. The original Francis Moore died in 1724, but the publication was still pursued as if under his supervision, and in 1775 a vigorous rival arose in another almanac claiming to be by the genuine Francis Moore. A great law-suit followed, which was decided against the monopoly of the Stationers' Company. A bill to renew and legalize the privilege was brought into the House of Commons by Lord North in 1779, but Lord Erskine most bril-

liantly exposed the absurdity and even indecency of the publication, and the bill was defeated. Although the privilege was thus destroyed, the Stationers purchased their rival, and continued to hold the field with a but slightly improved style of publications until 1828, when the Society for the Diffusion of Useful Knowledge published the British Almanac and demolished their predecessors with the able assistance of the daily press, which so vigorously assailed the Stationers' publications that the Company was constrained to follow the new example in the Englishman's Almanac.

The uniform price for an English Almanac for many years was a penny, but the monopoly increased the price, and the imposition of the stamp taxes after Queen Anne's time raised it still more. In 1781 Moore's Almanac was nine pence, two being for the stamp; in 1796 it rose to sixteen pence, and in 1816 to two shillings and three pence. Between 1821 and 1830 the duty produced an average yearly revenue of 31,000 pounds sterling to the government, but under William IV. this duty, then of fifteen pence per stamp, was abolished. In evasion of the stamp acts a shabby penny almanac was produced in England, and many are still sold for that price.

An almanac was established by Isaiah Thomas in Worcester, Massachusetts, which gained and established an extraordinary repute in 1780 from the happy accident that as it was being set up one of the boys asked what should be placed against the 13th of July. Mr. Thomas in careless haste answered, Any thing, anything! The lad, literally obedient, set up Rain, hail, and snow. The diligent readers were surprised, but when the day came the prediction was fulfilled—it really did rain, hail, and snow on the said 13th of July, and the fortune of the almanac was made.

The Almanach de Gotha, now one hundred and eight years old, is the best known of the German publications; the Connaissance des Temps has been a scientific authority to one class, as is the Nautical Almanac to another; and the Almanach des Gourmands has its devout students, as well as the innumerable publications of compacted facts published so numerously as the organs of special crafts, industries, and sciences.

Allen's Automatic Envelope Press.—This is a new American invention which has been successfully applied to the rapid printing of envelopes,—the rate of speed being about 6000 impressions per hour.

Alley.—The space between two opposite stands or frames. This is also sometimes called a corner.

Alphabet, The.—Dignified by the sonorous syllables of the Greek, this word is a mere translation of our nursery a, b, with the advantage of being composed of the more erudite and impressive alpha beta of classic learning. The accepted definition is simply the letters of a language, which leaves still open for discussion the point of what constitutes a letter, and whether the signs of the Chinese, the syllable writing of the Cherokees, and the hieroglyphic presentments of the Egyptians, can be classed as letters. If by the word letter, is meant an arbitrary sign representing a single vocal utterance, the most cultivated languages will be found defective in phonetic accuracy, and the modern system of phonography will come nearest to the true alphabet, in which every vocal sound must be represented by a distinctive symbol.

So much has been said and thought and written upon the origin and growth of written language, that the subject has been obscured by the very weight of the evidence adduced and the diversity of the deductions drawn therefrom. Modern investigation, in ascertaining some points with greater accuracy, has so generally deranged both dates and data as still more to confuse the discussion; and the technical students array themselves in solid phalanxes upon the banks of the Nile, the Euphrates, the Ganges, and the Hoang-ho, and discharge volleys of linguistic ammunition into each other's ranks, so full of sound and fire and fury as to wrap the combat in veiling smoke from the eyes of the unlearned observer.

The controversy was also long embittered by theological and metaphysical disputes, in which one party, comprising many learned men, strenuously advocated the doctrine that the construction of an alphabet is beyond the power of human reason, and that it was a direct gift from Heaven.

While the accumulations of learning were being ransacked for the arguments pro and con, the logical method of forming a written language received a curious exemplification in the creation of the Cherokee alphabet. This instance of the formation of an alphabet by the efforts of an individual, although perhaps familiar to many readers, will bear repetition on account of its value in the consideration of the subject.

The incident furnishes, in its minutest particulars, a singular condensation of the whole history of the origin and development of a written language, and is rendered only the more veracious and useful to the argument, by divesting it of that surrounding of romance by which many writers at first detracted from its probability by insisting that the author, Sequayah, or George Guess, was a wild, uncultivated savage, utterly unacquainted even with the fact that other nations possessed methods of written communication. Instead of this being the case, this famous Cherokee Cadmus was of mixed race, some of the blood of scholastic Scotland running in his veins, and his trade of silversmith giving still further assurance that he had possessed the advantages of intercourse with the white race. Notwithstanding these facts, it is still certain that he endeavored, unassisted, to form an alphabet for a hitherto exclusively vocalized language, and that circumstances compelled him to pursue his invention by a natural or progressive method, such as has most probably ordered the growth of those alphabets which have been formed by the course of centuries instead of months. That the Cherokee was

acquainted at least with the appearance of a variety of written symbols, is evident from his appropriating individual characters from various languages for his own service, although he has used them without reference to their established value in the alphabets to which they belong.

During the French and Indian wars a white prisoner was seized by a band of Cherokees. He had a letter in his possession which they compelled him to read, and, as was afterward proved, he had misled them as to its contents. This letter became the theme of much interest and discussion among the savages, many of them upholding the opinion that this means of communication was a gift from the Great Spirit to the white men, while some others, among whom was Sequayah, maintained that it was a discovery due to the white man's own intelligence. Frequently the young man meditated on this idea, without practical result, until many years afterward, when quite advanced in life, he became crippled. Then, in his enforced solitude, his mind reverted to his old problem. Following the natural method, he first attempted a system of picture-writing or hieroglyphics, but soon discarded it as cumbrous and inconvenient, and endeavored to establish a phonetic alphabet. Having systematized the Cherokee tongue under two hundred sounds, he undertook to make his daughter his first pupil. She showed remarkable aptitude for the study, and with her help he speedily reduced the number of characters to eighty-six, which remains as the number of the Cherokee alphabet. This alphabet, although containing so many characters, has been most methodically constructed: thus, five simple vowel sounds are first represented; the rest of the alphabet consists entirely of single letters which represent these vowel sounds preceded by a consonant. In this manner, after the simple vowel a, comes an array of other characters representing separately ga, ka, ha, la, ma, na, sa, etc.; and the same method is used with every vowel, so that the alphabet is really a systematic arrangement of the syllables of the Cherokee language. That the author, while he derived material assistance from his possession of copies of our letters, was entirely ignorant of their names, seems to be proved by the curious and incongruous selection of characters. Some of his letters are absolute inventions: thus he took the Roman capital D for a, W for la, R for e, T for i, H for mi, A for go, Z for no, Y for to, K for tso. Other Roman capitals are used in the same unsystematic fashion, while some other letters seem taken from the Greek; the Arabic numeral 4 represents se, and 6 stands for wo; a few look like modified German, and several appear to have been derived from an apothecary's prescription. This singular combination has, of course, made a most inharmonious text, in which upright angular k's and 4's stand in unseemly distinctness amid companions formed of flowing curves and convolutions.

Much learning has been lavished on the construction of tabular presentments, intended to prove that the alphabets of all other languages have been de-

ANCIENT EGYPTIAN (Monumental, Cursive)	PHŒNICIAN	ANCIENT GREEK	LATIN	MŒSO GOTHIC (Form, Sound)	CHEROKEE

LATIN

A, B, C, D, E, F, Z, H, —, I, K, L, M, N, —, O, P, —, Q, R, S, T

MŒSO GOTHIC (Form — Sound)

Form	Sound
λ	A
Ᏼ	B
Γ	G
ᴅ	D
Є	E
Ᏻ	F
Ç	G or J
h	H
ï or I	I
κ	K
λ	L
м	M
н	N
Ꝗ	O
п	P
⊙	HW
s	S
т	T
ψ	TH
п	U
u	CW
ѵ	W
х	CH
z	Z

CHEROKEE

a	o
ga ka	go
ha	ho
la.	lo
ma	mo
na hna Gnah	no
qua	quo
a sa sa	xo
da ta	to
dla tla	tlo
tsa	tso
wa	wo
ya	yo
e	u
ge	gu
he	hu
le	lu
me	mu
ne	nu
que	quu
se	su
de te	du
tle	tlu
tse	tnu
we	wu
ye	yu
i	v
gi	gv
hi	hv
li	lv
mi	nv
ni	quv
qui	si... sv
si	dv
di ti	tlv
tli	tsv
tsi	wv
wi	yv
yi	

rived from some one or other of the more ancient tongues; and certain similarities may be sufficiently marked to offer strong grounds for the wordy controversy by which each party traces the progress of language from the river to the ends of the earth, with only the difference as to whether the birthplace of learning be the river of Egypt or of Chaldea, of India or of China.

Whether it is believed that the dim and shadowy resemblances still lingering between the languages of nations now separated by oceans and continents, are to be traced back to the tongue spoken by the multitude upon the plain of Shinar, or that the original alphabet was expressed by Divine Power upon tablets of stone, the facts of history prove that the mind of man, craving the means of communicating with his comrades, first finds it in oral language; and eventually requiring to give his thought permanent existence in some form of visible sign, (either for preservation to future times or for communication to the absent,) he is compelled to use some method of delineation, which is naturally at first hieroglyphic in character, and gradually progresses into simpler, readier, and more convenient shapes, until it reaches the current handwriting of our present civilized nations.

So generally has this want been felt that nearly all nations have some method of representation, various forms of picture-writing being practiced by every tribe upon the American continent, excepting the inferior races at the extreme North and South, as well as by all other savages except the most degraded aborigines of Africa.

The first step in the progress toward a written language, consists in the mere rude delineation in which the savage emblazons the glories of a victory in a meagre outline upon the rocky precipice that overhangs the scene, or warns his friend of danger by a picture of a bird's feather, or offers peace to his enemy in the figure of a calumet.

The next step of progress will attach to these pictures more complex and symbolical meanings. The design that at first merely expressed a fact, will be required to convey a thought, and the subtleties of the hieroglyphics are gradually evolved by the necessities of the occasion. When these writings become numerous, and the records are more various and comprehensive, the symbolism grows burdensome as well as insufficient, and new ideas must demand new clothing, until the germs of an alphabet are at last developed. Thus, in the hieroglyphics of Egypt, the picture came to represent the first sound of the name of the figure used, after the fashion in which our juvenile readers are taught that

A was an Archer, that shot at a frog;
B was a Butcher, that had a big dog.

The theory that the alphabet has been produced by a gradual transition from the simply pictorial to the altered or conventional, and lastly to the phonetic, receives confirmation from the fact that in some languages certain of the letters resembled the forms of

the things of which they were at first the symbols. Thus, the Hebrew equivalent of our vowel a is called aleph, or the ox, and the original character itself bore a resemblance to the head and horns of an ox, so that in the nursery rhyme of the young Hebrew the a not only stood for, but veritably was, the aleph itself. In the same alphabet, the g, ghimel, signifying camel, resembled the long neck and head of that animal; while the d, or daleth, meaning a door, reproduced the door as delineated in Egyptian hieroglyphics. Similar, though less marked, resemblances have been found in other antique characters; and by following this course of reasoning, it is claimed that links have been established between the Egyptian hieroglyphics and the Hebrew and Phœnician alphabets, by which the ultimate origin of the shape and name of a number of our modern letters is traced back substantially as follows:

A to Aleph, or an ox.
B to a house, called Beth by the Hebrews.
Ch or K to a vase, named Kelol by the Egyptians.
D to a door or archway, called Daleth by the Hebrews.
G or Gh to a camel, called Ghimel by the Hebrews.
H to a hand.
I or J to a hand or a band and forearm.
K to the palm of the hand, called Kaph by the Hebrews.
M to a spot, or water, called Mem by the Hebrews.
N to a fish or serpent.
Ph or P to the mouth, called Phe by the Hebrews.
R to the head, called Resch by the Hebrews.
Sh or S to the teeth, called Shin by the Hebrews.
Z to a line, or blade, or sword, called Zain by the Hebrews.

In tracing an alphabet by this method, it would be unjust not to overlook a great amount of discrepancy as comparatively non-essential, by allowing for the almost unlimited variation possible in a written character. It is a fact daily verified, for notwithstanding the efforts of generations of schoolmasters and the laborious endeavors of students to form their calligraphy upon received models, individual handwriting has the singular peculiarity of offering one of the most certain methods of revealing personal idiosyncrasies, and varying with the endless varieties of the character of mind that finds unintentionally a sort of reflex in the character that flows from the pen.

The Jewish Rabbis claim priority for the Hebrew alphabet in the assurance that it was used before the flood (Josephus alleges that he had seen the writing of Seth), and that it is the parent of all written languages; while their opponents allege that the alphabet must be sought in that learning of the Egyptians of which Moses was a master, or in the labors of the Phœnicians, by whom it was transmitted through Greece to the rest of Europe. A school of modern philologists, by the evidence drawn from linguistic research, also trace back to Chaldea, where the shepherds, as they watched their flocks, were either wooed into poetic revery by the soothing breeze, or stimulated into studious observation by the evolutions of the stars overhead, and thus became the source whence learning spread in two streams, one turning westward to find its first resting-place in Egypt, and the other eastward to be welcomed by the contemplative Hindu.

There is little that is original or comparatively modern in our own alphabet. Still, like everything else connected with our language, it has undergone some modifications. The letter w is of comparatively modern origin, and it was formed by a union of two u's or v's, the early English v being identical with u in the Latin. In the last century, the English alphabet proper contained but twenty-four letters, for j and v consonant, although sometimes used, were not supposed to be entitled to the honors of a full admission. The names of some of the letters have also been materially changed. Thus, Z has been named Izzard, Zed, and Zee, by successive generations of American school-boys; and H, which we pronounce aitch, was up to a recent period, and perhaps is at present, called haitch by the best English authorities.

Independent of the grand divisions of the alphabet into consonants and vowels, subdivisions have been made by various authors. One work classifies g, e, d, t, b, p, as consonants; j, s, and z as sibilants; r, l, n, and m as liquids; and a, e, i, o, u, w, and y as vowels; and consonants have also been classified as dentals, labials, mutes, spirants, nasals, and semivowels, etc. (See CONSONANT, DENTAL, LABIAL, LIQUID, MUTE, SIBILANT, SPIRANT, and VOWEL.)

As the number of sounds and articulations differs in various languages, so the number of letters differs in the alphabets of different nations, although not in proportion to their respective copiousness. The English alphabet contains twenty-six letters; French, twenty-five; Hebrew, Chaldee, Syriac, and Samaritan, twenty-two; Arabic, twenty-eight; Persian, thirty-one; Turkish, thirty-three; Georgian, thirty-six; Coptic, thirty-two; Muscovite, forty-three; Greek, twenty-four; Latin, twenty-five; Slavonic, twenty-seven; Dutch, twenty-six; Spanish, twenty-seven; Italian, twenty; Ethiopic and Tartarian, two hundred and two; Sanscrit, fifty; Bengalese, twenty-one; Burmese, nineteen. The Chinese, properly speaking, have no alphabet, unless we call their whole language their alphabet.

Printed collections of more than two hundred alphabets have been made, by embracing different varieties or dialects.

The type-founders have cast Arabic, Armenian, Coptic, Domesday, Engrossing, Ethiopic, Etruscan, German, Greek, Alexandrian Greek, Gothic, Hebrew, Irish, Malabaric, Malayan, Bengalese, Burmese, Persian, Phonetic, Runic, Russian, Samaritan, Sanscrit, Saxon, Sclavonian (or ancient Russian), Script (imitation of writing), Swedish, Syriac, Tamul, Telegu, and Turkish, besides black letter, music, and a great variety of fancy types. The Imperial press at Paris is said to possess the type of fifty-six Eastern languages, being all that are known of the characters of Asia, ancient and modern, also the type of sixteen European tongues which do not use the ordinary Roman characters.

It is deemed sufficient, in this work, to give representations of a few of the most ancient or striking alphabets, and of those most likely to be used occasionally in American printing-offices.

German Alphabet.

Character.		Signification.		Name.
𝔄	a	A	a	Au
𝔅	b	B	b	Bey
ℭ	c	C	c	Tsey
𝔇	d	D	d	Dey
𝔈	e	E	e	Ey
𝔉	f	F	f	Ef
𝔊	g	G	g	Gey, or Gay
𝔥	h	H	h	Hau
𝔦	i	I	i	E
𝔧	j	J	j	Yot
𝔎	k	K	k	Kau
𝔏	l	L	l	El
𝔐	m	M	m	Em
𝔑	n	N	n	En
𝔒	o	O	o	O
𝔓	p	P	p	Pey
𝔔	q	Q	q	Koo
𝔯	r	R	r	Err
𝔖	fs	S	fs	Ess
𝔗	t	T	t	Tey
𝔘	u	U	u	Oo
𝔙	v	V	v	Fou
𝔚	w	W	w	Vey
𝔛	x	X	x	Iks
𝔜	y	Y	y	Ypsilon
𝔷	z	Z	z	Tset

The Greek Alphabet.

Figure.		Name.	Power.
A	α	Alpha	a
B	β b	Beta	b
Γ	γ ʃ	Gamma	g
Δ	δ	Delta	d
E	ε	Epsilon	e short
Z	ζ	Zeta	z
H	η	Eta	e long
Θ	θ ϑ	Theta	th
I	ι	Iota	i
K	κ	Kappa	k or c
Λ	λ	Lambda	l
M	μ	Mu	m
N	ν	Nu	n

Figure.		Name.	Power.
Ξ	ξ	Xi	x
O	ο	Omicron	o short
Π	π ϖ	Pi	p
P	ρ	Rho	r
Σ	σ ς [1]	Sigma	s
T	τ	Tau	t
Υ	υ	Upsilon	u
Φ	φ φ	Phi	ph
X	χ	Chi	ch
Ψ	ψ	Psi	ps
Ω	ω	Omega	o long

[1] σ, middle; ς, final.

The Hebrew Alphabet.

Name.	Figure.	Similitude.	Sound or Power of the Letters.	Num. ber.
Aleph	א	Fi- nals.	A *spiritus lenis*, or soft breathing, indicating the bare opening of the mouth, and simple emission of the voice.	1
Bheth	ב	ב כ	*bh*, very soft; with dagesh, ב b hard.	2
Ghimel	ג	ג ג	*gh*, very soft; with dagesh, ג g hard.	3
Dhaleth	ד	ד ד ר	*dh*, very soft, as in that; with dagesh, ד d hard.	4
He	ה	ח ה ת	a *spiritus densus* or thick, hard breathing.	5
Vau	ו	ו ו ו	v, or the digamma vv, s or s between vowels, as in *miser*.	6
Zajin	ז			7
Hbeth	ח		hh, a very hard or thick breathing, harder than ה, softer than כ, somewhat similar in sound to the Greek χ chi.	8
Teth	ט	ט ט	t.	9
Jodh	י		i or j.	10
Chaph	כ	ך כ	c or ch, harder than ה with a dagesh, it sounds like ך k.	20
Lamedh	ל		n.	30
Mem	מ	ם	m.	40
Nun	נ	ן	n.	50
Samech	ס	ס	s, sounds like the hissing of a goose or serpent.	60
Ghnain	ע	ע ע	sounds like the bleating of a calf in the absence of its dam.	70
Phe	פ	ף פ	ph or f; with a dagesh, פ p.	80
Tzade	צ	ץ ץ	ts, with a harder hiss than ן.	90
Koph	ק		k or q.	100
Resh	ר		r, the canine or larking letter, imitating by the quivering of the tongue, the snarling growl of a dog.	200
Schin	ש		sch, pointed on the right, it sounds sch (or sh, on the left s.	300
Sin	ש			
Thau	ת		th, as in thief, smith; with a dagesh ת t, hard.	400

Alterations.—It is the duty of the office to see that no proof of displayed work is submitted to the customer, unless it is done in a workmanlike manner. If it is badly or tastelessly arranged, the office should bear the loss of making the alteration. The customer should not, unless it has been done strictly according to his special directions. The office, as an expert, should decide what is, or what is not, workmanlike,—the standard being, not the productions of some specially skillful workman, but those of the average of ordinary good compositors. If the work is decided to be displayed fairly, then the customer should be charged with the expense of all alterations. Where the suggested alteration is trivial, it may not be worth while to insist on the claim; but in all cases the customer should be forewarned that he buys only the labor of good average workmen, and that the expense of all improvements he may suggest is justly chargeable to him.—*De Vinne's Price List.*

America, Early Printing in.—All writers on the history of printing agree that the first press in the New World was established in the city of Mexico, and that this event took place in the sixteenth century; but when details come to be considered, conflicting theories are set up and diverse statements made. One of these accounts claims that the first Spanish Viceroy of Mexico, Antonio de Mendoza, who went to Mexico in 1535, and who was distinguished for his devotion to literature, established a printing-office some years before 1551, and that the printer employed by him, whose name was Joannes Paulus Brissensius, or Lombardus, a native of Brescia, in Italy, was the first who plied the art preservative in America. For a time one of his books, a folio volume executed in 1549, was cited as the first book printed in America. Another and perhaps more correct theory is that printing was first established in Mexico by the Spanish missionaries, and the fact seems to be established that under their auspices a book, one mutilated copy of which is still in existence in a private library in Madrid, was printed in 1540, by Juan Cromberger, who died about 1544, and who was probably the first printer in America. The colophon of the work in question, as given in The Proof-Sheet by S. J. Hamilton, is as follows:

This Manual for Adults was printed in the great city of Mexico, by the command and at the expense of the most reverend men, Bishops of New Spain, at the house of Juan Cromberger, in the year of the nativity of our Lord Jesus Christ one thousand five hundred and forty. On the 13th day of the month of December.

It is quite certain that the printing-press was actively employed in Mexico in less than a century after the new art became generally known in Europe, and for nearly a century before a printing-press was introduced into the present limits of the United States. The second American city in which a printing-office was established was Lima, Peru, where a work designed to assist the priests in the study of the language of the natives appeared in 1586.

At Cambridge, Massachusetts, as Isaiah Thomas assures us, in January, 1639, printing was first performed in that part of North America which extends from the Gulf of Mexico to the Frozen Ocean.

The history of this first press opens with sorrow; the Rev. Jesse Glover, through whose exertions it had been secured, and who contributed largely to the purchase, died upon his voyage to the New World; and we find his heirs afterward suing their mother's second husband, their step-father, for the possession of the press, which was regarded as Glover's personal property, although worked for and subject to the authority of the College of Cambridge, the president of which was censor of the press and responsible for all publications, until licensers were appointed by law in 1662, the press never being enfranchised in Massachusetts until as late as 1755.

Glover's press was put into working condition in 1639 by Stephen Daye, who began his labors with the publication bearing the ominous title The Freeman's Oath. (See FREEMAN'S OATH.) Land was voted to Daye by the Government, some of which land he mortgages one year for a cow, a calf, and a heifer; next year finds him in prison on some unstated charge, and released on a bond for £100. That this unfortunate typo relinquished the responsibility of managing this press in 1648, and became foreman for his successor, Samuel Green, is not astonishing, if we judge of his prosperity by the fact that we find him in 1656 suing for £100 of unpaid wages, and petitioning, after sixteen years, for a confirmation of the original grant of land, on account of the services for which he had never yet any considerable satisfaction; and he dies two years afterward.

How Green (the second printer in the United States) fared in money matters we do not know, excepting that three hundred acres of land, wherever it could be found, was granted to him for his encouragement, in 1658; and this same land seems never to have been found until 1667, when it is recorded that three hundred acres of land were laid out to Ensign Samuel Green, of Cambridge, printer, in the wilderness on the north of Merrimac river.

The art of printing, true to its representative function, soon came into immediate relation with the two great problems of American society—the Indian and the negro. But just in the points where it would seem destined to come to grief, events consistent in their very inconsistency seemed to be especially fortunate, for an Indian boy, taught at the charity school of Cambridge to read and write English, was apprenticed in 1659 to Samuel Green, and forthwith became a worthy member of society, under the name of James the Printer, or James Printer. He rendered such effectual aid upon the Indian Bible, that, in the language of John Eliot, he had but one man, viz., the Indian printer, that was able to compose the sheets and correct the press with understanding; and the Psalter of 1709, in the Indian and English languages, bears the imprint, printed by B. Green and J. Printer for the Honorable Company for the Propagation of the Gospel among the Indians in New England. James seems to have conducted himself as a good citizen and industrious workman, only evincing his native characteristics once by secretly stealing off to join King Philip; but, as the war ended disastrously, James conformed to the condition of the amnesty proclamation of 1676, and exchanged his new title of James the Apostate for the more worthy one of James the Printer, and returned zealously to his work.

The negro appears first in an American printing-office under direction of Thomas Fleet, who fled to this country for refuge from the rage of an insensate London mob to Boston, where he established a printing-house with the sign of the Heart and Crown, in which his sons afterward also printed acceptably, changing the obnoxious crown into a Bible. Fleet owned several negroes, one of whom he taught not only to work the press but to set type. He found special profit in printing small books for children, and popular ballads; and these little books were rendered more attractive by the wood engravings cut for them by this negro artist. Cæsar and Pompey, the sons of this negro, born in Fleet's house, also became printers, and remained in the office of their master's sons.

The first firmly established newspaper in North America appeared in 1704, but full fourteen years before that date one number of a newspaper had been published in Boston, which was instantly suppressed by the authorities. To the publisher, Richard Harris, an Englishman with a deal of mercury in his natural temper, this was no new experience, for he had at home, in England, been fined for selling a Protestant petition, during King Charles's reign, and he had also fallen into trouble for printing a book with the dangerous title of English Liberties; besides this, he was once set in the pillory, but his wife (like a kind rib) stood by him to defend her husband against the mob.

Boston seems to have entered early upon the peculiar literary rôle that has been her distinguishing trait in modern times. The first attempt was made under the guidance of James Franklin, an older brother of Benjamin, who, in 1721, established a periodical which he made the organ of a company of literary gentlemen who seemed to have formed a mutual union of total dissent. It was intended, after the manner of its great successor, the Dial, to show the world generally the time of day by assaulting all established beliefs and conventional manners and customs. The objects of attack that the Courant struck currently were, of course, the Government, the preachers, and lastly, inoculation. The aged minister, Increase Mather, publicly protested against the iniquity of the vile Courant, and warned its supporters against being Partakers in other Men's sins. James Franklin was put in jail for a month, and forbidden to print or publish the Courant or any Pamphlet or Paper of the like Nature except it be first supervised; and he was finally obliged to end a stormy career in Boston, by following the example of his more distinguished brother Benjamin, and abandoning that city for a more liberal locality.

In Pennsylvania, also, printing began in tribulation. William Bradford had been apprenticed in London to an intimate friend of George Fox, and had espoused his principles. He was among the very first emigrants that arrived in 1682, before the first house was built in Philadelphia, and set up a press probably at Burlington, or perhaps at Chester. In 1689 he lived in Philadelphia, and became soon (1692) embroiled in a religious feud by publishing a pamphlet written by George Keith, a Scotch Quaker, who had been condemned by the Friends of Philadelphia. Keith, forbidden to speak, printed his own defence, and the printer was arrested, imprisoned, and his form seized. After a lingering trial and imprisonment, embittered with all the feeling of sectarianism, the locked-up form was examined as evidence, and a justice or juror, in the endeavor to lift it into a position where it could be conveniently read, tipped it over, and the unfortunate Bradford's case was at length concluded by the mishap of pieing his form. Bradford received an invitation to settle in New York, and retreated thither.

Samuel Keimer, a printer, also gave great offence to the Quakers, and the monthly meeting of September, 1728, published an advertisement explaining that although he had published a parable, in which he had used such a stile and language, as that perhaps he may be deemed, where he is not known, to be one of the people called Quakers: This may, therefore, certifie, that said Samuel Keimer is not one of the said People, etc. Franklin, who was a journeyman of Keimer's, described him as a French convulsionist or Jansenist.

Keimer was unsuccessful in Philadelphia, and went to Barbadoes and published the Barbadoes Gazette, where his ill-fortune continued to attend him, according to his own published lamentation, viz.:

What a Pity it is that some modern Bravadoes,
Who dub themselves Gentlemen here in Barbadoes,
Should, Time after Time, run in Debt to their Printer,
And care not to pay him, in Summer or Winter!
* * * * * *
In Penn's Wooden Country, Type feels no Disaster.
The Printer is rich, and is made their Post Master;
His Father, a Printer, is paid for his work,
And wal ows in Plenty, Just now in New York.
* * * * * *
In Maryland's Province, as well as Virginia,
To Justice and Honour I aim, sirs, to win ye,
Their Printer, I m sure can make it appear,
Each Province allows two Hundred a year.

Parks, the lucky typo of Virginia, so envied by Keimer for possessing Swift's ideal income of two hundred pounds a year, was sheltered by government patronage from many of the ordinary ills of the craft; yet his fortunes were endangered by that last, worst foe of the typographer, that fell Briareus of the profession, that seems ever lurking in ambush to clutch the unwary printer in his manifold grasp—the libel suit. A man convicted of sheep-stealing at Williamsburg

had retired into obscurity and the backwoods, to reappear after many years, prosperous and respectable, as a member of the House of Burgesses. For reviving the recollection of this gentleman's peccadillo after forty years of oblivion, the printer was brought to trial; but as the proofs of the truth of the charge were, by special favor, received as a sufficient defence, the fortunate Parks triumphed, and the Virginian legislator again found refuge in private life.

'Twere long to tell and hard to trace the history of the disasters that attended the establishment of printing throughout the vast extent of our domain; and almost every reader bears in his own remembrance the story of some of the pioneer presses of the West, that removed from place to place like harbingers of the wonderful harvest that was to follow them—rude, lumbering machines seemingly instinct with the desire to plant civilization upon the far frontier, which by their own efforts was ever moving before them, and calling upon them to follow, despite all dangers, and accomplish their appointed work.

Coggeshall's Newspaper Record says:

There was a printing-press at

New London in Connecticut, in	.	.	1709
Annapolis in Maryland,	.	.	1726
Williamsburg in Virginia,	.	.	1729
Charleston in South Carolina,	.	.	1730
Newport in Rhode Island,	.	.	1732
Woodbridge in New Jersey,	.	.	1752
Newbern in North Carolina,	.	.	1755
Portsmouth in New Hampshire,	.	.	1756
Savannah in Georgia,	.	.	1762

The first printing-press established in the Northwest Territory was worked by William Maxwell, at Cincinnati, in 1793. The first printing executed west of the Mississippi was done at St. Louis, in 1808, by Jacob Hinkle.

There had been a printing-press in Kentucky in 1786, and there was one in Tennessee in 1793—in Michigan in 1809—in Mississippi in 1810. Louisiana had a press immediately after her acquisition by the United States.

Printing was done in Canada before the separation of the American Colonies from the mother country. Halifax had a press in 1751, and Quebec boasted of a printing-office in 1764.

American Inventions.—(See INVENTIONS.)

Ames, Joseph, born at Yarmouth in 1688, died October 7, 1758. He is best known as the author of Typographical Antiquities; being an Historical Account of Printing in England, with Memoirs of our Ancient Printers, and a Register of the Books printed by them, from the Year 1471 to 1600, with an Appendix concerning Printing in Scotland and Ireland to the Same Time. London, 1749. Mr. Ames was originally a plane-maker, and afterward became a ship-chandler at Wapping, where he carried on the business until his death. He was early attracted to the special line of study which resulted in Typographical Antiquities. In 1741 he was appointed secretary to the Society of Antiquaries, which position was of great advantage in the prosecution of his researches; he was also elected to the Royal Society. Besides his most important work, he printed a catalogue of English Printers from 1471 to 1700; An Index to Lord Pembroke's Coins; A Catalogue of English Heads, or an account of about 2000 prints, describing the peculiarities of each; and Parentalia, or Memoirs of the Family of Wren. He was a great collector of coins, books, manuscripts, prints, etc.

Ampersand.—A corruption and contraction of the words and, per se and, i. e., and, by itself and. A word used to describe the character &.—The character itself was formerly a ligature combining the letters of the Latin word Et, and, and its present shape was not adopted before 1750. It is used most appropriately between the names composing a firm, as Fust & Schoeffer, and although many printers continue to employ it in the abbreviation of et cetera, (&c.) it is better to use etc. for this purpose.

Ana.—A suffix to names of persons or places, used to denote a collection of memorable sayings. Thus, Scaligerana is a book containing the sayings of Scaliger. The termination is sometimes used alone, as a noun; as in Hallam's saying that the Table-talk of Selden is worth all the ana of the Continent.

Anaglyptography.—The art of so engraving as to give the subject an embossed appearance as if raised from the surface of the paper:—used in representing coins, bas-reliefs, and the like.—*Art Journal.* Beautiful specimens of this description of engraving are contained in the fac-similes of the medals of the United States Mint, which were executed by J. W. Steel, of Philadelphia, for Hon. J. Ross Snowden's work on the medals of the Mint.

Anastatic Printing.—This process, by which fac-similes of any printed matter, whether engravings or letter-press, can be obtained, attracted much attention some years ago, but, probably on account of the real or supposed superiority of other methods for accomplishing similar objects, it has never come into general use. It is based on the known properties of the articles employed, viz.: 1. Water attracts water; oil attracts oil; but each repels the other. 2. Metals are much more easily wetted with oil than with water; but they will readily be moistened by a weak solution of gum. 3. The power of wetting metals with water is greatly increased by the addition of phosphatic acid. 4. A part of the ink of any newly-printed book can be readily transferred by pressure to any smooth surface beneath; if, for example, a corner of a newspaper be fixed on a white sheet of paper, and then pressed or rubbed with a paper-knife, the letters will be distinctly seen in reverse on the paper. The process is based on these facts. The printed paper, whether letter-press or engraving, is first moistened with very dilute nitric acid (one part in seven), and, after being placed between blotting pads to remove superabundant moisture, is pressed with considerable force on a perfectly clean surface of zinc until every part of the sheet of paper is brought in contact with the plate of zinc. The acid, with which the imprinted part of the paper is saturated, etches the metal, while the printed portion sets off on it so that the zinc surface presents a reverse copy of the work. The original being now renewed, the zinc plate, thus prepared, is washed or smeared with gum-water or weak solution of gum in weak phosphatic acid. This liquid is attracted by the etched surface, which it freely wets, while it is repelled by the oil of the ink in which the writing or drawing on the plate is traced. A leather roller, covered with ink, is then passed over the plate, when a converse effect ensues; the repulsion between the oil, ink, and watery surface over which the roller passes, prevents any soiling of the unfigured parts of the zinc plate; while the attraction between oil and oil causes the ink to be distributed over the printed portions. At this stage the danger of the ink adhering to the unprinted portions of the plate may be diminished by pouring over it a solution of phosphatic acid, by which a surface can be produced to which printers' ink will not attach. In this condition the anastatic plate is complete, and impressions are pulled from it by the lithographic press.

When it is required to apply the anastatic process to very old originals, which do not set off their ink on pressure, the page or print is first soaked in a solution of potash, and then in a solution of tartaric acid: by which is produced a perfect diffusion of minute crystals of bi-tartrate of potash through the texture of the imprinted part of the paper. As this salt resists oil, the ink roller may now be passed over the surface without transferring any of its contents, except to the printed parts. The tartrate is then washed out of the paper, and the operation of moistening with dilute nitric acid is commenced. It is alleged that by a similar process engravings or letter-press can be transferred to stone, tin, pewter, or type-metal, lead, copper, and glass, and that impressions can be obtained from such plates.

Drawings made on paper with lithographic chalk have also been transferred and printed by the anastatic process, but care must be taken to secure paper and pencils well adapted to the purpose. It is said that a metallic paper used for metallic pencils, has the required surface, and that the lithographic chalk should be of a hard quality and cut to a fine point.

Ancient Customs.—The following account of the customs common in old English printing-offices is extracted from Moxon's Mechanic Exercises, published in 1683, the first English work on printing, and although the modern unions have supplanted the ancient chapels in this country, it is interesting as a relic of the past:

Ancient Customs used in a Printing-house.

Every *Printing-house* is, by the Custom of Time out of mind, called a *Chappel*; and all the Workmen that belong to it are *Members of the Chappel*; and the Oldest Freeman is *Father of the Chappel.* I suppose the stile was originally conferred upon it by the courtesie of some great Churchman, or men, (doubtless when Chappels were in more veneration than of late years they have been here in *England*) who for the Books of Divinity that proceeded from a *Printing-house*, gave it the Reverend Title of *Chappel*.

There have been formerly Customs and By-Laws made and intended for the well and good Government of the *Chappel*, and for the more Civil and orderly deportment of all its Members while in the *Chappel*; and the Penalty for the breach of any of these Laws and Customs is in Printers Language called a *Solace*.

And the Judges of these *Solaces*, and other Controversies relating to the *Chappel* or any of its Members, was plurality of Votes in the *Chappel* It being asserted

9. If a *Press-man* leave his *Blankets* in the *Tympan* at Noon or Night, a *Solace*.

These *Solaces* were to be bought off, for the good of the *Chappel*. Nor were the prices of these *Solaces* alike; For some were 12d. 6d. 4d. 2d. 1d. ob. according to the nature and quality of the *Solace*.

But if the Delinquent prov'd Obstinate or Refractory, and would not pay his *Solace* at the Price of the *Chappel*, they *Solac'd* him.

The manner of *Solacing*, thus.

The Workmen take him by force, and lay him on his Belly athwart the *Correcting-stone*, and held him there while another of the Work-men with a Paper-board, gave him 10l. *and a Purse*, viz. Eleven blows on his Buttocks; which he laid on according to his own mercy.

ANCIENT PRINTING-OFFICE.

as a Maxim, *That the Chappel cannot Err.* But when any Controversie is thus decided, it always ends in the Good of the *Chappel*.

1. Swearing in the *Chappel*, a *Solace*.
2. Fighting in the *Chappel*, a *Solace*.
3. Abusive Language, or giving the Ly in the *Chappel*, a *Solace*
4. To be Drunk in the *Chappel*, a *Solace*.
5. For any of the Workmen to leave his Candle burning at Night, a *Solace*.
6. If the *Compositer* let fall his *Composing-stick*, and another take it up, a *Solace*.
7. Three *Letters* and a *Space* to lye under the *Compositers Case*, a *Solace*.
8. If a *Press-man* let fall his *Ball* or *Balls*, and another take it up, a *Solace*.

These nine *Solaces* were all the *Solaces* usually and generally accepted; yet in some particular *Chappels* the Work-men did by consent make other *Solaces*, viz.

That it should be a *Solace* for any of the Workmen to mention Joyning their Penny or more apiece to send for Drink.

To mention spending *Chappel money* till *Saturday* night, or any other before agreed time.

To play at *Quadrats*, or excite any of the *Chappel* to Play at *Quadrats*; either for Money or Drink.

This Solace is generally purchas'd by the Master-Printer; as well because it hinders the Workmens work, as because it Batters and spoils the Quadrats: For the manner how they Play with them is Thus: They take five or seven more in *Quadrats* (generally of the *English Body*) and holding their Hand below the Surface of the

Correcting Stone, shake them in their Hand, and toss them upon the *Stone*. and then count how many *Nicks* upwards each man throws in three times, or any other number of times agreed on: And he that throws most Wins the Bett of all the rest, and stands out free, till the rest have try'd who throws fewest *Nicks* upwards in so many throws; for all the rest are free: and he pays the Bett.

For any to *Take up a Sheet*, if he receiv'd *Copy-money*; Or if he receiv'd no *Copy-money*, and did *Take up a Sheet*, and carryed that Sheet or Sheets off the Printing-House till the whole Book was Printed off and Publisht.

Any of the Workmen may purchase a Solace for any trivial matter. if the rest of the *Chappel* consent to it. As if any of the Workmen Sing in the *Chappel*; he that is offended at it may, with the *Chappels* Consent, purchase a penny or two penny *Solace* for any Workmans singing after the *Solace* is made; Or if a Workman or a Stranger salute a Woman in the *Chappel*, after the making of the *Solace* it is a *Solace* of such a Value as is agreed on.

The price of all *Solaces* to be purchased is wholly Arbitrary in the *Chappel*. And a Penny *Solace* may perhaps cost the Purchaser Six Pence, Twelve Pence, or more for the *Good of the Chappel*.

Yet sometimes *Solaces* may cost double the Purchase or more. As if some *Compositer* have (to affront a *Press-man*) put a Wisp of Hay in the *Press-man's Ball-Racks*; If the *Press-man* cannot well brook this affront, he will lay six Pence down on the *Correcting Stone* to purchase a *Solace* of twelve pence upon him that did it; and the *Chappel* cannot in Justice refuse to grant it: because it tends to the *Good of the Chappel*: And being granted, it becomes every Members duty to make what discovery he can: because it tends to the farther *Good of the Chappel*: And by this means it seldom happens but the Aggressor is found out.

Nor did *Solaces* reach only the *Members of the Chappel*, but also Strangers that came into the *Chappel*, and offered affronts or indignities to the *Chappel*, or any of its Members; the *Chappel* would determine it a *Solace*. Example:

It was a *Solace* for any to come to the *King's Printing house* and ask for a Ballad.

For any to come and enquire of a *Compositer*, whether he had News of such a Galley at Sea.

For any to bring a Wisp of Hay, directed to any of the *Press-men*.

And such Strangers were commonly sent by some who knew the *Customs of the Chappel*, and had a mind to put a Trick upon the Stranger

Other Customs were used in the *Chappel*, which were not *Solaces*, viz. Every new Workman to pay half a Crown; which is called his *Benvenue*: This *Benvenue* being so constant a Custome is still lookt upon by all Workmen as the undoubted Right of the *Chappel*, and therefore never deputed; yet he who has not paid his *Benvenue* is no Member of the *Chappel* nor enjoys any benefit of *Chappel-Money*.

If a Journey-man Wrought formerly upon the same Printing House, and comes again to Work on it, pays but half a *Benvenue*.

If a Journey-man *Smout* more or less on another Printing-House, and any of the *Chappel* can prove it, he pays half a *Benvenue*.

I told you before that abusive Language or giving the Lye was a *Solace*: But if in discourse, when any of the Workmen affirm any thing that is not believed, the *Compositer* knocks with the back corner of his *Composing-stick* against the lower Ledge of his *Lower Case*. and the *Press-man* knocks the handles of his *Ball-stocks* together: Thereby signifying the discredit they give to his Story.

It is now customary that Journey-men are paid for all Church Holy days that fall not on a *Sunday*, Whether they Work or no: And they are by Contract with the Master Printer paid proportionably for what they undertake to Earn every Working day, be it half a Crown, two Shillings, three Shillings. four Shillings, &c.

It is also customary for all the Journey-men to make every Year new Paper Windows, whether the old will serve again or no; Because that day they make them, the Master Printer gives them a *Way-goose*; that is, he makes them a good Feast, and not only entertains them at his own House, but besides, gives them Money to spend at the Ale-house or Tavern at Night; And to this Feast they invite the *Correcter. Founder, Smith, Joyner*, and *Inck-maker*. who all of them severally (except the *Correcter* in his own Civility) open their Purse-strings and add their Benevolence (which Workmen account their duty, because they generally chuse these Workmen) to the Master Printers: But from the *Correcter* they expect nothing. because the Master Printer chusing him, the Workmen can do him no kindness.

These Way-gooses, are always kept about Bartholomew-tide. And till the Master-Printer have given this *Way-goose*, the Journey-men do not use to work by Candle Light.

If a Journey-man marry, he pays half a Crown to the *Chappel*.

When his Wife comes to the *Chappel*, she pays six Pence: and then all the Journey-men joyn their two Pence apiece to Welcome her.

If a Journey-man have a Son born, he pays one Shilling.

If a Daughter born, six Pence.

The *Father* of the *Chappel* drinks first of *Chappel Drink*, except some other Journey-man have a *Token*; viz. Some agreed piece of Coin or Mettle markt by consent of the *Chappel*: for then producing that *Token*, he Drinks first. This *Token* is always given to him who in the Round should have Drank, had the last *Chappel-drink* held out. Therefore when *Chappel-drink* comes in, they generally say, *Who has the Token?*

Though these Customs are no *Solaces*; yet the *Chappel* Excommunicates the Delinquent; and he shall have no benefit of *Chappel-money* till he have paid.

It is also customary in some Printing-houses that if the *Compositer* or *Press-man* make either the other stand still through the neglect of their contracted Task, that then he who neglected, shall pay him that stands still as much as if he had Wrought.

The Compositers are Jocosely called *Galley Slaves*;

Because allusively they are as it were bound to their *Gallies*.

And the *Press men* are Jocosely called *Horses*: Because of the hard Labour they go through all day long.

An Apprentice when he is Bound pays half a Crown to the *Chappel*, and when he is made Free, another half Crown to the *Chappel*; but is yet no Member of the *Chappel*: And if he continue to Work Journey-work in the same House, he pays another half Crown, and is then a Member of the *Chappel*.

The Printers of *London*, Masters and Journey-men, have every Year a general Feast, which since the re-building of Stationers Hall is commonly kept there. This Feast is made by four Stewards, *viz.* two Masters and two Journey-men; which Stewards, with the Collection of half a Crown apiece of every Guest, defray the Charges of the whole Feast; And as they collect the Half Crowns, they deliver every Guest a Ticket, wherein is specified the Time and Place they are to meet at, and the Church they are to go to: To which Ticket is affixed the Names and Seals of each Steward.

It is commonly kept on or about *Mid-day*: When, about ten a Clock in the Morning they meet at *Stationers Hall*, and from thence go to some Church thereabouts; Four Whifflers (as Servitures) by two and two walking before with White Staves in their Hands, and Red and Blew Ribbons hung Belt-wise upon their left Shoulders. Those go before to make way for the Company. Then walks the Beadle of the Company of *Stationers*, with the Company's Staff in his Hand, and Ribbons as the Whifflers, and after him the Divine (whom the Stewards before ingag'd to Preach them a Sermon) and his Reader. Then the Stewards walk by two and two, with long White Wands in their Hands, and all the rest of the Company follows, till they enter the Church.

The Divine Service begins, Anthems are Sung, and a Sermon Preached to suit the Solemnity: When ended, they in the same order walk back again to *Stationers Hall*; where they are immediately entertain'd with the City Weights and other Musick: And as every Guest enters, he delivers his Ticket (which gives him Admittance) to a Person appointed by the Stewards to receive it.

The Master, Wardens and other Grandees of the Company (although perhaps no Printers) are yet commonly invited, and take their Seats at the upper Table, and the rest of the Company where it pleases them best. The Tables being furnish'd with variety of Dishes of the best Cheer: And to make the entertainment more splendid is usher'd in with Loud Musick. And after Grace is said (commonly by the Minister that Preach'd the Sermon) every one Feasts himself with what he likes Best: whiles the Whifflers and other Officers Wait with Napkins, Plates, Beer, Ale, and Wine, of all sorts, to accommodate each Guest according to his desire. And to make their Cheer go cheerfuller down, are entertained with Musick and Songs all Dinner time.

Dinner being near ended, the Kings and the Dukes Healths is begun, by the several Stewards at the several Tables, and goes orderly round to all the Guests.

And whiles these Healths are Drinking, each Steward sets a Plate on each Table, beginning at the upper end, and conveying it downwards, to Collect the Benevolence of Charitable minds towards the relief of *Printers* Poor Widows. And at the same time each Steward distributes a Catalogue of such Printers as have held Stewards ever since the Feast was first kept, *viz.* from the Year of Christ 1621.

After Dinner, and Grace said, the Ceremony of Electing new Stewards for the next Year begins: Therefore the present Stewards withdraw into another Room: And put Garlands of Green Lawrel, or of Box on their Heads, and White wands in their Hands, and are again Usher'd out of the withdrawing Room by the Beadle of the Company, with the Companys Staff in his Hand, and with Musick sounding before them: Then follows one of the Whifflers with a great Bowl of White-wine and Sugar, in his Right Hand, and his Whifflers Staff in his Left: Then follows the Eldest Steward, and then another Whiffler, as the first, with a Bowl of White wine and Sugar before the second Steward, and in like manner another Whiffler before the Third, and another before the Fourth. And thus they walk with Musick sounding before them three times round the Hall: And in a fourth round the first Steward takes the Bowl of his Whiffler and Drinks to one (whom before he resolved on) by the Title of Mr. Steward Elect: And taking the Garland off his own Head puts it upon the Steward Elects Head. At which Ceremony the Spectators clap their Hands, and such as stand on the Tables or Benches, so Drum with their Feet that the whole Hall is filled with Noise, as applauding the Choice. Then the present Steward takes out the Steward Elect, giving him the Right Hand, and walks with him Hand in Hand, behind the three present Stewards another Round about the Hall: And in the next Round, as aforesaid, the second Steward Drinks to another with the same Ceremony as the first did; and so the Third Steward, and so the Fourth, and then all walk one Round more Hand in Hand about the Hall, that the Company may take notice of the Stewards Elect. So ends the Ceremony of the Day.

This Ceremony being over, such as will go their ways; but others that stay, are Diverted with Musick, Songs, Dancing, Farcing, &c. till at last they all find it time to depart.

Anderson, Alexander, M. D., who was born April 21, 1775, in New York, and died January 17, 1870, in Jersey City, was the pioneer Wood Engraver in the United States. The following facts relating to his history are condensed from a paper read by Benson J. Lossing before the Historical Society of New York:

Young Anderson evinced a love for art at a very early age. During his school-days he amused himself by copying engravings with India-ink. At twelve years of age he tried his hand in the engraver's art upon plates made of cents rolled out, and with a graver made of the back-spring of a pocket-knife. He soon cut small ships and other objects upon type-metal, and sold them to the newspaper publishers.

At the age of fourteen years he was apprenticed to Dr. Young, a physician of some eminence, who had been a surgeon in the Continental army. He remained with him as a student for five years. Meanwhile he employed in engraving every moment that he could spare from the duties of his professional studies and labors. He became so expert that, while he was yet a medical student, he was employed by all the publishers in New York, and by Dr. Mitchill; Philip Freneau, the poet of the Revolution; Hugh Gaine, the veteran newspaper publisher, and others. His earliest employers as an illustrator of books were William Durell and Evert Duyckinck.

Although he was licensed to practice medicine, and adopted that profession for several years, his love of art impelled him to abandon it, and to devote himself exclusively to engraving.

In 1793, when he was eighteen years of age, Anderson first learned the fact, from Bewick's Works, that box-wood was used for engraving. He found it so much more kindly than type-metal, that he employed it almost entirely afterward for pictures to be printed as type-metal ones were. And so it was that he became the first engraver on wood in America.

Anderson used both copper and wood, as occasion required, until about the year 1812, when he abandoned metal-engraving. His last picture of that kind, of consequence, was of the Last Supper, after Holbein, for a quarto Bible. Up to that time he had no competitor as a wood-engraver, and his initials or full name appear upon the pictures of almost every illustrated book published in New York during the preceding twelve or fifteen years. Then Abel Bowen began the practice of wood-engraving in Boston. Afterward, A. J. Mason, a skillful engraver, came from England, and remained as a practitioner of the art several years. Anderson instructed three pupils—Lansing, M. Morgan, and Hall—and about the year 1826, J. A. Adams, a self-taught artist, appeared.

Anderson was never tempted to depart from Bewick's general style of execution, which is the legitimate style of wood-engraving. Within a very few years it has been revived after a display of a vicious imitation of metal-engraving by elaborate cross-hatching. Fine specimens of Anderson's style may be seen in an edition of Shakspeare's plays published by Coolidge & Brother. They were engraved by Anderson when he was in the seventy-seventh year of his age. He continued the daily practice of his art skillfully until he was in his ninety-fourth year—a period from the beginning of his art-life of almost eighty-three years.

Mr. Lossing remarked in his paper that when he himself engaged in the business of engraving in New York—about 1840—there were not twenty professional wood-engravers in the United States. When the father of the art in America died, they numbered about four hundred.

Anglo-Saxon or Saxon Alphabet.—The Anglo-Saxon or Saxon alphabet contains twenty-three letters proper; the j, q, and v of the English alphabet being excluded from it. It also possesses single characters to represent, respectively, the sounds of th in thin and thine, as well as several words in common use; as and, that, etc. The forms and sounds of the Anglo-Saxon alphabet are shown in the following table, extracted from The American Printer:

Form.		Sound.	Form.		Sound.
Æ	... a	a as in bar	N	... n	n
B	... b	b	O	... o	o
C	... c	c as in choice	P	... p	p
D	... b	d	R	... p	r
C	... e	e as in feint	S	... ʃ	s
F	... r	f	T	... c	t
Ᵹ	... ᵹ	g as in gem	Đ Þ	... Ꝥ Þ	th
Ð Þ	... h	h	U	... u	u
I	... ı	i	Ƿ	... p	w
K	... k	k	X	... x	x
L	... l	l	Y	... ẏ	y
ᚱ	... m	m	Z	... z	z

Anglo-Saxon characters preserve their typographical importance, from the fact that they are occasionally used in reprints of ancient documents, like the Domesday Book of England, the Saxon Gospels, or the Saxon Chronicle, as well as in lines set-up or engraved for decorative printing. The use of the Saxon characters in England prevailed from the beginning of the seventh to the middle of the eleventh century, when they were supplanted by the Black-letter. This, in turn, was superseded by the existing alphabet, and it substantially embodies a pure form of the Roman letters. The Anglo-Saxon language has undergone in its gradual conversion into modern English, even greater modifications than the alphabet, as will be seen by the following extract from the will of Alfred the Great, manumitting his serfs; written in the ninth century:

And ic bidde on Godes naman and on his haligra, thaet nfnra maga nane né yrfewearda ne geswenco nán naenig eyrelif thara the io faregen'd, me Westsexena witan ió rihte gerehton thaet io hí mót lnctan sná freo swá theowe, swather ie wille; ao ic for Godes lufan and for mínre sáwle thearfe, wylle thaet by syn heora freolses wyrthe, byre eyres; and io on Godes bífendes naman beóde, thael by nán man ne broeie, né mid feos manunge, né mid naeninguin thinguin, thaet hie ne infean ecóaan swylcne mann swylce by wyllan.

And I pray in God's name and his saints that none of my kinsmen or heirs oppress any of my dependants, for whom I paid, and the West-Saxon Witan legally adjudged to me, that I might leave them free or slave whichever I would, but I for God's love and for my souls' need, will that they shall have their freedom and their choice; and I in the name of the living God command that no man disquiet them, either by demand of money, or with any other thing, so that they may choose such a man as they please (for an employer).

Aniline Colors.—See INKS.

Antimony.—This metal, which is used by all modern type-founders as an alloy in type-metal, is found in Saxony, the Hartz Mountains, Cornwall, Spain, France, Mexico, Nevada, Siberia, the Eastern Islands, and Martaban, in Pegu, but the chief source of commercial supply is Singapore, at which point it is received from Borneo. When pure, it is of grayish white color and has a good deal of brilliancy. It is about as hard as gold; its specific gravity is about 6.7; it is easily reduced to a very fine powder; its tenacity is such that a rod of one-tenth of an inch in diameter is capable of supporting ten pounds' weight. It is used in various proportions to lead in making type-metal, there being sometimes one pound of antimony to sixteen of lead, sometimes two pounds of antimony to ten pounds of lead, and sometimes even a greater proportion of antimony. It is rather a singular circumstance that while this metal has become indispensable in the manufacture of types which furnish food for the mind, it also furnishes the basis of so many medicines, for the relief of the ills of the body, that it has been said that in company with one or two associates, it will do much to supply all a physician desires in an apothecary-shop."

Antiquarii.—This name was applied to the monkish scribes who wrote or copied books before the invention of printing, and more especially to those who transcribed ancient books, the term librarii denoting those who transcribed new as well as old books.

The Anglo-Saxon monks were very celebrated as writers, and probably originated the small Roman letter used in modern times. The greatest delicacy and nicety were deemed essential in the transcribing of books, whether for the purposes of general instruction, or for the use of the convents themselves. Careless and illegible writing is therefore but seldom to be met with among the remains of monastic industry; and when erasures were made, they appear to have been done with the utmost care and skill. Ink, composed of soot, or ivory-black with gum, was used upon the vellum, for paper was not introduced until the tenth century. Hence the beautiful distinctness, as well as durability, of very ancient manuscript books. Indeed, such an important art was writing in those days considered, that Du Cange enumerates as many as a hundred different styles of writing in vogue among the learned. The predecessors of printers must have been quite numerous, for it is said that more than six thousand persons at Paris subsisted by copying and illuminating manuscripts, at the time when printing was first introduced into that city.

Antique.—This name has been applied to a large variety of fancy and job metal and wood letters, whose characteristic is uniformity in the thickness of each portion of every letter. While there is a marked deviation between the thickness of the ceriphs and other portions of other types, in the Antiques there is either no deviation whatever or a close approximation to uniformity. There is a large family of Antiques, for they include Condensed, Extra Condensed, Extended, Light, Open, Pointed, Shaded, Skeleton, and Tuscan, as well as other descriptions, of every size from Nonpareil to thirty-line Pica. (See JOB TYPE.)

Antiquities, Typographical.—The best collection in this country of the books of the ancient printers is probably to be found in the Philadelphia Library, and the learned and curious can readily feast their eyes, at that institution, upon the veritable products of the fathers of typography as well as those of the first printers in England and in the United States. In the Old World so much pains and money have been lavished by successive generations of the Spencer family in making a complete collection of the first works from the German, Italian, French and English presses, that their library at Althorp, England, splendidly illustrates the early history of the art of printing. A recent account (1870) of this remarkable library, in describing its contents, says it contains hundreds of Bibles, which represent all the great editions, from the Mazarin Bible of 1455, down to the Bibles in all languages of half a century ago. Here are the polyglot versions of Alcala, Antwerp, Paris, London, Hamburg, and Leipsic. Here are Greek Bibles, with the Aldine Princeps, and from the Strasburg, 1526, to the Oxford, 1798. Here are Latin Bibles—twenty of which were printed before 1480, and a magnificent series of vellum copies about 1476. Here are twelve choice editions of the sixteenth century; seven of the seventeenth; ten of the eighteenth. The early English Bibles are rare and choice, and valuable beyond price. Coverdale's Zurich Bible, 1535; the two London Bibles, 1537; that of Grafton and of Whitchurch, 1540; Cromwell's Bible, 1539; ten editions from 1551 to 1581; Tyndale's most rare Testament, 1536 (printed at Antwerp); the Southwark printed copy, 1538; the folio Testament (with Erasmian paraphrase), by Whitchurch, 1548; the octavo of Gaultier, 1550; and five editions between 1550 and 1600; the Crummer Bible, 1566; the Saxon and English Gospels, 1571; the Genevan Bible of Edinburgh, 1576-79 (the first complete Bible from the Scottish press, which Dibdin humorously described as in the Scottish language), combine to make one hundred copies of rare, remarkable, or choice editions of the Bible (or parts of the Bible) in English, now on the Althorp shelves. The nine German Bibles printed before 1495; the ten Italian Bibles (one with the autograph of Sixtus V.); the fifteen French Bibles; the four Spanish Bibles; the Sclavonic, 1581; the Delft Dutch, 1477; the Prince Radzivil's Polish Bible, of 1563, which cost Lord Spencer a hundred guineas to complete; the Bohemian Bible of 1596; the Livonian Bible of 1689, with European and Asiatic versions of all languages and dates, are beyond description for interest and value too.

In patristic and scholastic Theology there are fourteen rare editions of Thomas Aquinas, printed before 1480, and mostly from the presses of Schoeffer, Sweynheim (first printer in Rome), and Mentelin; thirty editions of St. Augustine, seventeen being between 1467 and 1490, and many being date-marks of typography; seven editions of St. Chrysostom, by Zell, and Laver, and Azzoguidi; thirteen of St. Jerome, including the celebrated Oxford Book, alleged to be 1468; the Adversus Gentes of Lactantius, the first book printed in

Italy, at the famous Subiaco press; eighteen of the earliest printed Missals, from 1475 to 1504; the fine Mozarabic Missal, printed by Cardinal Ximenes, in 1500; six Missals from the Naples press; many choice Breviaries, Psalters, etc., in all tongues, and of all dates.

In the gallery of one of the rooms of the library are scores, if not hundreds of quarto volumes, each containing a dozen to twenty of the little quarto tracts which did duty as newspapers in the great Civil War, and record the contests between Parliament and King.

All the other rooms of this vast library—for it numbers more than 50,000 volumes, nearly every one of which is a treasure to literature—sink into insignificance compared with one room alone. Range after range, press after press, shelf after shelf may attract the eye and bewilder even the coolest brain in its attempt to master even the titles of the treasures; but when room after room has been passed, when book after book has been noted, when anticipation has been dwarfed by facts, and wonder is wearied at the riches it has seen, one of the dummy panels in one of the side walls is opened, a noble hall is passed, a turn to the left is taken, and a lofty room is entered, where the morning sunlight streams in through the two windows on the right, and the tall presses, with tasteful wire-lattice work and neat white-painted doors, carefully closed, and secured by little brass padlocks, show that the sanctum is reached, and that we are at last in the presence of the choicest treasures of the Althorp shelves. A little upright glass-case on our left contains hundreds of microscopic editions of classics, from Didot's lovely little Horace backward—some in the choicest covers, the work of true artist-hands; some little volumes of manuscript, in Italian hand, and with glorious illuminations; and one curious little volume, with leaves of paper made from familiar English plants. Here in scholarly seclusion are the choicest editions—the editiones principes of the choicest authors of Greece and Rome. Here are the seventy editions of Cicero—nearly fifty of which were printed before 1473, mostly representing different texts, and thus practically as valuable as manuscripts now lost forever. Here are eight editions of Horace prior to 1480; here are copies of Ovid from all the Italian early presses of Parma, Venice, and Rome; here is Livy as printed by Sweynheim and by Aldus, in glorious tomes; here is Pliny, on vellum, from the press of Rome, 1471; while superb works of the Aldus press, the Stephens press, and Bodoni's Parma press are spread all around. Here is a rich case of Aldines, with the now familiar device; there is a row of the choicest works by Bodoni, who equaled even Baskerville in making printing an art. Here is the Florence edition of Homer, dated 1474; here is the most rare Horace, printed in Naples in 1476, by Arnoldus de Bruxella; here is the famous Terence of Riessenger, 1471, so curious from details of the early laws of Sicily and Naples, and for which two volumes, Lord Spencer was chiefly induced to buy Count Cas-

sano's library to enrich his shelves. Here on this Horace (of which there are so few copies that it contains Lord Spencer's pencil-note that it was the rarest, choicest classic he had known) is a curious bill of old Roger Payne, with all his minute details of the material, and the time employed in the binding of this rarest of books. Here, among nearly a dozen editions of Dante, is the magnificent edition of 1477—one of the eight editions between 1472 and 1484. Here is the first Roman Missal (a superb rubricated copy), on vellum, printed as early as 1477.

Here is the most famous single volume probably in the whole world—the volume which originally led the Duke of Roxburghe to begin book-collecting, and which sold at his great sale for £2260! It is only a small folio volume, some two inches thick, but it is an edition of Boccaccio, printed at Venice, by Valdarfer, as early as 1474, and no other perfect copy is known. Its very history is a romance. At the second Duke of Roxburghe's table some conversation on the book occurred. He remembered that it had once been offered to him for £100. He sought and found and bought it, and his son was so struck by the conversation that he became so great a collector, that the sale of his books in 1812 lasted forty-two days. When this famous volume was put up, Lord Spencer and Lord Blandford were both eager to possess it. It was started at £100, the price was doubled, then went to £250, and then jumped to £500. As the price advanced the bids were smaller, only £5 at a time. At last the lot was left to two competitors; Lord Spencer said £2250, and Lord Blandford £10 more, at which price the treasure became his own. Lord Spencer had resolved to give £1812 (the amount representing the date 1812), but having had a windfall of £438, he advanced to £2250; and although he lost the volume, he was lucky enough to secure it a few years later for £900. The description of the contest by Dibdin is one of the curiosities of literature, and the sale one of the most extraordinary in bibliomaniac annals, since the owners of Althorp, Blenheim, and Chatsworth competed for the possession of this unique and memorable book.

The Caxton press volumes in this room are quite unsurpassed in number and condition. Fifty-seven separate works from the Father of the English Press is a noble collection for a private library. Even the British Museum can boast only fifty-five, but of these eleven are unique, while Lord Spencer has only three unique. Here, in a quiet corner, are the first and second editions of Caxton's Game of Chesse, and two copies of his Chaucer's Tales, of excessive rarity and curious value; here are dainty little volumes with queer or reverent colophons, and in quaint old half-printing, half-manuscript letters, with ink still as black as a raven, and leaves as crisp as of a modern book. Here are the real treasures, the incunabula, the cradle books of the English press. Here are the materials for the history of the printing art. Here are the choice romances which delighted the days of Edward the Third. Here, too, are the works of Caxton's friends and pupils, a magnificent vellum folio of the Boke of St. Alban's by Dame Juliana Berners, printed by Wynkyn de Worde; here are Pynson's books by the dozen, and here are scores of rare, choice, splendid samples of the fifteenth century English press. In other presses of this noble room are the Block-Books which preceded books printed by movable type. Here is the earliest known wood-cut with a date, the Saint Christopher of 1423, which is a landmark in art. It has had reams written about it and its value; and its quaint old colored sketch of the good Saint crossing the stream and bearing the boy upon his shoulders, is curious and graphic in the extreme. Here, too, is a superb copy of the famous Mazarin Bible, supposed to have been printed as early as 1455 —a sumptuous copy, with sound and solid old paper, clean and clear and stainless; sharp and clear-cut old gothic letter, glossy raven ink, and brilliant rubrications, which have kept their color unfaded in all the chances and changes of four hundred years. Here, too, are not only the choicest classics, but real art-works of the binder's taste. Books bound by Roger Payne, and De Rome, and Padeloup, are crowded in the cases, in rich profusion, and delight the eye, and taste, and judgment of the bibliopegic connoisseur. Here, too, among the treasures, are choice copies of all the four folio editions of Shakspeare's Plays; a copy, in brilliant condition, of the excessively rare Sonnets, dated 1609; not to mention a copy of an edition of 1783, which is enlarged by a mass of illustrations selected from rare sources.

Beautiful and interesting as many of the works of early printers undoubtedly are, Bibliomaniacs, in their enthusiastic admiration, are apt to do injustice to modern typography, and to shut their eyes to the imperfections of the founders of the art. They ignore the regularity of spacing, of divisions, of orthography, and of punctuation, as well as the skillful blending of varieties of type, which are comparatively modern improvements, and forget that the fine effects produced by the best early printers were due in part to the use of vellum instead of paper, and to the assistance of illuminators.

A. P.—A technical abbreviation for Author's Proof.

Apocope.—The cutting off or omission of the last letter or syllable of a word; as, di. for dii.

Apograph.—A copy; as distinguished from an autograph. The word is sometimes applied to the ancient manuscript copies of books.

Apostrophe.—This point (') is used to denote the omission of a letter or letters in some elisions and contractions; to make the plural of letters and figures when they are used as nouns (as two l's or two a's); to distinguish the possessive case of nouns; and to indicate the end of a quotation.

In abbreviations the apostrophe can only be used appropriately when the proper pronunciation of the text corresponds with the contraction of the printed letters. Words used in familiar conversation, like don't, and can't, are properly printed in the form just given, because the pronunciation of the original words

do not, and cannot, is to be as much curtailed as the text. But when James is abbreviated as Jas. or Attorney as Atty. the use of the apostrophe would be improper, because no one in reading aloud is expected to say jas. or atty. Typographical emergencies may, however, justify the printer in using the apostrophe in abbreviations which are not contractions of sound, when there is a probability that it will give a better indication of the true nature of the shortened word than a period. If a word of twelve letters must be printed in some fashion in a measure barely wide enough to hold six letters, and a choice of evils is presented, it is probably better to use apostrophes to elucidate the true meaning, than to rely exclusively on the period. But this exception does not affect the general rule. It is justly contended, that even in poetry the apostrophe should not be used in pretended attempts to abbreviate such words as to, the, heaven, power, every, threatening, and others of a similar nature. If the poet must say 'gainst for against, or e'en for even, and the elocutionist is obliged to accept the abbreviations, the printer does his joint duty to both by printing 'gainst, or e'en, but he becomes a party to a useless sham, when he prints t' for to, or th' for the.

When the apostrophe is used to indicate the possessive case of singular nouns, it is placed before the final s, (as the Printer's Grammar), but in plural nouns after the final letter, as Printers' Unions. No additional s is added to plural nouns, but it should always be appended to the singular nouns, after the apostrophe, when the proper pronunciation of the word requires it, despite the usages in some offices, of dispensing with it in words like James's book, or Thomas's hat. The end to be kept constantly in view in abbreviations in which the apostrophe is used, is the representation of the appropriate sound, and since we say Jameses book, we should also print the additional s after the apostrophe. On the other hand, nouns usually ending with two s's, like goodness, do not require a third s when they are in the possessive case, for the reason already given.

The apostrophe is also used to mark the close of a quotation, two (") being ordinarily employed for this purpose, but only one (') when one quotation is included in another. Several vigorous protests have been made against the too frequent use of quotation marks in printing, and in some languages they have been abandoned. (See QUOTATION MARKS.) It is desirable that a better mode of distinguishing borrowed from original matter should be used in many cases (italics, or type smaller than the body of the text, for instance), and that when quotation marks serve no useful or important purpose, they should be typographically ignored.

Several authorities lay down the rule, that in composition no space is required before the apostrophe, but usage varies, and some good printers consider it advisable to insert a hair space between the final letter and the apostrophe, when the latter is not preceded by a point, or by a letter carrying a shoulder.

Appendix.—In a general sense, is something appended or added, but specifically, in printing, it implies matter added to a book which is not necessarily essential to its completeness; and it is thus distinguished from supplement, which is intended to supply deficiencies or correct inaccuracies.

Applegarth, Augustus, in conjunction with his brother-in-law and business associate, Edward Cowper, is the inventor of several of the most important improvements in presses and printing machinery made during the present century. They simplified and greatly improved Kœnig's power-press, both in the rolling apparatus and in the impression-cylinders, and it is even claimed that their machine was the first really useful one. These early efforts date back to 1818. In 1827 they made additional improvements, and constructed a press for the London Times, with four cylinders, which made from 4000 to 5000 impressions per hour; and, following up this success, Applegarth soon afterward constructed a much more rapid machine, in which the type was placed on the surface of a cylinder of large dimensions, revolving on a vertical axis. This was the first press of the world, until it was eclipsed by Hoe's American lightning presses, in which the type revolves on a horizontal axis. In 1853 Applegarth took out a patent for a four-cylinder press which he claimed would print at the rate of 12,000 perfect sheets per hour; but his best efforts could not prevent his presses from being supplanted in the office of the London Times, by those built by Hoe. (See PRESSES.)

Apprentice.—An apprentice, as defined in Bouvier's American Law Dictionary, is a minor who is bound in due form of law to a master, and who is to learn from him his art, trade, or business, and to serve him during the time of his apprenticeship. Apprenticeship of this description has been nearly abolished in recent years, and loose verbal or in some cases written agreements, far less binding than the old-fashioned indentures, are now adopted in a very large proportion of the contracts or business understandings with the boys who undertake to learn the art of printing. It was formerly the law of England that no person could practice any trade or calling to which he had not served a regular apprenticeship, either as master or workman, and there are instances on record of Englishmen who had not served a regular apprenticeship to the printing-business being prevented by the courts from establishing printing-offices. But this restriction has been repealed by statute. Its repeal, and the decadence of the old spirit of exclusiveness which formerly guarded the trades from unauthorized intrusion, as carefully as the professions are guarded at the present day, were quickly followed, there as well as here, by an abrogation of the strictness of the old forms of apprenticeship. This laxity has made the length of service of the learners of the art of printing little more than a matter of mutual convenience, the boy, in many cases, remaining with his original employer no longer than he conceives it to be his interest to do so. From this uncertainty, from the subdivision of the printing-business into various departments, from the diminution, in large printing-offices, of personal attention on the part of the owner or owners, and perhaps from other causes, has sprung up the great and growing evil of imperfect instruction; and while the number of journeymen printers is multiplying, very few men are skilled in both the leading branches of the business, and only a very small proportion of journeymen are either first-rate compositors or first-rate pressmen. Various remedies for this evil have been suggested, one of the most practical of which, in large offices, is the proposition that each boy should be placed for the first year of his apprenticeship, at least, under the special charge of an experienced journeyman, whose interest was secured by the receipt of a small percentage of the wages allowed to his pupil. This custom prevails in England, at the present day, in some offices, in the training of boys in press-work, and it might be advantageously extended to boys who are learning the mysteries of composition. In small offices, where few or no journeymen are employed, and where the office of instructor must be assumed, if at all, either by the elder apprentices, or the proprietor himself, there is perhaps no remedy except greater care and attention than have heretofore been displayed.

It should constantly be remembered, both by master and apprentice, that the first stage in the acquisition of the typographical art is a matter of primal importance, for the reason that, if the duties appropriate to this period are neglected, either by the instructor or the instructed, the loss to the latter is irremediable, and no after study or experience can ever fully compensate for the deficiency in the rudimentary education.

The time generally allotted to apprenticeship is really short for all that must be acquired in it, especially when we consider the vast variety of details necessary to the successful prosecution of the art; and it cannot be too strenuously urged that the youth who enters a printing-office should be fully impressed with the thought that upon his own conduct and zeal must depend his future fortunes. It is a profession in which he will not find greatness thrust upon him, but he must acquire it for himself by severe and persistent endeavor.

The apprentice must not shrink from the steady and patient fulfillment of all the work belonging to his place. These duties are often trivial and almost servile, such as the sweeping of the office, and the removal of the dirt and fragments, in which it is his business to find the type or other articles of value that have been accidentally dropped. But all these services must be performed with conscientious strictness, and a little just reflection ought to convince every apprentice that, in the worthy discharge even of these seemingly insignificant duties, he is laying the foundation of habits of order and accuracy, which will assist him in his future labors, as well as making for himself a reputation for carefulness, industry, and integrity that will be of the utmost value to him in after-time. These duties—disagreeable, monotonous, and apparently useless to his education—are all really necessary steps, and any carelessness in the discharge of them will be the subject of regret thereafter.

Thus, the composition of pi, an object of especial repugnance to apprentices generally, offers one of the best and most efficacious methods of learning to distinguish at sight, both with accuracy and rapidity, between the great variety of characters.

The holding of copy and reading it aloud to the proof-reader familiarizes the learner with the manuscript that he will afterward be called upon to compose. If this important duty be carelessly performed, the printer will often subsequently, when hesitating before his copy, bitterly regret his want of familiarity with the great varieties of manuscript, and those innumerable points of incidental information upon grammar, and the usages and niceties of language, which would have been acquired in such a training.

It is important that the apprentice should break himself successively to every kind of work, commencing with the most simple and elementary composition, and mounting gradually to the more difficult operations, and to those questions of taste which enter into the finer departments of printing. By means of these studies he will, in time, elevate himself above that sphere in which the uneducated workman must inevitably remain, suffering the disadvantages of an uncertain and moderate salary. Perfection in his work ought to be his aim, and it is absolutely necessary to ultimate success. Without aspirations toward exactitude and artistic perfection, he will inevitably remain a mere laborer—and, perhaps, a clumsy one—in a profession in which he might become an artist.

To reach this requisite perfection, the apprentice must studiously and zealously attend to all the instruction that falls in his way, never permitting himself to select the easy and avoid the difficult, for by this very indolence and carelessness he will shut himself off from success, making a willful choice of mediocrity. In typography there is no royal road to learning, and the good printer can only be produced by obedient submission to all the rules and even to the hardships of the trade; and such submission is the only price by which can be acquired the experience and information which will place the printer in that elevated rank in his own profession which should be coveted by every man.

The duties of the instructor are also arduous, and cannot be fitly fulfilled except by a person who not only conscientiously desires to do his own duty, but who is also inspired with a pride in his profession and a desire to elevate it above its present condition. Whoever accepts the duty of directing apprentices is bound by his office to counsel them seriously, to examine their work carefully and conscientiously, and to graduate their tasks with reference to their

capacity and advancement. It is only by such earnest efforts on both sides that the art of printing can recruit workmen worthy of a profession in which intelligence holds so conspicuous a part.

Many journeymen printers, in this and other countries, have favored a diminution of the number of apprentices, insisting that such a reduction would not only prevent an overstock of young printers but also insure more thorough instruction. The subject has repeatedly been agitated by local Unions as well as in the International Union, and in some cities the local Unions have insisted that the number of apprentices must bear a stated proportion to the number of journeymen who are regularly employed therein. The following rules were adopted by the Philadelphia Typographical Union, September, 1868:

RULE 1.—All boys entering a Printing-Office with the intention of learning the business, shall be held by indenture or written contract.

RULE 2.—Every boy shall be held under indenture or written contract for a period of not less than four years.

RULE 3.—The number of apprentices in an office shall not exceed the proportion of one to every five journeymen regularly employed: the average to be ascertained from the books of the office—say for one year.

RULE 4.—All apprentices in Book Offices shall be paid by the piece, at journeymen's wages, and fixed sums (as may be agreed upon by the contracting parties) shall be deducted by the employer as compensation for labor and expense incurred in instructing them in the art.

RULE 5.—When a boy shall have contracted with an employer to serve a certain term of years, he shall on no pretence whatever leave said employer and contract with another, without the full and free consent of said first employer: Provided, That such change may be made in consequence of the death or relinquishment of business by first employer.

RULE 6.—JOB APPRENTICES.—Job work being necessarily required to be done by the week, the apprentice shall receive such compensation for his services as his ability shall command. In all other respects he shall be governed by the same rules as apply to boys on piece-work.

The whole subject of apprenticeship, in all its bearings, deserves more careful attention than it has heretofore received from the printers of the United States. Greater pains should be taken to confine the choice of apprentices to bright and intelligent boys; more vigorous efforts to instruct the boys, both orally and by books, should be used; and if there is any way, since the abolition of the strict old apprenticeship system, of inducing boys to serve out their full time, and to make themselves well versed in the art before they undertake to practice it as journeymen, it should be speedily adopted. It is not at all unlikely that good usage, judicious treatment, and an extension of the opportunities for instruction will go far to solve even this difficulty.

One of the leading printers of New York read a paper on apprentices before the New York Typographical Society, a few years ago, which contained the following excellent suggestions:

I would have, as far as possible, a uniform business agreement—a contract signed by ourselves and the boy, and his parent or guardian, binding ourselves to fulfill certain obligations to the boy, and he certain obligations to us, and a forfeit of some kind in case of failure. I would have the boy not only afforded the opportunity of learning, but I would make it the duty of one who has learned the business thoroughly, and who possesses the rare quality of imparting to others what he has himself acquired, to take the special charge of instructing such a number of boys as he can do justice to, in all the details of the department in which he is engaged for the time being; and I would have some inducement given to this man, and such a responsibility thrown upon him as will give him a professional pride in their advancement, even as a professor of music, painting, or any science, feels personally interested in the honors justly accorded to any of his own pupils after they have passed beyond his teachings and become famous. Let the lad pass from one grade to the next no faster than he shall show by his work that he has merited advancement, and then advance him promptly from one department to another, and from one instructor to another, until he shall have acquired, by practice, as well as theory, and can expertly execute all the various kinds of work you have engaged to teach him. To encourage to application and enterprise, we should have rewards for well-doing, with their immediate benefits. A reasonably light task, with an opportunity to earn money by overwork, is the old plan, and is highly prized by some boys, while others care nothing about it. Some have a natural pride in excelling others in manifestations of skill, while others have a tremendous hankering after excursions, picnics, ball-playing, and boat-races, and if they can earn an occasional half day for such delicious enjoyments it will save them a wonderful amount of fibbing about sudden attacks of cramp in the stomach, dizziness in the head, or funerals of grandmothers. The particular disposition and inclinations of the boy should be carefully studied, and pleasantly, happily played upon, and if aught is discovered which is not good, it should be gently and judiciously restrained, not eradicated at one blow. Access to the Apprentices' Library should be afforded and encouraged, whether he has a particular fancy for reading or not. We should never feel above making ourselves familiar with a boy who is mannerly and respectful (and we should have no others), and should try, by kindness, to gain his confidence, that our influence over him for good may be the greater. When we feel that we have this confidence, we should use it for his benefit exclusively, for there are other ways enough to induce him to faithfulness in his business. Advise him as to what kind of reading he will wish he had

availed himself of when he comes to be a man and is talked of and nominated for some honorable position. Point him, as frequently as practicable, to the future, and always talk of something higher and better as attainable. Tell him, finally, if you have the courage to do so, especially if he is poor and ambitious, that skill, energy, enterprise, brains, and integrity are the masters of capital at all times, and that no man who possesses these qualities, in a fair degree, ever went roaming about the world complaining of his hard lot, of the misfortunes of his position or want of encouragement; but on the contrary, that he will find capital ever outflanked, begging him to enter in and possess.

Aquatint or Aquatinta.—A method of engraving on copper or steel plates, by which an effect is produced resembling a drawing in water-colors or Indian ink. It was invented by St. Non of France, about the year 1662, or, according to other authorities, by an artist, named Le Prince, who was born at Metz in 1723. This process has been supplanted, in a great measure, by lithography. A lengthy description of it is published in Knight's Cyclopædia, and brief descriptions are given elsewhere as follows: Etch the outline; but slightly in the distance and light parts; more strongly those near at hand. Clean the plate well to lay the ground, which is thus done: dissolve resin in proof alcohol; for distance, less resin is required. Increase the quantity for the nearest parts. Pour this mixture over the plate, run off the superfluous matter, and in drying it will form a granulation on the surface. This granulation is fine or coarse in proportion to the quantity, more or less, of resin contained in the alcohol. When the resin is in excess, no granulation will form. Stop out, bite, and rebite as in etching.

Arabic Numerals are so called because they were derived by the Europeans from the Arabs, who in turn derived them from Hindostan. The characters were originally the initial letters of the Sanskrit names for the nine digits, one, two, three, etc., and the cipher was a dot corresponding to our period. They have undergone great changes of form, and as used by the Arabs bear little resemblance to either our modern or old-style figures. In many descriptions of tabular work the old-style figures, after being temporarily banished, are again regaining favor, and as their diversities of shape prevent a uniformity which is apt to grow monotonous, it is not surprising that they have reacquired some of their ancient popularity. (See ARITHMETICAL FIGURES.)

Arbitrary Signs, used in writing and printing. (See SIGNS.)

Areopagitica.—Soon after the invention of printing, the princes and potentates of various countries established different forms of censorship over the productions of the press, and the first earnest protest against such censorship was that made by John Milton, in 1644, in his famous Areopagitica; a Speech for the Liberty of Unlicensed Printing. The following extracts from this work, show that it is not only the first, but one of the most forcible appeals ever made for Liberty of the Press:

He who is made judge to sit upon the birth or death of books, whether they be wafted into this world or not, had need to be a man above the common measure, both studious, learned, and judicious; there may be else no mean mistakes in his censure. If he be of such worth as behooves him, there cannot be a more tedious and unpleasing journey-work, a greater loss of time levied upon his head, than to be made the perpetual reader of unchosen books and pamphlets. There is no book acceptable, unless at certain seasons; but to be enjoined the reading of that at all times, whereof three pages would not down at any time, is an imposition which I cannot believe how he that values time and his own studies, or is of but a sensible nostril, should be able to endure. What advantage is it to be a man over it is to be a boy at school, if we have only scaped the ferula to come under the fescue of Imprimatur?—if serious and elaborate writings, as if they were no more than the theme of a grammar lad under his pedagogue, must not be uttered without the cursory eyes of a temporizing licenser? When a man writes to the world, he summons up all his reason and deliberation to assist him; he searches, meditates, is industrious, and likely consults and confers with his judicious friends, as well as any that writ before him; if in this, the most consummate act of his fidelity and ripeness, no years, no industry, no former proof of his abilities, can bring him to that state of maturity, as not to be still mistrusted and suspected, unless he carry all his considerate diligence, all his midnight watchings, and expense of Palladian oil, to the hasty view of an unleisured licenser, perhaps much his younger, perhaps far inferior in judgment, perhaps one who never knew the labor of book-writing; and if he be not repulsed or slighted, must appear in print like a Pupie with his guardian, and his censor's hand on the back of his title to be his bail and surety that he is no idiot or seducer; it cannot be but a dishonor and derogation to the author, to the book, to the privilege and dignity of learning. . . .

Debtors and delinquents walk about without a keeper: but inoffensive books must not stir forth without a visible jailer in their title; nor is it to the common people less than a reproach: for if we dare not trust them with an English pamphlet, what do we but censure them for a giddy, vicious, and ungrounded people, in such a sick and weak state of faith and discretion, as to be able to take nothing but through the glister pipe of a licenser! . . .

Behold now this vast city, a city of refuge, the mansion-house of liberty, encompassed and surrounded by His protection; the shop of war hath not there more anvils and hammers working to fashion out the plates and instruments of armed justice in defence of beleaguered truth than there be pens and heads there, sitting by their studious lamps, musing, searching, revolving new notions and ideas therewith to present, as with their homage and their fealty, the approaching

reformation; others as fast reading, trying all things, assenting to the force of reason and convincement. What could a man require more from a nation so pliant and so prone to seek after knowledge? What wants there to such a towardly and pregnant soil but wise and faithful laborers to make a knowing people, a nation of prophets, of sages and of worthies! . . . Where is much desire to learn, there of necessity will be much arguing, much writing, many opinions; for opinion in good men is but knowledge in the making. Under these fantastic terrors of sect, and schism, and wrong, the earnest and zealous thirst after knowledge and understanding, which God hath stirred up in this city.

Argenteus Codex, or Silver Book, is the name given to a curious ancient manuscript containing the four Gospels in the Mœso-Gothic language, preserved in the library at Upsala, in Sweden, and believed to be a relic of the Gothic Bible that dates back to about A. D. 360. This work has given rise to animated controversies among writers on the History of Printing, because it is alleged on the one hand and denied on the other that the letters it contains (which are all of silver except the initials, and they are of gold) were not written, but stamped or printed with hot metal types, in the same manner as bookbinders at the present day letter the backs of books.

Arithmetical Figures.—This name is generally applied in works on printing to the Arabic numerals, which in the new style in common use are formed as follows, viz.: 1, 2, 3, 4, 5, 6, 7, 8, 9, 0; and in the old style thus:

1, 2, 3, 4, 5, 6, 7, 8, 9, 0.

Army Press.—This title has been applied to a press manufactured by the Cincinnati Type Foundry,

and also to a small portable press, which, though too small for general use, was found very convenient in the printing-offices attached to many camps during the late war; and its name is derived from its adaptation to the use of movable army printing-offices or similar purposes. The small cut which is shown is known as the Army Press but is generally called the Adams Press, after the name of the maker. It will be readily recognized by amateur printers.

Asbestos.—A paper insensible to the action of fire has been manufactured in this and other countries, at various times, from the flexible fibre of the mineral called asbestos, which the ancients were in the habit of converting into cloth. Dr. Burman, Professor at Brunswick, published a treatise on this fossil, of which four copies were printed on asbestos paper. The process of fabricating this paper is described in the Philos. Trans., vol. xiv. p. 823. Asbestos paper has never come into general use, and perhaps never will, notwithstanding the fanciful proposition made by Signor Castaghattai, an Italian, some years ago, that by printing in gold on asbestos leaves, sewed together with threads spun from asbestos, and bound in thick asbestos binding, imperishable records could be made, and that books of this description, being subject to no changes from fire, water, or air, should be called Books of Eternity.

Associated Press.—The organization known as the New York Associated Press was formed soon after the magnetic telegraph became recognized as a success, and when the facilities of the lines were so limited that it was quite impossible to serve a distinct set of dispatches to each of the several New York Journals. The project originated with David Hale, then of the New York Journal of Commerce, who proposed to James Gordon Bennett, of the Herald, a combination of their two papers in the collection of news. Having agreed upon their plans, these parties invited and secured the co-operation of the Tribune, Times, Sun, and Courier and Inquirer; all of New York city. Out of that beginning has grown the institution which now collects the daily news of the entire world, by telegraph, and distributes it thence to every section of the Union. The present Associated Press is a partnership for the collection of news, and consists of the proprietors of the New York Herald, Tribune, Times, World, Journal of Commerce, Sun, and Express. These journalists own the Institution, and theoretically control its affairs, though its details in fact are managed chiefly by its General Agent (or Superintendent), acting under an Executive Committee, to whom the General Agent appeals for advice when necessary. Special agents are appointed in the chief cities of the United States, in which there are sub-organizations, composed of newspaper proprietors who receive news from the Associated Press, and who are admitted to full local membership; and they in

turn decide who shall share the news with them, and various other questions connected with local management. Besides these, there are hundreds of smaller cities and towns, where the local press is charged with the duty of acting as agents of the Association. The duties of these subordinate agents are, first, to collect and forward to the general agency the news of their respective localities; and, second, to receive the telegraphic news supplied by the New York office, and distribute the same to the press of their vicinity. The Association has its agents also in Europe and China, on the Pacific coast, in Central and South America, the West Indies, and the British Provinces of North America; everywhere, in fact, whence it is desirable to receive news by telegraph. Its collection of European news is superintended at London by Americans who engage such English and Continental aid from time to time, as they deem most useful and essential.

The Associated Press is governed by a set of by-laws, one of which forbids the members from taking news by telegraph exclusively for any individual journal, except from Albany, the capital of the State of New York, or unless the news relates to political conventions, sporting matters, or executions. But any member of the Association may order, through the General Agent, any special news which he may require, and use it alone, unless other members of the Association see fit to share it; in which event, the cost of obtaining the news is divided between them. Any special dispatch received by any one paper of the Association (unless within these exceptions) must be promptly sent to all the other members of the Association, to be paid for by whoever uses it. This regulation is to prevent useless competition between Associated papers, at the same time that each is left free to obtain any news which other members of the Association may not care to have.

Thus the news of the world is concentrated at New York primarily for the use of the Associated journals in that city. But the Association, having obtained the news, supplies it for a percentage of its cost, in such quantities as may be desired, to a vast number of journals in all portions of the Union.

By arrangement with the Telegraph Companies, the distribution of news is made simultaneously to all points desired to be served in a given section; and the Western Associated Press, while it acts in harmony, and receives news from the New York Associated Press, takes general charge of the distribution of news in the Western States, and at the same time furnishes the Western newspapers connected with it with news not published in the Eastern journals.

All the great dailies of New York, Philadelphia, Boston, and the larger cities of the Northwestern States, supplement the Associated news with special dispatches, upon which each journal expends a sum often larger than its share of Associated Press bills. The charges on such specials are settled directly between the offices using them and the Telegraph Companies, and therefore do not appear in the expenditures of the Associated. The Associated Press agents are rigidly restricted to reporting simple facts; always distinctly giving as rumor anything deemed of sufficient importance to notice at all, unless it is well authenticated. Opinions by telegraph are religiously tabooed; and the agent who ventures to put them upon the wires is sure to repent of his rashness as soon as his superior officer has time to communicate with him. The special correspondents—each catering for the particular journal to which he is attached—are restricted by no such rule, but travel unfettered in the realms of fancy, speculation, and gossip.

The American Press Association is a comparatively new organization (1870) established for purposes like those served by the Associated Press, and furnishing for the newspapers connected with it, domestic and foreign news, by a similar but not absolutely identical business arrangement.

The English Press Association, which was organized after the purchase of the English Telegraph lines by the Government, adopted some of the features of the Associated Press of America, but it made greater efforts to supply news to country journals, having one class of news which it undertook to supply for about one dollar per week. The plan adopted, as described in an English journal, was to fix a sum per annum for each kind of news it supplies, leaving the customer to cut his coat according to his cloth by taking only those kinds which he wants, and no more. Instead of saying, We will supply you with Reuter's, markets, monetary, sporting, and general news at so much a year, the Association says, We will supply you with Reuter's at so much, with markets at so much, with monetary at so much, with sporting at so much, and with general news at so much; and you may take which you please, or all together. It does more. It sub-edits its news into classes. It supplies Reuter's news entire; it supplies a summary amounting to one-half of the whole, and a shorter summary amounting to one-quarter of the whole. It supplies long and short Parliamentary news, and three different classes of general news. So that a paper which does not want, or cannot afford to pay for, long news may take short news. In the same manner, a paper which issues second editions may have the news supplied for use in those editions by paying for it, while a paper which issues no second editions, neither has the news nor pays for it. In this way the Association meets the case of higher or lower annual payments, while preserving a uniform tariff. It also furnishes a copious supply of general news three times a day; a midday supply of general news for evening papers and third editions of morning papers; and a London city letter of about two-thirds of a column daily. The tariff sets forth the charges in each class for tri-weekly, bi-weekly, and weekly papers. And so strict are the calculations upon which this tariff is based, that whoever receives the same class of news, be he the proprietor of a morning, an evening, a tri-weekly, a bi-weekly, or a weekly paper, he pays for it precisely the same sum per word. There is no handicapping—no favoritism. Every man pays for the news he has, and no more. Least of all does one man pay part of the price of another man's supply.

Assyrian Printing.—The earliest form of printing, except, perhaps, that of making impressions on various substances with seals, was the impression of pictures and characters upon clay, or some similar plastic surface. The Egyptians employed this process freely, but they did not carry it to such a high state of perfection as the Assyrians, and it is conjectured that some of the printed brick books of the latter are of even greater antiquity than the stamped Egyptian bricks of clay. Through the genius and industry of Wilkinson, Rawlinson, Layard, and others, a vast quantity of material illustrative of the labors of the Assyrian printers has been collected and explained. The characters used by the Assyrians are called cuneiform, on account of their wedge-like shape, which probably originated in the nature of the material used for printing purposes, as any instrument put into clay is apt to make a larger mark at the point where it is inserted than at the point from which it is withdrawn. Beginning, probably, with what were little more than rude attempts to write in clay, the Assyrians progressed until they devised engraved cylinders containing the letters or figures they wished to impress, and by these cylinders copies of clay tablets were readily multiplied. The art was used for purposes similar to those to which printing is applied in the present day. Agreements or deeds testifying to the sale of land or slaves, duplicated copies of proclamations sent to distant provinces, and books of considerable length are still extant. We append a few translations of the printed brick-book Assyrian literature, supposed to date back from seven hundred to eighteen hundred years before the Christian era:

HYMN TO THE FIRE GOD.

God of Fire, with thy bright fire,
In the house of darkness, light thou establishest;
Another name, Nabu, gloriously thou establishest;
Of iron and lead the melter art thou;
Of gold and silver the purifier art thou;
The tabbu of Ninkasi art thou;
To the wicked in the night the causes of trembling art thou;
The works of the man, the child of his God, do thou purify;
Like the heaven do thou brighten;
Like the earth do thou purify;
Like the midst of heaven do thou make shine.

ALMANAC OR ASTROLOGICAL PREDICTIONS.

When on the 14th day of the month, the Moon and Sun with each other [i. e. at the same time] are seen, the face shall be right, the heart of the country shall be good, the Gods of Akkad [Babylonia] to give blessings shall incline, joy shall be in the hearts of the people, the heart of the king shall be right, and the cattle of Akkad in the desert in safety shall lie down.

The next is a weather prediction: When the aspect of the moon is very cloudy, great floods shall come. Notes are sometimes added by way of explanation. Thus, after the mention of some of the names of Jupiter, we are told: The star of Marduk [Jupiter] at its rising [is called] the star Dunpauddu; when it reaches 5 Kaspu, 4 the star Sakmisa, when it is in the middle of heaven [southing] the star Nibiru.

INTERLINEAL TRANSLATION OF A TABLET DEPOSITED IN A RECORD CHAMBER AT NINEVEH.

Assur-bani-pal saru rabu saru dannu saru Assur-buni-pal the great king, the powerful king, *kissati saru mati Assur pal Assur-akh-iddina* king of nations, king of Assyria, son of Esarhaddon *saru mati Assur pal Sanakhi-irba saru mati Assur* king of Assyria, son of Sennacherib king of Assyria; *va ki pi duppi izlikusi duppi gabri mati Assur* according to the documents and old tablets of Assyria, *mati Sumri va Akkadi duppu suati ina tapkharti* and Sumri and Akkadi, this tablet in the collection of *duppani astur azniq abre va ana* tablets I wrote, I studied [?], I explained, and for the *tamarti saruti-ya kirib hekal ya ukin* inspection of my kingdom within my palace I placed.

sa sumu satri ipassitu sum su Whoever my written records defaces, and his own re- *isaddaru Nabu duppi satri gimri* cords shall write, may Nabu all the written tablets *sum su lipsit.* of his records deface.

Asterism.—In printing, three asterisks placed in this manner [*.*], to direct attention to a particular passage. In Astronomy, a constellation of stars.

Astronomical Signs.—See SIGNS.

Ascending Letters are all the Roman and Italic capitals; in the lower case, b, d, f, h, i, k, l, t. They are so called because they ascend to the top of the body of the type.

Asterisk.—The figure of a star, thus, *, used in printing and writing as a reference to a passage or note in the margin; to supply the omission of one or more letters or words; and as a signature on an inset. Asterisks are also used to indicate a hiatus or omission, especially of words, lines, or sentences, and were formerly frequently employed in England when it was considered desirable to clearly indicate the names of official personages without printing their names in full. Thus, a printer, anxious to establish a loop-hole for escape from a libel suit, would refer to Lord North as Lord N***h.

Asteroids.—Figures inclosed in a small circle, which by their number indicate various planets.—(See SIGNS.)

Astle, Thomas, born in Staffordshire, England, 1734, died in 1803. He acquired considerable reputation as an antiquary and man of erudition. He was appointed keeper of the records in the Tower; contributed to the Archæologia, and assisted in the publication of many manuscripts, catalogues, records, etc. To typographers he is particularly noteworthy as the author of The Origin and Progress of Writing, as well Hieroglyphic as Elementary, 1784,—a work of authority upon the subject.

Atkyns, Richard, born in Gloucestershire, 1615, died a prisoner of debt in Marshalsea, Sept. 14, 1677. He published, in 1664, The Original and Growth of Printing, collected out of History and the Records of this Kingdom: wherein is also demonstrated, that Printing appertaineth to the Prerogative Royal, and is a Flower of the Crown of England. This book is especially remarkable as having given rise to the famous Oxford controversy. Atkyns, in support of his argument that printing was a royal prerogative, maintained that Frederick Corsellis, a workman in the printing-house at Haerlem, had been secretly brought to England and established at Oxford fully ten years before the art was attempted in any other city except Mentz and Haerlem. This story, which disputes the just claims of Caxton to be considered the first English printer, has been vigorously and successfully combated, as well as the argument derived from it, viz.: that the king having by authority established the art at Oxford retained it as a prerogative; and Atkyns is worthy of mention merely as one identified with the history of printing who has rendered himself infamous by inventing a falsehood to maintain a false doctrine.

Author.—The author, from whom, primarily, springs the product of the printer, is defined by Webster to be, specifically, one who composes or writes a book; the composer of a work, as distinguished from a translator or compiler. The original Latin word auctor, from which author is derived, has the deeper signification of one who positively augments the already existing stock of human knowledge.

Author's Proof.—The clean proof sent to an author after the compositors' errors have been corrected.

Autography.—A process in lithography by which a writing or drawing is transferred from paper to stone.

Automatic Feeding-Machine.—This is an invention for supplying sheets of paper, at regular intervals, to printing-presses, which has been used in a few offices on long editions of weekly newspapers or similar publications where a speed of from 2000 to 4000 sheets per hour was required. The machine was described by the manufacturer as follows: A pile of sheets is placed upon an endless blanket, in the manner usual for hand-feeding. A number of small vertical cylinders are placed above the sheets, and parallel to the front edges. Each of these cylinders is closed at the top, and open at the bottom; inside of which is placed a piston, provided with a rod, which is long enough to reach the paper when the piston is down. In the rod is an elongated hole, through which the crank shaft is put. As the crank shaft revolves, the piston-rods are carried forward upon the paper, and lifted from the paper when carried backward. From the tops of the cylinders to the front edge, where the sheet requires to be moved to, are tubes, the bottom ends of which are flattened, and pierced with a small hole. The crank shaft revolving moves the pistons in the cylinder, and makes each one an air-pump, forcing the air through the tube as the piston rises, and drawing the air through it as it descends. The piston-rods, in sliding upon the paper, move the top sheet toward the ends of the tubes. As soon as the top sheet arrives at the tubes, the ingress of the air is checked, which causes a partial vacuum to be formed in the cylinders above the pistons, and the pressure of air below prevents the piston-rods working upon the paper, until the sheet is carried away. There are also fingers working upon the sides of the sheets, so as to obtain a proper register sidewise.

Autotypography.—A process similar to that of Nature Printing, for producing a metal plate from drawings.

Auxiliary Printing.—Publishers in New York, Chicago, Milwaukee, and several other American cities supply country newspapers with sheets of paper containing printed newspaper matter on one side, while the other side is left blank, to be filled with local news, editorials, advertisements, etc., at the local printing-offices, and this business is called Auxiliary Printing. One establishment in Chicago claims that it regularly supplies two hundred country printing-offices with auxiliary sheets, which are so arranged as to be adapted to newspapers of different sizes or different politics, and to accommodate editors who prefer insides as well as those who want outsides, the latter containing principally literary, agricultural, and scientific matter, while the former contain current news and market reports.

B.

Back-Boxes.—The boxes in the upper case not appropriated to either capitals, small capitals, or figures.

Backing.—In press-work, working the second side of the sheet; in Electrotyping, the process of filling in the back of the electrotype with metal.

Bad Copy.—Manuscript difficult to decipher is one of the greatest annoyances of compositors, and the extent of the evil, as well as an appropriate remedy, has been graphically described as follows:

A common simile, when speaking of bad writing, is that of a spider escaping from an ink-bottle and crawling over a sheet of paper. Certainly the hieroglyphics oftentimes placed in printers' hands do occasionally convey this impression to the mind, of a spider's presumptuous peregrinations; but nevertheless there are numberless instances where the fault is not so much in the slovenly formation of entire words as in the crude shape of particular letters, letters which, granting the remedying of that wherein they are defective, would cause an otherwise plain manuscript to become perfectly legible, instead of, as is the case, neutralizing the good parts, and making the whole illegible. These letters are four in number—i, n, t, u—and in the hands of careless writers are an endless source of mischief and vexation.

What the compositor asks—but at present cannot obtain—is, not that the n and u be made alike, but

that each have its distinctive shape; not that the t be made similar to l, but that it be crossed, or else formed after the fashion much in vogue—namely, a stroke more or less sloping, with a loop in the centre on the side farthest from the letter following it; and lastly, that the i be dotted—an omission which seems to meet with great favor amongst authors, though it is very tantalizing to the compositor, since in bad manuscript the undotted i may be taken to represent either c, e, or r, or even be supposed to form part of what in reality is the letter m. But, if the i's were dotted and t's crossed, few complaints would emanate from printing-offices, or indeed ever be heard, so great an aid is the due placing of these letter-belongings in the task of deciphering. Possessing these two requisites, it might be said still further that there is scarcely a bad manuscript you can place in an intelligent compositor's hands but what he will be able to read every word. Surely, then, in considering the sins of omission and commission recorded above, authors cannot fail to be impressed with the enormous importance of trifles, and to such an extent, it is to be hoped, as will induce them to cross and dot the specified letters. The extra trouble which such thoughtfulness implies is too insignificant to need mention; but the benefit its universal adoption would confer on compositors is incalculable; and if the thanks of a large body of men are not below accepting, then the assurance remains that such thanks will be unanimously accorded.

There are one or two instances, unfortunately, where even the carrying out of the above reforms will not admit of plain sailing in the matter of deciphering—where every letter is slovenly and wretchedly constructed. For this there exists no cure but a few lessons from a writing-master; and if authors consider such a proceeding to be somewhat derogatory, they should, rather than send such manuscript to the printer, place it in the hands of an expert, or turn it over to one of those numerous advertising gentlemen who make it their business to prepare manuscripts for the press, and doubtless it will then reach the printer in a presentable shape, as there is every reason it should do, both on the score of justice and also of humanity. For bad copy means depreciation of earnings, in spite of the enhanced price that here and there is obtained, which is meagre and inadequate.

Ball.—A circular piece of pelt, leather, or canvas covered with composition, stuffed with wool and nailed to the ball stocks, which was used before the invention of rollers to cover the surface of the article to be printed with ink,—two balls being generally used simultaneously. Moxon says they were occasionally stuffed with hair; and that if the ball stocks were six inches in diameter the ball leathers werecut about nine inches and a half in diameter.

Balls are now superseded, but, as a matter of historic interest, directions for making and using them, which were written for Savage's Dictionary of

4

Printing by an old pressman, who was familiar with the subject, are given below:

The pelt being well soaked, the pressman scrapes with the ball knife a little of the wet and filth off—twists it—puts it on the currying-iron, holding an end in each hand, and curries it, by pulling it strongly backwards and forwards, till it becomes warm and pliable, and the grease adheres to his hands, so that the pelt is in danger of slipping out of them while currying: without treading he cuts the pelt into two equal parts, across, and scrapes both sides of them; he then lays one of them on a press stone, or on any other stone that is large enough, and stretches it and spreads it well, with the grain side downwards: the pelt of an old ball being well soaked, he cleans it, scraping it partially, so that some of the moisture may remain in it, and spreads it on the new pelt, as a lining, but does not stretch it nearly so much as the new one, and then nails an edge of them to the ball stock: the wool, being previously carded or combed, he lays in single locks one upon another, crossways, till he has enough for the size of the ball which he is making. If it be for a newspaper, it must be very large; if for book-work, to be used with common ink, it must be smaller in proportion; but in both cases he brings the ends of the locks of wool into one hand, forming it into the shape of a ball very slightly, and puts these ends into the bowl of the stock; then, bringing the opposite edge of the pelt to that already nailed, he also nails that to the ball stock; then he nails two other parts of the pelt opposite to each other, between those parts before nailed; then he plaits the pelt, nailing it regularly on the ball stocks; and cuts off the superfluous edges of the skin. The linings ought to be large enough to be nailed to the ball stock equal with the skin. Then he makes another ball, exactly the same as the first; and if both have a full even face, with no billocks or dales, he has got a pair of good balls.

After having knocked up his balls, he washes both them and the stocks well, and lets them lie out of the water a quarter of an hour; then placing one edge of the face upon the edge of the bank, the coffin of the press, or upon any other convenient place, and the end of the ball stock against his breast, he takes the handle of a sharp table-knife in one hand, and the end of the blade in the other, and scrapes it regularly and rather strongly from the plaits to the face of the ball, at every scrape turning round the ball, which brings out such a quantity of grease and moisture, as obliges him at the first to wipe his knife at every scrape; he thus proceeds, till he can scarcely bring any more out of the skin. He then places a sheet or sheets of paper on the face of the ball, and rubs it well with his hands, till the ball is thoroughly dry, his companion doing the same to the other ball: they then begin to work the form.

If a pressman has to execute fine work with strong ink, he stuffs the balls harder with wool than he does for weak ink; because strong ink lugs or stretches the skin very fast, and soon slackens the balls, if not hard stuffed.

I was several years employed on fine work and strong ink, in an office where it was not allowed to tread a skin; this circumstance caused me to try the above-mentioned plan, and experience has taught me that it is by far the best method.

I also know by experience that a greasy skin is the best for strong ink, if treated in this manner; because it always keeps mellow until the balls are worn out, and there is less trouble in capping them.

Making balls is a nasty job; there is an old proverb in the trade, that The Devil would have been a pressman, if there were no balls to make; that is, the printer's devil.

Tanned sheep's skins, dressed with oil, have been used, to avoid smell, and for durability: they were more durable than pelts; but they were not calculated for producing fine impressions, not being soft; and, in consequence, not retaining dirt or other extraneous matter on their surface; this occasioned picks, and rendered them unsuitable for printing small letter or fine engravings with neatness.

When the pressmen leave work at night, the pelt balls are capped; that is, they are wrapped up, each in a blanket steeped in urine; and this is always done when they are not used; it keeps them soft, and in working condition; but they are to be scraped, and dried with paper, to get rid of the moisture, each time they are wanted. There have been many attempts to supersede the use of urine, on account of its disagreeableness and smell; but no substitute, to my knowledge, has answered the purpose so well with pelts.

Ballantyne.—The two brothers James and John Ballantyne are best known as the friends of Sir Walter Scott, his playmates in youth, his partners in prosperity, and his companions in misfortune and bankruptcy.

James Ballantyne,—born in Kelso in 1772, died in 1833—has frequently been styled the Jenson of the North for his exquisite printing, and ranks with Bensley and Baskerville as the foremost of British typographers. He was educated to the law, and commenced practice, but his fancy led him to abandon his profession and open a printing-office at Kelso, where his remarkably fine printing soon won him an extended reputation. In 1796, he commenced the publication of the Kelso Mail, a weekly paper, and on his journey to Glasgow, by coach, to purchase type he accidentally met Walter Scott, and renewed the intimacy begun years before when they were fellow-students in the Kelso Grammar School. This casual meeting led Ballantyne to become the publisher of Scott's early literary attempts. A small edition of the Ballads from the German attracted great attention by the superiority of the typography, and Ballantyne was induced to remove to Edinburgh, where he established what he styled The Border Press, and began his new career with Scott's Minsreby of the Scottish Border, which won great applause for the beauty of the typographical execution. From that time he printed all Scott's works, and from 1805 until his failure in 1826, Sir Walter Scott was a secret partner with Ballantyne, not only in the printing-business, but in the publication of the Edinburgh Weekly Journal.

Ballantyne, although in some respects careless, was a successful business man, printing Blackwood's' Magazine for many years, and issuing from his press, in the year 1822, 145,000 volumes, all from the pen of Scott. But unfortunately Scott also became, in 1808, principal in a publishing house of which John Ballantyne, James's younger brother, was the nominal head, and this connection, which lasted for five years, was the cause of great losses. Walter Scott's misfortunes, resulting from his purchase of land, and drawing bills on which heavy discounts were paid, involved James Ballantyne in the ruin.

In Lockhart's Life of Scott, James Ballantyne is blamed for having led the great novelist into his pecuniary difficulties, and a formal refutation of the charge was published in 1838, by the trustees and son of the late James Ballantyne. From the statements of both parties it appears probable that the true cause of the failure was Scott's constant demands for money, coupled with the rashness of the publisher, Constable, in drawing and accepting bills to meet the exigencies on both sides.

The friendship between Scott and the Ballantynes survived all monetary difficulties, and was only dissolved by death. Intellectually the trio must have been singularly congenial, for James Ballantyne was pronounced by Kit North to be the best declaimer extant, and was for a quarter of a century universally regarded as the best theatrical orator in Scotland, while he was at the same time a fastidious and candid critic, who freely and boldly corrected the rapid and careless style of Scott's hasty method of composition. John, the younger brother, was brilliant, eccentric, convivial, and so admirable a mimic and story-teller that, according to Lockhart, the elder Mathews was indebted to him for many of his best stories and imitations, which had been more brilliant from the lips of the first narrator than even from the histrionic skill of the great comedian.

A curious link between two generations of novelists is formed by the fact that James Ballantyne, the friend and confidential adviser of Walter Scott, married the sister of George Hogarth, author of the History of Music, and this gentleman, in after-years in London, became in his turn the friend, subsequently the confidant and father-in-law, of Charles Dickens.

Ball Tickets.—See JOB PRINTING.

Balsam of Copaiva.—This is a valuable article, without any preparation, as a varnish for printing-ink; but it must be old and pure. With this balsam, a due proportion of soap and coloring-matter, and a stone and muller, any printer may speedily make ink of superior quality without risk, and with very little trouble. The article sold by the druggists

as balsam of copaiva is frequently so much adulterated that it is of no value as a varnish for making printing-ink—being thin and weak, when it should be strong and viscid; and it should be remembered that ink prepared with this article is apt to impart an offensive odor to the printed page.

Bank and Horse.—The bank is a wooden table, usually about four feet long, two feet wide, and three and a half feet high, used by hand-pressmen to keep their paper on. About five inches from the bottom a board is fastened to the legs, which serves as a convenient shelf for worked-off heaps. The paper-horse, of a corresponding size, is also made of wood, and arranged so as to slant at an angle of about thirty degrees. It is placed on the end of the bank nearest the tympan, and is used for supporting the paper immediately before it is worked off.

Bank Books.—See JOB PRINTING.

Bank-Note Printing.—This work, which, from the necessity of avoiding counterfeiting, and the large current value of its products, taxes to the utmost the ingenuity of the best talent that can be applied to engraving and printing, has been revolutionized by American ingenuity.

Jacob Perkins, of Massachusetts, struck the keynote of a series of great advances, early in the present century, when he substituted steel for copper plates, and devised a method of making transfers of the original engraving in soft steel, which, by being subsequently hardened, could be printed from. Through his exertions, in conjunction with other American bank-note printers, the bank-notes of this country many years ago attained a superiority in mechanical and artistic execution over those of all other nations, which they have always since retained; and the improvements abroad are mainly due to the fact that Mr. Perkins went to London in 1818, and by his labors there, in conjunction with an eminent London engraver, Mr. Heath, gradually disseminated a knowledge of what was, in its inception, an American art, in Great Britain and on the Continent. In addition to the transfer process, important improvements have been effected in this country in the lathe-work by which the portions of the note designating its denomination are usually executed, and various new devices have been tried from time to time to baffle the counterfeiters, of which the latest and probably the most effective is that now used by the government, of printing notes, bonds, etc. exclusively on what is termed spider-legged paper, or paper which has small fibres of silk of various colors incorporated in its texture. The American Bank-Note Company, which is a consolidation of various Bank-note establishments, and the Treasury printing-office, have of late years done nearly all the Bank-note printing in this country. After the plates are prepared, extreme care is required in every process. The best ink, nicely ground and mixed, must be used, and the paper wetted with exact regularity. The best workmen can hardly print more than six hundred impressions in a day. After printing, the sheets are left to dry for several weeks, and they are then subjected to a heavy pressure in pressing machines. When a high polish is required, it is imparted by pressing the notes between hot metal plates, but this is said to weaken the paper. Impressions in red or green ink are sometimes printed on the face or back of notes (as in the famous greenback legal-tenders), but, while they increase the difficulties of counterfeiting, they do not furnish an absolute safeguard.

The Bank of England, after using steel plate notes for a time, adopted in 1853 an improved form of letter-press printing, which is thus described in an English publication: An original is first engraved in metal in relief. This is subjected to the galvano-plastic process, by which a matrix is obtained, and from this matrix a second cast is obtained in relief, a perfect fac-simile of the original engraved plate. From this plate the bank-notes are printed. The metal of which these plates are formed is exceedingly hard, frequently yielding nearly one million impressions without being worn out. The original engraving is never used for printing, but only for the production of matrices; consequently it always remains unimpaired, and thus perfect identity is maintained in the appearance of the notes.

The notes are printed on platen-machines possessing great advantages over the ordinary printing-machines, more particularly in the distribution of the ink. A tell-tale, or register, is attached to each machine, which marks the number of impressions. These registers are set by a clerk before the printing commences, and are checked by him at the close of the day, when the printer must account for, either in bank-notes or spoils, the number of impressions registered by the dial. The notes are printed upon dry paper, a process which has been very greatly accelerated by the recent improvements introduced into the ink by Mr. Winstone, who manufactures for the bank.

The number and dates of the bank-notes are added in an after-printing. This is effected by a very ingenious mechanism being attached to these machines which makes it impossible to commit any fraud by printing two notes of the same number. The apparatus consists of a series of brass discs, of which the rim is divided by channels into projecting compartments, each containing a figure. The numbers 1 to 9 having been printed in the course of the revolution of the first disc, the second disc then presents the figure 1, which, by combining with the 0 of the first disc, forms the number 10. The second disc now remains stationary until, in the course of the revolution of the first disc, the numbers 1 to 19 have been printed, when it presents the figure 2, and does not again move until another revolution of the first disc completes the numbers 20 to 29. Thus the two discs proceed until 99 notes have been numbered, when the third disc comes into operation, and, with the first two, produces 100. Consequently, the first disc performs one hundred revolutions to ten of the second, and one of the third. The notes may be numbered

independently by this process, without the possibility of error, the machine, meanwhile, being its own check.

Bar.—That portion of the hand-press which, in connection with the handle, acts as a lever for bringing down the platen and effecting the impression required.

Baskerville, John.—Born 1706, died 1775. This celebrated English printer and type-founder was a native of Wolverley, in Worcestershire. In 1726 he taught writing in Birmingham, and engaged in 1745 in the japanning business, in which he won celebrity for elegance of design and superiority of finish; this reputation led to the acquisition of considerable wealth. The peculiarities of taste and skill which had made him a chirographer and designer induced him to devote his matured skill and considerable wealth to improvements in printing, in which he sunk several thousand pounds with a greater return of honor than profit. His type was remarkably clear and elegant, being a great improvement upon the imported Dutch type in common use. He used Dutch paper, but is said to have generally manufactured his own, of a very fine quality, making it thick and rather yellow in color. His ink, also manufactured by himself, was remarkable for its rich purple-black tint, and the absolute uniformity of color. This fine and uniform lustre was produced by a constant succession of hot copper plates, between which the printed sheets were inserted the instant they were discharged from the tympan; the moisture was thus expelled, the ink set, and the gloss imparted simultaneously. His more delicate type is seen in his editions of Virgil, in the small Prayer-Book, and in the celebrated Horace of 1762. A quarto Milton of 1759, in a rather bold-faced pica, has won the highest praise from typographical critics. Baskerville's italic was unrivaled for its elegance, freedom, and symmetry. The publications from which he won special renown were his exquisite Bible in royal folio and his editions of the Common Prayer-Book. In order to gain the permission to publish the latter, he was compelled to pay the University of Cambridge twenty pounds per thousand for the octavo, and twelve pounds ten shillings per thousand for the duodecimo edition; the Stationers' Company also exacted thirty-two pounds for the privilege of printing one edition of the psalms in metre in order to complete the prayer-book. Baskerville retired from business in 1765, and endeavored ineffectually to find a purchaser for his types. After his death, in 1775, they were again offered in vain to the Universities, and to the London booksellers, who preferred the type of Caslon and Jackson. But his splendid material at last found a purchaser in 1779, in M. de Beaumarchais, who paid £3700 for the whole of Baskerville's punches, types, and matrices. Beaumarchais, at vast expense, established a printing-office at Kehl, and lost an immense sum of money on a magnificent edition of the works of Voltaire.

Bastard Title.—A condensed title preceding the general title of a work.

Bastard Type.—Type with a face larger or smaller than its appropriate body, as Long Primer on Bourgeois body.

Bath Note.—A folded writing paper, eight and a half by fourteen inches.

Batter.—An injury to the face of type, sufficient to render its printed impression imperfect.

Beard of a Letter.—That part of a type which is between the shoulder of the shank and the face.— *Brade.* The outer angles supporting the face of a type and extending to the shoulder.—*American Printer.*

Bearer.—This term is used both in press-work and composition for various appliances which serve the general end of protecting the type. It is applied to furniture, type high, placed on either side of a hand-press, when small forms are to be printed, to bear the impression off the form. Power-presses have pieces of iron extending over the sides of their beds to accomplish the same purpose, which are also called bearers; and strips of reglet pasted on the frisket to bear off the impression from a blank page or blank space, pieces of leather, cork, etc., tacked to the furniture to bear up the rollers, are called bearers.

In composition the regular bearer used in blank spaces of pages prepared for stereotyping is cast thus, ●, but worn-out type is often used for the same purpose. The original typographical dress in which type pages are cast at stereotype foundries presents a marked contrast to the printed page furnished to the public, on account of the presence of the bearers, as will be seen by the following specimen:

●●●●●●●●●●●●
●●　　　　　　●
●　AMERICAN　●
●　　　　　　　●
●　ENCYCLOPÆDIA　●
●　　　OF　　　●
●　PRINTING.　●
●　　1871.　　●
●　　　　　　　●
●●●●●●●●●●●●
BEARERS.

Bearer-lines.—The top and bottom lines of a page prepared for stereotyping or electrotyping. The bearer-lines, like the bearers, are removed from the plate before it is finished.

Beating.—Before the use of rollers, when balls

were employed, the process of inking the type was called beating. It formed a very important part of a pressman's business, the great object being to secure uniformity of color. The plan adopted was to lay the balls on the left-hand near corner of the form while the tympan was being lifted; they were then carried over to the near right-hand corner. In beating over the form, the elbows had to be kept rather inward, and the ball-stock handle inclining outward, in order that the balls might be perfectly upright. The beater then went up the right-hand side of the form and returned, leaving off at the left-hand near corner, taking care to make the form feel the force of the balls by beating hard and close. The balls were kept constantly turning round in the hands. Also, taking a proof with a mallet and planer, the latter being covered with cloth or felt.

Bed of the Frame.—The platform or ledge at the bottom of the frame.

Bed of the Press.—The flat, smooth surface on which the form is laid.

Bed and Platen Job Printing-Press.—This Job and Card Press, which is illustrated by the accompanying engraving, was patented by Seth Adams, and is manufactured by R. Hoe & Co. They

BED AND PLATEN JOB PRINTING-PRESS.

make several small sizes, to be worked either with a treadle or steam-power, and describe it in their catalogue as follows:

It is so arranged that it can be thrown out of action in an instant by a hand-lever, without stopping the press. The work is placed to the adjustable guides on the platen, which lies in a convenient inclined position, and is lifted up to the bed by means of a cam on the main shaft. The distribution is very good; the ink, being taken from the fountain by a ductor roller, is communicated to a metal cylinder on which a vibratory roller is kept continually traversing; the inking rollers, which are held in a sliding frame, receive a supply from the metal cylinder and then pass and repass smoothly over the form.

Bed and Platen Presses or Printing-Machines.—The general name of those power-presses which have a flat bed and a flat platen, in contradistinction to presses in which the impression is made by cylinders, etc. The term is applied not only to large book-presses (like the Adams'), but also to some card-presses constructed on a similar principle.

Begin Even.—See MAKE EVEN.

Bell, John.—An English publisher, who died February 26, 1831, in the eighty-sixth year of his age, and who was the first to set the fashion, soon generally followed, of discarding the unsightly and awkward long s in typography. This fortunate event occurred in the publication of the British Theatre, about 1795.

Bensley, Thomas.—Died in London 1833 or 1835. He was the son of a printer in the Strand, where he was himself first established, but afterwards removed to Fleet Street, where he succeeded Edward Allen, the warm friend of Dr. Johnson. When Bulmer published his magnificent Boydell's Shakspeare, Bensley followed with his splendid edition of Macklin's Bible, published between 1800 and 1815 in seven quarto volumes. These rival works were considered masterpieces of art, and were welcomed with enthusiastic admiration by the patrons of fine printing. Bensley published many very handsome works, among which Thomson's Seasons, in 1797, in royal folio, was ranked as chief by the critics of the day. He has, however, a greater claim upon posterity for his expenditure of labor and money in assisting Koenig in his great work of making power-presses.

Benzine.—Among the things used for washing ink from forms, nothing is so effective, especially in removing colored ink, which adheres with unusual tenacity, as benzine. It will cleanse type when lye and turpentine fail to do so. The chief objections to its employment are offensive odor and inflammability.

Bevels.—Slugs cast nearly type high, with a beveled edge, used by stereotypers and electrotypers to form the flange on the sides of the plates.

Bewick, Thomas, an Englishman, born August 12, 1753, died November 8, 1828, has been styled the father of modern wood-engraving. After the art had been supplanted by copper-plate engraving, in good publications, and had fallen into such a state of decay that only the rudest and roughest forms of wood-cuts were produced, he restored it to more than its pristine glory. In early life he displayed great skill in draw-

ing. This led to his choice of copper-plate engraving as a business, and at the age of fourteen he was bound apprentice to Mr. Ralph Beilby, a copper-plate engraver. Some time afterwards a mathematician who desired copper-plates to illustrate a work on mensuration, was advised by Mr. Beilby to employ wood-cuts instead. This advice being taken, Bewick executed in wood the mathematical illustrations so satisfactorily and successfully that he directed his chief attention forever afterward to the long-neglected art of wood-engraving. After his apprenticeship had expired, Bewick became a partner in his master's business. His brother John became their joint apprentice. Their illustrations of an edition of Gay's Fables afforded an opportunity to the Bewicks for displaying their talents in the higher branches of wood-engraving. One of these, the Old Hound, obtained the premium offered by the Society of Arts for the best specimen of wood-engraving, in 1775. A series of other illustrations from their skillful hands followed in quick succession. The publication of the History of Quadrupeds, which, after being carefully prepared, made its appearance in 1790, was the means of introducing Bewick to a gentleman who possessed a museum, remarkable for the number and variety of its specimens of winged and quadruped animals, living and dead, and of these Bewick was invited to take drawings, which tended greatly to enrich all his subsequent publications. The pictorial embellishments exhibit boldness of design, variety and exactness of attitude, correctness of drawing, and discrimination of general character. A spirit of life and animation pervades every figure, and thus a lively idea of each different animal is conveyed. A great and unexpected charm belonged to the History of Quadrupeds—this was the profusion of vignettes and tail-pieces with which the whole volume was adorned. These exhibited remarkable inventive genius, and a skill in catching the very lineaments in which the specific expression of the species resides, never before equaled. Under the auspices of William Bulmer, of the Shakspeare Press, London, the Bewicks embellished the Deserted Village of Goldsmith, the Hermit of Parnell, and the Chase of Somervile, all of which met with success. In 1797 appeared the first volume of the History of British Birds, comprising the Land Birds, the letter-press being furnished by Mr. Beilby. Before the publication of the second volume on British Water Birds, a separation of interests took place, so that its compilation and completion devolved on Mr. Bewick alone, with the assistance of a literary friend. In 1818, Mr. Bewick published the Fables of Æsop, and two or three years afterwards, a volume of Select Fables, the wood-cuts which were reproduced in many American editions being a selection from the earlier works of the Bewicks. The public were thus enabled to study the gradual advancement towards excellence which had been made by the revivers of this elegant and useful art. The number of blocks engraved by the Bewicks is almost inconceivable, and it is impossible to particularize the

The first Chapter.

The first boke of Mo- Eo.
see, called Genesis.

The first dayes worke.   The seconde dayes worke.   The thirde dayes worke.

The fourth dayes worke.   The fifth dayes worke.   The sixte dayes worke.

The first Chapter.

IN ý begyn
nynge God
created hea
uen & earth:
and ý earth
was voyde
and emptie,
and darck-
nes was v-
pon the de-
pe, & ý spi
te of God
moued vpõ
the water.

And God sayde: let there be a firmament
betwene the waters, and let it deuyde ý wa
ters a sunder. Then God made ý firmamẽt,
and parted the waters vnder the firmamẽt,
from the waters aboue the firmament: And
so it came to passe. And God called ý firma
ment, Heauen. Then of the euenynge & mor
nynge was made the seconde daye.

And God sayde: let the waters vnder hea
uen gather the selues vnto one place, ý the
drye londe maye appeare. And so it came to
passe. And God called ý drye londe, Earth:
and the gatheringe together of waters cal
led he, ý Sea. And God sawe ý it was good.

And God sayde: let ý earth bunge forth
grene grasse and herbe, that beareth sede:

various works which were embellished by Thomas Bewick and his pupils, of whom he had a continued succession. Some of these have done him great honor, and contributed to carry the art of xylography to a state of perfection at which he himself confessed he never supposed it was capable of arriving.

Beys, Giles, a celebrated Parisian printer, who died April 19, 1593, was the first after those who printed the works of Ramus, that made a distinction in printing between the consonants j and v, and the vowels i and u. Ramus was the inventor of this distinction, and employed it in his Latin Grammar of 1557, but it does not appear in any of his works printed after that time, nor in other books, until Beys adopted it.

Bible.—A large proportion of the typographical labor of the world has been devoted to the production of the Scriptures in whole or in parts; and many pious and learned men have expressed their belief that the invention, which for ages seemed to hover on the very brink of accomplishment, was withheld by Divine Beneficence until the moment that the human race was prepared, not only to throw off the errors of the past ages, but to accept with warmth the Word in its freedom and power.

Although the term *Biblia*, or The Books, had been ascribed to the Sacred Writings as early as the fifth century by Chrysostom, the number of the books had varied from time to time by the introduction or exclusion of those now known as the Apocrypha. But by the various councils and the labors of many students, the books contained in the present Vulgate had been arranged and accepted as canonical. The books had been divided into chapters in the thirteenth century, either by Langton, Archbishop of Canterbury, or by Cardinal Hugo; and this method of division had been adopted from the Christians by the Jews; while, on the other hand, a Spanish Rabbi, who, in 1445, wrote a concordance of the Hebrew Scriptures, introduced the present system of verses, which was accepted by the Christians. Thus the form and entirety of the volume, in all essential points, were accepted and established, both for the Old and New Testaments, by the time that the art in its gradual progression was fitted to reproduce and distribute it.

The present Old Testament originated in its united form in the collation of Hebrew Scriptures, translated into Greek for the Jews of Egypt, at Alexandria, in 285 B.C., and known as the Septuagint, from the fact that the labor was performed by seventy translators. Greek being the learned language of that period, this translation of the Old Testament was accepted and maintained by the Christian Church until the beginning of the second century, when a further popularization was attempted in translating it into Latin, with the addition of the books of the New Testament; this translation was known as the Itala, or old Vulgate (or vulgar tongue). The Itala was the standard version for two centuries, until it was revised in A.D. 405, by St. Jerome, and carefully amended by comparison with the Arabic, Syriac, and

Hebrew versions. This translation superseded the Itala, and became the recognized standard known in all subsequent time as the Vulgate.

Transmission from hand to hand by copyists, through centuries of ignorance and superstition, must have led to an accumulation of errors, which were so fully recognized by the Emperor Charlemagne, that he ordered Alcuin to revise the Vulgate early in the ninth century; and the same work was again attempted by Lanfranc in the eleventh century.

The infinite variations which occurred in the manuscripts may be inferred from the fact that at the Council of Nice, A.D. 325, it was stated that there were two hundred versions of the Evangelists, all differing considerably from one another. Copies of these numerous versions must have abounded, and they led to great confusion, even among the learned, while the other classes of society in all Christian countries were in possession only of detached portions of the Scriptures—favorite parts—such as the Psalms or the Gospels, and various collections and abridgments made by the clergy and scholars for common use.

The preparation of the Septuagint had been the first step toward the diffusion of the Scriptures in the vernacular tongues; the various emendations of the Vulgate continued the work; and in the early ages, other translations, such as the Ethiopic Scriptures of the fourth century, and the Gothic of Ulphilas, served the same purpose. Portions of the sacred writings had also been translated into the Anglo-Saxon, certainly as early as the eighth century; and vernacular versions were also used in Ireland, and probably in other countries, at an early day.

The Hebrew Scriptures, although more carefully preserved by the Rabbis, offered certain variations, and these were carefully collated and revised in the thirteenth century by Jews of distinguished learning.

Yet although so much labor and devout erudition had been devoted to the preservation and perfection of the text, it must be remembered that the expense and cumbrousness of the manuscript form made copies of the entire Scriptures very rare, even as late as the invention of printing—the block books, which marked the transition between writing and typography, being only small volumes containing portions of the Scriptures, or devotional abstracts suited to the daily devotions of the pious.

Contemporaneous with the popular insurrection of Wat Tyler, was the promulgation of Wycliffe's famous translation from the Vulgate (1380), which opened a religious war in England that was to continue for more than two centuries of interrupted strife. The story of the fifteenth and sixteenth centuries, both in England and France, is but a succession of bloody and tyrannous legislation on one hand, and of bitter, steadfast resistance on the other, centring upon the popular demand for the free use of the Bible in the vernacular; and in this struggle, printing immediately played a conspicuous part, by providing the means for the diffusion of the Scriptures.

It is supposed that Gutenberg had already attempted

to print an edition of the Vulgate before he solicited Johann Fust for the money necessary to complete the undertaking; and after their partnership was dissolved, the still unfinished work was continued by Fust and Schoeffer. Gutenberg, however, is believed by many authorities to have accomplished his design, at a later period, under the patronage of Adolphus of Nassau.

The specimens of early printing, which have been preserved, are destitute both of title-pages and dates; and many disputes have arisen, therefore, upon these editions. The first one, generally assumed to have been commenced by Gutenberg and completed by Fust and Schoeffer, is popularly known as the Mazarin Bible, for the reason that the first copy discovered was found in the library of that prelate; while the later one, ascribed to Gutenberg, is styled the Gutenberg Bible.

The new art was warmly accepted by the scholars as a most potent agent in the cause of learning. Portions of the Hebrew text were printed as early as 1477, and, as the typography was a laboriously accurate imitation of the ancient manuscripts, these works hold an authoritative position in Bibliology. The whole Hebrew Scripture was printed in 1488; and the Brescia edition of 1494 was that followed by Luther in his translation. Several editions, both in Hebrew and in Greek, appeared during the sixteenth century. Henry Stephens's Greek Psalms, of 1539, is famous as being the first divided, as at present, into verses; and the Bibles of this typographer are celebrated for their accuracy.

The labors of Tyndale in England and of Luther in Germany were contemporaneous. Tyndale published his translations in detached portions in various towns on the continent; and his Testaments, printed for him at Antwerp, by Grafton, in 1526, were sold in England at three shillings; the Dutch printers of the day pirated his work, and undersold him, offering them for two shillings and sixpence.

Luther completed his German translation in 1534, and in the next year it was published in Wittenberg, being the first complete Bible ever printed. Luther caused several cheap editions to be published, but was also anxious that some should be large and handsome, using his personal influence with his wealthy followers to engage their assistance in editions of two folio volumes, on vellum, in large character, and handsomely ornamented with capital initials cut in wood and illustrating the subject of the chapters. From 1535 to 1574, the production of Luther's Bible was immense, engaging the services of the printers in many cities; one office alone printing one hundred thousand copies during that period.

The English Bible was baptized in blood; Tyndale met his death on the scene of his work, ten years after its accomplishment; one of his assistants had preceded him from the fires of Smithfield; another was to follow by the same death in Portugal. John Rogers, his friend, survived to follow his example and meet his death at the stake, while Coverdale, the last comrade,

reserved for a happier fate, saw his own Bible offered freely in England by the same king (Henry VIII.) who had doomed his comrade to death. During the reign of his successor, Edward VI., eleven editions of the Bible were published in England. In the time of Mary, Coverdale and other English exiles prepared a version at Geneva, which was published immediately after her death, and became the favorite authority of the English Puritans and Scotch Presbyterians, passing through thirty editions between 1560 and 1616. Bishop Parker's version, known generally as the Bishop's Bible, was accepted by Elizabeth in 1568, and continued to be the standard until the present authorized version was published by order of King James I. in 1611. The Roman Catholic authorized English version is known as the Douay Bible, the New Testament being published at Rheims in 1582 and completed by the addition of the Old Testament at Douay in 1610.

In England the printing of the Bible and Prayer Book has been held under royal patent, claimed both by the University of Cambridge and by the King's printer—the University claiming under a patent or copyright, to print all manner of books approved by their Chancellor, etc., granted by Henry VIII. and renewed by Elizabeth and Charles I.

Richard Pynson was the first appointed king's printer, and held the office under Henry VII. and Henry VIII. Richard Grafton, his successor, was a zealous reformer, and received permission to print the English Bible (Coverdale's) from Francis I. of France. He was imprisoned in England for the offence, but was liberated upon giving a bond of one hundred pounds to print no more English Bibles until the king and clergy had settled a translation, and in 1540 received letters patent for printing an English folio Bible. Elizabeth, in the nineteenth year of her reign, extended a like grant to Christopher Barker, enumerating Bibles and New Testaments in the English tongue of any translation, and afterward extended the privilege to his son. James I. confirmed the right to the Barkers in the third and fourth generation, and empowered them to publish the version styled the King James's. In 1769, it was legally decided that the printing of the Bible in English was vested in the British Crown as the personal right of King James I. to the translation made by his order; and in 1819, Mr. Strahan published the Bible under his patent, as king's printer, in whom the privilege is vested, concurrent with the University.

The effect of this royal prerogative was felt in the American colonies, which were dependent upon England for the English Scriptures, although some copies were obtained from Holland, as in the earlier ages of the art. Translations of the Bible into the Indian tongues did not come within the limits of the royal copyright, and therefore several of them were successfully accomplished.

Christopher Sower, of Germantown, Pennsylvania, published, in 1743, a very handsome quarto German Bible; but no English version was publicly attempted until the War of Independence, when the first publication was made at Philadelphia, by Robert Aitken, in 1781—the undertaking being then considered so difficult and important, that the assistance of Congress was requested and received.

In the history of Bible printing, the Bible societies hold a prominent place. The Society for the Propagation of the Gospel in New England was established in England in 1661; and the celebrated Indian Bible, of Eliot, was published under its auspices and at its expense. A Society for Promoting Christian Knowledge, established in 1698, printed an Arabic New Testament, a Bible in the Manx language and another in Welsh; and a Scotch Society published the Scriptures in Gaelic. Difficulties arising from the inability or unwillingness of these societies to supply the great demand in Wales for the Bible in the vernacular, led to the establishment of the great British and Foreign Bible Society in 1804, which began its wondrous work with a Mohawk Bible. This society found such success, and such an extended field for its operations, that, in 1812, an agent was deputed to travel upon the continent, and nearly thirty auxiliary associations, embracing both Protestants and Catholics, were formed in the following four years; this number has increased until, in 1858, there were seventy-two societies, with numerous auxiliaries, agencies, and branches distributed in almost all parts of the inhabited globe.

In 1808 the first Bible society in America was founded in Philadelphia; the example was followed in other cities, and in 1816 the American Bible Society was formed with the intention of supplying the United States, and, according to its ability, extending its operations into foreign lands. The American and Foreign Bible Society, established in 1837, and the American Bible Union, founded in 1850, all labor to the same end, and are the means of distributing a vast number of volumes of the Scriptures.

The amount and variety of printing conducted under the auspices of these various societies, are almost beyond computation, and may only be imagined from the fact that the British and Foreign Bible Society has published the Scriptures in one hundred and sixty-six languages. The Serampore Society mentions the translation into sixteen dialects, with unpronounceable and unspellable names; while in Russia the Scriptures have been prepared in thirty-one dialects.

The Society for the Propagation of the Faith at Rome, established in 1622, supports the famous Polyglot printing-office, known as the Propaganda, which is furnished with types for all the principal languages, to the number, it is stated, of two hundred and fifty. This Bible House of the Roman Church was formerly considered the finest printing-establishment in the world; and in it the famous Bodoni received the training which gave him his great reputation.

The typographical labor which has been expended upon the republication of the Scriptures is beyond all computation, and the immensity of the amount can only be conceived by considering the vast issues of

the presses of Holland, Germany, and Switzerland, under the immediate impulse of the Reformation, added to the works of the Propaganda, the immense labors of the various Bible societies of the present century, and the incalculable quantity issued from the private presses in all countries.

To swell the vast aggregation, it would be but fair to add the great editions of such popular annotated forms as are received by various denominations of Christians, such as the Bible with the Commentary of Adam Clarke, Scott's Family Bible, Matthew Henry's Exposition, the Family Bible of Charles Beloved, and the pictorial edition by Dr. Kitto.

Bible Text.—This type, otherwise Great Primer, was so called because it was largely used in printing the Bible.

Biblical Allusions to Printing and Auxiliary Arts.—The Bible is frequently referred to as a source of information in regard to the ancient methods of engraving, preserving records, making books, etc. Below will be found some of its most striking allusions to such topics:

And he said, What pledge shall I give thee? And she said, Thy signet, and thy bracelets, and thy staff that is in thine hand.—*Genesis*, xxviii, 18.

So she wrote letters in Ahab's name, and sealed them with his seal.—1 *Kings*, xxi, 8.

And because of all this we make a sure covenant and write it; and our princes, Levites, and priests, seal unto it.—*Nehemiah*, ix, 38.

In the name of king Ahasuerus was it written, and sealed with the king's ring.—*Esther*, iii, 12.

And a stone was brought, and laid upon the mouth of the den; and the king sealed it with his own signet, and with the signet of his lords; that the purpose might not be changed concerning Daniel.—*Daniel*, vi, 17.

With the work of an engraver in stone, like the engravings of a signet, shalt thou engrave the two stones with the names of the children of Israel; thou shalt make them to be set in ouches of gold.—*Exodus*, xxviii, 11.

And further, by these, my son, be admonished: of making many books there is no end; and much study is a weariness of the flesh.—*Ecclesiastes*, xii, 12.

Then Darius the king made a decree, and search was made in the house of the rolls, where the treasures were laid up in Babylon. And there was found at Achmetha, in the palace that is in the province of the Medes, a roll, and therein was a record thus written.—*Ezra*, vi, 1-2.

The paper-reeds by the brooks, by the mouth of the brooks, and every thing sown by the brooks, shall wither, be driven away and be no more.—*Isaiah*, xix, 7.

Having many things to write unto you, I would not write with paper and ink; but I trust to come unto you, and speak face to face.—*Second Epistle of John*, 12.

Oh that my words were now written! Oh that they were printed in a book! That they were graven with an iron pen and lead in the rock forever.—*Job*, xix, 23-24.

Oh that one would hear me! behold, my desire is, that the Almighty would answer me, and that mine adversary had written a book.—*Job*, xxxi, 35.

The sin of Judah is written with a pen of iron, and with the point of a diamond; it is graven upon the table of their heart, and upon the horns of your altars.—*Jeremiah*, xvii, 1.

Bibliographer.—One acquainted with books, their authors, subjects, editions, and history.

Bibliography.—A history or description of books and manuscripts, with accounts of the various editions, the dates of publication, and such other information as tends to the illustration of the history of literature. In its Greek derivation the term merely signifies the writing or transcription of books, and a bibliographer in that language meant only a copyist. In France *Bibliographie* was formerly used to express only an acquaintance with ancient writings, and the art of deciphering them. In its more extended and modern signification, bibliography is the science of books, including a knowledge of the subjects, the relative rank, and reputed value, the material of which they are composed, and all such points as decide the position and classification of the volumes in the library.

Under this definition the field of this science is so extensive that it can rarely be covered by any single author; therefore writers have chosen particular sub-divisions; and from their united labors can be collected the varied and general information requisite to constitute the true bibliographer. It is estimated that a complete collection of the publications upon this science would reach to 20,000 volumes.

Among the best-known authors upon these multiform topics may be mentioned Dibdin, Horne, Astle, Ames, Haussard, Johnson, Savage, Lowndes, Timperley, Humphreys, Ottley, Sotheby; Isaiah Thomas being the acknowledged authority upon early printing in America.

In Germany and France special study has been devoted to this department of literature for many years, and the works upon the various topics are almost innumerable. Elementary works upon the subject have been written in French by Achard, Boulard, and Peignot; Maittaire, Meerman, Panzier, Santander, and Wolfius are considered authorities upon the vexed question of the origin of printing; and Ebert's General Bibliographical Dictionary is especially rich in early German literature.

A valuable work upon Spanish literature has been written by Ticknor, the American author, and of late years many extensive works have been published containing lists of books classified according to nationality, language, time, subject, etc.

Bibliology.—A treatise upon books, sometimes used to signify the literature of the Bible.

Bibliomania.—The rage for possessing rare and curious books.

Bibliomania, in its modern form, arose in Holland in the sixteenth century, whence it extended into England, where the fever assumed an especial virulence at the close of the eighteenth and the beginning of the nineteenth century. Manuscripts and books upon vellum were sold by eloquent auctioneers to ecstatic bibliophiles and enthusiastic noblemen for fabulous prices; while first editions, with all the glory of unshorn margins, awakened rapturous delight. Men are described as overcome with joy or plunged into despair by the fateful sound of the hammer; and under the impulse of this passing passion, a copy of Valdarfer's Decameron, of the date of 1471, and believed to be the only complete copy in existence, was purchased at the highest price ever given for a printed book, it being bought at a sale in 1812, by the Marquis of Blandford, afterward Duke of Marlborough, for £2260, that nobleman carrying the treasure off in triumph by outbidding Lord Spencer a mere trifle of ten pounds. Under this burst of fanaticism the early English printers gained new renown; a copy of Chaucer's Troylus and Creside, by Caxton, was bought for £252, while his Lyf of St. Katherin of Sienne was valued at £232.

One of the heroes of the hour was Bodoni, the celebrated printer of Parma. Rome entreated for his presence, England invited him to her shores, Eugene Beauharnais asked him to Milan, Murat besought his presence in Naples; he received gifts from Napoleon; and the Duke of Parma, to secure possession of the coveted artist, established him in a palace.

English bibliomaniacs boasted of the beauty and perfection of Baskerville's Horace of 1762, and decorated the Latin classics of Foulis, of Glasgow, with the most exquisite bindings; while Bulmer's Shakspeare Press was fostered by munificent patrons, who enjoyed the exquisite luxury of limited editions, magnificently illustrated and printed on white satin or vellum. Bulmer, thus protected, boldly challenged the world to equal his perfect typography, and Bensley strained every power to surpass him; while Dibdin became the trumpeter alike of the skill of the printers and the bounty of the patrons, and was well rewarded by the luxurious edition of his own Decameron.

The last years of the eighteenth century were in England marked by a veritable battle of the books, waged by Bulmer and Bensley, with Bewick as the chosen artist, while the alliteration was completed by the struggle centring upon Bulmer's Boydell and Bensley's Bible. Of this famous Bible we learn that one copy was insured in a London office for £3000, that another was valued at five hundred guineas, and still another bound for seventy-five guineas; while the binding of one copy of the Shakspeare amounted to £132 sterling. As a result of the mania, bookbinding became a matter of great importance; the names of Charles Lewis and Roger Payne were widely known, and a woman (Mrs. Weir) who showed especial skill in the renovation of old books, was honored with an admirable portrait in copper-plate. The type fever, as it was called, also led to the establishment of private presses, among which those of Hafod,

Lee Priory, the Grange, and Auchinleck are best known, and were generally devoted to the reproduction of limited editions of rare books in the possession of the owner of the press.

The fancy for fine printing extended to the throne; George the Third is quoted for extravagant praise of Bodoni and Bulmer; and Queen Charlotte erected a press for her own amusement at Frogmore. The Prince Regent became the patron of Whittaker, who achieved a great reputation by producing *fac-similes* of the text of Caxton, De Worde, and Schoeffer; but his crowning work was the Magna Charta from the original manuscript. It was magnificently illuminated and dedicated to the Prince Regent. The copies intended for royal libraries were printed on purple satin and purple vellum in letters of burnished gold, and the binding, of purple morocco lined with crimson silk, was profusely decorated with gold. This printer, so fortunate in catering to the foible of the time, also commemorated the coronation of his patron, George the Fourth, by a magnificent volume glorious with gold and purple.

From England, bibliomania spread into France, where the generals, who danced like bubbles in the wake of the great Napoleon, struggled for the possession of Bodoni; and Murat, in emulation of Louis XIV. and his Delphini, engaged the Parmese printer to prepare the French classics for his son. The French bookbinders of the sixteenth century had excelled those of England and all other nations in the elegance of their workmanship, and under this revival of interest, the names of Gascon, Desseuil, Padeloup, and Derome arose again in deserved pre-eminence. The works of the early French printers, with Verard, Jenson, and the family of Estienne, of course were the especial objects of national pride; and the collectors exhibited great enthusiasm for the jest-books and burlesque treatises of the sixteenth century.

The bibliomania excitement reached its utmost height in England in the summer of 1812, when the library of John Ker, third Duke of Roxburghe, who had died in 1804, was sold. This auction continued for forty-five days, and provoked a competition of prices hitherto unrivaled in the annals of bibliolatry. The original cost of the library was estimated at about £5000, and the proceeds of the sale amounted to £23,341. After the auction, a list of prices was published, both on small and on royal paper; and the whole affair was described by Dibdin in a rapture of eulogium. The famous rivalry for the possession of the Decameron was the great event of the sale, and to commemorate the event the Roxburghe Club was formed in London, consisting of thirty-one of the most eminent book-collectors in the kingdom, with Earl Spencer as President. Joseph Haslewood, one of the founders of the club, wrote an account of the annual festivities from 1812 to 1835, under the title of the Roxburghe Revels.

Bibliomania seems to have taken absolute possession of its victims and to have never relinquished them, for the collecting madness in England lasted out the generation in which it originated, attaining lusty strength a few years before the end of the eighteenth century, and lingering through increasing decrepitude a few years after 1820. The literature of the period exhibits the mania very fully, the Librarian, by Savage, being published in 1808, and in the next year Dibdin issued his Bibliomania, or Book-Madness, containing some account of the history, symptoms, and cure of the fatal disease, in an epistle to Richard Heber, Esq.; this gentleman being a noted collector and afterward one of the founders of the Roxburghe Club. The same year a poem with the same title and same dedication was published by Dr. Ferrier. In 1810 these essays were followed by Bibliosophia, or Book-Wisdom, containing some account of the Pride, Pleasure, and Privileges of that glorious avocation, Book Collecting. By an Aspirant. This pamphlet traces with keen sarcasm the symptoms of the madness through its varied stages of passion for large paper copies, uncut copies, illustrated copies, unique copies, until its last dangerous stages of first editions, true editions, and a general desire for black-letter. Dibdin's Bibliographical Decameron; or Ten Days' Pleasant Discourse upon Illuminated Manuscripts, and Subjects connected with Early Engraving, Typography, and Bibliography, appeared in 1817, and is at once a history of the bibliomania of the period as well as one of its finest products, containing color-printing and various styles of illustrations as the fullest exhibition of the ability of the famous Shakspeare Press of Bulmer.

In September, 1823, according to Dibdin, occurred the most marvelous phenomenon ever exhibited in the annals of bibliopolism, namely, an advertisement of four columns' length in the Times newspaper from Mr. Thorpe, containing the third part of his catalogue for the year. The influence of this literary excitement must also have extended to America, for in the same year, 1823, a delegation of printers and booksellers from Philadelphia attended the fourth centenary festival in honor of Laurence Koster in the city of Harlem. Hansard's Typographia appeared in 1824; and in the same year was published the Typographia of Johnson, who had been printer in Sir Egerton Brydges's private press at Lee Priory, and who dedicated his work to the members of the Roxburghe Club as an essay upon the Origin and Progress of the Art of Caxton, De Worde, and Pynson. As a tribute to the fashion of the hour, Johnson devoted his first pages to a genealogy of the house of Spencer, with a list of the members of the club, including Earl Spencer, the Dukes of Devonshire and Marlborough, Earl Gower, Viscounts Morpeth and Althorp, Sir Egerton Brydges, Sir Walter Scott, and twenty-three other untitled members of high standing as book-collectors. Lowndes's Bibliographer's Manual, published in 1834, was also an outgrowth of the excitement.

The fanaticism of the bibliophiles and the ostentation with which they rode their hobby before the public excited much lively criticism from the unsmitten masses, which frequently took the shape of poetic lampoons. One of the bitterest of these, assailing the leaders of the mania individually under the thin disguise of initial letters, and accusing them of theft, falsehood, and forgery in pursuit of their fancy, was ascribed to young Ireland. Many other publications of a somewhat similar character were burdened with ponderous notes in imitation of Dibdin, while others were dramatic fragments reviving Caxton and the early printers—breathing boastfully of black-letter.

The period was also remarkable for its literary imitations and forgeries. Whittaker's fac-similes of the early printers were received with great favor, and the gossip of the time contains stories of many delusions in the shape of forged specimens of rare books and manuscripts. Foremost among these may be ranked several copies of a newspaper styled The English Mercurie, which was introduced into the British Museum and accepted by Chalmers and others as an official publication of Queen Elizabeth with the date of 1588. The latter half of the eighteenth century is also responsible for three most remarkable forgeries, the ancient Scottish poems of Pinkerton, the still disputed Ossian of Macpherson, and the Shakspeare forgeries of Ireland; and the public interest in such efforts probably incited the Smith brothers to their admirable imitations styled The Rejected Addresses.

Bibliopegy.—The art of binding books.
Bibliophile. } —A lover of books.
Bibliophilist. }
Bibliopole.—A bookseller.
Bibliotheca. } —A library; used as a title of a
Bibliotheke. } book to signify catalogue; as, the *Bibliotheca Scoto-Celtica*, or Catalogue of Gaelic books.
Bienvenue.—An obsolete term, formerly used in England to designate the fee paid on admittance into a chapel.
Bill.—English type-founders call 3000 lower-case m's a bill, and proportion all other sorts by them; so that a bill of pica, including accents and italics, weighs 800 pounds. For every pound of Italic there are ten pounds of Roman. A full proportion of accents is not usually supplied unless they are specially ordered.

The term bill, in the type-founding sense, is not used among printers, who talk of fonts by their weight, and, when they do not order sorts, leave the type-founder to fix the proper proportion between the various letters supplied. The type-founder, in turn, is guided by the proportions of the bill, as nearly as possible, whether his customer wants to buy five hundred pounds or only fifty.

During the last hundred years the bill has varied comparatively little, except in minor particulars—the long s and the ligatures to which it gave rise having been abolished and a consequent increase made of the weight and quantity of other portions of the font. The bill of the modern English type-founders as given by Savage in 1841, and the bill of American founders as given in the American Printer, are nearly identical. The latter is appended here:

A BILL OF 800 LBS. OF PICA.

a	8500	,	4500	A	600	A	380
b	1600	;	800	B	400	B	200
c	3000	:	600	C	500	c	230
d	4400	.	2000	D	500	D	234
e	12000	-	1000	E	600	E	380
f	2500	?	200	F	400	F	200
g	1700	!	150	G	400	G	200
h	6400	'	700	H	400	H	200
i	8000	(	300	I	800	I	400
k	400	)	150	J	300	J	150
l	800	¶	100	K	300	K	150
l	4000	†	100	L	500	L	250
m	3000	‡	100	M	400	M	200
n	8000	‖	100	N	400	N	240
o	8000	§	100	O	400	O	200
p	1700	¶	60	P	400	P	200
q	500			Q	180	Q	90
r	6200	1	1300	R	400	R	210
s	8000	2	1200	S	500	s	250
t	9000	3	1100	T	450	T	326
u	3400	4	1000	U	300	u	150
v	1200	5	1000	V	300	v	150
w	2000	6	1000	W	400	w	200
x	400	7	1000	X	160	x	90
y	2000	8	1000	Y	300	y	150
z	200	9	1000	Z	80	z	40
&	200	0	1300	Æ	40	Æ	20
ff	400			Œ	30	Œ	15
fi	500	é	200				
fl	200	à	200		*Spaces.*		
ffi	100	è	2.0	Thick			18000
ffl	150	ê	200	Middle			12000
	100			Thin			8000
œ	60	All other accents, 100 each.		Hair			3000
				em Quads			2500
	150			en Quads			5400
	90			Large Quadrates, about			
	60			30 lbs.			

Billet Note.—A folded writing paper, six by eight inches.

Bill-Head Paper.—Paper of various sizes, as two, four, six, or eight to a sheet of cap or demy, ruled by a ruling-machine in white, blue, or fancy colored lines as it is likely to be wanted for bill-heads. In Europe a great deal of the work that serves a similar purpose is done on printing-presses with brass rule.

Bill-Heads.—Sheets of ruled writing paper, of various sizes, from the eighth of a sheet of cap to half a sheet, at the head of which the name of business firms, and generally their address, together with other matter similar to that usually put on business cards, are printed; a blank line being left for the insertion of the names of debtors.

Bills of Fare.—See JOB PRINTING.

Bills of Lading.—See JOB PRINTING.

Bind.—The effect produced when furniture is put carelessly together, so that it overlaps, and the pressure of the quoin is exerted on the furniture instead of the type; and also when a measure is so imperfectly made up that the appropriate rule, slug, or lead is longer than the accompanying matter.

Binny, Archibald, a native of Scotland, in which country he had, after becoming a printer, conducted the business of type-founding on a limited scale, at Edinburgh, emigrated to the United States about 1795, and in 1796, in conjunction with James Ronaldson, he established in Philadelphia the first type-foundry in the United States, and laid the foundation of the subsequently famous Johnson Typefoundry, which is now under the management of MacKellar, Smiths & Jordan. Before Binny's arrival in this country, Sower had made German type at Germantown, and Buel had made English type in Connecticut, but he was the first to put the business on an independent as well as a permanent basis. He not only made good type, but devised an improvement in the art of casting them which was the greatest advance step made after the invention of printing until the type-casting machine was invented. By a modification of the ancient mould, which he patented in 1811, Mr. Binny greatly increased rapidity of production, and at the same time rendered the labors of the caster less arduous. He subsequently made energetic but fruitless efforts to invent a machine for rubbing type. After a prosperous career, Mr. Binny in 1819, being then advanced in years, retired from business.

Bite.—A deficiency of ink on any part of the printed form which is caused by the frisket overlapping the type.

Black Ink.—See INKS.

Black Letter.—The name applied by printers, as well as by lawyers, when they talk of Black letter law books, to the old English type, which is otherwise called Gothic, and bears a close resemblance to the German type of the present day. Astle denounced the Modern Gothic, and contended that it did not originate with the Goths, but with lazy caligraphists whose bad taste prompted them to deteriorate the Latin writing. In the old English records, Roman characters, very similar to those now in use, preceded the Black letter, as they have followed it, but when Caxton commenced the first English books, Black letter was the fashion, and so continued until a purer taste restored the Roman characters. Even as late as 1784, the English statute books were still printed in Gothic or Black letters. The Dutch used it in their devotional books long after they had discontinued it in ordinary publications; and the Germans are now substituting in some of their publications the Roman for the Gothic characters.

The old Black letter, and more especially that form of it called Secretary, is represented in the fac-similes given elsewhere in this publication of a page of Caxton's Game of Chesse. Better Black letter, however, was subsequently made by the English type-founders. In this country, the chief use of Black letter has been to furnish to American founders the ground-work and title of a number of job and fancy types, among which are the following: Black Condensed, Black Ground, Black Open, Black Ornate, Black Ornate Shaded, Black Outline, Black Shaded, etc.

Blacks.—The name of an ink used in copper-plate printing, prepared from the charred husks of the grape, and residue of the wine-press.

Blaew.—William Jansen Blaew, the inventor of the press which bears his name, was a native of Amsterdam. Experiencing the inconveniences attending all the presses in use in his time, he caused nine improved presses to be made, each of which he called by the name of one of the Muses. As the excellence of these presses soon became known to other printing-houses, they were soon imitated, and in the course of a few years were almost general throughout the Low Countries, and from thence they were introduced into England. He was born in 1571, and died in Amsterdam in 1638. The peculiarity of the Blaew press, at the time of its invention, was: The carriage holding the form was wound below the point of pressure, which was given by moving a handle attached to a screw hanging on a beam having a spring, which spring caused the screw to fly back as soon as the impression was given. An engraving of this press will be found in the illustrations of presses contained in this volume.

The date of Blaew's invention is 1620, and it is notable not only on account of its being the first successful effort to materially improve the early printing-presses, but because it continued to be the best press extant for a long period. When Benjamin Franklin was a journeyman printer in London, a hundred years after the Nine Muses' presses had been put in operation, he worked on a slightly improved Blaew press, and this, in turn, was not surpassed before the invention of the Stanhope press.

In the early part of his life, Blaew was brought up to joinery, in which employment he served an apprenticeship. Being of an inquisitive disposition, he rambled to Denmark, about the time the famous Tycho Brahe established his astronomical observatory, by whom he was entertained, and under whose instruction he was employed in making mathematical instruments, which curious art he greatly improved; and it was generally reported that all or most of the sidereal observations published in Tycho's name were made by Blaew, as well as the instrument.

Before these observations were published to the world, Tycho, to gratify Blaew, gave him the copies of them, with which he went to Amsterdam, and there practiced the making of globes according to those observations. As his trade increased, he found it necessary to deal in geographical maps and books, and became so particularly curious in his plates, that many of the best globes and maps were made by himself; by his frequent connection with the printing of books, he obtained an insight into the practical part of the art, sufficient to set up a printing-office; he here soon found the inconveniences attending the structure of the old presses, and was thus led to contrive remedies.

Blank Books.—Bound sheets of unprinted writing paper in which records are kept, as, day-books or ledgers. Also books used for similar purposes, in public offices or large private business establishments, which have headings printed at the top of each page, or other printed matter interspersed with blank space left to be filled up with writing. Great improvements have been effected, during the present century, in the manufacture of blank books. The paper was formerly made by hand, in single sheets, with all the edges rough; and, being folded in the centre, it had to be broken down or opened flat and trimmed with plow and press; nor was it ruled before being bound,—many of the old Record Books now in the County offices of Philadelphia and other portions of the United States being unruled. Now the paper, as supplied by the paper-mills, is trimmed on all sides perfectly smooth and square; by the aid of machinery, lines are ruled across the sheets, to any pattern, in a variety of colors; and blank spaces are left for printing headings, or other matter at any portion of the sheet where printed matter is considered desirable. In binding, the improvements are equally marked. Blank books were formerly secured only on cords, being covered with vellum and tight backs. The sheets are now generally sewed on parchment slips, bound with patent or open spring backs, and covered with calf, or sheep-skin, Russia-leather, etc. By the application of machinery to the various processes of binding, the cost has been greatly lessened, and complete bound books can now be furnished for a smaller sum than the cost of the binding alone, a few years ago.

Blankets.—Whatever substance is fixed in the tympans to intervene between the type and the platen, in order, when the power is applied, to cause an impression, is denominated a blanket, and one of the most important duties of the pressman is to secure such blankets as are best adapted to the work in hand, and to see that they are kept in proper condition. You may have good type, good presses, good ink, and good rollers, and still produce very inferior results if you have either poor or inappropriate blankets; and among the manifold causes which lead to bad printing, want of proper care or of proper provision in regard to blankets is one of the most important. The general principles applicable to hand-presses have been stated as follows: There has been generally used a kind of blanket, manufactured for the purpose, of a more even fibre than ordinary blanketing, free from knots and having a very fine surface or pile; and to vary the impression as different kinds of work might require, very thin or Welsh flannel, cassimere, or fine broad-cloth was used. These are varied by the judgment of the master or pressman, according to the type, paper, ink, etc., with which he works: thus, for very close or heavy forms, small type, he must select the softest woolen blanket; for larger type and lighter work he must select the finer flannel or cloth blanket; and for yet larger type and more open work he must continue the change to a single cassimere. Again, a discretion will be required, according to the state or wear of the type: the newer the letter and sharper the ceriphs, the finer may be the work, the stronger the ink, and the harder the impression; while, on the contrary, in order to make type which has been worn appear well up to paper, additional softness must be given. The kind of press, also, at which the work is to be done requires

to be treated with a due degree of discrimination. In fact, nothing but observation, experience, and good mechanical common sense can well guide the judgment of the pressman in this most material point of making ready. By the various changes and combinations of his blankets, adding a soft to a hard, or a hard to a soft one, reversing them in regard to the one or the other falling next the type, adding a sheet of paper or glazed paper between, or under, or over, he must, with necessary judgment and patience, regulate his pull according to the various combinations of circumstances which may attend his work.

In cylinder presses the general principles described above should also be observed. What on them serves the purpose of the blanket of the hand-press is called by some a blanket (no matter what may be the nature of the material) and by others a tympan, the latter term being adopted in Hoe's Catalogue, which in its directions for making ready on a cylinder press recommends a pasteboard tympan [or blanket] for wood-cuts, for perfectly new type, and for the best kinds of press-work; a woolen blanket for old stereotype plates, for old type that has been rounded on the edges, for posters with large wood-type, and for all common work which requires a firm, solid, dull impression; thick paper for book-work, script circulars, and leaded forms; india-rubber cloth, or what is popularly known as the gum-blanket, for miscellaneous work, and for use when it is intended to make one blanket or tympan answer all purposes; and a combination of Welsh flannel over rubber, or thin rubber over pasteboard or under paper, for use when very good press-work is to be obtained from imperfect materials.

In many American printing-offices blankets are too much neglected. New type is repeatedly spoiled by the use of soft blankets, and the india-rubber blanket is made to do duty on occasions when substitutes better adapted to the work in hand should be used. In some of the best offices the gum-blanket is never used even on cylinder presses, and reliance is placed exclusively on packing or drafting paper, or tympan rolls, press-boards, muslin, etc.

On a hand-press a certain degree of softness is required in the blanket to lighten the labors of the pressman, but in a machine press this consideration may be utterly disregarded; and it is therefore possible as well as desirable to use on machine presses blankets more appropriate to new type than those which are practicable on hand-presses.

The French printers use blankets of cloth, cassimere, or silk. In ordinary impressions cassimere is used, but for careful work one of the blankets is replaced by two thicknesses of silk placed directly upon the tympan. One thickness of silk is often sufficient, but when great neatness is required a blanket of merino is added, and for special work two thicknesses of silk are advantageously used. When the type is worn or unequal in height, merino blankets are deemed absolutely necessary to produce good effects.

The blanket, of whatever material, should be well stretched, and, on hand-presses, turned and rubbed after the printing of each form, in order to obliterate the marks of the impression.

When a blanket has been used on one form for a long time, it will not do for a different form, as numberless imperfections will result in the impression.

A blanket has been patented by M. Delègue, composed of silk and wool, with a surface of caoutchouc. The patentee claims that it produces a finer impression and diminishes the wear of type, particularly in machine work, and that it is perfectly adapted to every variety of printing-press.

Blanking out.—The insertion of leads, reglets, or white lines, in titles or jobs, so as to open or extend the matter.

Blank Line.—A line filled with quadrats, reglets, or leads.

Blank Pages or **Blanking.**—When blank pages occur in a work, particularly in duodecimos and smaller sizes, the compositor should set them up to the exact size of the pages of the work, to insure good register, and to avoid trouble in the arrangement of the furniture.

Blanks.—See JOB PRINTING.

Blank Tables.—Tables in which only the headings are printed, leaving the columns to be filled up with the pen.

Blind, Printing for the.—The following article is contributed to this publication by Mr. Napoleon B. Kneass, Jr., a blind gentleman of Philadelphia, the publisher of a magazine for the blind, and the inventor of Kneass's system of printing for the blind:

The first successful efforts to introduce printing in raised characters for the blind, were made in 1784, by Abbé Valentin Haüy, at Paris, who founded the same year L'Institution Royale des jeunes Aveugles, which was the first institution for the instruction of the blind in the world.

The Abbé's experiments confirmed his hopes, that the blind were able to acquire an acute sensitiveness of touch which would render reading with their fingers by means of raised characters, practicable. He was not only the inventor of printing for the blind, but the founder of institutions for their instruction.

Since this benevolent man's time, much has been written and said upon the subject; theories have been advanced, experiments in various styles of characters tried, and improvements made, in relief printing.

Mr. Johnson, connected with the blind school in London, some years ago, in giving a description of how the blind read, said, The ordinary systems of embossed printing in present use, for teaching the blind to read, may be divided into two classes, one in which arbitrary characters are used to denote letters, sounds, or words, and a second in which the ordinary Roman letters are used, all alike presenting a raised surface to the touch of the reading finger.

Arbitrary.	*Alphabetical.*
1. Lucas's System.	1. Alston's System.
2. Frere's "	2. The American System.
3. Moon's "	3. French Alphabetical.
4. Le Système Braille.	4. Alston's Modified.
5. Le Système Carton.	

Lucas's system possesses great advantages for those who enjoy but an imperfect sense of touch or are employed in hard manual labor. It is justly considered to be easy of acquirement, and the least difficult of all the English arbitrary systems. It, however, has the disadvantage of being complicated in some of its details, while the abbreviations of words and syllables and the purely arbitrary formation of its characters render it troublesome for those with sight to teach, and difficult for the blind to understand. It is less bulky than some other systems, but more so than Alston's, the American, Braille's, or Carton's. It required thirty-six volumes to contain the Scriptures, while the Boston Alphabetic requires but eight. Besides the Bible, there have been probably not more than twenty other works, of smaller dimensions, published in it.

Frere's system is on the Phonetic principle, or combination of elementary sounds. Mr. Johnson says of this system, it is a matter of regret that he (Mr. Frere) should lend his valuable and charitable endeavors to a plan both difficult and arbitrary. The Scriptures required fifteen volumes; and there have been published in it probably from fifteen to twenty other works.

Moon's system may be considered as based upon Lucas's and Frere's. It professes to be an alphabetic arrangement, though decidedly of an arbitrary character, its chief recommendation being that it is the invention of a blind man, who, by industry and talent, became a teacher in the Brighton school. Mr. Moon's experience was but small, scarcely extending beyond the Brighton school, which in 1850 contained but twenty-four inmates, not all of whom could read. One feature of his system was borrowed from Frere's, that of preventing the constant recurrence of the finger to the ends of the lines, on the left side of the page. This is effected by printing every alternate line in a converse position, so as to admit of its being read backward, the first line being read from left to right, the second from right to left, and so on, a bracket guiding the finger from the end of one line to the beginning of the next.

This plan Mr. Johnson thought favorably of, but he fell into an error which many seeing persons are apt to make. There is no more necessity for the alternate lines to be printed backward for the blind, than for the seeing, as the finger of the blind reader can as readily retrace to the next line, where the bottom of the letters are all on a line (as in the American system), as the eye of the seeing.

Moon's system, which was both voluminous and expensive, was thus explained by himself: In order to avoid the complicated form of the Roman letter, and the still less discernible angular type, Mr.

Moon has invented an alphabet, each letter of which is formed of one or two lines only. Most of them have a partial resemblance to those in common use. Where this could not be obtained, the simplest possible form has been adopted. By the use of nine forms, turned in different directions, the whole alphabet and figures are represented; one form, for instance, serving for A, V, K, and X, and another form for E, L, M, Y. No contractions are used, except the common ones representing the terminations ment, ing, tion, and ness, by their last letters. L, G, J, and C, also, in the Holy Scriptures, stand for the frequently recurring names of Lord, God, Jesus, and Christ.

There have been probably twenty-five works, besides the Scriptures, printed in this system.

Braille's system has been adopted throughout France, in preference to all other systems, and after many years of merited success in raised alphabetical printing, the use of abbreviations renders it inferior to Abbé Carton's plan, and thus it is liable to the same objections as those of Lucas, Frere, and Moon.

The plan is rather simple, is not difficult to acquire, and is very convenient for purposes of correspondence, and for keeping accounts and memoranda. Its use in writing and reading is reversed: hence to make the letters they must be reversed from what they are for reading. Any blind person, with a small frame and stylum, can become his own publisher; but while great facility is no doubt attained in producing books, it still has the great fault of all arbitrary systems, the need of a peculiar course of training to both blind and seeing, ere it can be deciphered and understood. The principle is founded on dots from 1 to 6, in combinations. Carton's system is less arbitrary than Braille's, following more closely the form of the Roman letters (the system of pinpoint printing in use in this country may have been conceived from Carton's system), but it is liable to the very serious objection that applies to all dotted characters,—the want of durability, unless on very thick paper, which would make works too bulky. No other system is in use in Bruges, and the Belgians generally favor a dotted character.

Alston's system consists in a slight modification of the Roman capital letters. Mr. Alston's long experience convinced him that the simplest and most perfect system consists in the employment of ordinary letters, which those who can see can at once understand and use for the benefit of the blind. He says he has long been convinced that arbitrary characters, however ingeniously constructed, throw unnecessary obstacles in the way of the blind, and that an assimilation of the alphabet of the blind to that of the seeing, would, from its great simplicity, not only be free from all objections, but in the case of those who have lost their sight after becoming familiar with the Roman alphabet, it would be attended with manifest and peculiar advantages, whilst its similarity to the common printing would enable blind children, at a distance from any institution, to attend an ordinary school, without giving more trouble or inconvenience to the teacher than any of his other pupils. The advantages of a literature for the blind so simple, practicable, and easily taught, are obvious to every one. Besides the Bible, thirty to forty works, probably, have been printed in this system. Abbé Carton considered Alston's system as one of the best. The Rev. Wm. Taylor says that, after more than thirty years' close attention to the subject, no alphabet or system of characters that has come under his observation seems to possess (as a whole) so many advantages as the Roman alphabet (capitals and lower case), when divested of all useless ornament.

The principal American systems are Roman Alphabetic. J. R. Freelander, who founded the Pennsylvania Institution, devised a modification of the Roman capitals, which was adopted and to a small extent used throughout the United States. A number of valuable works—about twenty—were printed in this letter at the Pennsylvania Institution, among which is the only dictionary of the English language in raised letters.

Dr. S. G. Howe, the founder of the Institution at Boston, Mass. (which was the first of its kind in America), invented a lower-case angular letter (without the use of capitals, except the G and J, which are used to the exclusion of the corresponding lower-case letters) which is in use there, as well as in most of the other institutions in the United States. At the Boston Institution many valuable works (about fifty) have been printed. The Bible has been printed in the same letter, from stereotype plates, by the American Bible Society, in eight quarto volumes.

The French Alphabetic system is the common rounded lower-case letters with capitals, similar to the letters in which books were printed in England for Sweden, and also similar to what is known as the Bristol type.

The principal objection to these systems is, that the tails of some of the letters extend below the line, requiring longer type, throwing the printed lines further apart, and confusing the finger in retracing to the beginning of lines. The latter system was adopted by the Rev. J. Taylor. The compiler of this account, who is himself entirely blind, succeeded after long consideration and numerous experiments, in improving such of the capitals of the Alston system, and the lower case of the Howe angular system, as required more distinctness to the touch, and, combining the two characters, so improved, under the title of The Improved Combined Letter, introduced it to the blind, and to the Institutions for their instruction. By the blind, with but a few exceptions, the system has been approved and commended in pleasing and grateful terms, whilst nearly all the Institutions in the country are favorably impressed with it, though perhaps two or three would have preferred the omission of the capitals.

The founder of the system claims for it all that the Rev. Mr. Taylor claims for the Alston system,

and in addition that the Improved Combined Letter gives to the blind the same advantages from the use of capitals, as are enjoyed by seeing persons, as it marks the heads of sentences, proper names, etc., and thereby preserves a clearer sense of the context. A letter by Rev. B. G. Johns, chaplain of the school for the indigent blind in London, written to Mr. Johnson in 1853, upon the subject of reading for the blind, advocates so very strongly the advantages of a combined system, that it is quoted here as applicable to the claim of merit for the Improved Combined Letter:

All parties are, I think, now agreed that the blind, as a class, shall be educated, but, meanwhile, are most busily disputing on the very threshold of the work, viz., how the blind shall learn to read, whether by Brown's infallible stenographic, Smith's unrivaled abbreviations, Jones's unsurpassed contractions, Robinson's easy symbols, or by any other of the numerous perfect systems which, unfortunately for the blind, have been invented. For every one of these systems, eager and unwearied partisans labor night and day, each unalterably convinced of the infinite advantages of his own plan, and equally assured of the errors and mistakes of every other.

It is clear that, while matters remain thus, little will be in reality done in that good cause for which we are all so earnestly toiling, and the question is, How shall a change of circumstances be effected? There seems to be but one way of doing this, and that is, by the adoption of one common system. At present, to the learner of one system, all other systems whatever are incomprehensible and useless, until he has again toiled through a new alphabet, and a new detachment of elementary sounds or abbreviations. It is, in fact, almost like learning another language. The poor blind man, therefore, can read only the few books in his own system, and can be assisted only by the few who have already mastered it. His friend who drops in for an hour after his day's work, and would cheer his solitude with the words of the Holy Book, shuts it up in despair, when he looks at the mystic title-page, as unintelligible to him as the writing on a mummy-case.

It may be said, Why does not the blind man read for himself? I answer, Sickness or old age may have made his hand feeble, or trembling, or rough work hardened his fingers, or, possibly, the book he has had given to him is not on the exact system which he learned when a boy, and therefore puzzles him, or he may wish to earn his supper by making a basket while his friend reads, being perhaps obliged to work without intermission during the day to gain a livelihood. Any one of these causes may deprive him of the means of instruction and amusement.

The blind form a peculiar and almost distinct race of people; peculiar, as being deprived of one of the most important senses given to us by God, and distinct, as in a measure cut off from the visible

world, in which they still remain, in which their appointed work lies, and their fellow-men are engaged. On every account, therefore, it is most desirable not to render them more peculiar, or more distinct, but rather to make them, as far as may be, one in privileges, enjoyments, and duties, with those about them in the world.

From a consideration of these facts it is evident that the system of embossed printing for the use of the blind, for general adoption, must embrace at least the following features:

1. It must resemble, as nearly as possible, the type in ordinary use among those who have eye-sight.

(a.) That the blind scholar, in learning to read, may have every possible help from his remembrance of letters and words he may have formerly seen, but which now his fingers must decipher.

(b.) That he may derive help in learning from any one who can read an ordinary book, or, if needful, that his friend may be able to read it to him.

2. It must present the words correctly spelt in full, that when he learns to write he may do so in a correct manner, which others can read.

3. The raised characters must be clear, sharp, and well defined; that the finger hardened by long work, and the keen touch of the little child, may be equally able to observe them.

The only system which can ever offer such advantages as these, must clearly be some modification of Alston's and the lower-case type.

It remains to be seen whether science, which has done so much for all other readers, cannot help in providing for the blind a literature and typography which will aid in making them wiser and better men. Many thousands, in all parts of our land, are nobly working for this good cause; let us hope that all differences will soon be laid aside, and that, by working together, they will meet with the success which unity of action as well as of purpose can alone give. May God speed the work with the coming year!

Such evidence as this, alone, is sufficient to recommend an alphabetical system for general adoption; but should a doubt still exist on the subject, the conclusions of the Abbé Carton, even in the face of his own system, are yet to increase its weight. His letter may be translated as follows:

Indeed, if a character known to all readers is employed in printing in relief for the blind, these unfortunates will be drawn more nearly to other men than if they were taught to read a character unknown to those around them. Besides this, a common alphabet can be more readily learned by those persons who devote themselves to instructing the blind, while a new alphabet would raise an obstacle both to pupil and teacher, and render a mutual understanding more difficult.

The largest number of the blind are found among the poorer classes, and their sufferings are intensified by the feeling of isolation. All our efforts should be directed to removing these barriers, and to rendering instruction as easy as possible; and if the same character was used, the elementary works already provided for children could be used in their instruction, and the blind might even be admitted into ordinary schools, which would conduce to the more rapid development of their faculties than a course of instruction in peculiar institutions fitted only to their special needs and in the companionship of their fellows in misfortune.

The compiler of this article has been engaged for several years in the publication of books for the blind: among his first works were an English grammar, in two volumes, and some small books in the Roman capital system. Within a few years he has issued, in the Improved Combined Letter, quite a number of interesting and valuable works, among which are a Magazine of Science and Literature, the fifth volume of which is now in course of publication; poetical works of England and America; Shakspeare's Merchant of Venice (being, we believe, the first entire play of that eminent author ever printed in the raised letters); Milton's beautiful ode on the Nativity of Our Saviour; several valuable school-books,—Primer, Speller, Reader, Arithmetic, —and a number of small books on various subjects. He has also printed, for an association which he organized for publishing for the blind, a Dictionary of Musical Terms. There have been several attempts by various parties to form a method for embossing music. None as yet have been successful. The writer is now engaged in experimenting upon the subject, and hopes at no very remote day to accomplish a perfect system for this purpose, by which music will be printed from type and sheet-music furnished to the blind, at prices not varying much from the cost of that furnished to the seeing. One great advantage of music printed for the blind, will be the saving of the expense for a reader to the blind teacher.

Mr. Wm. B. Wait, Principal of the Institution for the Blind in New York City, has invented a system of an entirely arbitrary character, somewhat similar to the Braille—the dots being grouped from one to six—differing, however, from the position of the Braille, being but the space of two dots high. Mr. Wait claims that works printed in his system will be less bulky than in others; but this advantage will not counteract the numerous disadvantages of all arbitrary systems, particularly dotted ones.

For further information on the subject of printing for the blind, see Kneass's Philadelphia Magazine for the Blind, vol. i. page 2, vol. ii. page 2, and vol. v. page 2; and see, also, specimen page of the Improved Combined System, and of several other systems, printed for this publication by Mr. Kneass.

Block Books.—This term is used to designate works printed from wooden plates, containing both illustrations and text, but distinguished from those containing movable type.

These books were very numerous, especially in the Low Countries, during the years immediately preceding the invention of printing in its modern form, and are very valuable as showing the preliminary stages of the art.

Historically, the block books are traced to China, where they are found dating back to the tenth century, and even at that time decorated with illustrations of considerable merit. In 1295, Marco Polo described them as printed from tablets of wood, and probably brought some of them to Venice. Printing from blocks was already familiar to the manufacturing peoples of Europe in the preparation of woolen, cotton, and silk fabrics; but it is probable that Marco Polo, or other travelers, introduced or incited the establishment of the manufacture of playing-cards, which became so important a branch of business in Venice, that it was protected in 1441 against foreign competition. This legislation is supposed to have been directed against Holland, another maritime country, which might also have been indebted directly to China for the art.

That cards were printed in the Low Countries at an early date seems proved by an entry in the Burghers' Book of Augsburg, for 1418, mentioning Kartenmachers and Formenschneiders—card-makers and figure-cutters. Besides playing-cards, it is, however, probable that the art was used in preparing single sheets or cards containing portraits and figures of the saints with accompanying legends or text. There was an immense demand for such publications; even now they furnish a lucrative branch of manufacture; and it is probable that, at an early day, they were altered and improved into the primitive block book.

Upon the revival of learning, a widely-extended field opened for a cheaper and more popular form of literature than the ponderous and luxurious tomes of ancient Greece and Rome. Necessity had, at an early day, compelled the preparation of a few such works. As early as the beginning of the ninth century, Saint Ansgarius, a missionary to the Saxons north of the Rhine, had prepared a Bible for the poor,—the well-known Biblia Pauperum; and this book maintained an unbounded popularity for at least five centuries. A large number of manuscript copies still exist, varying much in the style of execution, not only in regard to neatness and accuracy, but as to the quality of adornment, showing that there was fully as much variety possible in a manuscript book as there is at present between a volume with proof illustrations, bound in turkey morocco, and the same on cheap paper with a muslin cover.

Much minute examination and careful comparison and collation have been devoted to the study of the specimens of the block books preserved in the great libraries of Europe, especially by those desirous of settling the rival claims of Koster and Gutenberg; but the subject presents many difficulties, as may be inferred from the fact that a very animated discussion arose in the present century over the question as to whether a certain Donatus, or grammar, was a specimen of the pure block book, or contained movable type; both sides were warmly espoused by learned

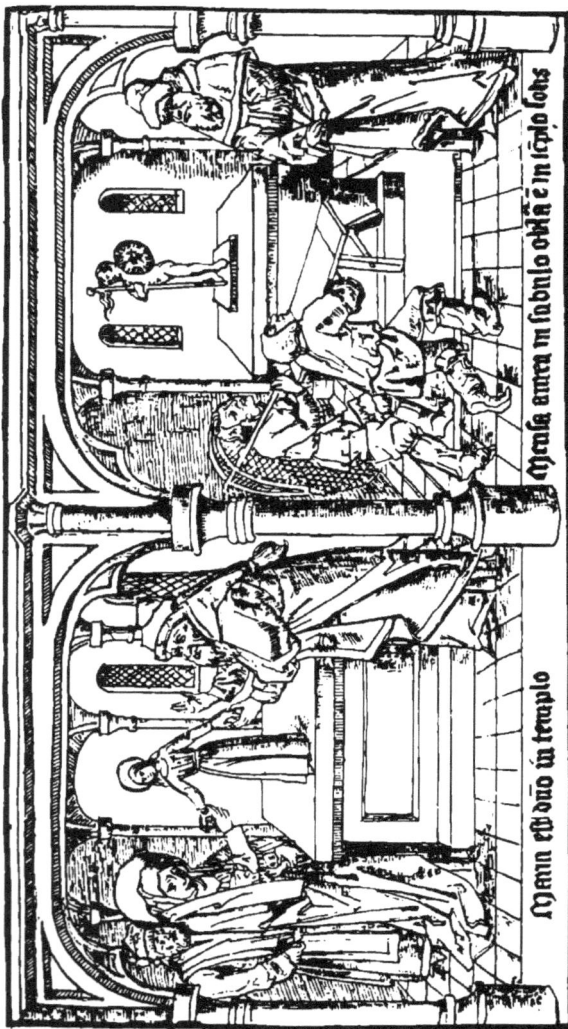

PART OF A PAGE OF A BLOCK BOOK, PROBABLY PRINTED BY KOSTER BEFORE 1430.

critics, when a third party stepped in and proved, to their utter confusion, that the pages in dispute were manuscript.

The Heroic Deeds of Alexander has been described as the earliest specimen of printing in Europe, and claimed to be a block book executed by the two Cunios, twin brother and sister at Ravenna, in 1285; but although the facts adhere, and the story is charmingly romantic, many authors believe the work to have been a forgery, executed about two centuries later than the assumed date.

The block books of Holland were superior in all points of style and execution, and were much more numerous than those of any other country in Europe. In what are believed to be the earliest specimens the illustrations are much finer than the text, there being apparently no effort to produce any improvement upon the style of writing usual to the period; some of the coarseness and irregularity of the type must also be ascribed to the material, it being extremely difficult to cut uniform and regular lettering upon wood. For these reasons the block books are usually inferior to the manuscript copies, and were probably regarded as a cheaper form and rude imitation of the original.

The gradual diffusion of learning, which marks the fourteenth and fifteenth centuries, can be traced, step by step, in the alterations which occur in the manuscripts and block books. In the case of the former, much of the old luxury is abandoned; the manuscripts, no longer restricted to the use of the wealthy and learned, are slowly popularized; instead of the illuminations, magnificent in gold and purple, plainer outline pictures are substituted, more or less elegant, according to the value of the work; and, as a still greater advance, paper supplies the place of vellum. The manuscripts appear to the casual observer to have become more rude and barbarous, but they were really the same boon to that age that cheap editions of standard works are to the vast reading public of the present day. The introduction of paper brought with it the next great step—printing from wood, which was impracticable with vellum. Paper, thinner and more pliable, could be laid upon the engraved block, which was already covered with distemper, and the impression was obtained by rubbing the back of the paper, just as the wood engraver does at the present day. The paper was printed only on one side, and the impression produced by the distemper was brown, frequently quite light, but occasionally gray or dark brown.

The Biblia Pauperum, already mentioned, appears to have been one of the most popular books, both in the manuscript and xylographic form. In the earlier copies it contained forty leaves, afterwards increased to fifty. A general idea of its appearance may be formed by imagining a rude but boldly designed wood-cut; in the centre, in a sort of apartment formed by gothic pillars, sits the Virgin, with a book on her lap, and her hands devoutly crossed on her breast; beside her stands the angel of annunciation,

with his legend upon a scroll, while from above, a ray issuing from the lips of the Almighty falls upon the head of Mary, bearing within it the descending dove, followed by the infant Christ bearing his cross. Panels of equal size, on either side of this central compartment, contain Gideon, a huge knight in full armor, praying that his fleece shall become miraculously moistened, and Eve beneath a tree with the serpent. In a division above the centre, Isaiah and David sit as in a church window, uttering scrolls bearing appropriate texts; and beneath, in a similar apartment, Ezekiel and Jeremiah perform the same explanatory office.

One of the rudest, but, at the same time, most popular of the block books was the Ars Memorandi, or art of remembering. This work probably constituted the library of the illiterate monks, as it furnished, in most condensed fashion, a complete key to the contents of the Gospels. In fourteen large, full-page pictures, a species of index is furnished—five pages being devoted to the Gospel of Matthew, and three to each of the other evangelists. One of the plates, embracing six chapters of Matthew, will sufficiently explain the method, which must have been a very efficient aid to the memory. The angel—the symbol of St. Matthew, in bold outline—covers the page, standing with outstretched wings. In one hand, as a curious expression of the contents of the eighteenth chapter, he holds the sun and stars, and a little child, while on the figures eighteen appended; above the head of the angel, two clasped hands, with the figures nineteen, recall the discourse on divorce in that chapter; the parable of the vineyard is represented by a bunch of grapes, labeled twenty, held in the drapery upon the breast; an ass's head, hanging like a pocket, with the figures twenty-one, indicates the entrance into Jerusalem, in the twenty-first chapter; at the feet of the angel, a spread table, with twenty-two affixed, expresses the parable of the wedding feast; and the twenty-third chapter is symbolized by an architectural fragment in the angel's other uplifted hand, as a representative of the prophecy of the destruction of Jerusalem.

The popular character of the block books can be gathered from the fact that one was a treatise upon palmistry, and another treated of planetary influences. Some seem to have served as tracts, such as the Ars Moriendi, or art of dying. The Mirror of Salvation, of Morality, and of History, were the precursors of a style of book which maintained a long-lived popularity; and the name has been, until recently, a favorite title for serial publications. It has been asserted that the statement of the associate of Gutenberg, repeated before the tribunals of Strasbourg, that they were engaged in manufacturing looking-glasses, was intended as a species of punning falsehood to conceal the fact that Gutenberg was endeavoring to produce, by printing, the Speculum Humanæ Salvationis, or, Mirror of Human Salvation.

The Mirabilia Romæ, or the Wonders of Rome, was a kind of illustrated guide-book for the use of visitors to the shrines of the city of Rome. Endkrist, or Antichrist, taken and drawn out of many books, how and of whom he shall be born, was a tract of twenty-six leaves, and it was generally accompanied by the Quindecim Signa, or fifteen signs preceding the day of doom. The Todtentanz was one of the earliest forms of that wonderful book, the Dance of Death. A popular German block book was the Zehn Bott fur die ungelernte Leut, or the Ten Commandments for the Unlearned.

A large number of books are usually styled the Donatuses, being the various editions, both in manuscript and in different forms of xylography and typography, of the popular grammar written by Donatus, the proper title being De Octo Partibus Orationis, or Of the Eight Parts of Speech: these, with the different Speculums, or Mirrors of Salvation, etc., have attracted special attention, as some of them are held by some authorities to have been printed from movable type previous to the time of the publications of Gutenberg, Fust, and Schoeffer.

The complications in the controversy arise, in a great degree, from the fact that the method of printing from wooden plates offered so many points of convenience, and was so economic for small editions, that it was still pursued even after the printing-press, as improved by Schoeffer, was in well-established use. The pictures used in the block books can be traced into works printed in the sixteenth century; and it is known that Veldener, in 1483, cut some of the plates already described as being drawn in panels or compartments, so as to suit the subdivisions to the requirements of a cheap octavo edition.

The absence of dates, names, and title-pages, in all the early books, compels the reader to rely on the mere appearance of the work, and makes the whole question a matter of nice discrimination. It is, however, believed that all the early block books were printed in distemper, that the impressions are therefore brown, and that the possibility of printing from wooden blocks in black oleaginous ink was not known until this composition had been used for some time with metal types.

Sotheby, one of the foremost authorities upon the subject, who personally examined the specimens in the principal libraries of England and the Continent, believed that he had found copies of five editions of the Apocalypse, three of the Biblia Pauperum, two of the Cantica Canticarum, and one edition each of the Ars Moriendi, Liber Regum, and Temptationis Dæmonis, pure block books printed in the Low Countries; while he held that specimens of the Donatus, Doctrinale, Abcedarium, Facetiæ Morales, and some others, including several editions of the Speculum Humanæ Salvationis, were books printed with movable wooden type.

In the numerous editions of the Speculum Humanæ Salvationis, it is contended, the proofs can be found that movable type was really used about the years 1430 and 1440, by some artist of Holland,—probably Koster, of Haarlem. Some copies of this work exhibit the illustrations in the original brown ink of the block books produced by the primitive process of rubbing, while it is contended that the lettering is in black oleaginous ink, clearly made by metal movable type; in some cases the text is upon paper pasted upon that used for the illustration; and in others, pages produced entirely by xylography are interleaved with pages produced probably with movable type. Some authors assert that there are copies of eight editions of this work extant, and that certain letters misplaced or reversed, as occasionally occurs in modern printing, exhibit complete proof that they were produced by movable type.

Blocked Up.—Letter is said to be blocked up when the whole of it is composed, and none can be sent to press so as to proceed with the work, owing to the author not returning the proofs regularly, the proofs not being read up, other work employing the same type, non-attendance of compositors, scarcity of sorts, pressmen not being able to work, etc.

Blotting-Paper.—Paper made without size, and capable of absorbing wet writing-ink, on which business advertisements are sometimes printed for distribution in counting-houses. Such products of printing are commonly known as Blotting-Pads.

Blue Ink.—See INKS.

Board Rack.—An arrangement of strong boards, with ledges nailed on the inside of the two sides, on which boards are placed to contain standing matter or forms of type.

Bodkin.—A pointed steel instrument, of various sizes and shapes, used to pick wrong or imperfect letters out of a page, and to push down spaces in correcting. Illustrations are given below of some of the bodkins in most general use:

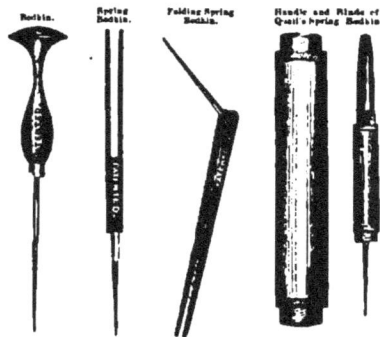

Bodkin. Spring Bodkin. Folding Spring Bodkin. Handle and Blade of Quail's Spring Bodkin.

Bodoni, John Baptist (in Italian, Giambattista), was born in Saluzzo, in Piedmont, 1740, died in 1813. This celebrated Italian disputed the honor of being the first typographer of his age against the rival claims of Baskerville, Bulmer, and Bensley of England, and Ibarra of Madrid. His father was a printer, and instructed him in the rudiments of the art. While quite young, he evinced a remarkable taste for design, and employed his leisure in engraving vignettes on wood. When eighteen years old, Bodoni and a school-fellow, Dominic Costa, left Saluzzo with the intention of trying their fortunes in Rome, hoping for assistance from the uncle of Costa, who was secretary to a Roman prelate. On the journey their funds failed, but Bodoni replenished the purse by selling some of his engravings on wood to printers. On their arrival at Rome the uncle of Costa advised the youths to return to their own homes, and Bodoni, greatly discouraged, was about to do so, when curiosity led him to visit the printing-house of the Propaganda. Bodoni's intelligence and vivacity attracted the attention of the Abbate Ruggieri, the superintendent of the establishment, and he engaged his services. Cardinal Spinelli, the head of the Propaganda, was also attracted to the youth, and became his patron, advising and directing him in the study of the Oriental languages. Ruggieri intrusted him in 1762 to print the Arab-Copht Missal and the Alphabetum Tibetanum, the work was so well executed that Bodoni's name was placed at the end of the volume.

Shortly afterwards Ruggieri committed suicide, and Bodoni was so strongly affected by the occurrence that he determined to leave Rome for England; on his way he visited his parents, and his further journey was prevented by a severe illness. In the mean while the Marquis de Felino offered him the superintendence of a press which he was about to establish in Parma, and Bodoni accepted the situation in 1768. Winning immense reputation, he, however, published comparatively few books. In 1788 he was invited to Rome to print the Greek, Latin, and Italian classics, but the Duke of Parma, unwilling to relinquish his services, established a model printing-office in his own palace, and from these royal apartments Bodoni issued his famous editions of the classics. Of these the most celebrated are the Horace, folio of 1791; Virgil, folio of 1793; Catullus, Tibullus, Propertius, and Tasso in 1794, and Tacitus in 1795. Bodoni's most magnificent work was the Homer of 1808, with a dedication to Napoleon in Italian, French, and Latin. Bodoni and his press had received marked protection from Napoleon when the French armies entered Italy, and in 1810 Bodoni personally presented the Emperor at St. Cloud with a copy of the Homer printed on vellum, and received a pension of three thousand francs. Eugene Beauharnois offered him the superintendence of the press at Milan, and Murat invited him to Naples, but he remained in Parma. In 1811 he received the Cross of the Two Sicilies from Murat, and undertook to issue a series of French classics for the young son of Murat, in imitation of the Delphine editions. This work was commenced with the Telemachus in 1812. Napoleon gave eighteen thousand francs to assist the enterprise, and nominated Bodoni a chevalier de la Réunion, but the successful typographer died shortly afterwards of gout. His widow continued the business for some years.

Bodoni was generally accepted as the prince of typographers, and the English so far acknowledged his excellence as to engage his services for some of their most luxurious publications. The Castle of Otranto was printed by him in 1791 in splendid style; Gray's Poems, in 1793, in quarto, the edition comprising only 100 copies on large paper and 200 on common; Gray's Elegy was also printed with an Italian translation in 1793, the edition only 100; Thomson's Seasons in 1794, 175 copies; and Lines to Victory, by Cornelia Knight, in 1793, a quarto edition of 100 copies.

Bulmer was believed by Dibdin and his companion book-fanciers to have received the highest compliment when George III. mistook some of his sheets for the work of Bodoni.

Body.—A term applied to the sizes of type; as Nonpareil body, Brevier body, Pica body, etc.; while the face is distinguished by special names, as Roman, Italic, Antique, Gothic, etc.

Body of the Work.—The subject-matter of a book, as contradistinguished from the preface, notes, index, etc.

Bogus Manilla.—A mixed wrapping-paper, inferior to the pure Manilla.

Bold-face.—The general name of many varieties of job letter of various sizes, the lines of which, while very thick in the shaded or heavy portions of the face, have hair-lines but little thicker than Roman letters. (See JOB LETTER).

Bond Paper.—An unusually strong writing-paper, generally thin and uncalendered, but of good writing surface, in common use for printing bonds and stock certificates.

Bonds.—See JOB PRINTING.

Book.—In its most general sense, a treatise of any length and form. In a more limited signification, a collection of blank, written, or printed sheets of paper or any similar material bound together; generally used to signify a work of considerable extent, as distinguished from a pamphlet or tract. Also a subdivision of a work, as the first book of Euclid, or the fifth book of Paradise Lost.

The word is usually derived from *boc*, beech-tree, the substance used by the Anglo-Saxons both in slabs or tablets, and in rolls formed from the bark. In a similar manner the Latins used the word *liber*, a book or scroll, from the bark of the tree; while *codex* was the tablet or square form cut from the body or trunk. *Volumen*, from which we derive volume, was a Latin word, signifying roll or scroll, and applied to the form whether in bark, skin, cloth, or paper.

Book is, therefore, the general term applied to the literary work and not to its material shape, and is equally applicable to the commandments delivered to Moses on tables of stone, to the Sibylline leaves, to the laws of Solon cut upon wooden planks, the poems of Hesiod on plates of lead, the wooden cubic blocks of the Scandinavians, the bricks of the Babylonians, the rolls of linen, vellum, or skin, the carved pillars of Crete, or a diamond prayer-book.

The tablets of wood, metal, or ivory were readily linked together by metal rods or leather thongs into a rude resemblance of the modern square book; and tablets folded in the middle to preserve the writing, or so hollowed out as to contain several sheets of wax, parchment, or papyrus, were the precursors of the present stitched volume. Upon the introduction of flexible materials, such as bark, skin, linen, and silk, the scroll form was used for convenience, the several sheets or segments being attached together in one long strip, which was fastened to a rod or cylinder around which it could be readily rolled and secured by a thong with an outer cover or case, to preserve the manuscript from injury. In long scrolls a cylinder was fastened at each end, just as is done at present with large maps, and the portions as read could be transferred from one cylinder to the other.

Among the learned classes of Greece and Rome books were not only valued for their intrinsic worth, but were lavishly adorned as a means of ostentation. Slaves were taught to serve as copyists and illuminators, and considerable private libraries were thus acquired. About the time of the Christian era the books of the Latins and Greeks were frequently superbly adorned with gold and color, written on richly-tinted vellum, and resplendent with jewels.

At the present day the author usually writes with his own hand, in the confidence that the printer will not only furnish him any number of copies, but also a convenient form for revision; but the ancient author was compelled in order to get out an early edition to dictate to a number of scribes, who were called *amanuenses notarii*, or hasty writers, equivalent to the short-hand writers of the present day. The work of these was revised or copied by trained hands, styled in Greek *Kalligraphoi* and in Latin *librarii*, or fine writers, and by the *bibliographoi* or copyists. Thus Paul in his First Epistle to the Galatians expressly states that it is written with his own hand, but includes the name of his amanuensis at the close of that to the Romans.

The esteem in which books were held in the first Christian century is well exhibited by the anxiety expressed by Cicero to purchase the library which Atticus was collecting by employing numerous slaves in copying the works in the Athenian libraries.

When the Saracens conquered Egypt in the seventh century, communication was destroyed between that country and Europe, and the supply of papyrus was interrupted. Greece and Italy were therefore compelled to depend upon parchment and vellum, which were scarce and expensive, and the number of manuscripts seems to have been sensibly diminished, while it appears to have become the custom to erase ancient manuscripts in order to substitute new works. This is said to have been frequently done by the priests, who destroyed the classic or profane writings to secure material for their missals. These re-writings are known as palimpsests.

This great scarcity of material continued for four hundred years, and its effect upon European literature is very marked, as is also the increase in books immediately upon the introduction of paper in the eleventh century.

About this period manuscripts, especially of the Scriptures, began to be multiplied by the priests, and certain portions of each day were allotted in the convents to copying from dictation, while such monks as were gifted with artistic taste devoted their talents to the pious labor of decorating the Scriptures or books of prayer.

Books, however, remained very expensive, as is proved by the fact that a Bible, fairly written, with a gloss or comment, was sold in England in the year 1274 for £33 6s. 8d., while in the same year the erection of two arches of London Bridge cost but £25.

In the thirteenth and fourteenth centuries, in Europe, there was a gradual and popular revival of interest in literature, as is exhibited by the multiplication of block books. The works of church service were also in increased demand, and, being profusely decorated, were included in the goods sold by the mercers or merchants.

It was to meet this growing demand that printing was so soon and successfully introduced, spreading rapidly from city to city and country to country. In its first stages, typography was intended to imitate handwriting, and the first Bibles of Fust and Schoeffer are believed to have been sold in Paris as manuscript. With this intention the books continued large and clumsy for a considerable period, and the letters were strictly conformed to the popular Gothic or Black-letter character in common use; but the more convenient and smaller Italic soon fought its way to favor, particularly in Italy, and the Roman was gradually accepted as both small and legible, and has been improved slowly into its present form.

Books also were gradually diminished in size and weight, from the ponderous tomes bound in solid plates of metal or thick planks of wood, through a great variety of styles of binding, until the acme of lightness was reached in paper-bound pamphlets.

Bookbinding.—This term is defined as the art by which the parts of a book are connected for convenience and protection; and if this is correct, the first form in use was probably the ancient method by which the scroll was attached to a cylinder, around which it was rolled and secured by thongs. A Greek, named Phillatius, is said to have invented the glue by which the strips of skin or papyrus were fastened together, and to have been honored by a statue for the invention.

The roll or scroll has been frequently styled Egyptian binding, but was used in very early times in many countries of the East. Rolls are mentioned in the Hebrew Scriptures at least seven centuries before the Christian era, and are still the form in which the books of the law are preserved in the synagogues, some of these documents, especially those upon goatskin, being probably very ancient.

The convenience of the square or oblong page for common use seems to have led to its introduction at an early date among the scholarly classes of all countries, and it was a short and necessary advance to attach the sheets of skin or papyrus to each other, and to an outer or heavier page of skin or wood as a still further protection; this once done, the modern art of bookbinding was in fact invented.

Great progress was made in the art during the first centuries of our era. The books of the Romans were covered with leather, colored in tints of red, yellow, green, and purple. The Gospels and missals of the Greek and Roman Churches were fastened in wooden boards, often nearly an inch thick, and carved and adorned with metal. In the sixth century, certain high dignitaries of the Irish Church are mentioned for their skill in binding in gold and precious stones. Pope Gregory III., in A. D. 731, had a copy of the Gospels bound in plates of gold weighing fifteen pounds; and the Bible, given by the learned Alcuin to Charlemagne, was written on vellum and bound in velvet, with a frontispiece and numerous illustrations painted in gold and colors. During the seventh, eighth, and ninth centuries, the art and industry of Christian scholars were lavished upon copies of the Scriptures and books of devotion, written with exquisite care upon vellum of yellow or purple tint, and often in letters of silver and gold, with illuminations in colors, and bound in velvet, gold, and ivory studded with jewels. The Jewish scribes made magnificent copies of the Old Testament, particularly distinguished by the beauty of the writing; and the Saxon monks also excelled in calligraphy, while the Spanish and Italians were famed for the beauty of their illuminations, and the Greek scholars for the luxury of their books.

Specimens of the binding of the fourteenth century are still extant, and in excellent preservation, exhibiting the care and industry with which the oaken boards were covered with vellum. Books were also covered magnificently in velvet and damask, with corners, clasps, and decorations of solid gold. White vellum also was stamped with gold, and morocco and calf were inlaid and adorned in all imaginable ways.

Printed books towards the close of the fifteenth century were frequently bound in calf with oaken boards and stamped with gold. A curious book of indentures, between Henry VII. of England and the convent of St. Peter, Westminster, has a cover of crimson Genoese velvet, edged with crimson silk and gold thread, with tassels of the same at each corner; the inside lined with crimson damask. On each side of the cover are five bosses made of silver, wrought and gilt; those in the middle have the crown and supporters gilt and enameled, and at the corners the figures of the portcullis in a similar style. It is fastened by two silver hasps enameled with the red rose of Lancaster.

Henry VIII. paid large sums for binding; but the art found a more liberal patron in his magnificent rival, Francis I., the personal friend of Robert Stephens. Grollier, a nobleman sent by Francis as ambassador to Rome, was one of the most celebrated patrons of the art. His library was most admirably bound in smooth morocco and calf, adorned with fine and delicate patterns, sometimes inlaid with morocco of different colors. This nobleman did much to elevate the style of binding in France; he is believed to have been the first to introduce lettering on the back; and he did even more, by impressing a similar taste upon Diana of Poitiers, who became a powerful aid to the industry. Her library was bound in tinted morocco, decorated in delicately graceful lines, with the interwoven initials of herself and her royal lover intermingled with the crescents, bows, quivers, and arrows which she bore so proudly in defiance of the criticism of the world.

Erasmus said of this age that the times had strangely changed, for it was the monks who were ignorant, and the women who loved learning. In proof of this, there are many handsome volumes still extant, showing the taste of Anne Boleyn, of Mary of England, of Mary Stuart, as well as the magnificent library of Diana, and the volumes embroidered by Queen Elizabeth herself.

Notwithstanding the attention of the queen, the art remained in England in a very incomplete condition, and the workmanship clumsy, while the binding in France during the sixteenth century was alike remarkable for its solidity, taste and accuracy of finish. Gascon, De Seuil, Padeloup, and Derome achieved a great reputation, Derome being particularly distinguished for beautiful workmanship in plain morocco with solid gilding, and Padeloup for a style of small dotted ornamentation which looks like gold lace upon the sides and back of the volume.

After reaching such artistic excellence, the art in France degenerated from the time of Louis XIV. until it became inferior to the English. The books of Napoleon's library, on which no expense was spared, were clumsy and disjointed, with coarse and unevenly worked decoration; they were usually bound in red morocco, lined with purple silk, impressed with the imperial bee.

During the sixteenth century, Caspar Ritter was one of the most famous binders of Germany, his work being solid, handsome, and square, frequently in red morocco, varied with colors and handsomely clasped. The Medici, of Florence, at this epoch, did much to cultivate a taste for luxurious decorations; and the family of merchant princes of Augsburg—the Fuggers—bestowed vast sums upon their books; De Thou had a fine library, admirably bound in deep-toned red, yellow, and green morocco; and the Chevalier d'Eon, in his passion for Etruscan art, decorated his books with figures drawn from the vases; but the heavy black and red dyes speedily corroded the leather.

During the earlier years of the eighteenth century, the English binding, with the exception of that of Cambridge, was exceedingly clumsy and tasteless. Some improvements in workmanship were, however, gradually introduced, but without any change upon the standard pattern of marbled sides, with brown backs and gilt lettering-pieces.

Toward the end of the century, the literary, or rather dilettanti, revival, led by Earl Spencer and proclaimed by Dibdin, produced a great effect upon the art. Two Germans, named Baumgarten and Benedict, were quite famous in London during the early years of the nineteenth century, their work being good and substantial in Russia, with marbled edges. But Roger Payne exactly met the requirements of the enthusiastic votaries of Bulmer, Bensley, and Bodoni. He exhibited much taste and fancy in adapting his ornaments to the literary character of the volume, and became one of the celebrities of the hour.

The French, who so excelled in the art in former times, have of late years been stimulated by the success of the English to renewed exertion, and Thouvenin founded the new school which so admirably combines substantial workmanship with delicacy of decoration. Technically, the bookbinding of the French is now distinguished for its solidity, squareness, freedom of the joints, firmness of the back and nicety of finish. The best material used for covering is a rich, soft Levant morocco; it is thick and heavy in texture, but the dexterity of the workmen prepares it even for small books, not only on the outer side but on the inside of the boards.

American bookbinding has won a just celebrity for its special excellence in stationery or vellum binding, suited to heavy ledgers and blank books. Admirable workmanship is here required, and the craft may well wear its honors proudly as achieved in one of the most difficult departments of the art. But more directly adapted to the demands of the home market is the beautiful and varied muslin and cloth binding so admirably adapted to our abundant ephemeral literature. The accidental protection granted by the scarcity arising from the war of 1812 turned the attention of American binders to the advantages of muslin, and subsequent improvements have produced such perfection, that it is difficult for eye or touch to detect the difference between the imitations and the costly and elegant covers in finely-worked morocco; but the English are said to have been the first to use muslin binding, as well as to devise methods for decorating it.

As the style of ornamentation depends solely upon the taste and dexterity of the artist and the fancy of the purchaser, there can be no limit to the variations in the decoration of a book; but the popular verdict has been for a long time in favor of what is styled half-binding, as the best combination of economy, durability, and neatness. The back and covers being covered with leather, renders it very strong, while the better quality of marble paper, with which the sides are usually covered, is as durable as the leather itself. The famous Vathek Beckford had his fine library at Fonthill half bound in olive-colored morocco, with marbled paper sides and insides, and no finishing except in the lettering and date. This style has furnished a favorite modern model, called Beckford or Fonthill. An excellent style of half-binding is familiar to Americans in many of the Governmental reports, and it seems the fitting garb for the standard works of reference.

Still stronger and more expensive is the long-popular Cambridge style, used especially for theological works. This binding is composed of brown calf with red edges, the back pieced with red Russia and very little gilding.

In full binding the Levant morocco ranks highest for strength, beauty, and expense, Turkey morocco holding the next rank. Calf is also very strong and handsome, but Russian leather soon cracks along the joint.

The finer styles of ornament have received various appellations: thus, the Aldine, appropriately named after the great Aldus, is a graceful and lighter modification in ungilt ornaments of the old monastic; the modern monastic or antique is, correctly, in divinity calf or brown morocco with very thick boards, and edges either red, brown, or matted gold; the decoration being in what is technically called blind tooling, or ungilt ornamental lines, and the design having a rather formal and rectilinear effect.

The modern fancy for the antique has produced many imitations, of which the oak, a favorite style for Prayer Books, is very handsome, as is also the iron, used for similar purposes.

The illuminated binding was invented by the French, and is a gorgeous combination of the graceful tracery of the moderns with the lavish color of the ancient illuminators. The paintings are executed by artists in high and lasting colors as a work entirely distinct from the bindery, and morocco of different tints is introduced to add to the brilliant effect.

It does not fall within the province of this work to give a detailed description of the various mechanical processes involved in bookbinding. A knowledge of the technical terms used by bookbinders, however, is often useful to printers, and we append the list given in Nicholson's Manual of the Art of Bookbinding, which furnishes, incidentally, some good indications of the manner in which books are bound:

TECHNICAL TERMS USED IN BOOKBINDING.

All-Along.—When a volume is sewed, and the thread passes from kettle-stitch to kettle-stitch, or from end to end in each sheet, it is said to be sewed all-along.

Asterisk.—A sign used by the printers at the bottom of the front page of the duplicate-leaves printed to supply the place of those cancelled.

Backing-Boards.—Are used for backing or forming the joint. They are made of very hard wood or faced with iron, and are thicker on the edge intended to form the groove than upon the edge that goes towards the fore-edge, so that the whole power of the laying-press may be directed towards the back.

Backing-Hammer.—The hammer used for backing and rounding: it has a broad, flat face, similar to a shoemaker's hammer.

Bands.—The twines whereon the sheets of a volume are sewn. When the book is sewed flexible the bands appear upon the back. When the back is sewn so as to let in the twine, the appearance of raised bands is produced by gluing narrow strips of leather across the back before the volume is covered.

Band-Driver.—A tool used in forwarding to correct irregularities in the bands of flexible backs.

Bead.—The little roll formed by the knot of the headband.

Bleed.—When a book is cut into the print, it is said to bleed.

Beveled Boards.—Very heavy boards for the sides chamfered around the edges.

Blind-Tooled.—When the tools are impressed upon the leather, without being gilt, they are said to be blind or blank.

Boards.—Are of various kinds, such as pressing, backing, cutting, burnishing, gilding, etc. The pasteboards used for side-covers are termed boards. The boards used for cutting books out of boards are called steamboat-boards. Tinned boards are used for finished work; while brass- or iron-bound boards are used for pressing cloth-work.

Bodkin or Stabbing-Awl.—A strong point of iron or steel, fixed on a wooden handle, to form the holes in the boards required to lace in the bands. Used also for tracing the lines for cutting the fore-edge.

Bole.—A preparation used in gilding edges.

Bolt.—The fold in the head and fore-edge of the sheets. Also the small bar with a screw used to secure the knife to the plough.

Bosses.—Brass plates attached to the sides of volumes for their preservation.

Broke up.—When plates are turned over and folded at a short distance from the back-edge, before they are placed, so as to enable them to turn easily in the volume, they are said to be broke up. The same process is sometimes applied to the entire volume.

Burnish.—The effect produced by the application of the burnisher to the edges.

Burnishers.—Are pieces of agate or bloodstone affixed to handles.

Cancels.—Leaves containing errors which are to be cut out and replaced with corrected pages.

Caps.—The leather covering of the headband. Applied also to the paper envelopes used to protect the edges while the volume is being covered and finished.

Case-Work.—Work in which the boards are covered and stamped. The volume is then glued upon the back and stuck into them.

Catch-Word.—A word met with in early-printed books at the bottom of the page, which word is the first on the following page. Now used to denote the first and last word in an encyclopædia or other book of reference.

Centre-Tools.—Are single, upright, or independent tools used for the middle of the panels by the finisher.

Clearing Out.—Removing the waste paper and paring away any superfluous leather upon the inside, preparatory to pasting down the lining-paper.

Collating.—Examining the signatures, after the volume is gathered, to ascertain if they be correct and follow in numerical order.

Corners.—The triangular brass tools used in finishing backs and sides. The gilt ornaments used on velvet books. Also, the leather pasted on the corners of half-bound books.

Creaser.—The tool used in marking each side of the bands, generally made of steel.

Cropped.—When a book has been cut down too much, it is said to be cropped.

Dentelle.—A fine tooled border resembling lacework.

Edge-Rolled.—When the edges of the boards are rolled. It may be either in gold or blind.

Embossed.—When a plate is stamped upon the cover, so as to present a raised figure or design, it is said to be embossed. Some inappropriately term this kind of work Arabesque.

End Papers.—The paper placed at each end of the volume, a portion of which is removed when the lining-paper is pasted down upon the boards. Also called Waste Papers.

Fillet.—The cylindrical ornament used in finishing upon which simple lines are engraved.

Finishing.—Is that department that receives the volumes after they are put in leather, and ornaments them as required. One who works at this branch is termed a finisher.

Finisher's Press.—Is the same as a laying-press, only much smaller.

Flexible.—When a book is sewn on raised bands and the thread is passed entirely round each band.

Folder.—This is a flat piece of bone or ivory used in folding the sheets and in many other manipulations. Also applied to a female engaged in folding sheets.

Fore-Edge.—The front edge of the book.

Foundation-Plate.—A plate of iron or brass upon which side-stamps are affixed.

Forwarding.—Is that branch that takes the books after they are sewed and advances them until they are put in leather ready for the finisher. One who works at this branch is termed a forwarder.

Full-Bound.—When the sides of a volume are entirely covered with leather, it is said to be full-bound.

Gathering.—The process of arranging the sheets according to the signatures.

Gauge.—Used in forwarding to take the correct size of the volume and to mark it upon the boards for squaring.

Gilt.—Is applied to both the edges and to the ornaments in finishing.

Glaire.—The whites of eggs.

Grater.—An iron instrument used by the forwarder for rubbing the backs after they are paste-washed.

Gouge.—A tool used in finishing, the face of which is a line forming the segment of a circle.

Guards.—Strips of paper inserted in the backs of books intended for the insertion of plates, to prevent the book being uneven when filled; also the strips upon which plates are mounted.

Guides.—The groove in which the plow moves upon the face of the cutting-press.

Half-Bound.—When a volume is covered with leather upon the back and corners, and the sides are covered with paper or cloth.

Hand-Letters.—Letters cut and affixed to handles, and adjusted singly upon the volume when lettering it.

Head and Tail.—The top and bottom of a book.

Headband.—The silk or cotton ornament worked at the ends so as to make the back even with the squares.

Imperfections.—Sheets rejected on account of being in some respect imperfect, and for which others are required to make the work complete.

In Boards.—When a volume is cut after the pasteboards are affixed to form the sides, it is said to be cut in boards. The term is also applied to a style of binding in which the boards are merely covered with paper.

Inset.—The pages cut off in folding and placed in the middle of the sheet.

Inside Tins.—So called from being placed inside of the boards when the volume is put in the standing-press.

Joints.—The projections formed in backing to admit the boards; applied also to the inside when the volume is covered.

Justification.—The observance that the pages of a volume agree and are parallel throughout, so as to insure a straight and equal margin.

Kettle-Stitch.—The stitch which the sewer makes at the head and tail of a book; said to be a corruption of chain-stitch.

Keys.—The little instruments used to secure the bands to the sewing-press.

Knocking-Down Iron, so called from having the slips, when laced in, pounded down upon it, so that they will not show when the book is covered.

Laced In.—When the boards are affixed to the volume by means of the bands being passed through holes made in the boards, they are said to be laced in.

Lettering-Block.—A piece of wood, the upper surface being rounded, upon which side-labels are lettered.

Lettering-Box.—The box in which the type are screwed up preparatory to lettering.

Lining-Paper.—The colored or marbled paper at each end of the volume.

Marbler.—The workman who marbles the edges of books, etc.

Mitred.—When the lines in finishing intersect each other at right angles and are continued without over-running each other, they are said to be mitred.

Out of Boards.—When a volume is cut before the boards are affixed, it is said to be done out of boards.

Overcasting.—An operation in sewing, when the work consists of single leaves or plates.

Pallet.—Name given to the tools used in gilding upon the bands, sometimes applied to the lettering-box.

Panel.—The space between bands; also applied to beveled and sunk sides.

Papering Up.—Covering the edges after they are gilt, so as to protect them while the volume is being covered and finished.

Paring.—Reducing the edges of the leather by forming a gradual slope.

Pastewash.—A thin dilution of paste in water.

Pencil.—A small brush of camel's hair.

Pieced.—When the space between bands, upon which the lettering is placed, has a piece of leather upon it different from the back, it is said to be pieced or titled.

Plow.—The instrument used in cutting the edges of books and pasteboards.

Points.—Holes made in the sheets by the printer; they serve as guides in folding.

Polisher.—A steel implement used in finishing.

Press.—There are various kinds of presses,—viz.: laying or cutting, standing, stamping, embossing, gilding, and finishing.

Rake.—An instrument used in forwarding, to harden the backs while being pastewashed in the standing-press.

Rasped.—The sharp edge taken off the boards.

Register.—The ribbon placed in a volume for a marker; also a list of signatures, attached to the end of early-printed works, for the use of the binder.

Rolls.—The cylindrical ornaments used in finishing.

Run Up.—When the back has a fillet run from head to tail without being mitred at each band, it is said to be run up.

Runner.—The front board used in cutting edges, &c.

Sewer.—The person who sews the sheets together on the sewing-press—generally a female.

Set-Off.—Designates the transfer of the ink to the opposite page.

Setting the Head.—Is covering the headband neatly with the leather, so as to form a kind of cap.

Shaving-Tub.—The paper cut from the edges of a volume are called shavings. The receptacle into which they fall while the forwarder is cutting the edges is termed the shaving-tub.

Signature.—The letter or figure under the footline of the first page of each sheet to indicate the order of arrangement in the volume; sometimes applied to the sheet itself.

Size.—A preparation used in finishing and gilding, generally made from vellum.

Slips.—The pieces of twine that project beyond the volume after it is sewn.

Squares.—The portions of the board that project over the edges.

Stabbing.—The operation of piercing the boards with a bodkin for the slips to pass through; also the piercing of pamphlets for the purpose of stitching.

Stamps.—The brass tools used in finishing to impress a figure upon the leather; they are distinguished by hand-stamps and stamps for the press.

Start.—When any of the leaves are not properly secured in the back, upon opening the volume they will project beyond the others, and are said to start.

Steamboating.—Cutting books out of boards, a number being cut at the same time.

Stitching.—The operation of passing the thread through a pamphlet for the purpose of securing the sheets together.

Stops.—Are small circular tools, adapted to stop a fillet when it intersects at right angles, to save the time used in mitring.

Title.—The space between bands, upon which the lettering is placed.

Tools.—Applies particularly to the hand-stamps and tools used in finishing.

Trindle.—A strip of thin wood or iron.

Turning Up.—The process of cutting the fore-edges in such a manner as to throw the round out of the back until the edge is cut.

Tying Up.—The tying of a volume after the cover has been drawn on, so as to make the leather adhere to the sides of the bands; also for setting the head.

Whipping.—The process of oversewing plates.

Witness.—When a volume is cut so as to show that it has not been cut as small as some of the leaves, their uncut edges prove this, and are called witness and sometimes proof.

Wrinkle.—The uneven surfaces in a volume, caused by not being properly pressed or by dampness, also caused by improper backing.

Book-Folding Machines.—Many efforts have been made to invent machinery to fold pamphlets and books, and the efforts of Chambers & Brother, of Philadelphia, in this direction, have been crowned with success, especially where large orders of uniform size are to be executed, or where machines adapted to each of the sheets of different sizes can be used. Cyrus Chambers, Jr., invented a machine to accomplish this object, and in 1856, Edwin and Cyrus Chambers established a manufactory in Philadelphia under the firm name of Chambers, Bro. & Co., to manufacture them. After many years of expensive litigation, and many fruitless and expensive experiments, they succeeded in producing machinery at once practicable and within the reach of publishers. They now manufacture thirty-eight varieties and styles of folding machines, which fold from an election-ticket to the finest and largest twenty-four-paged illustrated periodical, folding two separate sheets together, pasting the separate pages at the back, trimming the folded edges off, and leaving the margins of the front untrimmed. Some of the finest books in this country and Europe are now folded by these machines. They fold 8vo, 16mo, 12mo, both single and double with inset, cut off and set in as by hand, 32mo, 36mo, 48mo, etc.

They build machines cutting the paper into from two to five separate sheets, folding each piece prop-

erly and separately, and capable of executing accurately a great variety of work which formerly could be done only by hand.

The accompanying cut illustrates their Book-Folding Machine. (See FOLDING MACHINES.)

Book Paper.—Sized, or unsized, printing-paper above the grade of News. Medium or double-medium paper is more frequently used in printing books than paper of any other dimensions; and when such terms as octavo, quarto, folio, etc. are used, without qualification, to describe the size of a book, they mean that its pages are such as would be formed by making an octavo, quarto, or folio fold of a medium sheet. Paper of other dimensions, however, is frequently used in printing books, and in such cases the size of the paper is prefixed to the term indicating the fold, as, royal octavo, imperial quarto, etc.

Book-Perfecting Press.—A press which prints both sides of the sheets of book-forms simultaneously, or with only one feeding of the paper. In England and France several varieties of book-perfecting presses are extensively used, especially in printing large editions. In the United States, book-perfecting presses of various descriptions are also used, but only in a comparatively small proportion of the offices in which books are printed. The accompanying cut illustrates a Type-Revolving Book-Perfecting Press, of which four sizes, varying from 24 by 27 inches, to 33 by 50 inches, are manufactured by R. Hoe & Co. They describe it in their catalogue as follows:

As the name indicates, it is on the rotary principle, the forms being secured on the surface of the large horizontal cylinders. This system, as it does away with the reciprocating motion, admits of a greater speed in printing than any other. The distribution of the ink also is more perfect, there being room for from six to twelve inking-rollers to each form. It is equally well adapted to letter-press, stereotype and wood-cut work, and will print from 1500 to 2000 perfected sheets per hour, the only limit to its speed

TYPE-REVOLVING BOOK-PERFECTING PRESS.

being the capability of the feeder to supply the sheets. As it dispenses with the registering apparatus, and is furnished with a patent self-acting flyer, only one attendant is required for the largest-sized press.

Book-Work.—The tendency of modern times, especially in the United States, is to diminish the relative importance of book-work as part of the art of printing. At one period it was regarded as the only portion of the business worthy of serious attention, and even at this day this idea is exemplified in the German fondness for the term Book-making art. For centuries after Gutenberg and Fust had established a printing-office at Mentz, newspapers, in the present acceptation of the word, were unknown, and, though job-work was occasionally done, it formed but a very small proportion of the labors of the old printers. Now, in magnitude of operations, in this country, newspaper-work holds a pre-eminent rank; and job and fancy printing gives employment to more workmen than book-work proper,—the number of book offices being comparatively small. Book-work still holds a higher artistic rank in this country than newspaper-work, but it is questionable whether there is not in the aggregate less care, talent, and ingenuity bestowed upon it than upon the varied forms of job and fancy printing. Books, however, were long considered the choicest product of the printer's art, and, as they are intended for permanent use, the custom of displaying extra care in all matters relating to their manufacture has a good foundation.

In practice, the American compositor who can set a clean proof in a newspaper-office has little to learn to qualify himself for a subordinate position in a large book-office, except increased care in spacing, punctuation, divisions, style, etc. He need not know anything about making-up, imposition, order of the work, or signatures, such matters being left to the foreman or to assistants of his selection, and the average compositor being required only to do plain composition with greater nicety and exactness than in newspaper-work. Many printers are, unfortunately, contented with this limited stock of knowledge of a great branch of the art of printing, with the details of which all their predecessors were formerly obliged to be familiar. These details must still be understood, in whole or in part, by some one or more persons connected with every printing-office · that prints books or pamphlets, and it is to be regretted that all printers do not strive to understand them.

In the matter of composition, one of the most important things to be learned is the style (see STYLE) of the office in which the work is to be set up, as well as the special requirements of the authors of original works. The style affects not only punctuation, capitalization, divisions, and spacing, but nearly all things relating to typographical appearance; and it must be learned by all who wish to avoid dirty proofs. Directions applicable to each particular work are given when they are requisite, and the average compositor will usually have little difficulty in obtaining, comprehending, and observing them.

Before a book-form is ready for press, it is necessary that a proper estimate of the length of the copy (see CASTING-OFF COPY) should be made, that the different portions of the work should follow in their proper order (see CASE MEMORANDA), that the pages should be properly made up (see MAKING UP) and properly imposed (see IMPOSITION), that appropriate signatures (see SIGNATURES) should be inserted for the direction of the bookbinder, and that close attention should be bestowed upon all other details involved in the conversion of a mass of copy into a series of type forms from which a book can be correctly printed. In the United States book-work differs radically from book-work in England, in the fact that here the office usually undertakes making-up and imposition, through its foreman or weekly hands, while in England the piece-hands, working on the companionship plan (see COMPANIONSHIP), do everything relating to the preparation of the form for the press, except reading the proof. In England these additional labors are rewarded by a compensation for all the matter connected with the printed page, including head- and foot-lines, column-rules, etc., while in America the piece-hands are paid only for the matter actually composed, as in newspaper-work. It is claimed for the companionship plan that it promotes the interest of both the employer and the compositor, and as it is an extension of the piece-work system, in lieu of time-work, to imposition, etc., this claim may be well founded; but it is questionable whether the obvious difficulties in the way of its adoption in the United States will soon be surmounted.

Book-composition, at the prices usually current, is one of the most unprofitable branches of the printing business, unless it is allied either with stereotyping or electrotyping, or with press-work.

Book-Worm, a species of paper-eating moth which bores a narrow, straight channel directly through a volume. It was described by Hooke in his Micrographia, 1667, as a small, white, silver-shining worm or moth; its head is big and blunt, and the body tapers towards the tail. The existence and appearance of this insect have been matter of discussion; it is of rare occurrence, but is very destructive, eating alike through binding and paper. It is supposed to have been introduced into England in hog's-leather binding from Holland. There is now in a private library in Philadelphia a book perforated by this insect.

The word is generally used in a metaphorical sense for an indiscriminate reader—one who devours books, swallowing the contents without digesting them.

Borders.—This term is nearly a modern equivalent for what were formerly called flowers, and they are defined as types with ornaments cast on their face instead of letters, and used for borders round jobs, cards, pages, and wrappers of books; and for other embellishments. The term border also implies, in a general sense, anything used to inclose or surround the type which appears on the printed page or job, as brass or wooden rules, or engraved or electrotype borders.

The specimen-books of the type-founders and of manufacturers of wood type abound with an infinite variety of borders, many of which are exceedingly graceful and beautiful in design, and, in the hands of skillful compositors, they produce very pleasing effects. At this day type borders are used mainly in job printing, but formerly they were introduced freely into books and newspapers, being used in the latter where rules or double rules are used now, and in the former to construct head- and tail-pieces, to surround initial letters, to form borders to pages, and to divide miscellaneous subjects. Borders or flowers were made soon after the art of casting movable metallic type was invented, but they fell into comparative disuse after the early development of wood-engraving. When it became, in time, nearly a lost art, borders were again multiplied; but it was reserved for modern times, and for the demand created by diversified job printing, to witness the simultaneous production and use, on a wonderfully extensive scale, of type borders and wood-engravings.

Smith's Printer's Grammar, published in London in 1755, gives the following quaint suggestions for the construction of make-shift substitutes for borders:

For want of flowers, references and other sorts belonging to a font are sometimes made use of, to serve as well at the beginning as conclusion of work of a small size; such, for instance, viz.:

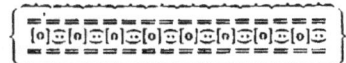

Botch.—An incompetent, negligent workman.

Botched.—Carelessly or badly executed work.

Bottle-arsed.—When a letter is wider at the bottom than the top.

Bottle-necked.—Letter that is thicker at the top than at the bottom. Types are now cast with such precision that this term and the preceding one have become almost obsolete.

Bottom Line.—The last line of the page, or that immediately preceding the signature or blank line.

Bourgeois.—A size of type smaller than Long Primer, and larger than Brevier. In some scales two lines of this letter are equal to one line of Great Primer, or four lines of Diamond. (See TYPE).

Boxed.—Any figure or other work inclosed within a border of brass rules.

Boxes.—The compartments in a case in which the several varieties of letters are kept. Thus, that in which the A is kept is called the A box, and so on with the rest.

Boxwood, Engraver's.—The best boxwood used in engraving is of a good yellow color, of a fine close grain, that has been of a slow growth, clear of knots and any imperfections, such as cracks or flaws. The finest lines may be engraved on this wood, as it is both hard and tough, and, with care in printing, the number of impressions that may be taken from an engraving on it would appear incredible. However, since the introduction of electrotyping, by which process the most perfect fac-similes can be taken, the originals are seldom printed from, being mostly preserved for electrotyping purposes alone. Papillon, in his History of Engraving on Wood, gives a specimen of an original wood-engraving, from which, he states, there had been upward of three hundred and seventy thousand impressions previously printed; and if the block had been carefully cleaned and well printed, it would still have produced respectable impressions. Boxwood of a dull bad yellow color, and of an open coarse grain, is not fit for engraving on, neither is wood that is of a blackish color at the heart; for in these cases it has begun to decay, is brittle and tender, and if engraved on the lines would not stand, but would fail in printing.

Braces.—The brace is a character (‿‿) composed of two pot-hook curves, joined by the foot of the first meeting the top of the second. It is used to embrace or group such particulars as have a common class or import, and thus avoids much tautology and circumlocution. The face of a brace is always turned to that part of an article which makes the most lines. Braces are generally cast two and three ems. Middles and corners (called cocks and hens) are also cast, by which, with the aid of dashes, a brace of any required length can be formed, thus, — — — — — —. These are called piece braces. Brass braces, however, are more beautiful and regular than piece braces, as will be seen by this specimen :

Bracket.—[ ] A character composed of three lines at right angles, and made to face right and left;

used by critics and editors to mark a word or phrase either supplied or rejected by them in matter written by other authors; and, also, sometimes in lieu of the marks of parenthesis.

Bradford, Andrew, born 1686, died 1742. The younger son of William Bradford, first printer in Pennsylvania. He was born in Philadelphia, and accompanied his father upon his removal to New York; after serving his apprenticeship, he became his father's partner for a short time, and then, in 1712, returned to Philadelphia to establish the second printing-office in that city. Until 1723 he was the only printer in the colony, his office being in Second Street, at the sign of the Bible, which was also the sign his father employed in New York.

In December, 1719, he established The American Weekly Mercury, the first newspaper in the province; his father commencing the first paper in New York six years later.

When Franklin visited Andrew Bradford in 1727, although he could furnish him no employment, he made him welcome to his house, where he boarded for some time, while he was serving as journeyman to Keimer, who had just opened a rival office.

In 1732, Bradford was postmaster of the city, and in 1735 became a considerable dealer in books and stationery. In 1741, he published a periodical, The American Magazine; or Monthly View of the Political State of the British Colonies. He was interred in Christ Church burying-ground.

The following bill against the Province of Pennsylvania will show the remuneration of the public printer a century and a half ago.

PHILADELPHIA, ANNO 1725.

Province of Pennsylvania, Dr.

To 14 Quires Paper from the 13th December to the 10th of August at 2/ - - - - }	£ 1 : 9 : 0
To 1 Blank Book - - - - -	0 : 3 : 0
To 1½ Sheet of the Laws for the year 1724 at 28/ pr Sheet - - - - - }	2 : 2 : 0
To Quills Ink and an Almanack - - -	0 : 2 : 1
To 1 Quire Demy Paper - - - -	0 : 3 : 6
To 8 Sheets of the Laws for the Year 1725 at 23/ pr Sheet - - - - - }	11 : 4 : 0
	15 : 2 : 7

To Printing the Votes and Proceedings of the House what the Honourable House please Allowed to make Even - - -	17 : 5
	16 : - : -

Errors Excepted: for me
this 12 Day of August 1725
ANDREW BRADFORD.

Andrew Bradford, being childless, adopted his nephew, William Bradford, born in New York, 1719, who, following the same business, commenced, immediately after the death of his uncle, a newspaper styled the Pennsylvania Journal and Weekly Advertiser, which was continued by his son, Thomas Bradford, until 1801; this periodical espoused the cause of the country, and from July, 1774, to October,

1775, the period of the agitation of the question of union among the Colonies, bore the device of a divided snake with the motto Unite or Die. Thomas Bradford in 1801 merged the Journal into a daily called The True American, which he conducted until 1819, when he sold it to be merged into its still existing successor, The North American and United States Gazette, thus closing a century (1719–1819) of journalism successfully conducted by three generations of the same family.

Bradford, William, born 1658 in Leicester, England, died in New York, 23d May, 1752 (his tombstone in Trinity Church-yard states his age as ninety-two). He was apprenticed in London to Andrew Sowles, a printer, the intimate friend of George Fox. Bradford married the daughter of Andrew Sowles, and with her joined the first Quaker emigrants to Philadelphia in the year 1682, bearing with him a letter from George Fox, introducing a sober young man whose name is William Bradford, who comes to Pennsylvania to set up the trade of printing Friends' books, and requesting that those to whom he writes shall let the Friends know it in Virginia, Carolina, Long Island, Plymouth Patent and Boston.

The first work known to have been issued from his press was an almanac with the following title:

KALENDARIUM PENNSILVANIENSE:

OR,

AMERICA'S MESSENGER.

Being an

ALMANACK

FOR THE YEAR OF GRACE 1686.

Wherein is contained both the English and Forragn account; the motions of the Planets through the Signs, with the luminaries, conjunctions, aspects, eclipses; the rising, southing and setting of the moon, with the time when she passeth by or is with the most eminent fixed stars: sun rising and setting, and the time of High Water at the City of *Philadelphia*, &c. With Chronologies and many other Notes, Rules and Tables, very fitting for every man to know and have: All which is accommodated to the Longitude of the Provence of Pennsilvania; Longitude 40 Degr. North: with a table of Houses for the same, which may indifferently serve *New England*, *New York*, *East* and *West Jersey*, *Maryland* and North part of *Virginia*.

By SAMUEL ATKYNS,

Student in the Mathematics and Astrology.

And the stars in their course fought against Sesera.—
Judg. 5, 29.

Printed and sold by William Bradford. Sold also by the Author and H. Murrey in *Philadelphia*, and Philip Richards in *New York*, 1685.

With this first publication began Bradford's difficulties with the Quakers, for he inadvertently described the Government as having been founded by Lord Penn. For this offence the author and printer

were both summoned before the meeting. The author was ordered to omit the offensive title, and the printer was warned not to print anything that was not licensed by the Council.

Bradford continued to reside in Philadelphia for nearly ten years, during which time he published about forty books and pamphlets, and was also interested with William and Nicholas Ryttinghuysen, since modified into Rittenhouse, in establishing the first paper-mill in America, at Roxborough, near Philadelphia, in 1690.

In 1692 difficulties occurred among the Quaker residents of Philadelphia, and Bradford, as printer, became involved in the quarrel. George Keith, a Scotchman, the Surveyor-General of New Jersey, was employed by the Society of Friends in Philadelphia, in 1689, to superintend their school. Keith became a speaker in their meetings, but was disapproved by many of the Friends, and was finally forbidden to preach in their assemblies; he appealed from this decision to the general meeting of the Friends, and printed and distributed an address in his own behalf. This pamphlet was declared to be seditious, and Bradford the printer was arrested, with a couple of the partisans of Keith who had distributed copies of the pamphlet.

A private session of the County Court was held by six justices, all Friends, who requested the attendance of two magistrates who were not Quakers. The avowed intention was to convict Keith and his party of sedition and condemn them without a hearing; but the two additional members reprobated the measure, declaring that the transaction was a mere dispute among the Friends respecting their religion, in which the government should take no part. They, however, advised that Keith and the rest of the accused should be put on their defence, and promised that if a case of sedition was proved against them they would unite cordially in the prosecution. The Quaker magistrates refused to comply with this proposal, and the two others in consequence left the court. The remainder then proceeded to prosecute Keith without a hearing, and proclaimed him by the public crier in the market-house to be a seditious person and an enemy of the King and Queen's Government.

Bradford and MacComb, who had been imprisoned, appeared before the court and requested to be brought to trial. They claimed, as free-born English subjects, the rights secured by Magna Charta, and Bradford, in particular, desired a speedy trial, because not only was his person restrained, but his working-tools, and the paper and books from his shop, were taken from him, and without these he could not maintain his family. The trial was postponed to the next term of court.

The offence of MacComb was his sympathy with Keith, and disposing two copies of the printed address to two Friends. For this he was imprisoned, and deprived by Lieutenant-Governor Lloyd of a license to keep an ordinary or house of entertainment, for which he had paid that official, but a few months previously, the sum of three pounds twelve shillings of the currency.

At the next session of court, Bradford was placed at the bar, the presentment being that certain articles of the pamphlet called An Appeal had a tendency to weaken the hands of the magistrates, and that William Bradford was the printer of the pamphlet in question. Bradford pleaded not guilty, and the jury, being unable to agree after more than forty-eight hours, was discharged.

It is worthy of remark that when one of the Quaker justices instructed the jury to find only whether William Bradford printed the pamphlet called An Appeal, and that whether the pamphlet was seditious, and whether it tended to the weakening of the hands of the magistrates, was a matter of law for the determination of the court, with which the jury were not to meddle, Bradford stoutly maintained that the instruction of the court was wrong; that the printing of the pamphlet was not the only fact which the jury were to find, but that they were to find, also, whether the pamphlet was seditious, and whether it tended to the weakening of the hands of the magistrates; for the jury, in criminal trials, are judges of the law as well as the matter of fact, the very point which awakened such intense interest in the trial of Jack Wilkes seventy years later.

Bradford attended at the next court, to know if the court would let him have his utensils and discharge him.

Justice Cook replied: Thou shalt not have thy goods until released by law. To which Bradford responded: The law will not release them unless executed. The Justice answered: If thou wilt request a trial, thou mayst have it; and Bradford closed with the pertinent query: Whether it be according to law to seize men's goods, and imprison their persons, and to detain them, under the terror of a gaol, one six-months after another, and not bring them to trial unless requested by the imprisoned? whether when a jury is sworn to well and truly try, and true deliverance make between the proprietor and prisoner, it is not illegal to absolve them from their oaths, dismiss them, and put the cause to trial to another jury?

The types themselves were at length brought into the court to witness against the unfortunate printer, and upon one of the examiners prying up the chase for examination the friendly type fell into pi, and exonerated their owner by destroying the evidence against him. Shortly after this session of court, Bradford was released.

The Governor of New York had previously invited Bradford to remove to that province, the inducements being forty pounds a year and the public printing, and under the pressure of this misfortune Bradford readily accepted the proposal, and became the first printer of New York as well as Philadelphia.

His first publication in his new residence was in 1693, and was an appeal in behalf of the son of Warner Wessels, and husband of Antie Christians, inhabit-

ants and sailors of the city of New York, in miserable slavery under the power of the Infidel. Subscriptions for the benefit of these unfortunate prisoners in Algeria were solicited and authorized under the hand and seal of Ben. Fletcher, at Fort William Henry, on the 8th day of June, 1693.

Bradford's second New York issue presents another striking picture of his age, being a proclamation declaring that:

Whereas there is actual war between our Sovereign Lord and Lady, William and Mary, . . . and the French king, and that the French have designed a squadron of Ships with Land Forces against the Province of New York, beacons were to be erected on the most prominent headlands of the coast, to be lighted on the approach of the enemy, and that upon such signal being given, the inhabitants were to drive their cattle into the woods, and repair, with arms and ammunition, to their respective places of rendezvous; [and ending], I expect a due compliance herein from all Persons, as they will answer the same at their utmost peril.

The only known copy of this proclamation is in the State Library at Albany.

Col. Fletcher having been removed in 1698, he was succeeded by the Earl of Bellamont, between whom and Bradford difficulties soon arose, and the printer, as he is styled by the noble earl, was reported to the Council as having neglected his duties for the past four months, and a proposition made that he be debarred from receiving any salary for that period.

At the earl's death, however, which occurred in February, 1701, Bradford was again received into favor, and his salary as public printer was increased to £75 per annum.

In his imprints Bradford styled himself Printer to their Majesties, at the Sign of the Bible.

His son Andrew was connected with him for a few years, but removed to Philadelphia in 1712, where he was very successful as a printer.

William Bradford continued to be during thirty years the only printer in the Province of New York, and was also printer to the Government of New Jersey from 1725 until his retirement from business.

In 1723, when the youth Benjamin Franklin left his home in Boston to seek for work, he applied to Bradford, the only printer in New York, who, having no employment for him, recommended him to his son Andrew in Philadelphia, thus introducing Franklin to the home of his adoption.

In October, 1725, when in his sixty-third year, he established the New York Gazette, a weekly paper, the first published in New York, his son Andrew having established the first newspaper in Pennsylvania, the American Weekly Mercury, in 1719.

Certainly as early as 1728, William Bradford owned a paper-mill at Elizabethtown, New Jersey; the date of its erection is uncertain, but it is supposed to have been the second mill established in British America, the first being the one he had assisted in founding near Philadelphia.

He continued his business uninterruptedly and prosperously until a few years before his death, which occurred in 1752, enjoying vigorous health until the last day of his life.

Brass Rule.—Strips of brass, of the height of type, used for forming lines. They are generally made in lengths of twenty-four inches, and of various thicknesses, and breadths of face. They are made single, double, triple, etc.; also, plain, curved, waved, dotted, and of various fanciful designs. The practice of cutting up rule to any necessary size, or according to the momentary caprice of the compositor, gives rise to great waste, both of time and material. To avoid this, type-foundries furnish rules cut to Pica ems, called Labor-Saving Rule, which, by competent workmen, can be used with great facility, as will be seen by the annexed specimens:

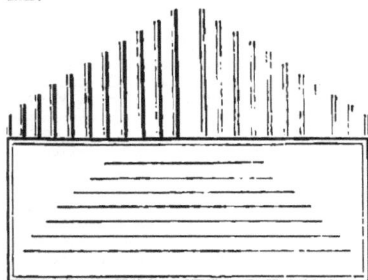

Brass Rule Cases.—Cases made specially for holding the various lengths of Labor-Saving Rule.

Brass Rule Cutter.—An apparatus for cutting up brass rule with greater readiness and accuracy than with the shears.

Brayer.—A small roller four to six inches long, used for spreading ink on the inking-table, and for applying it to the distributing plates or rollers connected with presses.

Break Line.—A short line; the end of a paragraph.

Breitkopf, Johann Gottlieb Immanuel, a German printer and publisher, who was also a skillful musician, is alleged to have invented movable music type in 1750. He also improved the shape of the German characters, and devised a method of printing maps, pictures, etc., from movable pieces. Johann Breitkopf was the friend of Goethe, and set his earliest poems to music, and the firm with which he was identified not only published Goethe's works, but the musical compositions of Beethoven and Mozart, as well as the productions of many other world-famous German authors.

Breve.—A curved mark (˘) used to indicate the short quantity of a vowel, or some particular quality of its sound.

6

Breviary.—An abridgment or compendium, generally used as the title of the book containing the canonical hours or divine office, recited daily by the Roman Catholic clergy, and formerly required also of the laity. The word is probably derived from the fact that the daily offices have been abridged from a longer service. It contains the eight daily services, viz., Matins, Lauds, Primes, Thirds, Sixths, Nones, Vespers, and Compline. In typography these books of devotion are especially important as specimens of decorative printing; in manuscript they were lavishly adorned with illuminations in gold and colors; and much of the early printing was intended as fac-similes of these works, for which there was great demand. The name of Brevier type probably originated from its having been employed in printing Breviaries.

Brevier.—A standard size of type, larger than Minion and smaller than Bourgeois. (See TYPE.)

Brilliant.—The smallest type that has yet been cast for practical purposes. (See TYPE.)

Bring Up.—To bring up a form is to place overlays on those parts in which the impression is defective, and to cut away those portions in which it is too heavy, so as to equalize the impression over the whole form.

Broadside.—A form of one page, printed on one side of a whole sheet of paper. Also, a poster printed in the largest measure the sheet permits, instead of the narrowest.

Broken Matter.—Pages of type thrown down and somewhat intermingled.

Bronstrup Press.—A hand-press, made by F.

BRONSTRUP PRESS.

Bronstrup, of Philadelphia, of three sizes, viz.: platen, 16 by 22 inches, 20 by 26 inches, and 22½ by 29½ inches. The material used is principally wrought iron, and the press stands securely without stay; it can also be easily worked, and moved and put up with facility. It is illustrated by the accompanying cut.

Bronze Powders, of various colors and qualities, are used with great effect in many descriptions of American fancy printing. The kinds in most common use are known as gold and silver bronze. In purchasing the latter, care must be taken to secure an undoubtedly good article; as inferior qualities are apt to change color, and to become nearly black after prolonged exposure.

Bronze Printing.—This is effected by printing a form with a light-colored glutinous ink or sizing, and, before it has time to dry, applying bronze to the printed surface by pads made of cotton, fur, or velvet, the surplus bronze being subsequently dusted off; and when particularly good effects are required, the bronzed sheet is subsequently burnished by being run between metallic rollers.

Bronzing Machines, of which one or more of American invention have been patented, are used in printing-offices where a large amount of bronze work is done, to supersede hand-labor, as well as to save bronze and to expedite bronzing operations.

Brothers of Common Life (The) rank among the early typographers, having printed books in 1474 at Vallis Sanctæ Mariæ, a convent in the Rheingau, a territory belonging to Mayence, and also at Brussels from 1476 to 1484, and probably at other places. This brotherhood, known as Fratres Vitæ Communis, a name better translated as the Fraternal Community, was an order instituted under the rule of St. Augustine, and marks the stages of transition between the ancient scribe and modern printer, by showing how naturally one succeeded to the other. The founder of the brotherhood, Albert Gerard, generally styled the Great, was born in 1340, and died in 1384. He received a fine education at Paris, but fell into dissolute habits, from which an earnest word of warning from a fellow-student aroused him as by a miracle. He thenceforth devoted himself to reclaiming men of evil lives, and was so successful in his devout labors that he instituted the Fratres Communis Vitæ, devoted to like duties, who lived with one heart, one soul, and one common property, under the obligation to support themselves by transcribing the Scriptures and other holy books. Successive popes confirmed and extended their privileges, and in 1402 the order possessed seven monasteries.

The priesthood were at that time the chief custodians of learning, being intrusted by the popes with the copying of the Scriptures, and of ecclesiastical works, as well as the bulls and edicts of the Church authorities. The monasteries also contained registers in which were entered accounts of public events, the royal succession, the accounts of the clergy, their succession in office, the deliberations of their councils, etc.,—in brief, the current history of the times.

The monks who were devoted to writing were classed as librarii, that is, the transcribers of old and new books; antiquarii, the copyists of old books; tachygraphi, short-hand or rapid writers, and calligraphi, or elegant writers. The Spanish monks were held to excel in beauty of penmanship; the Anglo-Saxon priesthood of England were also eminent, and the fine text of their running or cursive character is supposed by some authorities to have been the origin of the small, legible, and elegant Roman letter of the present day.

Brown Inks.—See INKS.

Brown's Patent Type-Setting and Distributing Machinery.—This is a new American invention, originating with O. S. Brown, of Boston, who in 1870 announced his readiness to supply type-setters adapted to the use of long primer or larger sizes of type, with a case for 60 letters, for $300, and a distributer with 30 receiving channels for $700. For every additional 10 letters required in the type-

setter an additional charge of $50 is made. The following description of the type-setter (for which a speed of 1200 ems per hour is claimed) is given in a pamphlet printed by Mr. Brown in 1870, which was set up and distributed by his machinery:

The Setter comprises a Case, a Stick, and a Justifier. The case consists of a series of grooves or channels ranged side by side, each just wide enough to receive a line of type. There is no limit to this case, either in the number of channels, or their length. In these channels, the types stand upon their feet, and the case is set at such an angle that they slide downward by their own gravity, and rest upon the bar which closes the lower ends. Across the foot a shield is placed, provided with openings for the types to pass through as they are set; and an index, showing the letters and sorts which the case contains. Corresponding openings in the rear allow the tongue, which forces out the letter, to enter.

Below and in front of the case, sliding back and forth upon a track at the will of the operator, is the Stick, or mechanical hand, which takes the letters from the case. The Stick consists of a semicircular groove for receiving the type, and a lever or key for operating it. The uppermost end of the stick forms an indicator, pointing to the index upon the shield. The key is provided at one end with a tongue, or plunger, for lifting the type, and the other forms a handle for working it. The whole weighing but a few ounces, it is moved with the greatest ease from letter to letter. The operator, seizing the handle with the thumb and finger, runs it nearly opposite the letter to be taken. It is so arranged with an adjusting gauge that no greater accuracy of stroke is required than in playing a piano. As the handle of the key is depressed, a type is thrust out into the stick. As the handle is raised again, a follower pushes the type just lifted sufficiently down the channel to allow the next one to be taken in the same way. This operation is repeated till the stick is full, when it is run to one end of the track, and the line slipped into the Justifier. The stick is then ready for another line; and, when several are set, they are broken up and justified by hand.

The leading advantage claimed for this machine is adaptation to the use of persons unskilled in type-setting. Below will be found what purports to be the first proof of the fifth hour's work, without alteration or correction, of a young lady inexperienced in type and type-setting machines:

Type setting should be so cheap that publishers can print books and papers in this ucountry, and sell them at the low prices which obtain in England. A London house has printed the Pilgrims Progress, in clear type, on good paper, so that the book can be retailed for a penny, News and illustrated papers are sogld in England atnearly proportionately low rates. We have not as yet, reached this point in this country, although in proprotion to our population, there are more readers here than in any other nation on the globe. We want the means of supplying the demand for reading matter. The inventive talent of our country produced the steamboat, the cotton-gin, and the elictic telegraph. It is fully equal to the production of the perfect type-setting machine, which shall rapidly and cheaply do the entire composition of the whole country. Nothing else so profitably suggests to the mind of the American inventors. We invite the press of the country to join in subscribing for a prize which shall be worthy the attention and competition of every skillful inventor in the country. The prize shall be less than half a million dollars; and, if the leading newspapers in the country can be induced to combine in such an offer, the World will gladly head the list with $25,000 as its own subscription. To the successful man, who produces the called-for instrument, a quarter of a million dollars will gladly be given by the publishers of the country. The rest of the prize should be distributed to the second, third, fourth, and fifth best machine.

Brown's Distributer is described as follows:

The Distributer consists of a rotating ring, about ten inches in diameter. At regular intervals in the edge of the ring are recesses for holding the types while being carried to their places. At one side is a galley, which receives the page to be distributed. Radiating from this ring are the channels, into which the types are distributed, and which, when full, are transferred to the Setter, and constitute a part of the case. From the galley, the machine takes one line at a time, and lifts it into a channel, in which it is fed towards the distributing-ring, but a little below. From the inner end of this line the types are lifted one at a time, and enter the distributing-ring. This ring has an intermittent motion, and each motion brings one of the recesses directly over the line. One after another the types are forced up into these recesses. A recess is large enough to receive the largest type, and is formed by cutting a larger slot in the ring, and inserting a set of levers. The levers are simply straight pieces of sheet brass or steel about two inches long, with a hole near one end, through which passes the pin on which they turn. These levers, placed one upon the other in sets of six or more, form one side of the recess. A slide or ejeetor, which forces out the letter when it arrives at its proper place, forms the back of the recess. When a letter is fed into the ring, it stands in this recess, and any nick that may have been made in the edge of the type will be opposite one of the levers. As the short arms of these levers shut against the edge of the type, some of them entering the nieks, the long arms take a corresponding position. It will be seen that a slight variation in the position of the short arms gives a much greater variation in the long arms. The relative position of these long arms, acting in connection with the keys, determines when the type shall be ejected. These keys slide out and in, and each motion of the ring brings each set of the levers successively in front of each key. The keys all advance a short distance, and try the ends of the levers; and, wherever the shape of the keys corresponds to the

position of the levers, the key advances farther, and, acting upon the ejector, forces out the letter. The operation is on the same principle as the common lever-lock; the levers with the type forming a certain combination, which will move around until it arrives opposite its own key. The lock will then be unlocked, and the letter forced out. The keys are the slides, which are placed in the stationary part of the machine, inside of the rotating ring, and radiating from the centre.

Bruce, David, born November 12, 1770, in Scotland, died March 15, 1857, at Brooklyn, New York, after serving an apprenticeship to the printing business in Edinburgh, emigrated to the United States in the spring of 1793, and immediately found employment in the city of New York as a pressman. He soon afterwards attempted to establish a printing-ink manufactory, but abandoned this undertaking on account of lack of capital. In 1806 he started, in conjunction with his brother George, a printing-office, and while prosecuting this business he became so deeply interested in what was then the new art of stereotyping, that he visited Great Britain in 1812, to acquire a definite knowledge of it. He there found, however, that the Earl of Stanhope, who was then an authority on this subject, could not be induced to impart the information which he had been expected to furnish, and although Mr. Bruce acquired some useful knowledge in regard to the process of moulding, in other respects he learned but little. On his return he instituted a series of experiments, and devised inventions or improvements, including the present planing or leveling machine, mahogany shifting-blocks, and the method of packing plates in boxes, which enabled him to successfully establish the new art in the United States, and David and George Bruce became the first to stereotype the Testament and Bible in this country. A combination of circumstances led the firm to abandon printing, and to engage in type-founding in conjunction with stereotyping,—David Bruce continuing to give special attention to stereotyping, until his withdrawal from active business life in 1822. Subsequently he made a series of experiments in type-founding, some of which led to useful results.

Bruce, David, Jr., of New York (a son of the David Bruce who, in conjunction with his brother, George Bruce, established the Bruce Type-Foundry), invented in 1838 the type-casting machine which, with a few modifications, is now in general use in the type-foundries of the United States and Europe. (See TYPE-CASTING MACHINES.)

Bruce, George, born in 1781, in Edinburgh, Scotland, died July 5, 1866, at New York. When a lad fourteen years of age, he emigrated to this country, arriving in Philadelphia in June, 1795. He served in that city an apprenticeship of two or three years to the printing-business. In 1803, he became foreman and occasional contributor to the New York Daily Advertiser. In 1806, he established, in conjunction with his elder brother David, a book printing-office in New York, and they used the first standing press for pressing sheets in that city. In 1812, they established a stereotype foundry, and soon afterwards they started Bruce's New York Type-Foundry, their first specimen-book being issued in 1817–18. In 1822, the firm was dissolved by the retirement of David Bruce, and George Bruce abandoned the stereotype business and devoted himself exclusively to type-founding. He undertook the difficult, laborious, and expensive task of harmonizing and graduating the size of the different bodies of type as they ranged in the eleven series, from Pearl to Canon, and introduced the Agate body for the first time into the series. After his nephew, David Bruce, Jr., invented the type-casting machine George Bruce devised a way to cool the mould by driving an artificial blast of wind through it, which he patented in 1854. In 1863, Mr. Bruce was elected President of the Type-Founders' Association, which position he continued to fill until his death.

Brune, William Maria Anne, a French journeyman printer who became a marshal and a peer of the empire. Like many others of the craft, and especially newspaper publishers, he has had two sets of biographers, one lavishing eulogies upon him, while the other heaps execrations upon his memory. The first is composed of those who admire the active participants of the French Revolution and heroes of the Empire, while the second denounces all who were prominently identified with the Revolution and with Napoleon. The contrast between these diverse versions of a printer's life is very striking, and well illustrates the conflicting views entertained of some prominent printers in the United States, as will be seen by the following extracts:

Timperley's Sketch of Marshal Brune.—He was born at Brivez la Gaillarde, in March, 1763. At the breaking out of the French Revolution, he was engaged as overseer of a printing-office at Limousin, and first became known by publishing some small works of his own composition. He afterwards devoted himself ardently to the cause of the Revolution, became a member of the club *des Cordeliers*, and played an active part in the tempests of that period. In 1793, he entered the military service in the revolutionary army in the Gironde, and soon gave proofs of intrepidity and military talents. Afterwards he distinguished himself as general of brigade in the Italian army, in 1797, in the attack of Verona, and in the battle of Arcole. In January, 1798, he received the chief command of the army sent against Switzerland: he entered that country without much opposition, and effected a new organization of the government. In 1799, he defeated the English in the north of Holland, near Bergen, and compelled the Duke of York to agree to the treaty of Alkmaer, by which the English and Russians were to evacuate the north of Holland. In January, 1800, he was made a counsellor of state, and was placed at the head of the army of the west. In 1803, he went as ambassador to the court of Constantinople, and

received from the Turkish ministry the highest marks of honor; and, during his absence, he was appointed a marshal of the empire. At the end of 1806, Napoleon appointed him governor-general of the Hanseatic towns, and soon after commander of the troops in Swedish Pomerania, against the King of Sweden. He drew upon himself the indignation of Napoleon, by allowing a personal interview with the King of Sweden, and also by favoring the English contraband trade in Hamburg. He was in consequence recalled, and suffered to remain without employment. After the revolution of 1814, he recognized Louis XVIII., and received the cross of Louis, but no appointment. This was the cause of declaring himself for Napoleon immediately upon his return from Elba, in 1815. He received the chief command of an important army in the south of France, and was made a peer. When circumstances changed again, he delayed a long time before he gave up Toulon, and sent in his resignation to the king. While retiring from Toulon to Paris, he perished, the victim of the most atrocious assassination, at Avignon, planned by the royalist reactionaries of that period, and directed by a well-known person, who, having betrayed his country in 1814, sought to recommend himself in 1815, by inflaming the passions and pointing the vengeance of a vindictive faction. The insurgents surrounded the hotel, and with loud shouts demanded the death of the marshal. In vain did the prefect and the mayor strive to defend him (as there were no troops in the city) for more than four hours, at the peril of their lives. The door was at last broken open, a crowd of murderers rushed into the chamber, and the unhappy marshal fell under a shower of balls, after a fruitless attempt to defend himself and justify his conduct. His body was exposed to the most shameful insults, and then dragged from the hotel to the bridge over the Rhone, from which it was thrown into the river. Thus perished Marshal Brune, of whom it is recorded, that during his command in Switzerland and Holland he displayed a noble disinterestedness rarely equaled. He approved himself a good citizen, and a good Frenchman; he deceived no friends, betrayed no cause, sacrificed no principle, and passed through the ordeal of the Revolution, and of the empire, without a stain on his character.

Sketch in the London Printers' Journal, November 4, 1867.—The extraordinary career of Field-Marshal Brune is worthy of record. In the year 1789 he was a journeyman printer, and married a washerwoman. Idle, profligate, and dissolute to a degree, his little earnings were spent in drunkenness; at the same time, the hard labor of his humble wife kept them both from starving. Like the majority of others destitute alike of prosperity and character, he rushed to the revolutionary standard which was just then unfurled in Paris. Here, with an audacity mistaken by some for courage, he preached to his followers plunder, proscription, and murder, in such a violent manner as to call forth the reproaches of such a character as even Marat. This ferocious regicide, Marat, then started the journal L'Ami du Peuple, and made Brune his printer. He continued as such until 1792, when the worst of the grand criminals became members of the Parisian commune. By that body he was nominated as aide-de-camp to Santerne, and he then commenced his military career by leading the ruffians who seized and destroyed the presses of all loyal newspapers. During the dreadful years of 1793–4 he figured prominently among the most sanguinary generals of the revolutionary army of Lyons and La Vendée. In the following year he was imprisoned as a terrorist, until Barras and Bonaparte liberated him to serve on the staff of the army of the interior. In 1798, he was prominently forward, more by craft than talent, in giving the death-blow to Swiss independence. His disgraceful success here, afterwards secured him the command in Holland, La Vendée, and Italy, in which countries he intrigued (necessitated, by courtesy) a vast deal more than he fought. In fact, he was ordered, in all operations, to act according to the opinions of the chief of the staff, his ignorance as a general being so notorious. The celebrated Moreau observed of him, when, in 1802, he was appointed ambassador to Turkey, that Brune's uniform of a general only covered the most mischievous and dastardly of intriguers, while his diploma as an ambassador protected the most active and dangerous of conspirators. Brune was the most tyrannical of upstart demagogues, and the most merciless of revolutionary marauders. He has been accused, in works printed on the Continent, of having assisted at the massacres of Paris in 1792, at Lyons in 1793, and in La Vendée in the spring of 1794; of having plundered, in 1798, two million livres (£80,000) in Switzerland; and of having robbed in 1800 his benefactor, Bonaparte, of one million livres, intrusted to him for disuniting the royalist chiefs in La Vendée. We bring this sketch to a close by remarking the curious freaks of fortune which made of a French journeyman-printer, under the name of a field-marshal, an inspector-general of German presses and printing-offices.

Buell, Abel, of Connecticut, was probably the first American who made a systematic attempt to cast English types. The following sketch of his career was given in The Printer of October, 1858:

Abel Buell, according to all facts that can be gathered, was a man of inventive genius, versatile in the direction of his mind, very erratic, self-willed, and enjoyed the character of being very eccentric. At one time we find him a bugler, an undertaker, teacher of a singing-school, and leader of the choir in the principal meeting-house; but he rendered himself very obnoxious in endeavoring to introduce a bass-viol, by way of improving the psalmody, which was very repugnant to professing Christians at that early period. He seems to have been of a restless, uneasy turn, and apt to get into trouble, either through patriotic impulses or some other cause. We are told that while attempting to make printing-types, in

which he was sustained by the State, he was denounced for treason, and that appearances were found strongly against him. The leaden equestrian statue of George III., which occupied the centre of the Bowling Green, New York City, was destroyed by a wild, infuriated, and rebellious mob, and Abel Buell was suspected of being one of the active leaders of the disaffected. This must have been prior to the final outbreak. Be this as it may, a large portion of it was found in his house (its head and shoulders), which he was detected in converting into type in pursuance of a sworn declaration, that either as bullets or types his majesty should be turned to a useful purpose, and make an impression. How he got out of this difficulty history is silent; most probably he fled. The next we hear of Mr. Buell is his being connected with the Boston tea-party, in which he took an active part, disguised as a Kickapoo Indian. We hear of him again at Salem, Massachusetts, where he was arraigned for open and profane swearing against the Commonwealth, with the additional charge of sorcery, but the jury not agreeing he was confined as insane—this becoming manifest by his asserting his disbelief in original sin. At Bunker Hill we hear of him again, where he got crippled in the knee. What brought him to New York is not told, but after a tedious confinement of seven weeks on board the old prison-ship Jersey, at the Wallabout, we lose sight of him for some time; probably he returned home to Killingworth, his native place.

Romantic and incredible as the above tradition seems to be, the following extracts from documents on file in the office of the Secretary of State, Hartford, somewhat strengthen the probability of the truth that he was a very singular character, and prove the fact that legislative aid was extended to Abel Buell.

It would seem from a memorial presented to the General Assembly of the Colony of Connecticut, etc., dated Killingworth, 8th day of October, A. D. 1766, by Abel Buell, that he petitions to be restored to his former rights and privileges, which he confesses he has justly forfeited, etc. In the said memorial he testifies his grateful appreciation of their clemency in so far compassionating his youthful follies as to give him enlargement from prison, where by the laws of the colony he was sentenced during life, and permitting him to dwell with his family in Killingworth, etc. Buell sets forth in his petition that he has made a great discovery in polishing crystals and precious stones, which will be a great advantage to the colony, and urges this fact as a kind of set-off against his misdemeanor against the colony, and as a reason why his petition should be granted.

Certificate of Justice of the Peace and townsmen to his good behavior, October, 1766.

He is restored to his privileges and liberties, by him forfeited, on giving bonds, etc.

In another petition, dated October, A. D. 1769, he sets forth his discoveries in type-founding, and says that through unwearied application for months past, and as a specimen of his abilities, he presents this memorial impressed with types of his own manufacture; that as the expense of erecting a proper foundry is great, and beyond his abilities, he humbly hopes for encouragement from this Assembly, either by granting him the liberty of a lottery, for raising a sum sufficient to carry on the same, or in some other way, etc.

On the favorable recommendation of the committee to whom it was referred and his apparatus examined, the Assembly voted a loan of £100, to be secured by bond, the money to be repaid in seven years; and the Treasurer was further ordered to pay said Abel Buell one other £100, after having pursued the business twelve months from date according to agreement.

Perhaps here come in some of his treasonable difficulties which break in upon his prospects, for we find a letter from his wife dated New Haven, August 8, 1777, directed to the Treasurer:

SIR:—The long absence of my husband makes me despair of ever seeing him again. When he left me, it was unknown to me that he was so much involved as he was; in a few days everything was seized from me. I have, by dint of industry, got together so much that I can now refund the money he had of the State. If, therefore, the £100 can be accepted in full for the demand against us, I am ready to pay it.

I am, etc.,　　ALETTA BUELL.

Assembly ordered the bond to be given up on payment of £100, August, 1777.

We are told by those who have examined the printed petition of Mr. Buell, in the archives of the office, that the type was more beautiful than any specimen shown at that period, and the printing exceedingly good. It was about the size of Brevier on Bourgeois body.

It is evident that Abel Buell never abandoned his love and predilection for type-founding through all his vicissitudes, or his hopes of some day successfully following the business, as many years after the Revolution something like a rude type-mold and a set of matrices, with a piece of the head of the statue of George III., were found in the ammunition-chest of an old field howitzer, to which he was known to have been attached during that memorable struggle, and which was used at the battles of Concord and Lexington. Some of the punches he carried about his person, probably in his hat, which was suspected to have had a false crown. What was remarkable, let the fashion change as it would, his hat always preserved its continental and revolutionary shape.

Bulk.—A platform or table affixed to the end of a frame, to hold a board containing wet matter for distribution.

Bullock Press.—Many attempts have been made from time to time, with varied success, to accomplish each of the following objects, viz.: 1. To print with extraordinary rapidity. 2. To dispense with feeders, or to supply the sheets to the press by machine instead of hand labor. 3. To make a perfecting press, or one which prints both sides of a sheet.

The Bullock Press, however, embodies the first successful effort to accomplish all these objects in one machine. Mr. Bullock, in carrying into practice his comprehensive conception, easily provided for feeding the paper from a continuing roll, as well as for a perfecting impression, and also soon mastered the difficulties arising from the necessity of separating the sheets from the roll, by equal and exact measurements. The latter object was first accomplished by making such a separation before printing, but by a subsequent modification, known as Kellberg's arrangement, the paper is cut after printing, and Bullock presses are made either way now, as parties desire. The company claim that by Kellberg's arrangement the utmost limit of production is reached, and that they can and will, if responsible parties desire, make a press capable of printing 20,000 perfected sheets of the size of the New York Tribune per hour, or, by a duplication of forms, 40,000 sheets of the size of the Philadelphia Ledger or New York Sun per hour. The Self-feeding and Perfecting machine has been practically applied to newspaper work, and is now in use in a number of American offices, as well as in the offices of the Daily Telegraph, and the Journal, in London, while one has also been extensively used on book-work in the Government printing-office at Washington. The Company also manufacture, in Philadelphia, Two-feeder and Single-feeder Perfecting presses, which are fed by hand. One of the former is in use in the office of Gray & Green, in New York, who, in a printed certificate, say that it perfects, per hour, in book or pamphlet work, four thousand sheets of 36 by 50 inches, thus making eight thousand impressions, and that the quality of the work is better than that usually done on a double cylinder.

The advantages claimed for the Bullock presses embrace compactness, speed, and great economy, and they are alleged to be not only essentially and thoroughly American, but the most original, the simplest, the most enduring and economical machines that ever printed paper.

Two features of the Bullock press—the arrangements for cutting the sheet, and for flying—are especially noticeable, on account of their ingenuity, completeness, and remarkably skillful adaptation to the desired end. The cutting is done, with great precision, by a serrated knife, which rarely needs sharpening, and the sheets are carried to their proper position by stout gum belting, to which iron grippers are attached. The arrangements for distribution are also at once simple and efficacious.

Bullock, William, born at Greenville, Green County, New York, in 1813, died April 14, 1867, at Philadelphia, learned at an early age, with his brother, the trade of iron-founder and machinist, and, being a close student, acquired a good theoretical as well as a practical knowledge of mechanics. After engaging in various pursuits, and making, among other things, hay and cotton presses, he commenced the publication of a newspaper, the Banner of the Union, in Philadelphia, in 1849, and subsequently removing this

BULLOCK SINGLE-FEEDER PERFECTING PRESS.

BULLOCK PRESS, WITH KELLBERG'S ARRANGEMENT.

establishment to Catskill, New York, in 1853, he there made for his personal use a wooden press, turned by a hand crank, to which a self-feeder was attached, which embodied the germ of his subsequent invention. Soon afterwards he went to New York City, The solution of the problem of constructing a press which should be at once be swift, self-feeding, and perfecting, however, was the master-triumph of Mr. Bullock's genius, and it engrossed his energies during his later years. It is a matter of profound regret

BULLOCK SELF FEEDING AND PERFECTING PRESS.

where he constructed a fast press on the planetary system for Frank Leslie, which enabled him to print with unprecedented rapidity a large edition of an illustrated account of the Heenan and Sayers fight, and also perfected the automatic feeding-machine. that while he was laboring on one of these presses, in Philadelphia, on the 3d of April, 1867, he was so severely injured by an accident, that his death ensued on the 12th of April following. (See BULLOCK PRESS.)

Bulmer, William, one of the most distinguished of British typographers, was born at Newcastle-upon-Tyne in 1746. He was apprenticed as a printer, and during this period formed a friendship with Thomas Bewick, the young wood-engraver, which lasted throughout their lives, to the mutual advantage of both. Bulmer always printed the first impressions of Bewick's blocks, and suggested to the artist the advantages to be derived from lowering the surfaces of the blocks where the distance or lighter parts were to be shown to perfection.

William Bulmer left Newcastle for London, and was engaged by John Bell, who was publishing beautiful miniature editions of the poets. An accidental acquaintance with George Nicol, bookseller to George III., led to the great triumph of Bulmer's life—the great Boydell Shakspeare. George Nicol had suggested to his relative Boydell a scheme for a magnificent edition of Shakspeare, and he found in Bulmer such fitness for the work, that premises were engaged and the Shakspeare Press established under the firm of W. Bulmer & Co. (the silent partner being Nicol). The first number of the celebrated edition of Shakspeare appeared in January, 1794, and Mr. Bulmer was immediately pronounced the first practical printer of the day, and began to reap the advantages of the passion for fine printing which was the pet hobby of the period. The magnificent editions of the Shakspeare Press were illustrated by the excellent engravings of his friend Bewick, and all possible luxury was lavished upon them; extraordinary care being taken in every department, and copies being printed upon white satin and upon vellum to meet the fancies of his patrons. The BIBLIOGRAPHICAL DECAMERON, by Dibdin, is one of the most celebrated publications of the Shakspeare Press, uniting many excellencies both in artistic illustration and mechanical execution.

Bulmer continued to print until 1819, when he retired with a considerable fortune, and was succeeded in the Shakspeare Press by William Nicol, the only son of his early friend. He died in 1830.

Bundle.—A package of paper consisting of two perfect reams, counting 960 sheets in America, usually, but sometimes increased, by special agreement, to 1000 sheets, which is the usual number in Great Britain.

Burin.—1. An engraver's tool, of tempered steel, with one end ground off obliquely so as to produce a sharp cutting point, and the other end inserted in a handle; a graver. 2. The manner or style of execution of an engraver; as, a soft burin, a brilliant burin.

Burr.—The roughness on types which have been imperfectly dressed, or on the sides of rules when first cut.

C.

Cabinet.—A stand or frame so arranged that cases of type put in it are protected from dust. It can be better understood by the annexed cut, than by a

CABINET.

verbal description. Cabinets are made of various sizes and materials.

Calendar.—An orderly arrangement of days, weeks, and months, forming part of an almanac.

Calender.—A machine or press, used to press cloths, paper, etc., for the purpose of making them smooth, even, and glossy, or for watering them and giving them a wavy appearance. It consists of two or more cylinders revolving nearly in contact, with the necessary apparatus for moving and regulating.

Calendered.—Paper is said to be calendered when it has been polished by a calender. When the pressure has been frequently repeated, the paper is said to be super-calendered.

Calico-Printing, by hand, is performed by applying the face of an engraved wooden block to a piece of woolen cloth stretched over one end of a sieve-hoop, and imbued with the coloring matter of a thin pasty consistence by means of a flat brush. The block is then applied to the surface of the cotton cloth while extended upon a flat table covered with a blanket, and the impression is transferred to it by striking the back of the block with a light mallet. As this method not only involves a great amount of labor but also causes many irregularities in the work, it has been almost universally superseded by machinery, the principal feature of which consists in having the desired design engraved on hollow copper cylinders, and then subjecting them to pressure in machinery or presses, so ingeniously constructed that three or four colors are printed on twenty-eight yards of calico per minute,—or nearly one mile in an hour.

Calligraphy.—The art of beautiful writing. Some of the scribes who made a profession of copying manuscripts, before the invention of printing, have been termed Calligraphers. Their art consisted not merely in writing, but also in embellishing their work with ornamental devices, although illumination was also practised as a distinct employment. The beauty of the printed works of Fust and Schoeffer is largely due to the fact that Schoeffer was a skillful calligrapher before he attempted, with such remarkable success, to print graceful letters and designs with type.

Campbell Press.—Several presses manufactured by Andrew Campbell, of New York, of various sizes, are known as Campbell presses, but one of the most celebrated, and most extensively used, is the Campbell Country Press. (See COUNTRY PRESS).

Canada Balsam.—This Balsam, as sold by reliable American druggists, is remarkably free from impurities, and it can be used advantageously, sometimes, in preparing printing-inks for fine work, more especially when it is not important that the ink should dry quickly.

Cancel.—To suppress and prevent the printing of a page, or other larger or smaller portions of composed type.

Canceled Work.—In composition, matter returned for distribution without having been printed. In press-work, all sheets condemned as unfit for publication. In book-binding, all sheets or leaves are said to be canceled which are not allowed to be bound.

Canon.—A type one size larger than Double Paragon; the body is nearly equal to four lines of Pica. (See TYPE.)

Capitals.—The large letters of a font of type. In manuscript, the words which are to be printed in CAPITALS have three lines drawn underneath them (≡); while words to be printed in SMALL CAPITALS are underscored with two lines (=). All authorities agree that capital letters should be used to commence the first word of every distinct sentence, the first word of every line of poetry or blank verse, the names of the Deity, of persons, and of places; and to print the pronoun I and the interjection O. Beyond these applications, there is a class favored by some writers and printing-offices, and rejected by others; and a class of words which are sometimes commenced with capitals, and sometimes with small initials. The want of a fixed standard in these particulars has caused an immense amount of vexation and confusion among compositors and proof-readers. Capitals, for instance, are used after exclamation and interrogation points, when they mark the completion of a distinct sentence, but not otherwise. Titles of honor and respect sometimes begin with capital letters, and sometimes with small initials, and the style of the office or the fancy of the proof-reader usually determines whether capitals should or should not be employed.

Adjectives derived from proper names are sometimes commenced with capital letters, and sometimes with small initials; and the rule authorizing the use of capitals at the commencement of words of primary importance or of special significance, opens an immense field for the fancy or discretion of writers and proof-readers.

The old system was to capitalize all nouns and all important words; this was succeeded, pretty generally, by a limitation of capital letters to words where their employment was obviously, and at all times, appropriate; and the modern tendency is to greatly increase the number of words which are occasionally, but not always, commenced with capital letters. (See PUNCTUATION.)

Caption.—The heading of a chapter, section, or page.

Card and Bill Head-Presses.—A number of presses are made by various manufacturers to be used, principally, in printing Cards and Bill-heads. S. P. Ruggles of Boston, was probably the first to make such presses. These, however, have been superseded by the convenient and beautiful card and bill-head presses invented by Gordon, Degener and others.

CARD AND BILL-HEAD PRESS.

Card-Cutting Machine.—A machine used for cutting card-board to any desired size. There are various patterns, prominent among which are: R. Hoe & Co.'s Card-Cutter for Printers, Cowles Patent Self-Feeding Card-Cutting Machines, Cowles Improved Combined Strip and Card-Cutter, and the Ruggles Rotary Card-Cutter. The price of these machines ranges from $13.50 to $200. (See page 91).

Cards.—The demand for various descriptions of pasteboard cards, for the use of printers, photographers, box-makers, etc., is so great in the United States that thousands of tons of paper are required to supply it. It is estimated that the annual product is at least 25,000,000 of sheets of 22 by 28 inches, most of which are cut up to sizes averaging eighty-eight to the sheet, so that the total is equal to more than 2,000,000,000 of small cards.

Cards are of various qualities and thicknesses, being sometimes homogeneous and sometimes made by a combination of stock of different grades. The china card, which is most frequently used by printers, is so called because its surface is enameled with a china clay obtained from the coast of England. This clay enamel, after being mixed with water and glue in proper proportions, and reduced to the consistence of thick cream, is, by means of a machine provided with revolving brushes, placed as a coating on the surface of the paper. This coated paper is then hung on a rack in a dry atmosphere. When thoroughly dry and hard, it is cut into convenient lengths, and pasted together in sheets, the enamel side being left out, and the sheets thus prepared are pressed firmly until all their parts are closely united. These united sheets are again dried and finished between the polished rolls of a calender, or in a plating-machine. The colored china cards are made by mingling pigments of the required colors with the china clay. Other kinds of enamel are also used to impart a metallic lustre to cards by means of heavy rubbing between steel plates.

Printers' blanks are formed by pasting sundry sheets of paper of different qualities and thicknesses together, and finishing them by processes similar to those already described. The fine Bristol boards used for visiting-cards, drawing-cards, etc., are also made in a similar manner, the quality depending upon the quality of paper used. The mounting-cards used by

cards are a clear, transparent substance; the snow-flake is produced by the crystallization of a harmless mineral substance on the surface of the sheet; and the wood card is a veneer of wood of various kinds, cut to suitable size.

Cutting-machines are generally used in dividing the sheets of card-boards into small sizes before they

COWLES COMBINED STRIP AND CARD-CUTTER.

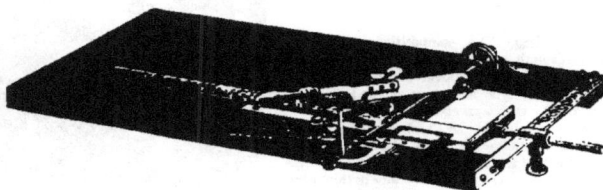

COWLES HAND-CARD CUTTING MACHINE.

RUGGLES ROTARY CARD-CUTTER.

CARD SHEARS.

photographers are generally thicker and heavier than the cards used by printers, and they are composed of very fine material. The tickets used for railroad purposes are also pasted cards, and of these one American manufacturer alone makes more than 30,000,000 annually. Gelatin, Snow-Flake, and Wood cards are also made and used to some extent. Gelatin

reach printers, and some of the power cutting-machines will cut from 300,000 to 400,000 of the small cards, per day, with great exactness.

Cards (Playing) were probably the first product on paper, or analogous material, of the printing-press in Europe. A demand sprang up for them in the fourteenth century, and there is little doubt that they preceded the early-printed religious pictures as well as block-books.

Heinecken, and some other writers, ascribe the invention of engraving to the manufacture of playing-cards; but this opinion is not supported. Mr. Ottley argues that the art came from the East; in support of which, he adduces the mode of printing practiced by the first engravers by the means of friction; and also the custom, which is still preserved in Germany, of fastening the design to be engraved on the wooden block. M. Bullet endeavors to prove cards to be of French invention, about 1376. Heinecken states that they were used in Germany in 1300, at which time they were drawn and painted; and about this period the outlines were made on blocks of wood; afterwards thin plates of metal with holes cut in them, were used for the purpose of finishing the cards with colors. Of these patterns, or stencils, it was requisite to have one for every different color. Mr. Singer supposes that they were invented in Italy, and that they found their way to Germany as early as the period stated by Heinecken. Stimulated by the high price paid for manuscripts, the engravers commenced executing works on wood, resembling those of the scribes; they were done in the most primitive way, no press being required, as they took their impressions by means of a roller or friction.

At the present day, playing-cards are usually formed of four layers of paper pasted together with great care, and subsequently subjected to a cool drying, a hot drying, and heavy pressure. The faces are sometimes stenciled, sometimes printed from engraved blocks, and sometimes both methods are combined.

Card-Printing.—The composition and press-work of cards both require the exercise of great care and taste, and the employment of good materials. Many varieties of type have been devised for card-printing, and by their appropriate use very beautiful effects can be produced. The best results, however, are obtained by an avoidance of glaring contrasts. One theory is that the stems of the type in every line should bear the same relative proportions in thickness; and this doctrine can frequently be advantageously carried one step further, so as to use only type of a uniform face, varied solely by diversities of size. The appearance of cards printed in well-stocked printing-offices is much more frequently injured by the use of too great a variety of faces than by a lack of variety, while lithographic or copper-plate cards often owe much of their beauty to the fact that they contain only a few diversities of lettering.

As cards are printed dry, usually on card presses, the forms must be made ready with great care; good inks only should be used,—blacks costing a dollar per pound, for instance; pains must be taken to regulate the impression properly, otherwise beautiful fonts of fancy type will speedily be disfigured, and cards cannot be well printed; and all the pains bestowed upon the finest descriptions of press-work will prove useful, if not absolutely essential, in card-printing.

Card-Presses.—Comparatively few presses are made to be used exclusively for printing cards. The annexed illustration represents the Patent Table Card Press, which is described in Hoe's Catalogue as follows: In this press the form is placed on an inclined bed, and receives ink from two rollers. The impression is given by a cam, and may be regulated by platen-screws. It has adjustable feed-guides, a large distributing cylinder, card-rack and receiver, and is well adapted for long service. The removal of a bar, easily effected, allows the platen and guides to be thrown back, uncovering the bed and rollers. Speed, from 1000 to 2000 per hour. Platen, 4 by 5 inches.

PATENT TABLE CARD PRESS.

Caret [∧].—A mark used in manuscript and proof-reading, to denote where words, letters, or points are to be inserted.

Carey, Mathew, born in Dublin, 1760, died in Philadelphia, September 16, 1839. The son of a man of considerable wealth, he was permitted to choose his own occupation, and at fifteen years of age, selected the congenial pursuit of printing and bookselling. When but seventeen, he made his first appearance as an author, in a pamphlet upon dueling, followed soon after by an address to the Irish Catholics, upon the severity of the penal code, for which he was compelled to find refuge in Paris from a threatened prosecution. Here he became acquainted with Franklin, and assisted in his printing-office at Passy. Returning to Ireland, after one year of absence, he edited the Freeman's Journal, and subsequently established the Volunteer's Journal, which he conducted so boldly in the opposition that he was committed to Newgate, and, to escape further prosecution, he embarked for Philadelphia in 1784. In this city his fame had preceded him, and General La Fayette welcomed and assisted him. With all this varied experience, Mathew Carey was not yet twenty-five when he established a newspaper, the Pennsylvania Herald, in Philadelphia, where he was destined to establish a family to be honorably known, through successive generations, as authors and publishers. A special feature of the Herald was its accurate reports of the legislative debates, furnished by Mr. Carey himself. His journalistic relations led to a duel with Col. Osborne, in which Mr. Carey was seriously injured. From this time forward Mathew Carey was one of the best-known men in the city, remarkable for his enterprise, public spirit, and benevolence, that caused him to be earnestly interested in all the civic, political, industrial, and literary questions of the day. He was one of the few original members who established the first American Sunday-school Society; he established, and conducted for some years, the well-known literary magazine called The American Museum, and his various writings upon politics, both American and Irish, and upon political economy, received much attention from the public. To printers he is well known for his interest in all matters belonging to the craft, his endeavors to establish book-sales in America, and the high style of his publications, continued through many years, one familiar incident being that he kept the entire Bible set up for several years, to serve for a succession of editions.

Carriage.—That part of the press by which the form is run in and out.

Case.—A general term used to designate the operations required to prepare type for the press,—composition, making-up, imposing, correcting, distributing, etc.,—in contradistinction to press-work. The two grand divisions of printing are case and press-work; and employment in the former is indicated by the phrase, He works at case.

Case-Memoranda.—There are necessarily variations, in some respects, in the order in which the various portions of a book follow each other, in consequence of a diversity in the usages of different printing-offices and the requirements of different publishers. In the absence of special directions, the following rules, laid down, under the head of Case-Memoranda, in Houghton's Printers' Every-Day Book, may be found useful:

1.—Where a half-title is required, it precedes the proper title, and contains nothing more than simply the name of the work.

The title-page looks best when set in plain thin type, the appearance of which, if judiciously chosen, is always neat.

When there is an advertisement to the edition, it follows the title, and always set in one or two sizes less than the body of the work, according to taste or convenience.

The dedication should follow the advertisement to the edition, if there be one, if not, the title; and is set, if short, in capitals and small capitals. If it be long, it is set in a size or two larger than the body, without folio. "Your very humble and obedient," etc., at the end of it, to be set in smaller type, with the name of the author in capitals of the same font.

The preface comes after the dedication, in a size larger than the body of the work, and leaded or double-leaded, according to circumstances, with folios in numerals in the middle of the line, if the work have no running heads. Otherwise, the preface also to have its headings.

The contents follow the preface, and are set in a size or two smaller than the text; also with running heads, if they be used in the work, and with numerals uniform with preface.

The errata also, if inserted, to come before the body of the work.

2.—The head-lines to the different divisions of the work, namely, Part, Chapter, Section, etc., to be set in different sizes, Part being largest, Chapter a size less, and so on.

The first word beginning the body of the work, and the Parts, into which it is divided, to be set with a two-line letter, without any indention, and to complete the word in full capitals of the type in which the work is to be printed. It is a matter of taste, whether this two-line letter range with the top or bottom of the line which it begins.

The first word of the chapter, section, etc., to begin with a capital and be completed in small capitals, without indention. The first line of every subsequent paragraph to be indented an em quadrat.

3.—The matter composed on book-work requires more care in spacing and justifying than is generally called for on either news or job-work. Even spacing is one of the characteristics of book-work, and constitutes an excellence in a compositor's work, and gives a uniformity in its appearance, upon which the beauty of the whole much depends.

4.—The dividing of words at the end of lines to be avoided as much as possible, the zigzag appearance thereby occasioned being offensive to the eye.

5.—The notes to be set two sizes less than the text.

6.—The running head-lines to be set in small capitals, or in capitals two sizes less than the text, with folios in the figures of the font in which the work is composed. If no running heads, the folios to be in figures a size larger than its own body.

7.—The white lines after the head lines to be in the quadrats of the text type. If the matter be leaded, two leads to be added to each such white line; the same also are added to each white separating the paragraphs.

8.—The length of octavo pages, etc., to be one and five-sixths of the width of the page, including the head-line and the signature-line; thus, if the width be eighteen ems pica, five-sixths of that measure—which would be fifteen ems—added to the width—eighteen ems,—would give thirty-three ems, and constitute the proper length of a page set in a measure eighteen ems wide, and bearing the same relative proportion as an octavo, and so on.

The length of a quarto page to be one and one-third its width; thus, if a quarto page was thirty ems

on short works or pamphlets, these lengths may be taken as the standard. (See BOOK-WORK.)

Case Rack.—A strong upright frame with ledges, in which to slide cases that are not in use.

Cases.—A set of boxes embraced in a frame in which type is kept for use in composition. Cases generally go in pairs, consisting of an upper case, in which capitals, small capitals, fractions, braces, etc.

AMERICAN UPPER-CASE.

AMERICAN LOWER-CASE.

wide, one-third of that would be ten, and ten added to thirty—the width—would give forty ems as the proper length of a quarto page.

Circumstances, however, may occur to prevent this principle being always adopted; for instance, when the matter is to be got in in a given number of pages, which may necessitate each page being a line or two shorter or longer than this. As this can only happen

are kept, and a lower case, used for the small letters, points, spaces, quadrats, etc. In job cases the upper and the lower case are combined. Triple cases are divided into three compartments, containing one-half more boxes than an upper case, but they are of smaller size. Labor-saving rule cases have boxes constructed to correspond with the various lengths of labor-saving rule. Wood-type cases are made without partitions between each letter,—lines of the type, only, being separated,—and they are sometimes called blank cases.

The common arrangement of the letter, or plan of the American Upper and Lower Cases, as given in The American Printer, is illustrated by the cuts on page 94.

Many offices deviate, however, in some minor particulars, from this arrangement. The capital letters, for instance, are frequently placed on the right side of the case instead of the left side, and there is considerable variation in the arrangement of the characters to which the three upper rows of the upper case are allotted. In the lower case, also, there are occasional deviations from the plan given above, in a few particulars.

The annoyances arising from confusing changes in the plan of the case are so great, that printers are very hostile to them, and no better evidence of this feeling is needed than the fact that every letter of the lower case in frequent use occupies, to-day, precisely the same box it did when Moxon wrote his work on printing, nearly two hundred years ago.

The upper case, however, has been radically changed during this period, by bringing down the capitals from the upper to the lower portion of the case; and the lower-case letters not in frequent use, such as j, k, q, as well as the double letters, some of the punctuation marks, etc., have had their position changed.

At the present day a strong disposition is manifested to make some important changes in the arrangement of the lower case, and it is strenuously contended that rapidity of composition can thus be accelerated.

The improved California lower case, originating in San Francisco, embodies one of these efforts. To adapt cases of the ordinary construction to its use it is only necessary that the h box should be divided into three parts, (one-half of it to be devoted to en quads, and the two remaining quarters to five-em and four-em spaces); that the e box should be divided into two equal parts (one being used for c and the other for u;) that the h box should be shifted to the present u box; that the en quad box be divided into two parts, one-half devoted to the dollar-mark ($), and the other to the short and (&); and that hair spaces and em dashes should find an abiding-place in the boxes devoted to the four- and five-em spaces. It is said that these changes reduce the distance traveled by a compositor's hand more than half a mile in a day's work.

Some years ago, Mr. Rooker,

of New York, patented a case which was approved by a committee of the National Typographical Union, but it has not been extensively adopted. Its leading idea was to combine the upper- and lower-case boxes in one case which was effected, without changing the position of the lower-case letters, by inserting at their sides small boxes devoted to capital and small capital letters. It was also part of this scheme to construct an Italic case of a corresponding form, in which the Roman upper-case sorts that are not in frequent use, such as references, etc., should be kept.

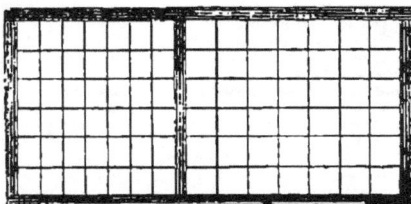

ROOKER UPPER CASE.

ROOKER LOWER CASE

Another case, shown in the accompanying illustration, has also been invented by Mr. Rooker, and it is manufactured by R. Hoe & Co. No changes are

COMBINATION CASE.—FRENCH.

made in the position of the boxes, but they are reduced in size and slightly changed in shape, so as to reduce the distance traveled by the compositor in distributing and composing type.

The Parisian printers, after using for centuries a case very similar to the English case, are now gradually introducing cases which contain both capital and lower-case letters—while the small capitals are placed in a distinct case. As the plan of the new French combination, or single piece case, might, with some obvious modifications, be worthy of consideration in some American offices, it is also given on page 95.

Casing the Letter.—When the types are to be used continually, as on daily newspapers, there should be a pair of cases for every fifty pounds of type in the font; because the capitals, figures, and sorts of like character may be required at any moment, and they should be where they can be taken and returned with the least trouble and most expedition. But in book-offices there need not be more than one pair of cases to each hundred pounds; the extra sorts being left in paper until required.

The best and most expeditious method of casing letter is: after having opened the paper of types, on the stone, so that the face will be downward, to take a small wooden galley, such as those used by type-founders, and place it so that its three ledges will be against three sides of the page of types; then to grasp the paper firmly at the side of the galley to which there is no ledge, the opposite side being pressed upon the stone to prevent the paper from slipping; then, with the other hand at the back of the galley, to turn it over by drawing the paper upward. The letter can then be taken out of the galley in lines; and, having put in case a sufficient amount of each sort, the remainder can be tied up again and put away until required. It will be found that it is better to do this than to fill the cases to repletion, as is generally done, and put the remainder of the sorts in papers, where they will be forgotten or mislaid; causing, when they are wanted, a loss of time in hunting them out of the corners of boxes or drawers, or any other place in which they may be kept.

Caslon, William, born in Shropshire, England, about 1692, died January 23, 1766, is often styled the Prince of English type-founders. He served a regular apprenticeship to an engraver of gun-barrel plates, and afterwards continued the business for himself, gaining considerable reputation for the dexterity and taste exhibited in his designs and devices. He also occasionally made tools for chasers of silver-plate and bookbinders. The attention of the distinguished printer, Mr. Watts, was attracted in 1716 by the excellence of some of his designs. He sent for young Caslon, and exhibited to him some of the fine types of the Elzevirs, and asked him if he could equal them. Caslon was anxious to make the attempt, and three distinguished printers, Watts, Bowyer, and Bettenham, lent him five hundred pounds to further his design. In 1720, Caslon was selected to cut the font of Arabic character for the New Testament and

Psalter published by the Society for the Promotion of Christian Knowledge. In 1722 he produced the Coptic type for Dr. Wilkins's Pentateuch, and was soon recognized as the foremost type-founder of England, supplying the home market with the type which had been previously imported from Holland. His most famous letter, generally known as old-face type, was based upon the fine, clear forms of the Elzevirs, but rounded, expanded, and made more elegant and distinct. This type maintained its pre-eminent popularity for nearly half a century, until 1772, when newer shapes became the fashion and continued to reign paramount until a gradual reaction during the last few years has brought it again into favor, and the identical punches cut by Caslon early in the eighteenth century, were again brought into service. In America the same reaction has given a recent popularity to the modernized old-face type.

Cassie Paper.—Imperfect paper; the outside quires of a ream. The term is rarely used in the United States.

Castaldi, Panfilo.—The Italians claim, but with little show of reason, that Panfilo Castaldi is the inventor of movable type, or that he at least suggested to Gutenberg and Fust the idea which they carried into practice. Their story, which is not accepted beyond the limits of Italy, was told by a writer in an Italian typographical journal a few years ago, as follows:

Panfilo Castaldi was born of a distinguished family of Feltre [where a monument honoring him as the inventor of printing was recently erected], in the early portion of the fifteenth century, and he had achieved a reputation by 1456. Castaldi attached himself to literary pursuits, and became one of the most learned of his time in the literatures of the Italian and the Latin languages, and was a poet of considerable merit. His principal claim to the regard of posterity is based, however, on very different grounds.

About the middle of the fifteenth century, Panfilo began to teach grammar, and acquired, in a short time, so great a reputation that students, not only from all parts of Italy, but from other countries, flocked to his lectures.

Enjoying the esteem of his fellow-citizens, not only for his wisdom, but his skill as a jurisconsult, he was frequently intrusted with the decision of difficult suits between private citizens, and, guided by a simple desire to do justice, rarely failed to render right to whom it belonged.

Endowed with great talents, Panfilo was not long in discovering that civilization had not progressed as it might have done, for the reason that, although Italy was not destitute of men of intellectual eminence, who had composed works of surpassing merit, their doctrines had not found the diffusion necessary for influencing the advance of humanity. And this was because but few copies of their works could be obtained, nor even these but at a very dear rate. It hence resulted that education was the sole privilege of the few whom fortune had favored. Perceiving this, Castaldi formed the resolution of applying his faculties to the discovery of some means of making known to all and every one the various products, splendid or useful, of the human intellect. He pushed on his endeavors with the perseverance and industry characteristic of superior natures, and succeeded at last in forming movable letters, first of all in wood, by means of which words could be composed and printed on paper, and thus several copies could be obtained of the same original at but little expense or trouble.

A little anterior to this epoch, Gutenberg, Fust, and Schoeffer, in Germany, were making their costly attempts at printing, not, however, with movable letters, but with engraved wooden blocks,—a procedure the employment of which involved time and labor.

It now happened that Fust, who had heard of Castaldi's reputation as a teacher, came to him for instruction in Italian, and learned from him, at the same time, the secret of his movable types, appropriating it without thanks or acknowledgment. Alas that ingratitude should be provoked in the heart of man by a blind-sighted and vain ambition! The name of this illustrious Italian—to whom the good of others was a greater object than his own fame—has thus been passed over without notice to our own times; and the merit of one of the most magnificent of modern discoveries has been attributed in its entirety to one to whom it belonged but in part, the more easily since in Italy there have never been wanting those to whom the national glory is of no concern. If now the skillful hands of Corti have raised an enduring memorial to Castaldi in Feltre, his native city, this is owing to the unwearied solicitude of that eminent lover of letters, the cavaliere Jacopo Bernardi, and to the journeymen printers of Milan, who gathered sufficient funds for the erection of this monument to the founder of their art.

Castaldi's title to the honor due for his invention is still contested, more particularly by the Germans. It cannot be wondered at that they should be unwilling to let go any part or parcel of an honor so distinguished; but we do wonder that Italians can be found who would deny an Italian honor to Italy. Whose arguments can be fairly opposed to those made use of by Bernardi, Valsecchi, and Zanghellini? or how can the matters contained in Cambruzzi's unpublished history of Feltre be explained away? What reason could this historian have had for attributing to Castaldi the invention of movable types, if this were not a fact? No one wishes to deprive the three Germans of the honor fairly due to them,—the honor, that is to say, of having made the primary experiments, and of having continued their researches with most exemplary perseverance, and at a great personal sacrifice, and of having been the first to bring Castaldi's work to perfection. But it is going too far to attribute to them the honor of an invention which is not theirs, and without which Gutenberg and his associates could not, at least for some time, have carried out their intentions.

Late in life, in a green old age, this illustrious citizen of Feltre closed his eyes forever, in the year 1470.

Casting off Copy.—The best method of casting off copy is: after having made up a composing-stick to the measure proposed for the width of the work, to take an average page of the copy, and set from it until a certain number of lines of the manuscript come out even with a number of lines of types. From this a calculation can easily be made for the whole of the work.

Suppose a manuscript of 250 pages, and 31 lines in a page, be brought into an office, and it is required to determine how many pages it will make in Long Primer, the page being 28 ems wide, and 40 lines of types in length; and it is found, by setting up a few lines, that 9 of the manuscript are equal to 7 of the types. Then:

250 pages manuscript.	9 : 7750 : : 7
31 lines in a page.	7
250	9)54250
750	4|0|602|7 lines of types.
7750 lines manuscript.	151 pages of types.

The number of sheets can be ascertained, by dividing 150 by 8, 16, or 24, according to the size of the signature in which the work is to be printed.

Another method, which will be found to be fully as accurate as that before given, is: to ascertain, by calculation, the number of words in the manuscript; then, as it has been found that 1000 ems average 380 words (that is, 2180 letters, spaces, and quads), if the number contained in the manuscript be divided by 380, the quotient will be the number of 1000 ems. Having done this, the number of pages it will make in any sized type and page can be found by ascertaining how many square inches there are in a page, and multiplying that number by the number of ems in a square inch of the size of type in which it is to be set; then, by dividing the number of 1000 ems in the manuscript by the number of ems in a page, the number of pages will be the answer.

The following is the number of ems in 100 square inches of the sizes of types from Pica to Agate, inclusive:

Pica,	3600	Brevier,	8836
Small Pica,	4900	Minion,	10404
Long Primer,	5625	Nonpareil,	14400
Bourgeois,	6889	Agate,	19680

The numbers given in the above list are based on the supposition that lines of the length of 6 ems Pica, 7 ems Small Pica, 7.5 ems Long Primer, 8.3 ems Bourgeois, 9.4 ems Brevier, 10.2 ems Minion, 12 ems Nonpareil, and 14 ems Agate, are equal to an inch. This is not strictly true; but the variation is so slight that it will not make a difference of 1000 ems in 100 pages of the common size.

Suppose it were required to determine, according to the above method, how many pages in Small Pica, 25 square inches to the page, a manuscript of 254 pages, averaging 263 words to the page, would make:

254	36,0)6680,2(176	25	1225)176000(144
263	36	49	1225
762	388	225	5350
1524	266	100	4900
508	220	1225	4500
66802	228		4900

In using either of the above modes of calculation, it must be borne in mind that such matter as tables, notes, or extracts set in types differing in size from that of the body, must be cast up separately.—*Lynch's Manual.*

Cast up.—To calculate the number of ems in a page, sheet, or column, so as to determine alike the sum that should be paid to a compositor, or by a customer, for the composition of the type occupying a given surface. The usual method is to multiply the number of ems in the width by the number of ems in the length of a page, column, sheet, or other convenient division, and, as an aid in ascertaining the number of ems, measuring-rules or tables are generally used. Work made up into actual pages of a certain prescribed size is generally charged by the page, while newspaper work is usually charged by the thousand ems, although it, too, is sometimes charged by the column.

Catalogues.—See JOB-PRINTING.

Catch-Line.—A short line placed between longer lines on a title-page, or in a displayed job; such words as of, and, or, the, when standing alone in the centre of long measures, being catch-lines.

Catch-Word.—The first word of the following page placed at the right-hand corner at the foot of the page. Catch-words are seldom used at the present day, except in law work or manuscript. The signature, when required, is placed in the same line.

Cave, Edward, born in Warwickshire, England, 1691, died January 10, 1754, is worthy of special mention as the founder and conductor of the first literary monthly magazine, a form of periodical literature which has since become so popular. Having received a fair education at Rugby School, he was apprenticed to a printer; his talents and application soon rendered him so skillful that his master made him the conductor of a weekly paper at Norwich. Working afterwards as a journeyman, he became known as the author of several successful pamphlets. He was made clerk of the franks, and detaining, with much boldness, the franks given by the members of Parliament to their friends, as an illegal extension of their privilege, was called before the House of Commons for detaining a frank given to the Duchess of Marlborough. He declined to answer questions, on the plea of his oath of secrecy, was dismissed by the House, and subsequently ejected from his situation. In January, 1731, he commenced the famous Gentleman's Magazine, announcing that it was to be continued monthly. His idea of this publication was borrowed from The Memoirs of the Society of Grub Street, a species of literary lampoon, which had appeared in numbers and been received with considerable favor. The magazine met with a rapid success,

and Cave introduced the modern idea of offering prizes for articles. In 1736 he began to publish the parliamentary debates, then prohibited by law. The matter was obtained by himself and one or two assistants, who, after listening to the speeches, met and compared their recollections, putting them into the form of crude notes, which were delivered over to Guthrie, the historian, to re-write into a more oratorical shape for publication, the names of the members being expressed by their initials. After continuing this method for two years, the publication was discussed by the House of Commons as a notorious breach of its privileges. To avoid prosecution, Cave in 1738 issued his reports as Debates in the Senate of Great Liliput. The increased public interest in the debates of 1740 induced Cave to discard Guthrie and give the work to the famous Dr. Samuel Johnson, as more capable of dressing up the fragmentary notes of the reporters into a suitable degree of classic and forensic eloquence; and the magazine continued to bring fame and fortune to the publisher, who was so assiduously devoted to its improvement that it was said he never looked out of the window without trying to see some new method of adding to its attractions.

Caxton.—Any book printed by William Caxton, the first English printer.

Caxton, William, born about 1410, died 1492—an Englishman famous for introducing and establishing printing in his native country, and for his zealous and long-continued efforts to improve the language. Caxton was born in the Forest of Kent, where the vernacular was spoken in its rudest and broadest form, but his parents furnished him with the best opportunities for education possible to their circumstances. He was sent at an early age to London, where he became the apprentice of Robert Strange, a mercer in high standing, who afterwards became Lord Mayor. Caxton remained with Strange, as assistant and subsequently as partner, for a number of years, and afterwards continued for a short time to act independently as one of the fraternity and fellowship of the Mercery.

In this situation, his avocations led him into constant familiarity with foreigners, and he studied the French language as the best means of communicating with them. This knowledge, united to his general intelligence, must have fitted him to support with great credit the agency to which he was appointed by the Mercers of London about 1445, and which caused him to reside for about thirty years in Brabant, Flanders, Holland, and Zealand, officiating in a capacity similar to that of the modern consul.

The Mercers of the fifteenth century were general merchants, trading in all kinds of foreign and domestic goods, including books; and it is therefore highly probable that Caxton, especially and keenly interested in all matters concerning literature, should have made himself conversant with the progress by which xylography was gradually rising step by step through the final stage of movable types, which only required

This fyrst chapiter of the fyrst tractate sheweth vnder what kyng the playe of the chesse was founden only
rathly. Capitulo .j. ...

Amonge alle the euyll condicions & signes that may
be in a man the fyrst and the gretteste is whan he ſ
reth not ne dredeth to dyſpleſe & make wroth god by ſynne
& the peple by ſpekyng diſordynatly / whan he retchyng not
not taketh hede vnto them that repreue hym and his wy=
ces But ſleeth them. In ſuch wyſe as dyd the emperoure
nero Whiche dyd do ſlee his mayſter ſeneque. For as moche
as he myght not ſuffre to be repreuyd & taught of hym. In
lyke wyſe was ſomtyme a kyng in babilon that was named

WILLIAM.

This first chappitre of the first tractate sheweth vn:
to vs what kyng the playe of the Chesse was founden and:
made .   Capitulo Primo

Amonge alle the euyl condicions & signes that may
be in a man the first and the grettest is . whan he fe
reth not ne dredeth to displese & make wroth god by synne
& the peple by lyuyng disordynatly / whan he retcheth not .
not taketh hede vnto them that repreue hym and his vy:
ces . But sleeth them . In suche wyse as did the emperour
nero . whiche did do slee his mayster seneque . for as moche
as he myght not suffre to be repreuyd & taught of hym . in
like wise was somtyme a kyng in babilon that was named

to be transmuted into metal by the genius of Gutenberg. His avocations and his taste would alike induce him to study with interest the rising art, especially in the very country where it was growing into such rapid perfection, and it is not surprising that when leisure and opportunity permitted he should urge the advantages of printing upon the attention of his learned friend and patron, Philip, Duke of Burgundy, and even be ready to devote his own old age to labors so congenial.

Caxton must have become favorably known in England during his residence abroad, for in 1464 he and Richard Whitehill were appointed as ambassadors and special deputies to conclude a treaty of trade and commerce between Edward IV. of England and Philip, Duke of Burgundy. Nowhere in Europe, then distracted with wars, could a student find so pleasant a refuge as at the court of Burgundy, where Philip maintained a little army of copyists and illuminators for his own pleasure, and extended a most hearty welcome to men of learning, and here Caxton soon found the opportunity that led to such happy results.

Raoul Le Fèvre, the chaplain of Duke Philip, had condensed and translated into French the stories of Homer's Iliad, and presented the volume, resplendent with illuminations, to his munificent patron. This new book became the sensation of the hour; copies of it were in great demand at the court, and all the clerks and transcribers were laboring to their utmost to supply the demand, when Caxton advised that recourse should be had to the wonderful new art of printing, and Le Fèvre's work was printed either at Cologne or Bruges some time previous to the year 1467, and by some authors is supposed to have been printed either by Caxton himself, or under his direct supervision.

The connection between Burgundy and England having been further strengthened by the marriage of Charles the Bold, the son and successor of Philip, with Margaret, sister of Edward IV., Caxton became still more closely connected with the court as a member of the household of the duchess, and appears at her instigation and with her assistance to have translated the famous Recueil des Histoires de Troyes, of Le Fèvre, into English, which was also printed at Cologne in 1471. This book is, therefore, the first specimen of printing in the English language, and is presumed to be the work of Caxton himself.

Caxton also translated and printed Jason, a species of sequel to the Histories of Troyes, also written by Le Fèvre, and these works were so well received in England that he determined to return there and establish the new art. The court of Charles the Bold was no longer a fitting abode for a man of peace, and Edward IV. and his queen were ready to welcome Caxton home, having become familiar with him while King Edward had been a penniless refugee at the court of Burgundy. The first book printed on English soil was the Game of Chesse. A facsimile of one of the pages of the second edition of

this work, exhibiting the grotesque but vigorous illustrations, will be found in this publication. The book is not, as its name would denote, a treatise upon the game, but a series of moral reflections deduced from it, and was dedicated to the Duke of Clarence, the colophon stating that it was fynysshid the last day of Marche, 1474.

Caxton's press received a most honorable welcome, and was established in the monastery of Westminster, where he continued in constantly increasing prosperity for many years, although it must have been difficult to disentangle printing from politics at a time when one of his books was dedicated to the poor little prince who met his mysterious death in the Tower, while the next must look for its patronage from Richard III., and his last five years' labor was performed under the reign of Henry VII.

Caxton is believed to have published at least sixty works; and when it is remembered that many of them were translated from the French, German, and Latin by himself, he is well entitled to a distinguished rank among those authors who have labored to enrich our tongue and reduce it into its present noble form.

The list of Caxton's publications shows not only his own literary taste and capacity, but great wisdom in adaptation to all classes of readers, for it embraces books of prayers, the lives and legends of the Saints, works on philosophy, and history, sentiment and chivalry, and even a primitive phrase-book for the convenience of French and English travelers.

Rarely does it occur that an individual holds so distinctly representative a station as that filled by William Caxton. His long life, in its mere extent of years, was almost coterminous with the fifteenth century. When his life began, the world had not emerged from the dark ages. He died in the year America was discovered, when the possibilities opened in a new world had been made practicable for mankind by the art of which he was one of the first masters.

Bred where his native tongue was most rude and uncultured, he lived to perfect it by stores drawn from the languages of the most enlightened countries of his own time, as well as the most cultured nations of antiquity. His representative function does not rest here, because he lived at a time when the nobility of England and of France were madly seeking self-destruction in insensate quarrels, while church and state at variance were mutually weakening each other, and his name may be chosen as one of the fairest and highest types of the intelligent people rising through all this anarchy to take their true station and power by the force of industry and education.

The last words from the pen of Caxton tell so well and so clearly what he had labored so zealously to perform, and reveal so plainly the difficulties of the task that he had undertaken, that they are worthy of careful perusal. They are taken from the preface to his translation of Virgil of 1490, viz.:

When I had advised me in this sayd booke, I delybered and concluded to translate it into Englyshe, and forthwyth I toke a pen and ynk, and wrote a leaf or tweyne, which I oversawe agayn to correcte it, and when I saw the fayr and straunge termes therein, I doubted that it sholde please some gentylmen which had late blamed me, saying, that in my translacyons I had over curyous termes, which coude not be understande of comyn people, and desired me to use olde and homely termes in my translacyons, and fayn wolde I satisfye every man, and so to do, take an olde booke and redde therein, and certaynly the Englisshe was so rude and brood, that I coude not wele understande it. And also my Lord Abbot of Westmynster ded do showe to me late certain evydences wryton in old Englisshe, for to reduce it into our Englisshe now usid, and certaynly it was wreton in such wyse, that it was more lyke Dutche than Englisshe. I coude not reduce ne bryne it to be understonden. And certaynly our langage now usid varyeth ferre from that which was used and spoken when I was born. For we Englisshe men ben borne under the domynacyon of the mone, which is never stedfaste, but ever waverynge, wexyng one season, and waneth and discreaseth another season, and that comyn Englisshe that is spoken in one shyre varyeth from another, insomuche, that in my dayes happened, that certayn merchauntes were in a shipp in Tamyse for to have sailed over the see into Zelande, and for lacke of wynde they taryed atte Forland, and wente to lande for to refreshe them, and one of them, named Sheffelde, a mercer, came into a hows and axed for mete, and specyally he axed for *egges*, and the goode wyf answerde, that she coude speke no Frenshe. And the merchaunt was angry, for he coude speke no Frenshe, but wolde have hadde *egges*, and she understode him not. And then at laste another sayd, that he wolde have *eyren*, then the goode wyf sayd, that she understode him well. Soo what sholde a man in thyse days now wryte, *egges* or *eyren?* Certaynly it is hard to playse every man, by cause of dyversyte and chaunge of langage, for in these days every man, that is in any reputation in his countre, will utter his communicacyon and matters in such manners and termes, that few men shall understonde them, and some honest and grete clerkes have ben wyth me, and desired me to wryte the most curyous termes that I coude find. And thus between playn, rude and curyous I stand abashed. But in my judgemente, the comyn termes that be dayli used, ben lighter to be understonde than the olde auncyent Englisshe.

Cedilla.—[ç] A mark used in French to denote that the letter is to be pronounced like the English letter s. Some printers who do not possess this sort, and do not care to purchase it, use an inverted 5, thus—ç.

Censorship of the Press.—A regulation which has prevailed in all monarchical countries, and still prevails in many, requiring that printed books, pamphlets, and newspapers shall be examined by officials, appointed for that purpose, who are empowered to prevent publication.

There are different modes of censorship; the uni-

versal previous censorship, by which all manuscripts must be examined and approved before they are sent to press; the indirect censorship, which examines works after they have been printed, and, if it finds anything objectionable, confiscates the edition, and marks out the editor or author for prosecution; the optional censorship, which allows an author to tender his manuscript for examination, in order to be discharged from all responsibility afterwards; and lastly, the censorship of newspapers, which has been continued in some countries after the censorship of books was abolished. All these forms imply the establishment of censors, examiners, inspectors, or licensers, charged with the duty of preventing obnoxious publications from reaching the public eye, and in this respect there is a wide difference between censorship and libel suits. When Blackstone wrote his Commentaries, he held that the English press was free, because at that time no advance official permission to print was requisite; and yet the English printers were then hedged round with a series of restrictions only one degree less galling than the chains of censorship. The latter is, however, the first and worst of devices to clog the press, to harass printers, and to arrest the dissemination of intelligence.

Before printing was invented, the practice of destroying writings obnoxious to dominant rulers or dominant parties had been followed by the ancient Greeks and Romans, and the councils of the Church had condemned such manuscript books as they deemed heretical, warning the faithful against reading them; but it is a noteworthy circumstance that among the Romans, even when they were under the rule of despotic emperors, proof of the truth secured exemption from punishment for obnoxious publications.

When printing first became known as a new art, in the latter half of the fifteenth century, it met with a gracious reception from learned bodies, ecclesiastical authorities, and every court in Europe. It was hailed by kings, courtiers, priests, and students as a valuable auxiliary, and some years were suffered to elapse before the idea of placing it under severe formal restraints was fully developed. Mentz shares, with her souvenirs of the glory of Gutenberg, the shame of having established the first formal censorship. In the year 1486, Berchtold, Archbishop of that city, in a mandate setting forth his high appreciation of the art of printing, claiming that it had its birth in Mentz, and pretending that his object was to preserve its honor by preventing it from being abused, forbids all persons subject to his authority from printing any work translated from a foreign language into German, unless it had been previously approved by the written testimony of certain doctors and professors of the University of Mentz, who were designated by the author of this mandate. The penalties incurred by a violation of this order were forfeiture of the books printed, a fine, and excommunication; and thus, in a generation after Gutenberg, Fust, and Schoeffer had triumphed over the mechanical difficulties of their art, it was enthralled in chains at its birthplace. For a short time other countries were somewhat slow in following the bad example of the Archbishop of Mentz; but in 1501 Pope Alexander VI. issued a bull which laid the foundation of censorship in all Catholic nations, and this was still further expressed by a decree of the Council of the Lateran, in 1515, setting forth that no books should be printed in any town or diocese, unless they were previously inspected and carefully examined, either by vicars, bishops, inquisitors, or other appointees of ecclesiastical authority; and any book not so examined and approved was to be burnt, and the author or editor excommunicated.

The principle of censorship thus broadly asserted was vigorously enforced for many years in Catholic countries; and even at the present day ecclesiastical censorship has not been entirely exploded. Protestant authorities imitated the system authorized by the Pope and the Council of the Lateran; and kings and politicians soon learned to fetter the press for reasons peculiar to themselves, even when they were indifferent to the character of the religious publications emanating from it.

The doctrine that a censorship of the press was necessary was so universally accepted, after its first promulgation, that Milton made his famous appeal for the liberty of unlicensed printing, in 1643 (see AREOPAGITICA), in vain, although he addressed Protestants and Republicans. Even in this country a censorship was imposed upon the Cambridge Press, in Massachusetts, by law, soon after it was established.

The general effect of the Reformation was rather to modify and diminish the rigors of censorship than to abolish it, and it has continued for four centuries, under various modifications, to press heavily upon nearly all printers except those of the United States and Great Britain. The attempts made to evade it, to defy it, and to destroy it, from time to time, have caused an indescribable amount of persecution, and many bold and self-sacrificing printers have suffered fearfully for their endeavors to secure approximate freedom for their art.

In England the licensing or censorship system was not abolished until 1692, and a relic of it still exists in the power vested in the Lord Chancellor to forbid the performance of any drama,—a power which was exercised as late as 1859, by an order forbidding the representation of Jack Sheppard.

In France, censorship was maintained alike by the old Bourbons and both Napoleons, but it has been commingled there, in modern times, with a system requiring large deposits of money from newspaper publishers as a guarantee that they will not print objectionable matter, while there have been occasional intervals of absolute freedom. The French Revolution of 1830 hinged on the question of the freedom of the press, and Charles X. lost the throne by his attempt to suppress it. When he first acquired power he gained momentary popularity by abolishing the

previous censorship, but on the 25th of July, 1830, he issued an ordinance declaring that no journal was to be published without a special authorization of the government, which was to be renewed every three months, and that all pamphlets or works under twenty sheets of letter-press were to be subjected to the same rule. In the revolution which quickly followed, the printers of Paris took a very conspicuous part, and a clear recognition of the doctrine for which they successfully fought was incorporated in the charter under which the Citizen King, Louis Philippe, ascended the throne.

The broad doctrine of the freedom of the press, as it is understood in the United States, however, has never been generally and permanently recognized on the Continent of Europe. Revolutions and reforms occasionally give new powers and privileges to European printers, but reactions often quickly follow, and the censorship is still an existing institution. Up to a recent period there was in Italy both an ecclesiastical and a political censorship. In France, before the late war, Napoleon III. instituted unceasing persecutions against French printers; in Germany a long battle for a free press has been attended with but partial success; and it is only in a few of the small European countries, like Belgium, for instance, that the principle of absolute freedom from censorship has been firmly established.

Ceriphs.—The fine lines and cross strokes on the face of a letter.

Certificates of Stock.—See JOB-PRINTING.

Chairman of an Office.—A printer selected by Typographical Unions in various American cities, to decide disputed questions as to charges and other matters regulated by Union rules, as well as to collect dues owing to the Union, etc.,—one chairman being appointed for each Union office. In some sections of the United States, the chairman is called the Father of the Chapel, and his duties approximate to those performed in England by that official.

Changeable Printing-Ink.—It is said that inks that change their color on the application of acid, and thus tend to prevent tampering with checks, may be made in the following manner:

Black.—Make a strong decoction of the best nut galls in water, having previously broken them into small pieces; when well boiled, strain the decoction from the galls, and mix with it about an equal quantity of a strong decoction of logwood, strained free from the chips and other extraneous matter. Add some sulphate of iron, which will precipitate a black powder by combining with the gallic acid; at the same time add some powdered alum, which will precipitate the purple coloring-matter of the logwood, which gives richness and intensity of color to the black precipitate of the galls and copperas; stir the liquid mixture until the alum and copperas are dissolved, then let it subside, and as the liquor becomes clear pour it off; after which dry the precipitate slowly, and there will remain an intensely black powder. Then take two parts of balsam of copaiva and one part of spirits of turpentine, and to these articles add as much of the black powder as will make the mass of a proper consistence for a printing-ink; after the ingredients are incorporated, grind them to an impalpable fineness, and the ink will be fit for use. On the application of oxalic acid to any lines printed with this ink they will change color in the same time and manner as the parts which are filled up with the ordinary writing-ink.

Crimson.—Lake of commerce ground with varnish will make an ink with which the tint-block or ground can be printed. It works free and clean, and changes color immediately on the application of an acid.

Chapel.—Among English printers this word is still used to designate a printing-office. It is supposed that this custom originated in the fact that when printing was first introduced into England, Caxton's office was established in a chapel in or near Westminster Abbey. An association of workmen in a printing-office is also called a chapel. To hold a chapel, is to have a meeting of printers for the purpose of considering rules and regulations, etc. In the United States the Printers' Unions furnish, in some of their modifications, the nearest American approach to the English chapel. (See ANCIENT CUSTOMS.)

Chapter.—A division of a book or treatise.

Character.—A distinctive mark; a letter, figure, or sign. The manner of writing or printing; the peculiar form of letters used by a particular person or people; as an inscription in the Runic character.

Chart.—A sheet of paper, pasteboard, or cardboard, on which information, arranged methodically or in tabular form, is printed. A marine map.

imposing-stone and press-bed. Cast-iron chases are sometimes used, but wrought-iron chases are preferred, especially for large forms. When two chases of equal size are worked together, they are called twin-chases.

Check-Book.—A book containing blank checks upon a bank or other custodian of the money of the drawer of the checks.

Check-Ends.—Ornamental designs placed at the left end of checks. They are frequently constructed of rule or border, and so arranged as to inclose the name or names of the parties ordering them.

CHECK-END.

Checkers.—Type cast to represent the men and kings used in playing checkers.

Check-Folio.—A flat writing paper, seventeen by twenty-four inches.

Checks.—See JOB-PRINTING.

Chemiglyphic.—Engraved by means of a galvanic battery.

Chemitypy.—A process used successfully in Europe, and, to a limited extent, in the United States, to make engravings, at comparatively small expense, that can be printed with letter-press. It is described as follows: Cover a polished zinc plate with an etching-ground. Bite the

CHASE FOR BOOK-WORK, WITH SHIFTING CROSS-BARS, SHOWING THE LOCK-UP.

Chase.—An iron frame intended to hold securely the pages allotted for a form. Its inner sides and the cross-bars should form exact right angles, and its under surface be finished so as to lie flat upon the

etching with diluted aqua-fortis, then remove the etching-ground, and carefully wash out the aqua-fortis. Heat the plate thus cleansed over a spirit-lamp, after covering with filings of a fusible metal, until fusible metal has filled all the lines of the engraving. When cold, scrape down to level of zinc plate, until none of the metal remains but what has entered into the engraving. Place compound plate in solution of muriatic acid; and as, of the two metals, one is positive the other negative, the zinc alone is eaten away by the acid, and the fusible metal which had filled the lines of the engraving is left in relief, so that it may be printed by the Typographic Press.

Chess Type.—Diagrams of games were formerly cut in wood, but now each character is cast as a separate type, for the use of newspapers and periodicals, to illustrate games of chess. The following is a complete assortment, consisting of sixty-four pieces:

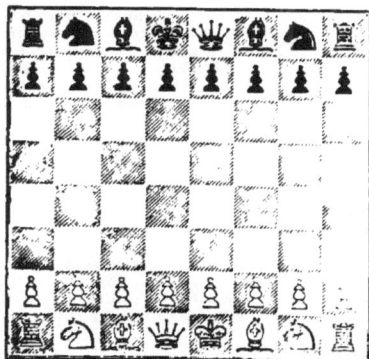

CHICAGO TAYLOR PRESS.

CHESS-TYPE.

Chiaro-oscuro.—A species of engraving invented in 1499 by a German, according to one account, while other authorities allege that it was invented by Ugo de Caspa, an Italian, in the sixteenth century. The operator takes two, three, or more blocks of wood; the first has the outlines cut upon it, the second is reserved for the darker shadows, and the third for the shadows which terminate upon the lights; and these are substituted in their turn, each print receiving an impression from every block. This mode of engraving was designed to represent the drawings of the old masters. Many excellent works in chiaro-oscuro have been produced in France; and in Italy it was honored with the performances of Titian and Parmegiano; but the attempts of English

engravers have not been equally successful; and in America, while it is common to use a number of blocks, successively, for a number of colors, it is a very rare occurrence for two blocks to be used to produce shadings of black.

Chicago Taylor Press.—A cylinder press made at Chicago, of various sizes, and extensively used in the Western States, which resembles the Taylor Press. (See TAYLOR PRESS.)

China, Printing In.—China claims just precedence over all other nations in the discovery of the art of printing from a pigment. The Assyrians impressed bricks, and the Greeks and Romans stamped coins, but despite the innumerable controversies which have arisen in reference to nearly every other important point connected with the history of printing, it has not been seriously denied, in any quarter, that the Chinese were the first to impress on paper, or similar substances, a reversed transcript of engraved characters, through the conjoint aid of ink and pressure.

Sir John Francis Davis, formerly British minister in China, says, there cannot be the least doubt of the art of printing having been practiced in China during the tenth century of our era. He fixes the period of its invention a short time before 950, A. D., when a minister of state, Foong-taou, (see FOONG-TAOU) introduced it to the notice of the Government. He gives the following description of the Chinese process: The block commonly used by the Chinese is pear-tree wood, called by them lymo. It is made of a thickness calculated to give it sufficient strength, is finely planed and squared to the shape and dimensions of two pages. The surface is then rubbed over with a paste or size, occasionally made from boiled rice, which renders it quite smooth, and at the same time softens and otherwise prepares it for the reception of the characters. The future pages, which have been finely transcribed by a professional person on thin, transparent paper, are delivered to the block-cutter, who, while the above-mentioned application is still wet, unites them to the block, so that they adhere; but in an inverted position, the thinness of the paper displaying the writing perfectly through the back. The paper being subsequently rubbed off, a clear impression in ink of the inverted writing remains on the wood. The workman then with his sharp graver cuts away, with extraordinary neatness and dispatch, all that portion of the wooden surface which is not covered by the ink, leaving the characters in pretty high relief. Any slight error may be corrected, as in our wood-cuts, by inserting small pieces of wood; but the process is upon the whole so cheap and expeditious that it is generally easier to replane the block and cut it again; for their mode of taking the impression renders the thickness of the block an immaterial point. A daily paper at Canton is imperfectly printed from a composition of the consistence of wax, in which characters can be more rapidly formed. Strictly speaking, the press of China would be a misnomer, as no press whatever is used in their printing. The paper, which is almost as thin and bibulous, or absorbent of ink, as what we call tissue paper, receives the impression with a gentle contact, while a harder pressure would break through it. The printer holds in his right hand two brushes, at the opposite extremities of the same handle; with one he inks the face of the characters, and the paper being then laid on, he runs the dry brush over so as to make it take the impression. They do this with such expedition that one man can take off a couple of thousand copies in a day. The paper, being so thin and transparent, is printed on one side only, and each printed sheet (consisting of two pages) is folded back, so as to bring the blank sides in inward contact. The fold is then on the outer edge of the book, and the sheets are stitched together at the other; which might lead an uninformed person to take any Chinese book for a new work, with its leaves still uncut. In folding the sheets, the workman is guided by a black line, which directs him in the same manner as the holes made by the points in our printed sheets direct the binder. The popular works of the country are very cheap, and three or four volumes of any ordinary work, of the octavo size and shape, may be had for a sum equivalent to two shillings.

In the year 1041, a Chinese blacksmith, named Pi-ching, invented a method of printing with plates, called ho-pan, or plates formed of movable types—this name being still preserved to designate the plates used in the Imperial printing-office of Pekin. The method is thus described: He made a paste of fine glutinous earth, forming regular plates of the thickness of the piece of money called tsien, and engraved upon them the characters most in use, making a type for each character. He then baked these types by the heat of a fire in order to harden them. He then placed upon a table a plate of iron, and covered it with a coat of very fusible mastic, composed of rosin, wax, and lime. When he wished to print, he took an iron frame subdivided by narrow perpendicular bars of the same metal—the Chinese writing from

above downwards. This frame was placed upon the iron plate, and the types were then arranged upon it pressed closely together. Each frame thus filled with type formed one plate or page. The plate being heated at the fire sufficiently to soften the mastic, a smooth piece of wood, serving as a planer, was then placed upon the composition, and the type was fixed into the mastic by pressure. By using two of these forms alternately, the impression of each page was produced with great rapidity.

He multiplied the types of the letters, and most frequently used signs, and finally produced types of words in common use, and preserved them from injury when not in requisition by wrapping them in paper. Letters of the same class were disposed in cases. When not supplied with a rare character, he would engrave it instantly, bake it by a straw fire, and prepare it for use in a very short time. When the printing from one plate was completed, it was heated again to soften the mastic, and the types were brushed with the hand, detaching them from each other and freeing them easily from the mastic.

When Pi-ching was dead, says the Chinese chronicler, his friends who inherited his types preserved them as very precious; which appears to mean that the inventor had no successor, and that the art fell again to the previous stage of printing from plates of wood. This loss of so valuable an invention has been quoted frequently by foreign authors as a disgrace to the Chinese nation; but it is mainly due to the peculiarity of the language. The immense number of signs used in the Chinese tongue, and the labor of search, of composition and of distribution, exact so much time, that it is often practically better in general to use wooden plates, or copper carved in relief, or to call in the aid of lithography. The printing-office established by the American missionaries at Shanghai, contains six thousand different characters of type, and, with the combinations that are made, more than thirteen thousand. Its chief advantage is the facility it offers for the correction of proofs.

Movable types have been occasionally used by the Chinese, and during the reign of Khang-hi, who ascended the throne in 1661, some European missionaries, who enjoyed the imperial favor, had two hundred and fifty thousand cast in copper, with which they printed a collection of ancient and modern works in six thousand octavo volumes. Of this edition, there are in Paris a History of Music, in sixty volumes; the History of the Chinese Language, in eighty volumes; and the History of Foreign Peoples known to the Chinese, in seventy-five volumes.

A printing-office has been in operation in the Imperial Palace of Pekin since the year 1776, in which a large number of works are printed every year upon movable types manufactured substantially as they are with us. The work of this office is much esteemed for its beauty and finish, and the type has received from the Emperor the graceful name of the assembled pearls.

Steel punches and copper matrices are a matter of great expense, for the reason that they are exposed to rapid deterioration by oxidation. The Chinese endeavor to avoid both these inconveniences by using punches of hard wood of a fine grain, and matrices of a sort of paste of porcelain, which is baked in the oven, and in which they make the type of an alloy of lead and zinc, sometimes mingled with silver.

It is a matter of controversy whether Europeans derived their first hints of the art of printing with a pigment from China, but it is known that Marco Polo returned from that country bringing with him printed paper money, only a short time before the art of printing playing-cards and religious pictures was practiced in Europe.

Chromatic.—Relating to color or colors. Thus, color printing is sometimes called chromatic printing.

CHROMATIC PRINTING-PRESS.

Chromatic Printing-Press.—A new American invention, patented and made by Suitterlin, Claussen & Co., of Chicago and New York, of four sizes, adapted to job work, from Eighth Medium to Medium. It is claimed that this press prints three colors from one form and at one impression, perfectly, and as rapidly as one color can be executed on any press. It is described in a circular issued by the manufacturers as follows:

The surface of The Inking-Cylinder is divided into three equal parts, which are supplied with adjustable sectors (or color strips,) of various sizes to correspond in width with any line or part of a line of type. Each part is supplied with a color from one of the distributing rollers. The cylinder has lines on its surface which are numbered to correspond with lines and numbers on the chase, making simple work for the pressman to set his sectors to correspond to the

lines of the type which he may wish to print in colors. Thus having the sectors arranged, they receive their proper colors and transfer them to the type rollers corresponding in width and position with the lines of the type to be printed. The Inking-Cylinder is very large; giving ample supply of ink to the various colors. Each color has its Vibrating Distributing Rollers, with lateral motion, giving as much distribution to each color as is given to the ordinary one-color job presses. No sectional rollers being used, any line of type or cut may be printed in two or three colors without blending, leaving the line of demarcation perfectly clear and distinct. The type and distributing rollers are similar to those of any job press. The type rollers can be detained from passing over the form at pleasure. The impression can be thrown on and off almost instantaneously, and is easily and accurately adjusted. No springing of the platen with the strongest impression. The form may be placed in any part of the bed and work equally as well as in the centre. Within one minute the press may be changed from two or three colors to one by means of throwing two polished shells or half cylinders over the color arrangements, (as shown in the accompanying cut,) which enables the pressman, if he desires,

HALF-CYLINDER OF CHROMATIC PRINTING-PRESS.

to use three times the amount of distribution and inking surface that he now has in any one-color job press. A very simple device securely fastens and easily unfastens the chase. The sheet is relieved from the type by grippers. They have great strength: being unusually solid and firm;—great simplicity: having less machinery than any other press;—perfect register: no variation in the movement of the platen being possible; and perfect and ample distribution. They run smooth and noiselessly, either by steam or treadle. Speed—1000 to 2000 impressions per hour, depending upon the ability of the feeder.

Chromatic Type.—Type made of metal or wood for color printing, and so arranged that there are duplicate or triplicate copies of each letter, which, after being printed, respectively, in different colors, on a given space, blend together in a harmonious whole. The specimens on page 106 are chromatic letters, intended to be worked over each other in different colors.

Chromo-Lithography.—See LITHOGRAPHY.

Chromotype Printing.—This work is not printing in the strict sense of the word; because part of it only is done at the printing-press, the remainder being finished by stencils and water-colors. Chromo-

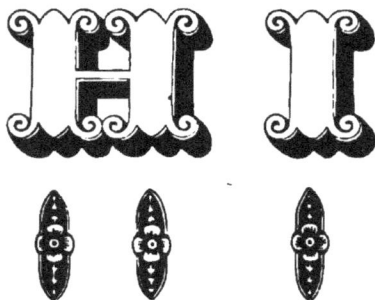

CHROMATIC TYPE.

type printing is employed to put in the colors of the maps in such jobs as the large cards printed for railroad companies, and for coloring parts of the borders of large cards. The latter kind of work is called illuminated printing.

The stencil is formed by pulling an impression of the job on a card, and cutting out the parts intended for one of the colors; a new stencil being cut for each of them. The colors must be laid on with a fine-grained sponge or soft camel-hair brush. Any color which can be used for maps may be applied to this purpose.

CINCINNATI CYLINDER PRESS.

Cincinnati Cylinder Press.—A press manufactured by the Cincinnati Type Foundry, of three sizes, their beds being, respectively, 28 by 40 inches, 31 by 46, and 34 by 52. The manufacturers in their description of it, say:

These machines are strong and compact. The workmanship and materials, throughout, are of the best quality. Distributes from a cylinder and not from a table; so that the rollers are always in motion, and always present a fresh service to the types. Front of press is open and easy of access. The feed-guides are a newly-patented device of great utility for making register. The fly piles the printed sheets with the utmost accuracy. The bed is shod with steel, and runs over steel rollers on steel ways, and contains spiral springs within itself, to arrest its momentum and start it back. It takes less power to run at same speed than any similar machine. Speed from 700 to 1000 per hour.

Circular Quadrats are used for printing curved lines. They are made from type metal of unusual hardness and solidity, carefully finished, and are of various sizes, so as to form circles or parts of circles from 1 to 24 inches in diameter. Each piece is marked with a distinct number, and is exactly one-eighth of a full circle, so that when combined with similar pieces, quarter, half, three-quarter, and full circles can be constructed. By reversing the combination of some of the pieces, serpentine and eccentric curves may be made of any length or depth. There are two kinds: Inner Quadrats, with convex surface, and Outer Quadrats, with concave surface. The curved line is produced by placing the convex and concave surfaces parallel to each other, so that when locked up they hold firmly the type inserted between them. The other sides of the quadrats are flat and right-angled, to allow a close introduction of type and an easy justification with common quadrats.

Circulars.—One of the subdivisions of job printing, embracing printed matter intended either to be addressed, as letters are usually addressed, to different individuals, or to be publicly distributed. They are printed on common news, writing, or sized and calendered paper, according to the use for which they are intended. They are printed with, and without a fly-leaf, and of varying sizes, which, however, rarely fall below half-note or go above a full folio-post sheet.

Circumflex.—The accent marked thus, ⌃. (See ACCENTS.)

Clay Process.—One of the processes for making stereotype plates. (See STEREOTYPING.)

Clean Proof.—A proof with but few faults in it; also, a proof pulled carefully after correction, to send to the author.

Clearing Away.—Taking out leads, heads, blank lines, and smaller type from the body of a work after printing, so that the type may be papered up and put away. The type should be washed, the chase and furniture put away, the pages lifted on galleys, and after the heads, blank lines, and all irregular matter are extracted and distributed, and leads, brass rule, etc. placed in their proper receptacles, the solid matter is tied up in convenient portions and put on a letter-board until dry, when it is papered up and marked with its proper name and description, viz.: solid, open, or figures.

Clearing Pi.—Separating various sizes or kinds of type from a confused mass, and placing each letter in its proper case and box. Not only does every distinct size require to be separated, but different fonts of the same size.

Clearing the Stone.—It is a rule in offices in England, that, after imposing or correcting, the mallet, shooting-stick, furniture, quoins, saw, saw-block, and shears, are to be returned to their respective places, type distributed, and bad letters put into the shoe, so that no impediment shall be offered to the next person using the stone. Any of these articles, or two letters left on the stone, will render the party offending liable to a fine. This would be a good rule for all printers to follow.

Clerical Errors.—Errors made in the copy by the transcriber or editor.

Cliché.—The impression or cast formed by plunging a die into metal or other substances in a state of fusion; a matrix. Cliché casting, is a method of casting in which the mold or matrix is forced suddenly and perpendicularly down upon the fused metal.

Clicker.—In England the clicker is one who, in a companionship, receives the copy and gives it out to compose, and attends to the making-up and correcting. The phrase is not used in the United States.

Clicking.—This is a term applied to the mode pursued in London of getting out work by the formation of a companionship, or selected number of men, who are appointed to go on with a certain work or works.

Close.—The end of a quotation. The copy-holder calls out:—close—to the proof-reader, when he arrives at the proper place for inserting the two apostrophes that mark the end of a quotation.

Close Matter.—Pages with but few breaks or blank lines, or without leads between the lines.

Close Spacing.—Putting as little space as possible between words.

Close Up.—When an article is divided into short takes, and the second take is emptied on the galley before the first is finished, the compositor setting the first take has to close up the opening, by pushing the subsequent matter up to his own; and so on, wherever an opening occurs. If, however, the first take is finished before the second is emptied, the second compositor is told to empty close up.

Clymer, George, the inventor and manufacturer of the Columbian printing-press, was descended from a Swiss family who left Geneva and settled in Pennsylvania long before the Revolution of 1776, and in that struggle for liberty they took an active part, for a Clymer appears among the signatures to the Declaration of Independence. Mr. Clymer's father was an extensive farmer of Bucks county, Pennsylvania. During his minority, George Clymer showed very superior mechanical skill in the construction of a plow, on a new and greatly improved principle, so infinitely superior to those then in use, as to attract the attention of scientific men. After many years spent at carpenter-work and cabinet-making, he turned his attention to the study of hydraulics, and he soon excelled most of his predecessors in the construction of a pump, the superiority of which was proved in clearing the coffer-dams of the first permanent bridge erected across the Schuylkill at Philadelphia. This pump was capable of discharging five hundred gallons of water per minute, together with sand, gravel, stone, etc. For this invention he obtained a patent at Washington, and subsequently one in England. The crude and defective condition of the printing-press next received his attention; and Mr. Clymer continued his improvements, till by great attention and anxiety he produced the Columbian, which he introduced into England in the year 1817. It was considered by many experienced journeymen printers far superior to all presses which had preceded it. Mr. Clymer, for his invention, received a gold medal of the value of one hundred golden ducats, from the King of the Netherlands, and a valuable present from the Czar of Russia, and his presses long remained popular in England, while some were also introduced into the United States. He died in London, on the 27th of August, 1834, at the advanced age of eighty years.

Codex.—Before more convenient materials were used, wooden tablets were written upon, and such written tablets were called codex. The ancients wrote first by making notches or indents in these tablets, but afterwards they covered them with wax and used a stylus to write with. From this custom the word codex eventually came to mean a book or collection of tablets, or sheets of writing on skins of parchment, and also a collection of laws, code being adopted for the last-named purpose in modern languages.

Collate.—To examine the signatures in each gathering of a book, to see that they are consecutive.

Collins, Tillinghast King, born in Philadelphia, October 14, 1802, died 1870. He lost his father at an early age, and before he was thirteen years old entered the printing-office of the celebrated Mathew Carey. He remained with this great publisher but a short time, and was then apprenticed to James Maxwell, from whose office he graduated with high repute as a skillful compositor and pressman. He then removed for a time to Washington, D. C., and upon his return to Philadelphia he entered the office of James Kay, the law publisher. In 1833 he united with Robert Wright in opening a printing-office with only one hand-press. This partnership existed about two years, when Mr. Wright retired, and Mr. Collins removed his office to No. 1, Lodge Alley, now No. 705, Jayne Street, where he formed a new partnership with his own younger brother, and the firm, under the name of T. K. & P. G. Collins, soon became known for the superiority of its typography. Many of the magnificent publications of our National Government were due to the skill of the Messrs. Collins. Dr. Isaac Lea's Naiades and also Fossil Footsteps in the Old Red Sandstone, justly celebrated for their beauty and perfection, and pronounced equal to the finest issues of any of the Government presses of Europe, were printed in this office; and many other splendid volumes attest the skill and care of this celebrated firm.

To the practical part of his special business, Mr. Collins paid much attention; and the patent roller-boy for hand-presses, and the immovable rules which surround the blocks on which certain stereotype plates are placed, are due to his inventive talents.

Colon.—The colon (:) is used to divide a sentence into two or more parts less closely connected than those which are separated by a semicolon, but not so independent as distinct sentences. Few writers use the colon too frequently. The prevailing tendency is in the opposite direction, as the semicolon, dash, or period is often employed where the colon would be more appropriately used.

Colophon.—An inscription at the end of a book. Generally restricted, by common use, to those post-scripts employed by the early printers, before the introduction of title-pages, containing the date and place of publication, and the name of the printer, with the customary addition of a text of Scripture or a valedictory verse. The device, or coat of arms, of the printer was frequently used, either in connection with an inscription, or alone; subsequently the word finis was substituted for the original colophon. The Latin noun colophon, meaning end or conclusion, furnishes a direct derivation precisely equivalent to the word finis.

In the absence of all other evidences of time, authorship, etc., the colophons of the early printed books become matters of great typographical importance, and that of the Psalter of 1457 holds the first rank, it being the earliest printed book yet discovered having an authoritative date, and its colophon containing the first formal announcement of the invention of printing. The inscription may be freely translated thus: Book of Psalms, decorated with elegant capitals, and sufficiently distinguished by its red letters, invented artificially, imprinted and characterked without the use of any pen, and for the service of God, carefully perfected by John Fust, citizen of Mayence, and Peter Schoeffer, of Gernsheim, Anno Domini 1457, upon the vigil of the Assumption. The second dated work printed by Fust and Schoeffer bears the same colophon, with the date altered to 1459, and the Bible, generally styled the Mentz, in contradistinction to the Mazarin Bible, and supposed to be their fourth publication, states that:—this present work was finished and perfected, for the service of God, in the city of Mentz, by John Fust, citizen, and Peter Schoeffer de Gernsheim, clerk of the same diocese, completed in the year of our Lord's incarnation, 1462, on the eve of the assumption of the Glorious Virgin Mary. The magnificent Bible usually known as Gutenberg's Bible, of which there are several copies extant, has no imprint or colophon, but a copy, preserved in Paris, contains at the end of the first volume a manuscript note, to the effect that:— Here ends the first part of the Bible or Old Testament. Illuminated, or rubricated and bound by Henry Albrech or Cremer. On St. Bartholomew's day, A.D. 1456. Thanks be to God. Hallelujah.

Some Latin verses appended to the imprint of the Institutes of Justinian, printed by Schoeffer in 1468, possess especial interest, from their bearing upon the origin of printing. The versification is very rude,

and may be translated thus:—Moses by the plan of the Tabernacle, Solomon by that of the Temple, only produced works of ingenuity; the Church shines with a brighter light. Greater than Solomon, she has renewed Bezaleel and Hiram. He who is pleased to create high talents has given us two great masters of the art of engraving, both bearing the name of John, both natives of Mentz, and both illustrious as the first printers of books. Peter advanced with them towards the desired goal, and, starting the last, arrived the first, having been rendered the most skillful in the art of engraving, by Him who alone bestows light and genius. Every nation can now procure its own kind of letters, for he (Peter) excels in the engraving types of all kinds. It is difficult to believe the prices which he pays to learned men to correct his editions. He has in his service Master Francis, the grammarian, whose Methodic Science is celebrated all over the world. I also am attached to him, not so much for the sake of vile gain, as for the love of the general good, and the glory of my country. Oh, if they could purge the text of all its faults!—those who arrange the letters, as well as those who read the proofs, the friends of literature would then infallibly award to them a crown of glory, who thus come in aid by their books to thousands of seats of learning.—These lines, written either by a proof-reader or printer in Schoeffer's employment, and placed in the colophon of one of Schoeffer's own publications, two years after Fust's death, must be accepted as evidence from the very inventors of the art,—the comparison made to Bezaleel, the worker in metal, and to Hiram, king of Tyre, who furnished the materials for Solomon's temple, being a remarkable testimony to John Gutenberg, the worker, and John Fust, who furnished the money that enabled both to become illustrious, as the first printers of books, while the tribute to Peter Schoeffer's skill gives him his due honor as the perfecter of the invention.

The Book of the Four Histories, printed by Pfister, of Bamberg, in 1460, contains a very complete specimen of the early colophon:—Every man desires in his heart to be wise and well instructed; but without a master and without books this cannot be. Moreover, we do not all understand Latin. These reflections having occupied me for some time, I revised and united the four histories of Joseph, Daniel, Judith, and Esther. God granted his protection to these four, as he always does to the good. This little book, of which the object is to lead us to amend our lives, was completed in Bamberg; and in the same town Albrecht Pfister printed it, in the year in which we count one thousand four hundred and sixty, such is the truth, a short time after the festival of St. Walpurgis, who is able to obtain for us abundant grace, peace, and eternal life. May God bestow it upon all of us! Amen!

Some of the difficulties with which the early printers had to contend may be inferred from the colophon added by Cenninus of Florence, in 1471, to his edition of Virgil, with the commentaries of Servius. It runs thus:—Bernard Cenninus, a most excellent goldsmith in the opinion of all men, and Dominic his son, a youth of extraordinary genius, having first made their steel punches, and afterwards cast their letters from them, printed this their first book. Peter Cenninus, another son of the same Bernard, corrected it, having first compared it with the most ancient manuscripts. It was his first care that nothing should pass under the name of Servius but what was truly his, or anything that was plainly from the most ancient copies to be his, lest anything might be maimed or wanting. But because many persons choose to write the Greek quotations with their own hands, and there were but few to be met with in the old copies, and also because their accents cannot be printed but with great difficulty, he thought proper to leave blank space for them. But as man can produce nothing absolutely perfect, it will be sufficient for us if these books be found, as we heartily wish, more perfect than any other.

A Latin couplet appended to The Pragmatic Sanction, by Bocard, in 1507, has been fairly rendered thus:—

> May this volume continue in motion,
> And its pages each day be unfurled ;
> Till an ant has drank up the ocean,
> Or a tortoise has crawled round the world.

Modest erudition and faithful industry are generally indicated as well as claimed in the early books, but Sixtus Russinger, a priest of Strasburg, who printed in Naples in 1472, was more boastful in his colophon:—

> Sixtus the copies printed with much care,
> Now twice revised by Dr. Oliviero;
> The happy purchaser in vain shall look,
> Yet find no error in this faultless book.

Colored Printing-Papers are made either by adding coloring-matter to the pulp, or, when peculiarly brilliant colors are required, by painting or staining the paper. By the use of both processes a great variety of shades is produced. In printing on colored papers, it should be remembered that the appearance of the ink is affected by the color of the paper. When black letters appear on a colored surface-ground, they lose the intense hue they have when printed on white paper. On blue they are telling; on orange (red lead) they are telling and brilliant, and assume a greenish bronze; on violet they are rich, in a greenish-yellow tone; the majority of yellows are weakened by black, which is thus rendered more intense. It should be remembered that—

1. Black Ink upon Red appears Dark Green.
2. Black Ink upon Orange, Bluish-black.
3. Black Ink upon Yellow is Black, with a slight tinge of Violet.
4. Black Ink upon Blue is Orange-gray.
5. Black Ink upon Green appears Reddish-gray.
6. Black Ink upon Violet appears Greenish-yellow-gray.

Color-Printing.—One of the most important things connected with color-printing is a proper understanding of the best methods of combining and contrasting colors. This work contains a colored illustration (which see) showing how the primitive colors, viz., yellow, red, and blue, in various combinations, produce orange, green, purple, and a neutral tint approaching black. The illustration not only shows how seven colors can be produced by three workings, but also indicates what colors can be most effectively placed in close contact with each other. The complementary colors, of corresponding shades, are mutually strengthened and heightened when printed in alternate lines, and it is worth remembering, that good results can be fairly anticipated from a contrast of red with green, or of blue with orange, or of yellow with purple. In practice, however, it is more common to see blue and red contrasted, a brown being formed when they are printed over each other,—or red and black contrasted. A variety of colors can also be produced by mixing a few inks as follows: Yellow and carmine produce vermilion. Carmine and blue produce purple. Blue and black produce deep blue. Carmine, yellow, and black produce brown. Yellow and blue produce green. Yellow and black produce bronze green. Yellow, blue, and black produce deep green.

In the present advanced state of ink-making in the United States, it is practically better for the printer, in nearly all cases, to buy his colored inks from some one of the numerous manufacturers, or their agents, than to attempt to make colored inks for himself. Ordinarily he will find sufficient difficulty in having the inks obtained in this way reduced or mixed with varnish, in the mode best adapted to the work in hand, to render it desirable to transfer the trouble of making inks to the ink-makers. If, however, he attempts to make colored inks for himself, either from necessity or choice, the following suggestions from Houghton's Printers' Every-Day Book may be found useful:

By the purchase of simple materials from the oil-shop, the ingenious printer has at his hand every color that fancy can require, at moderate cost, without delay. The appliances are few and cheap—a muller, a marble slab, and a palette-knife; the materials, a can of printers' varnish, to be purchased of the ink-makers, which will keep any length of time, and the raw colors hereafter given, which may be purchased from time to time; care, however, being taken that they are of the best quality, or they will fade and turn rusty in a short time, and be a deformity instead of an ornament to the work. If necessity forces the use of painters' common varnish, about a quarter of a pound of soft soap should be added to every pound of color, as this will keep the heavy-bodied colors much longer suspended in the varnish, and consequently will not so soon become hard.

Useful tints of red may be prepared of orange lead, vermilion, burnt sienna, Venetian red, Indian red, and lake vermilion. The pale vermilion is best for a bright tint, as the dark, when mixed with varnish, produces a dull red. Orange lead and vermilion ground together produce a very bright tint, which is more permanent than vermilion alone. The cheapest red, perhaps, may be prepared with orange mineral, rose pink, and red lead.

Yellows are prepared with yellow ochre, gamboge, and chromate of lead. Of these the brightest is the chrome; yellow ochre, when mixed with the varnish, produces a very dull tint, but grinds easily and is a good color where a dull yellow is wanted.

Blues are made from indigo, Prussian blue, and Antwerp blue. Of these, indigo, though exceedingly dark, and not very easily lightened, is a powerful and serviceable color, if not required bright. Prussian blue is a very useful and excellent color if ground perfectly smooth. This color dries quickly, therefore will require the roller or ball to be cleaned frequently. Antwerp blue is very light, and makes a nice, bright, smooth ink with little trouble. The shade of any of these may be varied with flake white.

Greens may be produced from a mixture of any of the blues and yellows, as gamboge, which is a transparent color, and Prussian blue, or chromate of lead and Prussian blue. These may be mixed in any proportions until the required tint is produced; but it must be remembered that the varnish has a considerable yellow tinge, and will produce a decided effect upon the mixture. With a slight portion of Antwerp blue, it will, without the mixture of any of the yellows, produce a decidedly greenish tinge. From verdigris and green verditure, greens may also be produced.

Purples of any degree of richness are made by judiciously mixing reds and blues.

Sepia produces a nice brown tint, burnt umber a very hot brown, raw umber a much lighter brown, bistre a brighter still. Neutral tints may be obtained by mixing Prussian blue, lake, and gamboge. In fact, every pigment that painters can use can be used in printing, avoiding, as much as possible, all heavy colors; and if the printer is desirous of imitating any particular color, or of producing any particular tint, he cannot do better than consult the nearest artist in oil or water colors (oil in preference), or, in default of that, the neighboring house-painter.

It is desirable that every color should be ground perfectly smooth, otherwise the form will be liable to clog and make the impression thick and imperfect; bestowing a little time and labor in grinding every color, therefore, is of the greatest importance; indeed, no color will work clear without it.

The necessary colors having been procured, the method of preparing them is very simple. Each must be well ground by the muller upon the slab, even although they may have been purchased well powdered. The color should then be well mixed with the palette-knife with the varnish, until the pigment has attained the required consistency, which will vary with the quality of the work to be executed; for if it be a posting bill or coarse job, the ink should be very

thin, and consequently a much larger proportion of varnish should be used. If, however, the work be a wood-cut or in small type, the pigment should be made as thick as possible. If the color required be a compound, the predominant tint should be first mixed with the varnish, and the lighter tint added in small quantities until the exact shade required be produced. Thus, if the color be a dark green, the blue should be mixed up first, and the yellow added; but if it be a very light green, then the yellow should be first applied, and the blue added. If the tint desired be exceedingly light, it will be found that the quantity of raw material to be employed will not make the mixture sufficiently thick to be applied to the type or wood-cut; in this case whiting is added to thin colors, and dry flake white to the heavier in considerable quantities, which must be adjusted in the course of mixing. To insure thorough combination, the mixture should be scraped into a corner of the slab, and a very small portion of it spread with a palette-knife, and well ground with the muller until no specks or lumps appear, then scraped up and placed in another corner. This should especially be done when white lead is used, as it will be found that every little lump when crushed will produce a white streak upon the slab. If this be not carefully done, independently of its tendency to clog the type, it will very materially alter the tint. When the pigment seems sufficiently mixed, it is better to bray it out with the muller instead of the usual brayer, and grind again each particular portion immediately before it is used. The ink should then be well distributed, and the form well rolled.

Preparing Forms for Color-Printing.—To prepare type forms for color-printing they are usually either skeletoned, as many distinct forms as there are colors to be worked being so made up that their respective impressions occur at exactly the right places; or the same result is reached by raising, in turn, all the portions of one form that are printed in one color, by placing underneath nonpareil reglet or a similar substance. The former method is adopted for large editions worked on power-presses, while the latter is successfully employed for fine work, in comparatively small editions, on the hand-press.

Press-Work.—A number of presses specially adapted to color-printing have been invented from time to time, some of which are illustrated and described in other portions of this volume. In ordinary printing-offices, however, the choice is restricted to some one of the power-presses in general use, or the hand-press, and by proper endeavors to secure good register, combined with good ink and good and clean rollers, good work can generally be produced. It requires, however, a skillful combination of the very best materials and appliances, with superior practical skill, as well as good taste, good judgment, and unwearied care, to produce masterpieces of colored letter-press printing.

To indicate the method employed by printers who aim at the highest results, the following article, written for Fournier's new work on printing, by Silbermann, a printer of Strasburg, who is one of the most successful and famous of modern letter-press color-printers, has been translated from the French, expressly for this publication:

THE FRENCH SYSTEM OF COLOR-PRINTING.

Printing in colors theoretically rests on principles that are very simple and easily understood, but their application presents great practical difficulties, which experience alone can surmount.

The principal labor is the preparation of the colored inks, for those made beforehand are frequently defective, some drying too soon and becoming pasty.

The choice of colors is of the greatest importance, as upon it depends success. It is necessary to select those of the first quality, and avoid those of a heavy specific gravity, as they are too easily precipitated, and do not combine completely with the varnish.

The varnish is also an essential matter. It must be pure, limpid, and of a strength proportionate to the work contemplated and the color employed. Frequently strong varnishes must be avoided, as they render the ink too thick, and should be used only as mordants. For ordinary work very weak varnishes are suitable, and for more delicate impressions the varnish should be increased in strength. That made of linseed seems to be the most useful.

The inks are made by successively amalgamating the colors with the varnish, by grinding with a stone upon marble. The quality of the ink depends much upon this labor, which should be a work of patience, so as to combine the colors and varnish into a consistence equal to that of the fine black inks. For it is with other colors as it is with black, the better and more thoroughly the color is mixed with the varnish the better the ink.

When a large number of impressions is to be produced, the colors should be prepared in proportion to the requirements, for some condense so rapidly that they soon become unserviceable, especially when the varnish is strong. One grinder can supply a hand-press in full work.

The inking is done as with black. It is always essential to avoid taking too much ink on the roller, as there is a great risk that the impression will be unequal and muddy. It is not the amount of ink which produces the darker shades, for they depend upon intensity of the color.

In general, color-printing exacts great care, the least negligence in any part being easily seen in the result. The rollers require to be in good condition, and at each change, either of color or shade, they should be carefully cleansed with spirits of turpentine or benzine. They should also, according to the colors used, be more or less elastic, and more or less dry or fresh,—practice alone being the guide in these cases.

For simple impressions, composed in one color, the process is exactly similar to a carefully produced impression in black.

But when several colors are used, the conditions are essentially different:

The Plates.—It is necessary that they should be made with great accuracy, and this is a serious drawback to most work of this order, for mathematical exactitude is necessary, and the word almost must be banished from the mind of the operator. Wood is subject to the atmospheric changes; a storm or sudden alteration in temperature, the dampness or dryness of the printing-office, all affect the wood, and sometimes to a very considerable degree. A storm, followed by a sudden cooling of the atmosphere, may cause such an extension in a single night, that the work already completed will not agree with that which is to follow; and we have known cases in which it has taken days of laborious experiments, by exposing the blocks to different degrees of temperature, to reduce them to their original dimensions.

It is better, therefore, to use plates in metal, and to make a stereotype from the original wood-engraving, to serve as a base for the blocks from which the different colors are to be printed.

Paper can be either sized or unsized, although the latter is preferable. In order to obtain good results, especially when the surfaces are large, the paper should be carefully smoothed upon a roller, and with plates of zinc. The impressions should always be dry, for the dampness destroys the brilliancy obtained by the glazing, and also causes shrinking.

It is, perhaps, unnecessary to add that the paper should be of good quality, equal in surface and perfect in color; any defect in this respect neutralizing the care taken in the impression.

Register.—This is the corner-stone upon which must rest all printing in colors, and it is this which gives typography an advantage over lithography. Thus, the typographic impression is made by a stroke, dry and straight, while that by lithography is executed by a friction which stretches the paper, by a movement more or less considerable in proportion to the thickness and consistency of the paper.

To preserve this superiority, exactitude of register is one of the most important means, and numerous processes have been attempted,—one of the best of which is to preserve for each impression a pair of special points.

For fine color impressions the presses need to be in perfect condition, the tympans covered with silk and not with either cloth or muslin, the blankets of thick and smooth satin, and everything in perfect unison. In a word instrument and workman should be equal to the work to be produced, and all depends upon the care, intelligence, and practice of the latter, and the perfection of the former.

Successive impressions seem essential to good work, the simultaneous impressions always leaving something to be desired. It is impossible to make the plates so perfect that no point of junction is visible, and in the next place this kind of impression requires as much time for the double or treble inking and the fitting together as is required for two or three successive impressions.

Color-printing is best done on the hand-press, for

the reason that the machine-presses by their own vibration prevent perfect register, and seem serviceable only when worked so slowly that they have no advantage over the hand-press, especially when consideration is made for time required in cleaning when there is a change of color. But in impressions in one color the machine-press offers a marked advantage.

The following are a few details upon the principal colors:

Gold.—For printing in this color there is used a mordant composed of very strong varnish and golden yellow ochre. While the mordant is fresh, sprinkle it with bronze of fine quality, and then allow it to dry. This sprinkling should be done with a hares'-foot with the hair on; an instrument to be preferred to brushes and pencils, because it requires less bronze. The bronze, being really only copper reduced to an impalpable powder, is very injurious to those who work in it, and serious diseases will often result unless all possible precautions are taken to prevent the operator from inhaling the atoms which are dispersed through the air. In order to avoid these consequences, it is well to use frames about a yard square, with glass above and at the sides, so as to permit the workman to see his work. On the front face a longitudinal opening can allow the introduction of the sheet of paper and the arms of the operator. A bandage can also be worn around the mouth, and with such precautions, workmen have followed the employment for years without suffering the least inconvenience. [In America the difficulty referred to is obviated by the bronzing machine.]

Silver is applied in the same manner as gold, except that for the mordant there is added to the varnish some white of silver. The finer qualities of silver are very expensive, but this can be remedied without serious injury to the effect, by mixing one-third of fine silver with two-thirds of imitation silver, which costs no more than bronze.

Blue. Ultramarine, is one of the most difficult colors to manage, and it seems impossible to unite it with the varnish without destroying some of its brilliancy.

When gold, silver, or ultramarine is well dried, wipe the pages with cotton and pass them under rollers, so as to fix the colors, and give them the required brilliancy. In order to obtain brilliant gold and silver perfectly polished, plates of steel are used.

Red.—The carmines are to be preferred to vermilion, because it is very difficult to obtain the latter in a pure state, and it frequently produces a color which darkens by exposure to the air. The choice of carmines is also difficult, as everything depends upon the manufacture. Experiment alone can be relied upon, and it is only in employing them that the better qualities can be discerned.

More recently the vermilions have, however, been improved in quality, and are serviceable for ordinary printing. Carmine may also be mixed with it, producing a fine color less expensive than carmine by itself.

French blue has the fault of drying too quickly; in this case it is necessary to add a little linseed oil; but the shade is, generally, to be preferred to Prussian blue.

Yellow.—Fine chrome yellow gives a good ink, easily handled, and very useful in many mixtures.

Green is made by a combination of French blue and chrome yellow, varied in quantity according to the preponderance of the shade. Green cinnabar is also useful in many cases.

Brown.—This useful color is made by a mixture of English red with black and yellow, shaded according to desire.

Sienna is employed advantageously, as also fine lake carmines, especially for rose color, black, etc.

All other colors are formed by combinations of the ones already mentioned.

Columbia Typographical Society.—An association of journeymen compositors and pressmen, founded at Washington, D. C., on the 10th of December, 1814, for benevolent purposes. In the first of a series of interesting articles, giving the history of its subsequent operations, contributed to the Printers' Circular by A. T. Cavis and E. Mac Murray, they say: It lived, extended its membership, and enlarged its powers to trade interests, and won a name, the pride of the profession here [in Washington] and elsewhere, always acting conservatively and justly, and ever drawing to its support, in the many conflicts which have marked its history, the zeal of its members and the sympathy and good wishes of the general community in which it was located, and to whom its benefactions were well known.

COLUMBIAN PRESS.

Columbian Press.—A hand printing-press invented by George Clymer, of Philadelphia, and completed about 1817. This press unquestionably exhibits the greatest amount of improvement ever attained in any one instance in hand printing-machines. Its strength of material and scientific combination of power took off an amount of wear from the pressman never before achieved. Its elbowed pulling-bar, its diagonal connecting-rod,

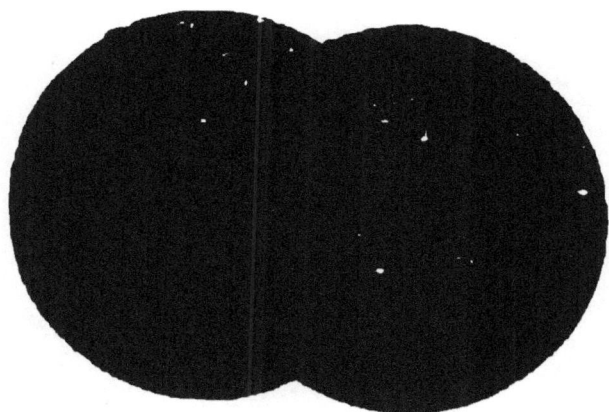

1. Lemon Yellow   2. Lake   3. Indigo

THE COMBINATIONS MAKING:

4. Orange   5. Green   6. Purple

7. A neutral tint apparently Black

COLUMBIAN PRESS.

Columbian Press.—A hand printing press invented by George Clymer, of Philadelphia, and completed about 1817. This press unquestionably exhibits the greatest amount of improvement ever attained in any one instance of a hand printing machine. Its strength of material and novel expenditure of power took off an amount of labor from the pressman never before achieved. Its elbowed pulling-bar, its diagonal connecting-rod...

COMBINATION OF COLORS.

I

1.Lemon Yellow.   2.Lake.   3.Dark Blue.

THE COMBINATIONS MAKING:

4.Orange.   5.Green.   6.Purple.

7. A neutral tint apparently Black.

which changed a horizontal movement into a perpendicular one, and its main lever, applying its weight directly to the form, commended it to all pressmen. The first press of this kind constructed in London was put up in 1818, and afterwards sent to Russia. (See GEORGE CLYMER.)

Columbier.—A flat writing-paper, twenty-three by thirty-three and a quarter inches.

Column.—A series of lines, separated from other matter by a rule or blank space, as a column of figures, the columns of a newspaper. A book which, like this publication, is set up in two measures on each page, is said to be printed in double columns.

Column-Galley.—A long narrow galley, used principally for newspaper work.

Column-Rules.—The rules that divide the columns of newspapers, books, etc.

Combination Borders.—Borders composed of several distinct patterns of face, most of which form separate borders of themselves; but when any or all of them are combined, some very tasteful and ingenious designs are produced.

Combination Leads and Slugs.—The following table, extracted from The Proof-Sheet, shows the combinations that can be formed by leads or slugs of six lengths only, not more than three pieces being required at one time. Indeed, only two pieces are used in eighteen of the thirty-eight examples given.

LENGTH IN PICA EMS OF THE PIECES EMPLOYED:—

4 7 9 13 15 20

4, 4	— 8		15, 13, 4	— 32
7, 4	— 11		20, 13	— 33
4, 4, 4	— 12		15, 15, 4	— 34
7, 7	— 14		20, 15	— 35
9, 7	— 16		20, 9, 7	— 36
13, 4	— 17		15, 15, 7	— 37
9, 9	— 18		20, 9, 9	— 38
13, 4	— 19		15, 15, 9	— 39
7, 7, 7	— 21		20, 20,	— 40
15, 7	— 22		15, 13, 13	— 41
15, 4, 4	— 23		20, 13, 7	— 42
20, 4	— 24		15, 15, 13	— 43
9, 9, 7	— 25		20, 20, 4	— 44
13, 13	— 26		15, 15, 15	— 45
20, 7	— 27		20, 13, 13	— 46
13, 13	— 28		20, 20, 7	— 47
20, 9	— 29		20, 15, 13	— 48
15, 15	— 30		20, 20, 9	— 49
20, 7, 4	— 31		20, 15, 15	— 50

The printer has also at command the six single pieces used, viz.: 4, 7, 9, 13, 15, and 20 ems.

By using four, five, or six pieces together, the above combinations may be extended, consecutively, to one hundred ems.

Comma.—This point (,) marks the smallest grammatical division in printed or written language, and in reading commonly represents the shortest pause. It is also more frequently used than any other punctuation mark, and in a great variety of sentences, especially those of a parenthetical cha-

racter, its employment is essential to a clear expression of the meaning. The following illustrations indicate the character of the errors likely to arise from its omission or its improper use: At a banquet this toast was given: Woman—without her, man is a brute. The reporter had it printed: Woman —without her man, is a brute. A printer, meddling with the verdict of a coroner's jury, struck out a comma after the word apoplexy, making it read thus—Deceased came to his death by excessive drinking, producing apoplexy in the minds of the jury. A clergyman was lately depicting before a deeply interested audience the alarming increase of intemperance, when he astonished his hearers by saying: A young woman in my neighborhood died very suddenly last Sabbath, while I was preaching the gospel in a state of beastly intoxication! M. Edward About wrote, in a report of the Fine Arts Exhibition: M. Lepère is skillful, educated, more than intelligent. M. Lepère inquired, by note, of the writer what he meant. What do you mean to say, sir? I am very much afraid you mean to say that I am better educated than intelligent, and that the comma signifies nothing. And even if it is there, it might not have been there. M. About replied: The comma proves, sir, that I look upon you as a man who is educated, and more than intelligent. M. Lepère was not satisfied, and appealed to the law to redress his grievance. M. About answered: I am challenged to explain and to say if that comma be a serious, solid, established, intentional comma, and if I meant to say that M. Lepère was both an educated man and a man of remarkable intelligence. I hasten to declare that I was still under that impression when I wrote my article,—that is to say, a fortnight ago. In the Imperial Dictionary, the word Tarn is defined as a small mountain, lake, or pool. The improper use of the comma here after mountain has made Tarn signify three things, (1) a mountain, (2) a lake, (3) a pool, instead of simply a mountain lake or pool.

In many other cases, however, where the comma is not absolutely required to express the meaning, it is, in practice, omitted or inserted, as the fancy of the writer, compositor, or proof-reader prompts an adoption or rejection of close punctuation. Lindley Murray laid down twenty rules to govern the use of the comma. Wilson, in his Treatise on Punctuation, gives nineteen, the most important of which are as follows: Two words of the same parts of speech and in the same construction, if used without a conjunction between them, are separated by a comma. In a series of words all of the same parts of speech, a comma is inserted between each. Expressions of a parenthetical or intermediate nature are separated from the context by commas. A word or an expression denoting a person or an object addressed, is separated by a comma from the rest of the sentence. With the exception of dates, figures consisting of four or more characters have a comma inserted between each class of hundreds.

Inverted commas are also commonly used to mark the commencement of a quotation, and it is said that a Frenchman invented them for this purpose, as a substitute for italic letters. In some modern French works, however, neither italic letters, inverted commas, nor anything else are used to mark the commencement of a dialogue or a quotation; and a writer in Once a Week made so strong a protest, a few years ago, against their abuse in the English language, that it is inserted, in part, below, not merely on account of its vigorous discussion of the question immediately under consideration, but because it incidentally furnishes a strong argument against all forms of superfluous punctuation:

Pray note two things to begin with. The first is, that there is not a single inverted comma in the Bible. I refer to the Bible now, not as of divine authority, but as a model of good English, on which printers have lavished their utmost skill. If the translators of the Bible could produce this masterly version, abounding in dialogue, in strange words and phrases, and in quotations of all sorts, without the use of one inverted comma, can it be necessary to sprinkle them so recklessly, as the present custom is, over the pages of books? The other is, that printing is but a device to represent to the eye what speech represents to the ear. The moment that typography attempts to represent more to the eye than the voice can to the ear, it attempts more than it can fairly accomplish, and passes into algebra. There are stops in the voice which printing can clearly represent, and there are words and phrases whose varying emphasis we can indicate in italics and capitals; but inverted commas convey ideas which are either not at all to be found in the inflections of the voice, or which are quite well enough expressed by other and more legitimate typographical devices.

But now we come to the most painful part of the subject—that use of inverted commas which indicates the degeneracy of the language and the feebleness of its writers. Let it be remembered that we live in an age when nearly every man writes. But, unfortunately, the greater number of those who write do not know the English language, and use many words which either they have no right to use, or they are afraid of using. In the olden time, when a man adopted a doubtful phrase—say a word too old, or a word too new, or any strange turn of words—he introduced it with a set apology, as, So to speak, or, If I may be allowed the expression. But now the language has become so colloquial and full of slang that it would be ludicrous to introduce the apology as often as it would be necessary, and so the page is crowded with words in inverted commas, in which we can hear the writer saying to us distinctly, I know that this is not English, but never mind, it must do. Likewise if the word is a remarkable one, as incarnadine, these half-educated writers, remembering that it occurs in Shakspeare, and not being sure whether his authority has prevailed so far as to

make it pass current, think it necessary to decorate it with commas. And if they should wish to speak of the rath primrose, they do not seem to understand that the English language, with all its wealth, is their heritage, and they put the old adjective into inverted commas, in token of the timidity with which they take possession of their inheritance. So, too, of every word and phrase which they can trace to a particular author, or to a particular occasion that gave it currency, they must needs touch it up with the commas, to show they know whence it comes. . . . . . .

Now, the state of things in literature which these inverted commas indicate is by no means to our glory. They indicate an epoch in literature, and if we look seriously into the matter, we shall see that these little commas, which now beset the pages of our literature, are a trifling sign of an immense fact. An age of inverted commas is essentially a degenerate one, and the inverted commas are the badges of our degeneracy. They imply two things chiefly—want of originality in thought, and want of grasp in language, with an infinite sense of borrowing and pilfering in both. They are the recognized sign of second-hand goods, and when they prevail in literature they necessarily mean that the power of originating has ebbed away, and that we are reduced to compilation. People can see that this is what they mean as regards the matter of thought; it may not so distinctly be seen that they imply a similar defect in the manner of expressing it—that is, in the language. Somebody has said of language that it is always best when it is like a pane of glass, so that you can see through it without thinking of the window. But a style fretted with inverted commas is a style afflicted with the vice of consciousness. It is a style in which the writer halts for words. He does not know what words are his by right of inheritance as an Englishman, and what are not. He does not know his mother tongue; he is obliged, in his weakness and ignorance, to insult the noblest of all languages by eking it out with borrowed plumes.

Commentary.—In literature, a word used in different significations:—1. In the same sense with memoirs, as a short narrative of particular events and occurrences, composed by an actor or spectator of those events, with the professed object of calling back the circumstances to his own mind, as, the Commentaries of Cæsar. 2. Critical observations on the text or contents of a book. These are either in the form of detached notes, containing remarks on particular passages; or they are embodied in what is termed a running commentary, or series of remarks written and printed in a connected form. The commentaries of this class most generally known are commentaries on the Bible or its respective books.

Commercial Letter.—A folded writing-paper, generally eleven by seventeen inches.

Commercial Note.—A folded writing-paper, generally eight by ten inches.

Commercial Signs or Abbreviations.—See Signs.

Communication.—Matter supplied to a newspaper by a writer not regularly engaged as a contributor, and which is deemed of sufficient importance and interest to be inserted without charge.

Companionships.—Temporary associations of compositors, which are organized in the large English book-printing-offices, while in nearly all our offices the opposite system of leaving the make-up to the office prevails. Companionships practically extend the system of piece-work to making-up, etc., while the American system restricts it to composition. The plan adopted here is advocated on the ground that it facilitates the progress of the work and secures uniformity; while, on the other hand, it is contended, in England, that under the companionship system all the pages are made up in a uniform style by the clicker, and that works of considerable extent are printed with great dispatch, and with a saving in the cost of production. The plan is described as follows: The clicker, on receiving copy from the overseer, calls the members of his companionship together for a few moments, and informs them what cases to put up and what letter to distribute; at the same time, he gives them any general directions which he may deem expedient for their guidance in composing. While his companions are putting in their letter, the clicker proceeds to get together what leads and other matters he may require for the making-up. He then draws out a table in a simple form. In the first column he sets down the name of each compositor as he takes copy; and in the second, the folio of the copy, so that he may be able to ascertain instantly in whose hands it lies. In the third column he notes down the number of lines each man has composed, opposite to his name, as fast as the galleys are brought to him. In the fourth, he sets down such remarks respecting the copy as may be necessary; also any circumstance that occurs in the companionship. When the companions are ready for their first taking of copy, the clicker deals it out in convenient quantities, giving the first two or three compositors rather less than those that follow. This plan is adopted to prevent any delay in the making-up. During the time the first taking of copy is in hand, the clicker sets the first page heading, the folios, and white lines, signatures, notes, poetry, and any other extraneous matter. As soon as he discovers that the first two or three takings are completed (of which he is informed by a second application for copy), he proceeds to the making-up of the first sheet. As he takes each man's galley, he counts the lines and enters the number against the compositor's name in the before-mentioned table, which serves as a check against the man's bill when he presents it at the end of the week. Having thus made up the first sheet, he lays the pages on the stone, and immediately informs the quoin-drawer overseer of it, who provides chases and furniture. The clicker then takes the cords off the pages, and locks up the form ready for the proof-puller. The companions are thus kept busily engaged at their cases, while the clicker goes regularly about the little jobs which so frequently take the compositors' attention off their work under the old system of each workman making up and imposing his own pages. The start being made, it only requires a plentiful supply of letter, leads, etc., and the work will proceed rapidly. If the clicker finds from any cause—such as abundance of notes, poetry, or other peculiarities in the work—that he cannot make up and impose the matter as fast as it is composed, he generally calls to his aid one of the companions who, in his opinion, is best capable of assisting him. Should this one not have finished his take, either the person next to him takes it and sets it up to himself; or, if there is a great deal to set, the man who took copy last finishes it for him. When this is the case, the clicker sets down the number of lines he has composed, and takes notice of the number of hours he is engaged on time, which he enters in the schedule referred to. As soon as the proofs are read, they are forwarded to the clicker, who immediately requests the person whose name appears at the beginning to lay up the form and correct his matter. The proof is then passed on regularly from one to the other, until all have corrected, the last one locking up the form and carrying it to the proof-press. This is the only instance in which the companions are called from their frames, and proves at once that a great saving of time to the compositor is effected thereby. When the last taking of copy is given out, it is the duty of the clicker to apply to the overseer for other work, so that the companions shall not be kept standing. Frequently, however, one companionship will have three or four works going on at the same time; so that, if there is a scanty supply of copy or letter of one work, the clicker uses his judgment by employing his companions on the others. But should it happen that all the work is nearly finished, and there is no more copy to give out, then, as soon as one of the companionship is out of copy, the lines of the whole are counted off and set down in the table, and every one does what he can for the general benefit, till all is completed. At the end of the week, the clicker makes out the bill, in the following manner: He first ascertains what amount of work has been done during the week; he then counts how many lines each companion has set, and divides them into hours. Having done this, he refers to his table to see how many hours of time-work have been charged, including his own time, which is generally about sixty or sixty-three hours per week, without overtime. He then adds the number of hours of composition, time-work, and his own together, which gives him the total number of hours to be paid for out of the bill. By reducing the sum total of the bill into pence, and dividing it by the number of hours, he gets at the price per hour at which the bill pays; so that it is to his interest to work well, in order to make the bill pay as much as possible. The fat, such as the title, blanks, short pages, folios, whites, and head-lines, is all made up by the clicker, and thrown into the general bill, so that each man gets his fair proportion of it when the bill is made out; whereas, by the old system, a considerable amount of time was wasted by the compositors, at the end of every work, in gathering round the stone and jeffing to decide who should have the title, who the blank, or any other fat matter, such as a piece of table-work, etc., often ending in disputes and angry feeling. Therefore, he who picks up the largest number of types, in the cleanest manner, comes in for the largest share of the fat. This is as it should be. But by the old system, one man may have a happier knack than another of throwing the quads, and will get the largest share of fat, when perhaps he has actually done the least portion of the work. Most companionships work on the same principle, although they have a different mode of paying the clicker. In some he is only paid for the time he is actually engaged at the work; another companionship will equally, not proportionately, divide all the fat; while others will allow the clicker to charge the same number of hours as the man who has composed the largest number of lines. The latter plan is bad on principle, as it affords ground for dishonesty; for it is very easy for a clicker to give the best and fattest copy to the compositor who can pick up the largest number of types. One of the largest London firms divides its work between three different classes of companionships, and pays its clickers established wages. The first-class companionships have all the best kind of work, and the companions are paid 7d. or 8d. per hour (or 1000 letters); the second-class companionships take the medium work, and are paid 6d. per hour, while the third and lowest class have to be content with the inferior work for which they get 5d. per hour. Each of these companionships receives the above prices irrespective of cuts, blanks, tables, or other fat, which is claimed by the employers as remuneration for the clicker's labor. The overseer generally places the compositor on being first employed in the third-class companionship. His manner of working is closely watched, and if he proves to be a quick and clean compositor, on the first opportunity he is drafted into the second-class; and if his abilities are still approved of and his conduct is good, he may ultimately be promoted to the first-class companionship. Here he will have a double advantage over his previous situation, for not only will he be engaged on the best work, but he will be kept constantly employed; for if a slackness occurs, the inferior work is taken from the third-class ship and given to the second; while the best ship is kept going with work from the others, rather than be suffered to stand still. Perhaps, however, the fairest and most equitable method is to let the companions choose their own clicker, and pay him out of the general bill. If he does not work to their satisfaction, they will soon replace him by a more competent man; thus the employer will have the satisfaction of knowing that his work is progressing with all the dispatch possible, and that he is only paying the actual worth of the labor performed.

Compendium.—An abridgment or epitome of a larger work.

Compo.—This word is sometimes used as the name of the composition of which rollers are manufactured.

Composing-Rule.—A rule made of brass or steel, of the length of the line to be set, and used to facilitate the placing of the type in the composing-stick. It has a small ear or nib projecting at one or both ends by which it can be conveniently taken from the stick when each line, successively, is composed and justified.

Composing-Stick.—An instrument in which letters are set, or arranged in lines. Composing-sticks are made of various designs. Those of the old-fashioned makes consist of the following parts: The plate, which forms the bed of the instrument; the flange, turned up from the plate at right angles, and five-eighths of an inch high above the plate, through which are bored holes, about one inch apart from each other, to receive the screw; the head, which is of the same height as the flange, but much stronger, securely fastened to it and the plate by rivets, dovetail, or brazing; the slide, having an opening in the lower leg, or part which rests against the flange, to admit the tenon of the nut, which is shouldered to fit into this groove, and which nut is to receive the screw on its being passed through one of the holes, to fasten the slide to any measure that may be required. This is done by means of the groove in the slide being moved backward or forward on the screw and nut, and by the screw being used at the hole convenient to the distance required, so as to set the slide at the point wanted from the head. Composing-sticks are made of iron, brass, or gun-metal; the latter, owing to their not being liable to corrosion, are best suited to warm climates. Recently, too, some composing-sticks have been plated with nickel. They are made of various lengths, from about four inches up to ten or twelve; above that size, for posters, they are generally made of mahogany. Sometimes the slide is split, and when the two parts are put asunder, they can be adjusted to a shorter measure, so that the compositor can have his work proceeding in two different measures at one time, without altering his stick. The usual depth of American and English sticks is about two inches, but French sticks are much smaller, frequently holding only six lines. The most usual defects in composing-sticks are, the slides and heads not being perfectly square to each other, and each of them to the plate; also, the slides and heads are sometimes not square, or at right angles to the flange. The following illustrations represent several of the varieties of composing-sticks now in use.

ENGLISH COMPOSING-STICK.

THUMB SCREW STICK.

SCREW STICK.

SCREW STICK.

COMPOSING STICK.

NEWBURY STICK.

SCREW STICK.

GROVER PATENT STICK.

QUAIL PATENT FRANKLIN STICK.

Composition.—Type-setting; also material for ink-rollers.

Composition.—The term composition includes the practical knowledge of picking up type, arranging them correctly into words, spacing, justifying lines, emptying the composing-stick, and embodying in a typographical form the matter embraced in manuscript or reprint copy. The leading objects of the compositor should be expedition, correctness, and, in the ornamental branches of the business, a manifestation of good taste. None of these objects can be attained if the compositor is not endowed with a fair degree of intelligence, and all the general knowledge he can acquire will help, incidentally, to promote speed, to guard against errors, or to set up a good title-page or a well-displayed card, poster, or advertisement. No man can become a fast compositor who does not at once readily comprehend copy, despite its comparative illegibility, and remember the text so well, that little or no time is lost in recurring to it. As the capacity of the most ingenious type-setting machine will necessarily be limited by the rapidity with which copy can be deciphered and readily remembered, so the first great duty of the compositor is to cultivate his intellect, perceptive faculties, and memory in the direction indicated; otherwise, he must inevitably waste many hours over his case, in efforts to understand or remember his copy. As the compositor is often required to correct orthography, punctuation, and capitalization, a double tax is thus imposed upon his intelligence, and it requires an extraordinarily quick eye and quick brain to achieve the best attainable results.

The best mental training, however, will not make a rapid and skillful compositor, if it is not allied to manual dexterity. The motions necessary to place the type in its proper position should be made with celerity, all superfluous motions being meanwhile carefully avoided. The general directions are to take up the letter at the end where the face is; if the nick be not upward, to turn it upward in its progress to the composing-stick; and to convey it to the line in the composing-stick with as few motions as possible. Very fast compositors economize time in each of these operations, while slow or indifferent compositors waste time in each. The fast compositor, for instance, is more apt to drop his type in his stick than to laboriously place it there; and while his right hand is picking up type his left is advancing (but not too far, as it rarely ventures beyond a circle corresponding with the central portions of the lower-case) with the stick to receive it.

The habit of making superfluous motions in setting type is so easy to acquire, and so difficult to break, that few compositors are free from it. These motions are classified by one writer as ridiculous, purposeless, and time-wasting, and he furnishes the following exemplifications of his meaning:

Look at one compositor, who accompanies the necessary movements of his right arm with a continuous shuffling of his right foot; at another, who clicks and knocks each type he picks up over and over again —two, three, four, five, and more times—against his composing-stick; or at a third, who makes a deep, reverential bow towards his cases whenever he lifts a type from them:—in fact, these purposeless movements are of so great a variety, and mostly so ridiculous, that I will not waste time in enumerating them, lest by so doing I should give to a few words, which

I desire to render impressive and earnest, a stamp of frivolity.

To expect the same speed in his work, and the same cleverness, from every compositor is a utopian and never-to-be-realized hope; yet what can be—and ought to be—expected, is the same quiet and thoughtful way of doing the work. And here it is not the ability,—it is the will of the man we have to deal with. Some may say, But what if a compositor has been spoiled during his apprenticeship?—to which I reply, If he will—earnestly will—reform bad and pernicious habits acquired when an apprentice, or through the bad example he had, in journeymen, before his eyes, he can do so!—nay, he must do so! Of course, what an earnest and sensible remonstrance would have prevented in the beginning, will, in later years, require more or less time to amend, always supposing that the good and earnest will to do so exists.

Then, besides the ridicule and the loss of valuable time, these purposeless movements will—some of them, certainly—affect the compositor's health, his chest, his legs, his feet; they will, indeed, greatly fatigue him before he has done half a day's work.

Before proceeding further, let us see how a compositor ought to do his work. This may be said in a few words. Standing perfectly upright before his frame, soldier-like, heels and knee-joints together; the upper part of the body erect, not curved; looking at a type before his right hand and finger grasp it, and then bringing it into the composing-stick with a simple, short movement—no curves, no clicking, no turning it up and down; not following with the whole body the advancing right hand towards an f or g, an s or k, but merely inclining just so much as is absolutely necessary towards that point of the case or cases where a type is to be taken up. The more quietly and with the less affectation or haste all these movements are practiced, the better for his exchequer will be the result ultimately; for his work will be all the more regular, and he will soon gain, in ems, in lines, in galleys or sheets, what he formerly spent in bows, in clicking, and in shuffling. He will be considerably less fatigued at the end of his day's work; and will thank me, rather than laugh at me, for this —he may call it sermon if he likes to do so!

Where are the reasons to be sought for that will account for the striking difference of compositors in productive power? In nothing so much as in the style of working, i.e., in the manner (so different!) of picking up type. One who causes a type to make two, three, or more curves through the air before he places it in the stick, or one who knocks it repeatedly (or even once only) against the stick, before he finally puts it down in the line, etc., etc., etc., is an evident loser in time, against one who, having grasped the type, places it quickly, in the shortest way, and without any further ceremony or reverential inclination, where it ought to be, looking out at the same time for the nick of its follower.

I can, therefore, only say to compositors who are guilty of these irregular and nonsensical habits, Reform! for if you realize a saving of only 10 per cent., i.e., if you, who formerly composed, in a given time, 10 types, can, by good and firm will, bring it to 11 in the same space of time, you will gain a hundred types in every thousand, say 700 or 800 daily, 4000 to 5000 in a week, 16,000 to 20,000 in a month—more than a month's pay in a year's time!

Conflicting opinions have been expressed in regard to the most convenient height of a stand or frame, but the standard advocated by Hansard and Houghton is the compositor's elbow. The former says that the height of a compositor and his frame should be so adjusted, that his right elbow may just clear the front of the lower-case by the a and r boxes, without the smallest elevation of the shoulder-point, and his breast be opposite the space, h, and e boxes; and Houghton states that personal experience of both methods has fully satisfied him that at a frame the height of the elbow, a compositor will do his work quicker, easier, and hold out longer than at a high one. Houghton, also, gives the following suggestions for facilitating fast composition:

When composing, the closer the elbows are kept to the body the better, both for expedition and ease. In putting the type into the stick, use the wrist-joint; there is no necessity to use the elbow-joint, except when the right hand, which the stick should follow to every box, is engaged at the upper case, or in those boxes of the lower case furthest out of reach. Another thing, equally important to a quiet compositor, and which equally requires his attention, is, that every type be lifted and put into the composing-stick by the first attempt. The time lost by compositors missing the letter they intended to raise, and trying twice, and even thrice, before they get hold of it, is incalculable. This must, by all means, be avoided; and that it may effectually be so, I would submit the following method. First, let the letter on which the eye first rests be picked up and secured in the fingers, before the eye moves to another box. Second, let the eye be fixed on the second letter while the right hand is bringing home the first; and fix it on the third while conveying the second, and so on. Again, let the time of picking up a letter be equal to the time of conuting two, and bringing it to the stick equal to one, counted at the same rate. If the compositor would extend his hand as if composing, and hold it so while he counts two, and again bring it back in the time he would count one, the movement that I would explain and recommend as the best to secure lifting up every type, would, perhaps, be better understood. Thus it will be seen that, to avoid missing any type, when the attempt is made to pick it up, two-thirds of the time of composing is occupied in securing it. It is immaterial at what rate the movement be tested, it will be the same relatively. This method of composing, once acquired, will doubly compensate for the trouble of learning it. When composing, take as much copy in the mind only as convenient; for it is better to take only half a line with certainty than a whole line with perplexity. The best time for taking copy in the mind is when inserting the last space in the preceding sentence, or when putting in the last space to justify the line.

It should constantly be borne in mind by compositors, however, that speed is only one of the important objects to be aimed at, and that, even if money is the sole end in view, it is often more apt to be secured by a reputation for careful, correct, and tasteful workmanship, than by negligent rapid composition. (See DIVISIONS, FAST COMPOSITION, JUSTIFICATION, PUNCTUATION, SPACING.)

Composition Kettle.—The utensil in which the glue, molasses, etc. used in making rollers is boiled.

Composition Rollers.—Of all the inventions of this century in connection with the art of Printing, none are so important as composition rollers and cylinder-presses. They can be properly mentioned together, because

COMPOSITION KETTLE.

without the former the latter would have been really impossible; a convenient instrument for putting ink upon the form being an indispensable adjunct of machine-printing. In England, the credit of introducing composition rollers is claimed for several persons, viz.: 1. For Bacon & Donkin, who used them in connection with a new machine-printing-press, which they patented in 1813, describing in their specification a mixture of glue and molasses, claiming it as a novelty for rollers to be used in printing, while admitting that a similar composition had been used for a long time previous in English potteries. 2. For B. Foster, who spread it in a melted state on canvas, and then formed it into balls of the old form. He is said to have derived his knowledge of its properties from its previous use in a cotton-factory. 3. A paragraph in a recent number of the Printer's Register asserts that the composition roller now in use was the chance discovery of Edward Dyas, printer and parish clerk of Madeley. The story is, that his glue-pot having been upset, and Dyas not having a pelt-ball ready at hand, he took up a piece of the glue, in a soft state, and inked a form with it so satisfactorily that he continued its use,—afterwards adding molasses to keep the glue soft. This theory, which is one of the latest, makes composition rollers a more legitimate descendant of the old-fashioned balls than any other, and is in that respect, at least, the most satisfactory. In the United States there is a still greater variety of theories in regard to the proper claimant of the honor of first using or introducing composition rollers in this country. It is quite certain that they did not come into general use here until some years after they are known to have been used in England; and yet patents for improved rollers were granted in this country at a comparatively early day.

Among the many other changes, of comparatively recent date, are the introduction of new substances into composition rollers,—glycerine and india rubber being two of the most important in this country, while a small amount of shoemaker's wax is said to have been used advantageously in England,—and a rapid increase of the custom of having rollers made wholly or in part by manufacturers of rollers and roller composition, instead of performing this labor in the printing-offices where the rollers are to be used.

Some recipes and directions for making composition rollers are given below, and any reader who wishes to make his own rollers can decide for himself, whether it is better to adhere to the beaten tracks or to attempt some of the new experiments. One thing should constantly be borne in mind, that defects in the raw material used will inevitably injure the quality of the composition, and that it is utterly impossible to make good rollers out of bad glue and bad molasses.

The following directions for making and preserving composition rollers are given in the American Printer:

Put the glue in a bucket or pan, and cover it with water; let it stand until more than half penetrated with water, taking care that it shall not soak too long, and then pour it off and let it remain until it becomes soft, when it will be ready for the melting-kettle. This is a double vessel, like a glue-kettle. Put the soaked glue into the inner vessel, and as much water in the outer boiler as it will contain when the inner vessel is placed in it. When the glue is all melted (if too thick, add a little water), the molasses may be slowly poured into it, and well mixed with the glue by frequent stirring. When properly prepared, the composition does not require boiling more than an hour. Too much boiling candies the molasses, and the roller, consequently, will be found to lose its suction much sooner. In proportioning the material, much depends upon the weather and temperature of the place in which the rollers are to be used. Eight pounds of glue to one gallon of sugar-house molasses, or syrup, is a very good proportion for summer, and four pounds of glue to one gallon of molasses for winter use.

For hand-press rollers more molasses should be used, as they are not subject to so much hard usage as cylinder-press rollers, and do not require to be as strong; for the more molasses that can be used the better will be the roller. Before pouring a roller, the mould should be perfectly clean, and well oiled with a swab, but not to excess, as too much oil makes the face of the roller scanty and ragged. The end pieces should then be oiled, and, together with the cylinder, placed in the mould, the upper-end piece being very open, to allow the composition to pass down between the interior of the mould and the cylinder. The cylinder must be well secured from rising, before the composition is poured in, by placing a stick upon the end of it, sufficiently long to reach above the end of the mould, and be tied down with twine. The composition should be poured very slowly, and in such a manner as to cause it only to run down one side of the cylinder, allowing the air to escape freely up the other.

If the mould is filled at night, the roller may be drawn the next morning; but it should not be used for at least twenty-four hours after, except in very cold weather.

To determine when a roller is in order for working, press the hand gently to it: if the fingers can be drawn lightly and smoothly over its surface, it may be said to be in order; but should it be so adhesive that the fingers will not glide smoothly over its surface, it is not sufficiently dry, and should be exposed to the air. In applying this rule due allowance must be made for the character of the work to be executed, and the nature of the ink to be employed.

Rollers should not be washed immediately after use, but should be put away with the ink on them, as it protects the surface from the action of the air. When washed and exposed to the atmosphere for any length of time, they become dry and skinny. They should be washed about half an hour before using them. In cleaning a new roller, a little oil rubbed over it will loosen the ink; and it should be scraped clean with the back of a case-knife. It should be cleaned in this way for about one week, when lye may be used. New rollers are often spoiled by washing them too soon with lye. Camphene may be substituted for oil; but, owing to its combustible nature, it is objectionable, as accidents may arise from its use. Benzine or turpentine may be advantageously used for washing rollers after they have been covered with colored inks.

A. E. Senter, pressman in Follett, Foster & Co.'s Printing and Publishing House, Columbus, Ohio, gives the following method:

Take seven pounds of Upton's frozen glue, put it into hard water, and let it soak until the water has struck half-way through it. In good frozen glue, this will be in ten minutes—in ordinary glue, considerably longer. Then take it out of the water and let it lie long enough so that it will bend easily; it is then ready for the kettle.

The kettle for melting and mixing should be so set as to heat and boil the composition by steam or a hot-water bath, in the manner in use by cabinet-makers. Let the glue heat in the kettle until it is all dissolved, or if there should be any pieces that do not readily melt, take them out, or they will make the roller lumpy. When the glue is all melted evenly, take four quarts of good sugar-house molasses or sorghum syrup, stir it in, and continue to stir occasionally for three or four hours, during which time the heat under the kettle should be kept up so as to give the composition a gentle boil. To try the composition, take a little out on a piece of paper, and when cool, if it is tough so as to resist the action of the finger without feeling tacky, it is ready to cast. A person can generally tell when it is done, by taking out the stirring-stick and holding it up, when, if the composition will hang in strings, it is done.

A very important feature of roller-making is in preparing the core. Strip off the old composition with a knife and scrape the core. Keep water away from it, and also sweaty hands. If water is used at all, let it be hard water, and let the core dry thoroughly before casting. If the core is likely to give the composition the slip, brush it over with lime-water newly made with quick-lime, and let it dry well, and the composition will stick fast.

Have the mould carefully cleaned and oiled on the inside, set it upright, with the core in its place in the centre, then pour in the composition hot from the kettle, carefully, upon the end of the core, so as to run down the core, and not down the inner surface of the mould, as that would be likely to take off the oil from the mould, and by flowing it against the core, would make it peel off when cast.

When the composition is cold in the mould, and ready to be drawn out, draw it steadily; trim the ends with a sharp knife, beveled toward the core, so that the ends will not be so likely to get started loose; take a hot iron and run it around the ends of the composition, soldering it to the core, which operation will prevent water, lye or oil from getting in between the composition and the wood, and making it peel at the ends. Do not wash a roller when it is taken from the mould; it will be all the better for two or three days' seasoning, with the oil on the surface. It is always good economy to have enough rollers cast ahead, so as not to be obliged to use new ones until they are seasoned. In washing, use lye just strong enough to start the ink, and rinse off with water immediately, and carefully wipe dry with a sponge. Rollers should always be kept in an air-tight box, without water, and in the room where they are worked. Sudden changes of temperature, as from a cold cellar to a warm press-room, will soon use them up.

The Chicago Specimen gives the following recipe, which, it says, has been used satisfactorily:

Rollers for Summer Use.—1 gallon sugar-house molasses, 2 ℔s. No. 1 Cooper bone glue, (@ 45c., 2 ℔s. Baeder common glue, (@ 19c., ¼ pint glycerine.

For Winter Use.—The only variation should be ¼ ℔. less each glue.

Soak the glues separately in woolen rags for, say, three or four hours, or until soft.

Boil the molasses first for about forty or forty-five minutes, skimming off the scum,—then put in the glue, continuing to boil for about fifteen to twenty minutes, mixing well; then put in the glycerine and boil for five to ten minutes, and then pour off.

Sugar-house molasses is better than syrup.

Compositor.—One who sets type, and makes up the pages and forms.

Compound Words.—Grammarians class as compound words those which are composed of two or more simple words; but of this mass of compound words only those which have their respective parts connected by a hyphen are compound in the printing-office sense. Unfortunately, the usage applicable to many words is conflicting, dictionary-makers and writers disagreeing, as to whether they should be printed distinctly, or be connected with a hyphen, or be printed as single words. Webster's and Worcester's Dictionaries designate, in each doubtful word, whether it is to be printed with or without a hyphen, but they do not explain on what principles their decisions are founded, and they do not always reach similar conclusions. Goold Brown, in his grammar, undertook to solve this problem by the doctrine that: Permanent compounds are consolidated; as bookseller, schoolmaster: others are formed by the hyphen; as, glass-house, negro-merchant. But Parker in his Aids to English Composition, in commenting on this doctrine, says that no better reason can be given for the use or omission of the hyphen than caprice. Wilson, in his Treatise on Punctuation, lays down some rules, yet he acknowledges that there are numerous exceptions to most of them, and he laments that the subject under consideration has been sadly neglected. Practically, the only safe course open now for proof-readers and compositors is to consult their favorite dictionary in all doubtful cases.

Condensed.—This general term is applied to various styles of job letter which are narrower than Roman letters of a corresponding size. Some of the English founders use in a similar sense the word **compressed.** (See JOB LETTER.)

Conner, James, born April 22, 1798, near Hyde Park, Duchess County, New York, died May 30, 1861, was the founder of the Conner Type Foundry of New York, which, since his death, has been conducted by his sons, under the firm name of James Conner's Sons. After serving an apprenticeship to the printing-business in a New York City newspaper-office, he worked for some years as a journeyman printer, chiefly in book stereotype offices, beginning his labors as a stereotyper in the office of Mr. Watts, who, in conjunction with Mr. Foy, was one of the first, if not the first, to stereotype successfully in the United States. Subsequently he started a stereotype establishment in New York, to which an extensive type-foundry was afterwards added, and he prepared plates of a number of valuable standard works, some of which he sold, while others he published on his own account. Later in life, after an adventurous career, his business attention was concentrated on his type-foundry, and he made strenuous exertions to increase his variety of faces as well as to improve the facilities for manufacturing type. A biographical notice of Mr. Conner, which appeared in The Printer of May, 1859, gives the following account of some of his experiments:

Among these, elaborated by the process of chemical precipitation, was the casting of letters from an electrotyped matrix. Previous to Mr. Conner's successful efforts in this direction, Messrs. Mapes and Chilton,

chemists, had experimented to produce a fac-simile of a copper-plate which Mapes wished to use for his magazine. Ascertaining the perfect success of the experiment under other hands, he was anxious to have their battery tried on a copper-plate. It was, to his and Mr. Chilton's joint delight, successful, and a very favorable report was inserted in many of the European scientific periodicals. So gratifying, in fact, were the results of the experiments made in this direction, that improvements were suggested from time to time.

In the course of his experimenting, Conner took a Long Primer Italic capital T, and inserted it through a piece of stereotype plate. This was attached to a copper wire by soldering; some zinc was attached to the other end of the wire; a weak solution of sulphuric acid was made and placed in a vessel; a solution of common blue vitriol in another apartment; then the matrix and the zinc were placed in their respective apartments, and the process of extracting the copper from the sulphate, through galvanic action, commenced, and the copper obtained was thrown on the intended matrix.

Conner and his assistants then took a small cut of a beehive, and, setting this also in the same way, obtained a perfect matrix, which is now in use at Conner's foundry. These successes encouraged him to other experiments on a larger and more valuable scale. Mr. Conner, therefore, ordered a fancy fount of type, which he originally had cut on steel, selecting therefrom a perfect alphabet, points, and figures, and then shaved a stereotype plate on both sides. This he lined off into sizes, equal to the matrices he desired to make. He then made the necessary openings through the plate, and inserted the types designed to be precipitated on, which he cut off and soldered on the back. This proved a highly successful experiment, as it gave him a perfect set of matrices at one precipitation. This plate is still to be seen at Mr. Conner's establishment, as originally made, and is regarded as a great curiosity—being supposed to be the first alphabet thus made, in this or any other country.

His next experiment was made on a more extended scale, and, to this end, the apparatus was enlarged so as to admit three founts of fancy types, which were placed in communication with the precipitated copper at the same operation. Between each letter was inserted a piece of wood, made to the height necessary to separate each matrix from the other as it came out, it being impossible to connect the wood along with the precipitated metal. Thus divided, each matrix would fall apart without the labor of sawing. This experiment, however, was by no means successful. From the circumstance of wood being introduced as dividing lines, and becoming wet, it swelled—such swelling causing the type to spring from the bottom of the trough. In the process of precipitation, only a very thin shell was formed on the face of the type; about the same quantity having found its way to the bottom, in consequence of the springing of the dividing lines, and the throwing of the types off their feet. All these difficulties have been since overcome, and his establishment has several thousand precipitated matrices that can scarcely be told from those made from a steel punch.

Consecutive Numbering-Machines.—Several machines are made by which tickets, checks, or cards can be numbered consecutively with great facility. They are extensively used in printing railroad tickets and tickets for secured seats in places of public entertainment.

Consonant.—An articulate sound which in utterance is usually combined and sounded with an open sound called a vowel; a member of the spoken alphabet other than a vowel; hence, also, a letter or character representing such a sound. Consonants are divided into various classes, as mutes, spirants, sibilants, nasals, semi-vowels, etc.

Contents.—A summary of the matter treated in a book, which usually follows the preface or introduction, but sometimes precedes it. When a work is divided into chapters, and the contents of each chapter are summarized at its head, these summaries are frequently printed at or near the beginning of the work, as contents; while in works not thus divided, and in which the summary assumes the shape of a minute alphabetical index, such an index is usually printed at the end of the book.

Context.—The parts of a composition which precede or follow a sentence quoted.

Co-operative Associations.—A number of co-operative associations of journeymen printers, formed for the purpose of enabling them to acquire an interest in printing-establishments, without abandoning their situations as journeymen, have been organized in various portions of the United States. The organization is usually effected under a general act authorizing the formation of corporations for manufacturing purposes. In one company, whose articles of association furnish, in some respects, a type of others, the capital stock is fixed at $5000; the term of the existence of the company is twenty-five years; the number of shares is twenty-five; the business is intrusted to the management of five directors or trustees; a small portion of the sum represented by the par value of each share of stock is paid at the time of the original subscription, and the balance in weekly instalments; members are prohibited from selling stock except to the association; and the members mutually agree that in case of difficulty or dispute they will rely for a settlement upon the honor of the board of directors, and the members of the association generally, instead of appealing to the courts.

Copper.—The immense number of impressions which electrotypes are known to bear without serious injury to their surface, has attracted increased attention to the value of copper as an ingredient of type-metal, and while a process of copper-facing type has been employed to a comparatively limited extent, many type-founders announce that copper forms an important portion of their alloy.

Copperplate Engraving.—This art is supposed to have been invented by Tommaso Finiguerra, a goldsmith of Florence, about or before 1460. It is said that he chanced to cast, or let fall, a piece of copper, engraved and filled with ink, into melted sulphur; and, observing that the exact impression of his work was left on the sulphur, he repeated the experiment on moistened paper, rolling it gently with a roller. His leading object is supposed to have been to obtain proofs or copies of the fine engravings he executed on gold and silver plates. In engraving copperplates they are cut with a steel instrument called a graver, the design being generally, either in part or entirely, etched upon the metal. This process is based on the chemical action of nitric acid. An etching ground, composed of white wax, burgundy pitch, and asphaltum, is laid upon the surface of the plate. This compound is tied up in a silk bag or roll, and, the plate being warmed, the wax is applied by rubbing over the surface—the heat of the metal causing the etching ground to ooze through the silk, and uniformity of thickness being caused by the application of a dauber. A drawing is made with a needle through this composition, until along all the lines the metal is laid bare. An edging of wax being placed around the plate, a solution of nitric acid is poured over it; this must be sufficiently strong to act readily, but not very intensely, upon the copper; this is technically called biting. The chemical action which ensues is the formation of an oxide of copper, which is rapidly dissolved off in the form of a nitrate of copper, there being at the same time some nitrous acid generated, which is visible in red fumes. When the acid has penetrated to a sufficient depth, its operation is arrested by an application that neutralizes it, and the plate is touched up by the graver. For a long period nearly all the illustrations used in books were copperplate engravings, but in modern times they have been supplanted, to a very large extent, by wood-engravings, mezzotints, and steel-plate engravings.

Copperplate Paper is usually made from the best stock, is unsized, calendered on one side and rough on the other.

Copperplate Press.—Many improvements have been introduced into this machine during the last few years. The copperplate press is employed in taking off prints or impressions from copper or steel plates, engraved, etched, or scraped as in mezzotint. It is a description of rolling press, and consists of two rollers or cylinders supported on a strong frame. These rollers are movable on their axes, one being placed just above the other. The table on which the plate to be printed is laid runs between the two. The upper cylinder is turned round by means of a cross fixed on its axis; the lower one is turned by the action of the upper on its surface. These rollers are so arranged as to admit of a greater or less amount of pressure—a woolen or india rubber cloth intervening between the upper roller and the engraved plate, acting as the blanket does in type-printing. Copperplate presses are made either to be worked solely by hand, or to be geared so that the pressure may be applied by machinery. Efforts are also being made to construct steam copperplate presses.

COPPERPLATE PRESS.

Copperplate Printing.—The processes formerly used in copperplate printing are now employed so frequently and generally in printing steel plates, mezzotints, etc., that even the name of the art has been gradually changed into Plate-printing; and it will therefore be described under that head. (See PLATE-PRINTING.)

Copy.—The subject-matter to be printed, whether it be an original work in manuscript, or a reprint: in the first case it is termed manuscript, in the second, reprint. From time immemorial, printers have been subjected to great inconvenience from imperfect or badly-prepared copy, and from the difficulty of knowing when they should or should not correct what they believe to be errors or imperfections in manuscript copy. Authors cannot be too careful in preparing their matter for publication, writing in a legible hand on one side of the paper only, whenever the work is of such length that more than one

compositor is likely to be employed upon it, and taking special pains to write with great distinctness names, words in foreign languages, or any other words which cannot be readily understood by the context. It is also desirable that they should pay at least some attention to punctuation, for, where points are necessary to elucidate the meaning, the authors ought to know better than any one else, where they are required. It is an old printer's rule to follow copy, but this is subject to many exceptions. Where copy is manifestly imperfect, it is better either to see that the author corrects it, to correct it in his presence, to obtain explicit authority for making the necessary corrections, or, where, as sometimes happens, the author is too ignorant to have any conceptions whatever of typographical accuracy, to make the printed job or work as nearly correct as possible at all hazards. A writer in The Printer told a story, a few years ago, of a rash vow, made by a Boston job printer, in consequence of a dispute which he had with a customer about a bill for alterations, that he would in future follow copy literally, and the result of this resolution was the following production:

A valuable house for Sale.

With ACKer of land and applss trees. It is anew house and nicely situated and Fiting for two famalys to live in there is foure Romes on the first floor and three up stairs there are all Large in Perpotion

It Stands on Souh Right In the sister of Both Depots Not five Minuts to Eighter and abot same to eighter of stores an It will sarce take Minut walk to Calulick Church.

Is to veew of the town

Plasse of Enqiery Marlboro Middle Sex
County mass
the Name and Oner Mr
Micheal keney
yours Respecfful friend
It is for the Purtcher Now and
Botween fust of June

On reflection, however, this gem of typography was amended before it was put to press; and as a considerable proportion of the copy furnished to American printers is in not much better shape than the extract given, the necessity of amending it, with or without the consent of the author, is obvious.

Copy-Holder.—The assistant of the proof-reader, who reads copy so that it may be compared with the printed matter in the proof. Also, an implement used to hold copy while it is being set up. (See GUIDE.)

Copying-Press.—A machine for taking, by pressure, an exact copy of any manuscript recently written.

Copying Printing-Ink.—A preparation has lately been invented, and patented by Mr. McIlvain, of Philadelphia, by the use of which copies of impressions from printing-inks of all colors can be taken as readily as copies of letters written with copying-ink. It is claimed that the invention will prove especially valuable to companies or individuals who wish to preserve exact copies of forms, bills of lading, or other documents which consist partly of printed and partly of written matter. Clear and distinct copies of the printed matter have been obtained months after the first impressions were made; and it is believed that this power will not be weakened or lost by time.

Copyright.—The property which an author or designer has in literary work, secured to him by law, for a limited time. The Copyright Laws of the United States were revised, consolidated, and amended by an Act of Congress, approved July 8, 1870, the essential portions of which are as follows:

All records and other things relating to copyrights, and required by law to be preserved, shall be under the control of the Librarian of Congress, and kept and preserved in the library of Congress; and the Librarian of Congress shall have the immediate care and supervision thereof, and under the supervision of the Joint Committee of Congress on the Library, shall perform all acts and duties required by law touching copyrights.

Any citizen of the United States, or resident therein, who shall be the author, inventor, designer, or proprietor of any book, map, chart, dramatic or musical composition, engraving, cut, print, or photograph or negative thereof, or of a painting, drawing, chromo, statue, statuary, and of models or designs intended to be perfected as works of the fine arts, and his executors, administrators, or assigns, shall, upon complying with the provisions of this act, have the sole liberty of printing, reprinting, publishing, completing, copying, executing, finishing, and vending the same; and in the case of a dramatic composition, of publicly performing or representing it, or causing it to be performed or represented by others, and authors may reserve the right to dramatize or to translate their own works.

Copyrights shall be granted for the term of twenty-eight years from the time of recording the title thereof in the manner hereinafter directed.

The author, inventor, or designer, if he be still living and a citizen of the United States, or resident therein, or his widow or children if he be dead, shall have the same exclusive right continued for the further term of fourteen years, upon recording the title of the work or description of the article so secured a second time, and complying with all other regulations in regard to original copyrights, within six months before the expiration of the first term. And such person shall, within two months from the date of said renewal, cause a copy of the record thereof to be published in one or more newspapers printed in the United States, for the space of four weeks.

Copyrights shall be assignable in law, by any instrument of writing, and such assignment shall be recorded in the office of the Librarian of Congress within sixty days after its execution, in default of which it shall be void, as against any subsequent pur-

chaser or mortgagee, for a valuable consideration, without notice.

No person shall be entitled to a copyright unless he shall, before publication, deposit in the mail a printed copy of the title of the book or other article, or a description of the painting, drawing, chromo, statue, statuary, or model or design for a work of the fine arts, for which he desires a copyright, addressed to the Librarian of Congress, and, within ten days from the publication thereof, deposit in the mail two copies of such copyright book or other article, or in case of a painting, drawing, statue, statuary, model or design for a work of the fine arts, a photograph of the same, to be addressed to said Librarian of Congress.

The Librarian of Congress shall record the name of such copyright book, or other article, forthwith in a book to be kept for that purpose, in the words following: Library of Congress, to wit: Be it remembered, that on the —— day of ——, Anno Domini ——, A. B., of ——, hath deposited in this office the title of a book (map, chart, or otherwise, as the case may be, or description of the article), the title or description of which is in the following words, to wit: (here insert the title or description,) the right whereof he claims as author, originator (or proprietor, as the case may be), in conformity with the laws of the United States respecting copyrights. C. D., Librarian of Congress. And he shall give a copy of the title or description, under the seal of the Librarian of Congress, to said proprietor, whenever he shall require it.

For recording the title or description of any copyright book or other article, the Librarian of Congress shall receive, from the person claiming the same, fifty cents; and for every copy under seal, actually given to such person or his assigns, fifty cents; and for recording any instrument of writing for the assignment of a copyright, fifteen cents for every one hundred words; and for every copy thereof, ten cents for every one hundred words, which moneys, so received, shall be paid into the treasury of the United States.

The proprietor of every copyright book or other article shall mail to the Librarian of Congress at Washington, within ten days after its publication, two complete printed copies thereof, of the best edition issued, or description or photograph of such article as hereinbefore required, and a copy of every subsequent edition wherein any substantial changes shall be made.

In default of such deposit in the post-office, said proprietor shall be liable to a penalty of twenty-five dollars, to be collected by the Librarian of Congress, in the name of the United States, in an action of debt, in any district court of the United States within the jurisdiction of which the delinquent may reside or be found.

Any such copyright book or other article may be sent to the Librarian of Congress by mail free of postage, provided the words copyright matter are plainly written or printed on the outside of the package containing the same.

The postmaster to whom such copyright book, title, or other article is delivered, shall, if requested, give a receipt therefor; and when so delivered, he shall mail it to its destination without cost to the proprietor.

No person shall maintain an action for the infringement of his copyright, unless he shall give notice thereof, by inserting in the several copies of every edition published, on the title-page or the page immediately following, if it be a book; or if a map, chart, musical composition, print, cut, engraving, photograph, painting, drawing, chromo, statue, statuary, or model or design intended to be perfected and completed as a work of the fine arts, by inscribing upon some portion of the face or front thereof, or on the face of the substance on which the same shall be mounted, the following words, viz.: Entered according to act of Congress, in the year ———, by A. B., in the office of the Librarian of Congress, at Washington.

If any person shall insert or impress such notice, or words of the same purport, in or upon any book, map, chart, musical composition, print, cut, engraving, or photograph, or other articles herein named, for which he has not obtained a copyright, every person so offending shall forfeit and pay one hundred dollars; one moiety thereof to the person who shall sue for the same, and the other to the use of the United States, to be recovered by action in any court of competent jurisdiction.

If any person, after the recording of the title of any book as herein provided, shall, within the term limited, and without the consent of the proprietor of the copyright first obtained in writing, signed in presence of two or more witnesses, print, publish, or import, or, knowing the same to be so printed, published, or imported, shall sell or expose to sale any copy of such book, such offender shall forfeit every copy thereof to said proprietor, and shall also forfeit and pay such damages as may be recovered in a civil action by such proprietor in any court of competent jurisdiction.

If any person, after the recording of the title of any map, chart, musical composition, print, cut, engraving, or photograph, or chromo, or of the description of any painting, drawing, statue, statuary, or model or design intended to be perfected and executed as a work of the fine arts, as herein provided, shall, within the term limited, and without the consent of the proprietor of the copyright first obtained in writing signed in presence of two or more witnesses, engrave, etch, work, copy, print, publish, or import, either in whole or in part, or by varying the main design with intent to evade the law, or knowing the same to be so printed, published, or imported, shall sell or expose to sale any copy of such map or other article, as aforesaid, he shall forfeit to the said proprietor all the plates on which the same shall be copied, and every sheet thereof, either copied or printed, and shall further forfeit one dollar for every sheet of the same found in his possession, either printing, printed, copied, pub-lished, imported, or exposed for sale; and in case of a painting, statue, or statuary, he shall forfeit ten dollars for every copy of the same in his possession, or which have by him been sold or exposed for sale; one moiety thereof to the proprietor, and the other to the use of the United States, to be recovered by action in any court of competent jurisdiction.

Any person publicly performing or representing any dramatic composition for which a copyright has been obtained, without the consent of the proprietor thereof, or his heirs or assigns, shall be liable for damages therefor, to be recovered by action in any court of competent jurisdiction; said damages, in all cases, to be assessed at such sum, not less than one hundred dollars for the first, and fifty dollars for every subsequent performance, as to the court shall appear to be just.

Any person who shall print or publish any manuscript whatever, without the consent of the author or proprietor first obtained (if such author or proprietor be a citizen of the United States, or resident therein), shall be liable to said author or proprietor for all damages occasioned by such injury, to be recovered by action on the case in any court of competent jurisdiction.

Nothing herein contained shall be construed to prohibit the printing, publishing, importation, or sale of any book, map, chart, dramatic or musical composition, print, cut, engraving, or photograph, written, composed, or made by any person not a citizen of the United States nor resident therein.

No action shall be maintained in any case of forfeiture or penalty under the copyright laws unless the same is commenced within two years after the cause of action has arisen.

The following are the official directions for securing copyrights under the Revised Act of Congress, which took effect July 8, 1870, viz.: *

1. A printed copy of the title of the book, map, chart, dramatic or musical composition, engraving, cut, print, photograph, chromo, or design for a work of the fine arts, for which copyright is desired, must be sent by mail, addressed,

LIBRARIAN OF CONGRESS,
COPYRIGHT MATTER.   WASHINGTON, D.C.

This must be done before publication of the book or other article.

2. A fee of fifty cents, for recording the title of each book or other article, must be inclosed with the title as above, and fifty cents in addition (or $1 in all) for each certificate of copyright under seal of the Librarian of Congress, which will be transmitted by return mail.

3. Within ten days after publication of each book or other article, two complete copies of the best edition issued must be mailed to perfect the copyright, with the address,

LIBRARIAN OF CONGRESS,
COPYRIGHT MATTER.   WASHINGTON, D.C.

If the above direction is complied with, both books

and titles will come free of postage, and postmasters will give receipt for the same if requested. Without the deposit of copies above required, the copyright is void, and a penalty of $25 is incurred. No copy is required to be deposited elsewhere.

4. Copyrights recorded at a date prior to July 8, 1870, in any district clerk's office, do not require reentry at Washington. But one copy of each book or other article published since March 4, 1865, is required to be deposited in the Library of Congress, if not already done. Without such deposit, the copyright is void.

5. No copyright is valid unless notice is given by inserting in the several copies of every edition published, on the title-page or the page following, if it be a book ; or if a map, chart, musical composition, print, cut, engraving, photograph, painting, drawing, chromo, statue, statuary, or model or design intended to be perfected and completed as a work of the fine arts, by inscribing upon some portion of the face or front thereof, or on the face of the substance on which the same is mounted, the following words, viz.: Entered according to Act of Congress, in the year ——, by ——, in the office of the Librarian of Congress, at Washington.

6. Each copyright secures the exclusive liberty of publishing the book or article copyrighted for the term of twenty-eight years. At the end of this period, the author or designer may secure a renewal for the further term of fourteen years, making forty-two years in all.

7. Any copyright is assignable in law by any instrument of writing; but such assignment must be recorded in the office of the Librarian of Congress within sixty days from its date. The fee for this record is fifteen cents for every one hundred words, and ten cents for every one hundred words for a copy of the record of assignment.

8. In the case of books published in more than one volume, or of periodicals published in numbers, or of engravings, photographs, or other articles published with variations, a copyright must be taken out for each volume of a book, or number of a periodical, or variety, as to size or inscription, of any other article.

9. To secure a copyright for a painting, statue, or model or design, intended to be perfected as a work of the fine arts, so as to prevent infringement by copying or vending such design, a definite description of such work of art must accompany the application for copyright, and a photograph of the same, at least as large as cabinet size, should be mailed to the Librarian of Congress within ten days from the completion of the work.

10. In all cases where a copyright is desired for any article not a book, the applicant should state distinctly the title or description of the article in which he claims copyright.

11. Every applicant for a copyright must state distinctly in whose name the copyright is to be taken out, and whether title is claimed as author, designer, or proprietor.

The following points have been decided, from time to time, by American courts, in suits brought for an infringement of copyrights, viz.: A fair abridgment is no infringement of copyright. Neither is the publishing an abstract of a work in a magazine or review,—especially if it appear that the plaintiff himself has published extracts in a periodical paper. Nor is it a proof of a piracy, nor sufficient to support an action, that part of the work of one author is found in that of another; the question is, whether such transcribing is fairly done, with a view of compiling a useful book for the benefit of the public, or colorably merely, with a view to steal the copyright of the plaintiff. But if so much is copied as to form a substitute for the original work, or if that which purports to be an abridgment consists of extracts of the essential or most valuable portions of the original work, it is a piracy; and it is not necessary that the whole, or the larger part of it, should be taken ; it is only necessary that so much should be taken as sensibly to diminish the value of the original work, or substantially to appropriate the labors of the author. And it is of no consequence whether the invasion of the copyright be by a simple reprint, or by incorporating the whole, or a large portion thereof, in some larger work. Where A published a Life of Washington, containing 866 pages, of which 353 pages were copied from Sparks's Life and Writings of Washington, 64 pages being official letters and documents, and 255 pages being private letters of Washington, originally published by Mr. Sparks under a contract with the owners of the original papers of Washington, it was held that the work by A was an invasion of the copyright of Mr. Sparks. A copyright does not protect the author against a translation of his work from the language in which it is originally written into another language.

The following copyright decisions have recently been made in England :

1. The proprietor of a newspaper has, without registration under the copyright act, such a property in its contents as will entitle him to sue in respect of a piracy. But the piracy of a list of hounds is not a case for an interlocutory injunction, as a correct list is easily got, and it is liable to frequent changes.

2. Plaintiff wrote an essay for the Welsh Eisteddfod, to prove that the English are the descendants of the ancient Britons, which he published. Defendant afterwards did the like. His book was plaintiff's in theory, arrangement, and, to a great degree, in the citation of authorities. The latter facts were explained by both parties having taken their references from Pritchard, and the theory by the occasion of writing. Two authorities were seemingly taken from the plaintiff, and certain results were based upon his tables. The writing was the defendant's. Held that plaintiff was not entitled to an injunction.

Defendant had a right to take authorities from Pritchard, even though sent there by plaintiff's book which took the same. An author has no monopoly in a theory propounded by him.

In cases of literary piracy the defendant is to account for every copy of his book sold, as if it had been a copy of the plaintiff's.

3. Although a rival publisher is not justified in copying slips cut from a directory previously published by another party, by having sent out canvassers to verify them, and to obtain leave of those whose names were on the slips to publish them in that form, he may use such slips to direct his canvassers where to go for the purpose of obtaining the addresses anew.

Corners.—Designs prepared in metal for the ornamentation of the corners of pages or of jobs. A great variety are supplied by American typefounders. Below are specimens.

Correct.—For correcting in metal, see CORRECTING. For correcting proofs, see PROOF-READING.

Correcting.—The correction of the errors in the types that the compositor has made, and also the typographical arrangement of such changes, modifications, or alterations as the author or editor, on mature consideration, deems necessary. In piecework, or matter paid for by the thousand ems, corrections of the class first named are made by the compositor at his own cost, while changes of the second class are termed office corrections, and are made either at the cost of the office (if it is a newspaper establishment) or at the cost of the author or publisher, in a book or job office. As soon as the proof has been read and given out, the compositor should lay up his form (unless his matter is on a galley) and unlock it all around, being careful not to leave the quoins too loose, as the matter may be squabbled, or types fall out at the ends of the lines. He should then set up the types required for the corrections in his stick, with a few spaces on a piece of paper, or, in a small tray with partitions in it, for this is more convenient. Taking his bodkin in his right hand, the corrector should place the point of it against the end of the line he wishes to correct, and with the middle finger of his left hand against the other end of the line, raise it altogether, high enough to give him a clear view of the spacing. He can then change the faulty letter, and make the necessary alterations in the spacing, before dropping the line. By this method the type will not be injured, as it often is when the bodkin is forced into the sides or heads, and regularity in the spacing may be secured, as well as much time saved. The best book compositors take the line out of the page and place it in their composing-stick, whenever the correction to be made requires an alteration in spacing, and thus secure absolute accuracy in justification. In tables, or in any matter in which rules prevent the type being raised in lines, the letters must be lifted singly, and great care will be necessary to avoid injuring the types. The bodkin should touch the neck of the letter, between the shank and the face, drawing it just high enough above the other letters to allow the taking hold of it with the forefinger and thumb of the left hand. In this operation as small an angle from the perpendicular as possible should be made with the blade of the bodkin, in order that it may not touch any of the surrounding types, as a trifling graze will injure the faces of the letters near it. It is better to use a pair of watchmaker's nippers.

Correspondent.—One who corresponds with, or furnishes information to, a periodical publication from comparatively distant points. Our own correspondent, regular correspondent, special correspondent, etc., play an important part in the preparation of matter for modern newspapers, and the matter they forward by mail or telegraph constitutes a considerable proportion of the copy furnished to such publications.

Coster, Laurentius.—See KOSTER.

Cotton Paper.—The most ancient manuscript in cotton paper, with a date, 1050, is in the Royal Library at Paris; another in the emperor's library, at Vienna, bears the date of 1095; but as the manuscripts without a date are comparatively more numerous than those which are dated, Father Montfaucon, who on these subjects is great authority, on account of his diligence and the extent of his researches, by comparing the writing discovered some of the tenth century. He contended that *charta bombycine*, or cotton paper, was discovered in the empire of the east towards the end of the ninth or early in the tenth century. In the march of improvement, cotton paper preceded linen paper, and in Europe its construction was the first transition step from vellum and parchment.

Cottrell & Babcock Presses.—These presses are of two general descriptions: first, first-class drum cylinders, made of various sizes from 19 by 24 to 41 by 60 inches; and second, country newspaper and job presses, made of two sizes, 31 by 46 and 32 by 50. The accompanying engraving illustrates the Cottrell & Babcock first-class drum cylinder.

In describing this machine the manufacturers enumerate among the most recent improvements they have adopted, the well-fountain so arranged as to

COTTRELL & BABCOCK FIRST-CLASS DRUM CYLINDER PRESS.

work with the smallest possible quantity of ink, and to be easily cleaned in a moment; an improved gripper motion, with registering rack adjustable by screw, insuring a perfect register; and a superior pointing apparatus, with discs in the feed table so arranged that they can be adjusted in a moment to suit any sized sheet.

Counter.—A small machine which, when attached to the printing-presses of various descriptions, indicates the number of sheets printed.

Counter-Proof.—In engraving, a print taken off from another just printed, which, by being pressed, gives the figure to the former, but inverted, and of course in the same position as that of the plate from which the first is printed, the object being to inspect the state of the plate.

who was the first American press-maker to engage actively in the manufacture of country presses.

Coupon Tickets.—See JOB PRINTING.

Cover.—In a general sense, that which is laid over something else. In bookbinding, the material used on the outer surface of a bound book; or, where only one substance is employed, the whole binding is sometimes called a cover; as, board covers. In printing, the outer leaves of bound or stitched pamphlets, magazines, and similar works, when they are of paper of a different quality or color from the inner leaves, are called covers.

Cover Paper.—Paper made for the covers of pamphlets, etc., many colors and grades being manufactured.

Cramped.—Work is said to be cramped when

CROCHET TYPE.

Country Presses.—This general term is used to designate cylinder presses made by different manufacturers, for use in country newspaper offices, where it is generally desirable that they should be driven by hand-power instead of by steam.

CAMPBELL COUNTRY PRESS.

The annexed cut illustrates the Campbell Country Press, made by Andrew Campbell, of New York,
9

blanks are used sparingly, short pages avoided, and the matter less spread than usual, to get a certain quantity into a given number of pages.

Crochet Type.—A type used to form pages representing patterns of crochet-work, many of which consist of pictures of flowers, animals, landscapes, etc. In the hands of a skillful compositor it can be made to give a fair representation of many objects. The accompanying illustration represents a design for the cover of a box to hold counters or cards, which was composed in crochet type by Mr. William F. Lacy, at the Collins Printing House in Philadelphia.

Cross-bar.—The long and short crosses of a chase, which are bars of iron, crossing each other at right angles, and dovetailed into the rim, dividing it into four parts.

Crotchets,—otherwise called brackets ([ ]), are

used to inclose a word or sentence intended to supply some deficiency or to rectify some mistake.

Crowd.—The name given to sub-organizations of the compositors in daily newspaper offices, regulating what portion of them shall be on duty at given periods. Such an organization is also sometimes called a phalanx.

Crown-paper.—Paper of a particular size, so named because it formerly had the water-mark of a crown. American crown-paper is 15 by 19 inches.

Cunabula.—The extant copies of the first or earliest printed books, or of such as were printed in the fifteenth century.

Cut-in Notes.—Side-notes let into the text, the lines of which are shortened to receive them.

Cuts.—See Wood Engravings.

Cutting Machine.—See Paper-Cutting Machines.

Cutting the Frisket.—Cutting off those parts of the frisket which would otherwise intercept the print.

Cylinder-Presses.—It is a remarkable fact in the history of printing, that the art was practiced for nearly four centuries before any better or quicker method of making impressions was devised than that afforded by a hand-press. The following article from the London Times of November 29, 1814, which was the first newspaper ever printed by a cylinder or power-press, affords a good indication of the wonder and admiration excited at that day by the new invention:

Our journal of this day presents to the public the practical result of the greatest improvement connected with printing, since the discovery of the art itself. The reader of this paragraph now holds in his hand one of the many thousand impressions of the Times newspaper which were taken off last night by a mechanical apparatus. A system of machinery, almost organic, has been devised and arranged, which, while it relieves the human frame of its most laborious efforts in printing, far exceeds all human powers in rapidity and dispatch. That the magnitude of the invention may be justly appreciated by its effects, we shall inform the public that, after the letters are placed by the compositors, and inclosed in what is called the form, little more remains for man to do than to attend upon and watch this unconscious agent in its operations. The machine is then merely supplied with paper; itself places the form, inks it, adjusts the paper to the form newly inked, stamps the sheet, and gives it forth to the hands of the attendant, at the same time withdrawing the form for a fresh coat of ink, which itself again distributes, to meet the ensuing sheet now advancing for impression; and the whole of these complicated acts are performed with such a velocity and simultaneousness of movement, that not less than eleven hundred sheets are impressed in one hour.

That the completion of an invention of this kind, not the effect of chance, but the result of mechanical combinations methodically arranged in the mind of

the artist, should be attended with many obstructions and much delay, may be readily admitted. Our share in this event has, indeed, only been the application of the discovery, under an agreement with the patentees, to our own particular business; yet few can conceive—even with this limited interest—the various disappointments and deep anxiety to which we have for a long course of time been subjected.

Of the person who made this discovery, we have but little to add. Sir Christopher Wren's noblest monument is to be found in the buildings which he erected, so is the best tribute of praise, which we are capable of offering to the inventor of the printing-machine, comprised in the preceding description, which we have feebly sketched, of the powers and utility of his invention. It must suffice to say that he is a Saxon by birth, that his name is Koenig, and that the invention has been executed under the direction of his friend and countryman, Bauer.

—At the present day thousands of American printing-offices have presses of greater capacity than that which excited the enthusiastic admiration of the Times, sixty years ago, while in hundreds of American newspaper offices it would fall infinitely behind present requirements.

Ever since the practicability of using a cylinder in press-work was demonstrated, improvements and extensions of this idea have been progressing, until at the present day there are two-, four-, six-, eight-, and ten- cylinder-presses,—presses in which the type or stereotype plates are placed on cylinders, and cylinder-presses on which very fine, as well as very rapid, press-work is executed.

In the United States, an immense amount of care, ingenuity, and talent has been displayed by various press-manufacturers, in improving cylinder-presses and in adapting them to various purposes; and the large number now in use is a sufficient proof of their popularity among American printers.

Cylinder-presses have nevertheless had to contend against some serious prejudices. It has been alleged that they are not well adapted to fine work, that they cannot be relied upon for accurate register, and that they wear out type more rapidly than bed-and-platen presses. Any force there may have been originally in these objections, however, has been much weakened, if not entirely destroyed, by modern improvements in cylinder-presses. At the present day, when they are supplied with a sufficient number of rollers, they print wood-engravings in a very superior manner. If the register becomes inaccurate, from the wear of the press, this is often owing, in a large degree, to carelessness, either in feeding, or in the arrangement of the nippers which hold the sheet, or to continued abuse of the press. The practice, which is far too common, of frequently putting on or taking off impression by shifting the position of the cylinder, on either side, is fraught with danger, and does more injury to cylinder-presses than any other single cause. The course adopted by careful pressmen, of increasing or diminishing impression solely by increasing or diminishing the thickness of blankets, paper, packing, or other matter between the cylinder and the type, is worthy of universal imitation. The enthusiastic advocates of drum-cylinder-presses contend that they never wear type more rapidly than bed-and-platen presses, except when a derangement of the machinery causes a slur. When this happens, the defect should be remedied as speedily as possible. At other times, it is alleged that as a harder blanket can be used on cylinder-presses than on bed-and-platen presses, the former, with proper care, wear out type less rapidly than the latter; and it is also said that, for a similar reason, type so much worn as to have no longer a presentable appearance when printed on a bed-and-platen press may be made to look passably well if printed on a cylinder-press.

D.

Dactyl.—In English verse, that measure in which an accented syllable is followed by two unaccented syllables—as in the word quantity. In Greek and Latin poetry, a metrical foot consisting of one long and two short syllables.

Dagger.—When used as a reference-mark, the dagger (†) stands next in order after the star. It is also called obelisk.

Dalton, Michael.—The oldest practical type-founder in Boston, Mass. He was born in Boston, May 23, 1800, and, leaving school at the early age of 14, was an apprentice to the business of making mathematical instruments from that period until he attained the age of 19, when he entered the branch type-foundry established by Elihu White in Boston. In that foundry he was first engaged as a caster, and subsequently as a dresser, fitter, mould-maker, etc. He has ever since been actively engaged as a type-founder, thus performing continuous service for a period of more than fifty years, and during a large portion of this time he was a member of the firm of Phelps & Dalton.

Dandy, or Dandy-Roller.—A roller sieve used in machinery for making paper, to press out water from the pulp and set the paper. The instrument used to form the water-mark in paper is also called a dandy.

Dash.—A mark or line, thus (—), in writing or printing, denoting a sudden break, stop, or transition in a sentence, or an abrupt change in its construction, a long or significant pause, or an unexpected or epigrammatic turn of sentiment. Dashes are also sometimes used instead of marks of parenthesis.

Two-em (——) and three-em dashes (———) are also cast: they are used under the headings in tabular work, and for various other purposes.

The dash most frequently used (—) is called, by way of distinction, em dash; while a dash of half its length (-) is called en dash.

A dash stands for a sign of repetition in catalogues of goods, where it implies ditto; and in catalogues of books, where it is used instead of repeating the author's name with the title of every separate treatise of his writing; but no sign of repetition should be at the top of a page, for there the name of the author or of the merchandise should be set out again at length. A dash likewise stands for to, or till: as, chap. xvi. 3–17; that is, from the third to the seventeenth verse, inclusive—an en dash being generally used for this purpose.

A great variety of brass, type-metal, and wood dashes, plain and ornamental, are made, which are used as dividing lines between articles, chapters, etc., or between different parts of various descriptions of job-work.

They are called small dashes, fancy dashes, telegraph dashes, news dashes, local dashes, etc. A plain-rule dash is formed of plain brass rule, thus:

A *Parallel dash*, of parallel rule, thus:

A *Double Rule dash*, is made of double rule, thus:

Date.—That addition to a document, inscription, coin, etc., which specifies the time of its delivery or execution; also the point of time at which a transaction takes place. In typography, dates are expressed variously, either by Roman or Arabic numerals, or by letters, according to taste and the requirements of the case.

Davis's Oscillating Power Press.—A press, formerly made in the United States, of various sizes, from half-medium to super-royal, in which no strings or tapes were used in taking the sheets in or out. Among the advantages claimed for it were good register, saving of time in making ready a form, and a convenient method of regulating impression.

Day, John.—An eminent English printer, born in 1522, died 1584. This name, famous among typographers, has been variously spelled Daye, Daie, and D'Aije. John Day began to print in 1546, and labored zealously in the cause of the Reformation. His device—a rising sun with a man awakening a slumbering figure in the foreground, and the motto: Arise, for it is Day—was intended to convey an expression of his religious devotion to the suffering cause, as well as a pun upon his name; and with the same intention his office was styled—at the sign of the Resurrection. Known as a friend of Rogers and Fox, and as a publisher of Protestant books, he was imprisoned at the commencement of Queen Mary's reign, and fled afterwards to the Continent, where he remained until 1556. On the accession of Elizabeth, Day became eminent as a printer, and held some of the highest offices in the Stationers' Company from 1566 to 1580. He was especially befriended by Bishop Parker, the editor of the Bishops' Bible, which became the accepted version under Elizabeth, and was employed by him in many of the controversial publications arising between the Catholics and Protestants. The English printing of the time was almost entirely in black letter, of a rude and uncouth style, Roman type being used only occasionally to mark quotations. Bishop Parker, a patron of fine printing, supplied Day with the means of casting what was called the Italian letter, and in consequence one of Parker's own works was printed in a full-sized, close, but flowing italic character. Under the Bishop's patronage, Day also cut the first Saxon letter, used in a Saxon homily published by Parker in 1567, and in the Saxon Gospels, edited by Fox under the patronage of the Bishop in 1571. This eminent printer also made many improvements on the Greek and Roman type. Two hundred and forty-five works are known bearing his imprint, among which were Tyndale's Bible of 1549, and Matthew's Bible, 1551. Many of his publications were handsomely illustrated.

John Day was twice married, and had by each wife thirteen children, one of whom, Richard Day, succeeded his father as a printer, devoting himself exclusively to religious publications, and using as a device three lilies surrounded by thorns, with the text from the Vulgate, *Sicut Lilium in Spinæ* (As the lily among thorns). Richard abandoned printing to succeed Fox as a minister at Reigate, and two other members of this numerous family also became clergymen and authors.

John Day was buried at Bradley-Parva, in Suffolk, and upon a curious mural entablature in the chancel are inlaid in brass the effigies of himself and his first wife, kneeling against a table, before which are two babes in swaddling clothes, while behind the figure of Day are grouped six sons, and behind his wife five daughters. Beneath are the following lines, cut in old English letter:

Here lyes the Daye, that darkness could not blind,
When popish fogges had overcaste the sunne,
This Daye the cruell nights did leave behind,
To view, and shew what blodi actes were donne.
He set a Fox to wright how martyrs runne,
By death to lyfe. Fox ventured paynes and health,
To give them light; Daye spent in print his wealth.
But God with gayne returned his wealth agayne,
And gave to him as he gave to the poore.
Two wyves he had, pertakers of his payne,
Each wyfe twelve babes, and each of them one more:
Als (i. e. *Alice*) was the last encreaser of his store,
Who mourning long for being left alone,
Set up this tombe, herself turn'd to a stone.
                                        Obiit 23 July, 1584.

John Day is supposed to be the ancestor of Stephen Daye, the first printer in the present limits of the United States.

Daye, Stephen.—The first printer in the American colonies, born in England, 1611, died in Cambridge, Massachusetts, 1668. Stephen Daye was engaged in England by the Rev. Jesse Glover to conduct the printing-press purchased in that country to be erected in conjunction with the college of Cambridge. Mr. Glover died upon the passage, and Daye established the press in January, 1639, his first issue bearing the singularly appropriate name of The Freeman's Oath. (See FREEMAN'S OATH.) He also published in the same year an Almanac,

by William Pierce, mariner, the well-known sailor, who had been in command of the Ann in 1623, and subsequently of the Mayflower and the Lyon. The first book was published in 1640, being the celebrated Bay Psalm Book, translated from the Hebrew by John Eliot and the Rev. Mr. Weld. It was a crown octavo of three hundred pages, bound in parchment, and very rude in execution. This version passed through seventy editions, and maintained its popularity for more than a century. The first edition in England was printed soon after its production in America, and the last in 1754. In Scotland it was also received with great favor, the twenty-second and last edition appearing in that country in 1759. Stephen Daye also printed the Body of Liberties, containing one hundred laws of the Colony, drawn up by the Rev. Mr. Ward, of Ipswich, author of The Simple Cobbler of Agawam.

The General Court of Massachusetts in 1641 granted three hundred acres of land to Daye as being the first that set upon printing; but he appears to have suffered from poverty, and sixteen years afterwards petitioned for the confirmation of the grant and for £100 of unpaid wages. Stephen Daye relinquished the conduct of the press in 1649 to Samuel Green, and continued to act as foreman to his successor. Stephen Daye is believed to have printed about a dozen books; but they all appeared without any imprint.

Dead-head.—A colloquialism in use in America to express any person who obtains something of commercial value without special charge; but generally restricted to such as receive free entrance into places of public entertainment, free passage in public conveyances, and gratuitous use of telegraph and express facilities. It is often applied to those members of the press who receive tickets free of charge as a means of prosecuting their labors as reporters or critics. An equivalent is found in the phrase—He has his hat chalked, and the word, in its abbreviated form, is written D. H.

Dead-horse.—Matter charged before it is set, or work for which a journeyman printer has been paid before the labor was actually performed.

Dedication.—A preface containing a complimentary address from the author to a particular person. By modern usage the dedication follows the title, and seldom exceeds one page. It is generally set in small capitals of different sizes, neatly displayed; the name of the person to whom the work is dedicated being in large capitals, and such terms as your humble servant, etc., in smaller type.

Dedications became customary in the first century before the Christian era, many of them being addressed to Mæcenas. Among the Romans the most famous were those of Horace, Virgil, Cicero, and Lucretius. In the degraded ages of literature the dedication was frequently a mere servile compliment to a wealthy patron as a means of gaining his bounty, and was often written by distinguished and impoverished authors for inferior writers, who hoped by a brilliant compliment to secure remuneration from a patron, who would never read farther than the dedicatory epistle eulogizing his own virtues. After the revival of learning in Europe, books were almost invariably preceded by dedications, and the custom has only been abandoned since, in the advance of modern progress, a Republic of Letters has been established, in which the enfranchised author need ask no patronage from the wealthy or the great, appealing only to the taste and discernment of an immense reading public. Of late years, dedications have been almost entirely abandoned, except as occasional tributes of love and respect, such as a graceful compliment from a child to a parent, from a husband to a wife, from one author to another, or from an author to the class he specially addresses, and the growth of literature might readily be traced by the gradual alteration in the tone of these prefatory letters exhibiting the stages by which the author has become one of the independent powers of the earth. A splendid specimen of the language of the time, as well as of the wonderful obsequiousness to rank, is presented in the extraordinarily labored dedication of the received English version of the Scriptures, beginning thus:

To the most high and mighty Prince, James. By the Grace of God, King of Great Britain, France and Ireland. Defender of the Faith. The translators of the Bible wish Grace, Mercy and Peace through Jesus Christ our Lord. Great and manifold were the blessings, most dread Sovereign, which Almighty God, the Father of all mercies, bestowed upon us as the people of England, when first he sent Your Majesty's Royal Person to rule over us. For whereas it was the expectation of many, who wished not well unto our Zion, that, upon the setting of that bright Occidental Star, Queen Elizabeth, of most happy memory, some thick and palpable clouds of darkness would so have overshadowed this land, that men should have been in doubt which way they were to walk, and that it should hardly be known who was to direct the unsettled State; the appearance of Your Majesty, as of the Sun in his strength, instantly dispelled those supposed and surmised mists, etc., etc.

King James, not satisfied with inducing the Dutch government to exile seven hundred families of Arminians, entered the controversial lists pen in hand, with a treatise dedicated thus:

To the honour of our Lord and Saviour Jesus Christ, the eternal Son of the eternal Father, the only theanthropos, mediator, and reconciler of mankind, in sign of thankfulness his most humble and obliged servant, James, by the grace of God, King of Great Britain, France and Ireland, Defender of the Faith, doth dedicate and consecrate this his declaration.

It may be interesting to printers to know that John Norton sturdily refused to print this book without being paid beforehand, and that the royal author was forced to comply with the demand.

But perhaps nowhere in English literature can be found more fulsome adulation than in the dedication in which Jeremy Taylor offers his two books, like the widow's two mites, to Charles II., and after quoting the appropriate scripture to describe the depths of disgrace reached by the nation under the Commonwealth, welcomes the Stuart back to his throne with a gratitude and obedience due only to Deity. Many a brave blow has been struck upon the battle-fields of literature between the day when a man of such learning as Jeremy Taylor so addressed the profligate Stuart, and our own time when the biblical student, Nathaniel West, dedicated the labor of a life of research, To all the lovers of God's Holy Word.

A curious incident in regard to the dedication of Castell's Polyglot Bible has given that work a special interest to book-collectors. Oliver Cromwell was so much interested in its publication that he ordered the paper to be imported free of all duties, and the work was dedicated to him. A large number of copies remained, however, unsold upon the accession of Charles II., and the thrifty and prudent editor continued to make them available by canceling the last two pages of the dedication, adding three new ones, and inscribing the whole to Charles. The ingenuity of the alterations to suit the time has rendered the book one of the curiosities of literature, the republican copies being quite scarce and the loyal ones numerous.

Scott afterwards deplored that the genius of John Dryden had fallen upon such an evil day; and every sincere lover of literature must look with especial shame upon the age immediately following the Restoration. It was notorious, during the period of Dryden's literary supremacy, that the dedication of a book was worth from twenty to fifty pounds, according to the rank and liberality of the patron, and from the time of the Revolution of 1688, to the accession of George I., dedications of plays could be readily bought at a price varying from five to ten guineas each, while some freak of fashion at the latter period suddenly caused a rise to double the former rates.

It is said that Pope was secured by his good fortune from the temptation to barter his poetry for pelf; but the number of noble and wealthy names crowded into his addresses would seem either to disprove this assertion, or to prove that he, too, dearly loved a lord, as, for instance, the lines to Lord Lansdowne:

Granville commands; your aid, O Muses, bring;
What Muse for Granville can refuse to sing?

Young said, very smoothly,—

Shall poesy, like law, turn wrong to right,
And dedications wash an Ethiop white?

Yet the long line of noble names that herald his own verses exhibit, in the strongest light, that thirst for office which disgraced his life and genius, even without the added proof of the flattering words,—

Dorset! lend your ear,
And patronize a Muse you cannot fear;
To poets sacred is a Dorset's name,
Their wonted passport through the gates of fame.

The first defense of his noble craft against venality in this particular is perhaps due to Dean Swift, who dedicated The Tale of a Tub to his Royal Highness Prince Posterity, and he pointed his meaning by adding another address, purporting to be from the bookseller to Lord Somers, complaining that the author had dedicated the work to a person not at all regarded by the present generation, and severely satirizing the customary panegyrics.

That the practice still continued to prevail, can be seen by the frequently quoted story of Dr. Johnson's refusal to dedicate his dictionary to Lord Chesterfield, and the surprise and admiration caused by the lexicographer's valiant conduct; and the knowledge of this fact throws new lustre upon the simple eloquence with which Oliver Goldsmith addressed the Deserted Village to Sir Joshua Reynolds:

I can have no expectation, in an address of this kind, either to add to your reputation, or to establish my own. You can gain nothing from my admiration, as I am ignorant of that art in which you are said to excel; and I may lose much by the severity of your judgment, as few have a juster taste in poetry than you. Setting interest, therefore, aside, to which I never paid much attention, I must be indulged at present in following my affections. The only dedication I ever made was to my brother, because I loved him better than most other men. He is since dead. Permit me to inscribe this to you.

In the middle of the seventeenth century, when every adulatory adjective was worth its weight in coin, Thomas Fuller contrived to arrange his Church History by an ingenious succession of title-pages and other subdivisions, so as to admit of separate dedications to about fifty patrons, and yet cleverly reserve four pages at the end for a patroness. Some years later, Motteux, an unlucky Norman, who followed authorship in England, was not able to spice his dish of flattery to the taste of his patron, and was compelled to bear the mortification of seeing the gentleman write the panegyric upon himself; but to add to his discomfiture, the patron was so unfortunate in his expressions that the affair became public, and poor Motteux had also to bear the obloquy of—being found out.

In France, at the same period, literature was in an equally degraded condition, and Cardinal Richelieu has been described as a gigantic baby of adulation crammed with the soft pap of dedications. The amount and quality that he was ready to swallow can be inferred from the following address selected from many of a similar kind:

Who has seen your face without being seized by those softening terrors which made the prophets shudder when God showed the beams of his glory? But as He whom they dared not approach in the burning bush and in the voice of thunders appeared to them sometimes in the freshness of the zephyrs, so the softness of your countenance dissipates at the same time and changes into dew the light clouds that veil its majesty.

It is not surprising that in a second edition of one of these works, published after Richelieu's death, the dedication was slightly changed and addressed to Jesus Christ.

When the fashion for addresses to eminent officials was at its height in France, the vexatious and ridiculous position of the literati was sharply satirized by an author who dedicated his book to the Brazen Horse on the Pont Neuf, in the confidence that he was a patron who would long remain in place. During the reign of Louis XIV. the dedications were contemptible in their servility, and it is stated that those addressed to the Dauphin were so exaggerated that his tutor refused to allow them to be presented, and upon discovering the young prince perusing one, ordered him to read it aloud, that he might feel to the utmost the utter impropriety of the panegyric. In 1699, the Duke of Shrewsbury presented Bayle with two hundred guineas for the dedication of his dictionary, but the author returned the gift with the explanation that he had so often ridiculed dedications that he could not consistently insert one in his own book.

Among the most elegant dedications in the English language are those prefixed to the Spectator by Addison; and equally remarkable for simple beauty and earnestness of feeling are the poetical addresses with which Walter Scott opened the several cantos of Marmion.

In the true spirit of literary equality, Lord Byron dedicated Cain to Walter Scott, the Giaour to Rogers, and opened Werner with these words:—To the illustrious Goethe, by one of his humblest admirers, this tragedy is dedicated;—and under the same impulse Judge Bouvier dedicated his law dictionary to Judge Story. The station of true dignity reached and held by the modern author is well shown by comparing the servility of Jeremy Taylor to Charles II., with the exceedingly moderate expression of loyalty by which the present laureate of England bases his dedication to the Queen solely on the hope that she will so continue to reign that the verdict of the future will be that

Her court was pure; her life serene;
God gave her peace; her land reposed;
A thousand claims to reverence closed
In her as Mother, Wife, and Queen;

And statesmen at her council met
Who knew the seasons, when to take
Occasion by the hand, and make
The bounds of freedom wider yet

By shaping some august decree,
Which kept the throne unshaken still,
Broad-based upon her people's will,
And compassed by the inviolate sea.

Degener & Weiler's Liberty Card and Job Presses.—These presses, of comparatively recent American invention, obtained prize medals at the London Exhibition of 1862, and the Paris Exposition of 1867. They are made of three sizes. Among the advantages claimed for them are clearness and distinctness of impression; simplicity, strength, and durability; convenience of making ready, adjusting, cleaning, and correcting. (See page 135.)

Dekle.—A thin frame of wood in a paper-making machine, set on the edge of the mould, along which the pulp passes; it serves to regulate the width of the sheet.

LIBERTY CARD AND JOB PRESS.

Dele.—A mark used on the margin of a proof, or in copy, to indicate that a letter, word, line, sentence, paragraph, or larger amount of matter should be blotted out or expunged. (See PROOF-READING.)

Delete.—To erase, blot out, or omit words or paragraphs in copy, or in proof.

Delphin.—The usual name given to the edition of the Latin classics prepared by order of Louis XIV., and styled *in usum Delphini*, or for the use of the Dauphin. These works were greatly esteemed for their accuracy, and were prepared under the personal supervision of Montausier, the governor of the Dauphin, with the assistance of Bossuet and Huet, the preceptors of that prince.

Demy.—Paper one size smaller than folio-post, and one size larger than crown. (See DIMENSIONS OF PAPER.) Pertaining to, or made of, demy paper, as a demy book.

Dental.—Formed by the aid of the teeth;—said of certain articulations, and the letters representing them; as, s and z are dental letters.

Derriey, Charles.—A Parisian type-founder of the present day, who has won an extended reputation for his ingenuity in devising new borders, ornaments, etc., and his skill in printing them. His color-work, especially, has been much admired, and it has rarely been equaled. He is also the inventor of circular quadrats.

Descending Letters.—The letters so called are g, j, p, q, y, of the lower case. In Italic fonts, the letter f is both ascending and descending.

Design.—Strictly, the idea formed in the mind of an artist on any particular subject, and which he intends to convey to some medium, as a means of making it known to others. The word is also frequently used as a synonym for picture or sketch.

Devices, Printers'.—In the earlier stages of the typographic art, emblems or devices were much used, serving as a species of trade-mark, but they have been gradually abandoned by the printers, and are now seldom seen except as used by the publishers, who still preserve the very patent emblems of the student's lamp, the book, the pen, and similar designs. During the period of their popularity much ingenuity was lavished upon their construction, and especially that peculiar wit which makes printers' puns so rich a department of literature. The use of devices was contemporaneous with the very birth of the art, for the great Mentz Bible is adorned with an emblem consisting of two shields linked together by and suspended from a tree-branch; upon these shields is displayed the printer's rule, chosen both by Fust and Schoeffer as the symbol most significant of the new art which they were exhibiting to a wondering world. Frederick III., Emperor of Germany, a man of learning, must have welcomed the new art with great warmth, for it is said that he himself designed the coat of arms which he granted to the German printers, and which is still used by them as well as by typographers in other countries as the heraldic arms appropriate to the art. This escutcheon bears the imperial eagle, holding in his right claw the copy-holder with copy, and in the left a composing-stick; above which is a large helmet surmounted by a crown, from which rises a griffin bearing the inking-balls. The precise date of the imperial recognition is not known; it was probably made soon after the art was discovered, and it must have been early, as Frederick died in 1493. The first emblems were of course simple and often very rude, frequently being merely a circle crossed or divided in some special fashion, and containing the initials of the artist. The arms of cities and countries were also used and varied according to the taste or necessities of the artist, as expressing his place of residence or in compliment to some powerful patron. Coats of arms were especially common in law books, where the printer often waived his privilege of using his own device, as in the case of Wynkyn de Worde. With the growing taste for such decorations, much skill and fancy were displayed in their invention; and it is but just to suppose that in some instances the play upon words incorporated in the devices was intended as a screen, or species of secret sign by which the printer of anonymous publications might escape the dangers of the penal code, while his handiwork would be recognized by the brethren of the craft. The emblems were generally merely fanciful creations of the typographers; but when the Emperor Maximilian granted a coat of arms to the son of Schoeffer, it furnished one of the first examples of the pictured puns which have since been so abundant in the profession. This coat of arms, embracing the original device of the printer's rule, added a shepherd (Schoeffer) with his sheep, as the illustration of the family name. That these devices were accepted as a trade-mark, is evident from a memorial published by Aldus in 1503, complaining that the printers of Lyons counterfeited his famous anchor and dolphin to facilitate the sale of their productions; while the preface to the Aldine Livy of 1518 ridicules the clumsy efforts of other imitators.

The classical simplicity of the dolphin gracefully

THOMAS WOODCOCK

WILLIAM VOSTERMANN

FUST AND SCHOEFFER

JOHN DAY, 1546-1584

ALDUS

WILLIAM CAXTON, 1478-1491.

JOHANN FROBEN

PRINTERS' DEVICES.

coiled around the anchor, was the appropriate device of the scholarly Manutius; and many other leading typographers followed in the same vein. The Elzevirs, many in number, multitudinous in works, assumed most significantly the prolific olive, crowned by Grecian fable as the greatest blessing to mankind and the gift of the wise Minerva. Great among the great, Plantin breathed the very spirit that directed his labors in the emblem of a hand and compass with the motto Labor and constancy. Froben used a crowned caduceus surmounted by a dove, which led

PRINTERS' COAT OF ARMS GRANTED BY FREDERICK III.

the learned Erasmus to say that the erudite typographer did indeed join the wisdom of the serpent to the simplicity of the dove. Several of the other learned printers of Basle used the palm-tree. The great family of Marnef assumed the pelican tearing her breast to nourish her young; and Destresius used the same emblem, making the moral more apparent by the motto, Without the shedding of blood there is no remission of sins.

Quaintness, rather than grace, seems to have been the aim of the early devices, many of them partaking

of the heavy Gothic style of the accompanying text, as in the huge, double-headed eagle of Vostreman; but in artistic beauty, the emblem of Oporinus has rarely been surpassed. The buoyant figure of Arion, poised upon the dolphin, seems borne upon the wind, while every line, replete with grace, conveys the inspiration of genius, and the purity and power in the image repeat the spirit of its legend, Valor and virtue surmount all things. Admirable, too, is the Saturn of Colinæus; and the bold and beautiful emblem of the Gioleti, with its grand eagle proudly facing the sun, and the motto, Ever the same. Full of grace and power, also, are the griffin of the Gryphii, and the splendid Pegasus on which the Wichels rode to fame. Worthy to be classed with these is the curious symbol of Jerome Scot, picturing a female figure resting upon the globe, which seems to obey the slightest touch upon the reins held in her grasp.

Among the largest of the devices ranks the three crowned figures of Eustace, probably intended to signify the Pope, the Emperor, and the King of France. Gigantic, too, are the savage lion of Mylius of Strasburg, and the three ferocious beasts of Brylinger, while the huge lion of Couteau rests peacefully upon a shield of flowers. The more romantic De Tournes displayed a Cupid shielding his eyes from the sun; and the Harduins selected Hercules rescuing Dejanira from the Centaurs.

More prosaic was the favorite English utilitarian fancy of drawing the device from the residence of the printer; thus, Byddell, living at the sign of Our Lady of Pity, took a female figure pouring from one hand Gratia, and from the other Charitas; Copeland, residing at the Rose Garden, garlanded his monogram with roses; Rastell, of the Mermaid, quartered her in his device; and Lawrence Andrew, at the Golden Cross, also contrived a small pun out of a cross of St. Andrew. The Frenchman Tory was more successful, transforming his cracked pot into a classic vase, shattered by a spear and surrounded by graceful symbols.

The emblems of the English typographers have been singularly rude and ungraceful, from the heavy design of Caxton until the final abandonment of their use; but they were often intended to convey a moral

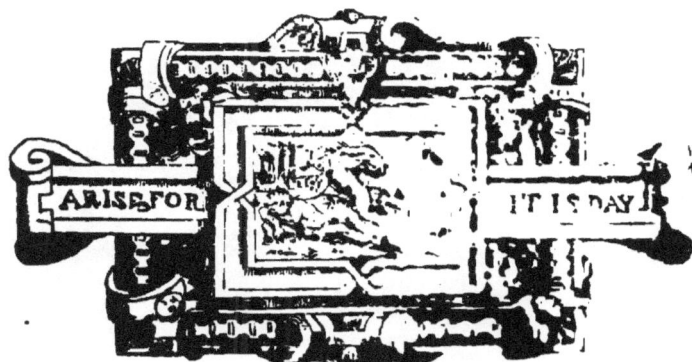

PRINTERS' DEVICES

THOMAS WOODCOCK

WILLIAM VOSTERMANN

FUST AND SCHOEFFER

ARISE FOR   IT IS DAY.

JOHN DAY, 1546-1584

ALDUS

WILLIAM CAXTON, 1476-1491

JOHANN FROBEN

PRINTERS' DEVICES.

or religious idea: thus, Tindale's sacrifice of Isaac was a sufficiently fair conception; and it is only the art that is to blame when we fear that the heavenly messenger will inevitably have his fingers cut off by Abraham's broad sword.

Certain plain and exceedingly patent emblems seem to have been held as a common stock among the typographers of all countries; thus, a globe was adopted by Oglin, Notary, Martens, Thanner, and Weissemburger. Short surrounded his book with a glory; Martens, of Loven, placed his in a window; and Scholar, of Oxford, displayed a volume wide open. The printing-press was chosen by Ascensius, Vascosan, Roigny, Schilders, and De Preux; while printers' balls were selected by Van Os of Zwolle. The cross, the star, and the anchor, were blended in every possible fashion; the serpent writhed its way through a multitude of devices; Time and Truth were most savagely mangled in every species of cuts; and even the cabbage found rival claimants in Italy and in Strasburg. The dull device of Doletus—an axe cutting a log of wood—reads into a fearful meaning when we remember that this Parisian printer found his dolorous ending on the funeral pile, vainly protesting, as the flames caught his dying breath, that there was that in his books which the readers had not understood.

English typography, while notably deficient in dainty devices, has reveled in puns, particularly in the sixteenth and seventeenth centuries. Hugh Singleton, dwelling at the Golden Tun, took a tun for his emblem; William Middleton put W. M. on the same barrel in the middle, with supporting angels on either hand; Richard Grafton, with the same idea, assumed a grafted tree growing out of a tun, with the motto, Receive the engrafted word; and William Norton finally used up the much-worn fancy by picturing the same hardly worked tun, inscribed with the syllable Nor, and serving as a root to a full-blossomed sweet-william. William Griffith, laboring under still greater disadvantages, followed on the well-worn track with a griffin holding a sweet-william in its mouth. Richard Harrison, very hard pressed for a fancy, used a sheaf of rye surmounted by a full sun and resting on a hare's head. The Barkers exhibited a man barking a tree; Thomas Pavier pictured a pavier at work, with the motto, Thou shalt labor till thou return to dust; and Dexter strove to mingle piety with punning in a right hand pointing to a flaming star, with the legend, Deus imperat astris. John Wight used his own portrait surrounded by the words, Welcom the Wight that bringeth such light; Reynard Wolf pressed a fox and wolf into service as supporters; John Day surpassed his contemporaries in taste as well as in skill, with his labored device of a landscape illuminated by a rising sun, while in the foreground a sleeping figure is aroused by an angel, and the whole pointed to the dullest comprehension by the words, Arise, for it is day. Perhaps worst of all was that of Garret Dewes, which pictured a house where two persons in a garret threw deuce at dice;

and the joke could hardly be worse if it is true that his name was really Gerard.

Among the quaint fancies should be classed the huge and horrent porcupine of Tinassius, and the tortoise of Cyane and Foucher. Kerver, the second, abandoned his father's graceful unicorns for a pair of fighting cocks; and Cavellet and Birkman prosaically contented themselves with very fat hens. The dragon-guarded cabbage of the Sabii seems to contain in itself that fatally short step from the sublime to the ridiculous; the mousing cat of the Sessæ has the advantage of being handsomely executed; and the ponderous elephant of Regnault gained much in the hands of his widow by the piquant declaration that she still remained an elephant. (See pictorial page illustrating devices.)

Devil.—Otherwise Printer's Devil, is a term applied to the boy who does the drudgery-work of a printing-office. In former years it was commonly used; of late its use has become less frequent, owing to the number of boys employed. On newspapers, the boy who waits on the editor for copy is generally termed the devil. In some offices, each new apprentice in turn, during the earlier period of his service, acts as devil. Various accounts have been given of the origin of this phrase. One is to the effect that, the early printer being supposed by superstitious persons to produce copies of manuscript with marvelous rapidity by the aid of the black art, the devil was deemed his natural assistant, and this word was, on this account, applied to printers' apprentices. Another story is that the term originated with Aldus Manutius, who, when he commenced the printing-business in Venice, had in his employment or his possession a small negro boy, who became known over the city as the little black devil. A superstition having spread that Aldus was invoking the aid of the black art, and that the little negro was the embodiment of Satan, Aldus, to correct this opinion, which was giving him sore annoyance, publicly exhibited his negro, making at the same time the following characteristic speech: Be it known to Venice, that I, Aldus Manutius, printer to the Holy Church and Doge, have this day made public exposure of the printer's devil. All those who think he is not flesh and blood, may come and pinch him. Another story is, that the first errand-boy employed by William Caxton, the first printer in England, was the son of a gentleman of French descent named De Ville, or Deville, and that the word devil, as applied to a printer's apprentice, in the English language, has this innocent origin. At a performance given some years ago at a London theatre, for the benefit of the Printers' Pension Society, an actor assumed the character of a printer's devil, and delivered an address written for the occasion, in which the position of the devil was thus described:

(Speaks behind the Scenes.)

What! I go on and thank the gentlefolks!
Go on the stage! A plague upon your jokes—
I cannot do it—I should die with shame!

Well, if I must—mind, you shall bear the blame.
(Enters, cleaning a Printer's Ball.)

Ladies and Gentlemen—I beg your pardon
For thus appearing here in Covent-Garden;
'Tis not my fault—I'd rather be at home,
But I was by the Printers *press'd* to some.
Having got all they can from you—'tis civil—
For thanks they coolly leave you to *the Devil!*
Start not—the Printer's *Devil!* that is me,
No *blacker* than I'm *painted*, as you see,
The Devil—that with *Fust* the first of Printers
(Called Doctor Faustus) had such odd adventures.
Every thing's thrown on me, but you shall hear—
Master, you know, commands the overseer,
The overseer he lords it o'er the men,
The men they fag the 'prentices, and then
The 'prentices blow me up—that's *not* civil—
So good or bad, all's laid upon the *Devil!*
For every thing they want, the pressmen call me,
And if I do not answer, they *block ball* me.
Nay, with abuse the very Authors cram me,
And when I go for copy, curse and damn me!

Dextrine.—The substance commercially known and sold under this name is potato starch, or a preparation of potato starch, from which is made the gum that coats the back of postage and revenue stamps, and similar articles. Printers who desire to use it, to coat the backs of labels or for similar purposes, can prepare the gum in the following manner: Add about ten pounds of dextrine to about two gallons of water, when the latter is boiling. Stir occasionally until the dextrine is dissolved, which would be in about twenty minutes if the boiling was done over a hot fire, and in about an hour if it was done over a comparatively slow one. In applying the gum to labels, care must be taken that the paper on which they are printed is not too thin. It should be sized, and of a grade but little inferior to writing-paper.

Diamond.—The name of a very small type. (See TYPE.)

Diamond Card Press.—A small press exclusively for printing cards, formerly built by S. P. Ruggles, Boston, Mass.; now nearly out of use in printing-offices.

Diary.—Properly, a note-book or register of daily occurrences, in which the writer holds a conspicuous part, or which have come under his observation. Also the name of a blank or note-book arranged with dates, etc., for convenient use as a diary.

Diaeresis, or Dieresis.—A mark consisting of two dots ["] placed over the second of two adjacent vowels, to indicate that they are to be pronounced as distinct letters; as, coöperation. (See ACCENTS.)

Dibdin, Thomas Frognall, D.D.—A celebrated author upon bibliography. Born in Calcutta in 1775, died in 1847. His father, Captain Thomas Dibdin, was the brother of the distinguished song-writer, Charles Dibdin, and the hero of his brother's well-known song of Poor Tom Bowline, the Darling of our Crew. Being left an orphan at an early age, Dibdin was sent home to England, where he received a fine education, and was prepared for the law, but decided in favor of the church, and was ordained in

1804. He became an author at an early age, writing essays, stories, and poems for the magazines, and some disquisitions upon legal topics; and editing various editions of the English, Greek, and Latin classic authors. Bibliomania, a poetic epistle addressed to Richard Heber, the great book-collector, by Dr. Ferrier in 1809, suggested to Dibdin his curious volume with the same title, which met a warmer reception from the numerous book-lovers of the period. This was followed by several works upon early printing, and especially the books in the collection of Earl Spencer; he also edited and enlarged Ames' Typographical Antiquities of Great Britain. These books attracted great attention, were splendidly printed, and catered directly to the bibliomaniac fancy of the time.

Dibdin's best-known work is The Bibliographical Decameron, or Ten Days' Pleasant Discourse upon Illuminated Manuscripts, and Subjects connected with Early Engraving, Typography, and Bibliography. This magnificent book was published in three large volumes in 1817, and is considered the crowning glory of Bulmer's Shakspeare Press, being adorned with the rarest illustrations in steel and copper-plate, and to add additional fame to the work the blocks were destroyed by the author and his friends in order to prevent the possibility of a reprint. The book is in fact a gorgeous monument raised to the bibliomania which raged through England during the first quarter of the nineteenth century, and which Dibdin did much to excite; to the general reader of the present day it can only be of interest as a bibliographic curiosity on account of its being written in the form of a cumbrous and wearisome series of imaginary conversations full of overwrought bibliomaniac ecstasies, while the real matter of the book is crowded into the notes which overburden every page. Dibdin continued to produce other works upon kindred themes, his bibliographical tours through France, Germany, and England being magnificently illustrated, and he lived to survive the book-collecting passion to which he had so ably ministered, and to bitterly bewail its extinction in an anonymous pamphlet published in 1831 under the appropriate title of Bibliophobia.

Dictionary.—A collection of words in one or more languages, with their significations, arranged in alphabetical order. In a more extended sense, any work professing to communicate information on an entire subject or special branch of a subject under an alphabetic arrangement of headings.

Didot.—The name of a family of eminent printers in France, who have pursued the calling with remarkable success from the year 1713 to the present day. François Didot, the first printer of this distinguished house, was highly esteemed for his fine publications, and instructed his sons in the art, giving them also an excellent classical education. He was succeeded by his sons François Ambroise (born 1730, died 1804) and Pierre François (born 1732, died 1795); these young men had been in-pressed by their father's enthusiasm, and devoted themselves energetically to the various departments of their avocation, François Ambroise making many improvements in type-founding and machinery, while Pierre established paper-mills at Essonne, near Paris. The collection of French classic authors printed by the order of Louis XVI. are still highly valued for their correctness and beauty.

At the close of the Revolution François Ambroise was succeeded by his sons Pierre (born 1760, died 1853) and Firmin (born 1764, died 1836). This third generation increased the fame of the house by their magnificent Louvre editions of the French and Latin classics, while Firmin deserves special mention for his elegant and correct cheap editions, his improvements in the processes of stereotyping, and his great success in the production of a series of scripts, which resulted in an unparalleled sale.

Among the sons of Pierre Didot the paper manufacturer, Henri became a type-founder famous for the microscopic types of his exquisite miniature editions, while his brother, St. Leger, devoted himself to paper-making, and introduced the present method of constructing it in a continuous web. Jules, a son of St. Leger, supported and increased the fame of the family by his skill as a punch-cutter.

Firmin Didot was succeeded by his sons Ambroise Firmin (born 1790) and Hyacinthe (born 1794,) who have increased the fame of their house by the adoption of all modern improvements and facilities; Ambroise Firmin Didot has acquired considerable reputation as an author upon subjects relating to typography. The firm now existing under the name of Firmin Didot frères also embraces Paul and Alfred, the sons of the two heads of the house; and the importance of their establishment may be judged from the fact that in 1859 they usually printed 140 reams of paper, or nearly seventy thousand sheets, a day.

Diesis.—The mark ‡;—called also double-dagger.

Digit.—One of the ten symbols 0, 1, 2, etc., by which numbers are expressed.

Digraph.—A combination of two letters to express a single sound; as ea in head, or th in bath.

Dilettante.—In popular use, an amateur, or one who devotes occasional attention to some art or science. The word is Italian in its origin, but has been adopted into the English, French, and German languages. In typography the term has a special significance as the name of the Dilettanti Society, celebrated for its publications upon art and science. This association was established in England in 1760, for merely social purposes, by a number of gentlemen who had traveled in Italy. The objects of the society were extended, and it became widely known for its liberal contributions to works of science and art.

Dimensions of Paper.—There was formerly, partly because all paper was made by hand, and partly because the English government levied a duty on paper that was regulated by the names of respective papers, great uniformity in the dimensions of the papers called by the various names. At present, however, these names afford an uncertain indication of dimensions, and they are little better than fancy titles. The sizes corresponding with each title vary not only in different countries, but in different sections of the same country; and while one manufacturer makes papers above, another makes them below the average standard. A due approximation to conformity has been preserved in medium and double medium printing-paper, medium printing-paper being nineteen by twenty-four inches, and double medium twenty-four by thirty-eight; but there is no similar uniformity in scarcely one other description of either printing- or writing-paper. Paper is bought and sold by weight, size in inches, and quality, and the names used have ceased to convey a specific meaning unless they are qualified by the addition of the name of some well-known manufacturer or by some local usage.

Charles Magarge & Co., give the following sizes of Blank Book Papers in general use in Philadelphia:

	Inches.		Inches.
Imperial	23 × 31	Census	18 × 26
Super Royal	20 × 28	Check Folio	17½ × 24½
Royal	19 × 24	Folio	17 × 22
Medium	18 × 23	Crown	15 × 19
Demy	16 × 21	Flat Cap	14 × 17
Extra Folio	19 × 24	"	13 × 16
		"	12 × 15

Inquiries among other Philadelphia paper-dealers resulted in the construction of the following table:

	Inches.		Inches.
Double Imperial	32 × 44	Folio	17 × 22
" Super Royal	27 × 42	Square Demy	17 × 17
" Medium 33 × 36 / 24 × 37½	24 × 38*	Demy	16 × 20
		Crown	15 × 19
Royal and Half	25 × 29	Flat Cap	
Imperial "	26 × 32	12 x 15–12½ x 15½	
" "	22 × 30	13 x 16–13½ x 16½	14 × 17*
Super Royal	20 × 28	Foolscap, varies	
Royal	19 × 24	accord'g to w'ght	12½ × 16
Medium (writing paper.)	18 × 23	Letter	10 × 16
		Packet Note	9 × 11
Census	18 × 26	Ladies' Bath	7½ × 11
Double Cap	17 × 28	Octavo	7 × 9
Large Check	19 × 24	Note	6 × 8
Check Folio	17½ × 24½	Billet	6 × 8

* Sizes in general use for printing purposes.

De Vinne's Price List gives the following table of the regular sizes of American papers, prevalent in New York:

FOLDED WRITING-PAPERS.

	Inches.		Inches.
Billet Note	6 × 8	Letter	10 × 16
Octavo Note	7 × 9	Commercial Letter	11 × 17
Commercial Note	8 × 10	Packet Post	11½ × 18
Packet Note	9 × 11	Extra Packet Post	11½ × 18½
Bath Note	8½ × 14	Foolscap	12½ × 16

Note is sometimes 8½ × 10¾ inches, Letter 9¾ × 10½ inches, Commercial Letter 10¾ × 16¾ inches, Foolscap 12 × 15 inches; but the dimensions given in the table are those in most general use.

FLAT WRITING-PAPERS.

	Inches.		Inches.
Law Blank..............	13 × 16	*Medium	18 × 23
Flat Cap..............	14 × 17	*Royal..............	19 × 24
Crown	15 × 19	*Super Royal........	20 × 28
Demy....................	16 × 21	*Imperial..............	22 × 30
Folio Post..........	17 × 22	Elephant......... ...	22½ × 27¾
Check Folio........	17 × 24	Columbier...........	23 × 33½
Double Cap........	17 × 28	Atlas..................	26 × 33
Extra Size Folio...	19 × 23	Double Elephant....	26 × 40

Extra-size Folio is sometimes 18 × 23 inches, and 19 × 24 inches.

Imperial is sometimes 23 × 31 inches.

Sizes above Imperial are never found on sale of American manufacture. They are made only to order, usually with some difficulty, and at extra price.

* Note the difference in size between writing- and printing-paper of the same name.

PRINTING-PAPERS.

	Inches.		Inches.
Medium	19 × 24	Double Medium....	24 × 38
Royal.... 20 × 24 or 20 × 25		Double Royal......	26 × 40
Super Royal........	22 × 28	Double Sup. Royal	28 × 42
Imperial........	22 × 32	" " "	29 × 43
Medium-and-Half.	24 × 30	Broad Twelves.....	23 × 41
Small Double Med.	24 × 38	Double Imperial..	32 × 46

Large sizes, like 34 × 46 and 36 × 48, as well as odd sizes, like 28 × 34, are not uncommon, but they are of too irregular supply to be considered as regular papers. The larger sizes are invariably of common quality, suitable only for posters and newspapers; the smaller sizes are usually of finer quality, adapted for books and fine job-printing.

Diphthongs.—A diphthong is a coalescence of two vowels into one syllable, as æ, œ. The English language does not require these twin types. Some printers, however, use them in such words as archæology, mediæval, manœuvre, etc., forgetting that æ, œ do not differ in sound from the simple vowel e; they are, in such words, utterly worthless, and no better than a mere pedantic incumbrance. They have already been thrown out of such words as cemetery, celestial, economical, ether, etc., but they may be retained in proper names, as Cæsar, Phœnicia, etc.

Diploma.—This word is usually restricted to a document containing the record of a degree conferred by an educational institution or a literary society. In its general sense, every kind of ancient charter, donation, bull, etc. It is derived from the Greek word to double, on account of the early emperors issuing such charters on a folded or doubled tablet, or diptych. These documents previous to the fifth century were inscribed on papyrus, and at a later period on parchment. Being intended for permanent preservation, great care and elegance are usually required in writing or printing and decorating them.

Diptych.—Among the Romans, a tablet of wood, metal, or other substance, used for the purpose of writing, and folded like a book of two leaves. The diptychs of antiquity were employed especially for public registers.

Directing Newspaper Wrappers.—Various contrivances are in use in the United States for directing newspapers, or newspaper wrappers, by having the proper addresses printed with type, either on the wrappers or on small slips cut and pasted on the wrappers. (See MAILING MACHINES).

Mr. Mackie, an English newspaper publisher, states, in a communication to the London Printers' Register, that he has successfully availed himself of the aid of lithography to accomplish the same object, and as he deems this a better plan than either the pasting or letter-press printing process, his description of his system is given below:

Printing covers from type is a slow process, if the covers are full size. Printing the names on strips of paper and then pasting them upon covers is not certain: they often come off. After trying both plans for a long time, I some years ago bethought me of lithography, and found a remedy for my annoyances. I wrote from thirty to sixty names and addresses on transfer paper, transferred them to the stone, and worked off my covers in thirties or sixties, just as if they were bill-heads, overlaying one another. To enable this to be done, the name and address appear on the cover as annexed:

In a few minutes any one learns to place the paper in such a position on the cover, when laid out blank side up, as will bring the title of the paper and the name and address together. I also print upon every cover the number which is opposite to the subscriber's name in my books, and then the posting clerk can see at a glance if any consecutive number is missing. No reading of names is thus required. Any lithographer will print covers in this manner far cheaper than they can be printed from letter-press, the headings being taken from type, and the names, etc. written by the postal clerk.

Direction Labels.—See JOB-PRINTING.

Direction Word.—A word formerly placed at the bottom of a page, on the right hand, to show the connection with the page following. Directions are now only occasionally used in law work. (See CATCH WORD.)

Directory.—The first Directory ever printed is said to have been The London Directory; or a List of the Principal Traders in London, for 1732. The originator of this work was Mr. James Brown, a native of Kelso, in Scotland, who, after laying the foundation, gave it to Mr. Henry Kent, a London printer, who carried it on, and got an estate by it. Mr. Brown was a scholar of some eminence, but is better known as a merchant and traveler in various parts of the globe. He was born May 23, 1709, died November, 1788.

Diseases of Printers.—While a considerable number of printers live to a green old age, the average term of life among compositors is less than that of persons engaged in many other indoor pursuits, or in agricultural labors. Statistical statements bearing on this point have been made from time to time in various countries. It is said that the average duration of the life of compositors on American morning newspapers is about forty-five years. A statement was made before the Typographical Society of Berlin, Prussia, some time ago, to the effect that of 1000 printers there had died in nine years 196, or nearly twenty per cent.; that of these, 126 died of consumption, and only 61 of other diseases; that more than one-third of those dying were from 19 to 30 years old, and that only two of those whose deaths were reported had reached the age of 80. A London physician who made an elaborate investigation of the sanitary circumstances of the printers of that city a few years ago, and who inspected the records of a number of printers' societies, found that the average age of their members at death was about 43 years. The Registrar-General furnished the physician referred to, with the following comparison of the rate of mortality among the printers of London and the agricultural laborers of England for 1860 and 1861:

ANNUAL MORTALITY PER HUNDRED PERSONS.					
Age	15 to 20	20 to 25	25 to 35	35 to 45	45 to 55
Printers	0.440	0.696	0.894	1.747	2.367
Agricultural laborers.	0.423	0.782	0.743	0.805	1.145

This table indicates that in early life, or from fifteen to thirty-five, there is very little difference between the mortality of printers and that of farmers. Out of a hundred of the former a small fraction more than two (2.032) die annually, and out of a hundred of the latter a small fraction less than two (1.928) die annually. After the age of thirty-five is passed, however, the contrast becomes startling, for then deaths become more than twice as numerous among the printers as among the farmers. Out of a hundred printers between the ages of thirty-five and fifty-five, more than four (4.114) die annually, while out of a hundred farmers of the same age, there are annually less than two (1.950) deaths.

Despite these statements, however, there is no good reason for regarding the printing-business as inherently unhealthy. Under favorable circumstances, compositors have repeatedly worked at it, steadily, for many years; and press-work is often more apt to be conducive to health than to be injurious. The thing most positively and directly inimical is the practice of heating type immediately after it is distributed, for the purpose of drying it, and then commencing composition before the type has become cold. Whether heat is thus applied by burning paper over the surface of the type, or by putting the cases near a stove or steam pipes, or by wetting matter for distribution with hot water, there is constant danger that pernicious effects will arise from the partial release of so subtle a substance as antimony. Although diseases directly traceable to this cause are comparatively rare, a sufficient number are known to have occurred to indicate that it is very dangerous to handle heated type. In some cases the lungs have been seriously affected by inhaling the fumes of hot type or melted type-metal; in others the hands or arms have been well-nigh paralyzed; and in others the whole body has been injuriously inflamed.

The most dangerous disease to printers, however, is manifestly consumption. Its fatal ravages among them may be due in part to the occasional inhalation of the dust accumulating in their cases, which has been called a poisonous dust, but it is owing mainly to the fact that a large portion of the work of compositors is performed at night, in badly-ventilated rooms, under blazing gas-lights, and that, after being exhausted by such labors, many compositors rush from overheated composing-rooms into the cold air without taking time to button up their overcoats or to protect themselves properly, by other precautions, against the inclemency of the weather. Even day-hands in book and job offices are often obliged by business exigencies to perform night-work, and few printers totally escape such exhaustive labors; so that the whole craft is more or less subject to industrial and sanitary conditions which have a strong tendency in themselves, and independent of the act of setting type, to breed consumption.

Display Letter.—See JOB LETTER.

Display of Type.—The art of displaying type is often erroneously considered as the exclusive function of the job printer. The book or news compositor is apt to think that a knowledge of this branch of the art is not a necessary part of his education. It is a mistake. He cannot be considered a good compositor who is incompetent to set up a good book title or a neatly displayed advertisement, for these are duties strictly within his province.

We have no reason now to complain of the poverty of our materials. It would be almost impossible to number or to strictly classify the distinct faces, sizes, and styles of modern types. Where the type-founders have done so well, it is not unreasonable in the public to look for a corresponding advance on the part of the compositor. It is much more difficult to be a good compositor now than it was one hundred years ago. The good presswork of the last century would pass muster with honor; but the good composition of that period would not now be tolerated.

The utility and importance of a knowledge of the best methods of display will not need any elaboration. However utilitarian any man may be in his tendencies, he cannot fail to note the superior merit of a properly displayed piece of composition. The subject-matter, the thought itself, of any form of printing, should be its chief attraction ; but there is no written matter so wise or so witty that the method of arranging the types, by which the wise or witty idea is conveyed to the reader, can be passed by as of trivial importance. A badly-arranged title-page, a profuse peppering of italics or capitals, or a neglect to proportion blanks, spaces, and margins, will repel an ordinary reader quite as effectually as dullness in the subject itself. How many persons would read accepted poems if they were run in solid? How many would read standard histories if they were set up in solid minion double columns? We have but to look at some of our old books again to perceive the necessity of a proper arrangement of type. Irrespective of subject-matter, the reading of one book is a pleasure, the reading of another a drudgery.

The superior attraction of a good modern book is due to its arrangement. In the old book there are no chapter-heads, no blanks, no paragraphs, no relief whatever to the eye. In the modern we have systematic divisions, displayed headings, paragraphs, capitals, italics, and suitable captions. This is one of the many forms of displaying types, the utility of which cannot be questioned. The first inference to be drawn is, that to make books look inviting and subject-matter attractive, there must be leads between the lines, frequent use of paragraphs, a systematic division of the subject in chapters and captions, and good broad margins. To sum all up briefly, there must be much more white than black on the page. This rule should be remembered, for it will apply almost as well to posters as to book pages.

Before the novice can reasonably hope to become expert in displaying type, it is important that he should have a clear idea of the effect he wishes to produce. He must first know what a good piece of display is, and what are the points that make it good. If he undertakes to study the matter, he will first perceive that in most pieces of display there are various sizes and styles of type. He will rightly infer that contrast is one of the methods by which the desired effect is produced—he will notice contrasts in the sizes, shapes, and shades of the type. He will see that a line of capitals is often followed by a line of lower-case—that a long line is preceded by a short line—that the prominent lines are black, while the catch-lines are small and light—that antique type appears all the blacker and bolder by reason of its juxtaposition with light-faced Roman—that the prominent lines are most prominent when they are not followed or preceded by lines of the same length. The inference would be, that bold and effective display can be secured only by using the best methods of making contrast,—that display itself is nothing but contrast.

To a great extent this is true; but it is not always correct. There are other kinds of displayed work than posters,—work in which violent contrasts are useless as well as in bad taste. Book titles would be disfigured by strict imitation of the method by which a poster is improved. The reason is obvious: the book is held in the hand, the poster is to be read, if need be, across the street; the book title needs no violent contrast to arrest attention, while the poster is ineffective without this violent contrast; the poster is an isolated piece of work, and need not agree with any

other, but the book title must be in some kind of harmony with the type in the text. It appears, then, that harmony in the grouping of type is as essential in one case as contrast is in another. And here we come to another rule: the finer, more artistic, and more elegant the class of work, the less need of contrast and the greater need of harmony. There may be contrast in the sizes of the type, and sometimes in the shapes of the type, but there must be harmony in the general effect. All the lines must look as if they were in some way connected.

We have, then, two distinct and apparently opposite qualities to be reconciled, so as to produce good effect. Let us first consider the methods of securing contrast.

1. *Contrast of Size*, from diamond up, which needs no explanation.

2. *Contrast of Style*, as may be shown in Roman, Italic, Antique, Gothics, Black, Ornamented, Script, etc. There are many varieties of all these styles. The radical difference between upper- and lower-case may also be classified under the contrast of style.

3. *Contrast of Shade.*—Most Roman type is light, while Antiques, Gothics, and Titles are black, in shade. By the skillful contrasting of these two distinct shades the most violent contrasts are produced. It is the blackness or lightness of any type, more than any other quality, that qualifies or disqualifies it for use. Ornamental types occupy a middle position between the extreme blackness of Antique and the lightness of Roman. Seen from a distance they look gray. It is this grayness, this dissimilarity in shade, quite as much as any grace of design, that makes Ornamental type attractive. An Ornamental line inserted between an Antique and a Roman not only gives greater prominence to each, by its difference in form, but serves also to harmonize both, by its approximation to each in shade.

4. *Contrast of Shape.*—The plain form, condensed, expanded.

Here, then, we have differences that can be combined in infinite variations. We must, however, study the points of difference to make good contrasts and proper effects.

If a poster is set up exclusively in light-faced Roman, even with a great variety of sizes, it will not be bold and effective. It has no blackness of shade or color; it cannot be read at a distance; it fails in its first purpose, the arresting of careless eyes. An effective poster should have mixed type, and that type should be bold.

If a book title is set in bold Gothic or Antique with ever so much care and judgment, no beauty of cut in type or skill in grouping can make it attractive. It is clumsy, for it is not in keeping with the text that follows, and is offensively and needlessly black.

Set up a large poster in mixed type; aim to make it as bold as possible; let every line be full, or nearly so; separate the lines by pica reglets only. The proof of such a job will show that the effect intended is defeated. The crowding of the type together to produce increased blackness and boldness has pro-

duced confusion only. There must be a certain
amount of white surface left to give relief to the eye
and perspicuity to the type. If this is neglected, the
stronger the contrast the more ineffective the display.
Set up a note circular with light Script and mixed
display of Ornamental type in crowded space. The
types selected may be most beautiful, but the job, as
a whole, will look weak and ineffective, for there is
no contrast of shade, and no relief to the eye. Remove
the Ornamentals; insert instead plain Italic caps, or
even Antiques, lead out liberally, and give the types a
fair field for show, and the job may look perfect. It
will certainly be more neat and tasteful.
Set up a poster in mixed type; let the first short
line be in condensed Antique, let the next following
line be in expanded Roman, and you will have a
violent contrast, but poor display, and in bad taste.
Put the inferior line in expanded type and the principal line in Antique (not condensed), and the
incongruity will not be so palpable. The expanded
type is not suitable in long lines, nor the condensed
type in short lines. The reversion of this plain rule
makes the contrast of shape in the type absurd when
considered with reference to the unequal division of
blank space around the types.
Again, set up a piece of displayed work exclusively
in Ornamental type, and let them be of the most
beautiful styles. In most cases the effect produced
will be quite unpleasant. The absence of contrast
in shape and shade will give a dull monotony to the
work that no beauty in the type can redeem. Remove
some of the Ornamental lines and put plain Romans,
Antiques, or Gothics in their place, and the effect will
be quite magical. The plain type will be clearer, the
Ornamental type more beautiful, and the work as a
whole much more effective. It follows that beautiful
type will not always make beautiful work,—that the
style of type used in one line must be in contrast to
and yet in agreement with the type in preceding and
following lines. This is the whole art of display,—to
make the work look effective.
This effect, however, cannot be produced only by
a balancing of long lines with short lines, or a
contrasting of large with small types. The use of
display is not to show a large and varied stock of
type, but to make the subject more clear and
readable. The job is best displayed that presents
most clearly and forcibly the purpose of the writer.
It is the effect wanted that is the object, and to this
object all artificial rules must give way.
If the compositor is ignorant of the effect that is
wanted, it is not possible that he can please. He
should, therefore, train himself to think over the
object of his work,—of the effect intended. If he
understands this clearly it will be of more importance
to him than the knowledge of any technical rules; he
will have but little difficulty in properly displaying
the most difficult copy. He should further be told
that this knowledge cannot be imparted by the foreman; it can be acquired only by cultivating habits of
perception.

Two displayed lines of the same size and the same
length should not be allowed together. Their proximity and uniformity prevent contrast and defeat
display. For the same reason, two displayed lines
of precisely the same size and style should not be
allowed together, unless the words or clauses intended
for display are so closely connected that they cannot
be divided. For example: the words Knickerbocker
Life Insurance Company may be required as a leading display line in a narrow measure. There is no
type sufficiently condensed, and yet sufficiently clear,
to give these words proper prominence. They must
be separated into two or more lines. It is usual,
in such a case, to make each line of a distinct face of
type. But there is no reason why the faces of type
should differ. The clause will not admit of it. The
name is one, and all the words constituting it should
be taken together and displayed alike; for there is no
one word in the clause that has any natural prominence over its fellows.
Every book title, poster, card, and almost every
variety of displayed work, should have one leading
line, superior to all others in size, clearness, and
effect. The leading line should consist only of the
word or words which embrace the pith and marrow
of the subject, and consequently most likely to arrest
the eye and give an insight into the object of the
work. In a poster for a transportation company, the
destination is the most effective line; in the show-bill
of a theater, the name of the chief piece, or principal
actor; in the title of a book, the words by which the
book is called. This rule is so simple that it needs
no enforcement by illustration. The word that gives
a key to all the other matter should have the greatest
prominence, and all else should be subordinate.
This leading line should never be divided by a
hyphen, nor should it be abbreviated so as to confuse
the meaning. To secure the greatest effect in display,
the shortest words or clauses are desirable; but these
are not always to be found in copy. But the wording
must not, for that reason, be contracted, or distorted,
to accommodate it to the type. The type must be
adapted to the words; it will not answer to make the
words fit a favorite style of type.
Example: Passengers are requested not to smoke
abaft the shaft. In this very common notice, the
words to smoke or smoke are sometimes made the
chief display line, the compositor disregarding the
negative not, which is certainly fully as important a
word as the verb it qualifies. The excuse that there
is no type in the office that will make a good full line
is inadmissible. If such is the case, the word not
should make a separate displayed line. The obvious
meaning of the copy should have its full expression,
no matter how odd it may appear.
The main display line should be located in the
center or at the head of the work. The compositor
will have but little difficulty in obeying this rule:
titles, posters, and show-cards are not prefixed with
dedications and introductions. There are occasions,
however, in awkwardly-constructed matter, where the

display line is placed at or near the foot. Where the compositor can do so, with confidence in its propriety and acceptability, he should alter it to a better position.

The leading display line appears to best advantage in capitals. There is a completeness and perfection in capitals entirely unapproachable by lower-case. What is applicable to a book title may be also applied to show cards and posters. In most cases it is a question of attainable materials. Of two lines—the one a weak line of capitals, the other a bold, showy line of lower-case—the compositor should select that which will produce the best effect. Where he has opportunity to decide between two of great prominence, the preference should be given to the capitals.

The leading display line in close or solid matter should be a full line. In loose or open matter it may be a short line. Where there is an unusual amount of matter, and few white lines or spaces occur in the body of a piece of display, the main display, if not full, has a bad appearance. The great white blanks on each side are in painful contrast with the density of the body. But where the body is loose and open, there is no such necessity, and it may be short to better advantage. There are words which no art can expand in a full line without increasing the size of the letter in a great disproportion to the body, and this would make the matter worse. It is better to give the true display-line a fair prominence, and no more. If it is not capable of sufficient extension, the adjoining lines must be arranged by spacing or crowding, so as to give it proper relief.

The leading display line must be supported by subordinate minor lines in a proper manner, to produce a good effect. It is generally a very easy matter to pick out the main line, but to lay off the minor points of display is no easy task. The word or words which are selected for the main line are those which are the most significant and definite. To find the minor lines the same rule should be followed, selecting them in the order in which they should stand, until the space is entirely occupied.

The minor displayed lines should be of irregular length. In light and open matters, if they are all made full, the effect is lost. How would a book title look in which every line was full? Even in more solid matter full displayed lines give an unpleasing appearance of squareness. A well-balanced irregularity of form in the outline of a job is as necessary to perspicuity as are variety in face and diversity in size of type. It is almost impossible to carry out this rule in jobs where an excess of display lines is introduced, and one of the reasons why a few lines of plain Roman text type is recommended is, that it avoids the necessity of taking in or spacing out of display lines to prevent this squareness and uniformity.

Every short display line should be placed in the center, thus giving a uniform blank on each side. This is needed to maintain the balance of the bill and give it sufficient precision and regularity.

When a number of displayed lines are grouped together, and all are required to be set in the same style of type, the effect is heightened by giving them an irregular indention, thus:

———

———

The prominence given to each word by the indention, and the well-balanced irregularity of the form in which they are arranged, give them a much better effect than they would have if arranged in the usual way. It has the additional advantage of permitting the use of thinner reglets between the lines.

Display lines should be made as nearly equidistant as the wording of the copy will allow. The proportions of a job are much better shown when the display lines are placed at even intervals. Nothing disfigures displayed work more than the huddling together of the leading lines.

Hints on Book Titles.—The proper size of the type to be used must be determined more by the effect than by names. A Two-Line Great Primer Condensed may appear lighter than a plain Two-Line Pica, for the condensing of the type contracts the width of the broad strokes and extends the hair-lines. The body of the first type may be larger, but the appearance will be more delicate. A large condensed letter may be used with perfect propriety where a smaller plain two-line letter would appear altogether too large.

The size of the type for display in titles is, in a great measure, determined also by the size of the text letter. If the body of the book is in brevier, the title should be set on a smaller scale than if it were set in pica. The style of the type selected for title display should also be in accordance with the peculiar cut of letter and general style observed in the book. If round old-fashioned type is preferred for text-letter, the title should also correspond.

The utility and superior beauty of condensed two-line Romans naturally commend them to an educated taste, but they should not be used indifferently or unthinkingly. When a book is long and narrow, as most books usually are, condensed type is in harmony with this shape. The type seems to have a natural adaptation to the shape of the leaf on which it is printed. But when the book is square, as in quarto form, condensed types should be used more cautiously. Plain type will give the best effect.

When a title is brief, no attempt should be made to expand it by undue spacing. An en quad of the body of the letter is the largest space which should be used, and this is seldom judicious. It certainly is desirable that there should be a full line. This cannot always be attained. When a letter of suitable size has been selected, and it does not make a full line, even with the aid of spaces, the compositor should not attempt to enlarge the letter or increase the spaces. It may not make a perfect title, but it will have a much better effect to enforce a perfect symmetry between the sizes than it would to unduly enlarge any one line. The title-page is almost invariably followed and preceded by a blank page, and where the title-page does not contain a full line, it may entirely escape observation; but an unduly spaced line will surely arrest attention and provoke criticism. When it is found necessary to space one line in a title, all other lines should also be spaced. It is not necessary that the spacing should be perfectly uniform throughout, but a decided separation should be shown in every line. It may be a three em space in one line and a hair space in another. A close line and a broad-spaced line in close proximity offend the eye by the want of symmetry; if both lines are spaced they cease to look singular.

The title should not be made to conform to any arbitrary shape. At one time it was fashionable to arrange titles in the form of a coffin, a wedge, an ellipse, etc. All such arbitrary designs are fantastic and unmeaning. If the display is based, as it should be, upon the relative importance of the clauses, it will appear easy and natural, and consequently beautiful. A title, or any other piece of display, is best composed when the arrangement appears so simple and easy as to preclude the idea of its being set up in any other manner.

The quickest method of setting up a title is to lay out the principal display lines first, irrespective of the length of the lines. For instance, the main line, it is assumed, will be Two-Line Small Pica Condensed—the next Two-Line Nonpareil, etc. With this mode it is rare that two lines will make the same length. When the plan is thus fairly laid out, it will be easy to group together the minor lines and arrange them properly.

Whether catch-lines do or do not occur, the same graduation of space should be maintained between all the main lines, and the catch-lines should be reckoned as blank.

The imprint of the book, containing the year, date, and publisher's address, should always be in small type. Where the title is very concise, the long line of the imprint should make nearly a full line, that the page may have a proper form. But when there are two or more long lines in a book, it is not necessary that the imprint-line should be a full one. The author's name should always be in a short plain line, and the word by should always be separate in a catch-line. The titles or descriptions which he may annex to his name should be set underneath in very small type, certainly no larger than the smallest catch-lines.

The spacing out of a title is not the least difficult portion of the work. All titles naturally divide themselves into two or more distinct parts, the chief of which are—the name; the extended description; the author and his titles; the imprint. The blank between these should be arranged according to their natural connection. Thus, the imprint is no necessary part of the title of the book; it should, therefore, be separated from the rest of the matter by the

widest possible space. But there is a natural connection between the name of the book and its extended description, and there is, therefore, a necessity for bringing them closer together. If the words second or third edition are thrust in, they should be clearly separated from all other clauses by wide blanks on each side. The name and titles of the author should also be closely connected.

The analysis of the title previously given will not suit all cases. The wide range of subjects forbids a precise generalization.

The use of dashes is forbidden in many offices. So far as this has been instrumental in banishing the thick double rules, or curiously curved brass dash lines, once so prevalent, it is an improvement; but it is absurd to reject so valuable a type arbitrarily and without a reason. There are not many titles where dashes are needed—there are those where their omission is fatal to a good effect. When a title is brief, and yet contains many distinct parts, such as the following: The complete works | of | Mrs. Hemans. | Reprinted entire from the last English edition. | Edited by her sister | With notes and an introduction by C. Griswold. | Vol. 1. | Second edition. | D. Appleton. | —the rapid change of the subject needs some further division than a broad blank, and dashes should be used to divide the clauses so as to make their relation more apparent to the reader. The differences in the sizes of proximate lines of type are trivial, and blanks are not enough to show their entire separation.

But in no case should any other than a plain straight line be used. Fancy dashes, waved and dotted rules, are entirely out of place.

The type selected for the main line should always be in proportion to the size of the volume. A title is intended to have a light and open appearance, and although the words of the main line may be few, the size of the type should not be increased, for all the other lines must be regulated by this main line. There must be harmony shown by the graduation of sizes. If all the other display lines are set in correspondingly large letters, the title loses all its case and symmetry. It is no more pleasing than a book advertisement.

The above article is condensed from a paper read a few years ago by Theo. L. De Vinne in the rooms of the New York Typographical Society.

Dissyllable.—A word consisting of two syllables only; as, pa-per.

Distemper.—A preparation of opaque or body colors, with size instead of oil. The original block books were printed with such preparations, and were usually brown in color. For some time after impressions from type were produced by oleaginous inks, the accompanying illustrations from wooden blocks continued to be printed with distemper, it being supposed that they could not be produced by the same ink.

Distich.—A couple of lines in verse making complete sense. An epigram of two lines.

10

Distributing.—In composition, the act of return-ing or replacing the types into the boxes from which they were taken when composed. Excellence con-sists in keeping each box clean or free from every other type but the particular sort it is intended to hold. This requires the joint coöperation of the mind, the eyes, the hands, and the fingers; each of which fills an important office, and demands training and practice to acquire skill in separating accurately and quickly the numberless combinations of types.

In distributing, it is immaterial whether the whole word or only a part of it be taken in the fingers at once. There is not the same liability to contract false and injurious habits in distributing as there is in composing, and therefore not the same necessity to guard against them. The best method of distributing is to take no more of the line than can be conveni-ently held, but always a complete word, with the space that separates it, when practicable.

Having acquired the habit of distributing cleanly, how to do so expeditiously ought next to be considered. The desire to do a given quantity of work in the least possible time, will produce exertion, and, aided by system, success. As every system is made up of apparently trifling observances, nothing must appear superfluous which tends to save time. Place the gal-ley, then, containing the matter for distribution, as near the case into which the letter is to go as con-venient. Before lifting a handful, the size of which must be regulated by the compositor's ability and inclination, press it on all sides and make it compact, that it may be raised with safety. Attention to this is a compositor's only security from accident, and safeguard against pi. A handful being lifted with the nick of the letter uppermost, and the face towards you, slant the matter a little, while holding it firmly in the left hand, that every word in the top line may be known or read, when it is taken in the fingers to distribute. When a word is once seen and taken from the line, avoid by all means looking at it again. Looking frequently at a word of only a few letters is the most fruitful source of losing time, and, great care is required to guard against it. Be careful, also, in sorting the spaces; in book-work, especially, it is essential that all the spaces should be placed in their appropriate boxes.

The inconvenience often experienced from water, which drains off the matter running down the wrist, is prevented by a small piece of sponge being held under the matter in the left hand whilst distributing.

Distributing.—In press-work, the process of dis-tributing the ink evenly over the surface of the rollers, so that they may, in turn, spread it evenly over the surface of the form. This is one of the most difficult tasks imposed on the manufacturers of power-presses, and on those who do the rolling on hand-presses.

Distributing Machine.—A machine for per-forming automatically the operation of type-distrib-uting. At the present time there are two descriptions in use in Great Britain—Mackie's and Hattersley's. In the latter the type is placed on a galley, whence it

HATTERSLEY DISTRIBUTING MACHINE.

enters, in long lines, upon a bridge. The operator, reading the matter as it approaches a certain point, touches the keyboard, and the letter which answers to the key pressed is instantly conveyed to a recep-tacle appropriated to that particular letter. By means of this instrument one operator can supply set-up or classed type sufficient for two composing machines. By a modification it may be used for dis-tributing into the ordinary cases. A column of type having been slid into the galley, it is placed in the machine. By the aid of a simple apparatus several lines are formed into one, there being no handling of the type, which is conveniently under the eye of the operator, who, reading the matter, presses the corre-sponding keys, and the mechanism in connection therewith causes different characters to descend from a given point to their respective receivers. The arrangement is such that the different keys may be pressed in rapid succession, without waiting the arrival of each character in its own receiver; as, although several types may be on the passage simul-taneously, self-acting mechanism directs each into its particular receiver. The machine works ordinary type, no special nicking being required.

MACKIE DISTRIBUTING MACHINE.

Mr. Mackie, of Warrington, England, has invented several distributing machines. Some years ago, he publicly exhibited one in Manchester. It consisted of a comb formed of steel needles, which entered notches in the type. All the a's were notched the 1-32d of an inch from the face of the letter, and on its back; the b's 2-32d, the c's 3-32d, and so on, thirty letters being thus classed on the back, and thirty (caps, etc.) on the front. On a row of 240 letters being laid before the comb, the points of the needles entered the notches in the a's; a forward motion was then given to the comb, which, of course, carried with it all the a's. The motion forward was just enough to draw out the a's, but the motion backwards was 1-32d of an inch more, so that the comb fixed upon the b's next time, and so on while a letter lasted, each time retreating 1-32d of an inch further than before. The caps, etc., notched on the front (printers' nick side), presenting no notch to the needles, were left, and, when sufficiently numerous, were reversed and distributed by themselves. The difficulty Mr. Mackie met with from types wanting to go, through the friction of the comb and of their fellows, when their turn had not arrived, delayed and tried him for a long time. At length, he found a remedy in a row of horizontal retarding needles, placed opposite the type, and working rather stiff between brasses.

Another distributor, by Mr. Mackie, dispenses with notched type, and distributes the common letter by merely altering his composing machine.

Another distributing machine has lately been patented by Mr. Kasternbein, in Paris, which has been pronounced there a decided success. A distributing machine was formerly connected with the Alden Type-Setting Machine, but in its latest modification, the Type-Setter and Distributor are distinct from each other; and distributing machines of various descriptions have been made to operate with a number of other type-setting machines. (See TYPE SETTING MACHINES).

Ditto.—The same, signifying the repetition of something already stated. In typography it is expressed by the abbreviation do., by two inverted commas, by the French quotation marks, and, in some works, by dashes.

Division of Words.—The method by which a word is continued from one line to the succeeding line, a hyphen being placed at the end of the first line, as a mark of separation. The early printers avoided a world of trouble, by either dividing words at the end of a line arbitrarily, without reference to syllabication, or by abbreviating one or more of the words embraced within any line. Such expedients, however, are inadmissible at the present day, and compositors are obliged, in all important works, to avoid, at once, unauthorized abbreviations, improper divisions, and unsightly spacing. Under the pressure of these conflicting requirements, the first question, in any given office, is, what deviation from the highest standard of excellence is most readily pardoned. In one establishment regularity of spacing is regarded as the most important consideration, while in others special stress is laid upon the avoidance of divisions.

The true rule, on this point, is to be sought in a golden mean. It is not worth while to insist, as has been done in some cases, that whole pages, and even entire works, should be printed without a single division at the end of a line; nor is it desirable, on the other hand, that unusual divisions should be made for the purpose of securing unnecessary and unappreciated uniformity of spacing.

Divisions being a typographical necessity, the want of well-defined rules to govern them is sadly felt by printers. Conflicting theories have been laid down by different grammarians and writers on typography; and as various proof-readers adopt or invent diverse doctrines applicable to divisions, the whole subject is in a deplorable state of confusion. The nature of some of the most important of these diversities is well indicated in a section of Webster's Dictionary devoted to syllabication, viz.:

Words are sometimes divided into syllables for the sole purpose of showing their proper pronunciation (as, a-dorn, o-void); and sometimes in order to exhibit their etymological composition merely, without the least regard to their pronunciati n (as, ad-orn, ov-oid). In ordinary cases,—as where a word requires to be divided at the end of a line,—these modes of syllabication are to a certain extent combined. In the United States, the etymological principle is allowed to operate only in separating prefixes, suffixes, and grammatical terminations from the radical part of the word, where this can be done without misrepresenting the pronunciation. In English practice, however, words are usually divided in such a manner as to show their constituent parts independently of the pronunciation (as, hypo-thesis, philo-sophy, belli-gerent, etc.), and a single consonant or a consonant digraph between two vowels goes to the latter (as, a-na-to-my, de-li-cate, ma-the-ma-tics, ele.). In this Dictionary, words are uniformly divided so as to represent their pronunciation in the most accurate manner; but very frequently the root of a word may be exhibited to the eye without violating the orthoëpical principle of syllabication, and, where this is possible, it has generally been done, more particularly in the case of accented syllables.

This extract furnishes the basis of a system which would materially assist in educing order out of the present confusion. The Dictionary itself, in its divisions of the respective words, however, does not afford an absolute guide, as it is not framed to serve this purpose. Words like abase and abandon, for instance, are divided thus: a-base and a-bandon,—while many divisions which are appropriate, and may become necessary, are not noted by hyphens, at all, in the Dictionary. Printers and proof-readers are thus thrown back upon their own resources, or forced to make a choice between rules laid down by conflicting authorities. But the best point to aim at is, nevertheless, well indicated by Webster, viz.: a division which represents the proper pronunciation of a word and at the same time exhibits its root. If such divisions do not necessitate the placing of only one or two letters in the first or second line in which portions of the divided word are placed, they fill the essential requirements of all important theories, and they are less objectionable than divisions of any other description. Many compound words can readily be divided under this theory, at the point or points where the original word or words are united.

When a choice must be made between a division which preserves the form of the original words, and one which corresponds with the proper pronunciation, it seems decidedly better to follow pronunciation than derivation. The force of this principle has been recognized by some English authorities, although their practice has not conformed to it, and even Lindley Murray quotes Dr. Lowth and others as saying that the best and easiest way to divide syllables is to observe the correct pronunciation, without regard to the derivation of words, or the possible combination of consonants at the beginning of a syllable.

Some American proof-readers rigidly enforce Lindley Murray's rule, that a single consonant between two vowels must be joined to the latter syllable; as de-light, bri-dal, re-source;—to which he makes only these exceptions, viz.: the letter x; as ex-ist, ex-amine; and words compounded, as up-on, un-even, dis-ease. This system is called dividing upon the vowel, and while it may have some advantages, it disregards pronunciation too frequently to be worthy of universal adoption.

The printer must seek, in divisions, to satisfy at once the eye, the ear, and the mind. His first necessity is to avoid unsightly divisions. Among these may be classed, those which put only one letter in the first or second line; in wide measures, those which leave only two letters of a word in one line; the repetition of more than two divisions in successive lines; and the division of a word at the bottom of a page, more especially if it is a page bearing an odd number.

In determining the conflict which prevails as to whether it is best to offend the ear or the mind, it should be remembered that while all intelligent readers are tolerably well acquainted with the pronunciation of words in common use, comparatively few readers store their memories with the derivation or origin of words. Divisions based on pronunciation will certainly be readily understood by the general reader, while divisions based on derivations may not only be a source of immediate inconvenience, but even of misapprehension.

Dodger.—Sheets of printed matter, usually relating to a star actor, a special play, or a new sensation, which are smaller than the programmes used to announce in detail the cast of characters and other particulars relating to theatrical perfromances.

Domesday, or Domesday Book.—This is an official English book framed by order of William the Conqueror (A.D. 1031-6), containing a general survey of most of the lands in England, which possesses a typographical interest from the fact that it gives the exact form of the letters used, and the mode of writing adopted, eight centuries ago. Several attempts have been made, under the authority and at the expense of the British government, to produce fac-similes of the Domesday Book, and, to execute this design, fonts of Domesday letter have been cast which differ from other Roman type mainly in the

large number of characters required to represent abbreviations. They were as numerous and varied as the letters now used in pronouncing dictionaries, and embrace some signs as unlike the letters of the alphabet as the marks used by phonographers at the present day.

Dominical Letter.—The letter which represents Sunday in the plan adopted by the framers of the Ecclesiastical Calendar. This is so arranged that the first seven days of each year are represented by the first seven letters of the alphabet, a, b, c, d, e, f, and g, and whichever of these happens to designate Sunday becomes the Dominical or Sunday letter for that year.

Donations.—It is impossible to obtain a full list of the donations made from time to time to local Typographical organizations in the United States. The most important, in this locality, are the bequests of Richard Ronaldson and Lawrence Johnson to the Philadelphia Typographical Society, and the gifts of George W. Childs to the same organization, in money and a deed for a valuable piece of ground known as the Philadelphia Printers' Cemetery. Attempts have been made in the Printers' International Union to organize an American Relief Fund, and to establish a home for disabled printers, but neither of these projects has been formally indorsed.

In London, a succession of donations has been made through a long series of years, for the benefit of London or English printers. Up to a comparatively recent period, the management of these bequests was generally intrusted to the Stationers' Company. Some of them were quite large. William Bowyer, an eminent London printer, left bequests in 1777, amounting in all to £6000, for the relief of compositors and pressmen. William Strahan, in 1784, gave £1000; Thomas Wright, in 1794, gave £2000; Andrew Strahan, in 1815 and 1818, gave £2225; and Luke Hansard, in 1818, gave £2500.

Of late years, a large proportion of the donations intended for the relief of London or English printers have been devoted to the support of the Printers' Alms House near London, or to a Printers' Pension Fund. In these organizations printers take an active part, as a small annual contribution gives them the privilege of voting for candidates for vacancies in the Alms House or on the lists of pensioners, as well as the right to become applicants for such benefits themselves. Some large donations have already been made to these funds by master-printers or booksellers, especially by George Biggs, one of whose bequests yields £300 per annum; and Earl Stanhope (a son of the Earl Stanhope who invented the Stanhope press) has taken a warm interest in the completion of the Printers' Alms House.

Donatus.—The Latin grammar of Donatus, being properly entitled,—*Donatus de Octo Partibus Orationis*. This school-book was one of the popular block books of Holland in the fifteenth century, and its various editions figure largely in the dispute as to the use of movable wooden type by Koster of Haarlem. Some copies of the Donatus supposed to be printed from leaden type on account of their blurred and indistinct appearance have been credited to Gutenberg, as being one of his earliest attempts at Strasburg. That many school-books of this kind were manufactured by different methods, and destroyed by use, is very probable, and numerous fragments are still in existence both in small folio and quarto form. The word donat or donatus seems to have been used popularly to express the elements of any art, as in Chaucer's line:

Then drave I me among drapers, my donat to learne.

The Prymar and the Plane Donat were the first grammars in the English schools, and in Scotland in 1568 a printer was empowered by writ of privy seal to print exclusively the buikes callit donatus pro Pueris Rudimentis of Pelisso.

Double Cap.—A flat writing-paper intended chiefly for blanks or blank books. (See DIMENSIONS OF PAPER.)

Double-Cylinders.—Presses with two cylinders over which paper is fed to one form.

Double Dagger.—A reference mark, thus (‡), which stands third in order, and follows the dagger or obelisk.

Double Elephant.—A flat writing-paper, usually 26 by 40 inches.

Double Imperial.—A printing-paper. (See DIMENSIONS OF PAPER.)

Double Letters.—Two or three letters cast on one shank, as fi, ff, ffi, ffl.

Double Medium.—A printing-paper. (See DIMENSIONS OF PAPER.)

Double Pica.—See TYPE.

Double Royal.—A printing-paper. (See DIMENSIONS OF PAPER.)

Double Super Royal.—A printing-paper. (See DIMENSIONS OF PAPER).

Doublet.—A word or phrase unintentionally and improperly set up a second time.

Dove-Tail.—A form made up of pages which do not follow each other in consecutive order.

Draw.—When a form has been badly locked up or the lines insufficiently justified, the action of the roller frequently causes one or more of them to be drawn up, either causing an out, if the letter is removed altogether, or a batter, if it falls upon the face of the form.

Dressing a Chase.—Fitting a chase or form with the proper furniture or quoins. (See MARGIN.)

Drive.—An impression driven in copper from a steel letter punch which has not been fitted up as a complete matrix. When a new font of letter is designed and cut, the type-founder who originates it frequently prepares drives in the manner indicated, and sells them to other type-founders, who convert them into matrices. Drives are also sometimes called strikes, or the originals of matrices.

Drive Out.—Matter is driven out when it is set widely, or branched out. Many compositors indulge

in the habit of spacing their matter widely near the end of a paragraph, in order to drive it out so as to secure a fat break-line. This system is reprehensible, as it disfigures the page, and should be checked by the reader marking it back on the proof. When, by reason of insertions in an author's proof, the sheet is overrun, the surplus lines at the end are termed driven-out matter.

Drum-Cylinders.—Single large cylinder-presses are called drum-cylinders, or drum-cylinder presses, partly because their cylinders resemble a drum in shape, and partly to distinguish them from the small cylinder. A large proportion of the new single-cylinder presses of the present day are drum-cylinders, and it is believed by many printers that they wear out type less rapidly than small cylinder-presses. (See page 150.)

Dryer.—Various preparations are used to insure the quick and perfect drying of ink on printed forms. One of the most reliable for fine grades of ink is the Japan Dryer, mixed in small quantities with the ink. Good turpentine, with a small quantity of balsam copaiba, is said to be an excellent mixture for the coarser grades of black and colored ink, and to act as a dryer, but it is said to have an objectionable odor. As a quick drying preparation for inks to be used on bookbinders' cases, the following compound is recommended: one ounce beeswax; one-quarter ounce gum arabic, dissolved in acetic acid sufficient to make a thin mucilage; one-quarter ounce Brown's Japan;—incorporated with one pound of good cut ink. A quick drying reducing preparation is also advertised and sold to the trade by C. E. Robinson, ink-manufacturer, of Philadelphia. Another preparation said to be useful as a dryer, as well as to impart brilliancy to inks, is the following: Demar varnish, one ounce; Balsam Fir, one-half ounce; Oil Bergamot, twenty-five drops; Balsam Copaiba, thirty-five drops; Kreosote, ten drops; Copal varnish, fifty drops. Use in small quantities.

Dry-Point.—A sharp point used in copper-plate engraving to draw fine lines, and to make fine points in stippling and engraving.

Dunk's Chromatic Press.—A press for printing in five or more colors at the same time has been patented by A. A. Dunk, of Philadelphia, who is now (1871) running it successfully on the ordinary colored work. Difficulties in former machines are overcome in this: overlaying is readily performed; register is perfect and easily adjusted; and the distribution of ink is well provided for. The sheet being firmly held in the nippers until it receives every color required, there is no loss of paper from careless feeders, and an important saving is thus made. There are two sectional cylinders revolving in unison, one of them carrying the required number of forms, and the other a corresponding number of tympans, while a skeleton cylinder contains the nippers. The sheet is retained until fully printed, in the same nippers, which present it to the successive forms, from each of which it receives an impression in a different color.

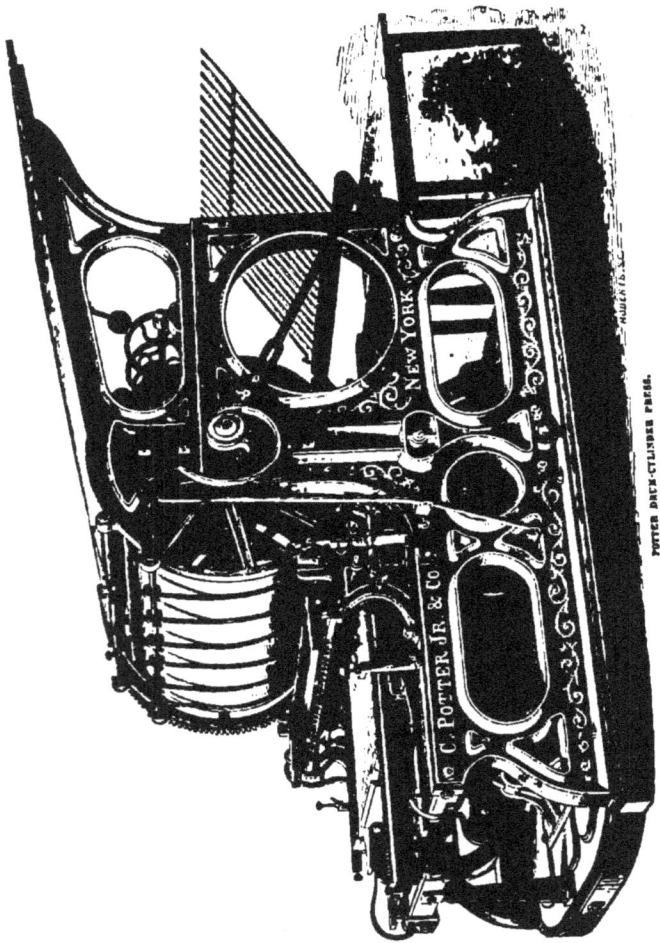

POTTER DRUM-CYLINDER PRESS.

There are four inking-rollers to each form, but where the full number of colors is not required, one of the forms may be rolled twice with four rollers, or, for printing in one color only, twenty inking-rollers might be made to ink one form. The feeding is done in the same manner as upon an ordinary cylinder press, and over 9000 sheets in five colors have been run in one day of ten hours, equal to 45,000 impressions, without the loss of a single sheet.

The supposed difficulty of printing one color upon another while the first was fresh, is surmounted in this machine. It has demonstrated that two colors or more can be printed, one on the other, where a different shade is required, without trouble; in fact, the inventor claims that this is the correct manner to print, when overlapping of colors is resorted to, to produce a new shade.

This press runs quietly, and requires, to drive it, no more power than any other press of the same size printing only one color at a time.

Duodecimo.—When a book is made up of a series of sheets folded into twelve leaves, or twenty-four pages each, it is said to be duodecimo, or, as this word is frequently abbreviated, 12mo.

Durer, Albrecht, born in Nuremberg, 1471, died in the same city, 1528, was an eminent German artist, whose fame is connected with typography by the great improvements which he introduced into the art of wood-engraving. After receiving considerable instruction from his father, who was a skillful gold-smith, Durer passed four years with an eminent painter at Nuremberg, and subsequently spent several years in the study of art in Germany and the Low Countries. In 1498 appeared his first great series of wood-cuts, illustrating the Revelation. The brilliant originality and power of his conceptions soon made Durer famous throughout Europe, and a Venetian artist counterfeited on copper a series of his wood-cuts, attaching to them his well-known monogram or stamp, of a large rudely-fashioned A surrounding a small D. Durer immediately hastened to Venice and appealed to the Senate, and that body compelled the offending artist to efface the mark, and secured its future use exclusively to its rightful owner. The earlier works of Durer were impressed with the prevalent taste for the fantastic, and his exuberant fancy crowded his groups with monstrous and grotesque figures; but later in life the artist earnestly espoused the cause of the Reformation, and his imagination was purified and exalted by the simple sublimity of his religious enthusiasm. He was the first German artist who taught the rules of perspective and insisted on the study of anatomy. In painting he elevated his art by his originality and grandeur of conception and richness of coloring, and he found engraving in its infancy and carried it to great perfection. The pictures of Durer and Holbein furnished the finest portion of the numerous admirable illustrated books of the fifteenth and sixteenth centuries.

Dusting Colors.—These colors are ground in a mill to a very fine powder. In using them for printing purposes, instead of being mixed with the varnish, they are dusted over it; that is to say, the form is rolled over with varnish, as with ordinary ink, and after the impression is pulled the colors are dusted over it with a broad camel's-hair brush or a clean hare's foot; some pressmen use wool. When the colors are well dried on the impression, the superfluous powder can be cleared off the sheet.

Dutch Gold.—The name in commerce for copper, brass and bronze leaf, used in Holland for ornamenting paper and toys; usually an alloy of eleven parts copper and two of zinc rolled into thin sheets.

E.

EAGLE CABINET.

Eagle Cabinet.—A Cabinet for holding cases of type, manufactured by Vanderburgh, Wells & Co.

Ear of the Frisket.—Otherwise, the thumb-piece. An iron projection at the edge of the frisket nearest to the workman. By taking hold of it he folds down, and also raises and unfolds, both the frisket and the tympan.

Eclectic.—Not original, but formed of selections chosen and combined without any special system. The term is used as a title for magazines made up of reprinted articles.

Ectypography.—A method of etching, in which the lines are produced in relief instead of being depressed or cut in.

Edition.—The number of copies of a work that are printed at the same time, or for one publication. To meet the requirements of the public, some of the leading daily journals issue successive editions of each number at stated hours, adding additional items of news, and sometimes altering the other departments of the paper.

Editio princeps.—The first edition of any work; frequently abbreviated into princeps.

Editor.—One who revises and prepares a work for publication; also the title of the conductor of a journal, magazine, or other serial publication, and of the heads of the minor departments, as news-editor, or fashion editress. The word in the former sense signified that preparation of a work which required critical taste and literary capacity, such as the writing of the preface, introduction, notes, indexes, and also the correction of the text; and, in the same manner, the editor of a journal not only revises and publishes the works of others, but prepares original matter.

Editorial.—That portion of a journal, magazine, etc., written by the editor or editors, consisting usually of comments on important current questions or events. In newspapers the editorial indicates the opinions of the editor, and is usually distinguished by being leaded and being placed under the sub-head. About the year 1739 several editors of newspapers in England undertook to insert short essays upon various subjects for the information and amusement of their readers. Mr. Raikes, the editor of the Gloucester Journal, commenced a series under the title of Country Common Sense, but so large a number of his readers were offended at what they considered as an interference with the news of the week, that he abandoned his design. Mr. Abreo, proprietor of the Canterbury News Letter, met equal opposition at first, but steadily continued the essays, and finally won the approbation of all his readers. Since then editorials have become an indispensable feature of vigorous newspapers.

Eidograph.—An instrument for copying drawings on the same or a different scale; a form of the pantograph.

Eighteenmo, or Eighteens.—A sheet of paper folded into eighteen leaves, making thirty-six pages. It is usually termed eighteens, from being written 18mo; and is sometimes called Octodecimo. The word also means, specifically, the size of a page proper for the eighteenth part of a medium sheet of paper.

Election Tickets.—See JOB PRINTING.

Electro-tint.—A method of engraving by an electrotype process. Smee, in describing it, says: A plain copper plate is procured, upon which the artist makes a painting with some substance insoluble in the solution of sulphate of copper. The plate is placed in the solution, and a reverse made, which is at once ready for the printer. A great many specimens of the electro-tint have been published at different times [in England] and of various degrees of excellence. . . . Sometimes the electro-tint cast is used to print from the hollows, at others from the elevations: thus, in one case it forms a kind of engraving, at another a surface similar to that of a wood-cut.

Electrotyping.—The art of separating the metals from their solutions and depositing them in solid form, by means of the electric current, excited by the Voltaic battery, so as to manufacture, by this process, copies of engravings, or forms of type, from which impressions can be taken by the methods usually employed in letter-press printing. This is, to printers, one of the most useful, interesting, and important of all modern discoveries. It accomplishes, in a superior manner, nearly all the ends attained by the various stereotyping processes. For duplicating wood-cuts or engravings it has practically superseded them, because it furnishes better and more durable copies. It is also better to electrotype pages of books, or forms of jobs from which large editions are to be printed, than to stereotype them, because millions of impressions can be made on electrotype plates, without serious diminution of the sharpness or legibility, while ordinary stereotype plates would be well worn by a much smaller number of impressions. It costs less to stereotype a given surface than to electrotype it, and the operation can be performed, especially by the papier-mache process, in a shorter time than electrotyping—so that when speed or cheapness of first cost is a paramount consideration, stereotyping is to be preferred to electrotyping,—but in all other cases where duplicate copies of a form are required, they are usually electrotyped.

Conflicting statements have been made in regard to the originators of the process of manufacturing electrotype plates for printing. It is alleged that the discoveries which led directly to it were made, about the same period, a short time before 1840, by Professor Jacobi, of St. Petersburg, Russia, by Thomas Spencer, of Liverpool, and by J. C. Jordan, of London. Joseph A. Adams, a wood-engraver of New York, also commenced experiments in electrotyping plates from wood-cuts in 1839, and produced a plate which was printed from in Mapes's Magazine in 1841. Smee, one of the best of English authorities on Electro-Metallurgy and Electrotyping, says that, so far as he knows, the London Journal for April, 1840, contained the first specimen of printing from an electrotype, by Newton, and that it was a small, rough sketch.

Savage's Dictionary of Printing, published in London in 1841, contains several specimens of good impressions of engravings, taken from electrotypes, and an impression of an electrotype of a page of Diamond type, which is quite imperfect, indicating that at that period good electrotypes of engravings could be taken in England, but that the art of electrotyping forms of small type was not well understood. The names which stand out most prominently in connection with the invention of Electrotyping are those of Jacobi, Spencer, Murray (who was the first to suggest the use of plumbago or black-lead as a coating for the forms and moulds), Smee, whose battery is in general use, and, in the United States, Joseph A. Adams, who has made several important improvements in electrotyping appliances, and Daniel Davis, of Boston, who is said to have been the first in this country to establish electrotyping as a distinct business. The latter event occurred in 1846, and soon afterwards, other electrotyping establishments were started in Philadelphia and other American cities, one of the first persons to practice the art in Philadelphia, as a business, being Thomas H. Mumford.

The galvanic battery, as improved and enlarged in its scope by Volta in 1800, furnishes the base of the art of electrotyping. Various improvements in the form and materials of batteries have been made, but all batteries are constructed on the principles laid down by Volta. The latest and probably the best battery is that devised by Joseph A. Adams, and manufactured by Hoe & Co. It is lined with glass to prevent leakage, and possesses other advantages.

position is made of the best unadulterated yellow wax, to which, in cold rooms or in cold weather, from five to twenty per cent. of virgin wax is added. The wax is boiled, to prepare it for use, and then poured into a moulding-case, which is a flat brass pan. The form to be electrotyped being placed on the bed of an

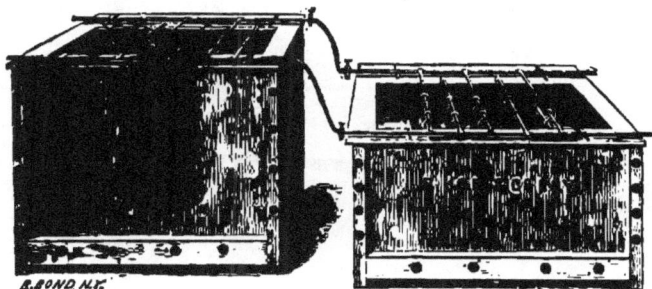

B.BOND N.Y.

ELECTROTYPE BATTERY.

It does not fall within the scope of this work to describe minutely the nature of the Voltaic pile or battery, and for present purposes it is only necessary to say that by its aid metals in solution can be firmly deposited on a properly prepared surface or mould, and that by the deposition of copper, in this manner, upon wax moulds of engravings or type forms, electrotype plates are made. The Voltaic pile or battery, however, was well known to scientific men for nearly forty years before it was used for electrotyping purposes. This application was hastened by a discovery of the fact that when copper or other metals were deposited on the sides of a Voltaic battery, and subsequently removed, they furnished an exact transcript of the inequalities of the surface to which they had been temporarily attached. This discovery furnished all the leading theoretical conditions for electrotyping which had not previously been explained by Volta and his successors; and it only remained to apply these principles effectually to the attainment of practical results, and to surmount a series of mechanical difficulties.

In preparing a form for electrotyping, the books say that type-high spaces and quadrats must be used; but this is not absolutely necessary, and in practice low spaces and low quadrats are often employed. The form, however, should be accurately justified, tightly locked up, and well protected on all sides by high slugs or type-high bearers. The first process of the electrotyper, after seeing that a type-high form or engraving is perfectly clean, is to cover it with finely powdered black-lead or plumbago, and to subsequently remove all excess of black-lead, by rubbing the palm of the hand over the surface of the type or wood-cut. This is done to facilitate the withdrawal of the form from the mould. The moulding com-

electrotyper's press, the wax in the moulding-case is placed upon the face of the form, and an impression taken. Several presses are used by electrotypers, and one of those commonly employed is represented by the accompanying engraving.

After this impression is taken and the form and mould are separated, the mould next goes through the process of building, which consists in dropping heated wax upon such portions as should be deeply sunk in the finished electrotype plate. Where there is a large body of quadrats, for instance, in a form, the corresponding part of the mould should be raised by a deposit of melted wax. Great skill is displayed by some electrotypers in building. They use a heated building-iron, or piece of iron shaped something like a poker, of convenient length, with a sharp point, which is applied to a strip of dry wax until some of the wax adheres to it; this wax is dropped, in a melted state, upon the portions of the mould which are to be raised; and it requires a steady hand to drop the melted wax exactly where it is needed, and to avoid dropping it upon any spot where it is not needed. After the building process is completed, the wax mould is next black-leaded,—very pure, fine, and lustrous black-lead being required for this purpose. It is also necessary that the entire surface of the mould should be very effectually covered with this substance, to insure a perfect deposit of the copper; and, to facilitate this operation, a black-leading machine is used, one of which is shown in the accompanying engraving.

After the mould is black-leaded, every particle of superfluous black-lead is removed by blowing it off, with a pair of bellows having a broad nozzle. The mould undergoes a further preparation, by having the back of the moulding-pan coated with wax, so

BLACK-LEADING MACHINE.

TOGGLE-PRESS WITH LIFTING HEAD.

that copper will not be deposited upon it, and also by attaching to a point near the face of the mould a bit of metal, or adopting some similar method for hastening the deposit of the copper on the black-leaded surface. It is then quickly immersed in one of the apartments of the battery, where the process of depositing a copper solution upon the black-leaded surface of the mould is continued until a solid plate is formed, which, though it is scarcely thicker than a man's thumb-nail, forms, when properly backed, the best and most enduring surface for letter-press printing that has ever been discovered. The battery itself is one of the marvels of modern science, being an offshoot of a long series of attempts to utilize discoveries appertaining to the mysterious domain of electricity. It will suffice here to say that in one of the chambers of the battery an acid bath is made of sulphuric acid dissolved in water; this solution is acted upon by zinc plates and other appliances; and a connection akin to the wonders of the telegraph is made by wires or rods, or both, with the chambers in which the forms are deposited, and with the form itself,—the result of all these and auxiliary processes being that copper, after its reduction to a liquid, is subsequently concentrated in a shape and consistency adapted to the printer's use.

One of the latest improvements in electrotyping is a process patented by Joseph A. Adams in January, 1870, for covering the surface of the wax with finely powdered tin, before it receives an impression from the type forms. It is claimed that electrotypes can be made much better and quicker by this process than by the use of black-lead alone. Mr. Adams also patented, April 19, 1870, an electric connection gripper, which is said to obviate the necessity of covering the back of the mould-pan with wax.

After the shell, as it is technically termed, is formed in the battery, it must next be carefully removed from the mould, and all wax taken from it. This is done by pouring hot water gently over the mould, or by placing it in a steam-heating table, and superfluous wax is removed by a heated solution of common potash. The other processes consist of trimming the shell, or soldering to it tin, and subsequently straightening, backing, shaving and finishing it. Tin adheres readily to copper; a backing metal composed of four parts of tin, five of antimony, and ninety-one of lead adheres readily to tin; and by a combination of these metals, the thin electrotype shell is thickened to the extent requisite for use as a plate.

Elegy.—A mournful or plaintive poem. Among the most famous elegies in the English language are Gray's Elegy written in a Country Church-yard, Milton's Lycidas, Shelley's Adonais, and Byron's Monody on Sheridan.

Elephant.—A large flat writing-paper. (See DIMENSIONS OF PAPER).

Eliot's Indian Bible.—This book, published at Cambridge, Massachusetts, in 1663, ranks among the typographical curiosities of America, having been the first attempt to translate the Scriptures into an Indian dialect. John Eliot, frequently styled the Apostle to the Indians, prepared a catechism in the Indian language, which was printed in 1653 at the expense of the English Society for Propagating the Gospel in New England. To further other publications of a like character, the society in 1655 sent over a second press, which was erected in the building occupied by Glover's press. The necessary type and materials were also supplied, and Marmaduke Johnson, a printer of London, arrived in 1660 to assist in the work. The New Testament, translated by John Eliot into the dialect of the Natick Indians, was issued in 1661. The entire Scriptures, together with the New England Psalm-Book in Indian verse, was finished in 1663, and printed in quarto form with marginal notes, having the joint imprint of Samuel Green and Marmaduke Johnson, and dedicated to Charles II. The work had lingered three years in press, owing to the irregularities and indolence of Johnson, and its completion was in a great degree due to the ability of an Indian apprenticed to Samuel Green. This Indian became a successful typographer, and his name appeared on the Psalter of 1709 in the imprint, B. Green and J. Printer. The original edition of Eliot's Bible is very rude in appearance, the paper poor and the type irregular. Although printing had been pursued in the colony for twenty years, the binding of this book, which is sheep-skin, is the first mentioned, John Ratcliffe being sent from England to complete it. According to a letter addressed by him to the Commissioners in August, 1664, he objects to the price paid for binding, and states that he cannot afford to do the work for less than 3s. 4d. per book, because each Bible requires a full day's work, and because he is required to furnish thread, glue, pasteboard and leather clasps to the value of one shilling," the prices being so much greater in America that he has to pay eighteen shillings for material which would cost but four shillings in England. The press-work on a part of the Bible was charged as follows: Sheets of the Old Testament, executed by Green alone, £3 10s. per sheet; with Johnson's assistance at £2 10s. per sheet. Title sheet, £1; Indian Psalms, £2 per sheet. The paper, which was fine post, was charged at 6s. per ream. It has been calculated from the various items that the whole expense of printing 1000 copies of the Bible, 500 additional copies of the New Testament, an edition of Baxter's Call, an edition of the Psalter, and two editions of Eliot's Catechism, all in the Indian language, including the cost of the types and the binding of part of the books, amounted to a fraction more than 1200 pounds sterling. The Corporation presented the materials to Harvard College after the completion of the work, the materials being valued at only eighty pounds. A second edition of two thousand copies of the Bible was printed by Green in 1685. Some idea of the language of the work may be derived from the following verse from the 19th Psalm:

1. Kesuk Kukootomahteaamoo
God wuttohsumoonk
Mamahchekesuk wunnahtohkon
Wutanakausoonk.

Elisions.—One or two contiguous words abbreviated by the substitution of an apostrophe for one or more letters, which are to be pronounced as printed in their abbreviated form, as I've, don't, you'd, o'er, 'em.

Ellipsis.—Marks denoting the omission of letters of a word, words of a sentence, or entire sentences, the reader being notified by them of a hiatus, which he may or may not supply from his own knowledge of the subject to which the omitted letters, words, or sentences relate. The characters used for this purpose are dashes (——), asterisks (* * *), and leaders (........). Dashes are most frequently used to denote omissions of letters in a word, as K—g for King, or C——s for Congress; but when it is desirable to designate the exact number of letters omitted, asterisks or leaders are generally employed, as G***t for Great. Asterisks were also· in great use, formerly, to denote the omission of words or sentences; but it is now considered better to use three periods an em apart for this purpose, as they have a neater appearance.

Elzevir.—The name of a family of Hollandish printers during the sixteenth and seventeenth centuries, famous for the elegance of their type, the excellence of their press-work, the accuracy of their text, and their successful efforts to introduce the duodecimo as an improvement upon the larger and more expensive forms. The type of this family was long and greatly esteemed in England, and furnished the basis of the famous type of Caslon. The Elzevir publications amounted to 1213 in number, of which 968 were in Latin, 44 in Greek, 126 in French, 32 in Flemish, 22 in the Oriental languages, 11 in German, and 10 in Italian. The most esteemed books of this series are the Pliny of 1635, the Virgil of 1636, certain classics dating between 1634 and 1642, and the celebrated duodecimo classics printed from 1626 to 1652. Of twelve printers belonging to this family at least seven were celebrated for special excellence.

· Louis Elzevir, the first printer of the family, was born at Louvain, established himself at Leyden in 1580, and continued to print in that city until his death in 1616. His five sons were all printers, the youngest, Bonaventure Elzevir, achieving the greatest celebrity as the publisher of the famous duodecimo classics. Louis, a grandson of the first Louis, was the founder of the Elzevir press of Amsterdam. His classic Latin authors in quarto, folio, and octavo are considered as the most splendid publications of the family; they appeared from 1655 to 1665. Daniel, the son of Bonaventure, achieved great fame in Leyden, and afterwards at Amsterdam, continuing to print until his death in 1689; his New Testament, published in 1658, is very beautiful and exact. The Elzevirs did not aim at luxury, like the Aldi and the Stephens, printing only one work upon vellum, but devoted their endeavors to furnishing accurate works

for common use. Some of their publications were issued without their imprint, because they were directed against kings and powerful corporations.

Elzevir.—The modernized name of types cut in imitation of those used by the celebrated family of Elzevir, type-founders and printers.

Em.—The square of the body of a type. In all piece-work, book and newspaper matter is counted by ems in the United States, the American system differing in this respect from the English and French systems, which aim, although by somewhat imperfect methods, at basing compensation on the exact number of letters set up. The use of the em as a basis of computation, in this country, arrives at substantially the same end, especially as unfairness or inequalities are guarded against by extra charges for composing unusually lean letter, or letter of inconvenient sizes, or for matter set up in unusually narrow measures.

Emblem.—A figurative representation which suggests to the mind an idea not expressed to the senses. Books of emblems, containing a series of plates, accompanied by explanations, were very common in Europe, especially in the sixteenth century. The most famous in England was Quarles' Book of Emblems.

Embossed Printing.—This description of printing is done by using metallic dies, into the surface of which the lettering has been cut or punched. The counter-die is made by cutting a piece of thick smooth leather to the size of the die; the side which is to receive the impression must now be moistened, and, being laid upon the surface of the die, a sufficient pressure must be given to it to make the leather go into all the cavities in the plate. The counter is then to be removed from the die, and its edges trimmed so that both will be of the same size, after which the leather must be adjusted to its place on the face of the die, and its back covered with a thick mucilage; another impression must be made, so as to transfer the counter to the tympan. A thin sheet of gutta-percha should now be warmed on one side, and laid upon the face of the plate, with the side which has been heated uppermost. An impression must again be made, by which the leather and the gutta-percha will become attached, the result being an elastic counter, which will retain sufficient firmness to throw up any part of the under surface of the card without breaking the parts at the edges of the letters. When the job is of large size, such as a show-card, the counter-die may be made by pasting ten or twelve sheets of smooth paper together with mucilage, and while they are in a damp state, to press the die into the pulpy mass, and leave it dry before they are separated. The printer must be careful in his choice of ink. Whatever color is used should be strong in body, and the roller must be passed over the form, in all directions, so as to secure a perfectly uniform coating of ink. The form must be cleaned, as occasion may require, by the application of spirits of turpentine with a brush.—*Lynch's Manual.*

Embossed Typography.—A system of printing for the use of the blind. Instead of the application of color, the surface of the sheet is embossed, and the characters can be distinguished by the contact of the fingers. (See BLIND, PRINTING FOR THE.)

Embossing Imprint.—An invention of Henry Wilson, of Chicago, which is attached to card- and bill-head-presses, and is used to emboss an imprint on cards, bill-heads, letter-headings, or similar jobs, at the same moment that the impression of printed matter is made.

EMBOSSING PRESS.

Embossing Press.—A press used in embossing by bookbinders, and in embossed printing. Various patterns are made by different manufacturers.

Em-Dash.—A dash (—) of the length of the em of the font of which it forms part.

Emendation.—An alteration or correction of the text, intended to improve the literary character of the work.

Emerald.—A type larger than Nonpareil, and smaller than Minion.

Empty Case.—When some of the sorts of a case are exhausted, so that a compositor can set no more matter from it, it is said to be empty, although there may still be in it many type of other sorts.

En.—Half the breadth of an em, in any body of type. In reckoning the work done by compositors, in England, the en is considered as the equivalent of a letter. Thus, if the measure of a page be twenty ems Pica, there are forty ens in it, and the breadth of an en being taken as the average breadth of a type, the compositor is paid for setting up forty letters.

Encyclopædia.—A work in which an art or science, or one particular branch of an art or science, is treated exhaustively under separate headings, usually in alphabetical order. The word is frequently written cyclopædia. The Greeks used the word to express a complete course of scientific education, and two lost works, one by a nephew of Plato and the other by Varro, are presumed to be the first books entitled to the name, which may also be applied to Pliny's work on Natural History. In the fourth and fifth centuries of the Christian era several compilations of a similar character were made, and during the middle ages, a number of erudite and comprehensive works were written with the intention of presenting the current knowledge. These repositories of scholastic science were styled Summæ (compendiums) or Speculæ (mirrors); the most famous being the Speculum Historiale, Naturale et Doctrinale of the thirteenth century, and the Summæ Theologiæ of Thomas Aquinas. The Novum Organum of Bacon, and the famous dictionary of Bayle, in the seventeenth century, introduced great improvements, both in the form and execution of these compendiums, which were still further systematized in Chambers' Cyclopædia, 1728. To this book may be ascribed the honor of being the model upon which were based the renowned French Encyclopædia, 1751, the Encyclopædia Britannica, 1771, and all the brilliant band of their successors in different departments of science.

En-Dash.—A dash (-) half the length of the em of the font of letter to which it belongs.

Engine Press.—A printing-press formerly made by S. P. Ruggles, in which the type was printed with the face downward.

RUGGLES ENGINE PRESS.

Engine-Sized.—Good papers of this description are specially well adapted to printed circulars. They require less labor in making ready, cause less wear to type, and take a finer impression than hard tub-sized papers.

English.—A type larger than Pica, and smaller than Great Primer. (See TYPE.)

Engraving.—The art of producing, by incision or corrosion, designs upon blocks of wood, plates of metal, glass, or other materials, from which impressions or prints upon paper or other substances are obtained by pressure. Some forms of engraving were practiced at very remote periods of antiquity. Thousands of years ago the Egyptians used wooden stamps, and the Assyrians engraved cylinders, to make impressions upon clay. Jewish knowledge of the art of engraving seals, tablets, etc. is recorded in the oldest books of the Old Testament. (See BIBLICAL ALLUSIONS TO PRINTING.) Many coins now in existence show that the art of engraving dies was practiced long before the Christian era. The Greeks and Romans not only engraved ornaments and monuments, but cattle brands, stencilled plates, etc. The Chinese, however, invented the art of making engravings on wood, and using them as forms to yield impressions by the aid of a pigment, as in the modern forms of printing. (See CHINA, PRINTING IN.) Marco Polo is supposed to have brought a knowledge of this art from China to Italy, about 1300; and it was soon afterwards practiced in various parts of Europe, for the purpose of producing playing-cards, religious pictures, and block-books, until it gradually led, by easy transitions, to the invention of the still more important art of typography.

From time to time new methods of engraving, and new plans for cheapening and improving the production of printed pictures, of various degrees of merit, have been discovered; and so many investigations and experiments appertaining to this subject are constantly being made, that new processes, of various degrees of utility, are frequently announced. Wood-engraving, which, as applied to printing purposes, precedes all others, still holds a front rank for popular purposes; and its utility has been immensely increased during the present century by the readiness and certainty with which perfect copies of an engraved block can be electrotyped, and the rapidity with which impressions can be made on machine-presses. Detailed descriptions of this art are given in another article. (See WOOD-ENGRAVING.) One of the most practical substitutes for wood-engraving is also explained elsewhere (see GRAPHOTYPE), as well as the art which approaches nearest in cheapness to wood-engraving for large editions, and is less expensive for small editions. (See LITHOGRAPHY.) References are also made elsewhere, under the appropriate headings, to various other descriptions of engraving. (See AQUA-TINT, CHEMITYPY, COPPER-PLATE ENGRAVING, ELECTRO-TINT, ETCHING, MEZZOTINT, STEEL ENGRAVING, ZINCOGRAPHY, etc).

Envelopes.—Envelopes, though now almost universally used to inclose letters, are of comparatively recent origin. They were used in France and England to a limited extent prior to 1839. In that year an act was passed in Great Britain, changing the old system of charging double rates when a letter

was composed of two pieces of paper, to a charge based on weight. The old system of folding the letter and sealing it with a wafer or wax, was then soon superseded by the new one of inclosing it in an envelope; and the records show that while in 1839 76,000,000 letters were posted in the United Kingdom, in 1841 fully one-half the letters sent through the post-office were inclosed in envelopes, and in 1850 100 out of every 112 were thus inclosed; their introduction into general use being at an earlier day and at a more rapid rate in England than in the United States. Warren de la Rue and Edwin Hill patented a machine for making envelopes in England in 1845, and again patented improvements to it in 1849, but this machine was not self-feeding; the blanks were cut out by a separate process; and the gum on the flap was applied by hand. Other machines were subsequently patented in England, but none so effective and productive as those which have been invented in this country.

For a number of years after the manufacture of envelopes was commenced in the United States, they were all cut out by ordinary chisels, and pasted and folded by hand, the gum having been first put on the flap by a brush. This was a very slow process, the quantity made by a single person in a day ranging from 2000 to 3000, according to size and shape.

The earliest patent on envelope machinery in the United States was taken out by Ezra Coleman, of Philadelphia. It is dated April 26, 1853 and in June of the same year, Mr. R. L. Hawes, of Worcester, Massachusetts, was also granted a patent for an improvement in envelope machines. Mr. Hawes spent a great deal of time and money in endeavoring to perfect his machinery, but was only partially successful.

Various patents were taken out from 1855 to 1859, for improvements in envelope machines, but, with the exception of one to M. G. Puffer, assigned to White and Corbin, and that of Duff and Keating, none of them was extensively used.

In 1863, Mr. Reay, of New York, obtained a patent for a self-feeding machine, which, with the exception of cutting out the blanks and gumming the flaps, will fold and complete about 18,000 envelopes a day. It is, perhaps, the best machine now in general use throughout the United States, and it has recently been introduced in England and Scotland. Prior to this invention, all envelopes, except those made under Pettee's patent, were gummed by hand, the process being to first cut out the lozenge-shaped blanks, by means of dies or cutters, and then to comb them out upon a board, and by passing a brush filled with gum over the flaps, to gum a number at a time, the envelopes being placed upon racks to dry, after they had been gummed. This process was tedious, and frequently many envelopes were spoiled or imperfectly gummed, through carelessness. To remedy this difficulty, Mr. Thomas V. Waymouth, in 1866, patented a machine so arranged as to gum the seal flaps of the envelope blanks at or about the same time with the lower or end flaps, after the blanks are placed in the machine, and before they are folded. This machine has since been extensively used only by the parties to whom the patent was assigned.

But the most interesting of all the improvements in envelopes and envelope machinery has taken place within a few years past, in connection with what is known as the Pettee patent envelope, and the machinery for making the same. On March 22, 1859, S. E. Pettee patented a new form of envelope, differing from any other previously made. The paper used is furnished in rolls of the proper width, and by cutting it so that the flap of one envelope is taken from a portion of another, and by an arrangement of narrow folds at each end of the envelope, more blanks are cut from the same quantity of paper than by the old form. This will be understood more fully by an examination of the cuts given below:

On July 10, 1866, Robert Park, of Philadelphia, a young and ingenious mechanic, patented a machine to make the improved envelope, and assigned all his rights to W. E. & E. D. Lockwood & F. J. Spangler. One end of a roll of paper, several thousand feet in length, being placed in the machine, the envelopes are cut out, creased, pasted on the sides, gummed on the flaps, and dried, before leaving the machine, coming out at the other end of it complete in all respects, and the machinery has been run for weeks at a time at the rate of 190 a minute. Experience has, however, demonstrated that 140 to 150 a minute is a better speed for the machines, although the envelopes made at this rate are no better than those made more rapidly. The gumming of these envelopes is done at the same time as the folding, and is much superior to the hand or machine gumming in the old form, being more uniform and even. The gumming and

The method of cutting the old style Envelope.

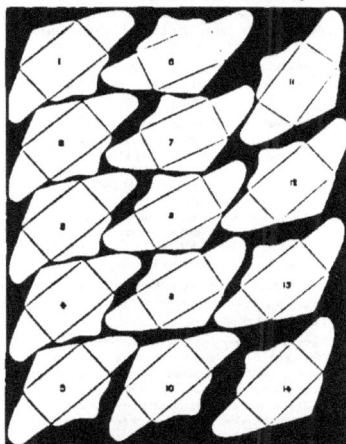

THE BLACK SHOWS THE WASTE.

The method of cutting Pettee Patent Envelope.

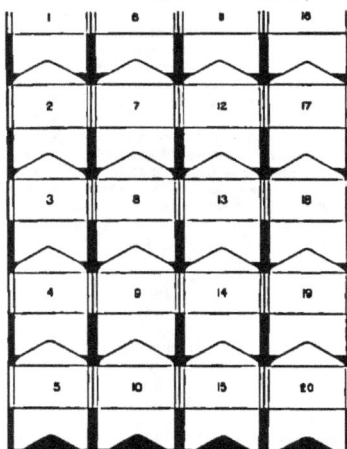

THE BLACK SHOWS THE WASTE.

It will be observed that both the above sheets of paper are of the same size, and that four of the blanks of the improved envelope are incomplete, the paper not being large enough, and that therefore there are not quite twenty full envelopes, although a great saving over the old style is effected.

That this envelope would save paper was apparent, but how to manufacture it as cheaply as the old style was a serious question. After several years of work and many experiments, the patent, after having been assigned and reassigned, finally fell into the hands of parties who, after expending large sums of money, perfected a machine entirely different from any ever before invented, which is a triumph of mechanism.

drying portion of the machine was the invention of John Armstrong, patented in 1862, making the completed machine, as now used, in reality the invention of Robert Park, John Armstrong, and John H. Cooper, who in 1867 patented certain improvements which have greatly increased its efficiency.

New York City, Philadelphia, Springfield and Worcester, Massachusetts, and Hartford and Rockville, Connecticut, contain the principal envelope factories in the United States; but envelopes are made to some extent in every section. The paper used in their manufacture is principally made at Philadelphia, Holyoke, Windsor Locks, Connecticut, and Lawrence, Massachusetts, and is itself a speciality. Two classes of paper are used, viz.: tub or animal-sized, and engine-sized. The former is generally loft-dried, feels harder and costs more than the latter, which is dried in the machine as it is made, and is not so brittle as the loft-dried. Recent improvements in engine-sized envelope paper have, however, made it difficult in some cases to distinguish it from the former.

To manufacture envelopes successfully, requires considerable capital, the machines being expensive, and the great variety of sizes and styles necessary to carry on the business requiring a heavy investment in paper and machinery.

There are two establishments in New York City and one in Philadelphia, which have facilities for manufacturing from 700,000 to 1,000,000 envelopes a day; but, as they make different sizes, it is seldom that all their machinery is kept running. Females are generally employed to manufacture envelopes and to attend the machines. Their wages vary from $4.50 to $10 a week, according to their skill, most of them working by the piece, or at so much per 1000.

The colors of papers used in envelopes are manilla, gold, dark and light buff, amber, cream, melon, dark blue, pink, dark and light canary, orange, and white. The papers vary in weight from 22 to 75 pounds per ream of 21 by 31 inches, and cost from 12 to 35 cents per pound, but average about 21 cents per pound. In envelopes of light weight and medium quality, the labor of making is about one-third their cost, while with fine heavy papers it is only about one-fourth to one-fifth. The business is steadily increasing, but during the last eight or ten years much new machinery was built, and the quantity now running is in excess of the requirements of the country.

Epic.—A poem of a particular form, elevated in subject and treatment, and descriptive of events of great importance. The principal epics are the Iliad and Odyssey of Homer, the Æneid of Virgil, the Paradise Lost and Paradise Regained of Milton. The title is also applied by some authors to the Niebelungen-Lied, the Romance of the Cid, the Divine Comedy, the Jerusalem Delivered, and the Henriade.

Epigram.—A short poem restricted to one subject and ending with a happy or witty turn of expression.

Epigraph.—A motto or inscription placed at the commencement of a work, or at the beginning of one of its divisions, consisting either of a quotation or of a sentence framed specially for the purpose.

Episode.—A digression or incidental narrative not strictly belonging to the subject under treatment, but naturally arising from it.

Epistle.—A writing directed to a person at a distance; but applied, in a religious sense, to the written addresses of the apostles to their Christian brethren, contained in the canon of Scripture.

Epitaph.—An inscription on a tomb in honor or memory of the dead; also lines commemorative of an individual, but not inscribed upon any monument. One of the earliest and best examples of the quaint use of typographical allusions in epitaphs is found in that of the Rev. John Cotton, who died in New England in 1652:

A living, breathing Bible; tables where
Both covenants at large engraven were;
Gospel and law in's heart had each its column,
His head an index to the sacred volume!
His very name a title-page; and next
His life a commentary on the text.
Oh, what a monument of glorious worth,
When in a new edition he comes forth!
Without errata, we may think he'll be
In leaves and covers of eternity.

This may have been an amplification of the epitaph of Christopher Barker, printer to Queen Elizabeth, who died 1599, viz.:

Here Barker lies, once printer to the crown,
Whose works of art acquir'd a vast renown.
Time saw his worth, and spread around his fame,
That future printers might imprint the same.
But when his strength could work the press no more,
And his last sheets were folded into store,—
Pure faith, with hope (the greatest treasures given),
Open'd their gates, and bade him pass to heaven.

Somewhat similar to these were the lines cut in black letter on the grave-stone of John Foster, a printer of Boston, who died in 1681:

Thy body, which no activeness did lack,
Now's laid aside, like an old almanack;
But for the present only's out of date,
'Twill have at length a far more active state;
Yea, though with dust the body soiled be,
Yet at the resurrection we shall see
A fair edition, and of matchless worth,
Free from errata, not in heaven sate forth:
'Tis but a word from God, the great Creator,
It shall be done when he says Imprimatur.

Another instance of the same species of wit is found in the epitaph on Geo. Faulkner, alderman and printer of Dublin, who died 1775:—

Turn, gentle stranger, and this urn revere,
O'er which Hibernia saddens with a tear;
Here sleeps George Faulkner, printer! once so dear
To humorous Swift and Chesterfield's gay peer;
So dear to his wronged country and her laws;
So dauntless when imprisoned in her cause;
No alderman e'er graced a weightier board,
No wit e'er joked more freely with a lord.
None could with him in anecdotes confer,
A perfect annal book in Elzevir.
Whate'er of glory life's first sheets presage,
Whate'er the splendor of the title-page;
Leaf after leaf, though learned lore ensues
Close as thy types, and various as thy news;
Yet, George, we see one lot await them all,
Gigantic folios, or octavos small:
One universal finis claims his rank,
And every volume closes in a blank.

Benjamin Franklin in his youth prepared for himself the following epitaph:—

THE BODY
OF
BENJAMIN FRANKLIN,
PRINTER,

(Like the cover of an old book, its contents torn out
And stript of its lettering and gilding)
Lies here food for worms;
Yet the work itself shall not be lost,
For it will (as he believed) appear once more
In a new and more beautiful edition,
Corrected and amended by
THE AUTHOR.

It is peculiarly characteristic of Franklin that he should have expended such care in condensing a sort of Poor Richard's epitaph for himself, in his early youth, and discarded it in his age, ordering that his grave should be marked with a simple slab, and the words:—Benjamin and Deborah Franklin, 1790; leaving, in all the security of conscious worth, his epitaph engraved upon the hearts of his countrymen.

Formed upon the same model is an inscription on a grave in Coventry, England, which reads thus:—

Here lie the mortal remains of JOHN HULME, printer, who, like an old worn-out type, battered by frequent use, reposes in the grave, but not without a hope that at some future time he might be recast in the mould of righteousness, and safely locked up in the blissful chase of immortality; he was distributed from the board of life on the 9th day of September, 1827, regretted by his employers, and respected by his fellow-artists.

But excelling all others in quaintness is the following:—

Sacred to the memory of
ADAM WILLIAMSON,
pressman printer, in Edinburgh,
who died October 3, 1832,
aged 72 years.

All my stays are loosed;
my cap is thrown off; my head is worn out;
my box is broken;
my spindle and bar have lost their power;
my till is laid aside;
both legs of my crane are turned out of their path;
my platen can make no impression;
my winter hath no spring;
my rounce will neither roll out nor in;
stone, coffin, and carriage have all failed;
the hinges of my tympan, and frisket, are immovable;
my long and short ribs are rusted;
my cheeks are much worm-eaten, and mouldering away;
my press is totally down!

The volume of my life is finished!
not without many errors:
most of them have arisen from bad composition, and are
to be attributed more to the case than to the press;
there are also a great number of my own;
misses, scuffs, blotches, blurs, and bad register:
but the true and faithful Superintendent has undertaken
to correct the whole.
When the machine is again set up,
(incapable of decay,)
a new and perfect edition of my life will appear,
elegantly bound for duration, and every way fitted for
the grand library of the Great Author.

Robert Goodby, an English printer, well known for his benevolence to the poor, left a bequest to the vicars of the town in which he lived, on condition of their preaching an annual sermon on the first Sunday in May upon the wonders of creation; and he also ordered the following words to be inscribed upon his tomb:—

In memory of Robert Goodby,
Late of Sherborne, printer, who departed this life
August 12, 1778, aged 57.
Death is a path that must be trod,
If man would ever come to God.
The fir-tree aspires to the sky,
And is clothed with everlasting verdure;
Emblem of the good, and of that everlasting life
Which God will bestow on them.
Since death is the gate of life,
The grave should be crowned with flowers.

One of the most curious of epitaphs is that written by Baskerville, the famous type-founder and printer, and placed by his orders upon a tomb of masonry in the shape of a cone:—

Stranger!
Beneath this cone, in unconsecrated ground,
A friend to the liberties of mankind directed
His body to be inurned.
May the example contribute to emancipate thy
Mind from the idle fears of superstition,
And the wicked arts of priesthood.

Epitome.—A compendium or abridgment.

Erasure.—An effacement or obliteration. The act of rubbing or scraping out letters or characters written, engraved, or printed.

Errata.—The printed list or table of errors occurring in a work, either in the impression, composition, or binding; inserted either at the beginning or end of the book, and usually on a separate page. Formerly tables of errata were very frequent, but modern printers have discarded them to a great extent, preferring, when possible, to correct the error in the body of the work, even when it entails the labor and expense of setting up a new form, or of altering a stereotype plate. The first printers corrected errors with a pen upon every copy, the alterations being frequently in red ink when the impressions were black; subsequently slips of paper were occasionally printed containing the correct word, and pasted over the misprint; and both these methods are used, in extreme cases, at the present day. In the Anatomy of the Mass, printed in 1561, containing 172 pages of text, the monkish editor seriously ascribes the fifteen pages of errata to the pernicious influence of Satan upon the minds of the printers.

Erratum.—An error or mistake in writing or printing. In the plural, errata.

Errors, Typographical.—The term error is used not only to express those typographical mistakes which appear in the book at its publication, but also those which have been discovered and corrected previously to the issue. All typographical inaccuracies, whether arising from incorrect reading, transposition, omission or substitution of letters, faults in punctuation, or in the selection of the different kinds of types, are classed under one general term, as errors. Errors must inevitably occur through the haste or carelessness of the compositor, and the inaccuracy or illegibility of manuscript, but the general accuracy of good modern publications is creditable to the skill of the present generation of typographers. The great printers of former times were proud to enlist the services of learned men as proof-readers, but this necessity arose in a great degree from the need of revision, required by the faulty manuscripts of the middle ages, and it may be safely said that the improved technical and mechanical processes of modern times insure a greater accuracy than could be secured by the assistance of erudite scholarship. The practical printer will readily believe, from his own experience, that in a Greek book, which had been revised with great care by an eminent scholar, a common proof-reader afterwards detected several hundred errors—the trained eye of the practical workman being much more efficient than the anxious observation of the learned linguist.

Errors, as a matter of every-day occurrence, are a fruitful theme of indignation to the author, of vexation to the printer, and sometimes of amusement to the public; as when a Pennsylvania paper in the midst of a hotly-contested campaign innocently referred to a tumultuous convention as the late Democratic Contention. In San Francisco, during the supremacy of the vigilance committee, an editor boldly inveighed against the outrages committed by lawless persons, and next morning found the effect of his indignant protest destroyed by the change of a single letter, for in his philippic, as printed, persons had become *parsons*, and he was himself known as a preacher! A distinguished member of the fraternity in Philadelphia amusingly insists that he was turned from politics in his youth to the profession which he now adorns, by a single misprint—he had most eloquently asserted that every marketable journal in the country was arrayed against him, but the treacherous types altered his pithy adjective into respectable, and overwhelmed him with confusion. The New York Times once felt called upon to explain that an article entitled the Metropolitan Excise Fraud had been intended to read Fund; a newspaper in the East Indies also apologized for apostrophizing the officers of the Survey as the Scurvy Commissioners; and an Arkansas editor respectfully requested his readers to refer to an article on the first page, and for dumsquizzle read permanence. A poetic reference to the scalds and sagas of the ice-cold north, read more prosaically when it appeared as the scolds and sages of the unsold earth; and Horace Greeley is reported to have indignantly reprobated a paragraph in which his own chirography intended to be read as Wm. H. Seward had been deciphered into Richard the Third.

At the anniversary dinner of the Printers' Pension, Almshouse, and Orphan Asylum, Dean Stanley presided, and related in his speech that he had once received a letter containing a very reasonable inquiry into the meaning of the passage, in one of his published works, of—the horns of the burning beast; and the author's own conjectures as to the possible significance of the phrase were unavailing until he chanced to recollect that he had written the words—the thorn of the burning bush.

Napoleon's wrath was once fearfully excited against the Imperial Printing-Office because in a bulletin, by a misprint of voleur for valeur, the Grand Army was described as performing tremendous deeds of theft instead of valor, and the terrified officials could only pacify the outraged warrior by conducting him to the office and showing him that in the compositor's case the o's were placed above the a's, and that the offending letter could have readily dropped from its legitimate station to the place below. The history of the Bible exhibits a long array of the most curious and important typographical errors. Pope Sixtus V., with an earnest desire to check the spread of the Reformation, personally superintended an edition of the Vulgate in 1590, prefixing a bull of excommunication against all printers, editors, etc. who in reprinting should make any alterations in the text. This edition was so extraordinarily imperfect that a multitude of scraps were printed and pasted over the erroneous passages, and the public strictures were so severe upon its inaccuracies that a succeeding Pope caused it to be suppressed. Clement VIII. revised and amended it, thereby subjecting himself to his predecessor's anathema, and promulgated his own, also exceedingly inaccurate, burdened with a similar anathema. The early English Bibles were notoriously incorrect, and governmental attention was attracted to the fact by Archbishop Usher, who made personal complaint to Charles I., that a text to which he wished to refer had been entirely omitted from one London edition. As a result of this protest, and shortly afterwards (1632), Barker, the King's Printer, was arraigned before the Star Chamber for the base and corrupt printing of the Bible, and fined 3000 pounds for printing an edition of one thousand copies omitting the word not in the Seventh Commandment. This famous edition has been since known as the Adultery Bible; and the same error occurred in an edition printed at Halle nearly a century later. In 1634, another edition was suppressed by the king for its egregious errors, as was also a Swedish version for the same cause and about the same time. In England, the received version made by order of James I. was allowed to lie unused, while the market was flooded with editions incorrect from negligence or design. Among the most notorious were the Bibles published by Field, the printer of the College of Cambridge, who is believed to have accepted bribes for alterations of the text made in the interest of some of the conflicting sects. The incessant attention required to assure accuracy in typography is well expressed in an anecdote of the great Erasmus. This learned man applied himself with scholarly diligence and enthusiastic devotion to the correction of sacred and classic texts for the office of Froben, the learned printer of Basle, who also regarded his work in the light of a religious duty; yet, notwithstanding their united endeavors, so many errors appeared in the publications that Erasmus declared that the devil himself must have interfered to prevent the perfection of their holy work.

Absolute freedom from typographical errors has been claimed for the quarto Virgil printed by Gering in 1498, and for the Corpus Juris Canonici of Rembolt. The Lusiad printed by Didot in 1817 is said to have contained only one error, and the same honor was claimed for a Horace by Foulis of Glasgow. The publishers of an Oxford Bible offered a guinea for every detected error, and as, after several years, only one correction had been made, it is supposed to be absolutely correct, as is also an American reprint of Dante. A good list of probable errors will be found in the following lines, purporting to be the wail of a suffering poet on reading his first poem as printed in a village newspaper, but evidently written by one conversant with the mishaps of the printer's case:—

Ah! here it is! I'm famous now—
An author and a poet!
It really is in print! Ye gods!
  How proud I'll be to show it!
And gentle Anna! What a thrill
  Will animate her breast,
To read these ardent lines, and know
  To whom they are addressed!

Why, bless my soul! here's something strange!
  What can the paper mean
By talking of the graceful brooks
  That gander o'er the green?
And here's a t instead of r,
  Which makes it tippling rill;
We'll seek the shad, instead of shade,
  And hell, instead of hill.

They look so—what? I recollect,
  'Twas sweet and then 'twas kind,
And now to think, the stupid fool
  For bland has printed blind!
Was ever such provoking work?
  'Tis curious, by-the-bye,
How anything is rendered blind
  By giving it an eye.

Hast thou no tears? the t's left out,
  Hast thou no ears, instead;
I hope that thou art dear, is put
  I hope that thou art dead.
Who ever saw in such a space
  So many blunders crammed?
Those gentle eyes bedimmed, is spelt
  Those gentle eyes bedammed.

The color of the rose, is nose;
  Affection is affliction;
I wonder if the likeness holds
  In fact as well as diction?
Thou art a friend,—the r is gone—
  Who ever would have deemed
That such a trifling thing could change
  A friend into a fiend?

Thou art the same, is rendered lame,—
  It really is too bad!

And here, because an l is out,
  My lovely maid is mad;
They drove her blind by poking in
  An eye—a process new;
And now they've gouged it out again,
  And made her crazy, too.

Let's stop and recapitulate:
  I've damned her eyes, that's plain—
I've told her she's a lunatic,
  And blind, and deaf, and lame.
Was ever such a horrid hash
  In poetry or prose?
I've said she was a fiend, and praised
  The color of her nose!

I wish I had that editor
  About a half a minute;
I'd bang him to his heart's content,
  And with an h begin it;
I'd jam his body, eyes, and bones,
  And spell it with a d,
And send him to that hill of his—
  He spells it with an e.

Essay.—A writing which treats of any particular subject; but it is generally understood to mean a composition less methodical and shorter than a treatise.

Estienne.—The name of a famous family of French printers in the fifteenth and sixteenth centuries, better known by their Anglicized name, Stephens. (See STEPHENS.)

Estimates.—One of the most difficult and important things connected with the management of a printing-office is the task of making out estimates or charges for the numerous descriptions of work which book- and job-printers are required to execute. De Vinne's Price List supplies a want long felt, by giving special directions applicable to nearly every kind of printing, which can be advantageously consulted alike by experienced and by inexperienced printers; and it also contains general directions, from which the following excellent suggestions are condensed:

For trivial orders, like cards, bill-heads, handbills, etc., you should be able to furnish prompt answers to all common inquiries. The promptness of an answer does much toward impressing one with the justice of the price. To hesitate or boggle, to ponder and calculate, does not impress a new customer favorably. Where he sees uncertainty in knowledge, he infers unreliability in price. But if you are not sure of the accuracy of your knowledge, never give the price till you are sure. For long and complex estimates, ask time for consideration. Avoid making such estimates in the presence of the customer, or at any time when you are likely to be disturbed. Analyze the work carefully. Where you have exact knowledge of cost of work, use the knowledge confidently and boldly; where you have not, defer to existing usage so far as you are informed. Do not be above asking advice or information where you know you need it. In so complex a business a novice should not be ashamed to confess ignorance of many matters.

It is not difficult to make estimates, even of complex work, if you commence properly. Keep this rule before you: Do but one thing at a time. Each item of cost must be fairly examined. For every ordinary job of printed work, you will have to compute the value of composition, paper, and press-work. For more complex work, you will have to compute items like electrotyping, binding, engraving, etc. In all cases, each item must be separately computed. Begin with paper, as the basis. You will have learned from the customer what quality is wanted. You have next to find the proper size and price. This is a matter for which no special directions can be given. The most useful knowledge about paper can be gained only by handling it and using it. Ascertain what fraction of a sheet, or how many sheets, each copy will require. Pay no attention whatever, at this stage of the work, to the number of forms, if it is a pamphlet, or to the number of impressions, if it is a job in colors, or if printed on both sides. This knowledge cannot aid you here. It will rather confuse you. All you have to know for this purpose is, how many sheets or what fraction of a sheet one copy will require. When you get this fact, the calculation is simple. If two or more kinds of paper are used, make special calculation for each.

You next proceed to compute the value of composition. If the work is open display, or of irregular form, it must be rated by time; if it is plain common matter, it should be rated by the thousand ems. If you are not a practical printer, or are not thoroughly conversant with the rules and usages of the trade, so that you can discriminate intelligently, take advice. Never make a price because the work appears to you to be no greater than that of similar work with the price of which you are familiar. Know to a certainty that it is no greater before you hazard a binding price. Very serious mistakes are often made by estimates based on a supposed analogy. For the fixing of time-work, consult a compositor or printer, if he can be had, but do not accept his estimate implicitly. It will probably be too little. Experience will teach you that the work that a compositor thinks may be done in ten hours will, in most cases, take twelve hours. In your estimate of time allow, if you think it expedient, for probable alterations or delays for which it may be injudicious to make special charge. If electrotyping is needed to cheapen the work, or for other reasons, ascertain how many plates can be used to advantage. In duplicating plates for a handbill or a check, you can make so many plates that the bill for press-work will be trivial. This should be avoided. You will also have to decide whether plates should be blocked or not. Of the relative advantage of each method you must decide. Here, too, you may need advice.

Your next step is to compute the press-work. If two or more plates are used for the purpose of cheapening press-work, you must calculate the number of impressions. For example: 20,000 copies of a handbill, medium 8vo., from one plate will make 20,000 impressions, for which the price would be $1.00

per 1000 impressions; from two plates there would be but 10,000 impressions, for which the price is $1.50 per 1000 impressions, for the edition is smaller and the sheet is larger; from four plates there would be but 5000 impressions, for which the price is $2.00 per 1000 impressions. If the work is to be printed on both sides, in the same color, you should estimate for press-work by one impression, in all cases where it can be done with advantage. If the form is very large, if paper or press of double size cannot be had, or if the number of copies is quite small, it will be more economical to print the matter on the back by a separate impression. Upon large orders, it is the usage to print work in large sheets, for it is both quicker and cheaper. In computing the value of press-work done in this manner on both sides, be careful to put down correctly the number of impressions that will be required. The caution is needed, for errors are frequently made at this point. Recollect, where both face and back are imposed together, that every impression makes one copy; if the job is set up or stereotyped twice, one impression makes two copies, etc. Forget, if possible, all about the number of plates (or the number of pages in the form), and think only of the number of copies that one impression will make. Divide the total number of copies wanted by the number of copies that are made by one impression. This will give you the entire number of impressions. Caution is needed here also. You must remember that the value of press-work increases with the size of the sheet.

These four items of paper, composition, electrotyping, and press-work are those that give most trouble in calculation. Ruling, binding, engraving, lithography, paging, gilding, and many other processes are needed to complete some kinds of work. Each of these should be examined in turn, and priced by the aid of the tables, and such other information as may be had from practical workmen.

Keep a record of every estimate, not only of the gross amount, but of the value allotted on each item. You will need it for reference on estimates of other work. If your estimate is accepted, it will be an instructive study to compare the actual cost of the work, after it has been done, with its estimated cost. There is no method by which you so readily acquire a knowledge of the real value of work.

Never give a detailed estimate to a customer. It is not your duty, nor is it good policy to expose your methods. The customer bargains only for a result, and not for methods of accomplishing that result. He may take no exceptions to the sum total; be probably will except to one or more items. That little knowledge, which is so dangerous a thing, is never more so than when used by a customer who knows a little about paper and a little about printing. You will have to waste much time in trying to explain matters to one who, from the nature of the case, has not sufficient knowledge to appreciate your explanation. His knowledge of the items will certainly be used to your disadvantage. The customer will buy the paper, and will probably get that which is unsuitable, or he will undertake to do the binding, and the result may be that you will have to complete his unfinished work at needless cost. By all means refuse detailed estimates.

Never make estimates for work you cannot do or choose not to do. Do not allow yourself to be made a tool of. It is a common practice with some tradesmen, when dissatisfied with one printer's bill, to go to another printer for a new estimate, giving the erroneous impression that the work for which the estimate is wanted is about to be ordered, and is to be an exact reprint of the copy. The fact that the first printer has spent many hours in expensive alterations and experiments is suppressed. The new estimate for a reprint work is made without allowance for time spent in alteration, and is consequently lower, and the first printer is unjustly accused of excessive charges. In this way many enmities are made, and fair prices are lowered. If you have reason to suspect such a state of affairs, decline an estimate altogether, until you have the request of both parties. It is not fair to price another printer's work from partial representations of the case.

Etching.—A manner of working upon copper and steel, or other substances, by which the lines of a picture or figure are eaten into the surface by the action of acid. A metallic plate is first coated with a waxen surface, which resists all action of acids; the lines intended to form the picture are then cut through the wax with a pointed instrument, and afterwards bitten or eaten into the metal by the application of acids. The invention of etching has been ascribed both to Francisco Muzzuoli of Parma, and to Lucas a Dentecum of Sutphen, about the year 1530; but the art was practiced at Nuremberg and Frankfort about the year 1512. Albert Durer's etchings were dated as early as 1518, and some authorities ascribe the invention to his instructor, Wohlgemoth, an artist of Nuremberg. Steel plates are now generally preferred to copper, the processes being similar in both metals, except that nitrous acid diluted with water is used for corroding copper, and nitric acid diluted with acetic acid or water is employed for steel. The coating of wax is of two kinds, one known as solid ground and the other as liquid ground. The solid etching-ground is formed of asphaltum, 3 parts, Burgundy pitch, 8 parts, and beeswax, 1½ parts, with a larger proportion of wax when additional softness is desired. This mixture is melted by heat, poured into hot water, and worked into balls of convenient size. The liquid ground is made by taking a ball of solid ground, formed as above, and breaking it into fragments, which are placed in a bottle with sulphuric ether. In applying a solid ground, the plate is first thoroughly cleaned with whiting or air-slaked lime, and then attached in a hand-vice. The plate is heated, and the ball of solid ground wrapped in a piece of silk, rubbed upon it so as to cover the surface with an even coating. If the plate cools during the process, it is again heated,

then turning the ground downwards, it is smoked by moving a lighted candle slowly back and forth, as near the surface as possible, without touching it with the wick. In applying the liquid ground, the plate is first cleaned with turpentine, and afterwards polished with whiting; the ground is then poured over evenly, or applied with a dabber, or with a ball of raw cotton covered smoothly with velvet; the evaporation of the ether leaving a clear, firm ground. In transferring the outline to the surface, one of the most modern methods is to obtain a daguerreotype of the exact size of the required picture; cut cleanly and smoothly with a sharp-pointed instrument into the copper over all the outline; remove the raised edges with the scraper, and get an impression from the copper. While it is damp, apply it to the etching-ground, and pass them through a printing-press. When the impression has been taken with red ink, the outline appears instantaneously; but if the impression has been made with black ink, the etching-ground must be dried, and a hair pencil dipped in vermilion passed lightly over it; the vermilion adhering to the oil from the impression only. Various methods have been used to transfer the outline; by one the outline is sketched upon oil-paper, from which it is transferred to the etching-ground by applying it to the surface, covering it with damp printing-paper, and passing them through the press, as before mentioned. The outline is also traced on gelatine paper with a sharp knife, which cuts into it. The cuts are filled with black lead or vermilion, and transferred, either by passing through the press as in the other methods, or with the gelatine dry burnish over the back sufficiently firm to set off the outline without breaking the ground. Strips of wood or leather are now fixed upon the margin of the plate with wax, and the etching or drawing is made with a steel point which is held lightly and easily like a lead-pencil, and permitting great freedom in drawing. Sufficient pressure is required to cut well into the steel, but not to prevent easy motion of the instrument. When the drawing is completed, all the unetched surface is covered with what is called a stopping-out varnish of asphaltum and turpentine. When dry, a well is formed around the work, by a wall of beeswax and burgundy pitch, leaving a spout or gateway for pouring off the acid.

The acid is then applied quickly, and removed quickly, lukewarm water being immediately poured over the surface, which is dried with a bellows. Small portions of the ground may be scraped away to judge of the effect produced by the acid, and the lines sufficiently eaten are carefully covered against the further ravages of the acid, which is applied again and again, until the picture is fully produced.

The easy processes of etching have rendered this branch of art especially attractive to amateurs, and it has become, at certain periods, a fashionable amusement, particularly in England. Tom Hood, while satirizing the fancy for the art, has so well described its processes, that it would be difficult to present them as clearly in any prose description. The operations already mentioned will be found most carefully and closely traced in his merry rhymes addressed to a lady, and entitled Etching Moralized, from which the following have been selected as the most essential to the description:

An art not unknown to the delicate hand
Of the fairest and first in this insular land,
    But in Patronage Royal delighting;
And which now your own feminine fantasy wins,
Though it scarce seems a lady-like work that begins
    In a scratching and ends in a biting.

Yet, O! that the dames of the Scandalous School
Would but use the same acid, and sharp-pointed tool,
    That are piled in the said operations—
O would that our Candors on copper would sketch!
For the first of all things, in beginning to etch,
    Are good grounds for our representations.

Those protective and delicate coatings of wax,
Which are meant to resist the corrosive attacks
    That would ruin the copper completely;
This cerements which whoso remembers the hue
So applauded by Watts, the divine LL.D.,
    Will be careful to spread very neatly.

Thus the ground being laid, very even and flat,
And then smoked with a taper, till black as a hat,
    Still from future disasters to screen it,
Just allow me, by way of precaution, to state,
You must hinder the footman from changing your plate,
    Nor yet suffer the butler to clean it.

But aloof from all danger by Betty or John,
You secure the veiled surface, and trace thereupon
    The design you conceive the most proper:
Yet, gently, and not with a needle too keen,
Lest it pierce to the wax through the paper between,
    And of course play Old Scratch with the copper.

Next let the steel point be set truly and round,
That the finest of strokes may be even and sound,
    Flowing glibly where fancy would lead them,
But alas for the needle that fetters the hand,
And forbids even sketches of Liberty's land
    To be drawn with the requisite freedom!

But prepared by a hand that is careful and nice,
The fine point glides along like a skate on the ice,
    At the will of the Gentle Designer,
Who, impelling the needle, just presses so much,
That each line of her labor the copper may touch
    As if done by a penny-a-liner.

So your sketch superficially drawn on the plate
It becomes you to fix in a permanent state,
    Which involves a precise operation.
With a keen biting fluid, which eating its way—
As in other professions is common, they say—
    Has attained an artistic station.

But beforehand, with wax or the shoemaker's pitch,
You must build a neat dyke round the margin, in which
    You may pour the dilute aquafortis.
For if raw, like a drain, it will shock you to trace
Your design with a horrible froth on its face,
    Like a wretch in articulo mortis.

But the acid has duly been lowered, and bites
Only just where the visible metal invites,
    Like a nature inclined to meet troubles;
And, behold! as each slender and glittering line
Effervesces, you trace the completed design
    In an elegant bead-work of bubbles.

But still stealthily feeding, the treacherous stuff
Has corroded and deepened some portions enough—
    The pure sky, and the water so placid—
And, these tenderer tints to defend from attack,
With some turpentine, varnish, and sooty lamp-black,
    You must stop out the ferreting acid.

But, before with the varnishing brush you proceed,
Let the plate with cold water be thoroughly freed
    From the other less innocent liquor—
After which, on whatever you want to protect
Put a coat that will act to that very effect,
    Like the black one that hangs on the vicar.

Then, the varnish well dried, urge the biting again,
But how long at its meal the eau forte may remain,
    Time and practice alone can determine:
But of course not so long that the Mountain and Mill,
The rude Bridge, and the Figures, whatever you will
    Are as black as the spots on your ermine.

But before your own picture arrives at that pitch,
While the lights are still light, and the shadows, though rich,
    More transparent than ebony shutters,
Never minding what Black-Arted critics may say,
Stop the biting, and pour the green fluid away,
    As you please, into bottles or gutters.

Then removing the ground and the wax at a heat,
Cleanse the surface with oil, spermatic or sweet—
    For your hand a performance scarce proper—
So some careful professional person secure—
For the Laundress will not be a safe amateur—
    To assist you in cleansing the copper.

And, in truth, 'tis a rather unpleasantish job,
To be done on a hot German stove, or a hob—
    Though as sure of an instant forgetting
When—as after the dark clearing off of a storm—
The landscape shines out in a lustre as warm
    As the glow of the sun in its setting.

Thus, your Etching complete, it remains but to hint
That with certain assistance from paper and print,
    Which the proper mechanic will settle,
You may charm all your friends—without any sad tale
Of such perils and ills as beset Lady Sale—
    With a fine India Proof of your metal.

Eulogy.—A formal address or essay in praise of the character or services of an individual; frequently used as the title of an oration in honor of a person recently deceased.

Euphony.—That quality in language which permits a melodious vocal utterance of all the members of a sentence, by preserving a just measure and harmony throughout all its parts.

Evans' Standing Press.—One of the Standing Presses in use in the United States.

Even.—See MAKE EVEN.

Even Headline.—The headline of an even page;

the compositor, in setting it, placing the folio at the near end of the stick.

Even Lines.—When copy has to be set up in great haste, especially for daily newspapers, it is frequently cut up into small divisions or takes, which do not correspond with paragraphs, so that many compositors may be at work upon it at the same moment; and in such cases they are required to resort to narrow, wide, or irregular spacing, so that their copy, as they set it up, may begin one line and end another. The process by which this object is attained is called making even lines.

Even Page.—A page whose folio consists of some even number, as the 2d, 4th, or 6th. It always stands at the left hand on opening a book.

EXCELSIOR PRESS.

Excelsior Card and Job Presses.—Presses patented and manufactured by William Braidwood, of New York, for small job-work, of eight medium, quarto medium, and half-medium sizes. Among the advantages claimed for them are great strength, good distribution, easy and complete supervision of all the principal parts of the press while it is in motion, and avoidance of slurs.

Exchange Cap.—This is a thin, semi-transparent, highly-calendered, hard, and strong paper. It is used for bills of exchange, certificates, and other blanks that must be of light weight and may receive hard usage. It is not so strong as Board or Parchment, but is better adapted for receiving fine impressions.

Exclamation, Note of, or Exclamation Point.—This character (!) is used to denote strong or sudden emotion; and as a sign of great wonder, or token of derision, it is sometimes repeated until three or more exclamation points follow each other, thus, ! ! ! ! !. It is usually placed at the end of an earnest address or invocation; (as: Whereupon, O King Agrippa! I was not disobedient unto the heavenly vision); and after interjections, words used as interjections, or clauses containing them. It immediately follows the printed word oh (!), but it is placed at the end of a clause or sentence containing O. It is also sometimes placed at the end of sentences of an interrogative character to which no answer is expected.

Excursion Tickets.—See JOB PRINTING.

Exordium.—The introductory part of a formal oration.

Expurgated.—Editions of books in which obscene or offensive words or expressions are omitted are called expurgated editions.

Extended Letters.—Letters which have a broader face than is proportionate to their height.

Extra.—An edition of a newspaper containing important news, and issued at an unusual hour of publication, is called an extra, especially if it is printed on a sheet of a smaller size than that commonly used.

Extra-Condensed.—Letters which have a much narrower face than is proportionate to their height, being even more condensed than condensed letters.

Extract.—A passage taken from a book or writing; a quotation.

Extra Packet Post.—A folded writing-paper, larger than Packet Post and smaller than Foolscap.

F.

Face of the Letter.—The surface of the end of the type which contains the letter. There are so many different faces cast on the same size of body, that two sizes of letters may not have any perceptible difference in face, when printed. The only way to obviate this, in ordering types, is to make the selection out of one series. By doing this, all the sizes will bear a relative proportion to one another—faces as well as bodies—and when two or more sizes are used in the same work, have a better appearance than if one of them had a heavy and the other a light face.

Face of the Page.—The upper side of the page, from which the impression is taken.

Fac-simile.—An exact reproduction; a copy which cannot be distinguished from the original; usually applied to works of art, engravings, printed pages, or books which closely resemble older pages or books, etc.

Falling Out.—A term generally applied to a page, or a quarter, or a whole form, which drops away from the chase, through the shrinking of the furniture and quoins. This accident can hardly occur without gross carelessness, if metal furniture and iron sidesticks are used.

Fancy-Type.—See JOB LETTER.

Fanning Out.—A term used in counting work. By taking hold of the right-hand lower corner of the paper between the forefinger and the thumb, and by a peculiar turn of the wrist (spreading out the upper part of the paper somewhat in the resemblance of a fan), the sheets can be counted with the greatest facility.

Fast Type-Setting.—Many American printers

desire to set up type with great rapidity, and they are stimulated to exertion not only by the prospect of an increase of compensation, but by special requirements for rapid work, either on newspapers, jobs, or books. Numerous extraordinary feats have been performed of which no accurate record was kept, and there are many fast compositors now quietly at work in various sections of the country, whose performances have never been published. To do justice to them all in this article would be impossible, and reference will be made here only to a few illustrative examples. John Fasey, of Philadelphia, familiarly known as Jack Fasey, was long considered the most rapid compositor in this city, and probably in the United States, and when in his prime he found 1700 ems per hour an easy task. A few years ago Charles K. Neisser, now employed on one of the daily newspapers of this city, won a prize offered for rapid composition on a City Directory, but he never received it, and no accurate account was kept of the number of ems set per hour, or per day,—the contest being for the largest quantity of type set by a single compositor upon an entire book. Similar contests in New York for prizes offered in the composition of Trow's Dictionary, have also induced fast typesetting, but accurate details of these performances were not published. In some of the California newspaper offices, there was formerly a great demand for rapid compositors, and the Sacramento Union office contained, in proportion to the number of men employed, more rapid compositors than any other office in the country. In 1864, the paper was all set in solid type, and the average earnings of each compositor amounted to one dollar for each working hour,—the rate of compensation being seventy-five cents per thousand. This would have necessitated the setting of 1333 ems per hour, which would not be poor work, even in this fast age. Many of the compositors working on the Sacramento Union could set a great deal more than this; and among the remarkably fast ones were S. B. Conklin, O. H. Tubbs, John Anthony, George N. Parker, and Thomas T. Sutliffe.

In or about 1852, the proprietors of a logotype patent called at the office of the New York Courier and Inquirer, to urge the adoption of a new system of logotypes, which, as they claimed, would enable compositors to set up 1500 ems per hour, an amount of matter which, they contended, the most expert workman could not compose in one hour if he did not use logotypes. At that period, 1500 ems per hour was considered very fast type-setting—the age of velocipedes not having yet dawned. In reply, the foreman of the Courier and Enquirer said that he had compositors then at work who, with the ordinary type, could set more than 1500 ems per hour. The proprietors of the patent were incredulous, and said they would like to see it done. This controversy led to a formal trial of speed. On a given day an editorial leader was cut from a newspaper, the type furnished, and the race commenced under the

following agreement: type, Nonpareil—solid; all paragraphs to be run in, and the whole article to be set up, provided it made less than 3000 ems. The result was that the compositor (Thomas T. Sutliffe) finished the article in one hour and thirty-one minutes, this time being ascertained and declared by judges present; and the article contained 2487 ems.

One of the greatest and best-attested feats of late years is that performed by George Arensberg, in the city of New York, in February, 1871. On a bet against time, in the presence of judges representing both parties, and holding stop-watches, as well as of a number of spectators, he set 2064 ems of solid Minion type in one hour, there being 6192 pieces of metal in the matter. The bet was that he could not set four stickfuls of solid Minion, each stickful to have one break-line containing two or more words; but this feat was performed in 55 minutes and 50 seconds, and by continuing his labors for the additional four minutes and five seconds he achieved the result already stated. The first stickful was completed in 13 minutes and 55 seconds; the second, in 13 minutes and 50 seconds; the third, in 14 minutes; and the fourth, in 14 minutes and 10 seconds.

A dispatch from Chicago to the Associated Press, dated November 5, 1870, said: Andrew W. McCartney, compositor in the Evening Post office, for six days ending yesterday, composed and corrected 95,600 ems. In four of these days he worked six hours and a half; the other two days, seven hours each. He thus achieved the extraordinary feat of setting 95,600 ems in forty hours without any extra fat. We annex the figures exhibiting the amounts of each day's work, which for rapid type-setting has probably never been equaled: Saturday, 17,200; Monday, 15,400; Tuesday, 19,100; Wednesday, 16,800; Thursday, 13,400; Friday, 13,700: total, 95,600 ems.

A correspondent of the Printer's Circular, writing from Albany, in February, 1870, who had kept a record of newspaper accounts of fast type-setting for several years, said: There is a long list of compositors who would set 2000 ems an hour, as they claimed, and their friends have asserted. Rapid compositors for an hour, however, do not always possess endurance. Yet there are not wanting instances of extraordinary endurance combined with great speed. For instance, in 1845, Mr. John J. Hand, deputy foreman of the American Republican, of New York, undertook, upon a wager, to set up 32,000 ems of solid Minion in twenty-four hours. He failed by 32 ems only. Mr. Robert Bonner—now the mighty man of the New York Ledger—was employed on the American Republican also, and is said to have set up 25,500 ems in twenty hours and twenty-eight minutes, without a moment's rest. Mr. George Dawson, now one of the proprietors of the Albany Evening Journal, was reported in the Rochester papers, where he was an apprentice, to have set up 27,000 ems of solid Brevier in ten hours. This being so incredible a performance—although published in the newspapers—I inquired of Mr. Dawson (begging pardon of the newspapers that published it), who asserts that it was an honest 22,022 ems, done in a day of something more than ten hours; he thinks thirteen hours. As Mr. Dawson has been ever since —probably about forty years—employed upon newspapers as compositor, foreman, editor, and proprietor, his assertion cannot be gainsaid. Mr. Henry Keeling, of Utica, N. Y., is said to have set up, distributed, and corrected, in six days of ten hours each, 100,950 ems. Mr. Wm. Mink, working upon the Eagle, at Pittsfield, Mass., in 1858, set 10,046 ems in four hours and forty-five minutes, solid Minion. A race between two compositors—A. J. Kenny, of the City Press, at Iowa City, and O. B. Bell, of the Nonpareil, at Council Bluff—resulted in each of them setting 4000 ems solid Bourgeois in two hours. Carlos Comens, of Rochester, N. Y., it is recorded, frequently set up sheriff's sales containing but little short of 1000 ems Nonpareil, in twenty minutes.

It is also reported that Charles McDonnell, foreman in the Portsmouth Tribune office, in 1853, set up 8240 ems in four hours, or 2060 ems per hour.

In a type-setting match at Toledo, Ohio, between George A. Barber, of Cincinnati, and C. C. Wall, of Toledo, Mr. Wall, commencing at two o'clock in the afternoon, set 4288 ems in two hours and forty minutes, while Mr. Barber set 4054.

Whatever may be thought of some of these reports, it is well demonstrated in Arensberg's case, if in no other, that more than 2000 ems per hour can be set up, and in a considerable proportion of the important newspaper offices of this country, compositors are to be found who can set up at least 1500 ems per hour.

In another part of this work (see COMPOSITION) will be found suggestions worthy of the attention of those who are anxious to become fast type-setters. The following article, condensed from an editorial in the Printer's Circular, also affords instructive hints: Systematic type-distributing, by giving the compositor confidence in his case, will be found to materially accelerate his speed. The action of a man working out of a dirty case is not unlike the walk of a blind man—hesitating, halting, and groping he knows not where, or upon what; while the action of one working at a clean case is like the firm tread and confident, forward step of the man blessed with sight. We have seen many butchers and space-benders who could rattle up their fifteen or eighteen hundred ems an hour out of a case that would disgust an ordinary compositor; but a sight of their proofs is sufficient to stifle any feelings of envy. A clean case, therefore, is one of the first elements of fast type-setting, enabling one to compose without stopping to sort out the case, or losing time afterwards in cobbling on what should have been nearly perfect.

A determination not to make any false motions, however fruitless it may at first appear, will in a day or week visibly increase the number of ems set; that is, by sighting the nick before the hand goes out to pick up the type, so that when it is taken by the thumb and forefinger, there need be no necessity for turning it around to see where the nick is, the arm meanwhile making a false or lost motion that would have sufficed to bring another type into the stick. These false motions not only consume time, but become chronic and increase in number and intensity, so that some men fairly shake themselves to pieces, and only set, probably, five or six hundred ems an hour. We have known men who acquired this nervous, jerky style in setting type, and making two or three motions for every type secured, almost entirely rid themselves of the superfluous shakes by adopting a slow and measured style, apparently unremunerative at first, but which gradually quickened into systematic speed. We therefore consider an avoidance of false motions essential to fast type-setting.

A guide, in newspaper- or ordinary book-work, is a drawback rather than an aid to the compositor. A peculiarity of most fast printers is their quickness of sight, enabling them to see from the corner of their eyes, as well as directly in front of them. This readiness of sight is diminished rather than cultivated by keeping the eye strained continually on a point directly in front; and the time supposed to be gained in always having the place, is more than counterbalanced by the time spent in arranging the guide. Besides, the effort to remember the place where he left off, compels a man to carry in his head the sense of what he is setting, resulting in well-punctuated, intelligent work. We cannot, at present, recall a fast printer addicted to the use of a guide, while the very slow ones invariably use them.

Fat.—Work yielding large wages for comparatively little or no labor. With compositors, light, open matter, and short or blank pages. With pressmen, light forms, wood-cuts, and short numbers for which a full token is charged.

Fat-face Letter.—Letter with a broad face and thick shank.

Fecit.—A Latin word, signifying he did it, frequently added to the name of the artist inscribed upon an engraving or picture, to indicate the designer.

Feet of a Press.—That part of the hand-press which is in contact with the floor.

Feuilleton.—That portion of a French newspaper which is devoted to light literature and literary or artistic criticism. It is usually printed on the lower part of the sheet, beginning on the front page, and carried over to the lower part of the subsequent pages when necessary. It is separated from the rest of the paper by rules running across the sheet and marking it off distinctly. The dimensions of the feuilleton are varied to suit the occasion, and it may occupy only a couple of inches at the end of each column, or half or even more than half of the page.

Fiction.—The general term for that portion of literature which includes works of imagination, particularly in prose, such as the novel, romance, tale, story, and sketch. Modern printing is largely indebted for employment to the ever-increasing demand for novels, magazines, and such periodicals and newspapers, as are chiefly filled with various forms of fictitious literature.

Field, Richard.—An English printer who practiced the art during the last years of the sixteenth and the beginning of the seventeenth century. Richard Field was born in Stratford-on-Avon, and was probably the friend of Shakspeare, for Venus and Adonis, Shakspeare's first work, was published by him in 1593, in a quarto of twenty-seven leaves. Field was celebrated as a printer, and is believed to have served his apprenticeship with Vautrollier, whose daughter he married in 1588, and in the following year, upon the death of his father-in-law, succeeded to his business, and adopted the same device of an anchor. The memory of Field is further connected with that of Shakspeare by his having published, in 1596, the Metamorphosis of Ajax, by Sir John Harrington, an objectionable lampoon, for which its author was temporarily banished from court by his god-mother, Queen Elizabeth, and which is alluded to in Love's Labor Lost.

The Art of English Poesie, by George Puttenham, published by Field in 1589, is remarkable for containing an excellent portrait of Queen Elizabeth.

Fine Printing.—This term in its general sense expresses excellence in any department of the art. It was formerly restricted in a certain degree to bookprinting, for the reason that the highest efforts of the typographer were then devoted to that order of publications; but in recent years usage has changed, especially in America, where books furnish but a small portion of the occupation of the trade, and the term fine printing, in popular use now, serves rather to denote superior job or color work. Excellence in the art is claimed for the early printers by those enthusiastic authors whose admiring eyes see perfection in Gutenberg, Schoeffer, Jenson, or Plantin, rather from the obstacles that they conquered than from the superiority that they achieved. Mechanical excellence in an art so largely mechanical as printing is, must inevitably progress towards perfection with the succeeding ages, and the best letter-press of the nineteenth century is, beyond dispute, far superior even to the highest efforts and the most loudly-vaunted triumphs of Baskerville or Bodoni.

In the earlier stages of the art, Jonson and the Elzevirs may be claimed as the fine printers, the latter especially becoming the model of the English, until in the early part of the 18th century, when Caslon, the type-founder, made the first great step in reform; in the middle of the century his work was continued by Baskerville, whose type and ink have been applauded to the echo by bibliomaniacs. But to the modern printer the books of Baskerville are valuable only as marking the transition from the old style to the new; his type lacking that perfect symmetry of line and curve which makes good fonts of the present day completely harmonious; while his ink, though preserving its blackness, is uneven in tone, the pages differing in shade. Didot, in France,

may be called the next devotee of fine printing, and his remarkable excellence is evinced by the Delphini classics, which exhibit a rather lighter-faced type than the bold face of Baskerville, but charmingly uniform in color. His ligatures also are an improvement upon those of Baskerville, but so sharp and delicate that they soon became worn. Didot supplies the link between the old and the new, by filling the period between Baskerville and the great typographical revival illustrated by Bodoni in Italy, Ibarra in Spain, and Bulmer and Bensley in England.

In the latter country this stage is marked by the labors of Miller Ritchie, of Scotland, who about 1780 began to exhibit remarkable elegance, showing an unrivaled richness and equality of coloring through every page, and pursuing his labors despite the failure of the necessary support from an unprepared and unappreciative public, until financial ruin compelled him to desist, to be followed by Bulmer, who was at least happier in his greater renown. The interest in fine printing which became a popular mania in England, was inaugurated by the magnificent edition of the Bible published by Macklin and printed by Bensley in 1800. The dedication to the king bears the date of 1791, and the long list of subscribers is headed by the names of the members of the royal family. This celebrated Bible was printed in double columns, upon heavy plate paper, and consisted of six large volumes; the page being eighteen and a half inches by fifteen, with a margin three inches wide; the type, a handsome bold-faced Roman, the capitals being a quarter of an inch in height, and the lowercase extending a little beyond the half. A note in the front of the book calls the attention of the reader to the fact that, in order to increase the typographical elegance of the work, the words usually printed in other editions of the Bible in italic are distinguished by a dot under the first vowel. The full-page illustrations are numerous, and in the very highest art of the day, both in design and execution.

The famous typographical rival of the celebrated Bible of Bensley was the Shakspeare which appeared two years later, with the statement on the title-page that it was revised by Steevens, and printed by Bulmer on types made by W. Martin. The plates of this work, bound separately, are considered unsurpassed, but, to judge from the typography, Bulmer must certainly yield to Bensley in general beauty and perfection. In France, the house of Didot has maintained its great reputation for fine printing, adding to its fame by the introduction of a variety of beautiful scripts, and at present the house of Memo is also renowned for its elegant composition and presswork.

In delicate and artistic color-work the French maintain the same superiority in printing that they have achieved in other decorative arts in which taste is especially required, and the specimen book of Derriey of Paris exhibits some of the choicest combinations of color ever displayed in this branch of the art. Although triumphant in color-printing, the leading French printers of the present day confess the superiority of the letter-press-printing of England; and it may be asserted, without danger of dispute, that the American job and fancy type, in turn, far excels the English. This marked superiority may arise in great measure from the immense demand for job-work in the United States; and under the same impulse the recent improvements in color-printing have been very great as well as rapid. Until the present day, large and cheap editions, principally, have been called for in this country, and attention has been turned particularly to supplying this demand; but the beautiful book-work occasionally produced, as well as the general superiority in job-printing, shows that the United States are fully prepared to compete with any other country in all grades of the art, even to the very highest.

Finiguerra, Tommaso.—A goldsmith of Florence, who is believed to have invented, in the year 1460, the method of obtaining a printed impression from an engraved copper plate, by filling the lines with ink and applying moistened paper, under gentle pressure from a roller. It is claimed by the Italians that the art was successfully practiced by several persons in Florence, and was thence transmitted to Antwerp, where it was prosecuted by Martin Schoen. But this origin has been disputed, the Germans claiming the invention for Stoltzhirs in 1450, others ascribing it to Stock, of Nuremberg, and the Dutch claiming it at a much earlier date. Some authorities have given the honor of the invention to Schoeffer of Mentz.

Finis.—A Latin word, signifying the end or conclusion, placed at the end of an English work. The word is separated considerably from the body of the text, and is printed in small capitals; the English words—the end, are also used in the same manner. This custom has been abandoned to a great extent, recently, and is rarely met, except in standard and important publications, which conform to the ancient usages.

First Form.—The form upon which the white paper is printed.

First Page.—The commencement of a book, or the first page of a sheet or signature.

First Proof.—A proof pulled immediately after matter is composed, for the purpose of comparing it with the copy and for the detection of literal errors. It may either be pulled on galleys or after the matter is made up into pages and imposed.

Fisher, Henry (died June, 1837). A distinguished English publisher, bookseller, and printer, chiefly remarkable for his praiseworthy endeavors to promote learning by the publication of works upon science and religion, in numbers, and at low prices. He was also celebrated for his handsome illustrated publications. After completing his apprenticeship with Jonas Nuttall, the founder of the Caxton Press, Fisher removed with that gentleman to Liverpool, and having suggested the establishment of depots in the principal towns, for the more effectual extension of the sale of standard works in numbers, was himself appointed, when 21 years old, manager of one at Bristol. His services were so valuable, that when but twenty-four years of age, Mr. Nuttall admitted him into partnership, with an independent salary of £900, for conducting the business. The popularizing of science by the efficacious method of publishing in numbers, attracted the attention of Dr. Adam Clarke to Fisher, and a friendship was formed which was greatly advantageous to both. Dr. Clarke's works were published by the firm of Nuttall, Fisher & Dixon, and Dr. Clarke assisted ably in the supervision of the standard and divinity works which were rapidly issued by the Caxton Press. In 1818, Messrs. Nuttall and Dixon retired upon handsome fortunes, leaving Fisher as the sole head of the Caxton printing-office, then the largest establishment in England. In 1818 the office was destroyed by fire, and- Fisher, accompanied by many of his employees, removed to London, where he opened a new press, and became widely known as the most extensive British publisher of elegantly illustrated works.

Flat Cap.—A writing-paper in very general use for blanks, the standard size being 14 by 17 inches.

Flat Papers.—Papers which have never been folded, and are therefore more convenient for printing.

Flock Printing.—Printing in which the sheets, after receiving an impression of the form in size or varnish, have the impressions subsequently covered with finely powdered wool or cloth, called flock.

Floor Pi.—Types which have been dropped upon the floor during the operation of composition or distribution. A careful compositor will pick up each type as he drops it, and thus prevent its being injured by being trodden upon. It is the duty of the person who sweeps the composing-room, before watering it, to pick up the floor pi near each stand separately, and place it, wrapped in paper, in the thick-space box of the case in use by the compositor occupying that stand, who should clear it away every morning before commencing work.

Flourish.—A figure formed by bold and fanciful lines, generally curved. A great variety of brass flourishes are now made in the United States, and extensively used in ornamental printing. The accompanying illustration is set up with brass flourishes:

Flowers.—Ornaments for embellishing chapter-headings, or forming tail-pieces to books; also a type-founder's phrase for what printers usually term Borders. In the early days of the typographic art, borders were composed chiefly of floral designs; at the present time they assume a variety of shapes, some of which are very beautiful.

FLY.

Fly.—An invention for taking off or delivering the sheets from a power-press. Acting automatically, they supersede the necessity of hand-labor in taking off the sheets, except in forms requiring a large amount of ink, like poster-forms, etc. The paper, coming over the tapes running round the small set of upper wheels, falls down to the lower set of wheels, but in front of the flies, which form a kind of great comb. The latter work on a rod axis, and alternately assume a perpendicular and a horizontal situation. The sheets cling to the flies while they are in the process of falling, and when they are horizontal they are laid regularly in a heap ready to be taken away. Nearly all the superior class of machines are now furnished with flies, as they effect an important saving of labor.

Fly-Boy.—A boy who takes off the sheet from the tympan as the pressman turns it up. This is seldom done now, as, when expedition is required, the form is usually worked on a power-press; but when, from the nature of a power-press, or the peculiarities of any form, it is requisite that boys should assist in taking the printed sheets, one by one, from the form or the press, this operation is called flying the sheets.

Fly-leaf.—A blank leaf worked with any single printed leaf. The second or back leaf of an 8vo or 4to circular. When single-page circulars are given to the pressman to work, it is usual for him to ask if it is to be fly-leaf or single.

Fly the Frisket.—To turn down the frisket and tympan by the same motion. This should always be done, as it saves time, on ordinary work; but not when very superior heavy or dry paper is used.

Folded Papers.—Papers folded in the centre.

Folder.—A person engaged to fold paper; also the instrument by which the folding is accomplished.

Folding.—Doubling the printed sheets so that the pages fall consecutively, and exactly opposite to each other, preparatory to binding.

Folding Machines.—Machines which fold news-papers, books, pamphlets, or other printed sheets of small sizes are now extensively used in this country as well as in England, the sheet as delivered from the press being fed at one place and taken out ready for mailing or for binding at another. (See BOOK-FOLDING MACHINE, FORSAITH FOLDING MACHINE, and NEWSPAPER FOLDING MACHINE.)

Folio.—The running number of the pages of a work. When there is no running title, the folio is placed in the centre of the head-line; when there is a running title, at the outside corner—the even folio on the left, the odd on the right. The preface, contents, index, and all introductory matter, usually have separate folios inserted in Roman lower-case numerals.

Folio Page.—A page which occupies the half of a full sheet of paper, as Post-folio, Demy-folio, etc. Two pages of folio are imposed together as one form, four pages being a perfect sheet. Post-folio and Foolscap-folio, however, are more frequently imposed as four-page forms, and printed on Double-post and Double-foolscap paper.

Folio Post.—A flat writing-paper, usually 17 by 22 inches.

Follow.—That is, see if it follows. This term is used by readers, compositors, and pressmen. By a reader or compositor, when he ascertains that the first line of a page or sheet agrees with the last line immediately preceding it, and that the folios numerically succeed each other. On newspapers in England—particularly daily—it is generally used by compositors when taking up copy of the Parliamentary reporters. They call out for the preceding folio to what they have in hand; and, when answered, say, I follow you. The pressman merely ascertains that the first page of the inner form follows the first page of the outer, or whether, in working half-sheets, he has turned his heap correctly.

Font.—This word is usually defined as a certain weight of letter cast at one time, of the same face and body; but in practice it is also applied to sets of types embracing all the letters of the alphabet, points, etc., although they may form not merely an incomplete font, but a very small portion of the type embraced in the cast of which they formed a part. The German equivalent of font means a cast or flow, and its original signification was probably all of the type made at one casting or series of castings, intended to embrace the manufacture of all the letters, points, figures, spaces, and quadrats necessary in printed matter. The orthography of the word is unsettled. In this work font is adopted mainly because it is believed to be more generally used by the printers of the United States than fount; but fount is also very extensively used, and is sanctioned by the dictionaries and good typographical authorities. Moxon, the earliest English writer on typography, used the word fount, but said that properly it should be called fund. This is an ingenious suggestion, but no reasons for it are given; and if the word font or fount were to be changed, the idea it is used to convey would be better expressed by cast or flow than by fund.

A complete font of letter is comprised under nine heads, containing the following sorts:—

1. *Capitals.*

A B C D E F G H I J K L M N O P Q R S T U V W X Y Z Æ Œ &.

2. *Small Capitals.*

A B C D E F G H I J K L M N O P Q R S T U V W X Y Z Æ Œ &.

3. *Lower-Case.*

a b c d e f g h i j k l m n o p q r s t u v w x y z æ œ ff fi ffi fl ffl.

4. *Figures.*

1 2 3 4 5 6 7 8 9 0

5. *Points, etc.*

, ; : . ? ! - ' ( ) [ ] * † ‡ § ¶ — ⁓

6. Four kinds of spaces.

7. Em and en quadrats.

8. Two- three- and four-em quadrats.

9. Accents.

Roman letter is now usually cast and put up according to schemes, arranged in pounds and ounces. The apportionment of weight or number of letters varies in some particulars in different type-foundries, but its general character is indicated under the headings BILL OF TYPE, and SCHEME. The sorts absolutely requisite for a font depend largely upon the character of the work for which it is to be used. Newspaper fonts require more capitals than ordinary book or magazine fonts; and there is an infinite variety of special demands upon the fonts used in job-work. Job-letter fonts are proportioned according to the number of letters likely to be required; and the size of the font varies with the style and size of the letter,—plain job letter, such as Antiques, Gothics, etc., being put up in larger fonts than fancy or ornamental job letter, and the small sizes containing more letters than the large sizes. Many varieties of job letter are put up in fonts composed exclusively of capital letters, but orders for such fonts should state specifically that capitals only are desired; otherwise, they will be construed to mean lower-case as well as capital letters. The size of job fonts is indicated by the number of a's they contain.

Font Cases.—Very capacious cases, used to hold the surplus sorts of large fonts.

Foolscap.—A folded writing-paper, usually 12 by 15 inches, or 12½ by 16. The name is supposed to have been derived from a watermark representing the cap and bells of the ancient jesters.

Foong-Tsou.—A Chinese minister of state in the tenth century, who is the reputed inventor of printing. It is said that this learned man, wishing to multiply the copies of a certain book, made various ineffectual attempts to make seals as stamps from which impressions could be multiplied, and finally dampened a written page and pressed it upon a smooth piece of wood. A transfer was thus produced, and when all the wood not impressed by the writing was cut away, he had reached his aim, and produced a tablet or seal, engraved in relief. The characters upon the tablet were then wet with ink, and successive sheets of thin paper applied to the surface with a light pressure. The immense number of characters required by the Chinese language precludes the general use of movable types, although they have been occasionally and successfully employed, and the method invented by Foong-taou is still in use. (See CHINA, PRINTING IN.)

Foot of a Page.—The bottom of a page.

Foot of the Letter.—The bottom of the type.

Footstick.—A piece of furniture, sloped or beveled from one end to the other, placed against the foot of the page. The slope allows the wedge-shaped quoins to be driven hard in between the footstick and the chase, and so secures, or locks up, the form or page.

Fore-edge.—The outer edge of a sheet of paper when folded to the proper size of a book.

Foreman.—The manager and director of the mechanical details of a printing-office which is not under the constant and immediate supervision of its owner. The duties of foremen vary with the character of the work they superintend, but to discharge their duties properly they should not only possess superior executive capacity, but accurate knowledge of everything relating to such branches of printing as are intrusted to their care. Whether acting as foremen of newspaper offices, of book offices, of job offices, or of press-rooms, the responsibility devolves upon them of discovering and remedying the manifold defects and delays which constantly arise from neglect, ignorance, bad workmanship, laziness, or thoughtlessness. An inefficient or inferior foreman is the worst barnacle that can be fastened on a printing-office; while a well-instructed, good-tempered, firm, and energetic foreman renders invaluable service.

Forgery, Typographical Safeguards Against.—Bank notes and government bonds are executed by bank-note companies, which profess to guard against imitation by the superiority of their workmanship; and the letter-press printer is chiefly interested in preventives of the forgery of such products as blank checks, corporation bonds, tickets, eating-house checks, perfumery and patent-medicine labels, etc.

Works designed for safety are seldom attempted in simple letter-press of one color. There is, however, a plan by which copying of this may be rendered very difficult. Get up a light tint, in some fancy small border, somewhat larger than one of the leading lines of the job. Put it under the press used for taking electrotype moulds, with a sheet of wax over it made hard with black-lead; and have bearers so arranged as to allow only a very slight impression on the wax. Having obtained a shallow mould, let the line previously chosen be placed under the same place, and impressed to just the same extent. The object of having the mould hard and shallow, is to prevent this second impression spreading out the wax so as to distort or spoil the first; heavy blanks may be easily chiseled out afterward. We now have a mould of the line of type set in a tint, and from this a plate may be taken which will print both at once. If, now, any one tries to do this again, he can not, for he can not bring the type line, in each stroke, to exactly the same part of the covered ground; and if he tries to do it by two impressions in black, which seems the easiest thing in the world, he will simply find that, what with spacing his type line exactly like the first, and then getting exact register, it can not be done; for a hair's variation in any part can be at once seen and detected.

To prevent a printed sheet prepared in this manner from being copied by either the anastatic or the lithographic process, it would be necessary to sprinkle the paper with a solution of india rubber, in naphtha, and then with a sulphate of copper. The product could still, however, be photographed, and although a photograph can be detected by cyanide of potassium, it is better to guard against photographic forgery by printing in two or more colors. To increase the utility of this preventive, it has been suggested that a series of inimitable ground tints, running into the matter, should be secured, and a paper read before the New York Typographical Society in 1864, by Alfred E. Parks, from which this article is condensed, concludes with the following directions for obtaining such tint-blocks:

Nature furnishes an infinite variety of products and processes from and by which printing surfaces may be obtained; each kind repeating itself somewhat in

general appearance, but never in detail; each beyond the ordinary power of man to imitate; and most of them exceedingly beautiful, so as to admit of being used in ordinary ornamental work. Take, for instance, a little sulphate of magnesia, commonly called epsom salts; make a strong solution, cover the face of a piece of plate glass, and let it evaporate very slowly. The glass will be covered with a foliated network of crystals, somewhat like window-glass on a frosty day, except that, properly done, the crystals will be separate, and not connected at the edges. A mould may be taken by pressure in wax, from which the salts can be washed out by water; then take an electrotype from this, which, in turn, is to be used as the mould from which to obtain the plate to be printed from, and you have a most beautiful picture of crystallization, which can not be reproduced by the same process, for the crystals will not dispose themselves alike twice, any more than the glasses in a kaleidoscope will; nor by hand, for it is too complicated to draw; nor by transferring nor photography, if it has been partly printed over with black lettering. Oxalic acid, similarly treated, gives a much finer crystal, and a plate which must be worked with the best black ink. Coarser, but still exquisite crystals may be obtained by soaking a slab of marble in water all night, and in the morning wiping the top dry and packing it in a freezing mixture. The water, forced up to the top, will freeze in beautiful foliated shapes. The mould from this might, perhaps, be taken in plaster; if wax is used, it must be quite cold. Again, make a solution of gum tragacanth, as in the marbling of paper. Have one oily solution, and one solution of ox-gall, which sprinkle precisely as for paper; if you like, you may add a few iron filings to one or both solutions. These solutions will spread just as colors do. Having got a surface to your mind, take it up on a piece of zinc instead of paper; expose the zincs to acids, as in the anastatic process, and the oil-covered parts will not be affected. You will have a beautiful marble ground. Well done, it will be next to impossible to copy this. Take a sheet of gutta percha; warm it; sprinkle iron filings on it and fold it over two or three times, kneading it slightly. Let it get cool and hard; then cut it carefully in two across the folds, and you will have a series of irregular layers of filings and gutta percha, the beauty of which will depend upon your skill in manipulating them. Try again, if not pleased at first; and when suited, dip the smooth face into nitric acid, which will cat out the iron and leave the gum. Take a plaster mould from this, and a stereotype plate. You can not take a wax mould, because the wax will stick in the roughness where the filings have been eaten out. Of course you may wave the lines as you please. Take a block of some knotty, irregularly-grained wood, and have it planed across in the direction in which the grain is most distorted. Then soak it in sulphuric acid, and the softer parts of the wood will be charred away faster than the hard ones, so that the grain will appear in ridges and hollows. This may be duplicated by a plaster cast and stereotype, and, on account of a peculiarity in the grain of most woods, will be absolutely incapable of reproduction—even by the same process and from the same block.

If a pane of glass be firmly held by one point, and sprinkled with fine sand or lycopodium seed, and then if a violin-bow be drawn across the edge so as to produce a musical note, the seed will arrange itself into very curious figures—stars, squares, triangles, and so on. These can not be reproduced exactly by the same process, without getting the same pane of glass, or at least one of the same shape, size, thickness, and density, holding it at the same point,

the leaf, which may be used as an engraved block, printing the leaf in white on a colored ground. It may, indeed, generally be used after the copper-plate fashion. Numbers of natural objects which never exactly duplicate themselves may be used in this manner to obtain tint-grounds of great beauty; such as feathers, the inner bark of trees, skeletons of leaves, leaves of the arbor vitæ, and so on; very few of which could be imitated, and all of which would be beautiful. A large feather, with every alternate vane cut out carefully and removed by combing, would form a splendid ground; for the barbs and hooks on the remaining vanes would appear finer than the finest engraving.

FORSAITH NEWSPAPER FOLDING MACHINE.

drawing the bow at the same place, and having the same quantity of seed sprinkled in the same manner. The figures, however, may be taken in a wax mould, and the seed eaten out of it by acid before taking an electrotype plate.

But the most valuable method of producing impressions of natural objects which can not be imitated, is that known as Nature Printing. If a soft object be pressed powerfully between two plates of metal even tolerably hard, it will nevertheless leave a full impression on them, which can be used for printing. Thus, if the leaf of a tree be placed between two plates of lead or copper, and passed through a rolling-mill, each plate will receive a perfect impression of

Form.—The job, page, or group of pages to be printed by one impression, or to be stereotyped or electrotyped from one moulding.

Form Lifts.—The condition of the form, when, on being raised from the stone or press, nothing drops out.

Forsaith Newspaper Folding Machine.—A machine for folding newspapers, patented and manufactured by S. C. Forsaith, of Manchester, New Hampshire. Machines of different sizes, with a varying number of folds, are built, which are said to be capable of folding from 2500 to 3500 sheets per hour, with the aid of a single operator. They are used by a number of American newspaper publishers.

Forties.—Sheets of paper folded into forty leaves or eighty pages.

Forty-eightmo, or Forty-eights.—A sheet of paper folded into forty-eight leaves or ninety-six pages.

Foul Proof.—A dirty proof—a proof with many errors or corrections marked in it.

Foul Stone.—An imposing stone or table which the compositor has not cleared after working at it. In well-regulated offices in England fines are inflicted for this neglect.

Founders' Measurement.—See PROPORTIONS OF TYPE.

Fountain.—The receptacle for ink, in power-presses, previous to its being conveyed to the form by distributing and composition rollers.

Fourdrinier Paper.—Paper made on a Fourdrinier machine.

Fractions.—A fraction is a part of a unit, written with two figures, with a line between, thus—$\frac{1}{2}$, or thus—$1/2$. The upper figure is called the numerator, the lower one the denominator. The fractions in general use are cast in one piece, as follows:

$\frac{1}{8}$ $\frac{1}{2}$ $\frac{3}{4}$ $\frac{1}{3}$ $\frac{2}{3}$ $\frac{1}{4}$ $\frac{5}{8}$ $\frac{3}{8}$ $\frac{7}{8}$.

Piece fractions enable the printer to form any fraction that may be required. They are made half the size of the body of the type they are to be used with, thus:

^{1} ^{2} ^{3} ^{4} etc., $_{1}$ $_{2}$ $_{3}$ $_{4}$, etc.

En and em quads of the same body are also cast, so that any fraction can be formed, as, $\frac{3}{4}$, $\frac{1}{16}$, etc.

Fragments.—Any pages left after the last full form of a work, and imposed with the title, contents, or any other odd pages, to save press- and ware-room work.

Frame.—See STAND.

Franklin, Benjamin.—Born in Boston, January 17, 1706, died in Philadelphia, April 17, 1790, holds deserved preëminence in the long line of distinguished American printers. The leading features of his useful and brilliant career as a statesman and philosopher are so well known that it is unnecessary to dwell upon them here. But it is worthy of remark that amid all his varied employments he never lost his deep interest in the art of printing and all that appertained to it. His lively picture of his labors as an apprentice, journeyman, and master-printer has awakened hope and inspired ambition in the breasts of thousands of young men, and a careful study of his writings only serves to confirm the exalted popular estimate of his talents and his character. A salutatory as editor of his brother's paper at Boston, written while he was still an apprentice, abounds with pungent wit, and his opening remarks in commencing the publication of his first journal at Philadelphia evince editorial ability of the very highest order. But his talent as an author never led him to be neglectful of mechanical excellence as a printer. His first important advancement in public life he attributes to the superior manner in which he executed a job of printing for the Assembly of Pennsylvania. He aided in the establishment of paper-mills; cut type or engravings with his own hand when they could not be readily obtained; invented a system of phonetic writing, resembling the phonetics of the present day; spent his happiest hours at the French Court in a private printing-office he had established near Paris; continued to retain a direct pecuniary interest in the printing-business during the whole of a long and prosperous career; bought in France many of the materials necessary for a type-foundry, in the hope that one of his grandsons would establish that business in the United States; displayed a lively interest in the development of the comparatively new art of stereotyping, if he did not contribute directly to its revival by information furnished to Didot; and finally, in making his will, described himself as Benjamin Franklin, printer, in the apparent belief that that was the most correct and comprehensive, if not the most honorable title he had won by a career that has deservedly elicited the warm and enduring admiration of civilized mankind.

Freeman's Oath.—The product of the first printing-office established within the present limits of the United States, which was at Cambridge, Massachusetts, was the Freeman's Oath; and this was, no doubt, the oath of allegiance prescribed for freemen by the colonial authorities of Massachusetts, in May, 1634. This oath, as given in the Charters and General Laws of the Colony and Province of Massachusetts Bay, was as follows:

I, A. B., being, by God's providence, an inhabitant and freeman within jurisdiction of this Commonwealth, do freely acknowledge myself to be subject to the government thereof, and therefore do here swear, by the great and dreadful name of the ever-living God, that I will be true and faithful to the same, and will accordingly yield assistance and support thereunto, with my person and estate, as in equity I am bound, and will also truly endeavor to maintain and preserve all the liberties and privileges thereof, submitting myself to the wholesome laws and orders made and established by the same; and further, that I will not plot nor practice any evil against it, nor consent to any that shall so do, but will timely discover and reveal the same to lawful authority, now here established, for the speedy preventing thereof; moreover, I do solemnly bind myself, in the sight of God, that when I shall be called to give my voice touching any such matter of this state wherein freemen are to deal, I will give my vote and suffrage as I shall judge in mine own conscience may best conduce and tend to the public weal of the body, without respect of persons or favor of any man. So help me God, in the Lord Jesus Christ.

Freight Tariffs.—See JOB PRINTING.

Friars.—Light patches caused by imperfect inking of the form.

Frisket.—A thin iron frame covered with stout paper, and attached to the head of the tympan by a joint. In hand-presses and the Adams press, spaces corresponding to the parts of a form that are to be printed, are cut out of the paper covering, and the frisket, being turned down upon the sheet on the tympan, keeps it flat, prevents the margin being soiled, and raises it from the form after it receives the impression.

Frisket Pins.—Iron pins passing through the joints of the frisket and connecting it with the tympan.

Frisket Stay or Catch.—A slight piece of wood fixed to support the frisket when turned up.

Froben, John.—A celebrated printer, of Basle, Switzerland, where he commenced the practice of the art in 1491, and continued it until his death in 1527. As apprentice of the pious, learned, and exact Amerback, Froben studied to pursue the same lofty aim, and became in turn one of the most celebrated of the learned printers of Basle. The eminence of Froben as a printer, and as a man of piety and learning, induced Erasmus to visit Basle for the purpose of publishing his works, and the acquaintance ripened into friendship. The first edition of the New Testament in the Greek language was printed by Froben and edited by Erasmus in 1516. It was printed in folio, in two columns, with notes at the end. This publication caused much severe criticism, Erasmus being blamed by many scholars for undue boldness in making such an attempt, and by others being accused of heresy. Froben was a man of great learning, and, in his anxiety to reach perfection in his texts, expended large sums in procuring manuscripts and in engaging scholars to read his proofs. Erasmus and others distinguished for learning and authorship, corrected his press, and were well remunerated for their labors. Erasmus said of him that he was well entitled to his chosen device, a caduceus surmounted by a bird, for that in his private character he did indeed blend the wisdom of the serpent with the harmlessness of the dove. Froben's name was sometimes Latinized into Frobenius.

Frontispiece.—The print, or engraving, which faces the title-page of a book—formerly the engraved title-page itself. The title-page was originally highly decorated, and has until recently frequently contained a picture or portrait set in the midst of the letter-press, making the title one of the pieces or illustrations; but modern taste has abandoned the fashion, and the name has been transferred from the title-page to the opening picture, now usually placed so as to face the title.

Fudge.—To execute work without the proper materials, or to finish it in a bungling or unworkmanlike manner.

Full Case.—A case completely filled with letters and spaces—wanting no sorts.

Full Form.—A form with no blanks or short pages.

Full Page.—A page containing its full complement of lines.

Furniture.—In England this term is applied to all pieces of wood or metal, exclusive of type and

12

rules, embraced within the chase when a form is locked up, and it includes reglet, side-sticks, footsticks, gutters, and quoins. In the United States the word has, in general usage, a more restricted meaning. Square or oblong pieces of metal, known as labor-saving quotation furniture, and hollow quad-

LABOR-SAVING QUOTATION FURNITURE.

rats are modern improvements now extensively used in filling up blank space, and for similar purposes. Cherry is generally used for wooden furniture, on account of its cheapness, but Cuba or San Domingo mahogany is much more durable, and less likely to warp or shrink; and in most cases it would be true economy, in the end, to use the superior material. Furniture is not usually well classified, and plans for cutting it in graduated lengths of Pica ems, and arranging it systematically, might often be advantageously adopted, especially in jobbing offices. Houghton, in his Printers' Every-Day Book, says that, after years of experience, he has found the system described below to be very useful, viz.:

The drawers in which the various lengths are deposited and kept are divided into compartments, which each hold pieces of equal lengths, of every thickness, broad, narrow, double-broad, etc., as well as the side-sticks. This plan simplifies the system and economizes space, without producing the least inconvenience in getting any size wanted. That every size may be again returned into its proper place after use, on the edge of each box is cut the proper length therein contained, which serves as a standard. For general purposes the following sizes, cut to Pica ems, will be found sufficient; namely,

12 ems, 16 ems,
18 ems, 21 ems, 24 ems, 27 ems, 30 ems, 35 ems,
37 " 40 " 42 " 45 " 47 " 50 "
52 " 55 " 57 " 60 " 62 " 65 "
67 " 70 " 72 " 75 " 77 " 80 "
82 " 85 " 87 " 90 " 92 " 95 "
97 " 100 " 107 " 114 " 120 " 130 "
and a few lengths as they are received from the joiners, for the largest-sized posting-bills. It is best to cut all the long lengths first, because what is thus cut off will perhaps come in for shorter lengths. It will be an advantage to cut the reglets, though kept in separate boxes, to some of the sizes of furniture, say 30, 35, 40, 47, 57, etc. The best way for cutting these lengths is by means of a slide being attached to an ordinary saw-block, something like that which belongs to a brass-rule cutting machine. With this, the lengths may be cut exactly.

The furniture thus cut, it will be necessary to have three drawers in the imposing-stone, divided into separate boxes, something like the following:

UPPER DRAWER.

		Waste cards.		
40	42		45	47
37	35	Quoins.	24	30
Furn.	Ditto.			
42	67	Broken Reglet.	35	37
Book.	Ditto.			

MIDDLE DRAWER.

70	72	75	77	80	82	85	87
50	52	55	57	60	62	65	67

LOWER DRAWER.

	120 and 130	
	107 and 114	
18	97 and 100	21
12	90 and 95	16

The edge of each box being cut by a gauge for every size, and every box containing its own, the furniture may now be used to advantage. For instance, suppose the form requires large blanks, and be set to any size in the furniture-drawer, it is evident that there can be no difficulty in making up the necessary blank with furniture, whatever it be, providing, of course, that there be a sufficient quantity of that size. Say the job is a foolscap folio, and set to thirty-five ems Pica (if that be too wide, it may be indented): the furniture for blanks and foot-stick will be found in the first drawer. The other furniture necessary to impose it will depend upon its length, but, for the sake of example, suppose it to be sixty-eight ems. It will be seen by a reference to the drawers that there is no size exactly of that length: therefore the next size, seventy ems, which is two ems longer, will be the proper length of the side-stick. The foot-stick being

exactly the width, there can be no fear of the side-stick being injured at the bottom end with locking, even though it is two ems longer than necessary, for it must be a very thin foot-stick that will not protect the length of two ems Pica. If the furniture, against which the form is locked, was an em or two longer than the side-stick and foot-stick, it would prevent both, in being locked, from slipping.

Fust, John (died in Paris, 1466).—A citizen of Mentz, closely connected with John Gutenberg in his first successful attempts in printing. The orthography of this name has been much disputed, being written variously Faust, Faustus, and Fust, but the latter is authoritative, as his name appears in the colophons of his publications thus:—Made by Johannem Fust, citizen of Mentz. One of the events attending the introduction of printing that is positively ascertained, is that John Fust of Mentz in 1455 gained legal possession of the printing-material of John Gutenberg in a suit for the return of certain money advanced, and that Fust thereafter pursued the art in partnership with his son-in-law, Peter Schoeffer. It appears probable, from a comparison of the various stories, that Gutenberg received assistance in money from John Fust, goldsmith, of Mentz, but having spent at least five years in experiments without producing any return for the investment, was sued, and the property adjudged to Fust, who, with the help of Schoeffer, carried the work to its conclusion, shown in their splendid Bible and the Psalter of 1457. Whatever be the respective share of credit due to the various members of this first firm of printers, no happier combination could have been made for the purpose of furthering their common design than was found in the united and varied capacities exhibited by Gutenberg with his inventive genius, the practical experience and skill in metals possessed by the successful goldsmith Fust, with the taste and dexterity of Schoeffer, a trained writing-master, who had been also apprenticed to the goldsmith. The amazing excellence and beauty of their earliest publications could only have resulted from such a union of special talents. The books with the imprint of Fust and Schoeffer are especially valuable on account of being accurately dated ; they are the Psalter of 1457, the Durandus of 1459, the Constitutions of Clement V., 1460, the Bible of 1462, the Decretals of Boniface VIII., 1465, and the Offices of Cicero, 1466. It is supposed that the struggle between Deither and Adolphus for the possession of Mentz prevented the publication of any important works between 1662 and 1665, but several other small works were published, to dispose of which it is believed that Fust visited Paris in 1666 and died of the plague in that city. The confusion of the name of Fust with that of the celebrated magician Faustus has its origin in a French story, which relates that shortly after the publication of the Bible, Fust took a large number of copies to Paris, and sold several of them to Louis XI. and the officers of his court as manuscripts. By some accident, several of the copies were minutely compared, and the absolute identity of the characters alarmed the superstition of the examiners, who accused Fust of witchcraft, and alleged that the beautiful red in the initial letters must have been written in blood. Fust was thrown into prison; but Louis XI. interfered in his behalf, and liberated him on the consideration that he should reveal the secret of his invention. The effect of the siege of Mentz was very injurious to the printing-office of Fust and Schoeffer, causing the dispersion of their workmen and apprentices, who fled from the unfortunate city and carried the knowledge of the new art with them. This is the old theory on the subject, and it is no doubt correct so far as the world in general is concerned; but it is now deemed quite certain that at least one famous printing-office—that of Pfister, at Bamberg—was in successful operation before the siege of Mentz.

A Latin book printed by Fust and Schoeffer, but without date, is preserved in the Philadelphia Library. The printed page is about three by five inches, and on tolerably good paper, with a fair margin. The type does not look much larger than that employed in this Encyclopædia, and is quite legible to the ordinary reader, although in Gothic character, or rather in what has been called the Secretary-gothic of the scribes. The ink is a good but not remarkably lustrous black, and the capitals, although distinctly made, are further distinguished by a red line run through them, apparently with a pen. The colophon is continuous with the text, but marked by being underscored with red ink. It may be translated thus:—Here ends the book of the blessed Augustine concerning Christian life. By so doing any one will obtain eternity.—The device of Fust and Schoeffer stands immediately below, printed in red. The only difficulty in reading the text arises from the abbreviations, which are, however, readily learned, as they conform to certain rules, and are marked by a stroke.

G.

Gage Paper-Cutter.—A machine for cutting paper, adapted to the use of printers and bookbinders, manufactured by S. C. Forsaith, Manchester, New Hampshire. It is recommended as a cheap and reliable Paper Cutter, which obtains a cut with great ease, smoothness and accuracy, through a depth of from four to five inches.

Gallery.—A term used frequently as the title to books of illustrations, being borrowed from the collections of pictures and statuary generally styled galleries.

Galley.—A thin, movable frame or tray used to hold types after they are set up, until they are made up in forms, jobs, columns, pages, etc. Galleys are made of various patterns and materials. Formerly wooden galleys were universally used, and they are still used to some extent in book and job offices. The ordinary wooden galley has ledges on only two sides, and matter cannot be locked up and proved on

GAGE PAPER-CUTTER.

it, nor conveniently transferred from it to an imposing-stone. The wooden slice galley was a natural and, for some purposes, a necessary accompaniment, for it provided means for sliding on to a stone forms of such size or construction that they could not safely be lifted after they were tied up. Brass galleys, which are now used universally in newspaper offices and extensively in book and job offices, provide facilities for proving matter before it is made up or tied up, thus lessening the difficulty of making corrections, and avoiding troublesome overrunning of pages; while the bottom of the brass galley is so thin that it can be withdrawn from long columns of type, and the matter be thus quickly and safely transferred to an imposing-stone.

The ordinary brass galley has three ledges, so arranged that the matter can be securely deposited, as it is supported by the head and lower ledge of the

BRASS GALLEY.

galley when it occupies an inclined position on a case or rest; and side-sticks and quoins of appropriate size and shape are interposed between the matter and the upper ledge of the galley when it becomes filled with matter, or when an article or job is finished, so that after the matter is thus locked up, the galley can be transferred to a press to be proved and be safely placed in a horizontal position, as on a level imposing-stone. A number of improvements have been made in the shape, size, and construction of galleys.

PATENT BRASS-LINED GALLEY.

The annexed cut represents a patent brass-lined newspaper or single-column galley, with a portion of the wood removed from the side-frame, showing the manner of attaching the side-lining. This patent galley is the strongest brass-lined galley manufactured. The improvement consists in soldering a tongue of metal to the brass lining, and letting the metal tongue into the wooden side (which is slotted), thus fastening, at one and the same time, by means of the screws in the bottom of the galley, the lining, side, and brass bottom, making a galley which presents, inside, a perfectly smooth side-surface. By this means the heads of the screws in the side-lining, which, in the old style galleys, sometimes project and make pi, are avoided. There is also a strip of brass across the head of the galley, which prevents the head and sides from warping or becoming loose.

Another invention, patented by Mr. P. Gray Meek, of Bellefonte, Pennsylvania, is illustrated by the annexed cuts, the advantages claimed for it being that it is self-locking, avoids the use of quoins, saves time, and secures uniform pressure.

MEEK PATENT GALLEY.

MEEK PATENT GALLEY.

A similar end is attained by another contrivance, in which side-sticks and quoins of the ordinary shape are used, and permanently attached to the galley, so as to render it self-locking.

Another modern form of galley is the making-up galley, illustrated by the annexed cut.

MAKE-UP GALLEY.

Galley Rack.—A rack made with runners, similar to a case rack, on which matter on metal galleys is placed after a proof has been taken from it.

Galley Rest.—An attachment to a stand made for the purpose of providing a convenient resting-place for galleys, so that they may not be placed on cases containing type.

Galley Roller.—A roller about five or six inches long, used at the proof-press.

Galley Slaves.—A derisive appellation for compositors.

Gallows.—The stay against which the tympan rests when the press is open.

Galvanoglyphy.—A modern process for engraving, which has been described as follows: Upon a plate of zinc, coated with varnish, a drawing is etched; then ink or varnish is rolled over. The ink adheres only to the parts it touches, every application, when dry, raising the coating, and consequently deepening the etched lines. From this original a plate is electrotyped that can be printed on a typographical press.

Galvanography.—A process for obtaining copper-plate engravings, described as follows: The artist covers a plate of silvered copper with several coats of a paint composed of any oxide—such as that of iron, burnt terra sienna, or black-lead—ground with linseed oil. The substance of these coats is thick or thin, according to the intensity to be given to the lights or shades. The plate is then submitted to the action of the galvanic battery, from which another plate is obtained, reproducing an intaglio copy, with all the unevenness of the original painting. This is an actual copper-plate, resembling an aquatint engraving. It may be touched up by the engraving-tools. This process has been improved upon by outlines etched in the usual manner, and the tones laid on with a roulette. A galvano-plastic copy of this sunk-plate is obtained. On this second raised plate the artist completes his picture by means of chalks and India-ink, and puts in the lights and shades; from this, a second galvano-plastic copy is produced. This second copy or sunk-plate, the third in the order of procedure, serves, after being touched up, for printing from in the copper-plate-press.

Galvano-Plastic Process.—A process for

obtaining electrotypes of fossil fishes and similar objects which can be printed on typographical presses. The method used in Austria is described as follows: By means of successive layers of gutta-percha applied to the stone inclosing the petrified fish, a mould is obtained, which, being afterward submitted to the action of a galvanic battery, is quickly covered with coatings of copper, forming a plate upon which all the marks of the fish are reproduced in relief, and which, when printed, gives a result upon the paper identical with the object itself.

Garamond, Claude.—A distinguished letter-founder of Paris. Francis I., in his anxiety to establish the University of Paris on the best possible foundation, showed special interest in the cultivation of the Greek, Hebrew, and Latin languages, and in 1538 ordered the erection of a printing-office (which was the foundation of the famous Imperial Printing-Office at Paris) to be devoted to the reproduction of important works in those languages. Garamond, then very celebrated as a letter-founder, made for it Roman type after the models of Jenson, and, by the advice and assistance of Robert Stephens, produced several exquisite fonts of Greek, in imitation of the beautiful Greek manuscript of Ange Vergèce, who held the office of king's writer in Greek letters. This type was so beautiful that it rescued France from the discredit of being far surpassed in Greek typography by the publications of the Aldi. The matrices made by Garamond were taken by Robert Stephens to Geneva, in 1551, when he fled from the persecutions of the Sorbonne, and it is believed that although a Royal Ordinance of 1541 had ordered him a kingly remuneration for his labors in preparing this type, it had never been paid, and that he considered the matrices of Garamond as his own property; the type and punches remaining in the Royal Printing-Office. Paul Stephens, the grandson of Robert, in 1612 pledged these matrices to the City of Geneva for a loan of 1500 crowns of gold, and they were brought back to Paris in 1621, by Antoine Stephens, son of Paul, and printer to the king and clergy, to be used on an edition of the Greek Fathers, they having been obtained from the Genevan government by Louis XIII. for that express purpose.

Garamond's type was celebrated throughout Europe, and the printers of Italy, Germany, England, and even Holland frequently recommended their publications as printed from Garamond's celebrated small Roman letter. Garamond died in 1531.

Gathering.—Collecting the sheets of a work in orderly succession for delivery to the bookbinder.

Gathering Table.—A long table on which printed sheets are laid, in the order of their signatures, to assist the operation of gathering them into perfect books.

Gauge.—In composition, a strip of reglet, with a notch in it, passed with the make-up, to denote the length of pages. In press-work, a piece of wood or other material, used sometimes to denote the proper margin on a sheet of printed paper.

Gazette.—A newspaper published at short stated intervals. In Great Britain, the official newspaper, which contains the authorized legal and state announcements and proclamations. The Acta Diurna has been already described as the Roman newspaper, and a similar official statement of events was established in Venice during the war with the Turks, about 1536; the sheet taking the name gazette, from gazeta, a small coin, which was its price. The Gazette continued to be distributed in manuscript in Venice, and similar manuscript sheets appeared also in other Italian cities, until suppressed by Pope Gregory XIII. The Gazette de France appeared regularly from 1631 to 1792, and was continued afterwards, although interrupted by political changes. The first Gazette in England appeared in London in 1642, removed with the court to Oxford during the plague, and returned permanently to London in 1666. In America the first newspaper bearing this title was the Boston Gazette, established in 1719; the New York Gazette was established in 1725, and the Virginia Gazette in 1735. The North American and United States Gazette is the present representative of the first daily paper printed on the continent, the Pennsylvania Packet, started in 1784.

Gazetteer.—A geographical dictionary; also, in some countries, an officer appointed by government to publish some classes of news in the official organ, styled the Gazette.

Ged, William.—(Born 1690, died 1749.) The reputed inventor of stereotyping. By birth a Scotchman, he was successful as a goldsmith, in Edinburgh, and was widely known for his inventions and improvements in his business. As a goldsmith, he became to a certain degree a banker, and was brought into connection with the trade by furnishing money for the payment of the printers. In the year 1725, one of the printers complained to Ged that he was seriously embarrassed by being forced to send to London for type, there being then no type-founders in Scotland, and that much of the English type was imported from Holland, and he urged the ingenious goldsmith to undertake the business of letter-founding; but Ged was struck with the idea of making plates from the composed pages, believing that it could be successfully done. He borrowed a page of composed type, and made many experiments with a variety of materials, but did not complete his invention until two years afterwards. Although in possession of some capital, Ged offered one-fourth interest in his invention to an Edinburgh printer, on condition of his advancing the sum necessary to establish a stereotype-foundry. This partnership lasted two years, but the printer, alarmed at the expensiveness of the undertaking, failed to fulfill his promises. A London stationer, named William Fenner, visiting Edinburgh, next offered to establish a foundry in London, in full working order, for one-half of the profits. Ged, now exceedingly anxious for the success of his invention, accepted these terms; disposed of his business in Edinburgh, and followed his new partner to London, to find himself again deceived. With many plausible pretenses, the stationer induced the unfortunate inventor to add a type-founder to their partnership, who furnished refuse type, which Ged rejected as totally unsuited to his purpose. Still undiscouraged, Ged applied personally to the king's printers, with a proposal to stereotype some type which they had recently introduced. The printers naturally consulted the type-founder who had made the type, and he as naturally denied the utility of the invention. An interview, however, was arranged, which led to the curious result of the founder laying a wager that he could make the stereotype himself. The foreman of the king's printing-house was made the umpire. Each of the disputants was furnished a page in type of the Bible, under the promise that he would furnish the stereotype in eight days. Upon receiving the type, Ged went immediately to work, and the same day finished three plates of the page, took impressions from them, and carried them to the umpire, who acknowledged his success with much astonishment. The fame of the invention soon afterwards reached the Earl of Macclesfield, who offered Ged and his partners the vacant office of printer to the University of Cambridge, with the privilege of printing Bibles and Prayer-Books by the new process. Ged eagerly accepted the position, and went to Cambridge, but the letter-founder prevented his success, by treacherously furnishing imperfect type, and even when Ged sent to Holland for new fonts he was again deceived, until, after struggling unsuccessfully for five years, without being able to complete a single set of plates, and encountering every possible form of opposition from the printers, as well as treachery from his own partners, he relinquished the undertaking, and returned, a ruined man, to Edinburgh. His friends in that city subscribed a sufficient sum for the stereotyping of a single volume, and the unfortunate inventor apprenticed his son to a printer, that he might no longer be subjected to the enmity of the trade. By the assistance of his son he produced, in 1736, after eleven years of endeavor, the first public proof of his success, an edition of Sallust. On account of the inferiority of the type, this volume was not a fine specimen of the art, but was sufficient to prove that the invention was completed. Ged's son devoted himself to acquiring a knowledge of printing, but just at the moment that he was fully prepared to effectually assist his father, the unfortunate inventor died. Although suffering so bitterly at home, Ged refused several offers, either to go to Holland, or to sell his invention to printers of that country, declaring that he only desired to serve his native land, and would not hurt it by giving the printers of another country such an advantage. The secret of his invention slumbered after his death until 1793, when it was revived or rediscovered in Paris.

Geometrical Signs.—See SIGNS.

German.—The pronunciation of the letters of the German Alphabet is given elsewhere in this work. (See ALPHABET.) The arrangement of the German

upper and lower cases in the United States, as given in The American Printer, is shown by the illustrations from that work on page 183.

Get In or Take In.—A term used when more matter is put into a line, page, or form than is in the printed copy which a compositor sets from; or when manuscript copy (as set up) occupies less space than was anticipated when it was cast up.

Giesecke and Devrient.—Printers of Leipsic. This house, famous for the variety of its productions, and for having received the highest honors awarded to printers by the French Exposition of 1867, was established in June, 1852. The partners were remarkably well prepared to achieve extraordinary success. Hermann Giesecke, the son of a distinguished type-founder of Leipsic, had studied printing practically with the celebrated publisher, Bernhard Tauchnitz; while the other principal partner, Alphonse Devrient, had served his apprenticeship with Friedrich Nies, a renowned Leipsic printer, and subsequently passed four years in the Imperial Printing-Office at Paris. At first the labors of the firm were limited to general book-printing, but an extensive lithographic department was opened in October, 1852, and the next year was added a copper-and steel-plate department for the production of bank-notes and other papers, intended to defy imitation. This department has been almost uninterruptedly employed in printing notes, checks, etc. for the Governments of Saxony, Switzerland, and other smaller States. In 1854 engraving in all the branches connected with printing was added, with complete electrotype and photographic apparatus. A new and extensive building sufficient for these requirements was built in 1857, and surrounded with a magnificent garden, similar to Mame's at Tours. In 1868 the establishment contained 36 copper-plate presses, 26 typographic presses, 20 lithographic presses, 5 embossing presses, 5 satinizing (or glossing) machines, 4 hot-pressing machines, 3 relief-copying machines, 2 guillotining (or waving) machines, 1 pantographic apparatus for microscopic purposes, and 10 letter-press printing machines, of the newest and best construction. The number of all the presses employed amounted to 93.

The first floor of the principal building forms a large press-room; the stereotype foundry is in the basement. The composing department, in another part of the premises, had, in 1868, 1823 cwts. of type of all descriptions. The lithographic and embossing department contained 4600 of the best litho-stones, 20 iron presses, 4 embossing presses, 3 satinizing machines, 3 cutting machines, and employed 66 persons under one overseer.

The copper- and steel-plate printing for bank-notes, etc. is done in one of the side aisles, on the second floor. To the right of the entrance a room is set apart for government officers, some of whom are constantly on the premises, as well as military sentries in the press-room, in the centre of which a space is most securely and strongly railed off for the protection of the produce of this department until it is handed over to the proper parties. Commencing with 18 presses, the increased demand on this department brought their number to 26 in 1866; and in 1868 to 30 copper-plate presses, 16 numbering machines, 3 printing machines, and 5 manual presses engaged in the production of the tasteful and complicated notes of the Saxon treasury.

of the proper number of printed sheets. The quantity of paper likely to be wasted must be estimated in advance, and added to the exact count necessary to supply any particular order, and in writing-paper allowance must be made for outside or imperfect sheets. It is usual for stationers to count 22 sheets as a quire, or 440 sheets as a ream, in fine blank books, whether they have printed headings or not,—

GERMAN UPPER-CASE.

GERMAN LOWER-CASE.

Girths.—Thongs of leather, or bands of stout webbing, attached to the rounce, and used to run the carriage of the press in or out.

Giving out Paper.—The delivery by a foreman, warehouseman, or other person in charge of paper, to a paper-cutter or pressman, of the paper intended for books, newspapers, jobs, etc. Great care is requisite in the discharge of this duty to insure the production

this rule being based on the theory that forty sheets will be rejected as outsides or wasted in ruling or printing. Of inferior papers, used for cheap blank books, sometimes 20, 18, or only 16 sheets are counted as quires. The average amount of waste in long editions of ordinary book and pamphlet printing is 32 sheets on crown work and 56 sheets on fine work. To insure 1000 perfect sheets of a book or

TABLE SHOWING THE
QUANTITY OF PAPER REQUIRED FOR ANY JOB
OF FROM 50 TO 10,000 COPIES.

Issued by Collins & M'Leester, Type Founders, No. 705 Jayne Street, Philadelphia.

(NO ALLOWANCE IS MADE FOR WASTE OR OVER COPIES.)

NUMBER OF COPIES REQUIRED.	44 to sheet Quires	44 Sheets	36 Quires	36 Sheets	32 Quires	32 Sheets	24 Quires	24 Sheets	20 Quires	20 Sheets	18 Quires	18 Sheets	16 Quires	16 Sheets	15 Quires	15 Sheets	12 Quires	12 Sheets	9 Quires	9 Sheets	8 Quires	8 Sheets	6 Quires	6 Sheets	4 Quires	4 Sheets	3 Quires	3 Sheets	2 Quires	2 Sheets
50	0	2	0	2	0	2	0	3	0	3	0	3	0	4	0	4	0	5	0	6	0	7	0	9	0	13	0	17	1	1
100	0	3	0	3	0	4	0	5	0	5	0	6	0	7	0	7	0	9	0	12	0	13	0	17	1	1	1	10	2	2
200	0	5	0	6	0	7	0	9	0	10	0	12	0	13	0	14	0	17	1	23	1	1	1	17	2	15	2	19	4	4
250	0	6	0	7	0	8	0	11	0	13	0	14	0	16	0	17	0	21	1	10	1	8	1	18	3	3	3	12	5	5
300	0	7	0	9	0	10	0	13	0	13	0	17	0	19	0	20	0	1	1	21	1	14	2	2	3	20	4	4	6	6
400	0	11	0	12	0	13	0	17	0	20	0	23	1	1	1	8	1	10	2	8	2	4	2	21	4	5	5	14	8	8
500	0	13	0	14	0	16	1	1	1	1	1	4	1	8	1	10	1	18	2	19	2	16	4	4	5	6	7	23	10	10
600	0	15	0	17	0	19	1	7	1	8	1	10	1	14	1	16	2	2	3	8	3	8	4	21	6	7	9	8	12	12
700	0	17	0	23	0	22	1	9	1	10	1	13	1	20	1	23	2	11	3	17	3	16	5	14	7	7	10	10	14	14
750	0	15	0	21	0	22	0	10	1	11	1	16	1	23	2	2	2	15	3	19	3	21	5	21	7	8	10	11	15	15
800	1	19	0	1	1	1	1	14	1	14	1	21	2	2	2	9	2	19	4	10	3	17	6	10	8	10	12	18	16	16
900	1	21	1	4	1	5	1	16	1	10	2	2	2	9	2	19	3	5	4	19	4	6	6	8	10	13	13	17	18	18
1000	1	8	1	11	1	8	2	5	2	13	2	8	3	7	3	14	4	12	5	23	5	10	6	23	13	15	9	20	20	20
1250	1	18	1	18	1	23	3	13	3	10	3	1	4	23	4	0	6	17	6	8	7	7	8	17	15	18	18	24	26	26
1500	2	8	2	1	2	8	3	13	3	8	4	16	5	5	5	8	6	10	8	15	8	10	9	17	18	21	20	31	31	31
1750	2	18	2	8	2	7	4	13	4	10	5	7	6	13	6	8	7	22	9	23	10	20	13	10	20	34	34	41	36	36
2000	3	5	3	8	3	22	5	9	5	5	5	20	6	13	7	8	9	17	11	18	11	18	14	20	26	41	41	53	41	41
2500	3	15	3	23	3	13	6	23	6	9	6	20	8	20	8	23	12	22	13	23	13	17	18	19	31	53	53	63	53	53
3000	4	8	4	16	5	7	8	17	8	8	8	7	9	7	9	17	12	17	14	18	15	26	19	11	41	63	63	84	63	63
4000	5	13	5	19	5	5	9	17	8	10	9	10	10	7	11	19	17	9	18	23	20	27	19	4	53	84	84	104	84	84
5000	8	9	6	19	6	1	10	8	10	10	11	11	13	7	13	17	17	10	23	17	26	20	11	10	69	104	104	128	104	104
10000	8	17	11	14	11	1	17	9	20	20	23	1	26	1	27	19	34	18	40	9	63	69	11	8	104	4	128	138	8	8

pamphlet printed on common paper, 43 quires of common paper should be given out, while on finer work 44 quires would be used or required; and a still larger number would be necessary in colored printing. In ordinary job-printing, which requires the sheets to be cut, an addition of five per cent. should be made for accidents, wastage, etc. Thus, while one hundred sheets cut into four equal parts would give four hundred sheets of white paper of the proper size, one hundred and five sheets, to be cut up into four hundred and twenty sheets of the size to be printed, must be given out if the customer is to receive four hundred printed copies of his job. A table showing the quantity of paper to be given out for jobs will be found on page 184; and although it makes no allowance for waste, that can be readily estimated.

Glair.—The white of egg, or any viscous, transparent substance resembling it. Glair is extensively used in bookbinding.

Glazing.—A thin coat of a transparent or semitransparent color over another color to modify the effect; also any thin coating which makes the surface of any substance smooth, lustrous, and glassy, as glazed cards, paper, etc.

Glazing Machine, or Calender.—A machine used for putting a polished surface on printed papers, or for burnishing gold and color work. It consists of two massive iron cylinders turned by a cog and flywheel, with power gear to increase the pressure. The sheets to be glazed are placed between polished copper plates, and so passed between the cylinders.

Globe Job Printing-Presses.—Presses manufactured of half-, quarto-, and eighth-medium sizes, by the Jones' Manufacturing Company, of Palmyra, New York. Among the advantages claimed for them are great strength, ease of running, perfect register and distribution, and superior devices for throwing off and dwelling on the impression.

GLOBE JOB PRINTING-PRESS.

Gloss.—A comment or note appended to a work as an explanation of the text.

Glossary.—A dictionary of words or phrases in any language, or occurring in a certain book or author; as, the glossary to Shakspeare.

Glycerine.—An extract from fatty substances, which has been used, to a limited extent, in the manufacture of printers' rollers. The privilege of

using it for this purpose is claimed as a patent right, but this claim is the subject of legal controversy.

Glyphography.—An electrotype process invented in England by Palmer, by which a coat of copper is deposited upon an engraved plate in such a manner that a copy in metal can be obtained with a raised surface suited to letter-press printing.

Glyptic.—The art of carving on stone, gems, or other hard substances.

Gold Composition.—A mixture of chrome and varnish, with which a form intended for bronze work is rolled previously to the impression. The chrome is well ground with a muller into the varnish, which gives the bronze a fuller tint—especially gold bronze—than if the form were rolled with the plain varnish only. This composition serves equally well for copper, citron, or emerald bronzes. Gold Size is the name frequently given to this preparation. For bronze printing, the roller should have a firm face, or the tenacity of the preparation may destroy it; yet it must have sufficient elasticity to deposit the preparation freely and cleanly on the type.

Gold-Leaf.—Gold beaten into thin leaves for gilding, used extensively in bookbinding.

Gold Printing.—This term implies printing in or with gold leaf instead of the more common process of using bronze or gold color. The types being made ready for press in the usual manner, the surface is covered in the ordinary way with gold size instead of ink, and the impression taken upon the paper. For a large job, remove only the back from a book of leaf-gold; for a small one, lay a straight-edge across the book, and cut it through, of the size required, with the point of a sharp pen-knife. This must be done before using the size. Slightly wet the end of the forefinger of the right hand, and, placing the thumb of that hand on the pile of gold, raise the edge of the paper with the forefinger sufficient to dampen it with the moisture of that finger; then press the moistened edge of the paper on the gold, and it will adhere sufficiently to enable the fingers to lift the gold and paper together and place it on the impression. Proceed thus until the size is entirely covered; gently pat the gold with the balls of the finger, or any soft, pliable substance, until it is set; then, with a very soft hat-brush, remove the superfluous gold, when a clear and beautiful impression will appear. Its sharpness will depend on the judgment of the printer in applying the size to the type.

Gold Size.—A thick, tenacious varnish. (See GOLD COMPOSITION.)

Good Color.—When a sheet is printed neither too light nor too dark, it is said to have a good color.

Good Work.—Fat, or well-prepared copy, by the composition of which high wages can be readily earned; or work performed in a correct and artistic manner.

Gordon Presses.—Presses of a variety of styles and sizes, used in printing small forms of job-work, many of which have been manufactured by George

P. Gordon, of New York. For a description of many of his numerous devices, see INVENTIONS, under the head PRESSES. One of the Gordon presses is illustrated by the accompanying cut.

GORDON PRESS.

Government Printing-Office.—The Printing-Office established by law and maintained by the public Treasury at Washington, in which the bills, resolutions, reports, etc. of Congress, and the letter-press work of the department, are executed, is called the Government Printing-Office, and it was recently described by a correspondent of the Printers' Circular, as follows:

The building is situated on the southwest corner of North Capitol and H Streets, is built of brick, four stories high, finely lighted, but not remarkable for its ornateness in architectural design. It is three hundred feet long; two hundred and forty feet of the length being sixty feet wide, and sixty feet of the length being seventy-five feet wide.

The Press-Room occupies some two hundred and seventy feet of the length of the first story of the building, and its entire width, except what is used for wetting and pressing the paper preparatory to its being printed. The presses are arranged on each side of a broad aisle, with the benefit of good light, and consist of one Bullock perfecting press, twenty-six Adams presses, fourteen Hoe cylinder presses, and thirteen Gordon and other small jobbing presses, making an aggregate of fifty-four printing-presses. The Bullock press has a capacity equal to sixteen Adams presses, and is used exclusively for printing the Agricultural Report, an annual work of some eight hundred octavo pages, with an edition of some two hundred and twenty-five thousand volumes.

These presses, together with the other machinery of the office, are driven by two steam-engines, aggregating fifty-horse power, both stationed in the press-room.

The east end of the ground floor, a room of 60 by 60 feet, is used as a drying-room, where the printed

sheets are placed upon racks and dried by steam apparatus. There are also in this room four hydraulic presses used for taking the impression out of printed work; and two cutting machines, driven by steam, in which the printed sheets are cut into proper sizes for folding and delivery.

There are, extending from this floor to the stories above, two elevators propelled by steam, by which forms, finished work, stock, etc. etc. are passed back and forth between the several stories, in the process of completion, and for delivery to the Capitol and the Executive Departments.

The Machine and Repair Shop, at which all the repairing of the presses and machinery, and the joiner-work, is done for the entire establishment, extends from the centre of the main building into the yard, some sixty feet. This department is in charge of experienced and skillful machinists and mechanics, who devote themselves assiduously and profitably to the necessities of the office in its various departments.

The Paper Warehouse extends on the south of the repair-shop, sixty by eighty feet, two stories high, through which all the papers pass that are required for the printing department. These premises are in charge of two trusty men, who, with such laborers as are needed, receive and dispense all the paper required for the public printing. There passed through this warehouse, for consumption, during the year ending September 30, 1870, 30,277 10-20 reams of printing paper, 32,679 16-20 reams of writing paper, and 994 reams of Post-Office paper, aggregating 63,951 7-20 reams of papers of all classes required for the public printing in a single year, which cost an aggregate of $418,974.21.

The Boiler-House is adjacent, but separated by a carriage-way from the other buildings. It contains two large boilers of sufficient capacity to furnish steam for the engines and for heating the entire building. These boilers consume some six hundred tons of coal per annum.

The Roller-House and Stables are adjoining the boiler-house. The roller-house is used for casting the composition rollers for all the presses in the office, and requires the constant services of two persons. The stables are used for the teams required for delivering the products of the printing-office and bindery. Faithful watchmen guard these entire premises night and day, the year round, to prevent intrusion and accident by fire.

The Business-Office and Composing-Room is on the second story of the main building. This contains offices for the Congressional Printer and his clerks, a room for the proof-readers, and the document, executive, and judiciary composing-rooms. The document and judiciary room occupies a space of two hundred and nineteen feet by sixty feet, and the executive room sixty feet by seventy-five feet, well lighted throughout. The stands are ranged on each side of a wide aisle, extending the full length of the composing-rooms. This aisle is occupied by imposing-stones, chase-racks, proof-presses, etc. There is now in use in the composing-rooms of this office more than sixty thousand pounds of type of all varieties. The physical force engaged in these composing-rooms is one foreman of printing, two assistant foremen, and two hundred and forty-one compositors, proof-readers, makers-up, their assistants and laborers, all of whom are employed in the type-setting, imposing, etc. for the printing service of the Government.

The Stereotype Foundry.—In the story of the repair-shop is a door opening out of the composing-room into the stereotype foundry. This department occupies two rooms, and employs a superintendent, assistant, two experienced stereotypers, and four laborers, who furnish all the stereotype plates required for the use of the office, and produce annually plates to the value of some $20,000. This department saves to the Government annually more than $10,000 in money, to say nothing of its marked convenience.

The Government Bindery.—This department occupies the entire third story of the building, and executes a large amount of binding of every variety; and some of the very best, in point of style and excellence, done in the world. There are connected with the operations of this department, one foreman of binding, two assistant foremen, one superintendent of ruling, and one superintendent of sewing, one hundred and thirty-one bookbinders, seventeen rulers, one hundred and three females engaged in sewing books and on the gilding tables, sixteen females feeding ruling machines, seven females on numbering and paging machines, five boys of all work, and laborers, in all aggregating a force of three hundred and ten persons.

The machinery used in the binding is of modern improvement and invention, and the most desirable and useful to be found in this country or in Europe. It consists of nineteen ruling machines, with modern improvements; eight numbering and paging machines, twenty-seven standing presses, three large cutting machines for paper and blank books, five cutting machines for printed books, six backing machines, one machine for cutting cloth, three board-cutting machines, three stamping presses, one smashing machine, one knife-grinding machine, and one machine for grinding colors. A large amount of ledger and cap papers, and binders' material of every description, is necessarily consumed annually in this spacious bindery, where every one is kept industriously at work.

The fourth story of the building is mainly occupied as a folding-room. After the printed sheets pass through the processes of drying and pressing, they are elevated to this room, where they are neatly folded and prepared for the sewing tables of the bindery. The employés of this department comprise a superintendent of folding, two assistants, two cutters, one hundred and seventy-nine female folders, and eighteen laborers, aggregating a force of two hundred and two persons.

The Specification-Room.—Some forty by sixty feet of the east end of the fourth story is occupied by a branch of the printing-office known as the specification-room, where the lists of patents, claims, and specifications of the Patent-Office are printed. This department is operated by the following force: one assistant foreman, two proof-readers, two copy-holders, twenty-eight compositors, one apprentice, and two laborers. There is in this room one power-press and one pressman. The press-work is now all performed in this room for a business that aggregates a product of more than $60,000 per annum.

The Government Printing-Office gives constant employment to about one thousand persons of all grades, from the Congressional Printer, who is an officer of the Senate of the United States, to the laborers who perform the more muscular but less onerous duties of the institution. It disbursed during the last year, in the compensation of service and the purchase of material, one million six hundred and nine thousand eight hundred and fifty-nine dollars and ninety-two cents. It consumed, during that period, more than seventy-five thousand reams of paper of all classes. It annually saves the Government in the expense of its printing and binding, under its present rapid increase, full half a million of dollars by its economics. It improves and elevates the character of the printing and binding for the Government, and presents to the world the spectacle of a printing-office which illustrates, in itself, the rapid growth of a nation that is yet in the first century of its history.

Grafton, Richard.—An English printer, celebrated for his connection with the publication of the Bible in English. Of his birth and education little is known, except that he was descended from a good family, and was a merchant of London. He is believed to have printed Tyndale's Testament, at Antwerp, in 1526. Under license from Henry VIII., Grafton, in connection with Whitchurch, printed Matthew's Bible upon the continent, in 1537. Only 1500 copies were published, and Henry VIII. requested permission of Francis I. that a second edition might be printed in Paris, by Grafton and Whitchurch. The privilege was granted, but just as the Bible was completed, the chief printer was summoned before the inquisitors, and Grafton and Whitchurch, the proprietors, and Coverdale, the corrector of the press, escaped by instantaneous flight. The Bibles were ordered to be burned, but the public officer who had them in charge, sold the whole edition to a haberdasher as wrapping-paper. Grafton returned to Paris, found and repurchased his Bibles, recovered his press and type, and, engaging the assistants of his first printer, removed to England, where the Bible was at length published, in 1538, as the Great Bible, and ordered by law to be exposed in every church. Cromwell, Earl of Essex, had long been the powerful advocate of this publication: his coat of arms appeared on the title-page, and it was frequently styled the Cromwell Bible. In 1540, when Essex was beheaded, it was urged by his enemies that as he had instigated the publication of the Bible in English, that work must also be treasonable, and Grafton was imprisoned in the Fleet, on the charge of printing the Matthew's Bible, and the Great Bible without notes. He was released under a penalty of £100 not to sell, imprint, or cause to be imprinted, any Bibles, until the king and clergy should unite upon a translation. He did not, however, lose the patronage of Henry VIII., for, in conjunction with Whitchurch, he received in 1543 a patent for the publication of several educational and religious works. Grafton was also appointed printer to Prince Edward, and on his accession to the throne received a patent for printing the statute books. By virtue of his office of King's Printer, Grafton published the proclamation of Lady Jane Grey (1553), and for this offense was imprisoned by Mary, deprived of his patent, and mulcted of the debt of £300 then owed him by the government.

During his imprisonment he compiled a history of England, which he appended to Hall's Chronicles, and published the work in 1562. Of the latter years of his life nothing is recorded but that he broke his leg in 1572, and continued lame until his death. Grafton published sixty-two works, most of them distinguished by his punning device of a grafted tree issuing from a tun, with the motto—By their fruits ye shall know them. His son Edward became eminent as a lawyer, received a coat of arms in 1584, and was retained as counsel for the Stationers' Company.

Grain.—The body of any substance considered with respect to the size, form, or direction of its constituent particles, as the grain of wood or stone.

Grained.—Colored in imitation of the grain of woods, marbles, etc., as in the ornamentation of marbled paper.

Graphotype.—A mechanical method of converting an artist's drawing into an engraved block ready for the printer, which is at once simple, speedy, and comparatively inexpensive. The process was discovered by Mr. De Witt C. Hitchcock, an artist and wood-engraver, in New York. Requiring, one day, to correct a drawing upon boxwood with white, and having none of that pigment ready at hand, he used the enamel of a common card. On removing this enamel, which he did with a wet brush, he found, to his surprise, that the printed characters on the card remained in relief, the ink used in impressing them resisting the action of the water, and so protecting the enamel lying underneath. The possible practical application of this at once suggested itself to him, and accordingly he began to make experiments. Ultimately he demonstrated that the process of producing relief plates direct from the drawings of the artist is as certain in its results as wood-engraving, with these special advantages: that it occupies at the very most one-tenth of the time, is less costly, and reproduces exactly, line for line, and touch for touch, the artist's own work. The process itself may be thus briefly described:—Upon a sheet of metal per-

fectly flat is distributed an even layer of very finely pulverized chalk, upon which is laid an ordinary steel plate, such as is used by steel-engravers; it is then placed in a powerful hydraulic press, where it is submitted to such a pressure, that on removal the chalk is found to have assumed a solid, compact mass, with a surface equal to an enamel card, and which is rendered still more solid by a strong coating of a peculiar composition or size. When dried the plate is ready to be drawn upon, and this is done with a chemical ink, composed principally of lampblack, gluten, and a chemical which gives the fluid the advantage of never drying until it comes in contact with the chalk plate. When the drawing is finished, instead of spending hours, as would have been the case had the drawing been made upon wood, in carefully picking out every particle of white, brushes are used of various degrees of stiffness, which by hand, and in some cases by machine, are caused to revolve on the surface, and in a very short time all the chalk untouched by the artist is removed, leaving the ink lines standing up in clear, sharp relief. All that now remains to be done, is to saturate what is left upon the plate with a solution which renders all as hard as marble, and it is then ready for the stereotyper or electrotyper, who, by the ordinary methods, produces a metal block from it, of which impressions may be taken to an unlimited extent. Graphotype has already been applied to book, newspaper, and magazine illustration; to the reproduction of colored drawings and paintings; to printing for transferring to pottery and japanned surfaces, etc. A company has been formed in London for carrying out this invention. They sell plates of certain sizes, on which the artist can make his drawing; he then returns his work, and the company complete the process, and in a short time produce a block ready for printing. Several publications are now issued, which are illustrated on the graphotype principle, but they are not first-class productions.

Grave Accent.—An accent formed thus, `. (See Accents.)

Graver.—An instrument for engraving upon hard substances.

Gray.—A color produced by the mixture of black with white. When printed matter is not distinctly black, the color is said to be gray.

Great Primer.—A large-sized body-type, which was formerly used for printing the Bible. (See Type.)

Greek.—It is said Greek types of correct proportion were first made and used by some unknown German printers, at a monastery near Naples, in 1465. The first Greek Testament was printed by Froben, at Basle, in 1516. The works of Homer were printed in Italy, in 1485. In former times, when a large proportion of the learning of the world was to be found only in the Greek language, type representing it was of much greater relative importance than at the present day; and printers and type-founders were then very proud of superior fonts of Greek type. The pronunciation of the Greek letters is given elsewhere (see Alphabet), and the modern plan of the

Greek Case, as given in The American Printer, is shown below.

Green.—A secondary color compounded of the primaries blue and yellow; and the complement or true contrast of red. Brunswick green is an oxychloride of copper; mineral green, a subcarbonate of copper; Scheele's green, an arsenite of copper; the green used in printing the legal-tender notes of the

tion with Marmaduke Johnson, and his own son. The most famous of his publications were Eliot's Indian Bible and Psalm Book. He had nineteen children, several of whom were printers, Samuel being one of the earliest printers in Boston; and another son, Bartholomew, being noted for establishing, in 1704, the Boston Newsletter, the first successful periodical in the Colonies. A grandson, Timothy

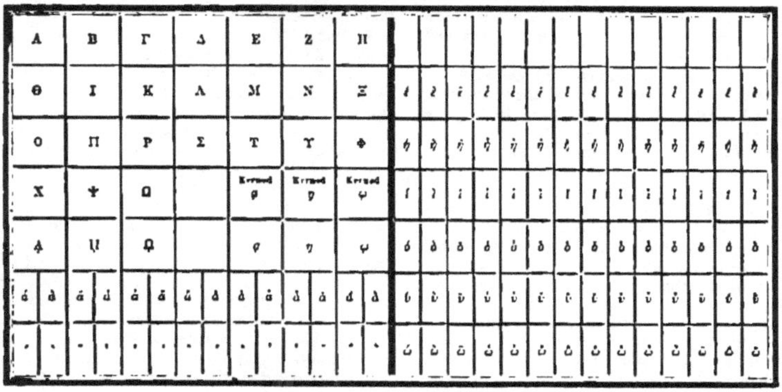

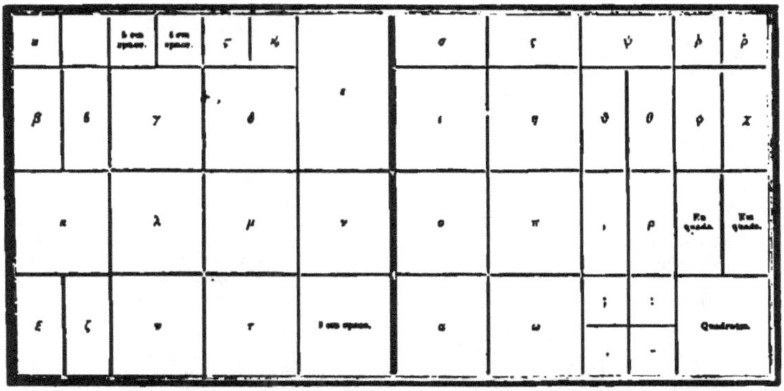

GREEK UPPER-CASE.

GREEK LOWER-CASE.

United States, or Greenbacks, was a compound of new and patented material.

Green, Samuel.—The successor to Stephen Daye, the first printer in the North American Colonies. Samuel Green printed from 1649 until his death, in 1702, and is believed to have published a hundred works during the fifty years that he conducted the Cambridge Press, including those issued in connec-

Green, became Government Printer in Connecticut, where his descendants pursued the same vocation for nearly a century.

Griffin, or Gryphon.—A fabulous animal, having the body and feet of the lion, and the head, wings, and claws of the eagle. A favorite figure in heraldry, as combining the highest qualities of the beast and bird, or strength and swiftness, with courage, prudence, and vigilance. It formed part of the armorial bearing granted to printers individually and collectively by Frederick III., Emperor of Germany. (See DEVICES.)

Gripper Machines.—Power-presses in which grippers, as contradistinguished from tapes, are used.

Grippers.—The metal claws of a power-press, which seize hold of the sheet of paper as it lies on the feeding-board and hold it while it receives the impression under the cylinder. They finally release it in order that the delivery apparatus may remove it from the machinery.

Groove.—An indentation on the upper surface of the short cross of a chase, to receive the spurs of the points and to allow them to make holes in the paper without being injured themselves.

Ground.—The principal colors of a composition or picture, to which all others are considered as secondary—the first layer of color upon which the others are placed. In a picture, the ground is the scenery, or objects introduced as a setting for the principal figures, the part nearest the eye being distinguished as the foreground, and the most distant as the background. In etching, the ground is the composition used to cover the plate. (See ETCHING.)

Group.—In art, an arrangement of figures which produces unity of effect either alone or as distinguished from other portions of the composition.

Grub-Street.—A term used to designate a low or venal order of literature, from the fact that Grub-Street, in London, was the residence of many impoverished authors, who supported themselves by writing poems, political squibs, lampoons, etc., at the order of occasional patrons. Seditious and libelous pamphlets and papers were written for a series of years by reduced authors living in the wretched tenements of this street, and the name became affixed to such anonymous publications. In 1730 an amusing and brilliant attack upon some of the authors of the day was published in a series of numbers, under the title of The Memoirs of the Society of Grub-Street, and the great success of the publication induced Cave to establish a literary serial, the famous Gentleman's Magazine, which became the prototype of the modern monthly magazine. Fox, the author of the Book of Martyrs, found shelter and security from persecution in this miserable street.

GUIDE OR COPY-HOLDER, INVENTED BY YOUNG.

Guide.—A piece of rule or lead, balanced by a light cord, to which a weight or large type is attached, which is laid upon the copy on the upper-case, to assist the compositor in keeping the connection. Many morning newspaper compositors never use a guide, partly because their takes of copy are generally short, and partly because guides are a hindrance to rapid composition. Various forms of guides have been invented, one of which is illustrated in the adjoining column.

Guillard, Charlotte.—The first celebrated female printer. As the wife and widow of two distinguished French printers, Rembolt and Chevalon, she was for a series of years interested in the art, and in the year 1552 testified that she had labored in the profession for fifty years. After the death of her second husband, Claude Chevalon, in 1540, she personally superintended her presses, and corrected the Latin publications, which were distinguished for their accuracy. For sixteen years she maintained a great renown for the beauty and exactness of her Latin and Greek books, publishing a fine Latin Bible, Erasmus Testament, and the works of the Fathers. The works of St. Gregory in two volumes is recognized as a typographical treasure, containing but three errors. Two works by Lippowan, Bishop of Verona, which were confided to her on account of her accuracy, were printed in 1546 and 1555, and were highly esteemed for the perfection and beauty of execution. A Greek lexicon, commenced by Bogard, was completed by Charlotte Guillard after his death, and, like her other voluminous publications, it was celebrated for elegance and accuracy. She died in 1556.

Guillemets.—In French, the marks of quotation, so called from the inventor, which are cast together, thus: « ».

Guillotine Cutting Machine.—This machine is of iron, with an iron or mahogany table on which to place the paper to be cut. A movable gauge is attached to a slide, which runs in a graduated scale, by which the size to be cut can be regulated to the sixteenth part of an inch. When the paper is in its place, it is held immovable by a platen and screw; a cog-wheel which moves in a ratchet attached to a large knife is turned, and the knife descends, cutting through the paper with great rapidity. The wheel is then reversed in its motion, and the knife ascends preparatory to a fresh cut.

Gutenberg, John, or John Gensfleisch.—The following sketch was translated by Mr. Jacob Glaser, of Philadelphia, expressly for this publication, from a recent article in Des Annalen der Typographie, a leading German typographical journal, and it embodies the version of Gutenberg's career which is now generally accepted in Germany.

John Gensfleisch, of Gutenberg, born 1397, was a member of a respectable patrician family of Mentz. His father, Frielo Gensfleisch, married Else, last branch of the patrician families in Gutenberg. The fruits of this marriage were two sons, Frielo and

John. Of his younger years and education nothing is known. Becoming involved in the strife between patricians and burghers, in Mentz, the Gensfleisch family removed (1420) most likely first to Eltville, in Rheingau, where they settled on an estate, and where the younger Frielo lived in 1434. From a document dated Strasburg, 1434, belonging to the Gutenberg family (this being the name by which it is best known), it appears for the first time with certainty that he was domiciled there. In this document he declares that the city clerk of Mentz was bound to him for the payment of an annuity due to him by the city of Mentz, but his claim was denied, because he did not return to Mentz when the authorities at Strasburg wished to retain him.

There is no clear development of his doings in Strasburg. The only authentic knowledge of him there, as well as later in Mentz, is drawn from the documents relating to his various law-suits. His name appears in the Acts of Strasburg, in 1436, in a suit at law against Andrew Dritzehns, in which suit mention is made of forms, presses, and printing. Probably Gutenberg was engaged in experiments and inventions of various kinds. In 1438 he organized an association for polishing stones and making mirrors. It appearing, however, that he possessed some secrets which he was reluctant to divulge, his associates entered into a new contract with him, in which, for a certain price, he was to disclose whatever he knew of the arts.

Among these arts was probably the printing of wooden tablets on the press, so that more than one could be printed at a time, and the leaves be printed on both sides, which was not customary, as far as is known, at that time, among those who produced a print by rubbing. It is also very probable that in Strasburg he attempted to introduce movable letters, without, however, arriving at any practical result.

During his sojourn in Strasburg, it also appears by public documents that he was sued by Anna of the Iron Door, for breach of promise of marriage, and that he probably married the plaintiff, as she was afterwards known by the name of Gutenberg. Whether they lived together subsequently, or were man and wife in name only, is not known. While these facts indicate that Gutenberg's first attempts to invent printing were made in Strasburg, it is in Mentz, whither we accompany Gutenberg, that the invention proper must be looked for; as there remain no traces of the products of his labor in Strasburg as a printer. Probably his continued financial embarrassment, and the prospect of procuring from his well-to-do relatives the necessary means for the prosecution of his plans, led him to Mentz. On the 23d of April, 1444, he was in Strasburg. Towards the end of the year 1444, or the beginning of 1445, accompanied by a faithful servant, Lorenz Beildeck, he must have arrived at Mentz.

Of the first five years of his residence in Mentz it is only known that his uncle rented to him a residence, and, further, that on the 6th of October, 1448,

he lent Gutenberg 150 guilders. He was probably engaged in experiments, by which his means were exhausted. In 1450 it was his fortune to find a wealthy and active partner in John Fust, with whom, on the 22d of August, he made a contract in pursuance of which Fust lent Gutenberg 800 guilders in gold, at six per cent. interest, for the purpose of purchasing material, and promised a yearly payment of 300 guilders for working capital. The profits were to be equally divided, and it was understood that in case the partnership was dissolved, the 800 guilders should be repaid to Fust, the business, stock, etc. being held as security for such payment.

Gutenberg's first works were probably alphabet cards, extracts from the Latin Grammar, the Catholicon, and a school-book, with precepts and examples. It is very likely that these publications were printed from wooden blocks, even after the invention of movable types. Gutenberg's first movable types were made of wood, and the earliest impressions of them are still extant. They were cut in pear-wood, and had a hole bored in them, so that by means of a thread or wire they could be kept in position. In printing, they were held together in an iron frame.

Although at this time the first steps had been taken, it is clear that the art was far from being completed. The wooden types were very susceptible to injury; they had to be cut of a very large size, and letters of a like character were not altogether uniform, for it was no easy matter to make them of a certain size and at the same time preserve the required firmness. The cutting in metal, however, must have caused a marked increase in the cost. The mind would naturally revert to the practicability of casting a type in metal, or impressing it on soft metal, in order to obtain a mould for casting type of uniform character. The fact that Fust, in 1452, advanced to Gutenberg an additional sum of 800 guilders in gold, indicates that at that time the invention had reached some degree of success, or the cautious tradesman would not have given such additional aid to further the enterprise.

The partnership had now progressed so far that they were enabled to undertake a great work, the *Biblia Latina Vulgata*, which was completed in 1455. This venerable monument of printing, contained in two folio volumes, 641 leaves (the copies in Munich and Vienna, with the record of the Rubric, containing 645 leaves) in double column, without folios, catchwords, signatures, and initials. With the exception of the first nine pages, which have 40 lines, and the tenth, which has 41, the pages have each 42 lines; hence the title—the 42-line Bible. (See Reduced fac-simile of an illuminated page of this Bible.)

The type used was called Missal-type; and it is supposed that it was cast in metal [but the appearance of the page indicates that some of the words were engraved logotypes, and that many of the letters were cut and not cast]. Two editions of the work were published; one on parchment, with brilliantly drawn initials, decorated with gold, the other on paper, with drawings of alternate red and blue initials. Six copies on parchment (one of which is in Leipsic, and another in Berlin) and nine on paper (there being one copy in each of the cities of Frankfort-on-the-Main, Leipsic, Munich, and Vienna) are known to exist.

Nearly all the early writers express a positive opinion that this 42-line Bible, and not the 36-line edition, was the first issued, and that the latter was the first production of the press of Albrecht Pfister, in Bamberg, although in later times T. O. Weigel and Zestermann have raised their voices in opposition to that version. The publication of the work without date or imprint indicates that the copies were sold at high prices, similar to those received for manuscripts. This business policy, however, does not necessarily imply any intention to defraud, as the leading motive of the inventors was probably an indisposition to proclaim their secret to the world.

In principle, the discovery was now ended; a great event had taken place; but in the subsequent progress much was wanting, and Gutenberg did not possess the capacity for dealing with details and overcoming the difficulties which from time to time presented themselves. The cast type, intended to supersede those made of wood, were very imperfect. The sharpness of face was soon lost, and the delineation and cut of the original letters were defective. The partners, for this reason, sought for a new power to overcome these difficulties, and found it in Peter Schoeffer, to whom, as the improver of the art, too much praise cannot be awarded.

Schoeffer was born in Gernsheim, between 1420 and 1430, and distinguished himself at an early age by his calligraphic efforts. Of his family and his younger years we know nothing more except that he applied himself for a time to studying law, resided afterwards in Paris, and was known as an accomplished illuminator and title-writer. In 1450 or 1451 he arrived in Mentz, and was employed by Fust as an amanuensis, probably in writing manuscripts and drawing initials, as well as in affording assistance in perfecting the types.

He beautified the forms (or shape) of the letters, made them more symmetrical, discovered a better composition for the type, and used for the matrices a harder metal. He cut the stamps in steel, by means of which he was enabled to punch the matrices, instead of casting them; in short, he introduced the casting of type, which, to this day, forms a vitally important auxiliary of the art. He also essentially improved the color of the ink by the addition of oil, which up to this time had been composed of lampblack, water, and lime.

That Schoeffer's labors were of great importance is shown by the fact that the wealthy and respectable Fust gave him his daughter Christina in marriage. This event occurred in 1454 or 1455; we can arrive at no truer date than this. (See SCHOEFFER.)

It is not improbable that the shrewd, calculating Fust contemplated, from the commencement of the partnership, depriving Gutenberg (whom he held in his power by his money advances) of his share in the business. And now, since he had established a firm alliance with the accomplished Schoeffer, he could go on unhindered in the accomplishment of his plans. The new improvements were not imparted to Gutenberg. In 1455 Fust instituted suit for the payment of the 1600 guilders he had advanced, with compound interest from date of loan, and the decision was, of course, unfavorable to Gutenberg. Fust demanded the delivery of the material and assets of the business, which had been pledged for the payment of the money, and Gutenberg saw himself defrauded of the fruits of his patient and, up to this time, unrequited toil.

His energy, in spite of this severe blow, however, was not lost. Under great trials and difficulties, he continued to make progress in the art, and in 1460 we hear of him in new enterprises. By the aid of Dr. Conrad Hummery, Gutenberg was again enabled to work on a satisfactory basis. He was also obliged to pledge his new printing-office as security for the money advances of Hummery, but was allowed to remain in undisputed possession of the same until his death.

According to all accounts, the business must have been carried on in Hummery's house. In 1460, the Catholicon, in large folio, printed with semi-Gothic type, was issued from Gutenberg's press. The type was certainly finished after the style of Schoeffer's improvements, but they lack the elegance of Schoeffer's. The work was comprised in 374 leaves, in double column, 66 lines to the column; it was printed in two editions, on parchment and on paper, with drawn initials. Signatures, catchwords, and folios are wanting. The printer is not named. There is no doubt that the book was printed in Gutenberg's office, as at that time he alone was in possession of the type.

On the 18th of January, 1465, Gutenberg was taken into the employ of the courtiers of the Elector, Adolph of Nassau, and removed to Eltville. The printing-office which he there organized he leased to Heinrich Bechter Münze. Gutenberg received an annual payment from the Elector of a new suit of clothes, twenty bushels of corn, and two tuns of wine. He did not, however, long enjoy his increased prosperity. On the 24th of February, 1468, he had ceased to exist, as is shown by a document of the above date, in which Dr. Hummery instituted an action against the Duke Adolph of Nassau, as Archbishop of Mentz, for certain printing-materials, which did not belong to Hummery, and which were claimed to be for the sole use of, and in, the city of Mentz. As Gutenberg is mentioned as a printer on the 4th of November, 1467, he must have died between that time and the 24th of February, 1468. He was buried in the Church of the Holy Franciscus, which was destroyed in 1742. No trace remains of any memorial to mark his exact resting-place; but on the site of the church there was erected, on the 14th of August, 1837,

٢٣

GUTENBERG

BASS-RELIEFS ON THE MENTZ MONUMENT

a bronze statue, by Thorwaldsen; and every printed book is a memorial of his world-moving discovery.

Gutta-Percha Plates.—Type-forms are sometimes stereotyped in gutta-percha, or a similar material which has been specially prepared for this purpose, and for such plates impressions are taken on tin, iron, wood, brass, or other hard substances. They can be used in printing on metallic surfaces which are not exactly level or even, or readily curved round cylinders. The mode of preparation is, to some extent, a trade secret, but it is said to be as follows: The matrix is taken by pressure from the form of type while the sheet of gutta-percha is hot and soft. When cold and hard, a second impression, or reverse of itself, is taken from this mould, and this, when cold and hard, is, after being blocked, ready for use on a typographical press.

Gutters.—The furniture separating two adjoining pages in a chase; as between folios 1 and 8 in a half-sheet of 8vo.

Gutter-Snipe.—A small and narrow printed bill or poster, which is usually pasted on curbstones.

H.

Haarlem, Haerlem, or Harlem.—A city of North Holland, which, as the residence of Koster, disputes with Mentz the honor of being the birth-place of printing by movable metal type. Situated on a navigable river only three miles from the sea, seventeen miles from Leyden, and but ten miles from Amsterdam, it has enjoyed for many centuries a conspicuous position in history, and great advantages in manufactures. It was once particularly celebrated for the success and magnitude of its printing, but this business has declined, although its type-foundries still maintain considerable reputation, especially as the principal source whence the Jews obtain their Hebrew type. The handsome public square contains a bronze statue in honor of Koster as the inventor of printing, and public festivals have been held periodically by the city in commemoration of his alleged claims to the invention.

Hagar, William.—An American type-founder, who was born in Rutland, Vermont, in 1798. In early life he was apprenticed to a watchmaker, and in 1816, after acquiring some skill in this pursuit, he went to New York, where, after searching in vain for employment in the business in which he had been partly trained, he found employment in Elihu White's type-foundry. He speedily became skilled in his difficult new occupation, and, after being promoted from one grade to another, obtained an interest in White's type-foundry. Subsequently, under various business connections, he continued the business of type-founding in New York, until a few years before his death, withdrawing from it only during one or two intervals of a long business career. At one time he was the owner of the patent right of the Bruce type-casting machine, and during this period he not only supplied American foundries, but introduced

13

the machines into England, France, Germany, the East Indies, and China (where one was furnished for missionary purposes). Mr. Hagar died in December, 1863, and his foundry is now owned and conducted by his sons, under the firm name of Hagar & Co.

Hair-Line.—Type having unusually thin lines on its face.

Hair-Space.—The thinnest of the spaces. On an average, ten hair-spaces equal one em, but occasionally they are made thicker, and sometimes thinner, than this, according to the body of the font. There are seldom less than seven or more than ten hair-spaces to the em.

Half-Case.—A case whose width is about half that of an ordinary upper case. The space between the uprights of a whole frame is usually equal to the breadth of one and a half cases. If a rack be fitted up within it, there remains a certain space unoccupied, and this is sometimes filled by a board or galley rack, or left vacant, with only a shelf at the bottom. Half-cases are made in order to utilize this space, and by fixing up a small rack for them, about ten may be conveniently accommodated. They are useful for holding title letters or fancy fonts. They contain forty-nine boxes.

Half-Sheet.—When a form is imposed in such a manner as to perfect itself, making two copies on a sheet, it is called a half-sheet.

Half-Tint.—An intermediate color, or a middle tint.

Half-Title.—An epitome of the full title, which is placed at the head of the opening page of the text of a book. It should be set in the neatest and simplest manner possible, and when the matter extends to three or more lines it should, if possible, be displayed in a similar style to the title-page, but in rather smaller type. The space occupied by the half-title will vary according to the width of margin in the succeeding pages, the size of the page, and the openness or closeness of the lines of the text. The degree of taste possessed by the compositor is invariably shown by the appearance of the title and half-title.

Hand-Bills.—Comparatively small printed bills, used chiefly to advertise auctions of real or personal property. In England they are intended for circulation by hand, and from this use their name is derived; but in the United States they are generally attached to the walls of frequented rooms of taverns, or other places of public resort. Like posters, which are of much larger size, they are also sometimes pasted on outer walls, or on trees or fences, in or near great thoroughfares. Any variety of type is permissible in a hand-bill, except small, ornate, and complicated letters, which are not easily read, and are, therefore, unsuitable for this class of work. In a circular the sizes of the types in the different lines should be duly proportioned to each other according to the importance of the words, and the whole should possess a certain harmony of appearance, both in regard to the character of the fonts employed and the thickness of the strokes of the letters. But in a hand-bill, a few lines may be thrown out very boldly, and their comparative importance may thus be advantageously exaggerated. The object of this is, that on a casual glance the reader may be at once struck with the novelty, usefulness, necessity, or advantage of the thing or occasion thus presented.

Handbook.—A small book for common use; generally a compendium or abstract prepared in a manner suitable for convenient reference. The word is theoretically a synonym for manual, but in practice there is generally a distinction in the class of subjects to which these terms are applied. Thus, publishers announce a Handbook of Travel, and a Manual of Typography.

Handle of a Press.—The extremity of the bar, and the part of the hand-press taken hold of by the pressman in running the carriage into and out of the position in which the impression is obtained. The handle is usually a wooden cylinder covering the bar, and is made of a size and shape that can be conveniently grasped by the hand.

Handling.—In art, the management of the instrument, pencil, brush, etc., within which the effects are produced. Thus, the handling of Albert Durer has been praised as spirited, bold, and free.

Hand-Inker.—A machine for diminishing labor and securing better work in rolling the forms printed on hand-presses. It is adapted to the use of one or two rollers.

HAND-INKER FOR HAND-PRESS.

Hand-Made Paper.—Paper manufactured by hand, in contradistinction to that made by machine.

Hand-Mould.—In type-founding, the small instrument or frame into which the matrix is fixed. The mould is composed of two parts. The external surface is of wood, the internal of polished steel. At the top is a shelving orifice, into which the metal is poured. The space within is set according to the required body of the letter, and is made exceedingly true. The melted metal, being poured into this space, sinks to the bottom into the matrix, and, instantly cooling, the mould is opened, and the type is cast out by the workman. Formerly the types were cast exclusively by this process; but the art has been gradually improved, until the type-casting machine (see TYPE-CASTING MACHINE) has entirely superseded the hand-mould in the United States, except in the manufacture of the very large sizes of types.

Hand-Press.—A press worked by hand, in contradistinction to one which works more automatically by machinery.

Handwriting.—Manuscript; also the peculiar style of letters formed by any individual. Handwriting seems to be an especially characteristic expression of individual peculiarities, and as such is infinitely varied, notwithstanding the prevailing style of certain countries or times; and a general acquaintance with the varieties is one of the earliest necessities of the printer.

Hanging Indention.—When the first line is brought full out to the commencement of the measure, and the second and following lines have a certain indention, the former hangs over, and the arrangement is called by some a hanging indention; by others the term used is run out and indent. This paragraph is an example.

Hanging Pages.—Pages of type which are found, after being locked up, to be out of the perpendicular. The remedy for this is, to unlock the quarter in which it is imposed, and to pat the face of the type with the fingers of one hand, at the same time pushing up the page with the other, until it regains its proper position. Sometimes the hanging of a page is caused by the page at its side being rather longer, or by the foot-stick binding against the furniture; in this case an extra lead or piece of reglet should be placed at the foot of the page before re-locking up, so as to be clear of the obstacle. When a form is unlocked, care should be taken not to leave the quoins too slack, as the operation of loosening the others may either squabble the matter or cause it to hang.

Hang up.—To place wet printed sheets, fresh from the press, upon drying poles or lines.

Hansard, Thomas Curson.—An eminent author on typography. He was the son of Luke Hansard, a successful and laborious typographer, who held for some years the office of printer to the House of Commons, and was very liberal in his benefactions to the printers of London. T. C. Hansard was an ingenious practical printer; he successfully founded an establishment called the Paternoster Press, in Paternoster Row, and was the inventor of a press and other articles of machinery applicable to his business. In 1825 he published his Typographia, a royal octavo of nearly one thousand pages, which has held an honorable station as one of the great authorities upon the history and practice of printing. It is a book written in a conscientious and careful spirit, and is well entitled to the fame that it has enjoyed. T. C. Hansard was also the author of the treatises upon Printing and Type-founding in the British Encyclopædia. He was born in 1776, and died in 1833.

Hard or Heavy Impression.—An impression taken when there is too much pull on the press, causing lines which should be soft and delicate to come up heavy and strong, and frequently injuring irreparably the face of the type.

HATTERSLEY TYPE-SETTING MACHINE.

Hattersley Type-Setting Machine.—An English type-setting machine, which stands on a space of two feet by three, and is worked by touching a key-board, like that of a piano. The type used is of the ordinary kind; and it is placed in the composing-stick direct, by only one motion. It is said that the keys have been worked at the rate of 26,000 letters per hour. The machine is simple and comparatively inexpensive, the price ranging from $375 (in gold) upwards.

Hat-Tip Press.—The accompanying illustration represents a hat-tip press, used in printing by the hot method, to obtain impressions in gold-leaf. In work of this description the forms must be composed of metal harder than type-metal, such as brass types, brass plates, or electrotypes. The presses are heated, so that the form to be printed may be kept hot. Hat-tips are prepared for working by being dampened with a solution of transparent shellac dissolved in spirits of wine; satin or velvet is powdered with the white of an egg dried in the sun, and subsequently ground very fine; to leather the white of an egg, mixed with a small quantity of sugar, is applied. In printing, better results will nearly always be obtained by laying the leaf on the face of the form than by putting it on the material; and the tympan should be quite hard.

TAYLOR HAT-TIP PRESS.

Headings.—The setting of words in the heads of ruled columns of ledgers, day-books, time-books, etc. The compositor, in setting them up, does not generally use a stick, but picks up the words in his fingers, and lays them along the bottom ridge of a long galley, to which he affixes the sheet, and spaces out the words so as to bring them into their proper positions. The pressman, in working headings, feeds his sheets to a particular line; for in ruling, some sheets may be a trifle out in the margin, although the lines will be exact; and by feeding to the same line at each impression, the headings are certain to fall right.

Head-Line or Head.—The top line of a page, containing the running title and folio. When there is no running title, the folio is styled the head-line. Chapter-lines are head-lines, as are also the titles of articles in periodicals and newspapers.

Head-Pieces.—Ornamental designs used at the heads or commencements of chapters. The early productions of the press were embellished with beautifully executed drawings in various colors, done by hand, and displaying the highest skill of the illuminators. Gradually, as books were produced more cheaply, wood-engravings were used; then metal ornaments were produced, and subsequently flowers or borders. The latter were superseded by simple brass rules, and some years ago even these were dispensed with, and head-pieces were seldom or never seen. The recent revival of old-style printing has brought with it not only the old faces of type, but the old ornamental head-pieces, and many of the newest and most tasteful works are now ornamented with *facsimiles* of head-pieces which were in fashion two centuries ago.

Head-Sticks or Head-Furniture.—Furniture put at the heads of pages, in composition, to make margin.

Heap.—The pile of paper given out and wetted down for any job.

Hebrew.—The names of the letters of the Hebrew Alphabet will be found elsewhere. (See ALPHABET.) The plan of the Hebrew upper and lower cases, with points, as given in The American Printer, is illustrated on this page. Hebrew, like several other ancient languages, is written and printed from right to left.

sometimes occur, either through the varying systems of different foundries, or through carelessness; and as the type is worn, its height diminishes. A letter or line of letter is said to be high when it is above the height of the letters surrounding it.

Heliotype.—A process by which an imprint of the characters or picture which are intended to be reproduced, is taken upon a bed of prepared gelatine;

HEBREW UPPER-CASE.

HEBREW LOWER-CASE.

Heliochromy.—The process of obtaining photographic pictures in their natural colors.

Heliography.—The art of fixing the images produced by the camera-obscura.

Height to Paper.—The distance between the face and foot of type. Bruce's Specimen Book states that American type are cast ninety-two hundredths of an inch in height. Variations from this rule, however,

from this imprint is then obtained a matrix which, when subjected to the galvanic battery, will produce a negative in copper, from which impressions can be made by the ordinary printing-press.

Hell.—The receptacle for broken and battered type. Modern refinement has almost expunged this expression from the printers' vocabulary.

Henry, David.—A printer and author, distinguished for being actively engaged in the Gentleman's Magazine for more than half a century, also as the particular friend of Benjamin Franklin while he was a journeyman in England, and as a near relative of Patrick Henry, of Revolutionary fame. Descended from a family of remarkable intelligence near Aberdeen, Scotland, he disappointed his father, who intended him for the Church, by leaving Aberdeen College for London, when but fourteen years of age, to follow his fancy for printing. Here he attracted the attention of Edward Cave, and married that gentleman's sister. While a journeyman, he was an intimate friend of Benjamin Franklin and William Strahan. Soon after his marriage, Henry established a newspaper in Reading, England, and in 1754, his name appeared as a partner in the Gentleman's Magazine. He is believed to have been a voluminous author, but a peculiar modesty made him avoid notoriety, and his publications were always anonymous. Remarkably successful as a printer and publisher, agriculture was his amusement, and, notwithstanding his other employments, he for many years practiced farming on a considerable scale, and wrote and published in 1772 a valuable practical work called The Complete English Farmer. He was also the author of a voluminous and excellent history of the voyages of discovery performed by English navigators, which was published from 1774 to 1786. David Henry died in 1792, at the age of eighty-two.

HENRY PATENT PRESS.

Henry Patent Press.—A press made of various sizes, suitable for printing country newspapers, books, or job-work. It was invented by John Henry, and is manufactured by the American Power-Press Manufacturing Company, at Newark, New Jersey. Among the advantages claimed for it are cheapness, simplicity, solidity, strength and durability. One feature said to be peculiar to this machine is a crank at the end of the shaft to which the level gearing is attached, which enables the pressman to get up and distribute ink without setting the press in motion.

Heroic Verse.—The measure usually employed in heroic or epic poetry. In English, the iambic of ten syllables, either with or without an additional syllable. A perfect instance is found in the following couplet:

A heap of dust alone remains of thee,
'T is all thou art, and all the proud shall be.

Hiatus.—A deficiency in the text of an author, as from an erasure, injury, etc.; also, in grammar and prosody, the occurrence of a final vowel followed immediately by an initial vowel of the next word, without an apostrophe and compelling a gap or stop for the full utterance of the words. This repetition of the same sound is a serious blemish in composition, although the short sound of a vowel may be permitted to follow the long one.

Hieroglyphic.—Writing by sculpture or picture, consisting of figures of animals, plants, and other material objects such as were employed by the Egyptians. A species of hieroglyphics were in use by the Mexicans at the time of their conquest by the Spaniards. By this method of writing, ideas are expressed by representations of visible objects; in the simplest form the word or thought is represented by the rude picture of itself, as when the American Indian drew the rude arrow-head to represent the weapon itself; but in a more complex system the same arrow was made to represent the idea of rapidity, war, or defiance, while in the highest or most scholarly hieroglyphics used by the priesthood of Egypt, as a secret language, the figure was used to express the first vocal sound in the name of the object represented. In Egypt the hieratic and demotic systems of writing were simplifications of the hieroglyphics suited to the requirements of the people. (See ALPHABET.)

History.—A narrative of events, particularly of facts respecting nations or individuals. This word as the title for a book is supposed to have been first used by Herodotus in the fifth century before the Christian era. In a broader sense, history is made to include the account of all events, and thus comprehends natural history, or the facts of the animal, vegetable, and mineral kingdoms. This extensive division of literature has furnished an immense field for all departments of typographical labor.

History of Printing.—Printing is the art of mechanically multiplying permanent copies of an original. The word implies pressure; but photographic pictures are said to be printed, although they are produced by the action of light. Typography is the art of reproducing written language or thoughts by means of movable types. Other varieties of printing are described under their appropriate heads. (See LITHOGRAPHY, ANASTATIC PRINTING, PLATE PRINTING, CALICO PRINTING, and PRINTING.)

Some forms of printing were practiced at the most remote periods of antiquity. One of the earliest methods was the pressure of engraved seals or signets into wax, clay, or other soft substance. This was understood thousands of years before the Christian era. (See BIBLICAL ALLUSIONS TO PRINTING.) It was also, probably, the first step in the art carried to such perfection by the Assyrians or Babylonians that they produced clay or brick books which are still in existence. (See ASSYRIAN PRINTING.) Coining money, by making copies of an original in gold, silver, copper, or other metals, was also practiced by the Greeks and Romans, and other ancient and civilized nations, several centuries before the Christian era, and some coins still in existence date back to about 600 B. C.

Printing, as contradistinguished from coining, and similar processes, however, usually implies, in the modern sense of the word, either the employment of a pigment, like printers' ink, or the use of chemical agencies (as in photography) which serve to produce copies in varied lights and shades of one or more colors. The Romans had metal stamps for marking names, goods, etc., to which it is supposed they sometimes applied ink, thus using them as hand-stamps are used at the present day.

Some writers have inferred from the nature of these hand-stamps, that the essential features of modern printing were understood by the Romans, and that it was either suppressed by the government, or that its development was retarded by the fact that copies of books, records, speeches, etc. were readily, rapidly, and cheaply multiplied by slaves who were educated to serve as copyists or scribes.

But the art of printing with the aid of a pigment is not known to have been applied to literary purposes, or to have been extensively practiced in any country, before its invention in China (see CHINA, PRINTING IN), in the tenth century, and it is probable that the first attempts to practice it in Europe were suggested by the knowledge of the Chinese processes, furnished by Marco Polo, at the end of the thirteenth century. He brought back with him to Italy, paper money printed in China, which was freely exhibited, as well as described in his published works; and as the Venetians are known to have adopted other Chinese inventions, it is plausibly conjectured that the skill they acquired during the fourteenth century in printing playing-cards and religious pictures originated in the information furnished by Marco Polo. During the fourteenth century, the art of printing playing-cards and religious pictures was practiced in Germany and Holland, as well as in Venice, and it led to the production of block-books. (See BLOCK-BOOKS.)

Italy, notwithstanding her skill in art, was surpassed by Germany and Holland in the knowledge of mechanical appliances; and it is a natural result of the state of European civilization in the fifteenth century that typography was a Dutch or German rather than an Italian, French, English, or Spanish invention. Many bitter and lengthy controversies have been waged over the disputed question of who was the European inventor of printing. The respective claims of the most important of these reputed fathers of the art, and the nature of their labors, are referred to elsewhere. (See GUTENBERG, KOSTER, FUST, SCHOEFFER, PFISTER, and CASTALDI.)

The most probable theory is, that printing had reached, in Europe, the advanced stage in which block-books were produced, before any of these reputed inventors attempted to practice it; that Koster made some marked advance in the art before Gutenberg's labors were commenced; that Gutenberg's long-continued efforts not only resulted in more marked success than those of any of his predecessors, but also in the development which brought printing prominently and directly to the notice of all the civilized nations of Europe; and that the superior excellence attained by the world-renowned efforts at Mentz, about the middle of the fifteenth century, was due to the strong combination of inventive genius, capital, command of varied mechanical appliances, and artistic knowledge, which was embodied in the joint efforts of Gutenberg, Fust, and Schoeffer.

The dispersion from Mentz, in October, 1462, of the workmen already initiated into the mystery of printing (see ADOLPHUS OF NASSAU) led to a wonderfully rapid extension of the art, which learned men of every nation seemed ready to welcome with delight; and the relative intellectual condition of the different parts of Europe can be fairly deduced from the bare chronology of the facts. Before the completion of the first half-century, printing had been established throughout almost the whole of civilized Europe, and the dates previous to the year 1500 are of special interest, as exhibiting the sturdy infancy of the art. (See INCUNABULA.)

England was one of the last of the civilized countries of Europe to establish a printing-office, many portions of Germany, as well as various towns in Italy, France, Switzerland, Poland, Flanders, Belgium, Hungary, Würtemberg, Bavaria, the Netherlands, and Spain, having had presses in operation before Caxton commenced his useful labors in Westminster Abbey. (See CAXTON, WILLIAM, and AMERICA, EARLY PRINTING IN.)

During this wondrous first half-century of typography, it was caressed as a prodigy, welcomed as a miracle by the Pope, kings, and courtiers, and petted as a new mechanical servant evoked for the special pleasure of the wealthy and the learned. But the true character of the art and its highest mission were soon revealed. Dire forebodings taught them that it was to be the grand liberalizing agent, especially intended to prepare the minds of the people for civil and religious liberty. Bigotry, royalty, and aristocracy combined against the newly-discovered foe, and the censorship of the press, in every land, endeavored vainly to battle with the inevitable, and blindly strove to destroy the power which it could only momentarily shackle, until in the far future it would rise in giant force and hurl tyranny from its throne. (See CEN-SORSHIP OF THE PRESS.)

Such extraordinary perfection had been reached by the united and peculiar talents of Gutenberg, Fust, and Schoeffer, that their immediate successors did little more than extend the art into foreign countries, where they gained popularity and wealth by multiplying the favorite manuscripts, block-books, etc. Gradually, however, the leading typographers established better and more uniform rules of orthography and punctuation. The virgule, or simple slanting line adopted from manuscript and corresponding to the present comma, was followed by a simple point, equivalent to a period, and two points, or a colon. After printing was more fully established, it became a less slavish imitation of manuscript; the abbreviations, and the cramped and crowded lines, common to the copyists on account of the expense of vellum, were gradually abandoned for a greater breadth of margin, and general roominess. Folios and signatures were invented, and a catch-word was placed at the bottom of each page. The use of the black-letter prevailed for a considerable period, being gradually modified by mechanical improvements upon its most common written form, known as the secretary-gothic. But just as Schoeffer had taken the finest handwriting of his time and country for his model, so the first Italian printers sought theirs in the elegant writing of the age of Augustus, and this Roman type was in some cases exquisitely made, particularly by Jenson, while the modern, or secretary-Italian, was copied by Aldus Manutius in his famous and beautiful Italic, at the close of the fifteenth century. Title-pages were not introduced in the earliest attempts at typography, the first appearing in 1488, and an ornamental one in 1498, but they were frequently printed merely in outline, for the illuminators to complete. The Aldine Livy of 1520, however, is a perfect and elegant book, with a full-page, well-displayed, printed title, almost precisely like the titles of the present day; the type of the body of the work is in handsome Roman, and the index is printed neatly in Italic at the front of the volume.

Under the auspices of many scholarly and erudite typographers, Hebrew and Greek type reached remarkable excellence during the sixteenth century, being based with conscientious and scrupulous care upon the best models.

There being as yet no vast reading public, editions usually consisted of only a few hundred copies, and the only works in much demand were elementary educational treatises or books of devotion. The first great demand for the services of printing arose from the religious excitement awakened by the publication of Tyndale's Testament at Antwerp, in 1526, and Luther's Bible, which followed it in 1534. As printing had responded to the necessities of the only universally educated nation of antiquity, and found its birth in China, it had again responded to the needs of the most intelligent races in Europe, on the great central ground, and, under happier influences,

spread slowly but surely, permeating from the educated classes to the illiterate, from the prince to the plowman, through a lingering growth of three centuries and a half, instilling lessons of knowledge and freedom, until it accomplished the first great step in its mission, and, at the close of the eighteenth century, in free America and enfranchised Europe, races in mature manhood were ready to welcome it to the maturity of its powers, and with one great leap printing, as if borne forward by the intellectual forces it had served to stimulate, at length grasped its fullest powers, and the brain of man, by endowing the printing-press with all the appliances of modern mechanics, at once repaid the debt it owed, and by the benefaction endowed its benefactor with new vigor. The education of the masses, which was only fairly commenced during the last century, multiplied readers, and it was not until they were numbered by many millions instead of a few thousands that the great modern era of printing fully commenced. Before this century, paper and type were made exclusively by hand, and all presses were worked by hand-power; and the increase of facilities gained by paper-making and type-casting machines and power-presses is so great, that at the present day there are single printing-offices which possess a productive power equal to that of all the printing-offices in existence seventy years ago, single paper-mills capable of manufacturing as much paper as all the paper-mills in existence in Europe and America previous to the year 1800, and single type-foundries capable of making more type than all the type-foundries of the last century. The increase in the magnitude and extent of printing has been scarcely greater than the improvements in every branch of the art. Entire departments, of immense importance, have been created. Lithography, Electrotypy, and Photography have been invented outright; Stereotyping has been extensively utilized and the variety of its processes enlarged; fonts and faces of type have been multiplied to an amazing extent; presses of every imaginable size, shape, and rate of speed have been extensively manufactured; and improvements and inventions applicable to printing and to its auxiliary arts have kept pace with the multiplication of the demands for their products. (See INVENTIONS.) Nearly all the great modern discoveries have been rendered useful in some way to the modern printer; and the triumph of mind over matter is nowhere so powerfully exemplified as in the daily workings of the multitudinous printing-offices of the present day. The most beautiful paintings are reproduced with wonderful fidelity by chromo-lithography; every object in nature is copied by the photographer; and typography responds to the demands of the age that she shall be the assistant, protector, instructor, critic, consoler, historian, and leader of mankind by surmounting all manner of literary and mechanical obstacles, and by becoming, instead of the mere art preservative of all arts, the employer of all arts, and the most powerful agent employed in human affairs.

Hoe Presses.—Presses of many varieties, sizes, and descriptions, manufactured by R. Hoe & Co., of New York, a number of which are described under their appropriate headings in this work. The most famous of these presses is the Patent Type-Revolving Printing Machine, which is described in Hoe's Catalogue as follows:

The Type-Revolving Printing Machine was invented by Col. Richard M. Hoe. It is, as its name indicates, on the rotary principle; that is, the form of type is placed on the surface of a horizontal revolving cylinder of about four and a half feet in diameter. The form occupies a segment of only about one-fourth of the surface of the cylinder, the remainder being used as an ink-distributing surface. Around this main cylinder, and parallel with it, are placed smaller impression cylinders, varying in number from two to ten, according to the size of the machine. The large cylinder being put in motion, the form of types is carried successfully to all the impression cylinders, at each of which a sheet is introduced and receives the impression of the types as the form passes. Thus as many sheets are printed at each revolution of the main cylinder as there are impression cylinders around it. One person is required at each impression cylinder to supply the sheets of paper, which are taken at the proper moment by fingers or grippers, and after being printed are conveyed out by tapes and laid in heaps by self-acting flyers, thereby dispensing with the hands required in ordinary machines to receive and pile the sheets. The grippers hold the sheet securely, so that the thinnest newspaper may be printed without waste.

The ink is contained in a fountain, placed beneath the main cylinder, and is conveyed by means of distributing rollers to the distributing surface on the main cylinder. This surface, being lower, or less in diameter, than the form of types, passes by the impression cylinder without touching. For each impression cylinder there are two inking rollers, receiving their supply of ink from the distributing surface of the main cylinder, which rise and ink the form as it passes under them, then again fall to the distributing surface.

Each page of the paper is locked up on a detached segment of the large cylinder, which segment constitutes its bed and chase. The column-rules run parallel with the shaft of the cylinder, and are consequently straight, while the head, advertising, and dash rules have the form of segments of a circle. The column-rules are in the shape of a wedge, with the thin part directed towards the axis of the cylinder, so as to bind the types securely. These wedge-shaped column-rules are held in their place by tongues projecting at intervals along their length, and sliding in rebated grooves cut crosswise in the face of the bed. The spaces in the grooves between the column-rules are accurately fitted with sliding blocks of metal, even with the surface of the bed; the ends of these blocks being cut away underneath to receive a projection on the sides of the tongues of the column-

rules. The locking-up is effected by means of screws at the foot of each page, by which the type is held as securely as in the ordinary manner upon a flat bed, and is much less liable to accident.

The speed of these machines is limited only by the ability of the feeders to supply the sheets. The Four Cylinder Machine is run at a rate of over ten thousand per hour; the Six Cylinder Machine, fifteen thousand per hour; the Eight Cylinder Machine, twenty thousand; and the Ten Cylinder Machine, twenty-five thousand.

The accompanying cuts illustrate this press; and also Hoe's Single Small Cylinder Press, from which from 2000 to 3000 impressions per hour may be obtained; a Single Large Cylinder Press adapted to fine newspaper and job-work; a Single Large Cylinder Press that can be run either by hand or steam power; and a Railway Newspaper Printing Press which is especially designated to supply newspapers of moderate circulation with a cheap but serviceable press.

Hoe, Robert, the founder of the firm of R. Hoe & Co., was born in 1784, in a sequestered district of Leicestershire, England. He was bound apprentice to a carpenter, but, purchasing his indentures, emigrated to the United States in 1803, and soon afterwards established himself in business—first as a carpenter, and subsequently in press-making, in partnership with Matthew and Peter Smith, who were his brothers-in-law, as he had married their sister soon after his arrival in this country. They were probably attracted to this pursuit by the fact that Peter Smith had invented what was subsequently well known as the Smith hand-press; but the business increased so slowly that when the two brothers-in-law died, in 1823, and Robert Hoe succeeded to it, he employed only a few workmen. Subsequently the demand for presses increased rapidly before Richard Hoe's retirement in 1832. He died in the following year; and his immediate successors were his eldest son, Richard M. Hoe, and Matthew Smith, son of his deceased brother-in-law.

Hogarth, William.—An English artist, ranking next to Albert Dürer as a popularizer of art, and as suiting it to the requirements of general literature. Richard Hogarth, the father of the artist, was by birth a yeoman of Westmoreland, because a schoolmaster in London, was occasionally employed in correcting for the press, and published a work on grammar in 1782. William, his only son, was born in 1697, and was apprenticed, when quite young, to an eminent silversmith, who employed him in engraving arms and ciphers upon plate. Having accidentally been present in a pot-house wrangle, young Hogarth was so amused at the absurdity of the scene, that he made a sketch of the group upon the spot; and the combatants and observers lavished so much praise upon the attempt that his attention was turned to developing his newly discovered talent, and on the conclusion of his apprenticeship he took some lessons in an art academy. He supported himself at first

TEN CYLINDER TYPE-REVOLVING PRINTING-MACHINE.

SINGLE SMALL-CYLINDER PRESS.

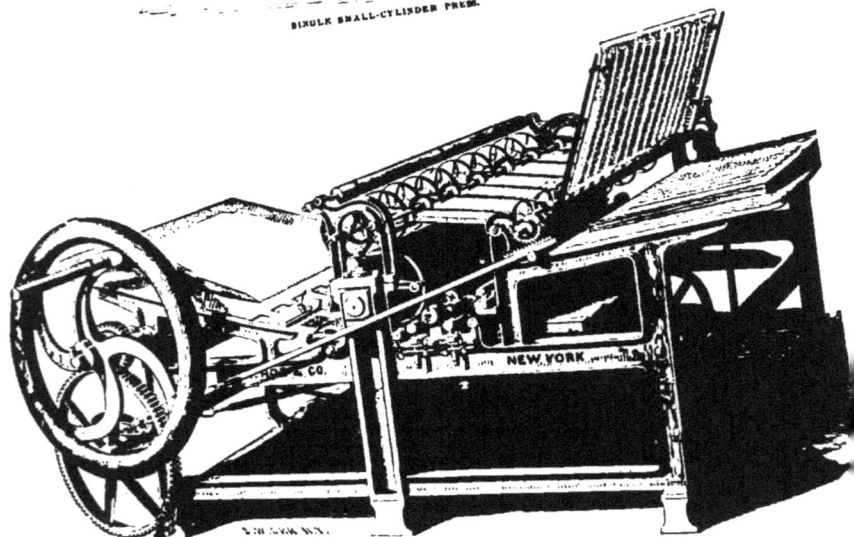

RAILWAY NEWSPAPER PRINTING-PRESS.

SINGLE LARGE-CYLINDER PRESS.

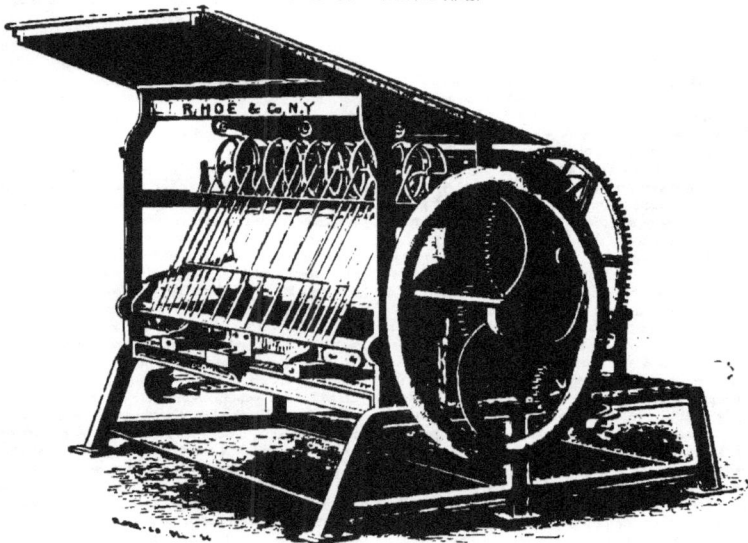

SINGLE LARGE-CYLINDER HAND-PRINTING PRESS.

by engraving arms and shop-bills, but soon found employment upon decorations for books; an edition of Hudibras giving him the first subject suited to his genius. In 1730, he eloped with the daughter of Sir James Thornhill, the painter, who opposed the marriage strongly until reconciled by the talent exhibited by the rising artist. To support his family, Hogarth painted a number of small groups, which he called conversation pieces, and which met with a ready sale on account of their novelty. His first great series of copper-plates, the Harlot's Progress, contained so admirable a portrait of one of the Lords of the Treasury, that it was exhibited by one of the members at the Board, and instantly became popular among the higher circles of society, was repeated on fans, etc., and appeared as a pantomime at the theatre. His subsequent works may be called comedies, constructed upon literary rules and in dramatic unity as satires upon the prevalent vices and follies of the time. Although his comic power won him popularity, a capacity of another kind is exhibited in his grand picture of Paul before Felix. Hogarth died in 1764, at the age of sixty-seven, and Garrick, the actor, inscribed upon his tomb the following appropriate lines:

> Farewell, great painter of mankind,
> Who reached the noblest point of art;
> Whose pictured morals charm the mind,
> And through the eye correct the heart.
> If Genius fire thee, reader, stay;
> If Nature touch thee, drop a tear;
> If neither move thee, turn away;
> For Hogarth's honored dust lies here.

Holbein, Hans.—A celebrated painter of the sixteenth century, especially famous for his numerous and admirable engravings on wood. It is supposed that he was born in Augsburg about 1495, and when a child accompanied his father, who was also an artist, to Basle, in Switzerland. This city was at that time remarkable for its scholarly printers, who were specially engaged upon religious and learned publications. Here young Holbein soon attracted attention by the excellence of his portraits, and his pictures upon Biblical subjects. He painted a remarkable portrait of Erasmus, which may probably have introduced him to Froben, for whom he executed a number of ornamental title-pages and designs, some of them illustrating the works of Erasmus. As a wood-engraver, Holbein is best known for his wonderful series called the Dance of Death, in which, in fifty-three successive pictures, death, as a ghastly skeleton, overtakes the unsuspecting mortal in every grade of life, from the pope to the pauper,—one of his victims, in these illustrations, being a printer. The superiority of the printers of Basle was so generally recognized, that Henry VIII. of England engaged Bebelius, a printer of that city, to execute a magnificent edition of Polydore Vergil's History of England, which for the elegance of illustration and beauty of type has been considered the most perfect volume published during the sixteenth century.

Some of the decorations and designs of this work were furnished by Holbein, and may have caused an invitation to England. He visited that country with an introductory letter from Erasmus to Sir Thomas More, who immediately presented him at court, where Henry VIII. made him court painter with a liberal pension, and induced the artist to remain in England, where he died of the plague in 1554. The portraits painted by Holbein of Henry VIII. and his queens, of Edward VI., and of the distinguished and illustrious personages of the time, have been relied upon as historical authorities.

Hollow Quadrats.—These are cast of various sizes, graduated to Pica ems. They answer many of the purposes of quotations, but are principally used as frames or miniature chases for circular or oval jobs.

HOLLOW QUADRAT.

Homily.—A sermon or religious discourse,—frequently used as the title of a published sermon. The Book of Homilies ascribed to Cranmer appeared in 1547, and a second work followed in 1562. These books were ordered by the Church of England to be read as a part of the service, where no original sermon was prepared.

Hornbook.—A name for the primer or first book used in learning to read. The term arose from the fact that in England, from the time of Elizabeth until the close of the eighteenth century, the primer in common use consisted of a single sheet of paper printed only on one side, which was fastened upon a board, and covered with a transparent sheet of horn to preserve the paper from destruction; and in some cases letters were cut or engraved on horns. A handle was often added to the board, making it resemble a rude paddle. A hornbook preserved from the seventeenth century contained the alphabet, a table of a, b, ab's, and the Lord's prayer.

Horse.—A sloping frame-work, or inclined plane, made of boards, which is placed on the bank used by hand-pressmen. The white paper is deposited on the horse before it is worked off or printed, so that the pressman can conveniently draw down the sheets with the nail of his thumb, or a piece of wood, bone, or ivory, and rapidly transfer them to the tympan.

Horsing it.—When a compositor or pressman charges more in his weekly bill than he has earned, or when he habitually resorts to devices to secure advances from his employer, he is said to be horsing it.

Hot-Pressing.—The act of passing or pressing printed sheets between hot metal plates. Hansard, in his Typographia, written at a time when hotpressing was being superseded by the present system, notwithstanding the popularity it had acquired by the brilliant artistic successes of Baskerville, Bodoni, and Ibarra, said:

Hot-pressing is usually executed by those who make a business of pressing cloths as well as paper. It is a process which costs some expense in the outfit, requiring very strong, powerful presses; glazed boards to be placed alternately with every sheet of the paper; furnace and oven to heat the iron plates, one of which is laid between each twenty or thirty sheets, till the press is full, and the whole is pressed down by a lever and windlass, or by Bramah's hydraulic machinery. This gives a smooth, glossy face to the paper and print, but is far from beneficial to either; the paper will yield, by the heat of the plates, something of its white bleached color, and turn brown or yellow; and the ink, unless of the finest quality, and well set by a length of time after printing, will run or spread on the surface of the paper, and very frequently, if the oil or varnish has not been well prepared, show a dark brown oily appearance, or shade, round the thick parts of the letter. It is, therefore, now the custom, to obviate such inconveniences, particularly since length of time is now neither the plan nor interest of printer or bookseller, to cold-press all fine work; that is, to effect the whole process by greater power, and the use of glazed boards only, abandoning the hot plates: consequently it is now more in the power of the printer's establishment to manage, than when the furnace, oven, and hot iron plates were necessary; for, by the addition of the glazed boards, to a powerful iron-screw standing press, and lengthened lever, or still greater power of an hydraulic press, he may manage to make the process pass tolerably well without sending his work to the hot-pressers.

Hours.—Prayers in the Roman Catholic Church appointed to be repeated at certain hours of the day. These books of devotion, before the introduction of printing, were often adorned with the utmost magnificence of decoration, written laboriously upon vellum, illuminated in the highest style of art, and ornamented with jewels. The early printers, particularly those of Paris, prepared editions in which the borders, capitals, and other decorations were presented in slightly shaded wood-cuts, that were afterwards colored by hand, and the demand was soon so great that sixty editions appeared between the years 1484 and 1498. All the early French printers, and especially Pigauchet, Verard, and Tory, exercised their utmost skill upon the production of these works, and they exhibit the transitionary condition of the art in curious completeness, the earlier editions being exclusively Gothic in the style of decorations, while the later ones introduced the

mannerism of the Italian school and of the French Renaissance. In some, the angular draperies and simple earnestness of German art are strangely blended with the architectural designs of the Italians, proving the effect produced by the powerful genius of Albert Dürer. The first edition of Hours executed entirely by letter-press was printed by Pigauchet, in 1486, in the reign of Charles VIII.; and in the subsequent and consecutive reigns of Louis XII., Francis I., and Henry II. the editions were almost beyond number, and became gradually less elaborate in finish, in order to meet the popular demand. The Books of Hours, called, in French, Les Heures, were usually of a small size, resembling a modern duodecimo, the elaborate margins frequently consisting of small designs, which, in different combinations, were often repeated. Mottoes or texts were frequently interspersed among these designs, as well as in the larger pictures, and the ornaments often exhibited an odd commingling of classic mythology with fanciful illustrations of the dogmas of the Church. The frontispiece of one of these books contains a large and elaborate picture of the device of Simon Vostre, surrounded by a handsome border, with the announcement that:—These present Heures, according to the ritual of Rouen at full length, with the miracles of our Lady, and the figures of the Apocalypse from the Bible, the triumphs of Cæsar, and many other histories from the antique, have been imprinted for Simon Vostre, Bookseller, residing in Paris.—An edition published by Vostre in 1510 is admirably printed on vellum, the central picture and four corner designs on the page being in high colors on a brilliant deep-blue background; the elaborate border is square and regular, with a high-colored scroll-work, and leaves of vermilion, blue, and green, on a rich gold ground. This work is preserved in the Philadelphia Library, and may be considered as a fair representative of this large class of publications.

Humphreys, Henry Noel.—A modern English writer, author of Illuminated Books of the Middle Ages, 1847–50; Art of Illumination and Missal-Painting, 1848; Ten Centuries of Art, 1851; Origin and Progress of the Art of Writing, 1852; A History of the Art of Printing, of which the second edition appeared in 1868; Master-Pieces of the Early Printers, and several other works upon coins, medals, and various branches of natural history. Mr. Humphreys also furnished the beautiful illuminations illustrating A Record of the Black Prince, The Book of Ruth, Sentiments and Similes of Shakspeare, etc. This author has done much to popularize the prosaic details of the history of printing by his attractive style, and his numerous and splendidly-executed fac-similes.

Hydraulic Press.—A powerful standing press used by printers for pressing their printed work, the pressure being given by means of water instead of the lever-bar, which works in a screw. The pumps and tank are fixed at the side of the press, and as they are worked, the piston is forced upward. Some hydraulic presses have only one pump; others have two. One pump is used at first, till the piston is raised high enough to cause a pressure, and when this becomes tight the other is applied, which increases the pressure still more. A long handle is then placed in the first pump, which gives greater power still; and, when placed on the second pump, two or three persons give their united strength till the required pressure is attained. The sheets are generally allowed to remain in the press all night; but sometimes it is necessary to fill the press twice a day. To release the sheets, it is only necessary to turn a tap, which lets the water escape back into the tank, and the piston is lowered in proportion as the water runs out. Its descent can be impeded instantly by fastening the tap again. Hydraulic presses are made by several manufacturers in the United States, of various sizes, and sometimes with a pressure exceeding seven hundred tons.

Hymn-Book.—A volume containing the hymns used by any religious society. The word hymn may be defined as a song of praise, confined in its modern and restricted sense to those addressed to the Deity. It is said that the Hebrews made no distinction between psalms and hymns, but among all denominations of Christians psalm signifies either the Psalms of David in the accepted prose translation, or versified and adapted to music; while the hymn is an original religious poem adapted to music, and suited to the requirements of church service, such as those of Addison, Bishop Heber, Wesley, and Watts. Modern hymn-books are usually divided into two parts, one containing a metrical version of the psalms, and the other a collection of hymns. The universal demand for books of this kind, and the great variety of styles in which they are produced have furnished much employment to the printers of every country and age, and for a more complete history of the subject the reader is referred to the articles PSALM-BOOK and PSALTER.

Hyphen.—A character [-] implying that two or more syllables, or two or more words, are joined. In printing, it is placed at the end of every line which terminates with a divided word (see DIVISION OF WORDS); in compound words (see COMPOUND WORDS) at the end of prefixes which terminate with a vowel and are followed by a vowel; and it is used in spelling-books and dictionaries to mark divisions of words intended to illustrate either their origin, pronunciation, or meaning.

HYDRAULIC PRESS.

I.

Iambic, or Iambus.—A favorite measure in English verse, consisting of a short syllable followed by a long one. Five iambics, or ten syllables, form the English heroic verse, as:—

Bē wīse tŏ-dāy, 'tĭs mādnĕss tŏ dĕfēr.

Six iambuses in English are known as the Alexandrine measure, as:—

Tait, like à woundèd snake, drags its slöw lèngth ă'öng.

The iambics of five feet, called heroic measure, are reserved in English, German, and Italian for serious composition, but among the French they are used as a lighter measure, the Alexandrine, or iambics of six feet, being the heroic or favorite serious measure in that language. The iambic was much used by the tragic writers of Greece, and also by the Latins.

Ibarra.—A native of Saragossa, who became printer to the King of Spain, and was widely celebrated for the accuracy and beauty of his impressions. He is credited with being the first printer who pressed the paper after printing, in order to remove the impression of the type. The committee upon printing at London, in 1851, visited the British Museum, to make personal and critical examination into the respective excellence of the masters of typography, and decided that the rivals for the highest honors were Ibarra, Bodoni, Bulmer, Bensley, and Didot. The finest specimens of Ibarra's typography, are his Bible, the Mozarabic Missal, Mariana's History of Spain, Don Quixote, and Gabriel's translation of Sallust. He invented an especially excellent printing-ink. Ibarra died in 1785, at the age of sixty.

Idem.—The same, a word taken from the Latin, and contracted into id.

Id est.—Two Latin words, signifying that is, usually expressed in printing by the abbreviation i. e.

Ideographics.—A system of characters intended to represent ideas instead of sounds, as the hieroglyphics of ancient Egypt. The characters of the Chinese language are ideographic, although the symbols formerly representing objects have become, by use, merely conventional.

Ideography.—A system of short-hand writing; also a treatise upon the same subject.

Idiom.—A form of expression peculiar to some individual language.

Idyl.—A poem expressing a quiet description of sentiment, or undramatic narrative, usually restricted to pastoral subjects, such as Goldsmith's Deserted Village, and Burns's Cotter's Saturday Ni ht.

Illuminated Letters.—Highly decorated letters, either in colors or black. In the first attempts at printing, the spaces for these letters were frequently left blank, that they might be supplied by the more delicate skill of the artists, but many specimens also show that the fondness for these illustrations caused them to be imitated in type at an early day. The taste for highly ornamented letters, especially of ancient and fantastic styles, has been revived for mottoes, cards, etc., and very elegant specimens have been produced by the type-founders to meet the demand for such novelties.

Illumination.—Strictly, the act of throwing light upon, and therefore formerly used as a name for such pictures as were intended to explain or throw light upon the meaning of the accompanying text. In the ancient manuscripts these illustrations were usually painted in brilliant colors, and the word was generally understood to express colored illustration, although it has been sometimes used in typography for highly ornamented initial letters, either black or colored. For many centuries the practice of the fine arts in Christian countries was almost exclusively devoted to the decoration of manuscripts, especially of the Sacred Scriptures; several Irish monks were famous for the beauty of their illuminations in the sixth century, and Saxon monks in England at a later period. In Italy the art was carried to great perfection, and was highly esteemed; two of the most renowned illuminators are thus mentioned in Dante's Purgatory:—

> O! I exclaimed,
> Art thou not Oderigi, art not thou
> Agobbio's glory, glory of that art
> Which they of Paris call the limner's skill?
> Brother, said he, with tints that gayer smile
> Bolognian Franco's pencil lines the leaves;
> His all the honor now.

Franco Bolognese, the last mentioned, achieved a great reputation about the year 1310, illuminated works for the Vatican, and established a school of art at Bologna. Don Jacopo, a monk of Florence, in the middle of the fourteenth century, devoted himself to writing choir-books on vellum, in a beautiful, large character, and a monk of the same monastery decorated them with pictures, together creating them into such works of art, that after their death the right hands of the two artists were preserved as sacred relics. The Corporation of St. Luke was a society established at Florence at the beginning of the fourteenth century, for the propagation of the art, and at the period of the invention of printing there were some very celebrated illuminators, especially in Italy. Mentelin of Strasburg, one of the alleged inventors of movable types, was an illuminator by profession, and much of the early and rapid success of typography must be ascribed to the skill of Schoeffer, who had been largely employed upon the writing and decoration of manuscripts, and especially to his taste in producing the gorgeous illuminated capitals, which were so favorite an adornment of the works of that age.

Illustrated Publications.—Before the invention of typography, manuscripts were profusely adorned with pictures, and the block-books, which marked the preliminary stages of printing, were decorated with them. The wood-cuts of these books were executed with considerable skill, and the same plates were frequently used afterwards in connection with letter-press, in the earlier specimens of typography. Copper-plate engravings are not known to have appeared in connection with typography until the publication of Dante's Inferno, by Botticelli, in 1481. The books of the sixteenth century were abundantly ornamented, both by pictures in wood and metal, Albert Dürer being one of the most celebrated artists in the early part of the century, followed by many others in Germany, Italy, and the Netherlands. Toward the middle of the century, the publications of Basle were especially famous for their illustrations, many of them due to the genius of Hans Holbein. During the seventeenth and eighteenth centuries, copper-plate engraving made great progress, and wood-engraving was generally neglected throughout Europe. In the early part of the eighteenth century, in France, the fantastic fashions of the court of Louis XIV. produced an elaborate style of engraving, which was carried to considerable perfection, both by German and French artists, who sought popularity by admirable delineations of plumes and laces. At the same period, in England, the portraits were also especially excellent, the other branches of art being imitated from the Dutch school, until the originality of Hogarth, about the middle of the eighteenth century, revivified the national art. But the great era of popular illustration, for the whole of Europe, commenced with the revival of wood-engraving by Bewick, in England, about 1785, this form of art being the best adapted to accompany letter-press, and especially suited to the requirements of the modern form of magazine and journalistic literature.

The British book fever, at the commencement of the nineteenth century, gave a great impulse to all forms of illustration, and under its influence much attention was directed to the expensive forms of steel-engraving, in the various styles of line, stipple, mezzotint, and aquatint; the latter of which was particularly adapted to represent the landscapes for which the British artists were so famous. A marked epoch in book-illustration in England commenced in 1822, with the publication of the first of the long line of Annuals, which for some years proved the most remunerative form of publication ever attempted in that country. The Annual, or a yearly publication containing a series of short articles in prose and verse, suited to the popular taste, made its first appearance in Germany in 1791, in a work styled a Year-Book of Social Amusement, followed shortly after by a Year-Book for Ladies; similar publications appeared annually, constantly improving in appearance, until the English publication in 1822 copied its appearance, as well as its name, the Forget-me-not, from a German prototype. These books, for a series of years, attracted the best talent, both literary and artistic, into their pages, and similar publications appeared in America, the first being the Atlantic Souvenir, published by Carey & Lea, Philadelphia, The Gift, by E. L. Carey, of the same city, and The Token, by S. G. Goodrich, of Boston. In England, Heath's Book of Beauty, in 1833, opened another style of publication, which became popular, and the general interest in illustration produced a great number of very fine editions of the poets, adorned with exquisite engravings.

The first comic paper also appeared in France, where it was an outgrowth of the great newspaper excitement attending the coronation of Louis Philippe. This paper, called La Caricature, appeared in 1830, with black and colored illustrations, and was published by Charles Philipon, who, the next year, established the famous Charivari. This paper, both in form and spirit, was the model upon which Punch, or the London Charivari, was started ten years afterwards, adorned with queer little grotesque silhouettes, by Leech and Doyle.

England, however, is entitled to the credit of the first attempt at producing cheap illustrated literature for the people, in the famous Penny Magazine, which was commenced in 1832, and followed the next year by a precisely similar style of publication, the Pfennig Magazin, in Germany. The English artists in the earlier part of the present century enjoyed an acknowledged pre-eminence in wood-engraving, and this excellence, probably, combined with the freedom of the press, led to what was then considered a remarkably daring venture, the attempt to combine illustration with the newspaper. This was accomplished in the Illustrated London News, in 1842, which was the forerunner of the vast number of illustrated weekly papers now published in Europe and America. Journals of a similar character, L'Illustration in Paris, and the Illustrirte Zeitung (Illustrated Times) in Leipsic, were started immediately afterwards. In Germany the illustrated weeklies met with remarkable success, and, although at first much inferior to the publications in England, they have been improving so steadily, that in many points of artistic perfection and accuracy they are now pre-eminent.

The first attempt in America was made by Ballou, and in 1853 the New York Illustrated News was produced in excellent style. The various illustrated papers published by Frank Leslie have attained great success. The publications of the Harpers are also remarkable for excellence, the Weekly achieving a great reputation during the late war for its representations of current events; and especially excellent in artistic perfection are the illustrations of Appletons' Journal. Another class of weekly newspapers has been immensely successful in recent years, both in Europe and America, in which a few illustrations are used to enliven the appearance of a sheet mainly devoted to serial stories and sketches.

Fashion magazines and journals illustrated in a variety of methods have been very numerous in France, Germany, America, and England; and the popular fondness for pictures has recently been transforming the established literary monthly magazines into picture-books, bent upon rivaling each other in the number of their illustrations.

Children's literature, always much adorned, has also been affected by the growing taste for art, and the illustrations have become more numerous and excellent, the German publications being in advance in this order of literature. Magazines and newspapers devoted to agricultural and mechanical pursuits are also more profusely illustrated than formerly.

All styles of illustration are at present exceedingly popular, although that upon copper- and steel-plates, while maintaining artistic superiority, has been superseded, to a great extent, for popular purposes, by wood engraving, and by the various improved methods of lithography. Photography is also introduced, and books are occasionally illustrated by photographs and chromo-lithographs.

Imperial.—A size of paper; writing being usually 22 by 30 inches, and printing 22 by 32 inches.

Imposing-Stone, or Bed.—The stone or plate on which forms are imposed and corrected. Formerly, imposing surfaces consisted exclusively of slabs of stone, generally marble, smoothed on their upper surface. Recently, plates of iron have been substituted to some extent, the advantages claimed for them being superior strength and smoothness. The superficial size of an imposing-stone varies, according to the description of forms to be laid upon it. Its height should be slightly over three feet. The frame on which the stone rests is usually fitted up with drawers for quoins, furniture, etc. Sometimes it contains a rack for locked-up forms; but the frequent vibrations from the locking-up and planing down of forms on the stone tend to loosen the quoins of those in the rack, and cause the matter to fall out. In England, printers assemble around the stone while a chapel is being held.

IMPOSITION OF HALF-SHEET QUARTO.

Imposition.—In job-work this term is used to denote the operation of preparing a form for the press, by securing the type in a solid manner in the chase, so that it can be lifted from the imposing-stone and placed on the press in such a state as to give an even impression. In book-work, in addition to the above, the term embraces the laying of the pages so as to read in progressive order when folded, allowing the proper margin between the front and back of the pages, so that, when trimmed, each page will be in its proper position on the leaf of the book, and the locking up, by means of side-sticks, foot-sticks, and quoins, be square and true, that the pages may give an exact register when backed.

The rules which apply to impositions for job-
14

printing are to be observed in imposing forms for stereotype or electrotype moulding, with the addition, in stereotyping and electrotyping pages for book-printing, of placing metal furniture, about one-eighth of an inch thick, beveled at the top, and reaching to the shoulders of the type, at the front and back of the page, so as to give a firm hold for the clamps of the ratchet-block when screwed up for printing, and in electrotyping job forms, of placing type-high bearers all round the form, to keep the wax mould from spreading on the outside edges of the form. The forms imposed for electrotyping are usually locked up tighter than for stereotyping, on account of the liability of the type to draw out when the wax mould is lifted from the form.

The art of imposing job, stereotype, or electrotype forms is, from its simplicity, easily acquired, more especially as the compositor is, in most job-offices, expected to set up his work and prepare it for the press, and only ordinary ingenuity is required to squarely lock up a form so as not to spring. The system followed in large book-printing establishments of having the making-up and imposing done by a few hands employed for that purpose, while going far to systematize and facilitate the getting out of work, has, in a measure, denied to the great majority of compositors the opportunity of learning by practice the art of completing their work, by imposing a book form in a workmanlike manner; and, notwithstanding the many able explanations which have been, from time to time, published on the subject, the matter seems to be shrouded in a cloud of mystery, which few care to penetrate, while knowing that a proper understanding of the subject is an important and remunerative requisite in the education of every printer. Before the introduction of stereotyping, the imposition of forms was performed entirely by the compositors, and each one was expected to have a knowledge of this important branch of the art. At the present time the finished pressman is often obliged to lay on pages, make margin, and lock up forms, while many compositors are not familiar with this branch of printing.

A complete list of all the plans that have been devised for the imposition of forms for book-work, comprehending, as it does, a great variety of schemes, as well as transpositions of pages, in order to throw the light pages on the inside of the form, so as to protect them from picks, or preserve them from a too great pressure of the rollers, and a consequent greater deposit of ink on the face of the type than is necessary, but all tending to the same result when the sheet is folded, would occupy more space than can be afforded in this book, and, as the explanations would not add to the reader's knowledge of the rules which govern the laying of pages, etc., we propose to give the fundamental principles, and illustrate them by a series of the smaller schemes of imposition, of which the larger are only duplicates, where the number of the pages to be printed on one sheet is doubled or quadrupled.

QUARTO.—Sheet turning lengthwise of the pages.

5	8
1	4

OCTAVO.—Sheet turning crosswise of the pages.

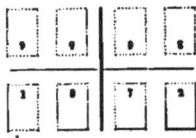

9	8	5	8
1	6	7	2

OCTAVO.—Sheet turning lengthwise of the pages.

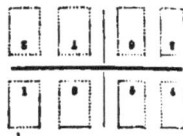

8	1	6	7
1	8	6	4

QUARTO.—Sheet turning crosswise of the pages.

1	4	5	2

OCTAVO.—Eight pages in a line.

1	8	5	4	3	6	7	2

OCTAVO.—First four pages placed in centre.

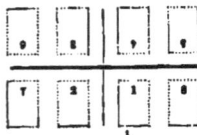

9	8	7	9
7	2	1	8

Form of 12s—sheet turning crosswise of the pages.

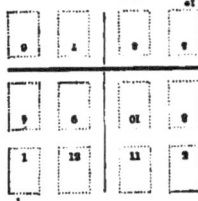

9	7	9	9
9	6	10	9
1	12	11	2

Form of 16s—with first four pages placed in centre.

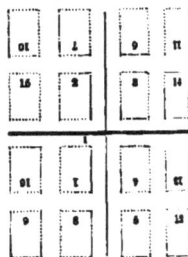

10	7	9	11
15	2	8	14
16	1	9	13
9	6	6	13

Form of Broad 16s, for printing books of music.

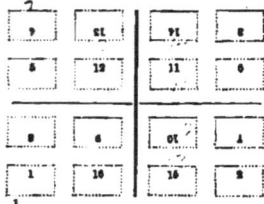

9	13	16	8
5	12	11	6
8	4	10	7
1	16	15	2

Form of 18s, transposing four pages.

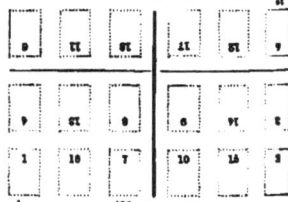

9	11	16	11	15	9
4	13	6	6	14	8
1	16	7	10	18	2

The method of transposition.

Form of 20s, with inset—sheet
turning crosswise of the pages.

Form of 48s, in three sections of 16 pages each—sheet turning
crosswise of the pages.

Regular form of 24s.

Form of 32s in one section—sheet turning crosswise of the pages.

Six page Leaflet. First page in centre.

Six page Leaflet. First page to the left.

Six page Leaflet. First page to the right.

Eight page Leaflet.
First page next to the left.

Eight page Leaflet.
First page to the right.

Eight page Leaflet.
First page to the left.

The materials used in imposing the book form are: First, the pages, the four sides of which are called the head, foot, front, and back; the head being that part which stands at the top of the leaf, the foot at the bottom, the front, if an odd page, at the right, and if even, at the left of the leaf, when the book is opened, and the back, at the reverse side of the front, or between the two pages. Second, the chase, the iron frame in which the pages are locked up for printing, having two bars dovetailed into the frame and crossing each other at right angles, called the long cross and the short cross. In forms printed without an inset or subsection, the bars are secured in the centre of the frame, while in 12mos the short cross, and in 24mos the long cross, is shifted to separate the inset from the main section of the form, thus dividing the chase into two unequal parts of one-third and two-thirds respectively. Third, the furniture used to make the proper margin between the pages; and the foot-sticks, side-sticks, and quoins with which the pages are locked up ready for press. The furniture used to make the head- and back-margin should be made of metal; or, if wood is preferred, the best San Domingo mahogany should be used, and kept well oiled when out of use.

The schemes for imposition are divided into two classes, each peculiar in itself, and adapted to as many pages as are required to be folded in a section of the book.

One of these classes is called a sheet, and comprises all those impositions which require an equal number of pages to be locked up in two forms, to back each other. These forms are called inner and outer, the inner form containing all those pages which are folded inside of the sheet, the outer all those outside of the sheet, making one complete section, and containing just double the number of pages that is expressed by the size of the sheet when folded; thus, a sheet of octavo requires sixteen pages of type, making eight leaves, a sheet of 12mo twenty-four pages, or twelve leaves, etc.

The other class is called a half-sheet, and contains the same number of pages in one form as are intended to be comprised in a section of the book, both sides of the paper being printed from the same form, both halves backing each other, and making two complete half-sheets. These are known by the terms, half-sheet of octavo, half-sheet of 12mo, etc.

The difference between these two classes is that while the sheet requires two forms to print one perfect copy of the section, the half-sheet requires but one form to print two perfect copies; each of the two copies of the half-sheet containing, however, only half the number of leaves and pages comprised in a whole sheet.

Laying the Pages.—In order to get a proper understanding of this subject, some knowledge of folding is necessary. When there is only one fold in a sheet, that fold must be through the back. When there are two folds, the first is between the heads, and the second through the back. In a sheet of three folds,

the first is at the front, the second between the heads, and the third through the back. In a sheet requiring four folds, the first is at the foot, the second at the front, the third between the heads, and the fourth through the back. These rules are only varied in the cases of a half-sheet of octavo imposed eight pages in a row, heads on a line, or in a form to turn lengthwise of the pages, and in a half-sheet of sixteens of oblong music pages. In the two former the first fold is at the front instead of between the heads; and in the latter the first fold is at the foot instead of at the front.

Form of 16—sheet turning lengthwise of the pages.

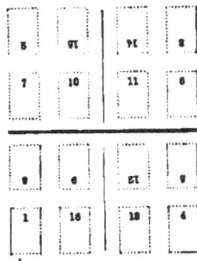

This may be illustrated by taking the scheme of imposition for a half-sheet of sixteens, or sixteen consecutive pages. The first page in a regular imposition should be laid at the left-hand lower corner, with the foot of the page toward you. All odd pages being backed by the consecutive even page, the next step is to ascertain where the second page is to be placed. In order to do this, it must be known how the sheet is to be printed in backing, which is in the direction of the length of the pages; the second page should be placed in the left-hand upper corner, with the head toward you, or in an opposite direction from the short cross to the position which the first page occupies. The first fold of this sheet being at the front of the pages at the long cross, it is necessary that the third page should be laid so as to face the second when folded, which would place it in the right-hand upper corner, head on a line with the second; page four, backing the third page, must be laid in the right-hand lower corner, with the foot toward you. The second fold of the sheet being between the heads, and as page five is to face four, you must place five head to head with four. The sixth page, backing page five, must be placed foot to foot with five on the opposite side of the short cross; the seventh page, facing the sixth in folding, must be placed on the opposite side of the form to that occupied by six, heads on a line; and the eighth page, backing seven, must be placed on the opposite side of the bar, foot to foot with seven. The succeeding pages can easily be laid by applying the rule that the first and last pages should stand back to back, heads on a line, the second and next to the last, the third and third from the last, etc.; if this rule is followed, the sum of the folios of every two pages standing back to back, will be equal to the sum of the folios of the first and last pages.

The only exception to the rule in regard to laying the pages for a form of this kind is found in imposing Hebrew works, the matter of which, reading from right to left, reverses the order of imposition by placing page one, in a Hebrew form, in the position occupied by page sixteen in an English form, and so on up to the last page, sixteen occupying the lower left-hand corner, with the foot toward you. In other words, a Hebrew book commences where an English book ends.

The laying of the pages having been proved to be correct, the next step to be taken is to adjust the margin so that the printed page will be in its proper position on the leaf of the book when bound. (See MAKING MARGIN.) After the blank space for margin has been inserted, the side- and foot-sticks should be placed in position. Great care should be exercised in this respect, to see that the furniture is of proper length to cover the sides and foot of the sections to be locked up, and that it may be free from contact, so as not to bind, as a neglect to provide for these contingencies is likely to cause bad register and crooked lines. The quoins having been inserted, the form should be planed down softly, and locked up by starting gently at the foot of each section, leaving the matter loose enough to allow some play in locking up the sides. The whole form should thus be tightened uniformly before the final lock-up is made, which should not be so tight as to cause the form to spring, or occasion the letters or pages to drop out in lifting from the stone or on the press. Give the form a final planing, and it will be ready for proof or press.

The printing of leaflets, or of forms of six, eight, ten, or twelve pages, to fold to the size of a single page, without stitching, so as to read continuously, having of late years become an important branch of job printing, we subjoin a few schemes showing the different positions of the first page in the form, which is guided entirely by the taste or choice of the customer; taking the position of the first page as a guide, the pages are imposed either in a row, heads on a line, or head to head, running from the first page to the right on the lower row of pages, and then from right to left on the upper row, until the form is filled, the manner of imposition depending on the length of the form, or the way in which the paper to be printed on will cut to the best advantage.

Imprimatur.—A Latin word signifying let it be printed, placed on the title-pages of books published in countries where there is a censorship of the press, to show that legal permission has been granted for the publication. It occurred frequently on the title-pages of English books during the sixteenth and seventeenth centuries.

Imprimerie Imperiale, or Nationale.—The government printing-office of France, established in 1640, and sustained to the present day. This renowned printing-office is said by some authorities to have been instituted by Francis I., but the statement has risen from a misapprehension of the facts. Francis I., in 1538, appointed Conrad Neobar royal printer of the Greek language, and shortly afterwards made Robert Stephens royal printer of Hebrew and Latin, creating them King's Printers by patent, but erecting no printing-office or establishment specially devoted to the purpose. Various privileges were secured to the royal printers with the rank of members of the King's household, and the office was maintained during the civil wars, but was neglected until the reign of Louis XIII., when the Royal Printing-Office was formally instituted in the Louvre by the exertions of Cardinal Richelieu; Sebastian Cramaisy, the King's Printer, being made its director. By its constitution, the Royal Printing-Office was appointed to print the acts of councils, to do the printing for the King's household, and also to be especially devoted to the extension of religion. The zealous attention of Richelieu caused the work to be carried on with great activity, and many handsome illustrated books were published under his direction. Louis XIII. and the Cardinal died shortly afterwards, and Louis XIV. pursued their plans with equal earnestness, ordering a thorough revision of the old types, and a supply of new fonts. This work was performed by Grandjean, engraver to Louis XIV. assisted by his pupil, Alexandre; the labor was begun in 1693, but was not completed until the reign of Louis XV., in the year 1745. In 1770, other new type was added by the famous founder Luce.

As an effect of the Revolution, the office changed its title to the National Executive Printing-Office, and afterwards to the Printing-Office of the Republic. In the third year of the Republic, it was removed from the Louvre to the Hotel Penthièvre, the property of the Duchess of Orleans, and its place in the Louvre was granted as a printing-office to Didot.

The institution received much attention from General Bonaparte, and at his request the Directory deputed members from it to establish an office in Greece, supplied with Greek type, one at Pondicherry supplied with Persian and French, and the Egyptian expedition was accompanied by one supplied with Arabic.

In 1804, the office changed its name for the fourth time, being styled the Imperial Printing-Office, and in 1809 was confirmed in the exclusive right to the printing of the departments of the ministry, the service of the Imperial Mansion, the Council of State, and the printing and distribution of the Bulletin of Laws.

In 1814 it retook its ancient name of Royal, and a member of the Anisson family was made Director in recognition of the fact that the office had been held by that family for almost a century before the Revolution, the last occupant losing his life for his loyalty.

In the Hundred Days this Bourbonist official temporarily disappeared, while his printers contributed liberally of their earnings to the armament of the Seine, and the office was ready in 1815 to change its title for the seventh time by retaking the name of Royal, and to welcome back its director. In 1823, an ordinance reëstablished it on the foundation of 1809. From 1825 to 1832, some fine types were made by Firmin Didot, Legrand, and Molé, known as the type of Charles X. As this last Bourbon precipitated his overthrow by legislation against the press, and his successor, Louis Philippe, endeavored to assure his own popularity by granting especial privileges to the journals, printing assumed a universal importance in public consideration, and the Royal Office was treated with great favor.

Upon the establishment of the Republic in 1848, the government office was styled the National Printing-Office, and Louis Napoleon altered it in 1852 again to the Imperial Printing-Office, a title which it maintained during his supremacy.

During many periods of its long existence, this government printing-office has achieved a great renown for the excellence of its labors, especially the publications authorized by Cardinal Richelieu, those during the Republic, the handsome work illustrating Bonaparte's Egyptian Expedition, and latterly by some of the books printed under Napoleon III.

By order of Francis I., Garamond with the assistance of Robert Stephens, made the long-celebrated Greek type Garamond also made some remarkable Roman, after the models of Jenson, in 1540. The first formal revision was performed by Grandjean and Alexandre in 1693, and their types were considered excessively handsome. Luce continued the work in 1740. The famous Firmin Didot added new forms in 1811; Jacquemin in 1818; other modifications were added by Marcellin Legrand in 1825 and in 1847. These modifications were all especially restricted to the Roman and Italic.

Besides claiming particular excellence for its Greek printing, and for the beauty and accuracy of its French works, the Imperial Office, in its official history published in 1861 by order of Napoleon III., exhibited specimens of its foreign types, embracing Egyptian hieroglyphs, and many of the languages of Asia and Africa, ancient and modern. The number of punches and matrices in the Imperial Printing-Office amounted in 1860 to 361,000, with an approximate value of 620,000 francs.

At the Imperial Printing-Office at Paris, great attention has been paid to the collection of a variety of characters, with the view of developing relations with the people of Africa and Asia. Among the grammars that have been printed are Tamul, Galla, Woloffe, Japanese, Mandarin, Thibetan, Anamite, Persian and French grammar for the use of the Arabs, and a Turkish dictionary. The series of complete fonts new includes Chinese, Canarie, Tamul, Telegan, Amharic, and are unequaled in the world in this particular.

Impress.—The imprint of a work; also used to express a device or emblem, from the fact that printers and publishers formerly used devices or coats-of-arms, instead of their proper names, in the imprint of books.

Impression.—1. The weight of the pressure applied by presses to forms. This is frequently reduced or diminished by various appliances, according to the nature of the work to be printed, and impressions may thus be rendered light or heavy. 2. The products of press-work. 3. The act of impressing or stamping, and thus producing in color, upon paper, or other substances, a copy of a prepared surface, like that of a form of type or the lines upon an engraving.—The main object of the true pressman is to apply a sufficient amount of color, and no more, to his types, and to take off said color completely, at each impression. This has never yet been fully attained, but great progress has been made toward such result. Besides the careful preparation of the ink, and its delicate application and removal, the moistening of the paper renders important assistance in the process; the water acts directly on the mass of the paper, separating its fibers and raising a minute nap on its surface, and the impression drives out the water from the parts in immediate contact with the type, while the ink readily takes its place, leaving the type comparatively clean, and when the whole sheet is freed from water and pressed between pasteboards, the fibers knit over the color, and thus add mechanical assistance to the adhesion already attained.

Imprint.—The name of a printer of books, newspapers, or other printed matter, printed on such book, newspaper, or job, and frequently accompanied by his place of business; also, the designation of the place where, by whom, and in what year a book is published. In England every printer is required, by law, to put an imprint, embracing his name and his place of business, upon every book or paper he prints, under a penalty of five pounds for each copy to which an imprint is not attached. In the United States, imprints are in general use, but they are often omitted for various reasons.

Incunabula.—The books printed immediately after the invention of printing, generally restricted to those published before the year 1500. The word incunabula signifies, in Latin, a cradle, and is used to express the infancy of the art. The books considered under this head have been subdivided for convenience into several classes, in the first of which have been included many of the block-books, which have been claimed to be produced from movable types. Among these are the books presumed to be printed. by Koster, and also several fragments ascribed to the early efforts of Gutenberg. In this class also are included the earliest ascertained examples of typography, such as the Letters of Indulgence issued by Pope Nicholas V., 1454, the Almanac of 1457, the Psalter of Fust and Schoeffer, bearing the date of 1457, with certain works ascribed to Pfister, of Bamberg, and Mentelin, of Strasburg, upon which have been based their claims as inventors of movable types. In a second class have been placed the first impressions in particular countries or cities, embracing books frequently as rare and valuable as those included in the first class. A third class embraces books in certain languages or type, such as the first works in Roman or Italic letter. Among these are enumerated the Cicero and Lactantius of 1465, as containing the first Greek words cut in wood; the Greek Grammar of Laskaris, printed in Milan, 1476, as the first work printed entirely in that language; the Hebrew work published at Soncino, 1484, etc. The fourth division contains editions from such presses as are famous for the rarity of their productions, as the Mentel editions of the old Roman classics. In the fifth class have been included books marking the stages of typographical improvement, such as the book published at Cologne, 1470, containing the first instance of numbered pages, and the work printed in the same city in 1472, containing signatures; the Cicero of 1465, claimed as the first quarto; Jenson's Offices of the Virgin, 1473, the first 32mo; and the first title-page, 1485. The sixth subdivision has been made to include the first instances of the application of the fine arts to typography, such as the work containing copper-plates, published in Florence in 1477, and books marking the introduction of special improvements in the arts of book illustration. A seventh class contains single copies celebrated as being on vellum, or in letters of gold, etc.; and the eighth and last class contains complete series of works of special kinds, such as the six Greek works printed in capitals by Alopa at Florence from 1494 to 1496; and the peculiar, round Greek type used in Milan from 1476 to 1499.

It will be seen that these classifications are essentially arbitrary, and have been adopted for certain reasons of convenience, notwithstanding the impossibility of exactitude arising from the fact that the same volume may belong at the same time to several of the classes. The standard authorities upon the interesting but perplexed question of the incunabula are considered to be Panzer, who is very complete and minute upon German printing down to 1534; Maittaire, who ranks high as an authority, but is more incomplete than Panzer; Santander, who supplements Panzer by adding an account of printing in Spain and the Low Countries, and Audiffredi, the acknowledged authority upon Roman and Italian typography. In England the works of Dibdin upon the incunabula of the Spencer collection have been very celebrated.

The extraordinary rapidity with which printing was extended throughout Europe, as well as the places where it was received, and by whom introduced, can be learned from the following table, which will itself furnish the most certain key to the list of works known usually as the incunabula. This table is nearly identical with that given in Johnson's Typographia.

1457.—Mentz, Gutenberg, Fust, and Schoeffer.
1460.—Bamberg, Albert Pfister.
1465.—Subiaco, Con. Sweynheim and Arn. Pannartz.
1467.—Rome, the same printers.
    Elfeld, H. and N. Rechtermuntze, and W. Spyes.
    Cologne, Ulricus Zel (or Zell) of Hanau.
1468.—Augsburg, Giuther Zainer of Reutlingen.
1469.—Venice, John and Vindeline of Spire.
    Milan, Philippus de Lavagna.
1470.—Nuremberg, Joannes Sensenschmidt.
    Paris, U. Gering, M. Crantz and M. Friburger.
    Foligno, Emilian de Orfinis.
    Trivi, Joan Reynardi.
    Verona, Joan. de Verona.
1471.—Strasburg, J. Mentel or Mentellus, H. Eggestein.
    Spire, Petrus Drach.
    Treviso, Girardus de Lisa, de Flandria.
    Bologna (Italy), Baldassare Azzoguidi.
    Ferrara, Andreas Belfortes.
    Naples, Sixtus Riessinger of Strasburg.
    Pavia, Anton de Carcano.
    Florence, Bernard Cennini and Son.
1472.—Cremona, D. de Paravicino and S. de Merlinis.
    Fivizano, Jam. Baptista (a priest) and Alexander.
    Padua, B. de Valdezochio and M. de S. Arboribns.
    Mantua, Petrus Adam de Michaelibus.
    Montréal, Ant. Mathias and Balth. Corderius.
    Sesl, Fridericus Veronensis.
    Munster (in Argua), Helias Heyle, or de Louffen.
    Parma, Andreas Portiglia.
1473.—Brescia, Thomas Ferrandus.
    Messina, Henricus Alding.
    Ulm, Joan Zainer of Reutlingen.
    Buda, Andreas Hess.
    Lauingen, printer's name not known.
    Merseburg, Lucas Brandis.
    Alost, Theodoricus (or Thierry) Martens.
    Utrecht, Nicholas Ketelaer and Ger. de Leempt.
    Lyon, Bartholomæus Bayer.
    S. Ursio, Joannes de Rheno.
1474.—Vicenza, Leonardus Achates of Basle.
    Como, Ambr. de Orcho and Dion. de Paravicino.
    Turin, John Fabri and Joanninus de Petro.
    Genoa, Matthias Moravus and Mic. de Monaco.
    Savona, John Bon (Bonus Johannes.)
    Esslingen, Conradus Fyner.
    Basle, Bernardus Richel and Bertholdus Rodt.
    Valls, Sanctæ Mariæ, Fratres vitæ communis.
    Valencia, A. F. de Cordova and L. Palmart.
    Louvain, Joannes de Westphalia.
    Westminster, William Caxton.
1475.—Lubeck, Lucas Brandis of Schass.
    Burgdorf, printer's name not known.
    Blaubeuren (or Blauberen,) Conradus Manes.
    Cagli, Fano and Bernardinus de Bergamo.
    Casale, John Fabri.
    Modena, Joan. Vurster.
    Perugia, Henricus Clays of Ulm.
    Pieve di Sacco, R. Mescullam, surnamed Kotsi.
    Placenza, Porcus de Ferratis.
    Reggio, Abraham Garton.
    Barcelona, Nicholaus Spindeler.
    Saragossa, Matthæus Flandrus.
1476.—Antwerp, Theodoricus Martins of Alost.
    Bruges, Colard Mansion.
    Brussels, Fratres Vitæ communis.
    Nova Plana, printer's name not known.
    Rostock, Fratres Vitæ communis.

1476.—Polliano, Innocentius Ziletus and F. Antiquarius.
Trent, Hermannus Schindeleyp.
Delft, Jacob Jacobs and Maurice Yemants.
1477.—Deventer, Richard Paffroet.
Gouda, Gerard Leu (or Leuw).
Angers, Joan. de Turre and Joan. de Morell.
Palermo, Andreas de Warmatia.
Ascoli, Gulielmus de Linis.
Lucca, Barthol. de Civitali.
Seville, M. de la Talle, B. Segura, and A. del Puerto.
1478.—Cosenza, Octavius Salamonius de Manfredonia.
Colle, Joannes Allemannus de Medemblick.
Chablis, Pierre le Rouge.
Geneva, A. Steinschawer, de Schninfordia.
Oxford, Theodoricus Rood.
Prague, printer's name not known.
Monast. Sorten, printer's name not known.
Eichstett (Neustadt), Michael Reyser.
1749.—Wurtzburg, S. Dold, J. Ryser, and J. Bekenhub.
Zwoll, Johannes de Vellehoo.
Nimeguen, no printer's name.
Pignerol, Jacobus de Rubeis.
Toscolano, Gabriel Petri.
Toulouse, Joannes Tentonicus.
Poietiers, J. Bouyer and G. Bouchet.
Segorbe, no printer's name.
Lerida, Henricus Botel.
1480.—Oudenarde, Arnoldus Cesaris.
Hasselt, no printer's name.
Nonantola, Georg. and Anselm. de Mischinis.
Friuli, Gerardus de Flandria.
Caen, J. Durandus and Egidius Quijone.
Saint Albans, no printer's name.
1481.—Salamanca, L. Alcumanus and Lupus Sanz.
Leipsic, Marcus Brand.
Casale, G. de Canepa nova, de Campanilibus.
Urbino, Henricus de Colonia.
Vienne (in France), Peter Schenck.
Auroch (in Wirtemberg), Conradus Fyner.
1482.—Aquila, Adam de Rotwil.
Erfurt, Paulus Widor de Hornbach.
Memmingen, Albertus Kunne.
Passau, Conradus Stahel and Benedictus Mayr.
Reutlingen, Joh. Otmar.
Vienna, Joh. Winterburg.
Promentour, Lonis Guerin.
1483.—Magdeburg, A. Rauenstein and J. Westval.
Stockholm, Joh. Snell.
Ghent, Arnoldus Cæsaris.
Troyes, Guil. le Rouge.
Schiedam, no printer's name.
Haerlem, Joh. Andriessen.
Culenborg, John Veldener.
Leyden, Heynricus Heynrici.
Pisa, Laurentius and Angelus Florentini.
Gironne, Matthew Vendrell.
1484.—Bois-le-Duc, G. L. de Noviomago (Nimeguen).
Winterperg (or Winterberg), Joannes Alacraw.
Chamberry, Antonius Neyret.
Bresand-Londébac (or Londéac), R. Fouquet.
Rennes, Pierre Bellescuiée and Josses.
Sienna, Henricus de Colonia.
Soncino, Joshua Salamon and partners.
Novi, Nicol. Girardengus.
1485.—Heidelberg, Fridericus Misch.
Ratisbon, J. Sensenschmidt and J. Bekenhaab.
Vercelli (in Piedmont), Jacobinus Suigus.
Pescia, Franc. Cenni.

Udine, Gerardus de Flandria.
Burgos, Fridericus de Basilea.
1486.—Abbeville, Jean Du Pré and Pierre Gerard.
Brunn, C. Stahel and M. Preinlein.
Münster, Johannes Limburgus.
Sleswick, Stephanus Arndes.
Casalo Maggiore, no printer's name.
Chivazio, Jacobinus Suigus.
Viqueria, Jacobus de S. Nazario.
Toledo, Johannes Vasqui (Vasques).
1487.—Besançon, John Comtel.
Gaeta, A. F. (Andreas Fritag).
Valeria, Juan de Roca.
Rouen, Guillaume le Talleur.
Ischar (Ixar, in Aragon), Eliezer filius Alanta.
1488.—Viterbo, no printer's name.
1489.—Hagenau, Henricus Gran.
Kuttenberg, Martin van Tischiniowa.
Lerida, no printer's name.
San Cucufato del Valles, no printer's name.
Lisbon, Samnel Zorba and Raban Eliezer.
1490.—Orleans, Matthew Vivan.
Ingolstadt, Joan. Kacholofen.
Porto, Barthol. Zanni.
Zamora, no printer's name.
1491.—Dijon, Petrus Metlinger.
Angoulême, by a printer unknown.
Hamburg, Joh. and Thomas Borchard.
Nozano, H. de Colonia and H. de Harlem.
1492.—Dole, no printer's name.
Leiria, Abraham Durtas.
Tsenna, no printer's name.
1493.—Alba, no printer's name.
Clugny, Michael Wenssler.
Friburg, Kilianus Piscator.
Lüneburg, Joan. Luce.
Nantes, Etienne Larcher.
Copenhagen, Gothofridus de Ghemen.
Valladolid, Joannes de Francour.
1494.—Oppenheim, no printer's name.
1495.—Forli, Hieronymus Medesanns.
Freisingen, Joann. Schaeffier.
Limoges, Joan. Berton.
Scandiano, Peregrinus de Pasqualibus.
Schoonhoven, no printer's name.
1496.—Barco, Gerson fil. R. Mosis Montulan.
Offenburg, no printer's name.
Provins, Guil. Tavernier.
Toura, Matth. Laterou.
Pampeluna, Arnoldus Gnillen.
1497.—Granada, Menardus Ungut.
Avignon, Nicol. Lepe.
Carmagnola, no printer's name.
Tübingen, Joan. Ottmar.
1499.—Tréguier (in Bretagne), no printer's name.
Montserrat, Joan Luchner Alemannus.
Tarragona, Joh. de Rosembach.
1500.—Cracow (Joannes Haller).
Munich, Joannes Schobser.
Amsterdam, D. Pietersoen.
Olmuta, Conradus Bomgathom.
Pfortzheim (in Suabia), T. Anselmus Radensis.
Perpignan, J. Rosembach de Heidelberg.
Jaen, no printer's name.
Albia, no printer's name.
Rheuon, no printer's name.

Indelible Printing-Ink.—It is said that an ink which, when printed on linen, cotton, or similar fabrics, would not be obliterated by washing, can be manufactured by thinning coal-tar, with naphtha, to the consistence of ordinary printing-ink.

Indention.—The blank space left at the beginning of the first line of a paragraph. Paragraphs are usually indented one em, although, if the work be set very widely, and with leads between the lines, or if the measure is very wide, two or three ems may be used.

Index.—An alphabetical table of the contents of a book. The index is generally placed at the end of the volume, and set in letter about two sizes less than that of the work. It is always begun on a right-hand page, unless space is unusually valuable, or the appearance of the work is not considered of consequence. In setting an index, the subject-line should not be indented, but if the subject make more than one line, all but the first should be indented about an em. Where several index figures are used in succession, a comma is put after each folio; but to save figures and commas, the succession of the former is usually noted by putting a dash between the first and last figures—thus, 4–8.

Index (☞) or Fist.—A symbol used to point out something which the author thinks of great importance. Among compositors, it is commonly known as a fist. The index is used chiefly in handbills, posters, direction placards, and in newspaper work.

Index Expurgatorius.—A catalogue of the works condemned as heretical by the Church of Rome, or for other reasons forbidden to be read. It is published annually in the city of Rome.

India Paper.—A Chinese paper used in fine or proof impressions of engravings. It is made by spreading the pulp with a brush upon a smooth stone, which gives the sheet a smooth and a rough side, the latter resembling the effect of paint rudely applied by an unskillful hand. It often contains particles of hard matter, like minute portions of stone, etc., which should be removed before it is applied to the surface of an engraving. The picture is always printed upon the smooth side of the paper. The best mode of dampening India paper is to let it remain for a few minutes in a heap of wet paper in proper condition for printing. India paper is held in high esteem by artists who wish to obtain superior impressions of either wood-engravings or plate pictures, and its alleged superiority, for such purposes, to plate-paper, was attributed by Professor Faraday to the peculiar nature of the fibre used in its formation. It is said to possess a singular degree of ductility, even in the dry state, so that the slightest impression of any hard body remains after the pressure is removed, while these marks, again, can be removed with extraordinary completeness by a second and obliterating pressure.

Hansard, in printing the illustrations for his Typographia, says he tried various papers, but found none equal to India paper. He says that in printing woodcuts he found it impossible, when using these substitutes, to give at once the same intensity of color to the black shades from the plane surface of the block,

and the delicacy of the lighter shades from the engraved part; while the India paper, on the contrary, by the flexibility of texture, and absorbent and congenial quality for fixing the ink, would take every light and shade, with much less color and pressure, and—what is of infinite importance in printing—allow the ink to set, or dry, in less time, than any other paper.

Inferior Letters.—Letters which are cast with their face low down on the shank, so that an unusual white space is left at the head when they are printed.

Initial Letter.—The first letter of a word. In the manuscripts which served as the model for the first printers, the initial letters were frequently elaborately ornamented, and often formed an illustration appropriate to the text. This was especially the case in copies of the Scriptures and devotional works, where the adornment of the text was regarded as a pious duty by the monk or devotee, and these ornaments were imitated closely by the early printers. A blank was frequently left, so that the initial could be afterwards supplied by a scribe or artist; occasionally the initial was printed in red, to distinguish it from the text, which was in black ink; and at a later day an outline ornamentation was given in black, to be adorned with color by the hand. The initial opening a chapter or division of a book was usually considered most worthy of decoration, and also the initial of each paragraph, while often the initial of each sentence was also ornamented.

The custom still prevails to a limited extent, the chapters of handsomely printed books and magazine articles being frequently introduced by a highly ornamental initial. The works of Thackeray were frequently so adorned, and often by appropriate sketches from his own artistic style. Ornamented initial letters of varied and beautiful patterns are manufactured by American type-founders, and occasionally used in various descriptions of job-printing.

Ink.—The coloring substance applied to type, engravings, or forms, by a roller, and subsequently transferred to paper, or such other material as may be chosen to receive an impression. The nature and ingredients of ink vary with the character of the work to be performed, there being considerable difference between the inks intended for plate, lithographic, and typographic printing, and also in the qualities of the various inks used in each of these branches of printing. Until recently, plate-printers and lithographers uniformly manufactured their own inks (see LITHOGRAPHY), and they still continue to do so to a considerable extent, but not universally. Typographic printers were formerly subjected to a similar necessity, partly on account of the limited extent of their operations, and partly because of the supposed difficulty of manufacturing an ink that could be kept ready for use from day to day; but no such necessity now exists, and scarcely a single typographer attempts, unless it be for special purposes or on extraordinary occasions, to manufacture black inks for his individual use. Colored inks are occasionally still made by those who intend to use them (see COLOR PRINTING), but even of these, nearly every desirable variety in price, color, and quality is furnished in convenient quantities by the ink-manufacturers of the United States, and it is unnecessary to make any additional reference to colored inks here, except to remark that printers should be cautious in their selection of colored inks intended for jobs they wish to print in fast colors, as some of the modern inks, and especially those made of aniline colors, frequently fade, while the brilliancy of good inks is rather heightened than diminished by exposure to atmospheric influences.

Black ink, however, is the standard color, and it may be readily obtained at nearly all prices, ranging from twelve or fifteen cents per pound to seven dollars per pound, the variations in quality, cost of ingredients, and character of the results produced on the printed page corresponding, in a large measure, to these wide diversities in price.

While the general character of the ingredients used in making ink, and the ordinary processes of manufacture, are well known, the business abounds with trade secrets, carefully guarded,—the ink-manufacturers of the present day, imitating, in this respect, the early printers who manufactured their own inks. That great improvements have been effected, during the last twenty or thirty years, in the art of making inks adapted to the special requirements of the age, as well as in the preparation of blacks, is plainly evident, and printers who are anxious to secure a superior quality of ink, regardless of price, can be as readily supplied as those whose wants are of such a nature that cheapness of first cost is a paramount consideration.

Hansard's Typographia says that the following method of making ink was adopted by Baskerville during the last century:

He took of the finest and oldest linseed oil three gallons: this was put into a vessel capable of holding four times the quantity, and boiled with a long-continued fire till it acquired a certain thickness or tenacity, according to the quality of the work it was intended to print, which was judged of by putting a small quantity upon a stone to cool, and then taking it up between the finger and thumb; on opening which, if it drew into a thread an inch long or more, it was considered sufficiently boiled. This mode of boiling can only be acquired by long practice, and requires particular skill and care in the person who superintends the operation, as, for want of this, the most serious consequences may occur, and have very frequently occurred. The oil thus prepared was suffered to cool, and had then a small quantity of black or amber rosin dissolved in it, after which it was allowed some months to subside; it was then mixed with the finest black that could be secured, to a proper thickness, and ground for use.

Savage recommends to printers who wish to prepare for themselves a superior black ink, without running risks, the following recipe:

Proportions for one pound. Balsam of copaiva 9 oz., Lampblack 3 oz., Indigo, or Prussian-blue, or equal quantities of both, 1¼ oz., Indian-red ¾ oz., Turpentine soap, dry, 3 oz.; to be ground upon a stone with a muller to an impalpable fineness, when it will be fit for use.

It is said that the objectionable smell which balsam of copaiva has may be entirely removed by putting three or four drops of kreosote in the above quantity of ink.

Printing-ink must be a mutable preparation, passing from the soft, adhesive state to that of a perfectly hard and dry substance, and this change of condition must have a certain rate of progress, and be to some extent under control. When prepared, some time generally elapses before it is used, and during this period it should not alter in the slightest degree; in fact, when the air is excluded from it, it should keep for almost any length of time. During its application to the type, its solidification should be as slow as possible, and unaccompanied by the emission of any unpleasant or deleterious odor. It ought not to affect the soft elastic rollers which are employed to convey it to the type, and which, unless the ink be a perfectly harmless preparation, are liable to considerable injury. The change of state should not be accompanied by the deposition of consolidated matter in the ink, as this impedes the pressman and proves a loss to the printer. Printing-ink should, moreover, have an oleaginous character; it ought to be very glossy, and perfectly free from any granular appearance. If, on the extraction of a small portion from a mass, it leaves but a short thread suspended, it is considered good, but the best test of its consistency is the adhesion it shows upon pressing the finger against a quantity of it. The requirements of a good printing-ink do not end here. Having been applied, its action must be confined to a very slight penetration into the paper—just sufficient to prevent its detachment without materially injuring the surface of the latter. It ought to dry up in a very short space of time into a hard, inodorous, unalterable solid. The ingredients of ordinary printing-ink are burnt linseed oil, rosin, and occasionally soap, with various coloring matters. The best quality of linseed oil is used in superior inks, and this is purified by digesting it in partially-diluted sulphuric acid for some hours, at a temperature of about two hundred and twelve degrees, allowing the impurities to subside, and then washing away the acid with repeated additions of hot water. The water, after this treatment, is pale and turbid, and if the freeing from the acid is complete, there is scarcely any odor. By rest, the oil clarifies, and has then a pale lemon color. It now dries much more rapidly than before. The purified oil is now partially rosinified by heat. For this purpose it is introduced into large cast-iron pots, and boiled until inflammable vapors are freely evolved. These are ignited and allowed to burn for a few minutes, after which they are extinguished by placing a tight cover over the boiler. Ebullition of the oil is continued until, on cooling, a firm skin forms on its surface, known by placing a drop on slate or other smooth, cold surface. Other drying oils besides linseed are occasionally used, but their cost, or other considerations, prevents their general adoption. Rosin oil is, indeed, pretty largely employed, but, apart from other disadvantages, its disagreeable and permanent smell prevents its entering into other ink than that intended for temporary or common printing, as newspapers, posters, etc. Paraffine oil, which has lately been used, is open to the same objections. Rosin is an article of considerable importance in the manufacture of printing-ink, since, when dissolved in the oil—after the latter has undergone ebullition and inflammation—it communicates body to the fluid. For many inks the quality of the common black rosin is sufficiently good; but some require the pale, clear, transparent rosin, obtained by remelting and clarifying the residue of the distillation of turpentine with water. The coloring matters of printing-ink demand great attention, as much of the beauty of typography depends upon them. The universal ingredient for black ink is lampblack. No expense is spared to get the most superior quality. Other black substances are occasionally used. Charcoal, from various substances, when reduced to an impalpable powder and mixed with other ingredients, furnishes a deep, blue-black ink that dries rapidly. The brown tint possessed by lampblack is not unfrequently neutralized by the addition of blue compounds, as indigo, Prussian blue, etc. In one of the most common systems of manufacturing of printing-ink, the rosin is dissolved in the burnt oil, in cast-iron pots or boilers, and the varnish thus prepared is introduced into what is termed the mixing-vessel, which is cylindrical, and in the centre of which bars or rods of iron, attached to a perpendicular shaft, revolve in a horizontal position. The coloring matter is then added to the hot varnish, and the whole, when thoroughly mixed, is drawn off through an opening in the base of the vessel. The pulp is next very carefully ground, by being passed between hard stones of a very fine texture, driven by heavy machinery, the motive power being steam, care being taken that the varnish of rosin and oil is clear and free from gritty particles, and that the black is in an impalpable state. The proportions and conditions of the various ingredients vary considerably, and great experience is required before an ink can be prepared to suit any one purpose. The oil has to be rendered more viscid, by burning, in some cases than in others; sometimes the quantity or kind of rosin requires to be varied; or perhaps different proportions of color are requisite. Newspapers printed on power-presses require an ink of less substance than that employed for book-work, which must be tolerably stiff. For wood-cuts, the ink must not only be very stiff, but very fine. The qualities of the material to which the ink is applied furnish an additional guide in this matter: thin paper must have a soft ink, which works clearly and is not too adhesive. A fine, stout paper, on the other hand, will bear a stiffer and more glutinous ink, and as rosin supplies these properties, so does it, in a great measure, communicate brilliancy, and the most perfect and splendid effects are by these means produced. Posters, with large wood type, require a semi-fluid ink, but one not surcharged with oil. Ordinary news-work requires a better quality, more tacky and finely ground. Good book-work should have a stiffer-bodied ink—soft, smooth, and easily distributed. Job ink, which is made expressly for press-work on dry paper, should be used only for such work. Book and job inks are not convertible; an ink for wet paper will not work well on dry paper, and vice versa. Very fine press-work, such as wood-cuts, or letter-press upon enameled paper, requires an ink impalpably fine, of brilliant color, of strong body, yet soft enough to be taken up smoothly on the inking-rollers. Every general printing-office should keep four grades of black ink—news, jobbing, book, and wood-cut. Fine press-work is impossible without good ink. To recapitulate: The cardinal virtues of good ink are, intenseness of color; impalpability; covering the surface perfectly; quitting the surface of the type or engraving when the paper is withdrawn, and adhering to the surface of the paper; not smearing after it is printed; and retaining ever afterwards its original color without change. Inks which are properly manufactured on sound chemical principles should possess the additional advantages of keeping the roller in good working order, distributing freely, working sharp and clean, and drying rapidly on paper; the color should be permanent, without a tendency to turn brown by age.

A few years ago it was announced that a new ink patented in Germany printed satisfactorily. Its composition is said to be as follows:—2½ oz. turpentine (Venetian); 2½ oz. liquid soap; 1 oz. olein (rectified); 1½ oz. burnt soot; ½ oz. Paris blue (ferro-cyanic acid); ½ oz. oxalic acid; ½ oz. water. Gradually warm the turpentine and the olein together; put the soap on a marble plate and gradually add, continually rubbing, the mixture of turpentine and olein; when well mixed, add the burnt soot, which must be well powdered and sieved before; then add the Paris blue, dissolved in oxalic acid, continually rubbing the composition on the stone, the Paris blue and oxalic acid having been mixed before with water in the above proportions. This ink is said to be beautiful. A solution of soda in water serves to cleanse the type.

In the United States various new methods of making ink were adopted during the late war, in consequence of the extraordinary increase in the price of rosin, some of which proved highly injurious to rollers. Methods have also been patented from time to time, some of which will be found described elsewhere. (See INVENTIONS, under the heading INKS.)

Ink Fountain.—See FOUNTAIN.

Ink-Block.—A block used to contain ink, and to afford a convenient place for partially distributing it, before it is conveyed to the distributing-rollers of hand-presses.

INK-BLOCK.

Ink-Slice.—An implement for taking ink out of kegs, casks, or tubs, and putting it on blocks, stones, or in fountains, etc.

INK-SLICE.

Ink-Table.—The surface upon which the roller is distributed, previously to being applied to the form. On those used for the old hand-presses, the back of the table is slightly raised, having two receptacles—one for ink, the other for the brayer. The ink is spread in small quantities along this raised portion by means of the brayer, so as to give an even supply to the roller across its entire length. The ink so spread, having been lightly touched by the roller, is distributed upon the face of the table until it is

INK-TABLE, STONE, AND MULLER.

covered evenly all over; it is then ready for inking the form. Various improvements have been made in the manufacture of ink-tables; some being supplied with an ink duct, similar to a machine, the feeding cylinder being turned by means of a handle or worked by a treadle. In job printing, an ink-table is also often used to prepare inks for working on presses of various descriptions. The annexed cut illustrates an ink-table of this kind.

Inner Form.—The form which contains the inner pages of a sheet, commencing with the second page. For instance, in a sheet of quarto the inner pages would be 2, 3, and 6, 7. The inner form perfects the first or outer form. The term is generally applied to the four middle pages of a 12mo form, which are necessarily folded separately and inset by the binder.

Insertion.—In printing, words or sentences added within the body of a text; also a term used to express the publication of an article in a newspaper or other serial publication, and especially advertisements, each publication of which is styled an insertion.

Inset.—That part of a sheet which, when printed, is cut off, and when folded is inserted in the middle of the other part, the pages, when thus united, being placed in regular and orderly succession.

Inscription.—A dedication, also any title, address, or name, written or engraved upon any object, intended to dedicate it to any special use or service.

Inside Quires.—The perfect quires of paper, containing twenty-four good sheets in each. They are thus designated to distinguish them from the outside or corded quires.

Inside Sheets.—The thin sheets used by pressmen for placing between the tympans of the press.

Intaglio.—Lines cut into a surface, as in copperplate engraving.

Interleave.—To insert leaves between other leaves. Books in the classic languages have been published in this way, accompanied by translations; it has also been done in many polyglot publications. The printed pages of a work are also occasionally interleaved with blank pages, intended to contain pictures, notes, commentaries, or other appropriate matter. In fine work, particularly when the paper is heavy, and the type large and black, set-off sheets are used to interleave the whole impression in working. This is also often done where large wood-cuts occur.

Interline.—To write between lines already written or printed, as a correction or addition; also to arrange in alternate lines, as in the text-books styled interlinear translations, in which each line of the original language is followed by a line of the translation, in order to present both at one view before the eye of the student.

Interlinear Translations.—In composing work of this kind, the lines must be spaced so that the translation will be under the centre of the text. In order to do this correctly, the compositor must set up the longest word or phrase in both until the line is filled, when it will appear thus:

Omnes the villages *atque omnia* the buildings, which *quisque*

The words of the translation must now be taken out, and the short words of the text justified in the centre of the spaces in the following manner:

Omnes vici atque omnia ædificia, quæ quisque
All the villages and all the buildings, which any one

Interpolation.—Words added to the original matter; generally used to express a spurious passage, intended to alter or injure the meaning of the original.

Interrogation, Note of.—A mark or sign (?) placed at the end of a sentence expressing a question. It is also used to express a doubt, in a sentence of questionable correctness, or to mark a query in proof-reading. In punctuation it should be placed at the end of every distinct question; but where several questions are so closely connected that only one answer, or no answer whatever, is required, only one note of interrogation, placed at the termination of the sentence, is necessary. The mark is often erroneously placed at the end of a sentence which merely states that a question has been asked. This should not be done, unless the substance of the question thus referred to is repeated in an interrogative form. The Spanish printers place an inverted interrogation mark (¿) at the commencement of an interrogative sentence, to assist the reader; but, although this custom has often been extolled by English or American writers, it has never been adopted in works printed in the English language. The meaning and use of the interrogation point are well illustrated by the following anecdote:

One day as Pope was engaged in translating the Iliad, he came to a passage which neither he nor his assistant could interpret. A stranger, who stood by, in his humble garb, very modestly suggested that as he had some little acquaintance with the Greek, perhaps he could assist them. Try it! said Pope, with the air of a boy who is teaching a monkey to eat red pepper. There is an error in the print,—said the stranger, looking at the text—read as if there was no interrogation point at the end of the line, and you have the meaning at once. Pope's assistant improved upon this hint, and rendered the passage without difficulty. Pope was chagrined; he could never endure to be surpassed in any thing. Turning to the stranger, he said, in a sarcastic tone, Will you please to tell me what an interrogation is? Why, sir, said the stranger, scanning the ill-shaped poet, it is a little, crooked, contemptible thing that asks questions!

Introduction.—The formal preface to a work, generally used by the author for special personal explanation, for summing up the conclusions arrived at in the work, or for presenting preliminary observations necessary to the complete understanding of the subject treated.

Inventions.—For a long period after the leading features of typographic printing were invented, the advance steps consisted chiefly in a gradual improvement in the faces of type, in the cutting of the alphabet of Greek, Hebrew, etc., and in the construction of a hand-press superior to that used by the early printers. A few improved methods of manufacturing paper and of binding books were discovered; movable types for printing music were invented, as well as types for printing maps and pictures; stereotyping processes were devised, but the art was not fairly established as a practical business; and with the exception of the patent granted to William Nicholson by the British patent office, in April, 1790, for a power-press, there is a deplorable dearth, from 1450 up to the present century, of original and useful inventions. Since the year 1800, printing has been frequently and wonderfully aided, in all its varied ramifications and departments, by discoveries of immense utility. After popular education multiplied readers, the facilities for printing increased as rapidly as the demand for the products of the press. Within the memory of living printers, Power-presses of amazing speed, Type-casting Machines, Lithography, Electrotyping, new and rapid Stereotyping processes, Photography, Paper-making Machines, Nature Printing, Anastatic Printing, new systems of Engraving, Composition-Rollers, Folding-Machines, Cutting-Machines, Small Job Presses, and thousands of devices for facilitating various operations in printing and its auxiliary arts, have been invented and utilized to a wonderful extent. Many of these inventions are described in this work under their appropriate headings, but, in order to present a general view of American progress, the following list and description of patents granted in this country has been compiled from official records expressly for this publication.

It is sufficiently complete to afford an excellent indication of the character of the labors of American inventors, and to mark the successive steps which have brought the art up to its present advanced condition. In the three grand departments of Press-Making, Paper-Making, and Type-Casting, the patents granted are especially numerous and useful; while many convenient appliances, implements, etc. designed to facilitate the various typographical processes have also been invented. Of the patents granted previous to 1836, an official record is kept only of those returned to Washington to be recorded after the fire which destroyed the original records, and Clymer's Columbian Press, and some other inventions famous in their day are omitted on this account.

ANASTATIC PRINTING.

C. F. BALDAMUS & F. W. SEIMENS, Berlin, Prussia, October 25, 1845.—The patent is for an improvement in the method of producing and multiplying copies of designs and impressions of printed or written surfaces, and consists in the process by which transfers or reversed fac-similes are secured upon metallic surfaces from designs in writing or lithographic ink, and from prints or printing in general, by means of treating the originals with acids of strength varying with the induration of the ink, and so pressing out the acid as to cause an etching of the blank spaces and a reversed impression of the originals. Also a process for reviving the ink on originals with caustic potash, or its carbonate, and tartaric acid, so as to form a cream of tartar on the paper, which prevents the adherence of fresh ink on the blank spaces, while the old ink is left in a state to take up an additional quantity of ink from a roller passed over it; and the process by which the adhesion of ink, during the operation of printing, to any parts of the plate required to remain blank, is prevented by acting upon such blank surface with an acid preparation of phosphorus.

CASES.

JOHN BELL, Harlem, N. Y., January 8, 1850.—An improvement in the manufacture of type cases, by grooving the bottom of the case for the reception of the lower edge of the partitions, and securing them in by glue.

WM. A. HUNTER, Bryan, Ohio, June 29, 1858.—The nature of this invention consists in constructing the bottom of the case of a metallic screen, or other perforated material, whereby it is kept constantly clear of the dust resulting from the abrasion of the types, and collecting the dust on a shelf or drawer, whence it can be removed when required.

THOMAS N. ROOKER, New York, April 5, 1859.—The invention consists in arranging the compartments of a type case, by placing at the side of the lower-case its corresponding upper-case, so that the movements of the body and travel of the hand of the compositor may be greatly reduced.

THOMAS N. ROOKER, New York, January 1, 1861.—This invention consists in forming the type case and its boxes of considerable depth, so as to hold a large quantity of type; the boxes being provided with movable bottoms arranged so as to be readily adjusted or raised as the types are taken out.

W. M. RANDALL and G. C. HOWARD, Belleville, Ohio, October 14, 1862.—This invention consists in arranging a type case in such a way that each box in the case may be adjusted in relation to the bottom, and that by sliding it down the type will be elevated to the top of the case, or as high as may be desired by the compositor.

LEONARD H. MILLER, Ottawa, Ohio, December 18, 1866.—The nature of this invention is the arrangement of movable boxes, made with curved sides toward the operator, and each box has an edge and slide curved over the upper edge of those in proximity to it.

CHARLES ALEXANDER, Washington, D. C., April 30, 1867.—By this invention the horizontal partitions, instead of being at a right angle to the bottom, are made oblique thereto, so as to be nearly vertical when in use.

CHASES.

WM. O. STODDARD, Champaign, Ill., July 9, 1861.—The object of this invention is to admit of the adjustment of the chase to any sized form of type smaller than the largest capacity, by the application of screws working simultaneously upon side-sticks, the side-sticks interlocking, and the combination of screws and side-sticks inside of the chase.

ALLAN M. BLANCHARD, St. Louis, Mo., Feb. 20, 1866.—This device is formed of four straight bars fitted together, so that they may be adjusted to any size of form required, without the use of quoins.

JOHN N. MURRAY, Chicago, Ill., July 9, 1867.—This invention consists in an adjustable sliding frame, supported in grooves in the stationary frame, by which means it is regulated to the size of the form, and is secured in position by clasps and set screws.

ROBERT DICK, Buffalo, N. Y., April 14, 1868.—This improvement consists in the construction and use of a sufficient number of suitably inclined planes, formed along the side and foot of an otherwise common chase, employed in combination with thin wedges of any suitable substance, operating between these inclined planes and a reglet of suitable material, so as to lock up a form in an eighth of an inch of chase room as easily and as efficiently as in two inches of chase room.

COLORS, PRINTING IN.

THOMAS F. ADAMS, Philadelphia, September 17, 1844.—A patent for Polychromatic printing, by which it is claimed any number of colors may be printed at one impression by a series of separate and complete inking fountains.

ALEX. D. MCKENZIE, Philadelphia, November 6, 1846.—This is an apparatus by which to work as many different colors as are required without taking the sheet of paper from the press before it is effected. It consists in the combination of a series of sliding tympans, with a corresponding series of plates for printing colors, so that a sheet when put on the machine shall receive successively an impression from each plate, the whole forming a vari-colored impression.

R. S. WEAVER, Maysville, Ky., October 28, 1851.—This invention is an adjustable ink-trough, provided with removable partitions and perforated side, so as to give out the ink in lines or belts, corresponding with the lines or size of the type in the form, in combination with receiving, distributing, and inking rollers.

JOHN DUNLEVY, New York, January 3, 1854.—The claim is for a method of producing intagliographic printing, and other plates, from forms of types, by surrounding the types, whilst in contact with a glass plate, or its equivalent, with plaster of paris, or some equivalent therefor, so that when set the surface of the plaster will be on the same plane with the surface of the types, and then stereotyping the form of types thus surrounded.

A. M. and G. H. BABCOCK, Westerly, R. I., October 31, 1854.—This invention aims to print different colors successively on the same sheet, as it is carried upon a revolving platen.

STEPHEN BROWN, Syracuse, N. Y., January 2, 1855.—This improvement is the employment or use of a series of platens, so that the forms of type on said platens may be inked simultaneously with separate and distinct colors, and operated or pressed simultaneously against the sheet.

CYRUS A. SWEET, Boston, Mass., November 27, 1855.—The rollers each receive its proper colored ink from a fountain; and as the cylinder rotates, the rollers will distribute upon the periphery of the cylinder belts of different colored inks, the width of the belt being equal to the width of the blocks.

WM. A. BAKER and GEO. J. HILL, Buffalo, Erie County, N. Y., June 2, 1863.—This invention consists in an arrangement whereby, by one passage through the press, a continuous sheet of paper or card-board may be printed in two or more colors. This is accomplished by an intermittent feed-motion in combination with the reciprocating motion of two or more cross-heads, each carrying a form of type with an inking apparatus attached thereto, which distributes the ink upon the face of the type during the intervals of the intermittent feed. The intermittent feed is obtained by feed-arms upon a rock-shaft, and the vertical reciprocating motion of the form-bearing cross-heads is given by cams of a peculiar construction attached to the press, and in combination with it are circular revolving cutters, by which a sheet or roll of paper or card-board may be cut into any required number of strips while passing through the press.

THOMAS L. BAYLIES and GEO. W. WOOD, Richmond, Ind., August 6, 1867.—This invention consists of an oscillating frame carrying a series of rollers, which are brought in contact with fountain rollers of a series of fountains, each carrying different colored ink; and the ink is communicated by another series of rollers to segmental rollers, which in turn, communicate the ink to a set of rollers common to all, by which the type is inked in strips of various colors.

JAS. W. SLATER, Richmond, Ind., June 16, 1868.—Adjustable inking tables are arranged in sets parallel with one another, each set receiving one color, and disposed upon corresponding lines of type. In traversing the ways, each roller is brought in contact with the face of its own table, without touching the others.

THOMAS L. BAYLIES, Richmond, Ind., July 14, 1868.—This invention is an inking apparatus designed for Chromatic Printing.

JOSHUA HUNT, Richmond, Ind., July 14, 1868.—This invention consists in the combination of the type bed, and two forms, and the inking rollers, and adjustable cam tracks, so constructed and arranged in relation to the ink-distributing rollers, that different colored inks, first disposed in bands on the type-inking roller, or on part thereof, shall be transferred simultaneously to the lines of type, and a single color be also transferred to the other form, so that by two impressions, the sheet or the form being reversed, two completed jobs may be printed in which the letter-press is printed in more than two colors, and the border in one color.

A. A. DUNK, Philadelphia, March 10, 1868.—The object of this invention is the arrangement of a press for printing in a variety of colors. To accomplish this, the nipper shafts are journaled in wheels of a larger diameter than the platen-cylinder, and the series of nippers outnumber the platen surfaces. The platen-cylinder has longitudinal recesses in its periphery into which the nipper shafts enter when in proximity

to the form-cylinder, and by the larger diameter of the nipper wheels the sheets are carried to a fresh surface at each revolution to receive the portion put on in fresh color. The inking rollers are moved radially, to bring them to their proper type, and to avoid the forms intended for another color, by cam grooves which give the necessary motion to their journal frames. The distributors have their reciprocation by the obliquity of their motive wheel.

COMPOSING-STICKS.

OLIVER S. GROVER, Middletown, Conn., July 15, 1855.—The invention consists in the application to the composing-stick of a guide to prevent the slide and bed from separating while adjusting the stick, and a clasp to secure and hold the guide in position when adjusted.

DAN. WINDER, Cincinnati, Ohio, April 7, 1857.—By this invention, the spring plate can be moved, adjusted, and held by a thumb screw, so that its end can be adjusted to any distance from the end of the stick, to suit any measure that may be required.

JAMES TIDGEWELL and WILLIAM TIDGEWELL, Middletown, Conn., June 2, 1857.—This invention consists in the application to the slide of a composing-stick, of a flange and screw, in combination with a washer, interposed between the point of the screw and the exterior surface of the foot or bottom stile of the stick.

ALEXANDER CALHOUN, Hartford, Conn., August 31, 1858.—The nature of this invention consists in the application of a clasping band, attached and combined with the sliding knee-bracket, to prevent springing back by the pressure of tight spacing or long-continued use.

STEPHEN W. BROWN, Syracuse, N. Y., May 22, 1860.—This invention consists in the use of an eccentric and elastic plate connected with the slide and applied to the side of the stick.

JOHN L. WAIT, East Cambridge, Mass., May 19, 1868.—In this stick the shoulder is provided with a clamp, which clasps the ledge of the composing-stick, and retains the shoulder in the position in which it may be set, the cam-lever being adapted to close the clamps with greater or less force.

CONSECUTIVE NUMBERING PRESSES.

GEO. BAILEY, Buffalo, N. Y., March 20, 1850.—The nature of this invention consists in the printing of coupon tickets for railroads, and numbering the tickets with their coupons in successive order or series, by one operation of the press; and, also, for feeding the paper under the types, in such manner as to perform likewise the operation of perforating or partially separating the coupons from each other and from the ticket, so as to be readily torn apart at the place of perforation.

JOSEPH EDMONDSON and CALEB HAWORTH, executors of JOSEPH EDMONDSON, deceased, Salford, England, May 23, 1854.—This invention was patented in England, March 19, 1850, and is intended to print on each of a number of tickets the same names of places, and to number them consecutively. The blank cards are placed in a feeding tube, from which they are fed, one by one, to a horizontal table, under a type box, containing the form, the impression from which is repeated on all the cards; the type is raised and lowered to receive the ink from the rollers, and to print the cards, which are held in place by guide-rails, which extend from the feeding tube to the receiving tube. The consecutive numbers are printed on the cards by the numbering-wheels, which have the numbers engraved on their circumference.

GEO. J. HILL, Buffalo, N. Y., September 7, 1858.—By this invention the press is operated in a common manner. The numbering machine is connected to the bed-plate, and moves with it.. As the bed-plate is moved inwardly, the spring pawl catches into the teeth of a ratchet, and causes the proper movement of the required number.

R. M. HOE, New York, March 8, 1859.—The inventor claims the invention of the peculiar mechanism for moving the registering disks on their axis at the proper times, by which means the tickets are numbered consecutively. Also, a separate inking apparatus, for inking in a different color the registering figures.

ELECTROGRAPHIC PRINTING.

A. W. THOMPSON, Philadelphia, April 26, 1845.—An improvement in the manner of preparing blocks or plates with raised designs, for the purpose of giving impressions in the same manner as those taken from type. This consists in preparing designs upon copper or other suitable metal, for the purpose of printing typographically, so that a plate in relief may be obtained therefrom by the electrotype process.

FEEDING APPARATUS.

JOHN P. COMLY, Dayton, Ohio, March 22, 1853.—This improvement in feeding paper, sheet by sheet, by means of atmospheric pressure. The principal features are an exhaust pump, attached by a flexible tube to a horizontal table, provided at the under side with small tubes. The paper is placed on an elevated table, which presses the paper against a roller; this runs out the top sheet of paper, which is sucked up by the exhaust tube, and by means of proper gearing is regularly fed and removed.

HENRY CLARK, New Orleans, April 25, 1854.—This invention consists in detaching or loosening the sheet of paper that is to be fed to the press from the sheets underneath it, by giving the sheet a backward and forward motion, previously to its being operated upon by the feed or pressure rollers.

GEO. LITTLE, Utica, N. Y., April 25, 1854.—The improvement is the mode for operating the feed tables of printing-presses, together with the guides, composed of india-rubber or other suitable resisting material.

WM. F. COLLIER, Worcester, Mass., June 27, 1854.—The object of this invention is feeding paper,—accomplished by means of a bellows, an elastic tube

or pipe, and a rotary lifter which is exhausted by the bellows. The paper is laid on an inclined table, from which it is taken by the lifter and carried forward towards the grippers, the sheets being kept separate by intermediate contrivances.

B. A. RUGG and E. H. BENJAMIN, Oakhill, Greene county, N. Y., September 5, 1854.—This is a frame, constructed with two endless aprons, rotated so as to feed the paper through rollers at graduated intervals, as the sheets of paper overlap each other. Thus but one sheet of paper is passed at one time to the apparatus for carrying the sheet upon the cylinder.

DAVID BALDWIN, Godwinville, N. J., January 2, 1855.—The improvement consists, 1st. Feeding sheets of paper to a printing-press, or paper-ruling machine, requiring the feed of a single sheet at a time, by means of a vibrating frame, having at its lower end a series of tubes, which, as the frame vibrates, pass over a portion of the cylinder, or other device for receiving the sheet; a vacuum being formed and destroyed in said tubes by means of an air-pump attached to the frame, for the purpose of conveying the sheets from the feed table to the receiving device of the machine. 2d. A self-adjusting feed table, constructed and arranged so as to be operated by the vibrations of the frame, and keep the sheets close to the ends of the tubes.

A. B. CHILDS and HENRY W. DICKSON, Rochester, N. Y., February 20, 1855.—The improvement claimed is the raising and delivering the sheets by means of inward and outward currents of air, said currents being produced and operated in one and the same trunk, by means of a fan, or its equivalent, in combination with a revolving trunk, by which the sheets are raised and separated.

JOHN BISHOP HALL, New York, April 10, 1855.—The object of this invention is to raise the sheets of paper from the feed-board by means of nippers, and convey the sheets so raised from the feed-board to the form to be printed, and also from the form when printed to the proper receptacle, by means of fingers attached to a tube and shaft, which is secured to endless bands or cords.

ISAAC B. LIVINGSTON and MILES WATERHOUSE, Barnet, Vermont, April 24, 1855.—The invention claimed is the using of angular guide ways, in combination with a cross-bar, and the use of a crank working in combination with levers and the cross-bar, for carrying paper forward, a sheet at a time, and feeding it to printing-presses.

A. H. ROWAND, Alleghany, Pa., July 3, 1855.—The invention consists in the employment of a swinging frame provided with rollers, in combination with a vibrating arm and clamp, or lip, operated by a slotted bar, which grasps the sheet and carries it to the press.

MOSES S. BEACH, Brooklyn, N. Y., December 23, 1856.—The object of the invention consists in turning the sheet, and delivering it to the cylinder for a second impression, by means of an extra or second cylinder.

R. M. Hoe, New York, November 10, 1857.—This invention relates to an improvement in that class of paper-feeding devices, in which the sheets are fed to the press through the agency or medium of drop-rollers, and consists in giving the drop-roller a constant and regular speed, corresponding at all times to that of the other running or working parts of the device.

William Bullock, Newark, N. J., September 21, 1858.—The object of this invention is to effect the feeding of sheets of paper to the press, with machinery, by which the hands, or their equivalents, used in feeding paper, shall have a greater capacity for moving the sheet than is necessary for the purpose. Also, effecting the progressive movement of the pile of paper by mechanism, whose operation is dependent upon the position of the pile, and moving the sheets of paper by automatic rubbing-bands, or their equivalents. And in operating the stop-cocks of the air-cylinder, and the flap-guides by a cam, or its equivalent, whose movement is coincident with, or bears a fixed relation to the movement of the fingers, which draw the paper into the press.

Moses S. Beach, Brooklyn, N. Y., November 9, 1858.—The object of this invention is to conduct sheets of paper from more than one impression-cylinder, or source of supply, into a single set of guide-tapes, and also to count them in desired quantities.

Lemuel T. Wells, Cincinnati, Ohio, October 19, 1858.—This invention consists in mounting the nippers on a frame having a limited motion concentric with, but independent of, the cylinder; the object being to insure a more perfect feed, by causing the nippers to seize the paper while in a quiescent state, or moving in an opposite direction to the cylinder.

Moses S. Beach, Brooklyn, N. Y., August 9, 1859. —This invention is, 1st. Feeding sheets to the impression-cylinder, by means of revolving arms or scrapers operating in combination with rollers. 2d. Retaining the paper in connection with the impression-cylinder, during the process of printing, by means of holders.

R. M. Hoe, New York, August 23, 1859.—The inventor claims as improvements, the combination of the feeding-mechanism, cutting-apparatus, and printing-machine, for the purpose of feeding the paper from a roll to the press, and cutting or partially cutting it into sheets as it passes along to be printed. Also, in combination with the cutting-cylinder, the employment of two pressure rollers for keeping the sheet distended.

Charles Potter, Jr., and C. B. Cottrell, Westerly, R. I., September 20, 1859.—The improvement consists in the securing of the registering-points firmly to a fixed portion of the machine, and releasing the paper therefrom, at the proper time, by elevating the adjacent surface. Also, depositing each sheet face upwards on the pile, by carrying it between a vibrating series of tapes; and, also, the arrangement of the cylinders.

John Hunt, New York, November 1, 1864.—The

object of this invention is to feed the paper to the press by atmospheric pressure, and to overcome the usual difficulty in thus feeding paper occasioned by the sheets adhering and dragging. Two pairs of bellows are used, and the paper seized at both ends and raised perpendicularly, when it is seized by mechanical means and carried forward.

FRISKETS.

Andrew Overend, Philadelphia, June 13, 1854. —The improvement consists in constructing a metallic frame, notched along its outer surface like saw-teeth, and then stretching longitudinally and transversely across the frame elastic strips, and having at each end a clamp. These clamps are intended to be, and can be, slid along the sides of the frisket-frame, or they will remain permanently in any position in which they may be placed. By this means a movable barrel frisket-frame is formed, which can be altered or adjusted at convenience, without involving any loss of material.

GALLEYS.

D. B. Dorsey and E. Mathers, Fairmount, Va., October 2, 1860.—The object of this invention is to facilitate the handling of composed matter without danger of knocking it into pi. To do this the inventors propose to set up the type in a permanent galley, where it shall remain until distributed. To this galley are arranged movable and justifying rules.

S. W. Brown, Syracuse, N. Y., March 12, 1861.— This invention consists of a metallic plate with ledges permanently secured on three sides, sufficiently high to retain the type within the galleys. The ledge is provided with a series of oblique projections corresponding with similar projections on a bar which is allowed a longitudinal sliding movement, and retained in proper position by means of guides formed on the surface of the ledge and fitting in grooves on the said bar. To the inner side of this bar is attached a metal bar which has a lateral movement, and, in connection with the bar to which it is attached, is made to clamp the type against a parallel stationary bar in the galley.

Alexander T. DePuy, N. Y., December 4, 1866. —The metallic strip which lines the inside edge of the galley is made to clasp the latter instead of being secured by screws to the face of the same.

Jasper Snyder, Burlington, Iowa, January 2, 1866.—By this invention the side of the column of type is regulated by an adjustable block, secured by guide bars and set-screws; an adjustable tail-piece clamps the foot of the column.

Jno. W. Baker, Warsaw, Ind., July 16, 1867.— This improvement consists in having a detachable end piece in combination with a side-stick, operated by screws.

P. Gray Meek, Bellefonte, Pa., November 19, 1867.—This invention consists in an adjustable side-stick having a series of springs attached to it, and bearing against the side of the galley, to render the

15

stick self-adjusting, thus securing the type in position.

CHARLES H. LAWRENCE, New York, N. Y., July 14, 1868.—The frame of the galley is of wood, slotted down its centre, along the inner side, to a depth of about two-thirds of its width, so as to receive a metal tongue which is soldered to the lining. The metal bottom is secured by means of screws which are put in from the under side, and pass up through the metal tongue, thus securing the frame, bottom and side-lining firmly, and in such a manner as to prevent the galley from warping or shrinking, and, by presenting a perfectly smooth surface on the inside lining, it prevents the type from being pied whilst moving and emptying the matter on the galley.

INKING APPARATUS, DISTRIBUTERS, &c.

ANDREW MAVERICK, New York, April 17, 1810.
W. J. STONE, Washington, D. C., October 20, 1829.
JOHN PRINCE, New York, December 3, 1829.
SAMUEL FAIRLAND, New York, October 25, 1830.
JOHN PRINCE, New York, April 23, 1830.
RICHARD WOOD, New York, November 4, 1830.
JOHN PRINCE, New York, December 3, 1831.
JOHN PRINCE, Philadelphia, Pa., November 19, 1833.
WILLIAM J. SPENCE, New York, April 30, 1834.
JOHN MAXSON, Schenectady, N. Y., January 9, 1835.
SAMUEL FAIRLAND and JOHN GILPIN, New York, March 27, 1835.
ELIPHAZ WESTON ARNOLD, Boston, Mass., September 21, 1837.
FREDERICK I. AUSTIN, New York, February 20, 1841.—This is a patent for an inking machine by which the rollers are thrown across the form by means of a pulley operated by a weight.
R. M. HOE, N. Y., April 17, 1844.—This invention combines the hollow roller with the inking fountain, to be heated by steam or otherwise, by which any quantity of steam or heated air may be made to pass through, and warm the ink upon the surface of the rollers.
THOMAS L. BAYLIES, Richmond, Ind., May 26, 1868.—This apparatus is intended to be employed in connection with a printing-press for the purpose of adapting it to print in different colors at a single operation.

INKS.

SAMUEL H. TURNER, Brooklyn, N. Y., September 6, 1853.—This improvement consists in the employment of colophonic tar, in connection with other materials, in the manufacture of printers' ink, and also in the manufacture of a varnish to be used by printers to modify the condition of their ink to suit the temperature of the weather and the kind of work to be executed. What the inventor denominates colophonic tar, is the tarry residuum remaining in the stills after the various stages of distillation commonly employed in obtaining colophonic oil. The ingredients and the proportions are as follows: Colophonic tar, 14 ℔; fine lampblack, 3 ℔; fine pulverized indigo blue, 8 ounces; fine pulverized Indian red, 4 ounces; yellow rosin soap, 1 ℔. The ingredients are mixed by the aid of heat.

CALEB A. THOMPSON, Adrian, Mich., April 17, 1855.—The object of this improvement is to produce ink which is tenacious and adhesive, and which, when dried, adheres firmly to the surface of the paper. The inventor takes for ordinary inks, four pounds of litharge, two pounds of acetate of lead, and forty gallons of linseed oil. Before using the linseed oil it is subjected to heat (600° Fahr.) after adding litharge and lead as dryers, for from 48 to 65 hours, according to the desired quality of the ink. The oil having been thus prepared, gum copal is added,—four pounds of it to one gallon of the oil (thus prepared). For news ink, fifteen pounds of the above oil, ten pounds of rosin (common), two pounds brown rosin soap, and five and a half pounds lamp-black. These proportions vary for other inks.

GEORGE MATTHEWS, Montreal, Canada, June 30, 1857.—This improvement consists in the use of the calcined green oxide of chromium, mixed with burned or boiled linseed oil, for making ink for plate or type printing.

GEORGE DURYEE, New York, June 27, 1865.—This ink is composed of 100 pounds of the dark-colored residuum resulting from the distillation of petroleum to which are added twenty-five pounds of the waste sulphuric acid which has been used in deodorizing petroleum. This compound is agitated until it becomes thick, tenacious, and nearly black. Water is then added to wash out the acid, and, if necessary, chloride of lime, to neutralize and destroy any unpleasant odor. The resulting substance is called petroline wax, which is substituted for linseed or other oils in the manufacture of printers' ink.

CHARLES MUSTIN, Lafayette, Ind., June 16, 1868.—This invention consists in the preparation of an ink for all the purposes for which printers' ink is used, in which the silicate of alumina, white clay, Jersey clay, or Kaolin, prepared with sulphate of zinc and with or without dilute sulphuric acid, is partially substituted for lampblack, blue, green, or other coloring matters, with drying materials and varnish.

MAILING MACHINES.

HENRY MOESER, Pittsburg, Pa., June 24, 1857.—The construction and arrangement of a machine for printing names of persons and places on newspapers, by means of a form containing the names, set up in type, and being brought under the action of a slide, moving by degrees, with the application of a slitted place, allowing the paper to be pressed down on the line right beneath the slit of the plate, and shielding the paper from the lines adjoining that under the action of the stamp.

EDWARD P. DAY, New York, June 6, 1854.—This is an improvement on Henry Moeser's invention for like purposes, whereby all the names of a subscription-list for one post-office, and the address of the post-office, may be printed at one operation.

STEPHEN D. CARPENTER, Madison, Wis., May 5, 1857.—In this machine the types are set on the circumference of a wheel. By pressing down a treadle the platen is forced down, causing an impression to be made on the newspaper. On releasing the treadle, a spring forces up the platen and treadle, and the cylinder is turned the length of one tooth, bringing a new name under the platen, ready for the next impression.

JAMES LORD, Pawtucket, Mass., September 7, 1858.—The nature of this invention consists in imprinting the name and address on newspapers and envelopes, by inserting type, expressing such name and address, in boxes secured spirally on the periphery of a revolving cylinder, and causing the newspapers or envelopes to be successively pressed against the types in the boxes, by means of a platen or follower, which is made to act in concert with the cylinder.

GEORGE SCHUB, Madison, Wis., April 26, 1859.—This improvement relates to that class of machines which are intended to substitute the process of printing for that of writing the addresses on papers intended to be mailed.

R. W. DAVIS and DANIEL DAVIS, Yellow Springs, Ohio, September 6, 1859.—The improvement consists in the arrangement of wooden blocks of suitable size for a single address, with indented letters in their faces, and attached by means of small tacks, or their equivalent, to a flexible band or belt, in close compact columns—the belt passing over a triangular, stationary bed-plate, by means of a belt-pulley, and the impression given by means of a lever.

GEORGE HUTCHISON, Alleghany, Pa., September 6, 1859.—The invention consists in the combination and arrangement of a metallic belt, furnished with a series of conveyors, pulleys, press-roll, inking roller, type or address frame and hopper, the whole combined and arranged and constructed for the purpose above named.

GEORGE HENDERSON, Alleghany, Pa., September 6, 1859.—This improvement consists in an arrangement and combination of a guide-table and pulley, press-wheel, conveying pulley, and inking rollers, with a type frame and open hopper, the whole being combined and arranged for the purpose of printing addresses on newspapers and envelopes.

JAMES A. CAMPBELL, Georgetown, Canada West, January 17, 1860.—This invention consists in printing addresses on the margin of newspapers simultaneously with the printing of the newspapers, by means of cells or boxes containing the address set up in type, and conveyed to the form, or to the bed thereof, by means of an endless apron, having an automatic intermitted movement.

M. and C. PECK, New Haven, and R. W. WRIGHT, Orange, Conn., January 12, 1864.—The purpose of this invention is, printing rapidly the name and address upon each paper, or bundle, from raised type, or wooden type-blocks, arranged in single column galleys. The wooden blocks upon which the letters are cut are beveled upon one side, so that a series of them, when placed in a column galley, shall form a continuous ratchet, of which each block is a separate tooth, and which may be fed forward at regular intervals, one or more teeth at a time, as may be required.

MISCELLANEOUS.

JACOB PERKINS, Newburyport, Mass.—Copper and Steel Plate Printing-Press.

JOHN EDWARDS, New York, August 22, 1816.—Printing and forming colors on hard substances.

GEO. J. NEWBURY, New York, February 1, 1821.—Printing with metallic and colored powder.

HENRY BETTS, Norwalk, Conn., September 14, 1833.—Printing paper on both sides.

THOMAS FRENCH, Ithaca, N. Y.—Printing both sides of a continuous sheet.

RICHARD HEMMING, Boston, December 16, 1845.—A patent for a new method of retaining types in their relative positions on a cylindrical bed by means of rules, or strips of metal, or other appropriate substance, fitting into recesses made for that purpose in the body or stem of the type.

JULIUS HERRIOT, New York, August 2, 1853.—The inventor prepares a mould of plaster, containing the requisite impressions or figures, into which he casts a substance or compound of three parts of cooper's glue and two parts of molasses. This substance, when well mixed, is poured into a mould, and, when cold, taken out, and is ready for use in printing on irregular surfaces.

SNOW MAGOUN, Newton, Mass., August 23, 1853.—A machine for cutting and beveling printers' rules, in which the strip of metal from which the rule is to be cut is placed upon the bed-piece and rigidly held by a set of screws. The tool-carriage is moved forward and back across the bed-piece. The tools are depressed, as the cutting progresses, by the screws, and raised up again, when the screws are relieved from the tools by the springs attached.

E. H. SPRAGUE, Zanesville, Ohio, June 13, 1854.—The improvement consists in locking and unlocking forms in the chase, by means of tapering bars, and intermediate wedges, extending lengthwise and crosswise of the chase on the side and end, and operated by a hand lever, by which the imposer is enabled to dispense with the usual sticks and quoins.

H. J. HEWITT, Brooklyn, N. Y., October 17, 1856.—This invention consists of a cylinder and other devices, whereby the operations of printing and ruling paper may be performed at one and the same time.

HENRY LOVEJOY and ROBERT WHEELER, Brooklyn, N. Y., September 14, 1858.—This invention consists in giving to the brush of the machine for coating electrotype plates a peculiar motion, by which its operation is rendered more thorough and perfect, and in combining with the operation of the brush a windblast, for the removal from the mould of the superfluous coating material.

J. HERON FOSTER, Pittsburg, Pa., July 22, 1862.—This invention relates to that class of presses in which

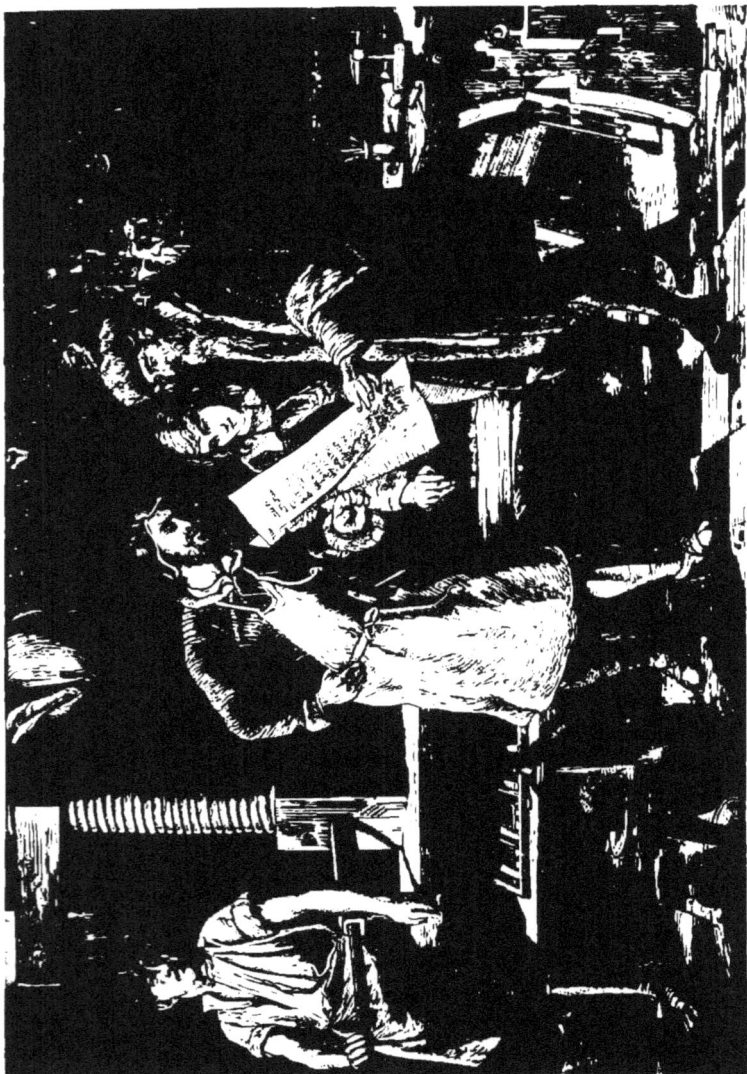

INVENTION OF PRINTING—GUTENBERG, FUST AND SCHOEFFER EXAMINING THE FIRST PROOF.

the form is locked up on a detachable or permanent segment of a continuous rotating or oscillating cylinder, called by compositors a turtle, and which constitutes the bed. The invention consists in stereotyping all but the latest news matter, while the columns in which it is desirable to make frequent changes are set up of movable type, in the form with the stereotype plate, and the paper printed therefrom, which arrangement admits of the expeditious changes necessary in a daily paper.

CHAS. N. MORRIS, Cincinnati, October 24, 1865.— This invention has for its object the production of lines of shaded metallic letters, or other characters of different sizes, from a single form of types, in such manner that each character will have the appearance of standing out in bold relief from the surface on which it is printed.

A. M. BOUTON, Newark, N. J., October 2, 1866.— This is a composition for removing ink from the type, which consists of the ammoniacal liquor distilled from bone, in the manufacture of bone-black, in combination with pearl-ash.

P. A. LA FRANCE, Elmira, N. Y., November 12, 1867.—A compositor's copyholder, in which the platform has a lateral movement on the case, and a folding presser with wire fingers to hold the copy, with a sliding indication bar, and side extensions.

MITREING MACHINES.

WM. McDONALD, New York, July 3, 1855.—In this machine the invention consists in a bed that can be raised and lowered to the required angle, and causes the rule which rests on said adjustable bed to be properly presented to the plane, so that the end of the rule may be beveled as desired.

OLIVER F. GROVER, Middletown, N. Y., and HENRY L. PELOUZE, New York, May 29, 1860.— This invention consists in the structure, arrangement, and combination of the parts of the mitreing machine, by which a machine is produced that is easy to be operated.

G. H. BABCOCK, New York, Feb. 5, 1861.—The improvement consists in the plate, constituting one arm of the vise, being made so as to have an adjustable movement on a segment placed below the emplate, that it may be fastened by a thumb-screw, so that both may be adjusted at any angle under the plate, and the rule mitred accordingly.

RICHARD WALKER, Milford, Mass., Dec. 3, 1867. —In this machine the cutters are placed opposite each other, the moving one being attached to a lever oscillated by a cam. Another cutter slides in a head, adjustable to any angle to cut the required mitre.

W. W. USTICH, La Crosse, Wis., July 21, 1868.— In this machine the cutter of the mitreing tool is formed with beveled edges having file teeth, the edges being at right angles with each other. The cutter of the grasping tool is similarly formed, except that its file edge is at an acute angle with the sides of the stock and of the cutter.

PAPER-MAKING.

LEMUEL W. WRIGHT, citizen of the United States, residing in London, Eng., March 27, 1847.—The arrangement of an apparatus by which straw and other materials, by the processes of bleaching, boiling, and bleaching, are reduced into pulp; and, also, the construction of an apparatus for converting the pulp into paper or mill-board, said apparatus consisting of a water-tight box, and of a deep frame, the movable bottom of which constitutes the paper mould.

JOHN M. HOLLINGSWORTH, Boston, April 17, 1849.—The improvement patented is a movable table, or sheet receptacle, in combination with a system of endless tapes, and their supporting rollers, applied to paper-making machinery, by which the sheets of paper are separated from the web and delivered to said system of tapes, or endless bands and rollers, and evenly packed or piled.

WM. CLARKE, Dayton, Ohio, Oct. 9, 1849.—The improvement consists in casting the bed-plates of paper engines in one piece, having the cutting or grinding edges arranged over the surface of the plate in diamond, or lozenge-shaped figures, or in curves, so as to present a number of angles or shearing edges for the rags to pass over between that surface and the roller above.

GEO. W. TURNER, London, Eng., Jan. 27, 1852.— The application to machines for making and sizing paper of the endless wire web, in combination with, and passing round the cylinder, and taking the pulp up from the vat and carrying it forward—taking the place of the fixed wire web and endless felt in the cylinder machines. Also the method of passing the paper through a trough of size between two endless felts, or other fabrics, thereby obtaining a perfect and uniform saturation of the paper, and protecting the paper from injury during the process of sizing and pressing.

JOSEPH KINGSLAND, JR., and NORMAN WHITE, Saugerties, N. Y., Aug. 10, 1852.—The invention claimed is the process of drying sized paper by passing it between a series of trunks perforated on two sides, and so arranged that the hot air, passing through these perforations, will come in contact with both sides of the paper, and then escape, and not run or be confined with the sheets.

JEAN T. COUPIER and MARIE A. C. MELLIER, of Paris, France, Aug. 2, 1853.—This improvement consists in the process of reducing straw and other similar vegetable matter into pulp for making paper. The process consists in applying and circulating the solution of the hydrate of soda or potash. Also in the circulation of hydrochlorates in the process of bleaching the straw, or similar vegetable matter, when prepared for the purpose of making paper.

JOHN HARTEN, New York, Aug. 9, 1853.—This invention consists in drying paper by conducting it between opposite series of equal-sized fans, revolving with equal velocity, causing the air to act simultaneously upon the opposite sides of the paper. The object is to give the paper a uniform and even surface.

SAMUEL G. LEVIS, Delaware Co., Pa., Feb. 14, 1854.—The nature of this invention is in an arrangement and combination of mechanism for simultaneously forming two fabrics of paper, and uniting them into one compound sheet by a continuous operation, so that these compound fabrics shall be inseparably united, while the thickness of the paper may be increased, and the strength and uniformity of the sheet preserved.

BENJ. A. LAVENDER and HENRY LOWE, Baltimore, April 4, 1854.—The improvement and claim consist in breaking down fibres of cane and other like plants, and dissolving the gummy and other foreign matter therefrom, by means of muriatic or sulphuric acid, of the strength of 10° Baumé, or thereabouts, preparatory to making paper-pulp.

CHAS. WATTS and HUGH BURGESS, London, Eng., July 18, 1854.—This is an English patent, and is restricted to the pulping and disintegrating of shavings of wood, and other similar vegetable matter, for making paper, by treating them with caustic alkali, chlorine, simple or its compounds, with oxygen and alkali.

E. and J. R. CUSHMAN, Amherst, Mass., Aug. 1, 1854.—This is a process for drying thick paper, and at the same time preventing it from warping out of shape by placing the sheets in a pulpy state upon heated tables or platforms, and allowing them to remain there until they harden to such a degree as to begin to warp out of shape, and then causing open or lattice weights to be let down upon them, and preserve them in flat positions until dry.

OBADIAH MARLAND, London, Eng., Dec. 5, 1854. —This is an English improvement in paper-making machines, and consists in vibrating the revolving cylinder-mould while immersed in the pulp, by which motion the fibres of the pulp, as they are successively laid on the cylinder-mould, are caused to overlie each other at angles dependent upon the relative velocities of the two motions of the cylinder, viz.: its vibrating and its revolving motion.

HORACE W. PEASLEE, Malden Bridge, N. Y., Jan. 23, 1855.—The invention consists in an improvement in machines for washing paper stock by the use of oblique curves in continuous succession round the open discharge end of a revolving screw cylinder, and forming channels between them to conduct the stocks continuously, as the cylinder rotates beyond the discharge end of the cylinder, when combined to operate together with elevating hooks within the cylinder, and serving to retain a copious supply of water in the cylinder for the proper washing of the stock, and to check the run of the stock through the cylinder to a speed in accordance with the conveying action of the cylinder, or its conveying hooks, to insure the regular and full action of the hooks on the stock.

OBADIAH MARLAND, Boston, Mass, Feb. 27, 1855. —The object of this improvement in rolls and driers is to produce a surface without blemish, the deposited metal being peculiarly adapted to give a superior finish to the surface of the paper, and to produce such roll or drier at a cost greatly less than that of the copper or composition rolls, and consists in a metallic foundation of the requisite thickness being made use of for the body of the roll, upon which a surface of copper or other suitable metal is deposited by galvanic or electric action.

MILTON D. WHIPPLE, Charlestown, Mass, May 29, 1855.—The invention consists in the process of preparing paper pulp from wood, by first grinding the block upon the surface of a revolving stone; and of maintaining the block in such position with respect to the stone, that the fibres of the wood shall lie in the direction of motion of the stone; also rotating the block during the process of grinding.

LOUIS ROCH, New York, Aug. 7, 1855.—This invention consists in the combination of a series of rollers, increasing gradually in diameter and speed, in proportion as the wood or fibrous substance is extended or pressed out—the face or circumference of one of every pair of the extending rollers having a greater speed than the face of its corresponding roller, by which the fibre is separated without destroying the same. This invention is for making pulp from wood and fibrous vegetable substances.

HARRISON LORING, Boston, Mass., June 5, 1855.— The object of this improvement in the apparatus for bleaching rags is the admission of steam to all parts of the revolving bleach at the same moment, by means of perforated pipe attached to the interior of the bleach—the rags are prevented from being forced into one end of the bleach, and thus the bleaching liquor is allowed to perform its functions more thoroughly.

HENRY GLYNN, Baltimore, Md., February 6, 1855. —The inventor introduces into 250 pounds of pulp, nine pounds of hydrated soap, either potash or soda, previously dissolved in boiling water; and when the soap is thoroughly incorporated with the pulp, he adds a mineral or metallic salt in such quantities as to render the introduced soap insoluble. The object is to prevent forgery, mildew, and the action of insects, rats, and vermin.

CHARLES C. HALL, Portland, Me., February 20, 1855.—This invention is a process of preparing paper pulp, using the entire substance of the bark of resinous wood, thus retaining the resinous and gummy matter, to act as a size or stiffening for the paper.

WM. CLARKE, Dayton, Ohio, May 6, 1856.—This invention is the boiling of coal tar in with the straw, or other vegetable material, for the manufacture of paper, for the purpose of neutralizing the lime used.

EDWARD B. BINGHAM, Brooklyn, N. Y., June 30, 1857.—The improvement claimed is the employment or use of endless aprons, one or more placed within the pulp vat adjoining the cylinder of paper-making machines. Motion is given to the endless aprons on their rollers, and the aprons knit or weave the fibres of the pulp together on the cylinder, so that a more compact paper is made.

MARIE AMÉDÉE CHARLES MELLIER, Paris, France,

May 26, 1857.—The improvement consists in placing straw or other fibrous matter, after being washed in warm water, within a rotary steam boiler, together with a solution of caustic alkali, and the material is boiled by steam introduced by means of pipes attached to the boiler. The invention claimed is the use of a solution of caustic alkali in a compartment of a rotary vessel separate from that which contains the steam heat.

COLUMBUS F. STURGIS, Dallas County, Ala., March 31, 1857.—This improvement is the process of manufacturing paper pulp from the bark of the root and the bark of the stalk of the cotton plant.

JULIUS A. ROTH, Philadelphia, Pa., July 28, 1857.—This invention consists in treating the fibres of wood with a sulphurous acid bath, either in liquid or gaseous form, preparatory to the application of the chlorine solution for bleaching the same, for the purpose of destroying the injurious effects of the relation of the chlorine bleaching agents to the nitrogen contained in the wood, by which the fibres are prevented from bleaching a pure white.

AZEL S. LYMAN, N. Y., August 3, 1858.—The improvement consists in the mode of separating the fibres of wood, flax, or other fibrous substances for paper, by charging the mass with hot water, steam, compressed air, or other elastic fluid, while in a cylinder, or other suitable receptacle, and then causing it to be projected from said receptacle into the atmosphere, or any space where it is subjected to a sufficiently less pressure to cause its disruption by the sudden expansion of the fluid within it.

STEPHEN ROSSMAN, N. Y., January 5, 1858.—The nature of this invention is in lifting the web of paper from the upper press roll by means of a lifting roll.

HENRY LOWE, Baltimore, Md., May 25, 1858.—The nature of this invention consists in the process of making paper pulp from reeds by disintegrating the reeds by boiling in a solution of potass, accompanied by agitation, and then reducing them directly to pulp without reducing to half-stuff by the machine called the rag engine.

CHARLES MARZONI, N. Y., December 21, 1858.—This invention consists in the abrasion or tearing of the woody fibre from the surface of wood, in combination with the use of steam and hot water during the process of converting the wood into minute particles adapted to its direct transformation into a suitable pulp for the manufacture of paper.

JOSEPH JORDAN, Hartford, Conn., May 18, 1858.—This is a machine constructed of a single conical grinder and outer shell, with pipes for the introduction of rags and size, and the reduction of both arranged with reference to the axis and ends of the grinder, so as to enable the grinder to operate to reduce the rags to pulp, and mix the sizing therewith.

THOMAS G. CHASE, Philadelphia, Pa., November 9, 1858.—The nature of this invention consists in the application of paraffine and naphtha to paper, by which it is rendered proof against the corrosive action of caustic alkali.

JAMES BROWN, London, England, May 10, 1859.—This invention consists in incorporating glycerine with pulps from which paper is to be made, or with paper at any stage of its manufacture, or in coating paper, after its manufacture, with glycerine.

EDWARD L. PERKINS, Roxbury, Mass., June 7, 1859.—This invention consists in feeding the paper from a roll outside of the drying chamber, to a series of rollers, and then conducting it over said rollers vertically, through the apparatus, and subjecting it, during its passage, to a gentle current of heated air.

SAMUEL S. CROKER and GEORGE E. MARSHALL, Lawrence, Mass., June 14, 1859.—The nature of this invention consists in the combination of internally heated drying cylinders, with a steam box, or boxes, arranged for the purpose of continuously first thoroughly drying paper, and then superficially moistening it, by the direct application of steam prior to calendering it.

JOHN MAYRHOFER, N. Y., November 1, 1859.—This improvement consists in making paper impervious to water, by mixing the alkaline solution of rosin with the pulp, and then adding what is known as English sulphuric acid, and after the sheets have been formed, drying them by contact with heated metallic surfaces.

J. B. PALSER and G. HOWLAND, Fort Edward, N. Y., November 22, 1859.—This improvement consists in boiling the straw or other stock for about four hours, under a pressure of from 110 to 120 pounds in a solution of caustic alkali, of a strength indicating from 3½° to 3½° Beaumé.

JOSEPH STORM, Woonsocket, R. I., Feb. 14, 1860.—This invention relates to improvements in that class of rag engines in which a rotary drum is employed to keep up a constant supply of rags to a revolving cutter cylinder operating against stationary knives, and consists in the employment of a conductor attached to the stationary knives, for the purpose of regulating the supply of rags to the cutters.

JOHN LOUIS JULLIM, Aberdeen, Scotland, May 8, 1860.—This improvement consists in the use of chloride or oxy-chloride of zinc, with glutinous matter, as a size for paper, and the use of compounds prepared by precipitation from watery or other solution of earths and acids, mixed with the sizing agent, to facilitate the absorption of writing and printing ink.

EBENEZER CLEMO, Toronto, Canada, July 10, 1860.—This invention consists in the employment of nitric acid, or the aqua fortis of commerce, in the conversion of straw and grasses into pulp for the manufacture of paper; it also consists in the use, in connection with nitric acid or aqua fortis, of a subsequent treatment with a solution of a hydrate or carbonate of an alkali for the purpose of reducing the stock to a fine fibrous pulp without subjecting it to beating or other mechanical operation.

F. DE CAMPOLORO, France, Aug. 7, 1860.—The

nature of this invention is the employment of the cobs of Indian corn, either alone or with the husks, for the purpose of producing paper pulp.

J. E. MALLOY, March 26, 1861.—The improvement consists in the process of separating fibre from fibre-yielding plants, consisting of the separate and successive steps of combining, rubbing, and washing the plants in cold water; the whole forming one continuous operation, performed while the plant is fresh and undesiccated.

A. RANDEL, New York, April 30, 1861.—The object of this invention is to separate the hard, worthless portion from the useful fibrous part of the vegetable material used for paper stock, before it is submitted to the bleaching process, by the combination of the differentially moving crushing cylinder and spiked concave.

JOHN HOYT, Cleveland, Ohio, July 23, 1861.—The invention consists of a method of drying sized paper by passing it over steam-heated cylinders provided with non-metallic guards to prevent the paper from coming in contact with the heated surface of the cylinder. The paper also passes over non-metallic rollers between heaters made to conform to the framework of the machine.

BENJAMIN LAMBERT, Surry County, England, July 23, 1861.—By this process the printed paper in its ordinary state is boiled in a closed vessel containing a weak solution of caustic alkali and then cooled. The lye or alkaline liquor is then removed from the paper, and a fresh supply of such liquor is substituted, and the whole boiled again. The boiled paper is then well beaten in the lye, to convert it into pulp. The lye is subsequently drawn from the pulp, and the latter thoroughly washed with water.

HENRY LOWE, Baltimore, Md., Aug. 20, 1861.—This invention consists in reducing the fibrous matter of many different paper-making materials having a very short fibre to a much greater subdivision than has heretofore been done for the manufacture of paper.

JAMES HARPER, East Haven, Conn., March 11, 1862.—This invention relates to improvements in the Fourdrinier machine, the improvements being intended to obviate a difficulty in couching from a wire cloth, by direct contact with an endless felt.

N. W. TAYLOR and J. W. BRIGHTMAN, Cleveland, Ohio, April 29, 1862.—This improvement consists of an apparatus by means of which sized or wet paper is first subjected to a moist heated atmosphere, and then conveyed gradually into an atmosphere of increased heat and dryness until it passes out of the dryer.

JOHN F. SCHUYLER, Philadelphia, Jan. 24, 1863.—The improvement consists in two rollers suitably journaled in standards, the lower one having a smooth surface, and heated by steam, the upper one having a slightly ribbed surface made by draw-filing longitudinally.

STEPHEN M. ALLEN, Woburn, Mass., March 31, 1863.—By this process wood is cut and sawed in

suitable lengths, and crushed longitudinally to preserve the fibres; it is then steeped and washed alternately in water of different temperatures. The mass is then boiled, bleached, and ground, and is then ready to be manufactured into paper.

HENRY PEMBERTON, East Tennessee, March 31, 1863.—This invention consists in washing the crushed stalks of sorghum to remove the saccharine and soluble matter, and then boiling in a solution of caustic alkali to extract the silicia, oily and coloring matter, and to open the fibre, and the stalks are again washed. They are next steeped in acidulated liquor, washed, and steeped in a solution of chloride of lime, washed, acidulated, and again washed. These operations reduce the stalks to a homogeneous white pulp, to be worked up by the ordinary mechanical means.

DR. ALOYSE CHEVALIER AUER DE WEBSBACH, Vienna, Austria, April 21, 1863.—The invention consists in boiling the husks or leaves of maize in a solution of lime or soda till the fibre is detached from the soluble matter, and precipitated; the fibre is then dried and carded, to be used for making paper. The soluble portion may be utilized for food.

JOHN F. JONES, Rochester, N. Y., May 26, 1863.—The object of this invention is to remove the water from the interior of cylinder moulds, so as to cause the pulp to adhere to the surface of the cylinder, and this is accomplished by introducing a pipe through the axis of the journal which draws off the water.

G. E. RUTLEDGE, Dayton, Ohio, May 26, 1863.—The improvement consists in causing the pulp in which the sieve cylinder rotates to move in a current in the same direction with the motion of the cylinder, to obviate the tendency of the fibres to be laid parallel by the dragging of the periphery of the cylinder through the pulp.

JONATHAN FAW, Lockland, Ohio, June 2, 1863.—The invention consists in providing deflectors, which are placed inside the cap of a rag engine, and which, in combination with the cap, deflect the stock in the engine, in the process of grinding, from the inside of a short circumference to the outside of a long circumference, and the object is to secure uniformity in the length of the staple which forms the pulp.

MORRIS L. KEEN, Royer's Ford, Montgomery Co., Pa., June 16, 1863.—The invention consists in connecting the main feed-hole in the shell of the boiler with the main feed-hole through the diaphragm by a perforated well or cylinder, so that the material can be charged through the well into the boiler without falling upon or clogging the perforated diaphragm; also in the valve and discharge-hole, through which the pulp is discharged under pressure.

J. L. SEAVERNS, Worcester, August 11, 1863.—This is an improvement in the arrangement of the bearing rolls which support the wire apron in the vacuum box under atmospheric pressure. The rollers rotate in checks which are inside of their bearings, and which are flush with the upper sides of the rollers, so that the wire apron makes a tight joint to preserve a vacuum beneath. The spaces between the cheeks and the sides of the box are filled with water, to preserve the packing and prevent leakage of air.

GEORGE ESCOL SELLERS, Hardin Co., Ill., October 6, 1853.—The essential feature of this invention is crushing the wooden fibre by pressure vertical to the line of the fibre; this is done by pressure on the end of a block, and then removing the disintegrated fibre, or by working on the thin laminæ of wood which have been removed from the block by a cut perpendicular to the line of the fibre.

AUGUSTUS H. TAIT, Jersey City, N. J., November 24, 1863.—By this improvement the straw is cut into lengths of three-quarters of an inch; it is then ground between burr stones, to divide the fibres, and separate in the form of dust the silicious and similar particles, which are removed by screening; it is then boiled, and the colored water run off; treated to a boiling solution of caustic alkali, and washed; treated to a boiling acidulous solution, and washed; then to a solution of chloride of lime; then again to the alkaline and acidulous solutions, and bleached.

GEO. ESCOL SELLERS, Sellers' Landing, Ill., January 5, 1864.—This invention consists in loosening incrusting or adhering non-fibrous matter by fermentation, and then washing the same from the fibre, leaving it in a condition to be bleached with a less amount of chlorine than would have been required without the fermentation and washing process.

A. K. EATON, New York, March 22, 1864.—This invention consists in subjecting straw to a grinding process soon after the hot alkaline solution has begun to act upon it, the grinding being continued in connection with the alkaline treatment. In order to recover the alkali of the waste liquor, it is passed through a filter of lime or charcoal a sufficient number of times; the liquor is then evaporated, and the residuum formed into cakes and burned, when a carbonated alkali will be formed, which may then be rendered caustic in the usual manner.

LUCIEN BARDOUX, Poitiers, France, April 5, 1864.—This invention consists in boiling, pounding, and washing the material of which paper is to be made, then treating it with sulphuric acid and bleaching liquor successively, until a fine fibre is obtained. The substances designated to be treated in this way, are potatoes, beans, peas, turnips, cabbages, bran, broom grass, ferns, and the stems and leaves of most trees.

GEO. A. CORSER, Leicester, Mass., June 7, 1864.—This invention consists of an angular bed-plate for working paper stock, composed of two or more sets of angular plates, arranged in such manner that the angles of the adjoining sets are inverted in relation to each other.

THEODORE BAKER, Stillwater, N. Y., June 28, 1864.—This invention consists in the employment of two adjustable cams, which are attached to the tops of posts on opposite sides of the frames (of paper-making machines) and having their edges rounded upward to facilitate the passage of the felt beneath them. The guide-roll is journaled in universal journal boxes, pivoted on and supported by arms at each side, so that, as the felt-cloth moves over the rolls, the cams are adjusted to felts of different widths, by bringing up the narrow or wide part of the cam to the edge of the felt, thus forming a self-acting guide.

HARRISON D. MUCH, Fort Edward, N. Y., September 13, 1864.—This invention consists in using a stationary boiler, with high temperature, sixty pounds to the square inch, with a soapy or alkaline liquor. The advantages over the same treatment in the rotary boiler, are that the fibres are thoroughly disintegrated without being ground and wasted in fine powder by the operation of boiling.

EUNICE N. FOOTE, Saratoga Springs, N. Y., Nov. 22, 1864.—The main object of this invention is to avoid the liability of fibres to become laid upon the face of the cylinder in directions parallel with each other. This is accomplished by giving the pulp, on its approach to the cylinder, the motion of the cylinder, by means of an endless band of slats acting in combination with the cylinder.

JOHN W. DIXON, Philadelphia, December 6, 1864.—This invention consists in heating wood with a strong solution of caustic alkali, and then using the residual liquor for treating straw for the manufacture of paper pulp; and using the residual liquor of the last operation for the manufacture of an inferior article of paper from straw.

REBECCA SHERWOOD, Fort Edward, N. Y., December 13, 1864.—This invention consists in adding grease or saponifiable fats to the alkaline liquor in which straw is treated for the manufacture of paper pulp. A part of the wash liquor of one boiling is treated with lime or other purifying agent, and added to the liquor for the next boiling.

JOHN W. DIXON, Philadelphia, December 20, 1864.—This invention consists in heating wood with caustic soda, of a strength of 18° Baumé, at from 212° to 290° Fahr. The liquor is then drawn off, and the pulp submitted to the action of chlorine, and the waste liquor, with the addition of a reduced percentage of caustic soda, is used for a fresh supply of wood.

HARRISON B. MUCH, December 20, 1864.—This invention consists in soaking the saw-dust in a solution of alkali and grease, after which it is boiled in a similar solution for a sufficient length of time. The surplus liquor is then discharged, and used to soak a new batch of saw-dust, and the boiled saw-dust, after being washed with clean water, is subjected to pressure, in order to dry it, when it is ready for the beating engines.

WILLIAM DELTON, New York, January 3, 1865.—This invention consists of a tank, in which there is a partition, provided with a gate. In the smaller portion of the tank is a series of perforated steam pipes, which radiate from a central pipe. In this portion of the tank the caustic alkali is prepared by means of lime, steam being admitted through the perforated pipes, in order to heat and agitate it, after which it is allowed to flow into the larger portion by raising the gate. From this tank the alkaline solution is conveyed to another tank, to operate on the fibrous material. This tank is made with a perforated bottom, beneath which are steam pipes, by means of which the contents of this vat may be heated.

HARRISON B. BEECH, Fort Edward, N. Y., January 10, 1865.—This invention consists in an improved arrangement of the pipes for introducing and withdrawing liquids from the boiler, and in an arrangement of the steam pipes, so that they will not be clogged up with the pulp.

JOS. G. FULLER, Brooklyn, N. Y., March 21, 1865. —This invention consists of a revolving wheel, composed of ranges of teeth, alternating with a rough or abraded surface, that draw the fibre from a hopper, tear up and rub the same, and also bring the fibre down into a washing vat, in which is a concave range of teeth that act to tear apart any fibres that are sufficiently long to reach from the stationary concave range of teeth to the revolving teeth.

SAMUEL DENHER and HALLEM H. SPENCER, Philadelphia, March 21, 1865.—An apparatus for washing paper stuff, which consists of the stuff tub, containing the agitators, and provided with an opening, through which the stuff flows. Beneath this opening is an endless band of wire gauge, moving over the drums; directly above this endless band is placed a tank, provided with roses, by means of which the stuff on the band is washed. The waste water passes through the sieves into the tank, and the stuff passes on and falls into the box.

JOHN F. JONES, Rochester, N. Y., April 25, 1865. —The object of this invention is to retain the water between the grinding surface, and thus keep the pulp from clogging. The bottom of the case is lightly inclined toward its outlet, the better to allow of the discharge of the pulp.

JAMES SCANLON, Lebanon, Pa., June 20, 1865.— In this invention a roller prevents the water issuing from the perforated pipe, and from running back upon the pulp; and the third felt operating in conjunction with the first one, the pulp passing between them, supersedes the ordinary roll-cloth; and being constantly washed clean, and the water pressed out of it in its circuit, allows the water from the pulp to pass upwards through it. A third polishing roller smooths that side of the paper which has been in contact with the first felt.

HENRY BETTS, Norwalk, Conn., August 1, 1865.— This invention consists in the manufacture of paper stock from the stalks and root of the plant known as sedge. The stalks are cut while green, and allowed to remain exposed to the air as long as possible without injury to the fibre. They are then cut in a straw cutter, and thoroughly washed in water, and then boiled in a solution of caustic soda; the roots are washed and converted into pulps in the same manner as the stalks.

JULIUS A. ROTH, Philadelphia, Pa., August 15, 1865.—This invention consists in treating fibrous materials, such as wood, hemp, manilla grass, and other similar fibres, after the same have been reduced

to small particles, with chlorine gas in a dry state and under continuous agitation.

M. A. CUSHING, Providence, R. I., October 10, 1865.—This invention consists of a liquor for treating flax, hemp, etc., prepared by mixing soda ash, borax, unslaked lime, and petroleum with boiling water. The mixture is allowed to boil for about fifteen minutes, and then cooled, after which the clear liquor is drawn off for use.

JOHN W. DIXON, Philadelphia, Pa., December 12, 1865.—This invention consists of a digester provided with a man-hole, and a perforated diaphragm near the top and another near the bottom. Below this diaphragm at the bottom is a coil of pipe which communicates with a steam boiler. The upper and lower parts of the digester communicate by means of tubes with a rotary pump, by which the water in the digester is caused to circulate from the bottom to the top of the digester. A pipe from the lower part of the digester passes through a tank in the form of a coil, and the tank communicates with the pipe, connecting the upper and lower parts of the digester by means of a tube.

JOHN W. DIXON, Philadelphia, Pa., December 12, 1865.—This invention consists in subjecting cornstalks to the action of a current of highly heated water in a close vessel, the waste water and the gummy matters being passed through a coil situated within a tank in such manner that the water contained in said tank will be heated by the refuse materials preparatory to being used in the digester for treating fresh material.

JOHN W. DIXON, Philadelphia, Pa., December 12, 1865.—This invention consists in subjecting the raw material of paper pulp to the action of a current of hot water under pressure, the refuse gummy matters and water being passed through fresh water in such a manner that it will be heated preparatory to further treatment.

JOHN W. DIXON, Philadelphia, Pa., December 19, 1865.—This invention consists in treating wood, straw, etc., with a solution of carbonate of soda in a digester, under pressure; the digester being so arranged that the current of a hot solution may circulate through the material contained in the digester, and the waste solution being passed through the coils contained in tanks in order to heat a fresh supply of the solution.

JOHN W. DIXON, Philadelphia, Pa., December 19, 1865.—This invention consists in bleaching pulp by subjecting it to the successive action of weak acid, or hyperchloride of lime, at a high heat, under pressure, the pulp being contained in a digester through which the fluid may be made to circulate.

JOHN W. DIXON, Philadelphia, Pa., December 19, 1865.—This invention consists in treating the fibre in hot solution of chloride of lime under pressure in a digester, so arranged that a current of the solution will constantly circulate through the material contained therein.

JOHN W. DIXON, Philadelphia, Pa., December 19,

1865.—This invention consists of a digester provided with, perforated diaphragms and communicating at top and bottom with a coil. The water is made to circulate through the digester and coil by means of a pump. A coil within a tank communicates with the digester, in such manner that the waste gummy matters and water may pass through the coil, and heat the fresh water contained in the tank.

JOHN W. DIXON, Philadelphia, Pa., December 19, 1865.—This invention consists in treating vegetable fibre with a solution of caustic lime in a digester so arranged that a current of the hot solution will constantly pass through the material contained therein, and the waste solution be used for heating a fresh supply of the solution.

JOHN W. DIXON, Philadelphia, Pa., December 26, 1865.—This invention consists in subjecting the fibre to the action of a current of highly heated water under a pressure of from 150 to 200 lbs., in a revolving digester provided with perforated diaphragms, the water being forced through one trunnion out through the other, a valve being arranged to open as fresh water is supplied to the digester, and allow the refuse to escape.

LORENZO C. DAVE, Lowell, Mass., January 9, 1866.—This invention consists in the employment of hard rubber rolls in pressing, sizing, and calendering paper.

JOHN W. DIXON, Philadelphia, Pa., February 10, 1866.—This invention consists in the employment of two boilers communicating with each other and the heating coil by means of pipes. The boilers are provided with perforated diaphragms, the upper one of which has an opening in it, provided with a cover. The lower diaphragm has an opening covered with a valve. The boiler being charged with the proper materials, a solution of caustic alkali is applied to it, and the liquid is caused to circulate through the boiler and heating coil, until the contents of the boiler are properly digested.

HENRY L. JONES and DUNCAN S. FARQUHARSON, Rochester, N. Y., March 14, 1866.—This invention consists of a vessel supported in bearings upon a frame and connected by a pipe with another vessel. The bleaching liquor is forced into the vessel containing the material to be bleached by a pump, or it may be allowed to flow into the vessel from an elevated tank.

H. B. MEEK, Fort Edward, N. Y., May 22, 1866.—By this process the vegetable matter is cut into pieces a few inches long, and treated in a rotary boiler with a watery solution of lime, soda ash, and common salt.

LEVI DODGE, Waterford, N. Y., July 31, 1866.—In this machine the rotary boiler in which the pulp is bleached has a smooth exterior surface in order that it may be used at the same time for drying paper which may be passed over it.

EDWARD B. BINGHAM, Newark, N. J., September 18, 1866.—This invention consists in the arrangement of two felts, and four pressure rolls, whereby the web

is pressed three times between the two felts, in combination with ducters within the felts, to remove the water from the rolls.

GEORGE W. HURLBURT, Fairhaven, Vt., October 16, 1866.—This invention consists in the use of pulverized clay, slate, or suitable stone as a material in the manufacture of paper to give it body, evenness, and finish.

HENRY and FRITZ MARK, Baltimore, Md., October 23, 1866.—In this machine several boxes are arranged around the periphery of the rough-faced revolving grindstone, and in each blocks of wood are forced edgewise against the grinding surface, by followers actuated by gearing and weights, while a stream of clear water is poured upon the surface. The pulpy result is assorted by a series of sieves and discharged into different receptacles, according to quality.

S. G. and G. S. ROGERS, Thetford, Vt., November 13, 1866.—The object of this device is to prevent the adhesion of the paper to the upper delivery roller, and its consequent liability to wind thereon, as discharged from the endless blanket.

JOSEPH E. HOOVER, Philadelphia, April 16, 1867.—The invention consists in coating paper to be used for printing with a size composed of starch 4 parts, water 240 parts, and lime 12 parts.

C. A. ROSE, Columbus, Ga., May 7, 1867.—This invention consists in the combination of pine leaves and cotton stalks, either with or without oak leaves and pine cones, as a material for making paper pulp.

JEAN B. BIRON, Carpentras, France, August 20, 1867.—By this process the wood is divided into cubes of two or more inches, and macerated in lime water until sufficiently saturated to sink. It is then crushed beneath a rolling stone, revolving in a trough containing lime water, then drained and washed. It is then treated in a vat with a solution of sulphuret of potassium, or penta-sulphuret of lime. After thorough impregnation, a solution of hydrochlorate of alumina is added. The acid combines with the alkaline base, and frees the sulphur to combine with the hydrogen of the coloring matter in the wood, and passes off in the form of sulphuretted hydrogen.

BENJ. C. TILGHMAN, Philadelphia, November 5, 1867.—This invention consists in the process of treating vegetable substances which contain fibres, with a solution of sulphurous acid in water, either with or without the addition of sulphites, or other salts of equivalent chemical properties, heated in a close vessel under pressure, to a temperature sufficient to cause it to dissolve the intercellular incrusting or cementing constituents of the vegetable substances, so as to leave the undissolved product in a fibrous state, suitable for the manufacture of paper pulp.

S. T. MERRILL, Beloit, Wis., November 12, 1867.—This invention consists in the introduction into a close-covered rag engine, or other close vessel, provided with an agitator, of chlorine gas, or the disengaging of the latter from a chlorine solution contained within the box of the engine, for the purpose of bleaching paper stock.

EDWIN WILMONT, Laona, N. Y., November 19, 1867.—By this machine the pulp is brought up from the vat by an endless gauge apron, and compressed with rubber rollers, and then taken from the apron to pass between other rollers to the drying cylinder.

JOSEPH A. VEAZIE, February 11, 1868.—This invention is designed to remove ink and colors from printed paper. To twelve pounds potash, in a boiling solution, are added fourteen pounds of tallow. After boiling three hours, add twenty-five gallons of water. The paper is boiled in this solution. The ink rises to the top and is allowed to flow off. The dirty water is then drawn off from the bottom, and fresh water is let in to wash the material.

ISAAC JENNINGS, Fairfield, Conn., July 7, 1868.—The object of this invention is to diminish the size of the roller after the paper has been formed in any convenient manner, so as to admit of the paper being removed without cutting.

E. T. FORD, November 3, 1863.—In this machine the wire cloth passes over and is supported by a perforated cylinder rotated in a box which is open at the top and provided with packing plates, the open edges of which hold rubber packing strips that support the wire cloth. The cylinder is provided with plungers which extract the water from the pulp, as the wire cloth progresses, and with concavo plungers between the cylinders and the box for preventing the passage of air or water.

JAMES VIXEY, Manchester, N. H., November 17, 1868.—In this machine a vacuum or partial vacuum, produced in the boxes, over which the apron bearing the paper pulp passes, extracts the water or moisture from the pulp. These vacuum boxes can be adjusted to the width of the paper to be made.

PHOTOGALVANOGRAPHIC PROCESS.

PAUL PRETSCH, Austria, August 25, 1857.—The following is the process patented: The solutions of nitrate of silver and iodide of potassium are mixed with a solution of clear glue in water. These are poured on a suitable plate so as to form a coating thereon when dry. A photographic impression is made on this coating in the usual manner, and when the original is removed from the coating, the photographic picture will be found to appear in relief, and, when sufficiently developed, must be washed with spirits of wine. The surplus moisture is then removed, and the plate is covered with a mixture of copal varnish diluted with oil of turpentine; before becoming dry, the superfluous varnish must be removed with oil of turpentine, and the plate immersed in a weak solution of tannin, from which the plate must be removed as soon as the design is sufficiently raised. The plate is then ready to be copied by the process of electrotyping.

PRINTING-PRESS.

APOLLOS KINSLEY, Connecticut, November 16, 1796.

JOHN DIXEY, New Jersey, January 24, 1798. (Printing Machine.)

JOHN B. SAWIN and THOMAS B. WAIT, Boston, Mass., February 1, 1810. (Circular Press.)

JOHN B. SAWIN and THOMAS B. WAIT, Roxbury, Mass., January 28, 1811. (Cylindrical Press.)

WILLIAM ELLIOTT, New York, February 17, 1813.

ZACH. MILLS, Hartford, Conn., February 20, 1813.

DAVID PIERSON, Newburyport, Mass., July 16, 1813.

OTIS TUFTS, Boston, Massachusetts, November 7, 1813. (Hand-Press Straightening the Toggle Joint.)

ADAM RAMAGE, Philadelphia, Pa., May 28, 1818.

JOHN J. WELLS, Hartford, Conn., February 8, 1819.

ABRAHAM O. STANSBURY, New York, April 7, 1821.

SAMUEL RUST, New York, May 13, 1821.

PETER SMITH, New York, April 6, 1822.

ADAM RAMAGE, Philadelphia, Pa., May 19, 1823. (Proof-Press.)

DANIEL NEALE, Philadelphia, Pa., November 15, 1825.

DANIEL TREADWELL, Boston, March 2, 1826. (Power-Press.)

DAVID PHELPS, Boston, September 15, 1826.

SAMUEL FAIRLAMB, New York, November 4, 1826.

SAMUEL COUILLARD, JR., Boston, July 14, 1827, and October 5, 1829.

J. C. HOLBROOK and E. H. THOMAS, Brattleboro, Vt., February 7, 1828.

CHARLES W. WILLIAMS, New York, May 29, 1829. (Cylindrical Press.)

SAMUEL RUST, New York, April 17, 1829. (Washington Press.)

JOHN J. WELLS, Hartford, Conn., June 29, 1829.

JONAS BOOTH, SR., JAMES BOOTH, THOMAS BOOTH, and JONAS BOOTH, JR., New York, September 1, 1829.

ISAAC ADAMS, Boston, October 4, 1830. (Power-Press.)

OTIS TUFTS, Boston, Mass., July 30, 1831.

ANSON SHERMAN, New York, February 26, 1831.

LUKE HALE, Hollis, New Hampshire, December 12, 1831.

SETH ADAMS, Boston, May 23, 1832. (Faustus Press.)

SERENO NEWTON, New York, February 26, 1833. (Double Napier Press.)

DANIEL NEALE, Philadelphia, Pa., February 13, 1834.

CHARLES F. VOORHEES, Newark, N. J., April 8, 1834. (Printing Machine.)

WILLIAM R. COLLIER, Washington, D. C., April 11, 1834.

OTIS TUFTS, Boston, August 22, 1834.

ADAM RAMAGE, Philadelphia, Pa., November 19, 1834.

J. LEMUEL KINGSLEY, New York, April 22, 1835.

SAMUEL KINGSLEY, New York, March 2, 1836.

ISAAC ADAMS, Boston, March 2, 1836. (Power-Press.)

HEZEKIAH CAMP, Trenton, Ohio, March 4, 1836.

F. J. AUSTIN, New York, October 8, 1836.

RICHARD WOOD, New York, November 4, 1836.

WM. and THOMAS SCHUERLY, Hagerstown, Md., September 7, 1839.

J. LEMUEL KINGSLEY, New York, October 31, 1839.

CHARLES J. CARR and ANDREW SMITH, England, Sept. 10, 1840.—An improvement in printing-machines by which the impression is obtained by locomotive cylinders passing over the type—securing register and regulating the supply of ink.

S. P. RUGGLES, Boston, Nov. 10, 1840.—The distinguishing feature of this patent is in arranging the form with the face of the type downward instead of the usual mode.

WILLIAM W. SMITH, New York, Feb. 1, 1842.—A patent for a particular mode by which the combined operation of the inking apparatus and that for taking the impression is effected upon presses used for printing cards and labels.

R. M. HOE, New York, May 20, 1842.—An improvement in the double-cylinder press, combining the most valuable properties of the Applegarth and Napier presses, patented in England.

JOEL G. NORTHROP, Cortlandtville, N. Y., Sept. 30, 1842.—An improvement combining with the press two or more forms of type placed on beds, and carrying them around, so as to bring them under the platen of a platen press, or the cylinder of a cylinder press.

R. M. HOE, New York, April 17, 1844.—A patent for an adjustable bearer, to be placed on each side of the bed of a cylinder press in combination with the enlargement of the cylinder.

R. M. HOE, New York, July 30, 1844.—A rotary combined cylinder press, denominated the Planetarium Printing-Press. The distinguishing feature is its being provided with any number of cylinders, from two to eight, or more, each of which receives a sheet, which is carried to the form to receive an impression.

ALONZO GILMAN, Troy, N. Y., Aug. 30, 1844.—A patent for an improvement in printing-presses by hanging the inking apparatus in a working frame provided for it, so that it may be easily adjusted in passing to the curve of the cylinder and the face of the type.

SETH ADAMS, Boston, Sept. 27, 1844.—A patent for an improvement in the hand-printing press, by which the bed, platen, and frisket frame and inking apparatus are so arranged, with respect to each other, as to be operated together.

JOHN L. KINGSLEY, New York, Jan. 4, 1845.—A patent for improvements in the bed and platen press, called Kingsley's Perfecting Press. The improvements claimed consist in the arrangement of the grippers, combined with the carrying belts, by which the paper is carried, held, and retained until it is perfected, by being printed on both sides and then deposited. These operations are effected by so combining the sheet apparatus with the inking rollers as to give to the carrying belts and grippers an intermitting progressive movement.

JOHN C. KNEELAND, Troy, N. Y., February 20, 1845.—This is a patent for an improvement in the printing-press, by an arrangement of the apparatus for governing the motion of the sheet on which an impression is to be made. This consists in arranging the machinery for gripping the sheet, which is placed on the feeding board, and for carrying it into the proper position for, and holding it whilst it is receiving the impression.

JOSEPH SAXTON, Washington, D. C., March 21, 1845.—This is a patent for the use and application of a flexible or elastic platen, and the application of pressure thereto, by means of a liquid or aeriform fluid, in printing-presses, copying-presses, lithographic presses, and zincographic presses, and the arrangement of machinery for the purpose of applying such pressure. The advantage claimed, is that the platen is equally acted upon over its whole surface, and may, therefore, be used in any position, to press upwards, downwards, or sideways. The platen is constructed of a thin plate of brass or other metal, varying in thickness from that of ordinary cap paper, to one-half inch, according to the dimensions of the platen, and of the vacant spaces between the columns or pages that compose the form.

JOEL G. NORTHROP, Cortlandtville, N. Y., April 26, 1845.—The improvement claimed by this patent is the manner in which the friskets and the parts by which they are made to traverse through the machine are combined, constructed, and arranged; and also the arrangement of the parts of the press by which the power is applied to the platen by a revolving shaft, which is made to operate intermittingly, and to carry arms which bear upon the back of the platen, by which the impression is taken.

R. M. HOE, New York, May 1, 1845.—This is a patent for improvements in the ordinary cylinder press. 1st. For the manner in which the fly-sheet-frisket, for delivering the printed sheets on the table, is adapted to the cylinder press. 2d. The manner in which a simple lever and cam-plate is arranged for operating the grippers. 3d. The manner by which the cylinder is raised from the form when it is desired an impression should not be taken. 4th. The manner of arranging a series of springs for arresting the momentum of the bed of the press. Extended seven years from May 1, 1859.

A. B. TAYLOR, New York, April 4, 1846.—A patent for the method of arresting the momentum of the carriage, which carries the form of types, in printing-presses, by means of plunges that compress the air in cylinders only, toward the end of the motion of the carriage.

WM. M. MARSTON, New York, September 12, 1846.—A patent for the use of the vibrating cylinder, or cylindrical segment, with two sets of grippers; also the application of revolving cylindrical brushes, to smooth the paper on its passage from the feeding-board, and likewise aiding in its delivery on the fly-board.

R. M. HOE, New York, July 10, 1847.—Patent for

improvements in the printing-press. 1st. Giving to the inking roller frame its motions independent of the motions of the frisket frame. 2d. Removing the printed sheet from the frisket, by passing a portion of the frisket between the rollers that remove the sheet and deliver it to the fly frame. 3d. The arrangement of finger bars in combination with the inclined planes on which the ends of the forward bar pass, and the lever which acts as an inclined plane to open the fingers, and then rises to suffer the tension of the spring to close them. 4th. The arrangement of either of the cams that operate the inking roller frame, cogged sector, and the train of wheels, in combination with the inking roller frame, giving the intermittent reciprocating motions more efficiently than by any other means. 5th. The arrangement of the cam, the sector, and train of wheels in combination with the frisket and finger frame.

R. M. Hoe, New York, July 24, 1847.—The method of securing the form of types on a cylindrical surface, with column-rules made thicker towards their outer than their inner edge, by connecting these grooves in the bed, by which they are permitted to approach and recede from each other, and at the same time kept down by the same radius, whereby prismatic types can be secured and held on a cylindrical surface as effectually as on a flat surface.

R. M. Hoe, New York, July 24, 1847.—The method of ending and commencing the alternating motions of rectilinear reciprocating movements, by means of two racks and cog wheel in combination with the vibrating levers; and the method of elevating and depressing the passing cylinder by means of the threaded sliding rods that carry the cylinder, in combination with the cogged nuts and sliding bar with a rack at each end, so arranged that the tracks and cogged pinions can be thrown out of gear for the adjustment of the cylinder.

R. M. Hoe, New York, July 31, 1847.—The mechanism for communicating motion to the carriage of inking rollers, in combination with the catch link or tilting shaft, by which the parts are thrown in and out of gear, to operate and stop the inking rollers; thus the motion may be transmitted to one or to the other of the spur wheels, which may be changed to carry the inking rollers over the form of types a greater or less number of times for each impression.

Joseph M. Marsh, New York, October 3, 1848. —A method of obtaining a reciprocating motion from a continuous rotary motion by combining with a cogged rack two cogged wheels, composed each of segments of different diameters.

James L. Burdick, Norwich, N. Y., March 27, 1849.—An improvement in the cylinder press, by combining two cylinders with their respective platforms, one immediately above the other, under an arrangement by which each of the cylinders is made to take impressions from the forms on the platforms to which it appertains; the lower cylinder perfecting the sheet which has been printed on one side by the upper cylinder and forms. This is accomplished by the peculiar construction of the sliding carriages, and of combining them with the platforms, and with the forms sustained thereon; by which construction and combination the form from which the impression has been taken is made to descend and pass back under the form last elevated, and is again elevated and forced forward.

George P. Gordon, New York, March 26, 1850.— The improvements claimed under this patent are: 1st, The peculiar manner of constructing the nippers, so that their upper surface shall be even with the surface of the paper, and their inclined or curved surface shall incline away from the surface of the paper. 2d, An adjustable table, to be adjusted to the nippers, the nippers being first adjusted to the type or form. 3d, A frisket operated by the motion of the carriage. 4th, The application of the vibratory power to the handle of the distributing roller. 5th, The combination and arrangement for opening the nippers when the carriage moves out with the printed sheet, and closing them just previous to its going in.

Isaac Adams, Boston, Mass., March 26, 1850.— An improvement in the apparatus for receiving and transferring to a pile sheets of paper from a printing-press and paper-machine—a cylinder in combination with roller and bands for receiving the printed sheets from the press upon a curved cylindrical surface, and by means of this curved or cylindrical surface transferring them, with their printed sides upwards, to the pile or table provided to receive them.

Charles W. Hanks, Boston, Mass., June 4, 1850. —An improvement on the toggle lever working on the stationary cam to raise the platen.

Bartholomew Beniowski, London, Eng., October 29, 1850.—A printing-machine in which the form of types or blocks is placed on the inner or concave surface of the cylinder or drum, which is made to revolve or carry the form or forms secured thereto, from the inking rollers to the printing or impression cylinders, all of which parts are mounted inside the cylinder or drum.

Stephen P. Ruggles, Boston, Mass., January 1, 1851.—The improvements claimed are: 1st. The gauge bar for cards, in combination with the vibratory platen and stop fingers, and crank which operates the same. 2d. The use of a segment of a cylinder, in combination with the stationary form bed, so that the inking apparatus may move over the form and then, after taking ink from the fountain, distribute it upon the said cylinder. 3d. The movable bearers on the side of the form bed, arranged so as to be moved outwards when the inking rollers are passing over the form, and drawn inwards when the sheet tympan is moved up to the form. 4th. Regulating the delivery of the ink by combining with the delivering roller a grooved ratchet wheel and weighted pawl band, operating with the lever stud, cam roller, and stop lever. 5th. Supporting the journals of one of the inking rollers on sliding bearers, so that it may be moved up against the delivering roll by means of studs on said bearers and cams.

GEO. P. GORDON, New York, August 5, 1851.—The improvements claimed, are: 1st. Giving the platen a rotary reciprocating motion, which enables it to assume two positions of receiving the sheet and the impression alternately. 2d. The affixing the vibratory bed on its own axis. 3d. The arrangement of two side-arms, so combined as to form a frame to hold and carry the inking rollers. 4th. The grooved cam-shaped arms or guides, or their equivalent, for carrying the frisket in the right direction, and holding it in the desired positions during the intervals of rest given to the platen. 5th. The combination of the bed, vibrating on its own axis, with the roller frame, composed of two arms.

JACOB WORMS, New York, September 23, 1851.—This is a French patent, obtained in France, May 19, 1849, and claims as an invention the combination with the ink troughs and printing-cylinder, the arrangement of the cam-cylinders, reciprocating cylinders, for receiving, carrying, and distributing the ink from the trough to the cylinder; also, the combination with the printing-cylinders, of cylinders provided with a sharp knife or saw, operated by a cam, for the purpose of severing the paper as it passes through the rollers.

JOHN R. HATHAWAY and JOHN P. STRIPPEL, Norfolk, Va., October 21, 1851.—The improvement claimed, is arranging upon a horizontally reciprocating carriage, a blanket frame, pressing cylinder, set of inking rollers, and sheet-flyer, in such a manner that the two ends of the pressing cylinder shall roll upon the side rails, thus constituting a pair of the carrying wheels of the carriage, and producing a rotary motion of the pressing cylinder as it passes over the form, whereby the requisite motion is given to the blanket.

HENRY MOESER, Pittsburg, Pa., January 20, 1852.—The invention is the tympan plate of a hand press, removable by hinges, and counterbalanced.

GEO. P. GORDON, New York, August 31, 1852.—The patent is for improvements in the printing-press, and claims as inventions: 1st. The arrangement and application of a cylinder which always remains stationary in its own position, as well while receiving the form, as when used as a distributing surface. 2d. The combination and arrangement of several sets of rollers in one frame, to traverse round the periphery of a cylinder, when these sets of rollers alternately, or consecutively, pass over the form, and admit an impression to be taken, between the time one of the sets leaves the form and the next set arrives to it. 3d. An improvement in the machinery for feeding a continuous sheet of paper, by the arrangement of the gauge, guides, pawl, cranks, and rod, pin and wheels in combination with the shears for cutting off the sheet after it is printed, and the cam from which it receives its motion.

CHAS. FOSTER, Cincinnati, October 5, 1852.—The improvement claimed, is the arrangement, in a hand-power-press, of guide-bars, resting upon adjusting points, or hinged at their rear ends, and guided at their front ends to a vertical vibration, concentric with said bar or hinge, so that the entire bed, guide-bars, and their appendages, shall move bodily upwards when giving the impression, and return by their own weight to a state of rest.

JOHN G. NICOLAY, Pittsfield, Ill., October 5, 1852.—The invention claimed, is the peculiar arrangement and combination of conical impressing cylinders, one or more in number, each provided with a set of conical distributing inking rollers, adapted thereto, and with a rotating wheel or disk, and the arrangement of the clamp which retains the paper at the required angle to receive the impression, and releases the same when the impression is taken.

LUCIUS T. GUERNSEY, Montpelier, Vt., October 19, 1852.—The invention secured is the combination of a reciprocating type-bed, with an impression cylinder which has the half rotary movement, and also a movement to and from the type-bed.

JOEL DINSMORE, Blooming Valley, Crawford Co., Pa., November 9, 1852.—The invention claimed, is the combination of the grippers for seizing the sheets, and holding them to the cylinder, the grippers being attached to shafts arranged longitudinally to the cylinder, and attached thereto, and being turned to give the necessary movements to the grippers, by the revolution or vibration of the cylinder, through the agency of cranks and rods, or their equivalents.

JOEL G. NORTHROP, Syracuse, N. Y., November 16, 1852.—The improvement patented, is such a combination and arrangement of a horizontal bed and cylinder, as will enable each forward movement of the bed to impart a revolution to the cylinder, for the purpose of taking or giving an impression, and permit it to remain stationary during the reverse movement of the bed. And, also, in combination with this movement of the cylinder, the inking and flying apparatus.

STEPHEN P. RUGGLES, Boston, November 16, 1852.—The improvements claimed, are: 1st. So hanging or balancing the bed which holds the form, and moves up and down for each impression, upon springs, that its own weight shall compress the springs to a great extent, and the entire compression of them be completed, by drawing the bed farther down, whilst in motion—the power to repeat its motion being applied near the termination of the movement. 2d. The arranging of the frisket and inking rollers in separate carriages, moving on the same ways with such relative velocity as not to interfere with each other. 3d. The pointing of the sheet by an automatic movement attached to some moving portion of the press. 4th. The application of a blast of air, or its equivalent, for the purpose of forcing the sheets upon the registering points, when the paper is being prepared for the reverse impression; and the removing of the sheet from the frisket, or from the press, by means of atmospheric pressure. 5th. Making the registering points adjustable in the paper table, by passing it through a friction plate, secured between two plates, so that it may be moved in any direction. 6th. The combination of the open toggle and adjustable eccentric shaft, or pin, which operates the bed, for the purpose of regulating the impression.

AARON H. CHAGIN, MARTIN BUCK, J. H. BUCK, F. A. JENNY, Lebanon, N. H., November 23, 1852.—The improvements consist of the arrangement and combination of the movements in connection with the bed, by which an extent of motion is imparted to the bed, much larger than that of the sweep of the operating crank, whilst the whole of the movements only occupy the space within the framework of the press below the bed; and the arrangement of the upper and lower tables, with the pressure cylinder, the bed, the conveying bands, the nippers attached to said bands, and the cams for operating the nippers, in such manner that an impression can be made at each right and each left movement of the form under the cylinder, and the sheets be deposited, after receiving their impressions, upon the lower tables.

CHARLES MONTAGUE, Pittsfield, Mass., November 23, 1852.—The improvement claimed is in placing the bed-plate in a vertical position, when a reciprocating motion is imparted to it, by which two impressions can be made at each forward movement of the bed-plate; also, the combination of the vertically acting bed, with a cylinder, or cylinders, arranged in such a manner that the forward movement of the bed will impart motion to the cylinder or cylinders, to give or take an impression, and allow said cylinder or cylinders to remain stationary during the return movement of the bed.

JEPHTHA A. WILKINSON, Fireplace, N. Y., Jan. 4, 1853.—This improvement consists in forming cylinders of metal with means to secure the type for printing upon their surface, combined with the means of cutting and folding the sheet when printed.

SETH ADAMS, Boston, March 8, 1853.—This improvement is the combination of the vibratory platen with the sheet-holders, arranged so as to be kept up a little distance from the platen when in position to receive the sheet, and moving with said platen to the form, in order to hold the sheets thereon, and draw them from the types; also the gauges for registering the sheets; also the moving or sliding tympan cloth in combination with a turning segment, to which an intermittent and reciprocating motion is imparted by means of a catch, a ratchet and spiral spring.

JAMES YOUNG, Philadelphia, May 10, 1853.—The patent is for the peculiar combination and arrangement for operating the inking rollers. Also a false bed hinged to a stationary one, and the mode of fastening the form to the bed; and the eccentric in combination with the platen, by means of which the latter can be adjusted while in motion, or thrown off.

WM. H. DANFORTH, Salem, Mass., June 21, 1853.—This invention consists in the employment of two parallel type forms, and two platens, in one printing-machine, so arranged one above the other that both platens can be operated together, so that a sheet of paper can be printed by each form at one impression. Also in the manner of feeding the paper into the machine between a series of gripping bars and bands, that hold it in place to receive the impression, and afterwards pass it forward; while the inking roller is so arranged as to follow closely after it, across the face of the type; and be followed in turn by the blank sheet which is to receive the next impression.

STEPHEN P. RUGGLES, Boston, Aug. 2, 1853.—The nature of this improvement consists in so arranging a series of diverging springs upon a plate extending across the rear or lower part of the platen, that they will make a guide for the paper when it is sliding on to the tympan; the springs are forced down by the paper-holders, so as to be condensed between the type and the furniture of the press.

JOHN LEWIS, Buffalo, N. Y., Aug. 9, 1853.—This invention is the construction of a swinging bail and a pressure bail, in combination with the lever power, in such manner as to bring the power upon the centre of the platen by one motion of the lever.

JOEL G. NORTHRUP, Syracuse, N. Y., Aug. 9, 1853.—This improvement consists in the combination of the series of intermittingly rotating platens with a vibrating bed, when so arranged that the delivery of the printed sheet is from the lower of the series of platens, so that it may drop from the platen on to the paper-table, or into a drawer.

VICTOR BEAUMONT, New York, Sept. 6, 1853.—This press consists of a printing cylinder, on a part of the surface of which are fixed the forms of type, the remainder of the surface being used as a distributing table. Around this large cylinder are fixed twelve impression cylinders, and between them are elastic inking rollers. Under the printing cylinder are the ink fountain, the rollers to distribute the ink on the distributing table, and the shaft by which the machine is made to revolve.

CHARLES MONTAGUE, Pittsfield, Mass., Sept. 6, 1853.—The invention is such a combination and arrangement of the cylinder and bed that, whilst one sheet is receiving its impression, the sheet to receive the next impression will be carried forward upon the cylinder nearly to the bed, for the purpose of being in readiness to commence the impression the moment after the bed starts on its next forward movement.

CHARLES MONTAGUE, Pittsfield, Mass., Sept. 6, 1853.—The combination of the intermittingly winding cylinder and feed-roller, or their equivalents, with the reciprocating pressure cylinder, bed, and rollers, arranged and operated in such a manner as to successively make an impression on the continuous sheet at each movement of the bed. Also, in combination with a double set of inking rollers, the arrangement of the arms for inking both sets of rollers from a fountain placed vertically below the impression cylinder.

STEPHEN P. RUGGLES, Boston, Feb. 28, 1854.—The invention claimed is in hanging the platen and the intermediate ink-roller to the same rock-shaft by their respective arms, so that the vibrations of the platen shall throw the intermediate roller first to the grooved ink-roller, and then to the ink-bearer, for

Incipit prologus sancti Ieronimi in parabolas Salomonis.

Iungat epistola quos iungit sacerdotium: immo carta non dividat quos Christi nectit amor. Commentarios in Osee, Amos, Zachariam, Malachiam quoque poscitis. Scripsissem si licuisset per valitudinem. Mittitis solatia sumptuum, notarios nostros et librarios sustentatis: ut vobis potissimum nostrum desudet ingenium. Et ecce ex latere frequens turba diversa poscentium: quasi aut equum sit me vobis esurientibus aliis laborare: aut in ratione dati et accepti: cuiquam praeter vos obnoxius sim. Itaque longa egrotatione fractus: ne penitus hoc anno reticerem et apud vos mutus essem: triduidui opus nomini vestro consecrani: interpretationem videlicet trium Salomonis voluminum: Masloth quod hebrei parabolas vulgata editio proverbia vocat: coeleth quem grece ecclesiasten latine concionatorem possumus dicere: sirahsirim quod in linguam

Parabole Salomonis filii David regis Israel: ad sciendam sapientiam et disciplinam: ad intelligenda verba prudentiae et suscipiendam eruditionem doctrinae: iustitiam et iudicium et aequitatem: ut detur parvulis astutia: et adolescenti scientia et intellectus. Audiens sapiens sapientior erit: et intelligens gubernacula possidebit. Animadvertet parabolam et interpretationem: verba sapientium et aenigmata eorum. Timor domini principium sapientiae. Sapientiam

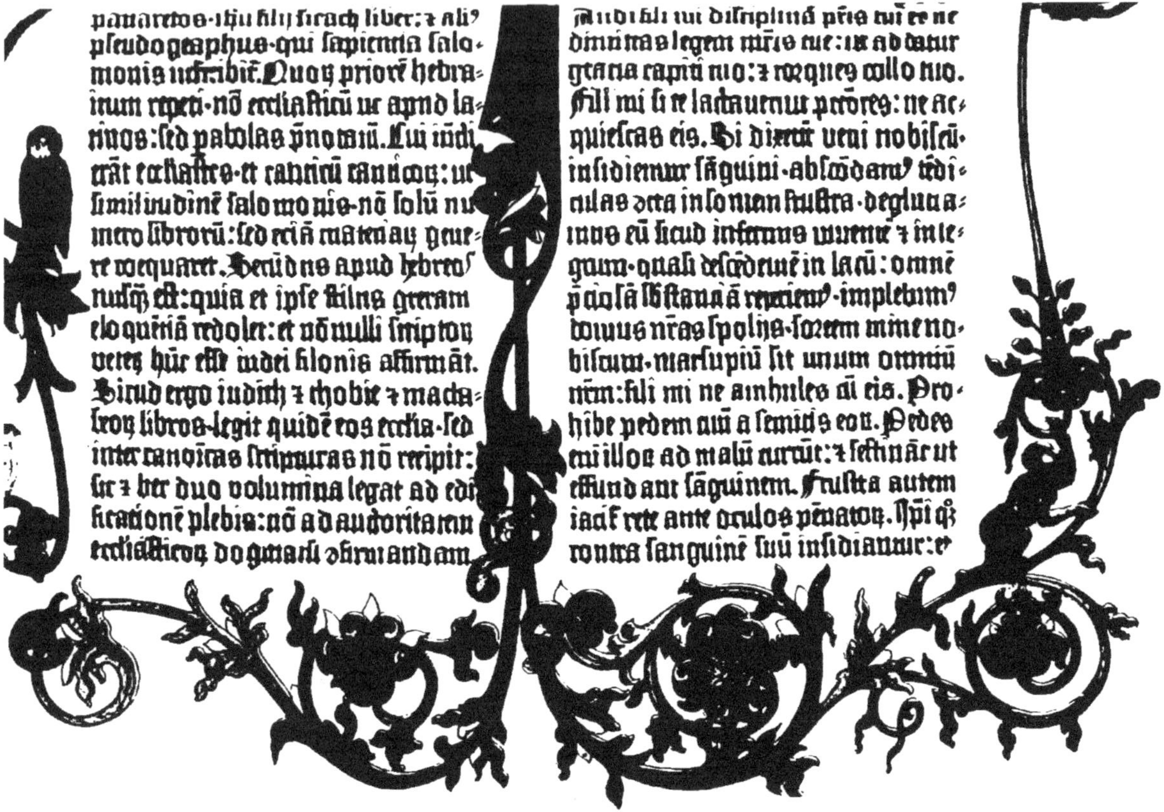

the purpose of receiving and distributing the ink from the ink-trough at every vibration of the platen.

CHAS. W. HAWKES, Boston, March 21, 1854.—The object of this invention is to remove the sheet from the form, after the impression has been given to it, by the use of improved nippers.

HENRY UNDERHILL, Canandaigua, N. Y., March 28, 1854.—The inventor claims as an improvement operating the platen by hand in connection with a reciprocating double frisket carriage, whose movement is derived from a continuous rotary motion, whether produced by hand or power, so that, as the carriage brings the frisket of each end under the platen, the latter may be made to descend at the will of the attendant, and independently of the movement of the carriage, so that its depression may be omitted if a blank sheet is not placed over the form.

ERVIN B. TRIPP, Concord, N. H., Oct. 3, 1854.—This is an arrangement for feeding sheets to the form, and removing them therefrom after having received the impression, and also for a device for applying ink to the form by rollers fed from the ink fountain by rollers receiving ink from oblique rollers, on an endless board.

SIDNEY KELSEY, Erie, Pa., Jan. 2, 1855.—The improvements are—1st. Feeding or conveying the sheets to the form by having the carriage formed of two parts, and arranged so that the edge of the sheet may be grasped between the two parts of the carriage as it is moved between the carriage and bed. 2d. The fly operated by means of a pulley attached to the carriage by a cord ; the pulley being hung on a shaft, which is provided with a spring. The spring throws the shaft around to its original position, the sheet being deposited thereby upon a proper fly-board.

LEMUEL T. WELLS, Cincinnati, March 21, 1855. —The object of this invention is to facilitate the feeding and accurate placing of the sheets. This is accomplished by having the platen hinged or pivoted to vibrating arms, in combination with stationary pins, or pins and retracting springs, or equivalent devices.

JUSTUS WEBSTER and SAM. H. FOLSOM, Lowell, Mass., March 25, 1855.—The nature of this invention consists in the employment of a printing-cylinder capable of printing paper of any desired length in a series of horizontal and transverse lines.

JOEL G. NORTHRUP, Syracuse, N. Y., June 12, 1855.—The improvement claimed is the manner by which motion is given to the bed of a printing-press by means of a vibratory connecting rod; one end of which is attached by a stud-pin, or wrist, to a stud that projects from the lower side of the bed; the other end being connected by a similar wrist to an endless chain, which passes around two wheels which revolve, thus producing an elongated crank-motion.

MERVIN DAVIS, New York, July 24, 1855.—The improvement claimed is an oscillating bed, having a plane surface, contradistinguished from a rotary bed, or sliding bed, by oscillating between two given

points, and the construction and operation of the platen in combination with said bed. Also the adoption and combination of the fly to the new construction and arrangement of the bed and platen.

DANIEL K. WINDER, Cincinnati, Ohio, October 9, 1855.—This invention consists in the double inclined bed, traversing form, and inking surface in combination with the lever and spring roller supports, and operating lever, of a card press.

DANIEL K. WINDER, Cincinnati, Ohio, October 16, 1855.—This invention is the double-armed rock shaft and outward pressing roller frame, or their equivalent, in combination with the platen and the springs actuating the arm of said rock shaft, constructed and arranged for operating the inking roller of a card press, combined with the supply roller actuated by the movement of the platen.

THOMAS HARSHA, West Union, Ohio, October 23, 1855.—This invention consists in attaching a box which contains the form (of a card press) to a lever, and connecting said lever with the inking rollers and feed rollers, so that when the lever is moved and the form brought over the ink-bed, the paper will be fed over the bed on which it is printed; and when the lever is moved over the bed in order to print the paper or cards, the charged ink rollers will pass over the ink bed, whereby the ink bed is kept properly charged with ink, and the paper fed over the bed on which the paper is printed, and the paper or cards printed by merely moving or operating the lever. Also in passing the paper or card-board between two knives, so arranged in relation to the lever that the printed paper or cards will be cut off in proper lengths as the form is pressed upon the paper—the knives cutting off a previous impression at each depression of the lever.

GEORGE P. GORDON, New York, January 1, 1856. —The invention consists in combining with the rotating disk for distributing the ink an annular disk, which shall revolve around, and in a contrary direction. Also, a rotating reciprocating cylinder, or segment of a cylinder, in combination with a reciprocating bed,—so placing the bed, when used with a rotating reciprocating cylinder, or segment of a cylinder, that it shall drop or pile the printed sheets underneath it.

MOSES PARKES and ALFRED PARKES, Brooklyn, N. Y., July 29, 1856.—The invention consists in a cylinder having flat surfaces on its periphery to receive the forms, in combination with printing-cylinders placed in sliding bearings, with reciprocating shafts, and stationary shafts, with tapes arranged, whereby two printing-cylinders can be fed from one feed-board.

A. NEWBURY and B. NEWBURY, Woodham Centre, N. Y., September 16, 1856.—The invention claimed is the rotating and reciprocating printing-cylinder operated by means of endless racks, and bars.

F. L. BAILEY, Boston, November 25, 1856.—The improvement consists in the combination of the sta-

16

tionary bed with the revolving distributing cylinder, when the two are placed within the circle of revolution of the ink rollers; and an impression lever in combination with the connecting bar; the two so arranged that they may be disconnected at pleasure.

PLATT EVANS, JR., Cincinnati, December 23, 1856. —The invention consists in so connecting the platen with the follower that the upward motion of the follower shall remove the platen from the ink-pad, and bring it back again; and during every alternate downward motion of the follower, the platen shall remain over the ink-pad and under the type follower.

G. H. BABCOCK, Westerly, R. I., December 25, 1856.—The improvement consists in attaching the bed and platen together by means of a joint, or its equivalent, when each is made to oscillate from a fixed centre, and giving an impression by means of the joint oscillation of the bed and platen, and operating the frisket by means of a weight, in combination with the motion of the platen.

HORACE HOLT, Winchester, Mass., March 17, 1857. —These improvements consist in a peculiar arrangement of parts; whereby the form is properly inked, the platen drawn underneath the form, the form pressed down upon the card on the platen, and the platen, after the card has received its impression, forced out from underneath the form. These movements are made by the operation of a single cam. There is also, in combination with the cam for operating the platen, a rotating and vibrating ink-distributing roller.

GEORGE P. GORDON, New York, November 3, 1857. —This improvement consists in the peculiar means employed for feeding a continuous sheet of paper to its proper place of printing, and in the use of adjustable shears or knives to cut off the proper length of paper or card, after the same has been printed, as fast as the printing is done, and by the same operation. Also, in providing side arms, or a frame, for the purpose of carrying the inking rollers in such a way as to give the same a continuous reversible motion as the rollers pass over the form, so that the impression may be taken at each alternate motion of the frame up and down, and this, in combination with the means employed in actuating the reciprocating bed-carriage, upon which bed the form is placed.

STEPHEN WILCOX, JR., Westerly, R. I., November 10, 1857.—The improvement claimed is the adaptation of the eccentric segment to the stationary bed, when the segment is held to the bed by radius bars.

R. M. HOE, New York, November 17, 1857.—The nature of this improvement consists in operating the fly-frame by means of cam shafts placed one at each end of the machine, and provided with cams, and used in connection with arms, rods, and springs, whereby the cams are made to actuate the fly-frames in a more direct manner, insuring a more perfect operation of the same.

J. M. JONES, Palmyra, N. Y., December 22, 1857. —The nature of this invention consists in an arrange-

ment of a hand-press by which the form bed is elevated a sufficient height to admit the ink roller to pass under and against the face of the type, and then readily brought down to the paper and a powerful impression given. Also, in hanging the inking roller by a rod and shaft, the shaft being under the platen in such manner that, in depressing the form, the ink roller is carried forward and against the face of the type. Also, in an improved method of suspending the bed on the lever bar.

THOMAS G. REYNOLDS, Athens, Ga., April 27, 1858.—The nature of this invention consists in—1st. The rotating segment in combination with the intermittingly rocking bed, viz., the segment having a continuous rotary movement while the bed rocks to and from the segment, and remaining, while in a vertical or nearly vertical position, stationary long enough to have the forms properly inked. 2d. Arranging the inking apparatus to operate conjointly with the segment and bed, so that the form can be properly inked during the dwell, or cessation of the movement of the bed.

GEORGE P. GORDON and F. O. DEGENER, New York, May 11, 1858.—This invention relates to an improvement in that class of printing-presses in which a continuous rotating cylinder that receives the sheet to be printed is used in connection with a reciprocating bed, on which the form is placed. The object of this invention is to simplify the construction of such presses, and also to give a positive or arbitrary movement to the cylinder and bed relatively with each other at the time the impression is given to the sheet.

GEORGE P. GORDON, New York, July 13, 1858.— The improvements claimed in this patent are—1st. One or more sets of grippers, independent in themselves, which shall revolve upon their axes, and carry the sheet from its point of feeding to its place of deposit. 2d. The stop for holding the grippers in the desired position, for the purpose of insuring an exact and regular feeding, registering, and delivering of the sheet. 3d. The combined action of the grippers, and the vibrating springs, strips or frisket, for the purpose of conveying the sheet to, and holding it in the proper position for the reception of the impression, and insuring its proper delivery after it shall have been printed. 4th. The vibrating double cam for throwing off the impression. 5th. A fly-board, with an adjustable ledge in combination with the grippers, to insure the even piling of the sheet.

E. EDWARD SNEIDER, New York, August 10, 1858. —This invention consists in the employment of a revolving segment frame which receives the blank sheets of paper, and serves at the same time to carry and support the inking rollers, and to communicate motion to the same; in the employment of a rocking bed, on which the form is placed, and between which and the segments the impression is given, said rocking bed being worked likewise from the segment frame, and provided with suitable ways on its under side, passing over rollers to produce the required impression; and also in the employment of a novel fly-motion, by which the printed sheets are brought upon the fly-board.

ERVIN B. TRIPP, New York, Sept. 14, 1858.—This invention consists—1st. In attaching to, and combining with, the type cylinder of a rotary printing-press a flattened plate or type bed which contains the type and revolves with the cylinder, and so attached to it as to move over the impression cylinder in a circular line, or in the arc of a circle. 2d. In a feeding roller operated by a positive movement, which can be adjusted in its movements to feed the paper to be impressed by the type at such given portion of the movement of the type cylinder as may be required to give the paper the requisite amount of margin; and 3d. In a feeding guide, up to and against which the paper is fed, and which is governed in its movements by the movements of the feeding roll, so that it is elevated to allow the paper to pass it, when the feeding roll is depressed and brought in contact with the paper to feed the press, and is depressed when the feeding roll is elevated and raised from the feeding table.

JAMES A. CAMPBELL, New Orleans, Sept. 14, 1858. —The inventor claims as improvements—1st. A set of teeth placed on a portion of the perimeter of a roller for the purpose of pushing the card through an opening above the perpendicular grooves used in feeding a card press, by the operation of these teeth on the surface presented by the front card of the pack. 2d. The arrangement of adjustable plates for the purpose of regulating the opening through which the cards have to pass, to the thickness of the card. 3d. The combination of the stationary arm, ball and ratchet, rod, sheet-arm, and the working-joints, for the purpose of giving the inking rollers a lateral motion.

CHAS. MONTAGUE, Hartford, Conn., Nov. 9, 1858. —This invention consists in such an arrangement of a horizontal reciprocating bed and revolving cylinder for impression that the surface of the bed or form placed upon it shall always travel in correspondence with the surface of the cylinder, and the cylinder is made to complete its revolution by other means independent of the motion imparted to it by the bed after the impression is given.

MOSES S. BEACH, Brooklyn, N. Y., Nov. 9, 1858.— The object of this invention is to dispense with the use of tapes in throwing the sheet out from the impression cylinder after it has received its impression.

DAVID E. JAMES, Utica, N. Y., Nov. 30, 1858.— This press is designed to furnish the means by which one person may, by a continuous operation, place the cards to be printed upon the press, print and remove them; inking the type by the same movement which carries and returns the paper, and doing the whole work completely and rapidly.

G. R. COTTON, Green Bay, Wis., Dec. 28, 1858.— This invention consists in—1st. Operating the form bed from the pressure cylinder by means of a cam, or eccentric, provided with pins; rack-bar provided with projection and roller; slide-bar and springs with the rack-bar, the whole being arranged to operate as set forth. 2d. A toothed sector which gears into the pinion of the roller, and is connected with the rack-bar and the arm of the sector provided with a pin and rod attached to the arm, the pawl attached to the arm, and the ratchet attached to the roller, the whole being arranged so that the inking apparatus will be operated automatically from the pressure of the roller. 3d. Having the bearings of the cylinder attached to rods, which are connected by tension nuts to straps that encompass the eccentrics of the shaft, for the purpose of readily raising when necessary the cylinder and regulating its pressure.

F. O. DEGENER, New York, Jan. 11, 1859.—The invention consists in arranging or hanging an oscillating bed, with an oscillating platen, in such manner that the motion of one will control the action of the other, so that by their forward movement they shall close and give an impression, and upon their reverse movement the form shall be inked, and the platen brought into the proper position necessary for the reception of the sheet, and thus alternate from one of their positions to the other. Also in the arrangement of the bed and platen, so constructed with a cam as to cause the frisket to assume the position necessary to hold the sheet of paper while it is conveyed from one position to the other.

GORDON MCKAY, Boston, Feb. 15, 1859.—The improvement is a combination of an impression cylinder and nippers operating in conjunction with a blast-pipe or mechanical means for producing an inequality of atmospheric pressure on the sheet when released from the nippers, and as the sheet is forced onwards by or with the impression cylinder in its rotary movement.

GEO. P. GORDON, New York, April 19, 1859.—The invention is—1st. The combination of one or more sets of revolving grippers, with finger-stops, for the purpose of piling the sheets of paper in an even and regular heap or pile. 2d. The combination of a vibrating feed-board, with the rotating or revolving platen, for the purpose of feeding the sheets regularly and with precision at each rotation of the platen, and the combination of a rotating reciprocating bed with a revolving platen.

S. P. RUGGLES, Boston, May 10, 1859.—The improvements claimed are—1st. The combination of two screws, having different-sized threads, and operating together so as to give a greater motion to a platen at one time, and more power at another. 2d. The connecting two such screws together, and to the lever or bar which actuates them, by a strong helical spring, that, by being wound up, becomes a clamp, so as to put the two screws in action, one after the other. 3d. Running out the bed on inclined ways, for the purpose of increasing the distance between the bed and platen, which gives a better entrance for the frisket, blankets, sheet, form, etc., by affording more space when they are run under the platen.

JAMES A. CAMPBELL, New Orleans, June 28, 1859. —This invention consists in the peculiar mode of constructing and operating the inking roller frame, and the distributing and impression cylinder of a card and job printing-press.

ANDREW DOUGHERTY, Brooklyn, N. Y., August 9, 1859.—This improvement consists in the combination of the inking apparatus at the side of the main cylinder of a press, with a carriage that can be moved from and towards the main cylinder, and with a stop that controls the position of the carriage.

GEORGE P. GORDON and F. O. DEGENER, New York, August 9, 1859.—The inventors claim as improvements: 1st. Combining with the tympan frame the sheet folding or relieving grippers, for the purpose of holding the sheet, and for relieving the sheet from the type. 2d. The combination of a cylinder, or segment of a cylinder, with its wheel bearers, the impression cylinder, roller, pendants, and the racks or gearing. 3d. A frictionless roller, in combination with the tympan frame, for the purpose of closing the tympan, and properly laying the sheet upon the form in advance of the passage of the impression cylinder. 4th. Operating the sheet-holding grippers by or through the motion of the tympan. 5th. Attaching a tympan frame to an adjustable bed in such manner that they, at all times, shall retain their relative positions towards each other; and 6th, Hanging, hinging, or attaching the inking apparatus to the frame of the press, or to the press, in such manner that it may be turned or swung, or set aside, so as to allow the workmen to get at the form to make any necessary alterations, or to make the form ready, or for the purpose of using the bed as an imposing-stone.

LEMUEL T. WELLS, Cincinnati, September 6, 1859. —The improvement claimed is the combination with stationary abutments on the ways, of an attachment to the bed of a closed cylinder, its position having a stroke relatively less than than of the bed, and acting to simultaneously condense and rarify the air at alternately opposite ends of the cylinder.

THOMAS H. BURRIDGE, St. Louis, Mo., December 20, 1859.—This invention consists in imparting the ordinary motion to the type-table of a printing-press by applying steam power directly to the table of the press, without complex machinery of any kind intervening between the table and the piston-rod of the engine, and causing the same piston that actuates the table to arrest its momentum.

GEO. P. GORDON, New York, January 10, 1860.— The improvements claimed are, the combination of the rotating, reciprocating inking roller frame, moving upon a centre, with the type or form bed, when such centre and such bed shall always sustain their relative positions towards each other; also the above combination, in combination with the rotating ink-distributing table. Also, the combination of a vibrating tympan with a vertical bed, or a bed placed out of a horizontal position, when the impression shall be given by a cylindrical surface.

VOSCO M. CHAFEE, Xenia, Ill., January 17, 1860. —This invention consists in the manner of feeding cards; distributing the ink on the rollers; imparting power to the printing-apparatus, by means of the combination of a cam and sliding frame; working the inking rollers, and counting the impressions.

CHARLES McBURNEY, Roxbury, Mass., January 17, 1860.—This invention consists in covering the blanket with successive layers of canvas or cotton cloth and india-rubber, and then covering it with an india-rubber compound that will vulcanize all the materials employed.

JOHN W. LATCHER, Northville, N. Y., January 31, 1860.—The nature of this invention is: 1st. The employment of two platens, arranged with two beds, and used in connection with a frisket, so arranged as to pass down between one platen and bed, to receive one impression, and then rise and pass down between the other platen and bed, to receive the other impression. 2d. In combination with the platen, bed, and frisket, so arranged an inking device, composed of the cylinder, distributing-rollers, dipping-rollers, and fountain-roller, in connection with the rollers attached to the frisket, the whole being arranged for joint operation. 3d. Securing the forms in or upon the beds, by means of movable jaws, fitted in the upper and lower parts of the beds.

FRANKLIN BAILEY, Boston, February 21, 1860. —This press operates as follows:—A card being placed on the platen, against the guide, motion is given by a crank; the platen is drawn upward, the nippers clasp the card in its upward motion towards the form; meanwhile, the cam, receding, allows the roller carriage to drop down, so that the roller will rest against the ink-cylinder just previous to the time that the platen reaches the form to take the impression. The upward movement of the platen being completed, it then falls back, the roller carriage again rises, the nippers lift from the card, allowing it to drop, and the platen comes to a state of rest as before.

F. O. DEGENER, New York, April 24, 1860.—The inventor claims as improvements—1st. The combination of a rotating ink-distributing table with a rotating, reciprocating type-bed. 2d. The combination of this mechanism for giving the desired movement to a type-bed hinged to a platen. 3d. In combination with a type-bed so constructed and operated, an eccentric, for the purpose of adjusting and varying the linear position of the type-bed and platen. 4th. Attaching a frisket, or gripper-frame, in such manner that it shall be carried by, and moved with, the type-bed. 5th. In combination with the bed and platen, an eccentric-pin, bolt, or shaft, for the purpose of suspending the taking of an impression.

GEORGE C. HOWARD, Philadelphia, June 26, 1860. —This invention consists in connecting the plate or table, by suitable mechanism, with a belt-shifter rod, so that at the proper moment the machine will stop itself; also, in connecting the shifter-rod with treadles, so that the press cannot be started in the wrong direction.

ALVA B. TAYLOR, Newark, N. J., June 26, 1860.—
The improvement consists in the combination of the
endless rack of the type-carriage with the cog-wheel
that imparts motion to it, by means of two pinions,
and a solid pinion-shaft, having boxes or bearings
that adapt themselves to the different positions which
the pinion-shaft assumes, in the operation of the
press.

JAMES A. SMITH, Fond du Lac, Wis., and ISAAC
ORVIS, Wisconsin, June 26, 1860.—The invention
consists—1st. In the arrangement of the form-beds,
and stationary platen, so that the impression may be
given simultaneously and by the same application of
power, and the under side of the upper form-bed be
made to serve as a platen for the lower one. 2d. The
arrangement of the form-beds and platen, with a roll
of paper, so that the paper may be printed from a
continuous sheet, and on both sides, during a single
passage through the press.

GEO. F. HEBARD, GEO. J. HILL, and S. D. ROCK-
WELL, Buffalo, N. Y., August 7, 1860.—This invention consists—1st. In the construction, application,
and use of an intermittent feed, so that cards, circulars, railroad-tickets, and the like can be printed on
long sheets or continuous rolls of paper. 2d. In so
arranging and combining the mechanism that each
card or ticket may be printed and separated or cut
from the continuous roll of paper by a simultaneous
operation of the machine.

WILLIAM H. BABCOCK, Homer, N. Y., October 23,
1860.—This invention consists in supporting a bed,
which vibrates in a line or arc perpendicular or
nearly perpendicular to the plane of its face, upon two
or more parallel radius rods, in such a manner that
the bed shall remain parallel to the face of the platen
in all portions of its motion.

CHAS. POTTER, JR., Westerly, R. I., March 5,
1861.—This improvement consists in the combination
of the oscillating platen and bed, connected, when
the former is provided with a pin, and the latter with
a corresponding socket, operated together, for the
purpose of securing an accurate register, and preventing slur.

A. S. ADAMS, Chelsea, Mass., March 19, 1861.—
The improvement claimed is—1st. The dog on the
tympan and stationary cam, for the purpose of automatically depressing the tympan before it reaches the
impression roll, when the form comes under from
either direction. 2d. The inking-roll, carried by a
bent U-shaped bar, which allows the roll to pass over
the bed, whilst the sliding part, which is supported on
the frame of the press, passes beneath the bed, where
it is out of the way, and may be readily operated by
a treadle.

GEO. P. GORDON, Brooklyn, N. Y, April 23, 1861.
—This invention consists—1st. In the use of a platen
having two distinct and separate motions, namely, in
a straight line to and from the type or form, for the
purpose of carrying the sheet to and from the impression, and rocking from such a line, for the purpose of receiving the succeeding sheet to be printed.

2d. In the use of a rocking platen, whose face, at the
time the nippers are receiving the sheet to be printed,
shall stand at an angle from a horizontal position,
for the purpose of allowing the printed sheet to slide
freely from the inclined surface of such platen. Moving with the rocking platen are automatic nippers,
for the purpose of taking the sheet to be printed from
the feed-table, and holding such sheet until the impression shall have been given, and for the further
purpose of lifting such printed sheet up from the
tympan at the proper time, and admitting a volume
of air between the sheet and tympan, in order that
the sheet, buoyed up by the air, may glide from the
tympan freely and surely.

GEORGE R. DEAN, Mayville, N. Y., May 7, 1861.—
This invention consists in an arrangement of parts of
the press, by means of which, as the lever is brought
down, the type rollers will pass over the form, and
run down upon the distributing table, out of the way,
while the fountain roller will run down to the fountain and take ink. The lever being raised, the rollers
will run up over the type, and the fountain roller to
the distributing table.

HORACE GOODRICH, Stoneham, Mass., October 1,
1861.—This improvement consists in arranging
cleats, upon which the upper corners of the frisket
frame rest, by which the frisket frame is prevented
from being forced down upon the inking roller, and
the hanging of the impression cylinder in spring
bearings, so that more or less pressure may be given
to it at pleasure.

F. O. DEGENER, New York, November 5, 1861.—
The nature of this invention is in constructing a
cylinder press in such manner that the printed
sheet, after it has been taken from the cylinder and
deposited on the pile-table, shall be brought in front,
and before the eyes of the operator.

CHAS. MONTAGUE, Hartford, Conn., December 10,
1861.—The nature of this improvement consists in
the combination of two cylinders, for letter-press
printing in different colors, whereby a sheet once fed
to the small cylinders is printed with the different
colors desired, before leaving the press, and also in
the use of interchangeable ink rollers, in combination
with the cylinders, to ink the different forms with the
colors desired.

GEO. P. GORDON, Brooklyn, N. Y., January 7, 1862.
—In this invention the tympan sheet is made of
paper, and arranged so as to admit of its being easily
replaced by a fresh one, as fast as it becomes charged
with the set-off ink. One end of the sheet is attached
to a vibrating nipper-carrying rod, and the other to a
roller, which, by the action of an elastic cord, rolls it
up, after each impression, for the purpose of delivering the printed sheet to the pile-table, situated beneath
the feed-table. The platen vibrates, and carries a
pair of nipper arms, provided with nippers, which
are caused to ascend and approach the feed-table
before each impression, to seize the sheet which is
drawn off the feed-table and down over the face of
the platen; the tympan sheet is also, by the same

method, unwound from the roller, and drawn down over between the face of the platen and the sheet of paper. The sheet gauges are so constructed as to present the edge of the sheet accurately to the nippers, and the ink-distributing surfaces comprise a revolving cylinder and a revolving disk combined, to secure a more even and thorough distribution of the ink than is possible by either device alone.

JAMES GORDON, Caledonia, N. Y., November 4, 1862.—This invention consists in the employment of a cylinder, having a form fitted in its periphery, and so operated as to have a reciprocating and partially rotating motion, and working in connection with a reciprocating bed, which receives the sheets, and upon which the sheets receive the impression from the form-cylinder, the same being used in connection with a reciprocating form bed and pressure rollers, all so arranged as to enable both sides of a sheet to be printed in passing once through the press, and the press to be fed at both ends, to render the printing operation continuous, the printed sheets being discharged, also, from both ends of the press.

ANSELL N. KELLOGG, Baraboo, Wis., July 6, 1863.—This machine is designed as an improvement in the press known as Newbury's machine jobber and card press, and consists in improvements in delivering the printed cards or sheets, leveling the platen more readily and firmly, and effecting a more perfect distribution of ink upon the ink-roller.

WILLIAM BULLOCK, Pittsburg, Pa., April 14, 1863.—This machine is known as Bullock's rotary self-feeding and self-perfecting press, and the invention consists in the following specifications setting forth its operation. The feeding of the paper into the machine from a continuous roll or web, by means of a feed-roller revolving in contact with the paper roll. The press being put in motion, the paper roll revolves and unwinds the paper, passing it between the two cutting cylinders, male and female, where it is cut the desired length. Grippers take hold of the cut end of the paper, and bring the severed sheet to the first impression cylinder, where grippers take hold of it and pass it between the said cylinder and first type cylinder, where it receives the first impression. It is then transferred to the second impression or main cylinder, where fingers take hold of it and bring it to the second type cylinder, presenting the white side, and there it receives the second impression. It is then transferred, printed on both sides, to the fly-belts, which bring it out on top of, or above, the fly-board, where it is delivered ready for the carrier. The inking apparatus is so constructed as to communicate an alterative lateral movement to the small ink-distributing cylinder, by giving a simultaneous reciprocating motion to one end of their bearings, thus securing a more perfect and uniform distribution of the ink. The form or face rollers, of which there are two to each type cylinder, are placed in bearings between the type and distributing cylinders, and receive a fresh supply of ink at each revolution of the form. The impression is regulated by means of

screws, and can be adjusted while the press is in motion.

GEORGE P. GORDON, Brooklyn, N. Y., September 29, 1863.—By this invention the platen is rocked from the horizontal position in which it receives the paper, and by the motion of a crank arm and roller in the cam groove of a cog wheel, it is made to assume the vertical position, in which it is locked while the bed, carrying the form, is vibrated on its centre by means of a link rod attached to the cog wheel, until it delivers its pressure upon the paper on the platen and retires, allowing the latter to be rocked back again, and the printed paper removed.

JOHN F. ALLEN and R. W. McGOWEN, New York, December 15, 1863.—This press is designed for printing with a plurality of colors simultaneously. It consists of a rotary cylinder in combination with a series of cylindrical forms or type cylinders, and a reciprocating form or type bed.

GEO. P. GORDON, Brooklyn, N. Y., March 8, 1864.—This invention consists,—1st. In an improvement whereby an unprinted sheet is taken from the feed-table, and presented properly to the type, to receive the impression, relieving it from the impression, and carrying it to and depositing it upon the pile-table, by the use of one and the same set of reciprocating automatic nippers. 2d. The combination of the automatic nippers with a cylinder, or segment of a cylinder, which shall have a part rotary with a return movement.

GEO. P. GORDON, Brooklyn, N. Y., June 21, 1864.—This invention consists of two revolving ink-tables, over which the ink-rollers pass in succession, to insure a perfect distribution of the ink, and also of a vibrating platen, in combination with a stationary bed, all connected with one source of motion, so as to have perfect coincidence of action.

STEPHEN D. TUCKER, New York, June 28, 1864.—This invention relates to an arrangement of machinery for delivering the sheets from the press, and consists of tapes, to carry the paper forward, so as not to require being turned over by the fingers as usual, but by a blast-pipe, to be separated from the tapes and dropped downwards towards the pile.

STEPHEN D. TUCKER, New York, June 28, 1864.—This improvement consists in mounting the inking roller of a rotary press, so that it shall bear continually against the distributing surface of the type cylinder, and at the same time remain in contact with the cylinder from which it receives ink, and in a nice adjustment of the pressure of the inking roller.

F. L. BAILEY, Boston, July 5, 1864.—The general object and nature of this invention consist in a rotating reciprocating or sweeping bed, whose flat plane surface for the type stands in a plane always obliquely to its centre of motion, and obliquely to the arc of a circle which any point on its surface may scribe as the bed moves to and fro on its centre or centres of motion, so that the lower edge of any form will scribe a smaller circle than any other part of the same; and a vibrating platen, which is so arranged that its face swings upwards for the reception of the sheets upon a hinge near its top edge, also the combination of the same with the bed; also giving the same a downward sliding or equivalent motion.

F. L. BAILEY, Boston, December 13, 1864.—This invention consists in a mode of distributing the ink in a lateral direction on the cylinder, to render the surface more equal, and in mechanical arrangements to make the press compact and efficient.

CULLEN WHIPPLE, Providence, R. I., November 8, 1864.—This invention consists in so arranging a secondary lever that it shall slide the bed of the press from over the ink-well, and at the same time depress the primary or printing lever to ink the type. The printing lever, being independent, can be depressed on to the printing bed, which remains over and covers the ink-well.

RICHARD W. MORAN, St. Louis, April 18, 1865.—This invention consists in a combination of impression cylinders and conducting tape rollers, by means of which both sides of continuous sheets of paper can be printed, by once passing through the press, and by a peculiar construction of the turtles and galleys.

JAMES SANGSTER, Buffalo, N. Y., June 27, 1865.—This invention consists of a movable revolving bed, with flat surfaces, with ink-rollers suspended between two springs, with a cylindrical impression roller, in combination with numbering wheels, revolving roller in the cylinder, upon the periphery or circumference of which the tickets or cards are printed.

MARTIN G. IMBACH, New York, May 1, 1866.—This invention consists in a two-bed press, arranged for printing both sides of the sheet simultaneously, by means of levers so arranged and connected with the beds that the latter will move simultaneously in opposite directions, and both give the impressions at once at opposite sides of the sheet, with inking and feeding mechanisms, proceeding automatically, with the necessary pauses, from a single shaft.

GEORGE J. HILL, Buffalo, N. Y., and STEPHEN GREENE, Philadelphia, August 28, 1866.—This press is arranged for printing cards in colors. The cards are pushed by a feed-slide from one box and received into another, which descends as the cards are fed from the former; the cards are printed in transitu by the descent of the cross-head which carries the form.

JAS. H. FRAY, and WM. HECKERT, Sharon, Pa., January 15, 1867.—This invention consists in so constructing and operating the platen that it shall move bodily in a right line up to and from the form-bed, and also assume an inclined position when at the terminus of its outer stroke, the platen performing these movements without revolving. The inking surface has an inner circular, and an outer annular plate, which revolve in opposite directions.

WM. BULLOCK, Philadelphia, February 12, 1867.—This improvement consists in endless belts, carrying nippers to transfer the sheets from the printing- or an intermediate cylinder to the fly-board. The fly is raised to allow passage to the sheet, and, descending at the point of its release, arrests it in place. The nip-

pers are raised by fixed cams, and depressed by spiral springs, on their axial shafts.

JOHN HENRY, Jersey City, N. J., February 12, 1867.—By this improvement, two fountains distribute the ink from two points, so that it may be spread in regular and small quantities. Revolving ink-disks are connected with an oscillating table.

ANSON JUDSON, Brooklyn, N. Y., July 30, 1867.—By this invention the bed is moved simultaneously with the cylinder by a straight rack on the former and a segmental rack on the latter. To effect the return of the bed during the continued rotation of the cylinder, a pin on the latter engages the jaws of an oscillating arm having a segmental rack engaging a spur wheel, whose shaft has a wheel engaging a rack on the bed.

B. O. WOODS and W. S. TUTTLE, Boston, August 6, 1867.—This invention consists in pivoting the tympan to the short arms of bell-cranks, whose outer edges are adjusted by set-screws parallel to the type bed.

STEPHEN GREENE, Philadelphia, and WALTER H. FORBUSH, Buffalo, N. Y., August 13, 1867.—The peculiarities of this press consist in the card tube being below the grooved guides, with a rising bottom operated by springs and weights, so that as the top card of the pile is pushed forward the next card takes its place. The front end of the card tube is hinged to its sides to allow throwing back to open the tube. The pusher arm extends beyond its pushing shoulder, and is hinged with a downward spring pressure to a vibrating lever. The extension, by resting on the moving card, causes the pushing shoulder to move parallel to the grooved guides. The lever carrying the pusher arm is adjustable on its shaft to suit the length of the cards and consequent movement required.

C. POTTER, JR., Westerly, R. I., August 20, 1867.—This improvement consists in arranging machinery by which the projections beneath the form-table take under friction rollers in oscillating spring levers, to hold the ends of the table down and prevent jar at the end of the movement.

HENRY BARTH, Cincinnati, October 22, 1867.—The improvements consist—1st. In the provision of the ink-table, or surface, arranged to admit of a greater or less reciprocation transversely to the path of the inking rollers, by means of a compound adjustable cam. 2d. In combination with a slotted ink-table, and inking rollers, an intermittent roller or shifter. This press is intended for colored printing.

HENRY C. CHANDLER, Indianapolis, Ind., November 5, 1867.—The nature of this improvement consists in having the segmental cog bars on the end of the revolving impression cylinder engage with straight cog bars on the edges of the bed to carry it under the cylinder in the process of making the impression. The bed has a quick return movement by means independent of that which carries it under the impression cylinder.

EDWIN ALLEN, Norwich, Conn., November 12,

1867.—The peculiarities of this press are: The type cylinder has a flat portion for the form, and the pressure cylinder a suitable convex portion to cause an even pressure thereon. The pitch line of the cog gearing agrees with the face of the cylinders. The form-cylinder shaft has friction disks whose inclined edges engage the broad-faced edges of adjustable disks on the inking roller shaft. This shaft is drawn toward the cylinder by spiral springs, and adjusted in distance thereon by shifting the broad-faced disks upon their shafts.

C. POTTER, JR., Westerly, R. I., January 7, 1868. —This improvement consists in journaling the cylinder shaft in two eccentrics, which have segments of gears that are engaged by segmental gears on the end of arms at both sides of the press. These arms are on a common transverse shaft, and are oscillated by a cam lever. The device affords means of raising the cylinder from the form.

C. POTTER, JR., Westerly, R. I., January 7, 1868. —By this improvement the guide is supported on the upper section of a box, which is clamped to the shaft by the adjusting screws of the guide.

EDWIN ALLEN, Norwich, Conn., February 4, 1868. —The nature of this invention consists in having one of the driving wheels of a rotary press provided with one or more adjustable segments or racks. The racks are adjustable in their length by set-screws. These racks are made straight, or nearly so, and the segmental racks engaging therewith are curved sufficiently to bring the pitch lines in coincidence.

LEMUEL T. WELLS, St. Louis, Mo., July 7, 1868. —This invention relates to an improvement in a former patent, and consists in adding a set of balancing springs to the movable platen, in order to counterbalance its increased weight, and adapt the machine to large as well as small presses.

WILLIAM BRAIDWOOD, New York, July 28, 1868. —By this improvement the motion of the roller carriage is independent of that of the platen, and the two motions may be regulated independently, to suit circumstances. The slots in the connecting rod, which impart motion to the platen, permit the platen, when the press is worked rapidly, to dwell sufficiently to admit of the adjustment of the sheets thereon; and the yielding bearings in the slots prevent shocks and concussions. When the platen moves forward the card drop is held in close contact therewith by the action of a spring arm, and as the platen recedes, after the impression has been taken, the card drop is raised, and the printed card permitted to drop off, and then the card drop is returned to the surface of the platen, ready to receive a new card.

SAMUEL J. BAIRD, Staunton, Va., November 24, 1868.—This invention consists of a frisket-frame made of flexible material, so that it may be bent, when used with a cylinder press, to avoid contact with the ink-rollers.

R. M. HOE and STEPHEN D. TUCKER, New York, December 1, 1868.—This is an improvement by which the sheets as they come from the press are directed alternately on opposite sides, so as to be delivered in two piles, either by two separate fly-frames, or a double acting fly-frame. The plates are clamped directly to the surface of the type cylinder, so as to dispense with the blocks and iron frames commonly used.

REGISTERING APPARATUS.

JOHN W. RICHARDS, Hoboken, N. J., May 10, 1853.—The nature of this invention consists in permitting the registering points to be passed through the feed-board at any point within a given area; which is accomplished by means of a circular plate of a size to include within its circumference all the area necessary for registering with a given size press.

JOHN NORTH, Middletown, Conn., March 8, 1859. —The nature of this invention consists in attaching to the feed-table of a printing-press two or more register points in addition to those commonly used, so as to make register points in the sheets to be printed, at the exact points required for the purpose of feeding the sheet in register, to the folding machine, to be folded.

STEPHEN T. BACON, Boston, March 8, 1859.—The invention consists in punching or cutting holes in sheets of paper, for the purpose of securing a more perfect and rapid register in printing and folding machines.

R. W. MACCOWAN, New York, Dec. 10, 1867.—By this invention pivoted pointers are snapped into the sheet by a spring, and held by it in position till the nippers of the cylinder draw the sheet, when the point automatically retires.

ROLLERS FOR DISTRIBUTING INK, ETC.

HUGH MAXWELL, Lancaster, Pa., Dec. 16, 1817.

G. W. CARTRIGHT, Mount Pleasant, N. Y., April 29, 1828.

JOSHUA LAIRD, Pittsburg, Pa., August 16, 1828.

ALEX. SCHIMMELFENNIG and JULIUS ENDE, Washington, D. C., June 8, 1858.—The improvement consists in the manufacture of ink-rollers out of elastic gums, such as caoutchouc or gutta-percha, or of compounds of the latter.

ALPHEUS A. HANSCOM, Saco, Me., June 29, 1858. —In the operation of this machine the roller or rollers are suspended in a rolling carriage, which is provided with nuts, by means of which the pressure of the rollers upon the type is regulated, thus making an adjustable hand-roller for inking type, with handles by which the carriage may be rolled backward and forward over the type.

ELISHA PRATT, Salem, Mass., Aug. 10, 1858.—The following are the ingredients used in making these improved rollers: Four pounds of glue, two ounces of gum shellac, in a sufficient quantity of alcohol to dissolve, and one tablespoonful of saleratus or sal soda.

JOS. H. OSGOOD, Peabody, Mass.—This is a process for recovering the discarded material of worn-out rollers; it is soaked in cold water, and the syrup is recovered by evaporation, and solidified by being placed in a tank with a false bottom, through which the saccharine matter percolates, while the glue remains, and is solidified by evaporation.

GEORGE LITTLETON, Cleveland, Ohio, April 7, 1863.—This improvement consists of an inking roller with a prepared India-rubber surface. The roller is made in two parts, one end being a collar on the other. Each end has an annular flange, and between them there are bearers to support the covering, which is stretched from one flange to the other. There are also wires under the covering to preserve the rotundity of the roller; the tension of the covering is adjustable by a temper screw at the end of the collar.

L. FRANCIS and F. W. LOUTRELL, New York, May 6, 1862.—This invention consists in the employment of glue properly combined with glycerine and castor oil, or any of the fixed oils, to form a composition from which inking rollers may be made.

LEWIS FRANCIS, New York, March 8, 1864.—This invention consists in making the inking roller of a composition consisting of glue, glycerine, castor oil or any of the fixed oils, borax, ammonia, and sugar.

LEWIS FRANCIS and F. W. LOUTRELL, New York, June 21, 1864.—This invention consists in combining glue, glycerine, and molasses to form a composition for the manufacture of inking rollers.

LEANDER K. BINGHAM, New York, Sept. 5, 1866. —The nature of this invention is the preparation of a roller composition, composed of glue, molasses, acetic or nitric acid, and alum, or sugar of lead.

WM. HARVEY, Portland, Me., Nov. 13, 1866.—This composition consists of glue 17 pounds, molasses 33 pounds, nitric acid 5 ounces, and sulphuric acid 5 ounces.

STEREOTYPING.

CLEMENT DAVISON, Saratoga, N. Y., November 26, 1844.—A patent for an improved method of moulding and casting stereotype plates, also cutting, chiselling, and finishing the same.

CHAS. HOBBS, New York, September 2, 1851.—The invention claimed, is the moulding in plaster of one or more forms, at one operation, in air-tight vessels, by means of exhaustion.

HOBART P. COOK, Albany, N. Y., August 3, 1852. —Casting stereotype plates by the application of pressure upon the surface of the melted metal. The pressure forces the melted metal through a tube, and upon the mould—the face of the mould being turned down to receive the metal making the casting.

JOHN L. KINGSLEY, New York, June 14, 1853.— The nature of this invention consists in making moulds for stereotyping of India-rubber or gutta-percha, by mixing the gums with metallic or earthy substances, and by expelling all air from the mould while it is being filled, to render the cast in all respects perfect.

WM. BLANCHARD, Washington, D. C., February 22, 1859.—The improvement consists in casting stereotype plates, by immersing a metallic mould-plate, with a mould or matrix formed upon and adhering to it.

M. S. BEACH, Brooklyn, N. Y., July 29, 1862.— The object of this invention is the production of a composite stereotype, of which one part is a stereotype or electrotype of the finer portions, made by any approved process, and the other part is made from papier-mache, or other matrix, which receives and embodies in itself the first-named part. Use is also made of a movable or adjustable bed or block made of type-metal or other similar, substantial, and yet yielding material, upon which the stereotype is placed, and under which, instead of under the stereotype itself, the underlays are adjusted.

CLEMOIRE F. CONFELDT, JR., and THOMAS T. PEARS, Philadelphia, June 7, 1864.—In this apparatus the melting-pot is suitably fixed in a furnace. Near the bottom of the pot is a pipe for conducting off the melted metal; at the end of this pipe is a device for regulating the flow of the melted metal.

J. D. McLEAN, New York, June 28, 1864.—The object of this invention is to obtain a machine of simple construction, by which moulds or matrices for producing stereotype or electrotype plates for letterpress may be formed directly from dies, for the purpose of avoiding the labor and expense of setting up type, and casting or forming moulds therefrom, and the invention consists in the employment of devices for effecting such object.

ARIEL CASE, New Haven, Conn., April 24, 1866.— A stereotype block. The stereotype plate is mounted upon quadrats set up in a chase; the clamps which hold the edges of the plate are inserted among the quadrats.

TYPES—CASTING, CUTTING, RUBBING, ETC.

WILLIAM WING, Hartford, Conn., August 28, 1805. (Casting.)

ARCHIBALD BINNEY, Philadelphia, January 29, 1811. (Type Mould.)

ARCHIBALD BINNEY, Philadelphia, February 4, 1811. (Type Rubber.)

ARCHIBALD BINNEY, Philadelphia, May 17, 1814. (Type Mould.)

GEORGE WEBSTER, New York, February 28, 1816.

GEORGE B. LOTHIAN, New York, December 18, 1816. (Type Mould.)

JOHN STURDEVANT and E. STARR, Boston, Mass., October 23, 1827. (Type-Casting Machine.)

WILLIAM M. JOHNSON, New York, August 21, 1826. (Casting.)

GEORGE F. PETERSON, New York, October 18, 1828. (Casting.)

WILLIAM R. COLLIER, Boston, Mass., February 9, 1830. (Casting and Setting.)

ELIHU WHITE (assignee), New York, January 7, 1831. (Casting.)

ELIHU WHITE (assignee), New York, January 7, 1831. (Rubbing.)

DAVID BRUCE, JR., Bordentown, N. J., March 10, 1838. (Rubbing.)

DAVID BRUCE, JR., Bordentown, N. J., March 10, 1838. (Casting.)

JAMES STEWART, New York, March 21, 1843.—An improved machine for casting, smoothing, and setting up type for examination.

DAVID BRUCE, JR., Williamsburg, N. Y., Nov. 6, 1843.—A machine for casting types. This patent was extended for seven years from Nov. 6, 1857.

DAVID BRUCE, JR., Williamsburg, N. Y., June 7, 1845.—A machine for casting types, by which the hand process is imitated as nearly as possible. This is done by having the mould placed upon a crane at an inclination of about fifty degrees from the perpendicular, by which greater freedom is given to the discharge of the type; and, as in the process of hand casting, the lifting of the matrix precedes that of the opening of the mould. Extended seven years from June 7, 1845.

THOS. W. STARR, Philadelphia, Aug. 4, 1845.—An improved formation of the matrix for casting the face of type, borders, and cuts therein, by means of a type, or cut, and a metallic plate, with an opening in the matrix with slanting sides. Thus prepared, it is placed in a solution of copper, and connected with the pole of a galvanic battery, in the same manner as practiced in electrotyping, and after receiving a sufficient deposit of copper is fitted up for use.

WM. P. BARR, assignee to Geo. Bruce and P. C. Cortelyou, New York, Sept. 4, 1847.—A machine for casting printing-types, so arranged as to move a matrix to and from the mould, and to discharge the type nearly perpendicularly, or at any suitable angle, without using the edge of the mould for a fulcrum.

JAS. L. DUNCAN, New York, Jan. 5, 1848.—A machine for rubbing types by means of the combination of stationary adjustable cutters with a revolving feed-plate.

JOHN L. STURGIS, New York, March 27, 1849.—The improvement in type-casting machines claimed is the conical plug, and arrangement of the chamber in which it works, in combination with the nipple and bath and well.

JOHN BACHELDER and S. D. DYER, Boston, July 27, 1849.—The improvement in type-casting consists in an endless chain and wheels, with a series of moulds attached thereto, with a suitable vessel or other suitable substitute for the metal, all made to operate together.

JOHN L. STURGIS, New York, Sept. 9, 1851.—The employment in type-casting machines of a lever, having adjusting slot, adjuster, and matrix spring-holder, and their combination with the horizontal slide, slide ways, and matrix spring.

WM. P. BARR, New York, Aug. 10, 1852.—The invention claimed is the employment in type-casting machines of an adjustable valve.

E. C. HARMEN, Troy, N. Y., Nov. 23, 1852.—The invention patented is a suitably formed elastic space for saving time in spacing out or thin spacing, and in correcting proof.

JOHN McCREARY, Chesterville, Ohio, Dec. 7, 1852. —The patent is for the combination of a lever, or crank, with an inclined plane on its side, to hold the dies in place, and the feeding lever, spring, dog, and tube or grooved piece on the side of the press, to move and guide the type wood to the place for receiving the impression, in a press for forming wooden type.

JOHN J. STURGIS, New York, June 14, 1853.—The nature of this improvement in type-casting machines consists in the use of the horizontal mould-block rest, in combination with the vertical and horizontal rock-shafts and cam, and the use of the lever and rod, in combination with the horizontal mould-block rest and matrix. Also, the use of the matrix holder, having a slot in it, to allow of a lifting motion on its centre-pin, and a notch on its back side for the end of a spring to act against, in combination with a spring, and inclined plane or cam, on the horizontal rock-shaft, and a pin for holding it, and a V-shaped bar secured to an adjustable end plate, attached to the outer end of the lower half of the mould-block.

CHAS. MÜLLER, New York, January 3, 1854.—The improvement in type-casting machines claimed is for suspending the mould below its axis of oscillation, whereby its tendency towards the centre of gravity will act in opposition to the momentum required, in its movement towards and from the mould, and its movement and degree of opening can then be reduced. Also, the combination of a cam, lever, and rod, for the purpose of opening and closing the mould.

DANIEL MOORE, New York, March 21, 1854.—An improved method of rubbing type, which consists in the use of a supply plate, from which the type are thrown, by centrifugal force, through a gutter or trough, into a conducting plate, that, by an elastic roller, supplies the type to a series of rotary fingers, that carry the types first over a stone, or similar rough surface, that takes off any small burs, or feathered edges, which, getting into the cutters, might cause the type to deviate from its course. Next, the type is carried through between a series of two or more cutters, that successively shave the sides of the type. The type passes, finally, between brushes, which clean or remove from the type the fibres or shavings of metal which have been cut from the type, and leave it ready for use.

GEORGE BRUCE, New York, November 14, 1854.—This invention consists in a blast to cool the type-mould, by means of a tube, in the operation of casting.

GEORGE SCHAUB, Hamburg, March 30, 1858.—The nature of this invention consists in manufacturing types for printing, by casting the stems or bodies of the types at the back of a sheet of type-heads, and, also, in the manufacture of spaces used in setting up type, by means of a movable frame.

JOSEPH CORDUAN, Brooklyn, N. Y., July 17, 1860. —This invention consists in an improved method of coating type-metal with brass.

WM. MOORE, Brooklyn, N. Y., September 23, 1863. —This invention is designed to remove the projection or burr attached to the cast type. The cutting plates, between whose edges the type are forced, are dressed so that one edge is thicker than the other, so as to make an interval or mouth between them when they are ranged side by side and confined by screws within the stock. Two of these stocks are ranged relatively to the bed, with a space between them to be traversed by the type, impelled by suitable machinery.

R. W. and D. DAVIS, New York, September 22, 1863.—The improvement consists of a mould, made of a series of detached strips, fastened by a connecting band, and passed through a box under a receiver filled with plastic material, and fitted with a plunger, whereby the material is pressed into the moulds, and cut off by a knife from the receiver, the registering of the moulds with the matrices being insured by projections on the mould.

JOHN J. C. SMITH, Philadelphia, July 19, 1864.—This invention consists of a machine for cutting types of all sizes from strips of metal which are cast or made of type-heads on one side. It is accomplished by a rotary saw, with clamps to hold the metal strips, and feeding arrangements suited to the purpose.

JOHN J. C. SMITH, Philadelphia, July 26, 1864.—The object of this invention is to obtain type by casting a strip of type-metal, which strip has on one edge a row of type-heads or faces, separated from each other by intervening spaces, sufficient to allow a saw to be passed between, to cut them apart into single type.

JOHN J. C. SMITH, Philadelphia, December 6, 1864.—This invention consists in forming the body of printers' type of rolled metal, drawn out to a uniform thickness and width, and in soldering a row of electrotype heads to one edge, and then cutting the strip into single type.

HORATIO J. HEWITT, Brooklyn, N. Y., October 8, 1865.—This invention consists in reducing the width of the body of script type below that of the top, or head, so that what is termed a kern projects from the top of the type. By this construction it is claimed that a saving of one-third of the type-metal may be effected, and more matter inserted in the same space.

THOMAS S. HUDSON, E. Cambridge, Mass., June 5, 1866.—By this process the letters are struck up from sheet metal, and the face ground off until the roundness is removed and definite square sides and angles are obtained.

DAVID BRUCE, Brooklyn, N. Y., July 28, 1868.—This apparatus is attached to a type-casting machine, so as to receive the type as fast as cast, and break off the jet or stem of metal adhering thereto, by a continuous consecutive operation.

TYPE-SETTING AND DISTRIBUTING MACHINES.

FREDERICK ROSENBURG, Sweden, September 9, 1843.—A machine for setting up type, arranging it for justification, and transferring it when justified to a galley with a distributor combined.

WILLIAM H. MITCHELL, New York, August 30, 1853.—This machine consists of means for distributing types from the form, and setting them up in rows, within grooves, a given letter in each groove or row, with the faces of the types upwards, and in a line. From these grooves the types are removed, each row of a given letter at a time, and placed within slides or conductors which supply them to an apparatus connected with finger-keys. The striking of any given finger-key drops one of the types upon a series of belts, which are moved by pulleys; the belts conduct the type to a composing wheel or conductor, in the order in which the keys drop them.

WILLIAM H. MITCHELL, Brooklyn, New York, May 16, 1854.—This is an improvement on the patent granted August 30, 1853, and applies to the parts for dropping the type from the conductors on to the belts which convey the type to the belt which carries it to the composing apparatus, and also comprises the invention of the wheel for setting up or composing type in line.

THOMAS W. GILMER, Charlottesville, Va., November 15, 1859.—This machine consists of three distinct parts, a case for holding the types, a composing-stick for withdrawing the type from the case and setting them in line, and a distributing-stick for the purpose of transferring the type from the line to the type cases.

HENRY HAEGER, Delhi, Iowa, June 26, 1860.—This invention consists in the arrangement of machinery in connection with the type case by which the types are fed to the composing-stick, and of an arrangement of fingers and levers in connection with the composing-stick, by which the types may be taken from the case and set in line.

D. B. RAY, Circleville, Ohio, January 28, 1862.—In this machine tubes are so constructed that the type, as they are being distributed into hoppers by hand, shall be made to arrange themselves in passing through the tubes with the notched edges all turned the same way. The arm is twisted for the purpose of reversing the position of the type as it passes down. Catches are placed at the bottom of each tube to prevent the type from sliding out, which tubes are operated, when necessary, by a key. The composing-stick is so constructed, with a spring and slide attached, as to bring the type into a perpendicular position at whatever angle they may be dropped into the stick.

O. L. BROWN, Boston, November 25, 1862.—This invention consists in placing the type in a case formed of cells of such a width as to admit of a single row of type, and using in connection therewith a sliding stick, together with a mechanism arranged in such manner that the stick may be shoved along below the case, and brought to a proper relative position with any of the rows of type in the case, the type to be discharged from the case and properly deposited in the stick.

H. W. ALDEN and W. MACKAY, New York, January 23, 1866.—This machine is too complicated to admit of a condensed explanation without reference to the specifications and drawings.

WILLIAM H. HUSTON, New York, March 17,

1848.—This machine cannot be briefly described; and it can be comprehended only by an examination of the entire specifications and drawings.

UNIVERSAL TYPOGRAPHY.

JOSIAH WARREN, New Harmony, Ind., April 25, 1846.—This is a patent for a composition to be used as a substitute for type-metal, composed of gum shellac, tar, and sand. Also a composition on which to take impressions of types, engravings, etc., or on which to form letters or drawings, thereby forming matrices or moulds, in which to form casts for type for printing made of this composition. This last composition is made of clay mixed with sand in various proportions, also with gum arabic, beeswax, stearine, tallow.

WETTING-MACHINES.

WM. OVEREND, Cincinnati, Jan. 24, 1854.—This machine is intended to give to paper the proper dampness, in order to prepare it for the press. A given quantity of paper is placed upon the table, and is fed into the machine by nippers, when it is carried forward between wetted blankets, passing between rollers, and is finally deposited on a pile beneath the machine, having received the required amount of moisture in its passage.

ANDREW OVEREND, Philadelphia, March 14, 1854. —This machine has two rollers, covered with felt or blanket. The lower roller is made to revolve in a trough of water, which is imparted by means of the felt cover to the upper roller. The paper is passed from an adjustable table, intermittingly between the rollers, by means of which both sides are wetted during its passage through the machine. It is then piled by means of a series of fingers on a receiving table.

JOHN A. LYNCH, Boston, April 27, 1858.—This apparatus consists of a hollow perforated cylinder covered with cloth, and containing water, and a second cylinder covered with floating paper, the two cylinders being connected by a handle, and revolving in a frame, whereby the sheets upon which an impression is to be made will be dampened by the water cylinder, and the superfluous moisture absorbed by the second cylinder at one operation.

ANDREW DOUGHERTY, New York, July 9, 1861.— The main feature in this invention is a roller covered with cloth for wetting a continuous roll of paper, and a brake for regulating the delivery of the dry paper from the roller. The brake consists of a block of wood placed vertically between the guides, its lower edge being rounded, and resting upon the dry roll to produce uniform friction, whether it be full of paper or nearly empty. The roller upon which the damp paper is wound moves a little faster than the dry-paper roller, on account of the increased length of the paper when wet.

Inverted Commas.—Commas having their faces inverted, two of which (") are placed at the beginning of a quotation, and one (') at the beginning of a quotation within a quotation. Two inverted commas are also often placed at the commencement of each paragraph of a quotation, and in some works at the commencement of each line of an extract.

Italic.—Types cast with an oblique inclination, thus: (this is Italic.) They were first made by Aldus Manutius, in imitation, it is said, of the close and careful handwriting of the Italian poet Petrarch. They were first employed in printing a small octavo edition of Virgil, issued in 1501, after the appearance of which Aldus obtained a letter of privilege, or patent, from Pope Leo X., giving him the exclusive right to use his invention. The chief recommendation of Italic type at that period was its compactness, and it was gratefully welcomed by the reading public because it tended to reduce the bulk of unwieldy volumes and assisted the efforts to reduce the number of abbreviations. Subsequently, after Roman letters of the smallest sizes desirable were cast, Italic letters were freely used in printing prefaces, in emphasizing words to which authors wished to direct special attention, and in the headings of chapters or pages. It is still in such general use that Roman fonts of body-letter are almost invariably accompanied with smaller fonts of Italic of the corresponding size; but it is rarely or never employed now in printing prefaces; and the proportion of words italicized in careful modern compositions is much smaller than in former times. Compositors working by the piece or thousand ems have a deep aversion to Italics, on account of the loss of time occasioned by journeys to and from an Italic case; and tasteful typographers object to it on account of the well-founded belief that its occasional employment mars the beauty of a page of Roman type. In the celebrated Bible printed with such extraordinary care for Macklin, the words usually appearing in Italic were designated by a small dot under their central vowel, and the beauty of that marvel of typographic excellence was greatly enhanced by this novel expedient.

For ornamental purposes, or for printing intended to imitate handwriting, Italic proper has been superseded by many elegant varieties of script invented by modern type-founders.

Item.—A Latin word meaning also, used in catalogues, etc., when an article is added. Item is also used to express the several details or subdivisions which combine to make a whole; the separate articles of a report of local news being called items, or local items.

Its Own Paper.—When one or more proofs of a work or job are printed on the paper that the whole is intended to be worked on, it is said to be pulled on its own paper. This is frequently done at the commencement of a work, when a proof of the first sheet is sent to the author or publisher that he may see the effect before the work is actually proceeded with.

Izzard.—A name for the letter Z, used in England, but generally abandoned in the United States, where the letter is commonly called Zee. The advocates of the change of name in America frequently illustrated its advantages by asking their opponents to spell the word lizard, which by the old established rule must be spelled thus:—l-i-izzard-liz-a-r-d, lizard.

J.

Jaggard and Blount.—Isaac Jaggard and Edward Blount are to be remembered as the printers of the first edition of Shakspeare's plays, the famous folio of 1623. The book was published under the direction of Heminge and Condell, two actors, who dedicated it to the Earls of Pembroke and Montgomery in these words:—

Since your lordships have been pleased to think these trifles something, heretofore, and have prosecuted both them and their author, living, with so much favour, we hope you will use the like indulgence toward them you have done unto their parent. There is a great difference, whether any book choose his parents or find them: this hath done both; for so much were your lordships' likings of the several parts, when they were acted, as before they were published, the volume asked to be yours. We have but collected them, and done an office to the dead to procure his orphans guardians, without ambition either of self-profit or fame: only to keep the memory of so worthy a friend and fellow alive, as was our Shakspeare.

This first edition contains a portrait for which authenticity may well be claimed, as the book was edited by two personal friends, and it has always ranked as the standard authority in questions of disputed readings, as presenting the original text accepted by the actors of Shakspeare's own age. It was sold originally for one pound. The book was entitled, Mr. William Shakespeares Comedies, Histories, and Tragedies. Published according to the true Original Copies. London, 1623. Folio.

Jeffing.—Throwing with quadrats, somewhat in the fashion in which dice are thrown, to decide disputed points in printing-offices, such as who shall receive a fat take of copy, etc. This ancient custom is still maintained, although it is now applied to a smaller number of objects than in former years. The usual plan is to take nine em quadrats or quads, which are shaken in the closed hands of each of the jeffing party, in turn, each person having three throws and the winner being usually the person who has thrown the largest number of nicks uppermost; although, under one system, a mollie, which consists of three throws without a single nick being turned uppermost, entitles the thrower to be declared winner.

Jenson, Nicolas.—An engraver of coins and medals in the Royal Mint at Paris, who was dispatched by King Charles VII. of France, about the year 1458, to Mentz, as a person specially suited, by his skill in metals, to study the art of type-making. Jenson accomplished his undertaking, but returning to France about the time of the death of King Charles, determined to establish himself at Venice, where printing was just introduced by John of Spires. Sweynheim and Pannartz, at Rome, in 1467, had made the first attempt at conforming their type to the character of the Roman or Italian manuscript. De Spira had made certain improvements in the same direction, and Jenson, with John of Cologne, pursued the same method. Jenson's type was remarkably excellent, and to him is usually ascribed the honor of bringing the Roman type to perfection. Jenson's first publications appeared in 1470, and were in Roman type; but in 1475 he introduced Gothic characters into his books, and engraved four different sets of that letter, which he employed in his Bibles, and books of divinity and law. His Gothic and Roman were considered equally excellent for their beauty and elegance of finish, and his Roman was assumed as the model for Garamond's famous French type. Being claimed as a Frenchman, Jenson has been especially celebrated by French authors; but his name and his close connection with the early German printers John of Cologne and John of Spires, have led some authors to conjecture that he was himself a German. Jenson's last publications appeared in 1481. A copy of his Pliny of 1476 preserved in the Philadelphia Library is a beautiful specimen of Roman, printed with a glossy black ink upon vellum with a handsome and wide margin.

Job-Hand.—A printer who generally confines himself to job-work. Skill in this department demands not only a knowledge of plain composition on newspapers or books, but a good comprehension of the style and effects of many descriptions of type, as well as of the multifarious details connected with the job printing of the present day.

Job Letter.—Under this head may be grouped all styles of printing-type, except Roman and Italic. This classification may not be regarded as strictly accurate. The types used for titles of books, etc. are generally known among printers as Title Letter, while the letter used on newspapers for the headings of articles is known as Head Letter, and that used in advertisements as Display Letter. Nevertheless, all the styles of type used on newspapers and in books are also employed in all other kinds of printing which are generalized as job-work; so they may all fairly be included under the head of Job Letter.

One distinct class of job letter—that made of wood —is described elsewhere. (See WOOD TYPE.) The smallest size of job letter made in the United States is Pearl, and the largest metal type is Twenty-one-line Pica, equivalent to three-and-a-half inches. Wood type, however, is made as large as One-hundred-and-fifty-line Pica, and as small as two-line Pica. Being less costly than metal type of large size, it is generally employed when letters of six-line Pica (one inch) or larger are required. The chief advantage of large metal type is its superior adaptation to printing on the surface of fine enameled cards, etc.

In no one particular is the contrast between the printing of the present day and that of earlier periods more marked than in the difference between the great variety of faces and sizes of type now used and the meagreness of the assortment of job letter possessed by the printers of former generations. There was no

Text Letters.

Black—Great Primer
Condensed Black—Great Primer
Sloping Black—Great Primer
Sloping Black Shaded
Modern Text—Great Primer
Scribe Text—Great Primer
Church Text—English
Boldface Borussian—Two-line Min.
Black Ornate Shaded
Eureka Text
Saxon Ornate
Medieval—Two-line Pica
Medieval Text—Two-line Small Pica
Allemanic—Two-line Long Primer
Fancy Text—Two-line English
Card Text—Two-line English
Card Text Shaded—Two-line English
Teutonic Extended
Teutonic—English

Scripts.

Graphotype—Cairo
Backslope—Charleston
Double Pica Script—Boston
Italic Script—Lancaster
Calligraphic Script—New Orleans
Payson—Philadelphia
2 line Small Pica—New York
Hancock Script—Baltimore
Garibaldi Script—Washington
Bulletin Script—Erie
Secretary—Cincinnati
Italian Script—Pittsburgh
Madisonian—Chicago
Great Primer Round—Brooklyn
Pica Script—The Smallest Size Made

PLAIN JOB LETTER.

ANTIQUE—Pica

ANTIQUE CONDENSED—Pica

ANTIQUE EXTRA CONDENSED—Pica

ANTIQUE EXT'D

ANTIQUE EXT'D

OLD STYLE ANTIQUE—Long Primer

TITLE—Long Primer

TITLE CONDENSED—Long Primer

TITLE EXTENDED

GOTHIC—Pica

GOTHIC CONDENSED—Pica

GOTHIC EXTRA CONDENSED—Pica

GOTHIC EXT'D—BREVIER

EXTRA CONDENSED—2 LINE LONG PRIMER

CONDENSED—English

LIGHTFACE

LIGHTFACE EXTENDED

LIGHTFACE CELTIC—BREVIER

CLARENDON—Small Pica

FRENCH CLARENDON—Long Primer

RUNIC—Pica

RUNIC EXTENDED—Long Primer

Engravers' Italic—Long Primer

CHAMFER CONDENSED—LONG PRIMER

BOLDFACE ITALIC—Pica

DORIC—2 line Nonp.

FANCY JOB LETTER.

PHILADELPHIAN

MINARET

MONASTIC—GREAT PRIMER

CONDENSED MONASTIC—BREVIER

BROADGAUGE SHADED

SMITHSONIAN—Pica

Greenback—Great Primer

TRIBIAL—Great Primer

STALACTITE—FUST

PEAKED—Great Primer

RAY SHADED

Rimmed Condensed

The following are a few of the varieties of Type called

ORNAMENTED:

Pica Ornamented

STOCKING KNITTLE

ELECTRIC MACHINE

LADIES' OXIGXOXS

RAIL FENCES

CENTRALIZATION

SHADY SLOPES

CREEPING TENDRILS

lack of talent among the early type-founders, nor of disposition to exercise it, but it was displayed only in varying the faces of letter used as text, in cutting the characters of foreign languages, and in making flowers, borders, etc. Job-work, as now understood, had no existence, and they were not called upon to devise fanciful styles for the plain a b c's of the English alphabet. It required the multifarious demands of plain and ornamental job printing, united with the modern facilities for cheap and rapid production, to incite modern type-founders to call into existence the bewildering variety of beautiful creations which adorn their specimen books, and subsequently give force and elegance to thousands of printers' products which were unknown half a century ago.

Rees's Cyclopædia (published in 1819), in its article on Printing, contains specimens of the printing-types of noted British founders of that day, in which faint streaks of the dawn of the new era appear. The list includes several varieties of Script; several styles of five-line letter; several sizes of open letter; one specimen called ornamented, which is only moderately embellished; and Blacks of various shapes and sizes, most of which had probably been originated for use in the text of the black-letter books of former times. A few years later, Hansard, in his Typographia, denounced as typographical monstrosities several new faces which did not conform in their proportions to his notions of propriety and excellence. In sorrow and in anger he said:—

One of these is called Antique or Egyptian, the property of which is, that the strokes which form the letters are all of one uniform thickness! After this, who would have thought that further extravagance could have been conceived? It remains, however, to be stated that the ingenuity of one founder has contrived a type in which the natural shape is reversed by turning all the ceriphs and fine strokes into fats, and all the fats into leans !

The Antiques and French Clarendon of the present day are improvements on the monstrosities that excited Hansard's ire. His work was published in 1825, and this may be taken as the date of the introduction of the style of letter named Antique, which now exists in many varieties, and is a standard job letter in daily use in every printing-office. Script type had been introduced long before, and Didot, the eminent French founder, had cast it as large as eleven-line Pica. (See SCRIPT TYPE.) The Didots were also probably the first to introduce fancy letter. Their earliest styles were called Gothique, Bâtarde, Coulée, and Ronde.

The Specimen Book of Binney & Ronaldson, of Philadelphia, issued in 1812, contained only six styles other than Roman and Italic, and but twenty-two sizes. In 1815 D. & G. Bruce, of New York, issued specimens of their type, consisting of fifteen plain faces from Pearl to Great Primer. They did not seem to think it worth while to show whatever job letter they had. The Specimen Book of Johnson

& Smith, of Philadelphia, issued in 1834, exhibited thirty-four styles and one hundred and fifty-five sizes. This includes the larger sizes of Roman and Italic, all the ornamented letter, and many fonts of wood type. As this book contained not only the styles manufactured by J. & S., but also selections from the manufactures of other founders, it may be regarded as presenting a close approximation to all the varieties of job letter made in the United States when it was issued.

There are now made in the United States more than two hundred radically different styles of job letter, besides about the same number which receive the common name of Ornamented, though each differs from the other. Including size and style, the varieties of metal job letter now in use far exceed two thousand, exclusive of Scripts, which number more than a hundred. Among the two hundred styles which have been called radically different, many differ as widely within themselves as from other distinct families. For example, the style called Antique is thus varied—

ANTIQUE   **ANTIQUE**
ANTIQUE   **ANTIQUE**
            ANTIQUE

The difference in Gothics is quite as marked—

GOTHIC   **GOTHIC**
GOTHIC   GOTHIC

Pages might be filled with similar examples. Including, then, the varieties that exist among the types simply called Ornamented, the American printer has nearly a thousand different styles of job letter from which to make a selection when fitting out his office. This is independent of wood type, which varies as much in style as metal type, and, by the scope it affords in size, may be extended to more than twenty thousand distinct alphabets.

Job Letter may be conveniently divided into Plain, Fancy, Text, and Script. The first includes such styles differing from Roman and Italic, as present regular forms without ornament. Fancy Letter includes all types highly ornamented or of grotesque or irregular shapes. Text Letter includes the Blacks of the early founders, in the original and in all their numerous modified forms. Scripts are those type which are made to represent modern handwriting.

The later forms of plain job letter—as Antiques, Lightfaces, Gothics, etc.—are generally more graceful than the earlier; and the fancy letter made within the last ten years has nearly banished from use that made previously. New styles follow each other with marvelous rapidity, and it requires a severe draught on the printer's pocket to enable him to possess all the new and beautiful types with which the founder constantly tempts him.

The most tasteful and useful of the fancy job letters now in use have been originated in the United States, and of both plain and fancy the variety is much greater here than in any other country. This is the case because our founders, in addition to the large number of styles originally produced by themselves, quickly and generally appropriate all new styles made elsewhere. This is accomplished either by purchasing drives from foreign founders, or by making electrotype matrices from type.

The purpose of the numbers attached to the names of different types is frequently misapprehended. A number simply denotes the order in which the founder who adopts it made the type to which it is attached. Thus, the Antique No. 5 of one founder may be identical with the Antique No. 2 of another. That is, it may be the fifth variety of Antique made by the one, and therefore called by him No. 5, and the second variety of Antique made by the other, and therefore called by him No. 2. It is important that the printer in ordering type should be careful to specify the number, if any is attached to the type he desires; and, as almost every printing-office is now supplied with specimens from various founders, he should also state from whose specimens his selection is made. In ordering sorts, a sample type should always be sent. When these precautions are taken by the printer, the type-founder will rarely make a mistake in filling the order.

The common name of Ornamented was for a long time given to nearly all fancy letter, the different styles being designated only by numbers. To such an extent was this carried, that one type-founder still has on his list forty-four different styles having the common name of Two-line Pica Ornamented, and distinguished from one another in title only by Nos. 1 to 44. Under this arrangement the name of a type conveys no idea of its distinctive character; and, as each founder uses different numbers, according to the order in which he makes a given style, the whole matter of ornamented letter is very confusing. Latterly, however, the nomenclature of job letter has been much improved. When a new style is now produced, the type-founder generally gives it a specific name, by which it soon becomes known to the printer. Thus, while Pica Ornamented No. 4 may mean a dozen different letters, made by as many different founders, no well-informed printer has any difficulty in recognizing Pica Philadelphian, Pica Rimmel Shaded, Pica Engravers' Open, Pica Phidian, and various other late styles.

It is to be regretted that this excellent plan is becoming deranged by the anxiety of some founders to make it appear, by the names they adopt, that they are introducing a new style, when in fact they are only reproducing what others have previously made. Thus, the Oblique Shaded of some founders is the Bank Note Italic of others; French Clarendon appears also as Egyptian; Fantail is identical with Arcadian, and so forth, until there is danger that the printer will soon be as completely confused by the various specific names for the same style of type as he has been by the multiplicity of ornamental letters distinguished only by numbers, which are varied by each manufacturer.

17

This is a matter of much importance to printers, and type-founders owe it to their customers to adopt an unvarying nomenclature for job letter; at least for that hereafter designed. A fair, rational and effective plan would be for them to enter into an agreement that the specific name given to any style by the original maker shall be adopted by all subsequent manufacturers.

Specimens of a few of the modern styles of job letter having specific names are introduced on pages 254 and 255.

Job Office.—An office in which job-work, mainly, is executed; the three grand subdivisions of modern typography being, book offices, newspaper or news offices, and job offices. Many American offices, however, are at once newspaper and job, or book and job offices.

Job Presses.—Presses constructed specially for printing job-work. They are intended to execute every kind of work that was formerly done on the hand-press, as well as new descriptions of printing of comparatively modern invention, with increased rapidity, economy, and ease. Nearly all the job presses now in general use in this country are described under their appropriate headings in this work.

Job Printing.—All kinds of letter-press printing, except the printing of books and of such newspapers as are printed in offices organized by their proprietors, are generally called job printing. Jobbing departments are attached to many newspaper establishments in the United States, and a well-equipped job printing-office is usually capable of printing either books or newspapers, while some book offices do some forms of jobbing; but there are, nevertheless, a considerable number of offices which confine their labors to some one of these departments, and are exclusively, either book, newspaper, or job offices. Job-work, of some descriptions, is as old as the art of printing. One of the first things printed by the early typographers was a blank form of Papal Indulgences; Fust and Schoeffer printed a poster for Diether, the Archbishop of Mentz, who was driven out of that city by Adolphus of Nassau; and the first printing executed in the United States was a blank form, to be sworn to and subscribed by each freeman of Massachusetts, known as the Freeman's Oath.

But, while activity in all branches of the art has been stimulated by the general spread of intelligence, job printing was the last to be developed into considerable importance by this powerful agent. Used to a great extent for business purposes, it was of limited utility before large masses of people learned to read; and the aggregate value of its products at the present day is so large, as compared with its products in former times, that it is virtually a modern creation. Its development has also been much hastened by the invention of many varieties of job presses and other machinery, as well as by the immense increase, during recent years, of the forms, faces, and sizes of types representing the alphabet. (See Job Letter.) In its diversified departments, it calls into requisition the highest skill of the compositor, pressman, paper-maker, ink-maker, type-founder, ruler, binder, engraver, and of all who manufacture materials or machinery to be used in a printing-office, or who are employed in typographical labors,—a long series of improvements having not only lessened the cost of production, but also educated the public taste to an appreciation of the finer qualities of printing.

While the hand-press, exclusively, was used for printing cards, circulars, posters, etc., as well as books and newspapers, it was a tedious, vexatious, and laborious operation to produce a fine job, especially from a small form, great effort being necessary to prevent slurring, and to give a sharp outline on the face of the card or sheet printed, with a slight show of impression on its back. But with the aid of job presses, and other modern appliances, specially adapted to fine work, the skillful printer is enabled to produce a clear and sharp outline, and at the same time to avoid slurs and injuries to the face of the paper,—so that the best products of typography will compare favorably with the products of the copper-plate press.

The great number of new styles of type, combination borders, and labor-saving·materials, united with the variety of inks, bronzes, papers, presses, etc., afford to a skillful printer a wide field for the display of taste and ingenuity in adapting his work to the varied wants of his customers, and in rendering it attractive and pleasing to the public. One of the most important branches of these labors is discussed elsewhere. (See DISPLAY OF TYPE.) While many fine specimens of skill in this department are exhibited, there are, unfortunately, very few printers who have given to it as much attention as it deserves, or who are capable of making the best use of the materials at their command. In the hands of a master, types are literally made to talk, and the meaning of the writer is conveyed with a force analogous to that displayed by a finished actor in representing passages of a great play. It was said of a very skillful Scotch compositor of the last century, that he combined in types such symmetry and elegance as might vie with the powers of a painter's pencil, although the varieties of type at his command would be considered exceedingly limited in number at the present day; and the highest attainable results now must, perhaps, be regarded rather as an inspiration of genius than as the emanations of even unusually well-trained skill. As the actor is told to suit the action to the word; so, in displayed jobs, superior compositors suit the type to the word or line to a surprising degree, even when they have a comparatively small number of fonts of letter at command, while inferior or unskillful workmen produce but poor results from an immense variety of job letter.

In the proper justification and locking up of jobs, especially such as are set with curved lines, initial letters, etc., there is a wide field for the exercise of that mechanical ingenuity which tends to save time and material, by inserting just enough space material to properly tighten a curved line, so as to preserve its

symmetry when locked up ready for the press, without bearing unequally on the ends of the straight line underneath, and causing it to hang either at the right or left, or to bow in the centre to such an extent as to cause a doubt, in the mind of the reader, whether the lines underneath the curve were intended to be straight, or the whole job set up in curved form, the upper line being only a base on which to build or set up the succeeding lines. The blocks on which initial letters are mounted are often out of square, and it remains for the careful job compositor so to set up his work that such defects will be entirely overcome. Much time can be saved by having the material used for spacing cut into proper lengths and kept in places within easy reach of the compositor while setting his job. In no department of the business is the rule of a place for everything, and everything in its place, of more importance than in job printing, and no other department calls for the exercise of so much vigilance in preventing the wanton destruction of valuable material by incompetent workmen. It would be well if, after sufficient material for the demands of the office had been cut up, that the saw, lead-cutter, and shears should be under the personal control of the superintendent or foreman, only to be used when the increased demands of the business require the stock of materials to be replenished. In press-work, the same rule might profitably be followed, in regard to the screw wrench in regulating the impressions on presses. In small job presses, more especially, where the impression can be increased or decreased by a greater or less number of sheets in the tympan, it would be well to set the impression even to the largest form that can conveniently be imposed in the chase, and then regulate the impression by the number of sheets which any other form requires to be placed in the tympan. The same rule might be followed with profit and economy on larger job presses, where the kind of work to be printed on them is of uniform quality.

In justifying poster forms, set with curved lines, requiring no proof previous to printing, gypsum, or plaster of Paris, is often used with advantage, and in the hands of a careful workman it is a valuable auxiliary in that department of job printing.

The proper adjustment of space between the lines of a job, or title to a pamphlet, is of great importance, and in this respect much depends on the judgment and taste of the compositor, and the character of the work. The new styles of letter furnished by type-founders, from time to time, by introducing new faces, have very materially changed the standard of excellence, in matters of taste, so far as the adjustment of light and heavy types is concerned, and there is a succession of new fashions in display, as well as in type.

No matter how well a job may be set up, however, it will necessarily be spoiled by bad press-work, while good press-work, good ink, and good paper will go far to redeem the imperfect or unsightly appearance of a form that has been badly balanced or poorly displayed. There would be an amazing difference in the appearance of two sets of sheets printed from the same electrotyped or stereotyped form, if great care was taken in the selection of the paper and ink, as well as in the press-work, of one set, while inferior material or inferior workmanship was employed upon the other. In view of the bewildering varieties of paper and cards, as well as black and colored inks, and styles of presses and press-work, there is, therefore, an immense field for the exercise of care, industry, taste, and talent, upon a job, after it leaves the hands of a compositor, and it requires due attention to all these details, in conjunction with artistic display of copy, to meet educated and exacting modern requirements. This is more especially necessary since lithography has competed successfully and victoriously, in some sections of the country, with typography, in various branches of job printing. To counteract the advantages lithography derives from the free scope it affords to the artist's pencil, the aid of wood-engraving is becoming more and more essential, with each new year, to city letter-press-job-printers,—and of late years there is also a marked tendency to divide the business into specialties, so that wood-engraving can be economically used, and various other aids to cheap production be secured. Thus, some job-printers direct their chief attention to railway printing, or to colored show-work, or to posters, or to the demands of some special trade or business, as druggists, tobacconists, grocers, auctioneers, merchants, etc.

It is still, however, the custom of the generality of job-offices to execute all, or nearly all, descriptions of job printing required in the localities in which they are established; and the demands of the public are exceedingly varied. The French term corresponding with job printing means, when literally translated, works of the city; and this phrase helps to suggest the appropriate and forcible idea, that miscellaneous printing is often required to accelerate the movements of all forms of intellectual and business activity. This will appear from the following partial list of its products:

Accounts Current, Account Book Headings, Advertising Charts, Anniversary Programmes, Advertising Pages, Almanacs, Acts of Assembly, Auctioneers' Catalogues.

Bill Heads, Bills of Fare, Blank Book Headings, Briefs of Title, Ballads, Bills of Lading, Bills of Exchange, Bank Notices, Bonds, Blanks of many descriptions.

Cards, including Business, Wedding, Announcement and Sample Cards, Ball Tickets, Ball Programmes, Checks for Balls, Professional and Visiting Cards, Railroad Show Cards, Time Tables, Price Lists, Rules and Regulations, Admission Tickets, Excursion Tickets, Conductors' Checks, Commutation Tickets, Coupon Tickets, Railway Passes, Restaurant Checks;—Certificates of Stock, Circulars, Bank Checks, Certificates of Deposit, Calendars and Catalogues of Books or Merchandise.

Deeds, Distributing Bills, Dodgers, Direction Tags,

Deposit Tickets, Diplomas, Diaries, Drafts, Designs from Wood-Cuts, Diagrams.

Envelopes, Election Tickets.

Gutter Snipes.

Hand Bills.

Insurance Policies, Invoice Blanks.

Lawyers' Briefs and Paper Books, Labels, including Direction Labels, Adhesive and Plain, Bottle, Liquor, Box, Can and Book; Letter Headings, Letter Circulars, Leaflets.

Manifests, Magazines.

Note Headings, Note Circulars, Notices of Dissolution, Co-partnership, Meetings, etc.

Order Books.

Pamphlets, Posters, plain and in colors, Promissory Notes, Pawn Tickets, Proclamations, Prospectuses, Papers, transient, weekly or monthly, Patterns for Garment Cutting.

Receipt Books.

Statements of Account, Survey Blanks, Survey Maps, Stock Lists, Sachets, and Show Work of many descriptions.

Way Bills, Wrappers for patent medicines or merchandise, etc., etc.

A rhyming advertisement aptly described some of the varieties of job-work as follows:

Printing by hand,
Printing by steam,
Printing from type,
Or from blocks—by the
ream.

Printing in black,
Printing in white,
Printing in colors,
Of sombre or bright.

Printing for merchants,
And land-agents too;
Printing for any
Who've printing to do;

Printing for bankers,
Clerks, auctioneers,
Printing for druggists,
For dealers in wares.

Printing for drapers,
For grocers, for all
Who want printing done,
And will come, or say,
Call.

Printing of pamphlets,
Or bigger books, too;
In fact, there are few
things
But what we can do.

Printing of placards,
Printing of bills,
Printing of cart-notes
For stores or for mills;

Printing of labels,
All colors or use, sirs,
Especially fit for
Colonial producers.

Printing of forms—
All sorts you can get—
Legal, commercial,
Or House to be Let.

Printing done quickly,
Bold, stylish, or neat,
At —— Printing-
office,
—— Street.

Johnson, John.—An English printer, author of Typographia, a valuable work in two volumes, published in 1824 by the Longmans of London. Although much of its technical and mechanical instruction is rendered obsolete by the rapidity of modern improvements, the work is still valuable as a book of reference on many of the numerous details of printing, and the first volume is especially interesting for its elaborate descriptions of the books published by the English printers down to the year 1600. Johnson appears to have been one of the victims of the book-mania of the time, and to have suffered great pecuniary losses from his connection with Sir Egerton Brydges in what is usually styled that gentleman's Private Press at Lee Priory. According to the statement of Sir Egerton Brydges, this press was established in 1813 by Johnson and a pressman named Warwick, with the understanding that the baronet was to have no share in the expenses, but that he was only to furnish them with copy gratuitously, chiefly of reprints from his library of rare old English books, and that the printers should run all the risk. This connection was broken in 1817, and Johnson quitted the establishment, which continued in operation until the end of 1822. In 1818, Johnson published the prospectus for a work upon the history of printing, but was compelled by want of funds to delay the publication until he received liberal pecuniary assistance from E. Walmsley, Esq. The work was afterwards expanded beyond the limits originally intended, and was published in 1824 as Typographia, or the Printer's Instructor. The difficulties arising from his connection with Leo Priory led to a lingering Chancery suit, and in his preface to Typographia, Johnson says that the task of writing it was undertaken as a relief from the mental affliction brought on by the cruel and unjust treatment experienced from those connected with the Press, and he further complains that the suit had already lingered eight years in Chancery. Johnson's Typographia owed its origin to the bibliomania of the time, and was dedicated—as a work upon the origin and progress of the art of Caxton, De Worde, and Pynson—to Earl Spencer, the president, and the members of the Roxburghe Club. Johnson was subsequently a master-printer in London.

Johnson, Lawrence.—One of the most extensive and successful type-founders in the United States. He was born January 23, 1801, in Hull, England, and was apprenticed to the printing-business in the office of John Childs & Son, at Bungay, England, at so early an age that he had served an apprenticeship of seven years before he emigrated with his parents to the United States, where they arrived in 1819, landing in New York. Here he worked with extraordinary diligence as a compositor in the printing-office of Mr. Gray, often protracting his labors sixteen or eighteen hours per day. About the year 1820, he became deeply interested in the comparatively new art of stereotyping, and with a view of obtaining a knowledge of it he worked for some months with B. and J. Collins, of New York, after which he removed to Philadelphia, where, with but a small capital and limited experience, he established a stereotype foundry. Despite numerous difficulties, he built up and conducted a large and prosperous business as a stereotyper, and after this had been successfully prosecuted for more than ten years, he added type-founding to his previous calling, by purchasing, in conjunction with Mr. George F. Smith, the type-foundry established by Archibald Binney and James Ronaldson, which was then (1833) owned by Richard Ronaldson. Ten years later

(1843) Mr. Smith withdrew from the business, and for two years both the type-foundry and the stereotype-foundry were under Mr. Johnson's exclusive care and ownership; but his indefatigable labors at length seriously affected his health, and in 1845 he associated with him Thomas MacKellar, John F. Smith, and Richard Smith, who, in conjunction with Peter A. Jordan, are the present proprietors of what is still widely known as the Johnson Type-Foundry, although the firm name is now MacKellar, Smiths and Jordan. Through the united efforts of the new firm, varieties of type were increased, an unprecedentedly large and attractive Specimen Book was published, the quarterly Typographic Advertiser was issued, and the operations of the foundry were greatly enlarged. Mr. Johnson died on the 26th of April, 1860, after an eminently successful business career, in which he gained the friendship, respect, and confidence of his associates, customers, and rivals, as well as of the entire community in which he lived.

John, St.—St. John the Evangelist was at an early day chosen as the patron saint of illuminators, scribes, etc. As the most learned of the disciples, as the author not only of the Gospel, but also of epistles and of the Revelation, and as the recipient of the Divine mandate, Write, St. John was always pictured as bearing a pen in his hand, and was the most fitting patron for the copyists, whose office of transcribing the Scriptures was considered as especially holy by the early Christian Church. The sixth day of May was devoted to St. John, in commemoration of his being miraculously empowered to endure without injury the torture of being boiled in a caldron of oil upon that day, at the gate of Rome leading to Latium, from which fact he is usually distinguished as St. John of the Latin Gate. The 6th of May was therefore celebrated by the illuminators, and accepted as the chosen anniversary by their successors, the early printers; but the birthday of John Gutenberg, falling upon the 24th of June, or the day appropriated to the memory of St. John the Baptist, has also been claimed to be the special anniversary of typography, having the advantage of occurring at a period when the printers are enjoying comparative leisure.

Jones, Griffith.—An English printer and editor, especially famous as the publisher of the Liliputian Histories for the Young, containing the popular stories of Goody Two-Shoes, Giles Gingerbread, Tommy Trip, etc. Griffith Jones was for many years editor of the London Chronicle, the Daily Advertiser, and the Public Ledger. He was associated with Dr. Johnson in the Literary Magazine, and with Smollett and Goldsmith in the British Magazine; he also translated much from the French, and his conversance with the literature of that language probably made him acquainted with the books for children, which were at that period more numerous in French than in English.

The stories styled Liliputian Histories were prepared by him with the assistance of his brother,

Giles Jones, and John Newbery, the author of Geography Made Easy for Children, a book republished in 1805. It is stated that Goldsmith also assisted in the work, and that he was the author of Goody Two-Shoes. Griffith Jones was born in 1722, served his apprenticeship with Bowyer, the celebrated printer, and died in 1786. He was the author of a number of anonymous works, several of which were very successful, especially one entitled Great Events from Little Causes.

Journal.—Strictly, a record of daily occurrences, but usually applied to the narrative, periodically or occasionally published, of the transactions of a deliberative assembly or society. It is also used as synonymous with magazine or periodical as the title of a serial publication, and is applied to newspapers appearing daily, weekly, or at greater intervals.

Journalism.—The profession of editing or writing for the public journals or newspapers. (See NEWSPAPERS.)

Journalist.—The conductor of, or contributor to, a public journal; also the author of a diary.

Journeyman.—A person of mature age working at a regular rate of wages. Usually, but not invariably, he has served, during his minority, some form of apprenticeship to the business in which he is thus engaged.

Justifying.—Spacing out a line so that it fits with a proper degree of tightness in the measure of the composing-stick; or placing a wood-cut or block in a page and filling up the vacancies with leads, quadrats, quotations, or furniture, so that when the form is locked up the whole shall be fast and firm. Correct and accurate justification is a cardinal point in good composition, as it is absolutely necessary. If the line is short, the letters will not stand properly on their feet, and it is then impossible to get a fair impression from the line. Besides, the letters are likely to drop out in lifting the form, and a column or a page may be easily broken through carelessness in this respect. Even if badly-justified matter can be sent safely to the press, the suction of the roller is likely to draw out letters, by which means many letters, or perhaps a valuable wood-block, may be battered and ruined. Indeed, carelessness in justifying is a fruitful cause of accident and damage of all kinds. Many chases, for instance, are broken by the form's being locked up too tight, to obviate the result of bad justifying and loose lines. Apprentices should be strictly cautioned against allowing themselves to fall into the bad habit, for when once acquired it becomes irksome to take the proper amount of care to justify a line properly. Some compositors adopt the plan of justifying their lines slackly, others tightly; but the latter is preferable; for no compositor can judge, in slack spacing, whether he has justified each line precisely the same as the previous one; whereas, if he adopts the principle of spacing each line as tightly as the measure will reasonably admit, he is sure to have every line alike; this is especially necessary in table-work.

Juvenile Literature.—Books and publications intended for the amusement of children, generally distinguished from text-books or school-books. The limits of this class of literature cannot be distinctly marked, as it begins at the lowest range in the vast variety of toy-books now printed in colors, and mounts up through Mother Goose and all grades of infantile lore to the higher range of romances claimed alike by the old and the young, such as the Pilgrim's Progress, Robinson Crusoe, and Gulliver's Travels. It is probable that books for children, or at least works intended to present knowledge in an attractive form for students, were attempted at an early day; but the first formal and regular endeavor to collect the popular fairy-stories into a permanent form was achieved by the learned Charles Perrault, the friend of the great Colbert, and the student to whose zeal and knowledge France is mainly indebted for her Academies of Inscriptions, Painting, and Sculpture. In 1697 he published, under the title of Contes de ma Mère l'Oye, or Tales of My Mother Goose, the stories still cherished among the chief treasures of the nursery, as, Blue-Beard, The Sleeping Beauty, Puss in Boots, Tom Thumb, Cinderella, etc. In 1704, Gallaud, a celebrated French traveler and Orientalist, published a volume of Contes Arabes, or Arabian Tales, which attracted great attention, and were accepted as original romances, until the author disclaimed the honor, explaining that the Tales were a translation of an Arabic manuscript obtained by him in Syria, and which he had found afterwards to be but the first of the thirty-six parts of the Arabic original, known in Asia under the title of the One Thousand and One Nights. These stories, now claimed by children, were thus introduced to Europe by a learned linguist as a faithful picture of Asiatic manners and customs, and were enthusiastically received, especially in France. They were soon afterwards translated into English, accompanied by the Mother Goose of Perrault, and aroused public attention to the value of the native legends at home and abroad, a field of literature hitherto much neglected. Among the hack writers engaged in England in translating the French stories, and preparing original ones, was Oliver Goldsmith, the reputed author of Goody Two-Shoes. Æsop's Fables were at an early day prepared for juvenile readers, with the addition of rude wood-cuts, and still preserve a foremost station even in the nursery, where they are welcomed in monosyllabic form by the most youthful readers. Pilgrim's Progress was published about 1672, but probably was reserved for adult readers for a considerable time. Robinson Crusoe, the great standard juvenile book, appeared in 1719. Gulliver's Travels was published in 1726, and, although intended as a political satire, soon became a popular book with the children, who must have been supplied with special publications, for about that time the novelist Fielding mentions a Mr. Newbery of St. Paul's Churchyard as providing picture-books for young readers. It was, however, only at the end of the eighteenth and the beginning of the present century that public attention was particularly drawn to the necessity of literature for children as the result of the effect produced throughout Europe by the teachings of Rousseau.

In England, the Liliputian Histories published by Griffith Jones, and to which Oliver Goldsmith is believed to have contributed, met with immediate success, which is still maintained by Goody Two-Shoes and her companions. Mrs. Trimmer's History of the Robins was one of the earliest stories expressly prepared for little children, and has rarely been surpassed in simple beauty.

Thomas Day, a distinguished writer upon political and philanthropic topics, was one of the first Englishmen to introduce practical instruction into juvenile literature, in his story of Sandford and Merton, 1783; and the same course was continued in The Evenings at Home, by Mrs. Barbauld and her brother, Dr. Aiken, in 1793; Miss Edgeworth followed with even greater success in her Parent's Assistant and Moral Tales. The Swiss Family Robinson, by Kampe, the tutor of Baron Von Humboldt, was also an excellent story of the same order, and the Germans have been especially successful in literature for the young, particularly in volumes of illustrated poetry for the nursery, many of which have been translated into English and circulated extensively in England and America. From the French have also been adopted into foreign languages St. Pierre's exquisite story of Paul and Virginia, Berquin's Children's Friend, and Madame Cottin's Exiles of Siberia. As writers for children in England, a high rank must be allotted to Mrs. Sherwood, Mrs. Hofland, and Mary Howitt. One of the most active pioneers in this field in America was Peter Parley; the Rollo Books of Mr. Abbot also were very well received by the public, and Hawthorne is usually classed with the Danish author Andersen as the foremost of modern writers for children. The brothers Grimm have also discovered many popular legends from the nations of Northern Europe, which have been formed into excellent story-books; and the works of Thorpe and Dasent contain much material of the same kind. Legends from the North American tribes have also been recently adapted to the same purpose, as well as stories from Hindostan and other Oriental lands. The imagination of children is always attracted by tales of travel and adventure, and the long-famous Robinson Crusoe and Gulliver head an army of stories true and false, in which Captain Parry, Captain Marryatt, and Mayne Reid have been especial favorites.

The supply of illustrated works for the young has immensely increased of late years, and many of the books, especially some of those printed in colors, may be classed among the triumphs of modern typography.

K.

Keep in.—To crowd matter into a limited space by thin spacing. The term generally used is bring in.

Kellogg's Improved Newbury Blank and Card Press.—A cheap small job press, which prints a sheet 14 by 17 inches, manufactured by A. N. Kellogg, of Chicago, Illinois, which is claimed to be a great improvement on the Newbury press, and to be well adapted to small job-work. (See page 263.)

Kern.—That part of the face of a type which hangs over one or both sides of its shank. In Roman, f and j are the only kerned letters, but in Italic, d, g, j, l, y, are kerned on one side of the face, and f on both sides. Many Italic capitals are also kerned on one side, as well as many kinds of job letter. This occurs especially with the fonts of which capitals alone were cast at first, and lower-case letters added subsequently.

Knife.—Several knives specially adapted to the use of printers have been made, two of which are illustrated below.

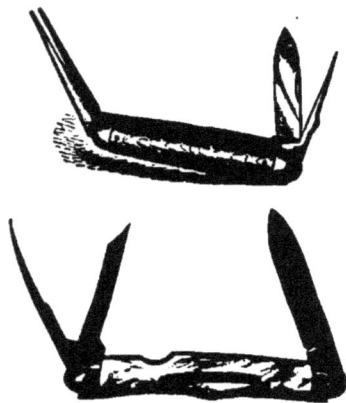

Knight, Charles.—An English printer, author, and publisher, distinguished for his indefatigable, varied, and intelligently directed efforts to promote the popular diffusion of learning, as well as for his interest in subjects relating to typography.

Among the great variety of Mr. Knight's publications may be mentioned as especially well known: The Library of Entertaining Knowledge, 43 vols.; The Penny Magazine, 1832–45, 14 vols.; The Penny Cyclopædia, 1833–58, 30 vols.; The Shilling Volume, 1844–49, 186 vols.; Half-Hours with the Best Authors, 1847–48, 4 vols.; The English Cyclopædia, 1854–62, 23 folio vols.; Popular History of England, 8 vols.; of these and many other important works he has been the responsible editor, contributing to them largely as author. Charles Knight has also written The Life of Caxton; Passages of a Working Life during Half a Century; Shadows of the Old Booksellers; several pamphlets upon subjects connected with book-

KELLOGG IMPROVED NEWSBURY BLANK AND CARD PRESS.

publishing, etc. As a publisher he has been especially active in the production of popular illustrated
works, such as the Pictorial Bible, 4 vols. quarto,
1838; Pictorial Prayer, 1838; Pictorial History of
England, 1840, 8 vols.; National Cyclopædia, 12
vols.; Shakspeare's Works, etc. He was born at
Windsor, England, in 1791.

Koenig, Frederick.—The inventor of the power
printing-press. He was the son of a small farmer at
Eisleben, in Prussian Saxony, where he was born in
1775. Exhibiting at an early age a strong desire to
become a printer, he was sent when sixteen to Leipsic, where he entered the printing-office of Breitkopf.
Here he invented the machine which has made his
name famous, but he was utterly unable to obtain
in Leipsic the assistance requisite to present his
invention in practical form, and he sought the
requisite aid in many other cities without success,
as the impending war with France was engrossing
the attention of all classes of Germans.

Koenig had, however, become known, and his
invention attracted some attention, for he received
an invitation from the Russian Government to organize a State Printing-Office in St. Petersburg. He

went to that city in 1806, but soon became disgusted
and disheartened by the official obstacles thrown in his
way, and determined to try his fortunes in England.
In that country Koenig found for some time difficulty
in obtaining sufficient work to support himself, but
with indefatigable energy he took every opportunity
to urge his invention upon the attention of the master-
printers. The only one to appreciate his project was
Thomas Bensley, who entered into a contract in
March, 1807, to furnish the money necessary to
construct the proposed machine. Koenig immediately began to construct a model, which occupied
him nearly three years, and a patent was taken out
for the invention, which is described as follows in the
official abstract of the specifications published by the
British Commissioners of Patents:—

A. D. 1810, March 29. KOENIG, FREDERICK.—A method of
printing by means of machinery. A table with a platen, as
in other presses, at one end. In the centre is an inking apparatus, consisting of several cylinders vertically arranged,
above which is an ink box, through a slit in which the ink is
forced by a piston, so as to fall upon cylinders by which it is
distributed. The two middle cylinders are for this purpose
of different diameters, so that when they are revolving the

points of contact may be constantly changed, and for the same purpose an alternating and opposite endwise motion is given to the two cylinders immediately below them, which furnish two inking cylinders revolving in opposite directions. The latter are fitted in a movable frame, and by the action of spiral springs the one and the other cylinder is alternately applied to the form. The inking cylinders consist of perforated tubes of brass, through axles of which, also perforated, steam or water is introduced to moisten their felt or leather clothing. The form is in a coffin, to which the tympan is hinged, so as to prevent its back to the press-head when thrown up. The frisket does not move upon hinges fixed at the top of the tympan, as is the case with the presses now in use, but has the same centre of motion as the tympan. In the common press the tympan is fixed close to the coffin; in my machine, coffin, tympan, and frisket have each two extending arms, one foot long, all meeting in a common hinge. The coffin runs to and fro along the table. On its return, after the impression, the tympan is raised by a chain attached to the press-head until it passes the vertical, when it falls back on and slides along a cross-bar. When the carriage is returning to the press the bar will force the tympan to rise to the vertical line, and, having passed the same, the tympan will sink down again upon the form by its own weight, guided by the end of the chain. The frisket has counter weights on its arms, by which it has a constant tendency to be erect. When the tympan is down, its superior weight overbalances these counter weights; but as soon as the tympan rises, the counter weights begin to act by lifting the opposite part of the frisket, and holding the same with the sheet close to the tympan until it passes the vertical, when it is acted upon by a weighted cord, which keeps it close to the tympan until the latter has arrived at a position in which the sheet will rest by its own weight, when the frisket rises to allow of its removal. The impression is given by means of a compound lever, which causes a crew to make one-quarter of a revolution. The motion of all parts of the machine is derived from a steam engine, or other first mover,—the description of the mill-work occupying a great part of the specification. There is a peculiar arrangement for producing the interrupted motion in the coffin and the compound levers which give the impression.

Koenig obtained the assistance of Andrew F. Bauer, an ingenious German mechanic, who became his ablest coadjutor and life-long friend and partner, and by their united efforts the first power-press was completed in April, 1811—the first work printed by it being sheet H of the Annual Register for 1810, at the rate of 800 impressions an hour, 300 being the highest rate usually reached at that time by the hand-press.

Koenig considered his machinery too complex, and immediately began to simplify it, and, having added to the firm two London printers, Taylor and Wood-fall, took out a new patent, Oct. 30, 1811. In this, several improvements were introduced, and it described a double machine on the same principle, the form alternately passing under and giving an impression at one of two cylinders at either end of the press. It also described a method by which a number of machines (the drawing contained 10 machines) might be combined into a system, by arranging them in a circle, the form continually running forward from one machine to the other, rendering every part of it productive.

He erected a single-cylinder machine by the patent

of 1811, and completed it in December, 1812. The proprietors of several of the leading London news-papers were invited to see this machine in successful operation. Mr. Perry of the Morning Chronicle refused to attend, doubting the possibility of success; but Mr. Walter of the Times, who had long been anxious to see the application of steam power to the printing-press, attended, and was so well satisfied with Koenig's description of the advantages to be derived from a double machine on the same principle that he ordered two double machines to be made for the use of the Times.

The single-cylinder machine was fitted for book-work, but the contemplated double-cylinder machines were intended expressly for the requirements of news-paper printing, and it took the combined ingenuity and experience of Koenig, Bauer, and Walter to conquer all the difficulties that arose during the progress of the work. The inventors had every reason to fear personal violence, or at least the destruction of their machinery by hand-pressmen, who were bitterly hostile to the invention, and the work was continued under all the disadvantages of enforced secrecy, with the additional difficulties arising from dependence on the services of inferior workmen, and the necessity of procuring or manufacturing the several portions of the machinery at distant places, which increased the frequency of blunders and mistakes. The obstacles were such that Koenig and Bauer at one time became utterly disheartened, and left the scene of their labors, so that Walter had to pursue them, and reawaken their zeal by the expression of his own confidence in the ultimate success of the undertaking.

Nearly two years were spent in this way, but their efforts were at last triumphant, and the Times of the 29th November, 1814, announced their success in glowing terms. (See CYLINDER PRESSES.)

This machine was capable of producing 1100 impressions in an hour, a number amply sufficient to the demands of the Times, and was employed in that office for many years.

Koenig took out a third patent July 23, 1813, which embraced considerable simplification in the mill-work, and other important improvements. The fourth and last patent taken out in England was dated Dec. 24, 1814, and specified arrangements by which the sheet was thrown out printed upon both sides, the improvement being adapted to single and double machines.

In 1816 a single-cylinder constructed for Bensley for book-work printed from 900 to 1000 sheets an hour on both sides. And under his fourth patent Koenig was able to produce from 1500 to 2000 impressions per hour, and was prepared to supply machines of four or eight cylinders, but found no demand for them.

By this time serious difficulties had arisen between Koenig and Bensley, the inventor considering that his partner wished to reserve the invention for the advantage of his own private printing establishment, and was in other ways hostile to Koenig's personal

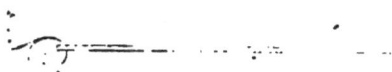

Koenig obtained ... of A... ... an ingenious ... ... addressed ... ... 5 to ... and ... ... efforts the ... ... No 1, 1811 ... ... of the Ve... ... the ... ... impression being ... ... actually ... ... by the handpress.

Koenig ... ... impelled to ... ... to the then ... ... full, took out ... ... several ... ... articled a ... ... form ad... ... ... pressed at the ... yon ... of the press. ... described ... ... manner of ... ... the details ... machines, arranging them ... their ... ... than one ... ... part of it press ...

... machine by the patent ...

of 18?? ... and it is ... 1812–13, ... proposed ... ... of the leading London news-papers ... ... to see this machine in operation. Mr. Perry of the Morning Chronicle ... but Mr. Walter of the Times, who had long anxious ... the application of steam power ... ... steam, and was ... satisfied ... Koenig's description of the advantages to be derived ... ... the machine on the same ... that he ordered two double machines to be made for use of the Times.

... one double steam machine was fitted for use ... were, but Messrs. ... of ... cylinder machines ... ... interested ... for the ... pursuits of newspaper printing, and it took the combined ingenuity ... ... of Koenig, Bauer, and Walter to overcome all the difficulties that arose during the progress of the work. The inventors had ... personal violence, or at least the destruction of their machinery by the pressmen, who were ... ... the necessity ... the work was carried on ... all the difficulties of enforced secrecy, with ... addition of those also arising from ... ... pressmen, ... workmen, and ... ... pretence of manufacturing the several ... ... away at ... ... which it ... ... together of ... and machinery. It ... ... were so, that Koenig and Bauer on their own ... ... Walter had to pay the same, and ... by the expense ... ... the ultimate success of the undertaking.

Nearly two years were spent in this way ... ... when ... at last triumphant, and the Times on the 29th November, 18??, announced their success, showing ... ... of the VALUE of STEAM in ...

... that ... capable of producing 1100 ... ... in an hour ... steady succession ... the records of the Times, and was employed there for many years.

Koenig took out a third patent July 2?, ... combined considerable improvements in the work, and after unusual improvements. The ... and last patent taken out in England was dated Dec 24, 1814, and specified arrangements ... which the sheet was thrown out printed upon ... ... improvement being adapted to single-cylinder double machines.

In this ... cylinder constructed ... ... work, printed from two to four sheets ... iron on both sides. And under his fourth p... Koenig was able to produce from 1? ... 2000 ... pressions per hour, and was prepared to supply machines of four or eight cylinders, but found demand ... them.

By this time serious difficulties had arisen between Koenig and Bensley, the inventor considering that his partner wished to reserve the invention for the advantage of his own private printing establishment, and was in other ways hostile to Koenig, personal

KOSTER

COMMEMORATIVE MEDAL

interests. Unwilling to commence a protracted suit in defence of his patent rights, Koenig abandoned England, where several rival claimants contested the glory of his invention, and retired with his friend Bauer, in 1816, to Germany, where they established themselves as press-makers in the little village of Oberzell, in Bavaria, the government giving Koenig a secularized monastery on easy terms to assist his new enterprise.

The editor of the Times always continued to uphold Koenig's claim to the entire honor of the invention of the power-press, keeping up constant communication with him, and requesting him to re-visit England in 1823, in order to build a new machine for the Times. Koenig, however, declined to do this, and the machine was constructed by Applegarth. In December, 1824, a leader in the Times made a most forcible and generous defence of Koenig's claims, with a personal explanation by Mr. Walter, of his own intimate knowledge and acquaintance with all matters relating to the construction of the machine used by the Times, and denying utterly that either Bensley or Nicholson had any claim to the honor.

In Oberzell the new invention at first also encountered ignorant opposition; but the undaunted inventor, with the assistance of his steadfast friend Bauer, was enabled to carry on the manufacture with the help of the inhabitants of the place, after the untrained laborers had been transformed into skilled mechanics. After four years of industry, two single-cylinder machines were completed, and sent to Berlin for the use of the State Printing-Office. The animosity of the trade proved a serious impediment for some years, but this opposition to improvement was gradually conquered, and by the end of 1825, seven double-cylinders had been constructed for the largest newspapers in Germany. A single-cylinder machine, constructed in 1823, printed 1200 impressions in an hour upon one side, and was so adapted to the needs of newspapers that hundreds of them were soon required, and the firm of Koenig and Bauer of Oberzell became widely known throughout Europe.

Frederick Koenig died in 1833, and was buried, in accordance with his own desire, in the orchard adjoining his factory. Bauer survived him, and in 1847 completed the six hundredth machine made at Oberzell, and capable of producing 6000 impressions an hour. Andrew Bauer died in 1860, and the business has since been conducted by the two sons of Koenig, under the old firm name of Koenig & Bauer, with great success, many varieties of presses being now manufactured by them.

Koster, Laurence.—The principal contestant with John Gutenberg for the honor of being the inventor of printing by means of movable types. Laureus Janszoon, of Haarlem, is usually surnamed Koster or Coster, for the alleged reason that he held the office of Keeper or Custodian of the Church; and he is upheld by the Dutch and also by some modern English writers as having invented movable types

shortly after the year 1420. The 10th of July is celebrated every year in Haarlem as the anniversary of the invention of movable type, and the same day is also celebrated by the printers of Dort and Amsterdam. His claims are further supported by a statue in the market-place of his native city, representing him in a civic robe, with a wreath of laurel on his brow, holding in his right hand a book, and in his left a cube, having thereon the letter A. The pedestal contains several inscriptions and bas-reliefs.

The residence of Koster was a handsome house in the market-place, and it is distinguished by the following inscription:

Memoriæ sacrum
Typographia, ars artium omnium conservatrix, hic, primum
Inventa, circa annum 1440,

which may be rendered: Typography, of all other arts the preserver, was here invented about 1440.

As the works ascribed to Koster bear no intrinsic evidence either of the time when they were printed, or of the person by whom they were manufactured, the whole subject has furnished grounds for much debate, and perhaps the most reliable typographical evidence upon the dispute can be gathered from the assertion of Ulric Zell, the first printer of Cologne, who was probably personally acquainted with the facts of the case. He made in the Cologne Chronicle of 1499 the following statement:

Item: this most revered art was first discovered at Mentz, in Germany; and it is a great honour to the German nation, that such ingenious men were found in it. This happened in the year of our Lord MCCCXL; and from that time, till the year MCCCCL, the art, and what belongs to it, was rendered more perfect. In the year of our Lord MCCCCL, which was a golden year, then men began to print, and the first book printed was a Bible in Latin, and it was printed in a larger character than that with which men now print mass-books. Item: although this art was discovered at Mentz at first, in the manner in which it is now commonly used, yet the first example of it was found in Holland, in the Donatuses which were before printed there. And thence is derived the beginning of this art, and it is more masterly and subtle than the ancient manner was, and by far more ingenious.

By some authorities it is stated that Koster, after becoming familiar with the method by which block-books had been successfully produced in Holland, conceived the idea of making movable letters in wood instead of entire plates. Taking the books already known and popular as block-books, he produced the Apocalypse, the Canticles, the Speculum Salvationis, the Donatus, and the Honorium between the year 1428 and his death in 1440. Specimens of the works are carefully preserved by the civic authorities of Haarlem, but many authors assert that they are mere block-books, exhibiting no evidences of having been produced by movable types.

Ranking next in importance to the evidence of Ulric Zell, already mentioned, is that deduced from a manuscript note or memorandum placed upon the fly-leaf of a Donatus by Mariangelus Accursius, a distinguished Neapolitan scholar of the early part of the sixteenth century. The note is in Latin to the

266 KOSTER, LAURENCE.

effect that:—this Donatus and confessional was the first actually printed in the year 1450. It was imitated from those previously printed in Holland from engraved tablets.

In the want of direct evidence upon the subject, it is important to notice that the rivalry between Haarlem and Mentz began at an early date, for in the preface to an edition of Cicero's Offices published in Haarlem in 1561, the author asserts, I have often been assured by well-informed persons that the art of printing was originally invented in Haarlem, although in a rude manner; the knowledge having afterwards been treacherously conveyed to Mentz by an unfaithful workman, and there brought to great perfection. The secret of the art was first made public in the latter city, and it therefore acquired the glory of the first invention, and our fellow-citizens obtain but little credence when they claim the honor for one of themselves.—A work of Guicciardini's printed in Antwerp in 1567 contains the statement that by the common tradition of the country printing and the casting of letters were both first invented in Haarlem, but that the inventor died before his work was fully perfected, and one of his workmen carried the secret to Mentz, where it was brought to perfection.

The whole story of Koster's invention, and the theft by one of his workmen, was fully told by Hadrian Junius, a native of North Holland, who commenced his studies at Haarlem, and subsequently attended other European universities. He was widely known for his learning, having lived for some time in England as physician to the Duke of Norfolk, and was afterwards appointed physician to the King of Denmark. In his History of Holland, written about 1568, he devotes considerable space to the evidence in favor of Haarlem, and the quotation is given at full length, as being the most important document yet discovered upon the subject, and containing the original statement from which all modern versions have been derived:—

I resume the history of our own city (Haarlem), to which, I assert, the chief henor of the invention of the art of printing is justly due; and which, I maintain, may be asserted with the greatest justice as of its own and native right. There is, however, an ancient opinion which alone eclipses our splendor, which is inscribed in the minds of some as if it had been burnt in by fire; so deeply rooted that no mattock, no wedge, no pick-axe, is able to eradicate or destroy it. In conformity with this opinion, they pertinaciously believe that the forms of letters with which books are printed were first discovered at Mentz, a celebrated and ancient city of Germany. Oh that I could obtain by a wish that incredible power of oratory which is supposed to have existed in Carneades, who is reported to have defended nothing that he did not prove, to have attacked nothing that he did not overturn,—so that I, the advocate of truth, might be able to recall from exile to its native right that fugitive praise, and to raise this trophy, which indeed I would not desire on any other account but that truth, correctly designated by an ancient poet as the daughter of Time, or (as I am accustomed to call her) the test of Time, may at length be discovered, and that she, although hidden, according to Democritus, in the deepest well, may be brought to light!

If the Phœnicians and Egyptians were not unwilling to engage in a glorious combat concerning the invention of letters: these arrogating to themselves their invention under the guidance of God, when they boast of their tables called in their language "written by God;" and the others glorying in having introduced letters (to the invention of which they assert a claim) into Greece at the time when Cadmus, transported in a Phœnician vessel, first instructed the ignorant Greeks: if, again, the Athenians claim the same praise for their own king Cecrops, and the Thebans for Linus; while Tacitus and Philostratus bestow the glory of the invention on Palamedes the Argive, and Hyginus attributes the invention of the Latin character to Carmenta, the mother of Evander: if, therefore, all nations have not blushed to seize for themselves, as the peculiar right of each, this glory, which is involved in so much doubt and controversy, what should hinder us from reseeking the possession of that praise which cannot be disputed, and to restore it to its ancient right, of which we have been deprived by the culpable negligence of our ancestors? I am indeed uninfluenced by any feeling of envy or malevolence, to assert any claim for one by calumniating or detracting from another. If, on the authority of Plutarch, the evidence of that man is most trustworthy, who, bound by no favors received, or by any partiality or friendship, speaks boldly and freely what he thinks, my testimony is surely entitled to credit, since I claim no relationship with the dead, his heirs, or his posterity, and have no favor or benefit to expect from them. In what I have undertaken I have been influenced solely by an act of justice to the memory of the dead. I shall therefore mention what I have learned from old men respectable for their authority, and distinguished by their public services, who have asserted that they had their information from the best authority, viz., their own ancestors, whose testimony ought to have due weight in determining the truth.

There dwelt in Haarlem, about 128 years ago, in a public edifice of some magnificence (as the fabric which still remains can attest), overlooking the market-place, opposite the Royal Palace, a man named Laurentius Johannes, surnamed Custos or Ædituus, because his family, by hereditary right, possessed an honorable and lucrative office distinguished by that title. To this man the world is indebted for an art more truly worthy of the laurel than that which blinds the brow, for by the clearest right, and by the most solemn assertion, he is entitled to the praise of being the inventor of printing.

Walking in a wood near the city (as was the custom of opulent citizens on festivals or after dinner), he began to cut letters on the bark of a beech-tree, which he, for the sake of amusement, pressed on paper, in an inverted order, for his grandchildren to imitate. Having succeeded in this, and being a man of talent and ingenuity, he began to meditate greater things, and being assisted by his son-in-law, Peter Thomas (who had four sons, who almost all attained consular dignity, and whom I mention to show that the art owed its origin, not to a low family, but, on the contrary, to men of distinguished rank and consideration), he invented a more glutinous and tenacious kind of ink, perceiving that the common ink spread and produced blots. He then formed wooden tablets, or pages with letters cut upon them. Of this kind, I have myself seen an anonymous work, written in the vernacular tongue, entitled Speculum nostræ Salutis, the first rude essay printed not on both sides but on opposite pages only, the reverse sides being pasted together to conceal their naked deformity. These types of beech he afterwards changed for lead, and after that for pewter, as being a more hard and durable substance; from the remains of which those old wine-pots were cast that are still visible in the mansion of which I have spoken, looking towards the market-place, and which was afterwards inhabited by his grandson, Gerard

Thomas, who died a few years since at a very advanced age, and whom I here mention with respect as a most honorable gentleman. The curiosity of men is naturally attracted by a new invention; and when a commodity never before seen became an object of gainful profit, the love of the art became more general, and work and workmen (the first cause of misfortune) were multiplied. Amongst those so employed was one John Faustus. Whether he was, as I suspect, ominously so called, faithless and unlucky to his master, and whether that really was his name, I shall not here inquire, being unwilling to disturb the silent shades of those who suffer from a consciousness of the sins they have committed in this life. This person, bound by oath to keep the invention a secret, as soon as he supposed he knew the mode of joining the letters together, the method of casting the types, and other matters belonging to the art, having seized the opportunity of Christmas Eve, whilst all were employed in the customary lustral sacrifices, puts together all his master's tools connected with the art, seizes all the types, elopes from his house, accompanied by one other thief as an accomplice, proceeds first to Amsterdam, then to Cologne, and at length settles at Mentz. Here he considered himself safe from the reach of his pursuers, as in an asylum where he might carry on a gainful trade with the fruits of his iniquity. Clear it certainly is, that, in about a year after this, about A. D. 1442, the Doctrinale of Alexander Gallus, a grammar in much repute at that time, and the Tracts of Peter of Spain, were brought out here with those very types which Laurentius made use of at Haarlem.

This is the account I have heard from venerable men, worthy of credit, to whom the story had been delivered, like a burning torch transferred from hand to hand; and I have myself met many other persons who corroborate and confirm their statements by the similarity of their testimony. I remember that the instructor of my youth, Nicholaus Galius, a man distinguished by an accurate and retentive memory, and venerable for his years and character, has mentioned to me that he more than once, when a boy, heard one Cornelius, a bookbinder who had been employed in the office, and lived to the age of eighty, relate with great emotion the whole transaction, describe the history and progress of the art, and all the circumstances connected with it, as he had received the account from his master. Whenever the conversation turned upon this subject, he would burst into tears and betray most violent emotion, both on account of the robbery committed on his master, and of the glory of which he was so unjustly deprived. He used to call down the most frightful imprecations on the head of the thief, and execrate the memory of those nights which he had passed with him as his bedfellow. This account agrees pretty nearly with that of Quirinus Talesius, the Burgomaster, who had it almost immediately from the mouth of Cornelius himself. The love of Truth, so generally the parent of envy and hatred, has induced me to enter into this detail, in the defence of which, so far am I from any desire to forfeit my recognizance, that, on the contrary, I feel more determined in proportion to the odium attached to it.

In defending it, our city will recover the honor to which it is justly entitled, and the arrogance of those who are not ashamed to lay claim to and possess the right which belongs to another, will cease. This truth, I fear, may perhaps be disregarded; but though prejudice may, amongst light and careless men, prevail above the argument which is founded upon authentic information, I shall ever derive consolation and delight from the recollection of having manfully defended the claims of this city and of the true invention.

So confident are the people of Haarlem of the substantial truth of this statement, that they have erected a monument in what they allege to be the grove in

which Koster conceived the idea of cutting movable type, and in one of the commemorative medals they have issued, Koster is represented in the very act of conceiving, or receiving from a ray of light, the project of cutting movable letters. (See portrait of Koster and fac-simile of commemorative medal.)

On the other hand, the claims of Koster have been severely criticised and unmercifully denounced. The modern judgment of his most generous German adversaries is expressed in the following extract from the Annalen der Typographie:

Koster is said to have been born in Haarlem, in the year 1370. One hundred years after Gutenberg was the attempt made to accord to Koster the priority in invention. According to the story, Koster, while walking in the woods, conceived the idea of cutting letters from the bark of trees, to amuse the children of his relatives. From this arose the idea of making practical use of the letters, by having a line set under his pictures. The first book printed by him from movable types was the ——— Mirror, and after this he resorted to the use of tin or leaden types. One of his pupils, named Gutenberg, took from him the materials, traveled to Mentz, and announced himself as the inventor of the art.

So goes the story. The Hollanders take the year 1423 as the time of discovery, and have erected a memorial to Koster, as the inventor, in the place where the first letters are said to have been cut.

Granted, that the vigor of the warm admirers of Gutenberg goes too far; granted, that, in spite of all attempts to white-wash the improbable story, a sexton, of flesh and blood, actually possessed, before Gutenberg, wooden as well as cast metal types: the discoverer never made more than the crudest beginning, and did not understand how to give the accidental discovery a form, or bring it to any practical result. This fact is indisputable, that the art, thirty years after Gutenberg, was introduced into Holland from Germany, as something new. The honor of the substantial discovery cannot, in any case, be taken from Gutenberg, and the fruitful benefits to mankind will remain his individual reward.

Without trespassing too closely on Gutenberg, a place could be accorded to Koster in the history of printing, the same as that occupied by Salomon de Caus and Papin in the history of the discovery of the steam-engine. A man might cherish the evidence that the great idea originated with him, while lacking the power of genius to overcome all obstacles in bringing his thoughts to practical utility; and herein lies the greatest consummation of the claims of the Hollanders. Even as James Watt, in spite of the many forerunners, is acknowledged as the creator of the steam-engine, which moves the physical world, so will Gutenberg, in spite of the many claims advanced by Hollanders, Italians, and Chinese, be to us the discoverer of the art, to whose flight of genius it was, is, and shall remain due.

L.

Label Borders.—Borders made and mortised by type-founders, and used by printers in printing labels.

Labels.—Inscriptions on bottles, boxes, drawers, merchandise, etc., describing their contents. A very large number of labels used by druggists, patent-medicine manufacturers, liquor-dealers, manufacturers of dry goods of various descriptions, etc., are printed in job printing-offices and by lithographers.

Labial.—A letter or character representing an

articulation or sound formed or uttered chiefly with the lips, as b, p, w.

Labor-Saving Quotation Furniture.

Metal furniture cast to Pica ems, which is extensively used to fill blank spaces in pages, and also as a substitute for wooden furniture in making blank spaces between pages.

LABOR-SAVING FURNITURE.

Labor-Saving Rule.

Brass rule of various thicknesses cut to various lengths, from one to fifty ems Pica, which is extensively and advantageously used in rule-and-figure work, and in many descriptions of job-printing. (See BRASS RULE.) Full fonts embrace mitred pieces for outside bordering. The plan of a labor-saving rule case is given below.

Latin, and Hebrew, by the collation, revision, and profound study of manuscripts prepared for the printer.

Latin remained the language of learned Europe for fifteen centuries, and the early chronicles of all the countries, northern as well as southern, were written in it. In Poland, Hungary, and Holland it was maintained until a very late period, the speeches of the Hungarian parliament having been delivered in it until very recently, and many Dutch professors lecturing in Latin even at the present day. Latin, in fact, was the universal tongue in which all Europeans met on a common ground, and as such it became a necessary part of polite education. Italian, the direct heir of the Latin, became highly cultivated soon after the introduction of printing, and was regarded as the fashionable and polite language in England during the reigns of Elizabeth and the early Stuarts, and was also accepted in France. The Spanish followed, under the prestige of Charles V., and was also a direct heir of the Latin; it was for a considerable time the court language of Vienna, and was cultivated in France, England, and Italy. Printing had received a warm welcome at the Sorbonne, and the kings and

LABOR-SAVING RULE CASE.

Language.

This subject has already been treated at some length under the heading Alphabet, and the scope of the present work will permit the mention only of a few of those points which directly tend to the apprehension of the present condition of our own language. Setting aside all those vexed questions of precedence which inevitably arise in the discussion of the origin or extent of the Asiatic languages, it is only important to say that when printing was invented the literature of Europe was confined to the Greek and Latin, both of which were in a degraded state, and that the first effect of typography was to excite attention among scholars, which led to a marked improvement in the condition of Greek,

court of France continued to befriend the art, which rose into great excellence, but especial regard was paid to the Greek and Latin languages until the mighty influence of Cardinal Richelieu was exerted in favor of the vernacular. French had, however, received a considerable degree of cultivation, and in it Caxton and all the early English printers were obliged to find their stores of classic lore, which, after being filtered through French translation, were reclothed in the new and unformed tongue which was to become English only towards the close of the sixteenth century, the early British printers being compelled to draw their literature from France, and their type and paper from Holland.

The Germans abandoned the Latin in the middle of the eighteenth century, and the enfranchised vernacular has since sprung into magnificent strength and varied beauty.

The youngest language that has acquired an extensive literature is that of Russia, whose literature only began in 1708, when Peter the Great issued his new alphabet as an improvement upon the clumsy characters of the Sclavonic, which was then abandoned for the spoken but unwritten Russian; and the growth of the language can be estimated by the fact that the library of St. Petersburg in 1850 contained 40,000 volumes in the Russian language. Imagination alone can picture the possibilities of the future, when it is remembered that in 1860 the English language was spoken by sixty millions of persons, and the Russian by sixty-five millions; while it was a Russian photographer who exhibited before a London audience a reproduction of the Codex of Strabo preserved with jealous care in the convent library of Mount Athos.

Latinism.—A Latin idiom or mode of speech.

Laws relating to Printers.—The printers of Europe are subjected to many annoying legal impositions and restrictions from which the printers of this country are fortunately exempt. The Constitution of the United States, as well as the Constitutions of the respective States, prohibits the passage of any laws restricting the liberty of the press, and no restrictions of any kind are imposed, except such as are embodied in the laws against libel (see LIBEL), and in a few State laws prohibiting the publication of advertisements relating to lotteries or analogous schemes, and to objectionable drugs or nostrums. Grossly obscene publications are also prohibited by some State laws. The general policy of this country has warmly encouraged the development of printing. It was only during a very short period of extreme national necessity that a tax was ever imposed on advertisements, and on the sale or circulation of newspapers,—while newspaper exchanges have been circulated free of postage for many years; during a considerable period all newspapers were sent free of postage to all the post-offices in the counties in which they are printed; and the national and State laws have, in various respects, promoted the interests of printers, by requiring the publication of contracts, laws, and many matters relating to elections, legal proceedings, etc.

Laying Cases.—Filling cases with new type.

Laying Pages.—The arrangement of the pages of a sheet on the imposing surface in their proper order. (See IMPOSITION.)

Laying Type.—Putting new type into the cases. The page received from the founder should be carefully unwrapped, and, after having been laid on a galley, should be soaked thoroughly with thin soapwater, to prevent the types from adhering to one another after they have been used for a short time; then, with a stout rule or reglet, as many lines should be lifted as will make about an inch in thickness, and, placing the rule close up on one side of the bottom of the proper box, the lines should be pushed off gently, taking care not to rub the face against the side of the box. Proceed thus with successive lines till the box is filled. Careless compositors are prone to huddle new types together, and, grasping them by handfuls, plunge them pell-mell into the box, rudely jostling them about to crowd more in. This is a bad practice. The type left over should be kept standing on galleys in regular order, till the cases need replenishment. A font of five hundred pounds of Pica may have, say four pairs of cases allotted to it; the same amount of Nonpareil, from eight to ten pairs. Fifty pounds of type fill a pair of cases.

Lay of the Case.—The system upon which the various letters, points, spaces, quadrats, etc. are distributed among the different boxes in a case. (See CASES.)

Lead-Cutter.—An implement used to cut leads.

Leaded Matter.—Matter with leads between the lines. In newspapers the editorials are nearly always leaded, while other portions of the paper are generally set in solid type, although special dispatches and important news of any description are also frequently leaded. A large proportion of new books are leaded, but new works or reprints in which it is desirable to crowd a large amount of matter into a comparatively small space are set solid, or in type containing no leads between the lines.

Leader.—The longest, most prominent, or most important editorial of a newspaper.

Leaders (. . . . or - - -).—These consist of two or three dots, similar to full points, cast on one type, to the em body; there are also two and three em leaders, the number of dots being multiplied according to their length. Hyphen-faced leaders are also made. (- - - -). These are sometimes preferred in book-work, and are always cast with Script type.

Leads.—Thin pieces of metal, lead being the chief ingredient, which are placed between the lines of matter, or composed type, to open it up; they are also used to blank out titles, jobs, and forms of various descriptions. Leads have been used for this purpose ever since the days of Schoeffer, who is said to have invented them, using them first in a work he printed at Mentz in 1465. Brass is now sometimes used as the material of newspaper leads, because it is less likely to break or bend than thin strips of lead, but brass is necessary only when the forms are to be stereotyped by the papier-mache process, as it affects injuriously leads of the ordinary kind. The height of leads is about the same as the height of quadrats, or a little more than four Pica ems. Their thickness is regulated by a Pica standard, as they are variously cast, so that 4, 5, 6, 8, or 10 of them, combined, will have the thickness of a Pica em; and they are sometimes made thicker or thinner than the sizes mentioned. The thickness most common, and most generally useful, is six to Pica. The length of leads varies with the purposes to which they are to be applied, as they are cast or cut to any measures desired for job-work, the pages of books, or the columns of newspapers. Among the measures most common for job-work, are 50, 42, 38, 36, 22, and 19 Pica ems. In book-work, the measures most frequently used are 22 ems, 19 ems, and 15 ems. The Proof-Sheet Tables give the following rules for ascertaining the weight of leads required for any work—the calculations applying to any measure, but being all based on the use of six-to-Pica leads:

The first table is for solid matter which requires to be leaded, viz.:

OF SOLID MATTER—

1000	ems	Pearl	require	7½	oz.	leads.
1000	"	Agate	"	8½	"	"
1000	"	Nonpareil ...	"	9½	"	"
1000	"	Minion	"	11½	"	"
1000	"	Brevier	"	13	"	"
1000	"	Bourgeois....	"	13½	"	"
1000	"	Long Primer .	"	15½	"	"
1000	"	Small Pica ...	"	16½	"	"
1000	"	Pica	"	19	"	"

Example.—It is estimated that the matter to be set will make 20,000 ems Small Pica solid. Required the weight of leads necessary to lead this matter. 1000 ems of solid Small Pica require 16½ ounces of leads. 16½ × 20 = 330 oz. = 20 lbs. 10 oz.

The second table gives the weight of the leads contained in 1000 ems of leaded matter, viz.:

OF LEADED MATTER—

1000	ems	Pearl	contain	5½	oz.	leads.
1000	"	Agate	"	6	"	"
1000	"	Nonpareil ...	"	7½	"	"
1000	"	Minion	"	9	"	"
1000	"	Brevier	"	10½	"	"
1000	"	Bourgeois ...	"	11	"	"
1000	"	Long Primer .	"	12½	"	"
1000	"	Small Pica ...	"	14	"	"
1000	"	Pica	"	16½	"	"

Example.—A page of leaded Long Primer contains 2000 ems. Required the weight of leads necessary to lead thirty-two pages. 1000 ems of leaded Long Primer contain 12½ ounces of leads. 12½ × 2 = 25 oz. per page. 25 × 32 = 800 oz. = 50 lbs.

Or, a column of Nonpareil contains 8000 ems. Required the weight of leads necessary to lead six columns. 1000 ems of leaded Nonpareil contain 7½ ounces of leads. 7½ × 8 = 60 oz. per column. 60 × 6 = 360 oz. = 22 lbs. 8 oz.

An allowance must of course be made for additional leads using for blanking out, and in standing matter. One pound of leads or slugs covers four square inches. Hence, when the space to be filled by leads or slugs is known, it is only necessary to divide the number of square inches by four, and the result will give the required weight in pounds.

Leaflets.—A description of circular or small pamphlet, rarely containing more than eight, and frequently but six pages, which is not cut, stitched, or bound in the usual manner, but is simply folded and unfolded at pleasure, so that only one page, or all the pages on one side of the paper may be presented to the reader. For the manner of imposing leaflets, see IMPOSITION.

Lean Face.—A letter of slender width compared with its height.

Lean Work.—The opposite of fat work—that is, poor, unprofitable work.

Le Bee, William.—A celebrated letter-founder and engraver of Paris. His father supplied Robert Stephens with paper, and young Le Bée was brought up in the household of that great printer, where he received the instruction which led to his subsequent success. Le Bée made, by order of Francis I., some of the type used by the Stephens, and he was employed by Philip II. of Spain to prepare the type for the Antwerp Polyglot. Le Bée went to Venice in 1545, where he was widely employed; he subsequently returned to Paris, and practiced his art with distinguished success until his death in 1599. His son Henry was successful as a printer in Paris, where several generations of the family continued in the same employment for nearly a century.

Ledger.—An account-book in which are collected and arranged, under their proper headings, the various transactions entered in the journal and day-book. As representing the systematized history and collection of the transactions of every day, this name was early chosen as the title of a daily newspaper, and has since been a favorite title for such publications.

Letter.—A synonym for type or types. Thus, a printer says he has a case full of letter, or in speaking of one set of types, says they are lean letter, while others are fat letter, etc.

Letter-Board.—A board upon which type-forms are frequently placed after they have been printed, when it is desired to keep the forms standing, or to distribute them.

Letter-Founders.—A name sometimes applied to Type-Founders, especially in laws passed by the British Parliament. (See TYPE-FOUNDERS.)

Letter Hangs.—If the matter transferred from the composing-stick to the galley does not stand perfectly square and upright, it is said to hang. It is usually the result of carelessness in emptying the composing-stick, but the phrase is generally applied to matter after it is made up.

Letter-Headings.—Lines printed at the head of sheets of letter-paper, containing the residence, and generally the name and place of business, of the party for whom such work is done.

Letter-Paper.— Writing-paper upon which letters, mainly, are written, the size being usually 10 by 16 inches.

Letter-Press Printing.—The method of taking impressions from letters and other characters cast or engraved in relief upon separate pieces of metal,— the inks used being always applied to the surface of the types, and the impressions being made by surface or cylindrical pressure.

Letter Rack.—A rack for containing wood and metal letters of such a size that it would be inconvenient to keep them in cases.

Lever-Sliding Knife Paper-Cutter.—A paper-cutting machine, for job printers and binders, which is manufactured by E. R. & T. W. Sheridan, in New York. It is said to be very strong, and not liable to get out of order.

LEVER-SLIDING KNIFE CUTTING MACHINE.

Lexicon.—A book containing the words of a language arranged alphabetically and defined, generally confined to dictionaries of the Greek and Hebrew tongues.

Libel.—A libel is a defamation expressed either in printing or writing, or by signs or pictures, tending to blacken the memory of one who is dead with intent to provoke the living; or a written or printed assault upon the reputation of one who is alive, with the intent of exposing him to public hatred, contempt, or ridicule. It may either charge the party injured with a criminal offense, or it may exhibit him in a ludicrous point of view, or state any thing which is calculated to drive him out of society. It has been decided that to say a man has a loathsome disease is a libel, but to say that he has had such a disease is not necessarily a libel, because his standing in society may not be affected by such a statement. If the matter is understood as scandalous, and is calculated to excite ridicule or abhorrence against the party injured, it is libelous, however it may be expressed; for ironical praise or insinuating interrogatories may be libelous. The publication of a libel consists in writing or printing and exposing the written or printed matter to the view of others, or in reading it to one or more persons; and it is an essential part of the offense that this publication should be malicious, but such malice may be implied; for where a man publishes a writing which on the face of it is libelous, the law presumes he does so from a malicious intention, and it is not necessary for the prosecutor to prove any circumstances from which malice may be inferred; and malice, in the legal sense, does not imply ill will toward the person libeled. Justification of libel consists in showing and maintaining a good legal reason for the publication complained of. The old common-law doctrine that the greater the truth the greater the libel no longer prevails, and it is a sufficient defense in most instances to prove that the defendant had a good motive or a reasonable excuse, especially when the publications are substantially true. Of thousands of libel suits commenced in the United States only a small fraction are successful. Verdicts in civil suits are most frequent in cases where parties have hastily, falsely, and on insufficient authority been charged with disgraceful or odious crimes or misdemeanors; and printers are not often convicted criminally of libel, unless they have carelessly or wantonly printed unjustifiable attacks upon private character.

Liberty of the Press.—By some English legal writers the liberty of the press is construed to mean simply freedom from censorship and the right to print any given document or article without obtaining a special license therefor. Practically, however, the real liberty of the press also requires exemption from all harassing and hampering restrictions, and absolute freedom in all respects except in the one particular that printers and publishers must be answerable to the courts for any abuse of their privileges. The importance of the liberty of the press to the welfare of a nation can scarcely be over-estimated. Of many forcible and eloquent statements of this truth which have been made, a few are given below:

The liberties of the press and the liberties of the people must stand or fall together.—*Hume.*

Give me a tyrant king—give me a hostile house of lords—give me a corrupt house of commons—give me the press and I will overturn them all.—*Richard Brinsley Sheridan.*

I have always considered the press as the protector of our freedom; as a watchful guardian, capable of uniting the weak against the encroachment of power. What concerns the public most properly admits of public discussion.—*Goldsmith.*

Without the free use of the press, any characters or designs unfavorable to liberty cannot be publicly known till it is too late to oppose them. Hence the greatest enemies to the press are characters notorious for entertaining those designs.—*Dr. Hayter.*

I acknowledge that abuses are sometimes committed in consequence of the unrestrained freedom of the press; but, after the observation of many years, I am confident that the advantages infinitely preponderate. The public is the dread tribunal before which every cause is judged. Every man is heard, and is free to vindicate his conduct. Had all lands such heralds, whose loud voice might awaken shame and fear; were common people of every country equally eager to read the public papers; then would discord, oppression, and bigotry soon be banished from their borders by a great majority of votes, and men that can read, and dare to write, would soon cease to be slaves.—*M. Wendeborn.*

The freedom of the press, however perverted at times or occasionally lowered in its influence by groundless and indiscriminate animadversions, was, at an early day, fully established here [in the United States], unchecked except by being made legally subject to punishment for flagrant wrongs. From Milton's speech for the liberty of unlicensed printing, published about the time many of our fathers emigrated hither, to the expiration of the celebrated sedition law, as well as since, the idea has grown with our growth that a still more effective remedy to prevent the licentiousness of the press, or the tongue through the press, is rather to be found in public intelligence and sound morals, than in the prison or the pillory, or in the personal violence inflicted thoughtlessly on its indiscreet conductors. However, then, we may lament its occasional prostitution,—mingled, it is admitted, with many excellences,—and however we may regret the manifold abuses of free discussion and liberty of speech, as well as of the press, yet they all rest on imperishable principles.—*Levi Woodbury.*

Library.—A collection of books of any extent, and also the apartment in which they are placed. As the caskets in which the gems of typography are preserved as the precious heirlooms of successive generations, the great libraries of the world must interest every printer. The first library of which there is any mention belonged to the King of Egypt, at Memphis, and is supposed to have existed fully fourteen centuries before the Christian era; and it is probable that collections were made by the Jews, the Hindoos, Chinese, and Persians, at a very early date. The first public library of Greece of which there is

any authentic account was founded about b. c. 540 by Pisistratus, who is credited with being the precursor of the vast army of Homeric editors. Alexander of Macedon carried with him on his journeys of military adventure the works of his tutor Aristotle, contained in a case luxuriously adorned, and from his countrymen the Greeks has descended the word bibliothica, which has been adopted into all the modern European languages in some form as the scholastic term for the English word library, which in itself reveals the old supremacy of the Latin tongue, in its derivation from *liber*, a book. The city of Alexandria, the first monument of the great Alexander, was the fitting seat of the first great library, which is believed to have contained 400,000 volumes when it was partially destroyed in the war with Julius Cæsar. In Pergamus was its only rival, a library of 200,000 volumes, which was presented with princely magnificence by Marc Antony to Cleopatra in order to restore the glories of her Alexandrian library, which by this addition was again raised to its old supremacy as the largest collection in the world, a position that it maintained until it was annihilated, A. D. 638, in the ninth century of its existence.

From Macedon also came the first library established in Rome, b. c. 167; and it is stated that Julius Cæsar planned the foundation of the first public library, but left it to be accomplished under his successor Augustus. Others were established at Rome, but were destroyed by fire in the latter part of the first century of the Christian era, and were replaced by the efforts of Domitian, who sent scribes to Alexandria for that purpose; and when Constantine established his library at Constantinople, A. D. 335, Rome already contained twenty-nine public libraries.

Alexandria became, for various reasons, one of the principal seats of learning, and here at the very time of the foundation of the great library was commenced that vast and wonderful work, the collection of the Hebrew Scriptures and its translation into Greek, as the vernacular of the Jews of Egypt, who were fast losing on a foreign soil the knowledge of the language of their fathers. The Alexandrian Library was necessarily especially rich in copies of the Scriptures and of the original manuscripts used in the compilation, and also in commentaries upon them written by the learned Jews of various countries; and it is probable that a knowledge of this fact led to the bitter antagonism that caused its destruction, for the same reason that a magnificent library in Syria was destroyed by the Crusaders in the twelfth century under the guidance of a European priest, who had discovered in it a whole apartment devoted to the Koran.

Of the Greek libraries there is a singular lack of careful records, when the civilization of that nation is taken into consideration, and it must be inferred that the books were treasured as the private property of the small class of highly educated persons who raised the national reputation for learning and art to so great an elevation, and that they were not collected in any manner which would be of advantage to the masses of the community. The more republican population of Rome demanded other treatment, and it is certain that Augustus founded two great public libraries, and that many of his successors followed his example, until, in emulation of the throne, the collection of books became one of the passions of the wealthy, some of whom received from the contemporary authors great praise for opening their treasures to the use of the learned.

During many centuries there is but little to be learned upon the condition of literature. Greece and Rome had fallen from their high estate, and the best modern authorities unite in doubting the glowing accounts given by the Arabs of the vast extent of their collections of manuscripts. But that libraries were common among various kingdoms of Asia, when Europe was plunged in ignorance, seems to be absolutely proven, and the Arabs of Spain certainly exhibited remarkable love of learning, adopting and combining the literature of Rome with the luxurious imagination and erudition of the East. Great libraries were collected by the Arabs in Spain, and it is only permissible to doubt that the collection of the Caliph of Cordova, who died after the close of the eighth century, was properly estimated at 400,000 volumes. In the same city, according to the Arab historians, a passion for book-collecting, a veritable bibliomania, raged during the tenth century, and every wealthy citizen boasted of being the fortunate possessor of some rare manuscript or autograph, exactly in the manner of certain literary circles of England, France, and Germany in the present century. In the middle of the thirteenth century, St. Louis of France, having learned in the East that the Sultan of the Saracens employed scribes, was prompted by this discovery to collect a library at great expense, and to gather up Bibles and religious books, on his return.

Most exaggerated accounts of the extent of libraries arose in Europe during the ages of general ignorance, and the reports have been handed down from generation to generation until it has become difficult to accept the truth that the libraries of the palaces and convents were more probably counted by scores than by thousands. The celebrated collection of the Sorbonne at the end of the thirteenth century reached but 1000 volumes, and the Royal Library of Paris, which enjoyed a sort of fabulous reputation, numbered in 1373, 910 volumes, and actually counted in 1791, amounted to but 152,868. The Vatican, founded in 1446, and long held as containing the entire literary treasure of Europe, has been recently computed at 100,000 printed volumes, although it is remarkably rich in manuscripts.

The principal collection of modern times is the Imperial Library of Paris, which contained in 1859 880,000 volumes. It was founded in the fourteenth century, and notably increased by Francis I., but the great impulse was given to it when Francis II., under the influence of Diana of Poitiers, ordered that a copy of every book issued in France should be deposited upon its shelves, while her fancy for fine books also impelled him to enact that the royal copies should be printed upon vellum, which has added much to the magnificence of the collection. The library was at first kept at Blois, then at Fontainebleau, until finally Henry IV. removed it to Paris to become a national glory. It was one of the boasts of Louis XIV. that he found the collection numbering 5000 and raised it to 70,000, although he left to his son the credit of opening it to the public in 1735,— Cardinal Mazarin having set the example in devoting to the public use his own private library, which was sold by the Parliament during his exile, and the proceeds offered for his capture dead or alive; but the able Cardinal returned to power, collected another library, and at his death, in 1661, left it by will to the public.

Under Napoleon I. the Imperial Library received great accessions, and he ordered in 1805 that when any book was found in any library, either in Paris or any of the departments, which was not contained in the Imperial collection, it should be taken from the minor establishment in exchange for some work possessed in duplicate by the Imperial Library, so that it might be said with certainty that if a volume was not contained in the Imperial Library it could not be found in France. Such an idea, and such a method of carrying it into execution, were assuredly Napoleonic, yet still an excellent means of obtaining that great national boon, a central, universal library of reference.

From the different methods of counting adopted by various libraries, there has arisen a conflict of claims for superiority, some counting by separate works, whether embracing single pamphlets or rows of folio volumes, and others counting by volumes, where uncertainty again arises in the counting of pamphlets and manuscripts. For this reason, although the first rank is given without question to the Imperial Library of Paris, the second place is claimed by the libraries of Vienna, Munich, St. Petersburg, and the British Museum. Between the two latter, the question is still undecided; but it is probable that the Russian Library is the largest, as its published catalogue in 1860 claims 840,853 printed volumes, 29,045 manuscripts, and 66,162 engravings, having added 200,000 printed volumes in ten years. This library was founded upon the Zabriskie library seized in Warsaw and transported to St. Petersburg in 1795. This collection, formed during his lifetime by a Polish bishop, with the assistance of another, was probably the largest ever formed by private expense, for, after suffering considerable injury in Poland, it was counted as 262,640 volumes when it reached St. Petersburg. The Warsaw library was neglected in Russia for some years, and in 1803 it had fallen to 238,633, and again suffered material injury, when it was hastily removed to an obscure place of security in dread of the all-appropriating grasp of Napoleon. The Russian Library is rendered exceedingly useful by being open from ten in the morning until nine in the evening, throughout the year.

18

Until rather recent times England has not possessed many remarkable public libraries. The Bodleian, founded at Oxford in 1602, was long esteemed by the British as the second library of the world, and almost universal in its contents; but its official return in 1849 made it number only 220,000 volumes. A great opportunity was given to this library in 1609, by its receiving the transfer of the privilege enjoyed by the Stationers' Company of one copy of every work entered at the Stationers' Hall; but the short-sightedness of the founder, Sir Thomas Bodley, destroyed this advantage by ordering the librarian to exclude almanacs, plays, and the infinite number of things daily printed unworthy of a place on the shelves. This sweeping charge was literally obeyed by a succession of librarians, who for two centuries simply destroyed every volume that they personally considered trivial, and, as a consequence, in 1674 the Bodleian contained neither the first nor the second folio Shakspeare, having only one copy of the great dramatist, the folio of 1664. Sir Thomas Bodley was himself a contemporary of Shakspeare, yet by his express order every copy of the plays was banished for more than half a century, and, as a consequence, the library in 1841 purchased one of the original editions of a single play of Marlowe's, remarkable for its historic value, for 131 pounds.

The Bodleian remained the great British library until about the middle of the eighteenth century, when Sir Hans Sloane by will offered his private library of 50,000 volumes to the British Government, on condition of a certain provision for his three daughters; the offer if neglected at home being renewed to the Emperor of Russia. Advantage was taken of this opportunity, and the Sloane Library was established in London in 1753, where it became the basis of the British Museum, which was increased in 1757 by the gift from George II. of the library of the Kings of England, and took rank among the first libraries of Europe, when in 1823 it received from George IV. the fine collection of George III., whose queen had been especially successful in gathering German and Danish works. Gifts, bequests, and purchases have increased the Museum to vast proportions, assisted by large grants from the Government, and it claims to possess the greatest variety of works, in the greatest number of languages, from the earthen cylinders of the Assyrian kings down to the last Irish newspapers.

The Imperial Library of Vienna, founded by Frederick III., the patron of the early printers, in 1440, was in 1789 the largest library in Europe, containing at that time 196,000 volumes, but it is supposed not to have advanced so rapidly as some of its rivals.

The impossibility of ascertaining with exactitude the extent of libraries is well exhibited in the fact that the Imperial collection of China contained, in 1790, 10,500 distinct works, no account being made of the volumes, although some of the separate works are known to contain a very large number.

Of the various national libraries of Europe it is impossible to make distinct mention. The library of Munich is very varied; that of Berlin is remarkable for its German literature; Leyden contains the largest collection of Dutch; Copenhagen has the finest library in the Scandinavian tongue; and Pesth, in Hungary, has a fine national collection. It is a curious fact that the French Imperial Library contains the best collection of the Dutch drama in the world, while Oxford has the largest known library of Hebrew. In France, outside of Paris, the finest collection was formerly at Strasburg, where the library, previous to the late war, contained 180,000 volumes. In Rome the Casanata is a very fine collection, while Naples, Milan, Bologna, and Ferrara contain large libraries.

The first public library within the present limits of the United States was founded at the College of Virginia, in 1620, by the donation, from an anonymous friend, of Sir Walter Ralcigh's Map of Guiana, and four large volumes, of what works is not stated. The library and college were destroyed in the Indian massacre in 1622.

The oldest American library now existing is that of Harvard College, established in 1638. It was destroyed by fire in 1764, but was re-established, and in 1869 contained 118,000 volumes. The first library for public use in New York was established in 1700 by the Chaplain of the King's forces, who bequeathed his collection expressly to found a public library; it continued without any considerable increase until 1754, when the city presented it to a thriving young subscription library, called the New York Society Library, which in 1793 contained 5000 volumes, and in 1869 contained 57,000.

The Library of Yale College was commenced in 1700, and thirty years afterwards received a fine gift of books from Bishop Berkeley; it numbered 50,000 volumes in 1869.

The Philadelphia Library owes its origin to Benjamin Franklin, in 1731, and was the first subscription library in America or England. It is especially rich in rare copies of early fine printing, both in Europe and America, and, although of limited extent, numbering 95,000 in 1870, it is a singularly fine collection, and perhaps the best general library in the country, for the reason that it has omitted burdening its shelves with the scientific works which are in Philadelphia gathered into the libraries of the Academy of Natural Sciences and the various Medical and other scientific schools and societies, and has devoted itself to the collection of what may be truly called the best style of standard literature. The Congressional Library at Washington was founded in 1800, and now ranks as the largest library in the United States, containing in 1869, 183,000 volumes, and 50,000 pamphlets. It had reached 3000 volumes when it was destroyed by the British in 1814, and the loss was made good by the purchase, by Congress, of the private library of President Jefferson, which reached 6700 volumes. In 1851 the library contained

55,000 volumes, when it was again burned, and a new and handsome fire-proof apartment was erected for it in the National Capitol. This library is the only one in the United States which enjoys the privilege of the Copyright Law, being legally entitled to a copy of every work copyrighted in the country.

The vast libraries of other countries have been built up by this means; the Royal Library of France has enjoyed this right for centuries; the Bodleian, now the second library of England, has increased by this means for two hundred years; and by law, since 1835, five libraries, the British Museum, the Bodleian, the Cambridge, the Advocates' of Edinburgh, and Trinity College, Dublin, are each entitled to a copy of every work published. The Boston Athenæum, founded in 1805, possesses an especially fine collection of American newspapers and pamphlets.

The increase in the libraries of America is so rapid that it is impossible to furnish accurate statistics, but some general idea of their respective size can be gained from the following table, prepared in the year 1869:

Congressional Library	. . . 183,000	volumes.
Boston Public "	. . . 153,000	"
Astor "	. . . 138,000	"
Harvard College "	. . . 118,000	"
N.Y. Mercantile "	. . . 104,500	"
Boston Athenæum "	. . . 100,000	"
Philadelphia "	. . . 85,000	"
New York State "	. . . 76,000	"
" " Society "	. . . 57,000	"
Yale College "	. . . 50,000	"

In the year 1859, the public libraries of the United States were computed to reach above twelve and a half millions of volumes.

The first circulating library in Great Britain was established by Allan Ramsay, in Edinburgh, in 1725. This style of library has increased rapidly throughout England, especially because the principal libraries do not allow the books to be taken beyond the walls of the establishment, but in America, where almost all libraries lend their books upon easy terms, circulating libraries are mainly restricted to a lighter and inferior range of literature.

While numerous libraries of general literature, of easy access to the inhabitants of different localities, constitute, of course, a most admirable and necessary means of public instruction, a single national library to be founded in a chief city, as the place of universal reference, is of equal importance. This idea of universality has, however, been but recently adopted; Sir Thomas Bodley, as has been stated, excluded plays; at the beginning of the present century, no British library admitted novels, and, as a consequence, thirty years after its publication the first edition of Waverley, after a long search, was discovered in private hands.

Newspapers, now regarded as a most valuable historic record, were for a long time excluded, and it is said that Sir Robert Peel strongly objected to the collection of the Colonial journals, as useless, and no collection of the English newspapers of India is known to exist. The value of these daily records is now so well understood that the British Museum preserves a vast number of them, and the library of Melbourne in Australia offered one thousand pounds for a complete set of the London Times. The remarkable and unexpected revelations made in recent years by the examination of state papers, have also attracted public attention to their value, and it has been proposed that all national archives and documents, of a date sufficiently remote to make them public property, shall be arranged in such manner as to make them available to historic students, so that such valuable information as Macaulay gained from the manuscripts of the Hague and the Vatican, or those astonishing discoveries made in the archives of Spain, may be continued until many of the mysteries of the past are explained.

Libretto.—Strictly a little book, but restricted by general use to a book containing the words of an opera.

Lift.—To lift a form is to remove it temporarily from the press, and thus to suspend the process of printing, in order that another form may be put on. In the wareroom, each separate portion of printed paper, whatever the number of sheets it consists of, that is placed upon the poles to dry, is termed a lift. A form is said to lift when it has been so perfectly justified and locked up that no parts of it drop out on being raised from the imposing surface.

Ligatures.—Letters cast together on one shank. The only ligatures now in general use are, Æ, Œ, æ, œ, œ, ff, ffi, ffl, fi, fl.

Light-Faces.—Numerous varieties of job type, in which the lines of the letters are unusually light or thin.

Line.—1. Composed types which fill the length of any given measure constitute a line of that measure. 2. When types are correctly made, the hair-lines at the top and bottom of each letter are said to line. One method of ascertaining whether the types of a font line or not is as follows: Take a lower-case m, and see if its hair-lines are even with the hair-lines on the other lower-case sorts of the font. Then see if its lower hair-lines are even with the corresponding strokes on the capital M, and, if they are, ascertain whether the capitals and small capitals line at the bottom with the last-named letter.

Liquid.—A letter which has a smooth, flowing sound, or which flows smoothly after a mute; as l and r, in bla, bra; m and n are also called liquids.

Literal.—Consisting of or pertaining to letters; as, the literal errors in written or printed documents. The word is more frequently used to express verbal exactness, or the exact following of an original word by word; as, a literal translation.

Literal Errors.—Errors in letters, as distinguished from verbal errors, which are errors in words.

Literary.—Pertaining to letters or scholarship.

Literary Property.—Ownership in copyrights, etc. (See COPYRIGHTS.)

Literati.—A Latin word adopted into English, and used to denote the learned class.

Literatum.—Letter for letter; the following of copy with literal exactness.

Literature.—The entire mass of the written or printed works of any epoch or country, or of the whole globe. It is sometimes used to express a knowledge of letters as distinguished from science, and also, in a more restricted sense, to denote polite learning, or belles-lettres.

Lithograph.—A print from a drawing on stone; also the act of engraving or etching on stone.

Lithography (λίθος, a stone, and γραφή, writing) is the art of drawing or engraving on stone and the process of taking impressions from the same.

Among the various methods of producing impressions, there are none that offer more varieties than lithography. 1st, we have the drawing on stone with prepared chalk or crayon. 2d, line drawings with pen or pencil with lithographic ink. 3d, the engraving on stone with steel-point or diamond. 4th, the drawing or writing on prepared paper for transferring on stone, which we will call autography. 5th, transferring on stone impressions taken from copper or steel plates, wood-cuts, or type. 6th, producing photographs on stone or glass to be printed by lithographic presses. 7th, drawings by lavis or wash on stone. And 8th, producing chromos, pictures resembling oil-painting, the highest attainment of lithography.

We propose to give a synopsis of these different branches, beginning with the origin and discovery of the art, and tracing its progress to the present day.

The process of lithography is founded—1st, upon the adhesion to the smooth face of a stone, of an encaustic fat, which forms the lines or traces; 2d, upon the power acquired by the parts penetrated by this encaustic of attracting to themselves and becoming covered with the printing-ink; 3d, upon the interposition of a film of water, which prevents the adhesion of the ink in all parts of the surface of the stone not impregnated with the encaustic; and 4th and lastly, upon a pressure applied by the stone sufficient to transfer to paper the greater part of the ink which covers the greasy tracing of the encaustic.

Lithography is a German invention, and, like many other useful arts, owes its origin to a simple accident.

In 1796 Aloysius Senefelder, a musician and composer, employed in one of the theatres of Munich, was in the habit of using pieces of slate or limestone, found in great quantity in the neighborhood of that city, on which to arrange for drawing his compositions previous to putting them on paper. While so engaged, he wrote with a pencil on a piece of this stone, for his mother, a memorandum of some clothes the washerwoman was about taking away, and inadvertently dropped it in a slop-bucket full of greasy water; hastily withdrawing it, fearful lest it should become effaced, to his astonishment he saw that every

letter had become coated with grease contained in the water, without affecting the other parts of the stone, and, on repeating the experiment, he invariably found the same result. This suggested to him the idea that some advantage could be derived from this singular phenomenon, and, being a man of ingenuity and perseverance, this simple accident led him to the discovery of lithography. He applied himself to the arrangement of suitable ingredients to compose a crayon and the proper acids to fix it upon stone, then to the construction of a press to take the impressions. This was not an easy task, for, being neither a chemist nor a machinist, and fearing to ask advice from any one, lest his secret should be revealed, he shut himself up, learned to draw, and persevered in experimenting for nearly four years, until he was able to produce samples sufficiently good to establish the validity of his discovery, and in the year 1800 he obtained the exclusive privilege of exercising his invention.

As soon as his discovery was made public, he received offers of large sums of money from all parts of Europe for the privilege of using it, or for entering into partnership to share the proceeds, but, like most inventors, he was so infatuated with his discovery that he refused all offers, wishing to reserve to himself the secret of his process. Being unable, however, to do all the work attending upon the operation of a lithographic establishment, he was obliged to employ assistants to aid him in various parts of the labor, and little by little his secret was revealed; and, as lithography sprang up simultaneously throughout every part of Germany, in 1801, Senefelder never derived any material benefit from his discovery.

It is said that a Mr. Mitterer, professor of drawing in the public schools of Munich, invented a composition for the chalk or crayon for drawing on stone. Messrs. Manlick and Aretin set up lithographic presses chiefly intended for the reproduction of fine-art subjects, and published part of the collection of drawings of ancient masters belonging to the King of Bavaria. It was only in 1802 that Senefelder himself set up an establishment in Vienna, while Mr. Delarmé, of Munich, settled in Milan and Rome. In 1807 André, of Offenbach, who had become a partner of Senefelder, made an unsuccessful attempt to obtain the privilege of establishing lithographic presses in London and Paris. It is said that the First Napoleon objected on the ground that the art furnished too many facilities for counterfeiting. In 1810 Mr. Hulmandel established the first lithographic press in London, but lithography did not enter France until the restoration of the Bourbons to the throne. In 1810 Mr. Engelman, who had an establishment in Mulhouse, set up branches in Vienna and Berlin, and in the following year in St. Petersburg, Madrid, and London.

In 1814 Mr. Martel de Serres, commissioned by the French Government to examine the manufactories in Germany, published some observations on lithography in his report, and explained, with great talent, the advantages of this new art; and his remarks attracted the attention of men of science.

In 1817 Count Lasteyrie succeeded in introducing lithography into France. He made several journeys into Germany to gain information, and studied the process until he became, in fact, a lithographer himself. In the interim Mr. Engelman established a branch in Paris, and, as he understood the business practically, he soon produced specimens which obtained an honorable mention from the Paris Institute. Paris then possessed two lithographic establishments. Unfortunately, Lasteyrie and Engelman became jealous of each other, and kept the whole process a

disinterested, he published the result of his experience in a treatise on the new art.

Thus lithography progressed slowly and with much difficulty, every practitioner keeping to himself the secret of his experience, and refusing to impart it to others. Every new beginner was aided only by a general theory, which was very insufficient when put in practice.

The government subjected the privilege to the Law of Censure, which compelled the lithographers to submit to a censor a proof of all their work before going on with the printing, and limited the brevets or licenses to three, but the number was increased

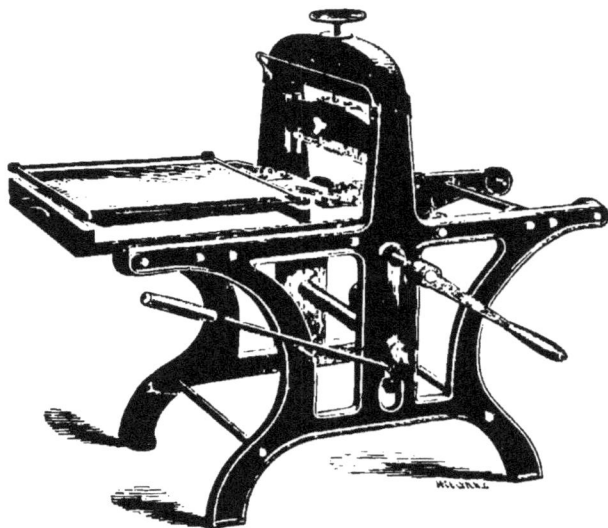

LITHOGRAPHIC HAND-PRESS.

secret; both had spent a fortune in fostering lithography. At this time the Royal School of France for Roads and Bridges obtained from the director-general permission to establish lithographic presses, and Mr. Harcourt, one of the oldest pupils, was intrusted with their management, but, being unacquainted with the process, and Lasteyrie and Engelman refusing to impart any information, he was at first entirely at a loss how to proceed, until Mr. Berigney, the director of the school, received from a learned friend in Germany several notes of information, which gave him some knowledge of the process, but left him still very deficient in practice; and it was only after repeated failures for more than a year that, by self-taught experience, he met with some success. Being

from time to time, and new brevets were granted to some applicants for special favors, and at the time of the revolution of 1830 the restriction was removed, and the trade became free.

Lithography was introduced into the United States in 1828 by Messrs. Pendleton Brothers, plate-printers and stationers in Boston, who added lithographic presses to their establishment. In 1829 John Pendleton, one of the brothers, came to Philadelphia, and set up a lithographic establishment in partnership with Mr. C. G. Childs, bank-note engraver, and a Mr. Kearney, under the name of Pendleton, Kearney & Childs. This firm existed but a short time. Messrs. Pendleton and Kearney going out of it, Mr. Henry Inman, a painter of great talent, then joined

Mr. Childs, and the establishment went under the name of Childs & Inman up to 1832, when the writer of this sketch, together with a Mr. George Lehman, an artist of merit, succeeded them, under the name of Lehman & Duval. Mr. John Pendleton, on leaving Philadelphia in 1830, settled in New York, and continued the business in that city for many years. The chief difficulty at that time was to procure practical artists and printers, and it impeded the progress of the art very materially.

An establishment was started in Baltimore in 1831, by an artist named Swett, but, owing to his decease, which took place a short time afterwards, the establishment was not continued, and no lithographic presses were set up in Baltimore until some years later. Another attempt was made in Philadelphia in 1831 by Messrs. Kennedy & Lucas, stationers, to set up lithographic presses, but, not being able to procure a practical printer, they abandoned the enterprise.

The establishment in Philadelphia produced some specimens of the art which made a very favorable impression. It may not be out of place to mention here that the principal lithographic artist in the United States at that time was a deaf-and-dumb young man named Albert Newsam, who had been instructed by Mr. Childs. Many portraits lithographed by this talented artist would bear favorable comparison with the best ones of the present time; he was remarkable for accurate resemblances.

We would like to mention the names of several artists and proprietors of establishments who contributed to the advancement of lithography in the United States, but this would extend our article beyond the limits intended, and we leave their productions, which are before the public, to testify to their merits. However, the progress of lithography was not without its drawbacks at the outset. Several publishers of prints, whose desire was for money rather than for the interest of the art, flooded the country with the commonest kind of pictures, wretchedly executed, which gave a very unfavorable impression of lithography. Not only the public, but the artists also, shunned an art which seemed to promise but mediocrity, and very poor pecuniary compensation. It was quite the opposite in Europe, where, at the start, artists of the highest merit, such as Isabey, Mauzaise Dubuff, Aubrey le Conte, Marin Lavigne, and a number of others, did not disdain to intrust lithography with some of their best productions, which gave it at once a rank among the fine arts. We beg pardon for this digression, and will now proceed with our subject.

In 1831 there were but three establishments in the United States, occupying about eight presses in all, while at the present time there are upwards of fifty-five establishments, occupying at least four hundred and fifty hand- and about thirty steam-presses. This great auxiliary to manual labor was only recently supplied to lithography. The first steam-press was invented in Paris in 1850, by a Frenchman, named Eugues. He sold the patent for England to Messrs.

Hughes & Kimber, press-builders of London, who made important improvements on the first pattern, and introduced it into the United States in 1866. It is

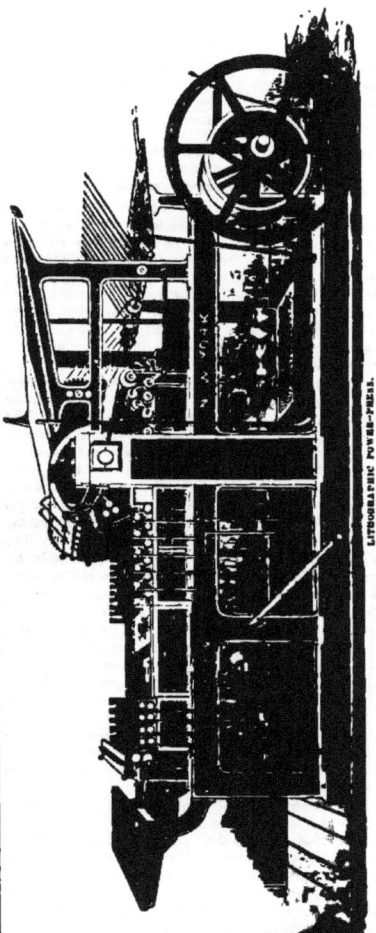

the pattern most in use at the present [...] there was one manufactured in [...] time previous, which is still in use [...] ments in New York and Boston. [...]

several patterns imported from Germany, and Mr. Hoe, the celebrated American press-builder, has also lately introduced a steam lithographic press. The need of steam-power had been felt for a long time in lithography, in consequence of the hard labor attending the work of the hand-press. In 1850 the writer of this notice, by a simple combination, added the steam-power to his hand-presses, but only so far as to save muscular labor, while the steam-presses in use at the present time do the work on the same principle as the typographic presses.

DESCRIPTION OF THE MATERIAL USED IN LITHOGRAPHY, AND THE MODUS OPERANDI OF THE DIFFERENT METHODS.

Before entering on the description of the different methods of lithographing, we feel it necessary to say to the practitioners of the trade, who will, no doubt, find our notice incomplete, that as there are varieties of combinations that can be used in making the different preparations, we do not propose to give more than one formula for each preparation, nor do we propose to enter into the explanation of all the imperfections that may occur, and the way in which they can be remedied.

Lithographic Stones.—The lithographic stones are calcareous, of superior texture, composed of carbonic acid, argil, and silex. They vary in color from light yellow to dark gray. They are susceptible of receiving very high polish, and a grain sufficiently close to admit of fine and sharp lines, and they have to be hard enough to resist the acidulation to which the drawing has to be subjected before printing, and yet sufficiently porous to be impregnated by the greasy substances of which the crayons are composed. The yellow, when sufficiently hard, are preferable for crayon drawing, as the artist can better see his work, while the gray, being harder, are better for engraving, the graver cutting cleaner and sharper lines. The pale yellows are generally very soft, and not suitable for any kind of fine work; the acid has too much effect on them, and the drawings are deteriorated by losing the fine tints in the acidulation; the grease of the ink also penetrates through the pores, and destroys the transparency of the drawing.

The best quarries of this stone are found at Solenhofen, in Bavaria, near Munich. Some have been found in the Pyrenees, and at Châteauroux, in France. They occur also in great quantities in the county of Pappenheim, on the banks of the Danube. They are found in the United States on the banks of the Mississippi. In 1854 the writer found several quarries in the city of St. Louis, and lately at Cape Girardeau; and he was told by a lithographer of St. Louis, recently, that in making the excavations for the centre piers of the bridge, now in construction opposite that city, a bed of lithographic stone was struck, at 90 feet below the surface of the river. But, in general, the Mississippi stones contain more or less pyrites of iron, which renders them unfit for fine work. They have been found, also, in the States of Kentucky and Indiana, but of very dark-blue color, and too hard, almost, for any use in lithography. The European stones are imported with rough dressing, and are finished in the lithographic establishments, by being grained or polished, according to the nature of the work for which they are intended.

The Graining of the Stones.—This operation, although apparently simple, requires the utmost care, as the success of the artist depends, in a great measure, on the quality of the grain of the stone. To be suitable for fine crayon drawing, and to enable the artist to produce clean and well-blended tints, it must be fine, close, and sharp. The crayon producing the drawing being laid on the top of each grain, if they are coarse and far apart, the drawing will be coarse, and produce rough impressions; if they are flat, the crayon will slip over the surface, preventing the artist from giving sufficient depth to the vigorous parts of his drawing and blending the fine tints, and the impressions will be monotonous and without effect. Simple as this operation may appear, but few hands succeed in producing a good grain.

The stone is grained in the following manner. One stone is placed on bars laid horizontally over a trough, fine sand is sifted over the face, then water is sprinkled on it, and a stone of smaller size is placed over the sand, and rubbed with a circular motion until the sand is ground; the top stone is then raised, new sand is added, and the rubbing is renewed; this operation is repeated until the grain is satisfactory. There are generally two or three grades of sand used, commencing with a coarser kind, so as to cut the stone more quickly, and the finest is used to produce the grain. The quality of the grain depends entirely on the motion of the hand of the grainer. If he moves the stone in a wide circle, the grain is generally flat, but by moving in a small circle, and reversing it from right to left, and left to right, alternately, a fine sharp grain is obtained. The last sand should not be used too long, as by rubbing the stone when the sand is reduced to mere mud, the grain would be destroyed. When the grain is satisfactory, the stones are washed with clean water, and dried, and if not to be used immediately, they should be kept wrapped in clean paper, to prevent the face from being soiled.

Polishing of the Stones.—When the stone is to be used for line- or pen-drawing, engraving or transferring, the face must be polished first with pumice-stone, and finished with a Scotch stone, such as is used in the marble-yards; it must be free from sand holes or scratches.

Lithographic Crayons.—The crayon must be composed so as to adhere to the stone, and penetrate it sufficiently to resist the acidulation and give adhesion to the printing-ink when the drawing is washed off with turpentine, so as to yield to the paper the ink received from the printing-roller. The crayon must be sufficiently hard to permit of its being cut to a fine point, so as to produce sharp and clean lines, and to bear a certain amount of pressure without bending or breaking. If too dry, it does not penetrate the stone sufficiently, and if too fat and greasy, it spreads in the pores, invades the spaces between the grain, and destroys the transparency of the drawing. The following composition will give the desired results:

Yellow wax (pure)	32 parts.
Mutton suet	4 "
White Castile soap	24 "
Salt of nitre	1 "
Fine calcined lampblack . . .	7 "

As the soap contains more or less water, according as it is more or less fresh, this proportion is calculated for dry soap. It is, therefore, best to cut it in thin slices and dry it before using it.

In manufacturing the crayon from these ingredients, the salt of nitre has to be dissolved separately (in a small copper or iron saucepan) in seven times its weight in water, and kept warm until the proper time, when it is to be added to the mass. The suet and wax are first melted in a copper or iron saucepan, then the soap is added in small quantities at a time, to avoid tumefaction. The composition must be stirred steadily, with an iron spatula, when these three ingredients are dissolved, the salt of nitre is added, also by small quantities at a time, to prevent too much effervescence. The black is next added, little by little, by stirring with the spatula, to incorporate it into the mass. The temperature is then increased until the mixture takes fire upon touching the surface with a piece of red-hot iron, and the flame is allowed to burn one minute. The saucepan is then covered to put out the flame, and taken off the fire; then the lid is lifted up and the fire set in again, but only to burn the scum formed on the surface. The mixture is then allowed to cool somewhat, when it is poured on a marble slab, divided into small lumps, and melted over again.

This second melting is done to incorporate the mass more thoroughly, so as to give a finer texture to the crayon. The degree of cooking is of the utmost importance: if too much, the stone is not sufficiently impregnated; and if not enough, it is too soft and greasy, and does not work clean, but produces heavy and muddy impressions: therefore this operation requires great care. Should the temperature rise too high, the mixture might be carbonized, and would then be unfit for use. It is best to proceed slowly, and from time to time take some of the mixture to cool, and try it. When arrived at the proper point, it is poured in a mould, or in an iron frame, over a marble slab, and cut with a thin-bladed knife, before it becomes cold. It is necessary to rub the slab with the soap, to prevent the crayon from adhering to it. As a greater quantity is mixed than can be poured at once, it is necessary to have the temperature of the mass high enough to keep it liquid, so that it may be poured again, until the whole is cut or moulded into crayon. It is customary to make three numbers of crayons, that is to say, crayons of three different degrees of hardness, so as to suit different tem-

peratures, and the different natures of drawings; these different degrees may be obtained by increasing the proportion of salt of nitre, or allowing the mixture to cook longer, but it is safer to obtain the difference by cooking, as too much nitre renders the crayon too brittle.

Lithographic Writing-Ink.—The manipulation is the same as that described for the crayon, with different ingredients. The following are the proportions:

Yellow wax	4 parts.
Mutton suet	3 "
White Castile soap	13 "
Gum shellac	6 "
Fine lampblack	8 "

The mutton suet and wax are dissolved first, the soap added, then the gum shellac; when the mixture is well incorporated, the temperature is raised until it takes fire, and the flame allowed to burn one minute; then the mixture is taken off the fire, to cool somewhat, and the lampblack is added, the whole being stirred steadily until it is well mixed. Then the saucepan is put over the fire again, and the cooking continued for a quarter of an hour; then the mixture is poured over a slab, which has been previously rubbed with soap; when cold, it is put again over the fire, and stirred as before, and when melted a second time, it is poured again over the slab, then cut in small pieces, convenient for use. It is best to keep it some time before using it.

Writing-Ink for transferring, or Autographic Ink.—The Autographic ink is composed as follows:

White wax	5 parts.
White Castile soap	5 "
Mutton suet	5 "
Gum shellac	5 "
Gum mastic	5 "
Copal rosin	5 "
Flowers of sulphur	3 "

No Black.—This ink requires great care in manipulation. Gum copal is melted first in a copper or iron saucepan. When heated to such a degree that it gives forth a crackling sound, the sulphur is added; the mixture then takes fire. When these two ingredients are liquid, the wax is added, then the suet; when these are well dissolved, the gum mastic, then the shellac; the mixture is kept burning until reduced to two-thirds of its original bulk, then allowed to cool somewhat, then poured on a slab and cut in sticks for use. This ink is very pale in color, but has an advantage over the lithographic ink in being much more fluid, and penetrates better into the stone. It may be preserved liquid for any length of time by dissolving over the fire 1 part of ink in 6 parts of water, boiling it until reduced to three-fourths the quantity, and then bottling it tight. Ink which has been manufactured for some time is the best for preserving liquid.

Ink for Lavis or Washes on Stone.—These drawings are made with crayon and three different sorts

... the ink requires ... a part of ...
... this ink ... That it is ...
... paste is added ... When these two are taken ...
... the well colored, then the subject ...
... will dissolve the gum paste ...
... the mixture about ... green colored ...
... swell to ... its original bulk, then allowed to ...
... some alum, then pass it on a slab and put in a ...
... this is very pale in color, but has ...
... over the language in ink in being ...
... and penetrates better into the ...
... the preserved for any length of time ...
... to soften over the great part of ink in 6 parts of
... water, until reduced to its soft ...
... quantity, and then making it tight. Ink which has
... been moistened for some time is the best for
... preserving it ... old.

Engraved drawings or Writing on Stone. These drawings are made with crayon and three different sorts

Alois Senefelder
Inventor of
Lithography

of ink, which we will designate as Nos. 1, 2, and 3. Ink No. 1 is composed as follows:

Castile soap	6 parts.
Mutton suet	4 "
Gum mastic (in tears)	4 "
Gum shellac	4 "
Lampblack	2 "

No. 2.—The same as the above, with the addition of one part of Venice turpentine.

No. 3 is the common lithographic writing-ink and the crayon, the same as for other drawings. The manipulation of this ink is the same as for the writing-ink, with the exception that it must be cooked very hard and dry.

Ink for Taking the Impressions from Plates to be transferred.

White wax	½ pound.
White Castile soap	½ "
Gum shellac	½ "
Burgundy pitch	¼ "
Mutton suet	½ "
Venice turpentine	½ "
Fine lampblack	1 ounce.

This printing-ink is made in the manner already described as applicable to other inks. It is also used for taking the impressions from engravings on stone to be transferred, with the addition of one-third of common printing-ink.

Line- and Pen-Drawings and Writing on Stone.—Line-drawings and writing are made on polished stones. Before commencing his drawing, the artist sprinkles a few drops of turpentine, which he spreads quickly and uniformly over the whole surface with a small piece of dry rag. This preparation facilitates the adhesion of the ink to the stone, and enables the artist to produce finer and sharper lines. The ink used is the same that we have described as lithographic ink. It is mixed as follows: The artist takes a small saucer, rubs the bottom with a piece of ink until it is well coated, then adds a few drops of water, and rubs with the ends of the fingers until the water has dissolved the ink and made it fluid; as soon as it becomes by evaporation too thick to flow, it must be made fresh. The pens used for this style of work are made of very thin bands of steel resembling watch-springs, mounted on small handles, which the artists generally prepare themselves. They are cut and split with fine scissors. This simple operation has to be learned by practice, and requires some perseverance.

The Engraving on Stone.—The engravings are also produced on polished stones, but the mode of preparing the surface for drawing is different. In this case the engraver prepares the face of the stone with a mixture of gum arabic and nitric acid, which he spreads uniformly with a camel's-hair brush over the surface, and, before allowing it to dry, he wipes off the surplus with a rag, so as to leave but a thin coating. The face of the stone may also be rubbed with oxalic salt

instead of gum and acid; with this preparation the graver cuts more freely. He then spreads some coloring powder, either red chalk or lampblack, uniformly over the face. Without this coloring it would be difficult to see the work on the stone. The gum should not be left so thick on the stone as to prevent the graver from cutting freely. The instruments used for engraving are steel points, manufactured for the purpose, and diamond points; the diamond cuts finer and sharper lines, but it generally cuts only in one direction, and for that reason is often inconvenient. The engraver having accomplished his part, the printer spreads linseed or palm oil over the face of the stone, which impregnates all the parts where the crust has been cut by the graver; the stone is then coated with the same ink used in taking the impressions for transferring, to which a few drops of linseed oil is added, to make it softer. The ink lodges in all the engraved parts, while the other parts, protected by the crust formed by the gum and acid, or oxalic salt, remain unaffected. The stone being then washed the engraving becomes perfectly clear. In taking the impressions of this style of work, the stone is inked with what the printers call a dauber, the roller being used only to take off the superfluous ink from the face of the stone.

Autographic Drawings, or Drawings on Paper for transferring.—Autographic drawings are made on prepared paper with autographic ink, and transferred to the stone in a manner which will be explained under its proper head. The ink is dissolved in the same manner as for writing on stone.

Crayon-Drawings on Stone.—As drawing is not to be taught by theory, we will only mention it in its relation to lithography, remarking that any artist who can draw on paper can, by practice, become proficient in drawing on stone.

The artist, having to execute a drawing on stone, makes a minute tracing, with soft conté crayons, of the design he desires to lithograph, and, having been supplied with a stone properly grained, makes an offset of his tracing on the stone; the outlines being thus transferred, he has a guide for his lithographic drawing. Great care has to be taken to keep the face of the stone perfectly clean and free from any contamination, as it is extremely sensitive when grained for drawing; the pressure of the hands or fingers will cause a stain in the printing, although it may not be detected on the stone previous to drawing upon it. The artist, while at work, should not keep his mouth too near the face of the stone, as the breath would affect it; small pellicles falling from the hairs will print as black as if steeped in ink. When the stone is laid on the drawing-table, blocks of wood are placed at each side, and a smooth board is laid across to support the arms and hands and prevent them from touching the stones. The lithographic crayon not being strong enough to bear the pressure of the knife, the point is made by cutting upward, the crayon reposing on the end of the finger. The manner in which the crayon is applied to the stone has a corresponding effect on the impressions; that is to say, if the artist touches with a timid hand, and does not apply the crayon firmly, although he may, by repeated touches, produce apparently the proper effect on the stone, the drawing will print ragged. The reason for this is that the first touch which covers the grain does not penetrate the stone, and interpose between it and the additional touches, and prevent them from impregnating it also, and when such drawings have been washed off with turpentine, which is indispensable in commencing the printing, they do not give sufficient adhesion to the printing-ink. On the contrary, when the crayon is applied with a firm and bold hand, it penetrates strongly and produces brilliant and vigorous impressions.

Drawings by Lavis or Wash on Stone.—This style of drawing has never been fairly brought into practice as yet, but we will describe it, in the hope that some artist may be induced to try it. Certain styles of drawing may be produced by this method in one-tenth part of the time that would be required by any other. The stone must be a dark-blue one, of the finest texture, grained very fine and free from sand holes or scratches. The artist begins by drawing lines on the margin of the stone and covering them with a preparation of gum and acid to limit the edges of his drawing; then with a camel's-hair pencil he lays the first wash rapidly over the whole surface with the ink we have described as No. 1. This first wash being intended to produce the half-tints only, it must be laid on very thin. When this first wash is dry, he proceeds to work the details with ink No. 2, blending with crayon the edges of the ink lines, and terminates by bringing up the vigorous parts with the ordinary lithographic ink, and producing the high lights with the scraper. In order to facilitate the rapid execution which is necessary for this style of drawing, the design may be first sketched upon the stone with lead-pencil, and, as it is important that the ink should not dry in places before being laid perfectly smooth, a basin full of warm water may be kept under or near the drawing-table, so that the vapor of the water shall reach the stone, keeping it moist and preventing the ink from drying too fast. Of course it requires promptitude and skill in handling the pencil, but not more than are required in drawing on paper with India ink. Drawings made by this process are fair imitations of aquatinta. They require no acidulation, but simply gumming before being charged with the roller, and are treated generally like transfers on stone.

Chromo-Lithography.—The chromos are without exception the finest products of the art of lithography. This method requires in the artist great intelligence in the management of the colors, as he has not, like the painter, the advantage of seeing the effect of each touch of the pencil as he progresses. He has to draw with black material each color on a separate stone, and, consequently, must bear in mind not only the effect that each touch will produce when printed with the proper color under or over a number of other colors,

but also the effect that each will have in modifying the tone of the adjoining colors. As the coat of color deposited upon the paper is very thin, it is only by the multiplicity of colors that the depth of tone, the harmony of colors, and the mellowness of an oil-painting are ultimately attained.

The artist proceeds in the following manner. First he designs on a stone an outline of his subject, and gets as many impressions printed of this outline as he intends to introduce colors in his chromo. The impressions, as soon as printed, and before the ink dries, are powdered with red chalk, so as to have the lines only coated with the chalk, and in that condition are transferred or set off on the stone intended for each color. These chalk lines serve as a guide to work the drawing for each color in its proper place. Then the artist proceeds with his work, commencing with the lightest color, and using a separate stone for each color, until the picture is brought to the proper tone and finish. To aid him in judging of the tone required for each additional color, proofs are taken of his drawing as he proceeds, the printing following in the same order.

Chromo-lithography, like the other branches of lithography, has been many years in attaining its present degree of perfection. In 1826, a Parisian lithographer, named Laeroix, exhibited at the industrial fair held at Paris in that year, specimens of large female heads printed in tints of different colors, by a process which he called lithochromy; but no attempts were made in these first specimens to produce anything better than the common colored lithographs. The drawings were badly executed, and the attempt produced an unfavorable impression among artists, and no further notice was taken of lithochromy.

In 1840, Messrs. Engelman, at their establishment in Mulhouse, produced several series of small landscapes printed in oil-colors, employing four colors only, yellow, red, blue, and black; the drawings were very artistically executed, and the colors judiciously combined, and they produced a very favorable impression among artists and amateurs.

They subsequently used a greater number of colors in their productions, and were quite successful. They also introduced this new style of lithographing into their establishment in Paris, where Mr. Schuessele (now Professor in the Academy of Fine Arts of Philadelphia) was their principal artist, and produced some remarkable specimens; but nothing of a very elaborate character was attempted, and the art was principally employed in the production of fine show-cards and fancy labels. Louis Philippe, then King of the French, gave Mr. Engelman a pension of twelve hundred francs a year, as a reward for his improvement in the art of lithography. In 1850, Messrs. Hannart and Brothers, who had succeeded Messrs. Engelman in London, introduced printing in colors in objects of art, and produced remarkable specimens which fairly elevated the process to a place among the fine arts. Subsequently the government of Prussia established lithographic presses in Berlin, under the direction of eminent artists, for the reproduction, fac-simile, of celebrated paintings of ancient masters. In 1849, the writer of this sketch engaged Mr. Schuessele, the talented artist above named, and introduced the chromo into his establishment in Philadelphia. Mr. Schuessele produced some fine specimens in chromo, among which were the portraits of Washington and Lafayette, which obtained the Silver Medal from the Franklin Institute of Philadelphia in 1849, the American Institute of New York in 1850, the Maryland Institute of Baltimore in 1851, and at the Metropolitan Fair held in Washington City in 1852, the Massachusetts Charitable Association in 1852, and the Bronze Medal of the World's Fair of London in 1850. Mr. Ewbank, then Commissioner of Patents of the United States, illustrated the Senate edition of his report on Mechanics with a frontispiece printed in colors, presented by the writer, which he designated as a specimen of machine-painting, for which he was highly complimented by the Art Journal of London. At that time the establishment with all its contents was destroyed by fire, and a large collection of chromos ready for publication were lost; nothing remained except a few proof-sheets then in possession of the artist. After that time nothing of any importance was attempted in chromo in the United States for nearly eight years. In 1850, Mr. Middleton, a lithographer of Cincinnati, produced very fine portraits of Washington and a number of other eminent personages of the United States, which had great success; his agents represented him as the only one in the country who possessed the secret of this style of picture, ignoring what had been produced previously. However, chromo-lithography, like most other new arts, has been improving steadily for the past few years, and the pictures now produced imitate oil-painting so closely that it requires a practiced eye to detect the difference. We now pass to the printing branch of Lithography.

The Acidulation of Chalk- and Pen-Drawings.— When the artist has completed his work, previous to its being printed, it has to be prepared or acidulated with a mixture of gum arabic dissolved in water and nitric acid, in the proportions of 8 ounces of gum, 32 ounces of water, and 1¾ ounces of nitric acid of the specific gravity of 35 degrees. This mixture is to be kept in a glass bottle, with a glass stopper to prevent the evaporation of the acid. Great care has to be taken to regulate the acidulation to the strength and style of the drawing and the quality of the stone. The pale yellow stone, being of softer quality, cannot stand strong acidulation; light drawings with delicate tints when the stone is slightly covered would lose their fine work if strong acidulation were used. The modification is effected either by the amount of preparation put on the drawing or by the addition of water. The preparation is put on the drawing in the following manner: the operator pours into a large bowl a sufficient quantity of the mixture, and with a large flat camel's-hair brush he lays it first on the margin of the stone outside of the drawing; then, with an additional

supply taken in the brush, he passes rapidly over the whole drawing; the brush in passing over the surface takes up the preparation on the margin, which has already expended some of its force. Thus the new supply is tempered and replenished without the artist being obliged to stop to take it from the bowl,—a very essential point, since the operation must be done quickly in order that the preparation shall act simultaneously over the whole drawing. This preparation has no power over the crayon, but simply acts on the parts of the stone which are not covered. It penetrates between the grains and keeps them divided by etching the stone and bringing the parts covered by the crayon slightly in relief, and at the same time prepares a lodgment for the water used in the printing to preserve the transparency of the drawing.

Washing the Drawings with Turpentine.—This operation, which is now considered indispensable, was not resorted to by the early practitioners; they used to charge the drawing with the printing-ink over the crayon, without washing it off, but the effect of this was to make the first impressions heavy and impasted, and it was only by using very stiff ink, and taking numbers of proofs, that this coat of crayon could be entirely removed from the stone, and the stiffness of the ink wore out the fine tints of the drawing and destroyed the mellowness of the effect. This is avoided by the washing off, as by removing the coat of crayon the impregnated parts of the stone are left free to the adhesion of the ink deposited by the roller. The operation is surprising to the uninitiated. The writer recollects an instance which came under his notice in the early days of lithography, which it may not be out of place to describe here. He had under his hands, for proving, a large and beautiful drawing of a female bust, drawn on stone by a lady artist, who had spent considerable labor upon it. As was customary in those days, the artist desired to be present at the proving of her drawing; and she was standing in front of the press, watching the operation with anxiety. When the sponge with the turpentine was applied to the drawing, and she noticed that it all disappeared, the stone becoming perfectly blank, she almost fainted, thinking that her beautiful drawing was destroyed; but she was quickly reassured, when told that it would all come right.

The washing is performed as follows. The preparation of gum having been washed away with clean water, the printer sprinkles some turpentine over the drawing, and spreads it with a sponge or fine rag, by rubbing gently, until the whole crayon or ink is dissolved; he then sprinkles some clean water over it, and with another piece of rag wipes it off; he next passes a moistened sponge over the face of the stone, and then applies the roller with the printing-ink. If the drawing be light and weak, it is best to allow some of the dissolved crayon and turpentine to remain, and to roll quickly over it; this promotes the adhesion of the ink to the fine parts of the drawing; but care must be taken not to let the turpentine dry upon any part of the work, as it would be extremely difficult to remove it without prejudice to the drawing. When this washing takes place, it will be found that all the parts of the stone which have been impregnated with the crayon give adhesion to the ink, while the parts unaffected retain the water, over which the ink has no power, and the drawing soon assumes its former tone. When the drawing is a new one, it is best to leave the stone laid under the gum after taking a few impressions; and in no case is a drawing to be left any time without gum. The gum closes the pores of the stone and confines the ink in its proper place, and thus preserves the transpareney of the drawing.

Printing.—This part of lithography being acquired by practice only, it is not necessary to enter into minute details of the mechanical operation of the process. We will simply indicate to the uninitiated the general modus operandi, prefacing our explanation with the remark, that to be a good crayon- or chromoprinter requires a great deal of care and good judgment. The printer should have some idea of perspective, and of harmony of tones, as much depends on him in bringing up the impressions, to produce the effect contemplated by the artist in making the drawing. It will be readily understood, when it is borne in mind that the drawing lies superficially on the fine grain of a stone, how difficult it is to charge it with printing-ink and preserve the tone and mellowness; the effect may be destroyed by overcharging it, or by failing to charge it to the proper point. The drawing is easily affected by bad judgment, in using acids or grease, or by tampering with it in any way. The important part contributed by the printer in producing fair copies of a drawing on stone, was so thoroughly appreciated at the beginning of lithography, that the artists of Paris volunteered to establish a night-school, to teach the printers the first principles of perspective and general effect. A good printer handles his roller over a drawing with the same feeling as that with which a violin-player handles his bow. By movements rapid or slow, and by greater or less pressure over certain parts, he charges the drawing to the proper tone. It happens frequently that portions of a drawing will become too heavy, and that others will be too feeble, or will disappear entirely. In these cases he uses acids or grease, as the case may require. A drawing is never to remain under the printing-ink without being gummed. The gum must be wiped dry to prevent it from accumulating in streaks or spots, which would crack and peel off, carrying portions of the drawing with it, if exposed to very dry temperature; while in a damp place it will become acrid and corrode the drawing. When the printer uses any greasy substances to support or nourish the delicate parts of a drawing, the stone must be kept wet, to prevent the grease from adhering to the white parts and destroying the transparency of the work. When the printing is completed, if the drawing is kept on stone for further printing, it should be charged with preserving ink, which is the same as that we have described for printing impressions for trans-

ferring. Drawings charged with this ink will keep, without drying, for any length of time, and when required to be printed again, will wash off as easily as new drawings.

Transferring on Stone.—The first attempts at transferring, in lithography, were made in Paris, in 1826, by a lithographer named Motte. He had contracted to furnish the illustrations for an edition of Buffon's Natural History, and, not being able to print a sufficient number of copies of each drawing on stone, resorted to transferring, to furnish the required number. Like other branches of lithography, the first operations were very rude. The present method of transferring is as follows:

The printer having taken impressions for transferring, he keeps them between sheets of damp paper. He then takes a clean stone perfectly polished, places it on the press, lays a sheet of clean paper over the face, so as to be able to set the pressure, and to ascertain that it presses equally over the whole surface, without soiling it; he then wipes the face of the stone with a clean rag saturated with turpentine, lays the impression over it, places over the back, first a sheet of wet paper and three or four dry sheets as backers, and runs the press through, first with light pressure, then three or four times more, increasing the pressure each time. He takes off all the backers, wets slightly the back of the impression without disturbing it, next passes the press through three or four times more in rapid succession, and the transfer is made. He then removes all the backers, soaks the paper of the impression with clean water, removes it from the stone, and the ink of the printed sheet is found to have left the paper adhering fast to the stone. The stone is then set aside for a few hours, to give time to the transfer-ink to impregnate it. In the next place, it is gummed for a few minutes, and then, the gum being washed off, is charged with the printing-ink. When the transfer is well coated, and all the work properly charged, it is acidulated with a weak preparation of gum-arabic and nitric acid and is ready for printing. When a piece of writing is made on paper without paste, the written sheet is saturated through the back with water and nitric acid to the strength of about ten degrees, and while it is wet the printer lays it on the stone, with the backers over it, and runs the press through, once only, with a heavy pressure. The sheet having no paste to make it adhere to the stone, if run through more than once it would be apt to shift, and spoil the transfer. The paper, in that case, leaves but a faint impression upon the stone; but it can be charged with a fine piece of sponge, and a fat ink, made thin with oil, and rubbing gently until all the lines are coated. The acid with which the paper is saturated, prevents the face of the stone from being soiled by the ink; the stone must be kept wet, as in all other cases, by applying greasy substances to it. The stone being thus charged, it is set aside for a few moments, then treated like other transfers.

When impressions are taken from type, or wood-cuts, for transferring, they must, of course, be printed with the transferring ink, and always on the side of the paste. Drawings or writings made on transfer-paper are treated in the same way as impressions from stone.

Raising Lithographic Works to be Printed by Typographic Presses.—Owing to the slowness of the lithographic presses, and the consequent cost of printing, it was formerly a great desideratum to raise works on stone so that they might be printed with typographic presses, and a method of doing this was devised; but the introduction of steam lithographic presses has rendered it useless, and we merely describe the process here, as being within the range of lithography.

For this method, the drawing may be made on stone or on zinc plates. Previous to being etched, the drawing has to be charged with the printing-roller, in the ordinary manner, with the following composition:

White wax	2 ounces.
Burgundy pitch	¼ ounce.
Black pitch	¼ ounce.
Bitumen of Judea, pulverized	2 ounces.

The wax and pitches are dissolved together over a slow fire in an earthen vase enameled inside, and when perfectly liquid the bitumen is added gradually. When the mass is well incorporated, it is allowed to cool a little, then is poured into a basin of lukewarm water, and while in the water it is made into small balls or sticks. When it is to be used, the quantity required is dissolved in essence of lavender, and the drawing charged with it; then a border of wax is made on the margin of the plate or stone inclosing the drawing, and a preparation of nitric acid and water of the strength of ten degrees is poured over it, and allowed to remain about five minutes. When this preparation is washed away, if the transfers are not raised enough, the stone or plate is again charged and etched, until sufficiently raised to print with the typographic press.

Stones used for this purpose should be of the hard blue variety, the better to resist the acidulation; as on soft stone the acid would cut away and undermine the drawing.

Photo-Lithography, or Photographs on Stone.—Since photography has become an important and useful art, photo-lithography has been aimed at as a means of saving expense in multiplying the impressions. As far back as 1850, M. Poitivin, a photographer of Paris, published in the Bulletin of Inventions of that city a process for photographing on stone, and within the past few years this new art has been developed, and there are at the present time establishments in this country and in Europe in full operation. The importance of photo-lithography will be appreciated when it is remembered that in a few minutes light will produce drawings the completion of which would occupy an artist for weeks.

Photo-lithographs may be produced in two ways,

by taking the impression from the negative direct on stone, and by taking it on prepared paper and transferring it to stone. In the first case, a stone finely grained is coated in the dark with a sensitive film of chromated gelatin and albumen from fresh eggs, and when dry the negative is laid on with a perfect contact, then exposed to light in the usual way. The action of the light decomposes the gelatin, which impregnates the stone sufficiently to give adhesion to the lithographic ink; the ink is spread over it with a soft sponge or camel's-hair brush, and then washed away with clean water; the parts affected by light retain the ink, and all the screened parts become perfectly clean; the stone is then gummed and treated by the usual lithographic processes.

When it is intended to retransfer a photograph, the impression of the negative is produced in the usual way on paper coated on one side with a mixture of anhydro-chromate of potassium, gelatin, and albumen from fresh eggs. The paper, having been coated with this mixture, is dried and smoothed in a dark room, and kept shielded from light. When the paper has received the impression, it is coated with lithographic ink; then the back of the sheet is floated over boiling water; the parts acted on by light retain the ink, and all the screened parts are washed away with a sponge and clean water; the parts remaining charged with the ink are then transferred to a lithographic stone by pressure, and treated in the usual lithographic way. (This transferring process is patented by Mr. Osborne, of Melbourne, Australia.)

There have been introduced lately two different methods, which are also patented, for producing photographs on plate-glass to be printed in the usual lithographic manner. The impressions produced by these processes compare favorably with those of the best photographs, and there is no doubt that they will, at no distant day, make an important addition to the art of printing.

Zincography.—Zincography is the process of drawing or transferring upon zinc plate instead of stone. The sheet of zinc is grained or polished like the lithographic stone, and the same crayon or ink is used for drawing. As there is a strong tendency in the zinc to oxidize while the graining or polishing is being done with sand and water, we would suggest the use of warm water instead of cold. When operating on a large sheet, the zinc thus heated dries quickly, and is prevented from rusting. When the drawing or transferring is completed, it is prepared with gallic acid. This preparation may be made by boiling half an ounce of ground nut-gall in a pint of water; when it has been laid over the drawing, the plate is gummed, and in the remaining operations it is treated like the lithographic stone. As the sheet of zinc would be too thin to print on a lithographic press without being backed, it may be laid on a lithographic stone, or a block of hard wood, to suit the bearing of the press.

Varnishes used for Lithographic Printing.—The varnishes for printing lithography are made of pure old linseed oil. Two or more gallons of oil are burnt in an iron pot with a lid shutting tight, and having a small valve on the top to let the vapor escape in case of the temperature becoming dangerously high. The oil should not fill more than two-thirds of the pot, to allow space for the effervescence without running over. These precautions having been taken, the pot is placed over a brisk fire, and, when heated nearly to the point of ignition, slices of stale bread and onions are fried in it, one slice and two or three onions at a time, to avoid too much tumefaction. When the bread is fried brown, it is taken out, and another slice is substituted, until 1½ pounds of bread and ½ pound of onions for each gallon of oil have been used. The bread has the effect of absorbing certain oily or fatty substances contained in the oil, which, if allowed to remain, would be injurious to the drawings; the onions clarify the varnish, and give it a drying quality. Some manufacturers add rosin, others rock-candy; but in our opinion these last two articles are useless. When the necessary quantity of bread and onions has been used, the temperature is increased until the oil takes fire from the application to it of a piece of burning wood or paper. From that moment the operation must be conducted with great care, for if the heat should become too great it would be difficult to manage the oil. When the oil ignites the pot is taken off the fire, and the flames are kept burning by agitating the oil with an iron ladle or a skimmer. The flames are kept in until the varnish becomes of the proper thickness, which is ascertained by taking some of the oil from time to time to cool and test it by placing it between the forefinger and the thumb and then quickly separating them. When sufficiently burned, the varnish will stick, and when the fingers are parted it will produce threads and a light crackling sound. Should the temperature fall too low to allow the flames to burn, the pot must be replaced over the fire to keep it to the burning point. The degree of the temperature may be estimated by the color of the flames; when moderate the flame is bluish, and when excessive it becomes white, and a thick froth forms on the surface of the oil; then the rise of temperature must be checked. As a measure of caution, it is prudent to keep at hand some of the oil cold, and when there is any danger of the varnish running over the pot a ladleful of the cold oil may be put in to subdue it. Varnish may be made without setting the oil on fire, but it takes a much longer time, and leaves the varnish too greasy for the purposes of lithography. It is customary to make three different degrees of thickness of varnish, to suit different classes of work; greater or less thickness is produced by more or less burning.

Lithographic Printing-Ink.—The printing-ink is made with lampblack mixed in the linseed oil varnish already described. It varies in quality according to the quality of the black and the fabrication of the varnish. The best black is made by burning linseed oil; next in quality is the black made from turpen-

tine. Gas also produces very good black, but all these are very expensive and rarely used. The black mostly used in lithography is made of rosin. When the black is prepared for lithographic use, it is calcined in a covered crucible placed in a charcoal fire and heated until the fire has communicated to the whole mass, when it is taken from the fire. It is essential to stop the burning at the proper point; if burned too much, it loses its brightness and becomes brown. The black, having been thus prepared, is mixed in one of the three kinds of varnish described, according to the degree of stiffness desired; as much black is put in as can be well incorporated; there is no danger of making it too stiff, as the printer can always modify it by the addition of varnish. It must be ground so fine that it shall leave no perceptible grain, and so smooth that when it is divided with a pallet knife and blown on, it will show a purplish hue like that of fine polished steel.

Printing-Paper for Lithography.—The quality of paper is a very important consideration in lithography. It will be readily understood that the stone and the drawing upon it, forming a kind of chemical affinity, are easily influenced by the quality of the paper. The want of good lithographic paper was long a great drawback to the progress of the art in the United States. Mr. Thos. Gilpin, of Brandywine Mills, was the first who succeeded in making paper that could be used with any satisfaction. Mr. James Wilcox and Mr. Chas. Magarge subsequently succeeded in making suitable paper, and at the present time lithographic paper is made in the United States equal to any manufactured in Europe.

The paper for printing crayon-drawing must have fine grain, be of soft and glossy mellow texture, and be free from acid or alkali. When it is to be used it is made slightly damp, to give adhesion to the printing-ink; for the printing of chromos it is used dry, and requires to be of very fine texture, firm and well calendered. For this kind of work sized paper is preferred, as being firmer, and not so liable to stretch in printing, which would be a serious obstacle in printing chromos, as it would prevent the colors from fitting in their proper place. For the printing of line-work or maps it is not of so much importance, provided that it does not contain substances injurious to the work on stone.

Live Matter.—Matter which has either not yet been printed, or which will probably be reprinted, and is therefore not intended for distribution.

Local.—In newspapers, the local editor has special supervision of the home or domestic news, and such intelligence is generally known as locals or local items,—that is, items of local intelligence.

Locking-Up.—Fastening a form in the chase. The quoins should first be pushed as far as possible with the fingers. Then, by the aid of the mallet and shooting-stick, they should be gently driven along, those against the foot-stick first, afterwards those against the side-stick. The several quarters of the form should be partially tightened before either quarter is finally locked up, otherwise the cross-bar may be sprung. The entire form should be gently planed all over the face before being locked up. If this be carefully done, a second planing is hardly necessary, provided the justification is perfect and the pages are all of the same length. Before lifting a form, after it is locked up, raise it gently a short distance and look under it, to ascertain whether any types are disposed to drop out.

Logography.—A method of printing in which types containing entire words are used instead of those containing only a single letter. (See LOGO-TYPES.)

Logotypes.—Types consisting of two or more letters, and forming either complete words or syllables, etc. They are intended to save the trouble of the compositor, for instead of lifting the word and in three letters, if cast as a logotype he picks it up as one. Earl Stanhope, of England, among other innovations, proposed to introduce eight new logotypes, believing that their regular and frequent occurrence would expedite the process of composition in a very considerable degree. The London Times, about the time it was first started, used logotypes for a short time, but soon abandoned them, because they proved useless, the compositors being able to set up more type in a given time by the old method, than by using logotypes. For some years, this, and a few other unsuccessful experiments, led to the total abandonment of the logotypes, but recently they have again attracted the attention of some American and English inventors. The combined letters stated to have been found of greatest value are:

be	com	oun	ent	ion	in
for	go	ing	ld	me	the
and	th	re	al	re	os

One of the latest systems is that introduced by Mr. W. H. Wilkinson, of Massachusetts, which was patented in 1868. It was tried in one of the largest printing-offices in London for the composition of a weekly periodical, and is, to some extent, in operation at the present time. The invention relates to the combined use of types consisting of words or parts of words, together with the ordinary letter or single character types. Words, roots, and parts of words, such as constitute a very large proportion of ordinary matter, are made up in types cast whole, or formed of letter-types united; these word-types are tabulated and arranged in cases in the order of their relative importance or frequency of recurrence. A set or series of cases or boxes is arranged partially around a central point occupied by the compositor, and divided into compartments for containing the types, which are arranged in tables so that their relative positions may be easily discerned by the eye; the said tables are placed strictly in the order of their relative values as calculated from the average number of words usually contributed by each table in the matter of composition, and each table is arranged in relation to the central point where the compositor stands, in such a position as to be accessible to his right hand in proportion to its comparative value. The ordinary letter-types, numerals, and other similar types, occupy the compartments of the cases at the left hand of the compositor, the rest of the space being occupied by the logotypes. The tables themselves are arranged with reference to their being learned step by step and used as auxiliary to the letter-types, until the compositor acquires the use of enough words to constitute the larger proportion of his work; these word-types then become the main feature in the system, the letter-types being used only as auxiliary.

The great objections urged against logotypes are the additional space or case-room they require if they are sufficiently numerous to be of material service; and the waste of type which would result from the necessity of destroying a whole word whenever a single letter was battered.

Long Accent.—A short horizontal line placed over certain vowels, as—ā, ē, ī, ō, ū.

Long Cross.—The long bar in a chase divided for octavo, etc. It is also the narrowest.

Long Letters.—Letters which fill the whole depth of the body, and are both ascending and descending, such in the Roman as Q and j, and in the Italic *f*.

Long Pages.—Pages of more than the proper length. Before fastening in the quoins, the compositor should carefully ascertain whether the pages of each quarter are of the same length; for the difference of a lead, even, will cause them to hang. To test their exactness, place the ball of each thumb against the centre of the foot-stick, raising it a little with the pressure, and if the ends of both pages rise equally with the stick, it is a proof that they will not bind. A similar plan should be adopted in locking-up newspaper pages, as regards the columns.

Long Primer.—A size of type between Small Pica and Bourgeois.

Loose Justifying.—The practice of insufficiently spacing the lines in the stick, thereby making them loose.

Lothian, George Baxter.—A celebrated type-founder of New York City, one of the experimental pioneers in machine type-casting and type-rubbing, and also in the present method of kerning types. He was the son of Dr. Robert Lothian, of Scotland, who made an ineffectual attempt to establish a foundry in New York in 1806, but, failing, sold his material to Binney and Ronaldson, of Philadelphia, and died shortly afterwards. The son, George B. Lothian, remained for some time with a bookseller in Philadelphia, where he became much interested in the theatre and appeared in public in a round of Scotch characters. In 1810 he was employed by John Watts, of New York, the first stereotyper in the United States; but Lothian's singularly irritable temper and license of speech led to a difficulty which resulted in his being committed to jail. He afterwards worked for Collins & Hanna, as a stereotype finisher, for about two years, leaving that employment to establish a type-foundry in Pittsburgh, Pennsylvania. Failing in this undertaking, he returned to New York, where his material was purchased by D. & G. Bruce, who also furnished him with employment. This engagement he abandoned in order to study for the stage, but was compelled to relinquish that pursuit on account of his defective verbal memory, although otherwise he was remarkably fitted for the theatrical profession. In 1822 he manufactured type for the Harpers and others, in partnership with Alfred Pell, but this connection was soon broken by a personal encounter, and Lothian's interest was purchased by Mr. Hagar. In 1829 he was again manufacturing successfully, and proposed a partnership with James Conner, a man of remarkable self-control; but in one of the preliminary conversations upon their affairs, Lothian used such exasperating expressions that Conner broke off the arrangements and nearly pitched Lothian out of the window. The Harpers continued to employ him, bearing with the eccentricities of his temper on account of the excellence of his type, and Mr. Hagar also undertook a partnership with him in 1840, but this connection, the last attempted by Lothian, was ruptured in less than half a year. Domestic sorrow was added to Lothian's business misfortune: his wife and children died, and in declining health his mind was seriously affected. He died in 1851, attended by a single female domestic. He left a handsome competency judiciously bequeathed.

Louis XI., King of France, was one of the earliest and most zealous friends of the art of printing. A prudent and practical man, Louis XI. earnestly assisted all the manufactures of his country, and at the very earliest opportunity displayed his interest in printing. Although, like the majority of his generation, a believer in magic, he personally interfered in behalf of Fust, when the printer was imprisoned on that charge in Paris, and is said to have obtained his liberation on condition of his revealing the secret art by which he had produced identical copies of the Bible. (See Fust.) After the death of Fust, Schoeffer established offices or depots for the sale of his printed books in several cities of France. His agent, died in Paris without having obtained any certificate of naturalization, and was, consequently, without the power of making a will. His effects, including the books owned by Schoeffer, were therefore seized and confiscated. Peter Schoeffer prevailed upon Frederick III. to interest himself in the question, and Louis XI. promptly ordered full restitution to be made. The amount claimed by the Mentz printer was eleven hundred francs, a sum which Louis XI. declined to pay at once, but the king gave directions to his receiver-general to pay to the printer eight hundred livres annually, until the entire claim should be discharged. Louis was also the earnest friend of Gering, Crantz, and Friburger, the three Germans who introduced printing into Paris in 1470, and was a great admirer of their works, which were printed in a large, bold Roman letter.

These printers met with bitter opposition from the scribes and illuminators, who were a large and well-organized body in Paris. Malignant and absurd charges of many kinds, including magic, were preferred against them, and finally the printers were brought to trial, and the Parliament ordered all their books and impressions to be confiscated. Louis XI. once more interposed, using his royal authority in behalf of the typographers. He forbade the Parliament to take any further cognizance in the affair, and referred it to his own special decision and that of his privy council, and in the end restored to the printers all their property.

Low Case.—A case which is short of its proper complement of type or in which the quantities in the different boxes are low.

Low in Line.—When the face of a type is lower (on the body) than that of its fellows, it is called low in line, in contradistinction to a letter which is higher than others in a line, and which is termed high in line.

Low to Paper.—When the impression of a type does not appear distinctly, from its not being of the same height as the body of a page or line, it is termed low to paper. This is observable when new sorts are mixed with an old font, the new sorts being, in that case, high to paper.

Lowe Press.—A small press, used chiefly by amateur printers.

LOWE PRESS.

Lower Case.—The case which stands below the capital case, in a pair of cases. It holds the small letters, double letters, points, spaces, quadrats, and other sorts, according to the lay adopted. These sorts are hence called lower-case sorts.

Lye.—A solution of alkalies, ashes, potash, pearlash, soda-ash, etc., used to wash the ink from a form. A preparation known as Concentrated Lye is frequently and successfully used for this purpose in many American printing-offices. It is essential that the lye should be neither too weak nor too strong, as, in either event, it fails to remove the ink. It is customary among many of those who make lye, to test it with their tongues—it being considered too weak when it does not bite, and too strong when it bites too much. When colored inks are used and lye fails to remove them turpentine and benzine are successfully employed for this purpose.

Lye-Brush.—A brush nine or ten inches long, by three inches broad, used for the purpose of applying

LYE-BRUSH.

the lye to the form and chase and cleaning it from ink. The bristles should be close, fine, and long, in order not to injure the type, and yet to allow sufficient force to be used to search every interstice in the letter to which the ink can have penetrated.

Lye-Trough.—A shallow trough in which type forms are placed in order to be cleansed from ink.

Lyric.—Among the ancients, poetry intended to be sung to an accompaniment of the lyre or harp; in modern usage, verses composed for musical recitation.

M.

M or Em.—A quadrat, the face or top of which is a perfect square, and the unit of measurement for the size of type used.

Machine.—In England, a printing-press in which the operations of laying on the sheet, inking the form, and effecting the impression, among others, are automatically performed, is called a machine; and this nomenclature has been adopted by some American press-makers; but it is the general usage in this country to call all printing-machines, by which an impression is given, presses.

MacKellar, Thomas.—Born August 12, 1812, in the city of New York. He is the senior member of the firm of MacKellar, Smiths & Jordan, typefounders of Philadelphia, and is the author of the American Printer, as well as of several successful volumes of poetry, and the editor of the Typographic Advertiser. He served an apprenticeship to the printing-business with the Harpers of New York, for whom he subsequently acted, for a short time, as proof-reader, but in 1833 he removed to Philadelphia, where he became foreman of the Johnson stereotype-foundry, and subsequently, in 1845, a member of the firm of L. Johnson & Co., the predecessors of the present firm. His Song of the Printer is the best poetic tribute to typography in English literature, and it is given below not only because it is a fine specimen of his poetic talent, but on account of its intrinsic interest and excellence.

> Pick and click
> Goes the type in the stick,
> As the printer stands at his case;
> His eyes glance quick, and his fingers pick
> The type at a rapid pace;
> And one by one, as the letters go,
> Words are piled up steady and slow—
> Steady and slow,
> But still they grow,
> And words of fire they soon will glow:
> Wonderful words, that without a sound
> Shall traverse the earth to its utmost bound—
> Words that shall make
> The tyrant quake,
> And the fetters of the oppress'd shall break;
> Words that can crumble an army's might,
> Or treble its strength in a righteous fight.
> Yet the type they look but leaden and dumb,
> As he puts them in place with his finger and thumb;

19

> But the printer smiles,
> And his work beguiles
> By chanting a song as the letters he piles;
> While pick and click
> Go the types in the stick,
> Like the world's chronometer, tick! tick! tick!
>
> O, where is the man with such simple tools
> Can govern the world like I?
> A printing-press, an iron stick,
> And a little leaden die,
> With paper of white, and ink of black,
> I support the Right, and the Wrong attack.
> I pull the strings
> Of puppet kings,
> And I tweak the despot's nose,
> Or let him alone
> Till the people groan,
> When I needs must interpose;
> Nor yet again
> Do I e'en disdain
> To talk of lowly woes.
> Then where is he,
> Or who may he be,
> That can rival the printer's power?
> To no monarchs that live
> The wall doth he give,—
> Their sway lasts only an hour;
> While the printer still grows,
> And God only knows
> When his might shall cease to tower.

Mr. MacKellar's remarkable and delicate appreciation of poetic and artistic beauty has also been charmingly illustrated in the Specimen Book of the Johnson Type-Foundry, where he has elevated the prosaic theme of a business catalogue into a work of art, wreathing the types into a garland of poetical fancies by the manner in which striking words and phrases are made to correspond to the form of the letter and infinite variety of types. The majestic and the minute, the grotesque and the graceful, each find the fitting word to express them both to the mind and to the eye, while the queer are displayed in quirks, and the pointed sharpened into puns. Page follows page, each singularly appropriate to the style of the text, until the observer is equally amazed at the taste, industry, and ingenuity of arrangement, exhibiting alike practical knowledge, literary culture, and artistic perception.

Mackie's Manifold Type-Setting Machine. —A new English machine for setting duplicates of, say, ten, twenty, or fifty. In either case the workman sets at half the speed he would set one column, so that in setting fifty duplicates he actually sets at the rate of twenty-five large columns, per day. The modus operandi is the following:—Upon thin brass rules with one edge and one end turned up, you place, say, twenty letters all alike, and on the flat. This you repeat with every letter and figure in the font, duplicating them scores or hundreds of times. When ready for setting, you empty one brass after another into a common setting-stick, with the following results. Suppose you wish to set the heading of this article, you empty one brass of cap M's into your stick the narrow way; then one of a's, one of c's, one of k's, one of i's, one of e's, one of s's, and so on, thus:—

Mackie's Manifold Type-Setting Machine
Mackie's Manifold Type-Setting Machine
Mackie's Manifold Type-Setting Machine
Mackie's Manifold Type-Setting Machine
Mackie's Manifold Type-Setting Machine
Mackie's Manifold Type-Setting Machine
Mackie's Manifold Type-Setting Machine
Mackie's Manifold Type-Setting Machine
Mackie's Manifold Type-Setting Machine
Mackie's Manifold Type-Setting Machine
Mackie's Manifold Type-Setting Machine
Mackie's Manifold Type-Setting Machine
Mackie's Manifold Type-Setting Machine
Mackie's Manifold Type-Setting Machine
Mackie's Manifold Type-Setting Machine
Mackie's Manifold Type-Setting Machine
Mackie's Manifold Type-Setting Machine
Mackie's Manifold Type-Setting Machine
Mackie's Manifold Type-Setting Machine
Mackie's Manifold Type-Setting Machine

By the time your stick is full you will have twenty lines of, say, fifty letters each, or one thousand in all, all set by fifty movements of the hand, i.e. by emptying fifty brasses. To be useful, the twenty duplicates are put on twenty different galleys, and form the first lines of twenty columns. It will be seen that the reading is very easy, any wrong letter being instantly visible. The distributing is done by reversing the last operation, and a slicing machine slices each row upon its own brasses—in rows of M's, a's, c's, etc. ready for further use. Mr. Mackie invented this system in order to supply duplicate columns to various newspapers, and for setting hand-bills, labels, short telegrams, etc. The mechanism required costs $100.

Mackie's Type-Setting Machine.—This is an English machine, invented by Mr. Mackie, publisher of the Warrington Guardian, and was completed in 1869. It is divided into two parts. One of these is a tiny instrument consisting of fourteen keys, by means of which narrow strips of paper are perforated by girls, either in the printing-office or elsewhere. The machine proper, consists, practically, of three horizontal rings, about three feet in diameter and two inches broad, the under one and the top one being at rest. On the top ring twenty pockets are inserted, each of which contains compartments for seven different kinds of type, and sufficiently open at the bottom to allow the proper apparatus to extract the bottom type from any one, or from all the seven divisions, as wanted. The middle or traveling ring has twenty pickpockets, each carrying seven of what are called the legs-of-man, and seven fingers. At the place where the machine may be said to commence operations, there is a drum, about two inches in diameter, with fourteen perforations across its upper surface, and over this drum the paper, previously perforated, is made to travel by a positive motion of one-tenth of an inch every movement. Over the top of the drum and paper there are fourteen levers with

pegs, which are always seeking to enter the perforations in the drum, but are only able to enter those which have corresponding perforations in the paper. One-half of the perforations regulate the legs-of-man, and the other the fingers. Two perforations are always made in the paper for the former, and from one to seven for the latter, so that a pickpocket is capable of taking type the same instant out of all the seven divisions of any pocket. On the type being extracted it remains upon the traveling ring till it has reached the delivery channel, when a pusher places it on a traveling belt, a few inches long, from which it is pushed down a syphon spout, one letter upon another, ready for being justified in lines. A ring carrying twenty pickpockets, each of which has seven fingers, may extract twenty times seven types in one revolution. The composing power of this machine is guaranteed at 12,000 an hour. The perforating can be done at the rate of 10,000 per hour, and the paper used many times. A proof is printed as the type is being set. The machine is in use at the Warrington Guardian office, driven by steam, but it may be driven by hand. (See page 291.)

Mackle.—When part of the impression appears double. If the frame of the tympan rubs against the platen, it will cause a slur or mackle. This is easily remedied by removing the obstacle so as to clear the platen. The joints or hinges of the tympan should be kept well screwed up, or slurring will be the consequence. When the thumb-piece of the tympan is too long, it always produces a slur; this can be prevented by filing off a part of it. Loose tympans will at all times slur the work, and great care must therefore be taken to draw them perfectly tight. The paper drying at the edges will also slur; this may be remedied by wetting the edges frequently with a sponge. Slurring and mackling will sometimes happen from other causes; it will be well in such cases to paste corks on the frisket, or to tie as many cords as possible across it, to keep the sheet close to the tympan.

Macron.—A short, straight, horizontal mark (ˉ) placed over vowels to indicate that they are to be pronounced with a long sound.

Madrigal.—A species of short poem of irregular measure, adapted to music, particularly popular during the sixteenth and seventeenth centuries. The madrigal was much cultivated in England during the reign of Elizabeth, and is by some authorities supposed to have originated in the pastoral love-songs of Provence, although the word has been derived from the town of Madrigal in Castile. The following may be considered as a fair specimen of the usual style of madrigal:

When Thoralis delights to walk,
The fairies do attend her;
They sweetly sing and sweetly talk,
And sweetly do commend her.
The satyrs leap and dance around,
And make their congos to the ground;
And evermore their song is this,
Long mayst thou live, fair Thoralis!

Magazine.—A periodical publication embracing some of the characteristics of the newspaper and the review, but containing more miscellaneous matter, as poetry, tales, etc.

This style of publication, now so popular, was first attempted in England in 1730, in the Memoirs of the Society of Grub-Street, a series of satires upon some of the popular authors of the time. The success of this publication induced Edward Cave to begin the issue of a pamphlet in 1731, called the Gentleman's Magazine, to be continued monthly. The periodicals previous to this date had been confined to politics or to foreign and domestic news, and the miscellaneous ber a harp, one of the first engravings of Thomas Bewick, the founder of modern wood-engraving.

The precursors of the modern fashion magazine are found in two Parisian periodicals styled the Courrier des Nouveautés, commenced in 1758, and the Courrier de la Mode, commenced ten years later. The present style of illustrated ladies' magazine had its prototype in the Cabinet de la Mode, with colored copper-plates, published in Paris in 1785; the Lady's Magazine of London having preceded it, being started in 1772. One of the first instances of a profusely illustrated article occurred in 1812, when the Poetical Magazine published the popular Tour of Dr. Syntax in Search

MACKIE TYPE-SETTING MACHINE.

literary character of the Gentleman's Magazine made it exceedingly popular. The London Magazine was established the following year by a party of booksellers, and the Scott's Magazine in 1739. These were closely followed by a number of others, three being started in the year 1761; and at the present time almost every department of knowledge, and every art, science, and industry, has magazines devoted to the consideration of its special topics, with articles of general interest interspersed to enliven the periodical and render it attractive to the casual reader. The Magazine of Ants, or Pismire Journal, which was established in 1775, and only reached its sixth number, is remarkable as containing in its fifth num-

of the Picturesque, with the admirable engravings of Thomas Rowlandson.

In the United States, magazines have always been a most popular style of publication, and the first of them all, a great venture, though a little book, cannot be dismissed without description. The title-page reads thus: The General Magazine and Historical Chronicle for all the British Plantations in America. [To be Continued Monthly.] January, 1741. Philadelphia: Printed and Sold by B. Franklin. The frontispiece exhibits the coronet of the Prince of Wales, with the motto:—Ich dien. The method and arrangement of this serial are indicative of the common sense of our most practical of philosophers. A synopsis of current history, abroad and at home, the proceedings of the British Parliament on all questions affecting the American Colonies, and the action of the Assemblies in the several Plantations, occupied more than half the space. Accounts of, and extracts from, new books published in the Colonies were followed by Essays culled from American newspapers, and original mathematical problems, with their answers. A small space was appropriated to what were styled Poetical Essays; and the final article was a condensation of news items, with the price of bills of exchange and prices current in Philadelphia. The one standing and only advertisement closing the last page was as follows: There is a ferry kept over Potomack (by the subscriber), being the Post Road, and much the nighest Way from Annapolis to Williamsburg, where all Gentlemen may depend on a ready Passage in a good new Boat and able Hands. By Richard Brett, Deputy-Post-Master at Potomack.—The second American magazine, intended as a rival of Franklin's, was commenced the same year by Andrew Bradford, but only reached its second number. Two years later, the American Magazine and Historical Chronicle was started in Boston, and was continued for three years and a few months. In Philadelphia, in 1757, The American Magazine, or Monthly Chronicle for the British Colonies, by a society of gentlemen, completed a volume, and was then discontinued. The same favorite title, The American Magazine, was chosen by Lewis Nichola for a publication maintained through the year 1769; and in 1771, the Royal Spiritual Magazine, or the Christian's Grand Treasury, survived a few months. Seven comparatively unsuccessful attempts, five of the number being in Philadelphia, had been made to establish an American magazine, when it was at last achieved in 1775, in a periodical which, in general arrangement, style, and method, bore a remarkable resemblance to those of the present day. The title-page reads thus: The Pennsylvania Magazine; or, American Monthly Museum. Philadelphia: Printed and sold by R. Aitken, Printer and Bookseller, opposite the London Coffee-House, Front Street. An engraved frontispiece represents Liberty surrounded by the symbols of the arts and sciences, with a cannon and a ship in the background, while the supporter on one side is the tree of liberty, with weapons of war resting against it, and on the other a mortar labeled Congress, with flags above it, and the motto: Juvat in sylvis habitare. Every number was accompanied by a full-page illustration, which in the first number displayed a variety of new inventions in machinery, and an engraved sheet of original music upon the death of Wolfe, but in June the illustration has another significance—The Harbor and Town of Boston, and parts adjacent; and thenceforward the implements of peace appear no more, and each succeeding number displays a battle-field, until the magazine abruptly closes in the darkest hour of the war without one word of warning, zealous in patriotism to the last. The

American Museum, published by Mathew Carey in Philadelphia from 1787 to 1792, forms a valuable record of the events of the time. Several magazines were attempted in Philadelphia, Boston, and New York about the beginning of the century, but were all short-lived, the Portfolio of Philadelphia being the most successful, continuing from 1801 to 1825. The Ladies' Magazine was established in Philadelphia in 1799, and was the first of the order in the country. Godey's Lady's Book, established in 1830, still continues to rank among the foremost of a number of magazines devoted to light reading and fashions. The first magazine devoted to children appeared in Brooklyn in 1806, and was followed by Merry's Museum, Parley's Magazine, and many others, the number increasing rapidly during late years. At present the literary monthly magazines are numerous, the best known being The Galaxy, The Overland, those published by Scribner, Appleton, and Harper, the Atlantic, etc. etc. As the special organs of religious denominations, of societies, of scientific associations, of the several arts and trades, monthly magazines are numerous and well supported throughout the United States, and the growing taste for illustrations causes them to be improved rapidly in that direction.

The monthly magazine has become an especially favorite form of publication in Russia, and it is stated that the demand for such literature is so great that each of the first-class magazines furnishes about 7000 closely-printed octavo pages annually.

Mailing Machines.—Contrivances of various descriptions to facilitate the operation of directing newspapers to subscribers. A number of the patents granted for machines designed to serve this purpose are described in the article on INVENTIONS, under the head of MAILING MACHINES. The one in most extensive use is that invented by Robert Dick, of Buffalo, New York, which, it is said, has addressed more than 6000 papers in one hour. More than twenty years ago Mr. Dick began to devise improved methods of addressing papers to regular subscribers, and first invented a machine for printing the addresses directly on the papers, but was prevented from resting there, by the consideration that direct letter-press printing made two movements, of every paper addressed, absolutely indispensable—to the type for impression, and then from the type after impression. Conceiving it to be possible, he at once resolved to invent a machine that would demand only one move of each paper in the process of addressing; he quickly saw that his aim would be achieved by inventing a machine that would take the separated and webbed columns of a paper impression taken from the type addresses, coat the back of the web with fluid paste at the rate needed, and in a single instant cut off each label, when so coated, and stamp it with the same motion on the paper to be addressed.

In working out the achievement of the conception so gained, 1st, he devised a shear that would practically cut off a label from its web, and stamp it on a

THE DICK MAILING MACHINE.

paper in one and the same act or single motion. 2d, he devised a roller movement, by which he made an endless apron descend into a fountain of fluid paste, and ascend therefrom between distributers, past which it could carry no more paste than it could give off to the back of the paper web of printed labels, when bedded upon it. 3d, he contrived to so unite the apron movement and the shear, that a move of the apron would propel a label over the edge of the inner blade of the shear, and so that the first downward motion of the outer blade must, at the same time, and in the same instant, cut off the label, and by the same motion stamp it on whatever paper or other article it touched. 4th, he so combined a reel with the parts just described, as to allow its web of addresses to be drawn from it as needed, by the forward motion of the apron in working the machine. 5th, he so constructed a wire frame, hinged back of the machine's centre, and so connected its movable front with the movable blade of the shear, as to cause it to cut off a label and stamp it on any paper, by simply touching that paper with the front left angle of the frame, thus enabling the left hand to coat with paste, cut off and stamp address labels on a pile of folded papers, one at a time, with as great rapidity and ease, as the right hand can ever be taught to twitch them off one at a time. And by thus accomplishing in the case of each paper the complete work of machine addressing, as instantaneously as a single move of each paper can possibly be made, he thereby rendered attainable double the speed that ever was attained by the use of any letter-press addressing machine.

Majusculæ.—Manuscripts written entirely in capital letters. This form of writing was of a very early date, and it is found in the ancient Latin manuscripts, and in those exhumed at Pompeii; it is of rare occurrence, either in instruments or books, later than the sixth century. The Majusculæ are also styled Capitales Literæ, and are highly esteemed as of undisputed antiquity.

Make.—In casting off copy or matter, it is said

that it makes so much—a galley, a stickful, etc.—that is, it occupies so much space.

Make Even.—When a long paragraph is divided into more than one taking of copy, the compositor setting the first portion is told by the one who follows him to end even. If, however, he cannot conveniently do so, he has to make even by overrunning a few lines of the second take.

Making Margin.—The art of placing matter or pages in position, so that, when printed, they will fall in their proper places on the sheet, and allow for the necessary trimming in binding the book; also, printing in certain positions on the sheet, in order to give the margin required.

This is a most important branch of imposition in book-work; for, if it is not properly done, it will throw the pages out of position on the leaf, and necessitate reducing the size of the book, or trimming so close as, in many cases, to leave the edges of the paper uncut.

There are several ways of making margin for book forms, each of which has its advocates. A good register, and a proper position of the page on the leaf, when trimmed, are the results to be obtained, and we will state a few of the methods, leaving the reader to judge as to the practical workings of each.

Before removing the strings, the pages should be placed as nearly as possible in their proper positions in the chase. Take a sheet of the paper on which the form is to be printed, or one of the same size, fold it at the short cross, and measure from the inside, or foot of the page next to that cross, to the outside, or foot of the outside page on the opposite side of that cross. The distance between these points should be just one-half the length of the sheet. Then fold the sheet again in the opposite direction, and apply the same process to the inside and outside pages, on opposite sides of the long cross. The distance between these points should be just one-half the width of the sheet. Then adjust the pages of one quarter of the form, so that the head and back margins will be equal, and the front and foot margins equal, but rather more than the head and back margins. The furniture may now be placed in position around the pages, and if this quarter is found, on measurement, to be correct, furniture of a like size may be placed around the other quarters.

In the 18mo or 36mo form, the sheet should be folded into one-third instead of one-half its width, taking the measurement from the front of the outside page to the front of the second page from it, so as to include one front and one back margin. If the measurement is made from the page at the long cross to the outside of the form, it will include one front and two back margins, and the proper proportions between the two will not be maintained.

Another method of obtaining margin, is to fold up a sheet of the paper to the size of the book to be made, and mark out the size of the page in its proper position on the leaf, then perforate the leaves on the four sides of the page as marked out. On opening the sheet, the holes will show the proper spaces between the pages of the form.

Another and very simple method is the following. To ascertain the margin between the backs, fold the sheet to the size of the work; then measure from the left side of the last page, letting the folded sheet extend over the left side of the first, to allow for the cutting which can be varied at will, according to the size of the book, from one-eighth to three-eighths of an inch. For the margin on the front, open the sheet one fold, and measure from the left side of the third page, to the right hand, to the left side of the first page, exactly even to the edge of the type. For the margin on heads, fold the sheet to the size of the work, then measure from the head of the page at the top of page 1, letting the sheet extend over the foot of page 1. For foot margin, open the sheet in the contrary way to that for gutters; then measure from the foot of the third page up, to the foot of the first page, exactly even to the bottom of the pages. The furniture may then be fitted in this quarter of the form, and, if found correct, the other quarters may be dressed with furniture of similar size.

We give below the manner of making margin, from a folio to a duodecimo, an acquaintance with which will enable the intelligent printer to adjust margin for a form of any number of pages:

Folio.—Having folded a sheet of the intended paper exactly in the middle, place the edge of the paper even upon the outer edge of the first page, and move the adjoining page to it till the fold in the paper will lie about half an inch upon it, when the folded sheet is laid upon the face of the first page.

The margin for the head of a folio, if imposed heads on a line, is arranged at press.

Quarto.—Fold a sheet of paper exactly into quarto; then lay it, thus folded, upon the first page, the fore edge of the paper being even with the left-hand edge of the type; bring the adjoining page toward the first page till the fold in the paper lies upon the left-hand side of it about three-eighths of an inch; this will make the back about right. Then place the lower edge of the paper even with the foot of the page, and bring the heads of the pages which adjoin at that part toward each other, till the fold in the paper covers the head-line and barely the first line of matter; this will make the head right. Then fit the furniture into the spaces.

Before we proceed to octavo, it will be necessary to observe that, in all sizes except folio and quarto, if there be not enough in the backs, the raw edge of the paper in the front margin will project beyond the folded margin, and this in proportion to the deficiency in the back; the same will take place in the length in duodecimo, and in smaller sizes where there are off-cuts, if there be not enough at the foot of the pages whence the off-cut is taken. The effect produced by these deficiencies is, that the binder is obliged to reduce the size of the book both in length and width, when cutting, in order to make the edges smooth.

Octavo.—Fold a sheet of paper into octavo, and lay it, thus folded, upon the first page, the fore edge of the paper even with the outer edge of the type. Then bring the adjoining page toward it till the other side of the octavo paper lies over the left-hand side of this page about a quarter of an inch; this will give the width of the gutter. Then open the paper out a fold, into quarto, and, laying it upon the two pages, bring the third page on the right hand sufficiently near for the right-hand side of the paper to lie upon the left-hand side of the page about an eighth of an inch; this will give the width of the back. Then fold the paper up again, and, laying it upon the first page, with the foot of the paper even with the bottom-line, bring the head of the page above it, so near that the top of the octavo paper will cover the head-line and barely the first line of matter; this will give the space at the head. Then fit the furniture as before.

Duodecimo.—After folding a sheet of paper exactly into 12mo, proceed as in octavo for the gutter, but let the fold lie rather less than a quarter of an inch over the edge of the adjoining page; proceed in the same manner for the back, but that the paper lie on the third page about an eighth of an inch will be sufficient; the fold in the head will just cover the top line of matter in the adjoining page above it, as in octavo. The off-cut is now to be considered: this is always imposed on the outside of the short cross, and the back and gutters are the same as those in the other part of the sheet; for the head of the off-cut, the space between the running title, or, where there is no running title, the head-line, and the middle of the groove in the short cross, must be exactly half the width of the head-margin; for, as register is made at this part, and the points fall into the groove and there make point-holes, the binder folds to these holes, and takes off the off-cut in accordance. Thus, when the sheet is folded, the off-cut inserted and knocked up, the head-lines of the off-cut ought to range with the head-lines of the other pages, and this should always be kept in view by the printer; the space between the bottom of the other pages and the middle of the groove in the short cross should be within a quarter of an inch of the outer margin at the foot of the pages, which will allow for any little variation in the size of the paper, and not affect the size of the book in cutting the edges.

We might go on still further, but, as the larger forms are only duplicates of those here explained, the principle remains the same, and we have given enough to illustrate the process.

In allowing the margin for front and backs, it should be borne in mind that there are two ways of binding books; one is called sewing, the other stabbing and stitching. In works intended to be permanent, the sections are sewed together, each section being sewed separately through the back, and fastened to cords, which run across the back and are attached to and secure the cover. In pamphlets and works of no permanent importance, the stabbing and stitching process is resorted to, which consists in punching holes through the back margin of the whole book, and stitching through the whole of it at once. As this latter process takes up more room in the back, the back margin should be proportionately increased, which would make the back and front margins about equal.

The introduction of metal furniture, now almost universally used, has greatly facilitated the work of the printer in adjusting the pages to a proper margin, and in the subsequent process of fitting the form with furniture after the margin has been obtained. The furniture, being mathematically correct and uniform as to size, has also obviated the necessity of placing card-boards in the head and front margins of the form, to allow for any defect in furniture, when register is wanted, which is often required to be done when forms are imposed with wood furniture of the ordinary make.

If two jobs, that are to be cut up, are worked together, it is usual to impose them so that the margin shall be equal on both sides. To effect this, fold the paper exactly in the middle, and, laying it folded upon the left-hand page with the edge of the paper even with the edge of the page of types, bring the other page to it till the left-hand side fairly touches the fold of the paper. This is termed being cut and out. When the paper is cut evenly in two, after having been printed, the side margins will be found to be even.

The following directions for making margin for two pages of different size, or for the imposition of deeds, insurance policies, or work requiring the first page and indorsement to print together, will be found very useful:

Lay the page or job on an exact line with the crease formed by folding the sheet in the centre—from the outer edge of the type to the edge of the sheet is seen all the white margin on the page; then fold the edge of the paper over till it strikes the outer edge of the type; crease it; draw the page over to the crease; keep the sheet to its place; lay the opposite page on a line with the centre crease, and proceed precisely as above. The open space between the pages thus laid gives the exact furniture which will be required between the pages when locked up for press. When imposing an indorsement to be worked at the same time with the face, proceed as above to secure the proper side margins for the face; after this is obtained, mark the spot on the edge of the half sheet on which the first line of the indorsement is to be printed below (or above) the folded crease, and move your type up (or down) till opposite the mark thus made.

The margin required for forms of leaflets of different sizes, depends on the whim of the customer, or the amount of margin the paper will allow between the pages. The only imperative rule to be observed is, that the margin on the outside of the pages should be rather less than one-half of that given on the inside, so that, in folding, no section of the sheet will double over.

Making Ready.—The act of getting a form ready to be printed; which includes the modes of overlaying, underlaying, and cutting out, to make up for any inequalities in the height or face of the type; putting up the rollers in proper order for printing the form, and adjusting the amount and quality of the ink to suit the form, and the paper on which it is to be printed. In addition to the above, in book-work, this term embraces making register, remedying any defects which may have arisen in imposing or locking up the form, to prevent the exact backing of the pages. In fact, making ready may be said to form the chief portion of the pressman's duty, to which the other matters pertaining to press-work are only auxiliary, while it very often requires the exercise of the highest skill, taste, judgment, and artistic excellence.

Hand-Press.—In hand-press printing, the form, if for a book, is placed in the centre of the bed of the press, so that, when an impression is pulled, the piston, to which the platen is attached, will fall exactly in the centre of the form. The form should then be securely fastened by means of suitable furniture and quoins. The tympan is then laid down, and paper or blankets put in according to the nature of the form to be printed. The drawer is then laid on, and fastened with the hooks for that purpose. A sheet of the paper to be printed is now folded into quarto, and the creases placed so as to fall in the centre of the long and short cross. The tympan is now dampened slightly, and brought down, and a slight pressure will cause the sheet to adhere to it, when it should be fully stretched, and pasted on the corners to the tympan. In a sheet of twelves the paper is folded into thirds, and the long and the short crease placed over their respective long and short crosses. The points are now screwed to the tympan. If for large paper, short-shanked points are used, and long-shanked for small paper. In printing an octavo, or form of like character, the off-point may be a little larger than the near one, as it enables the pressman to detect any error in turning the paper when working the second side. In printing 12mo forms, the points must be placed at exactly equal distances from the edge of the paper. The cutting out of the frisket is the next thing to be done. Having fastened the frisket to the tympan, lay it on the form, and rub the back of the tympan gently with the palm of the hand, so as to give a distinct impression. This is preferable to pulling an impression by means of the bar-handle, because, the frisket-paper having a rough, hard face, and being sometimes lumpy, there is great danger of injuring the face of the type if an impression is pulled on it. The frisket should now be laid on a board, and the marked parts cut out, at the distance of one-eighth of an inch from the edge of the printing, so that no part of the frisket will strike the edge of the type.

An impression is now taken, and examined to see if it be uniform throughout. As this is seldom the case, the form must be overlaid where light, and the

heavy parts cut out, to produce a uniformity of pressure and color over the whole form.

The overlaying is done with thin, unsized paper,
and where the impression is weak, a piece of paper of
the size of the weak part is pasted on it, and where
too strong, that portion cut out, to make it even with
the other parts of the printed sheet. A sheet is then
pulled to see the effect of the overlaying and cutting
out, and if not quite even, the same process is gone
over, wherever needed, until the pressure of the
platen is the same in every part of the sheet, and a
uniform shade of color is obtained. The unusual
height of parts of forms sometimes necessitates the
cutting out of the sheets inside the tympan, as well as
the making ready sheet, in order to make the impression even.

Where the same press does the whole or the greater
part of a work, it is generally preferable to overlay
on a sheet of stout, smooth paper, placed inside the
tympan. This sheet should be cut to fit the inside of
the tympan, so as not to move, which will keep the
overlays in their places while the form is being
printed. This system saves much time in printing
the succeeding sheets of the same work, as each one
will prove to have nearly an even impression on the
first sheet pulled, thus requiring very little making
ready.

Type-high bearers, placed across the narrow way of
the bed, one on each side, should be used where the
size of the form will admit. They should be placed
in such a position that the ends of the rollers will not
touch them when the form is inked, to prevent
tearing the frisket and soiling the tympan. The
impression can be regulated in any manner desired,
by placing cards or paper underneath the ends of the
bearers.

The bottoms of short pages, and the edges of pages
adjoining, will sometimes print heavy, and with a
dull impression. In such cases, bearers made of
reglet, to bear on some parts of the furniture or chase,
or hard paper rolled up, and pasted in proper position
on the frisket, will remedy the defect.

Slackness of the tympan, or very thin and soft
paper, sometimes occasions the paper to touch the form
partially when the tympan is turned down. To prevent this, cut an ordinary bottle-cork, so that, when
it is laid on the furniture, it will be about one-eighth
inch higher than the face of the form; place it on the
furniture near the matter which shows slurs, put a
little paste on the upper part, and it will become
attached to the frisket when the next impression is
pulled. The additional height of the cork will cause
the paper to remain in place until the platen is pulled
down, when, on account of its springing nature, it
will give way until the pressure is removed.

Register must be made before commencing to print
the form, no matter whether it be whole- or half-
sheet work. After the points have been made to
strike in the centres of the grooves, pull an impression, and, if the form be an octavo, or any other form
which is printed in a similar manner, turn the sheet

over, so that the edge which was at the top of the
tympan will be at the bottom; then put the spurs of
the points into the holes in the sheet of paper, and
pull another impression. If the points be in their
places, the pages and lines will back each other, and
the work can be proceeded with; but, if they do not,
one or the other, or both of them, must be moved up
or down, as circumstances may require. If the sheet
does not register, after the second side is pulled, leave
it on the tympan and observe in which direction it is
out,—the first or under impression being the one on
which the direction of the movement of the points
will depend. Suppose it be found that the lower
corner next the pressman is out of register one-eighth
of an inch, the first impression being the lowest; the
point at that side must be moved upward half that
distance, which will bring it to its proper position.
Print another sheet, on both sides, and examine as
before, and, if the register be correct, the pressman can
go on with the work.

In printing from stereotype or electrotype plates
mounted on ratchet-blocks, the position of the plates
should be marked, so as to notice any slipping which
may occur during the progress of the work.

Pins are sometimes used in printing the first side
of a book-form, to prevent the sheets from slipping.
A piece of card pasted at the foot of the tympan-
sheet, having a projecting tongue, under which the
sheet may be fed, is considered preferable by many;
but pin guides are indispensable where it is found
necessary to change the margin to suit a slight variation in ruling or cutting the paper, and they are specially well adapted for printing on dry paper.

The frisket for hand-bills, posters, and jobs requiring large quantities of ink, with narrow outside margin, is prepared by running cords across the frisket
frame, and tying them securely, so as to fall in the
space between the lines, and lift the sheet after the
impression is taken.

The rollers should be kept perfectly free from dirt,
pieces of paper, or other matter likely to cause bad
work. The ink should be rolled out thin on the ink-
block with a brayer, so that when applied to the
rollers it will be tolerably smooth, and the rollers
should be frequently turned on the cylinder, to keep
the ink well distributed before being applied to the
form.

As a uniform color is one of the great requisites in
good printing, it may be necessary to take ink at
every impression, where the form is large. Great
care should be exercised in supplying ink, before the
color is allowed to become gray, when the form has
been started with a full black.

In fine work, it sometimes happens that a form
should be rolled several times between each impression, using only a moderate quantity of ink.

Judgment and experience must be the pressman's
guide in this, as well as in the condition in which he
should put up his rollers to suit the quality of ink
and the work in hand.

Cylinder Press.—The bottom of the form and the

bed of the press should be perfectly free from dirt. The impression-screws should have an even bearing on the journals, and the cylinder should touch the bearers, which should be adjusted a trifle above ordinary type height.

The tympan should be selected to suit the class of work intended to be done, as upon this matter the perfection of the work, in great measure, depends.

The India-rubber blanket is best adapted where the press may be used for all kinds of work and it is not found convenient or profitable to change the tympan with each succeeding form. It combines, in a measure, the qualities of nearly all other tympans; and where it is designed to print book-work, posters, and general job and newspaper work on the same press, no better tympan can be obtained.

A tympan made of fuller's-board, or packing, is most suitable for new type, wood-cuts, and the finer kinds of press-work. A proper making ready on this surface will show a more delicate impression and a sharper outline than can be obtained with any other, and it will not wear the type round on the edges, and is less likely to dull the hair-lines on type or cuts. It requires a nice discrimination on the part of the pressman, and very elaborate making ready, to attain good results.

Tympans made of thick paper are more generally used for book-work, and for the lighter kinds of jobbing, such as script circulars, checks, etc. Paper is very serviceable on forms where the type is slightly and uniformly worn; it does not require the patient making ready of the hardest tympan, nor is it so destructive to the type as the softer kinds of tympan or blankets.

For posters, with wood type, old stereotype plates, or type which has been much worn, a woolen blanket is best adapted, and may be used on all kinds of common work, which requires only to be brought up fairly, as such forms can be made ready more quickly with this than with any other material.

The above are only given as general rules, as pressmen very often combine these materials, or use others, according to the kind of work in hand, and are guided in these matters by experience and judgment.

The tympan should be stretched very tightly over the cylinder, so as to present a smooth, even surface, as the time and labor spent in making ready are but thrown away, should the tympan be loose in any part. A woolen blanket can be secured at one end by the clamps on the impression segment of the cylinder, wound around the reel at the other end, and tightened with the pawl and ratchet. A rubber blanket, being less pliable, should be secured at one end of the cylinder by hooks, and holes punched in at the other end, about two inches apart, so that a piece of canvas may be sewed on, and wound around the reel in the same manner as the woolen blanket.

Packing or paper should be creased at the end, and laid on the flat edge of the impression segment of the cylinder; a piece of reglet should then be laid on the

crease, and all may be secured by bringing the clamps down on the reglet. A piece of fine muslin should then be laid over all, and secured in the same manner as a blanket, which will prevent a shifting of the overlays or tympan.

Great care should be exercised in keeping the bed of the press perfectly clean, and, when a form is laid on, to see that no type drop out on the bed, and the form should be rubbed over with a stiff, dry brush before the rollers are allowed to touch the face of the type. Neglect of these little particulars may cause serious defects, which it will take time and trouble to remedy.

The form having been placed on press, see that the nipper edge of the type is at the proper distance from the back end of the bed. This margin should be adjusted by means of a gauge, made the length of the distance between the back end of the bed and the point of the nippers, when the nippers are brought down so as slightly to lap over the back end of the bed. Next see that the type, chase, and furniture lie flat upon the bed, and if the form springs, loosen the quoins sufficiently to remedy the defect, and fasten the form so that it will not be moved by the action of the rollers. Push out the iron tongues at the edge of the feed-board, so that they will sustain the paper when fed down to the drop-guides. Slide the drop-guides along the rod, until they fall squarely over the tongues, and adjust them, so as to give the proper margin on the sheet, then secure them firmly to the rod by means of the screws. Set the side guide so that it will give a proper margin on the length of the sheet.

A fair, legible proof for revision should be pulled of every form, before the regular making ready is begun, and, if a book form, a register should be obtained. Attention to these matters will save much time and annoyance, if a form should require correction, or if a slight alteration should be found necessary to give a good register.

When the proof has been pronounced correct, proceed to regulate the impression by taking a proof with sufficient impression to take the ink from the face of the type and transfer it to the paper, but not so hard as to cause too much indention in the paper, as the difference in pressure can be more readily detected by the deposit of ink on the paper, than if the impression is full and solid over the whole form. A uniform impression should be produced before any attempt is made at overlaying. In making ready a type book form, avoid underlaying, unless the rollers do not charge the low parts with sufficient ink, as slight underlaying will often cause the type to work off its feet and show only a partial impression on the face, and, if carried too far, it will work up the spaces and furniture. A book form made up entirely or almost entirely of tabular work is an exception to this rule, as the inequalities of height between the rule and the type may be adjusted by an underlay under the whole form of a damp sheet of paper.

Old stereotype plates, being irregular in height, require more underlaying than other forms, and, when mounted on ratchet-blocks, the underlaying should be placed directly under the plate. Stereotype plates mounted on ratchet-blocks require watching, as the friction caused by the motion of the cylinder is calculated to make the plates slip from the position in which they have been imposed.

In job forms, set with large, bold-faced type, in connection with type of smaller body and lighter face, the large type should be underlaid to raise them above the level of the other parts of the form. This is done to give them extra rolling, and a greater impression to transfer the ink to the paper.

The impression should be made as uniform as possible before any underlaying is done. The bearers should be raised and lowered with the impression screws, in order to bear off from the force of the cylinder. The bearers should always be of even height, and the cylinder-shaft should always revolve on a true level. It would be well if, after the impression screws are set, and the bearers of an even height to give a fair impression, they were not tampered with, and all defects remedied by means of the tympan and making ready.

When the cylinder is adjusted to give a nearly even impression, cover the tympan with a sheet of thin, hard paper, take an impression on the tympan, and take two or three proofs on sheets of the same kind of paper. If any part of the form appears too high, cut out on the tympan in one or two thicknesses of paper, as the variation in height may require. The knife used for cutting should be very sharp, and the paper cut to taper towards the edge. Next raise the impression of those parts of the form where the type appears weak. Cut out these parts in different thicknesses of paper, as needed, and paste the overlays over the tympan smoothly, using very little paste. Should the overlays wrinkle, tear them off, and paste others on smoothly. Take another proof, and cut new overlays for any small defects, and proceed until a perfectly even impression is obtained.

A system of overlaying in use for cuts on newspapers is done by means of a card adapted for the purpose, having thin layers, on which proofs are taken; and as many layers as are necessary to produce the effect required torn or cut off for the light parts of the picture, while the extra impression given by the thickness remaining produces the heavy shading in the foreground, or wherever a dark effect is wanted to be produced. It is claimed that this method of making ready is more expeditious than the old method of cutting out and overlaying.

For ordinary poster- or job-work, overlaying is often unnecessary. After underlaying parts of the form, the tapes and fly may be set, and the printing commenced. But fine work cannot be done without overlaying, to give delicacy and finish to the impression.

The impression should be strong enough to transmit the ink from the type to the paper, but not of such force as to break the fibre of the paper. The character of the impression depends very much on the nature of the tympan, as a light impression from a blanket will show a greater indentation than a strong impression from a hard tympan; with a fine impression the amount of ink can be better regulated, the paper will not smear or set off, and the form is not likely to become filled up by surplus ink.

For short numbers on any form, the color may be kept up with a brayer or palette-knife, but in long editions the ink-fountain should be set or regulated, to insure a uniform flow of ink. The ink should be cut off evenly, and, when the form is ready, turned on until the required shade is obtained. The fountain should be kept covered, to protect it from paper dust, while the form is being printed.

The condition of the rollers for printing depends on the quality of ink used, and a thorough knowledge of this important matter is acquired only by observation and experience. While no absolute rule can be given, a form printed with thin or common ink will require a softer roller, with more suction than those printed with the finer qualities of ink. In the latter case the inks have a tendency to create additional suction in the roller, while working.

The inks used should be mixed ready for the different kinds of work. If the pressman is supplied with poster, book, job and wood-cut ink, he will not be at a loss, if necessary, to mix an ink of a proper consistency for any peculiar job, by compounding them, or reducing with varnish to suit the form or job in hand. The inks, whether colored or black, should be the best of their kind, as it is impossible to do good press-work without the best materials, properly used.

The form being ready to print, the tapes should be set by loosening the guide-pulleys on the upper shaft, and shifting them so that the tapes will rest on the outer margin of the sheet. Move the tape-pulleys so that they will rest on a line with the guide-pulleys, which should then be thrown back and tightened to the shaft, so as to hold the tapes tight. Run the tapes once around the cylinder, to make sure they are on a straight line.

The fly should be set by running through a sheet of paper to be printed, and allowing it to run down the fly just far enough to be barely held by the fly-pulleys. The cam on the side of the cylinder should then be set so that its point just clears the small roller on the connecting rod of the fly. Tighten the spring to suit the size of the sheet, and set the spring crank, to prevent the fly from striking too hard on the table.

Adams' Press.—The material for tympans, and the manner of making ready on an Adams' book-press, do not differ greatly from those in use on a cylinder for the same kind of work. The different construction of the press, and the mode of giving the impression by means of a bed and platen, render it remarkably well adapted for executing the finest kinds of letter-press and cut printing. By the use of friskets the blacking of the sheets from the space used for blank and short pages is entirely obviated, and, the impression being flat, it is believed by many printers that the type is calculated to remain in better condition for the same number of impressions than if printed on a cylinder press, where it is thought that the mode of giving impression has a tendency to grind the face of the type. As the platen can be rolled off, so as to leave the bed entirely exposed, the facilities for making ready and correcting on press cannot be excelled. In printing from stereotype or electrotype plates mounted on ratchet-blocks, the plates are not so liable to move from their positions, and should any movement occur, it can be more readily detected by the biting of the frisket, before any serious damage occurs.

For book-work requiring the finest effects, the most exact register, and where extra speed is not needed, this press is claimed by many to have no superior.

The tympans in general use are composed of fullers' board, covered with packing- or draughting-paper; or several sheets of draughting-paper, covered with fine muslin or billiard cloth.

Small Job-Presses.—The rules applicable to tympans for different descriptions of forms on the larger presses, also obtain in the making ready for the smaller-sized job-presses, with the exception that in working old type or plate forms several thicknesses of soft paper are used in place of the ordinary blankets. As the impressions can be arranged to suit the wants of any form by adding to or taking from the sheets in the platen, many offices adopt the plan of setting the impression level with a given number of sheets when the press is set up, and not allowing the impression screws to be moved in the subsequent making ready of any form. Care should be exercised in setting the nippers, so that they may not become loose and move in the direction of the face of the type and destroy that part with which they come in contact. A bend in the nippers will throw off the impression from the form, and cause it to slur. In forms having so little outside margin as not to allow the nippers to hold the sheet on the tympan after the impression is pulled, while there is plenty of margin running from end to end in the inside of the form, it is usual to make a frisket of paper or page-cord, taking the two nippers as side frames, and tying the cord or cutting the paper so as to press in the blank space. The almost imperceptible indentation of paper given by impressions on the small presses saves the pressing of small job-work, and only makes it necessary to lay the work out to dry the ink before packing for delivery.

Making Register.—The act of making the pages and lines fall exactly on the back of each other at press, when any work is perfected.

Making Up.—Making up a newspaper is the act of arranging the matter composed into proper divisions in a comprehensive form, and includes the knowledge of the successive order of the general head-lines, and of the particular place of every subject and paragraph under them; also of adjusting the columns to a proper standard, and of putting the required number of columns together to form a page. The width and length of such page are determined by the size of the paper and the manner in which it is folded. Though making up is a difficult operation, a few hours are usually deemed sufficient for this purpose, and it is generally, if not always, left as late as possible, with a due regard to the number to be worked, to the arrival of fresh news, or to any contingency that may arise before the time at which the forms must be at press.

The nature and number of the general standing heads must depend on the judgment of the editor, by whom they are filled up; but to see that every portion of information supplied be inserted under its own peculiar head, is the duty of the maker-up. To do this easily, certainly, and expeditiously, requires some experience; though a good system would largely obviate those inconveniences by which every new beginner is surrounded.

The first and principal essential to making up well, is a perfect knowledge of the several divisions into which a paper is divided, and the particular class of subjects included in each.

Making up a daily newspaper involves so many matters of detail, that it would be impossible to enlarge upon all of them in our limited space. We will assume that the editors and reporters have furnished the foreman with copy of their departments in good time: that functionary selects a competent assistant, to whom he gives general directions for making up the pages.

We will suppose the paper to be an eight-paged sheet (the most popular form at the present time). If the circulation is sufficient to warrant the proprietor in undertaking the expense of stereotyping, all of the pages can be kept open until a later moment than it could be if it were printed from types. Items of news can then be inserted with more regularity, under their appropriate headings; and if later editions are required, the new matter can be set up and inserted in its place, and new casts taken of the page required. But if the paper is printed from types, the inner form, containing the 2d, 3d, 6th, and 7th pages, must of necessity be put to press first, and many of the departments must be duplicated. It is the practice of many proprietors to permit their advertising patrons to dictate the place which their advertisements shall occupy; by this means rendering it impossible to observe any order or system in arranging the advertisements, and giving a vast amount of additional trouble to those who make up the paper.

The question of what should occupy the first page of a daily paper, does not admit of much dispute. The old idea that the first and last pages of a newspaper should be filled with advertisements, has been wellnigh exploded.

The public now demand that a newspaper should be filled with news, and it is found most profitable to place the best news on the first page. Hence the great struggle for publishing the paper in time generally takes place upon this page; the most attractive headings are here displayed, and here the public generally expect to find the most exciting news of the day. The second page would find its most fitting use in correspondence, which, in any daily paper of extensive circulation, can always be made interesting and important. The third page should be devoted to local matters; and the sixth and seventh pages can readily and appropriately be filled with foreign or domestic news. The arrangement of advertisements on these inner pages will necessarily vary with every different locality; but when a department is extensive, as For Sale, and To Let, and Wants often are, it is well to arrange the advertisements under these headings alphabetically. The fourth page of a daily paper is almost universally devoted, more or less, to editorials. The appearance of a paper is much improved if the fourth page is entirely filled in this way; but advertisers always evince a desire to appear on this page, and hence many publishers devote a portion of it to this profitable matter. The fifth page should be the place for Musical, Dramatic, or Art Criticism, together with Special Notices, or City Items. The eighth page should contain Financial and Commercial articles, Shipping Intelligence, Local News, Marriages and Deaths, etc.

Making up a Composing-Stick.—Adjusting it to the size desired for any particular work.

Making up Furniture.—Dressing a chase with suitable furniture, side- and footsticks, so that a proper margin will be given to the work when printed.

MALLET.

Mallet.—A wooden hammer, used to drive the quoins in locking and unlocking forms, in planing forms, and for other similar purposes.

Mame Printing-Office.—This establishment, famous for the extent, beauty, and cheapness of its publications, is established at Tours, in France, and is at present known as the firm of Alfred Mame and Company. At the close of the last century, the establishment was founded by Amand Mame, an ardent and indefatigable man, who had already achieved considerable success when he took into partnership his nephew, Ernest Mame, in 1830, and his own eldest son, Alfred Mame, in 1833. Ernest Mame retired in 1845, and has since held important and honorable offices. His retirement left Alfred Mame sole proprietor of the establishment, which had been greatly improved by his father, Amand Mame. An enthusiast in his profession, Alfred Mame determined to found a complete book-manufactory, combining all branches of the business; and this has been so fully accomplished, that, with the exception of the paper manufacture, all the processes connected with

printing and binding, including the arts of the designer and engraver, are provided, within its walls, for the production of about eight hundred different volumes, varying from the small prayer-book, valued, when bound, at 35 centimes, to the folio local history, splendidly illustrated, for 100 francs. The building erected for the purpose is a model for arrangement, spaciousness, thorough ventilation, and everything that can conduce to the health and comfort of the laborers. About 1000 men, women, and children are employed within the walls, besides almost an equal number employed at their own homes in the vicinity. The zeal and benevolence of the proprietor, assisted by his only son, Paul Mame, who entered the firm in 1859, have organized a complete community, in which the comfort of the working-people is assured by their being entitled to relief and medical attendance during illness, and to provision in old age. Suitable occupation is furnished to women who are kept at home by the care of young children, and in many cases father, mother, and children are all employed in the manufactory, the children all being guaranteed the opportunity of acquiring a fair primary education. Every window of the factory looks out upon greensward and trees, and in many of the rooms playing fountains sustain a perpetual current of fresh water in a circular trough, for washing; and the establishment proudly claims that women and children are provided with light work in a situation more healthy than their own homes.

The remarkable pecuniary success of this house must be ascribed, in a great degree, to the combination of all the auxiliary industries under one roof, and on the other hand, to the fact that the publications have been restricted to such works as must invariably meet a great demand. Great perfection in the result is thus reached, as well as remarkable cheapness. In 1851 the house of Mame received a prize medal at the London Exhibition for the extreme cheapness and great variety of the books printed, bound, and published. At the Exposition of 1855 it was also deemed worthy of especial mention, by the jury, that this establishment exhibited a book of prayers, in a volume of 636 pages 32mo, well printed, solidly bound in black sheep, with marbled edges, costing 80 centimes. It also carried off some of the most important honors of the French Exposition of 1867.

Manifest.—A list or invoice of a ship's cargo, or of the freight on a steamboat or railroad train, giving a description of boxes, bales, bags, etc., by marks and numbers, or their direction. The headings of manifests are usually printed, and they form an item of some importance in job printing.

Manilla Paper.—A colored paper of great strength, which is extensively used for wrapping newspapers, packages, goods, etc.

Manual.—A small book prepared as a work of reference or hand-book. Originally applied to the book of services in the Roman Church from its convenient size, as being readily carried in the hand.

Manuscript.—Anything written with the hand in contradistinction to printed matter. Previous to the sixteenth century, the period when printing came into common use, the study of the peculiarities of manuscript is important as the means of ascertaining the date of written documents. The earliest specimens of writing occur upon stone, metal, wood, and baked clay, and subsequently more flexible substances were used, such as wax, linen, the bark and leaves of trees, and the prepared skins of goats, sheep, and calves. The word parchment is supposed to be derived from the city of Pergamus, in which the skins of sheep were prepared for writing; and from the papyrus, a reed growing on the Nile, has been derived the modern word paper. The correct transcription of works both of sacred and profane history became so important that, previous to the fifth century, schools and associations of scribes were formed under definite and stringent rules. The famous copy of the Scriptures known as the Codex Alexandrinus, now preserved in the British Museum, was written by a female scribe, a member of the school of Alexandria, at the beginning of the fifth century. All the monasteries contained writing-rooms or scriptoriums, in which the monks wrote from dictation, the copy being revised by a competent person, and then placed in the hands of a miniator, or painter in vermilion, who decorated it and added the fanciful capital letters. The earliest writing was entirely in majuscule, or capital letters following each other continuously without any punctuation or spaces between the words. A smaller running character, called miniscule, began to appear occasionally during the fourth and fifth centuries, but was not frequent until the close of the eighth century. The vellum, or prepared skin of the calf, was also whiter and finer in the earlier ages; and the finest vellum yet discovered belongs to a period previous to the end of the eighth century. Uncial letters, a compound or transition style between the majuscule and the miniscule, prevailed from the sixth to the eighth century, when a fine Roman miniscule became quite common; a handsome illustration of which is still preserved in the Psalter of Charlemagne contained in the Library of Vienna. The miniscule is the prevailing character in the Latin manuscript of the ninth century, and in the Greek of the tenth. The Latin manuscript of the ninth century is delicate and slants to the right hand, while that of the tenth century is more upright, rounder and fuller in shape; the best specimen being a document written by St. Dunstan, conveying a grant from King Eadred to the church of Canterbury in the year 949. In the eleventh century, the very darkest period of the dark ages, parchment became very scarce, and it was usual for the monks to erase the manuscript copies of profane authors, in order to use the material for the sacred writings. This rewriting has been known as the palimpsest, and in modern times art has been able, in some cases, to remove the upper writing and recover the manuscript which lay beneath. In this century the handwriting became much smaller and more slanting, a change probably arising from the scarcity of parchment. In the twelfth century, especially in England, the letters became larger and the lines heavier, and towards the close of the century the angular character, generally known as the modern Gothic, began to take the place of the clear and beautiful Roman, and entirely superseded it in the thirteenth century. Abbreviations previous to this age had been simple and few, but they now became numerous and complex, and they are the chief distinguishing mark of the manuscripts of the time. In the fourteenth century the Gothic character still prevailed, but it became more broad, open, and legible, and the abbreviations were much less numerous, probably on account of the introduction of paper. In the fifteenth century the writing was almost universally Gothic, although of a more open and delicate character, and was so popular throughout Europe that the first printers, both in France and Italy, were compelled to abandon the Roman character, after a short struggle, and return to the Gothic black letter; the cursive or running style of which, known as the Secretary Gothic, was used by Caxton, and is well exhibited in the illustration already given in this work. The Roman character, however, soon triumphed in Italy, and its beauty and legibility made it a favorite with the printers of other countries, and it was gradually introduced. The chosen models for this character were taken from the Latin manuscripts of the age of Augustus Cæsar, and the Italic from the finest Italian penmanship of the fifteenth century.

Although the handwriting of the different centuries can be distinguished with considerable certainty, the peculiarities of ornamentation prevailing at different periods and in various countries are considered a more reliable means of deciding upon the date of manuscripts. The earliest style of ornament was the introduction of vermilion, a peculiarly brilliant and permanent red, called in Latin minium, and used to mark the titles or commencement of manuscripts. This red was afterwards used to distinguish the most important words, and such portions were customarily known as the rubricated, or red letters, from which is derived the modern word rubric, used to signify the order of the litany, both in the Roman and English Churches. Those scribes skilled in the use of the minium, and called miniators, introduced a delicate and minute ornamentation suited to the small sheets of vellum, and from these pictures and illustrations is derived the modern word miniature, a style of ornament especially suited to the requirements of manuscript and book decoration. Colored vellum was also used at an early date, that of the purple and rose tints being much more brilliant in the first Christian centuries, and losing brilliance and purity of tone in the eighth and ninth centuries. Purple manuscripts were unknown in England until the close of the seventh century. Writing in burnished gold and silver was also usual in the fourth and several subsequent centuries, the most ancient example known being the Codex Argenteus of Ulphilas, written on purple vellum at the close of the fourth century. The early Christian fathers, and particularly those who were employed in preaching the gospel among the heathen, decorated their manuscripts of the Scriptures with the utmost luxury, and lavished gold, silver, and even jewels upon them, as a means of exhibiting to the heathens the esteem in which the sacred works were held by the true believers. From this cause burnished gold was much used. Manuscripts written in gold and silver upon white vellum are chiefly confined to the eighth, ninth, and tenth centuries; and, although they occur even down to the fifteenth century, those later than the tenth century cannot properly be called written, the letters being formed by a process of gilding. The Byzantine style of ornamentation was a very elaborate, but rather weak, adaptation of classic forms, and continued from age to age with very slight modifications. It is a curious fact that the only original style of decoration arose in Ireland at a very remote period. Even earlier than the fifth century this style had reached considerable perfection, and was especially remarkable for its harmony of color, and precision and delicacy of execution. Intricate interlacings of narrow ribbons of color in symmetrical designs were used to form the letters, and sometimes covered the whole page. To these were added circular ornaments filled with delicate spiral lines springing from a centre, or wheels and concentric convolutions of colored lines or ribbons. Diagonals and straight lines were also occasionally introduced, and the whole was ornamented still further by the introduction of birds and animals in lavish profusion, coiled throughout the convolutions in general harmony with the design. The Book of Kells of the seventh century, preserved at Trinity College, Dublin, is a remarkable specimen of this style, the human figure being also introduced into it. This method of decoration was introduced by the Irish missionaries into England, and thence spread to the continent. The first improvement upon the Irish original began in England in the tenth century, when the architectural designs of the time, a species of rude and angular foliage, were introduced. During the tenth, eleventh, and twelfth centuries this style prevailed in England, thick, stalkless leaves springing from parallel bars of gold in the borders of the page, or grouped around the curves of the letters, colored with a barbarous profusion of tints, and occasionally intermingled with curved lines or heads of animals as a reminiscence of the Irish designs. This style was known upon the continent as the English, and in the twelfth century became very elaborate and splendid. The initial letters were very prominent, and the foliage luxuriant and graceful. The drawing of figures was also more exact and natural, and the draperies were highly artistic. At this time art in England was in advance of that of the continent, as being more artistic and original, while the other nations were following the worn-out styles of Byzantium. In the thirteenth cen-

tury the English began to exhibit that genuine love of nature which has developed recently into their fine school of landscape-painting; and the manuscripts show that the artists were abandoning the conventional forms of architectural foliage for a direct imitation of the natural forms. Burnished gold, scarlet, and blue were largely used. In the Philadelphia Library there is a manuscript of the thirteenth century which contains the Apocrypha; it is written on vellum, and slightly illuminated, the capital letters being all colored, and the writing clear and distinct. At this period the French constantly employed gold backgrounds in the miniatures, while the English used lower tones of color, sometimes relieving the backgrounds with small powdered patterns peculiar to the age and country.

In the fourteenth century the plain gold and heavy colored backgrounds were abandoned for rich checkered patterns, and the large masses of burnished metal were either broken into minute patterns or superseded by variegated color. The foliage also, used in the previous century to decorate the capital letters, was combined into graceful wreaths, which formed ornamental brackets, or encircled the whole page with a charming border of gold and color. In a Breviary of this period, in the Philadelphia Library, the illuminations are in gold, and the pauses in chanting are marked by short bands or ornamented blocks of red and blue; the contractions are also numerous, but simple, and readily understood, as apüis for spiritus, a waved line being placed over the two vowels to indicate the omission. That manuscripts were of very different styles, more or less ornamented according to the wealth or taste of the owner, is proved by the appearance of a large Bible taken by the English on the battle-field of Poitiers; it is not very abundantly illustrated, but contains a good many illuminated letters, with some miniatures. In the fifteenth century the style became very gaudy with flowers, fruit, and foliage, the strictly symbolic forms were abandoned for landscapes, which were also introduced as backgrounds into the miniatures, and the borders became more regular, serving as a framework for the central picture. A copy of the Psalms of David of this century, in the Philadelphia Library, is a handsome square volume written on vellum. The text is black, with highly illuminated initial capitals and margin; the marginal explanatory notes being in red. It contains many abbreviations, all designated by a mark resembling that of the Spanish ñ; and the pauses in chanting are marked by a colon. The illustrations are in deep, rich colors, and in one of them Goliath, a very big man in complete German armor, towers above an exceedingly thick-set, stout little David.

A Book of Hours printed upon vellum by Verard of Paris in 1510, as an exact imitation of the manuscripts of the period, is contained in the same library, and is especially valuable as a representation of the most acceptable style of the time. The marginal ornaments are square and regular, with a ground-work of gold, covered with high-colored scrolls, and leaves of red, blue, and green. To Italy the above description applies only to a limited extent, for, basing its style of illumination upon that of Byzantium, it gradually infused into it, without any marked period of transition, a national and more graceful style. In England, France, and Germany it may, however, be said that, in general terms, manuscripts may be known by the following rules, in the fourth, fifth, and sixth centuries, the ornamentation limited to red or gilded letters belonging to the text; in the seventh, eighth, and ninth, the introduction and perfection of the Irish style; in the tenth, eleventh, and twelfth, the prevalence of architectural forms; in the thirteenth, fourteenth, and fifteenth, foliage, at first architectural, but gradually more realistic; while in miniatures the thirteenth was the age of gold, the fourteenth of checkered backgrounds, and the fifteenth of landscape.

Manutius, Theobaldus. — A distinguished printer of Venice, and the inventor of the Italic letter, popularly known as Aldus. (See ALDUS.)

Map. — The delineation upon a plane surface of a portion of the terrestrial or celestial globe. Map-printing constitutes, with some publishers, a distinct business, and various devices have from time to time simplified and reduced the cost of the process. Formerly fine maps were all printed by the copper-plate process; now they are frequently lithographed, and sometimes printed from electrotypes on typographic presses.

Marble-Paper. — Paper which is stained with colors in imitation of variegated marble. This process forms one of the many adornments of bookbinding, and is used alike on the covers, linings, and edges of books.

Margin. — The part of a page, or the edges, left uncovered in writing or printing. The beauty of many works can be much heightened by broad margins; and, where fine effects are sought, regardless of expense, this subject deserves careful consideration. (See MAKING MARGIN.)

Marginal Notes. — Notes at the edge or side of pages running from top to bottom, and usually placed opposite to the matter to which they refer, when they are short. They are generally called side-notes by printers; and, when set in the body of the matter, cut-in notes.

Marinoni Press. — A French press, invented by Hippolyte Marinoni, of Paris, which is a rival, in speed, of the Hoe and Bullock fast presses. An illustration of it is given on the page of this work devoted to illustrations of presses. The Marinoni press is perfecting, and it is said to print 9000 sheets of large size per hour, on both sides,—the forms being stereotyped. One of its alleged advantages is its simplicity and comparative cheapness, the cost of one of the swiftest Marinoni presses being 40,000 francs.

Marks. — The alterations made by proof-readers, as well as some of the signs used in punctuation, especially those employed to indicate quotations.

Materials. — A general term for nearly all implements used in printing-offices, except presses and type.

Mathematical Signs. — See SIGNS.

Matrix. — That part of the mould in which types are cast, which contains a representation of the letter to be made.

MATRIX.

Matrix Compositor. — An invention of John E. Sweet, an American citizen, which attracted considerable attention at the Paris Exposition in 1867. It is designed to form the mould or matrix for stereotype plates, in a way that disposes with movable types and the labor of setting and distributing them. By operating on the keys of the machine (which are similar to the keys of a piano), impressions are made, in thick, soft, and dry paper, of the letters, figures, or characters required to form the words, lines, and sentences for a column or page. From the mould or matrix thus formed, stereotype plates are cast, which may be used on typographic presses in the usual manner. Although the end aimed at was achieved by the machine exhibited at the Paris Exposition, the work was imperfectly done,—there being inequalities in the depth of the impressions of the mould, and other defects; and it remains to be seen whether the invention can be rendered practically useful.

Matter. — Type composed, whether for jobs, books, or newspapers. If it has not yet been printed, it is called live matter; if it is ready for distribution, it is called dead matter; if it has once been printed, and is likely to be reprinted, it is sometimes called standing matter.

Measure. — The width of a line, page, or column of type. It is usually calculated in ems.

Measuring Type or Matter. — Ascertaining the number of ems square contained in a body of type set up, to determine the cost, or calculate the amount needed to fill a certain space.

The measurement is made by multiplying the number of solid ems contained in the length of any body of type, by the number contained in the width of the measure, and, unless otherwise specified, the gauge for measurement is an em of the type in which the matter to be calculated is set.

In book-offices, it is usual to count the matter appearing below the head-line in the manner given above, counting three ems in addition for the head-line with its blank and the foot-line, without regard to the size of type in which they are set; in measuring the subject-matter, anything in excess of an em and less than a half em or en is not counted, while an en, or an excess making less than an em, is counted as a full em. We will illustrate this by showing the number of ems contained in this page, as follows:

Length of matter . . . . 72 ems
Head- and foot-lines . . . . 3 "
                                    ————
                                    75 ems
Width of matter . . . .   50 "
                                    ————
Total . . . .   3750 ems.

Chapter-heads, blank spaces, or cuts occurring in the dimensions of pages are rated the same as though the space occupied consisted of type. It is also customary to count as type a cut occupying a whole page, when backed by a page of printed matter.

Quotations, poetry, and matter set in smaller type than the body of the work are always counted according to the size of type in which they are set, distinct from the larger type in the same page or body of matter, commencing at the first line, and extending to the first line of the larger type. Pages set in columns include all spaces between the columns, and bordered pages are measured from outside to outside of border, by the ems of the type which they inclose.

Side and centre notes, in Bibles or law works, are measured by the full width of the note and the full length of the page, in the type of which they are composed.

The mode of ascertaining the number of ems in a line is by laying as many of the letter m flatwise in the stick as will make the measure. This is usually done by the compositor when about starting on the work.

It is customary in many newspaper offices to count the rule set between the advertisements as a line of type, although it may not be of the required depth. This necessitates counting the lines, where a number are set together. The offices are generally provided with a scale, showing the total number of ems contained in any number of lines of the different sizes of type in which the paper is set, thus saving a vast amount of calculation.

Various tables have been published, having for their object the saving of time and labor in measurement, and obtaining ready results in calculating differences in proportion of the various sizes of type. Among these are Tables of Proportion of Type in length and depth; tables showing the number of ems in the various kind of types which will occupy the same space as 1000 ems in all the sizes from Pica to Nonpareil, inclusive; table showing the number of lines contained in 1000 ems, in all measures, from 10 to 100 ems wide; a Ready-Reckoner, for ascertaining with certainty and without computation the exact contents of any page or piece of matter of which the length and width are known; table of the number of pages which a sheet of one size of type will make, if set in a different-sized type. There are others, having similar scope, and all of them being excellent mediums for obtaining quick results. The tables intended for comparison of proportions must be accepted with some allowances, because the standard of size for each kind of book and newspaper type varies in different type-foundries.

Medal.—A piece of metal, in the shape of a coin, engraven with figures or devices, struck and distributed in memory of some person or event. A number of medals have been made at various times in honor of the reputed inventors of printing, especially of Gutenberg and Koster. A description of these medals, with fac-simile illustrations, has recently been published by Mr. Blades, of England.

Medical Signs.—See Signs.

Medium.—A size of writing- and printing-paper, the former being usually 18 by 23 inches, and the latter 19 by 24 inches. Medium and double medium (24 by 38) constitute the standard basis for sizes of books,—the usual designations of their size being predicated on the use of medium paper.

Memoir.—A biographical notice of an individual, or a short essay upon a special subject, particularly applied to essays or treatises read before scientific or literary societies.

Memoirs.—An account, by an individual, of his own life, interspersed with anecdotes and remarks regarding contemporaneous persons and events; often, but incorrectly, used for an irregular and descriptive biography, embracing a greater variety of subjects than is usually included in what is strictly termed a life, or a biography.

Mentz.—This word is written by the Germans Mainz, and by the French Mayence, and probably takes its name from the river Main, being situated on the Rhine near its junction with that river. It was called by the Romans Moguntia, or Moguntiacum, Moguntium being the name used in the colophons of Fust and Schoeffer, who always describe themselves as citizens of Moguntium, for the reason that the colophons were written in the Latin language. The city was enlarged by Charlemagne, and became famous under the direction of St. Boniface, who was Archbishop of Mentz in the eighth century. In the thirteenth century it was at the head of the confederation of Rhenish towns. In 1486 it was annexed to the electorate of Mentz, and during the Thirty Years' War was taken successively by the Imperialists, Swedes, and French. In 1792 it fell by treachery into the hands of the French, but was reconquered the next year by the Prussians. In 1801 it was assigned to France, and by the Congress of Vienna was allotted to Hesse-Darmstadt. The Rhine, as the great line of intercommunication between the nations of Europe, was the centre of intelligent industry, as well as of mercantile enterprise; here books were needed, and the requirements of trade understood, as well as the advantages of mechanical appliances: therefore printing naturally was first introduced here as the readiest means of multiplying manuscripts, and the region bordering on the Rhine justly claims the invention of movable type, whether the exact locality was at Mentz, Haarlem, or Strasburg. Mentz, as the residence of John Gutenberg, is considered by many authorities to have won the honor of the invention, and in a handsome public square, called Gutenberg Platz, there is a fine statue of Gutenberg, by

Thorwaldsen. Even if Gutenberg's claim is disputed, the city must rank foremost in typographical achievement as the place where the first ascertained and dated works were printed by Fust and Schoeffer.

Mercury.—A favorite title for newspapers from the earliest date, probably chosen from the name of Mercury, the deity of Greece and Rome, who served as the herald of the gods, and as the medium of communication with mankind. The origin of letters was also ascribed to him, and he was the patron of eloquence and of commerce.

Mercuriale was also the name given by the French, under the old régime, to the first Wednesday after the vacation of the parliaments, on which the people met to criticise the action of the members and discuss political grievances; the word being popularly used by the French in modern times to express an elaborate and regular reprimand for misconduct. Several occasional papers called Mercuries were at one time supposed to have been issued during the time of Elizabeth, especially conveying intelligence of the Spanish Armada (1588); but these documents have been since proved to be clever forgeries. As early as the year 1622, sheets, frequently in manuscript, appeared occasionally during periods of public excitement, and were sold in the streets of London by hawkers, called Mercury men and women. In 1642 a great demand arose for news, and several of these sheets appeared weekly, twice a week, or even tri-weekly, according to emergencies. The Mercurius Aulicus: a Diurnal printed at Oxford, appeared regularly every week, from 1st January, 1643, to 1645, after which it appeared occasionally. In 1643 a large number of quarto sheets appeared, some of them bearing the titles Anti-Aulicus, Mercurius Anglicus, Mercurius Rusticus, Wednesday's Mercury, Mercurius Britannicus, The Welsh Mercury, Mercurius Urbanus, Mercurius Aquaticus, Mercurius Vapulans, Mercurius Civicus or London Intelligencer, the latter being ornamented with a variety of wood-cuts, and a portrait of the Queen as an illustration.

About the year 1690 a small army of Mercuries sprang into existence, many of them bearing that name, and others calling themselves Pacquets of Advice, Intelligencers, News, Posts, and Flying-Post. In this year something of the modern method was attempted, for one of the papers was entitled The Coffee-House Mercury containing all the remarkable events that have happened from November 4th to November 11th, with reflections thereupon.

February 8th, 1696, The Athenian Mercury with its thirtieth number concluded the nineteenth volume, and announced that it would discontinue the weekly publication, and appear only in quarterly volumes, until the glut of news was a little over, the Coffee-Houses being at present supplied with nine newspapers every week, besides the Votes of Parliament every day. That many of the papers still appeared in manuscript is shown by the fact that in August, 1696, Dawk's News Letter appeared in a printed Italic

29

character, with the announcement that it was better than the written news, and contained more matter.

The London Mercury, or Mercuro de Londres, appeared in the same year, containing English and French in opposite columns. At the present day, Mercury, although a standard newspaper title, is not in very common use.

Metal Furniture.—Pieces of metal cast to Pica ems, or of other sizes, as Nonpareil, Brevier, Long Primer, etc., and cut to any requisite length. They are used in imposing forms, for furnishing the chase with the proper margins for books, for filling up blanks and short pages, for foot-lines, and for all other purposes for which wood furniture can be employed. All leads of a greater thickness than four to Pica are classified as metal furniture, as well as other kinds and shapes of metallic substances used as furniture.

Metal Rules.—English type-founders and printers apply this term to what Americans call one-, two-, or three-em dashes.

Metaphysics.—The philosophy of mind, as distinguished from that of matter. Commencing with its first use in the works of Aristotle, this science has embraced a large proportion of the written and printed matter in many countries.

Metre.—The measured arrangement of words in verse. Used in hymn-books to distinguish the varied measures, as long, short, and common metre.

Mezzotint.—A process of engraving so called because it was at first supposed to require a large amount of middle-tint or half-tone in the distribution of masses of light and shade. Prince Rupert, to whom the invention is usually ascribed, is believed to have drawn the idea from seeing a soldier polishing a rusty sword, from some parts of which the rust had been entirely removed, while on others it remained in all its original roughness, and others, again, were half polished. The diversified surface of the blade suggested the idea that a rapid and effective style of engraving could be produced if a metal plate were so roughened as to hold printer's ink. This roughening is now effected by a grounding-tool which resembles a chisel, two inches wide, cut all over one side with grooved straight parallel lines, equidistant from one another and of exactly equal depths. These run lengthwise upon the tool, so that when the end is sharpened to a bevel a saw-like edge is produced. This tool is held nearly upright, the teeth resting on the plate, and is rocked from side to side, advancing forward with a slightly zigzag motion. Guide-lines are drawn on the plate with a pencil or charcoal, parallel to each other, and not quite so wide apart as the breadth of the tool. The rocking operation is continued in one direction until all the spaces between the lines have been rocked through, and what is termed one way is completed. Guide-lines are then drawn in another direction and followed by the grounding-tool, and the same operation is again performed in a third direction, and so continued until a full black ground without a particle of polish is obtained. The outline of the proposed picture is then either sketched upon the plate with the end of the burnisher, or transferred from a drawing on paper by means of the copper-plate roller press. The ground is then scraped away to the various degrees of lightness, removing the roughened surface entirely for the high lights and leaving it untouched for the extreme darks. The bright lights are made with the burnisher, and the pure white lights are finished with it. The scraper is a simple band of steel, about three-eighths of an inch wide, and quite thin, although not

MINERVA PAPER CUTTER.

thin enough to spring or bend under use. A correct judgment of the effect of the work can only be gained by printing a proof occasionally as the work progresses. If the tints are made too light, the tint must be replaced by the use of the grounding-tool, by laying what is called a gauge ground over the defective part; that is, a ground produced by from five to seven crossings,—seldom more. The lights are then again produced by delicate scraping. If the dark parts of the picture need to be extended, the defect is remedied by puncturing a few rows of dots with the roulette, an instrument like a horseman's spur of minute proportions, and then removing the bur raised with a very sharp scraper. The process described belongs to simple mezzotint; but of late years a formation of etched lines and dots has been introduced before commencing the mezzotint ground. When this is done, the outline of the etching is faintly visible through the ground, and it need not be drawn with the burnisher. From the time of Tommaso Finiguerra, the Florentine goldsmith, who invented plate-printing in 1460, copper plate was chiefly used, until the introduction of plates of annealed or softened steel, about the year 1820, by which the application of mezzotint engraving was very widely extended.

Mill Boards or Milled Boards.—Thick, hard cardboard, used to form the sides of books, for mounting pictures, making boxes, and sometimes, when covered with white paper, for large printed cards.

Minerva Paper Cutter. —A paper cutter manufactured by Curtis and Mitchell, of Boston. It cuts thirty inches, and is recommended on account of its cheapness, great power, rapidity of operation, simplicity of construction, and its effectiveness in making a clean, smooth, and true cut.

Minion.—A size of type smaller than Brevier, and larger than Nonpareil.

Minionette.—A very small size of type, used chiefly in small ornamental borders.

Miscellany.—A collection of literary works or treatises; sometimes used as the title of a periodical publication containing miscellaneous articles. A publication called the Monthly Miscellany appeared in London in 1692.

Misprint.—An error in printing, caused either by accidents during the progress of press-work, by incorrect composition, or by mistakes in making-up a form. The most annoying and most frequent misprints in newspapers arise from the accidental transposition of lines, occasioned by the hurry in which they must be made up and sent to press, and the impossibility of careful revision.

Missal.—The book containing the prayers and ceremonies of the mass. These books were at an early day adorned with the utmost magnificence, and written upon vellum in the finest style of penmanship;

the great demand for such works caused them to become the model of the early printers, who endeavored to conform their types to the elegant writing of the scribes. Printed missals were issued both at Milan and Rome in 1475. John, Duke of Bedford, in the early part of the fifteenth century, was especially luxurious in his taste for books, and his missal has become famous both as a specimen of the art of the time and for its historic value. It was handsomely written upon vellum, and contained fifty-nine large and one thousand miniature pictures which have been accepted as authentic portraits, and as such used to illustrate histories of England. Many other missals have also supplied portraits. A missal belonging to Mary Queen of Scots, preserved in a Benedictine monastery in Flanders, is written on fine vellum, beautifully illustrated, and adorned with burnished gold. The book is covered with crimson velvet, with silver plates and clasps. Another missal which belonged to the same queen is in the Imperial Library of St. Petersburg; it is ten inches long, seven broad, and an inch and a half thick. It is written on rich vellum, highly illuminated with pictures of the saints, with inscriptions in Saxo-Latin; blank spaces left in various parts have been filled with private reflections written by Mary in prose and verse in the French language.

The word missal has been used by the Germans as the name of the largest-sized type, on account of large letters being frequently used in such works; and it is supposed that the French term canon, also used for a large type, has a similar origin; the English term primer has also been derived from primes, a prayer in the Roman Church.

Mitred Rules.—Rules which have their corners neatly joined, by being filed and carefully placed in their proper position.

Mitring Box.—A box used to facilitate the operation of cutting material that is to be mitred.

IRON MITRING BOX.

Mitring Machines.—Various machines made for the purpose of mitring rules neatly and accurately. By their use increased beauty and regularity are given to all work in which rules joined at corners are required. A brief description of some of the machines patented in this country will be found in the article on INVENTIONS, under the head MITRING MACHINES.

NEWBURY MITRING MACHINE.

PATENT UPRIGHT MITRING MACHINE.

PATENT MITRING MACHINE.

Modernized Old Style.—Types resembling those cut by Caslon in the early part of the eighteenth century, or the Elzevirian type, with slight modifications,—such as dispensing with the long s, etc. Of late years the demand for various faces of modernized old style has been very great, especially for books and magazines.

Monk.—A blotch of ink on a printed sheet, arising from insufficient distribution of the ink over the roller,—too much ink at one part of a form being called a monk, and too little being called a friar.

Monkey-Wrench.—A wrench or spanner having a movable jaw. It is frequently used in printing-offices which contain power-presses.

MONKEY-WRENCH.

Monody.—A mournful poem intended to express the lament of a single mourner. One of the finest illustrations is found in Lord Byron's Monody upon the death of Sheridan.

Monogram.—A character or cipher composed of one, two, or more letters interwoven, making an abbreviation of a name or the initials of a name. Monograms are found upon medals of the age of Philip of Macedon, and appeared only upon Greek coins. They formed the ornaments on seals, and thus became the customary impress upon legal documents, where they appear during the middle ages as the substitute for signatures. Monograms were assumed by artists and introduced into their works, and they have also been much used by engravers and printers. Book-publishers have adopted them for a trade-mark introduced into the title-page, and frequently impressed upon the binding; and a freak of fashion in modern times has made them a favorite adornment for writing-paper and envelopes.

Monograph.—A treatise upon a single subject in literature or science; frequently applied to scientific treatises prepared for learned societies.

Monument.—Any work of sculpture or architecture intended to transmit to posterity the memory of remarkable individuals or events. The monument to Gutenberg which adorns one of the public squares of Mentz, called Gutenberg Place, was executed by Thorwaldsen, the Danish sculptor, at Rome, in 1835, and cast in bronze at Paris. It was intended to erect the monument in 1836, to commemorate the four hundredth anniversary of the invention of movable type, but unexpected circumstances prevented, and the festival was postponed until August 14, 1837, when fifteen hundred strangers assembled in the city of Mentz, to do honor to the memory of Gutenberg. At eight o'clock in the morning a procession was formed, which moved with most respectful precision to the fine old cathedral, where high mass was performed by the Bishop of Mentz, and the first printed Bible displayed with the honor to which it is justly entitled. When the mass was ended, the procession proceeded to the adjacent square, where the deputations from all the great cities of Europe were seated in a vast amphitheatre, under their respective banners. The statue was unveiled amidst salvos of artillery, and a hymn was sung by a thousand voices. The festival was continued for three days. The statue is very handsome in its proportions, and graceful in its poise, Gutenberg standing with one foot slightly advanced, holding his Bible clasped to his breast with one hand, while several types are lightly grasped in the other. The peculiar robe or gown of the fifteenth century, with its fur collar, makes an effective drapery, together with the fur cap copied from authentic portraits. A series of bas-reliefs upon the pedestal exhibit the simple processes of the art in its earliest stages. In one where Gutenberg rests easily against the press, reading a printed sheet, and in another where he sits at a desk, examining a matrix, the figures display both vigor and grace. The inscription states that the monument was erected by the citizens of Mentz with the assistance of the whole of Europe.

In 1840 a statue of Gutenberg, by the celebrated French sculptor, David d'Anger, was erected in the market-place of Strasburg, now called La Place Gutenberg. The figure, full of life and spirit, stands erect proudly, holding forth a proof-sheet. Upon the pedestal four bas-reliefs illustrate the dissemination of knowledge by means of the printing-press, and on the front all the great authors of modern Europe are grouped about a printing-press; among them Shak-

speare, Dante, Bacon, Goethe, Corneille, and Voltaire are conspicuous.

A magnificent monument has been erected in the city of Frankfort. Upon a lofty pedestal of fine sandstone stand three colossal figures in bronze, the central figure being Gutenberg, with a type in his hand, while Schoeffer stands on his right, and Fust on his left. Four sitting figures upon separate pedestals represent Theology, Poetry, Natural Science, and Industry. Underneath these, four heads of beasts, representing the four quarters of the globe, serve as public fountains. Upon the central pedestal thirteen medallions contain the heads of celebrated printers.

In Haarlem a tablet has been placed upon the house in which Koster lived, containing, in Latin:—Typography, of all other arts the preserver, was here first invented about the year 1440. The citizens of Haarlem held a festival in 1823, as the four hundredth anniversary of Koster's invention, and placed a commemorative tablet in the wood where he is supposed to have first conceived the idea of carving letters upon beech bark. A statue of stone, painted white, stands on a pedestal in the market-place, representing Koster in a civic robe, and crowned with laurel, resting against a tree. His right hand holds an open book, and in the left, is a type with the letter A inscribed upon it. This statue was first erected in the Medical Garden at Haarlem.

Mordant.—Any substance which, having a twofold attraction for organic fibres and coloring matter, serves as a bond of union between them, and thus fixes dyes. Mordants are extensively used in calicoprinting, alum and copperas being two of the most common.

Mortise.—A cavity cut into a block or other material, and so arranged that new matter can be securely placed within it. Many wood-cuts, borders, rules, etc. are mortised for the use of printers,—the outer design remaining unchanged, while the lettering inside is frequently altered to suit varied purposes.

Motto.—A word or sentence added to a device, as the motto of John Day—Arise, for it is Day, or the E Pluribus Unum upon the American arms. The term is also applied to a sentence or quotation prefixed to a writing or publication.

Movable Types.—Types which, after being used in one line or page, can be distributed, and used again an infinite number of times, in forming new combinations of words, as distinguished from types cut together on a block, as in an engraving, which can be used only in one combination. The wordy controversies about the invention of printing, hinge on the point of who was the first to invent movable types, and a vast amount of erudition has been devoted to the championship of the rival claims of Gutenberg and Koster.

Moxon, Joseph.—An English mathematical instrument maker of the seventeenth century, who, during a portion of his life, cut punches used in type-founding, and who devoted one volume of a work entitled Mechanic Exercises, published in London in 1683, to printing. This was the first work in

FROM MOXON'S HISTORY OF PRINTING

Movable Types. Type which, after being used in one line or page, can be distributed and used again in future impressions of books, in forming new combinations, as well as distinguished from type set or cast or on a block as in an engraving, which can be used but once in combination. The wordy controversies waged over printing, turning on the point of views, as that to use movable types, and a vast amount of erudition has been devoted to the championship of the rival claims of Gutenberg and Koster.

Moxon, Joseph.—An English mathematical instrument maker of the seventeenth century, who, during a portion of his life, cut punches used in type-founding, and who devoted one volume of a work entitled Mechanic Exercises, published in London in 1683, to printing. This was the first work [on]

Case and Stand.

The manner of holding the Composing-Stick.

The manner of emptying a Stick of Letter.

Beating Balls.

Hanging up Sheets.

DUVAL & HUNTER, LITH PHILA

PICTURES FROM MOXON'S HISTORY OF PRINTING, 1683.

the English language relating to typographical literature, and, considering the remote period at which he wrote, it is one of the best. It is very rare, only three hundred copies having been originally printed. There are several in the United States, however, from one of which the illustrations representing the plan of the case used nearly two hundred years ago, the old method of making balls, and of hanging sheets, etc., have been copied for this volume. Moxon's work was well illustrated by a considerable number of good copper-plate pictures, and it abounds with quaint, terse, and faithful descriptions of the old method of printing, as will be seen by reference to the article ANCIENT CUSTOMS, which is extracted from it. Even in his day the modern tendency to a subdivision of labor had been so well developed, that he states that, —the number of founders and printers was grown so many, insomuch that, for the more easy management of typography, the operators had found it necessary to divide it into the several trades of the master-printer, the letter-cutter, the letter-caster, the letter-dresser, the compositor, the corrector, the pressman, and the ink-maker, besides several other trades, which they take into their assistance, as the smith, the joiner, etc.

M Paper.—Paper which is not quite up to the highest standard of the manufacturer, and which he prefers to sell under a general title as M, or em paper. The term probably denoted, originally, imperfect paper, and still implies inferiority, which, however, is generally so slight, that it can be noticed only by experts.

Muller.—A sort of pestle, usually of glass, used for grinding pigments used in ink, or in mixing them. (See INK-STONE AND MULLER.)

Music Type.—Among the products of Fust and Schoeffer was a Psalter representing the notes of the music of that day, but it was probably engraved, and not set from movable types. It was only during the last century that careful attention was devoted to the manufacture of type representing all the ramifications of printed music, and Breitkopf, of Leipsic, is credited with this invention. Type-founders, however, have gradually changed and improved the construction of music type from time to time, so that a series of great advances have been made. The following remarks on Music Composition, as well as the plan of music cases, are extracted from the American Printer:

A knowledge of the rudiments of music is essential to the correct and expeditious composition of music type; for, unless the compositor is acquainted with the relative time-values of the notes and rests, he cannot apportion them properly.

The manuscript copy is given to the compositor, with directions regarding the dimensions of the page required and the size of type to be employed. He counts the number of measures in the piece, and allots to each measure the amount of ems in length which the page will permit, so that there shall be a general equality of space throughout the piece.

In instrumental music, and in pieces which are not interlined with poetry, the compositor will set two or more staves simultaneously, ranging the leading notes in the under staves precisely under the corresponding ones in the upper staff; that is, a certain amount of space in each staff, in a brace must contain the same quantity of time-value. Where lines of poetry are interspersed, as in ballads and in church music, the staves are necessarily set singly; and in composing the second staff the workman must therefore constantly refer to the first, in order to make the staves correspond, proceeding in like manner with the third and fourth.

A good compositor will be careful to make the lines overlap each other, brick-wise, and not allow a joint to fall directly under another. Masters who aim to do cheap rather than good work have the music lines cast double or triple, to expedite composition. Such work has a very slovenly look, as the joints of the lines, coming under one another, are apparent in the entire depth of the staff. We have seen books set in this manner, in which all the lines seem to be composed of dotted rule, instead of a continuous stroke.

The compositor should be careful to make the stems of all the notes in a page of the same length, except those of grace-notes, which should be about half as long as the stems of the other notes.

Plan of Cases.—The plan of cases represented is adapted to MacKellar, Smiths and Jordan's Diamond Music No. 1, but, modified, will serve generally for the other new styles. The figures refer to the number of the characters, as printed in the music scheme furnished with fonts. (See pages 310 and 311.)

Mutton Quad.—A slang term, in English printing-offices, for em quad. It is rarely used in American offices.

N.

Naked Form.—A form without furniture.

Napier, D.—An English press manufacturer, who improved the power-press invented by Koenig by simplifying its construction and increasing its efficiency. He was specially successful in adapting it to newspaper work and in devising a perfecting machine. He obtained English patents dated 1825 and 1830, and his presses, or others of similar construction, were formerly famous in this country as well as in England, because they were used by several American newspaper establishments before satisfactory power-presses were manufactured in the United States.

Natural History.—The history of all the productions of nature, animal, vegetable, and mineral. Natural science and history form a large portion of the mass of written literature, and are especially important in typography as embracing many of the largest and handsomest books ever printed. In England works upon natural history were abundantly illustrated, and Bewick, the father of the modern improvements in wood-engraving, became widely known for the works now known as Bewick's Birds, etc. In America the works of S. G. Goodrich upon these subjects are very popular; and the publications in Germany, France, England, and animal, vegetable, and mineral. This department of knowledge, particularly of late years, has opened the widest domain for illustrated works, and many of the most magnificent books ever printed contain treatises upon these sciences, and the resources of illustration

MUSIC UPPER CASE.

MUSIC LOWER CASE.

America upon natural history are countless in number, and embrace many of the greatest triumphs of modern typography.

Natural Science.—Those branches of science which treat of the three kingdoms of nature, the have been lavished upon them in all kinds of engraving, lithography, photography, nature-printing, and color-printing. Many works upon ornithology have been especially splendid, as the brilliant hues and delicate forms of birds have given especial opportunity to the artist; books upon botany and its many subdivisions have been also very handsome. Nature-printing has recently been applied with great success, as in the splendid works published upon the ferns of Austria, and of Great Britain, etc. Audubon's Birds and Cassin's Ornithology may be cited as fine illustrations, also the plates accompanying the Reports of the Government Exploring Expeditions.

Nature-Printing.—A method of producing impressions of plants and other natural objects, in a manner so truthful that only a close inspection reveals the fact of their being copies. So deeply sensible to the touch are the impressions, that it is difficult to persuade those who are unacquainted with the manipulation that they are the production of the printing-press. The process, in its application to the reproduction of botanical subjects, represents an extensive scale in the Austrian Imperial Printing-Office.

The plant, perfectly dry, is placed on a plate of fine rolled lead, the surface of which has been polished by planing. The plate and subject are then passed between rollers, by the pressure of which the subject is forced into the surface of the lead. The leaden plate is then subjected to a moderate heat, by the action of which the subject is loosened from its bed and easily removed. This mould is then subjected to the galvano-plastic process, the second cast being a perfect fac-simile of the leaden mould. When the subject to be printed is of one color only, that pigment is rubbed in, and any superfluity removed; but when it is of two or more colors, the process is simple, but, it is believed, perfectly novel in any process of printing heretofore practiced. In the

MUSIC SIDE CASE.

the size, form, and color of the plant, and all its most minute details, even to the smallest fibres of the roots. The distinguishing feature of the process, compared with other modes of producing engraved surfaces for printing purposes, consists, first, in imprinting natural objects—such as plants, mosses, sea-weeds, feathers, and embroideries—into plates of metal, causing the objects to engrave themselves by pressure; and, secondly, in being able to take such casts or copies of the impressed plates as can be printed from at the ordinary copper-plate press.

The art is by no means new in idea, many persons having attempted something analogous to the present process, and produced results which were imperfect, merely because science had not yet discovered an art necessary to its practical development. It is to the discovery of electrotyping that the existing art of nature-printing is due, and it was first practiced on case, for instance, of flowering plants, having stems, roots, leaves, and flowers, the plan adopted in the inking of the plate is to apply the darkest color, which generally happens to be that of the roots, first; the superfluous color is cleaned off; the next darkest color, such, perhaps, as that of the stems, is then applied, the superfluous color of which is also cleaned off; this mode is continued until every part of the plant in the copper plate has received the right tint. In this state, before the plate is printed, the color in the different parts of the copper looks as if the plant were imbedded in the metal. The plate thus charged, with the paper laid over it, is placed upon a copperplate press, the upper roller of which is covered with five or six layers of blanket of compact fine texture. The effect of the pressure is, that all the colors are printed by one impression; for when the paper is removed the plant is seen quite perfect, highly embossed, with the roots, stems, and other parts, each of its proper tint.

Nautical Almanac.—The American Ephemeris and Nautical Almanac was commenced, in conformity with an act of Congress, in 1849, but the great amount of preliminary labor and the smallness of the first appropriations delayed its appearance, and the first volume, for the year 1855, was not published until 1852; since which time a volume has been issued annually, two years before the actual date. To prevent confusion, the arrangement of the British Almanac is adopted, the astronomical part of the work being calculated from the meridian of Washington. The British Nautical Almanac was begun in the year 1767, and has been continued annually, being published two or three years in advance of its actual date. The similar French publication called Connoissance des Temps was commenced in 1698.

part of advertisements, such as small pictures of houses, horses, pianos, ships, etc.

Newspapers.—A law of Congress, governing the decisions of the Post-Office Department, defines a newspaper to be any printed publication issued in numbers, consisting of not more than two sheets, and published at short stated intervals of not more than one month, conveying intelligence of passing events.

The title of many early newspapers contained a picture of a compass, on which were inscribed the letters N. E. W. S., as abbreviations of North, East, West, South, from which circumstance it has been conjectured that the term newspapers came to be applied to such publications. But the word news or newes was used in its present sense before English newspapers were printed; the publications preceding regularly printed newspapers, which related to current events, were frequently styled news or newes from the differ-

NEWBURY COUNTRY PRESS.

Newbury Country Press.—A cheap press intended for country newspaper, book, and job work, the size of bed being 31 by 46 inches, which is manufactured by A. & B. Newbury, Coxsackie, New York. It can be run by hand or by steam, and is said to do good work.

Newbury Paper Cutter.—A cheap paper cutter, warranted to be good, which is manufactured by A. & B. Newbury, Coxsackie, N. Y. (See page 313).

Newspaper Folding Machines.—Machines to fold newspapers are extensively used by daily newspaper establishments. For a description of one of them, see FORSAITH FOLDING MACHINE. A newspaper folder is also manufactured by Chambers & Bros., of Philadelphia. (See page 313).

Newspaper Cuts.—Electrotypes for the use of newspapers, and especially those intended to form

ent countries to which their contents referred; and the first regularly published English newspaper was styled Certain News of the Week, etc.: so that newspapers probably owe their present name to the fact that it was a convenient word for distinguishing them from ballads, books, and pamphlets. The official newspaper, first known to Europe by the publication issued by the Republic of Venice, was called Gazetta, or Gazette, and this term became, for a time, a common title for all newspapers. Three derivations of the word are given:—one, being to the effect that the price paid for reading or hearing the news from this source was an old coin, called the gazetta; another, that the name is derived from gazzera, meaning a magpie, or chatterer; and another, that it originated in the Latin word gaza, which when colloquially lengthened into gazetta would signify a little treasury

CHAMBERS NEWSPAPER FOLDING MACHINE.

NEWBURY PAPER CUTTER.

of news. The latter theory is accepted by the Spaniards, and is probably correct. The favorite German word Zeitung is, in derivation and meaning, equivalent to the English word tiding or tidings; so that the English, Italian, Spanish, and Germans have, by common consent, applied to newspapers a title descriptive of their contents,—by calling them either newspapers, little treasuries of news, or tidings. Long before the invention of printing, the Acta Diurna, a manuscript sheet issued at Rome, embraced many of the features of modern newspapers. (See ACTA DIURNA.) Soon after the Chinese invented printing, they established an official gazette, which was the first newspaper ever printed, and it has continued, through a long succession of centuries, to systematically publish an official record or registry, announcing such changes in office as occur from time to time, and giving such items of intelligence relating to laws, taxation, or public events, as the government desires to communicate to the people. This Chinese newspaper is printed at Peking. It is called King-Chau, or Court Transcripts, but is commonly termed by Europeans the Peking Gazette, and its contents are compiled from the proceedings of the general council of the Empire. Anybody is permitted to reprint or transcribe it without note or change, and in the provinces many persons find employment in copying and abridging it for sale to those who cannot afford to purchase a complete edition. Thus the Chinese newspaper is made up solely of matter analogous to that contained in the regular Associated Press dispatches from Washington, so far as Chinese matter of any kind can resemble the contents of American newspapers.

The Germans were the first European people to apply printing to the dissemination of current intelligence or the discussion of current questions; but even among them no such application of the art is known to have been attempted until near the close of the fifteenth century; and the first modern European approximation to the newspaper was the gazette issued by the Venetian Republic during a war which it commenced in 1563, against Solyman II., in Dalmatia; but although these gazettes contained military and commercial information, which was read at a fixed place or places by those who desired to learn the news, they were written and not printed, and continued for many years to be circulated in manuscript, notwithstanding the recognized utility and employment of the art of printing in the production of books. Singular as is this long-continued avoidance, in Venice, of the use of type and the press for the chief purpose to which they are now applied, a similar state of things occurred in England, for the people of Great Britain were principally supplied with such news as they received during a large portion of the eventful seventeenth century, by written news-letters, rather than by printed newspapers.

The first European attempts to establish printed and regularly published newspapers were made nearly simultaneously, in the early part of the seventeenth century, in Germany, France, and England. The first German newspaper, in numbered sheets, was printed in 1612. It was called Account of what has happened in Germany and Italy, Spain and France, the East and West Indies, etc. The first French newspaper was established at Paris, in 1632, by Renaudot, a physician, famous for his skill in collecting news to amuse his patients.

The first English newspaper was established in London, by Nathaniel Butter, in 1622. It was a small quarto of eighteen pages, called the "Certain News of the Present Week," and the editor or publisher solicited subscribers, by the following advertisement, at the end of his publication:

If any gentleman, or other accustomed to buy the *weekly* relations of newes, be desirous to continue the same, let them know that the writer, or transcriber rather of *this newes*, hath published two former *newes*, the one dated the second, the other the thirteenth of August, all which do carry a like title, with the arms of the King of Bohemia on the other side of the title-page, and have dependence one upon another: which manner of writing and printing he doth purpose to continue weekly, by God's assistance, from the best and most certain intelligence. Farewell, this *twenty-three* of August, 1622.

This is considered the first English newspaper, because it was the first publication of news which the editor publicly proposed to continue regularly. It had been preceded, however, by a number of transient publications, in London, descriptive of current events in various countries, two of which related to the American colonies. One of the latter, printed May 3, 1622, was called a Courant of Newes from Virginia, and other places; and another, issued June 19, 1622, was styled Newes from New England, by John Bellamie. Although copies of the English Mercurie in the British Museum, purporting to be printed in 1588, and to be the first English newspapers, are now considered, on good authority, literary forgeries, yet the forger, after all, only attempted to reproduce what probably had once a real existence, for an old English writer says that in the days of Queen Elizabeth papers were printed relating to affairs in France, Spain, and Holland, and as early as 1579 a small transient publication appeared which was called Newe Newes, contayning a Short Rehersall of Stukeley and Morice's Rebellion.

Nathaniel Butter continued his weekly newspaper

for several years before a rival appeared in the Mercurius Britannicus; but meanwhile he apparently provoked the ire of some of the wits of his time, either because the newspaper may have seemed to them likely to supplant, in a slight degree, the drama, or because it may have interfered with their occupation as writers of news-letters; for Ben Jonson's play, entitled The Staple of News, written in 1625, attempts to ridicule the mode of manufacturing news, and the following passage from it is supposed to be a direct attack upon the adventurous Butter, who was the sole editor of the period:

Cymb. We not forbid that any News he made,
But that be *printed ;* for when News is printed,
It leaves, sir, to be Nowes, while 'tis but written—
Fitt. Though it be ne'er so false, it runs News still.
P. jun. See divers men's opinions ! unto some
The very *printing* of them makes the Newes ;
That ha' not the heart to believe anything
But what they see in *print.*
Fitt. Aye, that's an error
Has abused many ; but we shall reform It,
As many things beside (we have a hope)
Are crept among the popular abuses.
Cymb. Nor shall the stationer cheat upon the time,
By *buttering* over again—
Fitt. Once in seven years,
As the age deals,
Cymb. And grows forgetful o' them—
His antiquated pamphlets, with new dates.

The exciting contest between the Puritans and Cavaliers, that finally brought Charles I. to the scaffold, led to the publication of many news pamphlets, and to the establishment of a number of newspapers. It also developed the political organ, and gave birth to the first influential political editor in the person of Marchmont Needham, who, after savagely attacking the king and court for a time, became an energetic champion of royalty, and subsequently deserted the king, when his fortunes waned, to become again an earnest advocate of the party of Cromwell and the Commonwealth. One of his effusions, during the interval in which he wrote in the interest of the royalists, was as follows:

When as we liv'd in Peace (God wot)
  A King would not content us,
But we (for sooth) must hire the Scot
  To all-be-Parliament us.

Then down went King and Bishops too,
  On goes the holy works,
Betwixt them and the Brethren blow,
  T' advance the Crowne and Kirke.

But when that these had reign'd a time,
  Rob'd Kirke and sold the Crowne,
A more Religious sort up climbe,
  And crush the Jockies down.

But now we must have Peace againe,
  Let none with feare be vext;
For, if without the King these reigne,
  Then heigh down they goe next.

But, despite a somewhat extensive newspaper development in England during the seventeenth century, which was stimulated by the long war of factions, the repressive laws enacted after the Restoration, the subservient severity of the judges, and the jealous tyranny of James II., crushed out utterly all these early efforts, and at the close of his reign the sole English newspaper was a strictly official organ called the London Gazette. It was a servile imitation of the Chinese Court Transcripts. It was edited by a clerk of the Secretary of State, and contained nothing which he did not wish to communicate. Macaulay, in describing it, says: It came out only on Mondays and Thursdays. The contents generally were a royal proclamation, two or three Tory addresses, notices of two or three promotions, an account of a skirmish between the Imperial troops and the Janizaries on the Danube, a description of a highwayman, an announcement of a grand cock-fight between two persons of honor, and an advertisement offering a reward for a strayed dog. The whole made up two pages of moderate size. Whatever was communicated respecting matter of the highest moment was communicated in a meagre and formal style. . . . The most important Parliamentary debates, the most important state trials recorded in our history, were passed over in profound silence. In the capital the coffee-house supplied, in some measure, the place of a journal. Thither the Londoners flocked, as the Athenians of old flocked to the market-place to hear whether there was any news. . . . But people who lived at a distance from the great theatre of political contention could be kept regularly informed of what was passing there only by means of news-letters. To prepare such letters became a calling in London, as it now is among the natives of India. The news-writer rambled from coffee-room to coffee-room collecting reports, squeezed himself into the Sessions House at the Old Bailey if there was an interesting trial, nay, perhaps obtained admission to the gallery of Whitehall, and noticed how the king and duke looked. In this way he gathered materials for weekly epistles destined to enlighten some country town or some band of rustic magistrates. . . . At the seat of a man of fortune in the country the news-letter was impatiently expected. Within a week after it had arrived it had been thumbed by twenty families. It furnished the neighboring squires with matter for talk over their october, and the neighboring rectors with topics for sharp sermons against Whiggery or Popery.

It seems almost incredible that more than two hundred years after Caxton had exercised the art of printing in England, her citizens were still compelled to rely upon letter-writers for their scanty supplies of genuine news. This result was due not to any lack of intelligence or enterprise among the printers, but to the tyrannical spirit of the government, and the inherent difficulties of publishing, regularly, a newspaper which a government is determined to suppress. Freedom is one of the necessities of its existence. It must proclaim the place where it is printed, and all the mechanical and literary labors involved in its preparation must be performed with

unvarying promptness—so that, even when arbitrary governments fail utterly to suppress free letter-writing and the occasional publication of anonymous pamphlets, they find no difficulty in suppressing obnoxious newspapers. During the very century that English kings crushed out daring journalism they were frequently baffled by printers of pamphlets containing violent and scurrilous attacks upon their doctrines or their dynasties; and while James II. had suppressed all newspapers save his government organ, his successor found it impossible to suppress the adverse ballads, pamphlets, and books of the Jacobites, which were issued in underground printing-offices, where precautions against detection and arrest were adopted similar to those used at the present day by those who print counterfeit money.

After newspapers had once gained a strong hold in public favor, however, as they did in England during the closing years of the seventeenth and in the eighteenth century; after a gradual change in the British constitution prevented a resort to purely arbitrary methods of destroying them in England; and after they had survived the stamp tax imposed by Queen Anne, a long series of battles were waged before juries, between successive English administrations and different newspaper proprietors, until finally, despite many unjust convictions, the freedom of fair newspaper comment on public questions has been finally established in England as the result of a series of parliamentary and legal contests lasting for more than two centuries.

The home policy of the British government during the latter portion of the seventeenth century was reflected in this country by the summary suppression of the first newspaper in the United States, and in the determined opposition of a Cavalier governor of Virginia to the establishment of a printing-press in that colony. The governor of New York, in 1690, graciously caused a reprint of the London Gazette, containing the details of a battle with the French, to be issued, which was probably the first thing resembling a newspaper ever printed in the present limits of the United States; but when Benjamin Harris issued, in Boston, on the 25th of September, 1690, a sheet of four small pages, one of which was blank, containing a record of passing occurrences, foreign and domestic, the legislative authorities at once prohibited future publications of a similar character, on the ground that it contained reflections of a very high nature, and because nothing whatever could be printed without a license previously obtained.

As newspapers multiplied in England after 1695, in consequence of a relaxation of some of the worst of the old restrictions, it was natural that the second newspaper venture in this country, especially as it was issued by an official, John Campbell, the postmaster at Boston, should also be tolerated. It was called the Boston News-Letter, and the first number appeared on Monday, April 24, 1704. It was printed on half a sheet of paper, being only about twelve inches by eight, and was made up in two pages, with two columns on each page, and so meagre were its contents that it was only after publishing a dull sheet of these contracted dimensions weekly, for nearly fifteen years, that the publisher proposed issuing it on a whole sheet, for the alleged reason that he found it impossible with half a sheet a week to carry on all the Publick News of Europe. A rival newspaper, called the Boston Gazette, was established in December, 1719, by a new postmaster, who represented Campbell; but it was only in the third newspaper of the United States, the New England Courant, established by James Franklin in 1721, that signs of live journalism in this country were developed; the Courant, under the management of James Franklin, assisted by his immortal brother Benjamin, being the first American newspaper that gave any signs of vigor or energy, or that was anything more than a dry rehash of safe and staple news. The Franklins speedily became embroiled, not only with their newspaper predecessor, Campbell, but with the clergy and the civil authorities, and, James being forbidden to continue his publication, it was published in the name of young Ben, then an apprentice in his teens, nominally on his own account, but really for his brother.

The single life of Benjamin Franklin practically embraces an epitome of American journalism from its first establishment until a period subsequent to the Revolution. His earliest effusions appeared in the New England Courant, and in his early manhood he established, in Philadelphia, the Pennsylvania Gazette, which continued for a long period to be the leading journal of the continent. But it is a noticeable feature of the condition of the press during the last century, that notwithstanding the prominence of Franklin's journal, and his extraordinary talent as a writer, few traces are left of his influence as an editor. He was content to publish a newspaper,—rarely or never seeking to influence public opinion by editorials. When he discussed grave questions, it was generally either in pamphlets or in communications; and a very large share of the vast influence he exercised was personal, arising from his official positions and his direct intercourse with the leading men of his time.

About the middle of the last century, however, a printer of New York was successfully defended in a prosecution for an alleged libel, which consisted of strictures upon the existing authorities; and this circumstance exerted a powerful influence in enfranchising the whole colonial press,—so that it was comparatively free to perform its great mission of awakening, strengthening, and consolidating the patriotic spirit of the American colonies. If there were comparatively few elaborate editorials, there was an abundance of pungent paragraphs, a series of incessant efforts to promptly apprise the people of every new form of aggression, and a very general republication of communications written by leading patriots, and of all telling attacks upon the oppressive policy of the mother-country. Tory journals, on the other

hand, which were sustained by government patronage, attempted to defend George III., his ministers, and his colonial governors, and, on a mimic scale, with a limited number of accessories, and before a comparatively small but intensely interested body of readers, a contest was conducted, similar, in many respects, to those which now occur during every Presidential campaign.

As the war waxed hot and fierce, its varying fortunes compelled the suspension, in one quarter, of Whig newspapers, and in another, of the organs of Toryism. But of the latter there were comparatively few, for in this, as in all similar well-defined contests, the bulk of the press, instinctively and necessarily, sided with the cause of freedom,—a devotion to popular rights, or what can, with a certain degree of plausibility, be made to appear the interest of a people, being essential to the life of all journals that are not sustained by official patronage. And patriotism was such a general attribute of the American country printer of the last century, that Freneau truly described him as one who

—— in his time, the patriot of his town,
  With press and pen attacked the royal side;
Did what he could to pull their Lion down,
  Clipped at his beard, twitched his sacred hide,
Mimicked his roarings, trod upon his toes,
Pelted young whelps, and tweaked the old one's nose.

Roused by his page, at church or court-house read,
  From depth of woods the willing rustics ran,
Now by a priest, and now some deacon led,
  With clubs and spits to guard the rights of man;
Lads from the spade, the pickaxe, or the plough,
Marching afar, to fight Burgoyne or Howe.

Meanwhile, although the Continental press continued to be enchained by censorship, the newspapers of England made steady strides towards independence. Wilkes, under the shield afforded by his position as a member of Parliament, attacked the British administration unmercifully, in the North Briton; and the letters of Junius, by their scathing invectives, astounding disclosures, and the universal interest they awakened, gave the people of England a foretaste of the coming power of journalism. There is little doubt now that these letters were written by Sir Philip Francis, at a time when he held an official position of considerable importance in the government he denounced with such matchless ability and unsparing severity. It is worthy of note, that the newspaper in which they originally appeared did not venture, on its own responsibility, to express similar opinions, and that, probably to ward off prosecutions, it simultaneously published energetic and abusive replies to Junius, as well as slavish eulogies of the men and measures he assailed.

In France, during the turmoil of the last century, newspapers also became, for the first time in her history, vehicles of free political discussion. In the upheaval of the old social and governmental system, many of the active men who aspired to power sought to gain it through the lever of the press; and Marat, through his newspaper, became the apostle of the Revolution. But the new-born liberty of writers, editors, and printers was so fearfully and dangerously abused, that the clear evidence furnished in Paris of the terribly bad uses to which free and unrestrained printing might be applied, and of the perils with which it might environ all interests, led to a reaction against the newspapers among timid and conservative men in Great Britain, and even in the United States. English juries became willing to convict editors of seditious libels whenever they dared to indulge in what would now be considered tame criticisms, and in this country the Alien and Sedition Law established, for a brief period, a similar system, under which there were a few similar convictions. For a time it seemed that even at the close of the eighteenth century, three hundred and fifty years after Gutenberg had commenced his labors at Mentz, the art of printing could not yet, in any locality, be freely applied to the production of a newspaper. But after a few intensely unpopular attempts to enforce the Alien and Sedition law it was repealed, and succeeded by Thomas Jefferson's liberal policy of encouraging the press, and of leaving truth to wage a free fight with error; while in England convictions for seditious publications gradually became more and more difficult.

After the freedom of the press was well established, newspapers rapidly multiplied in number, in circulation, and in the scope of their contents. In their infancy their mission was confined chiefly to a publication of news from distant or remote countries (exciting domestic topics being carefully avoided), or to a reprint of official news. When they ventured to treat public questions at all, they acted strictly in the interest of one or two powerful parties, or of some potent leader, able to protect them against censorship, sedition laws, and libel suits. During the last century the preparation of editorials or original leading articles formed no part of the regular duties of the editor. It was his business to collate the news,—more especially that arriving from foreign countries,—to keep open a poets' corner,—and to give place to such essays or communications as the wits or the politicians were gracious enough to contribute gratuitously to his columns. Local items were nearly unknown, the proceedings of important public assemblages were not reported, money articles had not been invented, and so much of the essence and life of all vigorous modern journals was lacking that it is scarcely surprising that a newspaper in those days would have been a curiosity in many households. At best, it was a thing of limited utility,—a luxury rather than a necessity,—and so small a proportion of the masses had been educated, that comparatively few could read. It was only by slow degrees that new attractions were added to journalism. A monthly magazine, which was rather a newspaper, however, than a magazine, in the sense in which that term is now used, ventured at last to report an abstract of the speeches of the British Parliament.

Editors slowly began to aspire to something better than stale compilations of foreign news. A few men of real talent were at last employed to write for the newspapers in the interest of the public, their contributions being paid for in sterling coin. The scope of advertising columns was enlarged, until they became a source of general interest. Able and vigorous editorials, on not merely partisan but on other topics, were written. And, strangest of all, a few adventurous publishers were finally emboldened to expend such large sums in obtaining intelligence of important events that they outstripped the swiftest government couriers, and became the instructors of the heads as well as the masses of great nations. Subscribers and readers multiplied. The old handpress, despite the duplication of forms and astonishing alacrity on the part of hand-pressmen, could no longer supply the demand for journals which excited such universal interest, and the newspapers, after making headway for so many years against ignorance, oppression, and prejudice, were threatened with a limitation of the sphere of their utility by mechanical obstacles. Other portions of this work describe how this danger was averted. A number of inventors, endowed with brilliant genius, and a series of enterprising press-manufacturers, type-founders, paper-makers, etc., have conquered each new difficulty as it arose, and the skill displayed in their conquests, together with the astonishing results achieved, form the grandest chapter in the history of printing.

Each new mechanical facility supplied to newspapers enlarged their sphere, cheapened their cost, and increased their attractions, until now they wellnigh absorb all other forms of printing, and embody every description of intellectual effort. As advertising mediums, their value cannot be overestimated, and they are indispensable thermometers and barometers of the whole business world. As collectors and distributors of news, their daily achievements outstrip the wildest dreams of the human imagination, and their success in telling the current history of the world, currently, to all the world is the greatest of modern marvels. The gist of the musty record of the past, so far as it is applicable to the present, is placed at the service of the newspaper reader whenever it is needed. The most carefully guarded secrets affecting public interests are disclosed. The greatest questions are discussed with freedom, and often with profound ability, by the press. It rarely fails to foreshadow every measure and event of real significance. In this country, especially, newspapers have exerted a boundless influence. They have made and destroyed countless reputations, elevated and deposed innumerable officials, furnished an indispensable prerequisite to genuine popular government, raised immeasurably the standard of civilization, diffusing far and wide its blessings, and, in view of their expanding power, he would be a bold man who would venture to affix a limit to their future achievements.

News-Work or **Newspaper Work.**—That branch of printing which is confined exclusively to newspapers. As they must be printed at a given time, punctuality and expedition are absolutely essential on daily journals, and the necessary labors on weekly journals must also be completed at regular stated intervals. On the morning newspapers, the compositors usually distribute their letter and set up a small amount of matter during the afternoon; but the question has lately been discussed whether it would not be better for all concerned to set no copy during the day, and it is contended that under this plan the compositor would be in better condition for his arduous nightly toil. The hands are usually divided into sub-organizations, commonly called crowds, all of whom work during the hours when copy is most plentiful, while usually only one crowd is retained for the late hours (often prolonged to two or three A. M.), when important copy may or may not arrive. During the period when the hands are required to be in the office they charge for such time, whether they are actually setting type or not, and out of this rule the practice originated of supplying them at such periods with what is termed punjob or punjaub, that is, copy of doubtful value, relating to stale or indifferent topics, which may or may not be printed. The foreman and one or more assistant foremen, who make up the newspaper, give out copy, etc., are paid for their labor by the week, while the compositors are all paid by the piece, or by the thousand ems of matter set up, and the amount of time (if any) which can properly be entered in a weekly bill. The labors on a morning newspaper are so exhausting that many compositors absent themselves from their accustomed posts on one or more nights every week; and to provide for such contingencies, as well as to have an available force at hand when an unusually large amount of copy is to be set up, many substitutes, or subs, are employed,—it being understood that whenever a regular hand is off duty he shall provide a sub to take his place during his temporary absence. Some compositors are employed during a large portion of their time, for a series of years, as subs, in various offices, without ever holding a steady situation. In some departments of a newspaper there is more fat (that is, larger wages can be earned in a given time) than in others, and it is customary to regulate the distribution of these profitable departments of work so that each hand may in turn receive a fair share. Speed being one of the most important qualifications of a news-hand, alike to himself and to his employer, newspaper work has tended to develop a race of rapid compositors, whose performances would astonish the printers of former times (see FAST TYPE-SETTING), and the abundance of newspaper work has also multiplied the number of printers whose labors have been confined so exclusively to plain newspaper composition that they are unskilled in all other branches of typography. Daily afternoon newspaper work is managed in much the same manner as the work on morning dailies, but the hours of labor are reversed, and there is often greater necessity for punctuality in getting the forms to press, as well as greater trouble in changing the forms for a succession of new editions. (See MAKING UP).

Nicholson, William.—An English author, inventor, and patent-agent, who, on the 29th of April, 1790, obtained a patent for a machine or instrument for printing on paper, linen, cotton, woolen, and other articles,—which embraces the first suggestion of self-acting, power, or machine presses. Although Nicholson never made a working machine, his failure to do so seems to have been due chiefly to a series of unpropitious circumstances, and to a waste of his practical efforts in attempts to accomplish what was one of the latest feats of modern times,—the task of curving type round a cylinder somewhat in the manner in which they are adjusted in the turtles used in the six-, eight-, and ten-cylinder Hoe presses. He imagined that, to accomplish this purpose, it would be necessary to have type cast or finished in a peculiar manner, and one of the specifications of his patent claims as part of his invention a mode of manufacturing type whereby provision is made for chamfering or sloping their tails, so that they may be firmly imposed upon a cylindrical surface, in the same manner as common letter is imposed upon a flat stone. Nicholson, for the age in which he lived, aimed at too much, rather than too little; and his patent probably covered a wider range of subjects, and embraced more original ideas, than any other single patent applicable to printing that was ever granted. Although this extensive claim was barren of direct results, Savage, in his Dictionary of Printing, published in 1841, defends Nicholson from the imputation of being a weak or visionary man. He says: I knew Mr. Nicholson personally, and I have no doubt that, had he lived, he would have carried his invention into effect; but he had a number of other pursuits which occupied his time. He published a work on navigation, which I have seen quoted as authority for its opinions; he was the author of a Dictionary of Chemistry, in two quarto volumes; he edited and published, monthly, Nicholson's Journal of Science, which was in high repute; he wrote the prospectus of the Royal Institution, on its establishment in 1799; and he likewise kept a large school in Soho Square, the leading feature of which was a scientific education. . . . . . In addition to his multifarious pursuits, he was agent to the late Lord Camelford, whose sudden death left Mr. Nicholson involved in difficulties from which he could never extricate himself.

It is said by one of Koenig's biographers, that when Koenig secured Nicholson's services as a patent-agent in obtaining a patent for his printing-machine, Nicholson said that he had patented a similar device seventeen years before, and that it wouldn't do.

The gist of that portion of Nicholson's patent which relates to the press or printing-machine is contained in the eighth clause, viz.:

I perform all my impressions by the action of a cylinder or cylindrical surface; that is to say, I cause the paper or cloth, or other material intended to be printed upon (and previously dampened if necessary), to pass between two cylinders, or segments of cylinders, in equal motion; one of which has the block, form, plate, assemblage of types, or originals, attached to, or forming part of, its surface, and the other is faced with cloth or leather, and serves to press the paper, cloth, or other material, as aforesaid, so as to take off an impression of the color previously applied, or otherwise. I cause the block, form, plate, assemblage of types, or originals, previously colored, to pass in close and successive pressure or contact with the paper, or cloth, or other material, wrapped round a cylinder with woolen. Or otherwise, I cause the last-mentioned cylinder, with the paper, or cloth, or other material wrapped round it, to roll along the face of the block, form, plate, assemblage of type, or originals, previously colored. Or otherwise, I cause a cylinder having the block, form, plate, assemblage of types, or originals, attached to, or forming part of, its surface, to roll along the surface of the paper, cloth, or other material intended to be printed, and previously spread out upon an even plane covered with cloth or leather; the said cylinder being supplied with color by means of a coloring-cylinder.

Nick.—A hollow, cast crosswise in the shank of the types, to enable the compositor to make a distinction between different fonts of type in distribution, and, in composition, to perceive readily the bottom of the letter as it lies in the case, as the nicks are always cast on that side of the shank on which the bottom of the face is placed. Printers should be careful to stipulate that the nick of each font should be different, more especially fonts of the same body; for a great deal of inconvenience frequently arises from the founders casting different fonts of type with a similar nick in each. Although this may, at the first sight, appear of little moment, yet it is attended with much trouble; and works are frequently disfigured in consequence, notwithstanding all the care of the compositor and the reader. For instance, where the nicks are similar, a compositor, in distributing head-lines, lines of Italic, small capitals, or small jobs, in the hurry of business, or through inadvertency or carelessness, frequently distributes them into wrong cases, when it is almost impossible for another compositor, who has occasion to use these cases next, to detect the error; and, with all the attention that the reader can bestow, a letter of the wrong font will now and then escape his eye, and disfigure the page. Even in fonts that are next in size to each other—for instance, Bourgeois and Long Primer, Long Primer and Small Pica, Small Pica and Pica, and Pica and English—head-lines, etc. are not unfrequently distributed into wrong cases, where the nick is the same; which always occasions loss of time in correcting the mistakes, and sometimes passes undiscovered. By going as far as three or four nicks, a sufficient variety may be obtained to distinguish one font from another without hesitation. Where there are a great number of fonts, it would add to the distinguishing mark, if consisting of more than one nick, should one of them be cast shallow; but where there is only one

nick, it ought always to be cast deep. In Russia, Poland, and some parts of Germany, the nick is placed on the reverse side of the letter, viz., the back of the type, it being considered by the printers of those countries an advantage in composing.

Niello.—A style of ornamentation upon silver and gold, used before the introduction of the modern method of printing from metal plates, and supposed to have been the origin of the art of copper-plate engraving. The Italian goldsmiths of the early part of the fifteenth century filled the sunken lines of engraved plates, both of gold and silver, with an indestructible black enamel; the surface of the metal was then burnished, and the design appeared upon it drawn in the lustrous black. It is stated that Tommaso Finiguerra, an artist in niello, when wishing to test the appearance of his work before completing it, filled the lines, as an experiment, with a mixture of oil and lampblack, and a pile of wet linen, having fallen accidentally upon the plate, received a printed impression of the design. This discovery led Finiguerra to attempt a like effect with damp paper. The whole method of copper-plate engraving was thus discovered, but was used by the artists for a considerable time merely as a means of testing the progress of their work.

Nimbus.—The circle of light around the heads of divinities, saints, and sovereigns in medals, pictures, etc.; it is often called the glory or halo. When the rays encircle the head merely, it is styled the nimbus; but when the light envelops the whole body, it is termed an aureola.

Nipper Gauge.—The adjustable gauge or gauges resting on the tongues of the feed-board of power-presses, used to give the proper head or side margin to the form, according to its position on the bed of the press.

Nippers.—The appliances used to grasp the sheet after being fed to the gauges, and to hold it in position until after the impression is received. On large power-presses the nippers are curved, and attached to the nipper shaft by means of set screws, so that they can be shifted to any position on the shaft. On some smaller presses a long, thin piece of iron is used for the same purpose, and attached to a frame on the lower part of the platen slotted to receive and hold it by means of a screw and nut, and may be removed or changed to any position on the frame. On others an iron tongue is made, specially adapted to hold the nipper when used, so as to fall over the head-gauge, and hold the sheet until the impression is taken.

Nom de Plume.—A French phrase, meaning, literally, name of the pen. A fictitious name assumed by an author who, unwilling to disclose his real name, desires to distinguish his publications from the mass of anonymous literature.

Nonpareil.—A size of type less than Minion, and usually half that of Pica.

Nonpareil Press.—A job press manufactured by the Cincinnati Type Foundry, of four sizes, from 6 by 12 (inside of the chase) to 15 by 25. It is said that all the sizes run easily by treadle, and superiority is claimed for the arrangement for distribution,—one peculiarity of the latter being the power to confine ink, in stripes, on any part of the rollers, so that different quantities or colors of ink can be simultaneously worked on different parts of the rollers.

NONPAREIL PRESS.

Nota Bene.—Note well, or Take notice; usually abbreviated into N. B., and placed at the head of an important explanation, especially one at the end of an article intended as a final explanation of the matter, or to correct any mistake or omission in the original statement.

Notes.—Matter descriptive of the text, illustrative of its meaning, referring to authorities or analogous paragraphs, etc., which is set in type smaller than the body of the page or column, the usual rule being to make foot-notes two sizes smaller than the text, while a greater diversity is permissible in side- or marginal notes.

Notice.—Any document containing formal, customary, or printed information, such as the printed announcement of the formal meeting of a society distributed among the members. Notices in the manner of remarks upon or descriptions of passing events, lectures, public amusements, building improvements, etc., form an important portion of the local items of the journals. Critical reviews upon current literature are styled book-notices.

Novel.—Prose fictitious composition, formerly indicating a short story, such as those in Boccaccio's Decameron, but now used to express a fictitious narrative of considerable length, and arranged according to certain established rules of art; it is distinguished from the romance by being more strictly confined to probability, and, while describing fictitious events, those occurrences must be made to appear natural and possible. As the chronicle, the epic, and the

drama have each had their age of popularity, so the novel is the form of literature best adapted to the present taste of the public, and a vast portion of current literature is devoted to this department, which is suited to all classes of readers; novels being divided into the religious, philosophic, historic, domestic, comic, sentimental, and sensational. The word novel, or new, was introduced about the time of Boccaccio, but the style of narrative intended as a new method of inculcating some moral or truth by fictitious occurrences more elaborate and realistic than the fable, is perhaps due to a Christian bishop of the third century, whose work was prepared with that avowed intention, and became a model of Greek narratives. In England the origin of the sentimental novel is ascribed to Richardson; that of the comic, to Fielding and Smollett; and that of the domestic, to Madame D'Arblay, Miss Edgeworth, and Miss Austen. Sir Walter Scott must be considered the originator of the true historic novel, and his unmatched success in various styles of narrative raised fictitious writing to the pre-eminence in public estimation which it has since held. In the general diffusion of education during the present century the prejudices of nationality have been to a great extent removed, and the immense reading public, especially in America, now receives with equal interest the works of the novelists of Germany, France, England, and our own country.

NOVELTY PRESS.

Novelty Press.—A cheap and simple press, of various small sizes, designed chiefly for amateur printers and business purposes, but also used, to some extent, in newspaper and job printing-offices. It is sold by Kelly, Howell & Ludwig, Philadelphia, who describe it as follows:

It is a Bed and Platen press operated by the power of a toggle joint with treadle attachment. The Bed (D) of the press is stationary and stands in nearly a vertical position, with its face slightly inclined towards the Platen (E). It is cast in one piece of iron with the frame and front (A), which secures for the press greater firmness and freedom from slurring than exists in any other press. The Chase (C), containing the form to be printed, is held in its place by two thumb screws (I), one at either end, which admit of its being moved laterally to perfect the gauge; and it is supported by two other thumb screws (K), one below each end, which may readily raise or lower either or both ends as occasion requires to adjust the gauge, and which are for the purpose the most perfect and convenient means in use. A square, direct impression is given on the face of all the type at once with the platen by the power of a toggle joint (H H) with a treadle (M) attachment in the Octavo and Quarto presses, and by a hand-lever (G) conveniently placed on the Duodecimo press.

Numeral.—A figure or character used to express a number; as, the Arabic numerals, 1, 2, 3, etc.; the Roman numerals, I, V, X, L, etc. In the English language these are the only numerals used in printing, the latter being employed only for a comparatively small number of purposes, such as the designation of the chapters of a book, or the order of succession of a series of kings bearing the same Christian name, as Louis XI., Louis XII., etc. It is a disputed point whether a period should be put after a Roman numeral. Common sense and analogy, as well as the usage of a few careful offices, condemn the use of the period, but it is generally employed. Capital Roman numerals are used in designating the order of succession of kings, in chapter-headings, and in indicating dates; while, when Roman numerals are employed as folios of a book, or to indicate chapters or verses referred to in the text, lower-case letters are used. There are very few occasions in which it is necessary or desirable to use the complete Roman system of numeration, but it is given below:

1	I	50	L
2	II	60	LX
3	III	70	LXX
4	IIII, or IV	80	LXXX, or XXC
5	V	90	LXXXX, or XC
6	VI	100	C
7	VII	200	CC
8	VIII, or IIX	300	CCC
9	VIIII, or IX	400	CCCC
10	X	500	D, or IƆ
11	XI	600	DC, or IƆC
12	XII	700	DCC, or IƆCC
13	XIII, or XIIV	800	DCCC, or IƆCCC
14	XIIII, or XIV	900	DCCCC, or IƆCCCC
15	XV	1000	M, or CIƆ
16	XVI	2000	CIƆCIƆ, IICIC, IIM
17	XVII	5000	IƆƆ, V
18	XVIII, or XIIX	10000	CCIƆƆ
19	XVIIII, or XIX	50000	IƆƆƆ
20	XX	100000	CCCIƆƆƆ
30	XXX	1000000	CCCCIƆƆƆƆ
40	XXXX, or XL,		

21

Arabic numerals are so obviously superior to the Roman numerals that there has been a steady tendency to diminish the frequency of the employment of the latter, and to confine their use to the few purposes in which they furnish an agreeable typographical variety; an illustration of this tendency being furnished by the modern substitution of Arabic for Roman numerals in the indication, on the titles of books, of the year in which they are published.

O.

Obelisk.—In printing, a mark of reference (†). It is also called a dagger, and is sometimes used as a mark of censure, or to indicate that a word is obsolete.

Obituary.—In journals, the notice of the death of an individual, whether a mere announcement or accompanied with remarks.

Octavo.—A sheet of paper folded into eight leaves or sixteen pages, frequently called an 8vo.

Octo-decimo.—A sheet so folded as to make eighteen leaves or thirty-six pages.

Odd Page.—The first, third, and all uneven numbered pages.

Odd Folio.—A folio consisting of an uneven number.

Ode.—A short song or poem. Among the Greeks and Romans the ode was usually accompanied by the lyre, from which has been derived the word lyric, but in the modern usage the ode is distinguished from the song by greater length and variety, and by not being necessarily adapted to music. It is also distinguished from the ballad by being confined to the expression of sentiment or thought upon subjects not admitting of narrative, as Dryden's Ode upon St. Cecilia's Day.

Off.—When a job is said to be off, it is meant that it is duly printed and finished.

Off-Cut.—Any part of a sheet which is cut off before folding.

Off its Feet.—Composed type which does not stand upright.

Old English.—A style of letter used in the early days of printing; it is commonly called Black, on account of its darker and heavier appearance than Roman.

Olio.—A medley or assemblage of unlike articles; occasionally used as the title of a varied collection of literary works, such as a magazine.

Old-Style Letter.—Roman and Italic letter of the design used previous to the present century, but which has been readopted to a great extent during the last few years.

Omnigraph.—A mathematical instrument for copying, which is also styled pantograph or pentagraph.

On-dit.—A rumor, from the French words On dit, they say.

On its Feet.—When letter stands perfectly upright, it is said to be on its feet.

Opening.—The space on the galley between two takes of matter.

Open Matter.—Widely leaded matter; matter that contains a number of quadrats, such as poetry, etc.

Opera.—A musical drama.

Operetta.—A short musical drama of a light or comic character.

Oration.—An address delivered in public upon some special occasion.

Oratorio.—A musical composition, of which the subject is generally taken from the Scriptures, as Handel's Israel in Egypt, or Haydn's Creation.

Ordinal.—Noting a number expressing order; as, second, third, fourth, etc.

Ornamental Dashes.—Dashes cast in metal or made of brass, and used chiefly in job-work. There is a great variety, of which a few samples are herewith given.

Ornamented.—A general name for many varieties of Job-Letter. (See JOB-LETTER.)

Ornaments.—Cast, engraved, or electrotyped designs, which, without representing any special object, are intended for the ornamentation of printed pages.

Orthoepy.—That part of grammar which treats of the pronunciation of words.

Orthography.—The art or mode of spelling words. No uniform and universally recognized system of orthography has ever been established in the English language, although the efforts of various lexicographers have been so far successful in noting the prevailing usage, and in correcting manifest absurdities, that a very large proportion of its words are spelled in a uniform manner in all careful publications. At the present day, in the United States, Webster's Dictionary is more of an authority than any other single work, but some of the innovations or changes proposed by Noah Webster have not been generally accepted (such as center for centre, mold for mould, etc.), and the preponderating usage was probably best represented by Worcester's Dictionary at the time of the publication of the quarto edition of that work. Since then, a revised and enlarged edition of Webster's Dictionary has appeared, representing current usage very fairly and fully, no undue prominence being given to that comparatively small portion of Webster's system which did not meet with general approval. Among authors, editors, and proof-readers, there unfortunately still remain great diversities of opinion in regard to the orthography of a considerable number of words, and it is not an uncommon thing, in some printing-offices, to have several works simul-

taneously in progress in which, by the direction of the respective authors, three systems of orthography, differing in various details,—as Johnson's, Webster's, and Worcester's,—will respectively be used. Different newspaper offices, or different proof-readers, also adopt diverse systems, so that the compositor may, in two different offices, or when he is employed on two different works, be required to spell a given word in one manner to-day and in another manner to-morrow. Many rules have been laid down for spelling certain classes of words, but as they are also, to some extent, subjected to the conflict of systems or authorities, and as they embrace many exceptions, it is scarcely desirable to publish an abstract of them here.

Otto, John.—The first bookseller who purchased manuscripts from the authors and had them printed by others, without possessing a press of his own. He established this business at Nuremberg, about the year 1516, and may therefore be considered as the first publisher. Steiger and Boskopf of Leipsic undertook the same employment in 1545. Previous to this period, the printers had executed all their works at their own expense, and sold them by their own personal exertions or by agents.

Out.—Anything omitted, and marked for insertion in the proof by the reader, is said to be an out.

Outer Form.—The form containing the first page of a book or newspaper.

Outline.—The exterior line by which any figure is defined; the general features either of a picture or any work of art; a sketch.

Out of Copy.—When a compositor has finished his take, he is said to be out of copy.

Out of his Time.—A youth is said to be out of his time when he has completed his apprenticeship. Hansard gives the following account of the old custom in the printing business of washing young men who have just completed their apprenticeship, before admitting them into the ranks as journeymen. The custom is still kept up in England; and for an hour previous to the clock striking twelve, great preparations are made, and brains set to work to discover by what means the greatest noise can be made. He says:—An old custom peculiar to printing-offices is termed Washing, and during the keeping up of this ceremony, if persons happen to reside in the neighborhood of the office, whose nerves are not made of stern stuff indeed, they will hardly fail of getting them shattered. Washing is had recourse to upon two occasions, either for rousing a sense of shame in a fellow-workman who had been idling when he might have been at work, or to congratulate an apprentice upon the hour having arrived that brings his emancipation from the shackles of his subordinate station and advances him to manhood. Upon the former occasion, the affair generally ends with a wash of one act; but upon the latter, the acts are commonly repeated with a degree of violence proportioned to the expectancies of a liberal treat at night. Perhaps the following description may afford some slight idea of the nature and effects of the performance. Every man and boy attached to the department of the office to which the person to be washed belongs, is bound in honor, upon a given signal, to make in the room as much noise as he possibly can with any article upon which he can lay his hands. A rattling of poker, tongs, shovel, and other irons, is harmoniously accompanied with running reglet across the bars of the case, shaking up of the quoin-drawers, rolling of mallets on the stone, playing the musical quadrangle by chases and crosses; and in the press-room, slapping the brayers upon the ink-blocks, a knocking together of ball-stocks, hammering the cheeks of the press with sheep's-feet, etc.; in short, every one uses the utmost means he can devise to raise the concert of din and clatter to the highest possible pitch of hideous discordancy, by means of the implements aforesaid; and then the whole is wound up with a *finale* of three monstrous huzzas. The apprentice is expected to treat the men in the office, either to a substantial luncheon, or to a supper in the evening, to which each man subscribes an additional amount, in which case a glass of ale only is partaken at noon, just to wash the dust out of their throats, caused by shaking up the quoin-drawers, etc.

Out of Register.—When the pages do not exactly back each other.

Outsides.—The outer sheets of a ream, which are disfigured by the cords.

Overlay.—A piece of paper fastened on the tympan-sheet by means of paste, to give more impression to a low part of a form. (See MAKING READY.)

Overrunning.—Carrying words backwards or forwards in correcting.

Over Sheets.—The extra sheets which are given out beyond what are actually required for the job, to provide against damages, bad impressions, etc.

Overture.—An elaborate orchestral introduction or symphony to an opera, oratorio, etc.

P.

Pack.—Fifty-two cards made up into a bundle.

Page.—One side of a leaf of paper; a sheet of writing-paper or a folio newspaper contains two leaves, or four pages.

Page-Cord.—A strong, thin twine used by printers for tying up pages of matter.

Page-Gauge.—A gauge used as a standard of the length of pages during the operation of making up pamphlets, books, etc.

Page (tying up a).—The proper way to tie up a page for imposing, is to begin at the left top corner of the page as it lies on the galley, wrap the cord round from left to right, and tighten each successive round at the right top corner. Passing it round about three times, and taking care to make the first end additionally secure each turn, draw the cord tight through that which is wrapped on the page, so as to form a noose, the end of which is left two or three inches out for the convenience of untying when imposed. A page thus tied, with the cord round the

middle of the shank, will always stand firm, and be in no danger of being squabbled while lying on the stone or letter-boards. Many compositors often pass the cord five or six times round the page before fastening it, and it is not secure then, for the very reason that they do not adopt any system, but carelessly overlap the cord at each turn; but if pains are taken to place each round of the cord immediately above the previous one, as neatly as cotton is wound round a reel, it will be found that three times round will be sufficient to bind the type securely; whereas, if one of the half-dozen overlapping rounds should slip—which is frequently the case—the others naturally become loose, and the page is likely to be squabbled in consequence. An advantage is also thus gained in imposing a form; for, instead of there being such a bulk of cord between the type and furniture, a single thickness only appears.

Paging or Pagination.—The marking or numbering the pages of a book or other written or printed work. This is done with the Arabic numerals, either in the centre or outer corner of the upper margin or below the last line of the page. The introduction, preface, index, supplement, notes, and other supplementary portions of a work, are frequently marked with the Roman numerals.

Paging Machine.—A machine for printing consecutive numbers with great rapidity on sheets of paper, check-books, cards, etc. The numbers are usually fixed on the circumference of a revolving cylinder, which is brought down to the paper by some mechanical appliance, by hand or treadle motion; and, after the impression has been effected, the cylinder takes a turn, and another number is ready to be printed. Paging machines usually ink themselves, and are made to print double, treble, etc.

Paging-up.—A phrase used in type-foundries for making letter into pages, and papering them up in the manner in which they are received by the printer.

Pale Color.—When the impression on a printed form is of a light color, it is said to be pale.

Paleography.—The art of deciphering ancient manuscripts and inscriptions, including a knowledge of the various characters used by the sculptors and writers of different nations. (See MANUSCRIPT.)

Palimpsest.—An ancient manuscript, from which one series of letters has been erased in order to make room for another, by rubbing the manuscript with pumice-stone and then smoothing it with a roller or polisher. Probably a protest against the prevalence of this custom was intended in the letter of Cicero, in which, while complimenting Tributius for his economy in having written his letter upon a palimpsest, Cicero continues to say that he would gladly know what had been erased as less important than the letter. The custom was very general in the ninth and tenth centuries, particularly among the Latins, and was carried to a great extent during the eleventh century. In Germany edicts were issued forbidding it during the thirteenth and fourteenth centuries. In some of the early-printed books ancient vellum manuscripts were used, and it is known that Jenson printed an edition of the Clementine Constitutions upon parchment from which the writing had been obliterated. The earliest discovery of a palimpsest was made in the Imperial Library of France in 1692, when a Greek Bible in the usual character of the sixth century was discovered beneath a Greek manuscript of the fourteenth century. Ulphilas, Bishop of Gothland in the fourth century, was known to have translated the whole Scripture into the vernacular, but nothing of his work was discovered, except the four Gospels contained in the Codex Argenteus, until his manuscript of the Epistle to the Romans was found beneath a Greek manuscript at Wolfenbuttel in 1755. In Milan some lost works of Cicero, the whole of the comedies of Plautus, and other classic writings have been found under Latin manuscripts. Cicero's De Republica, known only from quotations preserved in Latin authors, was found under a Commentary on the Psalms in a handwriting previous to the tenth century; the treatise of Cicero consisted of three hundred pages in double columns of fifteen lines each, and was in fine Roman uncials without divisions between the words. A number of important works have been discovered beneath Syriac writings of the ninth and tenth centuries, one of the most celebrated being an Iliad of four thousand lines in a Greek character not later than the sixth century. One of the most remarkable palimpsests was found at Verona by Niebuhr, who succeeded in deciphering the original manuscript notwithstanding that there were two others written upon it. The chemical agent used to render the palimpsest legible, although successful for a short time, frequently results in utterly destroying the faint lines of the original.

Palette Knife.—A long flexible knife, without sharpened edges, used by pressmen for taking ink out of kegs or cans, and mixing it with oil or with other inks, and, sometimes, for feeding it to rollers on power-presses and to distributing surfaces on small job-, or hand-presses.

Pamphlet.—A printed work consisting of but one or a few sheets, not exceeding in size five sheets octavo, and either stitched together or in a paper cover. Pamphlets, being a convenient method of publication, especially for treatises, essays, or strictures upon current events, were introduced at an early day. Written pamphlets were in use in England in the fourteenth century, and the word is written pamflet by Chaucer, and pamphletis and paunflet by Caxton. They appeared in large numbers during the political and religious disputes of the sixteenth century, both in England, France, and Germany. Before the establishment of newspapers, and through the long subsequent period during which the journals were subjected to severe censorship, this anonymous style of publication was the general form for political writing, and they present the best current chronicle of the history of parties and of political events. Old pamphlets are therefore regarded as important historical treasures, and a collection of

30,000 tracts found by a bookseller of London during the civil struggle from 1640 to the Restoration in 1660, was purchased by George III., and presented to the British Museum as a most valuable contribution to the history of the country. Many public libraries and some private collectors preserve the original paper cover in binding the pamphlets, as often containing important current information not readily found elsewhere. Collections of early American pamphlets have been attracting attention recently, and several valuable ones have been found.

Pantograph.—Sometimes written pentagraph. An instrument for copying maps and plans, either upon the same scale or larger or less than the original. Several instruments for this purpose have been invented in the United States, which are used extensively in the manufacture of wood type. The first plan of a pantograph was described by Christopher Scheiner in a pamphlet called Pantographia, in Rome, as early as the year 1631. The Eidograph, invented by Professor Wallace, of Edinburgh, has been highly approved for its accuracy and convenience. An instrument by M. Gavard, exhibited at the London Exposition of 1851, has also been highly commended. Pantographs have been manufactured in various shapes. One of the original styles consists of four brass rules or bars fastened to one another by joints, and moving readily upon castors. Upon one bar is fixed a movable pencil, and upon another a tracing-point, with which the lines of the original are followed while the pencil repeats similar movements upon another piece of paper; the proportion of the copy to the original being settled by the rule:—As the distance of the pencil from the fulcrum is to the distance of the tracer from the fulcrum, so will be the size of the copy to the size of the original. Simple in principle, the instrument presents considerable difficulties in mechanical execution, accuracy and ease of motion being absolutely essential; but many of the different styles have been found of much service to draughtsmen.

Pantomime.—A theatrical entertainment in which the action of the piece is represented by gesticulation, without the use of speech.

Paper.—In attempting to condense into a single article in this work a reasonable and intelligible amount of information on this subject, we feel that it is an act of presumption, requiring some explanation. Our first dim infantile recollections of any thing like mechanical contrivance are of the old Rittenhouse paper-mill, at Roxborough, on the Wissahickon near Philadelphia. There is no doubt that the processes then used there were the same as those used when, as the first paper-mill in this country, it was established in 1690. We have no means of ascertaining the limited quantity of paper then made by hand from the old materials.

At this present time we have obtained, from a friend best able to decide on such matters, an estimate of the quantity of paper now made yearly in the United States. He estimates the quantity of white paper of all kinds at about 225,000 tons per annum, and the quantity of brown and wrapping paper at about as much more, and that about one-tenth of the white paper is made of straw.

When it is seen that in this period of fifty-four years the production of paper has increased with us, from far less than there is now made of a material then unknown in this country and only just known and introduced in Europe, to the present enormous quantities, we can understand the importance of the subject. This country uses, and, sad to say, wastes, more paper than any other. In fact, its paper production is greater than that of France and England together.

If, then, in conscientiously endeavoring to treat of this matter, even only a few really useful hints are given, there may be some excuse for attempting to do so much in a small space. At the same time we are more than ever satisfied of the truth long ago felt and expressed by us, that it would be easier to fill a whole volume on this subject, than to condense the matter into the necessarily limited compass which the scope of this work affords. We see that many useful and, to some, important matters must be omitted, but in the course of selection can notice only those which have, in our judgment, the most useful application.

Substances used for Writing Purposes before True Paper.—We learn from ancient authors that various flexible materials (for it is only of such that we shall speak) have been used for writing upon, such as the inner bark of trees, their leaves, etc., and the skins or membranes of animals. The latter of these, the skins of animals, would seem to be one of the first in order of time among flesh-eating people. Of the early forms and modes of preparation we have no particular account until about 200 B.C., when, doubtless, merely an improved form was made at Pergamus, whence, through *pergamena charta,* our parchment. The numerous parchment manuscript writings contained in libraries are of no great antiquity. They are characterized by great inequality in the size of the material. Certain choice manuscripts are on a violet stained ground, with gold or silver letters. The remains of Mexican and other North American picture-writings are upon skins.

We can find no reference to the fact that animal substances being peculiarly liable to the attack of insects, may account for the loss of all very early records made upon skins, and even upon prepared parchment.

Parchment, or a similar preparation, vellum, has continued in use. Some of the first printed books are upon vellum, and parchment is still used, but generally only for official written records, such as deeds, charters, titles, diplomas, etc. Except for its property of not tearing readily, there is no reason why a really good paper should not take its place, and this only difficulty could be overcome by the best paper.

The use of the leaves of trees as writing-material is not familiar to us, as it has its origin in tropical climates, where palms and kindred plants afford an abundant supply of most beautiful writing material. As in such regions animal substances are prone to rapid decay, the use of leaves, commenced in earliest times, continues to this day. We have before us a characteristic specimen of leaf-writing from India. The substance is a portion of a leaf of the Talipot palm; its natural surface is polished, the body of the thickness of an ordinary card. Upon such a polished surface no writing could be made that would not be easily washed off. The writing is therefore done by a sharp-pointed iron or steel style, which cuts through the outer polished surface, and some kind of ink is then rubbed over the surface, and only adheres and penetrates where the cut has been made. The ink used being usually India ink, or some other form of suspended carbon, always employed by the Orientals, the writing is imperishable. (See WRITING-INK.) In this case, at first, it was difficult to recognize the character, which, however, was found to be that of one of the ordinary Indian languages, with beautifully rounded letters, which, however, from the parallel fibres of the leaf having caused the style to cut accordingly, had been converted into curiously angular letters, an instance where the nature of the material has modified the form of the character. A number of such manuscripts have been preserved in European collections. None of them, however, are of ancient date, and most of these are in English collections.

The skin or epidermis of certain large leaves also affords a suitable material for writing, as in that of the Mexican Agave, upon which, it is said, records have been made. A specimen in our collection would indicate that, being properly pressed, there would be no difficulty in obtaining sheets as wide as the leaf.

Another instance of a tissue taken directly from the plant is found in the Chinese so-called rice-paper, used for flower-painting, in making artificial flowers, etc. It is now known that this is made from the pith, or rather the pith-like wood, of the Æschynomene paludosa, or perhaps of other plants, which, by a spiral cut from the outside inward, allows the whole stalk to be developed to a flat sheet, which by pressure, slightly crushing the cells, remains permanently flat. This material, being eminently fragile, is limited in its use, and, from the conditions of the original source, of restricted size.

These, and others that might be given, are cases of what we may call natural paper. Before we can properly understand the nature and composition of artificial paper, even in its simplest form of papyrus, we must spend some time in considering the

Vegetable structure from which paper is made.—All parts of all plants are made up of cells. These cells in their natural state are entirely closed, and though minute, their structure, and the different substances in them, have the most important bearing upon the manufacture of paper.

The cell wall, when freed from all other substances, is found to be formed of a substance called cellulose, remarkable for its flexibility and its resistance to most reagents which destroy other substances; it is this, and this only, which should form good paper stock. It is best represented to us in old, worn, and well-washed linen or cotton rags.

As the, to us, modern, and what we may call chemical, mode of treatment has essentially modified the art of paper-making, we can afford to dwell upon the chemical properties of this interesting substance.

Strong sulphuric acid, if gradually added so as to prevent excessive heating, softens cellulose so that the cells are agglutinated and adhere together; if the action is arrested at this stage, the cellulose regains its original properties, but the physical structure is altered. This property is the foundation of the manufacture of PARCHMENT PAPER, which see.

If the action of the acid is continued, dextrine, a substance soluble in water, and identical with that made from starch, is obtained, whose uses are now so well known. If the action is still continued, the cellulose is converted into grape sugar, and as the action consists only in taking up the elements of water, we can understand that a pound of rags may make more than a pound of sugar.

Strong nitric acid used with proper precautions does not decompose cellulose, but actually enters into combination with it. When ordinary cotton wool is used, the result is gun cotton, now so much used for blasting purposes, and even, in some forms, for artillery. Even the microscopic structure of the cotton is not affected by this treatment; only with polarized light is the difference seen, but it has become soluble in a mixture of alcohol and ether, forming collodion, which when evaporated leaves a thin water-proof film. In this form it is now used in almost all photographic processes, being in fact but an amorphous nitrated paper of exquisite tenuity.

The moderate action of nitric acid removes all other substances from the vegetable cell, and develops the structure to be mentioned hereafter.

Caustic alkalies, potash, soda, or alkaline earth, as lime, in solution have no material action upon pure cellulose, but dissolve almost all other substances found in and around the vegetable cell. In fact, all salts having an alkaline reaction possess this property in a greater or less degree.

One other property of cellulose has been made known in recent times, that is, its solubility without decomposition in an ammoniacal solution of oxide of copper, from which it can be precipitated. This has been proposed as a means of water-proofing paper, by precipitating this solution upon already made paper. Its use under the microscope also adds an important one to our list of reagents.

All living and actively growing vegetable cells contain inclosed a substance containing nitrogen and quite like what we call animal matter, being liable to change and even fermentation or putrefaction under the combined influences of heat and moisture. This substance as the cells arrive at maturity may wholly or partially disappear, but in the condition in which

ordinary useful fibres are gathered much of it remains in them.

The presence of this nitrogenous matter in fibres as gathered, allows of that partial fermentation, which when limited in its action to the separation only of bundles of cells is technically known in flax or hemp, as rotting. The further continuance of this process may be carried far enough to involve the cellulose itself, and thus occasion a loss, as we shall see while treating of the preparation of rags.

The removal of this nitrogenous and fermentable matter is accomplished by the action of alkalies.

When certain cells attain maturity they become filled with what is called incrusting and sometimes, lignifying matter, as is seen in the heart-wood of trees, where it produces the difference between it and the sap-wood. Not only does this substance fill the cells, but it interpenetrates their cellulose walls and gives that rigidity which is characteristic of hard wood. Before such wood can afford cells fit for paper-making, all of this incrusting matter must be removed, a thing quite possible indeed, but, owing to the large percentage of this substance, utterly uneconomical. Here again we find caustic alkali to be the proper solvent. This agent, however, gives a brown or yellow color to the incrusting matter, and while the remaining portions may not interfere with the usefulness of the cells for paper-making, to obtain a white stock we must bleach with chlorine. Such wood paper may be recognized by the brown color which it regains on being treated with alkali.

But in paper-making we have not only to consider the cell itself and its contents, but we must study the nature of the substance which holds the cells together. This matter is known as the intercellular substance, and having been called gluten, and we know not what else, has improperly had properties assigned to it according to the names given.

A slight consideration of the results of modern investigation in vegetable anatomy will give us clear conceptions of this matter; leading at once to practical results. It is found by the application of suitable reagents, that this intercellular substance is not a homogeneous mass in which the cells are formed, but that a portion of it belongs to each cell. Now, it is known that the cells are formed by subdivision within older or mother cells, whose altered remains thus form the intercellular substance. In certain classes of plants we may trace this change in all its steps with the utmost ease, and we find the remains of these old cells more and more altered from pure cellulose with its power of resistance to ordinary agents, until it becomes soluble in hot water as mucilage, gum, etc. The investigations of chemists have led to the discovery, in this, of a host of matters having nearly identical chemical composition but different physical properties, and even these varying in the course of solution under their own hands. It is plain to see, therefore, that the intercellular substance is only cellulose which has become more and more attackable by reagents under the action of which pure cellulose remains unchanged. Many different substances will therefore effect the solution and removal of this matter, but no one is more economical and effectual than alkali, best, caustic for rapid action, and having also the property of removing all other adherent substances from pure cellulose.

We see, then, that for the entire separation of the vegetable cells from one another, and for their almost entire separation from all that affects their usefulness in forming paper stock, there is but one agent necessary, and that one, everywhere attainable. Without understanding the reasons for it, this has been known to the Chinese and Japanese for centuries, and, in fact, is the basis of their peculiar mode of paper-making. These nations, however, had no means of boiling at a temperature higher than 212° Fahr; whereas we, by means of inclosed boilers, can carry on the operation at a much higher temperature, and thus greatly expedite it. This process applied to rags, straw, rope, wood, etc., forms the great modern improvement in paper-making.

But there are different kinds of cells in plants. For our present purpose we may divide them into elongated cells, which only are useful in paper-making, and those short cells with nearly equal length and breadth, which for the sake of brevity we include under the name of pith-cells, and which, if they do accidentally appear in properly prepared paper stock, add nothing to its strength, and but little to its mass. It is therefore important to determine the relative proportion of these in a plant before we can ascertain the percentage of useful product. As the relative position of the various kinds of cells, and their different conditions all enter into the question, we must next look at

The grouping of cells in plants.—There are two great divisions of the vegetable kingdom, into which most plants suitable for paper-making fall. In one of these, the endogens, or inside-growers, there is no true bark, but the available elongated cells are found collected in bundles throughout the substance of the stalk, imbedded in more or less of pith cells. This we can readily see on examining a stalk of Indian corn. To the same class belong all the grasses, including the bamboo, cane, etc., the agave, or so-called aloe, the pine-apple, the banana, —the palms, including the rattan, etc.,—almost all tropical plants, and represented within our own territory, beyond the grasses, mainly by the palmetto and the yucca, known to us in one species as the bear grass. All of these plants afford long filaments, except in the case of the grasses, where the length is determined by that of the joints. These are, when separated from the surrounding pith cells, which can easily be done by mechanical means, at once, useful for all purposes requiring an elongated filament, and accordingly, in their crudest form, we find them directly made into some form of cordage. For instance, the Sisal hemp is from an Agave, the Manilla is from a Banana, and so on. These fibres being prepared by very cheap labor in this useful form of cordage, it is

best to let them take their usual course, do good work in that form, and then as old rope regard them as materials for paper-making, without seeking to derive at once, and at great expense, the material for paper stock from the original plant. As these are plants growing without our territory, there is no reason to fear a protective duty preventing them from being made into useful cordage, but inducing them to be made at once, and at great cost, into paper stock.

But the bundles of fibres in these plants, although strictly confined within a definite circumference, are themselves quite composite, and in any treatment necessary to make paper stock are quite altered; even for textile purposes they are greatly changed, and the nature of this change has, we believe, first been shown by us in an article on Vegetable Fibre, in the Agricultural Report of the U. S. Patent Office for 1859. It is enough to say that even in these bundles there is but a portion forming elongated cells, which, from their structure and function, are properly called by botanists bast cells, from their relation to those, so called, in the next class which we proceed to examine.

The next great division of the vegetable kingdom consists of plants which, as far as their wood is concerned, and they only form true wood, continue by annual growth to grow outwards, while the surrounding bark, increasing only on the inside, pushes out and gradually loosens the surrounding envelope. It is on the inside-growing surface of this bark that we find the strong elastic and pliable cells which form, what we call by the old Saxon name, the bast. It is this which prepared forms from the linum our linen, from the cannabis our hemp, from the Tillia or Linden the bast so largely imported from Russia. In finer and rarer forms, it is from Eastern species of Urtica, or rather Boehmeria, China grass, and similar products. The true wood of all these plants has cells far shorter than those of the far more useful bast cells, which in most cases are, in cultivated plants, the sole object; and, in fact, in these, being herbaceous plants, the shortness and weakness of the woody centre are essential elements in the ready mechanical preparation of the longer, stronger, and more valuable bast cells.

These cells, in general, are distinguished by their thick walls, with a more or less angular section, and, when isolated, by their great strength, elasticity, and pliability. One other most important property for their value in paper-making we shall consider further on. Bast cells are also distinguished from all others by their greater length; in flux we have found them as long as three inches, in the China grass seven inches or more. This length is far beyond our requirements for paper-making, but we shall afterwards show that the Chinese, Japanese, and their neighbors have availed themselves of it, for most useful purposes.

In the first treatment with weak alkaline solutions, the bast cells are only separated into bundles, as may be seen in our examination of specimens presented to the Flax Cotton Commission of 1864. It requires a prolonged or more active treatment to isolate the individual cells.

The wood cells of these plants are much shorter, but their properties, in a degree, are like those of all cells. In this connection, what we have said of the incrusting matter must be carefully borne in mind.

One other mode of occurrence of the vegetable cell remains to be considered, and that is, the single cells, which form the hair or down attached to seed. Of these, cotton is the eminent type, and cotton is the only single cell commercially known to us. For length, sometimes as great as three inches, and in its other properties, it is so like to bast cells that a distinguished botanist, in the examination of it, inadvertently classed it among them. But there is a host of these seed hairs, all by their tempting look inducing the hope of their useful employment as textile materials. On examination, however, they are found to be smooth and cylindrical, not capable of being interlaced, and breaking or bending with a sharp angle. This is caused by an outer coating penetrating the cell. Such hairs, useless in their ordinary form, are seen in the down of our Asclepias, milk or silk weed, and in the so-called silk cottons, the product of the Bombax and other tropical trees. The asclepias wool, which, from its tempting appearance, has induced so many to spend time and money on its employment, to the neglect of the really excellent bast of the same plant, is, as we have shown, practically useless for paper-making, although we have a specimen of paper made from it about one hundred years ago, but in the above named article we suggested that by the use of nitric acid it might be brought to a more useful resemblance to cotton. Since then we have seen a specimen so prepared, and, as predicted, it has become quite like cotton; the expense of the process, however, the difficulty of procuring the material, and its little worth after all, render this rather a matter of curiosity, as verifying a statement based upon scientific study of the substance, than any thing else.

There is another class of cells of moderate length, placed one above the other, with horizontal or slightly oblique ends, which, soon becoming obliterated in the plant, form continuous passages, and in the living plant are filled with air. Hence, such cells, or rather many of them, in continuous union, have the name of ducts. These add almost nothing to the strength of paper, but, being variously marked with rings, spirals, or pits in their walls, their remains in paper often enable us, under the microscope, to determine the origin of the fibre used.

We have now to consider a most important point in the structure of the cell wall, upon which, in fact, its usefulness for textile purposes and for paper-making is almost wholly dependent. If the cell wall were throughout of equal thickness, the cells would resemble a rod, which if twisted would untwist, and many of them mingled together in water would only lie together like so many jack-straws, without any

power to interlace. But, in fact, the cell wall grows unequally on the inside, having inward projections which take a spiral direction, and if they have pits or depressions they have the same direction; the cells, therefore, have a tendency to curve when suspended in water, and so to intertwine; and if their outer surface, as in most bark bast cells, is somewhat angular, they may be likened to screws of greater or less pitch. But if the cells are bruised, we find that throughout their substance they show still more strikingly this spiral structure: if they are not only bruised, but broken and bruised, their ends become frayed into fringes, each fibril of which, when freely suspended in water, retains its tendency to take a spiral direction. Hence the interlacement or agitation, which, when the water is withdrawn, leaves the material, as it were, felted.

It follows from this that if the individual cells are tolerably straight, as in endogenous fibres, they must be left very long to give the proper interlacement, if they are not broken. This extreme case is shown in Chinese paper (fig. 5), where with merely chemical action, and little if any mechanical abrasion, the entire cells enter into the composition of the paper.

On the other hand (fig. 4), we have a specimen of the condition of fibre in a French tissue-paper in which nearly all of the cells are broken up, and the interlacement depends upon the spiral tendency of the ultimate fibrils. Of course the latter is the weaker, the former the stronger paper; but the first requires a length of staple in the stock unknown to our processes of paper-making, while the latter is easily made by our existing paper-mills.

It is a curious fact that the first drawings of the condition of fibre, though presented to the Royal Academy of Sciences in Vienna in 1845, were not published until 1852, and in the next year Schacht published a work in which were given the further illustrations which we present. The above-given explanation of the reason why the vegetable cell could and did make paper, was given by us in the article in the Agricultural Report of the United States Patent Office in 1859. No other explanation had been made, or has since been made, although we believe it is now accepted without hesitation.

Copies of the excellent drawings of Schacht, to which we have referred, are given on page 329. It must be understood that the specimens have been torn apart, by needles, in water: the fibres have therefore been released from their interlacement, but their position after this treatment shows fully their adaptation to that end.

The peculiar characteristics of paper from different sources is worthy of remark. But we must state that with the method of boiling at high pressure with alkaline solutions, there will be found comparatively few useless, adherent cell-remains, though always enough, on extended examination, to identify the substances from which the paper was made.

From what we have said above, it must be evident in the first place that every plant can be made to

Fig. 1. Fibres from a fine, unsized printing-paper. The flat cells are those of cotton; the rounder ones, of flax; the finer mass below, the entirely frayed remains of both. Magnified 200 times.

Fig. 4. French tissue-paper, most of the cells frayed. Magnified 200 times.

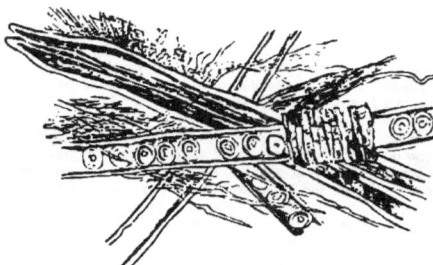

Fig. 2. Fibres from wood-paper. The round marks upon some of them are characteristic of the pine or other coniferous woods; the cross cells upon one of them show the remains of medullary rays (with cells). Magnified 200 times.

Fig. 5. Genuine Chinese paper. None of the cells are frayed; the remains of a few broken, dotted duct-cells are evidence of the origin. Magnified 200 times.

Fig. 3. New official Prussian hemp paper, some cells nearly entire, a few frayed. Magnified 120 times.

Fig. 6. Paper made from straw. The narrower cells are true bast cells; those with cross-marking are ducts, adding little to the strength; those with crenulate edges are superficial, epidermis cells, as shown by the stomates or air-openings —the larger and rounder are true pith cells. Magnified 120 times.

produce some kind of paper, and, in the second place, that the product in various kinds must vary in amount in proportion to the amount of useful cells, and also in strength, for the same reason. As we shall show in the history of more modern paper-making, the possibility of making paper from plants of all kinds has been demonstrated, the same or nearly the same process being used for all.

In fact, we find, at an early date, processes described as applicable to all vegetable substances; then we find others which refer only to certain families of plants, and finally to certain particular plants. It would hardly seem necessary to say that the Patent law of the United States was never intended to protect the claim of a monopoly over a certain species of plant which required no different treatment from any other. This would be equivalent to a claim for a certain species of tree as a fire-wood, because it could not be shown in print that some one else had previously used it for that purpose—and we all know that all wood may be burned. Again, it may be said that a certain kind of wood contains a great deal of moisture; the invention is not using it for fuel, but drying it first—but who has not heard the saying that it takes two cords of dry wood to burn one of green?

We state this almost self-evident proposition in order to combat a popular and wide-spread error. In the same direction, we find the error of considering as a new invention the application of a process to wood which had been used for straw, and, again, what had been done for rags as applied to other materials. All such views depend upon extreme ignorance of the history of the subject, as in the case of the famous decision granting a new patent for an old process on the ground that the man who converted a pine plank into a sheet of white paper should have some protection, while three-fourths of a century before good paper had been made from pine wood, whether a plank, or shavings, or saw-dust, does not seem to make much difference.

The great question in all such matters is not one of invention, but of economy, such as any reasonable person would entertain. It would be economical to select a plant or plants to form paper stock, where the growth was spontaneous and fuel cheap, to be used upon the spot; but the transportation of such plants, with, say, fifty per cent. to be wasted in their conversion, still worse the attempt to cultivate artificially such plants in a soil and climate to which they were not congenial, would be simply absurd. And yet such absurdity is every day proposed.

Having now set forth the principles upon which all paper-making depends, we may proceed to examine the history of artificial paper; and it is curious that up to this date, in most cases, the history has been written without this important prerequisite.

We have first to treat of the nearest ancient approach to our common paper.

Papyrus.—Without going into details, we may assert that this substance was known from a very remote antiquity. Pliny and other Roman authors give very circumstantial accounts of the finding upon the Janiculum of the books of Numa written upon papyrus, indicating, too, the means which had been used for their preservation. This would carry their date back to the seventh century B. C., a period for which the history of Rome is, at best, doubtful. But it is quite certain that these books were destroyed because they contained expositions of philosophy, possibly of religious belief, certainly of ritual observances, at variance with those held at the time when they were found. This would indicate their origin from an earlier people, and we know that on the site of Rome was a city before its so-called Roman occupation.

But we have still better evidences in the papyrus rolls found in Egyptian mummies of an undoubtedly older date. We have a fragment of genuine papyrus from the mummy now in the museum of the Smithsonian Institution; this mummy is believed by some to have been embalmed in the time of Moses, but we are unwilling to vouch for the accuracy of this statement.

All the circumstances show that the assertion that the discovery of papyrus was due to the conquests of Alexander the Great is in one sense true; the invention was vastly older, but the discovery of the source and existing mode of manufacture might well be said to have then been made.

The account of the mode of manufacture is mainly derived from Pliny, who accurately describes the stalks as triangular, and the slices as being split into very thin leaves by a needle, taking care to have them as broad as possible, the best taken from the inside; these were laid upon an inclined table side by side, as long as the slices from the papyrus would allow, and trimmed to equal length, being moistened with the Nile water, which, in a muddy state, was said to have the properties of glue. Upon these a similar row of strips was placed at right angles, and the whole pressed,—according to other accounts, beaten—together.

This account is evidently imperfect. We find, in fact, that no representation of their processes from such nations as the Egyptians, the Japanese, or the Chinese, are entirely reliable, partly from the misinterpretation of the foreign narrators, partly from the undoubted suppression of some particulars by the natives. But by the aid of modern science we can make a very fair discrimination between what is true and what is false. The gluey properties of the muddy Nile-water do not exist, but we find Pliny mentioning other forms of papyrus, in which he describes a right honest flour paste as used, and, moreover, gives quite particular directions for its formation. Then there is incidental mention made of the mallet by which it was beaten, showing that possibly the cross-layers were indeed incorporated by this instrument.

This is in substance about all that was known of the formation of papyrus. In this, as in other cases which we will point out, the solution of the problem depends upon microscopic examination. For papyrus this has first been done by Dr. Julius Wiesner—

Einleitung in die technische Mikroscopie—1867. He shows that the papyrus plant (Cyperus papyrus), like all solid endogens, has a solid pith, with continuous longitudinal cell bundles, and, more than this, with continuous air spaces in the pith cells, as in all water plants. Here we can understand that the continuous cell bundles give the strength in the two directions as they are crossed. But Dr. Wiesner has found that in all the specimens examined by him there were not two, but three layers, at once correcting the ancient accounts. But if we examine more closely, we can explain more: a needle, not a knife, was used to cut the layers; the former would pass between the cell bundles, while the latter might cut them. Still more, the pith cells around the air spaces would be severed, leaving their boundaries hanging free, and, in the process of beating, these would be more or less interknit. In a way, we might imitate this by slices of the pith of a corn-stalk; there would be the same element of longitudinal strength, but one thing would be wanting, the air spaces with the free edges of the surrounding pith, and from that the interknitting properties are obtained. We see, then, that papyrus is a pith paper, accompanied with the strength in two or three directions of cell bundles, which alone could give the paper real tenacity, while the interknitting remains of the ranges of pith cells would add to the strength or coherence, thus making, in one sense, one-half a pith paper, like the above-described Chinese rice paper, but supported and strengthened by successive layers at right angles to each other by complete long cell bundles. The tapa of the South Sea Islands, derived from the bast of the paper mulberry (Broussonetia papyrifera) has a similar structure.

It is distinctly asserted by Pliny and others that the outer rind of the papyrus was used only in the manufacture of cordage; this may be true, but that successive inner distinct envelopes were separated to make different qualities of papyrus cannot be true, for such layers do not exist.

At best, containing so much of pith cells, we can understand that the papyrus had no great strength. We learn from the ancients that only the best kinds were made without the writing running through to the reverse side, and we have the testimony of existing manuscripts to show that after every five or six leaves a sheet of parchment was interposed, to give strength to the rolls.

The continued use of the papyrus into more modern times, and in rivalry with true modern paper, was prolonged by the fact that certain official documents, papal bulls, etc., were continued upon it, instead of its more modern and more convenient rival.

The introduction of true paper, made from an intermixed pulp, is of doubtful origin. It is said that paper made from cotton wool, is first found in a manuscript of about 1050. But here the only true test, that of microscopic examination, is wanting. This kind of paper is said to have been originally derived from the Arabs, through Spain, and also from the East, by way of Samarcand. All these seem to point to an extreme eastern source, and one argument is, that the Chinese or Japanese made paper from cotton. Now, after an extensive examination of Chinese and Japanese papers, we have never found one containing cotton, and we can find no record of such.

This, however, reminds us of an experience which may help to solve the difficulty. Several years ago, a friend brought us a specimen of Japanese paper, which, when torn, showed long cotton-like fibres; together with a specimen of cotton; these we still retain in our collection in their original juxtaposition. On examination, the cotton was found to be true cotton, but the paper fibres, long bast cells, of angular section, and as unlike cotton as any such cells could be.

Another argument for the antiquity of cotton paper is that it was early made from Egyptian mummy-cloths, said to be made from cotton, but these have, in our own day, been proved to be entirely linen.

Our conclusion from the history given, is that the first manufacture of true paper was obtained from the East, and that it was from the isolated long bast cells of various plants, according to the Chinese or Japanese mode of manufacture, and that afterwards, perhaps suggested by the resemblance, cotton wool, and soon afterwards cotton and linen rags were used. The only true test can be by the microscopic examination of the material of the manuscripts on, what is supposed to be cotton paper, of the eleventh, twelfth, and thirteenth centuries. These have been judged only by superficial examination, and Spanish manuscripts, supposed to be of cotton, were asserted by Spaniards to be made of linen.

It would be useless to attempt to give in our limited space an account of the first establishment of paper-mills in each different country. As is usual in such matters, the first assigned date is always found to have some well-authenticated preceding effort, either successful or not. Variously, in different countries we may say that paper-making was introduced in the thirteenth and fourteenth centuries.

The early mode of paper-making was by pounding the material—generally linen, or mixed linen and cotton, rags—in a mortar, probably preceded by a process of fermentation, which helped to separate and partially disintegrate the vegetable cells. This gave as a result a material hardly finer than would now be called half stuff, and one of great strength, though not so fine as modern paper. It is undoubtedly from this cause that the earliest-printed books, about four hundred years old, and those published from that time on for a century or more, show a paper which, in spite of use and the effects of time, is in every way better and stronger than that found in books printed in the present century.

Having brought the history of paper up to what might be called the modern process of manufacture, we may stop to consider a far more ancient process, and one which, although it may be looked upon as superseded in many respects by modern methods, has yet in it some elements which may give hints for an improvement of these, which may lead to a far more extensive use of paper than we now deem possible.

Chinese and Japanese paper.—According to several European investigators among these nations, this paper had its origin about fifty years before our era; but there is good reason to believe that it was known centuries before.

In more modern times, however, we still have, in certain outlying islands, evidence of the most primitive forms of paper. One of these, in a specimen in our collection, probably from the Loo-Choo Islands, is worthy of a description. In this case the whole plant has been macerated, probably, in an alkaline lye, and perhaps, after a certain amount of pounding, has been laid into a sheet of paper, somewhat coarse, but yet tolerably strong. Here we see all parts of the plant represented; the broken or frayed wood cells, with the pith cells, seem to form the ground-work, but on the surface we can detect the long curls of white bast cells, unbroken, and over the surface are distinct fragments, even of the leaves. We are safe, then, in calling this a primitive kind of paper.

In general, among these nations a much more refined method is used. The material is usually stated to be the bast cells of the paper mulberry, and the endogenous cell bundles of species of bamboo, but it is almost certain that these are by no means the only sources of their paper material. These, or some of them, as in the case of other bast cells, are subjected to a mechanical treatment by hand, such as stripping the bark from the wood, processes which could only be adopted in a country overpeopled, and consequently with cheap labor abundant. They are next macerated in an alkaline lye from quicklime or wood ashes; and by the prolonged action of this, perhaps assisted by boiling, the individual cells are, for the most part, separated. They are then pounded in mortars until the stuff has the desired fineness. The rest of the process closely resembles that of our modern mode of hand paper-making, but instead of the wire for the bottom of the form or sieve, used in taking up the material, fine strips of bamboo are used. In some cases the product seems to have been transferred to, or couched upon, an absorbent material, as in modern hand-made paper, for we have specimens which distinctly show the exact structure of the form. But in other cases the paper is transferred to heated slabs of marble, perhaps of stucco made over a furnace; the paper is then further compacted by being pounded with a brush. Such paper betrays its mode of manufacture by one side being quite smooth while the other is rough. This, however, is of no consequence to these people, since writing or printing is almost always made on one side, the paper being folded so that each leaf is double, showing only the dressed side. The size for these papers is always vegetable in its nature, being

either some kind of mucilage or starch-paste. In this way sheets are sometimes made of great length,—it is said to the extent of sixty feet.

It is not possible however to give here in detail the processes used for different kinds of paper, which vary exceedingly, and in some can only, if at all, be inferred from the nature of the product.

The general characteristic of all these papers is that they are made of almost wholly unbroken cells, as is shown in Schacht's drawing of the material of genuine Chinese paper as seen under the microscope. (Fig. 5.) From such material was made the real India paper, which, from its softness, has been so much employed for proof impressions. In our times it is wholly replaced by a paper made in imitation of it, but in every respect inferior.

The sagacity and economy of these people are shown in their adaptation of different kinds of material to specific purposes: thus, in a bundle of Chinese fire-crackers, of which paper forms by far the largest part, we generally find about a half-dozen different kinds. So in a Japanese envelope for packing goods we find that part forming the sides made of stout paper, sometimes reinforced with a thin strip of wood, the gores, which require to be folded in another way, made of very thin, tough, and pliable paper, and the strings for tying are again made of another kind.

We can give but an imperfect representation of the various uses of this remarkable long-fibred paper. We find among Japanese papers some, the essential characters of which we will notice.

A thin gossamer paper, for what use we cannot say. The texture of this is remarkably open, not unlike that of lace. No such paper could be made of our ordinary short stuff.

Paper pocket-handkerchiefs of various figures, evidently made by marks in the mould, not unlike our water-marks.

Thick white papers of various kinds and for various uses. Among these we find one or two which have undergone great pressure, quite like paper which has been calendered.

But the use of these papers is again extended by the application of some drying oil of admirable quality. We have before us an overcoat made of this material, which has been worn by a friend who has tested its value. We have seen a similar article from China, where an officer in the United States Navy purchased them for half a dollar apiece, as the cheapest and best protection for his men on boat-service. These coats are made of as many pieces as, and quite after the fashion of, our ordinary overcoats.

In a Japanese woven fabric, our attention was drawn to what was apparently a golden thread used in the filling. On examination, this proved to be a very thin ribbon of gilt paper, or, rather, paper covered with silver, or, more likely, tin foil, which again was covered with a golden-colored varnish.

But the most remarkable fabric we have seen is a paper imitating leather. The outer surface is grained in various ways, and is prepared with a drying oil.

The sheet on the other side is plain, similarly prepared, but without any polish. Within there is another layer, over which is spread a mat of bast fibres, soaked in a non-drying oil, which, however, seems to have no effect upon the outer coverings. No such materials are known to us, for we can find no similar oil which would not penetrate the outer coverings and destroy them. The result is a paper quite like leather, which when folded does not crease, but at once regains its flatness when spread out. For bookbinding for pocket-books, etc., we can imagine no better material, for in some respects it is far superior to leather.

The above is but a slight outline of the uses of a kind of paper unknown in our manufacture. Of the difficulties, and yet the possibility, of its introduction among us, much might be said, but our limits forbid.

Before proceeding to describe the processes of paper-making, we may properly in this place examine what within a century have been proposed as

Various raw materials for paper-making.—From what has been said, we can understand that while all vegetable substances can be made into paper, there must be a great difference in economy, in the use of particular ones. One hundred years ago, the consumption of rags for paper-making was so great that there was a call for some substitute for them. In the year 1765, Dr. Jacob Christian Schäffer published the first of his experiments and specimens of paper made from various materials, either without, or with only a small addition of rags. In 1772 his six tracts were gathered in one in a second edition. The specimens were made in his own house, the materials only reduced to the condition of half stuff, and without the easy bleaching of, the then undiscovered, chlorine. His work has been misunderstood, his name, and even the language in which he wrote, have been misrepresented. For this reason we refer to the article Schäffer, J. C., where we propose to give a complete account of this most remarkable book, which has been the real instigation to all modern extensions in the way of paper material. The object of this author was simply to draw attention to the variety of vegetable substances from which paper might be made, using all that he could obtain, in fact, demonstrating the possibility of making some kind of paper from any vegetable substance, and, withal, giving us, from his extensive correspondence, such an account of what had been done before, that we can only complete the history of this branch of the subject from his work. The influence of the work was great, and many mere speculative patents were obtained in France and in England, which, after all, were but partial attempts to carry out what he had established.

In the year 1800, Matthias Koops published a work entitled Historical Account of the Substances which have been used to describe Events and to convey Ideas from the Earliest Date to the Invention of paper.—Printed on the first useful paper manufactured solely from straw, London. Printed by T. Burton, No. 31, Little Queen Street, 1800. With characteristic modesty, this work is published without the author's name on the title-page, in his formal dedication to King George III., or, in fact, anywhere else. The only identification of the author is from an inference drawn from reference to his well-known patent, which will be found to be based upon the alkaline treatment with quicklime. The paper is strong, but quite yellow. The subject is admirably treated, and for most purposes the book is superior to more recent authorities.

At the end of this work is an appendix printed upon paper made from wood alone, and the author refers to the possibility of using other vegetable substances. In this respect he is in advance of our recent judicial authorities, who seem to have considered that the same process may form the subject of one patent for wood, and of another for straw, possibly for any other vegetable substance, and again for each particular kind of grass (straw) or wood.

In 1801 there appeared a second edition, with the addition of—Printed on paper re-made from old printed and written paper. The author's name here appears upon the title-page. He had obtained a patent for cleaning written or printed paper, and upon this the first part of the work is printed. On the 237th page he refers to the work of C. A. Senger, who had discovered a natural paper, which, in fact, was only the matted and bleached remains of confervæ floating upon ponds. But long before, Dr. Schäffer had made paper from the same substance; and not many years ago, this substance caught up and carried off by the wind was renowned by the name of meteoric paper, and created a great sensation. The paper of the first part of this work is as white and good as ordinary paper, but on page 252 it is stated that—Part of this edition is printed on straw paper. Nevertheless, it is not easy, if it be indeed possible, to decide without microscopic examination where the ordinary paper ends, and the straw paper begins. There is much additional matter in this edition. The appendix is again printed upon paper made from wood alone,—not quite so white as the rest of the volume, but vastly superior to that of the first edition.

We have been thus particular, because these books show that in the year 1801 good and useful paper was made from straw and from wood, and in quantity.

In the year 1835, Louis Piette published a work, *Die Fabrication des Papiers aus Stroh und vielen andren Substanzen im Grossen* (The Manufacture of Paper from Straw, and from many other Substances, on a Large Scale.) In this work 160 specimens are given to illustrate the subject. First there are specimens of the various materials in their unbleached state, alone and mixed, then bleached, and afterwards mixed, and with the addition of rags. There is no doubt that this work gave the impetus to the modern manufacture of straw and similar paper. The bleached specimens are almost if not quite equal to the best work of our own day. A later work finished just before Piette's death, and a journal conducted by him, form our most valuable additions to the recent history of paper-making in this direction, as well as in others, especially on account of the liberal array of actual specimens. To do justice, however, to this most distinguished forwarder of this branch of modern paper-making, we must refer to the article PIETTE, where a more complete account of his valuable labors will be given.

A few specimens of paper made from unusual materials will be found in Herring's Paper and Paper-Making, London, 1855, and in the first edition of Munsell's Chronology of Paper and Paper-Making.

From our own collection we can produce an abundance of specimens of paper made from various materials.

The question then arises, What is the value of all this research and experiment? We answer, simply this: that it shows that paper of some kind can be made from any vegetable substance, but that in this, as in all other things, we must exercise common sense in the application. Mahogany will undoubtedly make a good firewood; in Brazil we have seen rosewood hacked by a rough tool into knees for a small vessel; but we would not recommend either of these substances for such purposes, because they are worth far more for something else. Again, in another way, some one has found that our common cudweed, or Life everlasting, will make a good paper. But if all the cudweed in the United States could be gathered together, Heaven knows at what cost, it would hardly suffice for a week's perhaps not for a single day's issue of one of our large daily papers. We have given an indication of the true course in the article of the Agricultural Report of the Patent Office, 1859, so often mentioned. We cannot economically use raw cotton, but after the cotton has gone through its use as a textile fabric we take its remains in the form of rags. So, too, for linen and for hemp. If in the manufacture of these, as a residue, there is cotton-waste, or tow, we might more economically use them, but even the cotton-waste is first used about engines, and after this employment we may take hold of it at lower price for paper-making, having previously to remove the grease and metallic impurity. Again, some have proposed to use the beautiful China grass as a material for paper-making. In the Agricultural Patent Office Report for 1855 we have shown that this plant affords in its bast the longest vegetable cells ever recorded, its compound filaments being much longer, the cells alone being about seven inches in length. Shall we chop up these admirable fibres to one-tenth or less of an inch to make paper, while if they are worth anything it depends, in another use, upon their extraordinary length? Our obvious course is to take only the residue of the manufacture of the long fibre, which, however, is quite limited, for it can be used only under certain restricted conditions. But, after all the amount of this residue is absolutely nothing, for the great work of paper-making; and for the benefit of those who are exercising ingenuity rather than invention in this direction, we may say that we can show them splendid specimens of paper made from this very China grass, Ramme, or Callocé.

Again, much depends upon the place in which fibrous plants are found. To use them economically with us, they must be reduced before transportation to the least volume and weight. A good instance is that of the banana. Calculations have been made of the enormous fibrous waste of this plant; for each year the old stalk is cut down and thrown away. If any one has done as we have done, taken a banana-stalk, as thick as a man's arm or leg, and kept it until dried and having the thickness of a walking-stick, even then only a small portion being useful for fibrous purposes, he can understand that it is far better to take the product of this or a similar banana, from which the fibre has been prepared in distant lands, by cheap and easy labor, so as to form what is called Manilla rope, and after that rope is old and worn to use it, as is done every day by our paper-makers, in the manufacture of paper.

We shall cite only one other misuse of material for paper-making. The husks of maize or Indian corn have been found to afford a good fibre for paper-making. Dr. Schaeffer gives specimens, but mentions that he has learned from one of his correspondents that good white writing-paper had been made in Italy from this material in the preceding century. Our own farmers know too well the value of such things for fodder, to be persuaded to spare them for paper-making. For this reason, in spite of the repeated attempts to use corn-husk for paper-making in the last two hundred years, it is still devoted to its more profitable employment as fodder. Within our own day, an attempt has been made to use the fibre for paper, etc., and save the nutritious portion for feed. Even so slight a knowledge of the subject as might be derived from what has been said in this article, would show that the alkaline lye used to separate the fibre would carry off all the nitrogenous and nutritious substance. But we have the results of a careful German experimenter, who has examined this supposed nutritious substance, and he finds it to be made up of the pith cells, without the least nutritious matter, the cellular walls being quite valueless as food.

In this connection we may say that direct experiment has shown that graminivorous ruminating animals, even with their multiple stomachs, cannot digest the pure cellulose; in fact, we hear that, based upon this fact, the dung of such animals has been used by tons for paper-making; but here the other excrementitious matters, so useful for fertilizing the soil, are wasted.

Following out our suggestions made in 1859, some have gone to Southern latitudes and used our great cane upon the spot, and have sagaciously produced a coarse but useful material, which they have found it profitable to send at once into the market, to supply a demand for just such material. But the time will come when this cane, a most nutritious food, eagerly sought by horses and cattle, will scarcely be spared for paper-making. We may say from personal knowledge that over the whole State of Kentucky, places whose local names of Cany fork, etc., indicating as they do the original fertility of the soil, always great where the cane grew, produce now only most diminutive specimens of cane. In fact, wherever cattle have access, the cane is kept down, though never quite exterminated. As soon as the nutritive qualities of this plant become well understood, paper-making from it will be at an end.

To show the loss sustained in resorting to the original materials, we need only refer to the fact that of one hundred parts of picked flax less than two parts can be used for paper-making. We can, therefore, in such a case, look only to the fibrous waste in the preparation of the flax for spinning into linen.

In the grasses, including Indian corn and our great cane, the most favorable results give but about fifty per cent. of fibre from the dry raw material. Some may exceed this, but most fall below, the loss depending upon the pith cells and adherent substances to be removed. This is not said to discourage the use of such substances for paper-making material, but to direct enlightened attention to the difficulties to be met.

At present straw is the only material in use with us which largely takes the place of rags; from the estimate given in the introduction to this article, we find that straw, forms probably, about one-tenth of the white paper made in the United States. We have in our possession excellent specimens of paper made wholly of straw. These are not selected for the purpose of show, but are taken at random from quantities made and used on the large scale. The harsh rattling, generally supposed to be characteristic of straw paper, is wholly wanting in this case.

In the case of wood, another difficulty has to be encountered,—the power required for the mechanical comminution before using chemical agents. This is a very important waste. We have yet to find that any one has taken our hint given in 1859, and, going to the site of the saw-mills of the West, which waste tons of coarse saw-dust, has made use of what others throw away. Wood cells are at best very short, and the ordinary processes for comminution make them still shorter. The proper way would be by well-known methods to split the wood at small cost into thin, tolerably long splints, and at once to subject them to alkaline action in the usual way, under high pressure, and consequently high temperature. We should then have the wood cells of their whole length, and the cost would be less than that of their purely mechanical comminution, while there would also be less waste.

For wood to be profitably used in paper-making, it must be porous, soft, free from resin, and of course with the least possible amount of incrusting material, attention being paid to the length of the wood cells, which in some plants is far greater than in others. So far as we are aware, wood fibre alone is not now used for paper-making; it, however, forms sometimes a useful addition to the stock, the value depending not merely upon its being wood, but upon its being the best kind of wood, that is, with the longest cells, other things being equal.

The microscopic examination of proposed paper material will often enable us to decide at once, whether, under existing circumstances, it will be profitable or not. Here the question is not one of invention, but simply of calculation. The real economy consists in using, as in the case of rags, what others throw away, and in the next place, in applying our material to the use for which it is best fitted. The greatest mistakes, which have resulted in the greatest failures, have been made by attempting to use coarse and inferior material, at once directly useful for certain purposes,—for the finest purposes, to which they are not adapted,—in short, using a vulgar but in this connection quite significant phrase, to try to make a silk purse of a sow's ear. The high value of rags, which must always be used for the finest and best paper, is not to be reduced by running in competition with them poorer materials at great cost, but by using these poorer materials, to supply a lower quality of paper, and so prevent the absorption of the better substance into a lower use.

Substances not vegetable used for paper-making.— In the work of Dr. Schaeffer we have a specimen of paper made from asbestos, which, although a mineral, has a somewhat fibrous texture, and we learn from other sources that alone, or mixed with vegetable fibre, its manufacture into paper has been continued. Known to the ancients, this substance was used for various purposes in textile fabrics, on account of its property of not being inflammable—chiefly for inclosing the bodies of the rich, for only such could afford the expense of the rare fabric, so that, after burning, their ashes and bones could be separately preserved. It is curious to note that the meaning of the word—*inextinguishable*—was derived from its use as the wick of lamps, which, with a perpetual supply of oil, never went out. In modern times it has been used in safes and elsewhere, because it will *not take fire.*

Wool has been used quite largely, especially in Germany, as an intermixture with other paper materials, probably because of a large supply of woolen rags. At present we find it represented in the very thick and almost pasteboard-like material of a grayish-blue color, with blackish spots, used on account of its body and flexibility for the covering of packages of German goods. Its use for this purpose, from the abundance of woolen rags, shows the nice adaptation of the means to the end, before noticed. The presence of wool in paper can always be readily detected by the animal smell on burning.

Leather finely comminuted, alone or mixed with rags, has been made into paper,—for what purpose we cannot imagine. A notice of specimens of these will be given under the article PIETTE.

Of special materials there remains only one of importance to notice,—the paper made from tobacco for the envelopes of cigarettes. In this case the original tobacco-leaf is subjected to the least possible solvent action of reagents, so that the paper made from it shall be, in a degree, homogeneous with the contained material. A similar end has been attained by soaking a pure porous paper in tobacco-juice.

We are now prepared to consider the more modern processes of

Paper-making.—In treating this subject, we are necessarily restricted to its consideration in a general way, for as we approach our own day we find that while mechanical improvements have been more and more confined to minute details, the number of inventions has increased in proportion.

Sorting the Rags.—The first operation required, when rags, rope, etc. are used, is the sorting of them according to quality of material, color, etc. It must be evident that raw, coarse material will undergo much more waste in treatment than fine well-worn washed rags, for the processes which would be required to bring the first to useful stock would almost destroy the latter. In Europe, where labor is tolerably cheap, a very minute classification is adopted, each kind of the poorer material being at once employed for inferior paper. With us, for finer paper, the general classification into about six sorts is adopted, and for the very finest only one or two kinds may be used.

Cutting the Rags.—This operation is performed by means of large-bladed fixed knives, placed with the back to the operator. There are two objects in this process,—the first to reduce the material to proper size, the next to pick out the seams, the buttons, hooks and eyes, pins and needles, and above all the India-rubber, for these will in the subsequent processes injure the machinery, or carry undesirable impurities into the paper, and, in spite of every precaution, there are enough of these retained to entail some loss in fine paper, while for certain purposes some of them, invisible at first in the finished product, may become visible on use, as we shall show in the article on straining.

In some cases a rapidly revolving machine is used in cutting; but this prevents the removal of the matters just mentioned.

Dusting the Rags.—This operation is performed in rotating wire drums with beaters inside. There is a slight loss in the cutting, but much more in this process; sand, dust, and adhering impurities are removed, and some fibre is also lost. The loss in cutting and dusting varies from six to ten per cent., the coarsest material losing most.

Fermentation.—Formerly the rags were next subjected to fermentation, the origin of which is found in the nitrogenous matters before referred to. While this operation diminished the power required for the subsequent mechanical comminution, it was found so wasteful that it has been abandoned. The loss from this source alone was found to be from twenty-two to fifty per cent., the coarser material again losing the most.

Boiling in Alkaline Lye.—This is the modern substitute for the last process; the saving as compared with the fermentation is from six to eighteen per cent., while the operation is far more controllable. The simple boiling at or about the ordinary atmospheric pressure has long been used. Next we find something like a large Papin's digester, in which the pressure and consequently the temperature could be raised to any desirable degree, the object of the elevation of the temperature being mainly to expedite the process. The introduction of this great improvement into paper-making was made by Schäuffelen of Heilbronn, a most active, ingenious, and intelligent mechanic, whose improvements in paper-making were but a part of his successful inventions. Schäuffelen died in 1848. It is added to his credit that, being an expert swimmer, he saved, in the course of years, twelve persons from drowning in the Neckar.

At present rotating cylindrical boilers are used, provided with means for rapidly charging and discharging them. From what has been said before, as to the chemical properties of the cell-wall and adhering matters, it can be readily understood that this process separates the adjacent cells, and removes the incrusting and interpenetrating as well as the contained matter; and this is as true for rags as it is for rope, for straw, or for wood. The temperature, the strength of the lye, and the duration of the boiling must vary with the quantity and nature of the material to be removed, rags, ropes, straws, and woods differing in their different kinds as much as one of the classes does from the other. It will then seem incredible that the use of this process has been deemed a distinct invention for each class of materials.

As the boiling greatly facilitates the separation of the cells, and so lessens the subsequent labor, the modern process is sometimes called the chemical, in contradistinction to the more purely mechanical treatment.

The treatment of straw at once, or after cutting, and of wood previously reduced in some way, commences at this process; but while the previous steps are saved, the loss of material and the cost of the alkali are, especially for wood, greatly increased.

Comminution.—The old mode of reducing rags and other material to paper pulp was by stamps or beaters acting in mortars, not unlike the ordinary stamps for reducing ores to fine powder. By this method the danger of injury to the material was quite slight; but the time consumed was enormous, as compared with that occupied for the same process by the engines now in use.

The modern engine was invented in Holland about the middle of the last century, although its introduction into other countries was but slow. It consists essentially of an oblong cistern with semi-cylindrical ends, having a partition in the middle as long as the parallel sides; this leaves a space of equal width through which rags or pulp suspended in water may be made to describe something like an elliptical path coming on one side and returning on the other. On one side of the partition is placed a roll or cylinder furnished with groups of blades arranged parallel to its axis. On a bed raised from the bottom of the cistern is secured a block below the cylinder and opposed to it, furnished with similar blades, but inclined horizontally to the axis. When the cylinder is set in rapid motion, the water and suspended material are set in rotation, drawn up an inclined plane, and the material is brought under the action of the opposed blades, the obliquity of those of the bed causing it to be drawn out in two directions. If the cylinder were fastened, its action would be constant and either too great or too little. To obviate this, its axis turns in bearings on beams which can be accurately raised or lowered at will. The first object of this machine is to thoroughly wash the material for this purpose; the cylinder is well raised, the clean water enters, and dirty water flows out by suitable arrangements. The next object is to open out the material, rather than to break up the individual cells. To accomplish this, the cylinder is gradually lowered and the material is reduced. It is this part of the treatment which is so much abridged by the previous boiling in alkaline lye. This is called the rag or washing engine, and there may be two cylinders or rolls instead of one, and if these revolve with different velocity, the drawing-out action may be greatly increased. The product of this engine is half stuff.

From this the material is transferred to a similar engine with more blades generally, and revolving with much greater velocity. This is the beating engine. The words knife used for blade, and cut for beat, in most descriptions of this machinery, lead to a wholly erroneous idea of its action. If each contact with the blades cut the fibre or the cell, the result would be an incoherent mass. The true action is to tear or fray out the cells, and in the case of long ones to break them up into short fragments, as indeed is in part done in the first engine. But, instead of being cut, they are rather bruised and frayed, and the whole action tends to bring out the tendency to the spiral structure, which forms the interlacement of the product. If the cylinder is rapidly lowered and brought close to the bed, the process is quickly finished, but the product is rather coarse, too short, and with little capacity for interlacement, yielding a weak but opaque paper. Upon the other hand, if the cylinder is lowered very gradually, and never brought very close to the bed much more time is required, the stuff is left much longer, it is more frayed than broken, and the paper will be more translucent.

Bleaching.—The product of these processes will, however, rarely be white enough to answer the requirement of modern taste. The causes of color are various. Many fibres, from the mode of treatment used, retain substances which under the influences of the air are gradually darkened to a brownish gray, which is not altered by the mere action of the alkaline lye. All cells which contain incrusting matter, as especially in the case of wood, are left brown

by the alkali, even if there is so little of this as not in the least to interfere with their useful employment as paper stock; then, too, rags colored by certain dyes could not be used for white paper, which by bleaching can be made as good as any other. It is true we find the paper of old books, made as far back nearly as four hundred years, of great strength, though rather coarse, of a not undesirable tint, which in fact is in a degree imitated artificially by our modern tinted paper; but such was made from select material, of which there would not be enough to supply our modern demand.

The discovery of chlorine and its bleaching properties, in the year 1774, was almost immediately brought to bear upon paper-making, and before long its more convenient combination with lime, in the form of bleaching-powder or bleaching-salts, extended the application. But this, like many other improvements when incautiously used, introduced new evils. In the early part of this century we find books falling to powder in a few years, and wrapping papers ruining metallic articles inclosed in them, and this in spite of thorough washing of the stuff. This mischief was caused by the actual combination of the chlorine with the stock, which by gradual change produced agents destructive to the paper. This led to the invention of the so-called antichlor, which combined with the contained chlorine and produced inert compounds which could be washed out. For this purpose sulphurous acid or its chemical equivalents are used.

We cannot afford to enter into the details of the various methods and apparatus used in bleaching paper-stock, which is operated upon in the condition of half-stuff. Whether the chlorine is used as gas, or in the form of bleaching-salt, as soon as the proper effect is produced, the antichlor is added, and, after it has acted, the resulting product is washed out. With what we have explained before in regard to the nature of wood, we can understand the uselessness of the proposed, uneconomical, alternate action of alkali and of chlorine, the whole work of which may be done by sufficient alkaline treatment to remove as much as is required of the incrusting matter, and by one treatment of chlorine to remove the color.

The action of chlorine favors the more complete separation of the cells; though used alone for this purpose, it is not economical, and injures the mere cellulose.

Hand-made paper.—The oldest way of paper-making, undoubtedly derived from the Orientals and introduced into Europe, and so into this country, is that of making sheets of limited size. This method has within late years rapidly gone out of use, even more rapidly with us than in Europe, where it is still retained for special purposes, and where cheaper labor and a greater demand for the special product maintain it. If this process is still continued in this country, it is only at one or two of the oldest establishments; the latest of which we have any knowledge is at the mill started in 1729, and which has been continued to this day by the Wilcox family, for our country an unexampled instance of the continuance of the same mode of manufacture in the same family—possibly there may be one other like it.

The method of making paper by hand was as follows. The pulp, suspended in water in a vat, was taken up by hand in a mould. This consisted of a hard-wood frame, over which was placed a series of very close parallel wires, supported at intervals by cross-wires. This produced laid paper, easily recognized by corresponding marks upon the paper. Another form was produced by a woven wire gauze, which made wove paper. To precisely limit the sheet, there was placed over this bottom a frame, the deckel, which upon the mould formed a shallow sieve. This was introduced into the vat so as to take up a certain quantity of the pulp, which by dexterous manipulation was so shaken as to cause the particles to interknit while the water drained through the sieve. The deckel was then removed, the sheet, being on a flat surface, was skilfully applied to the uppermost of a pile of felts, or couched, this felt with its sheet removed to form another pile, and so on in succession until a post was formed; these were then pressed to exclude the contained water, and after pressure, arranged in a new order, again pressed, and finally the sheets themselves, placed one upon the other, had a similar treatment. It is useless in this place to describe the mode of sizing, after which, when partially dried, the sheets were again pressed. If certain figures were wrought with wire upon the mould, they produced the water-marks.

This process is identical with that used by the Chinese or Japanese at a very early period, and they, too, as is now done in England, produced sheets of great length, requiring the help of many hands to manage the moulds. At the present time the largest hand-made papers are drawing-paper made with the water-mark of Whatman, one of the oldest existing firms in England; the smallest are those made by the Bank of England, two notes forming a sheet, and the one cut with three peculiar deckel edges, being one characteristic of their notes. All hand-made papers, if not cut, are distinguished by their selvage or deckel edges.

Machine paper.—The consumption of time in the intermittent method of making paper by hand led to various attempts to imitate the process by machinery, but it was not till 1799 that Robert, in France, framed the conception of our present method. The only useful result obtained was when the Fourdriniers in England took this up, and, by new inventions and a vast expenditure of capital, brought the thing into practical use, for they first produced machines which, within the space of less than one hundred feet, converted the paper-pulp into a continuous sheet of finished paper. Even at this day we can conceive of no more wonderful spectacle than the operation of one of their machines; and everything that depends upon the cheap and rapid production of paper

and all its manifold uses and misuses is owing to their efforts. Sad to say, however, their great and useful labors were accomplished at their own great loss, and the last of the original firm died in our own time, at the age of ninety, a poor man. It is a curious fact that at the age of sixty-five the daughter of Robert was found in a state of utter destitution, when, by the charitable efforts of French and German paper-makers, she was placed above want. Associated with the Fourdriniers were the Donkins, efficient engineers, who helped in the earliest construction of the continuous paper-machines, and who have devised and improved the more recent revolving boilers, for treating paper material in contact with alkali under high pressure, bringing the last century into the midst of this. We cannot conceive greater advance in the arts, than that due to the united efforts of Fourdrinier and Donkin.

The general plan of the Fourdrinier machine is to substitute for the single wire moulds and felts of the hand-made paper, continuous, or rather endless, wire webs and felts; while they are doing their duty on the upper surface, they turn on leaving the paper and return below, being kept extended by ingenious mechanical contrivances. It is in this way that the operation is made continuous, and that from the pulp at one end of the machine the finished paper rolls out at the other end, in almost as many minutes as the old process had required weeks.

But, simple as is this general plan, many important details are required for its successful performance. In the first place, the pulp must be cleared of all lumps or knots before being delivered upon the wire web; this is done by a peculiarly-formed sieve or knotter, an apparatus upon which a good deal of ingenuity has been expended. Of course this must be often cleared to keep up its efficient action, and when rags only are used, it is found that fragments of India-rubber constitute a large portion.

Then to distribute the pulp and interlace or felt it, the wire web upon which it is received has a lateral motion back and forth, imitating the manipulation of the workman in hand-made paper, and facilitating the draining off of the water. At the same time the width of the paper is determined by deckel straps, which revolve in close contact with the wire web and return above. During this stage the flat surface of the web is supported by a series of rollers over which it is passed. Just before the half-consolidated paper leaves the endless web, an upper roller impresses it with the designs required to form the water-mark, if such is desired, while partially exhausted boxes beneath, finish the consolidation and remove more of the water. It then passes to an endless felt, upon which it is pressed by a roller above and below, and so couched. Beyond this, the paper is taken off the felt, passes between pressure rollers, and variously, in different machines, passes to another felt, undergoes a succession of pressures by passing between rollers of different kinds, and finally between a further succession of hollow, steam-heated rollers, and issues as a continuous sheet of dry and finished paper. If, however, the paper is to be divided into sheets of definite size, machines are appended which cut the continuous sheet longitudinally, and, by reciprocating cuts, crosswise, so that the separated portions are cut off as fast as the paper is delivered.

A modification of the Fourdrinier machine, known as the cylinder machine, was invented by Dickinson. In this a hollow, finely perforated cylinder, covered with a wire web, revolves in contact with the prepared pulp, and, exhausted within, the pulp is quickly deposited and consolidated. This allows of great simplification of the machinery, but the felting of the fibres is interfered with, and paper made on this machine has little strength crosswise.

For certain purposes, two or more sheets of continuous paper are made separately, and, before their final consolidation, are brought together, and by the subsequent pressure are completely united, forming a double- or triple-webbed paper.

It would be impossible to give, within our compass, an idea of the details and refinements of this important machine; but there is no difficulty in understanding that, for coarser or finer papers, the parts may be profitably contracted or expanded.

Sizing.—The paper produced in the way above described, would still be deficient in some important particulars. If well made, its tenacity might be sufficient, but it could not be written upon, for the porous surface would cause the ink to run, – in short, it would be blotting-paper; nor could it well be used for printing-paper, as the adhesion of the ink to the paper would produce such a balance of forces that the paper itself would be liable to injury in parting. The old hand-made paper was sized by means of gelatine (glue), the sheets being dipped into the size, and afterwards dried by a tedious hand manipulation and a prolonged exposure to the air. At an early period in the history of machine-made paper, it was proposed to introduce the size into the last or whole-stuff machine. It was at once found that gelatine could not be used, for any excess not adhering to the pulp would be lost in the water. This led to the introduction of a peculiar size, made by the combination of resin with an alkali, a resin soap, which, being decomposed by alum, left a residue attached to the fibre. From this arose the modern process of engine-sizing, the pulp being delivered to the machine with its cells or fragments coated with an insoluble resinous compound. With a vast number of recipes, some containing starch in addition, this mode of preparation has been found quite sufficient for printing-paper and for the commoner kinds of writing-paper.

Here comes in a curious property of such substances as may be used for sizing. If to paper pulp, or even pure chalk, be added a wholly soluble size, it will be found, on slow drying, that the largest portion of the size has traveled to the outside, forming a hard exterior crust, and leaving a soft interior; but if the drying is very rapid, the size remains diffused

through the whole mass, so that while the strength is as great the surface is not much better. The engine-sizing, with a certain delay in the drying, attains the desired end, but for fine writing-paper we must have a better surface. Consequently, we must resort to gelatine size, which, as we have above shown, cannot be introduced into the engine. The paper is therefore made and dried and then drawn through a bath of size. If the process is not very rapid, the size penetrates, and when the paper passes through the heated drying cylinders, the size is left in the mass, while the surface is not so good as it should be, but if the drying is prolonged, the size comes outward and leaves a close and desirable surface. If, however, the drying be too much prolonged, the size, under certain atmospheric conditions, will decompose; and who has not had painful experience of this, in the intolerable stench of certain nice-looking writing-papers? But at the present day the necessity of rapid production leads to the quickest finishing of the product, and so, if the sizing materials are originally good, we have a fair chance, between the two extremes, of getting a good product; but a stinking size in the finished paper should not be tolerated, for its further action upon the ordinary writing-ink might be disastrous.

Earthy Matter added to Paper.—One of the first notices of such additions which we can find, is the statement of the fact that the French paper-makers fraudulently added whiting, washed chalk, or carbonate of lime to their stock. By this addition the weight of the paper was cheaply increased, but its strength and other useful properties were diminished. After this fraud had been long known, Sholl, in 1858, obtained a patent in England for paper so made, because it had the property of converting the writing made by pale ink at once to quite black marks. This property depends upon the immediate decomposition of the ink. The best inks containing iron are at first pale, and become dark only by exposure to the air, after they have been absorbed by the paper and have become intimately combined with it. If such inks become quite black, as they often do from the faulty and wasteful inkstands generally in use, the ink put upon the paper lies more upon the surface, and is far more easily removed. But the addition of chalk at once decomposes the ink and puts it into a worse condition for its future preservation. Here arises a curious question; a man adds chalk to paper fraudulently, but another man has found that this paper has a peculiar property, which, as we have shown, is after all undesirable, and he obtains a patent,—for what? for finding that a certain kind of fraudulent paper has this property. Should he have a monopoly of making this known paper simply because he has discovered one of its properties?

Then we find sulphate of lime, (or plaster of Paris) added to the paper; this, like the last-mentioned substance, does not combine with nor directly attach itself to the paper stock, and in no wise improves, but in many ways deteriorates the paper. Under the name of Annaline, etc., this has been greatly puffed in Europe, and specimens said to contain three hundred per cent. (!) of annaline have been circulated. But sulphate of lime is soluble in water, and, in the compounds as furnished to paper-makers, already contains a large quantity of water. So (to use plain English,) the paper-maker purchases an article to cheat his customers, and meanwhile he himself is cheated. We may illustrate this by an example given us by one of the oldest paper-makers in our country, not now living. Interested in a mill managed by the younger members of his firm, he found that they had been tempted by the asserted properties to purchase largely of one of these new named articles. After several thousand dollars had been expended, it seemed that the paper was neither improved in appearance nor increased in weight, and our friend, who was an old practical chemist, was called upon to explain the mystery. He took a sheet of the paper, and, after drying, weighed it, then burned it carefully, and weighed the ash: this weight he found to be but little more than that of the pure paper stock,—proving that this substance, with its wonderful properties, had been dissolved and carried off, going down stream with the thousands of dollars paid for it.

Sulphate of baryta is another substance which has been used for this purpose, as well as for adulterating white lead, on account of its great specific gravity. But it has no affinity for the fibre, and, on account of its great weight, it is very difficult to keep it in suspension with the paper stock, and what does go over with it falls to the under side of the sheet before it becomes consolidated, giving an unequal appearance to the two sides.

At present the only useful addition employed is kaolin or China clay, or some similar aluminous compound. This has the property of closely attaching itself to the paper stuff, and gives the desired opacity, and a good surface, while it takes well both printing- and writing-ink, and, above all adds to the weight of the paper. We doubt whether if it were not for this and its contributing to the present foolish fashion for a dazzling white and opaque paper, it would be used at all. But the use of this substance requires an increased quantity of size, and an excess is, for any really good paper, absolutely injurious. We have seen a series of specimens of paper, said to contain various proportions of kaolin up to one hundred per cent., the last we presume not meaning a paper made wholly of clay, but containing half clay and half paper stuff.

Coloring Paper.—The coloring of paper in the vat is said to have originated from the accidental dropping of an indigo-bag into a vat of paper pulp by the wife of a paper-maker, a fact kept concealed, until the desirable tint of the product giving it a greatly increased value, led to the discovery of the cause. Color is given to this story by the statement that the husband, in his delight at this successful hit, made his wife a present of a costly scarlet cloak, and, as

the very name is mentioned, we cannot avoid giving to Mrs. Buttenshaw the credit of having originated this process, which, under various forms, continues to this day.

The fashion of blue-tinting, soon led to the use of other substances than indigo. For many years this color was given by smalt, a sort of glass colored by cobalt and very finely ground. The use of this was kept up by the employment of the coarser particles of the material for dusting upon paint to make the groundwork to the gilt letters of signs, under the name of strewing smalts. Chemical science first detected the peculiar nature of the color of the precious lapis lazuli or ultramarine, and soon attempted its artificial reproduction. After a little while the result was a cheap, very cheap, reproduction of this desirable color, and now our signs blaze with this dazzling blue, and papers are colored with it. But the fashion for blue-tinted paper is passing away. Ultramarine is one of the most durable colors, under certain conditions; it even endures the heat of the porcelain furnace, and in old painting is one of the most lasting colors; but it is at once bleached by the action of acids. In most sizing methods, alum was added, and its acid reaction destroyed the color of the ultramarine. Various processes were devised to prevent this action, some of which were quite successful, but they involved the use of certain precautions which cost some trouble and pains. We believe that it is this, and this only, which has led to the modern fashion of tinted paper, in which a quite opposite tint—a delicate pinkish yellow—is used.

There are four ways in which paper can be colored in the vat. The first is by the intermixture with the pulp of solid insoluble substances, such as smalt and artificial ultramarine. These constantly tend to settle, and special contrivances must be used in the continuous paper-machine to avoid this difficulty, as it produces a difference between the two sides of the paper. This has undoubtedly helped to change the fashion.

The next process is to use some substance which will stain the paper; but here the body of the colored fluid remains, and is finally lost, while much of it goes over, staining the felts, and often acting upon the metallic parts of the paper-machine.

A more judicious and economical plan is to use rags already colored. But here arises the difficulty, that when mixed with white or colored rags, each particle maintains its own color, and while the general impression to the eye is good, close examination shows a difference displeasing to fastidious modern taste.

The fourth and best plan is to produce the color by two substances, which combined give the desired tint; first one is added which more or less combines with the paper stuff—then the other which causes the color to deposit, in an insoluble form, in and upon it. In this way is formed the usual buff, as for envelopes. A solution of the cheap sulphate of iron, copperas, is made to penetrate the stuff, then there is added an alkaline solution which deposits in and on the paper stuff an oxide of iron, which on exposure to the air quickly attains the desired tint.

Again, to heighten this color, or of itself to give a full yellow, or, when mixed, an orange tint, first a soluble salt of lead is used, and then the bichromate of potash, producing the beautiful yellow chromate of lead. Few persons, however, are aware of one dangerous property of paper so colored. When once set on fire, if the quantity of chromate contained is sufficient, the combustion of the paper is continued by the oxygen of the chromic acid, the paper is a true touch-paper, and if incautiously thrown down goes on to burn, and may do extensive damage. This whole subject of colored paper is so admirably illustrated in the remarkable work of Piette that we must refer to our special notice under his name.

Calendering and Finishing Paper.—With a general notice of the later operations of the paper-making machine, we have not dwelt particularly upon the final process, which, subjecting it to great pressure, and under the influence of heat, gives so much of the desired polish to the surface. Our modern use of steel pens—at best an abomination, for one good gold pen will far outlast its value in steel pens—requires the addition of China clay, from which no fibres can be carried off, and, above all, a highly-polished surface, which is best attained by subjecting the paper to the action of heated rolls, under great pressure. But if the paper is not surcharged with clay, a new set of appearances are brought out. The excessive pressure, welds together the vegetable fibres, and from being opaque they become translucent: the slightest increase of thickness in any one place, thus becomes apparent by a corresponding translucency, and the paper appears spotted; we have various specimens in our collection which show this. It is evident, therefore, that for these finer kinds of paper, subjected to such treatment, especial pains must be taken to distribute the pulp upon the machine with the utmost exactness. At the same time, the most inconsiderable fragments of India-rubber are spread out to produce a dark but transparent spot, and in fine paper this produces a corresponding loss.

Microscopic Examination of Paper and of Paper Material.—From what we have said above, and in the treatise already mentioned in the Agricultural Report of the Patent Office for 1859, it will be seen that it is only by the microscope, with the application of suitable reagents, that we can actually determine what there is in paper as made, recognize even the substances used, and, in a degree, the kind of treatment to which they have been subjected. It is by this means also that we can determine beforehand, with small quantities, and before any costly experiment, the properties and capabilities of any material proposed for paper-making, and so accept or reject materials as worthy or unworthy of more particular experiment. The microscope should be the constant companion of the intelligent paper-

maker, for without its aid he must remain ignorant of the quality and condition of the materials he uses. In such an investigation he cannot do without the works of Schacht and Wiesner, mentioned below.

Works containing Specimens, Drawings, or Special Information about Paper.—In the work of Harding, above mentioned, there are given specimens of paper taken at the various stages of the process. We know of no other work which so well illustrates this matter. Besides these, a variety of water-marks are given, with a few specimens of paper made of material other than rags.

The author gives one specimen which is worthy of especial notice. It has a water-mark, is tinted, and highly finished on the surface. One thousand such sheets together give a thickness of only three-fourths of an inch; each sheet is therefore 0.00075 of an inch thick; and yet a strip of this paper four inches wide supports twenty pounds.

The *Central-Blatt für deutsch Papierfabrikation*, edited by Alwin Rudel, is full of useful information, and gives a few specimens.

The works of Piette and of Schaeffer, with an abundance of illustrative specimens, will be more particularly described under their respective names.

The work of Dr. L. Müller, *Die Fabrication des Papiers*, Berlin, 1862, third edition, and in its earlier forms, will be found full of accurate information.

Of the two editions of Matthias Kopp's book, we have already given sufficient notice.

The various and exhaustive articles in the *Allgemeine Encyclopädie der Wissenschaften und Künste* of Ersch and Gruber, give up to the time of that volume, 1838 (for the work is still going on), an admirable summary of the history of the subject, under the heads of Paper, etc., and Papyrus. But we have seen that this, under the light of modern investigation, must be much modified.

The first work giving accurate microscopic representations of the condition of the fibre in paper was communicated to the Royal Academy of Sciences in Vienna, in 1845, but was not published in their transactions until 1852.

In 1853, Dr. Hermann Schacht published his work, *Die Prüfung der in Handel vorkommende Gewebe durch das Mikroscope und durch chemische Reagenten.* We give in this article all of his drawings, illustrating the condition of vegetable fibre in paper.

The latest and best work on this subject is Dr. Julius Wiesner's *Einleitung in die technischen Microscopie*, etc. From this work we have obtained the clue to the structure of papyrus, some of the doubtful points in the history of the manufacture being settled for us by his researches, although he has not himself touched upon them. The work is full of special instruction for the technical microscopic investigation of paper and paper material. This work and that of Schacht cannot be dispensed with by those who propose to go thoroughly into this branch of the subject.

The Microscopic Dictionary of Griffith and Henfry

gives many drawings of fibres, and under different treatment.

Astle, in The Origin and Progress of Writing, etc., gives many curious details in regard to ancient manuscripts, from those under his charge or in his own valuable collection.

Several other authors have written on this subject, and given specimens; but we have no personal knowledge of their works.

See, further, PARCHMENT PAPER, PIETTE, SAFETY PAPER, SCHAEFFER, SPLITTING PAPER, STAINING, WRITING- NK. See, also, DIMENSIONS OF PAPER, for the names and sizes of paper in general use; GIVING-OUT PAPER, for the amounts required for particular jobs, and that portion of the article on INVENTIONS which is devoted to PAPER-MAKING, for an account of the various processes, machinery, etc. which have been patented in the United States.

Paper-Boards.—Boards placed at the bottom and top of a pile of paper intended for a particular work or job, especially when it is dampened or wet down.

Paper-Cutter, or Paper-Cutting Machine.—A machine intended to cut paper. It is generally called a cutting-machine in printing-offices, and a paper-cutter by dealers in printers' materials. A paper-cutter of some description has become a necessary implement in all job-offices in which a considerable amount of work is done; and the large demand for paper-cutters in this country has led to the invention and manufacture of a great variety of styles. A number of these are described and illustrated in this work, under alphabetical headings corresponding to their respective names or the names of their manufacturers.

Papering the Cases.—Affixing pieces of paper to the bottom of the boxes. It is done by the manufacturers of the cases.

Papering-up Letter.—Wrapping up the pages of matter in paper, to be placed aside for future use. The type should be carefully tied up, and should be perfectly dry before it is papered; and on the outside of each package should be written the description of its contents.

Paper-Knife.—A knife used to cut up paper for printing. This work is now generally done on paper-cutting machines, the paper-knife being employed only to cut up the paper used on small orders, and in offices where paper-cutters have not been introduced.

Paper-Ruling Machines.—See RULING MACHINES.

Papier-Mache.—Mashed paper, a French term for a composition consisting of paper-cuttings boiled in water and beaten to a pulp, which is hardened by glue or size until it is exceedingly tenacious, and is used as material for ornamental articles of household furniture, inkstands, and portfolios, as well as in the system of stereotyping known as the papier-maché process.

Papier-Mache, or Paper Process.—An exceedingly quick method of stereotyping, used chiefly in stereotyping newspaper forms,—the whole opera-

tion being sometimes performed in fifteen minutes. (See STEREOTYPING.)

Papyrography.—A method of taking impressions from a sort of pasteboard covered with a calcareous substance.

Parable.—A fictitious but probable narrative taken from the events of ordinary life, to illustrate a moral or religious truth.

Paragon.—A type one size larger than Great Primer, and one smaller than Double Pica.

Paragraph.—1. A sign (¶), denoting the beginning of a new subject, or a new sentence, and also used as a reference mark. 2. A distinct section or a portion of a treatise or article relating to a particular subject. Several simple sentences may be embraced within a paragraph, and it is marked, both in manuscript and printing, by a blank space at the commencement of the first line. In printing, the first line of a paragraph is indented an em quadrat, of the type used; but in wide measure, two or even three ems improve the appearance, making the paragraph more strongly marked, the space of a single em being very slight in a long line. Authors differ greatly in their style of paragraphing, some using the division only to mark complete sections, or the commencement of an entirely new topic, while in the writings of others the paragraphs are almost as numerous as the sentences. Heavier styles of composition, and didactic treatises, generally require the long paragraph, while the lighter styles of descriptive, dramatic, or colloquial writing appear more vivid and lifelike when broken up into short ones. As a general rule, German and English writers prefer the longer paragraph, while the French, and some Americans, use the shorter as suited to a more vivacious style. In printing, a single word, or portion of a word, should be avoided, if possible, in a break-line; the final line of a paragraph should never stand at the top of a page; and the first line of a paragraph should not make the last line of a page when the work has blank lines between the breaks: to prevent this, the page may be shortened or lengthened, making the odd and even pages back, so that the difference shall not be perceptible.

Parallel.—A reference mark (‖) which follows the Section, and precedes the Paragraph.

Parallel Matter.—Matter printed in parallel columns, in such a manner that conflicting arguments or statements are brought into immediate contrast. In newspapers, parallel matter is usually printed in a measure only half as wide as the ordinary column; and in all parallel matter, efforts are generally made to have each paragraph commence on a line with the paragraph to which it corresponds in the opposite column.

Paraphrase.—The rendering of the meaning of a writing in other words, presumed to be more readily apprehended. A translation in which a new series of ideas and illustrations are made to express the same general meaning as the original, is also termed a paraphrase; also the rendering of verse into prose.

Parchment.—A writing-material formed of the skins of sheep and goats. The name is said to be derived from the fact that Eumenes, King of Pergamus, being engaged in collecting a large library, B.C. 250, excited the jealousy of Ptolemy of Egypt, who, fearing rivalry to the library of Alexandria, prohibited the export of papyrus. The King of Perganius therefore used skins prepared according to a manner then known to many of the Asiatic nations, but, introducing some improvements into the manufacture, it was called pergamena, a word afterwards altered into parchment. In Europe, at the beginning of the eighth century, parchment had almost entirely superseded papyrus, and all the public documents of the time of Charlemagne were written upon it. From that period until the general introduction of paper, books and documents were usually written or printed upon parchment, or a finer quality of prepared skins, called vellum (see VELLUM). In the handsomest ancient manuscripts, the parchment was colored purple or yellow, upon one or both sides; the purple having a gorgeous effect especially when the lettering was in gold highly ornamented with rich paintings, and even with jewels (see MANUSCRIPTS). Being more imperishable than paper, parchment is still frequently used for deeds, etc., and also in binding large and heavy volumes, such as ledgers and books of accounts. In the manufacture, the skins are prepared as if for tanning; they are then shaved down and rubbed with pumice-stone, and finally stretched and dried with great care.

Parchment Paper.—In the article on paper we referred to the action of sulphuric acid upon cellulose, as forming the basis of the preparation of what is now known as parchment paper. The experiment was made in 1846, by MM. Poumarède and Figuier, two well-known French chemists. They immersed a sheet of unsized paper in sulphuric acid for less than half a minute, and then put it into water to wash out the acid, the last traces of which were removed by soaking in water containing a little ammonia.

The paper thus prepared was found to have assumed the appearance of parchment, both when wet and when dry; and the discoverers at once suggested that it might be useful in the arts. They also suggested the probability of its identity with a peculiar paper made by Schönbein, the preparation of which was then a secret. We now know that this material was gun-cotton paper, made by immersing paper in a mixture of sulphuric and nitric acids. Its physical condition is identical with that of the paper prepared by MM. Poumarède and Figuier, but chemically it has the composition of gun-cotton.

In studying this action, it was found that on the removal of the acid the cellulose had its original composition unchanged. The action of the acid consisted in a temporary combination with the cellulose, at which time the fibres were so softened that they became as if fused together.

The moment of this change is indicated by a test which shows that, for the time, there is a real chemical alteration—for at this time the action of iodine produces the same blue color that it does with starch: on removal of the acid, however, this property disappears. About this time, the action of a strong solution of chloride of zinc was found to produce the same effect. Indeed, where used as a test under the microscope, the chloride is more convenient, and we have always employed it for that purpose.

In the year 1853, the process was patented in England, and, falling into the hands of enterprising men, the article was at once brought into the market. The only modification was the use of sulphuric acid diluted with about one-half its bulk of water; but it is found that the amount of dilution can be varied.

Patents have also been obtained for forming parchment paper with chloride of zinc.

When wet, as it is when first formed, this paper takes up water, but of itself it is water-proof, just as with animal membrane. When first made, on drying, it contracts enormously, and this produces a difficulty in the manufacture, since in a large sheet it is impossible to obtain quite uniform contraction. Care in the manufacture seems to have overcome this in some degree. Minute pin-holes are found in the paper, which are also owing to this contraction. Such holes are seen, too, in the gun-cotton paper.

One fault of parchment paper is its too great rigidity, being sometimes more like horn than parchment. This is prevented by using a small quantity of glycerine, or of other substance having somewhat similar properties.

There seems to be no reason why this paper should not almost wholly take the place of parchment, unless, indeed, for some purposes it might be too hard. It is said that it is now allowed to be used in England for documents required by law to be parchment.

For such uses as covering books, boxes, pocketbooks, and other matters where a stout paper or thin leather or dressed and glazed muslin is used, parchment paper, for its durability and other properties, seems to be the most suitable material, especially as it takes color well and is capable of being embossed. In the ninth volume of Piette's Journal des Fabricants de Papier there are several specimens, well illustrating this use.

From its resistance to moisture, it has been used to cover cartridges, to inclose confections and substances injured by exposure to air or to moisture.

Dr. Graham found it to be the best substitute for parchment in experiments on dialysis, by means of which crystalline substances and those called colloids, like jelly or glue, are separated from each other, the mixture being on one side of the membrane, and pure water on the other. In this operation, the crystalline substance passes into the water, while the colloid remains behind. The great and increasing use of this process is facilitated by the employment of parchment paper, which does not alter, as real parchment will under certain conditions. For this use, however, the pin-holes must be stopped, as with white of egg afterwards coagulated by heat.

The translucency of parchment paper makes it a good tracing-paper. This leads to the notice of an interesting fact in the history of this curious substance, and one which we have discovered only since preparing this article. Pierre Gerle obtained a patent in France for making paper transparent by means of sulphuric acid, on the 1st of March, 1839, seven years before the experiments of Poumaròde and Figuier, and fourteen years before the first English patent.

Parchment Tympans.—When the tympans and drawers of hand-presses are covered with parchment, care should be taken in the selection that it is of uniform thickness, and that the skins are free from imperfections and cuts. The parchment for the drawer may be a little thinner than that for the tympan.

Parenthesis, Marks of.—Two curved lines ( ), used to indicate expressions inserted in the body of a sentence, which break its unity by being either of an explanatory character, or so slightly connected with the context that they may be omitted without injury to its sense. In printing, they were formerly used much more frequently than at present, the comma or the dash being now employed to designate many clauses which would, in former times, have been inclosed in marks of parenthesis.

Parody.—A close imitation of the words of another composition, either in prose or verse, so as to produce a ludicrous meaning or adapt it to a new purpose.

Passing the Make-up.—Passing to the next hand in order the lines remaining (if any) after a compositor has made up his matter, together with the gauge and proper folio.

Paste.—A cement having the power to hold such substances as paper, etc. together, the term being usually applied in printing-offices to paste made of a mixture of water and wheat or rye flour, boiled, with or without other ingredients.

Pasteboard.—A thick stiff paper, made by pasting several sheets upon one another, or by macerating paper and casting it in moulds.

Pastel.—A crayon made of a paste composed of coloring matter and gum-water, used for painting on paper and parchment.

Paste Points.—Small brass or card points, pasted on the tympan for obtaining good register for cards, circulars, etc.

Paste-Pot.—A cup or other vessel used for holding paste in a printing-office.

Pastoral.—A poem descriptive of country life, of shepherds and their occupations.

Patents.—For the patents relating to printing which have been granted in the United States, see INVENTIONS.

Patois.—A provincial dialect.

Pawl Press.—A standing press, used by printers and bookbinders, which, next to hydraulics, is the most powerful standing press made.

Pearl.—A small type, one size larger than Diamond.

Peel.—An implement shaped somewhat like the

PAWL PRESS.

letter T, used for hanging up sheets on lines or slats. For a picture of the peel and the old mode of hanging sheets, see illustration of ANCIENT PRINTING-OFFICES.

Penny-a-Liners.—A name applied to a class of writers who furnish contributions to a newspaper, and sometimes to collectors of items or local reporters, from the fact that, at one period such contributions were paid for at the rate of a penny per line. Formerly, collectors of intelligence gathered at certain places in London, where they told their news to writers whose business it was to choose the most interesting items, commit them to paper, and prepare a number of copies, which they took to the journals, running the risk of their acceptance by one or several papers.

Penultimate.—Almost the last,—used to denote the last syllable but one of a word, the last syllable being known as the ultimate, the next preceding as the penultimate, and the second from the last as the ante-penultimate.

Perfecting.—Printing the second form of a sheet which backs, and thus completes, or perfects, the first form.

Perfecting Presses.—Presses which simultaneously, or by only one feeding, print both sides of a sheet of paper. Of the fast presses of the present day, three—the Bullock, Marinoni, and the Walter press—are perfecting; and a number of book perfecting presses have been invented. The latter are extensively used in England, and a few are in operation in the United States.

Period.—In punctuation, a mark or dot placed at the end of a completed sentence, or as a sign of abbreviation, as Dec.; Dr.; A. D. When used as a sign of abbreviation, it has no value in punctuation, except that, by usage, and as a matter of typographical neatness, the point is not doubled when it occurs at the end of a sentence. Periods or full points are sometimes used as leaders, in tables of contents, figure-work, etc.; but leaders can supply the place of the periods and quadrats, and save considerable time in composition.

Periodicals.—This term includes all publications continued in numbers, appearing at stated and regular intervals, but in recent usage it is confined to serial publications containing tales, poems, and essays on topics of popular interest, either literary, scientific, or artistic. The first literary periodical appeared in France, in 1665, with the title of Journal des Savants, and answered in description to what is usually now styled a critical review. A similar publication was commenced in Rome in 1668; in England the first attempt was made in 1681, but was unsuccessful, and several others failed, until, in 1699, a review devoted chiefly to continental works was established. Germany, although following England, in the fact that her first periodical was commenced a few months later, is really entitled to precedence, for the reason that the serial received an excellent style of communications, and was continued for almost a century. In Holland a similar publication was established in 1684. These early works in France, Italy, Germany, Holland, and England all resembled the modern review, and excluded that lighter style of literature now accepted as that of the periodical proper. Germany probably led the way in introducing sketches and illustrations into serial publications, but the first regular attempt at the modern magazine was made in the Gentleman's Magazine, in London, in 1731 (see MAGAZINES). How welcome such a convenient abstract of current litera-

ture was to the reading public, may be judged from the success of all the early periodicals, and the rapid increase both in number and in circulation. The service that they perform is well expressed in a tribute to the memory of George Miller, who, in 1812, established The Cheap Magazine, at Dunbar, in Scotland:—

Within thy native district first to rear
The Press, which, in thy hands, was doomed to wear
A chaster form:—No more, from door to door,
The lounging pedlar hawked his poisoned lore;
For now, subservient to one virtuous end,
Amusement with instruction thou didst blend.
And lo! where Brougham and Chambers blaze in day,
Thou went before, and gently cleared the way;
Unmindful of the magic of a name,
In secret toiled, and blushed to find it fame.

The peculiarities of American society led to the early introduction of literary serials, one after the model of the Gentleman's Magazine being attempted as early as 1741; and all styles of periodicals have rapidly increased in the country, especially during late years. About the end of the seventeenth century, serials devoted to the various arts and sciences began to appear. The Philosophical Transactions, commenced in London in 1665, and the Miscellanea Curiosa, commenced in Germany in 1670, are considered to be the first journals devoted to the natural and philosophical sciences. The first medical serial appeared in Paris in 1683, and the earliest upon jurisprudence in the same city in 1692. Germany introduced theological journalism in 1701, and the first publication on philology in 1715, continuing to this day to exceed all other countries in its number of publications connected with the study of languages. The first periodical upon agriculture appeared in France during the eighteenth century, and the agricultural publications of that country, and those of the United States, where they are particularly excellent and numerous, are regarded as excelling those of both Germany and England. The several serials devoted to mechanical industries commenced in England, but were rapidly introduced into France and Germany, where they have been carefully and successfully conducted; and they have been rapidly multiplying of late years, particularly in Germany and the United States. The number of periodicals published at present is beyond computation, although it was, in 1869, roughly estimated that the value of the sales in Great Britain and Ireland amounted to three hundred and seventy thousand pounds in gold, while the annual sales in the United States were supposed to be nearly equal to that sum. By actual count, there are published in London, in 1871, 473 periodicals, of which 338 appear monthly, 76 quarterly, 37 weekly, and the remainder annually, semi-annually, and bi-monthly.

Perkins, Jacob.—A distinguished American inventor, regarded as having introduced one of the greatest improvements in the art of plate-engraving. He was born in Newburyport, Massachusetts, in 1766.

Apprenticed at an early age to a goldsmith, he soon exhibited his inventive genius by introducing a new method of plating shoe-buckles, and was quite successful in the manufacture. When only about twenty-one years of age, he was employed by the State of Massachusetts to make dies for copper coinage. He next invented a machine for cutting and heading nails, patented in 1795, and shortly afterwards turned his attention to that branch of industrial art in which he afterwards gained so great a reputation. Copper had been, previous to this time, the only material used for plate-engraving, steel having been used but in one instance, in England, in 1805, in a print in a book entitled The Topographical Illustrations of Westminster. By the invention of Perkins, a steel plate engraved by the method used in copper-plate is hardened so as to transfer the design by pressure upon other plates of softened steel, which can in turn be hardened and used to transfer the design to an indefinite extent. A peculiar style of note, with a stereotype check, invented by Perkins, was in 1808, by a special law of Massachusetts, directed to be used by all the banks in the Commonwealth, as a thorough protection against counterfeiting; and it was used in some New England banks until a very recent period. His substitution of steel for copper, and his invention of transfers, were especially applicable to bank-note-engraving, and in 1814 Perkins removed to Philadelphia, and became associated with the firm of Murray, Draper & Fairman. Asa Spencer, also connected with the same firm, shortly afterwards succeeded in applying lathe-work to bank-notes, securing what was at that period considered an absolute protection against counterfeits. The directors of the Bank of England had endeavored, in 1800, to furnish notes secured from imitation; but forgeries had multiplied, and in 1818 they offered liberal propositions for competition.

Attracted by this opportunity, Perkins went to England, accompanied by Mr. Fairman and a number of experienced workmen. Unfortunately for his success, a London wood-engraver succeeded, after a number of efforts, in making a wood-cut copy of one of Perkins's pieces of lathe-work, and he was therefore compelled to withdraw from the contest, and the manufacture of the notes was awarded to Applegarth & Cowper, in 1820. Perkins, however, obtained the privilege of making the notes for the Bank of Ireland, and for this purpose entered into partnership, in London, with the distinguished engraver Heath, a connection which continued until the death of Perkins, in 1849.

Peroration.—The conclusion of an oration, in which the arguments are recapitulated in a rapid and brilliant manner, or a comprehensive conclusion is deduced, or an appeal made to the audience.

Perspective.—The method by which objects are delineated upon a plane surface, as they appear to the eye from any given distance or situation.

Petrography.—The art of writing on stone.

Pfister, Albrecht.—A printer of Bamberg, urged by some authorities as the inventor of movable types. The earliest work that can be positively claimed for Pfister is the Book of the Four Histories, the colophon of which states that it was completed in Bamberg; and in the same town Albrecht Pfister printed it, in the year in which we count one thousand four hundred and sixty. The colophon of a book called Belial, or the Consolation of a Sinner, also states that it was printed by Pfister at Bamberg, but has no date; and the Liber Similitudinis, an illustrated book of fables, dated at Bamberg in 1461, without any printer's name, has been with great probability ascribed to him. Contemporaneous writers have mentioned a fine Bible printed about this period at Bamberg, and this fact has caused what is generally known as the thirty-six-line Bible to be also ascribed to Pfister. The type of this work bears so close a resemblance to the Bible of Gutenberg that it has been claimed for that printer, other authorities urging that the type had been purchased from Gutenberg. This work is sometimes styled the Schelhorn Bible, from being first described by that author. A copy in the British Museum, and one in the French Imperial Library, are printed on paper, in three folio volumes, consisting of 881 leaves, and set in double column. Several other works have been claimed for Pfister, on the uncertain evidence of similarity of type, and some leading writers upon typography ascribe to him the Letters of Indulgence, dated 1454, the Appeal against the Turks, 1455, in nine quarto pages; the Calendar of 1457, and a Donatus of the presumed date of 1451. These works are in a large Gothic type, and have been ascribed both to Gutenberg and Pfister. The paternity of these early undated works has been, and still continues to be, a matter of dispute, and in some cases the question has even been complicated by the doubt as to whether some of them were not block-books. Two works, known as The Seven Joys of Mary, and The Passions of Jesus Christ, claimed for Pfister, are remarkable as containing illustrations from metal plates.

Philology.—The knowledge, study, or love of languages, and of the branches connected with them. According to general use, philology comprises etymology, grammar, rhetoric, poetry, and literary criticism.

Phonography.—A system of writing, by which each sound of a language is represented by a separate character or symbol; particularly, a method of short-hand writing used instead of stenography. Out of phonography has grown an attempt to reconstruct the orthography of the English language on phonetic principles, and to establish a new alphabet to be used in printing.

Phonotypy.—The art of printing by sound, or by characters or types representing the sounds of the human voice.

Photogalvanography.—A process (now little used) for transferring drawings, etc. to metal by means of light. A plate is rendered sensitive by gelatine and bichromate of potash, and exposed to light in contact with the photograph or drawing. A mould is then taken from this plate after exposure, and an electrotype impression taken from the mould. This electrotype is used for printing. The process is tedious, requiring some weeks for its completion.

Photoglyptic Engraving.—A process invented by Mr. Fox Talbot, by which, through the agency of light, photographic and other transparent designs can be transferred to metal plates. It is performed as follows: A solution of one part of gelatine in 40 parts of water is mixed with 4 parts of a saturated solution of bichromate of potash, and the mixture is poured over the steel or copper plates, and allowed to dry. It is then exposed, in contact with the object which it is desired to copy, in a printing-frame, to the action of light for several minutes. After this exposure to light, a little finely-powdered copal is strewed over the surface, and melted by the aid of heat. The design is now etched in by means of hydrochloric acid, saturated with peroxide of iron, and diluted with water. This attacks only the parts unacted on by light. When a sufficient depth has been obtained, the etching liquid is washed off, and the plate cleaned with soft whiting. It can then be employed for printing.

Photography.—The art of producing pictures of objects by the action of light on chemically prepared surfaces, or, in a more restricted sense, the art of producing such pictures on chemically prepared paper.

Photography has gradually risen, and assumed a scientific and practical form, from a series of accidental experiments and observations. In 1722, Petit observed that solutions of nitrate of potash and muriate of ammonia crystallized more readily under the light than they did in darkness. Scheele, in 1777, stated that a solution of silver in acid of nitre poured on chalk became black under the effect of the sunlight, and that chloride of silver became black soonest under the violet ray. Count Rumford, in 1798, wrote a memoir entitled An Inquiry concerning the Chemical Properties that have been attributed to Light, in which he endeavored to prove that the effects produced by sunlight upon metallic solutions were due to heat. This opinion was refuted by Harrup, in 1802, who proved that several of the salts of mercury were reduced by light and not by heat. Ritter, in 1801, showed the existence of rays in the solar spectrum which are to be found beyond its visible limits, and that these rays darkened chloride of silver. The effect of light and of the several colored rays now attracted considerable attention, and observations were made by Berard, Seebeck, Berthollet, Herschel, Englefield, Wollaston, Davy, and others. In 1802, a remarkable article was prepared for the Journal of the Royal Institution of Great Britain, by Thomas Wedgwood and Humphrey Davy, afterwards so widely known as Sir Humphrey Davy. The paper was entitled—An Account of a Method of Copying Paintings upon Glass, and of Making Profiles by the Agency of Light upon Nitrate of Silver; with

Observations by H. Davy. In the application of an optical instrument to imprint images of natural objects illuminated by the sunbeam or other source of light upon a sensitive chemical surface, this essay may be considered as containing the germ of the photographic art as at present practiced; and Davy concluded with these words:—Nothing but a method of preventing the unshaded parts of the delineations from being colored by exposure to the day, is wanting to render this process as useful as it is elegant. Although so fairly commenced, these investigations were not pursued, and nothing was done in photography in England until 1834, when Fox Talbot commenced experiments with the same view, but in absolute ignorance of what had been already accomplished. In France, in 1813, Niepce undertook a series of experiments with the same intention as those pursued by Wedgwood in England,—that is, to fix the images of the camera. He continued his experiments until 1827, when he achieved such success that he presented a memoir with specimens to the Royal Society of London; but no notice was taken of the matter, for the reason that he did not reveal his processes. In 1829, Niepce made the acquaintance of Daguerre, who had at that time acquired considerable celebrity for his dioramic paintings, and a partnership was formed, which continued until the death of Niepce, in 1833, when it was continued by his son Isidore Niepce. In January, 1839, Daguerre exhibited his first pictures, afterwards so widely known as Daguerrootypes, but kept the process a secret until the following July. Meanwhile Fox Talbot, in England, pursuing a similar train of investigations, presented a paper to the Royal Society, January 13, 1839, entitled—Some Account of the Art of Photogenic Drawing, or the Process by which Natural Objects may be made to delineate themselves without the Aid of the Artist's Pencil. Another communication upon preparing sensitive paper and fixing the images obtained was presented by him on the 21st of February; and he thus secured to himself the priority of publication of a method for the production of sun-drawn pictures. The original process of Daguerre received its first improvement from Figeau, and was greatly improved by Goddard, in 1840, who combined bromine with the original chemical iodine, and succeeded in rendering the plate much more sensitive. In the process of Talbot, iodide of silver was used, with nitrate of silver in excess, upon paper, to procure an image which remained latent until developed by a solution of gallic acid. The collodion process of Scott Archer consists of a film of collodion on glass, the collodion containing iodide of silver with an excess of nitrate, the image being developed by pyro-gallic acid, or by sulphate of iron, introduced by R. Hunt as a substitute for gallic acid. The elder Niepce, in the earlier years of his experiments, introduced a valuable process, which he styled Heliography, in which pictures were made upon a surface of bitumen laid upon a metal plate and afterwards engraved by acid; the bituminous surface being hardened by light so as to defy the action of the usual solvents, the shaded portions were affected by the solvents, and upon the removal of the shadows the plate was readily etched by aqua fortis. By a more recent process of Talbot, a sensitive film of bichromate of potash and gelatine is placed upon a steel plate; upon this surface a positive photograph is made, and the gelatine becomes almost insoluble wherever the light falls through the positive. The shaded parts of the plate can then be etched by acid, and an engraved surface obtained that can be printed from with printing-ink. Instead of etching the plate produced by the effect of light on the gelatine, Pretsch has used liquids, and obtained therewith a grained image in relief, a mould from which can be electrotyped to form a copper-plate surface that can be used to print from. Pretsch has also produced plates to be used like wood engravings. Impressions from these plates can be conveyed to porcelain or glass, and burnt in by the enameler. Chromium was first applied to general photographic processes by Ponton and Becquerel. Pauncey and others have introduced methods by which pigments and inks are made to adhere only to the altered gelatine and chromium compound surface, on stone, glass, paper, porcelain, or metals. Niepce de Saint-Victor presented, during the years 1851 and 1852, several papers to the Academy of Sciences of Paris, describing the method by which he made silver plates sensitive by chloride of copper, and reproduced upon them images in the natural colors of the objects. The method has been called Heliochromy.

Photography has already become a distinct branch of printing; some enthusiasts have ventured to predict that it will eventually be a formidable rival of all other forms of printing; but at present the slowness and cost of its processes seem to be insurmountable barriers to the fulfillment of this prophecy. It has, however, already proved a valuable auxiliary, as designs can readily be photographed on wood for the use of the engraver (this art having been perfected by Mr. Benjamin F. Taylor, of Philadelphia), and photographed on stone or zinc in a manner which makes them available to lithographers; while various attempts have been made to produce cuts capable of being printed on typographic presses without the aid of an engraver.

Photo-Lithography.—A method of printing on lithographic stones, by the aid of Photography, designs which can be printed by the ordinary lithographic processes. (See LITHOGRAPHY.) The Osborne process for accomplishing this object is thus described in one of the publications of the American Photo-Lithographic Company:

We desire to reproduce a given drawing. Taking it to the camera room, the photographer makes a negative of it, enlarging or reducing the size, or copying it equal scale, as may be required. This negative does not differ essentially from ordinary photographic negatives, save that greater care is used in its development, that every detail on the original

may appear in the copy. We next print from this negative, by sunlight, upon a sensitized paper, care being taken that the exposure is uniformly exact. Having by these two operations obtained a photograph, or sun-print, of the drawing, we now proceed to transform this print into a transfer-sheet, which is accomplished by the several processes of inking, floating, and washing-off,—thus completing the photographic part of the reproduction.

To transform the sun-print into a transfer-sheet, the entire surface is covered with transfer-ink, prepared expressly for this purpose. This being done, it is floated upon boiling water, that the several ingredients in the ink and paper may coagulate and harmonize, and the print made ready for washing-off, which operation removes all superfluous ink from the surface, leaving it clean and ready for the stone. We now have a photographic transfer-sheet, which, being placed upon the stone and transferred in the ordinary manner, gives us the desired photo-lithograph.

From this point forward all is plain lithography. Any kind of paper or ink ordinarily employed in lithographic printing can be used; or the stone may be kept as an original stone to retransfer from, if preferred.

Line engravings, wood-cuts, pen-drawings, engraved and drawn maps, manuscripts, architectural and mechanical drawings, music, printed matter, plans, etc., are copied full scale, reduced, or enlarged, as may be required. Each class of work will be a perfect facsimile of the original copy, and possess all its peculiar characteristics. If, for instance, a wood-cut be reproduced, no one would venture to assert that the reproduction was anything else than a wood-cut, every detail being so accurately preserved.

The scope of process embraces all drawn or engraved work which consists of black lines or markings upon white paper. Mezzotint engravings and photographs the process cannot grapple with. That is to say, we can produce any shade or tint possessing a distinct or recognizable structure, but not a wash or tint which manifests an unbroken, structureless gradation of light and shade. Upon close examination, it will be seen that the finest wood-cut consists of assemblages of lines, or markings, which are perfectly black in themselves, yet separated from one another by spaces of greater or less size, which are perfectly white. A photograph, on the other hand, no matter how greatly magnified, shows only tints of varying intensity, gradually passing into one another. The former can be photo-lithographed, the latter cannot.

Photo-Relief Printing.—A patented process for printing pictures resembling photographs, but which do not fade. It was discovered by Mr. Woodbury, of London, and is called the Woodbury process. It is now in successful operation in the United States as well as in England, and the modus operandi was recently described in The Photographer, as follows:

The top floor is divided and subdivided into sundry rooms for the different manipulations, one of which is an ordinary photographic skylight or atelier, in which are made copies of printings, drawings, furniture, machinery, people, or anything else, animate or inanimate, of which it is intended to produce pictures in quantity. In apartment No. 1 we see a pan of melting gelatine, such as is used for cooking-purposes, mixed with any desired pigment to give color to the gelatine, and a bichromate to make it sensitive to light. By a dexterous move of the hand, this liquid, when of the consistency of syrup, is poured upon a glass plate in quantity proper to make a thin sheet. This sheet is then placed in a drying-box. When it is dry, it is ready for printing. This operation is performed exactly in the same way as the photographic printer prints upon paper, only the gelatine sheet is substituted for the paper, and the bichromate used as a sensitizing agent, instead of nitrate of silver. An ordinary photographic negative is used, and used but once; for after we have exposed this little thin gelatine film, we have that which takes the place of the negative. We take our gelatine sheet, after exposure to the sun, into the second room, called the preparing-room, where we find that some parts of it have now been rendered insoluble by the light of the sun. It is well washed until all the soluble parts are washed away, and then, holding it up to the light, we have a perfect picture from our negative in relief. Place a white card in contact with it, and we see the most beautiful of pictures, full of delicate lights and shades made by the varied thicknesses of the sheet.

This limpid, shining film is taken into a third room, where it is again well washed in order to remove all the bichromate. It is then dried, and after that it appears to us a thin, horny sheet, hard and tough. It is, to all appearances, as fragile as glass, yet when in a tight place, so that it can't yield, it does its work valiantly. We call this the relief. We take it up and carry it down to the hydraulic press. We place it upon a steel plate lying ready for the work. A lead plate is then laid upon our relief, and the whole is pushed in the press. Now the assistant pumps away until the great jaws nearly meet. You rush to look at the gauge, and you see that already the press is exerting one hundred and sixty tons atmospheric pressure. A little more, cries the relentless Mr. Corbutt, and a crank is then appealed to, to increase the pressure. Ah me! you say, our little delicate relief is shattered into a thousand pieces, and the lead plate mashed to an unrecognizable jelly. Let us see. The turning of a half-inch screw releases the pressure, and those awful jaws slowly part and allow you to remove the plates, and the relief between them. We find the lead plate is whole, and apparently unharmed by that terrible squeeze. Turn up its face, and we see upon it the image of our relief, elegantly engraved in perfect detail, and not a line lost. The relief lies unharmed, ready and able to perform the same feat a dozen times without straining or distorting its tender form.

Now, from these impressed or engraved plates, which we shall, for brevity, call moulds, the prints are made; and we will proceed to the printing department and see how it is done. On one side of the room are two huge revolving tables. On each side of these stand six singular-looking pieces of machinery with one jaw thrown up like that of an alligator set for flies. In the mouth of one of these presses, level upon the lower jaw, we place our plates. Near at hand is a stand with a heating apparatus. The printer takes from this a bottle containing a warm solution of gelatine and pigment similar to that used in making the relief, only having no sensitizing agent in it. A little puddle of this solution is poured upon the plate, a piece of paper laid over the whole, and the upper jaw of the press brought down; this solution is thus made to spread in all directions, to fill in the depression of the mould, and to adhere to the paper firmly. While this is taking place, our printer turns his table, fills another press, and so on until six are filled. By the time he reaches the last, the print in the first is ready to remove. He catches the paper by one corner, pulls gently, and the separation of the picture from the plate is readily made. Thus we have a beautiful picture; but further treatment is needed. It is now dried on a muslin sheet. When dry, it is plunged into a solution of alum and water, which tans it and really makes leather of it. It is again washed, dried, and mounted upon the card in the same manner as a photograph.

Phototype.—A process by means of which it is proposed to supply cuts and plates for book-illustrations. It is based, as its name implies, on photography, the commencement of the process being a photographic plate either from a print or a drawing. From the photograph, after the employment of certain intermediate means, a raised printing-surface is obtained by the agency of the electrotype.

Phototypography.—One of the processes by which it is alleged that designs obtained by photography can be printed on typographic presses, without any aid from engravers. The following description of a method which is said to have been successfully employed was communicated to the French Photographic Society, in April, 1870, by Lefman & Lourdel, a Parisian firm who claim to have demonstrated its practicability:

We declare that the first expositions of our process depend on the discovery of M. Poitevin in relation to the properties of chromic salts. Not long since, struck by the inconvenient practices resulting from the necessity of having recourse to engraving in order to obtain the reproduction of the principal works of industry, we succeeded, by a series of peculiar processes, in obtaining some correct stereotype plates, with which any printer can hereafter, with the greatest rapidity, print any quantity of indelible copies with printers' ink. If the reproduction of photographs from nature still leaves something to be desired in the mode of execution, we shall endeavor to bring it to a state of perfection. But all the stamped reproductions, whether of wood, copper plate, aqua fortis, etc., can already be pr_duced with a perfection that leaves nothing to be desired. The possibility of reducing it to a mathematical scale will be of great service to architects, inventors, and engineers. Manufacturers will equally find in this study a valuable resource, because it supplies the means of affording, at little expense and with great rapidity, exact copies of their productions, whether in bronze, jewelry, furniture, machines, etc.

We shall close this communication with a few remarks on our method of proceeding: The gelatine (or mucilage), dissolved in its equivalent of water and saturated with bichromate of potash, is liquefied and spread on a sheet of paper. This paper, dried once, is stamped with a negative, then inked until it blends. The print obtained is traced upon a sheet of smooth zinc, and serves to economize the continual applications that would have been made by means of the azotic acid. One impression is sufficient, and there is nothing more to do but to mount the stereotype obtained upon wood of sufficient thickness, and the operation is complete; it is then ready to be delivered to the printer. The price at which we can deliver our stereotype plates is from ten to fifteen centimes a square—one-third inch.

Accompanying this communication, Messrs. Lefman & Lourdel submitted to the Society several typographical printed proofs, obtained on the zinc by means of the chromatic gelatine, with the methods they employ, and they also submitted a stereotype plate which was shown as a specimen of their work.

Photozincography.—A process for transferring accurate copies of manuscripts or drawings to zinc. Paper is washed over with a solution of gum containing bichromate of potash, and allowed to dry in a dark room. It is then placed in contact with the manuscript or design, and exposed to the action of light in a photographic printing-frame. After exposure, the whole surface of the prepared paper is coated with lithographic ink, and then a stream of hot water is sluiced over it. The parts that have been exposed to light have become insoluble in water, and remain unaffected, while the remainder is washed off. The outline thus obtained can then be at once transferred to zinc.

Phrase.—A manner of expression, either in written or spoken language. The word is also used to indicate a word or words used with some peculiarity of style, as an idiomatic expression quoted from a foreign tongue for its brevity and force, or as conveying an idea peculiar to the people from whom it is derived: thus, the English language has borrowed the phrase dolce far niente, or sweet doing-nothing, from the Italian, and beau-monde, or the fine world, or the world of fashion, from the French.

Pi.—A mass of letters disarranged and in confusion.

Pica.—A type one size larger than Small Pica. It is also frequently used as a standard of measurement, the size of leads, furniture, and wood-letter being indicated by their relation to a Pica em.

Pick.—A small quantity of dirt, or paper, or a piece of composition roller, which adheres to the face of the type, and causes an unsightly dark spot to appear on the printed form. In stereotyping, a small point of metal, resulting from a slight defect in the mould. Picks are removed by the stereotype-finisher by means of a sharp bodkin-like tool.

Pick-Brush.—A brush used to give parts of a form or cuts a more than ordinary cleaning, when clogged with dirt or ink. The best kinds of tooth- or nail-brushes are used for these purposes. In preparing cuts for stereotype moulding, any hard, greasy substances remaining between the lines of a cut are removed by rubbing spirits of turpentine over the face of the cut, applying fire thereto, allowing the turpentine to burn long enough to cause the heat to loosen the foreign substance, and, after extinguishing the flame, applying the pick-brush briskly over the face of the cut.

Picker.—A kind of spike or bodkin, used by type-founders for picking out imperfect letters.

Picture.—Any representation or likeness of one or more objects, generally, but not necessarily, restricted to a delineation upon a plane surface.

Piette, Louis, was born in Belgium in 1803. Intended for the bar, he studied at Metz, Strasburg, and finally at Paris, where he received his degree with distinction. Family reasons, however, obliged him to abandon his profession and take charge of his father's paper-mill, at Dilling, near Saar Louis, in Prussia. Finding no work to guide him in his new business, he soon collected the results of his own labors and observations, and published, for the benefit of others, his Treatise on the Manufacture of Paper, in 1831, written in French. For this the Berlin Society for the Encouragement of Industry and of the Arts and Trades made him a member and gave him a gold medal.

In 1838 he published, in German, his first remarkable work on straw paper, to be noticed hereafter. Other practical works followed; and it is noteworthy that several of them were in the interest of working-men. The King of Prussia gave him the order of the Red Eagle; and, to show that he could work as well as write, he obtained, at different exhibitions, medals for his paper. In 1853 he published his work on colored papers, which will again be mentioned.

In 1854 he removed to France and commenced his Journal des Fabricants de Papier. This work, continued after his death by his widow, and since her death by others, is one of the most remarkable technical journals of our day, and is distinguished by its abundant illustrations, with specimens of various kinds of paper and paper material. In fact, this is a characteristic of Piette's works. When the cost and trouble of this mode of illustration are remembered, it will be seen that such books could come only from one who had a labor of love to perform.

His greater work on paper of straw and other materials appeared, in 2 vols., in 1861, and still another in the same year. He died in July, 1862.

Without possessing a scientific education, his thorough earnestness, his clear-headed good sense, and his truthfulness, with his desire to inform others, enabled him to splendidly illustrate and to greatly advance his art.

Die Fabrication des Papieres aus Stroh und vielen andren Substanzen im Grossen, etc. Von L. Piette, Cöln, 1838.

This work gives a good idea of the processes then used for making straw paper, with many notices of other materials; but its great value consists in the one hundred and sixty specimens with which it is illustrated. Paper from each kind of straw is shown by itself, and unbleached, then in combinations, two and two, and finally mixed with rags. Afterwards, on pages of colored or unbleached straw paper, there are bleached specimens in a similar order.

There can be no doubt that this work had an important influence upon the introduction of straw paper. In one way alone an immense advance was made. With the specimens before him, each paper-maker could already start beyond this experience in any direction desired: in short, he was saved just so much of experiment. Notwithstanding the later and larger books on the same subject, this work, in our opinion has special value, and no paper-maker, especially of straw paper, can have his library complete without it.

With great good sense, the author seems to have avoided the now common error, of endeavoring to show that the best kind of paper can be made of every different substance, and has only aimed to show what could be done by simple treatment for each material. He had in his country a wider range of quality to supply, even for writing-paper, at a time when our wrapping-paper was required to be as white as the best writing-paper.

At the time this book was published, the author evidently had no great fancy for paper made of wood; he gives a handsome shaving as a specimen of something better. Since then we have seen cards printed on such slices, and by the machine invented long ago by Pape, of Paris, we can have slices of wood large enough to take the place even of wall paper.

Essais sur la Coloration des Pâtes à Papier et sur la Fabrication directe de Papiers de teinture après un nouveau Procédé, etc., par Louis Piette, etc. Paris, 1853. This work contains three hundred and fifty specimens. In the first place, it gives twenty-one specimens of the various qualities of rags,—or, rather, twice twenty-one, for each quality has its duplicate variation. We know of no other book containing such a representation of the whole scale of rags as known to commerce.

Next follows a very good account of the ordinary materials for coloring paper pulp. Then there is a series of three hundred and forty-one specimens of colored papers, made by one or more coloring substances, or by their mixture with originally variously colored rags. Each specimen has its precise formula recorded. In a scale embracing three hundred and forty-one distinct tints, it will be easy to detect any desired one, or the two between which it lies; this feature of the work renders it an invaluable guide to manufacturers of colored paper, saving them time and giving a direct indication for variation in any direction.

The next part of the book gives an account, with specimens, of a new mode of giving colored figures to paper in the act of formation. We cannot describe this, but it may be seen substantially in some of the later United States currency bills, with a wavy colored addition across the face.

At the end of the volume there is a very good set of illustrations of the contrast of colors as worked out by Chevreul, the specimens being made of strips of colored paper.

Die Fabrication des Papieres aus Stroh, Heu, etc., etc., im Grossen. * * Von Louis Piette. Cöln, Dresden, Paris, 1861.

This work is a natural outgrowth of the first similar one by this author. In it he describes the new processes, rotating boilers, etc.; he also introduces an account of new paper materials and correctly enlarges upon old ones. This part of the work alone is in every way excellent. But the highest merit lies in its illustrations by specimens. Of these there are more than three hundred. And by leaving out different degrees of bleaching of the same material, and introducing a large number of new substances, the total value is greatly increased. Besides the large number of straw papers, there are a dozen specimens of wood paper. Pine cones, leaves of trees, etc., are represented. Among the new materials we find Jute, Yucca, Pisang, Palmetto, Aloe, and others. Finally, there are fourteen specimens of paper made from leather, either without addition or with various additions of different materials. It is needless to dwell upon the value of this book to the paper-maker.

Pig.—A pressman was formerly frequently so called by compositors. The use of this class of words is, happily, growing less common every day.

Pigeon-Holes.—Unusually wide spaces between words, caused by the carelessness or want of taste of the workman. The word is used disrespectfully in this sense, but in cases of extreme hurry, as on news-paper work, where short takes have to be quickly justified to make even, pigeon-holes are unavoidable.

Pigment.—The coloring substance used in painting or in printing-inks.

Pile.—A heap of paper in the wareroom or press-room.

Placard.—A written or printed paper pasted up in a place of public resort.

Plagiarism.—A literary theft consisting in the appropriation of the ideas or words of another author and claiming them as original.

Planer.—A block of hard wood, perfectly smooth and even on the face, used for planing down the type in a form. A useful size for general purposes is nine inches long, four and a half inches broad, and two inches deep. For newspaper work larger sizes are occasionally employed. A groove usually runs along the two longer edges, to enable the workman to handle it readily.

Plantin, Christopher.—A printer of Antwerp, generally considered as the most successful typographer of the sixteenth century. He was born near Tours, in France, in 1514, and studied his art under the king's printer at Caen. He established himself at Antwerp, where he published, in 1555, a duodecimo volume, which he poetically styles, in the dedication, the first blossom from the garden of his printing-press. Plantin gradually extended his establishment, until in 1576, when he was visited by De Thou, celebrated as the patron of fine printing, he had seventeen presses in constant employment, and was spending above two hundred florins per day in wages to his workmen. His office was one of the ornaments of the city of Antwerp, and he became so celebrated for the excellence of his typography that the King of Spain conferred upon him the title of Archi-typographus, with a very handsome salary, and a species of patent for printing certain religious works, with which he almost exclusively supplied both Europe and the Indies. The King of France endeavored to prevail upon Plantin to return to France, but he preferred to remain in Antwerp, and finally established branch printing-houses at Leyden and Paris. Plantin was exceedingly liberal in his expenditures, retaining the services of a number of men of great learning as the correctors of his press, and lavishing large sums upon all the details of his business, in order to insure accuracy and beauty. He died in 1589, and left a large property to be divided among his children. He had no son, and his three daughters having married men connected with typography, either as practical printers or correctors of the press, Plantin left his three establishments to them as their dower. John Moret or Moretus, the husband of the second daughter, succeeded Plantin in the principal establishment at Antwerp, and the office was still in the possession of a direct descendant in the year 1817, being especially remarkable as retaining the old establishment without essential modifications, while all the modern improvements in the art had been introduced. One of the most remarkable productions of Plantin's press was the celebrated Polyglot Bible printed at Antwerp between the years 1561 and 1572, by authority of Philip II. of Spain, in Hebrew, Greek, Latin, and Chaldaic, in eight folio volumes. Only five hundred copies were printed, and a large portion of the edition was lost in a wreck at sea, on the passage to Spain. It has been said of Plantin that, although Jenson and Stephens had equal elegance, Aldus and Froben equal zeal, yet take the entire works of Plantin, they cannot be equaled, certainly not excelled.

Planting Sorts.—When certain sorts run short upon a particular work, and one compositor having a good quantity hides them from his companions, he is said to plant them.

Plate.—A page of stereotype, electrotype, or fixed metallic type.

Platen.—That part of the press which descends on the form (protected by the blanket, tympans, etc.) and effects the impression.

Platen Press or Machine.—A press in which the impression is effected by a flat platen, as distinguished from one in which it is made by a cylindrical or other impressing surface. Very few of the large power-presses are platen machines, the Adams Press being an exception to the general rule; but a large proportion of the small job presses are platen machines.

Plate-paper.—A heavy, spongy paper, manufactured expressly for printing from engraved plates. It receives the most delicate lines freely, and takes the impression of printers' ink readily.

Plate-Printing.—This term is now commonly applied to the description of printing formerly called copperplate printing, the name having been changed in consequence of the general substitution of steel for copper plates. It differs radically from typographical printing in the fact that the hollows of the plate used, instead of its elevations, are reproduced on the printed sheet,—the philosophy of the process being that pressure on the elasticity of cloth blankets forces moist paper to enter the indentations of a plate and take up all the black ink from it. The surface of the plate, after being supplied with a more liquid ink than that used in typographic printing, is carefully cleansed before each impression, so that no ink may be deposited upon the paper printed except that which sinks into the depressions of the plate. For an illustration of the press used, see COPPERPLATE PRESS. Plate or copperplate printing continues to furnish the highest type of artistic excellence, no other system of printing with black ink only being capable of producing specimens equal to first-class mezzotint and steel engravings. Some of its achievements are described under various headings in this work. (See BANK-NOTE PRINTING.)

Pleonasm.—The use of more words than are necessary; a redundant form of expression.

Pocket-Edition.—A publication in a form so small that it may be carried in a pocket; generally, a small bound book.

Poetry.—Metrical composition.

The lofty office of printing, as furnishing a permanent embodiment to thought, and not only preserving but multiplying its form of expression, has frequently become the chosen theme of the poets. Cowper vigorously and plainly described its power, both for good and evil, in his apostrophe:—

How shall I speak thee, or thy power address,
Thou god of our idolatry—the Press!
By thee Religion, Liberty, and Laws,
Exert their influence, and advance their cause;
By thee, worse plagues than Pharaoh's land befell,
Diffused, make earth the vestibule of hell;
Thou fountain at which drink the good and wise;
Thou ever-bubbling spring of endless lies;

Like Eden's dread probationary tree,
Knowledge of good and evil is from thee.

The security against loss which literature has gained from the invention and increase of printing, has frequently been expressed, and from the host of quotations, space permits the culling of only a few, viz.:

What numerous worthies whom with lyres high strung
In pompous strains frail manuscripts once sung,
To time's abyss are with their vouchers lost,
Nor one memorial of existence boast!
But living merit (still, alas! opposed)
Now sees the gulf of black oblivion closed;
Sees present envy impotently rave,
And pants for honest praise beyond the grave;
Firm and exalted o'er its wayward fate,
Sees the fair page for fame's impression wait,
And safe, in just posterity's reward,
Consigns its glory to the future bard.
The brave and good, prepared to live in death,
With unreluctant smiles shall yield their breath,
While latest times Newton entire shall boast,
Nor mourn a Bacon, Locke, or Milton lost.

Years are the teeth of Time, which softly eat,
And wear out curious books in manuscript.
Fire is the scythe, wherein he down doth mow
Ten thousand precious volumes at a blow:
Blest printing, best of all his rage withstands,
And often chains his feet, and ties his hands;
Rescued from whom here various authors meet,
And, all united, form a splendid treat.
So numerous flowers in one rich nosegay join.
And still more fragrant smell and brighter shine.

Science now dreads on books no holy war;
Thus multiplied, and thus dispersed so far,
She smiles exulting, doom'd no more to dwell
'Midst moths and cobwebs, in a friar's cell:
To see her Livy, and most favor'd sons,
The prey of worms and popes, of Goths and Huns;
To mourn, half-eaten Tacitus, thy fate,
The dread of lawless sway, and craft of state.
Her bold machine redeems the patriot's fame
From royal malice, and the bigot's flame;
To bounded thrones displays the legal plan,
And vindicates the dignity of man.
Tyrants and time, in her, lose half their power,—
And Reason shall subsist, though both devour.

The inevitable effect of printing in the diffusion of education among all classes was early foreseen, and before the close of the fifteenth century a French historian, a staunch conservative of his generation, sneered alike at the discoveries of Columbus and the invention of Gutenberg. His condemnation of the press may be fairly translated in the following lines:

I've seen a mighty throng
Of printed books and long,
To draw to studious ways
The poor men of our days;
By which new-fangled practice,
We soon shall see the fact is,
Our streets will swarm with scholars
Without clean shirts or collars,

23

With Bibles, books, and codices,
As cheap as tape for bodices.

John McCreery's poem, The Press, is one of the most elaborate tributes to printing; but it is at once so well known, and so lengthy, as to need only to be referred to for its acknowledged merit.

The printers of Edinburgh celebrated the 12th of July, 1837, as the fourth centenary of the invention of Gutenberg, and at the festival the following song, composed by one printer, was sung by another of the fraternity:—

When Liberty first sought a home on the earth,
No altar the goddess could find,
Till art's greatest triumph to Printing gave birth,
And her temple she reared to the mind.
The phantoms of Ignorance shrank from her sight,
And Tyranny's visage grew wan,
As wildly he traced, in the Volume of Light,
The pledge of redemption to man!

All hail the return of the glorious day
When Freedom her banner unfurled,
And sprung from the Press the Promethean ray
That dawned on a slumbering world;
When Science, exulting in freedom and might,
Unveiled to the nations her eye,
And waved from her tresses, refulgent in light,
A glory that never can die.

Great ark of our freedom! the Press we adore—
Our glory and power are in thee;
A voice thou hast wafted to earth's farthest shore,
The shout of the great and the free.
The slave's galling fetters are burst by thy might,
The empire of reason is thine;
And nations rejoice in the glorious light
Which flows from a fountain divine.

In Dublin, during the last century, among the poems chosen to be printed during the procession on the Lord Mayor's day, for distribution to the crowd, were the following lines by Mrs. Grierson, the wife of the King's printer, and herself a skillful compositor:

Hail, mystic art! which men like angels taught,
To speak to eyes, and paint embodied thought!
The deaf and dumb, blest skill, relieved by thee,
We make one sense perform the task of three.
We see—we hear—we touch the head and heart,
And take or give what each but yields in part;
With the hard laws of distance we dispense,
And, without sound, apart, commune in sense;
View, though confined,—nay, rule this earthly ball,
And travel o'er the wide-expanded all.
Dead letters thus with living notions fraught
Prove to the soul the telescope of thought;
To mortal life immortal honor give,
And bid all deeds and titles last and live.
In scanty life, Eternity we taste,
View the first ages, and inform the last;
Arts, History, Laws, we purchase with a look,
And keep, like Fate, all nature in a Book.

In America, Philip Freneau, in 1798, wrote an admirable description of the country printing-office.

354 POETRY.

Every stanza is excellent, but it is too long for insertion, and but a few lines must suffice:

Abreast the inn, a tree before the door,
A Printing-Office lifts its humble head,
Where busy Typo journals doth explore
For news that is through all the village read,
Who year from year (so cruel is his lot)
Is author, pressman, devil—and what not.

Fame says, he is an odd and curious wight,
Fond to distraction of his native place;
In sense not very dull nor very bright,
Yet shows some marks of humor in his face:
One who can pen an anecdote complete,
Or plague the parson with the mackled sheet.

Three times a week, by nimble geldings drawn,
A stage arrives; but scarcely deigns to stop,
Unless the driver, far in liquor gone,
Has made some business for the blacksmith's shop;
Then comes this printer's harvest-time of news,
Welcome alike from Christians, Turks, or Jews.

Each passenger he eyes with curious glance,
And, if his phiz be marked of courteous kind,
To conversation, straight, he makes advance,
Hoping, from thence, some paragraph to find,
Some odd adventure, something new and rare,
To set the town agape, and make it stare.

All is not truth ('tis said) that travelers tell;
So much the better for this man of news;
For hence the country round, who know him well,
Will, if he print some lies, his lies excuse;
Earthquakes and battles, shipwrecks, myriads slain,
If false or true, alike to him are gain.

Ask you what matter fills his various page?
A mere farrago 'tis of mingled things;
Whate'er is done on Madam Terra's stage,
He to the knowledge of his townsmen brings;
One while, he tells of monarchs run away;
And now, of witches drowned in Buzzard's Bay.

Some miracles he makes, and some he steals;
Half nature's works are giants in his eyes;
Much, very much, in wonderment he deals,
New Hampshire apples grown to pumpkin size,
Pumpkins almost as large as country inns,
And ladies bearing each three lovely twins.

One of the most popular and successful poems on the subject, in America, is Mr. MacKellar's admirable Song of the Printer (see MACKELLAR). A similar theme has received a different handling in the following:

A song for the Press—more potent far
Than the fiat of crowned king—
Than the cohorts of war—than the steel-clad men
That the mightiest chief can bring.
Kingdom and tower, and the palace-wall,
That have braved a century's might,
Crumble in ruin, and totter and fall,
When the Press wakes the giant Right.

A song for the Press! Like the armed men
That rushed over Rome's ivied wall,
When liberty swayed and trampled in dust
Cæsar's pride and judgment-hall:

So its silent step wakes the down-trod one,
'Mid his thraldom, his fear and gloom,
And thunders in wrath round the crowned king,
Foretelling of death and of gloom!

A song for the Press—the east-born star!
Of true religion—of liberty—power—
Untrammeled by wealth, by passion unswayed,
'Tis the index—the scribe of each hour;
And still shall remain—still the slender type
Shall click, and all nations bless,
And the last star from earth that ever fades out
Be the God-modeled Printing Press!

William Ross Wallace has also written a lay, which, in its true and lofty boast, makes a proud

SONG FOR AN AMERICAN EDITOR.

I'm of the Press! I'm of the Press!
My throne a simple chair:
I ask no other majesty
Than strikes the gazer there.
The horse of fire obeys my nod;
My couriers walk the sea;
The lightnings lift their flaming manes,
At art's command, for me.

I'm of the Press! I'm of the Press!
Do monarchs wear the crown?
I waft my pen across my page,
And crowns have tumbled down.
The clouds float on—the nations strive;
Without, the thunder rolls;
Within, I brood the quiet thought
That changes all the souls.

I'm of the Press! I'm of the Press!
The dead around me throng;
Their awful voices whisper truth!
Their eyes forbid the wrong.
From them I gather joy and strength,
Nor heed pale error's curse,
My faith in God large as the arch
He gave his universe.

I'm of the Press! I'm of the Press!
My host embattled types;
With them I quell the tyrant's horde
And rear the stars and stripes.
I give my hand to all my race,
My altar Freedom's sod:
I say my say, and bend my knee
Alone, alone to God.

The power of the daily press, and its effect upon society, are forcibly described in the following lines, which appeared originally in the Knickerbocker Magazine:

THE PRINTER.

He stood there alone at that shadowy hour,
By the swinging lamp dimly burning,
All silent within, save the ticking type,
All without, save the night-watch turning;
And heavily echoed the solemn sound,
As slowly he paced o'er the frozen ground.

And dark were the mansions so lately that shone
With the joy of festivity gleaming,
And hearts that were breathing in sympathy
Were now living it o'er in their dreaming;

Yet the Printer still worked at his lonely post,
As slowly he gathered his mighty host.

And there lay the merchant all pillowed in down,
And building bright hopes for the morrow,
Nor dreamed he that Fate was then weaving a wand
That would bring him fear and sorrow;
Yet the Printer was there in his shadowy room,
And he set in his framework that rich man's doom !

The young wife was sleeping, whom lately had bound
The ties that death only can sever;
And dreaming she started, yet woke with a smile,
For she thought they were parted forever !
But the Printer was clicking the types that would tell,
On the morrow, the truth of that midnight spell !

And there lay the statesman, whose feverish brow
And restless the pillow was pressing,
For he felt through the shadowy mist of his dream
His loftiest hopes now possessing;
Yet the Printer worked on 'mid silence and gloom,
And dug for Ambition its lowliest tomb.

And slowly the workman went gathering up
His budget of grief and of gladness;
A wreath for the noble, a grave for the low,
For the happy, a cup full of sadness;
Strange stories of wonder, to enchant the ear,
And dark ones of terror, to curdle with fear.

Full strange are the tales which that dark host shall bear
To palace and cot on the morrow;
Oh, welcome, thrice welcome to many a heart !
To many a bearer of sorrow;
It shall go like the wind and wandering air,
For life and its changes are impressed there.

Of the numerous excellent and amusing parodies
which appear in the contemporaneous journals, mention can be merely made; and the complaints in
which editors, proof-readers, and printers bewail their
griefs and give their sorrows words, appear, like much
of the other literature for which the world is indebted
to the printer, in an anonymous form. A large
number of fugitive verses show also their paternity by
being full to overflowing of the professional puns in
which printers are such adepts. One of the earliest
of these is a curious and elaborate poem which
appeared in London in 1752, under the title of—A
Contemplation on the Mystery of Man's Regeneration,
in Allusion to the Mystery of Printing: a few lines
will be sufficient to exhibit the quaint language employed, and the peculiar method of treatment:

> Great blest Master-Printer, come
> Into thy composing-room;
> Make, O make our souls and senses
> The upper and the lower cases;
> And thy large alphabet of graces
> The letter, which being ever fit,
> O haste thou to distribute it.

That graceful, convenient little superfluity which
closes the grand army of the alphabet was thus admirably apostrophised by Punch:

&

Of all the types in a printer's hand,
Commend me to the Ampersand,
For he's the gentleman (seems to me)
Of the typographical companie.
O my nice little Ampersand,
My graceful, swanlike Ampersand.
Nothing that Cadmus ever planned
Equals my elegant Ampersand !

Many a letter your writers hate,
Ugly Q, with his tail so straight,
X, that makes you cross as a bear,
And Z, that helps you with sounds to swear.
But not my nice little Ampersand,
My easily dashed-off Ampersand,
Any odd shape folks understand
To mean my Protean Ampersand !

Nothing for him that's starch or stiff;
Never he's used to scold or tiff;
State epistles, so dull and grand,
Mustn't contain the shortened and.
No, my nice little Ampersand,
You are good for those who're jolly and bland;
In days when letters were dried with sand
Old frumps wouldn't use my Ampersand !

But he is dear in old friendship's call,
Or when love is laughing through lady-scrawl,
Come & dine, & have bachelor's fare.
Come, & I'll keep you a round & square.
Yes, my nice little Ampersand
Never must into a word expand,
Gentle sign of affection stand,
My kind, familiar Ampersand.

Point-Holes.—Fine holes made by the points,
by which the second and succeeding impressions are
registered.

Points.—Two thin pieces of metal, each having
points projecting from one end. They are fixed to
the tympan of hand-presses and some power-presses,
to secure good register.

Points, of Punctuation.—In a general sense,
all the characters used in punctuation and as marks
of reference are sometimes called points; but this
term was formerly confined to the comma, semicolon,
colon, period, note of interrogation, and exclamation
point. Wilson, in his work on punctuation, divides
points into three classes, viz.: 1. Grammatical points,
including the comma, semicolon, colon, and period.
2. Grammatical and Rhetorical points, including the
note of interrogation, the note of exclamation, the
marks of parenthesis, and the dash. 3. Letter, Syllabic, and Quotation points, including the apostrophe,
the hyphen, and the marks of quotation.

Point-Screws.—Two small bolts with screws at
the end which go through holes in the tympan.
They are square-headed, with a nut on the upper
side, and serve to fix the points securely to the
tympan.

Polemics.—That department of literature containing controversial writings, especially upon theological subjects.

Poles.—Strips of wood fixed across a room, on which printed paper is hung to dry.

Polo, Marco.—A Venetian traveler, who returned to Venice from Asia in the year 1295, bringing with him a specimen of the printed paper-money of China, and a knowledge of printing from wooden blocks as practiced by the Chinese, which probably led to the introduction of the manufacture of playing-cards into Venice. Marco Polo, a nobleman of Venice, was born in 1250. Shortly after his birth his father and uncle sailed on a trading-expedition for Constantinople, where, changing their merchandise into the more convenient form of jewels, they proceeded into Asia, passed several years in Bokhara, and afterwards visited Cathay, where they were treated with great honor, and intrusted by Kublai Khan with an embassy to the Pope. They reached Rome just after the death of Clement IV., and, after waiting two years for the postponed election, set out again for the East in 1271, taking with them Marco Polo, then just twenty-one years of age. After a vacancy in the Pontifical Chair for nearly three years, Gregory X., at that time in Palestine with Edward I. of England, was elected Pope, and he immediately dispatched messengers, who reached the ambassadors in Armenia and supplied them with letters and presents for the Khan. Marco Polo was received into favor by Kublai Khan, appointed to an office near his person, several times sent as ambassador into northern and southern China and Thibet, and finally made governor of a city. Marco Polo and his father and uncle acquired great wealth in China and Cathay, and finally returned home with special honor, offering their fleet of fourteen ships as a conveyance for the daughter of Kublai Khan, who was affianced to the King of Persia. Thus officiating as the guard of honor of the princess and her train, they touched at various cities on their route, and upon their arrival in Persia were entertained with great magnificence for nine months. Thence they traveled by land to Trebizond, and reached Venice after an absence of twenty-four years. Maffeo, the uncle, became one of the chief magistrates of Venice. Marco Polo was intrusted with the command of a galley against the Genoese, by whom he was taken prisoner; and during this captivity he wrote an account of his travels, which was finished in 1298. It is believed that it was first written in French, and afterwards translated into Latin during Polo's lifetime. After several years' imprisonment, he returned to Venice, where he married and had two daughters. He died in 1324, asseverating to his latest breath the truth of his narratives, which were generally disbelieved, notwithstanding his high character and position, and it was only in after-years that travelers proved his extraordinary powers of observation and accuracy of recital. His travels in the original French and Latin were published in 1824 by the Paris Geographical Society.

Polyglot.—A book containing the same literary work in two or more languages, and so arranged in parallel columns, pages, or otherwise, as to be readily compared; the most familiar illustrations being the various polyglot Bibles.

Polygraph.—An instrument for multiplying copies of a writing.

Polysyllable.—A word of many syllables; used to express any word containing more than three syllables.

Polytypes.—Polytypes resemble stereotypes; but the means adopted in their production are somewhat different; for while a stereotype is taken by pouring molten metal on to the mould, the polytype is made thus. An electro is taken from a wood-block; from this a mould or matrix is formed. The matrix is then fixed to a weight suspended to a line running through a pulley, immediately over a steel plate. The metal, being ladled on to a sheet of writing-paper, is allowed to cool till it becomes of the consistency of dough, when the apparatus is inclosed, and the line loosened, which causes the matrix to fall on the metal, upon which it leaves its impression, similarly to that made upon a medal by means of a die. It is then trimmed round and mounted on wood or metal. The alleged properties of this invention are, that duplicates can be produced more rapidly, more economically, and deeper than by the stereotype process.

Portfolio.—A case, in the form and of the size of a book, intended for the preservation of loose papers, prints, etc.

Poster.—A printed bill, of a large size, each sheet being usually at least as large as double-medium, and generally of a size exceeding thirty by forty inches. The word poster is an abbreviation or modification of the term posting-bill, which is said to have originated in the fact that several centuries ago it became a custom to attach notices of theatrical performances, and similar matters, to posts on the sidewalk of Fleet Street, in London. Poster-printing has been brought to great perfection in this country, on account of the great demand for its products, arising from the large number of theatres, circuses, menageries, and museums, as well as the frequency of large meetings and agricultural exhibitions, and the disposition to advertise goods of various descriptions by posters. The standard theatrical poster is generally composed of three large sheets, pasted beneath each other. The colored posters used by traveling circuses and menageries frequently comprise a series of bills, which each consist of from nine to twelve sheets, and they elicit fine displays of the skill of artists, engravers, and printers.

Poster-Cuts.—Large engravings, usually of wood, from which impressions are obtained that form part, or the whole, of a printed poster.

Postfix.—A syllable, or a termination, added to the end of a word, or to the root of a word, to modify its meaning; an affix; a suffix.

Postil.—A marginal note; a name formerly given to a note in the margin of a Bible.

Postscript.—An addition made to a letter after it has been concluded and signed, usually marked at the commencement by the letters P. S. Also an addition of something omitted made to a literary work after it has been supposed to be completed.

Potter Presses.—Drum-Cylinder Power Presses with extraordinary rapidity. Formerly, the attention of Mr. Potter was concentrated chiefly on his country press, but in 1865 he formed a partnership with Mr. J. F. Hubbard, expanded his operations, and perfected arrangements for manufacturing his presses in an establishment entirely under the control of the

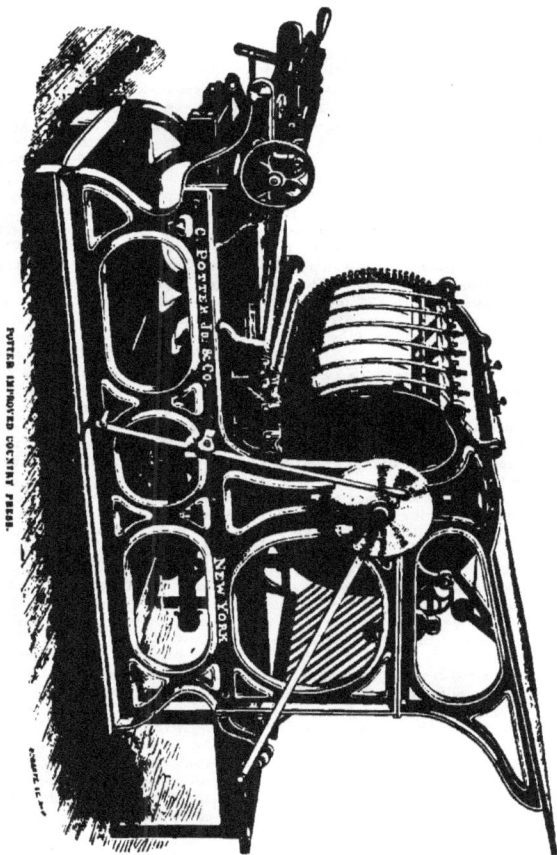

manufactured by C. Potter, Jr., & Co., of various sizes, one class being specially intended for country newspaper and job work, and another for the finest varieties of book and job printing. More than five hundred of these presses were in use in May, 1871, and the demand for them has increased, of late years, new firm; and since that period constant efforts have been made not only to improve the country press, but also to manufacture drum-cylinders of superior excellence. To promote this end, various new designs were made, combining beauty with convenience, great solidity, and strength, and several useful patents were obtained for improvements peculiar to the Potter press.

Preamble.—The introduction of a statute, bill, or act, setting forth its intent, and the circumstances which occasioned its passage.

Pre-Antepenultimate.—The last syllable but three of a word.

Preface.—Observations prefixed to a literary work, intended to explain its design, plan, or object, and addressed to the reader by the author or editor, as a means of personal explanation, and generally signed and dated. It is frequently used to describe the circumstances under which the work was written and the sources from which it was derived, and to convey a public acknowledgment of assistance received in its preparation. The preface is distinguished from the introduction, which is a preliminary essay treating of matters strictly belonging to the work, but which cannot conveniently be placed in the body of the book. Aldus Manutius, of Venice, printed the preface in Italic, and his example was followed by the early printers until it became a typographical custom. At present, Roman is used, generally of a size larger or a size smaller than that of the rest of the work. The running title of the preface is commonly set in the same manner as that of the body of the book.

Prefix.—A letter, syllable, or word placed at the beginning of a word to vary its signification or make a new word.

Pre-Raphaelism.—The theory of a modern school of artists, who profess to follow the method of the artists before the period of Raphael, by a close adherence to natural forms and effects.

Press.—This word has three meanings, according to its use, among printers. It is applied to the general body of journalism, which is called the press; to the machine which produces the impression—the press; and in a confined sense, to the operation of making printed impressions, which is called press in contradistinction to case, a term including the various processes connected with the art of composition.

Press-Bar.—The arm of the press to which the handle is attached.

Press-Book.—A book kept by the foreman of the press-room in a large printing-office, in which entries are made of the amount of paper given out by the warehousemen for the various works, the number printed, etc., as well as the names of the pressmen. The following form is frequently adopted:

When given out to wet.	Names of works.	No.	Sig.	Date when laid on.	Names of Pressmen.
1871.					
Feb. 27	History of Greece.	500	a	March 1	Wilson.
Mar. 2	Æsop's Fables	7000	u	March 4	Smith & Perkins.

Presses.—Machines used in pressing blank sheets of paper on type or plates to which ink has been applied, in such a manner that a reverse copy of the face of the type or plate is printed.

Various classifications of typographic presses have been made. Some are based on the nature of the machinery used, and others on the character of the work to be performed. The inventions patented in Great Britain are divided into classes descriptive of the shape of the cylinders and the surface pressed by them, as follows:

1. Flat-form pressing-cylinder.
2. Flat-form conical pressing-roller.
3. Prismatic-form pressing-cylinder.
4. Cylindrical-form (convex) pressing-cylinder.
5. Cylindrical-form (convex) flat pressing surface.
6. Cylindrical-form (concave) pressing-cylinder.
7. Flat-form pressing flat surface.

In the United States presses are, popularly, divided into newspaper, book, and large and small job-presses. Presses worked wholly by manual labor are called hand-presses, while self-acting presses are called power-presses, or steam-presses. Small job-presses are often styled Jobbers, or card and bill-head-presses. Another classification is based on size, as quarto, medium, double medium, mammoth, etc. A broad line of distinction is also drawn between bed and platen machine-presses, such as the Adams press, and cylinder-presses. The latter, in turn, are subdivided into classes based on the size or number of the cylinders, the small cylinders being distinguished from the large or drum-cylinders, and the number of cylinders of different presses being, respectively, one, two, four, six, eight, and ten. The term rotary is applied to presses in which the type or stereotype-plates revolve on a curved or cylindrical surface. Presses which print a sheet on both sides simultaneously, or with only one feeding, are called perfecting presses. Power-presses intended to be used mainly in country newspaper-offices are called country presses. Presses fed automatically are called self-feeding machines. There are, besides, other titles, some of which are purely arbitrary or fanciful, and some descriptive, as well as combinations of the titles already given.

In the primitive Chinese method of printing, no press is necessary, as copies of their engraved blocks are obtained by merely rubbing with a stiff brush the backs of the sheets of paper to be printed. But in printing from movable type, with stiff ink, it is necessary that a powerful impression should be given, and there is abundant evidence still existing that Gutenberg considered the construction of a machine for this purpose one of the essential parts of the invention of printing. Even before he commenced his typographical labors at Mentz, he had a press constructed at Strasburg; and in his business compact with Fust, presses are included as part of the property pledged for the repayment of money advanced by the goldsmith to the inventor. This early press was little more than a slight modification of the cheese- or wine-presses which had previously existed. In the illustration, on page 228, of the invention of printing, an artistic conception is given of the machine first used by Gutenberg at Mentz. A slight improvement on this rude device was effected at an early period, as will be seen by the representation of the press used in 1560, copied from a publication of that time, which is reproduced in the full-page illustration accompanying this article and devoted to various presses; but even it was little more than a common screw-press, with a contrivance for running the form of type under the screw after the form was inked; and as the screw must have come down with a dead pull, great care was necessary to prevent injury to the face of the type. This press, with perhaps a few minor modifications, was the only one invented until William Jansen Blaew devised, about 1620, a press considered so nearly perfect that for more than a century and a half no earnest effort seems to have been made to improve it. The Blaew press was rather above than below the standard of the requirements of the English printers of the last century, for Luckombe, an English writer on printing, whose work was published in 1770, says, There are two sorts of presses in use, the old- and the new-fashioned; the old sort, till of late years, were the only presses used in England;—and he proceeds to state that the new-fashioned presses to which he refers were those invented by Blaew, a century and a half before the date of his publication, while he adds that the presses on the old principle are still so common that it is unnecessary to describe them. (See BLAEW, and also full-page illustrations of presses.)

The Blaew press and the common press, in both of which a few minor improvements were gradually incorporated, were the only typographic presses in general use before the present century. The common press resembled in appearance the wooden Ramage press, which was formerly used extensively in this country, and the following names were applied to its respective parts: feet, cheeks, cap, winter, head, till, hose, garter, hooks, spindle, worm, nut, eye of the spindle, shank of the spindle, toe of the spindle, platen, bar, handle of the bar, hind-posts, hind-rails, wedges of the till, carriage, outer frame of the carriage, iron ribs, wooden ribs on which the iron ribs are fastened, stay of the carriage, coffin, plank, gallows, tympans, frisket, points, and point-screws. In lieu of an iron bed, the coffin served as a receptacle for a stone, usually of marble, which was the bed of the old presses.

A few attempts were made in the United States, during the last century, to improve the common press. Benjamin Dearborne, publisher of the New Hampshire Gazette, about the time of the Revolution, invented what was called the wheel-press, which possessed the new and desirable quality of impressing the whole side of the sheet at one pull of the lever; and this press was used for a time at Newburyport. A citizen of Connecticut also took out a patent for a power-press. But these efforts led to no general improvement.

Adam Ramage, who came to Philadelphia about

1790, and who for a long time was the chief press-builder in this country, was one of the first to construct iron beds; but his early presses, like those which had preceded them, were so small that only one-half of one side of a sheet of respectable dimensions could be printed at one time, and four distinct impressions were necessary to print both sides of a small news-paper.

It was only about the commencement of the present century that vigorous efforts began to be made to construct improved hand-presses, in which iron was substituted for wood as the principal material. The most successful of these efforts resulted in the Columbian press, invented by George Clymer, of Philadelphia (see COLUMBIAN PRESS), and the Stanhope press, invented by Earl Stanhope, the former, in its perfected condition, being by far the more powerful press of the two, and one of the first of the important inventions relating to printing which was made in this country. The Ruthven press, invented by John Ruthven, a printer of Edinburgh, Scotland, was patented in 1813, and it was soon afterwards manufactured by Adam Ramage, in Philadelphia. Its principal distinguishing feature consisted in the fact that the types remained stationary, the platen, or pressing-surface, being movable. Van Winkle's Printer's Guide, published at New York in 1818, in describing the presses then in use in the United States, deemed only four worthy of notice, viz.: The Columbian Press, the Ruthven Press, the Ramage Screw Press, and the Wells Press—the latter being then a comparatively new press, invented by John J. Wells, of which little is said by Van Winkle, except that two of them had been used for some time in Hartford and had given satisfaction. Subsequently (in 1822) the Smith hand-press was invented by Peter Smith, a brother-in-law of the founder of the firm of R. Hoe & Co., and in 1829 the Washington hand-press was patented by Samuel Rust. The Tufts press was also formerly a favorite in New England, its peculiarity consisting in a toggle joint, or a straightening of the toggle joint, and patents which probably related to this press were granted to Otis Tufts, of Boston, in 1813 and in 1831. Although various other hand-presses have been, and are now, made and used in this country, during the present century, American printing-offices were formerly supplied chiefly with the Columbian, Ruthven, Wells, Tufts, Ramage, Smith, and Washington press,—the modern Ramage press being in most general use until it was gradually supplanted by the improved Smith and Washington iron presses.

Self-acting power or machine printing-presses were totally unknown before the present century. The first conception of such a machine originated with William Nicholson (see NICHOLSON, WILLIAM), and the first to construct a working model was Koenig, whose labors are described elsewhere. (See KOENIG.)

Various patents for machine presses were also granted in this country before, and soon after, the dawn of the present century but they led to no important practical results. England was formerly the favorite resort of the ingenious inventors of printing machinery, Clymer and Treadwell (who was also an early American press-inventor) having gone there during the early part of the present century; and it was only after power-presses had been invented by Koenig, improved by Applegath, and simplified by Napier, and after some of Napier's power-presses had been built in or sent to this country, that the work of building power-presses was fairly commenced in the United States.

The Napier press was similar in appearance and construction to the small double cylinder-presses which were the precursors, in the American newspaper offices printing large editions, of Hoe's fast presses. It is elaborately described and eulogized in Hansard's Typographia, printed in London in 1825, the author, T. C. Hansard, having one of these presses then in use, and stating that its average speed was two thousand sheets per hour, but that it was capable of printing more. It is probable that the first power-presses made in this country were those manufactured by Dow, in Boston, for Daniel Treadwell. He had patented in England, in 1820, a press worked by a treadle, which was manufactured for him by Napier, and returning, a few years later, to the United States, he brought with him plans and descriptions of the original Napier press, from which Dow manufactured several working presses. But the printers of that day were so slow to purchase such novelties, that Treadwell could not sell his new presses. He then established a printing-office, running the presses by horse-power, but it was burned down, probably by hand-pressmen, who were intensely hostile to his invention; and it was only after he established a second printing-office, in which his presses were run by water-power, that a purchaser for similar machines was at last found, about 1825 or 1826, in Isaac Ashmead, of Philadelphia.

To Applegath, or Applegath & Cowper, the task was intrusted, of constructing machines to meet the increasing requirements of the London Times. It was supposed that Applegath had accomplished a wonderful achievement when, in 1827, he supplied that establishment with a four-cylinder-press, capable of printing, from one form, more than four thousand sheets per hour. Savage, in his Dictionary of Printing, published in 1841, in speaking of this press, says: The paper is laid on at four places, one form of which, consisting of four pages, is printed at the astonishing rate of 4320 an hour, at its ordinary rate of working, a fact which I have seen and ascertained myself, by counting its motions with a second-watch in my hand. Subsequently, Applegath made a press for the London Times, capable of printing between 10,000 and 11,000 sheets per hour; but it was afterwards supplanted in the office of that paper by one of the fast Hoe presses, which was used until it, in turn, was superseded by the Walter press, made under the immediate direction of the leading proprietor of the Times office. The fast newspaper presses of the pres-

ent day are the six-, eight-, and ten-cylinder Hoe Presses, the Bullock Press, the Marinoni and Alauzet Presses of France, and the Walter Press of England, which are described under their appropriate headings. It was some years after power-presses had been manufactured and extensively used in England, before any great demand arose for them in this country, and for a considerable period the firm of R. Hoe & Co. practically monopolized the business of making very fast newspaper-presses, while, of a series of attempts to construct power book-printing-presses, those embodied in the Adams press were decidedly the most successful. (See ADAMS PRESS.) But after the manufacture of power-presses was fairly established here it was prosecuted with characteristic genius, skill, and energy. An abstract of the specifications of patents granted by the American Patent Office, which will be found in a subdivision of the article on INVENTIONS, affords a good indication of the bewildering variety of advances made, as well as the order of the successive improvements, while the numerous illustrations given in this volume of the presses in present use indicate how wide a field for selection is now open to American printers, whether they are in search of fast or comparatively slow newspaper-presses, book-presses, or large or small job-presses. It would be no slight task to make a full enumeration of the distinct sizes and kinds of typographic presses now in use in the United States; and the total number in use, counting small and large, was estimated by The Typographic Messenger, in 1867, at 25,000.

Aside from the fast newspaper and book presses, a great deal of attention has been devoted, of late years, to the construction of machine-presses intended for country newspaper establishments, to small job-presses, and to the improvement of drum-cylinder-presses intended either for book-work or different varieties of fine job-printing on large sheets. Thousands of large drum-cylinder-presses have been made and sold in this country by the respective manufacturers, their varied capacities rendering them great favorites in many offices. The style of small job-presses has changed frequently, numerous improvements being made from time to time, one of the most important of which is the diminution of danger to feeders.

De Vinne's Price List contains the following estimate of the average daily performance of job-presses on editions of irregular numbers:

AVERAGE DAILY PERFORMANCE OF PRESSES,

On editions of irregular numbers, with a small allowance of time for making ready.

The estimates of the following table are for miscellaneous work, done in the usual manner, with little making ready, and under the favorable conditions of a busy season. It is supposed that the presses are at work full ten hours; that feeders and pressman are expert and diligent; that paper, rollers, steam-power, ink, etc. are in perfect order, and that there are no detentions or accidents.

These estimates are applicable only to a press in full employment.

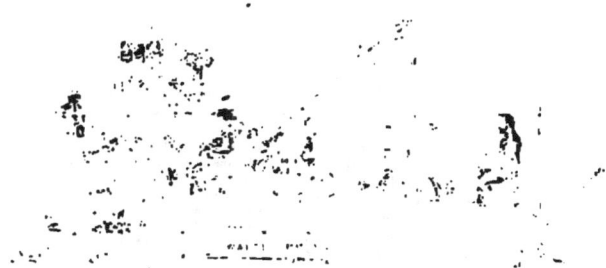

MARINONI PRESS

STANHOPE PRESS

BLAEW PRESS

PRESS ON WHICH FRANKLIN
WORKED IN LONDON

COLUMBIAN PRESS

WALTER PRESS

PRESS OF 1560

	Scale of Press. Number of Forms.	Time of Presswork, Hours.	Rate per Hour, Hours at Work.	Daily Per Pressman Impression.
	CARD PRESS.			
1	One Form of........7500 impressions	9	833	7500
4	Four Forms of......1000 "	8	666	4000
6	Eight Forms of.... 250 "	4	500	2000
	SMALL MACHINE PRESS.			
1	One Form of....... 6000 impressions	9	666	6000
5	Five Forms of..... 500 "	5	500	2500
8	Eight Forms of.... 100 "	2	400	800
	HAND PRESS.			
1	One Form of........1500 impressions	9	156	1500
4	Four Forms of.... 100 "	6	166	1000
	MEDIUM CYLINDER.			
1	One Form of......1500 impressions	9	833	7500
5	Five Forms of..... 750 "	5	750	3750
7	Eight Forms of.... 250 "	3	666	2000
	DOUBLE MEDIUM CYLINDER.			
2	One Form of........5000 impressions	8	666	5000
5	Three Forms of....1000 "	5	600	3000
7	Six Forms of...... 250 "	3	500	1500
	MAMMOTH CYLINDER.			
3	One Form of ......4000 impressions	7	570	4000
5	Two Forms of......1250 "	5	500	2500
7	Four Forms of.... 250 "	3	333	1000

The allotment of impressions to forms is not fanciful. The proportions are those of actual practice. In every job office small editions are always in excess.

Press-making has been brought to such perfection in this country, that the development of any well-defined demand quickly leads to a corresponding supply; and after any marked defect is discovered in an old press made for a special purpose, a remedy is promptly devised. A number of presses intended for printing in colors have been patented and made. Ingenious copying presses have been manufactured, and an immense number of them are in daily use in counting-houses. Presses specially adapted for fine wood-cut-painting have been made, one of the latest being Hoe's Stop-Cylinder. Ingenious railway-ticket and consecutive numbering machines have been devised. And, whether speed, size, cheapness, varied capacity, or superior execution is the object to be attained, the press-makers of this country have never failed, after due notice, to meet the requirements of American printers.

Press Goes.—When the press is properly at work, it is said to go.

Press Goes Easy.—When the run of the press is light, or when the pull is easy.

Press Goes Hard.—When the reverse of the above is the case. Paraffin oil has been found to possess good easy-running qualities for oiling the ribs of presses.

Pressing.—Removing the inequalities on the surface of a sheet caused by the impression of the types. This is done usually in Standing Presses or Hydraulic Presses. (See PRESS-WORK and HOT-PRESSING.)

Pressman.—A printer who does press-work,

especially one who devotes exclusive attention to this branch of the art.

Press-Proof.—A good impression of a sheet of a work, or of a job, taken so that it may be carefully read and corrected previous to its being put to press.

Press-Revise.—A sheet pulled after a form is laid on the press, to see that all corrections marked in the press-proof have been attended to, and that the form is in all respects correct.

Press Stands Still.—When the press remains unused from any cause, such as want of work, absence of pressmen, etc., it is said to stand still.

Press-Work.—The various operations required to take proper impressions, on paper or other substance, of a book-form or job, by means of the press and inking-rollers applied to the form, from the laying of the form on press to the delivery of the printed sheets; also the making of lye, and the manufacture of rollers and keeping them in a suitable condition for working.

To do good press-work, the press should be kept perfectly clean; the running-gear should be well oiled, to avoid friction; the parts which give the impression must be set with care, so as to have an equal bearing on the whole surface of the form, and the rollers put up in order suitable to the quality of ink used, presenting a smooth surface, free from cracks, lumps, or depressions. The ink to be used should be impalpably fine, of an intense color, freely covering the surface of the form when applied by the rollers, and as freely adhering to the paper when the impression is given, not liable to smear by ordinary contact with the other printed sheets, and retaining the color when dry. Before putting a form to press, the bed should be perfectly clean, and the back of the form brushed off, to remove any particles of dirt or other matter that may adhere to the bottom of the type. The brush for this purpose should be made of soft bristles. Paper or rags are not suitable, as they are apt to leave particles of the material on the form. After these requisites have been complied with, the making ready of the form tests the pressman's efforts to do good work. (See MAKING READY.)

In making ready a form of book-work on an Adams Press, too much care cannot be given to its position on the bed. If by any possibility it can be made to work on the centre of the bed (equidistant from its sides and ends), that is its proper place; if not there, then as near it as may be.

To determine the position of the form, the following rule is given:—Fold a sheet of the job in quarto form. Lay the folded edge to the ascertained centre of the bed, and see if the cut edge of the sheet will reach (with a quarter of an inch to spare) the longest nippers of the press. If nippers and sheet come together as above, you may safely proceed with making ready. If not, the form must be thrown out of centre that these relative positions may be attained.

To effect this object, the processes for type and stereotype are quite different. The inequalities of impression in stereotype may be more effectively remedied by underlaying than by overlaying, while type should be overlaid only, for obvious reasons. In underlaying, general results only are aimed at; which means, simply, a uniform impression of all the pages of a form. The imperfections of each page should be brought up by overlays.

It is customary to use one roller during the process of making ready for fine machine press-work, while the rollers intended for printing are put up when the proof is pronounced correct and the pressman is ready to proceed with the printing of the form, as the rollers are liable to get out of order during the time occupied in making ready. In hand-press work the rollers may be put in order when the making ready is commenced, while the distributing cylinder can be frequently turned during the delay caused by cutting out and overlaying.

If letters, quadrats, or furniture rise up and black the paper, they should be pushed down, and that part of the form should be locked up more tightly, or justified properly.

Iron bearers should be used across the bed of the press, as those made of wood will wear thin by long working.

Should the frame of the tympan rub against the platen, it will cause a slur or mackle; this can be remedied by moving the tympan so as to clear the platen. Slurring and mackling will sometimes happen from other causes; in such cases corks may be pasted on the frisket, or cords may be tied across it, to keep the sheet close to the tympan.

When the form gets out of register,—which will often happen by the starting of the quoins which secure the chase,—it must immediately be put in again, as there can scarcely be a greater defect in a book than a want of uniformity in this particular.

If picks, produced by bits of paper, composition, or film of ink and grease or filth, get into the form, they must be removed with the point of a pin or needle or with a pick-brush; but if the form is much clogged with them, it should be well rubbed over with clean lye, or taken off and washed: in either case, before the pressman goes on again, it should be made perfectly dry by pulling several waste sheets upon it, in order to suck up the water deposited in the cavities of the letter.

The pressman should accustom himself to look over the sheets as they are taken from the press; he will thus be enabled not only to observe any want of uniformity in the color, but also to detect imperfections which might otherwise escape notice.

Torn or stained sheets met with in the course of work are thrown out. Creases and wrinkles will frequently appear in the sheets when the paper has been carelessly wet: these should be carefully removed by smoothing them out with the back of the nails of the right hand.

Loose tympans will at all times slur the work, and great care must therefore be observed in drawing the tympans perfectly tight. The paper drying at the edges will also cause a slur: this may be remedied by wetting the edges frequently with a sponge.

The Press.—During the present century there has been an entire revolution made in the printing-business by the application of machinery to the execution of all kinds of press-work; and even after power-presses were first invented it was generally believed, by those who were supposed to be competent judges, that for job- and book-work the speed should not exceed a certain rate, or else the appearance of the work would not come up to the standard of good workmanship.

This idea seems to have grown out of the facts, that, in order to do fine work, it was necessary, when the rollers passed over the form, that the motion should be slow enough to allow the ink to cover the face of the types, and that when the bed and platen came together they should remain in that position long enough to allow the ink time to be transferred from the form to the sheet of paper. These were correct enough; but there are other parts of the operation which can be facilitated without having any detrimental effect: these are, the movements of the sheet before and after the impression is made, and the coming together and separation of the bed and platen after they have remained together long enough to make a slight dwell on the form.

The press, whatever kind used, should be in the best condition; and a fair knowledge of the construction and manner of putting up a press will enable a pressman to provide a proper remedy in case any of the parts should become misplaced, or have an unequal bearing during the motion of the press.

In putting together the several parts of a printing-press, it very often happens that, if the pieces be in pairs, they get transposed: for example, the legs of a hand-press. This should never happen, because the press-maker fits each piece to its proper position; and, should they become misplaced, it will cause much trouble to get them correct.

In the more particular kinds of work, where the paper is heavy and the types are large, set-off sheets are used to interleave the printed sheets while working, and are continued in it until the printed paper is taken down from the poles and put in the standing-press. These set-off sheets are put in when the white paper is working, and moved from one heap to the other during the printing of the second side. They prevent the ink setting off from one sheet to another, while they are newly printed, which it would be likely to do, on account of the weight of the paper, and also because fine printing is usually worked of a full color.

To produce press-work of a highly superior character, great care and much time are required; it is necessary to have a good press; to have new types, or types the faces of which are not rounded by wear; to have the rollers in the best condition; the ink should be strong, of a full color, the oil well burnt, to prevent it separating from the coloring-matter and tingeing the paper, and it should be ground so fine as to be impalpable; the paper should be of the best quality, made of linen rags, and not bleached by means of an acid which has a tendency to decompose the ink; the rolling should be carefully and well done; the face of the types should be completely covered, without any superfluity, so as to produce a full color; and the impression should be so regulated as to have a slow and hard pressure, and to pause at its maximum in order to fix the ink firmly upon the paper. These particulars observed, with paper only in the tympan, perfectly sharp impressions of the face of the types will be obtained.

Before the pressman leaves his work, he covers the heap of paper by first turning down a sheet like a token-sheet, to show where he left off, and then putting a quantity of the worked sheets and a paperboard on it, and, should the paper be too dry, it would be well to surround it with wet wrappers. The form should be washed with clean lye, and carefully gone over with a wet sponge.

After a type form has been worked and lifted from the press, the ink on its surface should be loosened with lye and thoroughly rinsed off with water. The brush used for this purpose should have the hairs about one inch in length, and set closely together.

Engravings.—When the workman puts the block on the press, he ought to be very gentle in the pull of the first impression, to prevent an accident, which has frequently occurred from thoughtlessness in this particular, by making the pull too hard and crushing some of the lines; by avoiding this he will be safe, and can proportion the impression to the subject. The only correct manner of doing this is, to take all the impression off, after which it should be put on, a little at a time, until the lightest part of the cut comes up with a proper degree of sharpness; then the heavier portions can be overlaid until the requisite amount of pressure is produced.

If a block be too low, it is advisable to underlay it, for the purpose of bringing it to the proper height, in preference to making use of overlays, for they act in some measure as blankets, being pressed into the blank places, and rendering the lines broader than they are in the engraving.

It will be necessary, sometimes, when the surface of the block is very uneven, to tear away parts of the paper in the tympan, to equalize the impression where it is too hard.

Some portions of the impression will frequently come up much too strong, and others too weak; it will then be necessary to take out from between the tympans a thickness of paper, and add an additional tympan-sheet, cutting away those parts that come off too hard, and scraping down the edges. Scraping away half the thickness of a tympan-sheet in small parts that require to be a little lightened will improve the impression.

The light parts require little pressure, but the deep shades should be brought up so as to produce a full and firm impression.

Neither the pressure nor the impression in an

engraving should be uniformly equal: if they be, the effect that is intended to be produced by the artist will fail, and instead of light, middle-tint, and shade, an impression will be produced that possesses none of them in perfection; some parts will be too hard and black, and other parts have neither pressure nor color enough, but will be obscure and rough, and without any of the mildness of the middle-tint which ought to pervade every part of an engraving.

To produce the desired effect, great patience and nicety are necessary. A few thicknesses of thin, fine paper are generally required over the salient points of a picture, the outline of the part overlaid being closely followed. The edges of all pieces that are to stand in strong relief should be carefully scraped down, that surrounding parts may not lose their individuality.

Engravings that are in the vignette form require great attention, to keep the edges light and clear, and in general it is necessary to scrape away one or two thicknesses of paper, in order to lighten the impression and keep it clean; for, the edges being irregular, and parts, such as small branches of trees, leaves, etc., straggling, for the purpose of giving freedom to the design, they may come off too hard, and are liable to picks, which give great trouble, and are difficult to be avoided.

When great delicacy of impression is demanded in a vignette, it will be found beneficial, after the engraving has been rolled, to take the superfluous ink from the extremities, by using a small piece of composition on which there is no ink. This will give the edges lightness and softness, particularly where distances are represented.

When highly-finished engravings are worked separately, cloth, or any other soft substance, should never be used for blankets, as the impression will sink into it; two or three thicknesses of smooth hard paper, or even a piece of glazed pasteboard, placed in the tympan, is better.

The rollers should be in the best condition for this kind of work; and the pressman should be very particular, in taking ink, that but little be put on at a time, and that it be thoroughly distributed before the rolling is done, or else he will not obtain a clear and uniform impression.

Should a wood-cut be left on the bed of the press or on the stone for any length of time, it is apt to become warped. When this happens, a very good method of restoring it to its original shape is to lay it, face downward, upon the imposing-stone, with a few thicknesses of damp paper under it, and to place a flat weight of some kind upon it; and in the course of an hour or two the block will be restored to its former position. This method is preferable to wetting the block with water, which is often practiced; for the latter swells the fine lines of the engraving, and consequently affects the impression. To retain the appearance as it comes from the hand of the artist, the block should never be wet with water; and, for this reason, when wood-cuts and types are worked together, the engravings should be taken out before the form is washed, and be cleaned with spirits of turpentine.

Lye should never be used to clean a wood-engraving. It will be found, in practice, that spirits of turpentine take off the ink more rapidly, and affect the wood less, than any other article used; and the facility with which the block is again brought into a working state more than compensates for the trifling expense incurred, as all that is required is to wipe the surface dry, and to pull two or three impressions on waste paper.

The pressman will find it a great advantage, if it be necessary to do full justice to an engraving, to have a good impression from the engraver, and place it before him as a pattern, and then arrange the overlays, etc. until he produces a fac-simile in effect.

Stereotype and electrotype cuts can be treated in the same way as wood-engravings, so far as making ready and overlaying are concerned. On account of the cheapness and durability of electrotypes, they should always be used in preference to the originals; because, if an accident should occur, the plate can be renewed at a small expense, and it obviates the necessity of keeping water from the cut, as it can be washed in the same manner as ordinary types.

Job-Work.—Paper should be used for tympans, in printing every description of job-work, the texture and number of thicknesses varying according to the character of the work. The impression should be put on just enough to bring up the types which are of the greatest height-to-paper, and then the indistinct lines must be overlaid, until the outline of each letter is perfect.

If a form be made ready in this manner, there will be no danger of the types being destroyed by too hard a pressure; because there is no more impression put on than is required to bring up the highest types. The impression should be taken off directly after the printing of one job, when it can be regulated, by degrees, until there is a sufficient amount put on for the next.

Washing the Form.—After the form is printed, it should be washed clean from every particle of ink. Care and attention to this particular are well repaid in the subsequent cleanly working of the same type when put on press. Much time is lost by not giving minute attention to the thorough washing and rinsing of forms.

The lye used for the purpose of cleaning a form is a solution of alkali in water; it ought to be made of the best pot- or pearl-ash, or, better still, of concentrated lye. It should be of sufficient strength to bite the tongue sharply in tasting. The usual proportion is, one pound of pearlash to a gallon of soft water; it should be stirred until the alkali is dissolved, which will soon take place. It is generally contained in a large jar, which should be kept covered, to prevent dirt and dust getting into the lye.

If hard water be used, it will require a greater amount of pearlash; as the acid in the water will combine with some of the alkali, to neutralize it; which, of course, will have the effect of making the lye weaker than if soft water, with which there is no such chemical combination, has been used.

The brush should be nine or ten inches long, by three inches broad; and the hair should be at least one inch in length, of a soft texture, and set as closely together as possible. By not having a good brush, more types are destroyed, on account of carelessness in washing, than by almost any other process which they are liable to undergo.

When a form is small, it may be rinsed by standing it on its edge in the trough and throwing water against the faces of the types; but if it be over half a medium sheet, it should be laid flat in the trough. In either case, plenty of water should be used; for a little care in this particular will always keep the types free from dirt.

Sometimes the counters of the letters become filled with ink before the working of the form is finished. In such cases, lye and water should not be used, as much time would be lost in drying the types. Spirits of turpentine and a soft brush will be found to take off the ink quickly, and the work can be proceeded with in a few minutes. When this article has been used, a few impressions must be made on waste paper, to remove the oil which remains on the types after the turpentine has evaporated; though, if alcohol be at hand, it will remove the oil more effectually.

Pressing the Sheets.—The paper being all printed, it must be exposed to the atmosphere a sufficient length of time to let the ink set firmly before the sheets are put in the standing-press.

The poles, upon which the sheets are placed to dry, should be two and a half inches wide, and made of one-inch white pine. They should be placed across the room, about fourteen inches from the ceiling and nine or ten inches apart, resting at each end on a piece of wood fastened to the walls of the room, in notches to retain them in their situations. They should be kept clean, and, if they have not had paper hung on them for some time, the dust must be brushed off before they are again used. As the weight of the paper would have a tendency to bend the poles, they should be turned over, as occasion may require, to keep them straight.

The number of sheets put in one place on the poles must be regulated by circumstances. If the work be in a hurry, or the poles be not in a favorable situation for drying, or the weather be rainy and the air charged with moisture, no more than three or four should be hung in a place; but, if the situation be favorable for drying, and the weather be warm, eight or ten sheets may be put in each place.

If the sheets be allowed to remain on the poles ten or twelve hours it will in most cases be found sufficient for the purpose of setting the ink or drying the paper.

They are now ready to be put in the standing-press. This is done by laying up a press-board, and putting on a pasteboard and one of the sheets of the work to be pressed, alternately, until all the sheets of paper are in the pasteboards. The pile must then be taken, fifty at a time, and placed in the centre of the standing-press, with a press-board at every two reams. The press must next be screwed down tightly, and suffered to remain in that condition ten or twelve hours; when it will be found that the sheets are as smooth as they were before being run through the press.

When highly-glazed paper or parchment is printed, the ink is liable to be transferred from one sheet to the other. In such cases sheets of common printing-paper should be put between them, and the whole put in the standing-press immediately after the job is printed.

If it be wished to give the surface of the print a glossy appearance, instead of proceeding according to the above method, each sheet of paper should be put between two sheets of zinc, to the number of twenty-five, and run forward and back, three or four times, between iron rollers similar to those of a copper-plate press. This will be found to give jobs done in gold and silver a brilliancy which cannot be obtained by the former mode of pressing.

Still another way is, to put the sheets of printed paper between sheet-iron pressing-boards, which have been heated previously; and then the whole is subjected to the power of a hydraulic press.

Although the last method mentioned is the best, it has not been brought into general use, on account of the expense and tediousness of the process. When, therefore, work is to be pressed in a manner superior to that which can be done by the common standing-press, the sheets of zinc and roller-press can be used with advantage.

Making Rollers.—This part of the pressman's business has undergone some modification of late years, owing to the fact that the increased demand for printing has made the manufacture of rollers a distinct branch of business in many large cities, and instead of the mixture of glue and molasses, or glue and sugar, rollers made of certain proportions of glue and glycerine, or glue, glycerine, and saccharine matters, combined with fixed oils, are now extensively and advantageously used. For directions in regard to the ordinary glue and molasses rollers, see COM-POSITION ROLLERS.

Preserving Rollers.—The washing of the rollers is an operation of great importance, as their preservation and good condition depend almost entirely on the care with which it is done.

When it is necessary to wash a roller, it should be done as quickly as possible, by first loosening the ink with lye and a sponge, after which clean water must be thrown upon it till all the ink is removed. This being done, and the lye being rinsed out of the sponge, which should be squeezed as dry as possible, it should be rubbed over the surface and ends of the roller, so that it will absorb any water that may have been left on those parts.

When rollers are new, they should not be cleaned with lye, as it will have an injurious effect on them, although the utmost care may be taken in its application. The best method of proceeding, in such cases, is to use spirits of turpentine to remove the ink; but, in default of turpentine new rollers may be cleaned by running them back and forth a few times over a dusty part of the floor which has previously been swept clear of all hard and large particles: the ink becoming absorbed by the dust, both of them can be removed by using a sponge which has been slightly dampened.

If a roller become too hard, and the surface is clean, dampening it with clean water will restore it to a proper condition for working; but, instead of doing this, it is preferable to put it in a damp situation, where it will gradually absorb moisture. It will often be found that sponging a roller while it is being used will make it work as well as it would if it were washed. When this is done, the roller must be kept in constant motion on the cylinder or stone until all the particles of water are absorbed.

When a roller gets too soft, it should be placed where a current of dry air will act on its surface. This will evaporate the superabundant moisture which it contains, and cool the composition, if the room has been too warm.

When rollers are not in use, they should be kept in an air-tight box, so made that water can be put in or taken out of it as occasion may require. With a box of this description, the rollers can always be kept in good order, by attending to the following directions: If the atmosphere be very damp, there should be no water left in the box, and the cover should be put down closely, so as to exclude the air; and if the atmosphere be very dry, water should be put in the bottom of the box, the cover being as before; in the intermediate states of the atmosphere, the cover may be left more or less open, as circumstances require.

Rollers should not be allowed to rest on the cylinder or stone for any length of time, as they will thereby become flattened, which will render them unfit for the uniform distribution of the ink; neither should they be exposed to the action of the rays of the sun in summer, nor to the direct heat of a stove in winter, as either will soften the composition so much as to cause it to run, and thus spoil the rollers.

Although rollers can generally be kept in good order by attending to the foregoing directions, yet it will sometimes be found that, no matter what care be taken, the rollers will work badly. This can generally be obviated by allowing them to rest for an hour or two.

Improvements in Presses, etc.—In the construction of presses, the genius of inventors has met with abundant success. An idea of the improvements in hand-presses may be gathered from the fact that in 1475 three hundred sheets, or six hundred impressions, was considered a good day's work. In the sixteenth century the number had increased to two thousand impressions, and in the early part of the nineteenth century, to twelve tokens, or two thousand eight hundred and eighty impressions; and in later years the last amount has been accomplished on job forms in eight hours. But the performances of power presses at the rate of two thousand impressions per hour, and the printing, perfecting, and cutting from continuous rolls of paper, at almost incredible rates of speed, seem to have left nothing more to be accomplished in the way of fast press-work.

It is a notable feature of the history of printing in this country, that a large portion of those who have successfully prosecuted the art have been celebrated for their superior knowledge of, and attention to, press-work. In Philadelphia, the late Mr. Sherman, Mr. Baird, of the firm of King & Baird, the late Mr. T. K. Collins, and the late Mr. Ashmead, may be cited as illustrations in point; while in New York, the success of the late James Harper, and of many others, teaches the same practical lesson. It is too much the habit of apprentices to devote their attention exclusively to composition; and, as a consequence, compositors are always plenty and good pressmen comparatively scarce. All the money and labor spent in purchasing fonts of letter, and in setting up type correctly or elegantly, are well-nigh useless when bad press-work mars the products of the type-foundry and the composing-room. We have great faith in modern machinery, in improved presses, roller-composition, etc.; but no machinery and no chemical combinations will cover up the blunders or carelessness of a poor pressman. An expert in this branch of the typographic art will produce fine, if not good, work on any press, and give a presentable appearance to fearfully battered type; while a botch will produce comparatively imperfect effects with splendid type, good rollers, and the best press that can be made.

Prices.—This subject has been ably and exhaustively treated in De Vinne's Price List, a work recently published, and now in the possession of a large proportion of those who are most deeply interested. The prices of labor and its products vary so much in different sections of the country, there are so many elements of cost in diversified job-printing, and so many fluctuations occur from various causes, that any elaborate discussion of this topic would necessarily be too extended for this publication. The usages of the trade, however, in book and newspaper work, are indicated by the following scales:

PRICES FOR LABOR IN NEW YORK IN 1871.

Book Composition by the Piece. Common Matter, Made up.

LANGUAGE.	MANUSCRIPT.		REPRINT.	
	Solid.	Leaded.	Solid.	Leaded.
Works in English........................	$ .53	$ .50	$ .50	$ .47
Latin, Spanish, and German......	.62	.58	.57	.53
French, Italian, and Portuguese..	.64	.60	.59	.55
Welsh, Indian, and African........	.67	.63	.62	.58
Greek, plain..............................	1.00	.96	.75	.65
Hebrew, if without points...........	.80	.75	.70	.—
Hebrew, kerned, with vowel points	1.60	1.55	1.55	1.50
Hebrew, kerned, vowel points and accents................................	2.00	1.95	1.95	1.90

Type larger than Pica to be counted as Pica. Pearl and Diamond, 5 cents extra per 1000 ems.

All matter leaded with a thinner lead than eight to Pica shall rate as solid.

It shall be competent for foreign-born compositors to work at composition in their native language at the same rates as specified for English.

By Reprint is meant printed copy free from alterations or interlineations, save remodeling of punctuation or orthography, which shall be done, if at all, before it is given out to compositors.

Thin fonts, from Pica to Bourgeois, the alphabets of which measure less than 12 ems; also all fonts smaller than Bourgeois, which measure less than 12½ ems, shall be paid for as follows: For every three-em space below the standard, 2 cents extra per 1000 ems shall be charged. A four-em space to count as a three-em space; less than a four-em space not to be counted.

Bastard fonts to be measured according to the body; but if the alphabet is less than the standard, the rule for thin fonts will apply.

In measuring the width of a measure, any fraction of an em less than an en will not be counted; an en or greater fraction will be counted as an em.

Each size of type used in a work to be measured and charged according to its own body.

All Blanks in matter in which different kinds of type are intermingled shall be reckoned as of the type of the text.

Extra Matter. Five Cents Extra per 1000 Ems.—Dictionary Matter without figured accents or marked letters.

Concordances, or any work in which abbreviations, italics, figures, capitals, etc. are profusely used.

Reading-Books with marked letters or spaced syllables.

Works on Natural Sciences, and school-books generally, when made up by the compositor, in which inset cuts are freely used, and which also have questions at bottom of pages.

Works in Old English spelling, contractions, etc.,

Works with an unusual quantity of references, which the compositor is required to change.

Indexes, in which italics, figures, capitals, and abbreviations are freely used.

Ten Cents Extra per 1000 Ems.—Arithmetics, Geometries, Surveying and similar Mathematical works. Grammars and Spelling-Books.

Dictionaries of a complicated character, with accented letters and frequent abbreviations.

Fifty Cents Extra per 1000 Ems.—Algebra Matter, with profusion of signs and formulas and algebraic fractions.

Greek and Hebrew Words.—Greek words shall be charged 2 cents each if not justified, and 3 cents each when requiring justification.

For Classical Works, Commentaries, and other works in which Greek words are freely used, the following schedule shall govern the price per 1000 ems, if the words are not justified.

For less than an average of 5 words per 1000 ems, the words may be counted.

If the words average from 5 to 7, 10 cents per 1000 ems extra; from 8 to 12, 15 cents per 1000 ems extra; 13 to 20, 20 cents per 1000 ems extra; more than 20, the words to be counted at 1 cent each. In no case, however, shall the price per 1000 ems exceed $1.00. If the words are justified, they shall count as 1½ words each.

Hebrew words shall rate double Greek words.

Side, Centre, and Cut-in Notes.—Side and Centre Notes in Bibles and Testaments to be counted the full length of the page (including the lead or one rule, which shall count at least one em), according to the type in which they are set, and to be charged 75 cents per 1000 ems. Cut-in Notes in the above works to be charged 5 cents extra each.

Side Notes in Law, Historical, and other works to be counted the full length of the page, according to the type in which they are set, and at the price per 1000 of the text. Side Folios in Law works to be counted by the maker-up. Cut-in Notes shall be charged at the rate of 5 cents per note. Seals 5 cents extra each.

Matter taking a greater price than the work in which it occurs shall be measured by itself, and have its own extra over plain matter added to the price of such work. For instance, French Grammar Tables should take the three extras of French, Grammar, and English Tables, according to this price list.

Grammars, Dictionaries, or other extra matter in Foreign Languages, will take the extra of the language and the kind of work; but when English exercises or reading-lessons are introduced as a regular feature of the work, such portions shall take the extra of the kind of work only.

Narrow Measures—Column Matter.—Matter eighteen ems or less in width shall be paid for according to the following schedule: Per 1000 ems extra.

18 ems...1 ct.	14 ems...7 cts.	11 ems...16 cts.	8 ems...30 cts.
17 " ...2 cts.	13 " ...10 "	10 " ...20 "	7 " ...40 "
16 " ...3 "	12 " ...13 "	9 " ...25 "	6 " ...50 "
15 " ...5 "			

Column matter (that is, matter made up continuously in two or more columns, not dependent upon each other for their arrangement, with or without rules) shall be paid for according to width of measure.

Tabular and Table Work.—This is matter set up in three or more columns dependent upon each other for arrangement, and reading across the page.

Three columns of figures or words, with or without rules, one-half extra.

Four or more columns of figures or words, with or without rules, double price.

When blank tables are introduced into a work, they are cast up as tables according to the size of the type in which the body of the work is set.

Short pages in a series of tables shall be charged as full table pages.

Small isolated tables occurring in works of a narrow measure, as in double column octavos, will be paid

for according to the time consumed in composing them, such time, however, not to exceed $1.50 per 1000 ems.

Making up.—In putting work in hand, the office shall decide whether it shall be made up by the compositors or by the office.

In all cases where the compositors make up, if they deem it necessary that matter should be made up by one person, they may appoint from among themselves, or authorize the employer to appoint, a person to perform that duty, on terms to be agreed upon between themselves and the person employed to make up; provided, however, that no more than three lines per page or three cents per 1000 ems shall be allowed for making up, imposing, taking necessary proofs, and keeping the schedule. The maker-up to have no privileges but such as are enjoyed by the other compositors on the work; copy to be given out in regular order, without selecting, and the matter to be charged in full pages, the compositors clearing away head-lines, blanks, leads, etc.

When made up by the office, the matter shall be measured and paid for on the galleys, deducting three cents per 1000 ems for making up, provided the employer allows the journeymen all cuts, blanks, and leads properly belonging thereto, except tail-pages and full-page cuts, the office clearing away head-lines, blanks, etc.

In all cases where matter is not measured and paid for by measurement on the galley, the tail-pages and other blanks belong to the compositor.

In book-rooms, the establishment has the right of claiming full titles and dedications; but in no case shall piece-paying establishments claim half-titles, or any other prefixed matter, nor cull the fat portions of any work.

Time-Charges.—Compositors employed by the week shall receive not less than $20.00 per week, not more than ten hours to be considered a day's work, and not more than nine hours on Saturday.

Time occupied by alterations from copy, by casing or distributing letter not used by the compositor, etc., to be paid for at the rate of 35 cents per hour. When compositors work beyond regular hours, they shall be paid at the rate of 50 cents per hour, or 10 cents an hour in addition to the matter set up, such extra time to be between the hours of 6 P. M. and 7 A. M. Sunday work will be paid at the rate of 70 cents per hour for day-, and $1.00 per hour for night-work. Composition by the piece, double the charges for week workdays. Holidays by mutual agreement.

The office must make its corrections according to copy on two proofs, but the compositor must make these corrections on further proofs, if any are rendered necessary through his neglect. But author's proofs and alterations from copy shall be paid for at the rate of 35 cents per hour.

Head- or sub-head-lines, giving a synopsis of the contents of each page, when filled up by the proof-reader or author, shall be considered as author's corrections, and shall be paid for accordingly.

When a compositor is required to turn for sorts, or to take out bad letters and replace them, in consequence of faults in the founder, miscasts, or worn-out fonts, he shall be paid at the rate of 35 cents per hour.

When a compositor (working by the piece) receives copy of contents, indexes, or any other copy, where more than the usual quantity of capitals, figures, periods, and italics are used, the establishment shall furnish the compositor with the necessary sorts.

When a compositor (working by the piece) is required to make up furniture for letter-press, stereotype, or electrotype forms, he shall charge for such work at the rate of 35 cents per hour.

Job-Work.—All men employed by the week shall be paid not less than $20.00—not more than ten hours to constitute a day's work—not more than nine hours on Saturday; when paid by the hour, the price shall be 35 cents per hour. When compositors work beyond the regular hours, they shall be paid at the rate of 50 cents per hour, such extra time to be between the hours of 6 P. M. and 7 A. M. Sunday work will be paid at the rate of 70 cents per hour for day-, and $1.00 per hour for night-work. Composition by the piece, double the charges for weekdays. Holidays by mutual agreement. All piece-work done in job-offices shall be governed by the book-scale.

Prices for Morning Newspaper Work.—Adopted by New York Typographical Union No. 6, Tuesday, October 29, 1867.

1. Compositors employed by the piece shall receive not less than 50 cents per 1000 ems for common matter, and shall be entitled to at least two hours' continuous composition between 1 and 5 o'clock P. M., and at least five hours' continuous composition between the hours of 6 and 12 P. M. When compositors are employed at night only, by the piece, they shall receive 55 cents per 1000 ems. Piece-hands after 3 A. M. shall be entitled to 40 cents per hour and all matter set after that hour.

2. Compositors employed by the week shall receive not less than $24 per week (six days), ten hours (at least two hours of which shall be between the hours of 1 and 5 P. M.) to constitute a day's work. When employed on night situations only—eight hours to constitute a night's work—the hours of employment shall be between 6 P. M. and 3 A. M., and they shall be paid $22.00 per week, and for all time after 3 A. M. time shall be charged. This article shall apply to compositors employed in reading proof.

3. Compositors may be employed during the day on Morning Newspapers at 45 cents per 1000 ems, or $20.00 per week—ten hours to constitute a day's work.

4. When required to remain in the office unemployed, the compositor shall receive not less than 40 cents per hour for such standing time. All men employed by the week shall charge 40 cents per hour after 3 o'clock A. M. Time occupied in distributing or casing letter not to be used by the person distributing or casing, alterations from copy, lifting forms, etc., to be paid for at not less than 40 cents per hour.

5. When bogus copy is given out in lieu of standing time, it shall not be of such a nature as to preclude the compositor from making fair average wages, viz., intricate or illegible copy, or copy containing great quantities of caps, small caps, italic, points, etc., or running on particular sorts.

6. When compositors are called before 10 A. M., in case of the arrival of a steamer, etc., they shall be paid not less than $1.00 each for such call, and be entitled to the matter they set. This is understood to apply to both week- and piece-work.

7. Tabular work, etc., containing three or four columns, either of figures or words, or figures and words, without rules, shall be charged a price and a half. All work, as above, with brass or other rules, or where there are five or more columns of figures, or figures and words, with or without rules, shall be paid double price. Headings to tabular column-work, in smaller type than the body of the table, shall be paid extra, according to their value.

8. For work done in any language foreign to the office, an advance of 5 cents per 1000 ems shall be paid.

PRICES FOR BOOK-WORK FIXED BY THE EMPLOYING PRINTERS OF PHILADELPHIA IN 1864.

All descriptions of work not enumerated in this Schedule, denominated extra or fine work, also paper extra large in dimensions of sheet, very thin paper, or very heavy fine paper, will be specially contracted for as heretofore.

COMPOSITION.

For Plain Composition, Book Work, Reprint Copy,	85 cents per 1000 ems.
For Plain Composition, Book Work, Manuscript,	90 cents per 1000 ems.
Alterations in Composition,	50 cents per 1000 ems.

(Tabular Work, Column Matter, Algebraic, Dictionary, and other work which has always commanded an extra price, to be charged at the same proportionate rate of advance.)

FOREIGN LANGUAGES:

Composition in all the occidental languages (except in German), Reprint, 95 cents per 1000 ems.

Composition in all the occidental languages (except in German), Manuscript, $1.00 per 1000 ems.

MUSIC.—Music composition varies so much in respect to size of type, close or open, character of the music itself, etc., that it is not deemed practicable to make a standard price.

COMPOSITION AND STEREOTYPING.

Pica, Manuscript,	$1 50 per thousand ems.
" Reprint,	1 45 "
Small Pica, Manuscript,	1 45 "
" Reprint,	1 40 "
Long Primer, Manuscript,	1 40 "
" Reprint,	1 35 "
Bourgeois and Brevier, Manuscript,	1 35 "
" " Reprint,	1 30 "
Minion to Nonpareil, Manuscript,	1 30 "
" " Reprint,	1 25 "

STEREOTYPING ONLY.

Pica,	65 cents per 1000 ems.
Small Pica,	60 " "
Long Primer,	55 " "
Bourgeois and Brevier,	50 " "
Minion and smaller,	45 " "

ALTERATIONS.—In Composition. . .   50 cents per hour.
        Stereotype Plates,   60   "
Materials destroyed to be charged.

PRESSWORK.

For ordinary Book Work, from Plates, 250 copies, 90 cents per token.

For ordinary Book Work, from Plates, 500 and 750 copies, 70 cents per token.

For ordinary Book Work, from Plates, 1000 to 1750 copies, inclusive, 65 cents per token.

For ordinary Book Work, from Plates, 2000 to 4750 copies, inclusive, 55 cents per token.

For ordinary Book Work, from Plates, 5000 or more copies, 50 cents per token.

For Book Presswork on Letter-press forms, add 5 to 10 cents per token, depending on quantity.

For forms (such as Pamphlets, etc.) of one or two tokens only, charge extra, depending on character of work and time employed.

For work on paper larger than 26 by 41, printed on either type or plates, charge from 5 to 10 cents extra per token, according to quantity.

For forms containing more than 36 pages (such as 48mo or 64mo Bibles and Prayer Books), from 50 to 80 cents per token to be charged, depending on number of copies; 10 cents extra on numbers less than 2000 copies.

PAPER ACCOUNT.

21 Quires to be allowed for each 1000 copies on a form, counting 19 Quires to the Ream.

Primer.—A small prayer-book used in the service of the Roman Church; also the preliminary book in which children are taught to read, probably called so from the fact that prayers from the devotional primer were reproduced in it, as the Lord's Prayer was usually appended to the alphabet in the horn-books.

Princeps.—An abbreviation of the words editio princeps, or first edition, used by bibliographers for the first edition of any book, especially of those early works particularly esteemed by book-collectors.

Printers, Distinguished.—The enrollment of famous printers is still unmade, and gigantic will be the volume that contains it. Far beyond the limits of the present work would extend a brief mention of those that have become known in the court, the council, and the camp, or that sadder array of names consisting of the martyrs in the cause of a free press. From the earliest age of typography, anonymous pamphlets and broad-sheets fought against power in high places. In Germany, France, Holland, and England, freedom in Church and State was taught by these fugitive sheets, and we know not how often the printer escaped, or how often he suffered as the readiest victim of the embittered authorities. Fiery death at the stake, and slower martyrdoms of poverty and contumely, are now hidden from honor as they were once sheltered from shame beneath many of those quaint imprints signed during the ages of persecution by Faith or Truth, and many another name feigned in the exigencies of the moment to screen the endangered printer. A few of the best-known victims alone can be mentioned. Among these stands Estienne Dolet, a man of remarkable learning, and author of twenty-four works, several of which were upon religious subjects. He printed at Lyons, and afterwards at Paris, where Francis I. accepted the dedication of one of his works, and in the latter city was accused of heresy, hung, and then burned, in 1546.

After Henry Stephens fled from Paris to save his life, the family of Morel became King's printers, and William Morel is accused by Stephens of having abjured the Reformed religion to gain the office, while it is known that a brother of Morel was burned in Paris, for heresy, in 1559. On the other hand, William Carter, a printer of London, who issued several anonymous tracts in favor of Mary of Scotland and the cause of prelacy, was hung, drawn, and quartered for printing a seditious work, in 1584. In 1526, Jacob Liesveldt, a printer of Antwerp, published a Belgic Bible, the translators of which were never known; but the unfortunate printer was beheaded on the charge that it was asserted in one of the annotations that the salvation of man proceeds from Christ alone. In 1693, William Anderton, of London, was accused of enmity to King William, and of publishing a treasonable libel entitled A French Conquest neither Desirable nor Practicable. Anderton's character for probity and integrity influenced the jury in his favor, and his conviction was obtained only by great exertions from the bench. He was tried on the 3d of June, and was executed for treason on the 15th of the same month; but in the September session of the same court a prisoner at the bar declared upon oath that he had himself printed the pamphlet for which Anderton had been executed. As late as 1720, a lad eighteen years of age, the apprentice of his mother, who had a printing-office in London, was executed at Tyburn for printing a Jacobite pamphlet. In France, the printers have been marked for sorrow as the representatives of the several parties in politics during the governmental revulsions, and the royal printers have frequently enjoyed privileges in one reign dearly bought by captivity or death in the next. It is a remarkable fact that nearly all the presidents of the revolutionary French National Convention of the eighteenth century were connected with the profession of journalism; and of the sixty-three who reached that honor, eighteen were guillotined, three died by suicide, eight were transported, six were imprisoned for life, four died madmen in Bicêtre, twenty-two were outlawed, and only two escaped without imposed penalties. By one mandate, in 1797, the French Directory imprisoned at La Force, the editors and printers of twenty-nine specified newspapers, and the retaliation from both of the internecine parties of that period in Paris fell heavily upon the profession.

The gayer crown of poesy has also been often granted to the printer, and the profession linked so closely to the masses, and so intimately cognizant of their feelings, has naturally produced many song-writers, among whom Béranger is the acknowledged poet of the people of France; Richard Gall's sweet lyrics have ranked him next to Burns in the love

24

of the Scotchmen; and while Woodworth's Old Oaken Bucket will long be remembered, Morris may justly claim a proud position as the song-writer of America. Among the students of natural science who have sprung from the typographical ranks, Franklin must hold the first historic rank, followed by the celebrated Hugh Miller, the distinguished American naturalist Dr. John D. Godman, John Lander, the African explorer, who with his brother discovered the source of the river Niger, and Professor Nuttall. Sir William Blackstone also practiced printing, as did Alexander Campbell, the celebrated theological author.

In England, but a few years ago, it was asserted that at least twenty of the actors of distinguished fame had been recruited from the ranks of the printers. Among these were Blanchard, the comedian, Keeley, who had served an apprenticeship to Luke Hansard, Davidge, the famous actor and manager, and Wilson, the Scotch singer, who had been corrector of the press to Ballantyne. In France, besides Béranger, typography claims Michelet, the historian, and Brune, one of the most celebrated of French marshals.

In the United States, the printers have furnished so many incumbents of offices of all grades, except the very highest, that pages might be filled with a list of printer Senators, Congressmen, Governors, Judges, Mayors, Legislators, Soldiers, and of active and influential printer editors, who have moulded public opinion, guided parties and administrations, and wielded the power which was nominally intrusted to their puppets.

Women have occasionally engaged in printing, since the earliest times. In 1481, female compositors were employed in Italy, and highly commended for their skill. There are numerous cases in all countries where women have conducted printing-offices, frequently working successfully at all departments of the employment. Charlotte Guillard (see GUILLARD), of Paris, was remarkable for the excellence of the Greek books printed under her own direct supervision, and for having followed the avocation for half a century, from 1506 to 1556. As a single instance of the active interest exhibited by women, the following inscription, copied from a silver service, may be quoted:

Presented
By the Reformers of East Cumberland
to
MARGARET JOLLIE,
One of the Proprietors of the Carlisle Journal;
The unflinching supporter of
The cause of the People,
June 7, 1834.

Among female printers, Mrs. Grierson was noted for her brilliant learning and accomplishments. She became an able compositor, and married the King's Printer for Ireland. Her son is mentioned by Dr. Johnson as a man of great learning and wit. A poem by Mrs. Grierson was chosen by the Dublin typographers to be printed in a car in the street as a part of the procession on the Lord Mayor's day, and it is one of the finest poetic tributes to the art that was ever written.

Printing is sometimes compared to the States which are said to be good places to emigrate from, and the success in new avocations of thousands who have abandoned typography indicates that it furnishes a good preparatory school. But many of those whose whole lives have been devoted to the art, as printers, editors, authors, publishers, etc., have rendered so much real service to mankind, and earned so much true fame, that in a better and higher sense they are, after all, the most distinguished of distinguished printers.

Printing.—This term, in an extended sense, formerly included every mechanical process necessary to convert blank sheets of paper into a bound book, thus embracing all the operations of type-founding and bookbinding, which were practiced by the early printers as an essential part of their business. At the present day more restricted definitions are given, which imply only the preparation of plates or forms, and the multiplication of copies of an original, by a press, or by other methods, as in photography. Different writers vary considerably in their interpretation of the exact scope of the word, as will be seen by the following extracts:

Printing is the art of taking one or more impressions from the same surface, whereby characters and signs, cast, engraven, drawn, or otherwise represented thereon, are caused to present their reverse images upon paper, vellum, parchment, linen, and other substances, in pigments of various hues, or by means of chemical combinations, of which the components are contained on or within the surface from which the impression is taken, or in the fabric of the thing impressed, or in both.—*T. C. Hansard.*

Printing, in the widest sense of the word, may be defined to be the art of producing copies of any writing, or other works, by pressure, either upon a substance so soft as (like wax or clay) to make the shape, whether in relief or by indentation, of the stamp applied to it, and yet not so perfectly fluid (like water) as to refuse to retain the form so given to it; or upon a substance sufficiently bibulous or otherwise attractive, as to receive color from some pigment with which the stamp is daubed. The essence of printing is the production of a copy by pressure. Correctly speaking, however, it is not an exact copy or fac-simile which printing produces in any case; so far from that, whenever the surface is raised in the stamp, it is sunk in the impression, and vice versa, and even a merely colored work is always reversed in form; but, what is alone of importance, all the impressions are exact copies of one another, and also bear a certain and perfectly assignable relation to the stamp or type.—*Charles Knight's English Cyclopædia of Arts and Sciences.*

Printing is the art of producing impressions from the surface of engravings in relief, whether those engravings are letters, diagrams, or pictorial engravings. This explanation applies to letter-press printing, in contradistinction to copper-plate printing.—*Savage's Dictionary of Printing.*

The act, art, or practice of impressing letters, characters, or figures on paper, cloth, or other material; the business of a printer; typography.— *Webster's Dictionary.*

Printing is the art of mechanically multiplying permanent fac-similes (inverted or direct) of an original. The fac-similes are usually termed impressions. The originals, according to the character of which the art is divided into various branches, are principally metal types, stereotype, wood-carvings in relief, metal and other plates perforated or engraved, paper writings, dies, and stone. The materials on which the impressions are taken are various. For literary purposes, that usually employed is paper.— *British Patent Office Abridgment of Inventions relating to Printing.*

The term printing, in its general scope of signification, has been brought into use as the primary name of an art which enables each present generation to accumulate and refine, while conveniently preserving (on vellum, card-stock, paper, etc.), such descriptive expressions of human language and pictorial effect as might be considered requisite for present utility, or worthy of future reference.— *W. M. Dolby.*

The History of Printing is discussed under that head (see HISTORY OF PRINTING); and of many tributes to its utility, one of the clearest and most forcible is contained in Babbage's Bridgewater Treatise, viz.:

Until printing was very generally spread, civilization scarcely advanced by slow and languid steps; since that art has become cheap, its advances have been unparalleled, and its rate of progress vastly accelerated. It has been stated by some, that the civilization of the Western World has resulted from its being the seat of the Christian religion. However much the mild tenor of its doctrines is calculated to assist in producing such an effect, that religion can but be injured by an unfounded statement. It is the easy and cheap methods of communicating thought from man to man, which enable a country to sift, as it were, its whole people, and to produce, in its science, its literature, and its arts, not the brightest efforts of a limited class, but the highest exertions of the most powerful minds among a whole community,— it is this which has given birth to the wide-spreading civilization of the present day, and which promises a futurity yet more prolific. Whoever is acquainted with the present state of science and the mechanical arts, and looks back over the inventions and civilization which the fourteen centuries subsequent to the introduction of Christianity have produced, and compares them with the advances made during the succeeding four centuries following the invention of printing, will have no doubt as to the effective cause. It is during these last three or four centuries that man, considered as a species, has commenced the development of his intellectual faculties; that he has emerged from a position in which he was almost the

creature of instinct, to a state in which every step in advance facilitates the progress of his successors. In the first period, arts were discovered by individuals, and lost to the race; in the latter, the diffusion of ideas enabled the reasoning of one class to unite with the observations of another, and the most advanced point of one generation became the starting-post of the next.

Printing Ink.—See INK. Colored inks are also referred to under the heading COLOR PRINTING, but additional particulars will be found below:—Colored inks, as a distinct manufacture, were first introduced into the United States about 1830, by Mr. William F. Prout, who confined himself to a few of the primary colors. They found little favor in the eyes of the printers, however, owing to the difficulty experienced in working them. Some ten years later, another manufacturer introduced a greater variety of colors, and somewhat improved their working qualities. Yet the printers found greater difficulty in using them than in using black ink, and consequently preferred to move on in the old way, rather than encounter the troubles of this new branch of the business.

In the year 1850 new efforts were made, by another manufacturer to promote the more general use of colors. It was necessary to make an ink of sufficient body to work readily, and yet not so strong as to pull the paper; to have it dry in a reasonable time after printing, without drying on the rollers; and numberless other details were equally perplexing. One great trouble with colored inks had been, that they became solid when exposed to the air. To prevent this, printers had been obliged to keep water upon the ink, a very unsatisfactory mode of procedure. This obstacle has been so far removed, that inks will now remain soft and pliable for years. At last, after great efforts, this branch of the business was perfected by making colored inks upon scientific principles, and thereby obviating the difficulties which had made them so distasteful to printers. Finding that they could be worked with the same ease as blacks, the printers no longer discountenanced them, and with their customers their brilliant hues rapidly found favor. After the manufacture of the colors already introduced had been perfected, carmine ink was introduced. This color was greatly admired, and notwithstanding its expensiveness, was sought after in large quantities, and yet reigns as the monarch of colors. This was followed by the introduction of lakes, finer qualities of red, tints of all shades, and aniline purple.

When the latter was first introduced, its rare, brilliant hue carried the craft by storm, and the demand for purple was astounding. It was found, however, to be a fickle beauty, sometimes flourishing but for a night, and then fading. Many a printer was astonished, after admiring the beauty of his job, to find in the place of his purple a faint slate tint; and purple, although still used extensively for transient work, has fallen into disfavor for expensive jobs.

Since the introduction of colored inks their sale

has increased immensely. Their use has become, to a certain extent, a fine art; the most beautiful combinations of colors being produced. They are used very largely for circus and theatrical posters, men and animals being faithfully delineated by a revolution of the press, as well as for many kinds of small jobbing.

By the aid of newly perfected machinery, several colors are printed at one impression, a feat which twenty years ago would have been deemed impossible. Our railways present their claims to the public by means of attractively printed show-cards, in colored inks. In short, wherever the printing-press revolves, colored inks are in requisition, and the funeral aspect of printing forty years ago has been replaced by the brilliant hues of the rainbow.

Printing without Ink.—This can be accomplished, so that a black or colored tint is given to the impression, by means of a Ribbon Hand-Stamp, and also by a simple method described in The Proof-Sheet, as follows:—A friend has shown us an impression of two octavo pages pulled on a Ramage press, without ink, by means of paper saturated with ivory-black and lamp-oil, the same as is used in the ordinary manifold paper. He lays the prepared paper over the form, and the paper to be printed over that, makes an impression, and thus produces a fair readable copy. From the sample before us, we are disposed to believe that this process may be made available for proving, especially in daily-paper offices, where time is valuable. Much will be gained if proofs can be taken on dry paper, without the trouble of inking and washing the types. We have made a few impressions on the ordinary roller proof-press with results that warrant us in recommending the method as worthy of consideration and trial.

Private Presses.—What may be styled amateur printing has had many votaries, especially among the wealthy scholars and the aristocracy of the Old World, who found in it an attractive occupation. For several years previous to the year 1600, Tycho Brahe maintained a private press in his castle of Oranienberg, for printing his own works. In Spain, the Bishop of Orihuela established a press in his palace, in 1602, and printed several works. Louis XIII. is described as taking great interest in his private printing-office, and Cardinal Richelieu published several fine works from his château near Tours. Louis XIV. maintained no press of his own, but he was interested in the art, and in the dedication of the Mémoires of Philippe de Comines, printed by Godefroy at the Royal Printing-Office in 1649, it is stated that the first sheet of the work was pulled by Louis XIV. for divertissement.

A work was printed at the Tuileries, with the following title:—Courses of the Principal Rivers of Europe, composed and printed by Louis XV., King of France and Navarre, Paris, in the Printing-Office of the Cabinet of his Majesty, directed by Jacques Colombat, printer-in-ordinary to the king, 1718. A press was established in the palace of Versailles by Madame la Dauphine, at which she personally assisted in printing a book of the communion service, in 1758. The Duc de Bourgogne also prepared with his own hands a book of prayer, for the use of the royal family, in 1760.

About this time Madame Pompadour established a press in her private apartments, from which she issued a tragedy of Corneille's, with a plate engraved by herself. Louis XVI., when Dauphin, in 1764, issued an edition of twenty-five copies of an octavo, written and printed by himself, entitled:—Moral and Political Maxims, extracted from Telemachus. Perron and Superintendent Fouquet also had private presses, at which they exercised themselves in typography. In England this fancy for amateur printing seems to have appeared at a later period, one of the first remarkable devotees being Sir Horace Walpole, who, impelled by his thirst for notoriety, established a press in his Gothic castle of Strawberry Hill, in 1757, and issued a considerable number of works in editions of 300, 600, and even 1000 copies. During the prevalence of bibliomania in England, several private presses were established. One of the first of these was that of Auchinleck, in Ayrshire, Scotland, by Alexander Boswell, who reprinted some rare works in black letter. Mr. Allen maintained a press which was named, from his own residence, the Grange, and from which he published interesting documents appertaining to the county of Durham. Mr. Johnes established a private press known as Hafod, for the printing of rare works translated and prepared by himself.

The book-fancy was at its height when Queen Charlotte erected a press at Frogmore Lodge, in 1812, from which two volumes of translations from the German, by Ellis Cornelia Knight, were issued, the edition being limited to thirty copies; upon a leaf following the title was this inscription: The gift of the Queen to her beloved daughters—Charlotte Augusta, Matilda, Augusta Sophia, Elizabeth, Mary, and Sophia: and, with her Majesty's permission, dedicated to their Royal Highnesses by the translator. This authoress, Miss Knight, also enjoyed the privilege of having a volume of her writings printed by Bodoni, the printer-hero of the day.

In 1813 a private press was erected at Lee Priory, the residence of Sir Egerton Brydges, the baronet supplying the copy and the advantage of his literary fame, while a couple of printers bore the pecuniary risk. This arrangement led to a chancery suit, in which Johnson, the printer, known as the author of the Typographia, suffered considerable loss (see JOHNSON). Among the books privately printed in recent years, the most remarkable are the numerous and handsome volumes of James Orchard Halliwell. Artists have frequently printed the impressions from their own engraved plates, and Rembrandt displayed a singular skill in printing his etchings, producing remarkable effects by increasing or diminishing the amount of ink in such a manner as to make some impressions of the same picture dark and gloomy, while others were in various degrees of color.

Proem.—A preface or introduction.

Profile.—An outline representation; also the contour of a human face, or of any other object, viewed from one of the sides.

Programme.—The outline or sketch of any entertainment, performance, or public ceremony; also the printed or written paper containing such outline description, with the names of the orators, actors, singers, etc., and the parts they intend to assume, or the topics upon which they will treat.

Prolegomena.—A formal essay introductory to a literary work.

Prologue.—A recitation, usually in verse, repeated before a dramatic performance, and intended as an introduction to it.

Proof.—A single impression of type matter, taken for the purpose of examination and correction by the proof-reader or author. The first impression taken for this purpose is called the first proof; the second, which is compared with the first to see that all the errors marked in it are corrected, is called the revise. In careful work other proofs are frequently taken, such as an author's proof, a re-revise, and a press-proof, obtained from the form after it is made up and placed upon the press on which it is to be printed. A foul proof is one containing many errors, and a clean proof one that is remarkably correct.

Proof-Brush.—A brush made of stiff bristles, about an inch long and closely woven together, which is sometimes used for the purpose of taking proofs.

Proof-Impression.—An early impression of an engraving, considered the best, as being first taken.

Proof Paper.—Paper used to pull proofs, it being usually of an inferior quality.

Proof Planer.—An ordinary planer, covered on the bottom with fine felt or cloth, and sometimes having an inner covering of parchment or muslin, used for beating proofs of forms or pages.

Proof Press.—A press for obtaining proofs from matter locked up in galleys. In the ordinary galley press in general use, the impression is given by passing a heavy iron roll, covered with felt, over the matter upon the galley, as it lies between the two tracks supporting the roll. (See READY PROOF PRESS.)

Proof-Reader.—A person whose duty it is to read proofs in a printing-office, for the purpose of correcting the errors that are unavoidable from the nature of the process of arranging type in words, lines, and pages.

Proof-Reading.—The detection and designation of typographical errors, and of defects in workmanship arising from battered type, careless punctuation or orthography, bad authorship, etc. The marks or signs used to designate the various classes of errors are indicated in the full-page illustration of a proof to be corrected, and the proper appearance of the page after these corrections is also shown. It will be perceived that a wrong letter in a word is noticed by drawing a short stroke through it, and making another short stroke in the margin, behind which the right letter is placed. A wrong word is corrected by drawing a line across it, and marking the right one in the margin, opposite the faulty line.

Where a word or words have been left out, or are to be added to the line, a caret must be made in the place where they are intended to come in, and the word or words written in the margin.

Where a space is wanting between two words or letters that are intended to be separated, a caret must be inserted where the separation ought to be, and two parallel lines with a horizontal line running through it, one at top and one at bottom, opposite the line in question in the margin. Where words or letters should join, but are separated, a stroke is drawn under, and a mark like two parentheses is made on the margin, signifying their junction.

When letters or words are set double, or are required to be taken out, a line is drawn through the superfluous word or letter, and a mark like an italic letter *d*, with a prolonged stroke of the pen, placed opposite in the margin.

A turned letter is noticed by making a stroke under it, and a turn-over (circular) dash mark in the margin.

Where a space sticks up between two words, it is noticed by a cross in the margin.

Where two words are transposed, the pen should be drawn half around the lower part of the first and up between them, and half around the upper part of the second, and the letters *tr* placed in the margin adjoining; but where several words require to be transposed, their right order is signified by a figure over each word, and the mark *tr* in the margin.

Where a new paragraph is required, a mark in the shape of a crotchet should be made, and the sign ¶ placed in the margin; also, where a paragraph should not have been made, a line should be drawn from the broken-off matter to the next paragraph, and in the margin should be written—No break.

Where several lines or words are to be added, they should be written at the bottom of the page, making a line from the place where the insertion begins, down to those lines or words to be inserted; but where so much is added as cannot be contained at the bottom of the page, write in the margin—Out, see copy.

If letters or words are to be altered from one character to another, a parallel line or lines should be made underneath the word or letter, viz.: for capitals, three lines; small capitals, two lines; and Italic, one line; and in the margin, opposite the line where the alteration occurs, should be written—Caps., s. c., or Ital., as the case may be.

When words have been struck out that have afterward been approved of, dots should be marked under such words, and in the margin should be written—Stet.

Where the punctuation requires to be altered, the period should be encircled when marked in the margin; the apostrophe should be marked above an inverted bracket, to distinguish it from the comma; the others should be plainly marked, and be backed by a stroke of the pen.

Where letters or lines stand crooked, they are noticed by drawing lines before and after them.

When a letter of a different font is improperly introduced, it is marked, and wf (standing for wrong font) placed in the margin.

The detection and indication of errors are variously known as the Correction of the Press, Reading, and Proof-Reading, those who adopt this pursuit being called Correctors of the Press, Readers, or Proof-Readers; but Proof-Reading and Proof-Readers, are the terms in general use in American printing-offices. Of all tasks connected with printing, proof-reading is one of the most important and difficult. Any tolerably well educated man, who has had some little experience as an author and frequenter of printing-offices, is apt to imagine that by a little practice he could easily become a very good proof-reader; but first-rate proof-readers are as rare as first-class poets or first-class orators. This fact will clearly appear when their peculiar duties and qualifications are duly considered.

A true proof-reader must be a printer. Only by long experience in the composing-room, by close attention to every step in the production of printed matter, is it possible to acquire the requisite technical knowledge and habitual observation of minute details.

He must not only be a printer, but one naturally endowed with a large share of critical acumen, love of order, quick perception, and sound memory, and with other intellectual gifts, in at least average development. As to acquired knowledge, there is no species of learning, no item of correct information, the possession of which may not at some time serve him a good turn. If he rival Addison in mastership of style, Mezzofanti in language, Gibbon in history, Newton in mathematics, and have all the science and philosophy of all the schools at his fingers' ends, so much the better; none of these will come amiss in a life-long devotion to correction of the press. If we would find such a walking cyclopædia, we need not seek for him at the reader's desk, however desirable his presence there may be; the honor and emolument it offers are too slight, too little above those of mere mechanical labor, to attract or hold him. But certain parts of such an education are indispensable to the honorable discharge of a corrector's duties. The structure and use of his vernacular tongue should be familiar to him in all their details, so that he may not only be able to detect a fault of orthography, grammar, syntax, or style, but to explain clearly why it is a fault. Even where a strict adhesion to copy, right or wrong, is the height of ambition, thus much and still more of attainment is requisite; for in order to follow copy, one must in many cases be able to understand copy, however abstruse. How often does it happen that, in obscure manuscript, the mis-reading of a single word, letter, or point will introduce utter confusion! and how often in printed copy errors of the press occur, to be detected only by clear comprehension of the language or the subject, which, if not corrected, will surely bring blame upon the reader of

the reprint! For the same reasons, some knowledge (the more the better) of foreign languages is necessary, especially of Latin and French, as they are of the most frequent occurrence. The use of the French accents should be clearly understood, for their misplacement, interchange, or omission often involves serious error. He should at least be familiar with the Greek and Hebrew alphabets, and possess a general acquaintance with scientific and technical terms, and with the leading facts and names of history, literature, geography, etc. And it is above all important that a reader should know where and how to find necessary information, which he may lack, in any emergency, and should be sufficiently self-distrustful to recognize his deficiency therein. In short, a thorough proof-reader requires knowledge much more varied than, if not in all points so thorough as, that of an average college graduate, in addition to a practical knowledge of the typographic art, and the special natural endowments before specified.

In addition to all other qualifications, a first-rate proof-reader can very materially assist the most careful authors. This task should be performed with great delicacy, by directing attention to questionable passages, rather than by reckless alterations of the phraseology of copy. That this valuable service is often rendered, is amply shown by the remarks of Charles Dickens at a meeting of the Proof-Readers, or Correctors of the Press, in London, in 1867, viz.: I know, from some slight practical experience, what the duties of the correctors of the press are, and how those duties are usually performed; and I can testify, and do testify here, that they are not mechanical, that they are not mere matters of manipulation and routine, but that they require from those who perform them much natural intelligence, much superadded cultivation, considerable readiness of reference, quickness of resource, an excellent memory, and a clear understanding. And I most gratefully acknowledge that I have never gone through the sheets of any book that I have written, without having had presented to me, by the corrector of the press, something that I have overlooked, some slight inconsistency into which I have fallen, some little lapse I have made; in short, without having set down, in black and white, some unquestionable indication that I have been closely followed through my work by a patient and trained mind, and not merely by a skillful eye. In this declaration I have not the slightest doubt that the great body of my brother and sister writers would, as a plain act of justice, heartily concur.

At the same meeting, another speaker, Mr. Harper, gave the following graphic description of a proof-reader's qualifications and duties: It might be asked, what would be our civilization without literature? and he might also ask, what would be our literature without printers' readers? There were compositors so bad, that if their work went out as it came from their hands, it would really astonish the natives. What must not a reader know? He must know all history, all biography, all isms, all ologies—he must

Raise line. Change to capitals.

Indent. Change to small capitals.

Wrong letter. Begin quotation.

Insert letter.

Omit word. End quotation.

Make compound word.

Transpose "he" and "soon."

Transpose lines. }

Do not alter. Change to comma.

Insert letters.

Word omitted.

Make space. Change to small letters.

Space evenly.

Make letters line.

Turn letters.

Bring out lines even. }

Change to full point.

No paragraph.

Insert apostrophe.

Is this correct ? Turned letter.

Close up words.

Push down space.

Wrong face or wrong fount type.

Change to Roman type.

End and commence sentence.

Wrong word. Make paragraph.

Transpose i and a.

Matter inclosed to go in succeeding lines. Straighten lines. }

Change to small y.

Change to comma and reduce space.

Words omitted. Refer to copy.

Change to capital E. Reduce space.

Imperfect type. Increase space.

Change to Italic type. }

Proof to be Corrected.

The old gentleman said he would go with me to the new printer; and when we found him, Neighbor," says Bradford, " I have bought to see you a young man of your business; perhaps you may want such such a one. He ask'd me a few questions, put a composing stick in my hand to see how I work'd, and he then said would soon employ me, old Bradford, whom he had never seen before, to be one of though he had just then nothing for me to do; and, taking the terms people that had a good will for him, entered into a conversion on his present undertaking and prospects; while Bradford, not discovering he was the other printer's father, on Keimer's saying he expected soon to get the greatest part of the business into his own hands, drew him on by artful questions, and starting little doubts, to explain all his views, what interest he reli'd on, and in what manner he intended to proceed. I, who stood by and heard all, saw immediately that one of them was a crafty old sophister, and the other a mere novice, Bradford left me with Keimer, who was greatly surpris'd when I told him who the old man was.

Keimers printing-house, I found, consisted of an old shattered press, and one small, worn-out font of English, which he was then using himself, composing an Elegy on Aquila Rose, before mentioned, an ingenious young man, of excellent character, much respected in the town, clerk of the Assembly, and a pretty poet. Keimer made verses, too, but very indifferently; he could not be said to write them, for his manner was to compose them in the types right out of his head. So there being no copy, but one pair of cases, and the Elegy likely to require all the letter, no one could help him. I endeavored to put his press (which he had not us'd, and of which he understood nothing) into order fit to be work'd with; and, promising to come and print off his Elegy as soon as he should have got it ready, I return'd to Bradford's, who gave me a little job to do for the, I lodged and dieted. A few days after, Keimer sent for me to print off the Elegy. And now he had got another pair of cases, and a pamphlet to print, on which he set me to work.—Extract from The Autobiography of Franklin.

...

...

...the company, that I

...

Bradford and I were...

...Keimer's going to...

of the business between his... the

question, and desiring little of...

whatever interest he could on...

pressed. I was struck by a... that...

that one of them was a... or

a mere novice. Bradford left me

greatly surprised when I told him...

Keimer a printing-house, I found... an old

tered press, and one small worn-out... of...

he was then using himself, composing an Elegy on... Aqua-

Rose, before mentioned, an ingenious young man of excellent

character, much respected in the town, clerk of the...

and a pretty poet. Keimer made verses too but very... in-

differently. He could not be said to write them, for his manner

was to compose them in the types directly out of his head.

So there being no copy, but one pair of cases, and the Elegy

likely to require all the letter, no one could help him. I

endeavored to put his press (which he had not used, and of

which he understood nothing) into order fit to be worked; and

ask, promising to come and print off his Elegy as soon as he

should have got it ready, took my leave, and returned to Brad-

ford's, who gave me a little job to do for the present, and there I

dieted. A few days after, Keimer sent for me to print off

the Elegy. And now he had got another pair of cases, and

a pamphlet to reprint, on which he set me to work. — *Extract

from the Autobiography of Franklin.*

[. . . . .]

at . . . . . v and g. . with me to the new

. . . . Samuel . . . . . Bra-

d. . . . .

. . . . . . t such ~~one~~ . one. He said

. . . put a . . . . it my head to see

. . . . said, would (soon) employ me,

. . . . he . . . ver seen before, to be one of

. . . . ng for me to do; and, taking

. . . . had a good will for him, entered into

. . . . . . a conversation and prawhen; while

. . . . . . svering, he was the other printer, father,

. . . . . . he expected, who tried (?)his greatest part

. . . . . . his own hands, drew him on by artful

. . . . . . uttering little praises to explain all his views,

. . . . he relied on, and in what manner he intended to

. . . . . was asked by and heard all, saw immediately

. . . . th one was a crafty old sophister, and the other a

. . . . Bradford left . . . with Keimer, who was greatly

. . . . I told him who I'm old now . . . .

. . . . printing house, I found, consisted of an old shat-

. . . . and one small, worn-out fount of English, which

. . . . . ing himself, composing an Elegy on Aquila

. . . . now joined. as Rose . . . a young lad, of excellent

. . . . much respected in the town, clerk of the Assembly

. . . . . . retty poet. Keimer made verses, too, but . . . in-

different, ... could not be said to write them, for his manner

. . . . to compose them in the types right out of the head . . . .

. . . . . . no copy but one pair of cases, and the Elegy

. . . . comprise all the letter, no one could help him. I en-

. . . . . to put his press (which he had not used, and of which

. . . . . knew nothing) into order fit to be work'd with; and,

. . . . come and print off his Elegy as soon as he

. . . . . . it ready. I return'd to Bradford's, who gave

. . . . . little job to do for the . . . I lodged and dieted. A few

. . . . after Keimer sent for me to print off the Elegy. And

. . . . he had got another pair of cases, and a pamphlet to

print on which he set me to work.—Extract from The

. . . . by of Franklin.

THE old gentleman said he would go with me to the new printer; and when we found him, "Neighbor," says Bradford, "I have brought to see you a young man of your business; perhaps you may want such a one." He ask'd me a few questions, put a composing-stick in my hand to see how I work'd, and then said he would employ me soon, though he had just then nothing for me to do; and, taking old Bradford, whom he had never seen before, to be one of the town's people that had a good will for him, entered into a conversation on his present undertaking and prospects; while Bradford, not discovering that he was the other printer's father, on Keimer's saying he expected soon to get the greatest part of the business into his own hands, drew him on by artful questions, and starting little doubts, to explain all his views, what interest he reli'd on, and in what manner he intended to proceed. I, who stood by and heard all, saw immediately that one of them was a crafty old sophister, and the other a mere novice. Bradford left me with Keimer, who was greatly surpris'd when I told him who the old man was. Keimer's printing-house, I found, consisted of an old shattered press, and one small, worn-out font of English, which he was then using himself, composing an Elegy on Aquila Rose, before mentioned, an ingenious young man, of excellent character, much respected in the town, clerk of the Assembly, and a pretty poet. Keimer made verses, too, but very indifferently. He could not be said to write them, for his manner was to compose them in the types directly out of his head.

So there being no copy, but one pair of cases, and the Elegy likely to require all the letter, no one could help him. I endeavored to put his press (which he had not us'd, and of which he understood nothing) into order fit to be work'd with; and, promising to come and print off his Elegy as soon as he should have got it ready, I return'd to Bradford's, who gave me a little job to do for the present, and there I lodged and dieted. A few days after, Keimer sent for me to print off the Elegy. And now he had got another pair of cases, and a pamphlet to print, on which he set me to work.—*Extract from the Autobiography of Franklin.*

be, in short, a peripatetic cyclopædia. He must also know all languages; and with all his care, he often met with very little civility or consideration from writers whose copy was of a character that ought to make them look with great charity upon an occasional slip. In a word, he maintained that the reader was the safeguard of his employer's reputation, a barrier against ignorant compositors, and a detective to look after the errors of literary gentlemen.

There is a stumbling-block in the road to correctness which ought not to be overlooked. The great problem in printing, as in all other business open to fierce competition, being how to do a maximum of work with a minimum of means, rushing naturally becomes the order of the day whenever work is abundant. The type must be rushed into the stick, on to the galley, into the form; the proof must be rushed through the reader's hands, often with the compositor or foreman standing over him to quicken his pace and distract his attention; it must be corrected and revised on the rush, and the form rushed into the foundry or on to the press. And with all this rushing, unless the proof-reader courageously stems the tide, there is apt to be very little discrimination between work that will bear such cavalier treatment without serious detriment, and work that will inevitably be well-nigh ruined by it.

On daily newspapers, especially, an immense amount of matter must be read and corrected with extraordinary celerity. The prime requisite of having a proof audibly read by copy is performed in a double-quick style, in which language is represented by a series of sounds that have been said to resemble, mum-mum-tuition, mum-mum-cution, mum-mum-mum-olution, mum-mum-eration, mum mum mum, and to consist of a string of syllables and polysyllables like the quavers and semi-quavers bubbling from the bosom and dancing from the strings of Ole Bull's violin.

Proof-Sheet.—An impression from types taken for correction.

Propaganda—Printing House of the.—The Congregatio de Propaganda Fide, or Congregation for the Propagation of the Faith, a society established at Rome by Pope Gregory XV. in 1622, has connected with it a printing-house, furnished with types of all the important languages in the world. This establishment for many years stood preëminent for the publication of the Bible and books of devotion in various languages, and claimed to be the most extensive and best-furnished printing-office in Europe. It was there that Bodoni, the celebrated printer of Parma, received his training.

Proportions of Type.—The relations of type of different sizes to one another. There is a variation in the sizes of the type known by the respective names, as made by the different type-founders of the United States, no common standard being recognized. The extent of the discrepancy is indicated by the following comparative scale of ems in the lineal foot, which was prepared a few years ago at Bruce's New York Foundry:

SIZE.	Bruce's New York Foundry.	A noted London Foundry.	A noted Philadelphia Foundry.	A noted New York Foundry.	A noted Boston Foundry.
Diamond..................	201.56	205.	204.50	....	....
Pearl.....................	179.59	178.	179.	....	....
Agate.....................	160.	....	165.	....	....
Nonpareil...............	142.54	143.	145.	....	....
Minion....................	126.99	122.	119.	128.	124.50
Brevier...................	113.13	112.50	109.	112.	115.66
Bourgeois................	100.79	102.50	103.25	102.50	104.50
Long Primer.............	89.79	89.	90.	90.50	90.
Small Pica..............	80.	83.	83.	86.25	84.50
Pica......................	71.27	71.50	73.	72.	72.
English..................	63.49	64.	....	....	....
Columbian...............	56.56	56.25	....	....	....
Great Primer...........	50.39	51.25	....	....	....
Paragon..................	44.89	44.50	....	....	....
Double Small Pica....	40.	41.50	....	....	....
Double Pica............	35.63	35.75	....	....	....
Double English........	31.74	32.	....	....	....
Double Columbian.....	28.28	....	....	....	....
Double Great Primer.	25.19	25.50	....	....	....
Double Paragon.......	22.44	....	....	....	....
Meridian.................	20.	20.75	....	....	....
Canon....................	17.81	18.33	....	....	....

Making due allowance for these variations, the proportions of type from any American foundry are indicated in the table from The Proof-Sheet, printed on page 377.

Proportions of Type to Space.—A knowledge of this subject often furnishes a useful guide to an employing printer in determining how much type should be purchased for a given purpose. The Proof-Sheet, of November, 1868, says:

The space occupied by a pound of average type may be stated as three and five-tenths square inches.

Suppose that a page of a weekly paper to be estimated measures 16 by 22 inches. We ascertain the square inches in it by multiplying the length by the breadth. Thus, $22 \times 16 = 352$ square inches. Now, as we have said, each 3.5 square inches contain one pound. Accordingly, by dividing the total number of inches by the number in a pound—adding an .0 to compensate for the decimal in the divisor—the weight of the page is ascertained.

In the case we have supposed—

3.5)3520(100 lbs. per page,
35

with 2.0 square inches over.

If but one page is to be set in a certain type, an allowance of 50 per cent. should be made for what will remain in the cases and for matter set up and left over. The greater the number of pages in the same size of type, the less the proportion of the extra weight of type needed. Thus, we should say—

For 1 page weighing 100 lbs.........150 lbs. will be needed.
" 2 pages   "   "   each...250   "   "   "
" 3   "   "   "   " ...350   "   "   "
" 4   "   "   "   " ...450   "   "   "

Therefore, if a newspaper of the size given is to be, say, half Brevier and half Nonpareil, 250 pounds of

each will be needed. If however, it is very prosperous, and columns are sometimes crowded out, of
course extra type must be purchased.

When presenting estimates, we are frequently met
with the objection, You make no allowance for space
occupied by column-rules, leads, dashes, etc. To this
we can only reply, that experience has shown that
estimates based as above give the minimum quantity
of type necessary for a weekly newspaper; standing
matter and letter remaining in case fully equaling
the space occupied by leads, rules, etc., as well as the
extra quantity of type allowed.

No special rule can be laid down for daily papers,
which vary so widely in the number of cases employed,
the average quantity of matter crowded out, or saved
for a weekly, and the style of composition. It may
be said, in a general way, that twice the weight of the
pages is the least quantity of type that will answer for
a daily alone, when worked most closely. What has

collection of hymns or religious poems adapted to
music. Psalms, as a fitting expression of devotional
feeling, have an origin beyond the limits of chronology,
and are discovered in the very earliest ages, in every
nation, those of the Hebrews, Hindoos, and Greeks
having been preserved with the greatest care. Among
Christians, the name psalm is restricted to those
ascribed to David, King of Israel in the eleventh
century before the Christian era. These psalms were
arranged for religious service, probably by Solomon,
and were again collected and arranged by Ezra, some
being added in the fifth century before Christ. The
Christian disciples adopted them from the Jews, and
they were chanted in the churches by direction of the
early Christian bishops. At first the whole congregation joined in the singing; but, as the Roman church
gradually increased the distinction between the clergy
and laity, the chanting of the psalms became almost
exclusively the office of the clergy. Luther was

	PICA.	SM. PICA.	L. PRIMER.	BOURG.	BREVIER.	MINION.	NONP.	AGATE.	PEARL.	SQUARE INCHES.
1000 ems Pica.............. =	1000	1323	1536	2005	2225	2703	4000	5263	6236	27.72
1000 ems Small Pica....... =	781	1000	1175	1556	1673	2085	3035	4000	4760	21.16
1000 ems Long Primer..... =	640	850	1000	1305	1446	1795	2576	3446	4000	18.20
1000 ems Bourgeois .... =	496	640	770	1000	1102	1366	1906	2373	3035	13.86
1000 ems Brevier.......... =	450	597	693	912	1000	1236	1805	2387	2797	12.60
1000 ems Minion .... =	366	485	562	731	810	1000	1432	1932	2265	10.10
1000 ems Nonpareil........ =	250	334	387	504	562	686	1000	1326	1545	6.93
1000 ems Agate .... =	194	250	294	387	422	522	703	1000	1188	5.29
1000 ems Pearl............ =	160	210	250	333	360	440	648	843	1000	4.55
One pound contains.....(ems)	130	170	200	270	290	360	520	690	800	3.5

TABLE SHOWING THE PROPORTION THAT ONE THOUSAND EMS OF EACH SIZE OF TYPE BEAR TO EVERY OTHER SIZE FROM
PICA TO PEARL.

been said, however, will afford a fair basis for calculations.

In book-offices, when the number and size of pages
to be set at one time are known, the quantity of type
needed can be ascertained as above; an allowance of
from twenty-five to fifty per cent. being made, according to the number of cases to be laid. A pair of cases
holds about fifty pounds of type.

Prose.—Language without metre or poetic measure.

Prosody.—That part of grammar which treats of
quantity, accent, versification, and the laws of harmony in metrical composition.

Prospectus.—The outline or plan of a proposed
undertaking, particularly of a newspaper, literary
work, or other publication.

Psalm-Book.—A book containing a metrical
version of the Psalms of David, as accepted by any
special denomination, and usually accompanied by a

anxious to introduce what is now styled congrega-
tional singing, and also psalmody, into private and
domestic devotions. With this intention he composed
the tune still known as Old Hundred, and several
others suited to psalms and hymns, which were so
highly admired by the composer Handel, that he
inserted many passages from them in his celebrated
oratorios.

In France, Clement Marot, a popular poet, and
groom of the Chambers to Francis I., translated
thirty of the psalms into the court language of the
day, and dedicated the volume, not only to Francis
I. but also to the ladies of France, with, as he expressed it, the design of adding to the happiness of
his fair readers, by substituting divine psalms for
amorous ditties, and inspiring their susceptible hearts
with a passion in which there was no torment, and
which would banish the fickle deity Cupid from the
world. No music was published with this holy song-

book, but it was known to be prepared for the harpsichord and voice, and was accepted by the court with delight. New editions were rapidly called for, and all classes of society caught up the words, adapting them generally to the popular ballad-music. Marot, encouraged by his success, increased the number of psalms to fifty, and the book was republished in Rome, by command of Pope Paul III., in 1542, in an octavo form, and Gothic letter. The work now became more popular than ever, especially at the court of France, where the members of the royal family, and the highest nobility, introduced the fashion of selecting psalms for their individual use and adapting them to music according to their fancy. The Dauphin, afterwards Henry II. who was passionately fond of the chase, went out to hunt caroling the words of the psalm As the hart panteth for the water-brooks; and a portrait of his favorite, the celebrated Diana of Poictiers, is still extant, bearing this verse of the psalm as an inscription. The queen adapted a lively popular jig to the words Rebuke me not in thy anger; and Anthony, King of Navarre, used a dancing-tune of Poitou as the measure for his chosen psalm, Stand up, O Lord, to revenge my quarrel. Diana of Poictiers selected From the depth of my heart. The immense success of Marot's Psalm-book induced Theodore Beza to complete the translation at Geneva, and the reformer Calvin engaged the best available musical talent to adapt the words to many of those grand and simple tunes now used in the Protestant churches. The enlarged publication, with the music, became even more popular than the first, and was freely accepted throughout France, until Calvin introduced it into the services at Geneva. The Sorbonne then interfering, the clergy, after great efforts, induced Francis I. to prohibit Marot's book, and Marot himself was compelled to seek safety in Geneva. The endeavor to suppress the book already sanctioned by the Pope, served only to increase the public interest, and the psalms spread from street to street, and from city to city, being particularly welcomed by the artisans of Flanders.

As a curious coincidence, it may be mentioned that an officer holding the same position in the household of the King of England followed the example of Marot, and a volume was published in 1549, dedicated to Edward VI., with the title:—All such Psalmes of David, as Thomas Sternehold, late grome of the Kinges Maiesties robes, didde in his lyfe time drawe into Englyshe Metre. Sternhold completed only thirty-seven of the psalms, and the work was continued by Hopkins and others, who prepared the version published in 1562 widely known as the version of Sternhold and Hopkins. The psalms of Marot, and those published afterwards at Geneva, increased in popularity throughout Germany, France, and Flanders, and were used so effectively in some of the popular insurrections of the time, that they were looked upon as incendiary in their character, and met with strong opposition from many of the highest clergymen of England, as being the

most powerful weapons of the Puritans. During the reign of Queen Elizabeth the introduction of psalms sung by the people, as distinguished from those chanted by the clergy, assisted by the congregation in responses or choruses, became a subject of much discussion, and is mentioned by Shakspeare in Winter's Tale, where the clown, describing the merry-making, adds among the tumultuous guests a Puritan singing psalms to hornpipes. In this state of public opinion, the psalms of Sternhold and Hopkins met with considerable opposition, and it is said that the book was really never fully admitted by legal authority, although it was asserted on the title-page that the version was set forth and allowed to be sung in all the churches.

The new version of the Church of England was prepared in 1598, by Tate and Brady. The Puritans afterwards offered many objections to what they stigmatized as the obsolete version of Sternhold and Hopkins, and a new metrical translation was published in 1641, by Francis Rous, under the approval of the House of Commons. Psalm-singing during public worship was unavoidably abandoned to a considerable degree during the years of religious persecution, and appears to have fallen into disrepute, from the fact that Benjamin Keach, in 1691, published a tract entitled The Breach Repaired in God's Worship; or, Psalms and Hymns proved to be a Holy Ordinance of Jesus Christ. Some of the Dissenting churches of London opposed psalm-singing until as late as 1720. The Presbyterians introduced psalms at an early date, and the old Scotch psalms were generally superseded by those published by John Patrickson, in 1604, and accepted by the Presbyterians and Independents, until they were, in turn, superseded by those of Dr. Watts.

Psalter.—A book in which the Psalms of David, or selections therefrom, are arranged for church service. Such works were found necessary, both for private and public devotion, at an early day, and several magnificent manuscript psalters have been preserved. Among them, that belonging to the emperor Charlemagne is a fine specimen of the handwriting known as the miniscule Roman, and a psalter made for Richard II. of England contains a calendar, tables, hymns, and the Athanasian Creed. The Psalter printed in 1457 is of especial interest to printers, as it is the earliest assured specimen of typography, containing in its colophon the express statement that it was made without the pen, in that year, by Johann Fust and Peter Schoeffer (see COLOPHON). Other editions of this work were issued in 1459, 1490, 1502, and, after Schoeffer's death, by his son, in 1566. It is in small folio, on vellum, accompanied by the Gregorian musical notes, the psalter occupying 135 pages, the recto the 136th, and the remaining 41 pages being appropriated to the litany, prayers, etc. The psalms are in a larger text than the rest of the work; and the principal capitals, cut upon wood, and printed in two colors, usually blue and red, have been much admired for their beauty and accuracy. A handsome psalter was printed by Gering in Paris in 1494, and the first one in England was issued by Wynkyn de Worde in 1499; another edition appearing in 1502.

Publication.—1. The act of publishing or making known; notification to the people at large. 2. That which is published or made known; especially any pamphlet or book offered for sale or to public notice.

Public Printing.—Printing executed at the expense of governmental treasuries; especially such work as is ordered by Congress and the Legislatures of the respective States. Popular institutions, and the prevalence of the franking system, have led to an unusually large development of this class of printing in the United States.

Publishing.—The act of putting forth or issuing to the public an engraving, book, or newspaper. It is distinct from the process of printing, and may be in a large degree distinct from a direct sale to the public. Many booksellers are not publishers; a considerable number of publishers are not printers; and some publishers dispose of their works solely to wholesale dealers, who, in turn, bring them to the notice of their final purchasers. In the infancy of the art, the departments of printing, publishing, and bookselling were united in all instances; and even at the present day, this rule still largely prevails in the printing, publication, and sale of books as well as of newspapers. Notwithstanding the constant tendency to a subdivision of labor, and the success of many who have made either printing, publishing, or bookselling a specialty, the most extensive and enduring triumphs have been reserved for those establishments in which all these operations are conducted under one business management, with no other aid than that given by retail dealers in disposing of their products.

In this country, the printing and publishing done in connection with newspapers far exceed in volume and pecuniary value all book-publishing; but the latter has also attained very large proportions.

Several effective methods of publishing and selling the products of printing are of comparatively modern origin. The sale of newspapers was formerly confined almost exclusively to the copies furnished to annual subscribers, but now immense numbers are disposed of through carriers, newsboys, agents, or news-venders. The latter obtain literary, weekly, and monthly publications mainly from News Companies, who derive their supplies from publishers, and whose transactions have attained great magnitude.

In the publication of books, the regular trade organization distributes its products mainly through numerous booksellers in various sections of the country. This business is so extensive that one of the leading American firms engaged in it (that of J. B. Lippincott & Co.) is said to make larger annual sales of books than any other establishment in the world. To facilitate exchanges between publishers, of their various products, trade sales were established some years ago, and they have since been steadily con-

tinued, at regular intervals. The business of publishing school-books is in itself very extensive, and recently a series of regulations for its better government have been devised and adopted by many firms.

It is usual, in publishing books, to fix retail prices, and then to allow to those in the trade a discount which ordinarily forms a considerable proportion of the sum paid by the final purchaser.

Independent of the sale of books by the regular trade, other methods are frequently adopted, such as the sale of large or expensively illustrated works in numbers, to subscribers obtained by agents or canvassers. The sale of complete books of a less expensive character by subscription, as it is called, is also extensively resorted to,—the plan being to engage canvassers or book-agents in various sections of the country, who have no fixed place of business, but journey from door to door soliciting subscribers or purchasers, and their efforts are frequently attended with great success. Books disposed of in this way are usually sold by subscription only, and a broad line of distinction exists between this method of publication and that pursued by the regular trade. (See STATISTICS OF PRINTING.)

Pull.—1. To take an impression of a form at the press, especially at the hand-press. 2. The character of the impression on the hand-press is also indicated by the words hard pull, meaning a heavy impression, and easy pull, a light impression.

Punch.—The original engraving of the face of type, cut on steel, and subsequently impressed into copper to form a matrix.

PUNCH.

Punch-Cutter.—One who engraves or cuts the punches used in making the matrices for casting type. This art is so difficult, in consequence of the extreme care necessary to maintain an exact relation between the faces of all the type in a font, that even at the present day an exceedingly small number of persons understand it, and it is nearly as much of a mystery as when it was first practiced by Peter Schoeffer.

Punctuation.—The art of dividing a written or printed composition, by points, marks, or stops, into sentences or parts of sentences, in such a manner that the meaning of the author, and the proper relation of the words used, may be readily understood. In this work the various points or punctuation marks, together with their appropriate use, are described under their respective names. (See APOSTROPHE, COMMA, COLON, DASH, etc.) No system of punctuation applicable to all cases has yet been universally adopted. In the infancy of the art of printing, the virgule, a slanting mark, supplied the place of the comma, and colons and periods were used at an early day. By slow degrees point after point was added by various printers, either in imitation of points used in the publication of Greek works, or on account of their inherent utility, but no rules were simultaneously adopted governing their use; and it has remained for comparatively modern authors to make a vigorous effort to establish anything approaching a comprehensive system of punctuation. The main point of divergence among those who pay close attention to this subject hinges on the question whether few or many points should be used. Some authorities are apparently ever on the alert to discover a pretext for introducing a point or mark into a sentence; while others oppose close punctuation. Printed matter may easily be over-punctuated, as well as under-punctuated, and the true course is to avoid burdening the reader with any extraneous point or mark that does not manifestly tend to assist his ready comprehension of the text.

It has been gravely recommended by writers on this subject that the punctuation of printed matter should be left solely to the printer; but in practice a compromise system generally prevails, in which such authors or preparers of copy as are not manifestly ignorant of the whole subject are suffered to exercise their own judgment, except when they perpetrate glaring errors or omissions, and the aid of a judicious compositor or proof-reader becomes essential to the rendition of their meaning; and absolutely correct punctuation, if such a thing can be presumed to exist, must be made wholly or in part by the author, for, when varied shades of meaning can be conveyed by varied punctuation, he alone is competent to decide authoritatively what peculiar idea he wishes to impress upon the minds of his readers.

The system of punctuation in most general use in the United States is that described in Wilson's Treatise. He divides the points used as follows:

1. *The Grammatical Points*, including the Comma (,), the Semicolon (;), the Colon (:), and the Period (.).

2. *The Grammatical and Rhetorical Points*, including the Note of Interrogation (?), the Note of Exclamation (!), the Marks of Parenthesis (( )), and the Dash (—).

3. *Letter, Syllabic, and Quotation Points*, including the Apostrophe ('), the Hyphen (-), and the Marks of Quotation (" ").

4. *Miscellaneous Marks and Characters*, including Brackets ([ ]), a Comma inverted ('), Two Commas (,,), the Index, Hand, or Fist (☞), Three Stars (*∗*), the Caret (⌃), the Brace (⌒), Marks of Ellipsis (——, ..., ∗∗∗), Leaders (. . . . . .), Accents, Marks of Quantity (ˉ, ˘, ˆ), the Cedilla (ç), the Tilde (˜), and Marks of Reference (∗, †, ‡, §, ‖, ¶).

Much less elaborate systems than that of Wilson are described in various grammars and similar works. Those who wish to comprehend the subject thoroughly must study its details in works devoted specially to this subject; but the gist of the prevailing system appertaining to the grammatical and rhetorical points is expressed in the following condensation of the rules laid down by Lindley Murray:

The Comma usually separates those parts of a

sentence which, though very closely connected in sense and construction, require a pause between them.

The Semicolon is used for dividing a compound sentence into two or more parts, not so closely connected as those which are separated by a comma, nor yet so little dependent on each other as those which are distinguished by a colon.

The Colon is used to divide a sentence into two or more parts, less connected than those which are separated by a semicolon, but not so independent as separate distinct sentences.

The Period.—When the sentence is complete and independent, and not connected in construction with the following sentence, it is marked with a period.

The Dash, though often used improperly by hasty and incoherent writers, may be introduced with propriety where the sentence breaks off abruptly, where a significant pause is required, or where there is an unexpected turn in the sentiment

The Interrogation.—A note of interrogation is used at the end of an interrogative sentence, that is, when a question is asked: as, Who will accompany me?

The Exclamation.—The note of exclamation is applied to expressions of sudden emotion, surprise, joy, grief, etc., and also to invocations and addresses: as, My friend! this conduct amazes me!

The Parenthesis.—A parenthesis is a clause containing some necessary information or useful remark introduced into the body of a sentence obliquely, and which might be omitted without injuring the construction: as, Know, then, this truth (enough for man to know): virtue alone is happiness below.

Punjaub or Punjob.—Copy given out on American morning newspapers merely to keep compositors employed at hours when they would, under existing rules, charge for time if no copy were furnished.

Q.

Quads.—An abbreviation of the word quadrats.

Quadrats.—Pieces of type-metal, of the depth of the body of the respective sizes to which they are cast, but lower than types, so as to leave a blank space on the paper, when printed, where they are placed. An en quadrat is half as thick as its depth; an em quadrat is equal in thickness and depth, and, being square on its surface, is the true quadrat (from quadratus, squared); a two-em quadrat is twice the thickness of its depth; a three-em three times, as their names specify. The first line of a paragraph is usually indented an em quadrat, but an em and an en, two ems, or even three ems, are more appropriate for wide measures. An em quadrat is the proper space after a full point when it terminates a sentence in a paragraph. En quadrats are generally used after a semicolon, colon, etc., and sometimes after overhanging letters. (See CIRCULAR QUADRATS and HOLLOW QUADRATS.)

Quarters.—Quarto, octavo, sixteen- and thirty-two-mo forms are said to be imposed in quarters, because they are imposed and locked up in four parts.

Quarto.—A sheet of paper folded in four leaves, or eight pages; a form of four pages being a quarto form.

Query.—A question, usually represented by an interrogation mark (?), asked on the margin of a proof, in regard to the correctness of a letter, word, or sentence.

Quire.—A quire of paper usually consists of twenty-four sheets; but in England a quire of the paper used by newspapers consists of twenty-five sheets, and this custom has been adopted, to a limited extent, in the United States.

Quoining a Form.—The putting of quoins in a form so that when it is locked up they shall, in an efficacious manner, wedge up and secure the type.

Quoins.—Short pieces of tapering wood, (usually hickory, dogwood, or boxwood, the latter being considered best,) of various widths, but of the same height as furniture, which are used to wedge up forms, the quoins being placed between slanting side-sticks and the straight lines of a chase. Several styles of mechanical or metallic quoins have been invented: these are used chiefly, but not exclusively, on the forms of newspapers printed on fast rotary presses. They are intended to obviate the necessity for shooting sticks, bevelled furniture, and wooden quoins, and to save the expense incurred by the destruction of these perishable materials as well as to economise time and labor, and to give additional security.

Quotation Furniture.—Quotations cast of various sizes in length and width, to be used for blanking and as furniture.

Quotation Marks.—(" "). Two inverted commas placed at the beginning of a quoted phrase, and two apostrophes at the conclusion. When a quotation occurs within a quotation, only one inverted comma and one apostrophe are used to distinguish it. (See COMMA.)

Quotations.—Large hollow quadrats, used in book-work for justifying marginal notes in their proper places at the sides of the pages, and for blanks at the heads and ends of chapters, as well as for the blank pages, and in job work, to justify the rules which run down the blank part of the sheet, in such jobs as bills of lading, etc.

R.

Racks.—Receptacles for cases or letter-boards.

Rag.—A term sometimes applied in type-founding to a bur on the edges of type.

Raikes, Robert.—The originator of Sunday-schools in England. He was the son of the publisher and editor of the Gloucester Journal, and, succeeding to his father's business, was very successful, his publications being elegant and accurate. His attention was attracted to the miserable condition of the county jail of Gloucester, where persons committed by the magistrates, out of session, for petty offenses, were associated with the worst felons, and almost entirely dependent upon the charity of chance visitors.

Robert Raikes effectively used his pen, his influence, and his fortune in their behalf, procured them sustaining employments, furnished them with books to read, and established Sunday-schools for their instruction. Observing that the children of the factory-laborers of the town were allowed to roam through the streets, and that they were very ignorant and depraved, he, with the assistance of the clergyman of the parish, established Sunday-schools in 1781, hiring women as teachers. The wonderful improvement soon exhibited by the children aroused the public interest, and the movement soon became popular, and rapidly spread to other cities throughout England.

Railroading.—Marks made at the end of a series of lines by a proof-reader, when he wishes a number of words or parts of words to be transposed to succeeding lines.

Railway Coupon-Ticket Printing and Numbering Machine.—A press specially adapted for the printing and numbering of Railway Tickets, and arranged to print either in sheets or continuous rolls. The machine is a modification of the cylinder press, but built more compactly. The form and numbering wheels are put on a traveling bed, receiving their ink from the same rollers. The impression cylinder is geared into the bed, turning forward and backward with it. Instead of fingers, it is furnished with cords, that run round in the spaces between the coupons. The feed table delivers the paper under the cords, by which it is carried down, and the body of the ticket is printed; then the motion of those cylinders is reversed, the ticket changes its position and is presented to the numbering wheels. In its course down and up, the ticket passes under prickers, and is deposited in a receptacle, printed side upwards. The press will print twenty-seven inches of matter, at the rate of 1500 sheets per hour. (See page 382.)

Railway Printing.—The improvement in modes of travel and transportation, caused by the introduction of railways, like nearly all other modern improvements, has necessitated the exercise of inventive genius, to provide the means for systematizing the large passenger and freight traffic opened up by the vast network of lines now spanning the country. In fact, the introduction of additional speed in printing is almost coeval with the advent of greater speed and conveniences in travel and trade. The production of printed matter for the special use of railway companies forms one of the most important departments of the printing business, employing a vast number of hands, and the most intricate machinery, while improvements are constantly being made to meet the requirements of this important new branch of the art. Much of this work calls into exercise the highest efforts of skill in printing and the auxiliary arts, whether in the shape of advertising cards, maps, time-tables, rates of freight, way-bills, or the innumerable quantity of coupon and local tickets, requiring to be consecutively numbered, and printed in one or more colors at a single impression. Some of the largest establishments in the country make railway printing a specialty to the exclusion of all other kinds of work, the business requiring a large supply of material for the rapid execution of orders.

Railway Rotary Ticket Machine.—A compact little machine, occupying a space of about two feet square, and designed for printing, numbering and cutting railway tickets from continuous rolls of paper or card board. (See page 383.) The tickets are printed at the rate of 10,000 to 12,000 per hour, numbered, cut, and deposited in regular order, at a single operation. The arrangement of the press can be changed with great facility to print the number in a different color from the body of the ticket.

RAMAGE PRESS.

ness, and its facilities for running in and out a form, a greater number of impressions can be obtained in a given time from the Ramage Press than from any other hand-press.

RAILWAY COUPON-TICKET PRINTING AND NUMBERING MACHINE.

Raisonné.—Accompanied by proofs, illustrations, or notices; arranged analytically or systematically: as, a catalogue raisonné.

Ramage Press.—A small hand-press, originally made of wood, by Adam Ramage, the most celebrated of the early press-makers of the United States, who is said to have constructed the first hand-press made with an iron bed and platen. A number of modernized Ramage presses are constructed and used for proof-presses, and various kinds of small work, not requiring speed; although, through its diminutive-

Rastell, John.—Printed, in 1530, the first abridgment of the English Statutes in the English language. The preface contains an interesting statement of the advantages to be derived by the people from the publication of the laws in the vulgar tongue. John Rastell died in 1536, and is known to have printed about thirty works. He was a scholar of considerable attainments, and a friend of Sir Thomas More, whose sister he married. His son William was also successful as a printer and author. The family adhered to the Catholic cause, and, although Elizabeth renewed the patent of William Rastell as Justice of the Queen's Bench in 1559, he retired soon after to Louvain, where he died in 1567.

Rat.—A compositor or pressman who works for less than the rate of wages established by Printers' Unions, or who refuses to be bound by the decisions of such Unions in the cities where they are in suc-

clamps on ratchet blocks, usually made of wood, with an attachment of brass or other metal, containing teeth of a proper size to fit in the small cog wheels of ratchet blocks, by which the plates

RATCHET.

RAILWAY ROTARY TICKET MACHINE.

cessful operation. The term has long been used in England, and is said to have originated in the idea that, as a rat undermines foundations, so a workman who labors for less than standard prices undermines the foundations of trade.

Ratchet.—An instrument used to loosen the

are loosened, or tightened to the block, the upper part making a convenient handle, while the comb or teeth act with a horizontal motion on the cog wheels.

Ratdoldt, Erhard.—A distinguished German typographer, who printed in Venice from 1476 to

1487, and n Augsburg from 1489 to 1516. He was the first to introduce ornamental capitals, called, from their adornments, flowering letters, in display-lines, in 1477. He was also the first to print in letters of gold, as seen in his famous edition of Euclid. In the Simplicius published by him in 1499, and in the Ammonius of 1500, the titles are in letters of gold.

Rat-Office.—A printing-office in which the requirements of Printers' Unions are not obeyed.

Ratting.—Working for less than the established wages.

Reader.—A person employed by publishers to read manuscripts or books, and to decide upon their merit or suitability for publication. In England the term is used for a proof-reader, or corrector for the press. Reader is also used in the United States for an elementary work containing exercises on the practice of reading.

Ready Proof Press.—A press specially designed for taking proofs of small jobs, or of matter on galleys for newspapers.

READY PROOF PRESS.

Ream.—Twenty quires of paper, each of which usually contains twenty-four sheets; but, by special agreement, paper intended for newspapers is sometimes made up in quires of twenty-five sheets each, in which case the ream contains five hundred sheets; and in England a perfect ream, for printing purposes, consists of twenty-one quires and a half, or five hundred and sixteen sheets, wastage being thus provided for.

Recitative.—Musical declamation used in the opera, to express action or passion, to reveal a secret, relate a story, etc.

Recto.—The right-hand page, opposed to verso, the left-hand page.

Red Letter.—Relating to or marked by red letters. In the ancient calendars, holy days were marked by red letters, and therefore a red letter became a phrase for a lucky or auspicious day.

References.—Marks or signs used in matter which has marginal or bottom notes, or notes at the end of the volume or any of its subdivisions, to direct the attention of the reader to such notes, the latter being always preceded by a mark similar to that used in the portion of the text to which it relates.

The common references are generally used in this order:—*, †, ‡, §, ‖, ¶, and where there are more than six notes in a page, two of each reference are sometimes put to the second series of notes; but this has an unsightly appearance. Italic lower-case letters are sometimes used, inclosed between parentheses (a), and sometimes figures (1). The letters, when they are used, are often continued through the alphabet, and then commence again with a. The neatest references are superiors, both letters and figures. Where the notes are at the foot of the page, letters are most frequently used, sometimes going through the alphabet, and sometimes commencing a superior * in each page in which notes occur. When the notes are placed at the end of the volume, figures (¹) are nearly always adopted in regular succession.

Register.—To cause the pages in a sheet to precisely back each other, an end which can only be attained by a careful arrangement of the marginal furniture, accurate feeding, and good press-work. (See MAKING READY.)

Register Color Points.—Points sometimes used for ornamental color printing, which are not fixed to the tympan, but screwed on to some part of the furniture of a form.

Reglet.—Wooden furniture of various thicknesses, from that of a Nonpareil type up to two-line Great Primer, used to fill out blank spaces in forms, and to make margin.

Reiteration.—The second form, which backs the form first printed.

Relief.—In the fine arts, the projection or appearance of projection of the figure above or beyond the place upon which it is formed.

Relief Associations.—It has long been considered one of the legitimate functions of the Printers' Chapels of England to assist sick members. The Printers' Unions of the United States make no formal provision for this purpose, but in some offices Relief Associations are formed to accomplish it in a systematic manner. The agreement and rules of one of these associations, which was organized by the compositors engaged in the office of The Press, in Philadelphia, in March, 1870, and has been in successful operation ever since, are as follows:

Agreement.—Believing it to be our duty to be charitable and to assist one another, particularly in the hour of distress and need, we, the undersigned compositors of the Philadelphia Press, do resolve ourselves into an association for our mutual benefit, and do solemnly obligate ourselves to strictly and cheerfully adhere to the rules governing the same.

Rules.—I. This association shall be known as the Press Relief Association.

II. Any compositor upon the Press who is well known as a resident of Philadelphia may become a member upon receiving a two-third vote of the Association.

III. There shall be a Collector, Assistant Collector, and a Visiting Committee of three, who shall be elected every three months.

IV. It shall be the duty of the Collector, upon the notification of the Visiting Committee, to collect the assessments and pay any disabled member the amount due him without delay.

V. It shall be the duty of the Assistant Collector to act in the absence of the Collector.

VI. It shall be the duty of the Visiting Committee to receive all notifications of disability, and to visit and inquire into the state and cause of disability, and see that the Collector receives and pays the assessments due, and to call all meetings of the Association.

VII. Any member shall receive benefits who shall be unable to perform his daily labor for the space of one week on account of sickness arising from natural causes or unforeseen accident. No member shall be entitled to benefits when sickness is produced by his own indiscretion.

VIII. The benefits of this Association shall be Ten Dollars per week for each disabled member, providing that it does not cause an assessment of over fifty cents per week upon each member in case of the disability of one or two members, and not over one dollar for three or more.

IX. Any member becoming sick or disabled shall give notification of the same to the chairman of or one of the Visiting Committee.

X. Any member refusing to pay the assessment, his name shall be stricken from the roll of the Association as unworthy of his fellow-workmen's charity, sympathy, and respect.

XI. No member shall be allowed to withdraw, save upon his disconnection with the Press office; and any member may remain a member so long as he continues to abide by the rules.

XII. Any of these rules may be altered by a two-third vote.

Amendment.—XI. Any member who wishes to withdraw may do so if he is not in arrears; provided, there are no sick members in the society.—*October* 24, 1870.

Reporter.—Strictly, one who records or takes down in writing the words of a speaker; but, in modern journalism, the province of the reporter extends also to accounts of current local events, etc.

The public interest in England in the proceedings of Parliament led, at an early day, to the distribution of written reports for the use of the London Coffee Houses and Clubs. A manuscript called the Votes of Parliament was circulated daily in 1691, but was a very meagre account. Remarkable debates or the history of special sittings of Parliament were published occasionally as personal reminiscences, often years after the occurrences described. More authentic reports were issued in the Historical Register during the reign of George I.; but the first effort to produce debates currently was made by Cave in the Gentleman's Magazine in 1736. Cave

had previously been interested in furnishing the manuscript reports for country circulation, and determined to introduce the speeches of Parliament as a feature of his magazine, hoping to avoid any legal penalty by publishing only after the conclusion of the session, and with the initial and final letter of the member's name. To accomplish this, Cave and one or two friends obtained admission into the gallery, taking notes when possible, and then consulting afterwards so as to form a crude abstract of the proceedings, which was given to Guthrie to present in more striking form. In 1738 Cave was brought before the House of Commons for this offense against the privileges of the Parliament, and thereafter omitted the names, and published the proceedings as The Debates of Great Liliput. During the great political excitement of 1740, Cave engaged Dr. Johnson to prepare the debates, and forthwith the public were amazed and delighted by the oratorical brilliance lavished profusely in the decoration of the outlines furnished by Cave and a few others,—Johnson never entering the gallery himself. Cave was again summoned for the same offense before Parliament in 1747; and such difficulties continued to attend the publication and preparation of the reports, that when William Perry assumed the editorship of the Gazetteer, in 1783, he found the parliamentary proceedings several months behindhand. By great exertions, he introduced a system of relays of reporters, and in a short time was enabled to present the debates of the previous night in the next morning's paper.

Perry afterwards edited for many years Debrett's Parliamentary Debates, and also purchased the Morning Chronicle, a journal upon which James Stephens acted as reporter, as a means of supporting himself while studying for the bar, an opportunity which he gratefully remembered years afterwards, when, as a wealthy member of Parliament, he told the story of his own exertions, as an effectual plea against a motion made to prevent barristers from being employed on newspapers. The Morning Chronicle is also celebrated in this connection as having been edited by William Woodfall, long distinguished under the name of Memory Woodfall, from the fact that when the rules prevented the introduction of a note-book into the House of Commons, he had been able to sit through a sixteen-hour session and write immediately afterwards a report sixteen columns long, without a particle of assistance.

Upon the Morning Chronicle was also employed as reporter Mark Supple, a gigantic Irishman, who for years delighted the House by the eloquence and wit with which he dished up the dullness of the Parliamentary disquisitions, with all the piquant relishes of Celtic rhetoric.

During the Speakership of Addington, who was remarkable for his prim propriety of demeanor, there occurred one evening an interval of absolute silence. Supple waited patiently, but the awful pause offered too tempting an opportunity, and in a ringing tone he called out most convivially for—A song from Mr.

25

Speaker! Addington, astonished, sat in grim consternation, while the House, led by Pitt, broke into peal after peal of irrepressible laughter. When at length a sergeant-at-arms was sent to the gallery to arrest the culprit, Supple, with absolute gravity, pointed out a very fat Quaker as the offender. The Quaker was taken into custody, but succeeded in shifting the responsibility to the right shoulders, and Supple, after a couple of hours of arrest, was allowed to escape upon promises of amendment.

In hard and valiant service in the same capacity, and for the same journal, Charles Dickens educated into rapidity and accuracy that minute power of observation and description which made him afterwards the most popular novelist of his time.

The improvements in short-hand writing, based on the invention and development of phonography, have in late years caused remarkable changes, by enabling the reporter to follow the speaker, word by word, with absolute accuracy; and in the United States many accurate phonographers report, with extraordinary fidelity, the proceedings of Congress, State Legislatures, public meetings, courts, etc.

The local reporter renders indispensable service to every modern daily, and to many weekly newspapers. Special reporters or correspondents are sent on errands as various as the new topics or objects of interest that arise from time to time in any portion of the world. Enterprising war correspondents give the first descriptions of great modern battles. Interviewers extract from garrulous public men, statements of their theories and purposes; and few facts or events of real significance escape the notice of the various descriptions of reporters who are now steadily engaged in the service of the newspapers.

Reprint.—A second or new impression or edition of any printed work, frequently used to describe the publication in one country of a work previously printed in another.

Resume.—A brief recapitulation or condensed statement—adopted from the French language.

Review.—A periodical publication consisting of critical essays. Analytical criticism in literature forms so obvious a need among students, that it is said that the Bibliotheca of the Patriarch Photius, a contemporary of Alfred of England, anticipated the plan of the modern review, and proves that the writer had access to two hundred and eighty authors. The germ of the modern literary accounts current, which have grown into the critical magazines, may be found in the periodical catalogue of the book-fair of Leipsic, in 1623; and in England in the reign of Charles II., Clavell's Lists served as a publishers' Circular. The first critical serial publication which has been styled a review was the Journal des Savants, commenced in Paris in 1665, and published weekly. This work was immediately translated in Germany, and followed in 1682 by an original work of similar character, which was the precursor of a multitude of others, this form of serial being especially popular in that country.

In England several publications of the kind were attempted, commencing with the year 1680, but they were all of short duration, until the Monthly Review was established in 1749. The name was adopted in 1704 by Daniel De Foe, as the title for the newspaper which he established during his imprisonment for publishing The Shortest Way with Dissenters. The paper appeared for two years as the Review of the Affairs in France, and was then changed to A Review of the State of the English Nation; it was continued by De Foe until 1713, when newly imposed taxes compelled him to discontinue it. The paper appeared first as a weekly, and afterwards three times a week, and has been considered as the forerunner and model of the Spectator.

The literary Review was introduced into Italy as early as 1668, and was very successful, all the principal cities supporting publications exhibiting a remarkable degree of erudition and scholarship.

The Edinburgh Review, commenced in 1802, and the Quarterly, in 1809, inaugurated a new era in criticism, and from that period such periodicals have been very generally adopted as the organs of sects and parties, in religion and politics, as well as literature. The articles preserving the character of reviews generally begin by specifying certain works at the head, although the books are not critically reviewed, but are only used as a species of text or excuse for a general essay. Parties, in church or state, in this manner are enabled to express their opinions or make statements of facts without assuming direct or personal responsibility. Although not necessarily appearing at any fixed period, reviews generally appear but four times a year, or quarterly, in England and America, and the articles are anonymous. In France the modern review contains tales and poetry, and corresponds more nearly to the English and American Magazine.

The first publication bearing the name in the United States, was the American Review of History and Politics, published in Philadelphia from 1811 to 1813. The North American Review, established in 1815 in Boston, is still continued. A very large number of the reviews in the United States are published by religious societies, and are both critical and theological in their character.

Revise.—A proof taken to examine whether errors marked in a previous proof have been corrected. The word is by some authorities applied exclusively to the last proof, taken on the press on which a form is to be worked.

Rhapsody.—A vehement and incoherent expression of thought or feeling, made impulsively and without logical connection either within itself or with the accompanying matter.

Rhetoric.—In its widest sense, the art of prose composition; in its more common use, the art of argumentative composition; and in its most restricted sense, the art of oratory. The first formal treatise upon rhetoric was by Aristotle, and the art received much attention in Greece and Rome, and has furnished the theme of many treatises both in ancient and modern times.

Rhyme.—The correspondence in sound in the final words or syllables of the lines in poetic composition. Rhyme was carried to great excellence in Arabian and Persian poetry at a very early day, but as the English were ignorant of the literature of Asia, it is probable that rhyme was derived by them directly from the Latin, it not being found in the Teutonic tongues, where alliteration was used as the means of producing melody.

Rhythm.—The division of time by a regular succession of motions, impulses, or sounds, so as to produce an agreeable effect, either in literary composition, in music, or in dancing.

Ribs.—The parts of hand-presses and of some power-presses which form a track in which the carriage or bed is run under and out from the platen or cylinder.

Rice Paper.—A material used by the Chinese for drawing or printing. (See PAPER.)

Richardson, Samuel.—A printer of London, and inventor of the English novel. Richardson was the son of a joiner in Derbyshire, and was born in 1689. His father was able to afford him only the limited educational advantages of the village school, but permitted him to choose his own occupation. Being fond of reading, he selected printing, and was apprenticed when seventeen years old to John Wilde, a printer of London. He faithfully and industriously performed the duties of this situation for six years, and continued as journeyman and proof-reader for six years more. In 1719 he established a printing-office for himself, with all the advantages of a reputation for integrity and industry, and the approval of John Wilde, whose daughter he married. While pursuing his vocation Richardson occasionally wrote prefaces and dedications, compiled indexes, and in various other ways established an intercourse with authors and publishers, acquiring a considerable reputation among his circle of intimate friends for his special faculty of letter-writing. He printed The Daily Journal, The Daily Gazetteer, and some numbers of The Briton. He was also the printer of the first edition of the Journal of the House of Commons, and attracted the attention of Speaker Onslow, who offered him a place at court, which Richardson declined, from a sincere devotion to his chosen avocation. His reputation as a letter-writer led to a proposal from a publisher to edit or prepare a collection of such compositions to serve as a complete letter-writer or book of models, and while engaged upon this task, Richardson conceived the plan of identifying the epistles with the experiences of one individual. With the business-like intention of preparing a work which would suit the requirements of the market, he was still, as always, conscientiously desirous of benefiting his kind, and with his earnest integrity and patient clear-sighted industry he found the right method of expression for his thought. The complete letter-writer assumed an entirely unexpected and original form, and became the first English novel, with the title of Pamela, or the Reward of Virtue. Never before did genius win such speedy and pleasing reward. In the year of its publication, 1741, it went through five editions in London, and was soon translated in France, where it met a reception as rapturous as that it had received at home. It was translated into German and Dutch, and the whole reading world of Europe accepted the gift with gratitude, returning the warmest thanks and most graceful compliments. Richardson deserved success both in fortune and fame, for it was not through erratic genius, but by industrious and conscientious endeavor, that he had constructed the new literary form, which was to furnish the most acceptable shape for popular instruction in succeeding times. He had reduced the romance, with its false and exaggerated descriptions of life, to the harmony of the true novel of domestic experience, full of wholesome instruction, and cleared the way for the great masters who were to follow him. Prosaic and tedious as the voluminous correspondence of Pamela, Clarissa, and Sir Charles Grandison may appear to modern readers, Richardson in those multitudinous volumes completed this work, balancing hero and heroine with the villain and his associates, and proportioning the weal and the woe, so justly, that it was only left for his successors to improve upon his scheme, without altering it in any essential. Besides his three novels, he edited and printed an edition of Esop's Fables, with reflections, contributed largely to the Christian Magazine, wrote a pamphlet upon the Duties of Wives and Husbands, a series of letters upon Duelling, and the only number of the Rambler that had a large sale.

Richardson continued to pursue his business with indefatigable perseverance, undisturbed by the extraordinary reputation acquired by his novels, and in 1754 was appointed to the honorable and lucrative office of Master of the Stationers' Company; soon afterwards he took down a row of old houses and erected an extensive and commodious range of warehouses and printing-offices, and in 1760 purchased the patent of law-printer in partnership with Miss Catharine Lintot. He died in 1761.

Riding.—Type at the end of a line catching against a lead; or leads and furniture so poorly adjusted that the form is likely to be bent or the type to fall out.

Riehl Patent Cutting-Machines.—Paper-cutters of various sizes and patterns made for the use of printers and bookbinders, by Mr. Riehl, of Philadelphia. They are said to be very strong and substantial in every part, and to embrace valuable improvements perfected with great care. An illustration is given of one of these machines on page 388.

Rise.—A form is said to rise or to lift when everything is properly justified, and when nothing falls out after it is locked up and lifted from the imposing-stone.

Ritual.—A book containing the rites or services of a church, or of some of the secret orders.

SMALL HAND ROLLER.

Roller.—A cylinder coated with composition, used to ink forms preparatory to taking an impression. (See COMPOSITION ROLLERS.)

in Portugal in the fourteenth century, and similar tales followed in Spain, Portugal, and France, becoming so popular that Don Quixote was written to ridicule them in 1609. A new and more domestic style of narrative appeared in Italy in the fifteenth century, called the Novelli, which in fact preceded Don Quixote in satirizing the absurdities of the romance. The Italian novelli was modified by Richardson in England, who in 1740 published Pamela, in which the romance was reduced to the due proportions of current experience and made to

RIEHL PATENT CUTTING-MACHINE.

Romance.—A species of fictitious writing, originally composed in metre, in the language corrupted from the Latin, or Roman, and spoken and written in the South of France and in Spain during the twelfth and thirteenth centuries. Chivalric adventures related in rude verse were popular in Northern France, and particularly in Normandy, from the twelfth to the fifteenth century, and thus became known in England. Prose writers compiled the substance of these songs and poems into tales, or romances, probably ascribing the deeds of unknown heroes to the popular knights Arthur, Charlemagne, and Amadis of Gaul. The romance of Amadis appeared

convey lessons of morality, thus becoming the precursor of the modern domestic novel. The distinction between romance and novel has never been clearly defined, but, according to common usage, the romance is restricted to tales of chivalric adventure, devoted to exaggerated descriptions of warlike incident or lover's intrigues, rather than to the events of the novel, which are preserved strictly within the limits of the probabilities of every-day life. Although it has been contended by some critics that Sir Walter Scott wrote romances rather than novels, he strongly indicated his desire to preserve one of the most important characteristics of the novel, when he carefully explained that he would endeavor to make his stories probable, and never allow his hero to spend a purse of gold without providing it beforehand, or the heroine to appear in the midst of a forest reclining at ease beside her harp immediately after escaping out of a window in the dead of night, at the risk of her neck. As an illustration of the distinction of terms, Goethe's Werther is called a philosophical romance, while Bulwer's What Will He do With It is a novel.

Romanesque.—A style of art in which fantastic and imaginary representations of natural forms are introduced.

Roman Letter.—Letter similar to that used by the ancient Romans, which, with minor modifications, forms the text of all printed matter in the English, French, Italian, Spanish, and various other languages. It possesses a manifest superiority to all other representations of an alphabet, in the fact that it is made up exclusively of figures mathematically accurate, consisting of straight lines, circles, and arcs of circles.

Roman Numerals.—See NUMERALS.

Romaunt.—A fanciful story without complex incident, told in verse.

Rondeau or Rondo.—A lyric poem containing a refrain or repetition, occurring according to a fixed law; also a musical composition either for voice or instrument, in which the first strain is repeated after each of the other strains.

Rotary Press.—A press on which type revolve on a horizontal cylinder.

Rounce.—The cylinder to which is attached the girth of hand-presses, used in running the carriage in and out.

Roundelay or Roundel.—An airy style of poem, formerly popular among the French, and adapted to music; it was of irregular measure, and contained a refrain. It was at one time popular in England.

Round Pick.—A dot in a letter in a stereotype plate, caused by an air-bubble.

Royal.—A size of paper. (See DIMENSIONS OF PAPER.)

Rubric.—In early manuscript and printed works, the part colored red, as the title-page or parts thereof; the title, initial letters, or any words printed or written in red. The directions and rules for the conduct of religious services were formerly in red letters, and hence rubric has been used as an ecclesiastical or episcopal injunction. In modern usage, italic character has to a great degree supplied the place of the ancient red letters.

Rucking.—The creasing or wrinkling of paper which sometimes occurs when it is printed on cylinder presses.

Ruggles Presses.—A series of presses of various sizes and patterns, made in accordance with designs invented by S. P. Ruggles, of Boston, who was one of the first successful inventors of small job-presses. A number of his presses are still in use, but they have been superseded to a considerable extent by later inventions. It is said that S. P. Ruggles invented the first American card press about 1830 or 1831.

Rule.—A rule type-high, of the same length as the measure of the stick in which it is used, made of various metals, such as tin, steel, brass, and sometimes silver, having short pointed projections at the top of both ends, which is used by compositors to retain type set, and type being set, in its proper position in the stick, as well as to empty matter, to lift matter, and to support matter held in the left hand, while it is being distributed by the right hand. Compositors on daily newspapers generally purchase their own rules, holding them as individual property. (See COMPOSING RULES.)

Rule and Figure Work.—Composition which involves the justification of rules and figures arranged in narrow columns.

Rules.—Strips of brass or wood made type height, so as to represent lines of various thicknesses in a printed page. (See BRASS RULES and LABOR-SAVING RULE.)

Rules and Regulations.—The necessity of rules and regulations, varying with the special demands of diversely organized printing-offices, is obvious; but the evils developed in a very badly managed office are so numerous that a faithful description of them may serve a useful purpose. Such an account was given by a correspondent of the London Printers' Journal, in describing a printing-office at Calcutta, in which the usual defects and difficulties were intensified by the employment of ignorant and indolent native workmen.

I will take the office in its several departments as it exists here:—

1. Readers and copy-holders.
2. Compositors and correctors.
3. Impositors and distributors.
4. Pressmen, inkmen, and fly-boys.
5. Dutries, or warehousemen.

To begin with readers. The marks observed by readers are the same as those used in England, with one or two exceptions. All matter is read first and second time in galleys, and then made up, imposed, and read a third time for press. It is a rare thing to meet with a good reader, that is, one who really understands what he is about, and will not make corrections merely for correction's sake, and thus give the poor corrector a great deal of unnecessary trouble. The reason of this paucity of good readers is, that few have ever been compositors (I know of only two or three in Calcutta), and they do not consequently understand the trouble they are giving. The first-proof reader's berth is certainly no sinecure, as the best of the proofs are bad. The following specimen will give you an idea how bad they can be. This matter was set up from very clear manuscript by a native convert who had been strongly recommended. I can vouch that it is a genuine production:—

13 The Cinese unhmu not coming from Honkong as expected (see P. W. docet No 1700 dp. 3. aps any reply No. 72 dates 13 Jdeea (i depimuce to desyated, the Big Mepna to Madias from wokpeople, as I saw, at once, Meet common coliea eonled make but little impussion cooles on the greatente store.

unpreed the duty of atlasting alone aukees and guany maul to at A, Seebe whome r aeute over to Madias in the Boy oteer

27 the aps which ardien which ondn hals the from more mate 6 and paemson and returning to Ballo(nuh aut 6 the l hade to any thought ahlitise in site if nothing letter apped on ving return This gone to with way of lodging out sheds for all laide down with reperoion to this lower level to duie a stapot down to duie athing a lower loavel to duie a stapot down lile we cause to the suppose opain thonseleave nakind got a fooe the knowledge after all work inguanyiag till conied got all th preaple wll

The above very elegant piece of composition was the result of only two hours and a half's work!

Readers do not have separate closets, three or four being generally located in some corner of the press- or composing-room. The hubhub and confusion going on in this spot are indescribable. Fancy reading a press-proof with three reading boys jabbering around you. In my office I have avoided this as much as possible; in the generality of offices, however, the above plan is invariably pursued. The pay of readers is too small to attract men of education.

Compositors form a motley group, whose vagaries are sufficient to exhaust the patience of a Job. Some few are Christians, but the majority are Hindoos and Mohammedans. They load a far easier life than I enjoyed during my apprenticeship. No imposition or locking-up for them; no lifting heavy forms on the stone or carrying them to the press; no hunting for sorts in the gloomy recesses of a store-room; no clearing pi; and last, though by no means least, no correction or distribution! The impositor must perform the first of the above, the proof pressman the next two, and the distributor and corrector divide the remainder. The compositor considers himself a veritable nawab; he cannot put his own case up, oh no! the distributor must do this. I have tried, but most unsuccessfully, to make compositors do all that properly belongs to their duty. They argue that locking-up and carrying forms are the work of coolies, and that their caste would be endangered by performing their duties. This bugbear caste has much to answer for, always standing in the way of progress. Some of the compositors are very fair hands, judged by the quantity turned out (seldom, by the way, an hour's work in an hour); look, however, at the quality, and you shudder. Totally regardless of spacing, and, of course, of sense and punctuation, they blunder on, their only object apparently being to fill up the galley. I have spoken numberless times about even spacing, and fined to a tremendous extent, all to no purpose; the excuse is that it takes up too much time. With a native compositor the thick and thin spaces always run out first, and you invariably find cases half full of letter, though quite denuded of the above-mentioned spaces. And then arises an outcry wild for the distributor—Oh, matee (the second syllable prolonged ad lib.), thick espace las (bring). And so on for everything that runs short. I had endless trouble in making compositors lead out their matter in the stick, and it was only by inflicting some heavy fines I succeeded in stopping their own insane plan of leading out in galley. Very few compositors understand anything of whiting out, and as for displays, unless you chalk the lines out and mark the type they should be set in, they will make a display that will astonish you. All compositors are bad hands at making up, and require assistance in every trifling difficulty. It is but fair to say that many of the hands can compose tabular statements in very good style, and I have more than once been agreeably surprised at the very neat and workmanlike way in which ticklish genealogical tables have been turned out in my own office. This is the description of niggling work that suits their attenuated fingers. Considering, however, the very poor training the generality of compositors get, it is a wonder that any of them are worth their salt. They serve no weary apprenticeship, and, working only from 10 A. M. to 5 P. M., are in blissful ignorance of what a day's hard work really is. The following is their mode of procedure:—A native boy gets into an office and picks up a slight knowledge of composing; after a few months' stay, he applies for a salary. At the end of about six months he again comes up with a pitiful tale of having to maintain a small wife and large family, with no end of relations, and requests an increase to his pay.

The correctors, who, by the way, are all natives, are always fully employed, as you may imagine, and correct their matter without a side-stick to the galley, the matter being generally pulled on wooden galleys. The justification is consequently bad. If the matter gets off its feet they can never succeed in putting it straight, but invariably make matters worse by ramming in spaces, and when the proof shows too plainly that all is not right, they endeavor to put the blame on the pressman's shoulders. Many of the bodkins used are curiosities in their way, and it is no uncommon thing to find correctors using an old nail, or, what is a great favorite, the pointed end of a setting-rule. In one office, to save the type, men were not allowed to use bodkins, but were provided with small pieces of bamboo, tapered off to a point.

All the impositors are natives, the head man generally being in charge of the distributors, and exercising control over the store-room. They want a great deal of training before they are worth anything, and in the event of the impositor being absent, it is useless expecting any one else to do his work. I remember telling one of the distributors, a man who must have seen hundreds of forms imposed, to impose a small job for me. He commenced by putting a side-stick on either side. I was in a great hurry at the time, and could not therefore allow him to complete the performance in his own peculiar style.

The distributors, also, are all natives, who place their cases on the ground, and then squat down before them. Their work is generally slowly and badly done.

The pressmen are, with very rare exceptions, Mohammedans—great rascals, up to any amount of roguery and laziness. Some of them can work very well when they choose, the misfortune being that they don't often choose. They have a most imperfect knowledge of their business, and making-ready is done in a very rough-and-ready style. It is often most disheartening to find that, after bestowing great care or attention upon the composing, the pressmen have spoilt all by their vile printing. This is often attributable to their insane way of dampening the paper, soaking it, in fact, and thus rendering it quite unsuited for printing.

The dustries (warehousemen) are also all Mohammedans, and a lazy lot, working very slowly and not over-carefully.

The most embarrassing and disheartening thing is the very great irregularity in attendance. Men will not attend office regularly, but absent themselves on the most trivial pretenses. My establishment numbers about seventy men, out of which the absentees generally amount to fifteen per day; a few days ago I had upwards of twenty absent. It is quite a red-letter day to have all present. It is unnecessary to enlarge on the inconvenience and delay thus caused.

The endless complaints about the most trivial matters are another cause of annoyance. It is more like having to deal with children than grown-up men. Complaints are made to you when men can't get, or are too lazy to search for, sorts, leads, chases, furniture, or anything else they may require. One man abuses another; up comes the injured party with his pitiful tale, and so on, till you are driven to the verge of insanity. In the hot weather, when I have been thus pestered, I have often felt inclined to make a rush in search of

A lodge in some vast wilderness,
    Some boundless contiguity of shade,
Where troubles of press-reading and foul proofs,

Of missing copy, or of absent men,
Might never reach me more.

It is needless to dwell upon the annoyance caused by the carelessness and stupidity of all around you. You may explain as carefully as you can, all to no purpose. If the thing can be done wrong, it will be. One instance is sufficient. I gave a man (a Christian, by the way) a letter-heading to compose. On the copy was written, Please supply 100 copies, and after that a signature. When the proof was brought, the heading was in its proper place, and in the centre of the sheet, in large type, the order for printing!

It is a matter of some difficulty to ascertain from compositors the position of their work, for a native's disregard of truth extends to everything he does. On one or two occasions I narrowly escaped getting into trouble from being too credulous. Experience has taught me to believe only as much as I see.

The best practical remedy for carelessness, idleness, ignorance, inefficiency, and destructiveness is probably to be found in the system of piece-work, under which it is the common interest of all concerned to maintain order and expedite business, as wages depend upon the amount of work performed. But apprentices and inferior weekly hands, when not closely watched, are apt to become only a few degrees less inefficient than the workmen in the Calcutta printing-office described above. Special rules frequently become necessary as special evils are developed, and the following standard rules are worthy of observance in all offices to which they are applicable:

1. Compositors are to receive their cases from the foreman or his assistant, free from all pi or improper sorts, with clean quadrat- and space-boxes, both Roman and Italic, which they are to return to him in equally good condition.

2. When a compositor receives letter, furniture, etc. from the foreman, he is to return any portion not used, in as good state as he received it, the same day.

3. When a case is taken out of the rack, the compositor is to return it into the proper place immediately after he has done with it.

4. No cases to be placed over others, or under the frames, or on the floor.

5. Compositors are to impose their matter and pull a proof as soon as made up, unless directed otherwise, and to correct the proof without unnecessary delay.

6. The proof, when pulled, to be given to the reader, the copy in regular order to accompany the first proof, and the foul proof the second.

7. Compositors are not to leave either type or furniture on the stone.

8. A compositor is not to detain an imposing-stone longer than the nature of the business may require.

9. Head-lines, or other useful materials, on galleys, used during the course of a work, to be cleared away as soon as the work is finished.

10. When a work is done, the compositor, before beginning another work, unless otherwise directed, is to clear away the forms, taking from them the head-lines, blank-lines, and odd sorts, as well as the leads

and reglets; which, with the furniture of each sheet, and the matter properly tied up for papering, are to be given to the foreman.

11. Sweepings of stands to be cleared away before one o'clock every day. Matter broken by accident to be cleared away on the same day.

12. The saw, saw-block, bowl, sponge, letter-brush, shears, bellows, etc., to be returned to their respective places as soon as done with.

13. Letter-boards, windows, frames, etc. to be kept free from pi.

14. No person to take sorts from the cases of another without leave, nor hoard useful sorts, not wanting or likely to want them.

15. Compositors employed by the week to work not less than ten hours per day.

16. Unnecessary conversation to be avoided.

Ruling-Machines.—Machines for ruling colored lines on paper. A small work was published in London in 1616, for the purpose of illustrating and describing what it termed, Two new inventions called Lineage and Fortage, whereby writing-paper and parchment are decently ruled and inclined, for to grosse or write upon, after a more dexterous and beneficial manner than is done or performed by the ordinary way of hand-ruling with plummet, ruler, or brass pen. For many years this invention and similar devices were used chiefly, if not exclusively, to rule writing-paper at the paper-mills, in a few given patterns, which were rarely varied, and there was no material improvement in ruling-machines. During the last quarter of a century, however, they have been greatly improved in the United States, and their powers so much enlarged that rulings of any width, pattern, or color can readily be made, as will be seen by the fine illustration of the capacity of the Pennsylvania Ruling-Machine which accompanies this article. This specimen page of modern ruling was prepared by John Jones, binder and paper-ruler, of No. 710 Sansom Street, Philadelphia, and indicates how many varied rulings can now be effected for the adornment of different classes of Job Printing, and for the convenient arrangement of Account Books, Blank Statements, Copy Books, Bill Heads, Note and Letter Headings, etc. The principle of the ruling-machine is simple. At each end of a frame a wooden roller is affixed, one of which is turned by a handle. Round these rollers revolves a broad endless band of canvas or cloth sufficiently smooth and elastic, and also a series of small cords so arranged that the paper may be kept in its proper position while it is being ruled. At one end of the machine is a table to which a gauge is attached in such a manner that accurate feeding of the paper can be insured, and after the paper traverses a short distance on the endless band it comes in contact with the ruling pens. They are firmly held in a broad clasp, formed of two pieces of wood, united by screws; and in the improved modern machines this clasp is so completely under the control of the operator that it may be readily moved either to the right hand or left, or slightly varied from its true rectangular position, so as to make the ruling correspond with the irregularities of imperfect paper, or with any description of ruling that may be required. The pens are formed of a peculiar quality of brass, and are simple channels, to convey the ink from its reservoir to the paper. The pens are arranged in sets, at various distances from one another, so that rulings of every desirable width can readily be made; and ingenious contrivances facilitate the ruling of lines in which several colors are very closely combined. The ink reservoirs are pieces of flannel, lying on the upper end of the pens, and kept thoroughly saturated by means of a small brush. The ink is made of pigments of various colors and materials, combined with fresh beeves' gall and alcohol, and when used, it is a thin liquid, flowing freely. When a sheet is to be ruled it is fed accurately, by the aid of the gauge, and as it passes under the pens it is held firmly by the ends in its proper position, on the endless bands. As it passes underneath the pens it receives from them all the rulings in one direction which are deemed necessary, several colors being sometimes simultaneously ruled; and the band in modern machines is made long enough to insure, with the aid of other contrivances, the drying of the coloring matter before the ruled sheet is deposited in the box in which it is finally delivered.

Runic.—A name for many sizes and varieties of job-letter, bearing a resemblance to the Runic characters used by the Teutonic and Gothic nations of Northern Europe. It is a matter of controversy among learned writers whether the original Runic alphabets are of great antiquity, or merely such a modification of Roman letters as would naturally be made by a people who found it convenient to substitute straight lines for elaborate curves when they undertook to carve inscriptions on wood and stone with rude implements.

Run in.—In press-work, to run the bed of a press under the platen or cylinder. In composition, to compress matter; the titles of the separate articles of this work, for instance, are run in to the lines containing the matter which immediately follows them, instead of being set in separate lines.

Running title.—The title of the book or subject placed at the top of the pages.

Run out.—To run the bed of a press from under the platen or cylinder.

Runs on Sorts.—When copy is of such a nature that it requires an unusually large quantity of particular letters or figures, it is said to run on sorts.

Ruthven Press.—A hand-press invented during the early part of the nineteenth century, which differed from presses previously made in having the bed stationary, while the platen was moved to and fro.

S.

Safety-Paper.—Under this title it has become customary to include all devices intended or proposed

to prevent the obliteration of written marks made upon such paper, or the change or counterfeiting of the marks themselves. In this broad sense it will be seen that the security of government stamps, written upon to prevent re-use, and bank-note paper, not to be imitated, are included.

For years, at the invitation of distinguished officers of the United States government, the writer has had ample means to investigate all questions connected with bank-notes, associated with and aided by the best technical and scientific ability of our own land, as well as of those who practically knew what had been done in other countries.

On another occasion, mainly by himself, the writer has had, also on government invitation, the opportunity of examining about two hundred plans proposed for the security of government stamps, with a view to prevent their illegal re-use.

The information thus accumulated and officially recorded cannot but be interesting, as well as useful. The fact that it has not in certain cases been used or even regarded, may be best explained by stating that the writer and his associates gave their services gratuitously, as government officers. Nevertheless, they have the satisfaction of knowing that they have been the means of saving the government from speculators' operations to such an extent that one of the highest authorities in the land has declared to our Chief Magistrate that they have saved to the treasury, directly and indirectly, some millions of money.

Of course it would not be right to reveal as the result of such information, the special tricks of rascals. But, in truth, these are very few, and are well known to all whom it may concern. It is, however, quite right that an intelligent community, themselves the real sufferers, should have a good general idea of this subject.

The first conclusion is, that capable men in the arts and sciences know far more than the counterfeiters and rascals, and can prevent most of their frauds. The second conclusion is, that the counterfeiters and rascals know far more than the speculators, who seek to furnish illusory protections, provided they are paid for them. In our experience, most of these men (there are honorable exceptions) are not unlike the ostrich, who hides his head and thinks his body is concealed. Quite honestly most of these men seek to attain one end, and do attain it; but they leave other weak points subject to a thousand attacks.

Few can understand the double mode of attack made upon the community by mere speculators. First we hear of strange stories of somebody, never found out, offering immense prices for old postage-stamps; next comes the plausible explanation that these stamps are really washed and used again; and after a convenient time we have from some ardent speculator a plan which is to prevent this enormous fraud, if the United States government will give him say $100,000 or thereabouts for his plan.

Now, we have taken the greatest pains, from the

-

The first plan proposed for a safety-paper for stamps
was to use such a miserable and even purposely
defaced paper that the stamp could not be transferred
from one document to another. The projectors forgot that such stamps must, in most cases, be carried
'fore they are used, and what will become of them
'he mean while? As to the transfer, he must be
' ignorant rascal who could not perform it.

'ext plan was to use a mere water-color ink,
v the slightest touch of water, and so not to
' from its original place without betray-
But what man, when the temperature
'° to 100° Fahrenheit, as it frequently
'er season, could affix a stamp with-
wing it to be a fraud? Besides,
uch colors.

'how the action of acids and
'ed; but, in our climate, few
't, would fail to be spoiled

'us, because uncertain,
ich, in most cases,
'osers themselves,
' fugitive colors,
'er that before
'ard to say,
and which
'cre, out
'distin-
the
're
'.

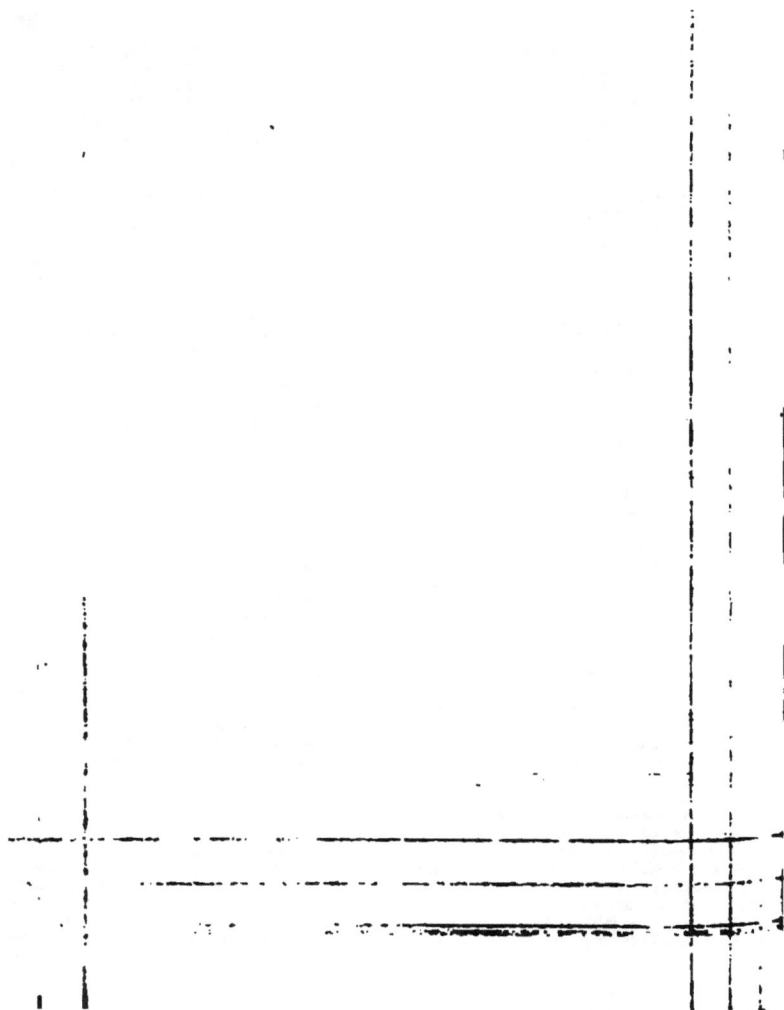

highest official sources, to investigate this matter, and we can safely say that there is no proof that the government has lost, by washed postage-stamps, a tenth or even a hundredth of what is proposed to be paid to some speculator for an infallible cure,—the infallibility of which is in no way demonstrated.

But here we must not for an instant be considered as pretending to say a word against the simple, honest-hearted people who, hearing that the country is suffering so great a wrong, have proposed possibly foolish but nevertheless well-meant contrivances to save their beloved country from the terrible loss to which they have heard it is exposed. Even from women we have seen such, the innocence and simplicity of which have drawn tears of joy from our eyes, showing as they did a simple-hearted patriotism which gave good promise for the bringing up of a great people, but which would never be regarded by the speculators who had informed them of the imaginary evil.

As to the idea of washing and re-using postage-stamps, we need only say that the poorest of our citizens would not find it profitable to collect, wash, and re-use old ones.

But the introduction of a higher stamp-tax, where not cents alone, but dollars and hundreds of dollars, were represented, created an additional necessity for Safety-Paper.

At the present time, high values are attached to some government stamps. Soon there came a report that such stamps were, after being canceled in the required manner, washed and re-used. Of the fact there could be no doubt, but it must be confessed that the greatest number and value of such old, cleansed stamps were found in the hands of projectors who proposed some cure for the evil. A possibly ill-advised proposal from the government led to an increase of the mischief and a host of proposals for its check.

The consideration by government request led to the investigation, the results of which will now be given as briefly as possible.

It would at first seem that a literature of such a subject could not be found, but here, as is often the case, it will be seen that men have quite uselessly retraced their steps. About the year 1830, the French government, feeling the need of such safeguards, invited proposals, and a commission of the most distinguished chemists and artists was charged with the investigation of the matter. The results of their investigations, and of the proposals sent to them, are matters of record.

To one engaged in such investigations, it would be quite natural to encounter what had been done before in such a line; and, even supposing it to be forgotten, the accidental reappearance, among the papers of a projector, of a more than thirty-years-old so-called safety-paper, led to the conclusion that the old mine was digged in, and the subsequent marvelous coincidence of old and new projects gave a good reason for considering them together.

The first plan proposed for a safety-paper for stamps was to use such a miserable and even purposely defaced paper that the stamp could not be transferred from one document to another. The projectors forgot that such stamps must, in most cases, be carried before they are used, and what will become of them in the mean while? As to the transfer, he must be a very ignorant rascal who could not perform it.

The next plan was to use a mere water-color ink, defaced by the slightest touch of water, and so not to be removed from its original place without betraying fraud. But what man, when the temperature ranges from 90° to 100° Fahrenheit, as it frequently does in our summer season, could affix a stamp without the risk of showing it to be a fraud? Besides, flies rapidly destroy such colors.

Colors prepared to show the action of acids and alkalies have been proposed; but, in our climate, few such, if carried in the pocket, would fail to be spoiled before being used.

Then came a more dangerous, because uncertain, mixture, the composition of which, in most cases, seemed to be unknown to the proposers themselves, except under the imposing title of fugitive colors, which so well maintained their character that before they were officially examined it was hard to say, even upon the same sheet, which was right and which was wrong. One most amusing case was where, out of compliment, the engraved portrait of a distinguished public officer had been placed upon the stamp. By the time that this had its turn the face of the honorable gentleman had such a comical black smudge over it, that laughter was irresistibly excited, and the amiable inventor who had wasted his ingenuity upon it quietly accepted the joke, and never appeared to claim the reward for his contrivance.

Then there were ingeniously contrived arrangements to produce marks to show the least touch of water, and so reveal the attempt at fraud. These, however, were easily cleaned out, and the paper made ready for an indefinite series of new reappearances.

One class of contrivances consisted in an attempt to fix the ink in the paper. The mere inspection of the paper was enough to show the old contrivance of a third of a century ago. But in one instance there was a captivating arrangement of fanciful colors, utterly useless for purposes of recognition, since no one could tell what they would be, a day, a month, or a year after; and over this was a great sprawling signature in common ink. The contriver, who had already shown himself fertile in reproducing old ideas, some of them in a not very reputable way, was boasting of the wonderful properties of his invention, the antiquity of which could be seen at a glance. Very quietly, while the talking was going on, the paper was neatly and cleanly cleared from the ink signature. When a doubt was expressed as to the possibility of the operation, a bit was cut in two, one-half of it was exposed to the same treatment, and, except on actual juxtaposition of the two halves, there could not be detected the slightest change.

The French Commission, however, arrived at a plain and good plan, capable, too, of considerable variation, especially with the knowledge we have acquired since their day; and this was, to print upon the stamp a design in an ink made mainly with the materials of ordinary writing-ink. The idea is a simple one, that whatever destroys the ink written upon the stamp will deface the stamp itself, and in most cases destroy it. Any reagent which will restore the one will restore the other. Abundant and careful experiments proved the entire success of this system.

The simplicity of this plan, and the fact that nobody is to be paid for it, are likely to lead to its public adoption; and there can be no doubt that individuals who need such a contrivance, taking advantage of the labors of those who have made these experiments for government, and who have surmounted the peculiar difficulties which belonged to it, will make use of it.

Bank Notes and Bank Note Paper.—The security of bank notes involves the prevention of the change of what is printed upon the note, either for the purpose of substituting for the name of a broken bank that of a good one, or of raising the figures on a note of small value to figures of higher value. The present plan of a national currency, entirely prevents this species of fraud, and the difference in design for each value, is at once distinctive. Every one sees this in the fractional currency, where the heads printed on them determine their value.

Another point is the prevention of counterfeiting. This is sought to be accomplished, either by the construction of the paper, or the character of what is printed upon it.

These safeguards are intended (providing the notes are constructed on old and well known principles,) not for experts, but for the ordinary public. Now, the conclusion to which we have arrived, in such matters, is this—that if the public mind is drawn to any such matter, attention is withdrawn from the ordinary and better tests, and if such safeguards are not infallible, the ordinary public is taught to lean upon a broken reed. Besides, the almost universal mode of judging bank notes is by looking at, or reading them, and it is the general impression which is the means of determination.

As to the peculiar structure of the paper, one of the first methods proposed, was that of Sir William Congreve; it consisted in the use of a paper of triple web, the inner one of which was marked with peculiar designs or colors. This was tried, and found to be quite too costly, and it is easily imitated. Many modifications of this idea have been proposed, none better than the original.

Since the use of bank note paper made on the Fourdrinier machine, the general direction of such contrivances has been for those which could only be made on such a machine, which was too large to be concealed, if engaged in making a counterfeit paper. The recent proposal to mark out a peculiar paper, not used for any other purpose, as peculiar to

government securities, for all plans proposed, is open to the objections which we shall show common to all, because they all depend upon the false idea that these devices cannot be imitated upon small pieces of already finished paper.

Dickenson, many years ago, proposed the introduction of fine threads of silk or other material, lying in parallel lines. This plan was tried in Prussian and Austrian official envelopes, and has been long since abandoned. It is hardly necessary to enumerate the disadvantages; they can be easily imitated in more ways than one, and for bank notes produce a weakness of the paper in one direction, which would involve the speedy destruction of the notes by handling.

The great reliance has been upon the water mark, and we have all read of trials in which forged papers have been detected by a more modern water mark than that of the date of the paper, and from this and from its being still used by the Bank of England, a certain sort of magic has been ascribed to such water marks.

Guided by four or five lines in a published work, we have succeeded at once in producing on finished paper the finest kind of water marks, and soon found another and easier way, which is known to counterfeiters. Moreover, in a bank bill, such marks are not noticeable in places covered with heavy engraving.

As to the matter printed, the first and great improvement was the introduction of designs obtained by the geometric lathe assigned to Asa Spencer, an American. The beauty and intricacy of these figures, and the mode of formation which renders their reconstruction impossible was a great advance.

The next and greatest improvement is also the invention of an American, Jacob Perkins. (See PERKINS, JACOB, and BANK NOTE PRINTING.)

In the Transactions of the Society of Arts, vol. xxxviii, London, 1820, in a full account of this process given by Messrs. Perkins, Fairman & Heath, they say:—The use of fine and delicate engraving for bank-notes has been objected to, in consequence of the difficulty of printing on such highly sized paper, But this objection is entirely got over by our method of printing in the water leaf, and sizing after printing. This improvement has a triple advantage —that of producing beautiful impressions, having on its surface, after printing, a better size, and preventing the ink from being so easily transferred.

This plan has been for years recommended in the published Reports of the Bank associations, and it seems worthy of a trial.

The foreign banks have their paper made of the best materials and in the best manner—most, if not all of it, is hand-made. In our own country, formerly the bank-note paper was made of new Russian duck, ground up with a small quantity of new bandanna silk handkerchiefs, giving a minute silk fleck, scattered all through the paper, but not projecting from its surface. (Projecting fibres cause the rapid destruction of the engraving and can easily be imitated by a well-known process).

The objection to all such well-made papers is, that they are too transparent, although much stronger than others. The old notes were printed only on one side, on a transparent paper—the printing on the two sides will interfere.

This difficulty can be met by having the printing on the two sides alternate, so that there can be no interference. Our present bank-notes are too crowded, and being less simple are less easily read, beside not being in the best taste.

Our idea of a good note consists in the best paper, with the best and most artistic designs. Properly

the Northern European races. Many of the sagas were arranged in the eleventh century in Iceland in a compilation called the Edda.

Salmagundi.—A collection of light, miscellaneous reading. A name taken from Italian cookery, signifying a dish of scraps made palatable by high spicing.

Salutatory.—An oration, letter, etc., introductory to other matter; as the salutatory address at the opening of the literary exercises at the Commencement of a college, or the first leading editorial prepared by a new editor of a newspaper,

SANBORN PAPER-CUTTER.

executed, such notes will last twice as long as those now in use, and the engraving will keep distinct and clear as long as the paper lasts.

Much has been said of counterfeiting by photography. The only specimens we have seen were made purposely for experiment by an accomplished photographer; but they could be detected by the feeling, without looking at them. A consideration of the modes proposed to prevent such counterfeiting would lead us beyond our limits.

Saga.—The general name of the ancient literary fragments containing the history and mythology of

in which he announces the course he intends to pursue.

Sanborn Paper-Cutter.—A paper-cutting machine, of original construction, intended to work by hand- or steam-power, manufactured by Messrs. George Sanborn & Co., of New York, who also make other paper-cutters of various sizes and kinds, bookbinders' machinery, various descriptions of standing- and hydraulic-presses of immense power, as well as embossing- and finishing-presses for book-binders' use, and card-cutters, shears, etc., for the use of printers.

Sanscrit or Sanskrit.—The learned language of Hindostan. It is not at present a spoken tongue, but is supposed by some authorities to have been imported by the conquering or Brahminical caste. The most ancient literature of the Hindoos is in this language, and in the drama the gods and saints invariably speak in Sanskrit, while the inferior personages speak the dialects of the country.

Sapphic.—A kind of verse consisting of five feet, the first a trochee, the second a spondee, the third a dactyl, and the fourth and fifth trochees, said to have been invented by Sappho, a Greek lyric poetess in the seventh century before Christ, who was remarkable for the grace, sweetness, and concentrated force of her expression.

Saspach, Conrad.—A turner of Strasburg, who, under the direction of John Gutenberg, made the first printing-press, in the year 1436.

Satin.—A superior fabric of silk, on which ornamental printing is sometimes executed for badges, bills of fare for fashionable dinners, etc.

Satin-Enameled Cards.—Cards having a highly polished, smooth, and glossy surface. Difficulties often occur in printing them, on account of the tendency of the surface to peel off. This may frequently be obviated by putting a small quantity of ultramarine powder in the ink when black ink is used, or carmine powder when carmine ink is used, etc. (See CARDS.)

Satire.—A species of composition, usually in verse, in which folly or vice is censured or exposed to contempt and hatred. It was especially popular among the Romans, and their satires have been frequently imitated by modern writers.

Saur or Sower, Christopher.—The first type-founder in the American colonies, and printer of the first Bible prepared for the European population. Christopher Saur, a German Protestant, settled with others of his countrymen in Germantown, near Philadelphia, and is said to have become a printer with the pious intention of supplying his fellow-immigrants with the Bible. In 1735 he commenced a quarterly journal in the German language, the first publication of the kind in a foreign tongue in America; it was afterwards changed to a monthly, and again altered in 1744 to a weekly paper, called the Germantown Gazette. Saur also published the first German Almanac in Pennsylvania, and extracts from the laws translated into German. The expense and delay attendant upon the importation of type induced him to establish the first foundry in America, and he there manufactured the German letter required for his Bible, and afterwards supplied other German printers. The Bible was commenced in 1740, and completed in three years, in a quarto of twelve hundred and seventy-two pages. It was the largest publication that had been produced in Pennsylvania, and was not equaled for many years after. The disinterested motives of the publisher were attested by his announcement that while its price in plain binding, with a clasp, would be eighteen shillings, to the poor and needy he had no price. The business was continued and enlarged by his son Christopher, who issued a second edition of the Bible, of two thousand copies, in 1762, and a third edition, of three thousand, in 1776. It is said that this last edition being unbound at the battle of Germantown was seized in sheets and used for cartridges. The book-manufactory under the conduct of Christopher Saur the younger was for many years the most extensive in the colonies, and employed several binders, a paper-mill, an ink-manufactory, and a foundry of German and English type. The name is printed Saur in the German imprints and Sower in the English.

Savage, William.—An English printer, and author of several valuable works on subjects connected with typography. He was born at Howden, in Yorkshire, where he commenced business with his brother James in 1790, as printer and bookseller. William removed to London in 1797, where he became distinguished as a printer, and published an excellent and handsomely illustrated work in 1822, under the title of Practical Thoughts on Decorative Printing. In 1832 he published another book, styled Preparations of Printing Inks, both black and colored; and in 1840 his best-known work, the Dictionary of the Art of Printing, appeared. This book is an octavo of 815 pages, written in a clear and practical style, prepared, in the words of the preface, in the hope that it might be placed in the hands of each printer's boy on entering the business. The author states that it is the work of his old age, and embraces all the information that half a century of practical experience has made him believe to be necessary to the practice of the art. William Savage died in 1843, at the age of seventy-three. His brother James was for many years engaged as an editor of journals and a contributor to the literary magazines; he was Assistant Librarian of the London Institute, and the author of a number of works, among the best-known of which is The Librarian, an account of scarce, valuable, and useful English books, manuscripts, etc.

Savant.—A man of learning. The word is adapted into English from the French, and frequently used in the plural as a term for the men of science, or literati.

Saxon or Anglo-Saxon.—The alphabet used in England from 596 to the middle of the seventh century. For the name and sound of the letters, see ANGLO-SAXON. A plan of cases of Saxon type, which is sometimes used in reprinting ancient records, the Saxon Gospels, etc., is given on page 397.

Scale of Prices.—The established wages of compositors and pressmen, as definitely and systematically arranged. One important and comprehensive American Scale is given elsewhere (see PRICES), and the variations from it, in other American cities, are mainly such as occur from difference 'in the cost of living, etc. The formation of detailed Scales of Prices is a comparatively modern movement. Timperley gives the following account of their origination in England, where compositors are paid by the thousand ens, which are supposed to represent the actual number of types composed, instead of the thousand ems, as in the United States:

The merit of forming the basis of the scale for regulating the price of the compositors' labor, certainly belongs to the [London] journeymen, who on April 6, 1785, submitted to the masters eight propositions imposing, correcting, etc., were more frequent. Antecedent to this time, whenever the compositor was paid by the thousand, he appears to have received for English type four-pence; for long-primer, three pence halfpenny; and for brevier, three pence farthing. In Scotland, at the same period, brevier type was paid two-pence halfpenny, and English type four-pence per thousand. Regarding Scotland, it appears

•	†	‡	¦	|	¶	☞							
								1 em	2 em	‿	⌣	⁓	
		]			–	—	1 em	2 em					
Æ	B	C	D	e	F	L	ꝝ						
Ð	I	K	L	œ	N	O	Þ						
P	Q	R	ſ	T	þ	ƿ							
X	Y	Z	Ð	U	]	)						hair spaces	

SAXON UPPER-CASE.

j	þ	3 em space	4 em space	·	k		1	2	3	4	5	6	7	8
þ					e									9
	b	c	ƀ				ſ		r	ſ	ʒ			0
ꝺ														
	l	m	n	h		o	ẏ	p	,	ſ	Eu quads.	Em quads.		
z														
x							;	:						
	ſ	u	ꞇ	3 em space.	a	ꝑ			Quadrats.					
ꝗ							.	-						

SAXON LOWER-CASE.

for this purpose, five of which were agreed to and three rejected by them, after they had been laid before them upwards of seven months. Previous to this year, the price paid for composition appears to have been regulated by the size of the type employed; upon the principle that the compositor was less liable to interruption when engaged in picking up his thousands of small type, than he was when employed upon large type, where the interruptions for making-up, that about the year 1763 a dispute arose in the office of Messrs. Murray and Cochrane, printers in Edinburgh, about the price of composition, when William Smellie, then engaged as a reader, devised a scale of prices for composition.

The first regular and acknowledged compositors' scale for the payment of piece-work is by one writer stated to have been agreed to at a general meeting of masters, who assembled in the month of November,

1785, to consider eight propositions submitted to them in a circular from the whole body of compositors, with a view to advance the price of labor. That part of the trade, however, who were most materially interested in the adjustment of the price of labor, namely, the compositors, do not appear to have been present when these propositions were discussed, or to have been permitted to offer any arguments in their favor; but the masters assumed the right to set a price upon the labor of others, although a short time afterwards they repelled with indignation an attempt of the booksellers to interfere with their decisions and profits. We are informed by another writer that the scale was not formed at a general meeting of masters, but by a committee who, after much labor and considerable discussion, agreed to a scale of prices which, although it has at different times been amplified and altered to suit the various circumstances of the times, and the different kinds of work as they occurred, has served as the basis of every other [English] scale.

In France the Scales of Prices are very elaborate, embracing many minute details. In November, 1868, a preliminary new Scale was formed at Paris, subject to revision by a mixed committee of masters and workmen, of which the following is a brief extract:

ART. 1.—The prices of composition are determined by the number of letters composed, taking for the base of the cast-up whatever letter recurs twenty-five times in the lower-case alphabet.

ART. 2.—Composition is paid per 1000 letters. Ordinary sizes of type range at 12½ cents (specie) per 1000 for MS.

ART. 3.—Any French work of which the orthography is different from modern usage will be charged as foreign—three cents extra.

ART. 6.—Foreign languages with accents. If the accents are not marked on the copy, the correction of them must not fall on the compositor. So for punctuation.

ART. 10.—Any work the cast-up of which does not exceed $10 (gold), to be cast up as manuscript.

ART. 11.—Copy badly written or arranged must be composed on time. The Commission arbitrale will decide disputed cases.

ART. 13.—Intercalations of caps and small-caps, italic, or any sort of type cast on the body of the font, are to be charged extra, at the rate of a half-centime a letter. (A long list exemplifying intercalations follows.)

ART. 17.—Corrections are paid at 12½ cents an hour at least.

ART. 21.—Distribution is paid at a fourth of reprint composition.

ART. 23.—Braces comprising two or three lines are paid, each, two cents; four or five lines, three cents.

ART. 29 regulates the prices payable for making up. The size of the paper and scheme of imposition are both taken into account. Sixty cents is paid for making up a sheet of ordinary 16mo.

ART. 30.—Making up to be done on the piece.

ART. 37.—Blank pages not to be deducted from the maker-up, except in folio size.

ART. 43.—Every note in a page is allowed 1 centime extra when the reference is in Arabic numerals between parentheses, and 2 centimes when superior figures, asterisks, or other signs are employed.

ART. 70.—The establishment wages fixed at not less than $1.12 (gold) for ten hours of work. Apprentices during the year following their apprenticeship, and old men, may fix their own price for their services.

ART. 71 treats of Sunday and night work. The former is paid five cents an hour extra. After midnight seven cents extra per hour; twelve and a half cents an hour is also allowed if the compositor is kept standing.

ART. 73 to ART. 85 detail the peculiarities of tables.

ART. 121.—A Permanent Arbitration Committee is to be constituted, consisting of an equal number of masters and journeymen, to settle occasional disputes.

ART. 125.—The present scale can be revised in five years from its taking effect. This revision to be conducted by a mixed conference of nine masters and nine workmen.

The Committee hope that no lad will be allowed to become an apprentice before the age of thirteen full years, nor unless he shows proof of having acquired sufficient education to enable him to follow the profession with advantage; and further, that his apprenticeship take place subject to the approval of the Committee of Arbitration.

Scenography.—The art of perspective, or the representation on a plane of an object as it appears to the eye.

Schedule.—A list of the names of compositors engaged on a given book, and the number of pages composed by them, systematically arranged. It was in universal use in American book-offices before the present make-up system was adopted, and was formerly passed with the make-up. Schedules are still used in all large book offices; being passed with the make-up when the compositors make up their own matter, and kept by the hand entrusted with this duty when he acts for the office. They constitute the standard record of the amount of work performed by each compositor, although matter is sometimes measured from galley proofs.

Scheme.—The system by which American founders proportion the weight or number of the respective sorts, letters, points, or characters embraced in a font of type. The equivalent for scheme in England is bill, and under that heading (see BILL) the English system of apportioning sorts is given. There is a slight variance in the schemes adopted by the different American type-founders, arising from a diversity of views, and a greater or less departure from old standards. It is impossible to cast to order a whole font of body-letter that will have exactly a given weight, and sorts are usually cast slightly in excess of the amount prescribed in the scheme.

Collins & McLeester's Scheme for a font of five hundred pounds makes the following allotment:

Lower case Letters	. .	263 pounds	13 ounces.
Points and References	.	19 "	6 "
Figures	. . . . .	13 "	12 "
Capitals	. . . . . .	36 "	10 "
Small Capitals	. . . .	17 "	—
Braces, Dashes, and Fractions	12 "	4 "
Spaces and Quads	. . .	97 "	14 "
Italic	. . . .	36 "	5 "

Total, 497 "

The details of this scheme are as follows:

SCHEME FOR 500 POUNDS.

Job-Letter Schemes vary materially with the size of fonts, and they are put up by count instead of weight. The general character of schemes for the smaller sizes of plain job-letter, is indicated by the Job Letter Scheme on page 400.

Schoeffer, Peter.—The assistant of Gutenberg and Fust, and the inventor of type-founding and other important improvements in printing. He was born in Gernsheim about 1430, and was a student in Paris in 1449, as is proved by a note-book in his handwriting, in which under that date he signed himself as Petrum of Gernsheim, alias Moguncia, student of the most glorious University of Paris. He was distinguished for his excellent penmanship, and became an illuminator in Paris, where the manufacture of manuscripts employed a large number of scribes, and where the decorative arts of illumination were carried to great perfection. The date of his return to Mentz is not known, but, as he was married to Christina Fust in 1455, it is probable that his connection with John Fust had commenced some years before, and it may be presumed that his special talents had been employed in furnishing the written decorative capitals to the first sheets of Gutenberg's Bible. When Fust, in 1455, obtained legal possession of the printing-material used by Gutenberg, he immediately took Schoeffer into partnership, and they published in 1457 the celebrated Psalter, which is remarkable for containing the date, the names of the partners, and the assertion that it was produced by the new art of printing. It also offers proof of the skill of Schoeffer in the fact that the capitals omitted in Gutenberg's Bible were printed

JOB LETTER SCHEME.

a	70	,	50			A	36
b	24	;	14			B	16
c	34	:	12			C	22
d	36	.	50			D	20
e	92	-	18			E	42
f	24	'	24			F	18
g	24	!	14			G	18
h	44	?	12			H	22
i	70	$	10			I	36
j	16	£	6			J	10
k	12					K	10
l	44					L	22
m	32					M	20
n	70					N	36
o	70					O	36
p	26					P	20
q	10					Q	8
r	70					R	36
s	70					S	36
t	70			1	16	T	36
u	34			2	12	U	20
v	12			3	12	V	10
w	20			4	12	W	12
x	10			5	12	X	8
y	24			6	12	Y	12
z	10			7	12	Z	8
æ	4			8	12	&	10
œ	4			9	12	Æ	10
fi	7			0	16	Œ	3
ff	7					Œ	3
fl	5						
ffi	4						
ffl	4						

in a most perfect and elegant style in two colors, and the rubric was also printed. Another edition of the same work, printed in three colors, was published in 1459. In the same year, the Durandus, a folio of one hundred and sixty leaves, in double columns of sixty-three lines each, must be considered as a special triumph of the new partnership, as it is in a new and finer type, more strictly conformed to the customary running Gothic penmanship popular at that time. Of this work, a single copy was sold in Venice in 1460 for about fifty dollars of our present money. The Constitutions of Clement V., printed in 1460, deserves special mention for the admirable method in which marginal notes are printed in a type smaller than the text. With the new type was also printed their great work, the Bible, bearing their names and the date 1462. This first dated Bible is sometimes styled the Mentz or forty-eight-line Bible, to distinguish it from the undated edition issued probably in 1455, styled the forty-two-line Bible (see GUTENBERG). This handsome work, splendidly adorned with colored capitals, contained one thousand and one pages in double column.

The siege of Mentz in 1462 interrupted the labors of the printers and dispersed their assistants, and Fust, availing himself of the enforced leisure following the fortunes of war, took a large number of the Bibles to Paris, where he died in 1466. The imprint of St. Thomas Aquinas, published in 1467, contains only the name of Schoeffer, and in the same year he signed a receipt for the sale of some books, styling himself proudly, impressor librorum, printer of books. In a poetical colophon to the Institutes of Justinian, published in 1468, Schoeffer took perhaps the first opportunity of presenting to the public a statement of the facts relating to the invention of printing, and it deserves especial consideration as being a record duly acknowledged by one of the inventors (see COLOPHONS). In the figurative and scriptural language of the time, it is asserted that Fust and Gutenberg furnished the material and the inventive skill, while Schoeffer introduced last into the work was the first to perfect it,—a boast which he might well make, in consideration of the remarkable mechanical skill, artistic taste, and inventive genius which he had exhibited. With equal zeal and talent Schoeffer continued his labors, which ended only with his life, for he printed a fourth edition of the Psalter in 1502, closing his career with the same book with which he commenced it, after nearly half a century of indefatigable industry. The work so well begun suffered no interruption, being instantly continued by his son, who with the name Johann Schoeffer assumed the honors inherited from the first generation of printers, and in 1505, in a dedication to the Emperor Maximilian, he reiterates with authority the true history of the invention, in words to the following effect:—May your Majesty deign to accept this book, printed at Mentz, the town in which the admirable art of typography was invented, in the year 1450, by John Gutenberg, and afterwards brought to perfection at the expense and by the labor of John Fust and Peter Schoeffer.

Obscurity veils all the facts regarding the origin of printing, and these doubts extend even to the orthography of the names of the inventors: that of Schoeffer appears occasionally in his own publications as Schoeffher, according to the German form, but as he usually wrote it in the more convenient shape of Schoeffer, the latter spelling has been generally adopted, and in the simpler form makes more evident its pleasant, peaceful signification,—a shepherd.

School-book.—A book intended for instruction in schools. This class of publications forms a very large proportion of the books printed in the United States.

Sciagraph.—The section of a building to exhibit the interior.

Science.—Any branch or species of knowledge, as moral science, natural science, physical science, etc.

Scientific Works.—Publications upon subjects relating to any of the sciences; the earlier books were upon rhetoric and the occult studies of astrology, etc. In modern times, works of scientific investigation, exploration, and discovery have furnished a vast amount of material for typographic labors and for the display of special skill.

Scrap-book.—A book in which scraps cut out of newspapers, prints, miscellaneous fugitive pieces, etc., are pasted for preservation.

*Schaeffer, Dr. Jacob Christian, was born at Querfurt in 1718, but removed to Regensburg, where, as clergyman and afterwards superintendent, he lived until his death in 1790. He is well known by his numerous works as an able and industrious naturalist. His work on the Fungi of Bavaria is still considered as a standard authority. We propose, however, to limit ourselves to the description of his work on Paper, before mentioned, and only refer to these particulars in order to show who he was, for some English writers on paper have treated him as an otherwise unknown man, writing in Low Dutch.

The title of his complete work is, *Jacob Christian Schäffer's Doctors der Gottesgelarkeit und Weltweisheit, etc., etc., etc., sämmtliche Papierversuche. Sechs Bände, Zweite Auflage. Nebst einundachtzig Nurstern und dreizehen theils illuminirten theils schwarzen Kuppfertafeln. Regensburg,* * * 1772. Or, *J. C. Schäffer's (LL.D., etc.) Complete Experiments on Paper. 6 vols., 2d ed., with 81 Specimens and 13 Copperplates, some of them colored. Regensburg,* 1772. The whole work is a stout small quarto, the volumes being but pamphlets, the text of the whole having 173 pages. As these appeared at different times, the early part was exhausted before the whole could be collected, and when so collected the title above calls it the second edition. Each of the separate volumes has a somewhat different title, and after the second volume the numbers begin again, but always specify the whole number of the entire series. We mention these particulars for the benefit of book-collectors who may find the volumes separately.

The fifth volume was intended to be the last, but the sixth was added to give a number of substances needing no special means of comminution previous to the beating—such as dye-wood after the color has been extracted.

The fanciful frontispiece represents all the operations of paper-making, naked little Cupids being the operators. Several elaborate plates represent the beating engine, which consists of a stout axis with pins or cams lifting the ends of levers carrying the beaters close to the cams and hinged at the other end. The beaters, five in number, operate in an oblong trough or mortar. The other plates, representing the plants employed, are colored, and, although somewhat rough, have enabled us to detect the plant, where an uncertain name was given.

These experiments seem to have been continued for about eight years; but the author was a very busy man in other ways. They were made in his own house and under his direct supervision. Three or four times, when he had a very tough material to deal with, he would send it to a neighboring paper-maker, whose stamps were much heavier than his own, and this was all of the work done out of his own house.

The mode of treatment is generally given with the utmost detail. The substances, according to their nature, were cut or chopped by hand. When woods are named, they were reduced with a toothed plane. In many cases they were put at once under the beaters. But quite often the milk of lime was used and the duration of the action noted. Where severer treatment was required, the material was left in a stiff lime paste for various lengths of time. Dr. S. notices the shortening of the beating produced by the lime treatment, as also the brown color produced by it on wood.

The author distinctly states that it was not his object to make fine paper, which would have required another engine, but that he left the materials in the condition of half-stuff, his object being only to prove the possibility of making paper from the various substances tried.

This should be kept in mind, for critics who have seen the specimens and not read the book have pronounced them to be poor paper.

Some of the specimens are sized, others are not, as the author considered that the nature of the stuff was better shown without size.

With most material one-twentieth part of rags was added.

It is quite curious to note the logical order in which substances were taken up—wasps' nests were already a sort of paper, he made paper from them; but the wasps got their material from wood, so he made paper of sawdust, the teeth of the saw representing the nippers of the wasp, and so on. Being engaged in an active correspondence, while his specimens were published, constant suggestions were made and experiments tried, so that no complete order for the whole could be observed.

It was frequently found that the same plant, collected at different times, gave quite different results, and if the supply was not sufficient the whole had to be done over again.

There is one quite curious instance of this. Experiments were made on potatoes, and it was found that paper could be made from the skins and also from the insides, but the author could not that year get potatoes enough to supply the quantity of paper needed for his specimens. To show how little known the potato then was (1767), we give a literal translation of the passage in which the author explains what it is and what are its uses (vol. v., p. 11):

The earth-apple [potato] is a kind of plant known particularly in Voigtland, France, Austria, and since some years also in Bavaria and the Pfalz, on whose fibrous roots there are produced, in the earth, uneven various-sized knotty and apple-like growths, which are known as earth-apples.

The earth-apples are an uncommonly useful vegetable for the kitchen and for all housekeeping, particularly where there is a scarcity of bread. Poor people in many places not only really eat these earth-apples, but the appetite is satisfied by them as well as by bread. They are used with certain preparations

* This article was received too late for insertion in strictly alphabetical order, but it appears here on a page very near its proper position.—ED.

26

as a not unpleasantly tasting vegetable; they are cooked with meat; they are made into a salad; they are also eaten raw, seasoned with a little salt and pepper; cakes are baked of them; meal and starch are made from them; and finally they are used as a good fodder for cattle. In a word, earth-apples serve for men and cattle as a good for everything [allerlei].

The book is full of useful information, and shows the observing and enterprising spirit of its author.

To make our notice of this curious work complete and useful for reference, we add a list of the specimens in each volume, the date of the volume being mentioned. The names are strictly the equivalent of the German names printed on the specimens; if the name given was generic, we have made it so, and add the species, if obtained from the book itself. The notes after the names refer to the peculiar part of the plant used, or to the mode of preparation.

Four of the specimens are marked as painted; these sheets form one of the curiosities of the book. The intention seems to have been the demonstration of one of the good properties of the paper, its capacity to bear color. The subject in all cases consists of flowers, wrought in body colors, in a rough but artistic way; each one is painted, and therefore original.

SPECIMENS OF PAPER IN THE WORK OF DR. J. C. SCHAEFFER.

Vol. I., 15th January, 1765.

1. Poplar down.
2. Wasps' nests.
3. Sawdust.
4. Shavings.
5. Beechwood.
6. Willow-wood.
7. Willow-wood without rags.
8. Tree-moss (a lichen. Usnea.)
9. Coral moss (a lichen. Cladonia.)
10. Aspen wood.
11. Hop vines, bark or bast.
12. "   " wood.
13. Grape-vine, outer bark.
14. "   inner bark and wood.
15. Fragments of nine of these papers.

Vol. II., 30th March, 1765.

1. Tow, hemp.
2. Mulberry tree, wood.
3. "   " inner bark.
4. Aloe leaves, A. Americana.
5. "   " fresh.
6. Clematis, bark.
7. "   wood.
8. Stinging nettle, bark.
9. "   " wood.
10. Willow, inner bark. ⎫
11. Cat-tail Typha, leaves. ⎬ Not in the
12. "   " ⎭ copy before us.
13. Earth moss, common moss.
14. Straw, barley.

15. Leaves of trees, wintered.
16. Blue cabbage stalks, red.
17. Scraps of uncolored specimens above.
18. "   " colored   "   "
19. Roof (sheathing) paper from tow.

Vol. III., 3d November, 1765.

1. Cyprian asbestos, mineral.
2. Seed down of woolen grass, cat-tail.
3. Thistle stalks, sized.
4. "   " unsized.
5. Burdock stalks.
6. Leaves of the lily of the valley, 1 day in lime.
7. "   "   "   "   " 6 days "
8. "   "   "   "   " 3 weeks rotted in water.
9. Seed down of the thistle.
10. Water moss, Conferva, with white rags.
11. "   "   "   " black "
12. Bavarian turf, (peat).
13. Hanoverian turf.
14. Poplar down thread, knit. ⎫ Fabrics.
15. "   "   " woven in colors. ⎪ two parts
16. "   "   " plain. ⎬ down, 1
17. "   "   " and printed. ⎭ p't cotton

Vol. IV., 1st January, 1766.

1. Silk plant, seed down of Asclepias.
2. Mallow.
3. Orache. Artiplex.
4. Spruce fir wood.
5. Artemisia, wood.
6. "   bark.
7. Indian corn husks, treated with lime.
8. "   "   "   " without lime.
9. Young grape-vines.
10. Mixed scraps from the foregoing.
11. Lace from Aloe fibre.

Vol. V., 13th April, 1767.

1. Genista.
2. Pine cones, painted.
3. "   " colored for sugar paper.
4. Potatoes, from skins.
5. "   from insides, painted.
6. Old shingles, painted.
7. "   "
9. Mixed scraps from all specimens of the 5 vols.

Vol. VI., 1771.

1. Reed.
2. Bean leaves.
3. Horse-chestnut leaves.
4. Tulip leaves.
5. Linden leaves.
6. Walnut leaves.
7. Genista, after extracting the dye.
8. Yellow wood, "   "   "
9. Brazil wood, "   "   "
10. Mixed scraps from the nine kinds above.

Scraper.—An instrument used by steel-engravers.

Scratched Figures.—Figures over which a line is drawn, represented by type. They are sometimes used in arithmetical or mathematical works; and are frequently called canceled figures.

Scrawl.—Unskillful and inelegant manuscript.

Screw-Press.—A machine for communicating pressure by means of a screw or screws; one class of standing-presses.

Scribble.—Writing which is careless either in appearance or expression of thought; hasty composition.

Scribe.—A public or professional penman.

Scrip.—A schedule or small writing; also a certificate given as evidence of property or interest possessed, as the scrip issued sometimes by corporations to their stockholders or creditors.

Script.—Types cast in imitation of various styles of writing. Nearly one hundred varieties of script are now made in the United States, a few of which are illustrated in the specimens accompanying the article on JOB-LETTER. Such peculiar difficulties attend the manufacture of script type, on account of the projection of the face over the shank, that it was scarcely attempted until the last century, and the first productions were exceedingly stiff, formal, and clumsy. In 1815, Didot & Sons, of Paris, devised a new method of casting script on a rhomboidal shank, with triangular blocks having a corresponding angle on one side, and the other two sides forming a right angle, with which to justify the beginnings and endings of lines. This and subsequent improvements in type-casting have enabled type-founders to make script of great freedom, beauty, and elegance, so that any regular style of handwriting can now be closely imitated. Script letters embracing very acute angles are now readily cast on oblong bodies, the projections being supported by kerns; and a number of styles of perpendicular script have been invented which do not require kerns. Bruce's Specimen Book contains a very large display of varieties, its list beginning with a Double Small Pica Script, cut by George Bruce, for which he obtained the first United States patent granted, under the act of August 29, 1842, for a design of new type. Among the names applied to various styles of script are the following: running-hand, copper-plate, Italian, national, Italian secretary, graphotype, title-script, meridian, meridian ornamented, caligraph, ronde, secretary, circular, Venetian, hair-line, Madisonian, paint-brush, etc.

Scrivener.—One who draws contracts and legal documents.

Scroll.—A paper or parchment usually containing writing and rolled up. This was an early form of manuscript, called by the Romans volumen, or roll, from which has been derived the word volume. Scroll is also used for the flourish made at the end of a signature, representing a seal.

Secretary-Gothic.—The easy or running style of handwriting prevalent in Germany in the fifteenth century, and imitated by Schoeffer in the smaller type

used first in the Durandus of 1459. It was also used by Caxton. (See FAC-SIMILE.) The secretary-gothic and the black-letter, or larger and more formal Gothic character, prevailed in Germany, France, England, and even in Italy, for some years after the introduction of printing.

Secrets of Printing-Offices.—The extension of education which especially marked the fifteenth century in Europe had made manuscripts very valuable, and some of the earliest specimens of printing were sold as manuscripts,—a species of extra remuneration which the printers were justly entitled to reap for a short time, as a repayment for the special difficulties under which they labored. The processes of what was long termed the art and mystery of printing were preserved as a secret, by Gutenberg, Fust, and Schoeffer, for a few years (their workmen being probably sworn or pledged to secrecy), but with no dishonorable intention, as may be inferred from the fact that the publications of 1457 contain a proud and almost boastful assertion that they were manufactured by mechanical means. Jenson was dispatched privately by the King of France to study the new art; but no greater secrecy is to be presumed from this than necessarily attends the introduction of any new and useful invention that simplifies the manufacture of any article in general demand. From time to time certain distinguished typographers have endeavored to preserve as secrets some special process, which they considered as giving them particular advantages: thus, it is said that Baskerville would not reveal the ingredients of the ink, which, in his day, was considered remarkable for its blackness, and that Ibarra of Spain imitated his example, while Bodoni refused his most honored visitors admittance into one room of his printing-office, in which, it is supposed, he adopted peculiar methods for pressing sheets. Even at the present day some trade secrets are still closely guarded, although many things are freely proclaimed.

Another species of secrecy—that relating to the careful supervision of confidential public documents, books printed for secret societies, and the authorship of articles or pamphlets—has been most honorably maintained. When treaties are prematurely published in newspapers, the copy is obtained from some leaky or venal official, and not from any of the printers who set up or work off the original. So, too, where it is desirable to conceal the authorship of articles or books, this is rarely or never disclosed by a printer who becomes acquainted with it in the exercise of his calling.

Most honorable to the profession is the story of Harding, the printer, who bravely bore imprisonment rather than reveal the authorship of the Drapier Letters; and the printer sitting in his cell calmly refusing the entreaties of his friends must stand in a far nobler light than the church magnate and celebrated wit, who, dressed in the disguise of a low Irish clown, sat by, listening to the noble refusal and the tender importunities, only anxious that no word or glance from the unfortunate printer should reveal that beneath the rough dress of a poor peasant was hidden Dean Swift himself, bent solely upon securing his own safety at the expense of the printer. Swift cowered before the legal danger which Harding boldly confronted, and, unequally as the world has allotted the meed of fame to the two combatants, the wit and the printer both fought the battle for the liberty of the press, until the sense of an outraged community released the typographer from the peril so nobly encountered.

Sir Walter Scott's authorship of the Waverley Novels, although known by twenty persons, including a number of printers, was so well concealed that the great novelist could not, even in his matchless vocabulary, find words of praise sufficient to express the sense of his grateful acknowledgment and wondering admiration for the matchless fidelity with which his mystery had been preserved.

In thousands of other instances, similar fidelity has been exhibited, and it is a part of the professional honor of a printer, not to disclose wantonly, or from venal motives, the secrets of any office in which he is employed.

Saction.—A mark (§) used to denote minor divisions of a book or chapter; and also a reference to notes.

Sedan.—A series of works much esteemed by book-collectors are known as the Sedan editions, being printed in Sedan, France, by John Jannon. They are highly valued for their accuracy and the beauty and smallness of the type, corresponding to the modern Diamond. Especially famous are the Virgil dated 1625, the Horace of 1627, and the Greek Testament of 1628, all in 32mo, and the Great Bible according to the Geneva version, dated in 1633, in two volumes duodecimo.

Sematology.—The doctrine of the use of signs, particularly verbal signs, in the operations of thinking and reasoning, comprehending the theory of grammar, logic, and rhetoric.

Semichorus.—A chorus sung by a part of the choir, much used in the Greek drama.

Semicolon.—A point (;) used to separate members of a compound sentence, when something more than a comma, and something less than a colon, is required to divide them.

Senefelder, Alois, or Aloysius.—The Inventor of Lithography. He was the son of an actor employed in the Theatre Royal at Munich, and was sent by his father, at an early age, to study jurisprudence, in the University of Ingolstadt. The death of his father compelled him to leave college, and for two years he endeavored to support himself upon the stage. Being unsuccessful, however, he abandoned the attempt, and for a short time met with a moderate success as a dramatic author. During the publication of his works, Senefelder became interested in the processes of printing, and especially in the invention of a substitute for type.

His first experiments were directed toward the discovery of a means of stereotyping. He formed a composition of clay, fine sand, flour, and pulverized charcoal, mixed with a little water into a stiff paste, with which he made a mould from a page of type. In a quarter of an hour the mould became so firm that he took a perfect cast from it in melted sealing-wax, by means of a hand-press, and it is said that pulverized plaster of Paris, mixed with the sealing-wax, made the composition very hard. He also experimented by writing with a steel pen upon a copperplate covered with an etching ground, and afterwards biting it in with aquafortis. The copperplate proving too expensive for his limited fortune, Senefelder supplied its place with Killheim stone, the surface of which is readily polished. One day, when practicing his skill in writing backwards upon the stone, his mother requested him in great haste to make out a bill for a washwoman; he hurriedly wrote it with his stopping-out ink, when the thought crossed his mind that the lines thus written could be raised from the surface by the action of aquafortis upon the rest of the stone. He subsequently built a wall of wax, covered the surface with acid, and in a short time found that the writing was distinctly elevated above the rest of the stone. After this first step in lithography, he spent much time and considerable money without reaching any remunerative results, until a chance examination of very badly printed sheet-music suggested a new application of that art. In connection with a musician of the Elector's band, he printed several pieces of music upon a copperplate press, and found a considerable sale. The invention of a press suited to lithographic printing next occupied his attention, and, after many failures, he finally succeeded in erecting one, with the assistance of a music-publisher. Step by step he improved his processes and machinery, and obtained the exclusive privilege of exercising his art in Bavaria.

Senefelder was pecuniarily successful for several years, but his inventive genius urged him to spend so much time in experiments, that he found himself losing ground in Germany, and in 1800 he visited London, with the intention of establishing a lithographic printing establishment there. After a few months he returned to Munich, to find that his privilege had been infringed during his absence, and he was induced to superintend, in Vienna, a calico-printing establishment, the operations of which were to be conducted according to the principles of lithography. After several years of application to this labor, he was again thrown out of employment, and was finally rescued from poverty and misfortune in 1809, by being appointed inspector of the Royal Lithographic establishment in Munich. This position enabled him to devote much time to the improvement of the processes of his invention, and in 1819 he published an illustrated work upon the Elements of Lithography. This book was translated into English by Ackerman, a Saxon bookseller of London, who published a number of handsome works with lithographic illustrations, and also introduced the annuals by imitating a German popular publication in the Forget-Me-Not in 1823. Senefelder died in Munich in 1834, at the age of sixty-three. (See LITHOGRAPHY.)

Sensational.—By modern usage, literary composition of a character exciting to the feelings and imagination, generally descriptive of thrilling events and adventures, as a sensational novel or drama. The word is also used to describe a highly-wrought style, abounding in superlative description and incident.

Sentence.—A series of words so combined by the rules both of grammar and logic as to make complete sense, and usually marked at the conclusion by a period; the place of which is supplied in an interrogative sentence by an interrogation mark, and in an exclamatory sentence by an exclamation point.

Sepia.—A pigment prepared from the black fluid secreted by the cuttle-fish, or sepia, which the fish ejects to annoy its adversary and to darken the water and facilitate its own escape. This coloring matter was used as an ink by the ancients. It is of a fine brown tint, and is much employed in landscape-drawing. The early block-books were printed with a brown ink resembling sepia in color.

Septuagint.—The Greek version of the Hebrew Scriptures, made for the use of the Jews of Egypt at Alexandria, about 280 years before Christ, and named from the fact that seventy persons were said to have been engaged upon the translation.

Sequel.—In literature, the continuation of a former work, which was apparently complete in itself. Thus, a history, narrative, or novel, which has ended at an event or incident furnishing a logical or artistic conclusion, may be resumed in a sequel and carried on to a further development.

Serial.—A publication appearing in successive parts, as a magazine, or book published in parts; also a tale or other writing continued in the successive numbers of a periodical.

Series.—1. A word sometimes adopted by typefounders as a mark of distinction between styles of type of a similar body and general description; as, the first, second, and third series of Long Primer, etc. 2. A number of works or treatises published in separate and consecutive parts, each of which is complete in itself, yet furnishes an essential portion of a whole, as a series of treatises upon arithmetic, prepared to carry the scholar from the elementary stage through the intermediate studies into the higher range of mathematics. A work is also said to be illustrated by a series of plates or engravings.

Sermon.—A discourse delivered in public, usually by a clergyman, intended to convey religious instruction, and predicated upon a text or passage from the Scriptures. (See HOMILY.)

Set.—To compose type. A compositor is said to set type; to set a clean proof, etc.

Set Off.—A printed sheet is said to be set off when some of its ink is transferred to any sheet upon which it is laid. This is apt to occur with any work newly printed, when it is subjected to pressure; and to guard against loss from this cause, the sheets of book- or job-work are interleaved with blank or waste paper before they are placed in a standing-press. Set-off sheets are also often placed on tympans, and oiled paper, or paper saturated with benzine, may be advantageously used for this purpose. It is said that set-off paper, of great utility in wood-cut and fine printing, where it is necessary not to deprive the first working of the least particle of color, is obtained by the following process. Make, in two separate vessels, and with rain or distilled water, saturated solutions of carbonate of potash (pearlash) and tartaric acid. First put the paper to be used for setting off into the alkaline solution till it is thoroughly saturated with it, and then treat it similarly with the acid solution. The paper is used while still damp. The combination of the alkali with the tartaric acid causes the formation of innumerable little crystals of tartrate of potassium upon and within the paper, which possess such a repelling power towards fat, that paper thus prepared does not take the least particle of color off the first working.

Set-Off Sheets.—See SET OFF.

Seventy-two-mo.—A sheet of paper folded into seventy-two leaves, or one hundred and forty-four pages.

Shade.—The darker portion of a picture, also the minute degrees or variations of color, as a light or dark tint or shade of red ink.

Shaded.—A general name for many varieties of job-letter, in which the main character is shaded.

Shading.—Such lines, etc. as produce in a picture the effects of light and shade, as the darker side of a letter intended to give prominence to the form, or to produce the effect of solidity in the figure; also the coloring used to fill up an outline. In colored job-printing, shading is often effected by taking two impressions of a given line, the position of the type being slightly shifted for the second impression, and the color used on it being darker than that used on the first impression.

Shank.—The square metal upon which the face of a type stands.

Sharp Impression.—A clear and firm impression, with little indentation on the paper.

Sheep's-Foot.—An iron hammer, with a claw at one end, used in locking up forms, and also by pressmen.

SHEEP'S-FOOT.

Sheet.—A piece of paper of any of the regular sizes, which, by folding in folio, is prepared for writing upon, as a sheet of letter-paper; or which is printed upon at one impression, and may be afterwards folded into any of the various sizes. Card-board, pasteboard, etc. are also originally manufactured in

8vo.

No.	Sig.	No.	Sig.
1......1	A	545......69	3 T
9......2	B	553......70	3 U
17......3	C	561......71	3 V
25......4	D	569......72	3 W
33......5	E	577......73	3 X
41......6	F	585......74	3 Y
49......7	G	593......75	3 Z
57......8	H	601......76	4 A
65......9	I	609......77	4 B
73......10	K	617......78	4 C
81......11	L	625......79	4 D
89......12	M	633......80	4 E
97......13	N	641......81	4 F
105......14	O	649......82	4 G
113......15	P	657......83	4 H
121......16	Q	665......84	4 I
129......17	R	673......85	4 K
137......18	S	681......86	4 L
145......19	T	689......87	4 M
153......20	U	697......88	4 N
161......21	V	705......89	4 O
169......22	W	713......90	4 P
177......23	X	721......91	4 Q
185......24	Y	729......92	4 R
193......25	Z	737......93	4 S
201......26	2 A	745......94	4 T
209......27	2 B	753......95	4 U
217......28	2 C	761......96	4 V
225......29	2 D	769......97	4 W
233......30	2 E	777......98	4 X
241......31	2 F	785......99	4 Y
249......32	2 G	793......100	4 Z
257......33	2 H	801......101	5 A
265......34	2 I	809......102	5 B
273......35	2 K	817......103	5 C
281......36	2 L	825......104	5 D
289......37	2 M	833......105	5 E
297......38	2 N	841......106	5 F
305......39	2 O	849......107	5 G
313......40	2 P	857......108	5 H
321......41	2 Q	865......109	5 I
329......42	2 R	873......110	5 K
337......43	2 S	881......111	5 L
345......44	2 T	889......112	5 M
353......45	2 U	897......113	5 N
361......46	2 V	905......114	5 O
369......47	2 W	913......115	5 P
377......48	2 X	921......116	5 Q
385......49	2 Y	929......117	5 R
393......50	2 Z	937......118	5 S
401......51	3 A	945......119	5 T
409......52	3 B	953......120	5 U
417......53	3 C	961......121	5 V
425......54	3 D	969......122	5 W
433......55	3 E	977......123	5 X
441......56	3 F	985......124	5 Y
449......57	3 G	993......125	5 Z
457......58	3 H	1001......126	6 A
465......59	3 I	1009......127	6 B
473......60	3 K	1017......128	6 C
481......61	3 L	1025......129	6 D
489......62	3 M	1033......130	6 E
497......63	3 N	1041......131	6 F
505......64	3 O	1049......132	6 G
513......65	3 P	1057......133	6 H
521......66	3 Q	1065......134	6 I
529......67	3 R	1073......135	6 K
537......68	3 S	1081......136	6 L

12mo and

No.	Sig.	No.	Sig.
1......1	A	325......28	2 C
5......1*	A*	329......28*	2 C*
13......2	B	337......29	2 D
17......2*	B*	341......29*	2 D*
25......3	C	349......30	2 E
29......3*	C*	353......30*	2 E*
37......4	D	361......31	2 F
41......4*	D*	365......31*	2 F*
49......5	E	373......32	2 G
53......5*	E*	377......32*	2 G*
61......6	F	385......33	2 H
65......6*	F*	389......33*	2 H*
73......7	G	397......34	2 I
77......7*	G*	401......34*	2 I*
85......8	H	409......35	2 K
89......8*	H*	413......35*	2 K*
97......9	I	421......36	2 L
101......9*	I*	425......36*	2 L*
109......10	K	433......37	2 M
113......10*	K*	437......37*	2 M*
121......11	L	445......38	2 N
125......11*	L*	449......38*	2 N*
133......12	M	457......39	2 O
137......12*	M*	461......39*	2 O*
145......13	N	469......40	2 P
149......13*	N*	473......40*	2 P*
157......14	O	481......41	2 Q
161......14*	O*	485......41*	2 Q*
169......15	P	493......42	2 R
173......15*	P*	497......42*	2 R*
181......16	Q	505......43	2 S
185......16*	Q*	509......43*	2 S*
193......17	R	517......44	2 T
197......17*	R*	521......44*	2 T*
205......18	S	529......45	2 U
209......18*	S*	533......45*	2 U*
217......19	T	541......46	2 V
221......19*	T*	545......46*	2 V*
229......20	U	553......47	2 W
233......20*	U*	557......47*	2 W*
241......21	V	565......48	2 X
245......21*	V*	569......48*	2 X*
253......22	W	577......49	2 Y
257......22*	W*	581......49*	2 Y*
265......23	X	589......50	2 Z
269......23*	X*	593......50*	2 Z*
277......24	Y	601......51	3 A
281......24*	Y*	605......51*	3 A*
289......25	Z	613......52	3 B
293......25*	Z*	617......52*	3 B*
301......26	2 A	625......53	3 C
305......26*	2 A*	629......53*	3 C*
313......27	2 B	637......54	3 D
317......27*	2 B*	641......54*	3 D*

18 MO.

649	55	3 E
653	55*	3 E'
661	56	3 F
665	56*	3 F'
673	57	3 G
677	57*	3 G'
685	58	3 H
689	58*	3 H'
697	59	3 I
701	59*	3 I'
709	60	3 K
713	60*	3 K'
721	61	3 L
725	61*	3 L'
733	62	3 M
737	62*	3 M'
745	63	3 N
749	63*	3 N'
757	64	3 O
761	64*	3 O'
769	65	3 P
773	65*	3 P'
781	66	3 Q
785	66*	3 Q'
793	67	3 R
797	67*	3 R'
805	68	3 S
809	68*	3 S'
817	69	3 T
821	69*	3 T'
829	70	3 U
833	70*	3 U'
841	71	3 V
845	71*	3 V'
853	72	3 W
857	72*	3 W'
865	73	3 X
869	73*	3 X'
877	74	3 Y
881	74*	3 Y'
889	75	3 Z
893	75*	3 Z'
901	76	4 A
905	76*	4 A'
913	77	4 B
917	77*	4 B'
925	78	4 C
929	78*	4 C'
937	79	4 D
941	79*	4 D'
949	80	4 E
953	80*	4 E'
961	81	4 F
965	81*	4 F'

16 MO.

1	1	A
17	2	B
33	3	C
49	4	D
65	5	E
81	6	F
97	7	G
113	8	H
129	9	I
145	10	K
161	11	L
177	12	M
193	13	N
209	14	O
225	15	P
241	16	Q
257	17	R
273	18	S
289	19	T
305	20	U
321	21	V
337	22	W
353	23	X
369	24	Y
385	25	Z
401	26	2 A
417	27	2 B
433	28	2 C
449	29	2 D
465	30	2 E
481	31	2 F
497	32	2 G
513	33	2 H
529	34	2 I
545	35	2 K
561	36	2 L
577	37	2 M
593	38	2 N
609	39	2 O
625	40	2 P
641	41	2 Q
657	42	2 R
673	43	2 S
689	44	2 T
705	45	2 U
721	46	2 V
737	47	2 W
753	48	2 X
769	49	2 Y
785	50	2 Z
801	51	3 A
817	52	3 B
833	53	3 C
849	54	3 D
865	55	3 E
881	56	3 F
897	57	3 G
913	58	3 H
929	59	3 I
945	60	3 K
961	61	3 L
977	62	3 M
993	63	3 N
1009	64	3 O
1025	65	3 P
1041	66	3 Q
1057	67	3 R
1073	68	3 S

24 MO.

1	1	A	457	20	U
9	1*	A*	465	20*	
17		A'	473		U'
25	2	B	481	21	V
33	2*		489	21*	
41		B'	497		V'
49	3	C	505	22	W
57	3*		513	22*	
65		C'	521		W'
73	4	D	529	23	X
81	4*		537	23*	
89		D'	545		X'
97	5	E	553	24	Y
105	5*		561	24*	
113		E'	569		Y'
121	6	F	577	25	Z
129	6*		585	25*	
137		F'	593		Z'
145	7	G	601	26	2 A
153	7*		609	26*	
161		G'	617		2 A'
169	8	H	625	27	2 B
177	8*		633	27*	
185		H'	641		2 B'
193	9	I	649	28	2 C
201	9*		657	28*	
209		I'	665		2 C'
217	10	K	673	29	2 D
225	10*		681	29*	
233		K'	689		2 D'
241	11	L	697	30	2 E
249	11*		705	30*	
257		L'	713		2 E'
265	12	M	721	31	2 F
273	12*		729	31*	
281		M'	737		2 F'
289	13	N	745	32	2 G
297	13*		753	32*	
305		N'	761		2 G
313	14	O	769	33	2 H
321	14*		777	33*	
329		O'	785		2 H'
337	15	P	793	34	2 I
345	15*		801	34*	
353		P'	809		2 I'
361	16	Q	817	35	2 K
369	16*		825	35*	
377		Q'	833		2 K'
385	17	R	841	36	2 L
393	17*		849	36*	
401		R'	857		2 L'
409	18	S	865	37	2 M
417	18*		873	37*	
425		S'	881		2 M'
433	19	T	889	38	2 N
441	19*		897	38*	
449		T'	905		2 N'

sheets. A printed book is said to be in sheets before it is bound, whether it is folded or unfolded.

Sheridan Patent Sliding Knife Paper-Cutter.—A recently patented, useful, and powerful machine for cutting paper. As indicated by the name, the paper is cut by a sliding motion of the knife, the parts being so nicely adjusted as to raise the knife after cutting through the last sheet of paper. This machine is used extensively throughout the United States, and is alleged to be one of the most complete labor-saving appliances for cutting paper. It is made of various sizes, and adapted to hand- or steam-power.

SHERIDAN PATENT SLIDING KNIFE PAPER-CUTTER.

Shooting-Stick.—An implement used, in conjunction with a mallet, to drive the quoins in locking and unlocking forms. It was formerly made wholly of wood (dogwood or young hickory being considered the best material), but many shooting-sticks now have brass sockets.

Short Cross.—The short bar, which, crossing the long bar, divides book-chases into four quarters.

Short Letters.—Type which have the face cast on the middle of the upper end of the shank, as a, c, e, m, n, o, r, s, u, v, w, x, and z.

Short Page.—A page not full of printed matter, like that which usually appears at the end of a book, and generally at the end of each chapter or similar subdivision.

Shoulder.—The upper surface of the shank of a type not covered by a letter.

Show-Bill.—A large printed sheet containing an advertisement or announcement, displayed in large type, and so decorated with color, pictures, etc. as to attract public attention.

Show-Cards.—Cards of a comparatively large size, to be put up in public places, descriptive of a business, article offered for sale, an entertainment, etc.

Sibilant.—A letter that is uttered with a hissing of the voice, as s and z.

Side-Boxes.—The small boxes on the sides of the lower case.

Side-Notes.—Notes or matter descriptive of the text, or referring to parallel passages, etc., placed at the side of a page or column.

Siderography.—The art or practice of engraving on steel.

Side-Sorts.—Type in the side-boxes and upper-boxes of a case, consisting of characters not in frequent use.

Side-Sticks.—Sloping pieces of furniture placed on the outside of pages of type, and forming, in conjunction with the inner side of the chase, a wedge-shaped aperture in which the quoins are inserted.

Sigla.—Notes and abbreviations used in ancient manuscripts, inscriptions, coins, etc.

Signatures.—1. Letters of the alphabet, or figures, inserted consecutively at the bottom of the pages (usually near the left-hand corner) commencing each form of a book, to assist and direct bookbinders in gathering the sheets in proper order, and also to serve as a convenient guide in printing. 2. Each printed form of a book, as the first signature, or signature A.

It is said that signatures were in occasional use by writers of manuscripts, and that they were sometimes used in block-books, before the invention of movable type printing. But they were not adopted by the first printers, who used neither folios nor signatures, and consequently exacted from their bookbinders great care and vigilance in gathering. It is generally supposed that Anthony Zarot first put signatures in typographic works, in an edition of Terence published at Milan in 1470. They are said to have been used in the same year by Helias de Slouffen, at Bern, in Switzerland; and the date of the introduction of signatures in Venice is supposed to be marked by their appearance in the middle of a work printed in that city in 1474, which indicates that the printer had only become acquainted with the new improvement when this book had been half printed.

Letters and figures are both used as signatures in the United States and in England, but figures are generally preferred in this country, while small-capital letters are preferred in England. Signatures representing an off-cut or part of a sheet are usually distinguished by an asterisk (*) when figures are used. The frequency of their occurrence in a book of course depends upon the number of folds in the sheets, and there are folio, octavo, twelvemo, sixteenmo, eighteenmo, and other signatures. A table of those in most general use is given on pages 406-7. In signaturing a work, it is usual to designate the first page of the body of the work as 2 or B, leaving the title-page, preface, etc. to form the first signature.

Signs.—Types used as symbols or emblems representing objects, phrases, etc. recurring frequently in printed works of various descriptions. They are often termed Arbitrary Signs. The following is a list and explanation of the most important:

I. ASTRONOMICAL SIGNS,

Used in printing Almanacs and Astronomical works:

The Sun and Planets.

☉ Sun.	⊕ Earth.	♄ Saturn.
☿ Mercury.	♂ Mars.	♅ Uranus.
♀ Venus.	♃ Jupiter.	♆ Neptune.

Moon's Phases.

● New Moon.	◯ Full Moon.
☽ First Quarter.	☾ Last Quarter.

Aspects and Nodes.

☌ Conjunction;—indicating that the bodies have the same longitude, or right ascension; as, ☿ ☌ ☉; that is, Mercury is in conjunction with the sun.

⚹ Sextile;—indicating a difference of 60° in longitude, or right ascension.

☾, or ☉ Quintile;—indicating a difference of 72° in longitude, or right ascension.

□ Quadrature;—indicating a difference of 90° in longitude, or right ascension.

△ Trine;—indicating a difference of 120° in longitude, or right ascension.

☍ Opposition;—indicating a difference of 180° in longitude, or right ascension; as, ☉ ☍ ◯; that is, the sun is in opposition to the moon.

☊ Ascending Node;—called also Dragon's Head.

☋ Descending Node;—called also Dragon's Tail.

In the sign ☌, the circle represents the zodiac, or the heavens, and the little mark at the top the meeting of two bodies in the same point or place; in the sign ☍, the circles touch at points opposite to each other, or 180 degrees apart; the signs ⚹, □, △, are symbolical of the derivation of the words sextile, quartile, trine, from the Latin words sex, six, quatuor, four, tres, three, being figures composed of six, of four, and of three lines respectively; the signs ☊ and ☋ represent a dragon, and originated in the fancy of the ancient astronomers, who saw in the deviation from the ecliptic made by a planet in passing from one node to another a figure like that of a dragon, the belly being where the planet has the greatest latitude, and the head and tail the points of intersection with the ecliptic.

Signs of the Zodiac.

Spring Signs.	1. ♈ Aries, the Ram.
	2. ♉ Taurus, the Bull.
	3. ♊ Gemini, the Twins.
Summer Signs.	4. ♋ Cancer, the Crab.
	5. ♌ Leo, the Lion.
	6. ♍ Virgo, the Virgin.
Autumn Signs.	7. ♎ Libra, the Balance.
	8. ♏ Scorpio, the Scorpion.
	9. ♐ Sagittarius, the Archer.
Winter Signs.	10. ♑ Capricornus, the Goat.
	11. ♒ Aquarius, the Waterman.
	12. ♓ Pisces, the Fishes.

The sign ♈ represents the horns of a ram; ♉, the head and horns of a bull; ♊, the ancient statues of Castor and Pollux, which consisted of two pieces of wood joined together by two cross-pieces; ♋, the claws of a crab; ♌, a corruption of the Greek letter Λ, the initial of the Greek equivalent for lion; ♍, a corruption of the Greek word for virgin; ♎, a rude picture of a balance; ♏, the legs and tail of a scorpion, or, according to some, the tail only, including the sting and two or three of the joints nearest to it; ♐, an arrow just leaving the bow, of which a small portion is to be seen at the bottom of the character; ♑, a ligature combining two letters of the Greek word for a goat; ♒, waves of water; ♓, two fishes tied together with a string.

Asteroids or Minor Planets.

These were formerly represented by varied signs, but are now designated by numbers, indicating the order of their discovery and inclosed in circles, viz.:

① Ceres,	⑰ Thetis,	㉝ Polyhymnia,
② Pallas,	⑱ Melpomene,	㉞ Circe,
③ Juno,	⑲ Fortuna,	㉟ Leucothea,
④ Vesta,	⑳ Massilia,	㊱ Atalanta,
⑤ Astræa,	㉑ Lutetia,	㊲ Fides,
⑥ Hebe,	㉒ Calliope,	㊳ Leda,
⑦ Iris,	㉓ Thalia,	㊴ Letitia,
⑧ Flora,	㉔ Themis,	㊵ Harmonia,
⑨ Metis,	㉕ Phocæa,	㊶ Daphne,
⑩ Hygeia,	㉖ Proserpina,	㊷ Isis,
⑪ Parthenope,	㉗ Euterpe,	㊸ Ariadne,
⑫ Victoria,	㉘ Bellona,	㊹ Nysa,
⑬ Egeria,	㉙ Amphitrite,	㊺ Eugenia,
⑭ Irene,	㉚ Urania,	㊻ Hestia,
⑮ Eunomia,	㉛ Euphrosyne,	㊼ Aglaia,
⑯ Psyche,	㉜ Pomona,	㊽ Doris,
㊾ Pales,	㊿ Virginia.	

(The number of Asteroids, as far as discovered up to 1871, is 112.)

Signs and Abbreviations used in Notation.

a, or α	Mean distance.
α; or A. R.	Right ascension.
β	Celestial latitude.
D.	Diameter.
δ	Declination.
E.	East.
e	Eccentricity.
h. or ^{h}.	Hours; as, 6h., or 6^h.
i	Inclination; especially, inclination to the ecliptic.
L, l, or ϵ	Mean longitude in orbit.
λ	Longitude.
M.	Mass.
m. or ^{m}.	Minutes of time; as, 6m., or 6^m.
μ, or m	Mean daily motion.
N.	North.
ν, ☊, or L.	Longitude of ascending node.
π, or ϖ	Longitude of perihelion.
ρ, or R.	Radius, or radius vector.
S.	South.
s, or ^{s}.	Seconds of time; as, 10s., or 10^s.
T.	Time; periodic time.
W.	West.

ϕ (*a*.) Angle of eccentricity, or the angle whose sine is equal to *e*; (*b*.) Geographical latitude.

° Degrees.

′ Minutes of arc.

″ Seconds of arc.

II. BOTANICAL.

㊉, ⊙, ○, or ① An annual plant.

♂, ⊙⊙, ◗, or ② A biennial plant.

♃, or △ A shrub or plant with a woody stem.

△ An evergreen plant.

⊙ A monocarpous plant; that is, a plant, whether annual or biennial, that flowers but once.

♂, or ♂ A staminate or male flower; also, a plant bearing such flowers.

♀ A pistillate, fertile, or female flower; also, a plant bearing such flowers.

☿ A perfect or hermaphrodite flower; also, a plant bearing such flowers.

♂ ♀ Unisexual; that is, having the male and female flowers separate.

♂—♀ Monœcious, or having male and female flowers on the same plant.

♀:♂ Diœcious, or having male and female flowers on different plants.

☿ ♂ ♀ Polygamous; that is, having hermaphrodite, or perfect, and unisexual flowers on the same or different plants.

) Turning or winding to the left.

(Turning or winding to the right.

O= Having the cotyledons accumbent, and the radicle lateral.

O‖ Having the cotyledons incumbent, and the radicle dorsal.

O> Having the cotyledons conduplicate, and the radicle dorsal.

O‖‖ Having the cotyledons folded twice, and the radicle dorsal.

O‖‖‖ Having the cotyledons folded thrice, and the radicle dorsal.

∞, or 00 An indefinite number; when applied to stamens, more than twenty.

0 Wanting; none; indicating the absence of a part.

° Feet.

′ Inches. ″ Lines.

? Indicates doubt or uncertainty respecting that to which it is affixed or prefixed;—applied to the names of genera or species, of localities, of authors cited, and the like.

! Indicates certainty;—used as a mark of affirmation or authentication, as of a genus or species, and the opposite or counterpart of ?. When appended to the name of an author, it indicates that he has examined an authentic specimen of the plant referred to, and when appended to the name of a locality, that the writer has seen or collected specimens from that locality.

III. CHEMICAL.

. One equivalent of oxygen;—written above a symbol representing an element, and repeated to indicate two, three, or more equivalents.

, One equivalent of sulphur;—used in the same manner as the preceding.

A dash drawn across a symbol having either of the foregoing signs above it, denotes that two equivalents of the substance represented by the symbol are joined with the number of equivalents of oxygen or sulphur indicated by the dots or commas.

+ Indicates, in organic chemistry, a base or alkaloid, when placed above the initial letter of the name of the substance.

— Indicates, in organic chemistry, an acid, when placed above the initial letter of the name of the acid.

Every elementary substance is represented, in chemical notation, by a symbol consisting of the initial or abbreviation of its Latin name; as, H for hydrogen, O for oxygen, Ag. (from Argentum) for silver, and the like, each symbol, when used singly, always indicating a single atom or equivalent of the substance represented by it; thus, O stands for one atom or equivalent of oxygen, C for a single equivalent of carbon, and the others in like manner. A compound body made up of single equivalents of its constituents is represented by the two symbols of the respective constituents written side by side; as, HO, a compound of one equivalent of hydrogen with one of oxygen, forming water. To express more than one atom or equivalent of a substance, a number is used, either prefixed to the symbol, or, more commonly, written after it, below the line; as, 2O, or O_2, two equivalents of oxygen.

A secondary compound, as a salt, is indicated by writing the symbol of the constituent compounds one after another, with the sign + between them, the symbol of the base being always placed first; thus, $CaO + CO_2$ represents carbonate of lime. A comma is frequently used instead of the sign +, commonly to express a more intimate union than would be expressed by that sign. The period is also sometimes used to indicate a union more intimate than that denoted by the sign +, but less so than that implied by a comma. A number written before the symbol of a compound designates a corresponding number of equivalents of that compound; as, 3 SO_3, three equivalents of sulphuric acid. When the formula of the quantity contains several terms, those to which the figure applies are included in parentheses or brackets, to which the figure is prefixed; as, 3 ($CaO + SO_3$), three equivalents of sulphate of lime.

IV. MATHEMATICAL, ALGEBRAICAL, AND GEOMETRICAL.

+ Plus; and; more;—indicating addition; as, $a + b = c$; that is, *a* added to *b* makes a sum equal to *c*; $6 + 4 = 10$;—used also to indicate that figures have been omitted from the end of a number, or that the latter is approximately exact; as, the square root of 2 is 1.4142136+.

— Minus; less;—indicating subtraction; as, $a - b$

$= c$; that is, a less or diminished by b is equal to c; $6 - 4 = 2$.

$\pm$ or $\mp$ Plus or minus; ambiguous;—indicating that the number or quantity to which it is prefixed may have either of the signs $+$ or $-$; as, the square root of $4a^2$ is $\pm 2a$.

$\times$ Multiplied by; times; into; as, $a \times b = ab$; $6 \times 4 = 24$.

Multiplication is also often indicated by placing a dot between the factors, or by writing the latter, when not numerals, one after another without any sign: as, $a \times b \times c = a . b . c = abc$; $2 \times 3 \times 4 = 2 . 3 . 4 = 24$.

$\div$, or : Divided by; as, $a \div b$; that is, a divided by b; $6 \div 3 = 2$.

Division is also very often indicated by writing the divisor under the dividend, with a line between them; as, $\frac{a}{b}$; that is, a divided by b; $\frac{6}{3} = 2$.

$=$ Is equal to; equals; as, $(a + b) \times c = ac + bc$; $6 + 2 = 8$.

$>$ Is greater than; as, $a > b$; that is, a is greater than b; $6 > 5$.

$<$ Is less than; as, $a < b$; that is, a is less than b; $3 < 4$.

A sign is also used which means is not less than; —the contradictory of $<$; that is, a is not less than b, or, a may be equal to, or greater than, b, but can not be less than it.

Another sign is used meaning is not greater than; —the contradictory of $>$; that is, a is not greater than b; or, a may be equal to, or less than, b, but can not be greater than it.

$\backsim$ The difference between;—used to indicate the difference between two quantities without designating which is the greater; as, $a \backsim b$; that is, the difference between a and b.

$\propto$ Varies as; is proportional to; as, $a \propto b$; that is, a varies as b, or is dependent for its value upon b.

: Is to; the ratio of;	
:: As; equals;	—used to indicate geometrical proportion; as, $a : b :: c : d$; that is, a is to b as c is to d; or, the ratio of a to b equals the ratio of c to d.
‥ Minus; the arithmetical ratio of;	—used to indicate arithmetical proportion; as, $a \cdots b :: c \cdots d$; that is, $a - b = c - d$.
:: Equals; is equal to;	

∞ Indefinitely great; infinite; infinity; used to denote a quantity greater than any finite or assignable quantity.

0 Indefinitely small; infinitesimal;—used to denote a quantity less than any assignable quantity; also, as a numeral, naught; nothing; zero.

$\angle$ Angle; the angle; as, $\angle A B C = \angle D E F$; that is, the angle A B C is equal to the angle D E F;—less frequently written $>$.

$\wedge$, or $\wedge$ The angle between; as, ab, or $A \wedge B$; that is, the angle between the lines a and b, or A and B, respectively.

By some geometers, the angle between two lines, as

a and b, is also indicated by placing one of the letters denoting the inclosing lines over the other; as, $\frac{a}{b}$; that is, the angle between the lines a and b; sin.$\frac{a}{b}$; that is, the sine of the angle between the lines a and b.

$\llcorner$ Right angle; the right angle; as, $\llcorner A B C$; that is, the right angle A B C.

$\perp$ The perpendicular; perpendicular to; is perpendicular to; as, draw $A B \perp C D$; that is, draw A B perpendicular to C D.

$\parallel$ Parallel; parallel to; is parallel to; as, $A B \parallel C D$; that is, A B is parallel to C D.

$\leftarrow$ Equiangular; is equiangular to; as, $A B C D \leftarrow E F G H$; that is, the figure A B C D is equiangular to the figure E F G H.

O Circle; circumference; $360°$.

$\frown$ Arc of a circle; arc.

$\triangle$ Triangle; the triangle; as $\triangle A B C = \triangle D E F$; that is, the triangle A B C is equal to the triangle D E F.

$\square$ Square; the square; as, $\square A B C D$; that is, the square A B C D.

$\square$ Rectangle; the rectangle; as, $\square A B C D = \square E F G H$; that is, the rectangle A B C D equals the rectangle E F G H.

$\sqrt{}$, or $\sqrt{}$ Root;—indicating, when used without a figure placed above it, the square root; as, $\sqrt{4} = 2$; $\sqrt{4a^2} = 2a$. This symbol is called the radical sign. To denote any other than the square root, a figure (called the index) expressing the degree of the required root, is placed above the sign; as $\sqrt[3]{a}$, $\sqrt[4]{a}$, $\sqrt[5]{a}$, etc.; that is, the cube root, fifth root, tenth root, etc., of a.

This sign is merely a cursive modification of the letter r, which was used as an abbreviation of the Latin word *radix*, root. The root of a quantity is also denoted by a fractional index at the right-hand side of the quantity, and above it, the denominator of the index expressing the degree of the root; as,

$a^{\frac{1}{2}}$, $a^{\frac{1}{3}}$, $a^{\frac{1}{5}}$; that is, the square, cube, and fifth roots of a, respectively.

——— Vinculum,	
( ) Parenthesis,	indicate that the quantities to which they are applied, or which are inclosed by them, are to be taken together; as $\overline{x + y}$; $2 (a + b;)$ $a \times (b + c [c + d]);$ $+\frac{x}{y} \mid z.$
[ ], or { }, Brackets,	
$\mid$ Bar,	

f, or F Function; function of; as $y = f(x)$; that is, y is, or equals, a function of x.

Various other letters or signs are frequently used by mathematicians to indicate functions.

d Differential; as dx; that is, the differential of x.

δ Variation; as δx; that is, the variation of x.

$\triangle$ Finite difference.

D Differential co-efficient; derivative;—sometimes written also d.

$\int$ Integral; integral of;—indicating that the expression before which it is placed is to be integrated; as,

$\int 2x dx = x^2$; that is, the integral of $2x dx$ is x^2.

$\int_a^b$ denotes that the integral is to be taken between the value b of the variable and its value a. $\int^a$ denotes that the integral ends at the value a of the variable, and $\int^b$ that it begins at the value b. These forms must not be confounded with the similar one, indicating repeated integration, or with that indicating the integral with respect to a particular variable.

M The modulus of a system of logarithms;—used especially for the modulus of the common system of logarithms, the base of which is 10. In this system it is equal to 0.4342944819+.

g The force of gravity. Its value for any latitude is expressed by the formula $g = 32.17076 (1 - 0.00259 \cos. 2 \lambda)$, in which λ is the latitude given, and 32.17076 (that is, 32.17076 feet per second) the value of g at the latitude of 45°.

° Degrees; as, 60°; that is, sixty degrees.

′ Minutes of arc; as, 30′; that is, thirty minutes.

″ Seconds of arc; as, 20″; that is, twenty seconds.

R° Radius of a circle in degrees of arc, equal to 57°.29578.

R′ Radius in minutes of arc; equal to 3437′.7468.

R″ Radius in seconds of arc, equal to 206264″.8.

′, ″, ‴, etc. Accents used to mark the quantities of the same kind which are to be distinguished; as, a', a'', a''', etc., which are usually read a prime, a second, a third, etc.; a b' c'' ┐ a' b'' $c + a''$ b c'.

When the number of the accents would be greater than three, the corresponding Roman numerals are used instead of them; as, a', a'', a''', a^{iv}, a^v, a^{vi}, etc. The accents are often written below also; as, $a_{\prime}$, $a_{\prime\prime}$, $a_{\prime\prime\prime}$, a_{iv}, a_v, etc. Figures, and also letters, are sometimes used for the same purpose; as a^1, $\overset{2}{a}$, $\overset{3}{a}$, $\overset{4}{a}$, a_0, a_2, a_3, a_m, a_x, and the like.

^{1}, ^{2}, ^{3}, etc. Indices placed above, and at the right hand of quantities to denote that they are raised to powers whose degree is indicated by the figure; as, a^1; that is, the first power of a; a^2, the square or second power of a; a^3, the cube or third power of a.

These signs are also often used to indicate the repetition of an operation; as d^2x, d^3x, d^4x, etc., indicating that the operation of differentiation has been performed upon x two, three, four, &c. times. As used to indicate powers, they are often preceded by the negative sign to indicate the reciprocal of the corresponding power, or an inverse operation; a^{-1}, a^{-2}, a^{-3}, a^{-4}, etc., which are respectively equivalent to $\frac{1}{a^1}$, $\frac{1}{a^2}$, $\frac{1}{a^3}$, $\frac{1}{a^4}$, etc.

sin. x. The sine of x; that is, of the arc represented by x. In the same manner cos. x, tan. x, cot. x, sec. x, cosec. x, versin. x, and covers. x, denote, respectively, the cosine, tangent, cotangent, secant, cosecant, versed sine, and coversed sine of the arc represented by x.

sin.^{-1}x. The arc whose sine is x. In the same manner cos.^{-1}x, tan.^{-1}x, cot.^{-1}x, sec.^{-1}x, cosec. ^{-1}x, versin.^{-1}x, and covers.^{-1}x, are used to denote, respectively, the arc whose cosine, tangent, cotangent, secant, cosecant, versed sine, or coversed sine is x.

This sign must not be confounded with the negative index, designating the reciprocal of a quantity, which would be applied to a parenthesis, inclosing one of these expressions; as, (sin. x)$^{-1}$, which is equivalent to $\frac{1}{\sin. x}$.

(See ARABIC FIGURES and NUMERALS.)

V.—MEDICAL SIGNS AND ABBREVIATIONS.

℞ stands for Recipe, or Take.

ā, āā, of each a like quantity.

℔ a pound.

℥ an ounce.

ℨ a drachm.

Ɂ a scruple.

i stands for 1; ij for 2.

ss. signifies semi, or half.

gr. denotes a grain.

P. stands for *particula*, a little part, and means so much as can be taken between the ends of two fingers.

P. æq. stands for *partes æquales*, or equal parts.

q. s. *quantum sufficit*, or as much as is sufficient.

q. p. *quantum placit*, or as much as you please.

s. a. *secundem artem*, or according to art.

In medical works, the quantities, in the formulæ, are set in lower-case letters. If the number end with an i, a *j* is always used in its place; as, *viij* instead of *viii*, *xj* instead of *xi*, etc.

VI.—MONETARY AND COMMERCIAL.

$ Dollar, or dollars; as, $1; $200.

ƒ Cent, or cents; as, 12ƒ; 33ƒ.

∕ Shilling, or shillings; as, ¼=1s. 8d.; ½=2s. 3d.

£ Pound, or pounds (sterling); as, £1; £45.

℔ Pound, or pounds (in weight); as, 1℔; 24℔.

@ At, or to; as, silk @ $2 per yd.; flour per bar. $8 @ $10.50.

₱ Per; as, sheep $4 ₱ head.

% Per cent.; as, discount 6% = $10.21.

℀ Account; as, J. Smith in ℀ with J. Jones.

A 1 The designation of a first-class vessel, in Lloyd's Register of British and Foreign Shipping; the letter denoting that the hull is well built and seaworthy, and the figure the efficient state of her rigging, anchors, cables, stores, etc. The figure 2 would imply that these were insufficient in quantity, or of an inferior quality. When a vessel has passed the age for the character A (four to fifteen years), it is registered A in red.

Æ The designation of a vessel of the third class, fit to convey perishable goods on short voyages only.

E The designation of a vessel fit for carrying on a voyage of any length, such goods only as are not liable to sea-damage.

I The designation of a vessel fit for carrying goods of the same sort on shorter voyages only.

M C Letters used to indicate that the boilers and machinery of a steam vessel have been inspected and found to be in good order and safe working condition.

XX Ale of double strength.

XXX Ale of triple strength.

@	to.	exch°	exchange.
ac., acct.	account	e | e	errors excepted.
₡ ᶜ	account current.	fm.	from.
Agt., Agᵗ	Agent.	gall.	gallon.
&	and.	h | a	his account.
at 3 m. dᵗᵉ	at 3 m'ths' date.	hhd.	hogshead.
bᵐ	bales.	Int.	Interest.
bᵗ	bought.	ldg.	loading.
brl., bbl.	barrels.	M.	thousand.
brot.	brought.	mdz.,mdˢ	merchandise.
bu., bush.	bushels.	mkt.	market.
bxs., bˣˢ	boxes.	mo., mos.	month, months.
cld., clᵈ	cleared.	No.	Number.
Co.	Company.	ord.	order.
Cr., Cʳ	Creditor.	oz.	ounce.
ct., cts.	cent, cents.	pble.	payable.
cwt.	hundred weig't.	° | ° p. ct.	per cent.
d dᵗᵉ	days' date.	pks., pᵏˢ	packages.
Dr., Dʳ	Debtor.	Recᵈ	Received.
dft.	draft.	Recpᵗ	Receipt.
disg.	discharging.	sld., slᵈ	sailed.
do.	ditto.	ᵗ,ᵃ	their account.
doz.	dozen.	tᶜᵉˢ	tierces.
ds.	days.	wt.	weight.
d st.	day's sight.	yd.	yard.
dupᵉ	duplicate.		

VII. MUSICAL.

Staff; the five lines with the four spaces between them, used to indicate the relative position of notes in the scale, as regards pitch.

When these are not sufficient, other lines are added above or below them, according to the necessities of the case, and are called leger lines, or added lines.

Bar;—the line drawn perpendicularly across the staff to separate measures of equal or given lengths. Double bar;—used to mark the larger divisions of a piece, especially in psalm or hymn tunes, songs, and the like, to mark the end of a verse or sentence.

Close;—used to indicate the end of a composition;—often written

Notes; characters placed upon the lines or spaces of the staff, indicating, by their form and position, the length and pitch of the tones which they represent. The notes here given are called, respectively, semibreve, minim, crotchet, quaver, semiquaver, and demi-semiquaver, each figure after the first indicating a tone of one-half the length of that represented by the figure immediately preceding it. A dot after a note adds to it one-

half of the length of the same note with the dot; thus, is equal to ; is equal to .

The stems of the notes are turned either upward or downward, as is most convenient in placing them on the staff; thus,

Besides these, the breve was formerly used, it being twice the length of the semibreve. It is still occasionally used in chorals and similar compositions. Two other characters, the long, equal to two breves, and the large, equal to two longs, or four breves, and the longest note ever used, were employed in ancient music. More than three strokes are sometimes attached to the stem of the note in very quick passages. When two or more tailed notes come together, they are often connected by the tails or strokes; as,

When many notes of the same kind are to be used, an abbreviated notation is sometimes employed. The strokes —, ═, ≡ etc., placed over a note, or written across the stem of it, signify that it is to be divided into quavers, semiquavers, demisemiquavers, etc., respectively.

These marks are also used to direct the repetition of groups of notes preceding them in the same measure.

₃, ₅, ₇, etc., are marks placed over groups of notes, and used to indicate that 3, 5, 7, etc. notes (all equal) are to be performed in the time of 2, 4, 6, etc. notes of the same kind respectively; as and which are performed in the same time as and respectively.

Rests;—characters indicating silence, or a pause in the performance, the length of the pause being indicated by the form of the character. Thus, the characters here given, taken in their order, indicate pauses of the same length as the following notes respectively.

More than three hooks or strokes may be attached to the stems of the rests, to indicate shorter pauses corresponding to the shorter notes. Rests may be lengthened in the same manner as notes, by placing a dot or two dots after them. A rest, or pause of a whole measure, is indicated by the mark ▬ placed upon the fourth line, the figure 1 being written above; and to express a rest of two, three, etc. measures, a similar notation is used; or sometimes, for the larger numbers, a heavy stroke in the measure, over which is written the number of measures included in the rest or pause.

G clef; —placed upon the second line, to indicate that every note upon that line is to be sounded as G of the natural scale;—called also treble clef. F clef;—placed upon the fourth line, to indicate that every note upon that line is to be sounded as F of the natural scale, an octave lower than the F of the first space of the treble clef;—called also bass clef.

C clef;—indicating that every note upon the line or space on which the character is placed is to be sounded as C of the natural scale;—called also tenor clef. This sign is not fixed like the preceding two, but may have four different positions on the staff.

Flat;—used to indicate that the note before which it is placed is to be sounded lower by a half-step than the same note without the sign. When placed on a line or space at the beginning of a piece, it signifies that every note on such line or space is to be sounded lower by a half-step than in the natural scale.

This character is a modification of the letter B, originally introduced to avoid the tritone, or sharp fourth, between F and B natural.

Double flat;—used to lower a note, already flatted, a half-step.

Single flat, as used after a double flat.

Sharp;—used to indicate that the note before which it is placed is to be sounded higher by a half-step than the same note without it. It is applied in the same way as the flat.

This character was originally designed to represent, by its four cross-lines, the four commas of the chromatic scale.—The sharps or flats placed at the beginning of a piece to determine the key or pitch are called the signature of the piece.

Double sharp;—used to raise a note, already sharped, a half-step.

Single sharp, as used after a double sharp.

Natural;—used to contradict, or counteract the effect of, a previous ♯ or ♭ either expressed or implied.

Repeat;—placed at the end of a passage to denote that it is to be performed a second time. Sometimes the dots are placed at the beginning of the passage. Heavy marks are occasionally added above and below the character, to enable the performer to distinguish the beginning or end of the passage to be repeated, or to call his attention to the repeat, as,

℃, or ℄ Characters marking common time; the former indicating two minims, the latter four crotchets, in a bar.

𝄋 Sign;—used to mark the point to which reference is made, or from which the repetition of a passage is to begin.

♩ or ♪ Appoggiatura, or leaning note; an embellishment consisting of a note placed before another note, one step or half-step either above or below the latter, and usually taking half the time of the principal note.

𝆷 An embellishment consisting of two appoggiaturas, moving by regular degrees to the principal note.

♪, or ♫ Acciaccatura;—an embellishment very similar to the appoggiatura, but performed much more lightly and quickly. When written with a stroke across it, as in the second example, it is performed very quickly, being, as it were, driven into the following note.

∿∿ A species of acciaccatura;—sometimes called double acciaccatura. It consists of two notes, the first of which is the same as that over which the character is placed, and the second a step or half-step above.

∾ Turn;—indicating an embellishment consisting of the note over which the character is placed, the note above it, and the semitone below it, performed in quick succession, generally as a triplet.

When the note above is flatted, the character is written ♭; when the note below is sharped, it is written. It may also be written with the natural sign [♮] ♯ in place of either of these, when the corresponding note should have that sign placed before it.

𝄒 Inverted turn, consisting of the same notes as the turn, performed in reverse order.

tr Trill; shake;—indicating that the note to which it belongs is to be rapidly alternated with the note above. A waving line is often added after it, indicating how far the shake is to be extended.

<<< or ～ Vibration;—indicating the rapid repetition of an emphasis upon the same note, as if three, four, or even a greater number of notes, somewhat staccato, were played instead of the note over which it is placed. It also sometimes denotes that the note is to be sounded in a tremulous manner.

𝄇 Arpeggio;—used in piano music, to denote that the notes of the chord before which it is written are not to be struck simultaneously, but in quick succession.

⁀ Pause, or hold;—indicating that the note or rest over or under which it is placed is to be prolonged at the pleasure of the performer. It is sometimes placed over the close, to denote that the strain which it ends forms the conclusion of the piece.

▭ Organ tone;—indicating that the sound is to be evenly and uniformly maintained, that is, with a uniform loudness;—not often used.

◁ Crescendo;—indicating that the volume of sound is to be gradually increased.

▷ Decrescendo; diminuendo;—indicating that the volume of sound is to be gradually diminished.

◁▷ Swell;—indicating a gradual increase or crescendo followed by a gradual decrease or decrescendo.

▷◁ indicates a gradual decrease followed by a gradual increase of sound.

> Sforzando, or Forzando;—indicating that the note or cord, over or under which it is placed, is to be struck with a force and an emphasis which are immediately diminished;—written also ∧, or ∨, or indicated by the abbreviation *fz* or *sf*.

The marks +, and ┬, are also sometimes used with the same signification.

< Pressure tone;—indicating that a sound begun soft is to be instantly increased to a loud tone.

' Staccato;—placed over or under a note, to indicate that it is to be struck with force, and performed in a short, sharp, emphatic manner.

" indicates that the note is to be performed in a manner similar to the staccato, but not so emphatically and sharply.

To indicate a still lower degree of emphasis and distinctness, the slur is sometimes written over the dots; as, ⁀······

⁀, or ⁀ Slur; tie;—indicating that the notes over or under which it is placed are to be performed in a smooth, connected manner. It is also used to connect two or more notes which are to be sung to one syllable, or to be united into one long note.

{ Brace;—used to connect those staffs of a composition or score which are to be performed together.

∿ Direct;—placed on that line or space at the end of a staff, which is occupied by the first note of the following staff, to indicate the position of the latter to the performer. It is now rarely used.

♩ = 80, ♩ = 60, etc. A notation used in indicating the proper time of a piece. Thus, ♩ = 80 ♩ = 60, etc., denote respectively that 80 crotchets or quarter-notes, and 60 minims or half-notes, are to be performed in one minute; or that each note of the kind indicated is performed in the time of one vibration of the pendulum of a metronome, when the nut is set at 80 or 60, etc., respectively.

✳, ⊕, or ☒. Characters used in music for the pianoforte, directing the use of the pedals. The last two are less frequently used.

✳, or ✳. A mark used after the preceding, and directing a discontinuance of the use of the pedals.

◻, or ∧ . Characters sometimes used in music for the violin, the former to indicate a down bow, the latter an up bow.

△ indicates a phrase, or incomplete musical idea.

⊐ indicates a section, or complete but not independent idea.

◯ indicates a period, or complete and independent musical sentence.

The ordinary marks of punctuation (, ; : .) are used by some composers instead of these three characters, or for a similar purpose.

ƒ Forte; with a loud sound.

ƒƒ Fortissimo; with a sound louder than a forte.

ƒƒƒ indicates a still louder sound, the loudest the voice or instrument is capable of producing.

ƒz Forzando, or Sforzando;—indicating that the note is to be struck with force and emphasis, which are immediately diminished; the same as > ,∧ ,∨ , or sƒ. It is also sometimes indicated by the letters ƒp.

m Mezzo; with a sound of medium strength or loudness.

mƒ Mezzo forte; with a moderately loud sound.

p Piano; with a soft or low sound.

pp Pianissimo; with a sound softer than piano, but firm and audible.

ppp is sometimes used to denote a very low or soft sound, softer than pianissimo.

rf, or rfz Rinforzando, or Sforzando; the same as >, ƒz, or sf.

sf Sforzando, or Forzando. See and ƒz.

VIII. TYPOGRAPHICAL.
See PUNCTUATION and PROOF-READING.

IX. MISCELLANEOUS.

&, &, & And.

&c. (Et cætera). And the rest; and so forth; and so on; and the like.

℟ Response;—used in Roman Catholic service-books.

℣ Versicle;—used in service-books in the Roman Catholic Church to denote the part recited or sung by the priest, or person who presides at the office or prayers.

* A character used in Roman Catholic service-books to divide each verse of a psalm into two parts, and show where the response begins.

✠, or ✠ A sign of the cross used by the pope, and by Roman Catholic bishops and archbishops, immediately before the subscription of their names. In Roman Catholic service-books, it is used in those places of the prayers and benediction where the priest is to make the sign of the cross.

↰ Broad Arrow; a British government mark, stamped, cut, or otherwise fixed on all solid materials used in the royal ships or dock-yards, in order to prevent embezzlement of naval stores.

×, or + A character customarily made by persons unable to write, when they are required to execute instruments of any kind, as deeds, affidavits, etc. The name of the party is added by some one who can write; as

John × Smith   his
mark.

4to, or 4°. Quarto; four leaves or eight pages, to a sheet.

8vo, or 8°. Octavo; eight leaves, or sixteen pages, to a sheet.

12mo, or 12°. Duodecimo; twelve leaves, or twenty-four pages, to a sheet.

16mo, or 16°. Sexto-decimo; sixteen leaves, or thirty-two pages, to a sheet.

18mo, or 18°. Octo-decimo; eighteen leaves, or thirty-six pages, to a sheet.

Other sizes are 24mo, or 24° (Vigesimo-quarto), 32mo, or 32° (Trigesimo-secundo), 36mo, or 36° (Trigesimo-sexto), 48mo, or 48° (Quadrigesimo-sexto), 64mo, or 64° (Sexagesimo-quarto), 72mo, or 72° (Septuagesimo-secundo), 96mo, or 96° (Nonagesimo-sexto), 128mo, or 128° (Centesimo et vigesimo-octavo). These sizes are of rare occurrence, and are not commonly known by their Latin names, but are colloquially called twenty-four-mo, thirty-two-mo, etc., or twenty-fours, thirty-twos, etc.

7ber, September; 8ber, October; 9ber, November; 10ber, December.

X. MASONIC SIGNS.

Silhouette.—A profile picture or portrait, made by cutting away the substance of the paper, so as to display a black surface beneath, thus making the picture appear in black. It is said that pictures thus produced by abstracting the material were named from Silhouette, a French minister of finance, in 1759, who introduced strenuous methods of retrenchment, while his opponents endeavored to make him an object of public derision by naming after him jackets without sleeves, pantaloons without pockets, cut-out pictures, outline pictures traced from shadows, etc. Silhouette portraits, cut out as above, enjoyed a temporary demand in some parts of the United States in the early years of the present century, and an imitation of them, in the shape of a profile presentment, printed in unshaded black upon white, has been recently much employed in wood-engraving, as a method of illustration. According to the latter use of the term, the figures upon the Etruscan vases, and the Egyptian hieroglyphic representations, might also be styled Silhouettes.

Simile.—A form of expression in which the subject is compared to another having some similarity, with the intention of rendering the description more clear and forcible. It frequently occurs, both in prose and verse, and is often as necessary to the explanation of the thought, as it is ornamental to the language. A comparison intended for illustration should be instituted between things of different species, so that the resemblance pointed out may appear surprising and striking.

Single-Cylinder Presses.—Presses having but one cylinder.

Sixteens, or Sixteen-mo.—A sheet of paper folded into sixteen leaves or thirty-two pages. Books of the size commonly termed octavo are now usually printed in forms of sixteen pages, on double-medium sheets of paper, measuring twenty-four by thirty-eight inches.

Sixty-fours, or Sixty-four-mo.—A sheet of paper folded into sixty-four leaves, or one hundred and twenty-eight pages.

Size.—A sticky substance, used in printing forms which are to be bronzed, and sometimes in mixing colored inks. The following is said to be a good recipe for making it. Take one pint of rosin oil, and six ounces of powdered rosin; and while the oil is boiling over a steady fire, pour in the rosin very slowly, until it attains the consistency of thick mo-

lasses—stirring it constantly. You can test its powers of adhesion, while it is boiling, by dropping a little upon a glazed card and allowing it to cool. It improves when kept closely boxed. When you are prepared to work, take a tablespoonful, and mull in a little ground Turkey umber. Colors must be mulled in also,—rendering down with burnt oil, Canada balsam, or copaiba balm. This preparation lends a pleasing brilliancy to colors, when worked upon a good surface, with ordinary care.

Sketch.—1. An unfinished or rough draught of any kind of literary composition or of a picture. 2. A short essay or writing of a descriptive character, but of a construction simpler than that of a tale, like those contained in Washington Irving's Sketch-Book.

Slice-Galley.—A wide galley with a double bottom, one of which is made to slide out through a groove, used for transferring large pages or jobs to an imposing-stone. (See GALLEYS.)

Slugs.—Pieces of metal of various lengths and thicknesses, but always thicker than leads, which they resemble in other respects. Slugs about a quarter of an inch thick are used at the bottom of newspaper columns as a protection to the type in locking up. In daily-newspaper offices another species of slug, cast with the various letters of the alphabet on the top, are used to distinguish the matter set up by the different compositors, and the latter are frequently designated, for business purposes, in the composing-rooms, as slug A, slug B, etc.

Slur.—A smear or blur on a printed sheet, especially such as is caused by a defect in the press or in the contrivances for presenting paper properly to the type while it is being printed. Slurs are frequently caused by inequalities in the thickness of tympans or blankets, and they are apt to occur whenever any presses get out of order. It is one of the important duties of pressmen to adopt effective measures for preventing them.

Small Capitals.—Capitals of a smaller size than the regular capitals, but cast on the same body. They are used frequently to set running heads, heads of chapters, the first words of sections or chapters, the titles of short newspaper paragraphs, subordinate lines of titles or jobs, and to add to words in the text one degree of emphasis greater than that represented by italic. In manuscript, two lines drawn underneath a word denote that it is to be set in small capitals. They are usually called small caps by printers.

Small-Cylinder Presses.—Cylinder presses in which the cylinders used have a comparatively small diameter.

Small Pica.—A type one size larger than Long Primer and one size smaller than Pica. It is very extensively used in book-work, especially in original editions and in law-books.

Smellie.—A printer of Edinburgh, eminent as a naturalist and author upon scientific subjects. He lost his father and became impoverished at an early age, but proved so indefatigable an apprentice that he was appointed proof-reader, with a weekly allowance of ten shillings in place of the stipulated wages of three shillings a week. His leisure time was spent in attending the classes of the University to such advantage that, when but eighteen years of age, he set up and corrected without assistance the 12mo Terence of 1758, which gained the prize offered by the Edinburgh Philosophical Society for the best edition of a Latin classic, the work being pronounced immaculate by distinguished philologists. Smellie's apprenticeship closed when he was nineteen, and he was immediately employed by Murray & Cochrane, of Edinburgh, as proof-reader and conductor of the Scots Magazine. During his engagement he studied Hebrew, in order to fit himself for superintending a grammar of that language then passing through the press. In 1760 he gained a gold medal from the University for the best essay on botany, and afterwards wrote and published a large work entitled The Philosophy of Natural History. Smellie also paid considerable attention to chemistry, which was at that time just beginning to assume its true station among the sciences. In 1765 he became a master-printer, the requisite capital being furnished by his admiring friends the professors of the University. In 1780 the learned printer was personally solicited by the Earl of Buchan to become a member of an antiquarian society which that nobleman was laboring to establish in Edinburgh, and he officiated as the secretary until his death in 1795. For this association Smellie prepared the admirable scheme of a statistical account of the parishes of Scotland, afterwards perfected by Sir John Sinclair. In 1780 he commenced the publication of his own translation of Buffon's Natural History, a version which has been highly esteemed for the value of the notes, illustrations, and observations added by Smellie. As a printer, Smellie became acquainted with many of the leading authors of the day, and his varied talents ripened the acquaintance in many cases into friendship. Of some of these he wrote memoirs relating the facts of his own personal observation: among them were Lord Kames, the author of the Elements of Criticism; Dr. Gregory, the physician, and author of the well-known Father's Legacy to his Daughters; and David Hume. He was also a special friend and comrade of Robert Burns, with whom he maintained a correspondence, which he destroyed as the history of a convivial episode in a long and useful life.

Societas Græcarum Editionem.—An association of French printers formed in 1588. They issued a number of handsome works printed with the royal types, and adorned with the figure of an ancient galley in full sail, which is the city arms of Paris. Anthony, the son of Paul Stephens, belonged to the association, and in conjunction with them printed the handsome octavo Sibyllina Oracula, dated 1599.

Solecism.—A word or expression which does not agree with the established usage of writing and speaking.

Solid Matter.—Matter without leads between the

lines; matter containing very few quadrats or break-lines is also said to be solid, in contradistinction to fat matter.

Solid Pick.—A letter in a stereotype plate filled up with metal.

Soliloquy.—A discourse uttered in solitude or addressed by a person to himself: frequently used in dramatic composition.

Solution of Silver.—This preparation can be advantageously used to cover copper-faced type or new electrotyped engravings, when vermilion or red inks are to be applied, as copper acts chemically on the color, causing it to become almost brown. This difficulty, as well as the danger of a deposit on the type, is obviated by the application of a solution of silver.

Sonata.—A composition for a musical instrument, usually of three or four distinct movements, each complete in itself, but united into a consistent whole.

Song.—A short poem designed to be uttered with musical modulations of the voice.

Sonnet.—A short poem of severely accurate structure, consisting of fourteen lines, the first eight of which form two quatrains, or measures of four lines each, and containing two rhymes each. The succeeding six lines are divided into two terzines, or measures of three lines and a single rhyme. This complex form was used among the Provençal poets, and was adopted from them into Italian literature, where it became and still remains very popular, being singularly suited to the melodious and pliable character of the language. Dante and his contemporary Tuscan poets introduced the sonnet to the popular attention at the beginning of the fourteenth century, when Italian literature held a commanding station in Europe, and it became a model for foreign countries, but it has never been very successful either in Germany or England, on account of the deficiency in rhymes in those languages, and it has never been really introduced into French. The masters of English versification have, however, all attempted the sonnet, and considered the form a triumph of their art; among these, Milton very successfully based his upon the Italian models. Sonnets of somewhat irregular form were written by Surrey, Wyatt, Sidney, Spenser, Shakspeare, Daniel, and other poets of that age, and have been imitated by some of the later writers. The Italian form used by Milton was followed quite successfully by Gray, Wordsworth, and Elizabeth Barrett Browning. In Germany, Uhland, Ruckert, Bürger, and some others have written sonnets, and Goethe wrote several in which he treated the structure of the verse itself as a species of artistic problem. In Spain, the artificiality of the structure gave it an exaggerated popularity during the sixteenth and seventeenth centuries. Although, in conformity with the fashion of the period, Shakspeare wrote sonnets, his taste for the natural and unaffected led him to describe the pedantic youth as laboriously constructing with mechanical accuracy a sonnet—to his mistress's eyebrow.

27

Sorbonne.—A college of the University of Paris, the members of which invited three German printers, named Ulric Gering, Martin Crantz, and Michael Friburger, to establish the first printing-office in that city, furnishing them for that purpose apartments in the college, where they pursued their labors from 1470 to 1473. The Sorbonne continued to exhibit great esteem for the printers, and accorded to Gering what was styled the privilege of hospitality,—that is, a right to an apartment and to a seat at the table, which compliment Gering amply returned by contributions of money. The Sorbonne was founded in 1252, by Robert de Sorbonne, the chaplain of St. Louis, as a gratuitous theological seminary for the poor students of Paris. The members, about thirty in number, were admitted after a severe scholastic examination, and received their maintenance from the college. Within a century after its establishment, the Sorbonne was largely endowed, and possessed many distinguished members; for about four centuries it was considered as the most eminent theological institution belonging to the Catholic Church, and was frequently called upon to decide the important theological disputes then disturbing Europe, and to act as adviser in the selection of the Popes. During the eighteenth century, its influence gradually declined, and after its suppression in 1789 it was never restored. The commanding position of the Sorbonne may be gathered from the fact that when Froben, the learned printer of Basle, wrote to Martin Luther in 1520, to congratulate him upon the success of his earliest treatises, Froben informed him that, having reprinted them in Basle, he had sent a large number into Paris, where they had been received with pleasure and approval by scholars, and even by some of the Sorbonnists. This favor was, however, not to last, for it was the assembly of the Sorbonne that censured Luther in 1521, and caused his books to be burned in the porch of Notre-Dame, ordering Jodocus Badius, one of their sworn printers, to print the censure with fidelity and exactness by virtue of his oath of obedience. The personal friendship of Francis I. shielded Robert Stephens from the animosity of the Sorbonne; but upon the accession of his son, Stephens fled secretly to Geneva, dreading that the long waiting vengeance of the irate doctors would be appeased only with his life.

Sorts.—All the characters in a font of type. When the letters belonging to one or more important boxes of a case are exhausted, the compositor using it is said to be out of sorts. If this deficiency arises from any unusual demand of the work in hand, orders are frequently sent to the type-founder for more sorts of the kind specially required. If there is no letter containing an abundant supply of the character specially needed to distribute, and the compositor wishes to continue his labors, he turns for sorts,—that is, he uses a type corresponding in thickness to the proper one, and turns its face to the bottom of his stick, so that instead of the face the foot of the type will be printed in proof. This practice, however, is injurious to the type so turned. A better plan is to turn the nick-side of the type down instead of up: the letter is thus thrown out of line and instantly catches the eye of the reader. Turning for sorts is at best an abomination, and should not be resorted to except in the utmost extremity.

Space Rules.—Fine lines, cast type-high, and of even ems in length, used sometimes in tables and algebraical work. In the headings of tables, they look better than two-em or three-em dashes, and in short columns they may sometimes be advantageously substituted for brass rules.

Spaces.—Low or short blank type, used to separate words, and to make a small blank space between a word and such points as the semicolon and colon. To enable the compositor to space even and to justify with nicety, they are cast to various thicknesses,—viz., five to an em, or five thin spaces; four to an em, or four middle spaces; three to an em, or three thick spaces; two to an em, or two en quadrats; and the hair space, cast remarkably thin, and found useful in justifying lines and assisting uniformity in spacing.

Spacing.—The adjustment of the distances between the words in a line, so that there shall not be any glaring disproportion; also extending a word or line of capitals or job-letter, by putting spaces between the letters. The appearance of all book- and important job-work is greatly improved by good spacing, and a neglect of this important matter is always noted by skillful proof-readers.

When the lines are very short, or the types are extended, all general rules, both of dividing and spacing, must give way to necessity; for in such cases it is impossible at all times to space regularly, or to divide the words after any given rule.

Regular spacing differs according to the character of the work. A careful compositor will endeavor to give to every line and every page an appearance of uniformity. Thickly-leaded matter should bear an average of an en quad, while solid matter will look best with an average of a thick space. When one or two letters require to be got in, or to be driven out, the difference between a thick space and a middling one is not perceptible to the naked eye, particularly if the compositor is careful to place the latter before or after a v or w, after a comma that comes before a v or w, or after a y; and, in like manner, an additional hair-space will not be perceptible if it comes after an f, or before a j; or if it comes between d and b, d and h, d and k, d and l, l and b, l and h, l and k, or l and l.

In setting a line of capitals, a careful workman will pay attention to the bearing off of different letters, for many of them, when they fall together, stand as if there were a space between them, and produce a bad effect. To remedy this inequality, hair-spaces, or bits of paper, are required between those letters that stand close. The inequality is still greater in many instances in a line of Italic capitals and, of course, requires the employment of similar means to remedy the difficulty.

In careful book-work, it would tend to facilitate regular spacing, if there were a greater number of hair spaces cast to a font than is now the case, or if what are called patent spaces were more generally called for by printers. For the information of those who are not familiar with these spaces, we will say that they are midway between a thick space and an en quad..

In poetry, the size of the type and the measure are usually so arranged as to admit the longest line to come into the measure. An opportunity is thus allowed for regular spacing—which is generally done with thick spaces, unless the matter is double-leaded, in which case it ought to be spaced with en quads.

A compositor will always find it advantageous to justify his lines to an equal tightness; and of this he must be sensible when he has to lock up his form. Carelessness in this respect will occasion considerable loss of time and great difficulty in getting his form to lift. And when it does lift, by means of sticking his bodkin into quadrats and spaces, to tighten those lines which are slack, it will never be safe, the suction of the rollers frequently drawing out the loose letters and creating a batter. The fact is, it is just as easy to do the work right as it is to do it wrong; and compositors should be ashamed to turn out their composition in a slovenly manner.

In all wide measures it is desirable to avoid having a lower-case f at the end of a line, or a lower-case j at the commencement of a line, as the projecting dot is almost certain to be broken off when the sheet is being worked; but in narrow measures the paramount object of uniform spacing must take precedence. The spaces inserted after points vary. After a comma, a thick space is sufficient; the colon and semicolon should be preceded by a hair space, and followed by an en quadrat. The exclamation point, and note of interrogation, should be preceded by a hair space, and followed by an en quadrat, except when they end a sentence, in which case they, like periods, are followed by em quadrats. These rules should be departed from only when a necessity for very narrow or very wide spacing requires a diminution or increase, proportionately, of the spacing between all the words of a line.

Special.—Not general, but designed for a particular purpose. A special telegraphic message is one sent as an item of news to a certain journal exclusively. A special correspondent is a letter-writer engaged for a certain paper.

Specimen Book.—A term used by type-founders for the bound collection of the printed impressions of their types, prepared for exhibition and to facilitate the transaction of business. The examination of the type itself would hardly be sufficient to the most experienced printer, and would be utterly impracticable in many instances, while the printed impression is not only convenient, but also presents exactly the effect intended to be produced. The necessity of such a work was so evident, that Caslon furnished printed specimens, and type-founders have since followed his example. In England, the specimen books, even at the present day, are remarkably plain, and devoid of ornament, being merely a simple display of the alphabet, well printed on good paper, with slight decoration in the way of flowers and borders. The first specimen books issued in this country were of a similar character, and contained little or none of the beautifully varied styles of character now known as job-letter. Some of these early publications have been already described (see JOB-LETTER). The first extensive book was published by the Johnson Foundry, in Philadelphia, in 1844, in an octavo volume of about four hundred pages, and the other foundries immediately followed the example by increasing the size of their publications. The same establishment issued the first quarto specimen book ever published, in 1849; the letters being for the first time arranged in appropriate words and phrases, making the sense suit the appearance of the type. This method of exhibiting their specimens has since been adopted by a number of the type-founders in the United States; and the skill with which the endless varieties of fanciful letters are shaped into sentences, produces excellent effects. The books of late years exhibit special characteristics. From the Western States the books come with wit and merriment scintillating through the lines; a vast amount of erudition upon the history of typography is ably condensed in the books of Bruce; a rare mingling of fun, fancy, and philosophy is lavished by MacKellar's brilliant pen upon the charming lines emanating from the Johnson Foundry; and Collins & McLeester have introduced, recently, the admirable plan of producing the rarest gems of English poetry, clothed in the fitting garb of those tiny instruments by which mind now rules the world. The magnitude of the design, and the splendor of its execution, have rendered many of the American specimen books almost too large for convenience; but any diminution has been rendered difficult, for the reason that it seems practically impossible to discard any of the old types, although every month produces new shapes to supersede them. After years of disuse, a type may at length be omitted, as if its mission has been accomplished, but a freak of fancy or fashion, ever seeking change, may chance to select it with all the vivacious admiration of a new discovery, as occurred in the recent revival of what is now called Old-Style, a form directly derived from the old-time Elzevirs of Holland, through the modifying hands of the English Caslon, to become, after a quarter of a century of oblivion, the favorite type of that newest of all things—an American magazine.

Serial publications intended to display specimens of newly-invented types also originated in Philadelphia, and have been widely adopted by the founders, who issue circulars, magazines, and sheets, either bi-monthly, monthly, quarterly, or irregularly, with the addition of more or less literary matter, or news interesting to typographers. At the present time there are at least twenty-five type-founders in the United States, most of whom publish some kind of serial, as a medium for the display of their new inventions, and among whom the following publish specimen books: in the city of New York, the foundries of Bruce, Conner, Farmer, Little & Co., Hagar, and Hemrick; in Philadelphia, the Johnson Foundry, Collins & McLeester, and Pelouze; in Boston, Phelps & Dalton, and the Boston Type Foundry; in Buffalo, Lyman; in Baltimore, Lucas; in Cincinnati, the Franklin Type Foundry and the Cincinnati Type Foundry; and in Chicago, Marder, Luse & Co. The manufacture of wooden type is an important industry in this country, large quantities of it being exported to Europe. The establishments of William H. Page, in Connecticut, and Vanderburgh, Wells & Co., New York, are extensive, and each publish a fine specimen book. While the metal founders are able to display every size of their types, the wood-letter is only exhibited in a few sizes, from the utter impossibility of embracing in any volume the huge and various lettering used on posters and other large sheets. The wood-letter specimen books, however, exhibit the fine variety of wood-letter and ornamentations intended for elaborate borders, showcards, hand-bills, and the innumerable styles of highly decorated posters now so generally used. The French specimen books, like the English, do not display fancy letter to so great an extent as the American, but are remarkable for the delicacy of taste exhibited in the exquisite blending and contrast of colors, revealing great beauty in the subdued harmony of the tinting.

Specimen Page.—A page composed and printed as a sample of the type and paper to be used for any work.

Spectacle.—By general usage, a public exhibition in which striking effects are produced by theatrical appliances.

Spectacular.—Representations appealing to the senses: thus, the spectacular drama depends for effect upon stage illusions, processions, large groups of figures, the introduction of surprising transformations, sometimes aided by colored lights, etc.

Speculum.—A Latin word signifying mirror, and included as a part of the title of many of the block-books. One of the most remarkable is the Speculum Humanae Salvationis, or Mirror of Human Salvation, which being produced in many editions exhibits the intermediate steps by which the engraving from wooden plates slowly progressed into the ruder forms of movable type. The Speculum Salutis, a quarto of sixty-three leaves of wood-cuts and text, printed on one side of the page, is asserted to be in part produced from movable type, and has been ascribed to Koster, but bears no internal evidence in the date, name, etc., confirmatory of the assertion, or of the proposed date of 1423. Many books of this order were produced in Holland and the Low Countries before the invention at Mentz, but their date and the method of their execution can only be conjectural. (See BLOCK-BOOKS.)

Speech.—A public address, usually extempora-

neous, as distinguished from an oration, which is presumed to have been prepared beforehand. Congressional addresses delivered impromptu upon the subjects of current business are called speeches. A speech, by strict construction, should never be written, but spoken without previous preparation, in a manner suited to transpiring events.

Speller, or Spelling-Book.—A manual or elementary work upon orthography, intended to serve as a text-book in the tuition of children.

Spilman, John.—A German, who acted as jeweler to Queen Elizabeth, and erected a paper-mill at Dartford, in Kent, about 1558, said to have been the first paper-mill built in England. A book with the following title was issued in 1558, and reprinted in 1588, with a dedication to Sir Walter Raleigh:—A sparke of friendship, and warm good will; with a poem concerning the commodity of sundry sciences; especially concerning paper, and a mill, lately set up near Dartford by a high German, called Mr. Spilman, jeweller to the queen's majesty. It is believed, however, that paper was made in England before this date, for in Bacon's History there is an entry mentioning a purchase made at a paper-mill on May 25, 1498.

Spira.—The name of two Germans who introduced printing into Venice, and who probably were born in Spira, taking their cognomen from their residence, as was done by John of Cologne, and others. John, the elder brother, is credited with introducing the direction-word at the bottom of the page. He died about 1470, and the business was conducted by Vendilin alone for several years, after which he entered into partnership with John of Cologne. Vendilin returned to Germany for a few years, but afterwards established himself in Venice, where, in 1477, he abandoned the elegant Roman character for the Gothic, in obedience to the demands of the popular taste. The beauty of the Cicero and Pliny published by the Spiras attracted the attention of the Senate, which granted to John the exclusive privilege of printing those works during his life-time. Some French authors have asserted that Jenson introduced printing into Venice, but it seems to be ascertained that the Spiras were established before his arrival, and that the death of John opened an opportunity of employment in Venice for many eminent typographers, who received liberal remuneration in that wealthy commercial emporium.

Splitting Paper.—This is rather a matter of curiosity than of use to honest men. About twenty years ago a number of advertisers in England offered to teach the art of splitting paper for a guinea. Happening to be out of the way of such instructors, and in the West, far from any aid, we devised a method of our own, and found, somewhat to our surprise, that the meanest and flimsiest paper that could be found —a quack's advertising pamphlet—could be readily split by a process, leaving each of the halves about as strong as the whole was originally.

The usual process is, simply, to paste a bit of cloth

or strong paper to the two sides of the piece to be split, and boldly pull the outside pieces apart, after which, when the paste is softened in water, the two halves are readily released.

There are but two practical applications to be made of the knowledge of this process. One hinges on the fact that the front and back of a document do not necessarily belong together, as an indorsement may not have been originally placed on the back of the paper on which it is found, and an actual indorsement may be removed.

Fortunately, however, as we have mentioned in our article on SAFETY PAPER, the rascals, after all, are deficient in knowledge and art. It is far more difficult to put two different halves together than to split an original sheet, and the putting together can always be readily recognized. We doubt, indeed, whether any frauds have been actually attempted in this direction. The warning once given will be quite sufficient to help the detection.

But there is another misconception of the structure of a given paper, which is involved in its capability of being split. If a sheet of paper be placed on a plate of glass, and thoroughly soaked with water, its upper surface can, by dexterous manipulation, soon be detached and gradually drawn off. This has been erroneously considered good evidence that the specimen in hand is a double-webbed part. In our article on PAPER, we have shown that properly applied sizing comes out to strengthen the two outer sides, and leaves the interior weaker. This quality favors the above-recited experiment upon a glass plate, and greatly helps all processes of splitting. The whole subject is worthy of notice only as a curiosity, as an indication of what might be done, and as a caution against a possible misconception in regard to the structure of a paper under examination.

Spondee.—A measure in versification consisting of two long syllables in immediate succession; as, pale morn.

Spring Back.—A term in bookbinding, used to describe the back of a book which has a curved piece of pasteboard or other stiff material fastened on the inside in such a manner as to make the leaves of the volume spring up and lie back flat.

Spring of a Form.—When a form contains a large quantity of furniture, and is locked up very tight, it frequently springs up in the middle so as to be in danger of falling into pi. To remedy this, unlock the form, plane it down, and tighten again very gradually, frequently planing it down while it is being locked up.

Springs.—Important parts of some hand-presses, such as the Washington, also of many power-presses.

Spur.—The point that pricks the hole in the paper at press, to insure register.

Squabble.—To twist or displace type. A page or form is said to be squabbled when some of the letters of one or more lines are accidentally shifted into adjacent lines, or when letters are twisted out of their square position.

Squib.—A censorious or sarcastic speech or publication, short and irregular in form, as distinguished from the more formal lampoon.

Stab.—In bookbinding, to puncture the sheets of a volume in order to introduce the binding threads which sew them together. Stabbing machines are frequently used for this purpose.

Staff.—A term sometimes used figuratively to describe the corps of assistant editors, correspondents, reporters, etc., engaged upon a large daily newspaper.

Staining.—In bookbinding, the coloring of the edges, fly-leaves, and backs of books, either in solid shades, or in the process styled marbling.

Staining and Spotting of Paper.—Every custodian of a large library must soon find, in books under his charge, notable and serious injury to the fair color of the paper. In purchasing old books he will meet with a larger range of mischief of this kind. Sometimes he will learn from the catalogues that, with few exceptions, the whole of an edition of a certain work is thus stained and defaced, and that the clean exceptions bear a high value.

In whole books any curative process is impossible, because the source of mischief lies in the very materials of the books themselves, as we shall soon show. But to valuable engravings, which are loose, or readily detachable, and to mere occasional and extraneous spotting in books, we may advantageously apply the resources of chemical science.

Ink-stains, from common writing-ink, can perhaps best be removed by the use of chlorine water, a solution of chlorine gas in pure water. The engraving should be wholly immersed in a very dilute solution, and, as soon as the marks disappear, be freely washed in pure water. Vegetable stains of most kinds will also yield to this treatment. As chlorine water cannot always be obtained, we may use, especially for mere local spots, a dilute solution of the hypochlorites of soda or potassa, the so-called Labarraque's fluid, or Eau de Javelle, or, in default of either (but less suitable), a solution of ordinary bleaching-salts, hypochlorite of lime. In all these cases there must be free washing with pure water. Grease-spots may be removed by the various kinds of hydro-carbon known as benzine, or in worse cases sulphide of carbon may be used. In such instances great care must be taken, for these solvents not only remove extraneous grease, but they attack the oil of the printing-ink, and if they act too long or too powerfully they set loose the whole of the material of the ink, and the print or engraving will be destroyed.

Another source of the staining of paper in books is their continued exposure to dust, and especially to smoke, even of gas-lights. The commencement of this mischief may be detected by the presence of a discolored edge surrounding the page, greatest at top, less at the sides, and least at bottom. There is no cure for this; but the evil may be prevented. If books are compactly bound, if the cut edges are gilt, especially on top, or even sprinkled with the usual preparation, the liability to stains of this kind will be greatly diminished. This gives a good reason for the fashion of gilt tops, but the open and loose free sides allow of the gradual introduction of the same evil. The old books bound with strong and tight clasps at once remove all such trouble. In fact, we have seen these with the edges burned with fire, and yet the inside quite free from any stain. The inside appearance of books called shop-worn depends upon this action of smoke and dust.

Strangely enough, when this action has uniformly penetrated throughout the whole page, and given a rich and creamy look to the paper, the very tint is produced which is sought to be imitated by our fashionable modern tinted paper.

The next and most serious extraneous cause of staining in paper is mildew. This is a true fungous growth; the plant, or its mycelium, remains imbedded in the paper, and, drying, leaves a brown stain, generally first seen in spots. The best that can be done in such a case is to stop the growth by keeping the paper perfectly dry. In one case, at least, we have traced the source of the mischief to an accidental sprinkling with rain-water, which seems to have introduced the spores of the fungus. Of course, well-kept books should not be exposed to such a risk, but in the transportation of papers they may encounter such an accidental sprinkling, and the danger and, above all, the chance of its propagation should be understood. The best cure is to expose such papers at once to the heat of a moderately hot oven, and keep them dry ever after.

In a similar way, books and papers may be injured, if not ruined, and caused to fall to pieces, when they are packed at a low temperature, perhaps below the freezing-point, such as would be the case when they were taken from an open wareroom in midwinter, and then sent to a hot climate. Quite new books and papers run less risk than those which have been handled: the latter, having received the saline and excessively alterable matters of the perspiration, are quite sure to be moulded, if not ruined. Great difficulty results from this cause, in the transmission of books and papers to India and similar climates. All such articles should first be moderately baked, and then inclosed in some air- and water-tight material; without such previous heat, the air- and water-tight envelope only aggravates the mischief.

Of the internal causes of the defacement of books, two are quite obvious. One is the striking of the ink through the paper, which is partly caused by a poor ink, but more frequently by the use of a very thin and badly-sized paper.

The next internal evil is from off-setting. Of course if the sheets are folded while the ink is quite fresh, we can easily see how this may occur; the hardly dry ink is pressed into contact with the opposite page, and the letters are more or less copied; but this would be the result of gross carelessness. We find, however, that the evil is not always obviated by great pains in drying and pressing sheets. In such instances, ordinary care having been taken, it seems

that some qualities of paper appear almost to compel the absorption of the opposed ink, while a well-sized paper resists it.

In a certain class of scientific books, the cuts have the ground black, and the figures are made in light lines upon this ground. Such cuts are very liable to off-set in time, unless the ink is of the very best kind; they should be guarded by slips of tissue-paper, perhaps still better by very thin tolerably well-sized paper. In a recent German work illustrated in this way, we find a special caution in regard to the binding.

An evil not very common, but one which we have sometimes seen, is that each letter is surrounded by a brown stain; this, except in the instances to be mentioned, is caused by the use of a poor, not well-burned ink.

But of all kinds of staining, we find none worse than that caused by the use of plate-paper, or the paper used for plate-printing, and this is peculiarly annoying because at the original time of printing nothing of it is seen, while the trouble begins at once and goes on to the perfect disfigurement of the book.

The simplest case of this kind that we have found (it may be seen in some of the plates of the American edition of Rees's Encyclopædia) is where the whole surface of the plate is discolored through and through, except that where the prints are made, and on the back beneath them, the paper is still white. There can be hardly any doubt that this is owing to imperfect wiping of the plate. The oily coating on the surface is gradually altered and browned by the action of the air, while the printed design prevents its penetration.

But in the examination of stained papers, we have encountered cases utterly beyond our powers of explanation, in which the disfigurement has been so great, that, if only for the purpose of warning, it seems necessary to try to find at least the evident cause, even if we cannot explain how that cause acts.

One of these cases is where a printed book shows throughout a fair and unstained page, except where an engraving is interposed, and then the ordinarily fair print is spoiled on both sides of the plate-paper, the damage being evidently not produced by off-setting, as it is quite independent of the engraved print. We will describe one extraordinary instance of this kind. A plate only partially covered by a portrait is wholly stained, not by the letters on the sheet at its back, but by the letters on the other side of that sheet, and these are carried through to the other side, stain the plate-paper, the tissue-paper opposite to it, and slightly the next printed page.

We can imagine that the porous plate-paper may exercise an absorptive action, but why this should select not the opposite sheet but its reiteration, is wholly inexplicable. In all cases, too, the action seems to have drawn the ink from the sheets back of the plate-paper, forward and through it even to the sheets in front.

The exceeding porosity of the plate-paper must be a leading cause of this disfigurement. A preventive might be found in the plan long ago used by Perkins,

Fairman & Heath, and mentioned in our article on SAFETY-PAPER, under the subdivision of bank-note-paper. This plan consists in printing on the soft plate-paper and sizing it afterwards,—of course sizing it on both sides. This would destroy the excessively absorbent power of the plate-paper, and we feel confident would do much to obviate the mischief.

But we can do more than this. In many cases it is quite obvious that the thin tissue-paper placed before the engraving has helped to do harm, sometimes carrying forward to the next page marks which do not show upon its own surface or in its substance. For this reason and for reasons given before, we recommend the disuse of tissue-paper before engravings, and the substitution of a delicate sized paper.

If we have not been able wholly to explain this strange disfigurement of books, we have at least traced it to its origin, and have suggested, we think, a reasonable remedy. But the whole investigation shows how excessively careful publishers should be in the selection of their materials, paper and ink.

Staining of Paper.—It was formerly an established custom of the master printers of London to dine together, annually, at some favorite hotel or other popular resort, in the vicinity of the British Metropolis; and one of the regular toasts always proposed and drunk with great gusto on these festive occasions, which typified activity and abundance of employment for all concerned in the various branches of typography, was the well-staining of paper.

Stamp.—A mark or impression made by pressure, and also the instrument with which such impression is made. A government stamp is an official mark affixed to articles subject to duty as evidence that the dues are paid, and devices, printed or stamped, are issued at fixed prices for general convenience, as postage stamps, revenue stamps, etc. As a means of obstructing the spread of newspapers, a stamp duty was placed upon them in England in the year 1712, and continued without interruption for one hundred and fifty-eight years. The highest rate required occurred in 1815, and it was gradually diminished from that date until its complete abolition in 1870. A considerable reduction in the rates in 1836 made that year the era of the establishment of a cheap press in England.

Stand.—The frame on which cases are placed. A single stand is one at which only one compositor can work, while a double stand affords space for two sets of cases and two compositors. Stands are usually made of wood, but improved iron stands are used in some modern offices. Stands are generally made three feet seven inches high at the side next the compositor; the inclined part, on which the lower case

rests, being six inches higher at the back than at the front. If the slant be greater than this, the types will fall from the upper boxes into those below them, when the case is full; and if it be lower, the compositor will have farther to reach, besides not being able to take hold of the types so readily when the boxes are nearly empty. The upper case, being higher on the frame than the lower, must have a still greater

STAND.

inclination, yet not so much as to cause the types to become pied. The space underneath stands is frequently fitted up as a rack for small cases, with a drawer for copy, etc.; or with ledges upon which boards may be placed for containing tied-up matter.

Standard.—A term applied to the rules adopted in different countries, or in various foundries, to regulate the size of type known by the respective names, as well as the relation of their sizes to one another. (See PROPORTIONS OF TYPE, and TYPE.)

Standing or Stand Still.—A term used by compositors and pressmen to denote that they are waiting for letter, copy, or a form to strike off.

Standing Matter.—Composed type remaining undistributed after it has once been printed, in the expectation that additional impressions will be required. The type used in advertisements which obtain more than one insertion in newspapers are, after their first insertion, one class of standing matter; and the forms of jobs or pamphlets are sometimes kept standing in a similar manner.

Standing Presses.—Presses used in book and job printing-offices to press out the inequalities produced on the surface of paper in the printing-press. Several varieties of standing presses are made, which are described elsewhere in this work. They are generally classified as Hydraulic, Pawl, Double-Pawl, Iron, and Screw Presses.

Stanhope, Earl of.—Charles Mahon, third Earl of Stanhope, the inventor, about the year 1800, of the first great improvement in the printing-press. Lord Stanhope, as a politician, carried the liberal principles of the Whig party of England to such lengths that for years he was distinguished as—the minority of one. His strong interest in the prosperity of the people turned his inventive genius into a useful direction, and, besides the famous press which bears his name, he invented considerable improvements in the locks of canals, and two excellent calculating machines. The interests specially engaging his attention may be inferred from the fact that his published writings, besides those upon the current questions of politics, were the Principles of Electricity, 1779; Securing Buildings against Fire, 1778; Rights of Juries Defended, 1792; Principles of Tuning Instruments, 1806; and Thunder Storms, 1787. He married as his first wife a daughter of the Earl of Chatham, and their eldest child was the famous Lady Hester Stanhope, who even in extreme youth was so aristocratic in her sentiments, and so proud of her station, that she rebelled against the liberal instructions of her father, and found a refuge with her uncle, William Pitt, with whom she lived, supporting the position of confidante and private secretary until his death, when Pitt consigned her to the care of the people of England. This curious charge was responded to by a pension of twelve hundred pounds, and, after living for a time in retirement in Wales, Lady Hester traveled in Asia, and so impressed the imagination of the people by her striking manners and lavish expenditure, that she was crowned queen on Mount Lebanon in 1813, and maintained her state and power until her death in 1839. The liberal father of this aristocratic daughter meanwhile devoted himself with steadfast zeal to the political and industrial advancement of the people of England, and, as one of the best methods of opposing the encroachments upon popular liberty, invented his improved press, of which he entered a notice or caveat at the Patent Office, but never permitted his improvements to become either a patent or a monopoly. In the construction of his press he engaged the assistance of an able machinist of London, named Walker; but his own zealous attention to the details may be inferred from the fact that he expended large sums in experimenting upon the inking-rollers, using every species of skin, and having them cured in various fashions, with an indefatigable determination to render them perfect. The Stanhope Press was first tried at the Shakspeare Press of Mr. Bulmer, and was immediately received as a remarkable advance in the art, and may be considered as the first real improvement upon the press as originally invented, having been preceded by the incompleted attempt in America afterwards perfected into the Columbian Press, and also in France by the plan proposed by Anisson. The Earl of Stanhope also revised and improved stereotyping. Although the processes of the art had been completed in Edinburgh by William Ged previous to the year 1736, the invention seems to have died with him, and no attempt was made to revive it for half a century. Tilloch and Foulis, of Glasgow, and Didot, of Paris, experimented upon it, but not very effectually; and Tilloch and Foulis had abandoned the pursuit for some years, when Earl Stanhope offered himself as their pupil, and paid eight hundred pounds for the instruction. He afterwards gained the assistance of Wilson, a London printer, and, after two years spent in experiments, an account of the invention was published, being ascribed by Wilson to Earl Stanhope, while he disclaimed the honor. Earl Stanhope also devised a system of logotypes, but his efforts to introduce them into general use were unsuccessful. He was born in 1753, and died in 1816.

Stanhope Press.—A hand-press, giving its power by a combination of the lever and screw, which was invented by Earl Stanhope, in the closing years of the eighteenth century. It was the first press made wholly of iron.

Stanza.—A distinct division of a poem, consisting of a number of lines regularly adjusted to one another. The Spenserian stanza invented by the English poet Spenser is charmingly adapted to the requirements of the language, and was used and modified into still greater perfection by Lord Byron. A stanza is frequently but incorrectly called a verse, the latter word meaning strictly a single line of a poetic composition.

Star.—The name by which printers usually designate an asterisk (*).

State Papers.—Papers or documents relating to public affairs, especially upon subjects of national or international importance, and those involving an account of diplomatic controversies.

Statements.—Blank printed bills or bill-heads printed monthly, or at other stated intervals, setting forth the indebtedness of customers.

Stationer.—By modern usage, a person who sells the materials required in writing, such as paper, pens, sealing-wax, wafers, ink, blotting-boards, blank-books, pencils, and the other articles that may incidentally be added to this list, frequently including certain papers and periodicals, generally of the lighter styles. The term was as early as the fourteenth century applied in England to booksellers, from the fact that they were distinguished from itinerant venders or pedlars by possessing permanent booths or stationary places of sale. Wynkyn de Worde, the second printer in England, in his will, dated 1534, styles himself citizen and stationer of London.

Stationers, Company of.—The history of this corporation is of especial interest, as exhibiting the rise and progress of the art of printing, and with it, of general education in Great Britain. By the authority of the Lord Mayor and court of Aldermen of London, the stationers of that city were, in 1403, formed into a guild, and assembled regularly under the government of a master and two wardens. The name stationer at that time was applied to the text-writers, who wrote and sold the Abecedariums, with the Paternoster, Creed, and such portions of the Bible as were especially called for, as the Psalms and the Gospels. These writers congregated in a district probably named from their avocation Paternoster Row, and in small streets in the vicinity, which for years after bore the names of Creed Lane, Amen Corner, Ave Maria Lane, etc. The Company of Stationers do not appear to have had any authority granted to them in relation to printed books, until they received their first charter from Mary in 1556, under the title of—the master and keepers, or wardens and commonalty, of the mystery or art of the stationers of London. This charter was renewed in 1588 by Queen Elizabeth, amplified by Charles II. in 1684, and confirmed by William and Mary in 1690. When the charter was granted, the public mind was familiar with the custom of hanging and burning persons for differences in religious opinion, and it was in harmony with the spirit of the age that the Stationers should be granted inquisitorial powers in regard to literary compositions, the right to search houses suspected of harboring books obnoxious to the State or to the interest of the Company, and the privilege of entry into any place, shop, or building belonging to any stamper, printer, binder, or seller of books, with the right of seizing and burning or converting to their own use any printed matter whatever which they deemed contrary to the form of any statute, act, or proclamation made or to be made. To the honor of a profession which was to act so directly for the enfranchisement of the people, typographers may proudly turn to the proofs that these privileges were rarely acted upon, and that the lives of the early English printers exhibit a spirit of liberality that places them notably in advance of the age in which they lived. The charter of 1556 was signed by ninety-four members of the commonalty or freemen, among the best-known of whom are Reynold Wolf, William Ryddall, Richard Jugge, William Norton, William Copland, and John Daye. The government was vested by the first charter, and afterwards continued, in a master, two wardens, afterwards increased by a court of assistants,—the trading business being managed by a regular committee, consisting of nine members. The coat of arms given by the Herald's Office to the corporation is thus described in technical language:—Azure, on a chevron Or, between three Bibles lying fessowise Gules, garnished, leaved, and clasped of the second (i.e. the clasps downwards), an eagle rising proper, inclosed by two roses Gules, seeded Or, barbed Vert; from the top of the chief a demi-circle of glory, edged with clouds proper; therein a dove displayed Argent; over the head a circle of the last. Crest: on a wreath, a Bible open

proper; clasped and garnished Or. Motto: Verbum Domini manet in æternum.

The common seal, used on certain occasions by the company, may be described in unscientific terms as a man crowned with a glory, bearing in one hand a vase from which issues a serpent, while a large bird stands beside him, and in front and below is a shield with eagles, Bibles, and vases. The expense of obtaining the charter is thus entered upon the records:

	£	s.	d.
Fyrste, for two tymes wrytinge of our boke before yt was sygned by the Kynge and the Queene's Majestie's Highness	0	18	0
Item, for the sygned and the prevy seale	6	6	8
Item, for the great seale	8	9	0
Item, for the wrytynge and inrolynge	3	0	0
Item, for wax, lace, and examenacion	0	3	4
Item, to the clerkes for expedycion	0	10	0
Item, for lymnyage and for the skyn	1	0	0
Item, payd to the screvener for wrytinge of the indentures of the surrender for the feffers of truste unto the Master and Wardyns of this Companye and thayre successors	0	14	0

At the first public dinner, held at their hall the next year, the typographers evidently worthily began the pleasant social meetings still maintained by the craft, with a bounteous spread of good cheer, which reads all the more ludicrously in the quaintness of the original account-book:

	£	s.	d.
Item, payd for 18 dosyn of breade	1	18	0
Item, payd for a barrell of stronge bere	0	9	0
Item, for a barrell of double bere	0	5	4
Item, payd for a stande of ale	0	3	0
Item, payd for 20 galons of wyne	1	0	0
Item, payd for 11 galons of Frenshe wyne	0	11	0
Item, payd for 37 lb. of beffe	0	4	7
Item, payd for 4 loynes of vele	0	4	8
Item, payd for a quarter of vele	0	2	0
Item, payd for 11 neckes of motton	0	6	6
Item, payd for 2 loynes of motton	0	2	0
Item, payd for 9 mary-bones	0	2	4
Item, payd for 25 lb. of suette	0	4	0
Item, payd for 38 punde of butter	0	9	8
Item, payd for a freshe samons	1	3	2
Item, payd for 4 dosyn of chekyns	1	0	1
Item, payd for 3 bushells 3 peckes of flowre	0	17	4
Item, payd for 20 pounde of cherys	0	8	4
Item, payd for 20 capons of grayse	2	13	4
Item, payd for 20 capons to boyle	1	2	8
Item, three capons of grese	0	9	0
Item, payd for 18 gese	1	4	0
Item, payd for 3 gese	0	4	6
Item, payd for 3 dosyn of rabbetts	0	10	6
Item, payd for 6 rabbetts	0	1	10
Item, payd for a galons of creme	0	2	8
Item, payd for bakynge of 20 pastyes of venyson	0	1	8
Item, payd for bakynge of 16 chekyn pyes	0	1	4
Item, payd for salte	0	1	0
Item, payd for venygar	0	1	0

	£.	s.	d.
Item, payd for vergis...................................	0	1	1
Item, payd for musterde.............................	0	0	4
Item, payd for goseburyes	0	0	10
Item, payd for a baskett..............	0	0	3
Item, payd for 10 dosyn of trenchers...............	0	1	9
Item, three dosyn of stone crusys.	0	3	0
Item, payd for tappes.................................	0	0	1
Item, payd for a pottie pycher.	0	0	2
Item, payd for 2 stone potts	0	0	2
Item, payd for pack thryde...........................	0	0	1
Item, payd for a hundredth of faggots..............	0	4	4
Item, payd halfe a thousand of bellets...........	0	4	4
Item, payd for 12 sacks of coles....................	0	7	6
Item, payd for flowres and bowes..................	0	1	3
Item, payd for garlands..............................	0	1	0
Item, payd for the carver............................	0	2	0
Item, payd to the minstrelles...................... ...	0	10	0
Item, payd to the buttlers.............................	0	6	8
Item, payd to the coke...............................	1	3	4
Item, payd to the under cokes to drink............	0	0	3
Item, payd to water berer...........................	0	3	10
Item, for 3 porters that carried over meat.........	0	0	6
Item, payd to the smythe.............................	0	0	2
Item, payd for the hyre of 3 garneshe of vessell	0	2	0
Item, payd for hundredth and 24 eggs.............	0	4	0
Item, payd for 2 strayners...........................	0	0	3

The spyce as folowethe:

	£.	s.	d.
Item, payd for 2 lb. and a quarter of pepper....	0	6	0
Item, payd for a quarte of pound of cloves.....	0	1	4
Item, payd for 4 pounde of dattes..................	0	4	0
Item, payd for 5 punde of currans..................	0	1	3
Item, payd for 23 pounde of prunys..............	0	3	8
Item, payd for safferon..............................	0	0	9
Item, payd for cynimon and gynger...............	0	3	8
Item, payd for a pounde of greate reasons.......	0	0	2
Item, payd for 10 lb. of curse sugar...............	0	8	4
Item, payd for 8 lb. of whyte suger...............	0	8	0
Item, payd for large mayse..........................	0	1	8
Item, payd for small mayse..........................	0	1	8
Item, payd for a punde of beskets and cary-wayes..	0	4	6
Item, a rewarde for bryngynge of a syde of venyson..	0	0	9
Item, payd for p'scan'ce.............................	0	0	8
Item, payd for wafers.................................	0	5	0
Item, payd for epycrys 4 galons....................	0	1	3

The first book recorded is in 1558, and it is entitled a ballet, called a Ryse and Wake. The importance of the society, as well as the special advantage of good looks to several members, is shown in an order from the Lord Mayor in 1589 requiring that the master, wardens, and the comeliest personages of the Company of Stationers attend him at the park-corner above St. James's, on horseback, in velvet coats, chains of gold, and with staff-torches, to wait on the Queen as she passes for recreation from Chelsea to Whitehall. In 1641 the officers are again required, and now it is with ten of their most graceful members, to attend on horseback, in their best array, with footmen, to receive the King, on his return from Scotland, and wait on him through the city. In 1654 they are bidden in their gowns and hoods to attend on the Lord Protector when he dines at Grocers' Hall. The Lord Protector, in his republican simplicity, demanded only a cloak and hood, but it is another matter in 1660, when the Company receives an order from the Lord Mayor to the effect that if the King, at his return to his kingdom, shall please to pass through the city, ten of the most grave, tall, and comely personages of the Company, well horsed, and in their best array or furniture of velvet, plush, or satin, with chains of gold, be in readiness to attend the Lord Mayor, aldermen, and other citizens, for his better reception. They were accordingly nominated, and ordered to choose each of them a footman to attend him. The wardens are to deliver them coats, ribbons, and truncheons, for the occasion. In a similar order, three years later, although the velvet coats, gold chains, and substantial horses are mentioned, nothing is said about good looks, and it is to be hoped that some of the homelier members had at last a chance to attend on royalty. It was in this year, 1663, that it was enacted by the English government that every printer should send three copies of every book new printed, or reprinted with additions, to the Stationers' Company, to be sent to the king's library, and the vice-chancellors of the Universities of Oxford and Cambridge; and the stationers in 1693 passed an order for the prosecution of all printers, booksellers, and others who neglected to comply with the injunction. That the Company was prosperous is indicated by the fact that they are reported as having lost two hundred thousand pounds at the Great Fire. Their quota of the forty-three hundred pounds levied on the city of London, to pay for the pageant at the coronation of Charles I., exceeded sixty pounds. In 1627 they pledged their plate at eight hundred and forty pounds for a loan to that unfortunate monarch, and in 1632 they furnished one hundred and fifty pounds towards the rebuilding of St. Paul's. The vast privileges enjoyed by the Company appear in the renewal of their charter in 1616, which reassures them in the sole right of printing Primers, Psalters, both in metre and prose, with or without notes, Almanacks, etc., in the English language; the A, B, C, with the Little Catechism and the Catechism in English and Latin by Newell. The valuable vested right in the Almanac was maintained by them until the memorable year 1775, when it was legally contested and the privilege lost by the Company. The Stationers' Company has, until a comparatively recent period, been intrusted with the distribution of the interest of nearly all bequests left by charitable men to the English printers;—new bequests being now frequently placed under the management of trustees of the Printers' Pension Fund.

Stationery.—The goods sold by a stationer, as the materials needed in writing.

Statistics of Printing.—In the absence of comprehensive authentic data, a number of statements, official and unofficial, compiled from a variety of sources, are given below, in the hope that they will assist in conveying an approximate idea of the amount of printing executed in this and other countries at various periods.

UNITED STATES.

The latest official statement furnished in a complete form is that based on the census of 1860. That portion of the volume of the census reports devoted to Manufactures, published in 1865, which relates to printing, says:

The number of printers and publishers in 25 States and Territories, exclusive of lithographic and copperplate printers, in 1850, was 673, and they employed capital amounting in the aggregate to $5,862,715. The number of employés was 8268, of whom 1279 were females, the annual cost of whose wages amounted to $2,737,308, and the cost of raw materials was $4,964,225. The value of the product was $11,586,549.

On the 1st of June, 1860, the book, job, and newspaper establishments, returned from 36 States and Territories, numbered 1666. They employed an aggregate capital of $19,622,318, and 20,159 persons, including 2333 females, at an annual cost of $7,588,096, and paid for materials the sum of $12,844,288. The total value of the product was $31,063,898, an increase of $19,477,349, or 168 per cent. over the value of the same industry in 1850. The increase in this branch of domestic manufactures is unprecedented in our previous history. The value of the printing done, though in the aggregate far short of the real value, both on account of the incompleteness of the returns from some States, especially in regard to the newspapers printed, and also because the profits accruing in the hands of the bookseller are in most cases not included in the total value, was, nevertheless, in the proportion of nearly one dollar to each individual in the Union.

[The above return of the number of newspapers in 1860 was very incomplete; it was subsequently corrected in the volume of the Census Reports relating to Mortality and Miscellaneous Statistics, published in 1866, which gave a tabular statement, showing that there were printed in the United States, in 1860, no less than 4051 newspapers and periodicals, of which 3242 were political, 298 literary, 277 religious or theological, and 234 miscellaneous, having an aggregate annual circulation of 927,951,548 copies.]

Of the whole number of printing-houses, the New England States returned 278, having an aggregate capital of $2,602,400, and giving employment to 3013 persons, 453 of them females, who received as wages annually $1,139,870, the raw materials costing $2,027,148, and the value of the work done amounting to $4,421,401, an increase of upward of 96 per cent. in ten years.

Of the establishments in these States, Massachusetts contained 150, against 112 in 1850; Maine 38; New Hampshire, 30; Connecticut, 28; Vermont, 18; and Rhode Island, 14.

The business in Massachusetts employed a capital of $1,755,200, and 1772 hands, and yielded a product of $2,989,416, an increase of 96 per cent. Of that amount 23 book- and job-printing establishments (three of them book-publishing alone) in Boston produced a value of $699,522, and 77 newspaper establishments in the same city, a value of $1,703,280.

Connecticut, with the labor of 522 hands, turned out an annual value of $675,528, the increment being in the ratio of 16 per cent.; and Maine produced the value of $261,874, an increase of 119 per cent.

The five Middle States and District of Columbia numbered 708 printing-offices, employing $13,056,750 in capital and 11,850 hands, including 1461 females, and paid for wages $4,355,856, and for material $8,585,413 annually. The value of printing done was $20,260,906, an increase over the product of 1850 of $11,789,274, or 139 per cent. in the value, and of 365 in the number of establishments. The value of the industry in that section amounted to 65.2 per cent. of the aggregate for the United States, and that of New York and Pennsylvania together to 60 per cent. of the whole. The value produced in those States was $18,639,982, and in the other Middle States and the federal district $1,630,924. The value of the manufacture in New York alone reached the sum of $12,617,105, which was upward of 40 per cent of the total product of the Union, and exceeded the total value of printing in all the States in 1850 by $1,030,-951, being 104.6 per cent. in excess of its own product in that year. The number of printing-houses in that State was 349, an increase of 149; and their collective capital amounted to $7,880,550, the cost of materials annually to $5,867,458, and of labor to $2,603,116, the last value being the cost of the labor of 6207 males and 1011 females employed. Of the total value of printing returned from that State, $10,438,155 was the product of 149 establishments in the city of New York, in which there were 51 newspaper establishments, with a total capital of $2,941,200 and 2486 hands, which printed newspapers and periodicals annually to the value of $6,182,946. Seventeen book-publishing houses, with capital amounting to $3,121,-000, and 2153 hands, printed books of the annual value of $3,225,551, and 81 book- and job-printing-offices, with $645,800 in capital, and 871 hands, produced work valued at $1,033,658. The value of the business in the second ward of that city amounted to $5,355,641, and included 134,116,800 copies of newspapers, valued at $3,574,493; $932,590 worth of books published, and $848,558 worth of book- and job-printing. One establishment issued 31,805,000 copies of newspapers, valued with advertisements at $800,000 per annum, and consumed 78,000 reams of paper, worth $400,000; another house in the same ward published 20,000,000 copies of newspapers; a third, 18,200,000 copies; and a fourth, 16,443,000 copies. The value of the printing done in the fourth ward of the city was $2,900,613, of which $2,143,613 was the value of daily, weekly, and other newspapers and periodicals, and $500,000 the value of 3,000,000 copies of books published by one house. The number of newspapers was 80,841,960 copies, of which 28,600,000 were from the Tribune office, and 16,000,000 from that of the Staats Zeitung. The number of magazines was 2,700,000, of which 1,500,000 were from one establishment. The value of printing done by four establishments in Albany county was $470,000, and Erie and Monroe each exceeded a value of $270,000 annually.

The number of establishments in Pennsylvania was 267, an increase of 165. They aggregated a capital of $4,137,850, employed materials of the value of $2,122,635, and paid for the annual labor of 3087 male and 315 female hands, $1,214,768. The value of the book, job, and newspaper printing done in the State amounted to $6,022,877, chiefly done in Philadelphia and Pittsburg. It was an increase of $4,305,265 in 10 years, or 250 per centum. Book-printing was executed by 42 establishments, to the value of $2,377,400, annually, employing a capital of $2,191,500, and 816 hands. Sixty-seven job-printing-houses, having invested $589,600, and employing 730 hands, executed work valued at $1,084,225; and 158 newspaper establishments, with capital amounting, altogether, to $1,356,750, and with 1847 hands, printed newspapers annually to the value of $2,561,252. Of the total value, upward of $5,000,000 was produced by 31 newspapers, about 40 book-publishing houses, and a large proportion of the job-offices in Philadelphia.

Sixteen newspaper establishments in Alleghany county (chiefly in Pittsburg) employed in capital $248,400 and 326 hands, and printed newspapers of the value of $538,103 annually.

In New Jersey 59 printing establishments employed a capital of $215,400 and 344 persons, producing work of the value of $303,669, which was a large increase upon the returns of 1850. From Delaware, which made no return in 1850, a value of $105,332 was returned by 7 establishments, and 26 in Maryland reported printing done of the annual value of $433,423. Eight establishments in the District of Columbia, having a capital employed of $471,250 and 405 hands, produced printed work of the value of $778,500, (chiefly government printing,) an increase of 322 per cent.

Eleven Western States and Territories contained 487 printing establishments, possessing a capital of $595,569, and employing, at a total cost of $1,393,922, 3646 male and 366 female hands. They expended for materials, $1,732,712, and the value of the printing done was $4,546,281, against a value of $676,186 reported in 1850, the ratio of increase exceeding 572 per centum. The largest amount of printing was done in Ohio, which numbered 141 printing establishments, with a collective capital of $1,224,374 and 1813 hands, which produced work of the annual value of $2,227,264, an increase of nearly 523 per cent. About $1,503,000 was the product of 32 printinghouses in Cincinnati, which employed a capital of $689,000 and 1043 persons; and 10 printing establish-

ments in Cleveland executed about the value of a quarter million dollars.

Illinois was next to Ohio in the number and extent of its printing establishments, of which there were in the State 84, with capital amounting to $487,200, and producing a value of $825,905, against $18,475 returned in 1850. The city of Chicago contained 19 of the whole number in the State, and the value of the work executed there was $525,000.

In each of the other Western States the increase was large. Returns were received in 1860, for the first time, from 13 printing establishments in Minnesota, which executed work of the value of $31,835; from 2 houses in Kansas, where work was valued at $4630; and from 5 in Nebraska, where the product amounted to $24,675.

From eleven Southern States returns were made of 151 establishments, having collectively a capital of $1,161,799 and 1014 hands, whose wages cost $417,912. The materials used cost $308,431, and the value of the printing done was $1,253,154, an increase of $1,080,149 over the returns of that section in 1850. The largest product was in Tennessee, where 21 printing-offices executed work valued at $443,120. Georgia and Texas each contained the same number of printing-houses as Tennessee, and the values returned by them, respectively, were $267,974 and $142,520. Virginia and Alabama each numbered 22 printing establishments, and the value of work done in the former was $102,959, and in the latter $63,100. No report of printing done in North Carolina, Florida, Texas, and Mississippi in 1850. In 1860 the first contained 13 establishments, producing a value of $87,950; South Carolina, a value of $15,295, by 5 establishments; Florida, $2000 in one office; and Mississippi, a value of $63,890, executed by 11 offices; while 6 in Arkansas produced a value of $16,650.

The Pacific States, since 1850, have brought into operation 42 printing establishments, with a total capital of $205,800 and 270 male hands, who received in wages $280,536, the materials consumed costing $140,584. The value of the work executed was $582,150. Of these establishments California reported 31, Oregon 9, and Utah 2; the first employing 219 hands, the second 31, and the last 20; and they produced, respectively, the following values, in newspaper, book, and job printing, viz.: California, $485,954; Oregon, $60,202; Utah, $36,000.

In 1791 the number of printing-presses in the United States was officially declared by the Secretary to be sufficient to render the country independent of foreign publishers for other books required, and to warrant a duty of 10 per cent. on books imported.

By the census of 1810, returns of printing done were made only from two States; one office in Vermont returned a value of $3194, and 108 in Pennsylvania executed work to the value of $353,517. The number of printing-offices in Philadelphia was stated to be 51, and the number of presses 153. They were supposed to print annually half a million volumes. There were two manufactories of printing-presses in the city, including that of Adam Ramage, long afterward known as a builder of improved presses. The number of newspapers printed in the United States at that date was estimated at upward of 22,000,000 copies annually.

The relative proportions of British and American books annually consumed in the United States in 1820 was estimated by the late S. G. Goodrich to be of American 30 and of British 70 per cent. of the whole. These proportions were reversed during the next 30 years, the American being 70 and the British 30 per cent. of the total consumption.

The following table, prepared and published by the same authority from official and other data, shows approximately the value of books manufactured and sold in the United States at different periods, and the several values of each class sold:

	1820.	1830.	1840.	1850.
School books.......	\$ 750,000	\$1,100,000	\$2,000,000	\$5,500,000
Classical books.....	250,000	350,000	550,000	1,000,000
Theological books.	150,000	250,000	300,000	500,000
Law books..........	200,000	300,000	400,000	700,000
Medical books......	150,000	200,000	250,000	400,000
All others...........	1,000,000	1,300,000	2,000,000	4,400,000
Total..........	2,500,000	3,500,000	5,500,000	12,500,000

By the same writer the value of the American book trade for 1856 was estimated at \$16,000,000, distributed as follows: City of New York, \$6,000,000; other parts of the State of New York, 600,000; Boston, \$2,500,000; other parts of New England, \$600,000; Philadelphia, \$3,400,000; Cincinnati, \$1,300,000; Northwestern States, \$100,000; District of Columbia, by the government, \$750,000; Southern and Southwestern States, \$750,000.

Printing-presses are now (1860) manufactured in two New England, two Middle, and one Western State to the value annually of \$943,450, by 14 establishments, which employ altogether a capital of \$1,015,000 and 707 men, at a cost for wages of \$289,684, and for materials of \$145,520.

In Massachusetts one establishment, with a capital of \$200,000 and employing 100 men, manufactured presses of the value of \$103,500; and one in Rhode Island, having 35 hands and a capital of \$26,000, reported a product of \$20,500.

Seven manufactories in the State of New York employed in this business an aggregate capital of \$758,000 and 530 hands, producing printing-presses valued at \$757,250, at a cost for wages of \$209,200, and for material of \$91,280, annually. Most of these are in the city of New York.

In Pennsylvania there were, in 1860, 4 small manufactories of printing-presses, with a total capital of \$16,000 and 17 hands, which produced a value of \$38,700.

One establishment in Cincinnati, Ohio, had a capital of \$15,000, and made presses of the value of \$23,500.

Type-Founding establishments in the United States in 1860 numbered 32, having invested \$1,113,600, and employing 795 male and 312 female hands, at an annual cost for labor of \$416,404, and for materials of \$357,600. They manufactured types to the value of \$1,276,570.

Of these establishments, 6 in Massachusetts, employing 166 persons, produced a value of \$176,770; 9 in New York, with 440 hands, turned out a product of \$540,400; 12 in Pennsylvania, having 263 hands, reported a product of \$308,300, of which a part was the value of stereotyping done by them. In Cincinnati, Ohio, three type-foundries, employing 182 hands, manufactured type of the value of \$210,000. One establishment in Chicago reported a value of \$24,600, and one in St. Louis a value of \$16,500.

In Connecticut two manufactories of wooden types, with a capital of \$26,500 and 39 hands, returned a value of \$25,000.

Stereotyping and Electrotyping employed, in three States, a capital of \$126,500 and 41 establishments, having 305 persons employed, and paying annually for wages \$120,840, and for materials \$60,507. They produced work of the value of \$286,300. One of these was in Connecticut, and with six hands produced a value of \$4000; 11 in New York employed 162 persons, and reported a value of \$66,360; and 29 in Pennsylvania, having employed 137 hands, executed work to the value of \$51,600.

Lithographic Printing.—Lithography employed in the United States on the 1st of June, 1860, 53 establishments, in seven States. The aggregate capital invested in the business was \$445,250; the number of persons employed, including 26 females, 786; the annual cost of wages was \$338,868, and of materials \$229,206; and the value of the product was \$848,230.

Of these establishments the States of Massachusetts and Connecticut each contained two; those in the former having capital amounting to \$10,500, and producing, by the labor of 24 persons, work valued at \$19,000, and the latter, with 23 hands and a capital of \$9500, the value of \$17,500.

In each of the States of New York and Pennsylvania there were 23 lithographic establishments; those in New York having invested in the art \$157,850, and producing work of the value of \$383,700 with the labor of 321 hands, and those in Pennsylvania, with capital amounting to \$255,600 and 382 hands (19 of them females), a value of \$386,300.

The States of Ohio, Indiana, and Missouri each contained one house for lithographic printing. The first employed \$10,000 in capital, and 29 hands, who produced work valued at \$38,000 per annum; the others, with capitals of \$800 and \$1000 respectively, and three and four hands each, produced work to the amount, severally, of \$2830 and \$900.

The first published specimen of American lithography may be seen in the twenty-fourth volume of the Analectic Magazine for July, 1819, which was but a few years subsequent to the introduction of the art into England from Germany. It was executed upon

Munich stone, by Benjamin Otis, of Philadelphia, who had also executed lithographic engraving upon stone from a quarry near Dick's River, Kentucky, obtained through Dr. Brown, of Alabama, and Judge Cooper, of Pennsylvania.

The number of lithographic and copperplate printers in the United States in 1850 was 26. They employed 375 hands, and executed work valued at $247,200. Since that time the number of establishments has nearly doubled, and the product has increased at the rate of 243 per centum.

Engraving.—This branch of art-manufacture employed, in 1850, 112 establishments and 480 workmen, whose labor produced a value of $566,005. In 1860 the establishments in 10 States numbered 191; their capital amounted to $431,650; the number of hands to 706 males and 18 females; the cost of labor to $330,524, and of materials to $157,171; and the value of engraving of different kinds done amounted to $829,140, an increase of over 48 per cent.

The value of this industry, in Massachusetts, Rhode Island, and Connecticut, which had, respectively, eight, four, and two establishments, was $45,100, of which $24,025 was produced in Massachusetts, $17,300 in Rhode Island, and $3775 in Connecticut. The first employed 18 hands, the second 25, and the third 5, and the total capital in those States was $11,800.

In the Middle States and District of Columbia there were 172 engraving establishments, having altogether employed a capital of $414,650, and 637 male and 16 female hands. The annual wages paid was $298,284, and the cost of materials was $147,586, the value of work executed amounting to $766,490. Of the whole product in those States, 97 in New York, having invested $138,100, and employing 406 persons, returned a value of $437,396, and 72 in Pennsylvania, with capital aggregating $271,000, executed, with the labor of 242 persons, engraved work valued at $322,400. In New Jersey two establishments produced work of the value of $2950, and one in the District of Columbia a value of $3744.

There were five in the Western States, viz., two in Illinois, two in Missouri, and one in Wisconsin. They produced work, respectively, to the value of $12,650, of $1000, and of $4000, and, together, employed 18 hands. This work is principally executed in the larger cities.

Bookbinding and Blank Books.—These branches of domestic industry employed [in 1860] 269 establishments, 2045 male and 2732 female hands, and a capital of $1,654,830, consuming materials of the annual value of $1,554,082, and producing, with an expenditure of $1,048,930 for labor, a yearly product of $3,729,080, an increase of a little over 14 per cent. on the product of 1850, which amounted to $3,255,678.

In the New England States there were 58 establishments, one-half of which were in Massachusetts. The business in these States employed a capital of $299,250 and 960 persons, and produced work valued at $863,223, which was a depreciation of $114,656 as

compared with its value in 1850. The falling off was in the States of Massachusetts and Vermont, the former of which manufactured to the value of $569,680, and the latter of $1200, a decline in the one of $234,740, or 78 per cent., and in the other of $8800, from the returns of 1850. In each of the other States there was a large increase of business. Eight establishments in Connecticut produced a value of $147,000, an increase of upward of 24 per cent.

The Middle States enumerated 132 binding and blank book establishments, having invested, as capital, $1,072,850, and employing 1318 males and 2053 females, at a cost for wages of $660,200. The value of their manufactures amounted to $2,273,449, the increase being 23.5 per cent.

All but $115,143 of the value in those States was returned by 120 establishments in the two States of New York and Pennsylvania. The former of these had 64 establishments, with a capital of $490,900, and 1140 operatives, of whom 527 were females, who received as wages $326,312, and manufactured goods valued at $1,173,628, an increase of 36.8 per cent.; and 56 concerns in Pennsylvania, having a capital of $518,900, and paying annually $297,816 for the labor of 641 male and 1474 female hands, made binding and blank books of the value of $984,678, which exceeded the product of 1850 in the ratio of 30 per cent. and upward. In New Jersey 7 manufacturers returned a value of $65,317, which was a falling off of nearly 50 per cent.; and in Maryland, which reported in 1850 a product of $52,850, one establishment returned a value of only $1700.

Fifty-nine establishments in the Western States employed in capital $194,680 and 362 persons, and paid for labor $101,562, and for material $219,055. They manufactured to the value of $460,608, an increase of nearly 16 per cent. in 10 years. Their business amounted to a little more than one-half that of New England, which had 3 establishments less.

Twenty-six of the Western manufactories were in Ohio, and employed a total capital of $77,780 and 202 hands, which made bindings and blank books of the value of $212,413, which was $9599 less than was made in that State in 1850. The product of 8 factories in Indiana was $104,800, an increase of over 214 per cent., and the same number in Wisconsin made work valued at $49,750, or 332.6 per cent. more than in 1850. Four establishments in Michigan produced a value of $40,600, and 6 in Illinois returned a product of $18,700, each having produced, in 1850, $12,000 worth.

From Missouri and Kentucky a large decrease in this branch, being reduced to one establishment each, was reported, while Iowa, which made no return in 1850, produced, in 5 establishments, a value of $26,545.

The shops in 5 Southern States numbered 17, combining a capital of $76,350, and paying for material $60,880, and for the labor of 66 males and 3 females $32,604. The value of their manufactures was $99,500, the increase being at the rate of 150 per centum. Of the total product in these States, $25,500 was returned by 8 establishments in Virginia, which, in 1850, returned only $2500; $49,000 by 4 in Louisiana; $17,500 by 8 in Georgia; $5000 by 1 in Mississippi; and $2500 by 1 in North Carolina. From the two last-named and from Louisiana there was no return in 1850; and from South Carolina and Alabama which in that year reported, the one a value of $4000, and the other of $23,500, no report was made in 1860.

California, in 1860, contained 4 binderies and blank book factories, having capitals amounting to $9700. They employed 9 males and 5 females, at a cost for labor of $6360, and for materials of $10,782, and produced work valued at $31,500. One small shop in Oregon, with a single hand, made $800 worth of binding and blank work.

The earliest bookbinding done in America, of which we have any account, was by John Ratliffe, an Englishman, who, in 1661, received £5, or 6d. each, for binding in leather two hundred copies of John Eliot's edition of the New Testament in the Indian tongue, and afterwards bound the same number of copies of the Bible in quarto, with clasps, for about 2s. 6d. each. He afterwards became a bookseller in Boston, where that class of tradesmen generally associated bookbinding with their business. Edward Ranger was a bookbinder and dealer in books in Boston in 1673, and of upwards of 90 booksellers who carried on business in that city previous to the Revolution, more than 30 are known to have had binderies connected with their shops, and many of them made binding a principal branch of their business. One of the number, Richard Fry, Stationer, Bookseller, Paper-maker, and Rag-merchant from the city of London, who, in 1732, kept on Cornhill, appears to have been one of the earliest blank book manufacturers in that city. He assured the merchants in a card that he would sell them all sorts of account-books, done after the most acute manner, 20 per cent. cheaper than they were accustomed to have them from London.

Bookbinding was carried on at Newburyport and Salem in 1761, and at New York, by Robert MacAlpine, in 1769, followed by others, soon after. Andrew Bradford, the printer, in 1718, and Benjamin Franklin, in 1729, and others in Philadelphia, and at least two in Charleston, South Carolina, executed binding, in connection with printing and bookselling, before the Revolution.

In 1810, returns were made of bookbinding from Pennsylvania only, where there were 102 bookbinders, whose manufactures were of the value of $107,183. In New Jersey one binder was reported, but the value of his business was not stated.

In 1840, the number of binderies in the United States was 447, of which 147 were in the New England, 190 in the Middle, 41 in the Southern, and 69 in the Western States. New York contained 107, Massachusetts 72, Pennsylvania 46, Ohio 41, New Hampshire 22, and the other States from 1 to 22 each.

The number of bookbinding and blank book establishments in the United States in 1850 was 235, and their capital $1,063,700. They employed 3468 hands, and the value of their manufactures was $3,255,678.

The principal improvements in bookbinding within the present century consist in the introduction of the cheaper materials of cloth and marbled paper for covering the boards, and in the greater use of machinery in the several processes of the bindery, of which last Americans make more use than European binders.

By far the larger proportion of all the books now published in the United States are put up in cloth binding, which, in addition to its cheapness and the rapidity with which work of that kind may be turned out, possesses considerable durability and capacity for ornamentation. Within the last ten years, bookbinders' muslin has been manufactured in the United States by at least one house, and marbled paper has been made for a number of years in Philadelphia of superior quality, in great variety of patterns, as well as by several manufacturers in other places. Their use has contributed to the growth of the publishing business of the country.

Bookbinders' tools for producing the ornamental work were manufactured in Philadelphia upward of forty years ago, by David H. Mason, who took out a patent in January, 1826, for ornamental rolls and stamps for bookbinders, and in partnership with M. W. Baldwin, the eminent locomotive-builder, introduced many new designs. Benjamin Gaskill, established as a bookbinder of the same place previous to 1812, was one of the first to use hydraulic presses and other machinery in bookbinding in this country. The improvements since made by Americans in the mechanism for folding, cutting, block-gilding, blind-tooling, embossing, backing, finishing, etc., and particularly in cloth binding, which employs machinery to a greater extent than other kinds, are very numerous and valuable, as well as those for ruling, paging, etc. of blank books.

Paper.—The total number of paper-mills in the United States in 1850 was 443. They employed an aggregate capital of $7,260,864, and 6285 hands, of whom 2950 were females. The annual cost of labor was $1,497,782, and of raw materials $5,553,929, and the value of the product was $10,187,177.

On the 1st of June, 1860, the number of paper manufactories in 24 States was 555. The total amount of their investments was $14,052,683, and the number of hands was of males 6519, females 4392—total, 10,911. The annual expenditure for labor was $2,767,212, and for materials $11,602,266. The total value of product was $21,216,802, which included the values of 131,508,000 pounds of printing-paper, 22,268,000 pounds of writing-paper, 33,379 tons of wrapping-paper, 8150 tons of straw board, besides 1,944,000 pounds of colored paper, 91,960 pounds of bank-note paper, and 3097 tons of wall paper—a total weight of 253,778,240 pounds. The average value per pound of the whole quantity was upwards of 8¼ cents (8.36). The increase in the value of the product over that of 1850 was 108.2 per cent. The quantity was in the proportion of 8.07 pounds to each person in the Union.

In the New England States the paper-mills numbered 204, which produced nearly one-half of the total value of paper made. Their aggregate capital was $6,533,460, the number of hands 5420 (one-half females), and the cost of wages was $1,875,790 and of materials $5,907,365 annually. The product was 56,105,300 pounds of printing, 17,298,000 pounds of writing, and 11,600 tons of wrapping-paper, 1568 tons of straw pasteboard, 1,720,000 pounds of colored papers, 67,000 pounds bank-note, and 2147 tons of wall paper, valued altogether at $10,502,069, an increase of upward of 109 per cent. in ten years. Considerably more than one-half the capital and product was reported by 99 manufactories in Massachusetts, employing 3339 persons, of whom 1845 were females, and making paper valued at $6,170,127, the increase being upward of 137 per cent. It was the value of 27,747,000 pounds of printing-paper, 15,598,000 pounds of writing-paper, 6443 tons of wrapping-paper, and 815 tons of straw board, besides colored and wall paper. In Connecticut there were 55 mills, producing paper of the value of $2,453,258. The manufactures consisted largely of printing-paper, of which 14,581,500 pounds were made, 1,500,000 pounds of writing-paper, 2848 tons of wrapping, 1,000,000 pounds colored, 375 tons of wall paper, and all the bank-note paper made in New England, namely, 67,000 pounds. The principal factories were at Hartford, where there were 21, and at Norwich. The Pacific mills at Windsor Locks, near Hartford, and those of the Chelsea Manufacturing Company, at Norwich, are among the largest establishments of the kind in the world.

In the other New England States the value fell below one million dollars in each. In Maine, which had 14 mills, it amounted to $990,000, and the manufacture in that State showed the largest rate of increase of all the New England States, viz.: 420 per centum. In New Hampshire there were 24 mills, and in Vermont 12, and from Rhode Island none were reported.

The Middle States contained 273 paper-making establishments, whose aggregate investments in the business amounted to $5,499,770. The labor was performed by 3971 persons, including 1188 females, whose annual wages cost $950,414, the cost of material being $4,292,358, and the value of the manufactures $7,908,437, an increase of 102 per cent. on the product of 1850. The quantity of paper in these States was 50,604,500 pounds of printing, 4,923,000 pounds of writing, 17,446 tons of wrapping, and 6582 tons of straw boards, besides miscellaneous articles.

The largest product was returned by 126 mills in New York, containing 1857 hands, and having a capital of $2,033,000. They manufactured 17,304,800 pounds of printing-paper, 1,772,000 pounds of writing-paper, 14,340 tons of wrapping-paper, and 2154 tons of straw board, besides 950 tons of wall-paper, valued

in all at $3,059,776, an increase of 87 per cent. Pennsylvania contained 84 paper-mills, having $1,917,970 in capital, and 1082 hands, who made 18,198,000 pounds of printing, 400,000 pounds of writing-paper, 1503 tons of wrapping, 1500 tons of straw board, and 24,960 pounds of bank-note paper, the total value of which articles was $2,367,268, which was an increase of 128 per cent. since 1850. New Jersey had 36 paper manufactories, with an aggregate capital of $990,000, 715 hands, and produced paper of the value of $1,582,703, the increase being over 78 per cent. These mills made 8,198,000 tons of printing-paper, 2,750,000 tons of writing-paper, 668 tons of wrapping, and 2928 tons of straw board, besides 224,000 pounds of colored papers. They turned out more writing-paper and straw board than were made in any other State in the Union. The principal mills are at Trenton, Paterson, and Newark, the Ivanhoe mills, at Paterson, being one of the most complete in the United States. Twenty-five mills in Maryland made paper of the value of $514,690, and two in Delaware made $385,000 worth of printing and wrapping papers, the increment in both considerably exceeding 100 per cent.

In the Western States there were 53 mills, of which 29 were in Ohio. The total capital employed in paper-making in those States was $1,386,603; the number of hands was 1109, of whom 362 were females: the annual cost of labor was $229,436, and of materials $1,074,168. The product amounted to $2,041,793, an increase of 104 per cent. It embraced 18,408,000 pounds of printing-paper, 48,000 pounds of writing-paper, and 3381 tons of wrapping-paper. The writing-paper was all made in Ohio, which also produced 12,590,000 pounds of printing-paper and 2500 tons of wrapping, valued altogether at $1,382,141, the rate of increase being upward of 197 per cent. The 29 mills in Ohio employed a capital of $875,500 and 724 hands. In Indiana there were ten mills, in Michigan and Wisconsin five each, in Illinois two, and in Iowa and Kentucky each one mill. In each of the three first named, and in Kentucky, between one and two million pounds of printing-paper, besides wrapping-paper, were made, Wisconsin producing the largest amount, or 1,724,000 pounds, and showing also the largest rates of increase in the value. In Kentucky the value of paper made showed a falling off from the product in 1850, and in Iowa, where no paper was made in that year, 170,000 pounds, worth $17,400, was produced.

The Southern States numbered, in 1860, 24 paper-mills, whose aggregate investments were reported at $572,850. They employed 397 persons (131 of them females), the cost of whose labor was $137,042 per annum, and of material the cost was $320,365. They manufactured 6,120,200 pounds of printing-paper, and 952 tons of wrapping-paper, valued in all at $724,503, showing an increase since 1850 in the ratio of 176.5 per cent. In Virginia nine mills made 1,940,000 pounds of printing-paper, worth $270,000. Six mills in North Carolina made 1,495,200 pounds, valued at $165,703, and four in Georgia produced nearly the same quantity and value. Three mills in South Carolina made 1,085,000 pounds of printing-paper, worth $96,500, and two in Tennessee made 200,000 pounds, worth $28,000, which was a decrease. From Alabama, which returned a value of $18,000 in 1850, no return was made. The increase in Georgia and the Carolinas was very large.

[For an estimate of the amount of paper now (1871) made in the United States see PAPER.]

Statistics for periods since 1860.—The following estimates of the amount of printing done in the United States since 1860, have been made by various experts:

In 1870 the total number of newspapers in this country was estimated at 5244, of which 542 were daily, and 4425 weekly.

The number of works or books of the various sizes and descriptions, which have been printed in the United States, and are now for sale by American booksellers, is roughly estimated at about 100,000.

The total number of new publications in the United States during 1868 was 2169, classified as follows:—

Fiction	754
Religion	258
Directories, Almanacs, etc.	173
Law	123
Biography, etc.	113
Poetry	105
Medicine, Surgery, etc.	97
History	85
Miscellaneous Literature	81
Arts, Trades, etc.	75
Education	70
Fine Arts	51
Travels and Geography	43
Sociology	40
Government and Politics	30
Natural Science	29
Philology and Learned Literature	17
Mental Philosophy	11
Military and Naval	5
Mathematics	4
Periodicals	5
Total	**2169**

Of these, 1866 were bound books. The number of new publications in 1867 was 2124, of which 1773 were bound.

During the year ending December 1, 1870, the Librarian of Congress reported that he had received, under the operation of the Copyright Law, the following publications, viz.:

Books	2734
Pamphlets and periodicals	3140
Musical compositions	2891
Engravings, photographs, and chromos	1175
Prints	1426
Maps and charts	146
Total number of articles	11,512

28

It has been estimated that five million children are in attendance upon the public schools in the United States; for whom there are each year manufactured twenty million text-books, costing 18,750,000 dollars.

The American Newspaper Directory for 1871, issued by Messrs. Geo. P. Rowell & Co., of New York City, contains the tables of statistics given below, which have suggested the following comments in Rowell & Co.'s American Newspaper Reporter, viz.:

A TABLE SHOWING THE NUMBER OF NEWSPAPERS AND PERIODICALS PUBLISHED IN THE UNITED STATES, TERRITORIES, DOMINION OF CANADA AND BRITISH PROVINCES OF NORTH AMERICA IN 1871.

	Daily.	Tri-Weekly.	Semi-Weekly.	Weekly.	Bi-Weekly.	Semi-Monthly.	Monthly.	Bi-Monthly.	Quarterly.	Total.
Alabama	9	2		66		1				78
Arkansas	4	2		41			4			51
California	34	2	6	129		2	12		1	187
Connecticut	17		1	51	1	3	13		1	87
Delaware	1		3	13			1			18
Dis. of Columbia	6			12			6		1	25
Florida	1	1	1	21			1			25
Georgia	14	5	7	86		2	9			173
Illinois	38	11	7	371	3	5	58	2	4	499
Indiana	20	3	3	209		3	25		1	264
Iowa	20	5	3	231	1	1	18		1	280
Kansas	14	3		85			8	1	1	112
Kentucky	10	2	5	76			12			105
Louisiana	9	2	3	71			3		2	90
Maine	6	1		48	1	1	9			86
Maryland	9			77			9		1	98
Massachusetts	21	1	13	165	4	5	60	1	10	280
Michigan	13	4		107	1	1	11		2	139
Minnesota	8	5	1	85			5			104
Mississippi	4	5	1	75		2	6			93
Missouri	21	5		227		5	29	1	1	289
Nebraska	7			31		1	7			46
Nevada	7		2	6						15
New Hampshire	7			39		2	8	1	1	58
New Jersey	21		1	98	1	1	16			138
New York	89	3	18	568	2	25	167	2	20	894
North Carolina	8	3	4	43	1	1	5			65
Ohio	25	9	5	306	1	9	53	2	1	411
Oregon	5			25			1	1	1	32
Pennsylvania	61	2	1	410		17	82	3	8	584
Rhode Island	6		1	18			1			26
South Carolina	5	4	2	42			4		2	59
Tennessee	12	2	1	79	1		9			104
Texas	11	8	7	95			2			123
Vermont	3			39			2			44
Virginia	16	8	8	71		2	11			116
West Virginia	3	1	1	49		1	3			58
Wisconsin	16	2	3	165		6	9			201
	581	102	108	4330	16	98	676	13	59	5983
Territories	13	3	4	50	1	1	1			73
New Brunswick	3	1		16	1		1		1	26
Nova Scotia, D.C.	3	5		20	1		3			32
Ontario, D.C.	21	1	2	166			21	1	1	213
Quebec, D.C.	13	5	7	43		1	12			82
	40	12	9	247	2	2	37	1	3	353
British Colonies	3	1	8	15	2					29
Totals	637	118	129	4642	21	101	714	14	62	6438

The whole number of periodicals issued in the United States is 5983, with 73 to be added for the Territories, and 353 are printed in the Dominion of Canada, and 29 in the British Colonies, making a grand total of 6438, of which 637 are daily, 118 tri-weekly, 129 semi-weekly, 4642 weekly, 21 bi-weekly, 100 semi-monthly, 715 monthly, 14 bi-monthly, and 62 quarterly. New York has the largest number of publications, 894, of which 371 are printed in New York City, and Nevada has the smallest number issued in any State—only 15. Nevada has more

second, with 61. Next comes Illinois, with 38, and California has 34, being the fourth on the list. Delaware and Florida have each 1 daily paper. Kansas has as many as Vermont, West Virginia, Mississippi, and Arkansas combined. Nebraska and Nevada have each more dailies than either Oregon, Rhode Island,

A TABLE SHOWING THE AVERAGE CIRCULATION OF THE NEWSPAPERS AND PERIODICALS PRINTED IN THE UNITED STATES AND DOMINION OF CANADA.

	Daily.	Tri-Weekly	Semi-Weekly	Weekly	Bi-Weekly	Semi-M'nthly	M'nthly	Bi-M'nthly	Quarterly	Total.
Alabama	1,960	838		944		1,500				1,070
Arkansas	788	250		652			600			650
California	3,387	2,500	1,077	1,308		1,500	3,519		2,000	1,846
Connecticut	2,160		1,080	1,632	700	410	10,425		1,500	3,000
Delaware	1,488		763	1,278			2,000			1,247
District of Columbia	7,275			4,260			2,500		500	4,323
Florida	450			635						616
Georgia	2,095	876	587	1,050		438	3,273			1,270
Illinois	4,383	3,294	464	2,249	4,000	7,756	6,069	5,500	1,504	2,907
Indiana	2,490	450	628	1,129		587	4,102		3,000	1,490
Iowa	1,102	480	734	983	500		1,862		750	1,013
Kansas	1,539	309		1,024			10,665	5,000	5,000	1,828
Kentucky	3,348	500	1,080	1,768			2,880			1,968
Louisiana	3,903	400	1,000	846			2,833		1,168	1,220
Maine	1,436	348		2,377	480	720	2,763			2,257
Maryland	4,920			1,831			2,075		1,500	2,077
Massachusetts	10,436	600	1,983	4,541	1,267	1,670	8,852	4,009	6,174	5,709
Michigan	2,354	1,301		1,429	800		3,318		980	1,654
Minnesota	1,126	480	225	1,124			2,056			1,121
Mississippi	881	480	4,000	719		1,068	1,179			758
Missouri	4,511	2,997		1,633		7,900	3,111	1,050	1,500	2,104
Nebraska	910			885		1,000	1,021			913
Nevada	660		575	493						516
New Hampshire	961			1,760		400	6,880	1,000		2,194
New Jersey	2,164		300	1,146	200	500	2,646			1,475
New York	10,714	1,007	4,950	6,390	900	5,332	10,899	38,700	3,162	7,411
North Carolina	694	233	1,181	835	300	2,500	650			814
Ohio	6,148	663	1,720	2,888	2,000	2,748	4,140	1,400	500	3,154
Oregon	1,264			1,257			5,000		500	1,352
Pennsylvania	7,789	5,000	5,000	2,938		2,671	10,175	2,717	3,400	3,704
Rhode Island	4,410		1,000	2,066			900			2,489
South Carolina	1,686	906	490	1,054			5,338			1,354
Tennessee	2,483	1,150	1,700	1,383			1,305			1,747
Texas	628	704	443	721			980			701
Vermont	963			1,465			25,600			2,528
Virginia	1,651	772	986	1,001		950	1,389			1,107
West Virginia	1,267	350	216	801		600	1,550			842
Wisconsin	2,044	1,600	2,050	1,200		1,383	2,009			1,317
Territories	733	222	645	933		1,000	960			868
New Brunswick, D.C.	2,367	400		1,600	2,000	5,000	700		1,500	1,700
Nova Scotia, D.C.	1,367	1,610		1,165	400		2,283			
Ontario, D.C.	3,046	1,100	700	1,594			3,267		8,000	
Quebec, D.C.	3,154	1,647	1,596	2,687		14,500	1,492		900	
British Colonies	367	350	556	758	700					
Total Average	2,717	1,057	1,272	1,598	1,096	2,741	4,081	7,421	1,95?	

daily than weekly papers, and is unique in this respect, every other State having from three to twelve times as many weeklies as dailies. Tri-weekly papers are more common in the South than semi-weeklies, while in the Northern States the reverse is the case.

The largest number of daily papers published in any State is 89, in New York. Pennsylvania is

South Carolina, Vermont, West Virginia, Arkansas, Delaware, Florida, Maine, or Mississippi.

Of the 73 publications issued regularly in the Territories, 13 are daily and 50 weekly, 3 tri-weekly, 4 semi-weekly, 1 appears monthly, 1 semi-monthly, and 1 bi-weekly.

The papers of New York State have the largest

circulation, averaging 7411 each issue. Massachu-setts is second, with 5709 average; then comes the District of Columbia with 4323. Nevada has the smallest average circulation, only 515, while Florida averages 616, Arkansas 650, Texas 701, and Missis-

would appear if inserted once in all. The same ad-vertisement, if continued one year, would be printed the enormous number of 1,499,922,219 times. The total number of publications printed in an entire year in North Carolina will supply only four copies to each

A TABLE SHOWING THE AREA, POPULATION, ANNUAL CIRCULATION OF ALL NEWSPAPERS AND PERIODI-CALS PRINTED IN THE UNITED STATES AND DOMINION OF CANADA, AND THE NUMBER OF COPIES PRINTED EACH YEAR FOR EACH INHABITANT.

	Area in Square Miles.	Population.	Total Annual Circulation.	Average Number of Copies Printed Yearly for each Inhabitant.	Average Area for each Publication in Square Miles.
Alabama	50,722	1,002,240	8,891,432	9	676
Arkansas	52,198	474,818	2,438,716	5	1,065
California	188,891	559,742	45,869,408	82	1,032
Connecticut	4,750	537,418	15,697,320	29	60
Delaware	2,120	125,015	1,596,480	13	118
District of Columbia	60	131,706	11,637,400	89	3
Florida	59,248	176,741	841,880	5	2,693
Georgia	58,000	1,188,857	14,447,388	12	489
Illinois	55,410	2,548,337	102,086,204	41	116
Indiana	33,809	1,642,451	28,515,862	17	130
Iowa	55,045	1,193,083	19,344,636	16	204
Kansas	81,318	361,961	12,465,768	35	726
Kentucky	37,680	1,309,128	17,392,044	13	369
Louisiana	41,346	717,026	14,628,028	20	954
Maine	35,000	630,719	9,082,596	14	538
Maryland	11,124	779,750	19,461,660	25	122
Massachusetts	7,800	1,457,351	107,691,952	74	30
Michigan	56,461	1,184,266	17,513,120	15	425
Minnesota	83,531	432,387	2,811,120	7	811
Mississippi	47,156	859,006	4,403,440	5	518
Missouri	65,350	1,722,102	37,737,564	22	233
Nebraska	75,995	116,888	3,147,120	27	1,302
Nevada	81,539	42,667	1,714,960	40	5,436
New Hampshire	9,280	317,603	5,711,720	18	179
New Jersey	8,320	902,980	19,766,104	22	63
New York	47,000	4,370,848	492,770,868	113	57
North Carolina	50,704	1,074,235	4,220,676	4	805
Ohio	39,964	2,662,681	93,592,448	35	101
Oregon	95,274	90,922	3,658,304	40	2,977
Pennsylvania	46,000	3,611,543	233,380,532	67	83
Rhode Island	1,306	217,393	10,048,048	46	50
South Carolina	84,000	735,000	5,804,136	8	586
Tennessee	45,600	1,237,412	15,712,236	13	456
Texas	274,356	885,000	6,813,432	7	2,345
Vermont	10,212	330,235	4,486,944	14	232
Virginia	38,350	1,195,278	13,790,788	12	342
West Virginia	23,000	442,000	3,372,668	8	396
Wisconsin	53,924	1,052,878	20,577,396	20	277
Territories	1,041,366	297,934	3,820,121	13	14,465
New Brunswick, D. C	27,105	319,091	3,961,808	12	1,043
Nova Scotia, D. C	18,660	391,073	3,838,784	10	583
Ontario, D. C	121,260	2,000,000	33,757,528	17	680
Quebec, D. C	210,020	1,400,000	21,812,560	16	2,561
	3,380,254	42,617,960	1,499,922,219	35	550

sippi 753. The average circulation of all the daily papers published is 2717, of the weeklies, 1598, and of the monthlies, 4081. The average edition of all the papers printed is 1842, which, multiplied by 6438, the entire number of publications, gives 11,858,796 as the number of copies in which an advertisement

inhabitant, equivalent to one paper to every soul once in three months. Mississippi, Florida, and Arkansas do but little better, furnishing five copies per year, Alabama, Minnesota, South Carolina, Texas, and West Virginia all print less than enough to give each inhabitant a paper once in five weeks, while California gives 82 copies per year, exceeding every other State except New York, which prints 113 copies per year for every soul within its borders. As New York papers circulate everywhere, while those of California do not go very much out of the State, it is evident that the papers issued there have a better local support than those of any other State of the American Union.

In the District of Columbia we find that one newspaper is published for every three square miles of territory. Massachusetts has one to thirty square miles, and Rhode Island one to fifty; then comes New York with one to 57; Connecticut has one to 60, New Jersey one to 63, Texas one to 2345, Florida one to 2693; while in the Territories one newspaper spreads its circulation over no less than 14,465 square miles.

There are 548 papers in the United States which print more than 5000 copies each issue, and 11 which print more than 100,000. The New York Weekly has the largest circulation given; among the political mediums the New York Weekly Tribune takes the lead, and among the agricultural weeklies Moore's Rural New-Yorker stands first. The New York Independent is the largest paper, and has the largest circulation of any religious paper. Nearly 1000 papers are printed on the auxiliary plan—that is, on sheets purchased from New York, Chicago, and other centres, with one side already printed. This number has more than doubled within one year. More than 1000 new newspapers have been established since the first of March, 1870, and the number of new ones announced since January 1, 1871, has averaged nearly four per day. The number of suspensions is about one-fourth as large as that of the new issues announced. Messrs. Geo. P. Rowell & Co. assert that the number of newspapers issued has fully doubled within six years.

In looking over the publications devoted to specialities (or class publications) we find the religious largely predominate over any other class, which shows the interest the public press takes in the moral and religious welfare of the country. There are in the United States 283 publications advocating evangelical or sectarian ideas, and 22 in the Dominion of Canada, with none either in the territories or the colonies. Of this number New York City has 44, Philadelphia 23, Boston 21, while Florida, Kansas, Nevada, and New Jersey are entirely unrepresented.

The farmers, horticulturists, and stock-raisers have their interests represented by an agricultural press numbering no less than 106 publications, many of which are gotten up at great expense and are very extensively circulated.

The medical profession enlightens its members through the columns of 72 publications, of which 5 are weeklies, 50 monthlies, 3 semi-monthlies, 3 bi-monthlies, and 11 quarterlies.

Nearly all the schools of medicine have their representative organs, each of which circulates among its admirers, and is criticised severely by its cotemporaries, whose views differ from it about the healing of the nations, while there are a number that furnish intelligence of interest to all medical men, as well as the general reader, without taking sides for or against any particular school of medicine.

Most of the colleges, and many of the State Boards of Education, have each their representative organ; besides which there are several publications that treat educational matters in a general way. Of this class there are 84 in the United States, and 6 in the Dominion of Canada. They are mostly monthlies, with an occasional weekly, bi-weekly, and quarterly.

The large cities have their commercial papers, which are nearly all issued weekly.

Insurance is discussed through the medium of 19 special publications, 12 of which are issued monthly, a number of them being noted for their superior typographical appearance.

Freemasonry, temperance, odd-fellowship, music, mechanics, law, sporting, real-estate, and woman's suffrage, have each their representative organs, many of which are edited with ability, have extensive circulations, and net large incomes to their enterprising publishers.

The list of class publications is increasing rapidly of late, its ratio of increase being greater than that of the entire press of the country taken together, owing, probably, to the fact that the increase of wealth and population of the country makes it possible and profitable to publish class papers where, but a very few years back, they could not have been made self-supporting.

The number of papers published in other languages than the English is growing rapidly, owing to the immense immigration from foreign countries, especially Germany, France, Scandinavia, and Italy.

The publications printed in the German language in the United States number 341, and in the Dominion of Canada 5, and are over three times as many as the sum of all the other publications in foreign languages combined.

The publications in the French language are confined principally to Louisiana and the Province of Quebec, where the language is in common use.

The Scandinavian publications number 18, and are confined entirely to the West and Northwest (with a single exception, that of a daily, semi-weekly, and weekly in New York City), the immigrants from Denmark, Norway, and Sweden having principally settled there.

In the Spanish language there are but 7, Hollandish 6, Italian 4, Welsh 3, Bohemian 2, Portuguese 1, Cherokee 1, none of which have a very wide circulation.

GREAT BRITAIN.

The following statements indicate the amount of printing done at various periods in Great Britain:

In 1599, the number of master printers in the whole of London was twenty-two; the journeymen numbered about sixty. No other printers were allowed in the kingdom, except in the Universities of Oxford and Cambridge. The number of persons who exercised the art in England, from its introduction in

1474. to the end of the sixteenth century, was about two hundred; in Scotland, eleven; in Ireland, two; and in Wales, one.

In 1666, the total number of working printers then residing in London, who had served a regular apprenticeship, was 140.

The following official returns were made of the number of newspapers stamped, and of the amount of duties received for stamps and advertisements, in Great Britain, during various periods in the eighteenth century:

1753	7,411,757	1779	14,105,842
1760	9,464,790	1780	14 217,371
1774	12,300,000	1790	14 035,639
1775	12,680,000	1791	14,791,152
1776	12,830,900	1792	14,791,198
1777	13,150,512	1793	17,073,621
1778	13,240,059		

1796. The number of newspapers sent through the London post-office during this year was 8,600,000.

1797. Stamps on newspapers: England, £144,940 14s. 10d.—Scotland, £9482 12s. 9d.—Total, £154,423 7s. 7d.

1798. The net duty received on advertisements in the United Kingdom was, for newspapers, £82,104; on pamphlets, £153; for stamps on newspapers, £154,423; England, £215,154; Scotland, £15,521; Ireland, £6103.

1799. Advertisements in newspapers paid £102,990; in pamphlets, £168; stamps on newspapers, £180,240; England, £200,831; Scotland, £17,694; Ireland, £4873.

1800. Advertisements in newspapers, £79,508; in pamphlets, £233; stamps on newspapers, £184,204; England, £238,817; Scotland, £18,754; Ireland, £6,-873.

The number of all the new publications published in London during the year 1800 was 693, and the cost of a single copy of each work, in boards, was £230 5s.

The number of new publications issued in Great Britain from 1800 to 1827, including reprints altered in size and price, but excluding pamphlets, was, according to the London Catalogue, 19,860. Deducting one-fifth for the reprints, we have 15,888 new books in twenty-seven years; showing an average of 588 new books per year, being an increase of 216 per year over the last eleven years of the eighteenth century.

In 1831, according to the census returns of that year, there were 3628 printers in London, and in Ireland 914 letter-press printers.

In 1833, the number of newspapers published in England was thirteen daily; six two or three times a week; thirty-six once a week; and one hundred and eighty provincial:—in Scotland, fifteen twice or three times a week; thirty-one weekly:—in Ireland; in Dublin, five daily; seven three times a week; and fifty-seven provincial:—in British Islands, Guernsey, Jersey, and Man, two twice a week, and eleven weekly—total, 369. The total number of newspapers

which passed through all the post-offices in the United Kingdom and Ireland, in 1833, was 41,600,000.

In 1833, the commercial value of literary works published in England amounted to £415,300; and adding to this the amount of daily and weekly papers, reviews, and magazines, the general sale of English literature was then estimated at £2,420,900 sterling. There were published two hundred and thirty-six monthly periodical works; a single copy of each cost £17 12s. 6d.

In 1837, the number of weekly periodical works (not newspapers) issued in London was about fifty, of which the following is an analysis: -Religious, 6; literary criticism, 2; musical criticism, 1; medical, 4; scientific, 2; for the advocacy of peculiar opinions,—one advocating opinions similar to those in the works of Carlyle, and one by the friends of co-operation, 2; miscellanies, 18; tales and stories, 5; attempts at fun, some of them called forth by the success of the Pickwick Papers—mostly trash, 7; and sporting slang, 1. Two hundred and thirty-six monthly periodical works were sent out on the last day of each month, to every corner of the United Kingdom, from Paternoster Row. There were also thirty-four periodical works, published quarterly, making a total of 270. Of the monthly periodicals, including the weekly issued in parts, fifty-eight were devoted to general literature; forty-eight to various branches of science, natural history, etc.; forty-six religious and missionary—many the organs of particular sects; four histories of England, appearing periodically; seventeen works issuing in volumes—a few in parts; twenty to the fine arts—picture-galleries—topography; six to the fashions. Of the remainder, many were very cheap periodicals, addressed chiefly to children.

The census returns of 1861 stated the number of printers (counting apprentices and minors, and females as well as males) to be, in England, 30 590; in Scotland, 4470.

The London Printer's Register for March, 1868, said, The one fact that must strike all readers is the marked and continuous increase of literary activity which has characterized the last few years; an increase which, as evidenced by the number of newspapers published in the British Isles, has gone on at a rate vastly more rapid than the coincident increase of the population. Between 1851 and 1861, the census showed an advance of 14 per cent. In other words, for every 100 persons to buy papers in the first-named year, there were 114 in the last. But, taking the years 1857 and 1867 as standards of comparison in newspaper matters, we find that the growth of the press as a power has been immensely greater than the mere numerical increase of the nation. In January, 1858, there were 866 journals; in 1868 there are 1324. In 1858 there were 41 dailies; in 1868 there are 85. So that while the population has only increased by 14 per cent., the number of newspapers has increased by nearly 60 per cent., and the daily press especially by more than 100 per cent. Surprising as are these figures, they do but partially represent the development which has taken place. The number of copies sold by the press of to-day is, we should think, at least ten times as large as that of ten years ago. Then the Times held the foremost place, not only in influence, but in circulation. Now, whatever be thought of its power, its constituency is confessedly more limited than that of several of its rivals. The Standard and the Telegraph each issue every morning nearly three times as many copies as the Leviathan of Printing-House Square, while it would be easy to point to powerful and well-conducted provincial papers, which would run him very hard if they had to pit their impression against his.

In 1869, according to Mitchell's Newspaper Press Directory, there were 1372 journals published in the United Kingdom, distributed as follows:—

England—London 260
Provinces . . . 779
————1039
Wales 51
Scotland 136
Ireland 131
British Isles 15

There were 89 daily papers published in the United Kingdom, distributed as follows:—

England 63
Wales 1
Scotland 136
Ireland 131
British Isles 15

The Magazines then in course of publication, including the Quarterly Reviews, numbered 655, of which no less than 248 were of a decidedly religious character.

The number of new works published during 1867 in England reached 3516 vols., amounting to £1089 9s. 11d. at the publishing price. The number of reprints of books previously published was 1422 vols., at the sum of £429; amounting in all to 4938 vols., at a cost of £1518 9s. 11d.

The London Publishers' Circular stated that 4581 new publications and reprints appeared in Great Britain during 1868. The American Literary Gazette placed the number at 4439, against 4144 in 1867, and 4204 in 1866.

Longman & Co.'s Catalogue for 1870 stated that there were in that year published in London, of monthly magazines and serials, 361; of quarterly, 70; of transactions of various societies, 39; and of newspapers and other periodicals, 299; making a total of 769. In the year 1869, there were—monthly, 372; quarterly, 72; transactions, 89; and newspapers, etc., 298; total, 781.

The London Publishers' Circular of December 31, 1870, gave the following analytical table of books published in Great Britain in 1870, a denoting new books; b new editions; and c American importations:

Theology, Sermons, Biblical, etc............ { a 548 / b 208 / c 55 } ——— 811

Educational, Philology, Classical, etc...... { a 406 / b 142 / c 20 } ——— 568

Juvenile Works and Tales.................... { a 486 / b 171 / c 38 } ——— 695

Novels and other Works of Fiction........ { a 200 / b 162 / c 19 } ——— 381

Law, Jurisprudence, etc...................... { a 64 / b 39 / c 20 } ——— 123

Political and Social Economy, and Trade and Commerce............................. { a 77 / b 26 / c 16 } ——— 119

Arts, Science, and Fine Art Works........ { a 205 / b 83 / c 58 } ——— 346

Travel and Geographical Research.......... { a 245 / b 52 / c 41 } ——— 338

History and Biography...................... { a 235 / b 106 / c 55 } ——— 396

Poetry and the Drama...................... { a 212 / b 134 / c 20 } ——— 366

Year Books and Bound Volumes of Serials { a 313 / b 13 / c 12 } ——— 338

Medicine and Surgery...................... { a 106 / b 49 / c 38 } ——— 193

Belles-Lettres, Essays, Monographs, etc... { a 155 / b 71 / c 23 } ——— 249

Miscellaneous, including Pamphlets, not Sermons..................... .... { a 125 / b 23 / c 11 } ——— 159

Total.................... 5082

Summary for each month:	New Books.	New Editions.	American Importations.
January................................234	88	58	
February..............................301	112	21	
March..................................309	113	43	
April...................................267	120	26	
May....................................261	108	39	
June...................................254	117	35	
July....................................252	96	25	
August.................................159	76	26	
September..............................178	82	35	
October................................340	107	41	
November..............................375	129	45	
December 447	131	32	
	3377	1279	426

Making the total during the twelve months, of 5082 new publications.

FRANCE.

In November, 1864, *L'Imprimerie*, a Parisian Typographical journal, said, There are 85 licensed printers in Paris, exclusive of the Imperial office and that of the *Moniteur Universel*.

The value of their production in 1860 was 31,883,-720 francs. Three firms produced work of the value of 2,000,000 francs; three others less than 25,000 francs.

The number of workmen is 6158, viz., men, 5308; women, 408; boys over 16 years, 249; apprentices, 190; girls, 3. Of these workmen, 1300 worked by the day, and 3923 by the piece. The average of daily wages is from 4 to 5 francs; 446 receive from 2½ to 3 francs (these are sheet-flyers, wheel-turners, stitchers, and paper-cutters); 551 from 3½ to 3½ francs; 1307 from 4 to 4½ francs; 1376, 5 francs; 1153 from 5½ to 6 francs; 207 from 6½ to 7 francs; 112 from 7½ to 8 francs; 133 from 9 to 10 francs; 21, 12 francs; 1, 15 francs; 1, 20 francs. In the latter classes are the proof-readers, makers-up, overseers of presses, fancy job-printers, and swift compositors.

Of women, 147 work by the day, and 261 by the piece. Their wages range from 1 to 3 francs—the average about 2½ francs. Boys earn about 1½ francs, and girls about 1½ francs, daily. Apprentices average 1½ francs.

The working day includes 11 hours—from 6 to 7 in summer and from 8 to 7 in winter. 60 printers state that they have had no dull season; with the others the dull season lasts through July, August, and September.

Of the 5307 male workmen, 4658 kept house or boarded, and 650 lived in furnished rooms; of the 408 female workmen, 382 kept house or boarded, and 26 hired furnished rooms. All the apprentices are sons of the workmen; 173 of them are not indentured. The lowest term of service for an apprentice is 3 years.

These printers employ 417 hand-presses, and 339 machine-presses, and 57 steam engines.

Type-Founders.—Their number in 1860 was 53, of whom 15 were punch-cutters, 30 type-casters, and 8 stereotypers. The entire value of their work is 2,880,300 francs, of which 165,500 francs are exported to America. They pay out in wages 71,060 francs.

The number of workmen is 825, viz., 660 men, 120 women, and 45 boys, including 18 apprentices. 108 work by the day, and 552 by the piece. Their average wages is 4½ francs. The working day is 12 hours, from 6 to 6 in summer, and 7 to 7 in winter—this includes 2 hours for meals.

Lithography and Copperplate Work.—There are 367 of this class of printers, the annual value of whose work amounts to 12,766,320 francs. The number of workmen is 3119, viz., 2540 men, 230 women, 445 boys, including 266 apprentices. 867 men work by the day, and 1677 by the piece. Their wages average 5 francs.

According to official intelligence (blue books) laid before the French Chambers, there were, on the 1st January, 1867, published, all over France, 336 political newspapers, 64 in Paris, and 272 in the departments; of non-political, there were 1435, 710 in Paris, and 725 in the departments; altogether, therefore, 1771 papers. On the 31st of October the number of political papers had risen to 384 (an increase of 48), 74 of which were being published in Paris (an increase of 10), and 310 in the departments (an increase of 38); the non-political papers stood, at the same date, thus: all France, 1692 (an increase of 257), of which 886 were published in Paris (increase of 186), and 806 in the departments (increase of 81).

According to an official return of French journals made in 1869 (which probably embraced only those published in Paris), there were at that time 932, classified as follows:—Catholic organs, 62; Protestant, 25; Jewish, 3; instruction, 28; jurisprudence, 48; administration, 25; political, 45; political economy and commerce, 47; medical science, 58; natural, physical, and mathematical science, 40; agriculture and veterinary art, 32; horticulture and arboriculture, 10; military art, 20; marine and colonies, 12; geographical history and heraldry, 24; fine arts, painting, sculpture, music, and theatres, 65; architecture, 9; archaeology, numismatics, 19; railways, bridges, roads, and mines, 29; financial journals, and Bourse returns, 28; technology and popular science, 65; literature, 86; journals of ladies, young ladies, families, and children, 35; fashions and ladies' work, 65; racing, fishing, shooting, and play, 25; freemasonry, 5; spiritualism, 5; bibliographical, 16. One religious monthly paper has a circulation of 50,000; and the *Journal de St. Joseph* sells 56,000 copies.

GERMANY.

The following table, compiled in Steiger's *Monatsbericht*, gives a comprehensive summary of the book-trade of Germany (Austria, Prussia, and all the German States, being probably counted as part of Germany) for the years 1868 and 1869:

	1868.	1869.
General Literature	196	262
Theology	1440	1607
Law, Politics, and Statistics	970	1141
Medicine	528	517
Natural Science and Chemistry	636	675
Philosophy	126	127
Educational	966	1131
Juvenile	246	322
Classical and Oriental	440	471
Modern Languages	322	335
History and Biographies	710	634
Geography	290	269
Mathematics and Astronomy	124	124
Military Science	281	308
Commercial Treatises	425	424
Architectural, Engineering, and Shipping	190	213
Forest Culture and Mining	83	93
Agriculture and Horticulture	280	305

	1864.	1869.
Belles-Lettres	958	999
Art, Music, and Stenography	437	435
Popular Pamphlets	237	335
Free Masonry	14	8
Miscellaneous	381	364
Slavonian and Hungarian	48	62
Maps and Charts	225	144
Total	10,563	11,530

In a speech made by Herr Frank at a meeting of the Historical Society at Leipsic, in 1869, he gave the following particulars of the printing-trade of that city. In the year 1709 only 355 works were published there, whilst in 1859 the number had increased to 1582, and at Berlin to 1299. In periodical literature Leipsic can only boast of 178, whilst at Berlin 194 are published. In 1867 the quantity of printed matter issued at Leipsic weighed 130,000 centners. The Gartenlaube alone, with its circulation of 280,000 copies, uses up 4000 bales of paper annually. The 47 printing-establishments at Leipsic, which are continually extending the sphere of their operations and obtain considerable printing orders from England and Russia, work with 98 hand-presses, 214 simple machine presses, and 4 large double machine presses. They give regular employment to 1000 workmen, 300 apprentices, and 450 women.

The postal statistics of the North German Confederation give some information respecting the circulation of newspapers. According to these, 1983 newspapers were transmitted by post during the first quarter of 1869, 581 of which were political and 1402 non-political. Of the political newspapers, 505 had a postal subscription of under and up to 1000 copies; 32 over 1000 and up to 2000; 13 from 2000 to 3000; 10 from 3000 to 4000; 8 from 4000 to 5000; 7 from 5000 to 6000; 2 from 6000 to 7000; 2 from 7000 to 8000; 1 from 8000 to 9000; none from 9000 to 10,000; and finally one (the Cologne Gazette) from 10,000 to 15,000.

In all Germany (including Austria) there were published, a short time before 1870, 2297 newspapers or journals, 198 being published in Berlin, and 159 in Vienna.

Recently published statistics show that there were at Berlin, in 1811, 24 master printers, which number declined to 21 in 1816, probably from the effects of the wars of 1813–15. It rose to no more than 32 in 1835, and to 42 in 1842. From that year the numbers have steadily increased, and they were 60 in 1850, 85 in 1860, and 115 in 1868. There were at Berlin, in 1811, 31 publishers; in 1816, 26; in 1835, 70; in 1842, 87; in 1850, 154; in 1860, 210; and in 1868, 230. The lithographic art was seemingly not much known before 1840, as our statistics show lithographers to have numbered 33 in 1842, and 69 in 1850. From 1860 to 1868 they nearly doubled their numbers, being 140 in the former and 208 in the latter year.

On January 1, 1867, 291 newspapers were published in the little kingdom of Saxony.

In 1868 there were published in Austria 178 political and 481 non-political newspapers and journals, 381 of which were printed in the German and 107 in the Hungarian language, the remainder being made up by the polyglot composition of the Austrian empire.

Other portions of Europe.—In Holland there are 156 paper-mills, 318 printing-offices, 935 booksellers, 30 music-sellers, 80 lithographers, 11 wood-engraving establishments, 54 trade bookbinders, 10 stereotypers and type-founders, and 10 printers' and bookbinders' brokers.

The number of newspapers and periodicals now published in Warsaw amounts to 33; in the other districts of Poland, to 12, among which are 2 in the German language; in the whole kingdom, therefore, there are 45 published.

Switzerland has 394 newspapers, of which 46 are dailies.

A large amount of printing is also done in Russia, Italy, Spain, Greece, Portugal, Norway, Sweden, and Turkey. Newspapers as well as books are printed in all these countries. A few years ago 33 journals were printed in Constantinople, in ten languages; and recent political events have given a great impetus to journalism in Italy and Spain.

MISCELLANEOUS.

The following estimate of the number of newspapers and their proportion to population was made in 1870:

	Population.	Newspapers.	Inhabitants.
France	37,000,000 has	1640	1 paper per 23,000
Great Britain	28,000,000 "	1260	" 23,000
United States	35,000,000 "	5000	" 7,000
Prussia	18,000,000 "	700	" 26,000
Italy	22,000,000 "	500	" 44,000
Austria	38,000,000 "	365	" 15,080
Switzerland	2,500,000 "	400	" 6,250
Belgium	4,700,000 "	275	" 15,000
Holland	3,500,000 "	225	" 16,000
Russia	66,000,000 "	200	" 330,000
Spain	15,000,000 "	200	" 75,000
Swd'n & Nor'y	5,200,000 "	150	" 36,000
Denmark	2,000,000 "	100	" 20,000
Turkey	30,000,000 "	100	" 300,000

The number of paper-mills in the principal states of Europe is estimated as follows: Great Britain, 408; France, 276; Germany, 243; Austria, 78; Russia, 40; Italy, 30; Belgium, 26; Spain, 17; Switzerland, 14; Sweden, 8; Turkey, 1. The annual production of paper in Europe is 8,956,000 cwt., valued at £15,004,400.

Six newspapers are now published at Honolulu, the capital of the Sandwich Islands, three of them being in English and the rest of them in the Hawaii language. There is an average circulation of 7800 of the native papers and about 2200 of the English, making a total average circulation of 10,000 for a population which consists of 600,000 natives and 5000 foreigners.

New South Wales (of which Sydney is the capital)

has a population of 400,000 inhabitants, and has now 49 newspapers; two of them are dailies, and one an evening paper, published in Sydney; all the rest are published once, twice, and three times a week. Victoria (of which Melbourne is the capital) has a population about one-third larger than New South Wales, and possesses 60 newspapers. Three of these are dailies, published in Melbourne, and two or three dailies are also published at the diggings; the remainder are issued at various intervals, as at Sydney.

A modern catalogue of the titles and editions of the books printed before the year 1500—made with all the conciseness of a German bibliographer – by Hain, in his Repertorium Bibliographicum, occupies four good-sized octavo volumes, printed in small type, and with all possible abbreviations, enumerates 16,312 publications, consisting of different works, or different editions of the same works, made in about the space of forty years. It has been estimated that an average edition with the old printers was about five hundred copies. Supposing that these 16,312 editions consisted each of five hundred copies, this would give us eight million one hundred and fifty-six thousand volumes printed and offered for sale in Europe within a space of little over forty years. In this view of the case, the publishing activity of the fifteenth century will compare not unfavorably with that of the nineteenth.

In 1828 M. Adrian Balbi estimated that upwards of three thousand one hundred and sixty-eight periodicals were published in the world. Of these, two thousand one hundred and forty-two were published in Europe, nine hundred and seventy-eight in America, twenty-seven in Asia, twelve in Africa, and nine in Oceania. The United States of America, with a population of eleven millions, had eight hundred journals, whilst the British empire, with a population of one hundred and forty-two millions, had but five hundred and eighty-eight periodicals.

In 1841 Henry G. Bohn, a London bookseller, published a catalogue of 330,000 volumes, comprising books of recognized merit in the fine arts, natural history, classics, and in the German, French, Spanish, Portuguese, Northern, Oriental, and Hebrew languages.

Statute.—An act of the legislature of a state or country; usually, in the United States, applied to Congressional enactments in force over the whole Union; the enactments of the several states being generally distinguished as state laws.

Steam Power.—This is one of the most important auxiliaries of modern printing, as it propels the presses of all offices in which a large amount of press-work is executed; and many offices are designated as Steam-power Printing-offices.

Steel Engraving.—The art of producing, by incision or corrosion, designs upon steel plates, from which impressions or prints may be obtained by pressure. Various methods are applicable to the treatment of steel, and have already been described under the separate heads of COPPER-PLATE, ETCHING, MEZZOTINT, etc. Steel was made especially available

for the requirements of art by the inventions of Perkins, the American engraver, and has since almost superseded copper.

Stencil.—A plate or sheet of any material with the pattern cut out so that by the aid of a color-brush the figure can be marked upon some surface beneath.

Stenography.—The art of writing in short-hand, by using abbreviations or characters in place of the entire word. Various systems of stenography were invented and much used before the introduction of phonography.

Stephens.—The Anglicized name of the family of Estienne, which furnished a continuous succession of famous printers for nearly two centuries; at least twelve members of the family excelling in typography in Paris and Geneva during the sixteenth and seventeenth centuries. Some confusion has arisen in the history of this princely line of printers from the repetition of the same name through several generations, and they are generally distinguished in royal fashion, as Henry the First or Second, Antoine the Third or Fifth, etc. The most famous printers in the line were Henry Estienne, the first printer of the name, and his three sons, Francis I., Robert I., and Charles. Robert I., who assumed the name Stephens, had three sons known as printers, viz.: Henry II., Robert II., and Francis II.; Henry II., being followed in direct lineal succession by his sons Paul and Joseph, grandson Antoine, and great-grandson Henry III. Robert II., was succeeded by his son Robert III. Francis II., had two sons also printers, named Gervaise and Adrian.

Of Henry Estienne, the first of this long line of typographers, not much is known with certainty, but that he was a learned man of noble birth, who alienated himself from his family and abandoned his title in his enthusiastic admiration of the new art which offered a mechanical method for reproducing the stores of the student for the education of all classes of society. Impelled by this admiration, he practiced printing with intense devotion, and for this engagement in a mechanical industry lost his position and rank, apparently without regret, for neither he nor his descendants ever endeavored to regain their relinquished position, but worthily and proudly maintained the honorable title of erudite typographers which they held uninterruptedly through so many successive generations. It is not known where or when Henry acquired his practical knowledge, but he was officiating in conjunction with Wolfgang Hopyll, as printer to the University of Paris, as early as the year 1496. His name also appears in conjunction with those of Jean Petit, Denis Roce, and Jodocus Badius, respectively. He began to print by himself in 1504, latinizing his name in Henricum Stephanum, and published more than one hundred distinct works. He generally used Roman letter, but sometimes employed the new popular character, a semi-gothic and abbreviated letter, imitated from the manuscripts of the period. His publications were all in Latin, and upon scholastic and scientific subjects; the last being dated in 1520. He used the arms of the University with the addition of his own initials.

FRANCIS I. printed with Simon de Colines, who married the widow of Henry Stephens. After separating from his step-father, he printed alone, and enjoyed a great reputation as a typographer, especially from 1537 to 1547. He was a sworn printer to the University of Paris. His type in Roman and Italic was both handsome and accurate. He published two works entirely in Greek, the Psalter of 1542, the Horæ Virginis of 1543, and is believed to have issued ten other works. His mark or device was a pedestal surmounted by a closed volume, on which stood a vase containing a vine. In some of his publications Greek mottoes or verses were also added, which may be rendered,—

> Transient the rose's bloom! when past and gone,
> Seek you the flower?—you'll find the bush alone.
>
> Of all things, the most difficult is to please everybody.

ROBERT I. was born in 1503, and therefore was seventeen years of age at the death of his father, and had probably received instruction from him. With his elder brother Francis, mentioned above, he worked under the instruction of their step-father Simon de Colines, and Robert subsequently acted as the director of his press. In 1524, Robert became sole proprietor of his father's printing establishment, and from that time until 1552 continued to publish works remarkable for their typographical perfection. He married the daughter of Jodocus Badius, a woman of remarkable learning, who made her husband's corps of scholarly proof-readers especially welcome to her house. The various members of this circle belonged to different nations, and, as the only means of common and convenient intercourse, used the Latin language, which was fluently spoken by the wife of Robert. It was amid such daily associations that her children were educated into the remarkable scholarship which they exhibited in after-life. Finding a new dictionary of the Latin tongue much needed by the University, Robert Stephens undertook the labor himself in 1528, and labored on it so indefatigably, day and night, for two years, that he kept two presses in constant exercise. His remarkable erudition and professional ability and zeal attracted the admiration and esteem of the King of France, Francis I., who was then anxiously endeavoring to introduce the study of the Greek language, and he appointed Robert Stephens Royal Printer of Hebrew and Latin, and afterwards of Greek. (See IMPRIMERIE IMPÉRIALE.) Defended by this friendship, Robert continued prosperously until the death of that monarch; but Francis's son and successor ordered the Bibles published by Robert Stephens to be examined by the faculty of theology. The doctors of the Sorbonne censured some of the marginal annotations; and Robert, fully aware of the dangerous influence of the enemy he had to encounter, secretly dispersed his family, sending them by different routes outside of France, and then fled himself for safety to Geneva, where most of his family joined him. In that city Robert Stephens printed with great zeal and industry, adding to his original reputation under the assumed or rather Anglicized name which he formally adopted as a means of security. After a short time, his son Henry, one of the most distinguished printers and authors of the family, returned to Paris, using the name of Estienne, enjoyed all the honors of personal intimacy and friendship with the king, and kept his father completely acquainted with the affairs of Paris, which information was frequently of great service to the Calvinists of Geneva, with whom Robert had been almost forced into sympathy by the persecution of the Sorbonne. Robert died in Geneva in 1559. In the language of the historian De Thou, Not only France, but the world owes more to him than to the greatest warrior that ever extended the possessions of his country, and greater glory has redounded to Francis I. from the industry of Robert Stephens than from all the illustrious warlike and pacific undertakings in which he was engaged.

CHARLES the Third, son of the founder of the family, was even a finer scholar than his brothers Francis and Robert, who have been already mentioned. During his youth, he traveled much throughout Europe, increasing the vast stores of his learning upon scientific and artistic subjects, and became a particular friend of Paul Manutius. On his return from his travels he became a physician in Paris, and was much distinguished in the profession, writing several important works upon medicine. About the time that his brother Robert fled to Geneva, Charles, impelled by his inherited tastes, abandoned the profession which he was adorning, and established himself as a printer. He produced a very large number of books, which not only appeared with extraordinary rapidity, but are held by some critics to have surpassed those of the rest of his family in elegance of workmanship. His great merit won him the title of King's Printer, which was never granted to Henry, the son of the recusant Robert. Charles remained King's Printer from 1551 to 1561; he also wrote a number of works upon scientific subjects, and others upon various topics tending to the promotion of critical and grammatical studies and the advancement of general learning. Charles is accused of being jealous of his brothers and nephews, and inimical to their interests; but it is probable that the religious controversies of the age affected their personal relations, and that the learned printer of Paris, satisfied with his scientific studies and his comfortable fortune, derived mainly through the friendship of the King and the Sorbonne, did not wish to embroil himself in the difficulties of his heretic brother in Geneva.

HENRY II. was born in Paris in 1528, when his father was writing his dictionary. The scholarship of the household affected Henry to such an extent that he became at a very early age a remarkable Greek scholar; he enjoyed the advantages of the courses of lectures upon languages established by Francis I., and assisted his father in the preparation of Greek books for the press. This precocious learning injured his health, and he spent three years and a half in travel in Italy, studying her art and antiquities. In 1550, Henry visited England, and received a warm welcome from the learned and gentle Edward VI. He returned home through Flanders; and the intercourse with Spaniards in that country and in England attracted his attention to the literature and language of Spain. He must have reached Paris just as his father made his escape, and soon afterwards established himself in his place, and enjoyed the friendship of King Henry, just as his father had enjoyed the confidence of Francis; and although the office of King's Printer was given to his uncle Charles, Henry received and published under the protection of a privilege from the king. His first publication, an Anacreon, in 1554, ranks as an extraordinarily elegant and perfect book; he introduced the work by a letter and poem in Greek from his own pen. He visited Italy again, and engaged successfully in diplomatic intrigue in a public position at Naples, while he secretly visited Geneva to see his father. On his return to Paris he again engaged industriously in typography, and edited with great skill and erudition the works which he published. In 1558, Ulric Fugger, the merchant prince of Augsburg, made Henry Stephens his private printer, with a munificent salary. Henry, like his father, married a woman of remarkable learning, the daughter of a Greek professor, and her son Paul was a man of great learning. In 1569, Henry published a list of the books issued from his press, apparently on the plan of the modern publishers' circular, and preceded it with some humorous verses explaining to his friends and the public the reasons why he preferred this method of announcement to sending his books, as he had previously done, to the fair at Frankfort.

In 1572 Henry published his magnificent original work, the Greek Thesaurus, inscribed to the Emperor Maximilian, Charles IX. of France, Elizabeth of England, John George, Marquis of Brandenburg, and the academic institutions of their domains. This splendid publication bears the date of the eve of St. Bartholomew, and it is supposed that it was in part executed in Geneva, for it is hardly possible that Henry, suspected of Protestantism, could have escaped if he had been in Paris holding a conspicuous position. From the exigencies of the times, Henry published books in Geneva, Paris, London, and several other places; and the perfection of his typography is amazing, when it is considered that war and the rumors of war frequently interrupted his printing-press while in full operation, and compelled him to seek peace and safety in a speedy retreat. Henry used as a device the olive-tree adopted by his father.

FRANCIS II., son of Robert the First, was a remarkable linguist, and, having embraced the Reformed religion, practiced printing in Geneva from 1562 to 1582. He published the works of Calvin, a Bible in French, and the New Testament in French and Latin, besides other works. He finally settled in Normandy, where he married, and two of his sons, Gervaise and Adrien, were printers or booksellers in Paris.

ROBERT III., the son of Robert the Second, printed in Paris for about half a century; his last publication bears the date of 1640. He received the title of Poet and Interpreter of the King for the Greek and Latin languages; and a considerable number of his Greek and Latin epigrams have been preserved. As King's Interpreter, he translated into French a part of Aristotle's Rhetoric.

PAUL, son of Henry the Second, was born about 1566, and received his education chiefly at Geneva, under the care of his grandfather. He traveled extensively during his youth, as one of the most effective means of completing his education and introducing him to the world, and his father, who directed his journeys, also employed him at intervals in his own printing-office, so that he was from extreme youth familiar with the mechanical processes of his future profession. Henry also sent Paul to spend a considerable time under the instruction of the distinguished Commelin of Heidelberg and Tornasius of Lyons, just as he had himself had the advantages of instruction from Manutius. Paul paid much attention to Greek verse, and became a proficient. Upon the death of his father, in 1598, Paul succeeded him, and continued to print for many years.

ANTOINE, the son of Paul, was born in Geneva, but was educated at Lyons and Paris, where he abjured the Reformed religion about 1612. He was a printer and bookseller in Paris, and afterwards became King's printer and held various offices, enjoying several pensions. His handsomest works are those published in conjunction with the Societas Græcarum Editionem. He was distinguished for his learning, especially in Greek literature. Antoine became decrepit and impoverished, and died in a hospital at Paris at the age of eighty. His son Henry, a printer and bookseller in 1646, was afterwards King's printer. With the last-named Henry the uninterrupted succession of printers in this family is believed to have closed; but in the year 1826 Firmin Didot was introduced to a young man named Paul Stephens, a lineal descendant of the race; this youth was apprenticed to the Didots, and proved himself so worthy of his descent that he became the director of the mechanical presses of that famous establishment, and again revived in the same profession a name rendered illustrious in the annals of typography three centuries and a half before. Foremost among the high honors to which this family is entitled, is their publication, during the ages of severest religious persecution, of forty-five editions of the Bible in various languages.

Stereotype.—The word is derived from the Greek words stereos, fixed, and typos, form, type; the literal meaning therefore signifies a fixed form of metal. There are at the present time three modes of stereotyping successfully practiced, known as the plaster, clay, and paper or papier maché methods; stereotyping in copper may properly be said to constitute a fourth (see ELECTROTYPING). Of these various processes, the plaster, the oldest as well as the most perfect method, may be thus briefly described.

The pages of type, being imposed in the composing-rooms in an iron stereotype chase, are sent to the casting-room and placed by the moulder upon the moulding-stone. The face of the type is first rubbed with fine olive- or sperm-oil, in order to prevent the adhesion of the plaster mould. Around the form, and fitting closely to it, is placed a metal frame-work of about three-quarters of an inch in depth, called a

with others, is next placed, with the face down, on the floater, a plate of metal fitting on the inside of the pan. The pan, as its name implies, is a large shallow cast-iron dish or box. The lid of this pan is screwed down on the back of the moulds, and by means of a crane the whole apparatus is steadily lowered into the casting-kettle containing the molten metal. Into the open corners and sides of the pan the metal rapidly runs, filling up every hollow space and the minutest interstice in the plaster mould. When at the end of ten minutes the pan is raised

STEREOTYPE MOULD DRYING PRESS FOR PAPER PROCESS.

flask, and into this, plaster of Paris, in a semi-liquid state from admixture with water, is poured. While the mixture is still soft, it is well rolled or spread evenly over the surface of the type, for the double purpose of giving a uniform thickness to the mould and also of expelling as far as practicable, the minute air-bubbles, which if not driven from the mould would cause picks or small imperfections on the surface of the stereotype cast. In a few minutes the plaster hardens into a compact mass; the mould can then be lifted from the type. This mould,

and cooled off upon the cooling-trough, the stereotype casts, fac-similes of the type from which the mould was taken, are secured. The stereotypes are then sent to the finishing-room for examination and approval, and the backs twice shaved in the leveling-machines, to obtain that perfect and regular thickness so absolutely essential to good press-work. They are side-planed, chiseled, and thoroughly gone over for picks, or other imperfections, which the most careful casting will not always prevent. A plate-proof is taken, and read by a proof-reader for errors that may have escaped former readings. Finally the plates are put in boxes, containing each from sixteen to ninety-six plates, according to their size, and delivered ready for the printer's use.

In stereotyping by clay the form is placed upon the movable bed of an iron moulding-press, somewhat similar to that used in electrotyping. A flat iron plate is screwed upon the inside of the lid of the press, and upon this plate a thin layer of prepared clay is spread. Preliminary impressions are taken to obtain the outlines of the type and to remove the dampness from the mould. The surface of the form of type is rubbed with benzine, and the lid of the

IRON TOP BEATING TABLE FOR PAPER PROCESS.

press then being closed and clamped securely by means of a lever, the movable bed of the press is raised carefully and the mould thus obtained by pressure. The press-lid is next unclamped and raised, and the moulding-plate is unscrewed, and with the mould upon it is placed in a slow oven to dry. This occupies but a few minutes, and, separated by a thick wire bent in shape to fit the bottom and sides of the moulding-plate, the latter is clamped fast to a companion plate of equal size. Into the opening between the plates, formed by the wire, molten stereotype-metal is poured, and the stereotype cast by the clay method is formed. This mode of stereotyping has the advantage, not possessed by the plaster, of taking

a mould from low spaces and quadrats without filling them up. It was first introduced about ten years ago at Washington, and has been extensively employed on government work ever since. The Congressional Globe, the Census Reports, and many of the large volumes issued by the national government are stereotyped by the clay process, which is in practical operation in New York, Philadelphia, and other cities.

The Papier Maché mode of stereotyping is of French origin, and its successful application is of comparatively recent date. Four or five sheets of dampened sized tissue-paper, called papier mache, lightly pasted together on a sheet of plate-paper, are laid upon the surface of the type, and struck with a heavy brush until the soft paper maché has taken an exact impression of the type. On this matrix, as it is then called, a sheet of plate-paper is spread and beaten in by another application of the brush. This completes the matrix, which is then dried and hardened by being placed upon a steam-press, and a heavy pressure brought to bear upon it by means of a screw and platen. This is done to retain a perfect impression while in process of drying. Casts can be taken from the mould thus obtained by simply placing it in a flask and pouring upon it stereotype-metal by means of a ladle. A careful workman can take a large number of casts from the same mould. Steam-power has recently been employed to facilitate the beating in of the matrix.

The simplicity and quickness of the papier maché method have induced its extensive adoption, particularly among newspapers having a large circulation; for with its aid they are enabled, by duplicate stereotype plates, rapidly to supply the desired number of printed sheets.

STEREOTYPING IN THE UNITED STATES.

It is a noteworthy fact, that though the art of stereotyping was known and practiced in Europe more than a century ago (see GED, WILLIAM), the process was so awkward and imperfect that it interfered very little with the usual mode of letter-press printing. The Old-World people were slow in making improvements on the original rude and defective methods—a serious drawback to the use of the first stereotype plates being their want of uniformity in thickness, which caused both labor and vexation in the printing, and disposed the old-fashioned press-men to set their faces against the innovation. Comparatively few books were therefore stereotyped, and for a long period the art lay in abeyance.

But when, about half a century ago, stereotyping was introduced into the United States, our skillful and ingenious mechanics soon placed it upon a very different footing. Discarding the bungling turning-lathe, whereby the English were wont to shave their plates, the American stereotyper substituted at once a simple machine of easy operation, which did its office so well that during the more than fifty years which have elapsed since its introduction, scarcely any essential improvement has been found necessary. The early antagonism to the art of stereotyping was further abated by another very important improvement. This was made in the packing of the plates. Incredible as it may appear, when we consider the great proficiency of Europeans in most of the arts, their stereotypers awkwardly placed the plates in wooden racks, thus occupying large spaces for each work, and so encumbering the printing-offices as to preclude the reception of many sets of plates. The first set of stereotype casts of a Bible sent from England to Philadelphia, for one of the religious societies of that city, may be remembered by the older printers as occupying the entire side of a moderate-sized room; and if the stereotype plates at present in the large cities were to be stored in this old-fashioned way, entire blocks of warehouses would be needed for the purpose. Packed in boxes, as they now are in the compact American method (likewise devised in the very origin of American stereotyping), a cellar or a vault suffices for the accumulated plates of a large publishing-house or an extensive printing-office.

Though we derived stereotyping and electrotyping from Old-World inventors, the decided improvements made by our countrymen entitle us to a large share of the general merit. The stolidity with which our cousins of Britain cling to their antiquated methods is amusingly illustrated by the following reminiscence. A prominent American stereotyper and printer, visiting London, called on one of the largest stereotyping firms of that city for a friendly conference, and by chance saw in the yard of the establishment two of Hoe's American shaving-machines. They stood exposed to the elements, crumbling to rust and ruin under complete neglect. Our countryman inquired into the reason of this strange disuse of such excellent machinery. The Englishman answered that such was the disinclination of his stereotype-finishers to adopt new improvements of any kind, and such also his own reluctance to urge his workmen against their will, that he had never had the machines placed in his foundry, and consequently they lay unused and decaying.

To David Bruce, a Scotchman by birth, but for many years a resident of New York, belongs the honor of introducing stereotyping into America. (See BRUCE, DAVID.) In the year 1812 he visited England, and, becoming acquainted with the success of the experiments in stereotyping then being made by Earl Stanhope (see STANHOPE, EARL), a nobleman well known at that period for his interest in inventions appertaining to printing, Bruce acquired by purchase a general knowledge of the art, and in 1813 brought it to this country. Associated with his brother George, under the firm name of D. & G.

Bruce, the brothers commenced the business in the city of New York. Meeting with the many obstacles always encountered by those who attempt a peculiar and untried mechanical business, the Bruces made the most strenuous efforts to introduce and perfect the new art. Their ingenuity, resolution, and skill finally triumphed over adverse circumstances; all opposing difficulties were one by one vanquished, and in 1814 the first work stereotyped in America, a New Testament in Bourgeois, was completed.

In the latter portion of the year 1815, Jedediah Howe, of Connecticut—a shrewd and energetic New Englander—hearing of the success of the Bruce brothers in the newly-invented art, came to New York and commenced a stereotype foundry on Thames Street. Mr. Howe obtained his fair proportion of the limited and uncertain stereotyping of that early day. But in the course of eight years other foundries started, and an exceedingly keen competition followed. Mr. Howe was thence induced to remove his establishment to Philadelphia, which he did in August, 1823. The late Lawrence Johnson was already there, having commenced a stereotype-foundry about the year 1820.

Adding type-founding to stereotyping, Mr. Howe formed a partnership with Mr. Johnson (which continued until the death of the former in 1834). Although partners, the two foundries were carried on by the new firm as if they were separate establishments.

The publishers of Philadelphia had, previous to the arrival of Mr. Johnson, sent their orders for the few books they ventured to subject to this process to the stereotype founders of New York. There was a reluctance to incur the extra expense of casting after setting up the types, for at that time this caused a double expenditure, and capital was hardly abundant enough to afford such a locking up for future benefit. Nothing, perhaps, could more forcibly show the necessity of such a process as stereotyping, than the nature of the rude, imperfect, and expensive system which preceded its advent. Only half a dozen years before, Mathew Carey, of Philadelphia, had set up in type all the pages of a quarto Bible and Testament, keeping the forms continually standing in a fire-proof room, and printing editions as sales demanded. It is probable that this enterprise cost Mr. Carey four or five times as much as the price of a set of stereotypes for the same work, and yet we believe the venture was a successful one in its material results. It may interest printers and type-founders to note that about a dozen years ago these old forms of type were sold as metal to Mr. Isaac Ashmead, and that from the minion side-notes he collected several casefuls of good type, the unexposed portion of which still retained much of its original hardness and sharpness—a fact reflecting great credit on the manufacture of Messrs. Binney and Ronaldson, from whose foundry the fonts were purchased.

Bibles and school-books were the first to be stereotyped, and then gradually came books of great and continued popularity, including the English classics in prose and verse, and the books of popular authors like Washington Irving and J. Fenimore Cooper.

The slow and cautious manner, however, in which American publishers availed themselves of this new invention was rather discouraging to the new beginners. Gradually, however, the booksellers were led into the stereotyping, though at first not very profitably; for the first large work stereotyped by J. Howe, for W. W. Woodward—Scott's Commentary on the Bible, in five quarto volumes—proved so heavy an undertaking that Mr. Woodward broke down under it, and left the plates on the hands of Mr. Howe, to his great embarrassment.

Mr. Johnson was more fortunate in stereotyping a book not very dissimilar in character and magnitude, Henry's Commentary on the Scriptures, undertaken by Tower and Hogan, and carried on successfully to a remunerative result.

On the death of Mr. Howe in 1834, John Fagan, who had been employed in the stereotype foundry for some time, purchased, enlarged, and continued the establishment.

Gradually the business increased, until almost every class of books was included, as well those of standard value, as others whose sanguine authors or publishers hoped they would become so. The cost was diminished also, as the competition of young and enterprising stereotypers caused a considerable narrowing of the profits, and induced a great extension of the new art.

When the process was supplemented by the new art of electrotyping, or stereotyping in copper, a still further inducement was offered to abandon the letter-press mode, in all books where wood engravings were used; for the new method brought up in beautiful distinctness those fine lines which in mere stereotyping were apt to be imperfect or blurred. This aid to the pictorial art has also conduced much to displace the expensive copper and steel engraving which in the olden time rendered the illustration of books so costly.

These successive steps in the advancement of stereotyping and its companion art of electrotyping, contributed much to recommend their use; and now even periodical journals came to be stereotyped. The rapidly increasing readers of newspapers had so multiplied the subscribers to the daily press that even the improved presses, aided by steam-power, were inadequate to the printing of the numerous impressions within a reasonable time. This necessity brought forth its appropriate invention; for now came forth Hoe's improved cylinder press, which dispensed with the flat form, and permitted type or a stereotype plate to be curved around a cylinder, and thus printed from with unprecedented rapidity. Soon the type for this purpose gave way to the stereotype plate, cast by the quick process of the papier-maché moulding, and bent round the cylinder with certainty and facility.

The saving in the wear and tear of type was a positive gain of great importance; but the practicability of printing large editions within the brief space of

time essential to a daily newspaper, was even a greater advantage than this economical one. Newspapers of very large circulation are now generally printed in this way; and thus has been realized a typographical triumph, which, had it been but proposed in Franklin's time, would have made that old printer and philosopher give utterance to his strongest expression of doubt or denial.

Not only has stereotyping now become the usual method in printing such books as Bibles and classical standards, but even such as require alterations within short periods, as Geographies, Medical Dictionaries, Gazetteers, are done in this way, it being deemed better to print off smaller editions to save interest on purchases of paper. At the end of five years or thereabouts, the publisher can afford to melt up his plates and cast them anew, incorporating into the text of his new editions the changes or discoveries which are continually occurring in this active era of the world. It would be difficult to estimate exactly all the advantages which have resulted from the art of stereotyping. It has facilitated immensely the business of publication, and permitted a cheap and rapid diffusion of knowledge, intelligence, and art appreciation, which would have been altogether impossible under the old and imperfect modes of printing.

Stereotype Blocks.—Blocks on which stereotype plates of books are temporarily fastened while they are being printed. Small or unusually large plates are blocked, or permanently attached to blocks of wood of such thickness that, when it is added to the thickness of the plates, type-height is formed. But to avoid bulkiness and unnecessary expenditure, stereotype blocks of the various regular sizes are made to support in succession any requisite number of stereotype plates of pages of books. These blocks are usually of mahogany, bound with brass, and they have catches or claws to hold the plates firmly in their true position, so arranged that they can be conveniently tightened or loosened by a ratchet.

Stet.—A word written on the margin of a proof when a proof-reader has inadvertently marked out a letter, word, or sentence which, on second consideration, he prefers to leave unchanged. It is derived from the neuter verb sto, meaning to stand, to endure, or abide.

Stick.—1. A common term for the implement in which type are composed. (See COMPOSING-STICKS.) Lynch's Manual suggests that the sticks should be selected according to the character of the work to be done. For newspapers, instead of having them so that they could be altered, the sticks should be riveted, to obviate the possibility of their being changed to suit the notions of the compositors. If this be not done, the types set up by the different persons will be found, very often, to vary in width, thus preventing the form being locked up evenly, and allowing the looser portions to drop out, when it is lifted from the stone; or to be drawn out by the rollers, when on the press. For book-work, the stick made after the old plan is the best; because the movable part, being held in its place by a screw, is not so liable to be shifted as if it were held by a spring. For job-work, the stick which can be altered from one measure to another in the easiest manner will be found the most convenient; and, for this reason, the one which is retained by a spring is the best.

2. When letter which is rinsed or laid up for distribution, adheres so closely that it is separated with difficulty, and the compositor's fingers are made sore by pressing the types against the edge of the case in order to distribute them, they are said to stick. All new letter is difficult to separate and distribute if it remains long in chase after it is worked off, from the lye penetrating the interstices of the letters. New type should always be saturated with a solution of soft soap and water before being laid into case. This not only prevents sticking, but takes off the extreme brightness which is so unpleasant to the eye, and renders the type more agreeable to the hand. Old type will stick the harder if the ink is not properly washed off, and the form well rinsed before the types are put away.

Stigmatypie.—Literally, printing with points, but by present usage the word is applied to a species of printing with points which consists of their arrangement in pictures. A number of efforts have been made to construct representations of varied objects with movable type, and to invent type especially adapted to this purpose. There is no doubt of the practicability of some of the systems devised, but it is more economical and more effective to employ engraving or electrotyping in so many cases, that Stigmatypie has never been extensively employed. It is said that Conrad Sweynheim, one of the earliest printers, invented the art of printing maps with movable types, at the time he was preparing maps for the Cosmography of Ptolemy; and this art, after being practiced for some time during the sixteenth century, fell into disuse, to be subsequently revived and improved by Breitkopf, of Leipsic, about 1777, and by Firmin Didot, of Paris, in 1829. In 1623, a book, now very rare, was printed at Amsterdam, which contains a number of curious cuts formed with type, instead of in the common mode. By crochet type (see Crochet Type), designs specially adapted to patterns for crochet-work can be conveniently composed. But Stigmatypie proper uses much smaller characters than those employed in crochet-work. They consist of six varieties of periods, cast on bodies the size of one-sixteenth of a Brevier em, being the smallest type made, and capable, by skillful management, of producing beautiful effects, a fact illustrated by a stigmatypic portrait and flower piece set up by Carl Fasol, a printer of Vienna, for which he obtained a medal at the Paris Exposition in 1867.

Still-Life.—In painting, the representation of inanimate objects, such as fruit, flowers, dead game, and animals, etc.

Stippling.—Engraving in dots. It is the only mode of engraving which is supposed to have been the invention of the Italians. Agostino de Musis,

better known by the name of Augustine of Venice, a pupil of Mark Antonio, used it in several of his earliest works, but confined it to the flesh, as in the undated print of an old man seated upon a bank, with a cottage in the background. He flourished from 1509 to 1536. We also find it in a print of a single figure standing, holding a cup and looking upwards, by Giulio Campagnola, who engraved about the year 1516. The background is executed with round dots, made apparently with a dry point. The figure is outlined with a stroke deeply engraved, and finished with dots, in a manner greatly resembling those prints which Demarteau engraved at Paris in imitation of red chalk. The hair and beard are expressed by strokes. Stephen de Laulne, a native of Germany, followed the steps of Campagnola; and many of his slight works are executed in dots only. John Boulanger, a French artist, who flourished in the middle of the sixteenth century, and his cotemporary, Nicholas van Plattenberg, improved greatly on this method, and practiced it with much success. John Lutma executed this kind of work with a hammer and a small punch or chisel.

In this style of engraving, Francis Bartolozzi stands pre-eminent in modern times; he contrived to execute it so beautifully as to assist in seducing the public taste from the superior and legitimate style of line engraving. He was born at Florence in 1728, and died at Lisbon in 1815. He resided for some time in England, and executed many prints for Boydell's Shakspeare, which are exquisite specimens of taste and execution.

Stitching.—The operation of sewing or uniting together, by means of thread, as the sewing of leaves of paper together so as to form a pamphlet. (See Bookbinding.)

Stock.—The supply of material necessary in any business, called by English printers the plant.

Stone.—See Imposing-Stone and Ink-Stone.

Stop-Cylinder Hand Newspaper Printing Machine.—A country newspaper press, made by R. Hoe & Co., designed to run exclusively by hand, at a rate of 700 or 800 impressions per hour.

Stop-Cylinder Wood-Cut Printing Machine.—A comparatively new press, made by R. Hoe & Co., which is especially designed for fine printing, and for the superior execution of wood-cut work. It is made of ten sizes, varying, in size of bed inside of bearers, from fourteen by seventeen, to forty-five by sixty-one inches, and is described as follows in Hoe's Catalogue. The distribution is either by an inking table or vibrating cylinder, as may be desired, and the number of form rollers, from two to ten. The bed is driven by a crank, without bed-springs, and without the slightest jar. The impression-cylinder is stationary during the return of the bed, and the fingers close on the sheet before the register points are withdrawn; the cylinder then revolves, and as it gears directly into the bed, perfect register is obtained. The fingers never require shifting, whatever the size of the form, and no tapes are used. When so ordered, the

bed is arranged to be run either once or twice, thus passing the form under the inking-rollers either two or four times to each impression, as may be required.

Stopping-Out.—A term used in etching, for a varnish antagonistic to the acid and used to protect parts of the surface from its action. It is frequently composed of asphaltum dissolved in turpentine or gum resins, or scaling-wax dissolved in alcohol.

Story.—A narration of real or imaginary events, by common usage applied to a composition shorter and less regular than a tale; the word is also frequently used as a synonym for anecdote.

Story-Book.—A volume of short tales or stories, generally intended for children.

Strahan, William.—A Scotch printer, who rose to wealth in London, and was elected a member of Parliament, as colleague of Charles James Fox, in 1775. His father held a small place in the customs, but Strahan, fortunately, had full opportunities of availing himself of the excellent grammar-schools of Edinburgh. He served his apprenticeship in Scotland, and at its conclusion removed to London, where he worked as a journeyman in the same office with Benjamin Franklin, with whom he established relations of friendship. Sober, diligent, economical, and attentive, he slowly but surely worked himself upwards in his profession, and was one of the most flourishing printers in London in 1770, when he purchased from Mr. Eyre a share in the patent of King's printer. The emoluments of this office, united to those from his own flourishing private business, rendered him quite affluent, and he devoted his leisure to politics, in which he had always taken a deep interest. He served in Parliament from 1775 until 1784, when he lost his seat by the dissolution. He employed a large portion of his wealth in purchasing the copyrights of the celebrated authors of the time, and led the way in offering terms of remarkable liberality. In 1774 he was elected Master of the Stationers' Company, and at his death left a considerable sum to be distributed yearly to poor printers, under the supervision of that corporation. Strahan, always keenly alive to the

29

interests of his country, anxiously regarded the events which directly preceded the American Revolution, and in 1769 wrote a series of most apposite queries upon the causes of the dissatisfaction prevailing in the Colonies, and addressed them to Dr. Franklin. The friendly relation maintained between them is exhibited in the following extract from one of the latest letters addressed to Strahan by his distinguished American friend and cotemporary:

But let us leave these serious reflections, and converse with our usual pleasantry. I remember your observing once to me in the House of Commons, that no two journeymen printers within your knowledge had met with such success in the world as ourselves. You were then at the head of your profession, and soon afterwards became a member of parliament. I was an agent for a few provinces, and now act for them all. But we have risen by different modes. I, as a republican printer, always liked a form well *planed down;* being adverse to those *overbearing* letters that held their heads so high as to hinder their neighbours from appearing. You, as a monarchist, chose to work upon *crown* paper, and found it profitable; whilst I worked upon *pro patria* (often indeed called *foolscap*) with no less advantage. Both our *heaps held out* very well, and we seem likely to make a pretty good day's work of it. With regard to public affairs (to continue in the same style), it seems to me that the compositors in your chapel do not cast their copy well, nor perfectly understand imposing; their forms are continually pestered by the outs and doubles that are not easy to be corrected. And I think they were wrong in laying aside some faces, and particularly certain headpieces that would have been both useful and ornamental. But, courage! The business may still flourish, with good management, and the master become as rich as any of the company.

Passy, near Paris, Aug. 19, 1784.   B. FRANKLIN.

Straw Paper.—Paper of which straw forms the principal ingredient. (See PAPER.) Various accounts are given of its first introduction in the United States. One of the most interesting of these statements was published a few years ago in the New York Tribune. The following extracts are taken from it:

So far as we can trace it back in this country, the idea originated with Judge Henry Pettibone, of Wilkesbarre, Pennsylvania, about the year 1821–22. Although not one-tenth of the amount of paper was then used that is now, the subject of paper stock was a good deal talked about, and what could be used for stock as a substitute for rags.

While the subject was one day fresh upon the mind of Judge Pettibone, then at Meadville, Pennsylvania, he was passing by a leach-tub that had just been emptied of its contents, among which was a handful of straw that had been placed at the bottom to serve as a strainer of the lye, as it leached from the ashes. He took a little of this in his hand, and the idea at once suggested itself to him that it possessed all the qualities of a strong fibre, which the lye had softened until it was in a semi-pulpy state. He took this straw to a paper-maker, who manufactured paper from it with such success that he was induced to continue the experiments. Of course this paper was straw-colored, and only fit for coarse wrapping, and was very brittle, but it served a purpose, and came rapidly

into general use a few years later, as it was manufactured by a great many mills in various parts of the United States.

The first white paper made from straw, to any considerable extent, we believe, was by John and David Ames, of Springfield, Mass. They commenced operations in 1849. but all that they or others made before 1854–55 was a very inferior quality compared with that now in use, and even for six years more the business was not successful, because the quality of the paper was not good. It generally had a harsh feel, was brittle, and did not take a good impression.

Paper-merchants in New York say that white straw paper has been in the market since 1852. It was not until 1854 that the discovery was made in France and patented there, and subsequently here (in 1857) by Coupier and Mellier, that an increase of heat progressively facilitates the action of alkalies in disintegrating the organic forms of all fibrous substances, and consequently enables the bleacher to effect his purpose upon them by application of chlorine, either in the gaseous or liquid form. But their discovery, far in advance as it was of all that had preceded it in making paper of straw, still lacked something very essential to render the process economical. Some paper-makers who purchased the Coupier & Mellier patent, and incurred large expense in working after it, relinquished the business as unprofitable. The paper was not of a quality to make it readily salable.

An important step, however, had been made in the right direction by these Frenchmen, which soon led Yankee ingenuity to accomplish all that the others had failed in. The French patent contemplated the use of caustic alkali, and boiling in a closed, steam-tight boiler, but not at the high pressure since used. We believe that the discovery of the effect of boiling at a high temperature is due to Coe S. Buchanan, Rock City, Saratoga County, N. Y., as late as the year 1857 or 1858, and the first paper made under this system was at Fort Edward, Washington County, N. Y.

The discovery of Buchanan was to the effect that boiling under a pressure of 130 lbs. in caustic alkali of 3¼ to 3¾ degrees completely disintegrated the straw and rendered soluble the silex that coats it, and breaks down all knots, which at first it was thought necessary to crush with iron rollers. Under this system it was found that clean straw was not essential—the boiling and powerful alkali cured all such defects as dirt, knots, etc.

The alkali is made by one formula now before us, as follows:

Soda-ash of 93 per cent., 788 lbs.; caustic lime, 637 lbs. Dissolve in hot water and settle. Draw off part of the liquor and stir up the sediment, and add more water to get a lye of less strength. Another formula gives 535 lbs. soda-ash to 300 lbs. of lime.

The liquor of the right strength, being stored in a tank six feet in diameter, requires a depth of seventy-two inches to a boiler of straw, of 20 cwt. or 21 cwt.

In the first experiments at making straw paper, the

straw was boiled in lime alone, and always in open vessels, and when closed boilers were first used, seventy lbs. pressure was all that was thought necessary. In some of the first attempts to carry the pressure up to a hundred pounds or higher, great fears of a blow-up were entertained. The rotation of the boiler can never be dispensed with, because if it did not rotate the inert mass of straw would settle down upon the boiler over the fire so compactly that the liquor could not penetrate it, and therefore it would become a mass of charcoal. The relative proportion of soda-ash and lime to a given quantity of straw is necessary, and so is the strength of the solution, to produce the most economical results, because, if it is used too diluted, it will require much longer boiling. When the alkali is right, the sooner the boiling reaches 130 lbs. the better, for that is all that is necessary. At 100 lbs. it will make white paper, but it will lack softness and strength of texture. At a still lower temperature the paper will betray its origin at once.

The first rotary boiler that we can find any account of was at Jeffreys, Scotland, by John Martin, about 1841–42; and the first in this country at Butler's paper-mill, at Paterson, New Jersey, in 1843, to boil cotton waste and rope. Another was shortly after started at the Rainbow Mill, in Connecticut, and two more at the Pequonnock Mill, perhaps in 1853–54, and the next year at Derrickson's Mill, in New Jersey, and in 1857–58, at Fort Edward. None of these were intended to boil straw at the pressure that we have indicated as necessary to produce first-rate white paper, because that secret had not yet been discovered.

Mr. Butler believed in the advantage of high pressure, and tried to get his men to work up to 90 lbs., and went himself and stood by the boiler while it was heated to that point, to show them that there was no danger. It was found that high pressure killed the seeds in the cotton waste, and the shives in the hemp bagging and rope, which, if not killed, appeared as black specks in the paper. This is also the case with straw, as may be seen in paper made from stock that was not well boiled. In such paper little pieces of straw are found, as perfect in texture as though never manipulated by the paper-makers. The progress that has been made in straw paper manufacture since the issue of the Coupier & Mellier patent in May, 1857, is, indeed, wonderful, when we consider the great expense necessary to fit up a straw mill or to change a rag mill into a straw mill.

Streamers.—Large posters intended to be placed side by side, instead of above and beneath each other. They usually consist of one word or series of words, set in very large type, as, Dan Rice's Great Show.

Stretchers.—Bills or placards, printed in colors, or in ornamental style, mounted on frames of wood.

Strike.—An abandonment of work by journeymen compositors or pressmen, to enforce compliance with their requirements respecting wages or matters appertaining to the management of offices.

Strong Ink.—Ink made with a powerfully binding varnish, and usually of superior ingredients, so as to prevent the separation of the coloring matter, and the spread of the varnish in the paper.

Stump.—A roll of paper or leather cut to a point, and used for rubbing down the harsh or strong lines of a pencil or crayon, or to mingle them in a softer effect of shading, or for applying solid tints to paper from powdered colors. Stumps are also made of fine cork.

Style.—1. The mode of expressing thought in language, whether oral or written; rhetorical expression. 2. The custom of respective printing-offices in regard to unsettled or disputed points relating to orthography, division of words, spacing, compound words, capitalization and display of certain classes of words, etc.

There is a lack of uniformity in so many matters that it is highly important for a compositor to thoroughly familiarize himself with the style of the office in which he is employed, as well as the style adopted for any special work, in book-offices, or for peculiar articles in newspaper-offices. Much time is lost in conforming to arbitrary and unnecessary rules, or in changing composed type so that it may conform to them. Matter that would be considered correct in one office would be unmercifully scored by the proofreader of another establishment. Styles are as various as the tastes and caprices of editors and publishers. One style insists upon even spacing, no matter how words are divided; another style demands unexceptionable divisions, no matter how great may be the irregularity in the spacing of different lines. One style follows Webster in orthography, invariably; another, partially; another abjures all his reforms. In punctuation, great diversity of usage prevails. In compounding and capitalizing words, as well as in the selection of clauses of words or phrases to be set in Italic, small capitals, etc., there is no fixed law; and of thousands of printing-offices it would be difficult to find two in which absolute uniformity of usage prevails.

The character of these discrepancies and their evil effects are partially illustrated by the following extracts from various sources:

After a compositor has been at an office for years, where, habituated to the style of the house, he sets up words in type as follows,—now-a-days, anything, bye-the-bye, jewellery, connexion, etc.,—he has, on transporting himself to a fresh establishment, to take cognizance of another style, which, among other matters, comprises the following metamorphoses of the above words: nowadays, any thing, by the bye, jewelry, connection, etc. By dint of much exertion, he at length obtains a clear comprehension of these changes and of many others. By the time, however, this fresh style is ingrained on his memory, slackness of work, or some other cause, may necessitate his removal to new quarters. Here, again, all has to be undone; for he now meets with now a days, by-the-by, jewelery, and so on.

Another writer, in a communication to an American

Typographical Journal, says: In our daily city papers you behold a heterogeneous mixture of capitals, small-capitals, Full-face, Italic and Roman, of all sorts and sizes of type, from Brevier to Agate, and sometimes from Bourgeois to Pearl. Now, this arrangement might be well enough for the exhibition of type-founders' specimens; but for the poor compositor, who has to walk about twenty-five yards—as in many of our large offices—to set a word of Italic or a line of Full-face—will it pay?

For example: A compositor gets an obscurely-written take of copy, and goes to his case, where, by his light, he deciphers enough to know that a Title heading is needed. Having walked the length of the office to get it, and back again to his stand, he commences his second line—a date line, of small type, part of which is small-caps, and he has frequently to hunt over twenty-five yards more of space for sorts to set that. He returns to his stand; finishes the line; changes cases; and, on looking at his copy, finds that the steamer Vixen has run foul of a shad-pole, etc.; and, in many offices, he must run for the Italic Vixen. This Italic case being usually in a dark corner by day, and poorly lighted at night, when Typo gets back to his stand, where the gas-burner is better looked after, he discovers that he can now see a c, where he intended an c, and must tramp back for the altera-tion. Once more at his stand—the first line of the body of the article set—he changes cases, and con-tinues the article in smaller type. Two lines set, and he learns that Senor Don Spaniola lost a fine parrot through fright at a collision; and, if the accented letters, as in many offices, are kept in the Italic case, away goes Typo for the Spanish n. Back to his case—a few more lines set—and he learns that the editor of the Chronicle was also a passenger; and the name of the distinguished paper must be chronicled in Italic. Back again to his stand—a few more lines set, and the compositor is gratified with the closing infor-mation that the Vixen arrived safe, and is discharging freight at her depot—involving, perhaps, two more unlooked-for tramps after Italic and accents.

Thus, through the whims of reporters and editors—who, as often happens, know little and care less about the styles of italicising, accutuation, etc.—and from other evils combined, the compositor is often com-pelled to walk about two hundred yards, and change cases three or four times, to set two-thirds of a stick-ful, or about five hundred ems. Pursuing such aggravating and time-consuming styles throughout the day, the week, and the year, it is little wonder that compositors are kept poor, hand-to-mouth mortals forever.

If editors, reporters, and authors generally, would rely a little upon the common sense of their readers, and less upon a hodge-podge arrangement of type, their meaning would, doubtless, be understood quite as well, to say nothing of the saving to the composi-tor, or of the neat appearance of a book or newspaper. What a stupid blockhead any one must be, who would not readily know what was meant by saying: the editor of the Picayune; the editor of the Chron-icle; or, to use another mode of expression, the Herald says: etc.; the steamship Arago, etc. Of late years, in many offices, compositors have to contend with an additional and more aggravating loss of time, through the style of setting names of persons—no matter how obscure or insignificant—in small capi-tals.

In several European countries the evils arising from a confusion of styles, which are complained of by American and English printers, exist only to a very moderate extent, in consequence of the success of efforts to establish uniformity; and it is to be regretted that effective means have not been adopted to restrict the domain over which style exercises arbitrary sway in the United States.

Stylus.—The pointed instrument of brass or iron used by the ancients in writing upon waxen tablets, the reverse end being left blunt in order to make erasures by smoothing the surface of the wax. From this instrument has been derived the modern English term, meaning the manner of expression peculiar to each individual.

Sub.—An abbreviation of substitute, meaning a compositor occasionally employed on a daily paper, to fill the place of an absent regular compositor.

Sub-heads.—Words or expressions placed above or at the commencement of chapters, sections, or paragraphs, to indicate their contents.

Subject.—The theme of a proposition or discourse, or the topic brought under thought or examination: the word has a similar use in the fine arts, being the topic or thought represented to the eye by a sculptor or painter.

Subscribe.—To express assent by signing one's name to a document; thence, by signing a name as an agreement to the terms specified as the price of a book, a person becomes a subscriber.

Subscribers.—Patrons or purchasers of news-papers who obtain them regularly, daily, tri-weekly, semi-weekly or weekly, for stated periods.

Subscription.—The signing of a name as an agreement, and thence the sum promised by such an act of signing as the price paid by previous agree-ment for a book or journal. The term is generally distinguished from the word price by showing that, for some reason, an agreement is necessary in the trans-action instead of an instantaneous exchange or purchase: thus a serial publication is purchased by a subscription, or a transaction in which the publisher promises to furnish a number of continuous works on certain conditions and for a given remuneration.

Subscription Books.—Books for which orders are solicited by canvassers or agents, their sales being usually restricted to copies disposed of by this method of publication. Hartford, Connecticut, is the head-quarters for this trade, no less than twelve or fourteen firms in that city being engaged in it. In the eight years 1861-68, there were issued from Hartford alone about 30 subscription books, the other cities pub-lishing, perhaps, enough more to make 100. The business in Hartford amounted during that time to $5,000,000, and employed 10,000 agents in disposing of 1,426,000 copies. The character of the works which have been sold in this manner, and the extent of sales, may be gathered from the following statistics: Greeley's American Conflict, 225,000 copies; Nurse and Spy, a tale of the war, 175,000; Kettell's Rebellion, 120,000; the late A. D. Richardson's Field, Dungeon, and Escape, 100,000, and his Beyond the Mississippi, 90,000; Stephens' War between the States, 62,000; Frank Moore's Women of the War, 60,000; Prof. Stowe's Origin and History of the Books of the Bible, 60,000; Mrs. Stowe's Men of Our Times, 55,000; Mark Twain's Innocents Abroad, 60,000. A work by Rev. Matthew Hale Smith, called Sunshine and Shadow, has had a sale fully equal to the average of those just named. Other adventurers in this field have been Dr. Holland; the historians, Abbott, Lossing, and Headley; newspaper correspondents, like Junius H. Browne, Thomas W. Knox, and George Alfred Townsend; editors, like the late H. J. Raymond, Samuel Bowles, and Augustus Maverick; law professors, like Chamberlain and Parsons; together with Mr. Beecher, Mr. Parton, Mr. P. T. Barnum, and a few other persons of some note as lecturers or writers, including, among the latest, Miss Olive Logan. Religious books, embracing a Cottage Bible, medical works, and books for making every man his own lawyer, represent what may be called the natural staple of the subscription business.

Suffix.—A letter or syllable added to the end of a word to modify its meaning; as print-er, print-ing.

Summary.—A reduction into a small compass or into few words of a number of items or thoughts previously stated.

Super-Calendered.—Paper highly polished by repeated pressures between steel rolls.

Superiors.—Small letters or figures cast upon the upper part of the shank or the body of type, so that they range with the top of the letter to which they belong; as **°°°°°°**, **°°°°°°°**. They are frequently used as references, and occasionally in abbreviated words.

Super-Royal.—Writing and printing papers, the former being usually twenty by twenty-eight, and the latter twenty-two by twenty-eight inches.

Superscribe.—To write at the top, on the outside, or on the surface.

Superscription.—That which is written or engraved upon the surface, outside, or upon the top, as the words engraved upon a monument, or the address written upon a letter.

Supplement.—1. An addition of one or more pages or sheets to the number usually contained in a newspaper, which is published with the regular edition, and is issued chiefly on account of a pressure of advertisements or news. 2. In a general sense, as applied to printing, supplement has a signification similar to Appendix, but their meanings are not quite identical.

Suspension Rings.—Metallic rings which can be conveniently attached by their claws to show-cards, business cards, calendars, etc., the object of this patented invention being to facilitate the suspension of printed matter of the kinds enumerated, on hooks, nails, etc.

Swash.—A term formerly applied to unusually long projections or kerns of some classes of type.

Sweepings.—Type found on the floor when composing-rooms are swept.

Sweynheim and Pannartz.—The names of Conrad Sweynheim and Arnold Pannartz always appear in conjunction, as having introduced printing into Italy in the year 1464. Torquemada, afterwards Inquisitor-General of Spain under Ferdinand and Isabella, was at that time Administrator of the monastery of Subiaco, a town near Rome, and, intelligently appreciating the value of the invention lately promulgated from Mentz, influenced the monks to invite the two German printers to settle within their walls. The siege of Mentz which destroyed the printing-office of Fust and Schoeffer had occurred in October, 1462, and it is highly probable that these two Germans belonged to the apprentices dispersed by that event, and that Sweynheim had acquired his skill as an engraver of types from Schoeffer, as well as that ready apprehension of the conditions and requirements of his new situation which enabled him to immediately prepare in Italy a letter suited to the country, while his educated taste led him to select the best classic models. The first publication of Sweynheim and Pannartz was a Donatus or Grammar for boys, and they completed the Lactantius in 1465. It was a grand folio volume, of a type never before attempted, and differing absolutely from the angular Gothic letter of Schoeffer. The German or Gothic character had prevailed in Italian manuscript during a portion of the thirteenth and fourteenth centuries, but a revolution had then occurred in favor of the Roman letters, and the scribes had again adopted the fine, rounded character of the earlier periods. This style, modified slightly from the older forms, was a graceful, rounded letter, and in copying it Sweynheim prepared the originals of the present type so widely used and known as Roman. The first Greek printed from movable type also occurred in this book, the quotations used by Schoeffer having been cut on wooden blocks, which were entirely sufficient for the few phrases required. It seems probable that it had been originally intended to supply the Greek by manuscript additions, as was done in subsequent works by other printers, and the blank spaces for the purpose were prepared in the earlier sheets; but later in the book a fine movable type appears, imitated from the manuscript of the seventh and eighth centuries. Two other works were printed by the Germans at Subiaco, both excellent in typographical execution and for the fine blackness of the ink. They soon afterwards removed to Rome, probably at the instance of Pope Paul II., who appointed John Andrea, the secretary of the Vatican, to supervise their works. Here, in 1467, they issued the Letters of Cicero in an entirely new set of types, more nearly resembling the current Roman manuscript, from which fact it has been supposed that the monks of Sabiaco claimed possession of the fonts already made at their expense. The Letters of Cicero was the first of a series of works poured forth with unexampled rapidity, for, according to their own statement, they produced on an average more than eight volumes per annum in the five years succeeding 1467. These works were generally of classic authors, and were very handsomely executed, having the advantage of all the stores of the Vatican in the choice of the best original manuscripts. In seven years they published twenty-eight different works, some of which were very voluminous and handsome; but either the great expense or the difficulties in sale caused them great financial distress. The partnership was annulled, and Sweynheim appears to have been afterwards successful as an engraver. The originality of his genius is again exhibited in the maps which he engraved on copper for an edition of Ptolemy, this book being one of the first works illustrated with copper-plates. Pannartz continued to print on his own account, and both he and Sweynheim died in 1476.

Syllabication.—The division of words into syllables. (See DIVISION OF WORDS.)

Syllable.—A single elementary sound, or such a combination of sounds as can be uttered at one impulse of the voice, and therefore making the lowest subdivision of articulate speech.

Syllabus.—A compendium or abstract containing the heads of a document or discourse.

Symphony.—A harmony or consonance, either in vocal or instrumental sounds. In music, the term is restricted to an elaborate instrumental composition intended for a full orchestra.

Syncope.—An elision of one or more letters or of a syllable from the middle of a word.

Synonym or Synonyme.—One of two or more words in the same language, which are the equivalents of each other, or which have very nearly the same signification, and are liable to be confounded.

Synopsis.—A general view or collection of the heads or parts of a writing or argument, so arranged as to exhibit a general view of the whole.

Syntax.—The due arrangement of words in sentences in their necessary grammatical relations and according to established usage.

T.

Tablature.—In painting, a composition within regular circumscribed limits, such as the adornments usual upon ceilings or walls. In music, the term formerly meant the expression of notes by letters of the alphabet.

Table.—The arrangement of figures, etc. in parallel columns of regular proportions, so as to present a general view of a subject to the eye, as is done in mathematical or astronomical works, statistical publications, etc.

Table- and Tabular-Work.—Matter consisting partly of rules and figures, or matter set up in tabular form. Under the English system, matter in which there are five columns or more ranks as table-work, for the composition of which double the rates for plain matter are paid, while a series of only three or four adjacent columns rank as tabular-work, for which only a price and a half is paid; and a similar distinction is made in some portions of the United States. Houghton defines table-work as composition consisting chiefly of rules and figures, and tabular-work as matter arranged in tabular form, which consists chiefly of names or other words. The words are often used, however, as synonyms. The following valuable practical directions for composing table- or tabular-work were given in The Proof-Sheet of November, 1867:

When a compositor receives copy for a table, the first thing he has to do is to cast it off—that is, to ascertain whether it will come in in a given measure, in the type intended to be used, and, if not, how it can be best arranged. The table may be set in smaller type, divided, or widened and run into the margin. The foreman or employer will of course decide which method shall be adopted; but it is the compositor's business to measure and calculate the matter so as to be able to suggest the best plan. He will gain in reputation in proportion to his ability to do this intelligently. We do not pretend to give full instructions on this point; but, as a convenient mode of illustration, we here introduce a table of the simplest form, numbering the columns so that we may refer to them in the remarks which follow.

PARTIAL STATISTICS OF PRINTING IN THE UNITED STATES DURING THE YEAR ENDING JUNE 1, 1860.

	1	**2**	**3**	**4**	**5**
STATES.	**Books.**	**Jobs.**	**Papers.**		**Total.**
Maine..........	$84,000	$63,536	$177,103		$284,939
New Hampshire	....	120,080	124,790		244,879
Vermont.......	9,975	36,450	53,276		99,701
Massachusetts.	397,500	529,347	1,979,069		2,905,916
Connecticut...	467,900	36,000	117,600		641,500
Rhode Island...	20,500	70,082	114,700		205,282
New York...	6,970,102	2,574,529	13,422,254		22,916,885
New Jersey...	24,161	43,469	149,678		217,270
Pennsylvania..	2,264,250	1,905,306	2,112,122		6,281,567
Delaware......	....	81,600	23,932		105,532
Maryland......	68,000	122,800	169,355		360,155
Michigan......	4,500	53,281	122,948		929,729
Illinois.........	13,900	327,925	412,148		733,973
Wisconsin.....	15,419	74,070	90,655		180,444
Iowa..........	15,000	76,077	49,136		140,213
Missouri......	10,000	119,753	130,996		260,749
Kentucky......	64,000	49,500	191,100		304,600
Ohio	673,800	632,606	844,377		2,150,783
Indiana	....	62,123	73,292		135,415
Tennessee......	175,750	133,300	182,270		491,220
Aggregate......	**$11,508,459**	**$7,141,713**	**$20,540,371**		**$39,389,542**

In casting off this table, we first place six rules in the stick. Then, glancing at the aggregates at the bottom of the figure columns, we see that columns 2, 4, and 5 require over 5 ems each, while column 3 takes an en less. Preferring, in a table like this, that the columns shall be of equal width, we allow 5¼ ems for each. Placing these in the stick against the rules, we find that 8 ems remain for column 1. Now, setting up the longest line in this column, we find that it requires a hair space more than 8 ems, besides which we need a 3-em space between the outer rule and the beginning of the line. We look again at the figure columns, and see that they can be reduced to 5¼ ems each, but at the same time we notice that if so reduced there will be a great deal of unnecessary trouble in setting the table so as to allow space between the right-hand side of the figures and the rules. We therefore abandon the intention of making the columns the same width, and reduce column 3 to 5 ems, remarking that the blanks will now be equal, and that this is quite as important as that the columns shall be of one width. We now have 8¼ ems for column 1, the space that it requires, and the table is cast off.

It frequently happens that the headings materially affect the apportionment of space to the different columns, and the compositor must be careful to examine them at the outset. In the example here given, however, a glance at the copy shows that the headings will come in, and measurements are unnecessary.

It may be here stated that, as a rule, headings should be set in type two sizes smaller than the body of the table, and some sacrifice in the regularity of the width of columns and of blanks may at times be made in order that they may read across. Tables in Nonpareil or smaller type frequently look as well with the headings—if they be short—in the same type as the body. In the above table, we use Agate over Nonpareil. If it were solid, we should use Nonpareil only, as the body would then look heavier than now.

The width of the columns and the arrangement of the headings being decided, the compositor's next care should be to collect an ample supply of the sorts that will be needed. Those who are not in the habit of so doing, but who habitually grub out of an empty case, cannot understand how much they lose by so doing.

Having made every necessary preparation, we now begin the composition of the above table.

We make up a stick for the first column. But the measure (8¼ ems Nonpareil) is too narrow for convenient working, and we increase it by placing Pica quads, sideways, in front—to be removed when the stick is emptied. (If the table were solid, we should simply use a Nonpareil quad at the end of the line.) We now set the heading of the first column, and then all the other headings before proceeding with the body of the table. Next we cut the two cross rules in column 1. We wish to use an en quad flatwise above and below these rules, and, the column not

being even ems, we make an em-and-a-half en quad by cutting down a Pica 4-em space, and, foreseeing that we shall need several of these, we at the same time cut all that will be wanted. No one need be alarmed at the trouble of making spaces of this kind. Lay a lead on the bed of the cutter, which make up as much longer as the space required—in the present case 1½ em Nonpareil. Then lay the space to be cut against the lead—which makes room for the finger between the slide and the knife—and you can easily cut it to the required size. With ordinary care in saving these odd spaces, enough will soon be accumulated for any occasion.

Column 1 admits a 3-em space in front. This we run down continuously, by the en quads that separate the lines, thus leaving a trifle over 8 ems to be covered by them. But as eight of these, flatwise, can be used, the blanks are a trifle shorter than the matter, but not enough to affect the table in any way. The irregularity might be avoided by using the odd spaces above mentioned. But it is just as important to waste no time as it is to use all that may be requisite to produce good work. Arriving at the bottom of the column, we substitute a lead for the 3-em spaces that are on the outside, because they might slip when the table is handled. We use a Pearl line at the foot of the column, and, while at the case, set those for the other columns Now, first making sure that we have not left an out, we cut all the rules that are required, making those for the sides the thickness of two rules longer than the column—this being required for mitering.

If the columns were even ems, we should now make up a stick the width of the four remaining ones, and set across as in plain matter. But, as three of them are uneven, we set each separately.

Column 2 is 5¼ ems wide, and there is a 3-em space to spare in the longest line—the aggregate. As all the other lines are shorter, we place this space at the end of the line, thus keeping the figures from contact with the rule on either side, and bringing all as near the centre of the column as is practicable. En quads are used continuously down the front of the column (as the 3-em space is used in column 1), leaving 5 ems, across which the en quads are laid between the lines. Columns 4 and 5 are set in the same way; while in Column 2, which is even ems, the blanks are simply set across. The table is now in type. Carefully mitering the outside rules, we ascertain that it lifts as readily as plain matter, and pronounce the job finished.

The tasteful workman will avoid the use of ordinary dashes under the headings, substituting rule for them, which gives uniformity to the lines in the table. At first sight this may be supposed to involve a great deal of non-paying labor. But this is not the case. Good work always pays, sooner or later. Rule dashes, of say four ems Pica and upwards, can be cut as readily as the column rules, while smaller sizes are made without great trouble. For example, a number of 2-em Brevier dashes are required. Take some scraps of rule and cut them to one length—say two inches. Then, without moving the slide of the cutter, place two Brevier ems against it and recut the rules. The pieces you now cut off are the required size. Now reset the cutter to the size of the shortened rules, replace the two ems, cut as before, and so continue until the rules become too short to be held in place.

The best rule-cutter will turn the corner of the face of the rule and make a burr on the side. The compositor should have a large fine file, and a small one, known as a watchmaker's—and he should own them. An office file is generally worthless. The large file is to be used for taking the burr off the side of the rule, for filing down when necessary, and for mitering. The small one—the finer the better—is used as follows:—

Lay the turned corner of the rule on the index finger of the left hand, holding the rule with the thumb and fingers, and, keeping the file parallel with the rule, pass it carefully over the corner. The turned portion of the rule can thus be taken off without perceptible injury to the face. We have found this method much preferable to that of rubbing the face on the stone.

We have not forgotten Labor-saving Rule; but while considering it indispensable for jobbing purposes, and as answering very well for an occasional small table, we do not think it applicable to general tabular-work.

The printer who is an adept in this class of work will doubtless find much to except to in the directions here given. We have avoided discussing the other plans with which we are acquainted, desiring simply to present one which the learner can safely adopt, and which the writer successfully followed for many years.

Houghton, in his Printers' Every-Day Book, an English publication, advocates a system of composing tabular-work which he claims to have originated, and which he describes as follows:

It consists of the lines, connected with each other in the successive columns, being set in one stick in the order in which they read across the page, and emptied the same as ordinary or common matter. The proper and exact width of the columns is preserved by justifying each against various-sized pieces of brass rules or leads of the required widths; while the proper length column-rules are inserted between the columns after the matter has been read and corrected in the usual way. In this way, tabular copy may be given out in small or large takings, to any number of men, join up and be made up into pages as common matter, without the least inconvenience, extra trouble, or loss of time. And those who have had to do with setting tabular work in single columns to any extent will know how to appreciate these advantages. I well recollect my own pleasurable feelings when the idea first occurred to me, and I had satisfied myself of the possibility of this system being practicable. Since then, my superintendence

of the Lancashire county register, year after year till 1858, with only a very few exceptions, has afforded me ample opportunities for perfecting it.

This register is set in Long Primer, and forms two thick royal quarto volumes; one, containing the names of persons in the south, whose property qualifies them for voting, used to make from ten to twelve hundred pages; while the other, containing the voters in the north, made five or six hundred. In 1861, these two columns had expanded over more than 2000 pages, each page having six columns, with Minion and Nonpareil running headings of different widths, and five rules to separate the columns. Both of these used to be got out with ease, on this system, with eighteen or twenty compositors and comparatively little overtime, in about five weeks. The following example of the work will supply an illustration to show more clearly the working part of this new system of setting tabular work.

The specimen proposed consists of six columns, and our first object is to get the measure and the proper lengths of the rules or leads against which the columns are to be justified. Let us suppose it to be printed on the same-sized pages as this book, the measure of which is 17 ems Pica. [This is not strictly, but very nearly, the measure of one column of The American Encyclopædia of Printing.] This width being divided into six columns will give 3 ems Pica for five and 2 ems for one. As this is extremely narrow, there is a necessity to ascertain the lightest and the heaviest column, with the view of so adjusting the different widths as to prevent as much as possible the lines turning over. This done, the relative width of each column may be supposed as follows:—

1	2	3	4	5	6
To Poll	No.	Name.	Abode.	Qualification.	Where Property is situated.
2 ems	1 em	3½ ems.	3 ems.	3 ems.	3½ ems.

The narrowness of these columns necessitates an encroachment on the margin to the extent of the width of No. 1 column. There being only the name of a town inserted occasionally in this, it may be left with advantage till the other columns are up, as well as give an additional em to the fourth and an en to the sixth column. Five columns and four down rules now remain to be got in the 17 ems Pica measure. The stick to set them in is made up as follows:—first make a stick up to the proper width of the page; in this instance it is 17 ems Pica. This done, fill the stick with Pica lower-case ems, using an en where the column divides the en, and insert four small pieces of brass rule the thickness of the column-rules, thus:—

2	3	4	5	6
No.	Name.	Abode.	Qualification.	Where Property is situated.
1 em	3½ ems.	4 ems.	3½ ems.	4 ems.

Or thus:—

☰ ☰ ☰ ☰n☰ ☰ ☰ ☰ ☰ ☰ ☰ ☰n☰ ☰ ☰ ☰ ⁞

These four rules being less than a Pica em, put such spaces into the third column as may be found necessary to justify the whole of the 17 em measure. This done, the rules are taken out, and the stick made up tight to the Pica ems, including the space put in the third column to justify them. The exact measure in which all the columns are to be set across is now obtained.

The rules or leads against which each column is to be justified are the next consideration. Referring to the above example for the proper measure, it will be seen that the No. column, which contains figures only, needs no justifying, and that the first which requires it is the name column. The first justifying rule or gauge wanted, therefore, is to be the exact length of the abode, qualification, and property columns, namely 4, 3½, and 4 ems Pica. These together make 11½ ems Pica, and constitute the justifying rule or gauge, to be put into the stick that the name column may be justified to its proper width, thus:—

Justifying gauge 11½ ems.

9473Moore, Joseph⎯⎯⎯⎯⎯⎯⎯⎯⎯

The name column being thus properly justified, this gauge is taken out of the stick, the abode column set, and another gauge, the width of the two last columns, 7½ ems pica, is put into the stick, and this column like the former justified against it, thus:—

Gauge 7½ ems.

9473Moore, Joseph 43 Gorst street⎯⎯⎯⎯⎯

This 7½ ems gauge is then taken out of the stick, the next, or qualification column, is set and the rule or gauge the width of the last column—4 ems pica—is used to justify it, thus:—

Gauge 4 ems.

9473Moore, Joseph 43 Gorst street, Freehold shop⎯⎯

In the space left the last column is then set and justified, and the first line of this piece of tabular-work is completed, and the setting-rule put in for the next line, thus:—

9473Moore, Joseph 43 Gorst street, Freehold shop Nos 7, 8 and 9.

The doubles are then set as they occur in each column and thus justified against the respective gauges, line after line, until the stick is full. The appearance of the matter, as emptied on the brass galley, when proved, will be as follows:—

9473Moore, Joseph	43 Gorst street, in this parish	Freehold shop and houses	Nos. 7, 8 and 9. Bank terrace, Lancaster	
9474Moss, John	8 Spring Street	Freehold land	Brewery field	
9475Myres, Thomas Richard	Bank parade	Freehold land	Seed street	
9476May, Timothy	Winckley street in this parish	Freehold house	Lancaster road	
9477Naylor, John	Russell street	Freehold house and shop	Berry street	
9478Nickson, Amos	Marsh lane	Freehold land	Snow hill, John White tenant	
9479Night, Samuel George	Thomas street	Freehold shop	Saul street	
......Newgair, John	Tuxleth park	Leasehld shop	Deepdale road, Lancaster	

In this example, it will be seen that the lines which

turn over in the different columns appear only as common indentations. It is, however, the accuracy required in justifying these indentations by their proper gauges which makes all the difference. A line of common matter is justified only once, but a line of this tabular matter is justified every column.

The down rules are put at the end, as well to justify the full measure as to show in what manner, after this matter is made up into pages, the proofs are pulled for reading and correcting. It is much easier to correct the matter in this state than with the rules in their proper places, especially should there happen to be outs, etc.; as any line may now be taken out, additions or alterations made in any column, and the line replaced without interfering with any other. When corrected, the down rules are then inserted for the revised proof. But before showing how to insert the rules, I would say a few words about the headings.

Column headings are supplied to every page; a sufficient number of which are set up to perfect all the proofs, until the forms are worked and the headings are again returned to the compositors on the work. Whether there be few or many set, therefore, will depend upon the number of hands, and the number of forms returned from press. There should always be sufficient to keep both case and press going. The only peculiarity about these headings is, that they are confined between two long cross rules with short down rules that separate the head of each column, thus:

To Poll at	No.	Voter's Name	Place of Abode	Nature of Qualification.	Situation of Property, &c.

This exhibits the running heading to the entire work, and is set complete and justified within itself, for the special purpose of being lifted conveniently and entire out of the forms worked off before the pages are distributed. For extensive works, therefore, like this, this method of setting them is decidedly the best, on account of the facility they afford and the security they guarantee in lifting them to other pages in a hurry. This may suffice for the headings.

Supposing now the matter previously set to be read, corrected, and sufficient to make a page, the down rules, as seen at the end of the lines in the example, are put into their respective places between the columns. This is done easily, by turning the galley with its head next the body and insinuating between each column at the head the point of a bodkin, the left hand holding steadily the bottom of the column to be opened. The columns are thus moved and the rules inserted as soon as so many leads could be in ordinary matter. Should the matter be thought too near the column rules, leads on each side of them will improve their appearance; but it is best to use thick rules with beard sufficient on each side of them to obviate the necessity for leads. With the rules in, the page would be finished, and when proved appear thus:

To Poll at	No.	Voter's name	Place of Abode	Nature of Qualification.	Situation of Property, &c.
	9473	Moore, Joseph	48 Great street, in this parish	Freehold shop and houses	Nos. 7, 8 and 9, Bank terrace, Lancaster
	9474	Moss, John	2 Spring street	Freehold land	Brewery field
	9475	Myres, Thomas Richard	Bank parade	Freehold land	Seed street
	9476	May, Timothy	Winckley street, in this parish	Freehold house	Lancaster road
	9477	Naylor, John	Russell street	Freehold house and shop	Berry street
	9478	Nickson Amos	Marsh lane.	Freehold land	Snow hill, John White tenant
	9479	Night, Samuel George	Thomas street	Freehold shop	Saul street
Preston		Newgate, John	Toxteth park	Leasehld shop	Deepdale road, Lancaster

This system of setting tabular-work may be adopted with advantage in an endless variety of forms, and for setting any number of columns. The only difference would be, that, in matter containing many columns, two or three sticks of different measures might be required to take in the entire width of copy, and add to the convenience of setting.

Table-Book.—A volume used for memoranda, and frequently consisting of tablets or leaves of ivory clasped together.

Tablet.—A smooth piece of metal, wood, ivory, etc., on which lines or characters can be engraved, written, or traced. The following lines, from a French metrical romance written about 1376, prove that waxen tablets continued to be occasionally used till a comparatively late period:

> Some with antiquated style
> In waxen tablets promptly write;
> Others, with finer pen, the while
> Form letters lovelier to the sight.

There are many ample and authentic records of the royal household of France, of the thirteenth and fourteenth centuries, still preserved, written on waxen tablets.

In an accompt-roll of Winchester College for 1395, there is an article of disbursement for a tablet covered with green wax, to be kept in the chapel, for noting down with a style the respective courses of duty alternately assigned to the officers of the choir. Shakspeare alludes to this mode of writing, in his Timon of Athens:

> My free drift
> Halts not particularly, but moves itself
> In a wide sea of wax.

Tabular.—An arrangement in tables, or in columns, etc., so as to present a synopsis.

Tabula Rasa.—A Latin term adopted by English metaphysicians to express an absolute blank, or tablet upon which no lines have ever been traced, but which is prepared for their reception. Thus, Locke calls the human mind a tabula rasa.

Tachygraphy.—Stenography, or the art and practice of rapid writing by the use of symbols or abbreviations.

Tags.—Pieces of stout paper, card-board, paper combined with linen, etc., cut into convenient shapes and sizes, and eyeleted, so that they can be readily attached by a string to bundles, packages, etc., to serve as direction-labels. A very large number of tags are now used, many of them containing printed matter setting forth the business and address of the party by whom they are issued.

Tail-Pieces.—Ornaments placed at the lower portion of a short page at the end of chapters, etc. They were formerly in almost universal use, then totally abandoned, and are now inserted occasionally, especially in illustrated works, or works printed in old-style letter.

Take.—A subdivision of copy. Thus, when an article a column long is received at a late hour in a morning newspaper office, and cut into twenty parts, each one of which is given to a a different compositor, these parts are said to be takes.

Take Ink.—To give a new or increased supply of ink to composition-rollers.

Take-Up.—To take or lift matter with a composing-rule, for the purpose of distributing it, or to transfer it in making up.

Taking Copy.—A compositor receiving copy from the foreman or other person who has charge of it, to compose.

Talbotype.—A kind of photograph, named from its inventor, Fox Talbot, an Englishman. By this method a sheet of paper rendered sensitive by being impregnated with a mixture of iodide of silver, nitrate of silver, and organic matter is exposed in the camera to rays of light proceeding from the object, the picture being afterwards developed by means of gallo-nitrate of silver, or some other substance.

Tale.—A fictitious narrative less elaborate in design and execution than a novel: thus, according to modern usage, Sir Walter Scott was more correct in entitling his historic sketches the Tales of My Grandfather, than when he used the same word in the series of Tales of My Landlord, The Heart of Mid-Lothian being in all respects a novel.

Taped Work.—A description of bookbinding in which the sections are stabbed in the back, with long flat stabs, through which tapes are inserted and fastened on the covers.

Tautology.—The repetition of the same idea in different words or phrases, not necessary for emphasis, and injurious to the elegance and effectiveness of the style.

Taylor Presses.—Presses of various sizes, and adapted to various kinds of press-work, which are manufactured by the A. B. Taylor Printing-Press and Machine Company, established at New York in 1842, —Mr. Taylor being one of the oldest press-makers in the United States. These presses include nine sizes of an improved drum-cylinder, intended for fine book-, job-, and cut-work; a country news- and job-press; a small job-press; and rapid single small- and double-cylinder newspaper presses. See pages 459-60.

Technical.—Belonging to art, to the arts, or to any particular art, profession, or handicraft; denoting a word, term, or phrase used exclusively, or in a particular sense, in any art or science.

TAYLOR PRESS WITH FOUNTAIN ON BACK END.

A. B. TAYLOR   PATENT   NEW YORK

TAYLOR NEW DRUM-CYLINDER BOOK- AND JOB-PRESS.

TAYLOR JOB-PRESS.

Technicality.—A word or phrase used exclusively or in a peculiar sense in any art, science, or handicraft.

Technology.—A description of, or treatise upon, the arts; also a collection of the terms used in any art or handicraft, with an explanation of their meaning.

Telegram.—A message carried by the magnetic telegraph.

Telegraph.—Any mechanical contrivance for the rapid communication of intelligence by signals; but the term is at present, by common use, restricted to the electric-magnetic telegraph invented by Professor Morse, an American, and first put in operation by him between the cities of Washington and Baltimore in 1844. In the printing electric telegraph, a mechanism produces the impressions of the letters of the alphabet upon paper, by means of printing-type.

Telestich.—A poem in which the final letters of the lines taken consecutively form a name; the reverse of an acrostic.

Telotype.—A magnetic telegraph which prints the messages it conveys.

Tenet.—Any opinion, dogma, doctrine, or principle maintained by any person or persons.

Tense.—The various forms of a verb made by inflection or the addition of auxiliary words so as to indicate the time of the action expressed by the verb.

Term.—A word or expression; usually one that denotes something peculiar to an art or science.

Terminology.—The terms or nomenclature of any art, science, or handicraft; also, a treatise upon such a nomenclature.

Terse.—Elegant and concise in expression: applied to style in language.

Terza Rima.—A complicated and peculiar method of versification, constructed by the Troubadours, and borrowed from them by the Italians. Every three alternate lines rhyme in regular succession, with the exception of a couplet at the beginning and end: thus, the first and third lines rhyme; the second, fourth, and sixth; the fifth, seventh, and ninth. Although very difficult in construction, the effect is pleasing, by the constant interconnection of rhymes producing a consistent and regular flow in the measure, without the distinction of stanzas, which in other measures often necessarily break the sense by enforced structural division. Dante's Divine Comedy is written in this measure, and it has been imitated in some of the English translations of that work with but moderate success. Byron adopted it in his Prophecy of Dante, but the complex involvement of the rhymes seems to render it unsuited to the English language.

Testimonial.—A certificate intended as an evidence of character; also, by common usage, any gift or public manifestation of any kind, intended to express esteem for an individual.

Test-Paper.—In chemistry, paper colored with litmus, or blue cabbage. Paper colored by an infusion of blue cabbage is a valuable test, as it becomes instantly bright green on the application of an alkali, and bright red on the application of an acid.

Tetrameter.—In poetry, a line consisting of four feet.

Tetrastich.—In poetry, a stanza or epigram composed of four lines.

Tetrasyllable.—A word composed of four syllables.

Text.—1. A generic name for many varieties of job-letter. 2. The substance or body of a literary composition, as distinguished from notes, comments, etc. The word is also used to express a quotation from the Scriptures or any other work made the subject of a discourse.

Text-Book.—A hand-book for students, containing the principles of a science, or of any branch of learning.

Text-Hand.—Handwriting in large size, formerly used to distinguish the text of a book from the annotations, etc., written in a smaller hand.

Text-Pen.—A pen used for engrossing.

Theme.—The subject of a discourse; also, the essay of a student or pupil written upon a subject prepared by a teacher.

Theology.—The science which treats of the existence, nature, and attributes of God. This division of literature embraces a vast number of works, furnishing an immense field for typography.

Thermography.—Printing by heat;—an invention for taking impressions, or fac-similes, showing the grain and general appearance of different kinds of wood. The process consists in slightly wetting the surface of the wood to be represented, with a diluted acid or alkali, and then taking an impression on paper. The impression is at first invisible, but by exposing it for a short time to a strong heat it becomes more or less distinct, according to the strength of the alkali.

Thesaurus.—Literally, a treasure: used as the title of a dictionary, or treasure-house of words and information.

Thesis.—A proposition, affirmative or negative, intended as a theme for argument; also, the subject proposed for an academic essay, and the essay itself.

Thick Space.—A space one-third of the thickness of the em quadrate of the font to which it is attached; it is also called sometimes a three-em space.

Thin Space.—All spaces thinner than three-em spaces and thicker than hair spaces may, in a general sense, be called thin spaces; but five-em spaces can perhaps be specially designated as thin spaces with more propriety than spaces of any other size.

Thirty-six-mo.—A sheet of paper folded into thirty-six leaves, or seventy-two pages.

Thirty-two-mo.—A sheet of paper folded into thirty-two leaves, or sixty-four pages.

Three-quarter.—A size of portraits measuring thirty inches by twenty-five; also applied to a portrait extending downwards to the hips.

Threnody.—A song of lamentation; especially a short occasional poem composed for a funeral.

Tickets.—Many varieties of job printing, the list including card—or paper—certificates of the right of entry to places of amusement, as well as ball, commutation, coupon, deposit, dinner, election, excursion, passage, and railroad tickets.

Time-Table.—A register of specified hours, as of the recurrence of the tides, the departure and arrival of railway-cars, steamboats, etc.

Time-Work.—Work paid for by the day or hour, in contradistinction to that paid for by the piece or amount of labor actually performed. Nearly all book and daily newspaper work is now paid for by the piece, while nearly all classes of job-work and the making up, etc. of books and newspapers are time-work.

Timperley, C. H.—A practical printer of Manchester, England, and author upon Typography. He was born about 1794, and was apprenticed to an engraver and copper-plate printer. In 1810, when but little over fifteen years of age, he became attached to the 33d regiment of foot, and remained in the British service until 1815, when he was discharged in consequence of wounds received at the battle of Waterloo. On his return to Manchester he resumed the business of copper-plate printer, but relinquished it in 1821 for the practice of letter-press printing, under indentures to the proprietors of the Northampton Mercury. In 1828 he delivered a lecture upon the Origin and Early History of Printing before the Warwick and Leamington Literary and Scientific Institution, which was so favorably received by the public that he was encouraged to devote his leisure to a further study of the subject. He afterwards published a collection of poems upon typography, entitled The Songs of the Press, which was followed in 1838 by a work of practical instruction, with the title of A Printer's Manual. In 1839 Timperley published his excellent and useful compilation styled A Dictionary of Printers and Printing. This work is a model of industrious devotion, and is arranged on a most effective plan, containing a brief statement of facts relating to printing and printers, in chronological order, under the appropriate dates, beginning with the fifteenth century, and bringing it down to the

year 1838. Valuable tables are also added, and a voluminous introduction upon the state of literature from the earliest period to the invention of printing.

Tint.—Any shade or modification of a primitive color, produced in oil-colors by the addition of a white pigment, and in water-color by the addition of water.

Tints.—Many of the finest effects of modern job-printing are produced by the use of tint-blocks, from which impressions are taken in various light or neutral colors, to serve as a ground-work for printed matter in black or other dark-colored inks. Checks are very frequently printed in this manner. Tints are occasionally employed to decorate nearly all kinds of ornamental jobs.

Title.—The inscription placed at the head of any literary work, intended to describe the subject treated, and usually including the name of the author. The title of a work is intended to express its character, condensing into few words a description of the contents of the volume: thus, every nation places at the head of its literature its sacred writings under the pre-eminent title of The Book, a meaning expressed equally by Koran, Scriptures, and Bible. The difficulty of combining into one short line a summary, and also a pleasant and attractive name suited to the literary fancy of the hour, has compelled many authors to use the trite title of history, essays, miscellanies, or works, in order to avoid the labor of seeking names more aptly and peculiarly suited to their writings. In works of imagination the name of the hero or heroine has been chosen as the best method of avoiding difficulty, and even Shakspeare placed such convenient, ready-made titles as Macbeth, Hamlet, and King John to the majority of his dramas, although he exhibited his powers in the apt titles of Measure for Measure, The Taming of the Shrew, The Comedy of Errors, Love's Labor Lost, Much Ado about Nothing, and The Merry Wives of Windsor. Excellently descriptive as are these titles, the great dramatist seems to have been seized with despair when he named the chief of all his comedies As you Like It, and petulantly threw down his pen in entitling another Twelfth Night—or, What you Will! Richardson, Fielding, and the novelists that succeeded them generally followed the same method, and merely labeled their works as Pamela, Joseph Andrews, or Tristram Shandy; Sir Walter Scott rarely departed from this rule, although The Talisman and The Betrothed are more fairly descriptive, and The Heart of Mid-Lothian is one of the earliest of those delusive titles in which sense is sacrificed to sound in order to attract public attention. The genius of the great authors has, however, so clothed these titles with living warmth that it is difficult to remember that but a mere name stands as an apology for a title at the head of such works as Othello, Don Quixote, Robinson Crusoe, Rob Roy, Zanoni, or David Copperfield. The Iliad means but the tale of Ilium; the Æneid, the story of Æneas; the Divine Comedy of Dante receives its quaint title from its sombre beginning and happy end. Milton and Tasso were more fortunate in entitling their epics

Paradise Lost and Jerusalem Delivered; and the early poems of Scandinavia are happily called the Edda, or legends told by a Grandmother. Ancient stories have in many countries been strung together on a thread of narrative with such names as The Thousand and One Nights, The Decameron, and the Canterbury Tales. Many great books have, however, found fitting titles. The Dance of Death seized the imagination of a despairing multitude; the Fairy Queen well expressed the delicate fancies of Spenser; and the Pilgrim's Progress promised peace to many an aching heart. Among the Latins, instead of direct dedications, authors frequently used the names of their friends as the title of a book: thus, Cicero gave his treatise on Orators the title of Brutus; that upon Friendship he called Lælius; and one upon Old Age, Cato. Tasso in imitation affixed the name of his friend Manso as the title to his dialogue upon Friendship, and there have been other modern instances, although a better taste impelled Tennyson to call his wail of sorrowing friendship In Memoriam, without violating the sacredness of private life by obtruding too prominently the name of the friend so lamented; and the same feeling furnished the impulse of the exquisite laments in which Milton mourns for Lycidas, and Shelley wept the death of Keats in the Adonais.

In England, in the sixteenth and seventeenth centuries, the fancy for quaint and queer titles was carried to an almost inconceivable extent. In 1585 a book was published called The Anatomie of Abuses: being a Discourse or Brief Summarie of such Notable Vices and Corruptions as now reign in many Christian Countries in the World, especially in the Country of Ailgna: Together with the most fearful judgments executed upon the Wicked for the same—very Godly. To be read by all True Christians everywhere, but most chiefly to be regarded in England. Made Dialoguewise, By Philip Stubbs. In 1559 a publication appeared with the following name and motto:—The Key to Unknown Knowledge, or a Shop of Five Windows;

Which if you do open,
To cheapen and copes,
You will be unwilling,
For many a shilling,
To part with the profit
Which you shall have of it.

Another publication bore as its title these words:

Gentlemen, look about you!
Read this over if you're wise,
If you're not, then read it twice:
If a fool, and in the gall
Of bitterness, read not at all.

The Puritans affected especial quaintness, as in a treatise styled Eggs of Charity, layed by the Chickens of the Covenant, and boiled in the Water of Divine Love—Take ye and eat. The fancy of the time seems to have been especially pleased with this device, for another work, 1653, was styled Some Fine Biskets baked in the Oven of Charity, carefully conserved for the Chickens of the Church, the Sparrows of the Spirit, and the Sweet Swallows of Salvation. While a third boasted the variation of being A Reaping-Hook well tempered for the Ears of the Coming Crop; or Biscuits baked in the Oven of Charity, carefully conserved for the Chickens of the Church, Sparrows of the Spirit, and Doves of the Soul. There were also Crumbs of Comfort for the Chickens of the Covenant, and, more comforting still, Hooks and Eyes for Believers' Breeches; and High-heeled Shoes for Dwarfs in Holiness. But unapproachable in quaintness was the treatise entitled Salvation's Vantage Ground; or, A Louping-Stand for Heavy Believers. Poverty-stricken Puritans were offered A Sixpennyworth of Divine Spirit, while the wealthier were welcomed to A Bank of Faith, and the ailing to the Shop of the Spiritual Apothecary. Even the silver-tongued Silvester, from whom we have received hymns matchless in their simple fervor, influenced by the fashion of the time entitled a poem Tobacco battered, and the Pipes shattered about their Ears that idly idolize so loathsome a Vanity, by a Volley of Holy Shot thundered from Mount Helicon. William Penn directed an answer to Fox and his follower Burrowes as—A Fox digged out of his Burrowes; and De Foe found that A Short Way with Dissenters lodged its author promptly in jail.

The Puritans carried the same taste with them into New England, and one of their favorite catechisms was entitled Spiritual Milk for Boston Babes in either England. Drawn out of the Breasts of both Testaments for their Souls' Nourishment. But may be of like use to any Children. By John Cotton, B. D., late Teacher to the Church of Boston in New England, Cambridge. Printed by S. G., for Hezekiah Usher, at Boston in New England, 1656. A pamphlet against the Duke of Orange in 1703 contained this bitter lampoon upon his personal deformity:—The Deformity of St. Cured, a sermon preached at St. Michael's, Crooked Lane, before the Prince of Orange, by the Rev. J. Crookshanks. Sold by Mathew Denton, at the Crooked Billet, near Cripplegate, and by all booksellers. Text—Every crooked path shall be made straight. Fuller, the author of the Holy War, was a royalist, so devoted to the cause of the king that when Charles quitted London, in 1642, he risked his personal safety among the Puritans by preaching from the text, Yea, let him take all, so that my lord the king may return in peace; yet the quaint fancy of the period was also impressed in his successive works entitled Good Thoughts in Bad Times (1640), Good Thoughts in Worse Times (1645), and Mixt Contemplations in Better Times (1660). Robert Greene, in 1617, wrote A Farewell to Folly sent to Courtiers and Scholars, as a President to warn them from the Vain Delights that drawe Youth on to Repentance; and his last work, called A Groat's Worth of Wit, bought with a Million of Repentance, immediately preceded his death from a feast of pickled herring and Rhenish wine. Lovell, the naturalist, published at Oxford, in 1661, a work entitled Panzoologicomineralogia.

For called his great work The Acts and Monuments of the Church, or the Book of Martyrs, but in the last clause we find the title by which it acquired its celebrity. Sir Walter Scott chose melodious and appropriate names for The Lay of the Last Minstrel and The Lady of the Lake. Burns gave his matchless poem its perfecting touch in calling it The Cotter's Saturday Night, and Coleridge's impressive lines are suitably ushered by the quaint title of The Rime of the Ancient Mariner. The Pleasures of the Imagination, of Memory, and of Hope, and the Sentimental Journey, struck the fancy of their day as surely as the name of the Tale of a Tub met the humor of its time, or that of Hood's Own, that of a later generation. Byron found a good name for his detached poems in Hours of Idleness, and his pungent wit made a true title for his sarcastic bitterness in the brief but telling name of British Bards and Scotch Reviewers, and the still keener title of The Irish Avatar. Fenimore Cooper was particularly fortunate in attracting the public attention to volumes with such winning names as Homeward Bound, and Home as Found, or the more sentimental ones of The Last of the Mohicans, and the Wept of Wish-ton-Wish; and Goethe prepared his audience to weep by the very name of The Sorrows of Werter. That there is, indeed, much in a name is proved by the fact that an excellent novel which was utterly overlooked in England under the title of The Champion of Virtue, afterwards became very popular as The Old English Baron; and Horne Tooke brightened a topic as dull as grammar by styling his treatise the Diversions of Purley.

Sir Walter Scott, who regarded the subject not only as a poet and a novelist, but also with the keen business instinct of a Scotchman, defended his custom of using the names of the principal characters as the title of his fictions, on the ground that such names, giving no foretaste of the style of the story, left all to the imagination of the expectant reader. Notwithstanding this plausible reason for a generally accepted method of nomenclature, fashion has ruled the titles of books to a great extent; and that of an extraordinarily successful one has always found imitators: The Mysteries of Udolpho was followed by the Mysteries of Paris, and that in turn by the Mysteries of London; while Japhet in Search of his Father was mated by Cœlebs in Search of a Wife.

Another class of attractive names embrace such as The Pirate, The Antiquary, The Absentee, The Monk, The Marooners, Partisan, The Pioneer, Bravo and Bandit, The Spy, and The Scout, while in poetry similar titles are The Minstrel, The Hermit, and The Wanderer.

A very large number of novels have been published under such pleasing catchwords as Patronage, Progress and Prejudice, Pride, Discipline and Discretion, while the Lord of the Isles and the Lady of the Manor have marshaled a host of followers. The

taste for descriptive titles has increased during recent years: thus, Dickens, who in his early days was content with the Pickwick Papers or Burnaby Rudge, afterwards selected such names as The Haunted Man, Hard Times, Great Expectations, and Our Mutual Friend. Bulwer began his long career with the staid old-fashioned title of Pelham, or the Adventures of a Gentleman, but, altering with the altering times, took afterwards the pleasing title of My Novel, and the still more effective one of What Will he do With It? —which has provoked imitation in the striking titles of Can You Forgive Her, and, Put Yourself in His Place. Victor Hugo, in a similar manner, named an early book The Hunchback of Notre-Dame, and his later ones, Les Misérables and The Man Who Laughs. Kit North's euphonism of the Lights and Shadows of Scottish Life has also been frequently imitated. In modern German literature, some thoughtful novels have been thoughtfully named as Debit and Credit, Hammer and Anvil, and Through Night to Light; and Auerbach has treated lofty topics in On the Heights. In popular English light literature, striking titles also prevail, as The Yellow Mask, Scouring the White Horse, Very Hard Cash, Never too Late to Mend, The Woman in White, Man and Wife, Woman's Kingdom, The Book of Snobs, Yellow-Plush Papers, Vanity Fair, and The Dead Secret. In the very varied literature of the United States every species of title has been used, from The Mystery of the Scarlet Letter to Sam Slick of Slickville. Neal's dashing manner was well reflected in the name Charcoal Sketches, and Willis's elaborate sprightliness was curiously styled Dashes at Life with a Free Pencil. Effective titles for popular books have been Moby Dick, Ten Nights in a Bar-Room, The Wide Wide World, Alone, An Old-Fashioned Girl, Ginx's Baby, and The Innocents Abroad. In dramatic literature the especial necessity for effective and striking titles has been felt from the earliest times. An ancient Hindoo play was called the Toy-Cart, and the first comedy in the English language Gammer Gurton's Needle; in later times there have been The Broken Heart, Every Man in his Humor, A New Way to Pay Old Debts, She Stoops to Conquer, and, still more recently, Money, Still Waters Run Deep, London Assurance, The Last Man, Delicate Ground, Extremes, The Marble Heart, and a multitude of others equally suited for effect upon a hand-bill or display on a poster. In periodical literature the same difficulty has been experienced as in the selection of titles for books. The first review was styled the Journal des Savans, but was compelled to counteract the unfavorable impression conveyed by its title by explaining that even the humblest laborer could find profit and pleasure in perusing its pages; the subsequent titles of The Tatler, Spectator, Rambler, Idler, Lounger, and Connoisseur cannot be regarded as especially suitable selections, and the same objection is applicable to such indefinite titles as Blackwood, Edinburgh, the Two Worlds, and the North American. Recently the same endeavor after effect has been displayed among periodicals in adopting such names as

Household Words, All the Year Round, Every Saturday, Temple Bar, London Society, and the Atlantic and Overland Monthlies. The magazines, however, still generally preserve titles made from the names of the proprietors, as Harper's, Lippincott's, and Scribner's Magazines. In newspapers, in every country, titles have been used equivalent to Mercury, Courant, Times, Tidings, News, News Letter, Journal, Gazette, Sun, Messenger, Post, Advertiser, Chronicle, Ledger, Post-Boy, Herald, Press, Telegraph, Register, and other expressions for a periodical compendium of news. The fondness for certain names is illustrated by the fact that among the newspapers of London, in 1870, there were thirty which contained in the title the word Gazette, twenty-eight using the word Journal, twenty-five News, twenty-two Times, fifteen Chronicle, and fifteen the word Review.

Title-Page.—The page of a book, generally the first, devoted to a full statement of its title, together with the names of the author and publisher, and the year of publication. It is one of the most difficult tasks of a tasteful typographer to set up a good title-page. For general directions on this subject, see DISPLAY OF TYPE. The American Printer makes the following valuable suggestions:

As men whom nature puts in the fore-front of all other men are noted for an intellectual simplicity of life and style, so the title-page, that heralds all the inner pages of a book, should be printed in a style of elegance severe and unadorned : no fancy type, except a line of Scribe Text, or Old English,—no italics, unless perchance a single-line motto in Pearl caps,—no bold-face type, nor Antique, nor Gothic,—but plain, clear, light-faced letters, that seem the embodiment of the soul of thought. All experienced printers incline to this simple style; but publishers sometimes interfere with this province of art, legitimate only to a typographer, and insist on the indulgence of a taste which certainly owes no allegiance to any of the laws of beauty; and the printer or stereotyper who executes the book receives credit for a title-page which he would fain utterly repudiate.

We add a few hints which may assist the learner. 1st. Having divided the title into lines, and decided upon the size of type suitable for the principal one, begin by composing those of the second and third class, both in ascending and descending order. 2d. Avoid having two lines of equal length to follow or come in contact with each other. 3. Catch-words should be set on a very reduced scale, and proportioned according to the strength of the preceding and succeeding lines; for bold catch-words detract from the general effect of the title. 4. Close attention should be given to those title-pages which are acknowledged to be displayed with true taste and judgment.

Authors should endeavor to make their title-pages as concise as possible; for a crowded title can never be displayed with elegance or taste.

Toasts.—Sentiments or names of persons, countries, officials, etc., in whose honor a company is invited to drink. A few toasts, offered on various occasions in honor of printing and those connected with different branches of the art, are given below:

Printers, Publishers, and Proprietors—May neither ever throw a wet blanket upon the other, to damage the good impression which, when united and harmonious, they always make upon the world.

The Military—May the shooting-stick of the printer render obsolete the shooting-stick of the soldier.

The Printer—The master of all trades. He beats the farmer with his Hoe, the carpenter with his rules, and the mason with setting up tall columns; he surpasses the lawyer and doctor in attending to his cases, and beats the parson in the management of the devil.

The Editor and the Lawyer—The devil is satisfied with the copy of the former, but requires the original of the latter.

The Triple Brotherhood—Gutenberg, Fust, and Schoeffer, whose genius gave to their age the type and the press, enabling us of the present to hold communion with the soul of the past. Let Time, as he waves his pinions over the ages to come, transmit the history of our now uncounted brotherhood, in words that may give fire to the mind, eloquence to the tongue, and friendship, freedom, and morals to the universal heart of mankind.

The National Typographical Union—The golden chain that binds the press-gang of the nation.

Compositors—Better off when they stick to a plain rule than when they attempt to cut a swell dash.

The Printers—May their social position rise higher and higher until it takes a stand as noble as the art they represent.

The Newspaper Correspondent—He photographs everything, analyzes everything, epitomizes everything, is welcomed everywhere, is dead-headed in this world, and expects to be in the next.

The Press—The tongue of nations—the terror of tyrants.

Movable Type—May they ever move onward as the vanguard of human rights, and aid in elevating mankind to the highest destiny which humanity is capable of reaching.

The Editor—The helmsman of public opinion.

Type and Ink—Bullets for the upholders of despotism—ointment for the eyes of ignorance. May they be everywhere dispensed and everywhere successful.

The Printers—The greatest of scholars, for they have had all the books of the world at their fingers' ends.

Union—As wine for Printers as for States.

Our Fathers in the Art—They builded wiser than they knew; they founded an Order that will be honored when the claims of noble birth shall be forgotten.

The Graphic Arts and their Contributors.

　　Beneath the rule of men entirely great,
　　The pen is mightier than the sword.

Token.—This word was formerly used to designate ten quires or half a ream of paper. By some it is now construed to mean two hundred and fifty sheets;

by others, two hundred and forty sheets; and in England it signifies half a ream of perfect paper, or two hundred and fifty-eight sheets.

De Vinne, in his Price List, objects to the use of the word by printers in dealings with customers, on account of its ambiguity. He says, In New York, token means two hundred and fifty or two hundred and forty impressions; in New England it means five hundred or four hundred and eighty impressions. To a customer the word is unintelligible; its meaning and use as a unit of calculation are explained and defended with difficulty. He is puzzled when told that two hundred and fifty impressions are one token, and that two hundred and seventy-five impressions are two tokens, and is aggrieved if charged double or nearly double price for twenty-five added impressions.

Token-Sheet.—In wetting paper, the last sheet of each token is often doubled down, so that the corner projects; this projecting sheet marks the division of the pile into tokens, and is styled the token-sheet.

Tome.—A word adopted into English from the Latin, to express the word volume, and generally applied to classic works, and to the ponderous books of the early printers.

Topic.—The subject or theme of a discourse or writing; in rhetoric, an axiom, or a general head to which the author refers all the proofs adduced in his essays,—generally used in the plural.

Tops.—In piling away the printed sheets of a work, after they have been dried, the warehouseman of English printing-offices takes a few sheets of each signature, and lays them at the top of the pile; these are called Tops, and enable him, with little trouble, to deliver copies of all signatures printed, when they are required, without having to take down all the piles.

Tornaesius, John, or Detournes.—An eminent printer and bookseller of Lyons, France, and head of the family of typographers generally known in France as the Detournes, who for two hundred and forty years maintained a distinguished reputation as printers in the cities of Geneva and Lyons. John Tornaesius, the first printer of the name, studied his art under Sebastian Gryphius, and established an office for himself in Lyons in 1540. His publications were remarkable for correctness, and were usually preceded by dedications and prefaces written by himself in the Latin language. He was for some years King's Printer, continuing so till his death in 1564. His business was continued by his son, John Tornaesius or Detournes, who was also King's Printer at Lyons. His editions were remarkably correct and elegant, and he had acquired a well-deserved celebrity, when in 1585 he was compelled to leave France and find refuge in Geneva on account of his Protestantism. He was very successful in his new home, being made a member of the Council of Two Hundred, in 1604, and continued to print in that city until his death in 1615. The remarkable inferiority of the paper used in

Geneva detracted much from the appearance of the works which he published in that city. His descendants continued as printers and booksellers in Geneva, and in 1726 John James and James Detournes purchased the stock of a famous firm of booksellers in Lyons, and obtained permission, notwithstanding their Protestantism, to return to that city. They still retained their printing establishment in Geneva, but resided in Lyons, and in 1740 Wolff dedicated his work entitled Monumenta Typographica to them, as the oldest printing and bookselling house in Europe. The sons of John and James Detournes, having acquired considerable wealth, sold their establishments in 1780, and retired from the profession in which their family had been engaged for nearly two centuries and a half.

Torquemada, Tomas de.—Famous as the organizer of the Spanish Inquisition. Torquemada was born in Valladolid in 1420, and became a devotee of the severe order of the Dominicans. Possessing extraordinary ability, he rose rapidly to distinction, and was the Administrator of the monastery of Subiaco, near Rome, when his attention was so strongly attracted to the advantages of the new art of printing that he used his personal influence with the monks to make them unite in inviting Sweynheim and Pannartz, two German printers, to that monastery. An undated Donatus, or Latin Grammar, is supposed to have been the first work, printed in 1464, and the first dated book was the Institutes of Lactantius of 1465. In this work a new and remarkably fine style of Greek letter was used, and it is probable that the printers received efficient assistance from the monks in working the press. The German printers remained in the monastery only three years, and then removed to Rome under the patronage of the Pope, probably at the instance of Torquemada, who thus became the real instrument of the introduction of Printing into Italy, and probably one of the influential improvers of the art, especially by the assistance furnished to Sweynheim in producing the type in which he abandoned the shapes used by Schoeffer and imitated the Italian writing of the period. Torquemada subsequently became Inquisitor-General of Spain in 1484, and died in 1498.

Tory, or Torinus, Geoffroy.—A Parisian printer of the sixteenth century, distinguished for the artistic perfection of his work, and for his book, entitled Champ Fleury, published in 1526, in which he proposed a systematic method of producing uniformity and beauty in the shape of the letters. Tory was born in 1480, of poor parents, in the province of Berry, but fortunately obtained patronage which enabled him to attend the best schools in the neighborhood. He afterwards traveled in Italy, where he had admirable opportunities for pursuing his studies. In 1505 he began his literary career in Paris by issuing Pomponius Mela, a work dedicated to a member of the Privy Chamber of Francis I. The work was published by Jean Petit, and it is probable that the influence of its patron obtained for Tory the position

30

466

of instructor in the Collegium Du Plessis. He afterwards prepared Æneas Sylvius and other works for Henry Stephens the elder. Having a special fondness for art, Tory began to practice wood-engraving, and finally relinquished his professorship in order to pursue the study of art in Italy. Here he became much interested in printing, and, in order to meet his expenses, supported himself by miniature-painting, then much used in the adornment of manuscripts and printed books. As a wood-engraver, he was soon recognized as one of the chief artists of his time; and the plates marked with the cross of Lorraine, and ascribed to him, are now considered worthy of the first place in every choice collection. His excellent manner was imitated by other wood-engravers, and he is regarded as head of a school of art. Tory was admitted to membership in the guild or corporation of booksellers, which also included the illuminators and wood-engravers, and, as a means of introducing his special style into the adornment of books, he engraved initials, characters, and borders for Simon de Colines. The Books of Hours offered at that time a profitable opportunity for fine illustration; and a Book of Hours of the Virgin, published by Simon de Colines and signed in full with the name of Geoffroy Tory, shows that the artist was acquainted with all the resources of his art. The style of the arabesques is drawn from the finest classic forms, while the supple grace of the figures shows the influence of French taste.

Tory is also supposed to have engraved the elegant antique script used by Henry Stephens. The active intellect of Tory led him to consider that the undue pre-eminence given by scholars to the Greek and Latin languages was producing a disastrous effect upon the vernacular of his own country, and the result of his considerations upon this topic was the publication, in 1526, of a remarkably original work, styled Champ Fleury. The book was divided into three parts. The first of these parts contained a dissertation upon the proper use of language. The second treated of the origin of capital letters, and instituted a curious and fantastic comparison between them and the true proportions of the human face and frame, with a series of ingenious wood-cuts to illustrate the theory. The third part contained accurate drawings of the letters, produced upon a species of chart or diagram, in the form of a square, divided into ten lines, perpendicular and transverse, making one hundred square compartments, upon which circles drawn by the compass served to produce the exact shape of the letters. This division of the book also treated of the pronunciation of peoples of different districts and nations, and presented a large number of alphabets of various kinds, as well as fanciful letters in arabesque, etc. The result of this work was an immediate and complete revolution in French typography and orthography—the abandonment of the Gothic and the adoption of a new cut of antique type. Robert Stephens forsook the shapes favored by his father, and Simon de Colines introduced essential alterations, and the

faces of type thus produced were used until near the close of the eighteenth century.

The Champ Fleury also attracted general attention to the proper use, in French, of the accents, apostrophe, and marks of punctuation, resulting in a remarkable and immediate improvement in the general appearance of the national typography. The publication of this work won for its author the title of King's Printer, from the scholarly Francis I., who, despite his especial devotion to the Greek language, recognized the value of such labors in the perfection of the vernacular as an additional mark of distinction. Tory was elected one of the sworn booksellers of the University of Paris, and although the regular number, twenty-four, was already full, an additional or extra membership was provided in his honor, to be held by him during his life, and to expire at his death. The richly Illustrated Books of Hours published by Tory are distinguished by a combination of antique art with French grace, and an abandonment of the prevalent Gothic method of ornamentation. A publication in 1533 introduced his own improved system of orthography, the improvements in the use of capitals being especially marked. Tory died about this time, and his widow completed and published in 1535 a remarkably fine edition of Diodorus Siculus, which he had commenced.

Totem.—The picture used by the American Indians as the symbol of an individual or a family, thus forming a rude species of picture-writing or hieroglyphics.

Tour.—A journey of observation, in which various places are visited. The word tour and tourist are frequently used in the titles of works of travels.

Tracing-Paper.—Paper made transparent, and used in copying drawings or engravings. Various modes of manufacturing it are adopted, among which are the following:

Moisten a sheet of paper with benzine, applying it with a sponge. The paper becomes temporarily transparent, and lines may be traced through it. In a few hours the benzine evaporates, and the paper again becomes opaque.

A permanent tracing-paper can be made by mixing, with the aid of gentle heat, an ounce of Canada balsam and a quarter of a pint of spirits of turpentine, and washing one side of the paper with this mixture.

Tract.—A short essay upon some particular subject, generally religious, and usually printed in pages of some one of the smaller book-sizes.

Tragedy.—A dramatic composition, representing human passions or misfortunes in such a manner as to excite horror, pity, or indignation, and generally applied to a drama written in a lofty style, conforming to regular rules, and ending with some touching or terrible catastrophe.

Tragi-Comedy.—A dramatic writing combining the characteristics of comedy and tragedy. According to some critics, all the plays of Shakspeare, except the Merry Wives of Windsor, are described under this head, on account of the intermingling of humorous with serious incidents. The strict rules of the classic drama, advocated by some French and German authors, have, however, never been adopted in England and America, where tragedies are generally diversified by the introduction of some humorous character or incident.

Transcript.—A copy,—generally applied to a copy of words; frequently used as the title of a newspaper, to imply that the news conveyed is a faithful copy or rehearsal of the events described.

Transfer.—In engraving, a mode of placing a picture on a plate, so that the lines may be engraved without being drawn by the artist, the copy being made by a species of off-setting.

Transfer-Paper.—A species of paper used in copying-presses, and in lithography for transferring impressions.

Translation.—The rendering of a literary work from one language into another. This is performed by two methods,—either by an exact substitution of one word for another, precisely equivalent, forming what is called a literal translation, or by selecting such terms and expressions as produce a similar effect in another language. Thus, the line of Aristophanes, literally translated, They scolded like bakers' wives, would, in conformity to an English phrase, be better translated, They scolded like fish-women.

Transpose.—When letters, words, lines, or pages of printed matter are not in proper order, compositors are directed to transpose them to their true position, the proof-reader's mark, in such cases, being tr., an abbreviation of transpose.

Travels.—A work containing an account of the occurrences of a journey, and the observations made thereupon by the author,—used as a general term for a large division of publications, styled books of travel.

Treatise.—An elaborate essay or disquisition of considerable length, generally restricted to scientific works.

Trialogue.—A discourse in which three persons are engaged, as distinguished from dialogue, or a discourse between two, and a monologue, or soliloquy.

Trilogy.—A work, usually a drama, consisting of three parts, each of which is complete in itself, although forming a constituent portion of the whole. The dramas of Æschylus and Shakspeare's Henry VI. are examples.

Trio.—A musical composition for three parts.

Triphthong, Trigram, or Trigraph.—Three letters united in one sound, as in the English word eye, or as eau in beau.

Triplet.—A form of verse in which three sequent lines conclude with the same rhyme; as,

Is ever a lament begun
By any mourner under sun,
Which e'er it endeth suits but one?

Triptych.—A writing-tablet made in three leaves, so that the two outer ones fold over the middle one, forming a book. This classic shape of tablet was one of the earliest models of the modern book or volume, and was adopted to preserve the face of the wax from injury. Pictures were formerly painted upon panels

in the same manner, the middle one being usually the principal scene, and the lateral ones intended to accompany or explain it.

Trite.—That which has become hackneyed or commonplace from over-use; often applied to phrases of speech.

Trisyllable.—A word containing three syllables.

Tri-weekly.—Occurring three times a week; frequently applied to newspapers published at such intervals.

Trochee.—A measure in versification, consisting of feet of two syllables, the first long and the second short; as,

But a trouble weighed upon her,
And perplexed her night and morn.

Trope.—Literally, a phrase or expression turned from its proper meaning or use, in order to give freshness or emphasis to the style. The figures called metaphor, allegory, metonymy, etc. are classed as tropes.

Turnebus, Adrian.—King's Printer in Paris, for a few years, about the middle of the sixteenth century, and regarded as the greatest scholar of his age. Turnebus is believed to have descended from an English family named Turnbull, who altered their name in France to Tournebeuf, occasionally written Turnebe, and at a later period, by the family of the printer, to Turnebu. Turnebus was born in Normandy in 1512. When nine years of age he was taken to Paris, where he became, even in his boyhood, widely known for his proficiency in the learned languages. His prefaces, annotations, commentaries, and criticisms upon classic authors exhibited such a rare combination of vast learning with fine judgment, that the German professors at a late date recognized his remarkable superiority by touching their caps in respect at the mention of his name. De Thou mentions that in his youth he had been once in the presence of Turnebus, whose appearance made such an impression upon his mind that his image recurred to his memory repeatedly in after-life; and Montaigne gives a similar tribute in saying that his vast learning was absolutely free from pedantry, and that his manner was affable, his speech prompt and genial, his decisions rapid, and his judgment accurate. Turnebus's great book was the Adversaria, a work upon criticism, pronounced by De Thou as worthy of immortality. It was published in three volumes, the first appearing in 1584, and the last in 1573. Turnebus held the Greek professorship at Paris, and his interest in Greek literature led him to accept the position of King's Printer, and with the assistance of William Morel he published several Greek works of singular beauty, which are esteemed very highly by book-collectors. He died in 1565.

Turned Letters.—Types placed in such a position that their feet instead of their face are printed. When matter runs upon sorts, such as capitals, figures, signs, etc., and a character is thus exhausted before the case is empty, it is usual to put in the composing-stick a type of the thickness of the one lacking, so that an impression is taken of the feet instead of the face, thus, ▆ ▆ ▆ ▆ in proof, and that the peculiar appearance caused may direct the attention of the compositor to the necessity of putting the proper type in the place temporarily occupied by its substitute, after necessary sorts are procured from a type-foundry or by distribution.

Turn Over.—In England, an apprentice, especially one connected with the printing business, who, after serving for a short time with one employer, and before the completion of his apprenticeship, obtains a situation with another master-printer.

Turtle.—The bed of Hoe's fast Rotary Printing Machine, in which the forms of daily newspapers are made up. It is divided into sections corresponding to the number of pages to be printed, each forming the arc of a circle, which are removed from the press to the composing-room to have the type made up in them and transferred back to the press when the forms are to be printed. The turtle and its appendages constitute one of the most ingenious, interesting, and important inventions devised to facilitate fast printing.

Twelve-mo.—A sheet of paper folded so as to make twelve leaves, or twenty-four pages.

Twenty-four-mo.—A sheet of paper folded into twenty-four leaves, or forty-eight pages.

Twenty-mo.—A sheet of paper folded so as to make twenty leaves, or forty pages.

Two-line Letters.—Fonts of capitals that are equal to two bodies of any specific-sized type. They embrace Two-line Agate, Two-line Nonpareil, Two-line Minion, Two-line Brevier, Two-line Bourgeois, Two-line Long Primer, Two-line Small Pica, Two-line English, and Two-line Great Primer; and are used for lines in tables and jobs, and frequently as the initial letters of chapters and advertisements.

Tying up a Page.—See PAGE, (TYING UP A).

Tympan.—1. In hand-presses, a frame covered with linen cloth, silk, parchment, or other material, according to the character of the work to be done, on which the sheet of paper to be printed is placed. This is the outer tympan; the inner tympan fits into it; and between the two, blankets and making-ready sheets are placed. 2. In many varieties of automatic or power-presses the substance upon which the paper to be printed is laid is called the tympan, and India-rubber cloth, a woolen blanket, calendered printing-paper, pasteboard, packing, or a combination of these or other materials, is employed. (See BLANKETS, MAKING READY, and PRESS-WORK.)

Tympan-Hooks.—Small hooks fixed on the upper side of the outer tympan of hand-presses, which assist in keeping the inner tympan in its place.

Tympan-Joints.—The joints by which the outer tympan of hand-presses is attached to the carriage on which it works.

Tympan-Sheet.—A sheet of paper pasted on the tympan of the hand-presses by the corners, as a mark by which to lay the sheets even in working.

Tyndale, or Tindall, William.—The translator and publisher of the first Bible in the English language, for which he was strangled and burned at the stake in Brabant, in 1536, under a law promulgated by the Emperor of Germany, and at the instance and with the assistance of Henry VIII. of England, the College of Louvain, and the clergy and magistracy of Brussels. William Tyndale was a descendant of the Barons of Tindale; he was born in Gloucestershire about 1484, and was educated at Oxford, where he officiated for some time as a tutor. He afterwards took orders as a priest at Cambridge. While acting as an instructor at Bristol, he became interested in the works of the Reformers, especially in those of Erasmus, and, finding himself an object of suspicion, began a life of wandering by seeking the freer opportunities of London. In this city he commenced the translation of the New Testament, but, fearing for his personal safety, removed to Hamburg, where he completed his task. He visited Luther in Saxony, and is supposed to have had parts of the Testament printed at various places. He finally found a safe residence among the English Reformers at Antwerp, with the advantages of a free press, and here his first edition of fifteen hundred copies was completed in 1525, by Richard Grafton. The book was a duodecimo, without title-page, and contained no name, date, or place by which its printer or editor could be discovered. It consisted of 350 leaves, besides an address To the Reder, and a list of The Errours committed in the Prentynge. The marginal notes which were afterwards printed were in this edition in manuscript, and the initial letters were handsomely gilt and illuminated. The books were burned publicly at St. Paul's Cross, London, in the same year, by Tunstall, Bishop of London, who was so energetic in the purchase and collection of them that only one copy is now known to exist. The public destruction of the books attracted so much attention, that some Dutch printers hastily prepared two editions of inferior style, with the aid of George Joye, an English refugee, and published them in 1527. Tyndale also prepared a second edition at Antwerp in 1534. In Brussels, Tyndale's translations were interdicted under the severest penalties, and by a public ordinance all persons possessing copies, who did not deliver them to the public officers to be burned, were condemned to death. A similar law was enforced in England, and many persons suffered death on the charge of purchasing, possessing, selling, reading, or hearing them read. The Emperor Charles V. issued a like order in 1546.

Tyndale also completed a translation of the Pentateuch, but on his way to Hamburg by sea the ship was wrecked and the manuscript lost. He recommenced his task immediately, and with the assistance of Miles Coverdale completed it in a short time. The book was published in small octavo, and from the different types used appears to have been printed at various presses. Some copies bear the imprint of Hans Luft, 1530, at Marlborough in Hesse, a fictitious name for the town of Warburg. Tyndale afterwards translated the Prophecy of Jonas. He was repeatedly invited to England, but he wisely refused to comply. John Fryth, who had assisted him in the publication of 1526, ventured to visit England, and was burned for heresy at Smithfield in 1533. Tyndale's other assistant, William Roye, was also burned in Portugal, and Tyndale suffered completion of his martyrdom just ten years after his first publication, and near the scene of his early labors. The edition of 1526 was reprinted verbatim in 1836, by George Offor, of London, and published by Bagster.

Type.—1. A raised character, such as a letter, mark, or sign, cast in metal or cut in wood, of such dimensions and proportions that it is adapted for use in printing. 2. Types in general,—as the whole quantity of letters in a font, collectively.

Different Parts of a Type.—Different parts of a type are designated as the face, the counter, the beard, the shoulder, the shank or body, the pin mark, the nick, the groove, and the feet. It is worthy of note that a considerable portion of this nomenclature is similar to names applied to the human frame. The face *b* is the part from which an impression is taken, and various portions of its surface are called stem, ceriph, and kern. The straight flat stroke of a straight letter is a stem; the fine lines at the top and bottom of a letter are ceriphs; and a projection over the shank or body, like that at the top of the letter f, is a kern. The counter is the space between the lines of the face. The lower portion of a type, on which it is supported whenever it is doing service as part of composed matter, is divided by a groove, (*e*) made by the type-dresser, and, probably on account of this division, is called the feet instead of the foot. The nick (*d*) is a hollow cast in the shanks or bodies of type, one or more nicks being inserted in various fonts, and their position being varied. While the nick in all American and English type is always cast on the same side as the bottom of the letter, and while the number and position of the nicks used in any one font are uniform, a wide diversity is purposely made in the number and position of the nicks of different fonts of letter. (See NICKS). In England the body of the letter is called the shank. This word is not in general use in the United States, but it serves a good purpose in drawing a clear distinction between the sizes of type established by the respective standards and the metal which supports the face of a letter. By some writers that portion of the type not occupied by the face is called the shoulder, while others call this part of a type the beard. The true system seems to be to call that portion of the type directly opposite *c* in the accompanying engraving, the shoulder; while that portion represented by ruled lines which runs up from the shoulder to the face is the beard. The pin mark is a small circular indentation on the side of the shank, near the face, made in the process of manufacture by a small pin, which forms part of a type-casting machine.

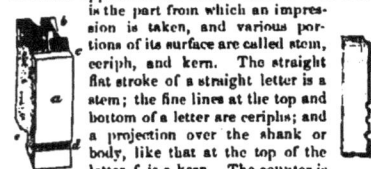

Type-metal.—The component parts of type-metal have varied considerably at different periods; even at the present day they vary in different foundries; and in any given foundry metal of different degrees of hardness is employed in manufacturing type of various sizes. Lead is now, and always has been, the principal ingredient of metallic type, but, as it is too soft for durability, various alloys, such as iron, steel, brass, tin, copper, and antimony, have been employed from time to time. In the seventeenth century types were made, in England, of lead hardened with iron stub nails, mingled with antimony, twenty-five pounds of lead mixed with three pounds of iron and antimony, mingled together, being used to make twenty-eight pounds of type-metal. In Germany, about the middle of the eighteenth century, type-metal consisted of steel, iron, copper, brass, tin, lead, and antimony. A modern French writer described French type-metal as a compound of lead and regulus of antimony, melted together in various proportions, the most usual being eighty pounds of lead added to twenty pounds of regulus of antimony already melted; but for small characters, requiring a greater degree of hardness, seventy-five pounds of lead were combined with twenty-five pounds of regulus of antimony; and for unusually large type the proportions were eighty-five pounds of lead and fifteen pounds of regulus of antimony. He considered it highly important that only the purest regulus of antimony, or that which is freest from sulphur, should be employed; because, when there was an intermixture of sulphur, that substance acted upon the lead, giving it a dull appearance, and causing the letters to become brittle and lose their force. He also suggested that tin added to the lead and antimony insured a much greater degree of hardness; and tin now almost always forms part of type-metal.

Various alloys, used in various proportions, are employed in different type-foundries at the present day, the exact combinations being trade secrets. Lead, antimony and tin seem to be universal ingredients, while copper is sometimes added. One composition, which is especially hard, consists of fifty parts of lead, twenty-five parts of tin, and twenty-five of antimony. In another, known as Didot's metal, one part of copper is added to three each of lead, tin, and antimony. It is said that a new type-metal has been made in Humboldt county, Nevada, by separating silver from one of the ores of that region, leaving a compound consisting of about thirty parts of lead and seventy parts of antimony. Type-foundries frequently designate by different names the various qualities of metal used in manufacturing type of different sizes, etc. They may be known in one foundry as ordinary metal, hard metal, and extra-hard metal; and in other foundries they may be divided into four or five grades, which are sometimes designated by the names of various sizes of type. Comparatively soft metal is generally used for spaces, quads, leads, slugs, and very large type, while a harder metal is used for small type. A slight variation in the metal used in a given font of type is also sometimes caused by the difficulty of maintaining a thorough and uniform fusion of all the ingredients during the entire process of casting.

Bodies of Type.—The various sizes or bodies of type are represented by the specimens given below:

BRILLIANT;
abcdefghijklmnopqrstuvwxyz ABCDEFGHIJKLMNOPQRSTUVWXYZ

DIAMOND;
abcdefghijklmnopqrstuvwxyz ABCDEFGHIJKLMNOPQRSTUVWXYZ

PEARL;
abcdefghijklmnopqrstuvwxyz ABCDEFGHIJKLMNOPQRSTUVWXYZ

AGATE;
abcdefghijklmnopqrstuvwxyz ABCDEFGHIJKLMNOPQRSTUV

NONPAREIL;
abcdefghijklmnopqrstuvwxyz ABCDEFGHIJKLMNOPQRST

MINION;
abcdefghijklmnopqrstuvwxyz ABCDEFGHIJKLMN

BREVIER;
abcdefghijklmnopqrstuvwxyz ABCDEFGHIJKLM

BOURGEOIS;
abcdefghijklmnopqrstuvwxyz ABCDEFGHIJ

LONG PRIMER;
abcdefghijklmnopqrstuvwxyz ABCDEFG

SMALL PICA;
abcdefghijklmnopqrstuvwxyz ABCDEF

PICA;
abcdefghijklmnopqrstuvwxyz ABC

ENGLISH;
abcdefghijklmnopqrstuvwxyz A

GREAT PRIMER;
abcdefghijklmnopqrstuvw

The larger Roman letters (used generally on hand bills and posters) vary materially in the style of the faces—the sizes are as follows:

PARAGON;
abcdefghijklmnop

DOUBLE SMALL PICA;
abcdefghijklmn

DOUBLE PICA;
abcdefghijklm

DOUBLE ENGLISH;
abcdefghijklm

DOUBLE GREAT PRIMER;
abcdefghij

CANON;
abcdef

The larger sizes of metal type are rated by their relation to Pica, being known as four-, five-, six-, seven-, eight-, nine-, ten-, eleven-, and twelve-line Pica, while the larger sizes of wood letter extend to one hundred and fifty-lines Pica. The American names for type conform substantially to the English names, except that a size between Nonpareil and Pearl, first made about 1820, is called Ruby in England and Agate in the United States; and a size between Nonpareil and Minion is known in England as Emerald and in this country as Minionette.

Standard of Type.—The exact dimensions of the bodies of type and their relation to one another constitute what is termed the standard; and while there is an approximation in the standards used in American type-foundries, they do not exactly conform to one another,—so that while all the Minion, Brevier, Bourgeois, or Long Primer made at one foundry conform to the special standard of that establishment, these types are not precisely of the same size as the types of corresponding names made at many other American foundries. A diversity of this description originated in England years ago, partly on account of the desire of some printers to obtain type differing slightly in size from all other type; and, although this diversity has been partially corrected in England, it has been widened in American foundries. English founders agree, with one exception, that the Pica shall be one-sixth of an inch; that two Nonpareils shall be equal to one Pica, two Pearls to one Long Primer, two Diamonds to a Bourgeois; but beyond this there is no relation between one body and another, and each founder differs from his fellows in the exact size of the types called by the respective names. The ideal English standard was stated by Hansard, half a century ago, to consist of the following number of ems or lines in a foot:

Canon	18½
Two-line Double Pica	20¾
Two-line Great Primer	25½
Two-line English	32
Two-line Pica	35
Double Pica	41½
Paragon	44½
Great Primer	51½
English	64
Pica	71½
Small Pica	83
Long Primer	89
Bourgeois	102½
Brevier	112½
Minion	128
Nonpareil	143
Pearl	178
Diamond	205

This standard is not now respected, however, and an idea of the existing diversities between various American foundries, and between American and English foundries, may be formed from the table appended to the article on PROPORTIONS OF TYPE.

In France, uniformity has been established. A modern English writer, familiar with the subject, says:

Many years ago, by common consent of the printers, through their Trade Council, the Chambre des Imprimeurs, a definite standard was adopted, and the founders are obliged to conform to the rules laid down, so that, from whatever source obtained, the type of a given body is of uniform dimensions. The evil of the want of such a system was recognized and remedied even as early as 1730. Fournier, in establishing his foundry, determined to put an end to the confusion that then prevailed among the French founders, as in our own. The plan he adopted is the basis of that which now universally prevails. He took two inches as his standard measure, which he called his Prototype, and divided these into twelve parts, which he called lines, and each of these again into twelve parts, which he named Points, thus forming one hundred and forty-four divisions. To apply this in practice, he assigned to each body a definite number of Points. Thus, the body Cicero, corresponding to our Pica, was twelve points, and it was rendered exactly of these dimensions by laying twelve Cicero types on the two-inch standard, and dressing them until they exactly fitted the required space. Nonpareil, half a Cicero, was six points: so that in dressing this body twenty-four had to be made to fill the Prototype. Leads were made to a certain number of points; and thus any body worked with another without justification. Fournier's standard is still that used in the Imprimerie Impériale, but it was modified by Didot, who adopted as his Prototype—or Typomètre, as it has since been called—a definite portion of the metre, and thus brought type-founders under the French decimal system of measurement.

An English compositor who had worked as a journeyman in a Parisian printing-office furnished the following description of the practical workings to a London typographical journal:

The French have taken the Pica and divided it into twelve parts, called points; and, having discarded the old names, they call the type after the number of points it contains: thus, Nonpareil is six, and Long Primer is nine. The leads and rules are named in the same way: so that in justifying tables and other work requiring great exactitude, all they have to do is to reckon the number of points in the type, and add the remaining points in leads, without adopting the system of trial and error necessary in England.

The practical difficulties involved in the establishment of a uniform standard in the United States are well-nigh insurmountable, for while each founder is willing to have his particular standard adopted by all other founders, each naturally shrinks from a voluntary assumption of the immense labor and expenditure involved in procuring an entirely new set of moulds. It is, also, questionable whether an absolutely regular series of gradations would be satisfactory to printers if it were carried through the smaller sizes of type. The Chicago Specimen, in discussing this subject, says:

It is generally believed and averred by printers that all type should be made so that in the case of three

bodies following each other, two lines of the intermediate size should be equivalent to one line of the size preceding it and one of that following it. This is generally the case in the sizes ranging from Pica to Nonpareil. Thus, two lines of Small Pica are equal in body to one Pica and one Long Primer; two of Long Primer, to one of Bourgeois and one of Small Pica; and so on. Now, as every printer knows, Pica is the standard of measurement among all printers and founders. Small Pica is about one-twelfth less than Pica; Long Primer, one-twelfth of Pica smaller than Small Pica; and so on to Nonpareil, decreasing about one-twelfth of Pica with each successive grade. To carry this gradation through would make Brilliant of the body of a six-to-Pica lead, while now it is a trifle more than a four-to-Pica lead. It seems to us that a more regular gradation would be to reduce each size one-twelfth of the body of the size preceding it —making Long Primer a twelfth less than Small Pica, Brevier a twelfth less than Bourgeois, Nonpareil a twelfth smaller than Minion, etc. An inch on a man's nose is a good deal, and while the present one-twelfth difference between Pica and Small Pica is all well enough, it becomes too sudden a descent when applied to the sizes below Long Primer or Brevier. The gradations should be relatively the same in each case, in order to secure the proper proportion of faces.

Height to Paper.—Discrepancies also exist in the height of type to paper, or the distance from the face to the feet of type made by some of the American foundries (the usual height of a letter being eleven-twelfths of an inch); but these discrepancies are less common and less glaring than those relating to the size of type. (See HEIGHT TO PAPER.)

Measurement of Alphabets.—In addition to the differences in type arising from the number of established sizes, and the variations of those sizes occasioned by the non-existence of a uniform standard, a wide diversity is created by a difference in the width of varying fonts, some faces being fat and others lean. The character of a type, in this respect, is estimated by the number of ems required to embrace all the lower-case letters, and the application of this test is called a measurement of the alphabet. Thirteen ems (that is, a type so proportioned that all its lower-case letters can be set up in a measure equivalent to thirteen ems of its body) are commonly considered a fair average measurement for newspaper type; but many fonts are thicker, measuring from fourteen to sixteen ems to the alphabet; while some fonts intended for book-work measure less than twelve ems. Thin or lean fonts are comparatively rare, partly because an extra price per thousand is charged for composing them, and care is usually taken to avoid such charges. The difference between alphabets of letter of the same body is illustrated by the following variations in types manufactured by Collins & McLeester:

AGATES.
abcdefghijklmnopqrstuvwxyz
abcdefghijklmnopqrstuvwxyz
abcdefghijklmnopqrstuvwxyz
abcdefghijklmnopqrstuvwxyz

NONPAREILS.
abcdefghijklmnopqrstuvwxyz
abcdefghijklmnopqrstuvwxyz
abcdefghijklmnopqrstuvwxyz
abcdefghijklmnopqrstuvwxyz
abcdefghijklmnopqrstuvwxyz

MINIONS.
abcdefghijklmnopqrstuvwxyz
abcdefghijklmnopqrstuvwxyz
abcdefghijklmnopqrstuvwxyz
abcdefghijklmnopqrstuvwxyz
abcdefghijklmnopqrstuvwxyz

Scheme or Bill.—The apportionment of the respective sorts, characters, or letters in a font of type is described elsewhere. (See SCHEME and BILL.)

Names for Different Classes of Letters.—Various names designate different classes of letter in the fonts of type used as the text of books and newspapers, such as ASCENDING LETTERS, DESCENDING LETTERS, LONG LETTERS, SHORT LETTERS, SUPERIORS, CAPITALS, SMALL CAPITALS, and ITALICS, which are described in separate articles under these headings, respectively. A distinction is also sometimes made between regular- and irregular-bodied letter, under which Great Primer, English, Pica, Long Primer, Brevier, Nonpareil, and Pearl are called regular-bodied letter, and Paragon, Small Pica, Bourgeois, Minion, and Agate are called irregular, because they are of intermediate sizes to letter of regular bodies. When a type having a face corresponding to that of a given size is cast on a body larger or smaller than that to which it is usually applied, it is called a bastard type. Another wide and constantly increasing diversity is produced by a rapid succession of new faces, embracing a bewildering variety of text, title, condensed, extended, and ornamental type, which are described under the heading JOB LETTER. The multiplicity of characters, irrespective of those representing letters, is indicated by the article on SIGNS. Types are also now manufactured to print works in every important written language possessing a distinct alphabet.

The Quality of Type is determined by the appearance of its face, or the cut; the shank or body, whether it be true or otherwise; its alignment or accurate range with all other types of the same font, in the upper- as well as the lower-case; its equal and uniform height; the character of the metal, which should be neither too hard nor too soft, too pliable nor too brittle; the depth of the face; the depth, number, and position of the nicks, etc.

Manufacture of Type.—Few arts have been brought to greater perfection than the manufacture of type, and, while its leading principles have not been materially changed since the days of Schoeffer, nearly all its processes are now conducted by methods which by their rapidity would greatly astonish the type-founders of the last generation. In devising an entirely new type, if it be intended for the text of books or newspapers, the first step is to prepare a steel punch. (See PUNCH.) This task requires, at the present day, even greater skill and accuracy than were requisite in former ages, when the production of a new face was a notable event in typography, on account of the severe requirements of cultivated modern taste; but one set of punches may be made to do duty in many foundries, through the sale or interchange of drives, or impressions capable of being fitted up as matrices. Many new fonts of Job-Letter are now produced for which punches were never cut,—the originals having been letters engraved on type-metal. It is also practicable to make matrices for job-letter from a font of type in good condition, by the aid of an electrotype battery; and by these methods the processes preliminary to the preparation of matrices have been expedited as much as the operation of casting type. The fitting up of the matrix (see MATRIX) requires extreme nicety of adjustment, to prevent the possibility of inequalities or irregularities in the height or alignment of type, and in this operation scrupulous care is necessary to make the matrix for each distinct character conform to those for all the other characters.

After the matrix is found to be absolutely correct, the next step is to adjust it properly to the mould, and, the combined mould and matrix being applied to the Type-Casting Machine, type are readily manufactured, at the rate of from one hundred to one hundred and seventy-five per minute, instead of from four to five hundred type per hour, which was the ordinary product of an expert workman when the hand-mould exclusively was used. (See TYPE-CASTING MACHINE.) The hand-mould is now seldom used in this country, except for casting large metal or kerned type. Each type, when first cast, has a small piece of metal attached to its base, called the jet, which is made of the surplus metal poured into the mould, and this is broken off by boys at the rate of from 2000 to 5000 an hour. The flat sides of the type are next rubbed upon a piece of gritstone, to render them free from roughness, by Type-rubbers. They are then set up in thin brass sticks, with astonishing rapidity, and laid on long wooden frames, the nicks and faces being placed in regular position. These lines are passed to the Type-dresser, who corrects inequalities on the front and back of the shank or body, and planes a groove in the centre of the base, at the point originally occupied by the jet—thus forming the feet. The type being now smooth on all sides, the dresser next examines each line with a magnifying glass, and discards any type that appears defective in the face. He next arranges the proper proportion of each letter (according to a prepared scheme) in small galleys, holding a type-founders' page, which measures six by four and a half inches. These pages he then papers, and marks with the name of the type, the letters that each contains, and also with figures and letters unintelligible to the printer, but serving to inform the type-founder, what face and nick the contained type is; what mould it was cast in, by whom it was cast, and by whom dressed. This information is retained in a memorandum by the type-founder, after the font is sold, and enables him to trace the responsibility for any error that may afterwards be discovered. When the dresser has paged the font—i.e., made it up in

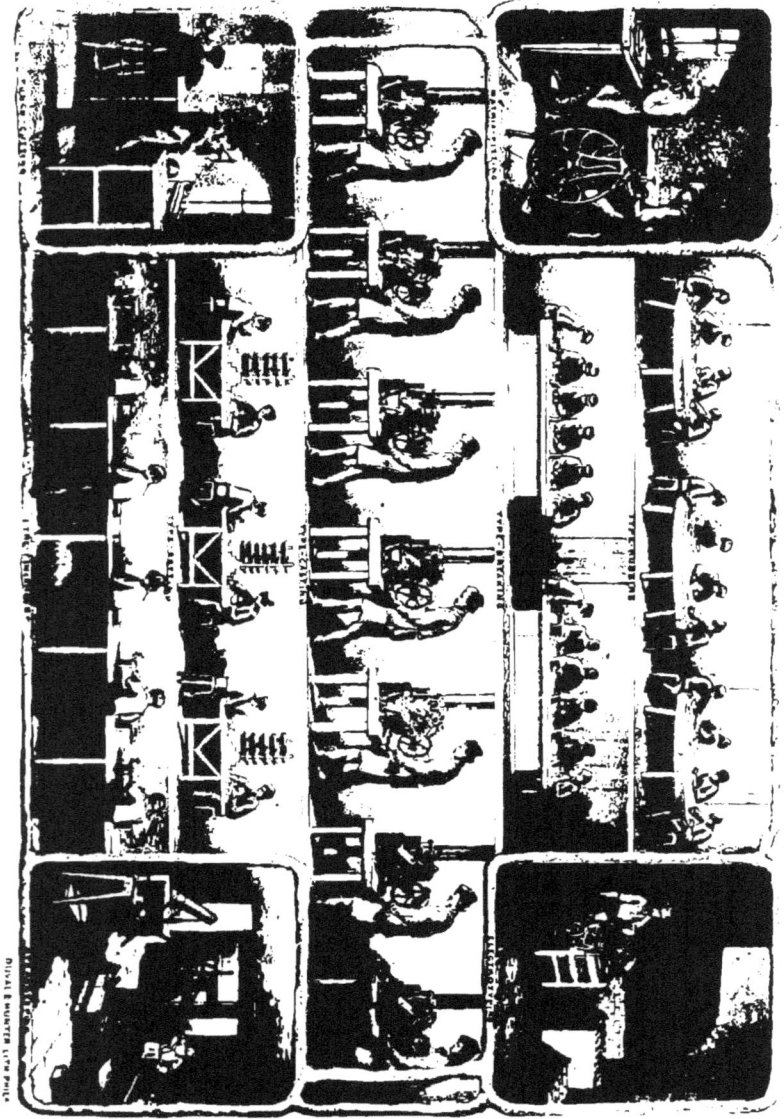

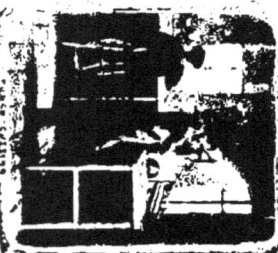

pages—it is ready for sale; but in well-regulated foundries, an examination is subsequently made in the wareroom of the apportionment of the sorts. (See full-page illustration of the operations involved in modern type-founding.)

Many efforts have been made to radically change the present mode of manufacturing type, the heads of type having been electrotyped and soldered on shanks, and type having been cut by machinery out of steel or brass, instead of being cast; but none of these experiments have been attended with commercial success. Efforts have also been made, with somewhat more satisfactory results, to perform the operations involved in rubbing type, as well as the finishing or dressing processes, by machinery, but the foundries nearly all adhere to a system substantially similar to that already described.

Type-Founding.—Other portions of this work describe some of the labors of the early type-founders of Europe as well as of the United States. (See ALDUS, BUELL, BINNEY, BRUCE, CONNER, JOHNSON, LOTHIAN, GARAMOND, JENSON, SAUR, SCHOEFFER, SWEYNHEIM, TORY, WELLS, etc.) Peter Schoeffer, the son-in-law of Fust, and the associate of Fust and Gutenberg, is believed to have brought the art, in its infancy, to such an advanced state that for centuries no important improvements were made. It is said, however, that some, and perhaps all, of the early punches were cut in copper and struck in lead, instead of being cut on steel and struck in copper as at the present day. The first printers were their own type-founders, as the business of printing originally included every process, from the cutting of a punch to the binding of a book. It is said that Caxton, the first English printer, had five distinct fonts prepared for his personal use; and he was succeeded by a line of English printers and type-founders, until, by the seventeenth century, type-founding was established in England as a distinct business, for a decree of the Star Chamber, issued on the 11th of July, 1637, ordered (for political reasons, arising from a desire to restrict the number of presses) that there should be no more than four type- or letter-founders. In Holland type-founding was meanwhile conducted with such energy and skill, that a considerable portion of the type used in England was manufactured by the Dutch, and it was only some years after the commencement of the eighteenth century that England became capable of manufacturing all the type needed for her own use, through the skillful labors of William Caslon. He established a foundry in London in 1716, which is still known as the Caslon foundry, and is conducted by his descendants, its one hundred and fiftieth anniversary having been celebrated in 1866. Some of his punches furnish matrices for old-style letter used at the present day. (See CASLON, WILLIAM.)

During the colonial era of American history nearly all the type used in this country was imported from Great Britain. Christopher Saur, or Sower, commenced the manufacturing of German type about

1735, at Germantown, Pennsylvania; an abortive attempt was made to establish a foundry at Boston, about 1768, by a Mr. Mitchelson, from Scotland; soon after Abel Buell commenced his labors in Connecticut (see BUELL, ABEL); and at the close of the Revolutionary war, John Baine, a type-founder of Elinburgh, came to this country, and conducted the business until his death in 1790. But type-founding as a distinct and permanent business was then only about to commence in the United States; and its subsequent history is so well sketched in an article contributed to the Typographic Messenger by David Bruce, that his account is here given in a condensed form:

The history of type-founding as a business [in the United States] dates no farther back, strictly speaking, than the year 1798. It is true, the introduction of various parcels and portions of type-founding implements dates almost coeval with the introduction of the earliest printing establishment, simply for the purpose of supplying sorts to particular offices; but type-founding as a self-sustaining business did not exist in this country prior to the above date, when Messrs. Binney & Ronaldson established themselves successfully in Philadelphia.

Their struggle for existence in the then limited condition of printing in the United States was, indeed, very severe; and had not the State of Pennsylvania generously donated them the sum of five thousand dollars, it is doubtful if they could ever have survived the depressing difficulties they had to encounter. But competency at last crowned their labors, and, after a successful career of many years, they withdrew from the business.

Among those who brought type-founding materials from abroad for his own convenience in casting sorts, was Dr. Franklin. These tools,—purchased in France, —after the doctor's death, fell into the possession of Mr. Duane, a relative of the philosopher, who, generously appreciating the assiduity with which Messrs. Binney & Ronaldson strove for success, kindly offered them the loan thereof. Mr. Ronaldson examined them, and was so struck with their great superiority over some of their own, and apprehensive that Mr. Duane might change his mind, that he at once borrowed a wheelbarrow, and lost no time in personally trundling such as he selected to their foundry, during one of the hottest days in the summer of 1806.

Mr. Binney acknowledged that they received many valuable suggestions from these tools; thereby conclusively proving that the type-founding art, as it existed at that period, was at a much higher state of perfection in France than in Scotland or the United States. Mr. Binney, being a practical Scotch workman, with a considerable American experience, was fully competent to judge.

Still, from the examination of drawings, documents, apparatus, moulds, matrices, and methods of manipulation, all which have passed down to us from the earliest period of type-founding,—that is, the casting of type by hand-mould and spoon,—little material improvement had taken place down to the year 1828, excepting, perhaps, a closer approximation to accuracy and higher finish. The punch was the same elaborated piece of steel; the mould, matrix, and spoon were the same in general form, plan, and fashion; the method of casting was the same spasmodic jerking motion of the body; the rubbing, finishing, and preparing for the wareroom were all substantially identical; and the very tools for testing the accuracy of the whole business varied in not a single essential particular.

It must not be inferred, however, from the apparent non-progressive condition of the art for so long a period, that there had not been at all times a fair amount of thought, ingenuity, and talent bestowed upon it in order to bring it up to a higher standard of perfection. But there seems to have been a decided timidity on the part of all artistical and mechanical investigators about departing far from the beaten track.

The impression that would almost invariably strike a thoughtful visitor on beholding for the first time the process of type-casting by the old hand-mould system, would be the apparent waste of time and labor in producing such an insignificant result—the casting of a single type! it requiring at all times great and continuous labor over a pot of molten metal. Hence, all projectors of improvement were apt to be caught in the snare of multiplying the number of types at one cast, and, from their ignorance of the peculiar accuracy required, sought to give expedition by increasing the number of moulds to be filled by the same operation. The records of the Patent Office show that much time, money, and thought have been uselessly expended, before inventors were convinced of the peculiar necessity of casting but one type at a time, and that in the same mould and matrix.

The first individuals who boldly attempted improvement in this direction—that is, a deviation from the hand process—were Mr. Elihu White and Mr. William Wing, in Hartford, Connecticut, in the year 1794. These gentlemen commenced under very unfavorable circumstances, being totally ignorant of the common process, except from verbal description and information gathered from itinerant workmen. We find their patent dated August 28, 1805.

This attempt at improvement—bold, energetic, and ingenious as it was—was based also upon casting a multitude of types at the same operation, and, consequently, was a failure. After many discouragements and singular expedients to acquire even a tolerable knowledge of the ordinary process (inasmuch as Messrs. Binney & Ronaldson, who were the only type-founders of the United States at that time, looked with great suspicion on these Hartford Yankees, and thought it most prudent to exclude all visitors, and thus prevent all competition), type-founding as a business with Mr. White trembled in the balance of uncertainty and abandonment for some time. He had lost much money; but in his

experiments he certainly gained its equivalent in experience, which he felt could be turned to profitable account in a properly arranged foundry on the old system. But here was the rub: neither himself nor any of his workmen, on summoning a solemn advisory council, were found to possess any reliable conception of the common type-mould.

At this memorable meeting, Mr. Edwin Starr—one of his principal workmen, and a very ingenious man—remarked, If I can only get a glance at an ordinary type-mould, I am certain I can make an exact copy. In his dilemma, and despairing of obtaining by fair purchase this vitally important knowledge, Mr. White had recourse to a ruse, which may as well be here related—the humor of the story fully redeeming any want of fairness.

By prearrangement, Mr. Starr presented himself for employment at the foundry of Messrs. Binney & Ronaldson, Philadelphia. Starr ingenuously admitted that, although White had made some very valuable improvements in type-founding, and was enabled to manufacture type with great rapidity, yet, from some unreasonableness in his temper and disposition, he found it impossible to continue longer in his employment, thus artfully blending a reason for his discontent so plausibly together with the (supposed) great value of White's inventions as to excite in the minds of Binney & Ronaldson a like desire to become surreptitiously possessed of the secret of his valuable improvements.

While Messrs. Binney & Ronaldson were hesitating as to the advantage of giving Mr. Starr employment, and thus, at a very cheap rate, getting possession of these Yankee Notions, a letter was received from Mr. White, complaining of Mr. Starr's contemplated violation of confidence, and hoping they would not encourage such treatment, as honorable men—concluding with a caution not to put in practice any of the secrets he (Starr) might communicate.

Messrs. Binney & Ronaldson then hesitated no longer. Mr. Starr was immediately employed; and, in justice to him it may be said, he freely communicated the wonders of this type-casting abortion in all its crudeness, and received in return all he wanted—a glance at a common type-mould. Mr. Starr fulfilled his engagement with these gentlemen faithfully, which was of very short duration, and returned to the employ of Mr. White with valuable experience. They next removed, with their establishment, to the city of New York, in 1810, where they resumed business with renewed vigor and satisfactory profit.

Two years subsequent to this, Mr. Starr, with his brothers, entered into business for themselves in the same city. But they were unsuccessful for want of sufficient capital, and their materials fell into the possession of Messrs. D. & G. Bruce by purchase.

From the year 1806 to 1825, no material change or attempt at improvement took place in the method of casting—the founders expending their energies in a quiet rivalry, and in increasing their business facilities on the settled old plan; turning a deaf ear to all suggestions of even ordinary advancement; not stopping to discuss the arrival of certain epochs, or the manifest destiny of man, bearing him onward in the grand current of progress with a view to certain important accomplishments. Certain it is, with the year 1826, the period seemed to have arrived when this happy old-fogy tranquillity was to be disturbed by the meddlesome spirit of progress. And what to philosophers is worth noting in these matters, is, as in most all revolutionary changes (whether in the arts, the sciences, or opinions in politics or theology), intelligent improvement was initiated and forwarded by an outsider—one practically unacquainted with the business.

William M. Johnson, of Hempstead, Long Island —a man full of mechanical resources—from his observations of the ordinary process, conceived the idea that type could be cast by machinery. But in his interviews with some of the leading founders of that day, he was discouraged from the attempt. However, throwing himself in the way of Mr. Elihu White, in the course of a few interviews he succeeded in reviving the old ambition of this gentleman to the accomplishment, under more favorable circumstances, of the glory of his younger days—the production of type by a more rapid process than the one that was universally followed.

Although Johnson, with all his opportunities, was unsuccessful in reducing his ideas to practical utility, still to a certain extent he demonstrated the possibility of improvement. His machines were a failure as a matter of profit, but they begot a rebellious spirit against the old hand-mould process, which never seemed to die out.

At the same time that Johnson was experimenting, Messrs. Starr & Sturdevant, of Boston, and Messrs. David Bruce, Sen., and G. B. Lothian, of New York, were giving the subject an examination. The most insurmountable difficulty with all, was the porousness or lightness of the type; a fount ranging from ten to fifteen per cent. lighter than common type.

The experiments of Starr & Sturdevant, under the patronage of the Boston Type and Stereotype Foundry, an incorporated company, promised at one time to be very successful; so much so, that at one period they had in operation several machines of their construction, and felt encouraged that they would be able to overcome every difficulty, and soon present to printers, if not perfectly solid, at least reliable, merchantable type. But they were disappointed, and after the loss of a large portion of their capital they abandoned altogether the use of machinery, and fell back into the old system of hand-casting.

But with Mr. White there was no retrogression. Perplexing as were the difficulties, doubtful the profit, and prejudiced the printers, he succeeded, by the employment of such inventive talent as he could procure, and at great expense, in surmounting some of the difficulties and objections to machine-cast type, and kept his article before the public in fair competition.

As a matter of profit, the type-founders seemed to view machine casting with doubt. Although Mr. White made considerable effort to sell rights of his patented improvements, none embraced his offers; and with the exception of those foundries in which he was interested—New York, Buffalo, and Cincinnati—thus stood the position of machine type-casting at the day of his death in 1838.

Our observations now bring us down to the year 1839, by which time the number of foundries had increased from the three mentioned in 1812, to sixteen, and along with this increase it was natural to expect active competition would give an additional spur to improvement; but, in truth, improvement in type-founding, as in wood-engraving, had been held somewhat in check by the hopeless condition of the art of printing. Of the old pelt balls and rollers there could be little hope. It was a standing reproach upon the printing-business, that they could not do the type-foundries justice, even in printing their specimens. We want better printing, was the general complaint. But the aspect of affairs was now fast changing. The introduction of the present composition roller and balls, by the elder Mr. Booth, in 1826, coming now into general use, the superior quality of the printing was readily observed, and the cry was changed to, We want finer cut type and finer engraving.

Encouraged partly by this decided advance in printing, and the vastly increasing demand for type, inventors were once more induced to enter the field, and among them none were so entirely successful as David Bruce, the inventor of the present generally used type-casting machine; it being used, either in part or wholly, throughout Europe and America.

Looking into a type-foundry now, and beholding the rapidity and ease with which type is cast, either turned by steam or hand, the mould throwing out at an average rate of one hundred types per minute, contrasts strangely with type-founding in 1832, when the casting was performed by the hand process, and the highest average speed of an expert workman was but fifteen per minute!

The introduction of type-casting by machinery enables the founder to produce uniformly a better article than formerly, and also to attempt a higher grade of ornamental work, altogether unapproachable by the old process. And what is also worthy of remark is, that while it has superseded the old, tedious, and unhealthy jerking process, a very satisfactory increase in workmen's wages has happily been one of its beneficial results.

It is with peculiar pride that the philanthropist can look around him and note these real evidences of a nation's glory: inasmuch as any matter appertaining or giving facility to the typographic art gives assurance that the means of developing the human mind receives ample reward. As intelligence —popular intelligence—is the only means through which man can be elevated to his highest perception of enjoyment, even so it is pleasant to witness each improvement in type-founding and printing, as another rapid stride toward harmonizing the human family.

In respect to style and fashion of American type, we find, by reference to ancient and modern specimens, that the American article has always compared favorably with that of Great Britain, whence we take our models. But we find that even in these grave symbols of thought and knowledge, the capriciousness of fashion has more to do than one would at first suspect. Much has been said of the Scotch face, the turned or filled-in corner, as adding beauty, grace, and durability to the type; and now that the eye has become familiarized with its appearance, we begin to think, as in the matter of ladies' crinoline, that there really is a grace, ease, and utility in the change, however startling it may at first have been to our staid fogyism. Hogarth's lines of beauty have been quoted in support of the change, and square corners pronounced as decidedly offensive to the eye. We have before us specimen-books of some of the old British type-founders, dating as far back as 1805. In one of these they were congratulating themselves and the public on having surmounted some of the gross vulgarisms of former specimens, among which was the turned corner. We remember with what pleasure we gloated in admiration over these specimens—some from the foundries of Messrs. Caslon and Messrs. Fry & Steel of London—and thought they had arrived in some of their faces to the highest point of classic proportion and artistic finish. We have since compared these specimens, which so much entranced our youthful mind, with the more modern turned corner, and, admitting equal beauty in execution, are inclined to ascribe any absolute improvement in appearance rather to the love of change and the whimsicalities of fashion.

'The main secret seems to be that the great improvement in printing—the ability to take a better and more truthful impression of the face—compelled type-founders to remodel the cut of their letter to conform to this improvement. It is evident that the present stubbed cut and prolonged length of hair-line of our modern type would be quite as unsuitable for pelt balls, a Ramage press, and weak ink, as the best ancient type would be if worked on a modern press. In the former case it would be an unsightly, continuous, black, incongruous mass, while in the latter it would have the appearance of worn-out type, minus its hair-lines, and altogether curtailed of its fair proportions.

American founders have always evinced a laudable zeal to be foremost in the exhibition of good taste, even when not driven thereto by direct rivalry. Thus, Messrs. Binney & Ronaldson's early specimens, issued in 1806, show favorably their exertions in this direction. Mr. Elihu White, directing his attention more particularly to increasing the facilities of manufacture, did not, however, neglect attention to a correct style of faces, and had many that were highly prized.

Messrs. D. & G. Bruce, drawn into type-founding

through the desire to prosecute the then new art of stereotyping, of which they were the first successful introducers, certainly by their example incited a more lively ambition to attain a higher artistic finish of face. Once in the business, they saw at a glance the necessity of taking a foremost position in the allurements of style, and to this end paid the cutters of those days liberally for thousands of punches which were canceled before they were submitted to the inspection of printers.

As new type-foundries sprung into existence, as a matter of course, each endeavored to offer additional inducements and attractions to procure business: thus we find the few letter-cutters fully employed in experiments in style, to arrest the attention of the printer, and with more or less success. Thus, while one took the square and symmetrical proportions of the Caslons as his beau-ideal of the pure Roman alphabet, another would adopt the same model, and venture on a slight change, either in weight of face, increase of relative size, or, perhaps, wishing to please some economical printer, give it a slight contraction, for the purpose of taking in; all of which experiments, although very costly to the founders, added much to their variety, and gave printers full as much choice as they could reasonably desire.

Mr. James Conner, about the year 1828, desiring to add greater facilities to his business of stereotyping, which had greatly increased, determined to cast his own type; but, through the natural opposition of the founders, he found great difficulty in procuring the necessary materials. But there is no keeping down a man of determination. Securing to himself the services of a letter-cutter, he soon gave a new impulse to type-founding, in presenting to the admiration of printers generally, in a well-arranged and beautifully printed sheet, his series of light-face type.

The advantages of this light-face series were judiciously set forth—as being easier to read, taking less ink, in stereotyping easier to mould, and requiring less labor from the pressman. There is no doubt that these points, to a certain extent, were sustained in practice; and certain it is that James Conner was the successful introducer of a beneficial change, and this was the advent in this country of the light-face era, which has ever since prevailed. (See SPECIMEN-BOOKS.)

Type-Casting Machines.—The first type-casting machine invented in the United States was patented in 1805, by William Wing, of Hartford, Connecticut. The patent was sold to Elihu White, but as it was based on the system of casting a number of type simultaneously,—twenty or thirty type being made at once, and projecting from a shank like the teeth of a comb,—the patent, after the expenditure of large sums in efforts to perfect it, was finally abandoned. Subsequently the idea was conceived that a machine might be constructed to cast type singly, on the principle of the hand-mould. William M. Johnson, of Hempstead, Long Island, made the first American effort in this direction. He was followed by Starr and Sturdevant, of Boston. George B. Lothian, an American type-founder, invented an ingenious machine, which overcame the difficulty arising from the danger of the mould overheating, in rapid casting, by sending a continuous stream of water through the mould. But to David Bruce, Jr., the honor is universally awarded of having invented the first and only thoroughly successful American type-casting machine. It was patented March 17, 1838, after years of study and experiment; and after being subsequently improved, it became the model of

TYPE-CASTING MACHINE.

all American as well as a large proportion of European type-casting machines. It can be, and is in some foundries, worked by steam as well as hand-power. A representation of it accompanies this article. The American Printer thus briefly but graphically describes it:

The metal is kept fluid by a little furnace underneath, and is projected into the mould by a pump, the spout of which is in front of the metal-pot. The mould is movable, and at every revolution of the crank in the hand of the workman it comes up to the spout, receives a charge of metal, and flies back with a fully-formed type in its bosom; the upper half of

the mould lifts, and out jumps a type as lively as a tadpole. You don't see how the letter is formed on the end of the type? True, we had forgotten: well, this spring in front holds in loving proximity to the mould a copper matrix, such as you saw just now in the fitting-room. The letter a, for instance, stamped in the matrix, sits directly opposite the aperture in the mould which meets the spout of the pump; and when a due proportion of a's is cast, another matrix with b stamped in it takes its place; and so on throughout the alphabet. Slow work, you say, one at a time? Well, the world is peopled after that fashion; and it fills up fast enough. But just time this machine: it is making small, thin type. Count the type made in a minute. One hundred and seventy-five, you say. One hundred per minute will probably be the average of the ordinary sizes of printing type.

While many of the Bruce type-casting machines are used in European type-foundries, machines to cast type were also invented years ago in Germany; Henry Didot, of France, invented a machine in 1823, which has been used to cast or manufacture hundreds of letters at one stroke of the plunger; and in England J. R. Johnson, in 1853, invented a machine which, with subsequent improvements, and the addition of an apparatus for rubbing and dressing type, is said to now form one complete instrument, in which the metal is melted by a jet of gas at one end, and perfect type is set up on a stick at the other, without having to be touched by hand. This machine is operated by an English Patent Type-Foundry Company; but as it has never been introduced or practically tested in this country, some of the American type-founders are incredulous in regard to its alleged capacities.

Type-Founder.—One who manufactures or casts type.

Type-Gauge.—A triangular wooden gauge, with the length of a considerable number of lines of type of various bodies, marked thereon, which is used to facilitate the measurement of advertisements or matter. (See illustration on page 478.)

Type-Line Formers.—A device to facilitate the formation of curves, patented by Charles N. Morris, of Cincinnati, July 20, 1869. A full set contains eighty pieces, embracing all the usual and convenient sizes of curves, arranged for circulars, bill-heads, cards, letter- and note-heads, newspaper advertisements, and all work of a similar character,—each piece consisting of brass curves, closed at

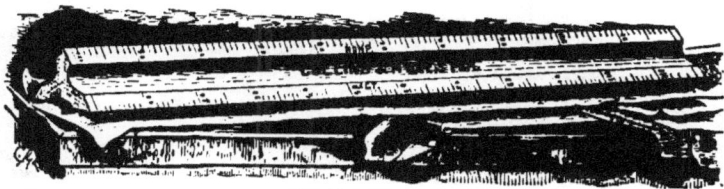

TRIANGULAR TYPE-GAUGE.

both ends, and forming a frame for the curved line.

Type-Metal.—A metallic compound used in the manufacture of type. (See TYPE.)

Type-Rubbing Machines.—Many efforts have been made to invent machinery to perform the operation of rubbing type immediately after it is cast. One of the most famous of these originated with Mr. Welch, an American citizen. He exhibited it at the Paris Exposition of 1867, and received for it one of the medals or prizes awarded for superior inventions. There seems to be little doubt that this machine could be advantageously used in all cases where a type-founder had large orders for type of a uniform size and quality to supply; but no machine can be of much service in manipulating an endless diversity of faces, sizes, and varieties of small fonts. Mr. Welch's machine was described by a Paris correspondent of the London Printer's Register, during the progress of the Exposition, as follows:

The first operation, after breaking off the jet, is to set the letters in lines of six inches body-wise and leaded; in this manner they are pushed from the movable or setting-galley into the receiving-galley of the machine, in a body of twelve or more inches; by the action of the machine they are pushed forward a line at a time, and laterally through an adjustable channel provided with shoulder and body knives governed by fine-threaded set-screws, thus enabling the operator to give the exact rub or dress required. The parallelness of the knives is governed by the jointer in sharpening. The leads are disposed of by dropping through the table into a box at the instant the delivery of a line to the channel and knives is completed. By leading the lines after being rubbed, they can be delivered to the machine for dressing, with the exception of cutting out the jet, an addition Mr. Welch has not deemed it best to add at present, his chief object being to produce a perfect rubbing-machine—an object which, we consider, he has accomplished. The shoulder-knife is constructed of four blades, which may be set, graduated, and moved to the desired angle by horizontal set-screws. It is cut from one piece, and the blades may be multiplied, if desired. One side of the channel is movable in and out by means of a thumb-screw, and fastened in its desired position by a similar upright one. The change from one body to another can be effected in a

moment. So nice is the set of the machine that the scale or chill on the letter can be divided. The thinnest characters are protected from all bending or marring—in fact, are straightened, if by any means bent. An exact uniformity of thickness and body is obtained in the sort being dressed; a desideratum in figures. The face is never touched after the type is set for the machine. Its capacity is wonderful. Mr. Welch has rubbed Bourgeois type upon it at the rate of five pounds per minute! and considers a thousand pounds in ten hours a moderate estimate. Every provision is made for breaking the lines of different bodies, and for the lean of the ascending and descending letters. The machine can be learned in a few hours; it is simplicity itself. It can be worked by hand or steam. Mr. Welch claims that he can so adjust his jointer and sharpen his knives as to rub a line of type that will, without any spreading, set solid around any sized cylinder.

ORIGINAL ALDEN TYPE-SETTING MACHINE.

Type-Setting Machines.—It is sometimes considered a matter of astonishment, in view of the extraordinary success of efforts to make paper, cast type, and run presses by machinery, that the operation of composing type has not been simplified to a corresponding extent, and that type-setting machines have not superseded hand-labor. A little reflection, however, readily suggests powerful causes for the failure, in a commercial sense, of promising type-setting machines. Inventors are confronted, at the outset, with the necessity of devising a contrivance to facilitate the composition of every description of written or printed matter, and of every imaginable combination of letters, syllables, and words. The tasks to which machinery is successfully applied so as to insure an enormous increase in rapidity of production generally possess such unvarying uniformity that the labors of one hour are substantially similar to those of any other hour; while a type-setting machine might be in use for years without ever being required to repeat, letter for letter and word for word, any considerable portion of its service. It is to be remembered, also, that human supervision will constantly be necessary to compose the copy furnished; that no machine can be made to set type correctly with greater rapidity than the operator can intelligently read it; and that a large proportion of the manuscripts sent to printing-offices is so badly prepared, and so nearly unintelligible, that many compositors can set it up by hand about as rapidly as they can decipher it. Much of the type composed on daily newspapers is set up from short takes, given out at late hours, under circumstances scarcely admitting of the use of a machine; and a large proportion of all printed matter is thickly interspersed with either Italic, capital, or small-capital letters, two-line letters, job-letter, leads, dashes, rules, etc., which would often preclude the advantageous and economical use of the most ingenious machine that could possibly be constructed.

There are other difficulties to be confronted; and unless the machine is simple and inexpensive, annoying delays, liability to derangement, and the interest on its cost go far to counterbalance any slight advantage gained by it.

Nevertheless, a great deal of ingenuity, labor, and money has been expended in efforts to substitute machine- for hand-labor in composing type, and these efforts have not been wholly fruitless. The following list of patents granted in the United States and England indicates the earnest attention attracted to this subject:

A LIST OF PATENTS GRANTED IN THE UNITED STATES FOR TYPE-SETTING AND DISTRIBUTING MACHINES.

Inventor.	Date of Patent.
Fred. Rosenberg	1840
Young & Delcambre	1841
Fred. Rosenberg	1843
O. T. Eddy	1850
Wm. H. Mitchell	1853
Wm. H. Mitchell	1854
Victor Beaumont	1854
W. S. Loughborough	1855
J. J. Koenig	1856
Wm. H. Mitchell	1857
W. H. Houston	1857
Timothy Alden	1857
J. B. Gilmer	1859
H. Harger	1860
C. W. Felt	1860
D. B. Ray	1862

O. L. Brown	1862
C. W. Felt	1863
C. Baer	1866
Alden & Mackey	1866
John Paulding	1866
Wm. H. Houston	1867
M. M. Nelson	1867
J. E. Sweet	1867
—— Harper	1867
J. Thorne	1868
J. T. Slingerland	1868
J. McNair	1868
M. Umstadter	1869
J. T. Slingerland	1870
Manoel de la Pena	1870
O. L. Brown	1870
W. Wheeler	1870
J. T. Slingerland	1871
J. Jones	——

A LIST OF PATENTS GRANTED IN ENGLAND FOR TYPE-SETTING AND DISTRIBUTING MACHINES.

Inventor.	Date of Patent.
Wm. Church	1822
Robt. Gaubert	1840
J. H. Young & Adrien Delcambre	1840
J. Clay & Fred. Rosenberg	1840
J. Clay & Fred. Rosenberg	1842
Duncan & Mackenzie	1848
Wm. Martin	1849
J. H. Johnson	1852
W. H. Mitchell	1853
Jean T. B. F. Caillaud	1853
Moses Poole	1853
Adrien Deleambre	1853
Alphonse C. de Simencourt	1854
Wm. H. Mitchell	1854
Martin Wiberg	1854
J. P. Humaston	1855
Louis Pierre Coulon	1856
Wm. E. Newton	1856
Isadore Delcambre	1856
Timothy Alden	1856
Robt. Hattersly	1857
James H. Young	1858
Alfred V. Newton	1859
Charles W. Felt	1860
James H. Young	1860
John Cumming	1862
Wm. Young	1863
Wm. E. Gedge	1864
Mackie, Garside & Salmon	1865
W. Clark	1865
A. & W. Young	1865
A. Mackie & J. P. Jones	1865
Alden & Mackey	1866
J. T. Slingerland	1870
J. T. Slingerland	1871

Also a machine by one Sorenseu, exhibited at the London World's Fair, 1851.

Some of these machines have already been described in other portions of this work. Those which are now exciting most attention in this country are the Alden (see ALDEN TYPE-SETTING MACHINE), and the Brown Type-setting Machine (see BROWN TYPE-SETTING MACHINE). More labor and money have

will be thoroughly successful. It has been in practical use, by Messrs. Appleton, the New York publishers, on book-work, for several years. Its capacity is rated at 3500 ems per hour,—one person being

ORREN L. BROWN'S PATENT TYPE-SETTING MACHINE.

been devoted to the Alden machine, in its various styles, than to any other invention of this description; and energetic labors to perfect it are still being prosecuted by Mr. J. T. Slingerland, in the hope that they

employed to play upon the machine, or compose, while another justifies the matter. Type of ordinary manufacture can be used, but each character must have a nick peculiar to itself, to facilitate distribution in the distributing machine, and fifteen logotypes are employed, representing such combinations as tb, re, at, en, ed, or, al, ell, it, etc.

The Brown machine is illustrated by engravings accompanying this article. It is comparatively sim-

a few months previous, measuring nearly eighteen hundred ems.

Of the type-setting machines invented by William H. Mitchell, of New York, Appleton's Cyclopædia, published in 1861, said that ten had for some time

GREEN L. BROWN'S TYPE-DISTRIBUTING MACHINE.

ple and inexpensive, and the inventor recently forwarded us a proof taken from type set up in this machine in fifty minutes, by a woman-compositor, of the same matter which George Ahrensberg had set up in one hour in the office of the Printer's Circular,

been kept in operation in the printing-house employed upon that work, as well as a number of distributing machines, and that the use of these machines was found to be economical. Bruce's Specimen Book says it has been in use for ten years in a New York

31

printing-office. Another American inventor, Mr. Felt, has attempted to justify as well as to set and distribute matter. Mr. Sweet, another American, was one of the first, if not the first, to attempt to devise a new system, based on the idea of manufacturing a mould or matrix from which a stereotype plate could be formed, instead of composing type. He exhibited an ingenious machine, designed to accomplish this object, at the Paris Exposition of 1867, where it attracted considerable attention; but though he succeeded in producing stereotype plates by his process, they were somewhat imperfect, and the rate of progress was comparatively slow.

The latest English machines, the HATTERSLY and MACKIE machines, are described under their appropriate headings. The Hattersly machine has been used, to a limited extent, for more than a dozen years; and the description of it in Chambers's Encyclopædia says that type has been put into the composing-stick attached to it at the rate of 25,000 per hour, although a young and comparatively inexperienced girl working at it did not usually set up more than 23,000 to 24,000 brevier types during nine hours.

It is a demonstrated fact that type-setting machines can, under favorable circumstances, be advantageously employed on plain composition; but, for various reasons, very few printing-offices have attempted to use them, partly because their construction is still in an experimental stage, and partly because the gain or saving they effect is comparatively slight, as well as for the reasons above given.

No machine has yet been devised which is well adapted to miscellaneous newspaper- and job-work. A machine was exhibited at the Paris Exhibition of 1855, which had been used for some time in composing a Copenhagen (Denmark) newspaper, but it was probably made up principally of plain composition. This machine was invented by Christian Sorensen, and it made so favorable an impression upon Charles Knight, of England, and M. Didot, of France, and other competent judges, that they united in the opinion that it approached nearer to the accomplishment of the object sought than any machine previously made. Two operators, one of whom justified the matter, were enabled, according to the statement of the exhibitor, to set up and distribute about six thousand type per hour.

Typo.—A familiar term for a compositor.

Typographer.—A letter-press printer; written in French typographe, and in Spanish and Italian tipografo.

Typographical Literature.—A complete catalogue of the works already published in this department would considerably exceed eight hundred in number, and it is only possible to present such a list as will show the constantly increasing interest in the subject displayed by the leading civilized nations. Books and treatises upon printing or upon its various branches were published soon after the introduction of the art; but the work of the learned and artistic French printer Tory (see TORY) may be selected as the first remarkable and general practical essay upon the subject. We append the date of Tory's publication, as well as the dates of publication of a number of his most distinguished successors:

Upon the origin of printing some of the best-known works are those by Maittaire, Santander, Seiz, Seemiller, Zapf, and Wurtwein. The introduction of the art into Paris has been treated by many authors, among whom are Chevallier in 1694, Delandine 1817, Gresswell 1818. Crapelet 1836; the introduction into Spain, by Mendez, 1799; into Ghent, by Vanderhaeghen, 1853; into Augsburg, by Mezger, 1840; into Holland and Belgium, by Vander Meersch; while the introduction into England has been extensively treated by Dibdin, Lucombe, Johnson, Hansard, Savage, Timperley, Knight, Humphreys, Blades, etc.; Thomas' History of Printing being a standard book of reference for the United States. The introduction of printing into Normandy, and its subsequent history, was the theme of a work by Frere; and the same task has been performed for Sweden by Alnander; Brescia by Lechi; Florence by Bandini; Ferrara by Baruffaldi, and Lorraine by Baupre. Sotheby's splendid work upon Block-Books also tends directly to throw light upon the question of the origin and originators of the art.

The earliest works upon printing are specially valuable as treating of its origin in Europe, its introduction into various countries, and the appearance of the early books; but the matter of these books has been so carefully studied by recent authors, that it is hardly necessary for the general reader to seek for Maittaire, Santander, Chevallier, Alnander, Wolffius, or even Moxon, unless as a matter of curiosity. For the zealous reader in quest of the facts and dates of the subject, a mine of wealth is opened in Timperley's Dictionary of Printers and Printing. The method of arranging all the facts chronologically makes this book invaluable to the student, but seriously inconvenient and unattractive to the casual reader, who desires the conclusions drawn from facts rather than the facts themselves.

In typographical, or rather bibliographical, literature, the works of Dibdin have been especially popular, the fine illustrations of the Bibliographical Decameron making it particularly attractive; but, although the works of this author contain a vast amount of information, it should always be remembered that Dibdin assumed the position of chief trumpeter to the great bibliomaniac movement led by the Roxburghe Club, and that he wrote in the interest of parties engaged in stimulating public curiosity as a means of increasing the market value of certain classes of books. The first work in the English language upon typography was the admirable treatise of Moxon, published in 1683, to which Lucombe and other authors have been largely indebted. Ames brought his careful training as an antiquary to bear upon the history of printing, and his Typographical Antiquities, published in 1749, is careful and accurate in statement, especially in regard to the early history of the art in England. Johnson's Typographia of 1824, and Hansard's Typographia of 1825, both contain very fair condensed historical accounts as matter introductory to the practical instruction in the art, which occupies a large portion of both works. Savage's Dictionary of Printing, 1841, is a work excellent in arrangement, clear and practical, but burdened with unnecessary details. Smith's Printer's Grammar, 1755, found favor in its day as a practical manual; and Stower, in 1808, made it the foundation of a new work, which has, in turn, been modified to suit the improvements in the practice of printing, both in the United States and England—the work of Smith thus furnishing the basis of numerous manuals

and books upon the practice of the art, published in the English language. The practical works upon printing in the French language have been criticised as being incomplete, with the exception of a Manual by Brun, in 1824, and Lefèvre's Compositor's Guide. A typographical manual in the shape of a dictionary of printing was published in France in 1847, and Henri Fournier, apprentice, and afterwards foreman, to Firmin Didot, and subsequently director in the Mame establishment at Tours, published in 1870 a third edition of his treatise upon typography, much enlarged and improved. The names of some of the principal German authors have been stated in the foregoing lists, and several valuable journals devoted to the subject appear in that language.

Mentz, Strasburg, and Haarlem are not the only cities which have striven to enrich their annals by claiming the glory of the invention of printing; certain authors have urged Antwerp, Augsburg, Basle, Bamberg, Cologne, Dort, Feltre, Florence, Lubec, Nuremberg, Rome, and Venice as claimants for the honor, and a vast amount of authorship has been expended not only in the original presentment of these claims, but also in subsequent discussion and criticism, based upon them. Such disputes generally result in partisan animosities, and much of the debate upon the subject has degenerated into a wordy warfare, too voluminous to be either interesting or valuable to any but the anxious student; and it is but just to say that the whole subject, as at present understood, can be gathered from a careful perusal of the Typographia of Johnson and that of Hansard, with the dictionary of Timperley and the works of Humphreys. Another valuable book of reference is the laborious and faithful work of Cotton, in which the establishment of every printing-house, with the locality and date, has been entered in chronological order, and much information not elsewhere to be found is embraced in the volume of Abridgments of Specifications relating to Printing, published by the British Commissioners of Patents in 1859.

Typography, as the most complete form in which human language is now conveyed, preserved, and disseminated, becomes so inextricably involved with a vast variety of other topics, that its successful treatment requires a rare combination of practical knowledge with literary research, and the difficulties arising at every stage are curiously illustrated in the account of the preparation of Palmer's History of Printing, as given by his assistant Psalmanazar. Samuel Palmer was one of the most successful London printers of his time; he had served his apprenticeship with John Dunton, and accompanied him to America. Palmer afterwards established himself in London, and Franklin worked for some time in his office. As a skillful printer, and the introducer of many improvements and inventions, Palmer determined to present his knowledge to the public in a printed work, and decided upon dividing it into a preliminary historical treatise, to be followed by a portion conveying practical instruction upon printing and its necessary branches. Palmer met warm encouragement from the Earls of Pembroke and Oxford, and other wealthy and distinguished literary men, who freely offered him the use of their libraries, and he undertook his task under the engagement that a complete plan of the whole work, with one or two specimen numbers of the first, or historical part, should be ready for the inspection of his patrons at the end of a year. Full of hope and enthusiasm, Palmer commenced his labors, but soon became convinced that he had overrated his own capacity, and that he was entirely unequal to the task. Unwilling, however, to abandon so promising an undertaking, he engaged the services of an Irish bookseller, with whose literary talents he was highly delighted, and relinquished the work entirely into his hands. Nearly nine months of the specified time had passed, when Palmer discovered that the only work accomplished was some miserably faulty translations from the standard French authorities upon the history of printing; these Palmer claimed from his incompetent assistant, and gave them to George Psalmanazar, who, as an accomplished author, readily perceived the drift of the proposed book, and, as he himself stated, tossed it together by clever piecing and splicing from a dozen of the principal books upon the subject.

Current periodical publications upon typography were introduced by Thomas MacKellar, of Philadelphia, and have spread so rapidly that they now appear in almost every principal city both of Europe and America, and latterly in Australia. The number in America amounts to about fifty. These periodicals contain the news of the craft, and also, in many cases, literary matter of excellent character, upon subjects connected with printing; the specimens of new types, ornaments, machinery, color-printing, etc., which are included in many of them, whether as advertisements or otherwise, forming an essential and necessary portion of the information required by the readers.

From the above has been rigorously excluded mention of all books which do not primarily treat of printing from type, but which might, however, be included in typographical literature, such as the numerous practical works upon paper and paper-making, bookbinding, book-illustration, etc., also a number of historical and compilations upon newspapers, and that most interesting theme, the liberty of the press.

Typographical Societies.—Typographical Societies (using the phrase in an enlarged sense) in the United States may be naturally divided into the following classes:—1. Those embracing alike master-printers and journeymen, such as the Philadelphia, New York, and Columbia Typographical Societies. A leading object of these organizations is to provide for the relief of worthy indigent members in times of sickness or distress, as well as to relieve their widows and orphans in case of death, to promote social union, and to advance the art of printing. 2. Associations of master-printers, electrotypers, and stereotypers, for the promotion of their mutual interests,

and the removal of reckless and destructive competition. There are very few permanent organizations of this description, the combinations occasionally made, being usually of temporary duration. In New York city, however, the Typothetæ was organized in 1865, with the intention of rendering it a permanent organization. 3. Organizations among the journeymen employed in large printing-offices, especially daily newspaper offices, to provide by mutual contributions a fund for the relief of sick members. (See RELIEF FUND.) 4. State Editorial Associations, composed chiefly of the editors and publishers of country newspapers, which have for their object the promotion of social union, the mitigation of the harshness of political and personal newspaper controversy, and the advancement of mutual business interests. 5. Associations of publishers of daily newspapers for obtaining news. (See ASSOCIATED PRESS.) 6. Co-operative Societies, formed by journeymen printers who desire to acquire a pecuniary interest in printing establishments, and who contribute a small sum weekly, monthly, or at other stated periods to form a capital to purchase material, etc. 7. Printers' Unions, the most powerful and most thoroughly organized of all American Typographical Societies, as a very large proportion of all journeymen printers of the United States are members, and as a complete connecting link is formed between the local unions of this country and those of the Dominion of Canada by the International Union. (See UNIONS, PRINTERS'.)

There are Typographical Societies, having objects similar to those stated above, in nearly all European countries. In England, combinations of journeymen are called Chapels (see ANCIENT CUSTOMS and CHAPELS), and they combine the objects of the Printers' Unions of the United States, with those contemplated by the Relief Fund Associations.

In France the principle of association has been more elaborately developed and more minutely classified than in any other country, as will be seen from the following list of the organizations in Paris a few years ago, viz.:

1. Le Cercle des Maîtres-Imprimeurs (Masters' Association), 86 members. 2. La Socié é fraternelle des Protes (Brotherly Association of Foremen), 50 members, and 20 honorary. It has sick and pension funds, library, and weekly social meetings. 3. La Socié é des Correcteurs (Proof-Readers' Association), 90 members, sick and pension funds. 4. La Société Typographique Parisienne, which has 2400 members, and is the nearest French equivalent for the Printers' Union of the United States. It has a sick and pension fund, an officer for procuring work for such of its members as are out of employment, an accumulating fund for the purpose of efficiently sustaining the price tariff, called the resistance fund, and, lastly, a loan fund for members in need. 5. La Socié é de Gutenberg, ou des Conducteurs (Association of Power-Pressmen), 160 members, sick fund, and fund for keeping up the prices. 6. La Société

des Imprimeurs (Pressmen's Association), 350 members, sick, invalid, and resistance funds. 7. La Société des Margeurs et Receveurs (the English equivalent of this would be—Machine-Boys' or Feeders' Association, but in Paris the layers-on and takers-off are adults), 420 members, sick and resistance funds. 8. L'Association de l'Imprimerie Nouvelle, or the joint association of members of all the branches of the profession, with a view to establish a printing-office on the co-operative principle. 9. L'Association Générale Typographique (General Typographical Association), 850 members, which is also organized with a view to the establishment of a co-operative printing-office.

Typography.—The art of impressing words upon paper and other surfaces with pigments, inks, etc., by the use of movable metal or wooden types.

Tytler, James.—A Scottish printer, and one of the principal contributors to the Encyclopædia Britannica. The plan of this great Encyclopædia was devised by William Smellie (see SMELLIE). It originally appeared in 1771, in three quarto volumes, entirely written and compiled by Smellie, for which he received only two hundred pounds from the publishers,—Andrew Bell, an engraver, and Colin Macfarquhar, a printer. A second edition was commenced in 1776, under the editorship of the eccentric James Tytler, a man of remarkable talents, who remained almost in beggary on account of his intemperate habits. By the labors of Tytler, the Encyclopædia was extended from its original size of three volumes to ten. In 1772, while in the sanctuary of Holyrood, Tytler also wrote a remarkable work entitled Essays on Natural and Revealed Religion. While laboring upon the Encyclopædia, he received so petty a remuneration that he was forced to lodge in the house of a washwoman, and wrote his articles surrounded by his children, with an inverted wash-tub for his table. The whole family lived in one small mean room, in which stood a press made by Tytler's own hands, and resembling that afterwards perfected by John Ruthven. Tytler often stood at a case of type, composing pages, or condensing matter from a volume lying before him. In this manner he prepared the first volume of an abridgment of the Universal History, which he never completed. He also commenced a periodical called the Weekly Review, but, being unable to support it, it passed into other hands, Tytler continuing to be the chief contributor.

U.

Ultimate.—The last syllable of a word.

Ultramarine Blue.—A description of the coloring matter frequently used in the blue inks with which bright showy work, tints, and posters are printed. In shade it holds a medium rank between light and dark blues.

Uncial.—A style of written character found in Latin manuscripts from the third to the tenth century, which combines the more ancient capital letters with the more modern miniscule or small letters. This transitional style of writing slowly altered into the easy, small running character, and in its most improved stages is known as the semi-uncial. The miniscule began to prevail in Latin manuscripts of the ninth century, and the Greek of the tenth. This style of writing was formerly termed unciales literæ, or text letters, the term being probably derived from the Latin word uncia, or an inch, descriptive of their large size.

Underlays.—Pieces of paper pasted on the bottom of an engraving, stereotype plate or block, or type, to raise it to a proper height for good printing. (See MAKING READY.)

Underscore.—To draw a line below—as is done in manuscripts to call especial attention to a particular passage. In some of the earliest printed books, words now distinguished by the use of italic were marked by an underscored line in red, apparently added by hand.

Uneven Page.—Any page having an uneven number, such as 1, 3, 5, 7, 9, etc.

Unions, Printers'.—In all the cities and large towns of the United States and the Dominion, the journeymen printers have associated themselves in Subordinate Unions, which, while acting independently on minor questions, form part of, and are in harmony with, the International Typographical Union. This organization holds annual sessions, at which nearly all the subordinate Unions are usually represented by one or more delegates; and during the recess or intervals between its sessions, it is the duty of the President to exercise a general supervision over the Subordinate Unions, to decide doubtful questions, and to exercise other executive powers. The chief object of the Subordinate Unions is to maintain such a rate of wages as they deem equivalent in the respective localities; and to accomplish this purpose they fix a scale of prices, from time to time, and no member is allowed to work for a smaller remuneration than that established in this manner. Members of the Union are also required to abstain from working in any printing-office which does not conform to the requirements of the Union; those who lose their situations in consequence of their acquiescence in a resolution of Subordinate Unions are supported, while out of work, by a contribution from the funds of the local Union to which they are attached, or sometimes, when a long strike occurs, by moneys received from other Subordinate Unions. Deliberations on reports from various printing-offices, etc. are kept secret, and entrance into the meetings of the Unions can be obtained only by a knowledge of a password, changed from time to time, which is communicated to each member in good standing. The International Union grants charters to such new Subordinate Unions as are established in various localities, and it forms a common bond, giving additional efficacy and strength to all the Subordinate Unions. The number of the latter reported at the annual session of 1870 was one hundred and forty.

The total number of members of the Subordinate Unions officially reported in 1868 was 6974, of whom 6095 were in good standing, and there has since been a considerable increase in the number of members, as well as in the number of Subordinate Unions.

Unities, The.—In the fine arts, those qualities in any work by which the parts are kept in due subordination, and made to minister, to the general design. In the classic drama the unities of time, place, and action were accurately preserved.

Unit Lines.—Ruled lines in blank-books, intended to form a division between figures representing different commercial values.

Unique.—Without an equal; singular—used to describe a copy of a work supposed to be the only one in existence, as a single copy of an edition printed in some special manner, as on vellum; also the only copy remaining of an ancient work, as the copy of the first edition of Tyndale's New Testament preserved from the public burning, or the only perfect copy of the Decameron printed by Valdarfer, and purchased by the Marquis of Blandford at the Roxburghe sale in 1812 for 2260 pounds. A London bookseller secured himself a unique copy by binding the History of James II., written by Fox, in fox-skin; and Askew, the bibliomaniac, had a volume bound in human skin.

UNIVERSAL PRINTING-MACHINE.

Universal Printing-Machine.—A half-medium job-press, manufactured by Gally, McNeal & Hamilton, Rochester, New York, for which are claimed great strength, durability, compactness, simplicity, and capacity to speedily produce the best descriptions of work.

Unlock the Form.—To loosen all the quoins.

Upper Case.—The case having the highest elevation on a stand, and containing capital and small-capital letters, references, etc., which are called upper-case sorts.

V.

Vade-Mecum.—Anything, but especially a handbook, carried about the person for daily use or reference; used as a title of a manual.

Valediction.—A farewell, or a formal speech of dismission.

Valedictory.—In the colleges of the United States, the farewell address delivered by one member of the graduating class as the formal and public farewell of the students to the Faculty and to their fellow-students; also applied sometimes to the farewell article of a retiring editor.

Valentine.—An anonymous letter containing professions of love, sent upon the 14th of February, or St. Valentine's day, and generally highly decorated with pictures, etc. Comic valentines usually consist of a burlesque picture printed on a single sheet of paper, with lines of rhyming verse. Upon the finer ones, distinguished as sentimental valentines, every imaginable style of miniature decoration is lavished, and they vary in value in the common styles from five cents to five dollars, mounting upwards to ten, twenty, fifty, and even one hundred dollars.

Vantage.—The name formerly applied to those remunerative descriptions of work now called fat.

Variorum.—An abbreviation of the Latin words *cum notis variorum*, meaning with notes from several persons. These words are frequently placed upon the title-pages of books, which are therefore called variorum editions.

Varnish.—A useful ingredient in mixing inks; printers' varnishes, especially adapted to this purpose, being frequently employed in job-printing.

Vaudeville.—In French, ballads or short comic songs, and also theatrical performances in which such songs are abundantly introduced.

Vellum.—The skin of very young or abortive calves prepared to be written upon, and much used in the finest of the ancient manuscripts, also occasionally selected for printed works, and for the binding of heavy volumes, such as ledgers, account-books, etc. In the earliest Christian centuries vellum was exquisitely stained in tints of rose color, purple, blue, yellow, and green, and furnished a splendid background for illuminations in gold and brilliant paints. The tinted vellum of the eighth century was inferior in beauty to that which had preceded it, and from that time white vellum was mostly used, that of the ninth and tenth centuries being remarkably fine. The magnificent missals of the fourteenth and fifteenth centuries were written upon vellum, and, as Paris was the principal seat of their production, it is probable that the skill of the Parisian artists in the manipulation of those skins led the first printers of that city to continue to employ them. The handsomest of the printed Books of Hours were printed upon vellum, and many of the finest works of Verard and others. Diana of Poitiers' admiration for fine printing led her to influence Henry II. to enact that a copy of every work published in France should be sent to the Royal Library printed upon vellum; and this kingly order laid the basis of the splendid collection of vellum books in the Library of Paris. During the bibliomaniac fancy at the close of the eighteenth and the beginning of the nineteenth century, in England, books were printed upon vellum, but not very successfully, and the attempt has been made occasionally of late years to print a very limited number of copies. The finest recent specimens were exhibited in the Paris Exposition of 1867, from the printing-house of the Wards of Belfast, Ireland, in the shape of magnificently illuminated books, decorated after the manner of illustration which placed the Hibernian artists foremost in Europe during the seventh, eighth, and ninth centuries.

Vellum Paper.—A fine paper occasionally used for expensive books.

Verbal.—In grammar, derived from a verb—as, a verbal noun; also oral, as distinguished from written, —as, a verbal message. By common custom, the word is used to denote anything relating to words, as a verbal alteration in a manuscript or proof conveys the idea that the changes embrace only such corrections in words as do not affect the general construction of the language.

Vermilion.—A brilliant and permanent red color used by the illuminators and early printers, called miniore, from which is derived miniature, or that species of elaborate and minute drawing suited to book-illustration. In much of the red ink used in printing, vermilion forms the pigment at the present day.

Vernacular.—Belonging to the native land; generally restricted to language—as, the vernacular, or common popular language, of a district or country.

Verse.—Language in poetic measure, arranged according to the rules of composition and either with or without rhyme. A verse is correctly a single line of a poetic composition, but the word is generally used to describe a subdivision or stanza. In the same manner the shortest subdivisions of the Scriptures are called verses.

Version.—A translation into another language—as, Tyndale's version of the New Testament; also such change in the expressions of the original language as produce an alteration in the meaning.

Verso.—A left-hand page.

Victoria Press.—A printing-office established in London, in 1859, under the auspices of a Society for Promoting the Employment of Women, for the purpose of giving to women an opportunity of learning and practicing the printing-business, and more especially composition. In 1869, after the office had been in operation nearly ten years, the London Printers' Register gave an elaborate description of it, stating

that about twenty-five girls were then employed, three of whom had been working in the office for nine years, one for eight years, and two for seven years. Their weekly earnings ranged from six to twenty shillings.

Vienna, Imperial Printing-Office of.—This printing-office has gained a world-wide celebrity, and attracts multitudes of visitors from all quarters of the globe. In magnitude, diversity of work, and completeness of arrangement, it has no superior.

The entrance-hall contains an interesting exhibition of the fine arts, consisting of samples of the numerous classes of work executed in the institution, and classified in a tasteful and appropriate manner.

The press-rooms, bureaus, warerooms, composing-room, drying-room, foundry, etc., occupy five buildings, from four to six stories in height, formerly used as a Franciscan convent, on Singer Street, Vienna, the printing-office proper occupying an area covered by a roof of iron and glass, and so arranged that it can be thrown into one large room.

The Imperial Printing-Office usually gives employment to at least 1000 persons, and uses yearly over 200,000 reams of paper. It contained in 1864 over 175,000,000 letters or characters (of which 12,000 were Chinese), weighing over 350,000 pounds. Two hundred machines are constantly at work in the various departments. The type-foundry contains 25,000 steel punches and 89,000 matrices. The facilities are being rapidly augmented and improved in every branch of the institution. Tracks are at work in subterranean railways in bringing coal to feed engines used to propel the various machines. Heat is applied to the rooms by means of 1062 feet of steam-pipes. Through 5000 feet of gas-pipe there streams daily 24,000 cubic feet of gas for supplying 700 burners, for lighting, soldering, warming, and other purposes; and hot and cold water is supplied through the whole building. From the central office of the directors, fourteen copper speaking-pipes convey orders to all parts of the establishment. The composition department embraces over 600 kinds of German and Roman letters, which have been designed, cut, and cast in the building. In the casting-room are numerous furnaces and casting-machines of ingenious construction, manufacturing twenty different faces of Roman, and nearly as many of Italic, besides 200 kinds of ornaments for various uses, and 100 fonts of script and alphabets, embracing the regular English scripts, the alphabets of the Middle Ages, black-letter writing, gothics, and a large quantity of book faces, with an assortment of over 100 corners and borders.

Besides the 500 different native alphabets, the institution contains over 120 alphabets of foreign tongues,—in short, an alphabet of all the written languages. Here may be seen the curious Chinese and Indian characters, side by side with the ancient monumental letters on the ruins of Babylon, Nineveh, and Persepolis, the various square-shaped letters of the Hebrew alphabet, the ornamental, carved, and dotted Arabian and Persian characters, the angular

Northern Runic, with the round form of the Ethiopian, Etrurian, and Coptic alphabets, besides a multitude of others, with strange countenances and unheard-of names, mostly Asiatic. Large rooms are required for the proper storage of the paper, as well as the laying out of the printed sheets. One of the rooms is occupied by 120 compositors and correctors, while another is used as a wash-house, where the printed types are placed in copper receptacles, to be cleaned with lye; farther on are the printing-presses of all shapes and sizes. Very much like a church is the five-story dry-house, with its galleries and communicating halls, where the sheets, hung upon lines, are dried by means of warm air ascending through openings in the floor. Here is a standing-press, capable of pressing sheets piled to the height of four or five feet; farther on is the smoothing-machine, in which the sheets being placed between metal plates and passed through two cylinders become perfectly smooth; then follows the bookbinding with its apparatus. The Imperial Printing-Office turns out various kinds of work brought to perfection by all the methods employed in book and artistic printing; gathering triumphs of human genius, in the domain of printing, from the ordinary wood-cut to the finest oil-color and nature printing, and representing the history of printing in all its branches and periods. In the department devoted to the printing of bonds, bank-notes, and state papers, part of the impressions are taken by means of hand-presses, and part by lithographic and steam power-presses. Forty-six machines have at busy seasons been used for this description of work alone.

Photography is brought into requisition for many purposes, among which is the reproduction of old and rare prints, engravings, manuscripts, etc., which are portrayed with singular fidelity.

An interesting portion of the work in this institution is embraced in the production of embossed letters, words, and maps for the blind, whereby these unfortunates are enabled to read through the sense of feeling. Besides these, the means for writing are supplied to them in the shape of alphabet dies or stamps, which can be used by the blind to stamp on paper, and thus preserve their thoughts and ideas in the same manner as their more fortunate fellows. These alphabets for the blind are also made to suit the language of Eastern countries.

The copper-plate presses are fitted with steam attachments for giving the impressions, thus saving time and labor, but are restricted in the capacity for much more work than the hand-presses, by the delay occasioned in rolling the plate, which is manipulated by hand.

The art of nature printing, the discovery of a director of the Imperial Printing-Office, Dr. Alois von Auer, has here been brought to a high state of perfection. The process is simple, and consists in attaching a pattern of lace to the surface of a highly-polished steel or copper plate, on the top of which is laid a polished plate of pure lead, and the plates and pattern thus laid are subjected to a cylindrical pressure of from 80,000 to 100,000 pounds, when the pattern will be found to be imbedded in the leaden plate. The pattern being carefully removed, the plate may be rolled with suitable color, and impressions taken therefrom on a letter-press, which will show the pattern in white on a colored ground. A stereotype may be taken from the lead plate, which will furnish a greater number of impressions than the original could give, or the original may be placed in a galvanic battery and a perfect electrotype taken therefrom.

The style of impression may be reversed by treating the plate as an ordinary copper-plate.

The forms of leaves, etc., are also preserved without taking the impression in the manner described above. A cast of the object is taken in gutta percha, and the gutta percha covered with a facing of silver, to assist the electrotyping therefrom of the most faithful counterparts of the originals. In this manner tender plants, insects, etc. are treated, if the forms are nearer flat than round.

Another interesting part of nature printing is the taking of impressions from stones or minerals. Certain minerals, on being ground, show beautiful and characteristic crystals; others show lines of varied shapes and sizes, or the forms of fishes, insects, plants, etc. The different parts of the stone do not possess the same power of resistance to acids, some parts being more easily acted upon than others, and thus, by a system of etching with acids, a uniform face of raised and depressed surfaces may be obtained, and it only remains to cover the surface with ink and take an impression on paper, in order to obtain a picture showing the different strata, etc. of the stone.

This system of printing has been made the subject of great research in the institution, and the flora of the Austrian empire is embodied in a work of 500 folio and 30 quarto pages. While the plants and leaves are all printed in brown, instead of their natural variegated colors, it would be impossible to produce more faithful pictures than are contained in this work, as the most minute fibres are faithfully portrayed, and the formation and growth of the plants can be as well studied from them as from the originals.

View.—A representation of a scene, either by picture or verbal description; thus, a series of landscapes are styled views, and a work on travels has been entitled Views a-foot.

Vigesimo-Quarto.—A sheet folded into twenty-four leaves, generally written 24mo.

Vignette.—A small ornamental engraving, used as the decoration of a page; formerly the decorative capital letter, which, standing at the head, spread its flourishes like the branches of a vine.

Visiting-Cards.—Cards used for social purposes, and containing only a name, or a name and residence. The finer qualities are usually printed from plates or copper-plate presses.

Visorum.—An implement formerly used by compositors as a guide or copy-holder. Moxon describes it, and the method of using it, as follows: Pricking the point of the visorum, most commonly upon the border or frame of the upper case, on the left hand, compositors fold the leaf of copy they compose by, so as the bottom of it may rest upon the square shoulder near the bottom of the visorum; then, with two pieces of scale-board tied together at one end, they clasp both the copy and visorum between these two scale-boards, which pinch the copy and visorum tight enough to keep the copy in its place, and at the same time also serve as an index to direct the eye to every line, as the compositor moves it downward.

Volume.—A number of printed sheets in one cover, whether including a part or the whole of a work or of several works. Volume and book are both used indiscriminately to describe the whole or a portion of a work: thus, it is usual to state that a certain edition contains two volumes of a work bound in one. In like manner the book of Paradise Lost is divided into many books. Standard English novels appeared for a long time in three volumes, and these books are now usually bound together in one cover, with the several title-pages, introductions, etc. retained in their proper places.

Vowel.—Webster's Dictionary defines a vowel to be a voice sound; a constituent of the spoken alphabet, other than a consonant; also, a letter or character which represents such a sound; an utterance of the human voice, made through a more open position of the organs than that with which a consonant is uttered. In the English language, the written vowels are a, e, i, o, u, and sometimes w and y. The spoken vowels are much more numerous.

Vulgate.—The Latin version of the Scriptures, being the translation from the Greek into the vulgar or common tongue of Italy.

W.

Wafer.—A thin leaf of paste, generally circular, used to seal letters, and for official impressions or seals upon documents. Wafers, as a convenient substitute for sealing-wax, were formerly in common use, but they have been superseded, to a great extent, by self-sealing or gummed envelopes.

Wall-Paper.—Paper pasted upon the inner walls of houses, for their adornment and protection—frequently termed paper-hangings, from being regarded at first as a substitute for the draperies of cloth, silk, and tapestry which were formerly used to conceal walls, and called hangings. It is stated that paper was first printed expressly for the ornamentation of walls by a Frenchman named François, at Rouen, in the year 1620, and a patent was taken out for the manufacture, in England, in 1634, by Jerome Lanyer, to whom is attributed the invention of velvet- or flock-paper. In 1755 Rubre patented in England a method by which paper, first prepared with successive coatings of glue, followed by linseed oil and sugar, could be printed, painted, gilded, etc. in an especially brilliant and durable manner.

In the earlier stages of the manufacture, an outline was printed from wooden blocks, and afterwards colored by hand; stencil-painting was also used, and subsequently wooden blocks for each color; but all these processes were expensive. Wall-paper was first offered for sale in America in 1737, but was only introduced into the houses of the wealthy. The manufacture was commenced in this country in 1763, and in 1787 there were several manufactories in Pennsylvania, New Jersey, and Boston. In 1810 four establishments in Philadelphia produced 140,000 pieces, valued at $97,417, and during the war of 1812 great improvements were introduced in imitation of the superior styles of French designs, the finest domestic paper being still made in Philadelphia.

In 1813 a patent for making satin grounds was taken out, and glazed grounds were produced in 1824. The introduction of the Fourdrinier machine marked a great improvement in the manufacture, by producing rolls of paper of great length, usually 1200 yards long, and from twenty to forty inches in width. The remarkable increase in the manufacture in this country can be seen in the fact that in 1860 there were twenty-six manufactories, producing a value of $2,148,800. The cheaper qualities of wall-paper are printed by machinery, the patterns being engraved upon cylinders, as in ordinary calico-printing; the finer kinds are printed by the hand-press. Machinery has been substituted in America for many of the preliminary processes usually performed by hand, and a series of cylinders driven by steam is also used in the final polishing and glazing. Curtain-papers, printed in the piece, in patterns suited for window-shades, are also largely manufactured.

Walter Press.—A fast newspaper press of modern construction, used in the office of the London Times. It is illustrated on the full page devoted to presses. In a circular describing it, J. C. MacDonald, its manufacturer, says:

It is a Perfecting Machine—printing on both sides at the rate of 12,000 copies per hour, or from 10,000 to 11,000, including stoppages. Ample provision has been made for overcoming the difficulties of set-off; and, as there are only four composition rollers used, and great care has been taken to make the cutting and delivery processes certain, the liability to interruption is reduced to a minimum. When changing from one reel to another, the arrangements are such that the delay scarcely exceeds a minute, and the reels are kept as large as possible for convenient handling.

The labor employed when the Walter Press is in operation consists of two lads taking off, who suffice to inspect and count each sheet, and a striker to start the machine and look after the reels as they are unwound. One overseer can easily superintend two presses—capable of turning out, with six unskilled hands, perfected sheets at the rate of 20,000 to 22,000 per hour, stoppages included. With four of these presses—twelve lads and two overseers—The Times is now printed at the rate of more than 40,000 copies per hour—i. e. in less than half the time, and with one-fifth the number of hands, required by the fastest and best printing-machines previously in use. More-over, layers-on, who are highly-trained workmen, and must be paid accordingly, are entirely dispensed with.

Attention is directed to the extreme simplicity of the Walter Press in all its details. There is nothing about it liable, with the usual ordinary care, to get out of order; while a practically unlimited rate of production is secured by the repetition of stereotype plates on additional machines to any extent that may be required. Thus, newspapers of large circulation can be printed with maximum economy of time and labor, and with a freedom from risk in the process of production never before attainable. The waste of paper may be stated at ⅓ per cent.; but, in connection with the change of system, newspaper proprietors and printers will at once find that they obtain a knowledge of the kind of article which is supplied by their paper-makers—how it counts and weighs per ream, and with what degree of uniformity it is produced—never before realized. There is a considerable saving of ink also, and in blankets and rollers. The exclusive use of stereotype plates releases the ordinary type from all wear and tear; so that a font lasts at least ten times as long as it could under the former system. It is hardly necessary to add that with the Walter Press the register must be practically perfect.

Warehouse or Wareroom.—A department of a large book-printing office, devoted to the reception and safe-keeping of paper before it is printed, and to the proper management of printed sheets while they are being dried and pressed.

Warehouseman.—One who has supervision of the warehouse or wareroom.

Wash.—A term applied to an old custom in printing-offices, of evincing doubt or disbelief by a loud drumming at or near the case or press of the person who tells an improbable story. (See OUT OF HIS TIME.)

Washing Lists.—Blank forms of lists of clothing sent to the laundry.

Washing the Form.—Cleansing type immediately after it has been printed, or during the process of printing, if it becomes clogged up with picks, etc. (See PRESS-WORK.)

Washington Press.—A hand-press invented by Samuel Rust. As it is in very general use in the United States, the following directions for setting it up are given:

All the connecting parts being marked, or indented by points, if these be observed carefully, the press may be put together without difficulty.

After setting the frame upon its legs, and putting on the ribs and bed, lay the platen on the bed, placing under it two bearers about type high. Then put the springs in their places, and the nuts over them, and pass the suspending-rods through them, observing to place the rods so that the number of indentations on them correspond with those on the platen. Give the nuts two or three turns, then run in the bed so as to bring

WASHINGTON PRESS.

the platen under the rods, and screw them fast to the platen; after which, put in the bar-handle, standard, and lever (or wedge and knees, if a Smith press). Turn the nuts on the suspending-rods, so as to compress the springs just enough to give the platen a quick retrograde motion, observing at the same time to get the surface of the platen parallel with the surface of the bed.

After having put the press together and leveled it by means of a spirit-level, be particular not to raise the end of the ribs by the gallows, but let it go under rather loose, which will have a tendency to make the bed slide with more ease on the ribs.

Waste.—The surplus sheets of a work, which are not necessary to fill an order for printing. They are often called over-sheets.

Watermarks.—Indentations made on paper, in various shapes, during the process of manufacture, the pulp of the paper being compressed by an engraved instrument called a dandy. A new process for accomplishing a similar result has been devised by Col. Charles Reen, of Philadelphia, who has prepared by it the accompanying illustrations in this work, which imitate not only the old watermarks, but show what superior effects can now be produced. Mr. Reen compresses the fibre of the paper after all the manufacturing processes have been completed. He engraves a raised drawing on a metal plate, and passes the paper between this plate and a steel roller.

Watermarks have been carefully studied as a means of arriving at the facts in regard to the early manufacture of paper in Europe, and still further as offering a key to the problematic questions of the block-books and earliest specimens of printing from wooden and metal types. Paper-mills worked by water were established in Tuscany about the beginning of the fourteenth century, but it is not known whether watermarks were introduced by them. The earliest known watermark is a globe surmounted by a cross (see illustration), found in an account-book at the Hague, bearing the date of 1301. This mark is very

si.nilar to the devices used by John of Cologne, Jenson and Scot, when printing in Venice, and may prove the Italian origin of the paper. A bull's head, similar to that in the illustration, but three inches in length, appears in the watermark of an account dated in the year 1310, which might also be of Italian origin, as a similar design was used as the arms of Pope Calixtus III. in 1455; this mark never being found in the Flemish block-books, but appearing in the Mazarin Bible, in Fust and Schoeffer's Bible of 1462, and in the publications of Ulric Zell at Cologne. Many early undated Italian manuscripts contain a cross as the watermark. Antwerp must have been largely engaged in the manufacture at an early date, for records of purchases of paper made in that city are entered at the Hague and Haarlem under the date of 1352, and the watermark of a tower (see illustration) found at the Hague in a manuscript dated 1354, is doubtless the tower of Antwerp, used also as an emblem by Gerard Leeu in 1470. This tower also appears frequently in German and Italian manuscripts of the fourteenth and fifteenth centuries. A hand is also displayed upon Leeu's emblem, as pertaining to that city, and may probably have been the origin of the watermark of a hand common in the Dutch block-books. The fleur-de-lis, the Peter's cock, and the paschal lamb (see illustration) are all found in the public account-books at the Hague, bearing respectively the dates of 1366, 1380, and 1356, the fleur-de-lis probably referring to Philip of Burgundy, who bore it on his arms, and the lamb being the insignia of Rouen, and also of other bishoprics. The rude outline of the postman's horn (see illustration) is exactly copied from the mark upon a letter dated in 1421, and this mark, afterwards very common, is supposed to have given the name to post paper; while the almost unrecognizable fool's cap, with its feather and bells (see illustration), is taken from Caxton's Golden Legend, the same mark, afterwards improved, giving the name to foolscap paper. The unicorn and also the shield (see illustration) are supposed to prove a Flemish origin, the unicorn being the supporter of the arms of Philip, Duke of Burgundy, and the shield being the arms of Compiègne, bestowed upon Philip in 1429 by King Charles of France, and confirmed to him in 1430 by Henry VI. of England upon his coronation in France. The unicorn, the shield, and also the marks of P and Y, either separately or together, are all presumed to be proofs of Flemish manufacture, the P crowned with a fleur-de-lis having been used by Philip, Duke of Burgundy and Count of Compiègne, who reigned from 1349 to 1361; and P and Y being adopted afterwards by his descendant, Philip and his wife Ysabel, who were married in 1429, the Y appearing first in an account dated 1431. The marks of the dolphin and anchor seem to point to some maritime country, both being used by Aldus Manutius at Venice, but they are equally applicable to the chief cities of the Low Countries. The dolphin appears first at Haarlem in a manuscript dated 1418,

also at the Hague in 1423, and in a letter to the Bishop of Durham dated at Melun in 1420. The anchor, afterwards in common use, appears first at the Hague in a writing dated 1396. A pot or jug was a favorite early mark, first known with the date of 1352, and giving its name to pot-paper. The account-books preserved in the archives of the Netherlands, and from which many of the accompanying illustrations have been accurately copied, show that the small folio paper employed in them was the same used in the block-books, and for account-books in Germany and Italy about the middle of the fourteenth century; and the same paper is found in the printed works of Fust and Schoeffer, Zell, Veldener, and in the publications of John of Westphalia at Louvain, although no printed German or Italian books are known to contain it. Soon after the introduction of printing, a larger size of paper was used, and of better quality, as is seen in the early Bibles, the Catholicon of Balbi of 1460, and the Pliny of 1469. The difficulty of obtaining large quantities of paper is shown by the variety of watermarks often included in a single volume of the block-books, and also of the early printed works; the first Bible printed in Delft, 1477, being remarkable as exhibiting nearly all the watermarks previously used in the Netherlands. One of the modern arguments advocating the theory that printing was invented in the city of Haarlem is founded upon proofs deduced from watermarks, but the evidence only settles conclusively that paper was made at an early period in the Netherlands, and its use cannot prove the place of the publication of any work, because Flemish paper was largely used at Mentz and Cologne, and Caxton, Lettote and Macklinin depended chiefly upon the paper of the Lowlands, a few occasional sheets of Italian or German manufacture being introduced by Caxton into his works. Watermarks began to be used as the private sign of the manufacturer at the close of the fifteenth century.

Water-Proof Paper.—A water-proof paper can, it is said, be made by passing paper rapidly over and in contact with the surface of a solution of oxide of copper in ammonia, by means of properly placed rollers moving with speed. The paper on leaving is pressed between two cylinders, and next dried by drying cylinders, similar to those in use in paper-mills. The action of the solution is to dissolve the cellulose of the paper to a very slight degree, and to form an impenetrable varnish.

Way-Bill.—A writing or instrument containing a list of the passengers carried in a public conveyance, or a list of goods carried in a similar manner. Such documents are usually printed, leaving the necessary blanks to be filled as occasion requires.

Wayz-Goose or **Way-Goose.**—A term applied in England to the annual dinner customary among the printers of that country, which is usually held on a Saturday in the month of July.

Weak Ink.—Ink in which the varnish possesses comparatively little tenacity.

Webb's Mechanical Quoin.—An American invention, designed as a substitute for wooden quoins in locking up forms.

WEBB'S MECHANICAL QUOIN.

Wells, Horace.—A celebrated Cincinnati type-founder. The following sketch of his career is condensed from an account written for the Typographic Messenger by David Bruce:

In the early days of Elihu White's business of type-founding, among the skillful mechanics he gathered around him in Hartford, Connecticut, was Oliver Wells,—a Yankee clock-maker of those comparatively primitive times,—to whom, in the course of events, were intrusted the mechanical direction and management of his branch type-foundry in Cincinnati, Ohio, a position he filled with eminent ability and success. Horace Wells was the oldest son of Oliver, born at Hartford in 1797. Receiving such an education as the schools of his native place afforded, at the age of sixteen he was apprenticed to the trade of cabinet-making, of which he became a master.

In the spring of 1820, when a selection of workmen was made for the foundry at Cincinnati, Mr. Wells was chosen as the best-qualified man to undertake the wood-work of the establishment; for in those slow-coach times every article sold had to be made on the spot, and cases, stands, and galleys afforded ample scope and employment for a man of experience, and even the old two-pull Stansbury press—composed of hard-wood frame, stone bed, and iron leverage—came within the range of his abilities. Several months were consumed on the journey and in preparation for business, and the arrangements were completed and the business patriotically inaugurated by casting the first type in Cincinnati, July 4, 1820, amid the jubilations of all interested in the new establishment.

The versatility of young Wells found a wide field for display. His industry soon produced a surplus stock of stands, cases, galleys, and even presses—the iron parts of which he discovered he could forge in a more satisfactory manner than any operative blacksmith then in that vicinity. Indeed, he even took an apprentice to learn the trade of a blacksmith, and one of the oldest devotees of this herculean profession in Cincinnati looks back with great satisfaction to the time when Horace Wells taught him his trade. The type-dressing also fell to his lot for a time; then, as business grew and other men were found to take charge of these simpler operations, we find him fitting matrices, making moulds, and, finally, cutting letter-punches, sets of which, of his workmanship, are still in the possession of the Cincinnati Type-

Foundry; and with all these manifold employments he found time to help in the office in cases of emergency, and for a short period kept the books of the concern; and finally, when Mr. Foote, the original business agent, retired, Horace and his father, Oliver Wells, divided between them the whole management of the foundry and business, which had developed into an interest of considerable importance. Their united management was as successful financially as it had been mechanically, and so continued for several years thereafter, when he retired to a farm, chiefly induced by the ill health of his wife, whom he had married within a year after his arrival in Cincinnati. He sold out his interest in the foundry for a sum which insured him a moderate competence in those inexpensive days, and entered upon the duties of a farmer among the beautiful hills which surround the Queen City of the West.

In 1837, however, the even tenor of his peaceful life was seriously interrupted by the failure of his banker and several other parties who were indebted to him; and some embarrassments attending these losses still hampered him when, in 1842, he again took charge of the Cincinnati Type-Foundry.

At this period, quite a change had taken place in the foundry. Oliver Wells had sold his interest in 1833; Mr. White still retained his interest, but had all his attention and care absorbed in his New York business; and the other shares, and the management of the foundry, were in the hands of men totally unconversant with the practical details of type-founding. Under such untoward circumstances, the business of the concern rapidly declined, even to the verge of bankruptcy, and Mr. Wells was enabled to purchase the largest portion of the stock on almost his own terms. His untiring industry, combined with his sound practical experience, produced marvels in the way of resuscitation. His first move was to issue a small Specimen Book, in the most condensed manner, showing all the faces of the foundry; his next, to circulate them extensively among the trade of his section; his next, to introduce as rapidly as possible the new and useful in type and ornament as they appeared in the older foundries. In this manner he reintroduced himself to the trade in the most acceptable way; his old customers, and many new ones, rallied around him, and the old prosperity of the Cincinnati Type-Foundry rapidly returned, enabling Mr. Wells to clear off the responsibilities of the concern in the most satisfactory manner, as well as his personal liabilities resulting from the financial trouble of 1837.

But the ways of Providence are inscrutable. In the moment of his triumph over the business difficulties of farm and foundry the fiat had gone forth, and Horace Wells's earthly labors were declared at an end. It seems that Oxford is a seat of learning; that there is a scholastic institution located there of some note; that the usual number of young and thoughtless men frequent the principal hotel of the place; that one of them was carelessly handling a rifle; and that Mr.

Wells (on a visit to his farm, and while passing in front of the hotel in question) was accidentally shot dead on the spot. This mournful event occurred about 1851.

Wetting Machines.—Several machines designed to wet paper have been invented and used successfully, one of which is used in conjunction with the Bullock Press, to dampen paper on long continuous rolls. Another machine applicable to paper of the regular sizes is illustrated by the accompanying engraving. It is very simple in operation. The bundle of paper is placed on the bank, and fed in quires, either open or folded, to guides on the feed-table. At the proper time the table advances, and enters the paper between two cylinders covered with felt, the lower one of which runs in a trough of water. As the paper issues from these cylinders, it passes between a top and bottom sprinkler, by which addi-

good presses, cannot be obtained by impressions on dry paper.

Houghton gives the following directions for wetting paper: Before the paper is wet, it is requisite to know two things: first, the nature of the form,—is it solid or open? second, the nature of the paper,—is it spongy or hard? If the form be solid and the paper be hard and well sized, of course it will require much more water than it would if spongy. Again, for an open form the paper, though hard, would take much less water than it would for a solid one, and still less if spongy, because the softer the paper is made with water the thicker and heavier is the impression when pulled.

The nature of the form and the quality of the paper being ascertained, the number of times the paper should be wet every quire may then be determined. Hard well-sized paper may be wet three, four, five, or

WETTING MACHINE.

tional water can be put on, and the quantity regulated at pleasure. The paper is then conveyed by cords to a sheet-flyer, which lays it on a table suspended on springs. These springs are quickly adjustable to suit the weight of the paper, so that the table falls as the weight increases, and thus keeps the top of the pile always at the same height. There are three sizes built, to wet paper 36 inches long, 48 inches, and 60 inches.

Wetting Paper.—All paper used in printing was formerly dampened or wet; even cards and plate-paper were dampened, as this operation was considered essential to good work. At the present time a large proportion of the paper used on newspaper and book work is still wet or dampened, but the proportion of matter printed dry in job-offices is very large, and it may well be questioned whether the best results with superior paper, new type, good ink, and

even six times a quire, while soft spongy paper should not be dipped more than twice or once in a quire, or perhaps should only be sprinkled every quire and a half or two quires. How many times a quire should be wet, the pressman himself must decide, according to the quality of the paper and the form for which it is intended; and for this a little observation will sufficiently qualify any one.

After deciding the number of times a quire should be wet, lay a clean wrapper on the wetting-board, on which lay a few dry sheets of the first quire. This done, draw the remainder of the quire through the water, and, laying it on the few dry sheets left on the board, turn up the bottom corner with the left thumb, and count the number of sheets that will make the first portion of the quire, and open it out straight. For instance, if a quire is to be wet twice, it will be two portions of twelve sheets each, there being twenty-four sheets in the quire; if wet three times, count eight sheets in a portion; if four, six sheets, and so on. This will make the heap regular throughout. The first portion of the quire being wet, proceed with the second and third, etc., and turn over the last portion of every quire, after leaving the last wet sheet on the heap, so that its back will be opposite that which is on the heap; this will break the back of the paper and make it straight. Proceed in the same way to wet the remainder, and turn down token sheets to save counting. The whole of the paper being wet, lay the heap in its proper place, cover it with another wetting-board, and leave it about half an hour to soak. After that time, if not in a hurry, press it with about half a hundred-weight for an hour, then add as much more weight as is at hand; for the heavier paper in this state is weighted the better. The heap, thus pressed for twelve hours, should then be turned and well mixed throughout, and again pressed the same number of hours. If it be wanted in a hurry, screwing it down between the wetting-boards, in a standing-press, for a short time, will forward it considerably.

If the heap be too wet, putting dry sheets between every four, five, or six wet ones, and pressing it in a standing-press, will materially improve it. If too dry, sprinkling about every half-quire or so, and pressing as above, will also be found advantageous.

It may be observed, in conclusion, that, in wetting paper, drawing it through the water slowly, without draining it afterwards, will make paper much wetter than if it were drawn through the water quickly and then shaken, even though it were wet the same number of times.

Wharfedale Press.—A modern English press, said to be well adapted to newspaper work requiring a speed of from 3000 to 3500 impressions per hour.

Wheel.—A cylinder, also called girth wheel, and drum, on which the two girths of hand-presses wind and unwind alternately as the carriage is run in and out.

White, Elihu.—One of the early type-founders of the United States, was born in Bolton, Conn., July 27, 1773. He came of good old New England stock, being a descendant, in the sixth generation, of Elder John White, who landed in this country the 16th day of September, 1632, and was one of the first settlers of Cambridge, in Massachusetts, of Hartford, in Connecticut, and of Hadley, in Massachusetts. The subject of the present sketch first began active life in Hartford, Conn. After a few years' residence in that city, he removed to New York, and established a type-foundry there in 1810.

Not confining his enterprise to the city of his adoption, however, he early recognized the importance of the growing cities of what was then the Far West, and started type-foundries in Buffalo and Cincinnati, which were probably the first establishments of the kind in either of those cities. He was a man of great ingenuity, and made valuable improvements in the art of type-founding. He was also, for several years,

a bookseller and publisher. In his business relations, as well as in private life, he was highly esteemed for his intelligence and uprightness.

An evidence of the general esteem in which he was held is found in the fact that he was appointed on the Committee of Mechanics and Artisans of New York City to wait upon President Jackson in reference to the financial troubles which overwhelmed the nation in 1832.

He married a daughter of Hon. John Trumbull, Judge of the Supreme Court of Connecticut, and author of a famous political satirical poem, directed against the British and their sympathizers in this country, entitled McFingal. He died at the age of 63, on the 7th of November, 1836.

White Ink.—An ink used for making tints, of which it forms the body, small quantities of inks of various colors being added to and mixed with it.

White Line.—A line of quadrats, reglet, leads, etc.

White Page.—A page containing no printed matter.

White Paper Register.—An impression taken without ink, or with a sheet of waste paper between the form and the paper, intended for a mark, for the purpose of ascertaining that the furniture is right.

Wide Spacing.—Such spacing between the words of a line, or in the lines of a page, as exceeds the usual average; the uniform use of an en quad or two thick spaces between words being generally considered wide spacing.

Wolgemuth, Michael.—An artist of Nuremberg, who introduced marked improvements into the art of wood-engraving, and to whom has been ascribed the invention of engraving by the process of etching. He is particularly known as the art-master of Albert Dürer. Anthony Koburger, styled the prince of printers, introduced typography into Nuremberg in 1472, and published a variety of magnificent works. Among these were thirteen folio editions of the Bible, twelve of them in Latin, and one in German. The most splendid of his publications was the German folio Bible, published in 1483. It contained eighty-three wood-cuts, some of which are ascribed, in the preface written by Koburger, to the artist Wolgemuth. Koburger, in 1493, published the famous Nuremberg Chronicle, containing over two thousand wood-cuts, which were engraved under the supervision of Wolgemuth. Koburger was the godfather of Albert Dürer, and it is probable that the learned printer introduced the artistic young goldsmith to the notice of his artist-friend, Wolgemuth. The illustrations of the Nuremberg Chronicle contain the first examples of cross-hatching.

Wood-Cut Printing.—The following directions for underlaying and overlaying wood-cuts are extracted from an address read by H. J. Crate, a New York pressman of great skill and experience in working wood-cuts, before the New York Typographical Society:

When an impression is taken from a cut, the extremities sink into the paper, and print heavy from the want of a sufficient bearing, while the centre has not sufficient impression to bring the ink from off the solids, which are generally in the centre of the picture. It is the business of the wood-cut printer to reverse all this, and to have just as much impression on every part of the cut as is necessary to bring off the ink perfectly—and no more. Some of the old school of engravers tried to obviate this difficulty by lowering the extremities of the block before the drawing was made, and that, too, with such good effect that I have made ready some cuts (by Chapman and others) that required nearly as much overlaying at the extremities as they did in the centre. It is true the cuts were small, and not nearly so fine as those of the present day.

The first thing to be done is to level the cuts, or to bring them to the same height all over, and this should be a little lower than type. This process of underlaying requires considerable care and judgment. There should be as few pieces of paper used as possible, to produce the desired effect, as too much paste will sometimes cause the cut to warp or crack. The cut should be raised a little in the centre, or under the principal solids, but not too much, as that may injure the cut. If there are any hollows or inequalities in the under surface of the cut (as is frequently the case), they must be carefully filled up, or the wood will give, and the effect will soon show itself on the face. In short, a judicious underlaying is of the utmost importance, and every half-hour spent in underlaying a form ought to save an hour in the overlaying. Stereotype and electrotype plates must be leveled in the same way, and, if the plates are blocked, it is far the best way to take them off the blocks and put the underlays between the plates and the blocks. Small hollows and inequalities may be reached and remedied which could not possibly be through the wood, and, once done, they last as long as the plate lasts, without the possibility of the underlays being washed or rubbed off.

The principle of overlaying wood-cuts is very simple, and is the same for every variety of printing-press and every size and quality of cut; being, as already stated, the putting just as much impression on every part of the cut as is necessary to bring off all the ink, and no more; but the practice varies with almost every workman, and ranges all the way from a tissue-paper to a card-board, from a great piece of thick paper, which covers a double-pica more than the object, dabbed on somewhere near where it should be, to a piece of thin paper so minute that it can hardly be seen, taken up with the point of a penknife, and put in its place with the utmost exactitude.

Some excellent workmen use a certain number of pieces (four or five), of the same thickness, for their overlays, using a very thick piece for the ground or base, and scrape away a good deal on the lights. I prefer to have two or three impressions on three different thicknesses of paper, such as thin, medium, and thick, using the thin as the ground, and cutting out

the lightest parts in that. I find these afford a sufficient variety for every degree of shade or solidity; but whatever different modes different workmen may have, this I hold to be an axiom, that the thickness of paper, and the number of layers used, must depend on the size of the cut, the size and boldness of the solids, the fineness or coarseness of the engraving, and the time allowed to be spent on the making-ready. This is, I believe, allowed by all, that the finer the cut the thinner should be the paper used; the details must be left to the judgment of the workman. I have used little else than tissue on some cuts, and pretty thick paper on others; card I have never used, and I do not wish to use it, as I see no advantage in it over paper, and several disadvantages.

For the ordinary run of cuts, and the ordinary run of workmen, I would recommend four thicknesses of thin paper; the first, as the ground, should have sufficient margin to allow of its being pasted on the sheet outside the engraving; the extreme lights may be cut out of this. Then commence with the solids, the smallest and deepest shades first, then the second in size and color, and the largest and lightest last—all to be cut with the greatest neatness, and put on exactly in its proper place. This mode of putting on the courses is, I am aware, different from some others, but it has this advantage, that by putting on the larger pieces last the smaller are kept from falling off. The paper used should be of the best quality, (sized and calendered), and free from specks or spots. As little paste as possible should be used.

Although the proper overlaying of a cut is absolutely essential to the proper working of it, it must not be forgotten that, if first-class work is required, there are other things of almost equal importance, namely, good ink, good paper, a good roller, a good workman, and sufficient time allowed to do good work. If either of these are lacking, good work may be had, but the best of work cannot.

Wooden Furniture.—Furniture made of wood, sizes adapted to every type under Great Primer, and, above that, up to twelve ems Pica, being manufactured. It is used in large jobs, such as hand-bills and posters, instead of leads, on account of its cheapness, and also because, being of less weight, it can more readily be lifted from the stone than large quantities of metallic furniture. (See Furniture.)

Wood-Engraving.—The art of cutting designs on wood, so as to leave the lines in relief, the engraver following every line of the drawing, cutting away the whites and leaving the blacks. This form of art is especially important to the printer for the reason that the wood-cut can be produced in combination with type at a single or simultaneous impression.

Although carving in wood was practiced by almost all nations, in some form, at an early day, it only became an art when means were invented to obtain a printed impression from raised surfaces, such as the block-printing of China, and the similar manufacture of playing-cards in Europe. Card-makers and figure-cutters are mentioned as a class in the Low Countries at the beginning of the fifteenth century. The figure of St. Christopher, with the date of 1423, was for a long time considered the earliest engraving from wood with an ascertained date; but a picture was afterwards found at Brussels dated 1418, and a manuscript has recently been discovered with two plates printed upon it bearing the date of 1406. The History of Alexander, alleged to have been printed from wooden blocks in Italy in 1284, has been accepted by some authors, and, although it is highly improbable that it was completed at so early a date, it is not impossible, for the reason that only a few years later Marco Polo published a description of Chinese printing, the knowledge of which might have been previously acquired by the merchants of Venice in their intercourse with the East. The block-books of the Netherlands are the first important European specimens of wood-engraving, and they seem to have been printed exactly after the Chinese method. Although the dates of these books cannot be ascertained with accuracy, there is strong confirmatory proof in the fact that one edition of the Speculum Humanæ Salvationis is in the dialect spoken in the Low Countries at the end of the fourteenth century, and the testimony of Ulric Zell upon the use of printed educational and religious books may be regarded as conclusive. Many of the pictures of these books illustrate the manner of Van Eyck, the leading artist of the Netherlands during the latter portion of the fourteenth century. Many things in these works also exhibit the influence of the customs, tastes, and fashions of the Dukes of Burgundy, whose initials and other insignia appear in the watermarks of the paper (see WATERMARKS). The remarkable originality of Flemish art was maintained during the fourteenth and fifteenth centuries, but an admiration and imitation of the Italian manner became very injurious in the sixteenth century, and continued its influence until, under the great masters Rembrandt and Rubens, originality and nationality were restored. In Italy, wood-engraving did not, as in other countries, precede engraving in metal, and the art improved very slowly. The Hypnerotomachia Poliphilii, printed at Venice by Manutius in 1499, contained some wood-cuts of such excellent style that they have been ascribed to the artists Mantegna and Bellini. The sermons of Savonarola, published at Florence the day after they were delivered, were illustrated by fine cuts, which afterwards appeared in the Art of Happy Dying, published in the same city in 1513. The printers of Venice were the foremost patrons of wood-engraving in Italy, and the finest specimens are found in the publications of that city, especially about the year 1550. A history of St. Veronica, published at Milan in 1518, contains some admirable illustrations.

In Germany, the earliest wood-cuts resemble the Flemish, but are later in time, and the Biblia Pauperum, one of the most remarkable of the early block-books, is claimed by both nations. The celebrated Albert Pfister, sometimes urged as the inventor of type-printing, established himself in Bamberg about 1458, and printed a number of works with wood-cuts. The Bible printed by Koburger contains eighty-six cuts, some of which are attributed to the preface to Wolgemuth, the teacher of Albert Durer. Dürer also engraved upon wood, and did much to elevate that branch of art in Germany, his fame extending also into Italy, where his manner was widely copied. Lucas Cranach, the warm friend of Martin Luther, was also a famous wood-engraver, and he furnished the illustrations for Luther's pamphlets. The designs of Hans Holbein were engraved upon wood by an artist who styled himself Hans Lutzelburger, formschneider, and whose remarkable talent is proved by the excellence of the execution of the plates published as the Dance of Death, at Lyons, in 1538, and Holbein's scriptural illustrations. Many of the splendid books published at Basel, by Froben and his compeers, were elegantly illustrated by wood-engravings from Holbein and other artists. In the publications of Caxton, the illustrations are extremely rude, as if executed by very inferior artists, and the wood-engravings in England continued to be of marked inferiority until the sudden impulse given to that department of art by Bewick in 1770. In France playing-cards were manufactured at a very early day, although the date is not accurately ascertained, and a rude and almost barbarous style of print, with texts or mottoes in French, is probably of an early origin. The Romance of Fierabras, published at Lyons in 1480, is one of the first illustrated books, but it was far excelled by the rude but powerful scenes of the Dance of Death, published by Verard in 1485. The remarkable superiority of the miniature painting used in France for the adornment of books of devotion had created a taste for illustrations, and the Books of Hours, Missals, etc. published by Vostre, Verard, and other printers prove the employment of high artistic talent in the preparation of their first publications,—a demand for cheaper books causing the subsequent deterioration. During the sixteenth century in France much taste was exhibited in book-ornamentation, such as borders, capital letters, tail-pieces, etc. About 1540, Tory, widely known as one of the first great improvers of typography, became also famous as a wood-engraver, and founded a school of art much in advance of any that had previously existed in France. The immense popularity of wood-engravings during the sixteenth century gave rise to much inferior workmanship and a general deterioration in style, upon which there was no marked improvement until after the great advance made by England in the latter part of the eighteenth century.

In the United States wood-engraving was not cultivated as an art before the present century, and the first professional wood-engraver of this country died quite recently. (See ANDERSON, ALEXANDER.) Of late years, however, such an extraordinary amount of labor and talent has been devoted to wood-engraving here, that it may be questioned whether any other country excels the United States either in the quantity or the quality of its wood-engravers.

It will be perceived that wood-engraving has not been steadily progressive. Although its productions were distinguished for excellence of design and freedom of execution at a comparatively remote period, mere mechanical labor was subsequently substituted for the talent of artists; after which change wood-engraving, as a means of multiplying works of art, rapidly declined, and it remained for Bewick to revive it. (See BEWICK.)

At the present day, impressions of the products of wood-engraving are in universal circulation. They appear alike in the child's first book, in works in the useful arts, and in volumes devoted to science, religion, history, travels, poetry, geography, and to every other theme capable of illustration.

Practice of Wood-Engraving.—The pieces of wood used are called blocks. In fine engraving they are invariably of the box-tree. Mahogany, maple, and pear-wood are used in executing the common styles of wood-cuts, after they are prepared in the same manner as box-wood. Large poster-cuts, such as are used to advertise theatrical exhibitions, etc., are engraved on pine, upon the side of the grain, with carvers' tools instead of gravers. Many of these cuts are good specimens of art; and their use as posters was for a long time peculiarly American.

In preparing box-wood, the tree is cut across in slices with a fine saw, and the slices, after being planed smooth on the surface, are cut into square blocks of the required size. The blocks should be exactly the height of the printing-type in which they are to stand. When a block of more than from six to eight inches square is wanted, it is necessary to join two or more pieces together, as the box-tree is too limited in diameter to furnish blocks of a large size. Blocks are prepared in this manner, of any requisite dimensions, by at least one establishment which devotes special attention to this business,—that of N. J. Wemmer, of Philadelphia.

The best box-wood is smooth on the surface, perfectly level, perfectly dry, and of a uniform yellow color, without knots or flaws.

Tools.—The following articles are required by the engraver on wood:—

1. A round flattish pad, made of leather, and filled with sand, on which to rest the block while engraving it.

2. Gravers. A graver is a tool about four inches long, made of steel, with a small head or handle of wood. One side of the handle is flat, to allow the tool to rest steadily when set down. The blade or steel part of the tool is various in shape; some blades are much thicker than others. As it is the point of the blade which cuts, the sharper the blade is, the finer may the edge be ground in proportion. Six or eight degrees of fineness are usually

A SLIGHTLY BENT GRAVER.

employed; the finest being for the more delicate lines and markings, and the broader-pointed for cutting broad and bold lines. One or more of the gravers require to be slightly bent in the blades, to permit the excavating of hollowed parts. The shape of the point of this tool, as seen on its upper side, is here represented.

3. Tint-tools. These are tools of various degrees of fineness, suitable to the fineness or coarseness of the tint required to be cut. While it is the object of gravers to cut lines in various directions and of various lengths, and markings of a miscellaneous kind, tint-tools are chiefly employed to cut parallel lines close together, representing the tints of the sky. The tint-tool has a thinner blade than the graver, and, as is shown in the annexed cut, is much more tapering and sharp at the point.

4. A flat or gouge tool, for cutting away blank spaces at the edges, and trimming the cut.

5. A hone or Turkey stone, on which to sharpen the various tools and bring their edges to any required degree of slope.

6. A burnisher.

7. An inking-slab, a dabber, and a small quantity of fine printing-ink.

8. India paper, on which to take proofs.

9. Two or three fine and hard black-lead pencils.

Drawing.—Preliminary to engraving, the figures must be photographed, transferred, or drawn on wood; and the ability to draw with neatness and precision, as well as a knowledge of effect in light and shade, is very useful to the amateur wood-cutter and indispensable to those who desire to rise in the profession. Designers generally place the drawings on the blocks, when they are not transferred or photographed; but a general knowledge of drawing is always useful, and often indispensable, to an engraver. Sometimes the designs are made by black-lead pencils, and sometimes by various shades of India-ink, laid on with camel-hair pencils. In either case the effect of the shading must be brought out by the engraver, by means of lines and marks of different kinds.

Besides mere drawing, there is another branch of this department of art, called lowering, which consists in scraping away the surface of the block upon those portions of the design that are to be printed lightly. This practice was at one time extensively adopted, the whole surface of the block being more or less lowered in accordance with the shade desired, except the positive blacks; but lowering is now confined chiefly to the softening of the edges of vignettes, the edges of skies, and the surface of light tints where they adjoin positive whites. The necessity for other lowering has been obviated, in a great measure, by the skill possessed by modern printers in making ready cuts for good and faithful impressions.

The surface of the block being too smooth to receive the markings of a pencil, it is roughened

32

and at the same time delicately whitened all over with moistened powder of fine brick and flake white, and the palm of the hand is afterwards passed over the block, to remove from it any gritty particles. When dry, it is ready for the drawing, which is now put upon it, care being taken that nothing is marked which is not to stand in relief. On being finished, the drawing appears to be a minute and perfect sketch on a white ground.

Besides being able to draw, the learner should be acquainted with the practice of copying and reducing from prints. Photography is now used extensively by professional engravers, not only in reducing the object to be engraved, but also, whenever practicable, in putting the design, by peculiar processes, directly upon the wood, ready to be engraved. Old cuts are reproduced by the transferring process. The impression from the cut is soaked in a solution of caustic potash and alcohol until the ink is sufficiently soft, when it is transferred to the block by pressure in a copying-press. The old method of reduction is as follows:—For example, a wood-engraving three inches long by two inches broad is required to be made from a print twelve inches long and eight inches broad. In this, as in all other cases, it is necessary to copy everything in exact proportion. A square frame, on which threads are stretched lengthwise and crosswise, leaving square openings, is laid on the print. Small squares to the same number are now lightly traced on the wood, and whatever parts lie within any opening in the frame are copied within the corresponding opening or square on the wood: thus a copy in exact proportion is obtained.

As pencil-drawing is very apt to be blurred or partly effaced by touching with the hand, it is necessary to cover the block, while working upon it, with a piece of paper. A slip of smooth wrapping-paper is best for this purpose; it should be neatly folded over the edges, after they have been rubbed with beeswax, and fastened thereto by rubbing the portion folded over with the thumb-nail. On beginning to engrave, tear off a piece of the paper from the part to which the tool is to be applied, and so remove the paper as the work proceeds.

First Exercises.—Persons with weak sight use a strong magnifying glass when engraving, or when closely examining the appearance of their work. We would recommend beginners to avoid using a glass, if possible, for it injures the sight with the naked eye. Persons with ordinary eyesight require no glass in wood-cutting.

The work can be best executed with a strong steady northern light. In cutting by lamp-light, a shade should be employed, to throw the light down, and the light may be concentrated by being made to shine through a globe of water, the light coming to a focus on the block.

The engraving is done at a table or bench of convenient height, placed below or near the light just mentioned. The engraver, seated on a chair, holds and moves about the block on the pad with the left hand, while he operates with the tool in the right, as is represented in the annexed cut. Great steadiness

Fig. 1.

of hand is of the utmost importance, for the least cut in a wrong direction may mar, if not ruin, the effect to be produced. Until the learner becomes familiar with his tools, he should proceed gently and patiently, pushing the graver cautiously forward at a uniform depth, and clearing out small chips or thread-like parings.

In painting, innumerable tones, tints, lights, shades, nearness, and distance, are produced by applying a variety of colors, and any error can be rectified by a new touch of the brush. In wood-engraving, every kind of effect must be produced by a mere variation in the marking, first with the pencil, and afterwards with the graver; the result in printing being a variety of dark marks and lines on a white ground. The skill of the wood-engraver is therefore tested to no mean degree. On the careful and judicious disposition of his lines, and the lightness and strength of his masses of darkened parts, depends the entire effect of his labors.

In engraving a wood-cut, the parts drawn upon remain, and the blank spaces which the pencil has not touched are cleared away.

The first lessons of a learner should consist in engraving straight parallel lines with a tinting-tool, as is exemplified in Fig. 2. The degree of darkness is regulated by the thickness of the lines, and the spaces cut out between them. Let the lines be cut smooth and clean, and free from ruggedness or breaks.

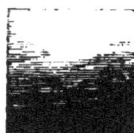

Fig. 2.

Not till he is pretty well grounded in the art of cutting straight parallel lines, should the learner proceed to the next steps in advance, which will consist in cutting bent and waving lines. Figs. 3, 4, and 5 show the nature of this progression.

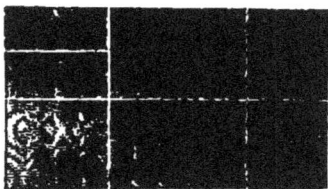

Fig. 3.

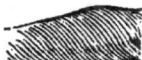

FIG. 4.   FIG. 5.

Having cut one or more of these early exercises, the parts of the block not to be printed must be lowered with a flat or gouging tool, so as to leave no parts so high as the lines.

Perfected in the art of cutting lines straight, bent,  and waved, the learner may proceed to cross-hatching, which consists in cutting lines at different angles, and of different lengths, across other lines, with the view of expressing graduated depths of shade. The varieties of hatching are endless, from light tones up to the darkest shadows. Fig. 6 represents a familiar kind of cross-hatching.

FIG. 6.

These specimens are given more for the purpose of showing what cross-hatching is, than of inducing learners to prosecute this kind of engraving. Cross-hatching should always be sparingly employed, and in no case should it be used when an effect can be attained by simple lines; for it introduces complexity, and often too much minuteness of detail.

In drawing on wood it is easier to produce a shade by this means, but in engraving on wood it is precisely the reverse, for it is easier to leave a thick line than to cut out the interstices of lines crossing one another. Nothing is more common than for persons to refer to the frequent cross-hatchings in cuts as a proof of their excellence. There is not a wood-engraver of the least repute who cannot cut fac-similes of any cross-hatching that is to be found. The execution of cross-hatching requires time, but very little talent; whereas the rendition of shades washed in with India-ink not only calls for artistic talent in the engraver, but also, in a majority of subjects, gives greater tone to the picture. Cross-hatching is judiciously used in delineating drapery, by many of the first artists of the present day, in shaded drawings on wood. Upon examination of some of the finest wood-engravings executed during the last twenty years, especially the shaded performances of Doré, we find that the manner in which they are engraved is comparatively simple; there is little or no labored and unnecessary cross-hatching where the same effect might be obtained by simpler means, and no time is wasted in mere mechanical execution, which in the end displays not so much of art as of simple patience and labor.

With this caution, it should be mentioned that, if cross-hatching is found indispensable, the learner must execute it with particular care; for there is a difficulty in cutting out the whites so as to leave continuous lines sweeping across, as in the above figure. If possible, rest the tool on the whites afterwards to be cut away; and when nothing remains

as fulcrum, a small piece of card may be laid on the block as a protection. Take care also not to undermine any already cut lines; for if undercut, they may break off in printing.

Apparent faults in wood-engravings can with great difficulty be remedied; and it is better to allow them to remain, or to execute another engraving, than to attempt improvement. Experienced engravers are sometimes able to correct errors in their cuts by what is technically called plugging. A small piece of wood is dexterously drilled out of the block, and a new piece is inserted in its stead, and glued, to prevent shifting. On this new piece the correction is executed.

Taking Proofs.—When an engraving is finished, the workman will be gratified by seeing how it looks on paper, and this gratification he can afford himself without the aid of the printing-press. The materials necessary for this operation are a small quantity of the finest printing-ink; a smooth stone or slab to distribute it on (the back of a large strong earthenware saucer will, however, answer the purpose); a dabber, composed of wool, tightly tied up in white leather or fine silk; some India or Chinese paper; a burnisher; and a piece of card. Having smeared a small quantity of ink on the dabber, beat it for some time on the stone, that it may be distributed equally over the surface. Holding the cut steadily on the sand-bag, strike it gently with the dabber, taking care not to use any pressure whatever; the ink will thus be imparted evenly upon the surface of the lines, without descending to their sides. Having cut a piece of India paper to the required size, breathe upon its smoothest side, lay it on the block, place the card on the back of the paper, and commence rubbing the back of the card with the burnisher. A very steady hand is requisite to do this effectually, for if the India paper be allowed to move the lines will be blurred or doubled. When every part of the object on the block has been sufficiently rubbed, the operation is finished, and the proof may be removed.

A precaution may be necessary in taking proofs by the above plan, which is, to leave a border of the whites standing round the edge of the block, as something for the hand and the burnisher to bear upon. To prevent the black mass (which will of course be inked with the rest) from appearing on the finished proof, a rough one must be taken first, and the subject of the engraving cut out of it with scissors. After inking the block for the clean proof, the black border must be covered with what is left of the first impression, which protects the former from the ink during the burnishing process. Of course the border on the block must be cut away in finishing the wood-cut for press.

After using, the slab should be cleansed with lye of potash, or turpentine, and the dabber must be kept clean and soft. If these precautions are not attended to, the proofs will soon become coarse in appearance, and the cuts will be clogged. Cuts are best cleaned with turpentine, and they should be dried before being put aside, always on their edges.

Outline Figures.—In commencing to cut figures and scenes, it is advisable to copy from wood-engravings of a simple and expressive kind. Almost all beginners commit a serious mistake in attempting to imitate the finer class of wood-engravings, which abound in minute marking. They should learn to bring out an effect in light and shade with as few lines and hatchings as possible, never making two or more small marks where one of a bolder stretch would answer. The first figures attempted should only be in outline, as is exemplified in the annexed engraving of the leaves of a plant.

Fig. 7.

Here it will be observed what effect is produced by a few thin and thick lines, with a very slight shading. Other outline figures, such as the above,

Fig. 8.

may also at this stage of advancement be engraved; after which figures with shading, or small groups of rural objects, as in Figs. 8 and 9, may be executed.

Fig. 9.

Another class of exercises consists in cutting sketches of round and oval objects, in which there are strong depths of shadow and strong lights, as in Fig. 10.

Fig. 10.

It will be observed in these examples, as well as in other cuts of a simple class, that three gradations of shade require to be studied. After the pure white comes the lightest shading, consisting of only a few scratches. Next we have the gray or middle tone. Lastly we have this mid tone shading down to the pure black. Pure blacks are portions of wood scarcely, if at all, touched by the graver.

About this stage of advancement the learner may exercise himself in drawing and cutting foliage of different kinds. As is well known to the draughtsman, foliage is represented differently, according to the nature of the tree. In Fig. 11 the willow is repre-

Fig. 11.

sented by perpendicular markings, terminating in a point, to give the idea of its pendent foliage. A broad mass of light is usually preserved, and an increase of markings is given to one side of each subdivision of foliage, with considerable power of characteristic markings on the shade-side of the tree, besides an occasional repetition of touch for effect.

The fir has been represented by short angular markings connected with each other, much like the zigzag scratch with a pen to obliterate an incorrect word. These markings are continued in agreement with the projections of the branches, and repeated with increased power on the shade-side of the tree, and a few slight markings are given on the extremities, and beneath the masses, to indicate foliage on the farther side of the tree. The elm has been represented by escalops in a semicircular direction, so distributed as to give the idea of thick foliage.

The oak has been represented, as in Fig. 12, by a character which partakes of angular and broken circular markings, intermingled with dots and sharp

Fig. 12.

touches. The lighter parts are penciled tenderly, and the shade portions are repeated upon, with additional power given by sharp angular markings.

We mention these varieties for the purpose of showing that foliage is not to be represented by distinctly portraying every leaf, but by a bold grouping and superficial outlining; the purpose being served by merely a general representation. Suppose a tree is to be selected for placing in the foreground of a drawing, where its peculiarities are required to be displayed. Let the growth of the branches be observed; a straight line is rarely to be seen, nor do they spring from each other with uniformity; there is usually an undulating line, often graceful, or a wild luxuriance, ever pleasing, in these supports to the foliage. Let the effect of the leaves which may compose a principal mass be indicated, not the outline of a leaf or leaves, which would prove labor in vain, but what is seen as much by the imagination as by the eye; that is, not the detail, but the effect. If too much regularity appear, destroy it by projecting a touch or two on the extremities, and attack any formality by additional markings, in conformity with the character adopted. Oftentimes the mere waving of the pencil, or a powerful repetition with the broad point, will not only remove a monotonous appearance, but communicate characteristic spirit and effect.

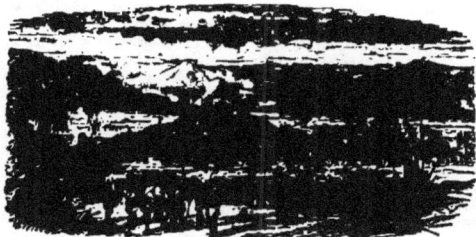

Fig. 13.

Advanced Exercises.—After outline and shaded figures, the learner may proceed to figures with shadings and backgrounds, requiring a variety of light and dark lines. In beginning figures or objects with backgrounds, it is necessary to cut an outline round it, as a boundary to other lines coming against it; but this outline should not be seen in the impression of the engraving. This outlining prevents the figure from appearing to adhere to the background, and is indispensable.

In this department of study the learner may engrave human figures, animals of different kinds, and rural and street scenes with skies; as, for example, views like that in Fig. 13; in this, however, as in many other things, much must be left to the taste, the patience, and the skill of the engraver.

Color Blocks.—The art of engraving wood blocks from which pictures in various colors are to be produced, has been brought to great perfection, and where large editions are desired it is more economical than lithography. In producing color blocks the design is first engraved in the usual manner, except that there is less than the ordinary amount of shading. Impressions are then taken from the first block and transferred to the other blocks—one block being necessary for each color used. All parts of each block are then cut away, except those which are to be printed in the respective colors. The blocks are then printed successively, the lighter colors being usually printed first. Thus, a design in yellow, red, blue, and black, would be run through the press, in the order mentioned, four distinct times; the whole number of impressions required in each color being printed before work commences on the succeeding color. Some modern machines, however, now print different colors in such rapid succession that they are, practically, printed simultaneously.

Wood Paper.—Paper of which wood forms an important ingredient. Large quantities of wood paper are now made in the United States and in Europe. At the Paris Exposition of 1867, Voelter and Decker, of Würtemberg, who have been actively engaged for more than twenty years in manufacturing wood pulp, and in constructing machinery to be used for that purpose by numerous European paper-mills, exhibited their most recent patents, in operation. The process, as described by one of the British Commissioners, was as follows:

Wood pulp is mixed with rag pulp, in proportions varying from 18 to 80 per cent., according to the quality of the paper—namely, 15 to 50 per cent. for good writing- and printing-paper; 50 to 70 per cent. for ordinary writing-, printing-, and wrapping-paper; 50 to 80 per cent. for common paper-hangings and cardboards. Pasteboards may be made entirely of wood pulp.

Pine and fir wood give the best fibre, while ash and lime produce the whitest pulp; all woods of similar character may, however, be used; and, indeed, any wood will produce pulp. Birch and beech have been used extensively in both Belgium and France.

It is very desirable that the water used in the process be clear; if dirty river-water be used, it must be filtered, or the pulp will be colored. Hard water containing lime is not only not unfit, but very suitable for the purpose. An expenditure of 5-horse power effective is required for twenty-four hours to produce 1 cwt. of wood pulp air-dry. Therefore, a 40-horse power mill, working day and night, will produce eight cwt. of pulp. An excess of power, even on that liberal allowance, is, however, recommended. For the production of 1 cwt. of pulp 2 cwt. of wood is required. Young wood, from three inches to twelve inches in thickness, is preferred, and it should not be kept in store more than six months before being used. The wood must be cut into pieces about twelve inches long, and all the knots, bark, and other impurities removed. Waste pieces of wood, provided they are not too small, may be utilized.

For every cwt. of pulp made a water supply throughout the twenty-four hours has to be kept up of from one-half to three-fourths of a cubic foot per minute.

Besides the foreman, each hundredweight of pulp made in the twenty-four hours requires one man. From the price-list, a 60-horse power machine will weigh nearly nine tons, and cost £515, irrespective of packing, delivered in the manufacturer's yard. It is likely that, besides the above sum, a heavy bill for extras would have to be paid, irrespective of driving power.

From the above details it will be seen that, with a 60-horse power machine, working day and night, twelve cwt. of air-dry pulp will be produced, at the cost of the wages of twelve people, irrespective of foremen, engine-drivers, and stokers, if steam be used, to which must be added the price of power and wood, depending on the locality; and, further, the charge of transporting the pulp to the paper-machine, unless the pulp- and paper-mills happen to be close together.

Messrs. Voelter and Decker state that they have tried to use wood pulp for the manufacture of picture-frames, statues, and the like, as a substitute for papier-maché, and that fairly satisfactory results have been obtained. I believe there is a chemical means of reducing wood to the form of pulp, but I have not heard that as yet it has been practically successful. It is said that the fibre of the wood, on which its value depends, is destroyed by the process, while, by mechanically reducing it, the fibre remains uninjured. The machine by which the above operation is effected may be described as a big, vertical grindstone, against which the wood is to be ground is pressed, while a stream of water assists the operation and at the same time keeps the working parts cool. The wood thus ground down is passed through successive sieves until the residue is of the required degree of fineness.

At the Exhibition the mill is driven by three portable engines, of about fifteen or seventeen horse power each, two of which are kept running together. It would, however, require the power of all three to work the mill up to its full productive power. The grindstone is of the ordinary description, with a hammer-picked face, the one in the Exhibition being about four feet in diameter, and making from 150 to 180 turns per minute. Around its periphery are fixed five boxes, or hoppers, which receive the wood to be ground, and which has been previously cut into proper lengths by a circular saw. These boxes are fitted with sliding covers, which are gradually forced forward by screws, as the stone wears the wood. The amount of feed (which is necessarily very small) is regulated by a governor similar in principle to those which are used in connection with water-wheels. It is driven from the main shaft, and causes an increased or diminished feed to be given, according to the velocity of the stone, and, consequently, the pressure of the wood against it. A simple arrangement permits of the slow motion of the feed-screw being dispensed with, and the cover rapidly withdrawn by means of a rack and pinion, when it is required to renew the charge of wood.

The first process reduces the wood to a mass of pulp and splinters of different degrees of fineness. To separate the larger from the less, the whole, profusely mixed with water, is passed into a trough containing a revolving cylindrical strainer, permitting only of stuff of a certain degree of fineness passing through it. All those pieces which from their coarseness adhere to the outside of the cylinder are thrown away as useless. The pulp then undergoes a similar process again, but the strainer is much finer, and the pieces of wood which it separates are worth being further dealt with. As they are separated by the action of the revolving strainer, they are carried with a stream of water to the centre of the upper of a pair of ordinary horizontal millstones, where they are reduced by grinding to the same condition or quality of fibre as that coming direct from the grindstone. It remains now only to separate the pulp into three degrees of fineness, according to the purpose for which it is intended. This is done by passing it through strainers of various degrees of coarseness, that which separates the very finest pulp having a mesh with 40,000 holes to the square inch. The pulp is then dried partially by the action of the air and partially by being pressed between rollers, when it is ready for use. If, however, it has to be transported, as a matter of economy the drying process must be completed.

In Germany wood pulp sells for about 36 francs per 100 kilos (or nearly 15 shillings per hundredweight). In France it is worth 50 francs per 100 kilos (or nearly £1 per hundredweight). The condition of the matter is air-dry—that is, containing some 10 per cent. by weight of water. In Germany rag pulp costs double wood pulp, or 72 francs per 100 kilos.

Wood Type.—Type made of wood; generally of cherry, cut end-wise; nearly every imaginable size, from two- or three-line Pica, up to one-hundred-and-fifty-line Pica, and of a great variety of shapes and designs, being now manufactured in the United States. The only establishments now in active operation in this country are those of W. H. Page & Co., of

Greenville, Connecticut, and Vanderburgh, Wells & Co., of New York, which not only supply the home demand, but also export large quantities to Europe. The Monthly Review says that the first font of wood type cut on the section of the wood was made in 1827, when Darius Wells, a New York printer, after making several fonts for his own use, commenced manufacturing wood-type as a distinct business.

The tools, patterns, and processes used by him at first were of the most primitive kind. The simple slide-rest and chuck were employed to reduce the wood to an equal height; and first paper, then sheet-brass, and afterwards cast-brass patterns with raised outline, were successively used to secure the delineation of letters upon the face of the blocks. Then, to cut away the surplus wood (outside and counters) the mallet, gouge and chisel, and finally the more delicate chisels, gravers and files, were used in finishing up the face of the type.

Soon another improvement was invented by Mr. Wells. It was the application of a revolving, vertical spindle, carrying a cutter, by which the surplus wood was speedily and neatly cut away. To this process Mr. Wells gave the technical term of routing, a term now universally known among printers and wood-engravers.

It will be seen that the process of turning down blocks to an even height for type would be equally adapted to preparing blocks for wood-engravers and stereotypers. This also was soon adopted by them, and this may properly be denominated an era in the progress of that kindred art. Hitherto each wood-engraver had been content to purchase of the dealer in boxwood, a log, which he usually took to a cabinet-maker, by whom a slice was sawn off and planed down as well as it could be. But it would so happen, in many instances, that these blocks would be thinner on one side than the other, and defy the best skill of the printer, by overlays or underlays, to do justice to the engravings.

The blocking of stereotype plates upon blocks thus prepared, for like reasons, immediately followed, and thus every branch connected with the printing-business fully participated in this improvement.

No young printer, who now witnesses the universal use of wood type, and is accustomed to turn over the ample pages of the existing wood type specimen-books, can appreciate the difficulties which at that time stood in the way of an introduction of this hitherto untried article. A few individuals only could at first be found who would venture to attempt their use. But the great consequent superiority of their posters, soon compelled others to imitate their example, and thus the use of wood type soon became universal.

About the year 1830, an Englishman, named John Lomax, became a competitor with Mr. Wells, so far as to make regular fonts of type on side-wood, but they never attained much popularity.

In 1834, William Leavenworth commenced the manufacture of wood type, in Allentown, New Jersey.

He was a man of decided genius; but, not being a practical printer, he did not succeed in giving his type all the requisite qualities, and he finally disposed of his business to Mr. Wells. He introduced the pentagraph, which was a most important improvement, both for marking and routings, as it obviated the necessity of making patterns for every size, as formerly.

The next effort to manufacture wood type, after that of Mr. Leavenworth, was by Mr. Allen, of Norwich, Conn., who copied the most of Mr. Leavenworth's methods, except that of facing the wood. The only characteristic difference, perhaps, was that, instead of the grooved pattern of the former, Mr. Allen adopted a raised pattern, being of easier execution.

Home-Made Wood Type.—A contributor to a Western typographical journal recommends the following as a cheap and convenient method for manufacturing home-made wood type in times of emergency. Select a board of clear, well-seasoned bass-wood, or white-wood (cucumber-wood is still better, if it can be had), one inch and a quarter in thickness—the width the size you would have the type, and have it dressed with a machine planer, having it a little more than type-high in thickness. Sandpaper the face of it well, and it is ready for the pencil. When a line is wanted for a poster, draft it on the prepared board; cut away from the outline of each letter, then have them sawed apart with a burr saw, and it is a very easy matter to finish them up for the press. This style of type will require less impression and less ink than type cut on hard wood, and will leave the ink on the sheet smooth and even. It should not be washed, but put away after using, in a clean place, standing each letter on its edge.

How to Treat Wood Type.—To prevent warping, all very large wood type should be set up on the edge when put away, so that both sides may be equally exposed to the air. In cleaning it, neither lye nor water should be employed. Turpentine, camphene, benzine, or kerosene oil may be used; but turpentine and camphene are the best. Procure a small, shallow pan; lay the form flat on a board; pour about six tablespoonfuls of turpentine into the pan; touch the face of the brush to the turpentine, and pass it quickly over the form before it evaporates. From six to eight spoonfuls of fluid will be found sufficient to clean a large form, if thus used.

Word.—A single component part of human language, either spoken or written, used as the expression of an idea. The Scriptures, as the revelation of God, are frequently called the Word of God, or the Word.

Word-Book.—A vocabulary or dictionary.

Worde, Wynkyn de.—A celebrated printer, the successor of Caxton in England. He is believed to have been a native of Lorraine, to have assisted Caxton in printing at Bruges and Cologne, and to have accompanied him to England. De Worde continued with Caxton, and succeeded to his business, printing for some years in Caxton's own house. In a work published in 1494, De Worde mentions the death of Caxton, and also the patronage extended to himself by Queen Margaret, the mother of Henry VII. Immediately after Caxton's death, De Worde cut a number of new and remarkably excellent fonts of type, not only for himself, but for other printers. The introduction of the Roman character in England has been claimed for both De Worde and Pynson, but it is certain that De Worde made use of it at first in the same manner as Italic is now employed. In 1523 he published a work in Roman character, with marginal notes in Italic, which book contained the first Greek ever printed in England, it being in movable type, while the Arabic and Hebrew were cut in wood. De Worde printed four hundred and eight books, generally using the device of Caxton, with the addition of his own name. In law-books, etc., he used other devices composed from the armorial bearings of the houses of Tudor and Plantagenet. A copy of his Bartholomæus, as the first book printed upon paper manufactured in England, was bought at the Roxburghe sale for £70, 7s. De Worde died in 1534.

Worked, or **Worked Off.**—When a job, newspaper, or a sheet of a book is printed, it is said to be worked, or worked off.

Working in Pocket.—When the hands share equally the earnings on a work.

Wrappers.—Products of job-printing, which, in the appearance of their printed matter, resemble labels, but differ from them in having larger margins, so that they can inclose or wrap up a bottle of patent medicine, a bar of soap, etc.

Writ.—An instrument in writing, or in writing and printing, in which a court of justice, or some sovereign power in a government, commands some act to be done by the person to whom it is directed. Printed blank forms are generally used.

Writing-Ink.—From history and documents we find that the oldest material used as ink consisted of finely divided carbon, generally some form of lamp-black, mixed with some mucilaginous substance. This seems for ages to have been sufficient for the wants of mankind. In a modified and improved mode of preparation, this, under the name of India-ink, is still almost universally used by the Chinese, sometimes with a pen-shaped reed, but oftener with a camel's-hair pencil, the latter, in skillful hands, admirably adapting itself to the formation of the Arabic and other Oriental characters. We have seen a copy of the Koran made in this way, which for beauty and regularity of form of letters could not be excelled.

The formation of India-ink, with some variations, seems to be as follows: A fine lampblack is mixed with some vegetable mucilage, and sometimes scented with camphor. The essential excellence of the ink depends first upon a nice selection of materials, and next upon the pains taken to render it as compact as possible; this requires a more laborious method of rubbing it up for use, which leaves the particles of carbon in the finest possible state.

But while such inks were imperishable, unless put upon an absorbent substance, they could be washed off from smooth surfaces, and at an early period—how soon we cannot ascertain—our ordinary iron inks came into use, and have continued to this day. Such inks are made substantially as follows. A cheap salt of iron, generally the protosulphate, is mixed with galls or some similar astringent substance. In the first case a mixed gallate and tannate of iron is formed, which is generally soluble at first, but, as part of this becomes insoluble in time, some gum is added to keep it suspended, and, as the organic matter present is quite favorable to the formation of mould, a little of some highly-scented oil, such as oil of cloves, is added; a small quantity of carbolic acid would be cheaper and better. This is, in fact, the substance of the thousands of receipts which can be found for ordinary ink. In some of them, however, a little sulphate of copper is added, and other astringents are added to the galls, the most important being the extract of logwood, which imparts its own color to the compound.

By whatever receipt made, these inks at first are to a great extent real solutions, and in this consists their especial value: they are absorbed by the paper, penetrate it, dye its fibres, and then become insoluble and grow black. Hence all good inks of this kind are at first pale, and then gradually become black. But if, by undue exposure to the air, such inks become black before being used for writing purposes, the coloring matter is only suspended in the fluid, and, instead of dyeing the fibre of the paper, it only remains deposited upon it, and of course is much more readily erased. Of the immense quantity of really good inks made by well-known makers, ninety-nine hundredths are spoiled before they are ever put to paper. This is owing to the faulty structure of our ink-stands, which are often made to be mere ornaments, instead of being constructed with a view to the preservation of the useful fluid they are intended to contain.

Every ink-stand for really good ink, should have the great bulk of the ink protected from the air, and only as much exposed as will fill a dipping-cup with sufficient ink to supply the pen dipped into it. Even this ink, after prolonged exposure, should be removed, and the pen at intervals wiped on a sponge; and in this way only can the best writing be done with the best inks. A very little exposure to the air produces in these best inks a sticky gummy consistence which prevents clean writing.

The wonderfully low price of steel pens in modern times has caused the quill to disappear. It was soon found, however, that the ink corroded the steel pens. Efforts to obviate this led to the use of a poorer ink, and now we have corroded steel pens used and rapidly wasted, with half or wholly spoiled ink. For public service or for private use, wherever it can be afforded, a gold pen tipped with the well-known osmium or iridium points should be used, and the best inks should be most carefully protected for use in their best condition.

A blue ink was introduced by Mr. Stevens of London. This was made by washing Prussian blue with hydrochloric acid and then dissolving it in oxalic acid. This ink was for a while exceedingly popular, but has now almost entirely gone out of use. Its endurance was perhaps quite equal to that of ordinary iron inks, and there were few disadvantages about it, except its action on steel pens.

A green ink, afterwards turning nearly or quite black, has been brought into use in modern times. This needs no gum, its own material supplying the proper substance to the compound. These inks are made by the action of a small quantity of chromate of potash upon extract of logwood. Such inks are about as permanent as ordinary iron inks, and have some advantages but many disadvantages.

A dark purple ink made, apparently, largely from extract of logwood has become, even for official use, quite a favorite, simply because it is a copying-ink, a property which can be given quite readily to any good writing-ink by the addition of a little glycerine. The ink in question, however, soon becomes so intolerably thick and gummy, that we consider its continued use a brave persistence under difficulties rather than a judicious selection of material.

The recently used pale blue or violet aniline inks are merely abominations. Eminently fugitive, even under sunlight, their use should be strictly forbidden, in all official documents.

The restoration of old and faded iron inks is sometimes required; the new-fangled modern fancy inks have not lived long enough to need restoration, and when they are faded they are gone forever. The fading of good iron inks is sometimes caused by a gradual decay of the gallic and tannic acids or other organic matter, leaving only an oxide of iron, but, while this is left so pale as no longer to give legible characters, it has become so dense and insoluble that it does not give, with the ordinary re-agents for iron salts, any very good marks. We have had some experience in trials of this kind, especially upon parchment, the documents being about one hundred years old. Tincture of galls, prussiate of potash, and other salts have been recommended, but we cannot say that any one perfectly answers the purpose of reducing the iron, on account of its insolubility. Perhaps the best way would be to act first with a strong solution of a sulphur salt, and then, if necessary, with any of the other re-agents.

In India, this destruction of iron inks is said to be very rapid. This should be borne in mind, in the hotter parts of our own country.

An Imperishable Black Writing-Ink.—For the knowledge of this most invaluable material, we are indebted to the Commissioners of the French Government on the subject of Safety-Paper. It was known that India-ink was imperishable, but it could rather easily be washed off the paper. It was Dumas, we think, who first proposed India-ink held in suspension by hydro-chloric (muriatic) acid but this destroyed steel pens and did not answer for resin-sized paper.

He then proposed India-ink held in suspension by some alkali, possibly soda as best. For thirty years we have used no other writing-ink, trying alternately caustic soda, caustic potash, and sometimes ammonia, but finally we have come to the simplest, best, and most ready means of suspension, and that is a saturated solution of borax, always to be obtained and free from any objection in its use. Any good Chinese or Japanese India-ink (we think the latter rather the blacker) rubbed up with this saturated solution of borax gives an ink which leaves nothing to be desired. It flows so freely that the pen does not cease to mark until all visible ink has disappeared from it, and the freedom of writing is marvelous. We are certain that in these thirty years we have comfortably written twice as much as we could have done with ordinary ink; and we also find that, with the same material, the most elaborate pen-and-ink drawings may be made by skillful hands, with the same facility that we find in writing.

The advantage which a rapid thinker and writer would derive from such an ink is incalculable. The only trouble is the grinding of the ink. This is a *sine qua non*, and that, too, not upon a rough but a tolerably smooth surface, such as a porcelain plate. Upon this depends the fineness of the product. No doubt it would be quite easy to arrange a simple contrivance for the rapid grinding of such an ink: a porcelain grindstone, if not turned so rapidly as to throw the fluid off by centrifugal force, would be the simplest.

It has been proposed that such an ink should be used for the cancellation of stamps. If always used, it would be a perfect preventive of fraudulent re-use.

Every banker or man of business, however, should use such an ink to fill his checks and to write all important papers and documents. Certainly all important official papers should be written with it, for the ink will remain unchanged forever, and while by various re-agents the paper may be injured the ink will remain unaltered.

By the addition of a little glycerine, and possibly of some other coloring matter, this may be converted into a copying-ink, if this somewhat doubtful advantage is desired.

X.

Xylography, (and Xylographic Printing.) —The term xylography is almost pure Greek, but it came to us from the French. It is a modern coinage, and from its derivation it should mean engraving upon wood; this, however, is not its signification in the United States, where it was introduced to express the

ornamental work upon labels for perfumery, imported direct from Paris, about 1830. The distinctive style of the engraving is that of the Geometric Lathe, at first applied as an ornament to watch-cases, and afterwards extended to fine-grained wood, and then to printing-plates of copper, steel, and type-metal. Its structure is composed of circles and other curves, and arcs of these, intersecting by an exact graduated change of centre, by the passage of the surface under a fine steel point, thus producing figures of great beauty, suitable for borders, and damask ground-work and endings for checks and drafts. It has reached its highest application in our present national currency. Its original use in this country is principally due to Edmund Morris, Esq., formerly of Philadelphia, whence the work was dispensed almost throughout the continent, in labels, show-bills, and commercial blanks. It is adapted properly to fancy colored inks—its lines being too heavy for black inks; but no other style of ornamental printing embraces such capacity for critical accuracy, coupled with almost kaleidoscopic variety. The execution of the printing requires skill and judgment, the contrasts of the surface demanding difference of treatment as to quantities of both color and impression, in securing which, exact overlays on the tympan are the surest resource. It could not have preceded the invention of the elastic inking-roller—the skin balls being wholly inadequate for the purpose. The hardest stereotype castings, taken from originals of softest type-metal, are preferable for general work; electrotypes give finer lines, and have other valuable points, when backed up sufficiently to stand the heavy pressure, but precaution must be taken to prevent them from spoiling all varieties of vermilion colors. Xylographic printing is now supplanted, to a great extent, by lithographic work.

Y.

Year-Book.—A work published annually, such as a report or summary of the occurrences, statistics, etc. of a year, and intended to be used as a book of reference.

Z.

Zarot, Anthony.—The supposed inventor of signatures. He commenced the printing-business in Milan, Italy, in 1470; and no other printer is known to have used signatures before the appearance of his edition of Terence. Zarot continued printing until 1500, when he is supposed to have died.

Zell, Ulric.—A printer of Cologne, during the fifteenth century, whose name is frequently mentioned in the controversies relating to the origin of printing, on account of the direct testimony he furnished in regard to some of the facts involved. (See KOSTER.)

Zincography.—Engraving on zinc.

Zinc, Printing on.—Plates of zinc are drawn upon and printed from by a process similar to that employed in lithography. They are said to be specially useful when only small editions are required, or where it is desirable to avoid the expense of large lithographic stones. Various methods of engraving on zinc plates, by an economic process, that will render them available for use on typographic presses, have also been devised, some of which are described in other portions of this work. In Frank Leslie's official report, as American Commissioner at the Paris Exposition of 1867, on the Fine Arts, he describes the following methods:

The Gillot Process.—On a plate of zinc, polished, a transfer is made of an ordinary lithographic drawing, either by pen or pencil. The plate of zinc is covered on the back by a layer of oil varnish, and submitted to a bath of sulphuric acid diluted with water. Every part of the plate not covered, either by the ink of the transfer, or by the varnish, is bitten or hollowed out by the acid, and leaves in relief the covered parts, which, mounted on wood, form a cast replacing an engraving on wood. This process is very quickly executed, and offers great advantages for illustrations which will not bear delay. It offers, also, this considerable advantage, that all drawings executed in lithography of all kinds, etchings, engravings on steel, plates of music, etc., from which can be taken a proof on paper, are rapidly transformed into a cast, and can be printed with text. The most marked disadvantages of this process are: 1. Breaking down of the lines in the operation of transfer, however delicately this operation may be performed. This thickens and blots the delicacy of the original work. 2. Difficulty of obtaining the tints when the work is taken directly from lithography in pen and ink. The blotting is very apparent when it is a lithographic drawing.

The Conte Process.—Instead of transferring the drawing to a plate of zinc, the plate is covered with a white water-varnish, sufficiently adherent for a tracing, and sufficiently soft to be easily cut away, without scratching the zinc, by a point of wood, ivory, or whalebone. The artist then proceeds as for etching, with this difference of result, that the zinc uncovered is again covered by oil-ink, and, instead of being incised as in etching, remains in relief in the acid bath, which is the same as in the Gillot process. This process is very convenient for artists, who can judge of their work as if they were drawing on paper by means of a black-lead pencil. The lines do not thicken, but remain delicate. The varnish can be removed or put on with a camel's-hair pencil, so that any part may be corrected at any time by the artist.

Different processes of the same nature have been tried by persons who endeavored to substitute for zinc copper, steel, and other metals, but without success.

Zoography.—A description of animals, their habits, forms, etc.

Zoology.—The science which treats of animals, their habits, forms, etc. This division of literature embraces many very large and handsome publications, elegantly and abundantly illustrated.

CONTENTS.

507

www.ingramcontent.com/pod-product-compliance
Lightning Source LLC
Chambersburg PA
CBHW022126020426
42334CB00015B/786